W9-DDR-376

PRESENTING THE LATEST "HOT" TOPICS

THE WORLD OF MANAGEMENT

MANAGEMENT INFOTECH

WORKING WITH DIVERSITY

TODAY'S MANAGEMENT ISSUES

THE QUALITY CHALLENGE

Management

6TH EDITION

Management

Ricky W. Griffin

Texas A & M University

Houghton Mifflin Company

Boston   New York

For Glenda (The "new" Dr. Griffin)
My lifelong partner and my best friend

Sponsoring Editor: Kathleen L. Hunter
Associate Sponsoring Editor: Joanne Dauksewicz
Project Editor: Elizabeth Gale Napolitano
Senior Production/Design Coordinator: Jill Haber
Senior Manufacturing Coordinator: Priscilla Abreu
Marketing Manager: Juli Bliss

Cover Design: Minko Dimov

Library of Congress Catalog Card Number: 98-72034

ISBN: 0-395-89351-8

123456789-WOC-02 01 00 99 98

Brief Contents

End-of-Part Video Cases

Contents

6   The Cultural and Multicultural Environment   166

Planning and Decision Making   196

7   Basic Elements of Planning and Decision Making   198

8 Managing Strategy and Strategic Planning   230

Preface

Since the publication of its first edition in 1984, well over half a million students have used *Management* in preparation for their careers in business. *Management* continues to be used in hundreds of universities, graduate programs, community colleges, and management development programs throughout the world. Indeed, the last edition of the book was used in over forty countries and translated into several foreign languages.

In this edition, I have strived to retain all the elements that have contributed to the book's success in the past while also taking a clear look toward the future—the future of business, of management, and of textbooks. Writing a survey book poses a number of challenges. First, because it is a survey, it has to be comprehensive. Second, it has to be accurate and objective. Third, because management is a real activity, the book has to be relevant. Fourth, it has to be timely and up-to-date. And fifth, it needs to be as interesting and as engaging as possible.

Users of previous editions assert that I have done an effective job in meeting these goals. I am convinced that this edition achieves these goals even more effectively. Previous users of the book will be pleased that I retained the essential ingredients while adding a variety of new elements and perspectives. People new to this edition will be drawn to the solid foundations of management theory and practice balanced with new and exciting material.

■ Improvements in the Sixth Edition

The sixth edition of *Management* is a significant revision of the earlier work. Rather than simply add the "hot topics" of the moment, I continue to thoroughly revise this book with the long-term view in mind. There is a newly created chapter on multiculturalism; significant revisions of other key chapters; an increased emphasis on quality, ethics, global management, and information technology; and an integrated organization of chapters. These changes reflect what I believe and reviewers have confirmed students will need to know as they enter a brand new world of management. Several new pedagogical features, such as Management Implications sections, video exercises, and skill development exercises, will also prove to be invaluable.

Integrated Coverage

Many books (including early editions of this one) set new and emerging topics off from the rest of the text by creating a separate section at the end of the book called "Emerging Trends," "Special Challenges," or something similar. Unfortunately, by setting the material apart this way, it often tends to be ignored or receive low-priority treatment. In the previous edition I eliminated this separate section. Simply put, I decided that if this material was really worth having in the book to begin with, it needed to be fully integrated with the core material. Thus, all material has been integrated in order to provide more uniform and integrated coverage of the entire field of management. This change also helped streamline the book's overall organization by moving from seven to six major parts. Because reviewers and students responded so favorably to this approach, it has been continued in the sixth edition. Further, more cross-referencing strengthens the integrated coverage throughout the text.

Improved Chapter Organization

This integrated approach also resulted in an improved chapter organization. In this edition, a bit of fine-tuning has improved things even more. For example, the discussion of corporate culture previously found in Chapter 3 and workforce diversity found in Chapter 14 have been combined into a new Chapter 6 entitled "The Cultural and Multicultural Environment." By moving this material into a single chapter and placing it in Part II, "The Environmental Context of Management," the complete discussion of the environment of management is now integrated into a single section.

New Material for a Brand New World of Management

A variety of topics are new to this edition, and coverage of other areas has been increased. Highlights are noted below:

Chapter 1: **Managing and the Manager's Job** An expanded managerial skills framework incorporates technical, interpersonal, conceptual, diagnostic, communication, decision-making, and time management skills.

Chapter 2: **Traditional and Contemporary Issues and Challenges** An expanded discussion of contemporary applied perspectives introduces the work of Senge, Covey, Peters, Porter, Hammer, and Adams. A revamped section on contemporary management challenges introduces trends in downsizing, diversity, demography, change, technology, alternative models of organization, globalization, ethics and social responsibility, quality, and the service economy.

Chapter 3: **The Environment of Organizations and Managers** A new section on the physical work environment is discussed as part of the organization's internal environment. A new section provides examples of effective organizations and illustrates that different criteria of effectiveness result in different classifications.

Chapter 4: **The Ethical and Social Environment** The section on individual ethics has been streamlined. There is new coverage of triggers for unethical behavior, and the previous discussion of organizational constituents has been re-framed to reflect contemporary models of organizational stakeholders. New terminology is used to describe different approaches to social responsibility.

Chapter 5: The Global Environment The previous discussion of developing economies has been revised and recast to focus on high potential/high growth economies, while a new section has been added describing Hofstede's framework of cultural differences.

Chapter 6: The Cultural and Multicultural Environment This newly created chapter includes an introductory section presenting an explanation of culture and providing a rationale for its inclusion as a major topic.

Chapter 8: Managing Strategy and Strategic Planning This chapter includes new coverage of deliberate and emergent strategy.

Chapter 10: Managing Entrepreneurship and New Venture Formation This chapter provides new coverage of entrepreneurship and international management. Coverage of intrapreneurship has been removed and placed in a later chapter.

Chapter 12: Managing Organization Design This chapter includes new coverage of the team organization, the virtual organization, and the learning organization.

Chapter 13: Managing Organization Change and Innovation The coverage of models of change and reengineering has been streamlined and revised. Coverage of intrapreneurship has been moved to this chapter.

Chapter 14: Managing Human Resources in Organizations This chapter includes revamped coverage of change and human resource management as well as new coverage of ADA.

Chapter 15: Basic Elements of Individual Behavior in Organizations This chapter contains new coverage of the "big five" model of personality, affect and mood in organizations, and individual creativity in organizations.

Chapter 16: Managing Employee Motivation and Performance This chapter includes new coverage of the goal-setting theory of motivation, employee empowerment and participation, and new forms of working arrangements.

Chapter 17: Managing Leadership and Influence Processes This chapter contains new coverage of impression management.

Chapter 18: Managing Interpersonal Relations and Communication The coverage of communication in teams has been revised and reframed, and coverage of electronic communication has been integrated.

Chapter 20: Basic Elements of Control The discussion of budgets and financial control has been streamlined to achieve better clarity.

Chapter 21: Managing for Total Quality in Organizations There is now a clearer integration between quality, productivity, and operations in this chapter.

Chapter 22: Managing Information and Information Technology This chapter includes new and expanded coverage of the Internet and corporate intranets.

In addition to these content changes and additions, all in-text examples have been carefully reviewed and most have been updated or replaced.

■ Features of the Book

Basic Themes

Several key themes are prominent in this edition of *Management*. One is the global character of the field of management. Examples and cases throughout the book reinforce this. Another timely theme is quality. Although we cover quality and quality-related material in detail in Chapter 21, quality is also woven into the discussion of several related topics throughout the book. Still another theme is the balance of theory and practice. Managers need to have a sound basis for their decisions, but the theories that provide that basis must be grounded in reality. Throughout the book I explain the theoretical frameworks that guide managerial activities, and then I provide illustrations and examples of how and when those theories do and do not work. A fourth theme is that management is a generic activity not confined to large businesses. I use examples and discuss management in both small and large businesses as well as in not-for-profit organizations.

A Pedagogical System That Works

The pedagogical elements built into *Management*, Sixth Edition, are effective learning and teaching aids for students and instructors.

- *Learning objectives and a chapter outline* serve to preview key themes at the start of every chapter. *Key terms* and concepts are highlighted in boldface type, and many are defined in the margin next to where they are discussed. Effective *figures*, *tables*, and *photographs* help bring the material to life.

- A new feature in this edition is called *Management Implications*. Each major section in every chapter concludes with a highlighted paragraph that clearly and succinctly reminds the reader of the specific application value of the preceding discussion.

- Three kinds of questions are found at the end of every chapter, designed to test different levels of student understanding. *Questions for Review* ask students to recall specific information; *Questions for Analysis* ask students to integrate and synthesize material; and *Questions for Application* ask students to apply what they've learned to their own experiences.

- Video cases and exercises conclude each part in the book. These video segments explore various aspects of the management process as they relate to the particular section where they are presented. The video exercises challenge students to think critically about the issues raised in the videos, and they provide numerous points of departure for lively class discussions or homework assignments. In addition, a popular video follow-up section provides a listing of recent movies that also illustrate the concepts presented and challenges students to think of other examples.

■ Each chapter also concludes with three useful skill development exercises that have been based on the managerial skills framework developed in Chapter 1. Students are able to measure their technical, interpersonal, conceptual, or diagnostic skills within various management situations and learn how they can work to improve those skills in the future.

Applications That Keep Students Engaged

To fully appreciate the role and scope of management in contemporary society, it is important to see examples and illustrations of how concepts apply in the real world. I rely heavily on fully researched examples to illustrate real-world applications. They vary in length, and all were carefully reviewed for their timeliness. To give the broadest view possible, I vary examples of traditional management roles with nontraditional roles; profit-seeking businesses with nonprofits; large corporations with small businesses; manufacturers with services; and international examples with U.S. examples. Other applications include:

■ *Opening incidents at the beginning of every chapter.* These brief vignettes draw the student into the chapter with a real-world scenario that introduces a particular management theme. Most opening incidents were revised for this edition.

■ Each chapter also includes two or three boxed inserts. These boxes are intended to briefly depart from the flow of the chapter to highlight or extend especially interesting or emerging points and issues. Altogether there are five different featured boxes represented throughout the text:

- "Management InfoTech" (new technology and its role in management)

- "Working with Diversity" (the role of diversity in organizations)

- "Today's Management Issues" (current controversies, challenges, and dilemmas facing managers)

- "The World of Management" (global issues in management)

- "The Quality Challenge" (the increasing importance of quality)

■ *End-of-chapter cases.* Each chapter also concludes with a detailed case study. Virtually all the cases in the sixth edition are new and have been especially written for this book.

An Effective Teaching and Learning Package

■ *Student and Instructor Web Sites.* With the sixth edition, I am delighted to introduce our new student and instructor web sites, which provide additional information, guidance, and activities that will help enhance the concepts presented in the text.

The student site includes term paper guidelines, job and career information, interactive personal self-assessments, Internet exercises with hyperlinks related to each chapter, interactive chapter quizzes, and links to companies and chapter-related resources that expand the concepts and examples in the text.

The instructor site provides lecture notes, PowerPoint slides, case notes, comments on the Internet exercises, and a downloadable PC Study (our computerized Study Guide) that can be saved and distributed to students on disk. An online Instructor's Resource Manual is also provided for instructors adopting the *Exercises in Management* supplement. In addition, special material on Production and Operations Management is included for those instructors who would like to explore this area in more depth.

- *Annotated Instructor's Manual.* Available in loose-leaf format, the *AIM* combines the elements of an Instructor's Resource Manual and an Instructor's Annotated Edition to provide the instructor with a complete teaching tool. Every page of the AIM contains three elements: (1) a reduced version of the corresponding page from the student textbook, (2) a detailed lecture outline that corresponds to the material on that page, and (3) a series of marginal annotations that help make class presentations easier to prepare and provide more opportunity for enrichment experiences for students. On appropriate pages, answers to end-of-chapter and case questions are included in the margin. The *AIM* also has ample space for the instructor's personal notes and materials. I have prepared all material in the *AIM* myself in order to ensure consistency with the main text.

- *Power Presentation Manager.* This CD-ROM will provide instructors with a number of tools that can be used to create attractive, lively, and informative classroom presentations. Instructors will be able to easily build classroom lecture presentations by choosing appropriate line art, PowerPoint slides, pieces from the overhead transparency program, and selected video clips as part of a "script." In addition, instructors may create completely original presentation slides or copy and edit text from the lecture outline files provided.

- *Test Bank.* Carefully revised and expanded to well over 4,000 test items, the *Test Bank* includes true/false, multiple-choice, completion, matching, and essay questions. Questions have been assigned a level of difficulty and are labeled according to whether they test knowledge, understanding, or application.

- *Computerized Test Bank.* This electronic version of the printed *Test Bank* allows instructors to edit or add questions, and select questions or generate randomly selected tests. The program also includes the On-Line Testing System described below.

- *On-Line Testing and Grade Book.* This feature of the *Computerized Test Bank* allows instructors to administer tests via a network system, modem, or personal computer, and includes a grading function that lets them set up a new class, record grades from tests or assignments, and analyze grades and produce class and individual statistics.

- *Color Transparencies.* 130 full-color transparencies illustrate every major topic in the text. The package consists of several key figures from the book as well as new materials that can be used to enrich classroom discussions. Four types of transparencies are included. *Chapter Text* transparencies reproduce key chapter figures. *Chapter Enrichment* transparencies provide images not in the text that will enhance chapter material. *Text Transition* transparencies introduce material in each of the six parts. *Supplemental Resource* transparencies provide general information that can be used when and as the instructor chooses.

- *Video Package.* Six professionally developed videos have been integrated with the book to correspond to material at the end of each part of the sixth edition. These videos explore various aspects of the management process, including the various levels and functions of managers, the importance of organizational culture and the differences in culture between different organizations, the global environment as a framework for growth and expansion, the complexities of the organizing function, the crucial role of motivation in the leading process, and the importance of information and information management in effective control.

- *Study Guide* (Joe G. Thomas, Middle Tennessee State University). The *Study Guide* has been updated to optimize student comprehension of definitions, concepts, and relationships presented in the text. Each chapter contains an expanded chapter outline to facilitate note taking, multiple-choice and true/false questions, and targeted questions that ask students to integrate material from lectures and the text. Annotated answers appear at the end of the Study Guide.

- *PC Study.* This is an electronic version of the printed *Study Guide* that can be downloaded from the Instructor's Web Site onto a disk. This menu-driven, user-friendly program supports a mouse, and includes a help screen containing complete documentation. It allows students to choose questions in the order given or in random order, and it contains a timer that indicates how long it takes them to complete a test. As students work through the questions, the program tells students why incorrect answers are wrong. At the end of the test, students can print their score, the questions, and the answers. A screen indicates the percentage and number of questions answered correctly, and the number of attempts that were made to answer each question correctly. Students can also work on and print out the expanded chapter outlines.

- *Exercises in Management* (Gene E. Burton, California State University—Fresno). This student manual provides experiential exercises for every chapter. The overall purpose of each exercise is stated, along with the time required for each step, the materials needed, the procedure to be followed, and questions for discussion.

I would also like to invite your feedback on this book. If you have any questions, suggestions, or issues to discuss, please feel free to contact me. The most efficient way to reach me is through e-mail. My address is <u>rgriffin@tamu.edu</u>.

R. W. G.

Acknowledgments

I am frequently asked by my colleagues why I write textbooks, and my answer is always "because I enjoy it." I've never enjoyed writing a book more than this one. For me, writing a textbook is a challenging and stimulating activity that brings with it a variety of rewards. My greatest reward continues to be the feedback I get from students and instructors about how much they like this book.

I owe an enormous debt to many different people for helping me create *Management*. My colleagues at Texas A&M have helped create a wonderful academic climate. The rich and varied culture at Texas A&M makes it a pleasure to go to the office every day. My staff assistant, Phyllis Washburn, deserves special recognition for putting up with me and making me look good.

The fine team of professionals at Houghton Mifflin has also been instrumental in the success of this book. Kathy Hunter, Susan Kahn, Joanne Dauksewicz, and Liz Napolitano each had a major role in the development and creation of this edition of *Management*. Jennifer Speer, my former sponsoring editor, was also instrumental in planning this edition. Marcy Kagan and June Waldman also played key roles in the production of this edition.

Many reviewers have played a critical role in the evolution of this project. They reviewed my work with a critical eye and in detail. I would like to tip my hat to the following reviewers, whose imprint can be found throughout this text:

Ramon J. Aldag
University of Wisconsin

Dr. Raymond E. Alie
Western Michigan University

William P. Anthony
Florida State University

Jeanne Aurelio
Stonehill College

Jay B. Barney
Ohio State University

Richard Bartlett
Muskigum Area Technical College

John D. Bigelow
Boise State University

Allen Bluedorn
University of Missouri

Marv Borglett
University of Maryland

Gunther S. Boroschek
University of Massachusetts—Harbor Campus

Joseph Cantrell
DeAnza College

George R. Carnahan
Northern Michigan University

Ron Cheek
University of New Orleans

Thomas G. Christoph
Clemson University

Charles W. Cole
University of Oregon

Elizabeth Cooper
University of Rhode Island

Carol Cumber
South Dakota State University

Joan Dahl
California State University, Northridge

Carol Danehower
University of Memphis

Satish Deshpande
Western Michigan University

Gregory G. Dess
University of Kentucky

Gary N. Dicer
University of Tennessee

Nicholas Dietz
State University of New York—Farmingdale

Thomas J. Dougherty
University of Missouri

Shad Dowlatshahi
University of Wisconsin—Platteville

John Drexler, Jr.
Oregon State University

Stan Elsea
Kansas State University

Douglas A. Elvers
University of South Carolina

Dan Farrell
Western Michigan University

Charles Flaherty
University of Minnesota

Ari Ginsberg
*New York University
Graduate School of Business*

Norma N. Givens
Fort Valley State University

Carl Gooding
Georgia Southern College

George J. Gore
University of Cincinnati

Stanley D. Guzell, Jr.
Youngstown State University

John Hall
University of Florida

Mark A. Hammer
Washington State University

Barry Hand
Indiana State University

Paul Harmon
University of Utah

John Hughes
Texas Tech University

J. G. Hunt
Texas Tech University

John H. Jackson
University of Wyoming

Neil W. Jacobs
University of Denver

Arthur G. Jago
University of Missouri

Madge Jenkins
Lima Technical College

Gopol Joshi
Central Missouri State University

Norman F. Kallaus
University of Iowa

Ben L. Kedia
University of Memphis

Thomas L. Keon
University of Central Florida

Charles C. Kitzmiller
Indian River Community College

William R. LaFollete
Ball State University

Kenneth Lawrence
New Jersey Institute of Technology

Clayton G. Lifto
Kirkwood Community College

John E. Mack
Salem State University

Myrna P. Mandell, Ph.D.
California State University, Northridge

Patricia M. Manninen
North Shore Community College

Thomas Martin
University of Nebraska—Omaha

Barbara J. Marting
University of Southern Indiana

Wayne A. Meinhart
Oklahoma State University

Melvin McKnight
Northern Arizona University

Aratchige Molligoda
Drexel University

Linda L. Neider
University of Miami

Mary Lippitt Nichols
University of Minnesota

Winston Oberg
Michigan State University

Michael Olivette
Syracuse University

Eugene Owens
Western Washington University

Sheila Pechinski
University of Maine

Monique Pelletier
San Francisco State University

E. Leroy Plumlee
Western Washington University

Ray Polchow
Muskigum Area Technical College

Paul Preston
University of Texas—San Antonio

John M. Purcell
State University of New York—Farmingdale

James C. Quick
University of Texas—Arlington

Ralph Roberts
University of West Florida

Nick Sarantakas
Austin Community College

Gene Schneider
Austin Community College

H. Schollhammer
University of California—Los Angeles

Harvey Shore
University of Connecticut

Marc Siegall
California State University

Nicholas Siropolis
Cuyahoga Community College

Michael J. Stahl
University of Tennessee

Charlotte D. Sutton
Auburn University

Robert L. Taylor
University of Louisville

Mary Thibodeaux
University of North Texas

Joe Thomas
Middle Tennessee State University

Robert D. Van Auken
University of Oklahoma

Fred Williams
University of North Texas

James Wilson
University of Texas—Pan American

Carl P. Zeithaml
University of Virginia

I would also like to make a few personal acknowledgments. The fine work of Andrew Lloyd Webber, Elton John, Phil Collins, Eric Clapton, Johnny Rivers, and the Nylons helped me make it through many late evenings and early mornings of work on the manuscript that became the book you hold in your hands. And Stephen King, Tom Clancy, James Lee Burke, Peter Straub, and Carl Barks provided me with a respite from my writings with their own.

Finally, there is the most important acknowledgment of all—my feelings for and gratitude to my family. My wife, Glenda, and our children, Dustin and Ashley, are the foundation of my professional and personal life. They help me keep work and play in perspective and give meaning to everything I do. It is with all my love that I dedicate this book to them.

R. W. G.

Management

PART ONE

An Introduction to Management

1

Managing and the Manager's Job

OBJECTIVES

After studying this chapter, you should be able to:

- Describe the nature of management, define management and managers, and characterize their importance to organizations.
- Identify and briefly explain the four basic management functions in organizations.
- Describe the kinds of managers found at different levels and in different areas of the organization.
- Identify the basic managerial roles that managers may play and the skills they need to be successful.
- Discuss the science and art of management and describe how people become managers.
- Summarize the scope of management in organizations.

It once seemed as if there might one day be a McDonald's restaurant on every street corner. But although there are certainly a large number of the venerable hamburger restaurants around today, Starbucks Corporation has, at least for the time being, replaced McDonald's as the highest-profile and fastest-growing food-and-beverage company in the United States. Starbucks was started in Seattle in 1971 by three coffee aficionados. Their primary business at the time was buying premium coffee beans, roasting them, and then selling the coffee by the pound. The business performed modestly well and soon grew to nine stores, all in the Seattle area. The three partners sold Starbucks to a former employee, Howard Schultz, in 1987. Schultz promptly reoriented the business away from bulk coffee mail-order sales and emphasized retail coffee sales through the firm's coffee bars. Today, Starbucks is not only the largest coffee importer and roaster of specialty beans but also the largest specialty coffee bean retailer in the United States.

What is the key to the phenomenal growth and success of the Starbucks chain? One important ingredient is its well-conceived and well-implemented strategy. Starbucks is on an amazing growth pace, opening a new coffee shop somewhere almost every day. But this growth is planned and coordinated at each step through careful site selection. And through its astute promotional campaigns and commitment to quality, the firm has elevated the coffee-drinking taste of millions of Americans and fueled a significant increase in demand.

Starbucks has also created an organization that promotes growth and success. As long as they follow the firm's basic principles, managers at each store have considerable autonomy over how they run things. Starbucks also uses a state-of-the-art communication network to keep in contact with its employees.

"One reason a lot of youths don't find corporate America so attractive is because of the IBM image: I'll become a blue suit. Starbucks makes you feel like a partner."

Karen Hunsaker, Starbucks employee, quoted in Fortune, December 9, 1996, p. 196.

Another ingredient of Starbucks' success is its relationship with its employees. The firm hires young people and starts them at hourly wages somewhat higher than those of most entry-level food-services jobs. The company also offers health insurance to all of its employees, including part-timers, and has a lucrative stock-option plan for everyone in the firm.

Yet another key to Starbucks' success is its emphasis on quality control. For example, milk must be warmed to a narrow range of 150 to 170 degrees, and espresso shots must be pulled within twenty-three seconds or else discarded. And no coffee is allowed to sit on a hot plate for more than twenty minutes. Schultz also refuses to franchise, fearing a loss of control and a potential deterioration of quality.

Starbucks remains on the alert for new business opportunities. In 1996, for example, the firm opened its first two coffee shops in Japan and another in Singapore, and most observers suggest that there is a world of opportunity awaiting Starbucks in foreign markets. Another way the company can grow is through brand extension with other companies. For instance, the firm has collaborated with Dreyer's to distribute Starbucks coffee ice cream to grocery freezers across the country. Starbucks has also collaborated with Capital Records on two Starbucks jazz CDs. And Redhook Brewery uses Starbucks coffee extract in its double black stout beer. All things considered, then, Starbucks' future looks so bright that its employees may need to wear the sunshades the firm might soon begin to sell![1]

oward Schultz is clearly a manager. So, too, are Philip Knight (chief executive officer [CEO] of Nike), Jill Barad (CEO of Mattel), Shinroku Morohashi (president of Mitsubishi Corporation), Sir David Wilson (director of the British Museum), Debbie Fields (president of Mrs. Fields Inc. cookie stores), Rick Pitino (president of the Boston Celtics), Bill Clinton (president of the United States), John Paul II (pope of the Roman Catholic Church), and Mark Ferguson (owner of Contemporary Landscape in Bryan, Texas). As diverse as they and their organizations are, these managers all confront many of the same challenges, they strive to achieve many of the same goals, and they apply many of the same concepts of effective management in their work.

organization A group of people working together in a structured and coordinated fashion to achieve a set of goals

For better or worse, our society is strongly influenced by managers and their organizations. Most people in the United States are born in a hospital (an organization), educated by public or private schools (all organizations), and buy virtually all their consumable products and services from businesses (organizations). And much of our behavior is influenced by various government agencies (also organizations). We define an **organization** as a group of people working together in a structured and coordinated fashion to achieve a set of goals. The goals may include such things as profit (Starbucks Corporation), the discovery of knowledge (Florida State University), national defense (the U.S. Army), the coordination of various local charities (United Way of America), or social satisfaction (a sorority). Because they play such a major role in our lives, understanding how organizations operate and how they are managed is important.

This book is about managers and the work they do. In Chapter 1, we examine the general nature of management, its dimensions, and its challenges. The chapter explains the concepts of management and managers, discusses the management process, presents an overview of the book, and identifies various kinds of managers. It also describes the various roles and skills of managers, discusses the nature of managerial work, and examines the scope of management in contemporary organizations. Chapter 2 describes how both the practice and theory of management have evolved. As a unit, then, these first two chapters introduce the field by presenting both contemporary and historical perspectives on management.

An Introduction to Management

Although defining "organization" is relatively simple, the concept of "management" is a bit more elusive. It is perhaps best understood from a resource-based perspective. As we will discuss in greater detail in Chapter 2, all organizations use four basic kinds of resources from their environment: human, financial, physical, and information. Human resources include managerial talent and labor. Financial resources are the capital used by the organization to finance both ongoing and long-term operations. Physical resources include raw materials, office and production facilities, and equipment. Information resources are usable data needed to make effective decisions. Examples of re-

Organization	Human Resources	Financial Resources	Physical Resources	Information Resources
Shell Oil	Drilling platform workers Corporate executives	Profits Stockholder investments	Refineries Office buildings	Sales forecast OPEC proclamations
Iowa State University	Faculty Secretarial staff	Alumni contributions Government grants	Computers Campus facilities	Research reports Government publications
New York City	Police officers Municipal employees	Tax revenue Government grants	Sanitation equipment Municipal buildings	Economic forecasts Crime statistics
Susan's Corner Grocery Store	Grocery clerks Bookkeeper	Profits Owner investment	Building Display shelving	Price lists from suppliers Newspaper ads for competitors

sources used in four very different kinds of organizations are shown in Table 1.1.

Managers are responsible for combining and coordinating these various resources to achieve the organization's goals. A manager at Royal Dutch/Shell Group, for example, uses the talents of executives and drilling platform workers, profits earmarked for reinvestment, existing refineries and office facilities, and sales forecasts to make decisions regarding the amount of oil to be refined and distributed during the next quarter. Similarly, the mayor (manager) of New York City might use police officers, a government grant (perhaps supplemented with surplus tax revenues), existing police stations, and detailed crime statistics to launch a major crime prevention program in the city.

How do these and other managers combine and coordinate the various kinds of resources? They do so by carrying out four basic managerial functions or activities: planning and decision making, organizing, leading, and controlling. Management, then, as illustrated in Figure 1.1, can be defined as follows:

TABLE 1.1
Examples of Resources Used by Organizations

All organizations, regardless of whether they are large or small, profit-seeking or not-for-profit, domestic or multinational, use some combination of human, financial, physical, and information resources to achieve their goals. These resources are generally obtained from the organization's environment.

> **Management** is a set of activities (including planning and decision making, organizing, leading, and controlling) directed at an organization's resources (human, financial, physical, and information) with the aim of achieving organizational goals in an efficient and effective manner.

The last phrase in our definition is especially important because it highlights the basic purpose of management—to ensure that an organization's goals are achieved in an efficient and effective manner. By **efficient**, we mean using resources wisely and in a cost-effective way. For example, a firm like Toyota

efficient Using resources wisely and in a cost-effective way

effective   Making the right decisions and successfully implementing them

Motor Corporation that produces high-quality products at relatively low cost is efficient. By **effective**, we mean making the right decisions and successfully implementing them. Toyota also makes cars with styling and craftsmanship that inspire consumer confidence. A firm could produce black-and-white console televisions very efficiently but still not succeed because black-and-white televisions are no longer popular. A firm that produces products that no one wants is therefore not effective. In general, successful organizations are both efficient and effective.[2]

With this basic understanding of management, defining the term "manager" becomes relatively simple:

> ▪ A **manager** is someone whose primary responsibility is to carry out the management process. In particular, a manager is someone who plans and makes decisions, organizes, leads, and controls human, financial, physical, and information resources.

FIGURE 1.1
Management in Organizations

Basic managerial activities include planning and decision making, organizing, leading, and controlling. Managers engage in these activities to combine human, financial, physical, and information resources efficiently and effectively and to work toward achieving the goals of the organization.

Today's managers face a variety of interesting and challenging situations. The average executive works sixty hours a week, has enormous demands on his or her time, and faces the increased complexities posed by globalization, domestic competition, government regulation, and shareholder pressure. The task is further complicated by rapid change, unexpected disruptions, and both minor and major crises. The manager's job is unpredictable and fraught with challenges, but it is also filled with opportunities to make a difference.[3]

Many of the characteristics that contribute to the complexity and uncertainty of management stem from the environment in which organizations function. For example, as shown in Figure 1.1, all the resources used by organizations to create products and services come from the environment. Thus it is critical that managers understand this environment. Part II of the text discusses

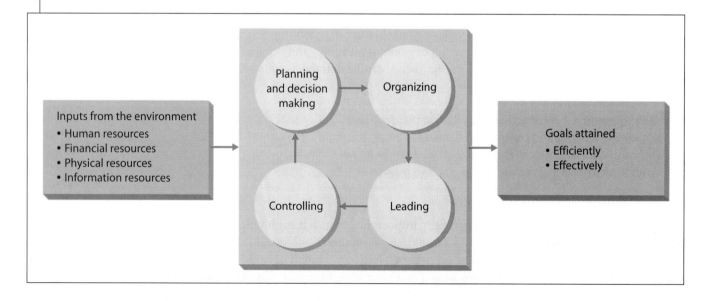

Inputs from the environment
• Human resources
• Financial resources
• Physical resources
• Information resources

Planning and decision making → Organizing → Leading → Controlling →

Goals attained
• Efficiently
• Effectively

Management is a complex, challenging, and exciting process. Jeong Ju Wha, shown here on the right, is a production manager at Samsung Motors. He and other managers at Korea's Samsung Group are creating this new automobile company for the parent organization as part of its strategy for entering new businesses and markets around the world. The new automobile company makes use of a wide array of resources, such as Samsung Group's financial investment, factories and warehouses, aluminum engines, quality standards and measures, and production workers. Their responsibility as managers is to use these resources efficiently and effectively so as to help meet Samsung's goals for the new enterprise.

the environmental context of management in detail. Chapter 3 provides a general overview and discussion of the organization's environment, and Chapters 4 through 6 address specific aspects of the environment more fully. In particular, Chapter 4 discusses the ethical and social context of management. Chapter 5 explores the global context of management. Chapter 6 describes the cultural and multicultural environment of management. After reading these chapters, you will be better prepared to study the essential activities that comprise the management process.

The Management Process

We noted earlier that management involves the four basic functions of planning and decision making, organizing, leading, and controlling. Because these functions represent the framework around which this book is organized, we introduce them here and note where they are discussed more fully. Their basic definitions and interrelationships are shown in Figure 1.2. (Note that Figure 1.2 is an expanded version of the central part of Figure 1.1.)

Recall the details of Starbucks discussed earlier. Howard Schultz has created a clear set of goals that articulate what he wants Starbucks to be. He has set up an effective organization to help make that vision a reality. Schultz also pays close attention to the people who work for Starbucks. And he keeps a close eye on how well the company is performing. Each of these activities represents one of the four basic managerial functions illustrated in the figure—setting goals is part of planning, setting up the organization is part of

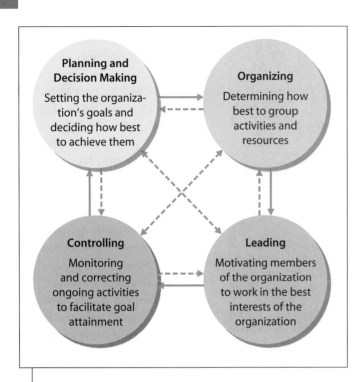

organizing, managing people is part of leading, and monitoring performance is part of control.

It is important to note, however, that the functions of management do not usually occur in a tidy, step-by-step fashion. Managers do not plan on Monday, make decisions on Tuesday, organize on Wednesday, lead on Thursday, and control on Friday. At any given time, as illustrated in the cartoon, a manager is likely to be engaged in several different activities simultaneously. Indeed, from one setting to another, managerial work has as many differences as it has similarities. The similarities that pervade most settings are the phases in the management process. Important differences include the emphasis, sequencing, and implications of each phase.[4] Thus, the solid lines in Figure 1.2 indicate how, in theory, the functions of management are performed. The dotted lines, however, represent the true reality of management. In the sections that follow, we explore each of these activities.

FIGURE 1.2
The Management Process

Management involves four basic activities—planning and decision making, organizing, leading, and controlling. Although there is a basic logic for describing these activities in this sequence (as indicated by the solid arrows), most managers engage in more than one activity at a time and often move back and forth between the activities in unpredictable ways (as shown by the dotted arrows).

planning   Setting an organization's goals and deciding how best to achieve them
decision making   Part of the planning process that involves selecting a course of action from a set of alternatives

■ Planning and Decision Making: Determining Courses of Action

In its simplest form, **planning** means setting an organization's goals and deciding how best to achieve them. **Decision making,** a part of the planning process, involves selecting a course of action from a set of alternatives. Planning and decision making help maintain managerial effectiveness by serving as guides for future activities. For example, managers at Coca-Cola are aggressively pursuing a goal set by the firm's CEO of controlling 50 percent of the U.S. market for carbonated soft drinks by the year 2001.[5] These goals help everyone at Coca-Cola to focus on the need to constantly strive for new market opportunities and to seek every conceivable avenue for growth. Thus, the organization's goals and plans clearly help managers allocate their time and resources.

Four chapters making up Part III of this text are devoted to planning and decision making. Chapter 7 examines the basic elements of planning and decision making, including the role and importance of organizational goals. Chapter 8 looks at strategy and strategic planning, which provide overall direction and focus for the organization. Chapter 9 explores managerial decision making and problem solving in detail. Finally, Chapter 10 addresses planning and decision making as they relate to the management of entrepreneurship and new venture formation, which are increasingly important parts of managerial work.

■ Organizing: Coordinating Activities and Resources

Once a manager has set goals and developed a workable plan, the next management function is to organize the people and other resources necessary to carry out the plan. Specifically, **organizing** involves determining how activities and resources are to be grouped. To help achieve its goal of market share growth, Coca-Cola has established a number of new organizational groups. One group seeks new opportunities for partnering with other businesses in selling soft drinks. Another looks for opportunities on college campuses. Still another concentrates on identifying new and more efficient distribution networks for Coke products.

Organizing is the subject of Part IV. Chapter 11 introduces the basic elements of organizing such as job design, departmentalization, authority relationships, span of control, and line and staff roles. Chapter 12 explains how managers fit these elements and concepts together to form an overall organization design. Organization change and innovation are the focus of Chapter 13. Finally, processes associated with hiring and assigning people to carry out organizational roles are described in Chapter 14.

organizing Grouping activities and resources in a logical fashion

leading The set of processes used to get members of the organization to work together to achieve the goals of the organization

controlling Monitoring organizational progress toward goal attainment

■ Leading: Motivating and Managing People

The third basic managerial function is leading. Some people consider leading to be both the most important and the most challenging of all managerial activities. **Leading** is the set of processes used to get people to work together to advance the interests of the organization. For example, Coca-Cola's CEO constantly encourages the firm's managers to keep pushing for growth. The firm has also established motivational incentive systems for rewarding managers who meet or surpass their own growth goals.

"Do you mind? I happen to be on the phone!"

Leading involves a number of different processes and activities, which are discussed in Part V. The starting point is understanding basic individual and interpersonal processes, which we focus on in Chapter 15. Motivating employees is discussed in Chapter 16, and leadership itself and the leader's efforts to influence others are covered in Chapter 17. Managing interpersonal relations and communication is the subject of Chapter 18. Finally, managing work groups and teams, another important part of leading, is addressed in Chapter 19.

■ Controlling: Monitoring and Evaluating Activities

The final phase of the management process is **controlling,** or monitoring the organization's progress toward its goals. As the organization moves toward its goals, managers must monitor progress to ensure that it is performing so as to arrive at its "destination" at the appointed time. A good analogy is that of a space mission to Mars. NASA does not simply shoot a rocket in the general direction of the planet and then look again in four months to see whether the rocket hit its mark. NASA monitors the spacecraft almost continuously and makes whatever course corrections are needed to keep it on track. Controlling helps ensure the effectiveness and efficiency needed for successful management. When Coca-Cola's growth goal was set in 1995, the firm had a market

Managers are constantly engaged in many different activities. The types and sequences of activities are often difficult to predict from one day to the next, however, and managers often do their work in impromptu settings or on airplanes, in taxis, over meals, or even when walking down the street. The manager shown here, for example, may be helping a colleague develop goals for the next quarter (planning), discussing a proposed company restructuring (organizing), praising a subordinate for outstanding performance (leading), or checking on last month's sales information (controlling). The pace of this work may be stressful for some people, and exhilarating for others.

share of 42 percent and by mid-1997 had bumped its number up to 43 percent—a clear increase but still far from the ultimate goal. Thus, managers have increased their efforts to gain a bigger market share and will continue to monitor their progress as the clock ticks toward 2001.

The control function is examined in Part VI. Chapter 20 explores the basic elements of the control process, including the increasing importance of strategic control. Managing for total quality, an increasingly important concern for all organizations today, is explored in Chapter 21, along with productivity and operations management. Finally, Chapter 22 addresses the management of information and information technology, still other critical areas of organizational control.

MANAGEMENT IMPLICATIONS Managers should thoroughly understand all the basic functions—planning and decision making, organizing, leading, and controlling—that constitute their jobs. Managers should also recognize that although each function is important in its own right, effective managers are skilled in performing every function, must be capable of moving back and forth among the functions as circumstances warrant, and must often juggle multiple functions and activities simultaneously. Managers cannot afford to be effective in or to enjoy performing only some of the functions, since all are important.

Kinds of Managers

Earlier in this chapter we identify as managers people from a variety of organizations. Clearly, there are many kinds of managers. One point of differentiation is among organizations, as those earlier examples imply. Another point occurs within an organization. Figure 1.3 shows how managers within an organization can be differentiated by level and area.

■ Managing at Different Levels of the Organization

levels of management The differentiation of managers into three basic categories—top, middle, and first-line

Managers can be differentiated according to their level in the organization. Although large organizations typically have a number of **levels of management**, the most common view considers three basic levels: top, middle, and first-line managers.

Top Managers Top managers make up the relatively small group of executives who manage the overall organization. Titles found in this group include president, vice president, and CEO. As described more fully in "Working with Diversity," most top managers today are men. However, a cadre of outstanding female executives stands poised to break into the ranks of top managers in a variety of companies in the very near future. Top managers create the organization's goals, overall strategy, and operating policies. They also officially

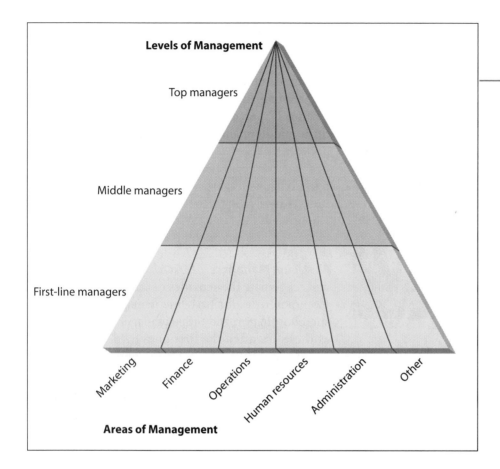

FIGURE 1.3
Kinds of Managers by Level and Area

Organizations generally have three levels of management, represented by top managers, middle managers, and first-line managers. Regardless of level, managers are also usually associated with a specific area within the organization, such as marketing, finance, operations, human resources, or administration, or some other area.

represent the organization to the external environment by meeting with government officials, executives of other organizations, and so forth.

Howard Schultz at Starbucks is a top manager, as is Deidra Wager, the firm's senior vice president for retail operations. The job of a top manager is likely to be complex and varied. Top managers make decisions about such activities as acquiring other companies, investing in research and development, entering or abandoning various markets, and building new plants and office facilities. These people often work long hours and spend much of their time in meetings or on the telephone.[6] In most cases, top managers are also very well paid. In fact, the elite top managers of very large firms sometimes make several million dollars a year in salary and stock.[7]

Middle Managers Middle management is the largest group of managers in most organizations. Common middle-management titles include plant manager, operations manager, and division head. Middle managers are primarily responsible for implementing the policies and plans developed by top managers and for supervising and coordinating the activities of lower-level managers.[8] Plant managers, for example, handle inventory management, quality control, equipment failures, and minor union problems. They also coordinate the work of supervisors within the plant. Jason Hernandez, a regional manager at Starbucks responsible for the firm's operations in three eastern states, is a middle manager.

Organizations need many different kinds of managers. Steven Jobs is the top manager at Apple Computer. He recently returned to the firm he founded back in 1976 in an effort to save it from bankruptcy. Jobs is very effective at inspiring other managers and motivating them to work harder. His charisma also helps inspire confidence in customers, investors, and other employees. While Apple Computer may have a difficult time returning to its earlier prominence in the industry, with Jobs as the top manager many observers believe that the firm at least has a fighting chance.

areas of management   The differentiation of managers according to the area in which they work—for example, marketing, financial, operating, human resource, administration

In recent years many organizations have thinned the ranks of middle managers to lower costs and eliminate excess bureaucracy. Even though middle managers represent only around 5 percent of an average company's workforce, they accounted for around 17 percent of total layoffs in recent years.[9] Still, middle managers are necessary to bridge the upper and lower levels of the organization and to implement the strategies developed at the top. Although many organizations have found that they can indeed survive with fewer middle managers, those who remain play an even more important role in determining how successful the organization will be.[10]

First-Line Managers   First-line managers supervise and coordinate the activities of operating employees. Common titles for first-line managers are supervisor, coordinator, and office manager. Positions such as these are often the first ones held by employees who enter management from the ranks of operating personnel. Wayne Maxwell and Jenny Wagner, managers of Starbucks coffee shops in Texas, are first-line managers. They oversee the day-to-day operations of their respective stores, hire operating employees to staff them, and handle other routine administrative duties that the parent corporation requires. In contrast to top and middle managers, first-line managers typically spend a large proportion of their time supervising the work of subordinates.[11]

■ Managing in Different Areas of the Organization

Regardless of their level, managers may work in various areas within an organization. In any given firm, for example, **areas of management** may include marketing, finance, operations, human resources, administration, and other areas.

Marketing Managers   Marketing managers work in areas related to the marketing function—getting consumers and clients to buy the organization's products or services (be they Ford automobiles, *Newsweek* magazines, Associated Press news reports, flights on Southwest Airlines, or cups of latte at Starbucks). These areas include new product development, promotion, and distribution. Given the importance of marketing for virtually all organizations, developing good managers in this area can be critical. Jill Barad, CEO of Mattel, started her career as a marketing manager.

Financial Managers   Financial managers deal primarily with an organization's financial resources. They are responsible for activities such as accounting, cash management, and investments. In some businesses, such as banking and insurance, financial managers are found in especially large numbers. Duane L. Burnham, CEO of Abbott Laboratories, spent much of his career as a financial manager.

WORKING WITH DIVERSITY

Shattering the Glass Ceiling?

The executive ranks of America's largest companies have always been dominated by men. So scarce are female top executives that the recent ascension of Jill Barad to the top spot at Mattel—making her the first woman to be promoted to such a position at a major company—made national headlines. This phenomenon has long been called the glass ceiling, an unseen boundary that apparently keeps women from reaching the top.

But there are clear signs that the glass ceiling is cracking, at least in some companies. A cadre of talented, skilled, and motivated women stands ready to move ever higher up the corporate ladder and is certain to join Jill Barad among the ranks of corporate leaders in the very near future. At Pitney Bowes, for example, five of the top eleven managers are women. Motorola has thirty-eight female vice presidents. And 44 percent of the top management positions at Avon are held by women.

Several women executives, in particular, are poised to compete for the top spot at their respective companies. Gail McGovern was recently named head of AT&T's $26 billion consumer business, perhaps the second most important job in the company. Lois Juliber runs Colgate-Palmolive's North American and European operations. Irene Rosenfeld is a top vice president at Kraft Foods. Ellen Marram, executive vice president at Seagram, runs the company's $2 billion nonalcoholic beverage business.

On their own, the numbers are still sobering: women hold only 10 percent of the top management jobs in the largest five hundred companies in the United States. But the middle ranks are more balanced. And as enlightened firms continue to seek the best people—not men, but people—to assume key leadership positions, more and more women are certain to break through the glass ceiling. Perhaps one day it will be only a dim memory.

"Women are in the pipeline in droves."

James E. Preston, CEO, Avon*

"Progress is being made, but it's painfully slow."

Rene Redwood, U.S. Labor Department official and former director of the Federal Glass Ceiling Commission **

References: *"Watershed Generation of Women Executives Is Rising to the Top,"* Wall Street Journal, *February 10, 1997, pp. A1, A6 (**quote on p. A6); and "Breaking Through,"* Business Week, *February 17, 1997, pp. 64–70 (*quote on p. 64).*

Operations Managers   Operations managers are concerned with creating and managing the systems that create an organization's products and services. Typical responsibilities of operations managers include production control, inventory control, quality control, plant layout, and site selection. Gordon Bethune, CEO of Continental Airlines, started his career as an operations manager.

Human Resource Managers   Human resource managers are responsible for hiring and developing employees. They are typically involved in human resource planning, recruiting and selecting employees, training and development, designing compensation and benefit systems, formulating performance appraisal systems, and discharging low-performing and problem employees. Mike Bowlin, CEO of ARCO Chemical Company, was in human resource management early in his career.

Administrative Managers   Administrative, or general, managers are not associated with any particular management specialty. Probably the best example of an administrative management position is that of a hospital or clinic administrator. Administrative managers tend to be generalists; they have some basic familiarity with all functional areas of management, rather than specialized training in any one area. Donald Graham, CEO of the Washington Post Co., spent much of his career as an administrative manager.

Other Kinds of Managers   Many organizations have specialized management positions in addition to those already described. Public relations managers, for example, deal with the public and media for firms like Philip Morris Companies, Inc., and Dow Chemical Co. to protect and enhance the image of the organization. Research and development (R&D) managers coordinate the activities of scientists and engineers working on scientific projects in organizations such as Monsanto Company, NASA, and Merck & Co., Inc. At The Prudential Insurance Co. of America, internal consultants provide specialized expert advice to operating managers. In other organizations, such as Eli Lilly and Rockwell International Corp., specialized managers coordinate many areas of international management. The number, nature, and importance of these specialized managers vary tremendously from one organization to another. As contemporary organizations continue to grow in complexity and size, the number and importance of such managers are also likely to increase.

MANAGEMENT IMPLICATIONS   Managers can be found at all levels and in all areas of an organization. A career path up the organizational ladder might be primarily within a single area or might span several areas. Thus managers should try to understand where their current position fits into the organization and what path they may want to pursue to advance their career goals. Cutbacks in the ranks of middle managers also mean that lower-level managers in major corporations may have to wait longer for a promotion, since there are fewer jobs at the higher levels for them to enter.[12]

Basic Managerial Roles and Skills

Regardless of their level or area within an organization, all managers must play certain roles and exhibit certain skills if they are to be successful. The concept of a *role*, in this sense, is similar to the role an actor plays in a theatrical production. A person does certain things, meets certain needs in the organization, and has certain responsibilities. In the sections that follow, we first highlight the basic roles managers play and then discuss the skills they need to be effective.

Category	Role	Sample Activities
Interpersonal	Figurehead	Attending ribbon-cutting ceremony for new plant
	Leader	Encouraging employees to improve productivity
	Liaison	Coordinating activities of two project groups
Informational	Monitor	Scanning industry reports to stay abreast of developments
	Disseminator	Sending memos outlining new organizational initiatives
	Spokesperson	Making a speech to discuss growth plans
Decisional	Entrepreneur	Developing new ideas for innovation
	Disturbance handler	Resolving conflict between two subordinates
	Resource allocator	Reviewing and revising budget requests
	Negotiator	Reaching agreement with a key supplier or labor union

TABLE 1.2
Ten Basic Managerial Roles

Research by Henry Mintzberg suggests that managers play ten basic managerial roles.

■ Managerial Roles

Henry Mintzberg offers a number of interesting insights into the nature of managerial roles.[13] He closely observed the day-to-day activities of a group of CEOs by literally following them around and taking notes on what they did. From his observations, Mintzberg concluded that managers play ten different roles, as summarized in Table 1.2, and that these roles fall into three basic categories: interpersonal, informational, and decisional.

Interpersonal Roles   Three **interpersonal roles** are inherent in the manager's job. First, the manager is often asked to serve as a *figurehead*—taking visitors to dinner, attending ribboncutting ceremonies, and the like. These activities are typically more ceremonial and symbolic than substantive. Second, the manager is also asked to serve as a leader—hiring, training, and motivating employees. A manager who formally or informally shows subordinates how to do things and how to perform under pressure is leading. Finally, managers can have a *liaison* role. This role often involves serving as a coordinator or link between people, groups, or organizations. For example, companies in the computer industry may use liaisons to keep other companies informed about their plans. This type of communication enables Microsoft, for example, to create software for interfacing with new Hewlett-Packard printers while those printers are being developed. At the same time, managers at Hewlett-Packard can incorporate new Microsoft features into the printers it introduces.

interpersonal roles   The roles of figurehead, leader, and liaison, which involve dealing with other people

Informational Roles   The three **informational roles** flow naturally from the interpersonal roles just discussed. The process of carrying out these roles places the manager at a strategic point to gather and disseminate information. The first informational role is that of *monitor*, one who actively seeks informa-

informational roles   The roles of monitor, disseminator, and spokesperson, which involve the processing of information

tion that may be of value. The manager questions subordinates, is receptive to unsolicited information, and attempts to be as well informed as possible. The manager is also a *disseminator* of information, transmitting relevant information back to others in the workplace. When the roles of monitor and disseminator are viewed together, the manager emerges as a vital link in the organization's chain of communication. The third informational role focuses on external communication. The *spokesperson* formally relays information to people outside the unit or outside the organization. For example, a plant manager at Union Carbide Corp. may transmit information to top-level managers so that they will be better informed about the plant's activities. The manager may also represent the organization before a chamber of commerce or consumer group. Although the roles of spokesperson and figurehead are similar, there is one basic difference between them. When a manager acts as a figurehead, the manager's presence as a symbol of the organization is what is of interest. In the spokesperson role, however, the manager carries information and communicates it to others in a formal sense.

decisional roles The roles of entrepreneur, disturbance handler, resource allocator, and negotiator, which primarily relate to making decisions

Decisional Roles The manager's informational roles typically lead to the **decisional roles.** The information that the manager acquires as a result of performing the informational roles has a major bearing on important decisions that he or she makes. Mintzberg identified four decisional roles. First, the manager has the role of *entrepreneur,* the voluntary initiator of change. A manager at 3M Company developed the idea for Post-it Notes but had to "sell" it to other skeptical managers inside the company. A second decisional role is initiated not by the manager, but by some other individual or group. The manager responds to his or her role as *disturbance handler* by handling such problems as strikes, copyright infringements, or problems in public relations or corporate image.

The third decisional role is that of *resource allocator.* As resource allocator, the manager decides how to distribute resources and with whom he or she will work most closely. For example, a manager typically allocates the funds in the unit's operating budget among the unit's members and projects. A fourth decisional role is that of *negotiator.* In this role the manager enters negotiations with other groups or organizations as a representative of the company. For example, managers may negotiate a union contract, an agreement with a consultant, or a long-term relationship with a supplier. Negotiations may also be internal to the organization. The manager may, for instance, mediate a dispute between two subordinates or negotiate with another department for additional support.

■ Managerial Skills

In addition to fulfilling numerous roles, managers need a number of specific skills if they are to succeed. The most fundamental management skills are technical, interpersonal, conceptual, diagnostic, communication, decision-making, and time-management skills.[14] "Management InfoTech" explains how firms like Price Waterhouse are using the latest technology to help their managers develop some of these important skills.

MANAGEMENT INFOTECH

Technology Boosts Management Skills

Businesses have long sought ways to help managers effectively learn and develop the fundamental skills necessary for the competitive environment. Continuing breakthroughs in information technology are opening new paths that some progressive firms are using to promote skill development among their managers. One popular method of developing skills, management simulations, is getting a new spin, thanks to the emergence of new technology. Simulations are essentially "games" in which teams of "players" run hypothetical companies, make competitive decisions, and then get feedback about their performance. This feedback is generated by a computer program that compares company decisions against one another and parameters built into the program itself. Until recently these simulations were often very narrowly focused on a few very objective pieces of information and usually lacked any means for incorporating the more intangible elements of management.

Price Waterhouse, an international accounting and consulting firm, is among several firms now using Tango!, a new form of business simulation that goes far beyond most of its predecessors. Tango! is focused on the management skills needed to lead knowledge-intensive companies. The objective of the game is to build market value, not profits. Among the more ingenious components of Tango! are provisions for building intangible assets, allowing firms to head hunt from one another, and allowing companies to steal customers from one another—all common goals and events in today's business world.

How is a computer simulation able to create such realistic conditions? In just the way that a computer can beat a chess master. The power of today's computers has grown to the point where their capabilities are often limited only by the imagination of programmers and operators. Memory, speed, and multimedia interface capabilities enable Tango! to function in ways undreamed of only a few years ago. And using this technology to its fullest, Tango! and other new-generation simulations like it are providing a novel and exciting vehicle for developing a wide array of critical management skills for the twenty-first century.

> *"This isn't easy. We don't have a lot of experience managing the balancing act between money and know-how."*
>
> Price Waterhouse manager, while playing Tango!*

References: *Thomas A. Stewart, "The Dance Steps Get Trickier All the Time,"* Fortune, *May 26, 1997, pp. 157–160 (*quote on page 158); and Bill Toner, "One Terrific Place to Work,"* CA Magazine, *October 1996, pp. 33–35.*

Technical Skills   **Technical skills** are the skills necessary to accomplish or understand the specific kind of work being done in an organization. Technical skills are especially important for first-line managers. These managers spend much of their time training subordinates and answering questions about work-related problems. They must know how to perform the tasks assigned to those they supervise if they are to be effective managers.

technical skills   The skills necessary to accomplish or understand tasks relevant to the organization

Interpersonal Skills   Managers spend considerable time interacting with people both inside and outside the organization. For obvious reasons, then, the manager also needs **interpersonal skills**—the ability to communicate with, understand, and motivate individuals and groups. As managers climb the organizational ladder, they must be able to get along with subordinates, peers, and

interpersonal skills   The ability to communicate with, understand, and motivate both individuals and groups

those at higher levels of the organization. Because of the multitude of roles managers must fulfill, a manager must also be able to work with suppliers, customers, investors, and others outside of the organization. Although some managers have succeeded with poor interpersonal skills, a manager who has good interpersonal skills is likely to be more successful than one who doesn't.[15]

conceptual skills The manager's ability to think in the abstract

Conceptual Skills **Conceptual skills** depend on the manager's ability to think in the abstract. Managers need the mental capacity to understand the overall workings of the organization and its environment, to grasp how all the parts of the organization fit together, and to view the organization in a holistic manner. These skills enable managers to think strategically, to see the "big picture," and to make broad-based decisions that serve the overall organization.

diagnostic skills The manager's ability to visualize the most appropriate response to a situation

Diagnostic Skills Successful managers also possess **diagnostic skills,** or skills that enable them to visualize the most appropriate response to a situation. A physician diagnoses a patient's illness by analyzing symptoms and determining their probable cause. Similarly, a manager can diagnose and analyze a problem in the organization by studying its symptoms and then developing a solution.

communication skills The manager's abilities to both effectively convey ideas and information to others and effectively receive ideas and information from others

Communication Skills **Communication skills** refer to the manager's abilities to both effectively convey ideas and information to others and effectively receive ideas and information from others. These skills enable a manager to transmit ideas to subordinates so that they know what is expected, to coordinate work with peers and colleagues so that they can work well together, and to keep higher-level managers informed about what is going on. In addition, good communication skills help managers listen to what others say and to understand the real meaning behind letters, reports, and other written communication.

decision-making skills the manager's ability to correctly recognize and define problems and opportunities and to then select an appropriate course of action to solve problems and capitalize on opportunities

Decision-Making Skills Effective managers also have good decision-making skills. **Decision-making skills** refer to the manager's ability to correctly recognize and define problems and opportunities and to then select an appropriate course of action to solve problems and capitalize on opportunities. No manager makes the right decision all the time. However, effective managers make good decisions most of the time. And when they do make a bad decision, effective managers usually recognize their mistake quickly and then reverse it with good decisions that enable their organizations to recover with as little cost or damage as possible.

time-management skills the manager's ability to prioritize work, to work efficiently, and to delegate appropriately

Time-Management Skills Finally, effective managers usually have good time-management skills. **Time-management skills** refer to the manager's ability to prioritize work, to work efficiently, and to delegate appropriately. As already noted, managers face many different pressures and challenges. A manager can easily get bogged down doing work that he or she could easily postpone or delegate to others. Unfortunately, more pressing and higher-priority work may get neglected unless a manager uses effective time-management techniques.[16]

Effective managers recognize both the multiplicity of roles inherent in their jobs and the array of skills they need to perform those jobs. Few managers have equally strong skills in all areas. However, it is very useful for managers to understand their own strengths and weaknesses and to use this understanding to capitalize on their strengths while also working to overcome their weaknesses. For example, a manager with weak time-management skills might be sure to hire an especially effective assistant to help maintain an efficient schedule, whereas a manager with weak decision-making skills can use group decision-making techniques whenever possible to enable him or her to utilize the skills of others.

The Nature of Managerial Work

We have already noted that managerial work does not follow an orderly, systematic progression through the workweek. Indeed, the manager's job is fraught with uncertainty, change, interruption, and fragmented activities. Mintzberg's study, mentioned earlier, found that in a typical day CEOs are likely to spend 59 percent of their time in scheduled meetings, 22 percent doing "desk work," 10 percent in unscheduled meetings, 6 percent on the telephone, and the remaining 3 percent on tours of company facilities. (These proportions, of course, are different for managers at lower levels, and may also be quite different today.)[17]

In addition, managers perform a wide variety of tasks. In the course of a single day, for example, a manager might have to make a decision about the design of a new product, settle a complaint between two subordinates, hire a new secretary, write a report for the boss, coordinate a joint venture with an overseas colleague, form a task force to investigate a problem, and deal with a labor grievance. Moreover, the pace of the manager's job can be relentless. Managers may feel bombarded by mail, telephone calls, and people waiting to see them. They may have to make decisions quickly and formulate plans with little time for reflection.[18] "Today's Management Issues" notes how these characteristics of managerial work, especially in larger companies, may be driving some individuals to pursue different kinds of careers than those sought by earlier generations. But in many ways, these same characteristics of managerial work also contribute to its richness and meaningfulness. Making critical decisions under intense pressure, and making them well, can be a major source of intrinsic satisfaction. And managers are usually well paid for the pressures they bear.

■ The Science and the Art of Management

Given the complexity inherent in the manager's job, it is reasonable to ask whether management is a science or an art. In fact, effective management is a

Following the Dream ... But Whose Dream?

In the past, most people aspiring to a business career had a clear vision of how to measure success: get a job with a big company, work long hard hours, and hope to move up the corporate ladder. Getting into the "corner office" or the "executive suite" were the basic career goals for most of these individuals. And if their dreams didn't come true, they still had a reliable paycheck and job security.

But a growing number of managers now entering the workforce appear to have a different set of dreams. Although many business school graduates still want the status, security, and allure of a big corporate job, others want something different. For example, one recent study found that only 1 percent of the one thousand adults surveyed listed a job as a corporate manager as their first choice for a career. Similarly, the percentage of graduates of Stanford's MBA program who took a job with a big company declined from 70 percent in 1989 to 50 percent five years later.

So what do the people who spurn a corporate career choose instead? Some start their own businesses. Others look for a small start-up company to buy. Still others go into consulting. And among those who do opt for a corporate ca-

> *"If your aspiration is to be a bureaucratic infighter, you may be well suited for a large organization. But you've got to swallow more than I care to. On some level, you can't be who you really are during the workday"*

Daniel Grossman, talented manager who chose to start his own business.*

reer, quite a few say, at least in private, that they only want to earn enough money to have some financial security. Then they, too, plan to pursue their dreams in a different arena.

But why are some people so turned off by big companies? Most offer one or more of the following reasons: (1) Some big companies reward the best politicians, not the best performers. (2) In a big company you may get pigeonholed or stuck in a dead-end job. (3) It takes too long to get responsibility and authority. (4) Big companies impose too many constraints on when and where you work. (5) Top managers at big companies are too cautious and discourage risk and innovation.

Of course, these generalizations represent the perceptions of only some people, and even if they are true, they don't apply to all companies or to all settings. But they do explain why some people are seeking nontraditional career options and why the entrepreneurial spirit is stronger today than ever before.

References: *Kenneth Labich, "Kissing Off Corporate America,"* Fortune, *February 20, 1995, pp. 44–51 (*quote on p. 44); and Anne Fisher, "Six Ways to Supercharge Your Career,"* Fortune, *January 13, 1997, pp. 46–48.*

---

blend of both science and art. And successful executives recognize the importance of combining both the science and the art of management as they practice their craft.[19]

The Science of Management   Many management problems and issues can be approached in ways that are rational, logical, objective, and systematic. Managers can gather data, facts, and objective information. They can use quantitative models and decision-making techniques to arrive at "correct" decisions. And they need to take such a scientific approach to solving problems whenever possible, especially when they are dealing with relatively routine and straightforward issues. When Starbucks considers entering a new market, its managers look closely at a wide variety of objective details as they formulate their plans.

Technical, diagnostic, and decision-making skills are especially important when practicing the science of management.

The Art of Management   Even though managers may try to be scientific as much as possible, they must often make decisions and solve problems on the basis of intuition, experience, instinct, and personal insights. Relying heavily on conceptual, communication, interpersonal, and time-management skills, for example, a manager may have to choose a course of action from several equally attractive options. And even apparently objective facts may prove to be wrong. When Starbucks was planning its first store in New York, market research clearly showed that New Yorkers preferred drip coffee to more exotic espresso-style coffees. After first installing more drip coffee makers and fewer espresso makers than in their other stores, managers had to backtrack when the New Yorkers lined up clamoring for espresso. Starbucks now introduces a standard menu and layout in all its stores, regardless of presumed market differences, and then makes necessary adjustments later. Thus, managers must blend an element of intuition and personal insight with hard data and objective facts.[20]

▐ Becoming a Manager

How does a person acquire the skills necessary to blend the science and art of management and to become a successful manager? Although there are as many variations as there are managers, the most common path involves a combination of education and experience.[21] Figure 1.4 illustrates how managers generally acquire their skills.

The Role of Education   Many of you reading this book right now are doing so because you are enrolled in a management course at a college or university. Thus you are acquiring management skills in an educational setting. When you complete the course (and this book), you will have a foundation for devel-

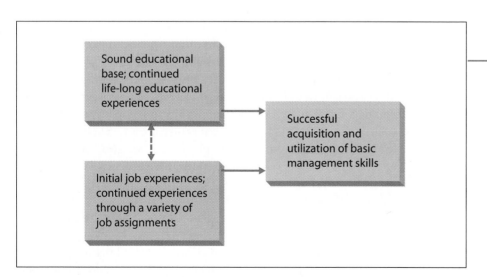

FIGURE 1.4
Sources of Management Skills

Most managers acquire their skills as a result of education and experience. Though a few CEOs today do not hold college degrees, most students preparing for management careers earn college degrees and go on to enroll in MBA programs.

oping your management skills in more advanced courses. A college degree has become almost a requirement for career advancement in business, and virtually all CEOs in the United States have a college degree. MBA degrees are also common among successful executives today.[22] More and more foreign universities, especially in Europe, are also beginning to offer academic programs in management.

Even after obtaining a degree, most prospective managers have not seen the end of their management education. Many middle and top managers periodically return to campus to participate in executive or management development programs ranging in duration from a few days to several weeks. First-line managers also take advantage of extension and continuing education programs offered by institutions of higher education. A recent innovation in extended management education is the Executive MBA program offered by many top business schools, in which middle and top managers with several years of experience complete an accelerated program of study on weekends. Finally, many large companies have in-house training programs for furthering managers' education.

The primary advantage of education as a source of management skills is that, as a student, a person can follow a well-developed program of study, becoming familiar with current research and thinking on management. And many college students can devote full-time energy and attention to learning. On the negative side, management education is often too general to meet the needs of a wide variety of students, and specific know-how may be hard to obtain. Further, many aspects of the manager's job can be discussed in a book, but cannot really be appreciated and understood until they are experienced.

The Role of Experience   This book will help you gain a solid foundation for enhancing your management skills. Even if you were to memorize every word in every management book ever written, however, you could not then step into a top-management position and be effective. The reason? Management skills must also be learned through experience. Most managers advanced to their present position from other jobs. Only by experiencing the day-to-day pressures a manager faces and by meeting a variety of managerial challenges can an individual develop insights into the real nature and character of managerial work.

For this reason most large companies, and many smaller ones as well, have developed management-training programs for their prospective managers. People are hired from college campuses, from other organizations, or from the ranks of the organization's first-line managers and operating employees. These people are systematically assigned to a variety of jobs. Over time, the individual is exposed to most, if not all, of the major aspects of the organization. In this way the manager learns by experience. The training programs at some companies, such as Procter & Gamble, General Mills, and Shell Oil, are so good that other companies try to hire people who have gone through this training. Even without formal training programs, managers can achieve success as they profit from varied experiences. For example, Herb Kelleher was a practicing attorney before he took over at Southwest Airlines. Of course, natural ability, drive, and self-motivation also play roles in acquiring experience and developing management skills.

Most effective managers learn their skills through a combination of education and experience. Some type of college degree, even if it is not in business administration, usually provides a foundation for a management career. The individual then gets his or her first job and subsequently progresses through various management situations. During the manager's rise in the organization, occasional education updates, such as management development programs, may supplement on-the-job experience. And increasingly, managers need to acquire international expertise as part of their personal development. As with general managerial skills, international expertise can also be acquired through a combination of education and experience.

MANAGEMENT IMPLICATIONS Students should recognize that even if certain material in a course does not seem relevant, they are still building an intellectual foundation for future growth. They should also recognize, however, that knowledge alone is usually not sufficient for success in the business world. Finally, students should also understand that their education doesn't end when they walk across the stage and receive a diploma. People already in the business world, meanwhile, should not forget the importance of continuing to learn, regardless of how or where this learning occurs. ▬

The Scope of Management

When most people think of managers and management, they think of profit-seeking organizations. Throughout this chapter we use people like Howard Schultz of Starbucks and Jill Barad of Mattel as examples. But we also mentioned examples from sports, religion, and other fields in which management is essential. Indeed, any group of two or more persons working together to achieve a goal and having human, material, financial, or informational resources at its disposal requires the practice of management.

■ Managing in Profit-Seeking Organizations

Large Businesses Most of what we know about management comes from large profit-seeking organizations because their survival has long depended on efficiency and effectiveness. Examples of large businesses include industrial firms such as Tenneco, British Petroleum, Toyota, Xerox, Unilever, and Levi Strauss; commercial banks such as Citicorp, Fuji Bank, and Wells Fargo; insurance companies such as Prudential, State Farm, and Metropolitan Life; retailers such as Sears, Safeway, and Kmart; transportation companies such as Delta Air Lines and Consolidated Freightways; utilities such as Pacific Gas & Electric and Consolidated Edison of New York; communication companies such as CBS and the New York Times Company; and service organizations such as Kelly Services, Kinder-Care Learning Centers, and Century 21 Real Estate.

Management is important across a wide variety of different kinds of organizations. Purple Moon, for example, is a new start-up business based in Palo Alto, California. Purple Moon is creating software and other computer-related products primarily targeted toward girls. One of its first products was software that allowed users to design fashions for a digital Barbie. Brenda Laurel, the firm's co-founder and lead designer, carefully researches the market and its interest in her new products before launching them. Because Purple Moon is small, Laurel must ensure that its resources are used as efficiently and effectively as possible.

Small and Start-Up Businesses   Although many people associate management primarily with large businesses, effective management is also essential for small businesses, which play an important role in the country's economy. In fact, most of this nation's businesses are small. In some respects, effective management is more important in a small business than in a large one. A large firm such as Exxon or Monsanto can easily recover from losing several thousand dollars because of an incorrect decision; even losses of millions of dollars would not threaten their long-term survival. But a small business may ill afford even a much smaller loss. Of course, some small businesses become big ones. Compaq Computer Corporation, for example, was started by three men in 1982. By 1998 it had become one of the largest businesses in the United States, with annual sales of more than $16 billion.

International Management   In recent years, the importance of international management has increased dramatically. The list of U.S. firms doing business in other countries is staggering. Exxon, for example, derives almost 75 percent of its revenues from foreign markets, and Coca-Cola derives more than 80 percent of its sales from foreign markets. Other major U.S. exporters include General Motors, General Electric, Boeing, and Caterpillar. And even numbers like Ford's are deceptive. For example, the auto maker has large, European-based subsidiaries whose sales are not included as foreign revenue. Moreover, a number of major firms that do business in the United States have their headquarters in other countries. Firms in this category include the Royal Dutch/Shell Group (the Netherlands), Fiat S.P.A. (Italy), Nestlé SA (Switzerland), and Massey-Ferguson Inc. (Canada). International management is not, however, confined to profit-seeking organizations. Several international sports federations (such as Little League Baseball), branches (embassies) of the federal government, and the Roman Catholic Church are established in most countries as well. In some respects, the military was one of the first multinational organizations. International management is covered in depth in Chapter 5.

■ Managing in Not-for-Profit Organizations

Intangible goals such as education, social services, public protection, and recreation are often the primary aim of not-for-profit organizations. Examples include United Way of America, the U.S. Postal Service, Girl Scouts of the United States of America, the International Olympic Committee, art galleries, museums, and the Public Broadcasting System. Although these and similar organizations may not have to be profitable to attract investors, they must still employ sound management practices if they are to survive and work toward their goals.[23] And they must handle money in an efficient and effective way. If the United Way were to begin to spend large portions of its contributions on administration, contributors would lose confidence in the organization and make their charitable donations elsewhere. Indeed, this very thing happened a few years ago. United Way officials had to engage in extensive "damage control," and still incurred a downturn in contributions for the next year. Fortunately, things did get straightened out and contributions bounced back quickly.

Government Organizations   The management of government organizations and agencies is often regarded as a separate specialty: public administration. Government organizations include the Federal Trade Commission, the Environmental Protection Agency, the National Science Foundation, all branches of the military, state highway departments, and federal and state prison systems. Tax dollars support government organizations, so politicians and citizens' groups are acutely sensitive to the need for efficiency and effectiveness.

Educational Organizations   Public and private schools, colleges, and universities all stand to benefit from the efficient use of resources. Taxpayer revolts in states such as California and Massachusetts have drastically cut back the tax money available for education, forcing administrators to make tough decisions about allocating remaining resources.

Health-Care Facilities   Managing health-care facilities such as clinics, hospitals, and health maintenance organizations (HMOs) is now considered a separate field of management. Here, as in other organizations, scarce resources dictate an efficient and effective approach. In recent years many universities have established health-care administration programs to train managers as specialists in this field.

Management in Nontraditional Settings   Good management is also required in nontraditional settings to meet established goals. To one extent or another, management is practiced in religious organizations, terrorist groups, fraternities and sororities, organized crime, street gangs, neighborhood associations, and households. In short, as we noted at the beginning of this chapter, management and managers have a profound influence on all of us.

MANAGEMENT IMPLICATIONS   Management is applicable to all organizations. Thus, when a manager leaves work and goes to a weekly meeting of a civic or church group, to an organizing meeting for a child's youth soccer league, or to a volunteer job in a political campaign, he or she should keep in mind that many of the same functions used in a business can be used in these other organizations. And although each organization has its own unique goals and mission, effective management can help every organization accomplish its goals and more successfully realize its mission. ■

Summary of Key Points

Management is a set of activities (including planning and decision making, organizing, leading, and controlling) directed at an organization's resources (human, financial, physical, and information) with the aim of achieving organizational goals in an efficient and effective manner. A manager is someone whose primary responsibility is to carry out the management process within an organization.

The basic activities that constitute the management process are planning and decision making (determining courses of action), organizing (coordinating activities and resources), leading (motivating and managing people), and controlling (monitoring and evaluating activities). These activities are not performed on a systematic and predictable schedule.

Managers can be differentiated by level and by area. By level, we can identify top, middle, and first-line managers. Kinds of managers by area include marketing, financial, operations, human resource, administrative, and specialized managers.

Managers have ten basic roles to play: three interpersonal roles (figurehead, leader, and liaison); three informational roles (monitor, disseminator, and spokesperson); and four decisional roles (entrepreneur, disturbance handler, resource allocator, and negotiator). Effective managers also tend to have technical, interpersonal, conceptual, diagnostic, communication, decision-making, and time-management skills. The manager's job is characterized by varied, unpredictable, nonroutine, and fragmented work, often performed at a relentless pace. Managers also receive various intrinsic and extrinsic rewards.

The effective practice of management requires a synthesis of science and art—that is, a blend of rational objectivity and intuitive insight. Most managers attain their skills and positions through a combination of education and experience.

Management processes are applicable in a wide range of settings, including profit-seeking organizations (large, small, and startup businesses and international businesses) and not-for-profit organizations (government organizations, educational organizations, health-care facilities, and nontraditional organizations).

Discussion Questions

Questions for Review

1. Name the four basic activities that managers perform. How are they related to one another?

2. Identify different kinds of managers by both level and area in the organization.

3. Briefly describe the ten managerial roles identified by Mintzberg. Give an example of each.

4. Identify the different important skills that help managers succeed. Give an example of each.

Questions for Analysis

5. The text notes that management is both a science and an art. Is one aspect more important than the other? Under what circumstances might one ingredient be more important than the other?

6. Recall a recent group project or task in which you have participated. Explain how each of the four basic management functions was performed.

7. Some people argue that CEOs in the United States are paid too much. Find out the pay for a CEO and discuss whether you think he or she is overpaid.

Questions for Application

8. Interview a manager from a local organization. Ask how he or she performs each of the functions of management, the roles he or she plays, and the skills necessary to do the job.

9. Locate a recent business management publication, such as *Fortune*, *Business Week*, or *Forbes*. Read an article in the magazine that profiles a specific manager or executive. Identify as many examples in the

article as you can that illustrate management functions, roles, or skills.

10. Watch a television program that involves an organization of some type. Good choices include *N.Y.P.D. Blue, M*A*S*H, Spin City,* or *E.R.* Identify as many management functions, skills, and roles as you can.

EXERCISE OVERVIEW

Technical skills are the manager's abilities to accomplish or understand work done in an organization. More and more managers today are realizing that having the technical ability to use the Internet is an important part of communication, decision making, and other facets of their work. This exercise introduces you to the Internet and provides some practice in using it.

EXERCISE BACKGROUND

The Internet, or "information superhighway" as it is sometimes called, is an interconnected network of information and information-based resources using computers and computer systems. Electronic mail was perhaps the first widespread application of the Internet, but applications based on "home pages" and "search engines" are increasingly popular.

A home page is a file (or set of files) created by an individual, business, or other entity. It contains whatever information its creator chooses to include. For example, a company might create a home page that includes its logo, its address and telephone number, information about its products and services, and so forth. A person looking for a job might create a home page that includes a résumé and a statement of career interests. Home pages are indexed by key words chosen by their creators.

A search engine is a system through which an Internet user can search for home pages according to their indexed key words. For example, suppose an individual is interested in knowing more about art collecting. Key words that might logically be linked to home pages related to this interest include art, artists, galleries, and framing. A search engine uses these key words to provide a listing of all home pages that are indexed to them. The user can then browse each page to see what information they contain. Popular search engines include Yahoo, Lycos, and WebCrawler.

EXERCISE TASK

1. Visit your computer center and learn how to access the Internet.

2. Using whichever search engine your computer center supports, conduct a search for three or four general management-related terms (for example, management, organization, business).

3. Now select a more specific management topic and search for two or three specific topics. (If you cannot think of any terms, scan the margin notes in this book.)

4. Finally, select three or four companies and search for their home pages.

Building Effective Diagnostic Skills

EXERCISE OVERVIEW

Diagnostic skills enable a manager to visualize the most appropriate response to a situation. This exercise encourages you to apply your diagnostic skills to a real business problem to assess the possible consequences of various courses of action.

EXERCISE BACKGROUND

For some time now college textbook publishers have been struggling with a significant problem. The subject matter that constitutes a particular field, such as management, chemistry, or history, continues to increase in size, scope, and complexity. Thus, authors feel compelled to add more and more information to new editions of their textbooks. Publishers have also sought to increase the visual sophistication of their texts by adding more color and photographs. At the same time, some instructors find it increasingly difficult to cover the material in longer textbooks. Moreover, longer and more attractive textbooks cost more money to produce, resulting in higher prices to students.

Publishers have considered various options to confront this situation. One alternative is to encourage authors to write books that are briefer—and thus more economical to produce. Another option is to cut back on the complementary supplements that publishers provide to instructors (such as videos and color transparencies) as a way to lower the overall cost of producing a book. Another option is to eliminate traditional publishing altogether and provide educational resources via CD-ROM, the Internet, or other new media.

Confounding the situation, of course, is cost. Profit margins in the industry are such that managers feel the need to be cautious and conservative. That is, they cannot do everything, and must not risk alienating their users by taking too radical a step. Remember, too, that publishers must consider the concerns of three different sets of customers: the instructors who make adoption decisions, the bookstores that buy educational materials for resale (at a retail markup), and students who buy the books for classroom use and then often re-sell them to the bookstore.

EXERCISE TASK

With this background in mind, respond to the following:

1. Discuss the pros and cons of each option currently being considered by textbook publishers.

2. Identify the likely consequences of each option.

3. Can you think of other alternatives that publishers in the industry should consider?

4. What specific recommendations would you make to an executive in a publishing company regarding this set of issues?

EXERCISE OVERVIEW

Conceptual skills reflect the manager's ability to think in the abstract. This exercise will help you extend your conceptual skills by identifying potential generalizations of management functions, roles, and skills across several kinds of organizations.

EXERCISE BACKGROUND

This introductory chapter discusses four basic management functions, ten common managerial roles, and seven vital management skills. The chapter also stresses that management is applicable across many kinds of organizations.

Identify one large business, one small business, one educational organization, one health-care organization, and one government organization. These might be organizations about which you have some personal knowledge or simply organizations whose name you recognize. Now imagine yourself in the position of a top manager in each organization.

Write the names of the five organizations across the top of a sheet of paper. List the four functions, ten roles, and seven skills down the left side of the paper. Now think of a situation, problem, or opportunity relevant to the intersection of each row and column on the paper. For example, how might a manager in a government organization use diagnostic skills to engage in planning? Similarly, how might a manager in a small business carry out the organizing function and play the role of negotiator?

EXERCISE TASK

1. What meaningful similarities can you identify across the five columns?

2. What meaningful differences can you identify across the five columns?

3. Based on your assessment of the similarities and differences identified above, how easy or difficult might it be for a manager to move from one type of organization to another?

Building Effective Conceptual Skills

CHAPTER CLOSING CASE

The Sky's the Limit

Back in 1975, two high school friends got together and decided to start a business in the embryonic software market. The first commercial microcomputers were just coming to market, and the two friends had fallen in love with both the technology and what they saw as its long-term potential. Their first product was a version of the programming language BASIC. The fledgling business grew steadily as they modified and extended their BASIC programs for new computers just entering the market. In 1979, the two friends, William Gates and Paul Allen, moved the business—called Microsoft—to Seattle. And the rest, as they say, is history.

Microsoft's big break came in 1980 when IBM selected Gates and Allen to write the operating system software for its new line of personal computers. Gates and Allen bought the rights to an existing program for $50,000, modified it a bit, and named it MS-DOS (for Microsoft Disk Operating System). Even though IBM was a relative latecomer to the PC market, its dominance in the computer industry brought it instant respect. And because other software developers wanted their products to run on IBM computers, MS-DOS quickly became the industry standard.

Paul Allen became seriously ill in 1983 and left the firm in Gates' capable hands. For the next seven years, Microsoft developed relationships with other computer manufacturers and began introducing new application software like Word (for word processing), Excel (a spreadsheet), and Power Point (a presentation package). When the firm made its initial public stock offering, Gates became the PC industry's first billionaire. Popular new products such as Windows, Windows 95, and Microsoft Office and deals with new industry giants such as Compaq and Dell cemented Microsoft's place at the top of its industry. Today, Word controls 90 percent of the worldwide market for word processing, and Excel has 87 percent of the spreadsheet market. Windows and Windows 95 together have 83 percent of the operating systems market. And the firm's total annual revenues are approaching $10 billion.

Because of the clout Microsoft has throughout the industry—and perhaps because of its continuing success—both the firm and Gates are widely feared and criticized in some quarters. For example, other software developers complain about unfair business practices. Some computer manufacturers fear that they may become too dependent on Microsoft as the sole provider of software for their products. And even the government keeps a wary eye on Microsoft for possible antitrust practices.

But Gates himself keeps his eye on the future and Microsoft headed unwaveringly toward it. For example, he personally oversaw the fifteen-year development of the firm's newest success story, Windows NT, an operating system for computer networks. And he actively participates in every major decision made by the firm's top managers. He also fosters communication throughout the organization, however, and stresses the need to keep the firm lean and nimble, always wanting to avoid the bureaucratic procedures that saddle many big companies. And he keeps a close eye on the bottom line at all times, closely analyzing monthly and quarterly sales reports.

In many ways, however, Gates' biggest role at Microsoft today is as its public persona. He appears at all major news conferences, makes all major announcements, and travels extensively to keep in touch with suppliers, computer manufacturers, customers, strategic allies, and government officials. He typically works sixteen hours a day, and seldom takes any time off. Even when he is "away from work," he keeps up with things via e-mail. And in every corner of the globe, Microsoft employees look at Gates with something bordering on awe. Some, for example, visibly copy his mannerisms. They also clearly recognize that because of his own personal work habits and schedule that he surely expects no less from each of them.

The sky, then, does seem to be the limit for Gates and Microsoft. The firm's dominance in its core software markets continues to grow, and its products are gaining ever-wider recognition and acceptance. But a few thunderclouds are on the horizon. For one thing, Microsoft faces formidable competition from firms such as Netscape in the emerging markets related to the Internet. And for another, computer giants like IBM and Compaq are seeking new alliances to avoid being too much at the mercy of Microsoft. But like many weather forecasts, the chances of these thunderclouds actually raining on Gates' parade are really quite slim.

Case Questions

1. Identify as many examples as you can in this case to illustrate the four management functions and ten management roles.

2. Which management skills do you think have played the biggest role in Bill Gates' success?

3. What future events could derail Microsoft?

Case References: "Microsoft's Future," *Business Week,* January 19, 1998, pp. 58–68; David Kirkpatrick, "He Wants All Your Business—And He's Starting to Get It," *Fortune,* May 26, 1997, pp. 58–68; *Hoover's Handbook of American Business 1997* (Austin, Texas: The Reference Press, 1996), pp. 926–927; Brent Schlender, "On the Road With Chairman Bill," *Fortune,* May 26, 1997, pp. 72–81; Randall E. Stross, "Manager Gates Builds His Brain Trust," *Fortune,* December 8, 1997, pp. 84–98; and Brent Schlender, "Microsoft—First America, Now the World," *Fortune,* August 18, 1997, pp. 214–217.

CHAPTER NOTES

1. Jennifer Reese, "Starbucks—Inside the Coffee Cult," *Fortune*, December 9, 1996, pp. 190–200; "Starbucks Does Not Live by Coffee Alone," *Business Week*, August 5, 1996, p. 76; and "Starbucks: Making Values Pay," *Fortune*, September 29, 1997, pp. 261–272.

2. Fred Luthans, "Successful vs. Effective Real Managers," *Academy of Management Executive*, May 1988, pp. 127–132.

3. Stanley Bing, "Help! I Need Somebody," *Fortune*, March 4, 1996, pp. 41–43. See also "The Top 25 Managers of the Year," *Business Week*, January 12, 1998, pp. 54–68.

4. Sumantsa Ghospal and Christopher A. Bartlett, "Changing the Role of Top Management: Beyond Structure to Process," *Harvard Business Review*, January–February 1995, pp. 86–96.

5. "A Coke and a Perm? Soda Giant Is Pushing into Unusual Locales," *Wall Street Journal*, May 8, 1997, pp. A1, A8.

6. Henry Mintzberg, *The Nature of Managerial Work* (New York: Harper & Row, 1973); see also Ford S. Worthy, "How CEOs Manage Their Time," *Fortune*, January 18, 1988, pp. 88–97; and Patricia Sellers, "Does the CEO Really Matter? *Fortune*, April 22, 1991, pp. 80–94.

7. "The Prize," *Forbes*, May 19, 1997, pp. 166–169.

8. Rosemary Stewart, "Middle Managers: Their Jobs and Behaviors," in Jay W. Lorsch (ed.), *Handbook of Organizational Behavior* (Englewood Cliffs, N.J.: Prentice-Hall, 1987), pp. 385–391.

9. Wayne Cascio, "Downsizing: What Do We Know?" *Academy of Management Executive*, February 1993, pp. 95–103; "Casting for a Different Set of Characters," *Business Week*, December 8, 1997, pp. 38–39.

10. Anne Fisher, "Six Ways to Supercharge Your Career," *Fortune*, January 13, 1997, pp. 46–48.

11. Steven Kerr, Kenneth D. Hill, and Laurie Broedling, "The First-Line Supervisor: Phasing Out or Here to Stay?" *Academy of Management Review*, January 1986, pp. 103–117; and Leonard A. Schlesinger and Janice A. Klein, "The First-Line Supervisor: Past, Present, and Future," in Lorsch (ed.), *Handbook of Organizational Behavior*, pp. 358–369.

12. Brent B. Allred, Charles C. Snow, and Raymond E. Miles, "Characteristics of Managerial Careers in the 21st Century," *Academy of Management Executive*, November 1996, pp. 17–27.

13. Mintzberg, *The Nature of Managerial Work*.

14. For a classic discussion of several of these skills, see Robert L. Katz, "The Skills of an Effective Administrator," *Harvard Business Review*, September–October 1974, pp. 90–102.

15. See Thomas Teal, "The Human Side of Management," *Harvard Business Review*, November–December 1996, pp. 35–44.

16. For a recent discussion of the importance of time-management skills, see David Barry, Catherine Durnell Cramton, and Stephen J. Carroll, "Navigating the Garbage Can: How Agendas Help Managers Cope with Job Realities," *Academy of Management Executive*, May 1997, pp. 26–42.

17. Mintzberg, *The Nature of Managerial Work*.

18. James H. Davis, F. David Schoorman, and Lex Donaldson, "Toward a Stewardship Theory of Management," *Academy of Management Review*, January 1997, pp. 20–47.

19. Gary Hamel and C. K. Prahalad, "Competing for the Future," *Harvard Business Review*, July–August 1994, pp. 122–128.

20. James Waldroop and Timothy Butler, "The Executive as Coach," *Harvard Business Review*, November–December 1996, pp. 111–117.

21. Walter Kiechel III, "A Manager's Career in the New Economy," *Fortune*, April 4, 1994, pp. 68–72.

22. Shelly Branch, "MBAs Are Hot Again—And They Know It," *Fortune*, April 14, 1997, pp. 155–157.

23. James L. Perry and Hal G. Rainey, "The Public-Private Distinction in Organization Theory: A Critique and Research Strategy," *Academy of Management Review*, April 1988, pp. 182–201; see also Ran Lachman, "Public and Private Sector Differences: CEOs' Perceptions of Their Role Environments," *Academy of Management Journal*, September 1985, pp. 671–680.

2

Traditional and Contemporary Issues and Challenges

When the Steven Spielberg blockbuster *The Lost World* opened on Memorial Day weekend in 1997, the question wasn't whether the movie would succeed, but, rather, how much money it would make. Movie fans had been whipped into a fever pitch for months as they were peppered with promotions, merchandise tie-ins, teasers, magazine articles, and carefully leaked rumors about the film. And to no one's surprise, the movie set a new opening weekend box office record by taking in over $90 million in ticket sales. But although the movie itself reflected state-of-the-art technology, Universal Studio's strategy to boost the film's revenues to astronomical levels can be traced back several decades to well-known management pioneer Henry Ford.

In the 1920s, the Ford Model T was the best-selling automobile on earth. The car was manufactured at thirty-four assembly plants in the United States, as well as twelve more in Europe, Asia, and South America. More than half of the cars on the road at the time were Model Ts, and Henry Ford himself was a veritable legend. So when Ford shut down its assembly plants in May 1927, the world seemed to hold its breath. Everyone knew that Ford was planning a replacement for the venerable Model T, but no one knew much about when the new model would appear or what it would be. And when the factories simply shut and locked their doors, the suspense began to mount.

Almost immediately rumors began to circulate about the new Ford. One day Ford was planning a major new kind of engine, whereas the next day the rumors dismissed the engine and focused on some radical new design or interior that might be used in the car. But the truth was that no one really knew what was happening inside the locked Ford factories, because Henry Ford himself was still figuring it out. As the days turned into weeks and the weeks into months, the excitement about the new Ford—whatever it was going to be—grew daily. Meanwhile, inside the plants the new model design was finalized in August and test models began trickling off the assembly lines in October.

Finally, on November 28, 1927, Ford officially announced that its new car, dubbed the Model A, would be unveiled one week later. Within days, 125,000 Americans put down deposits for a Model A, even though no one knew what it looked like or how much it would cost. In Detroit, more than 10,000 people were waiting in line to be among the first to see the Model A when it was unveiled at the convention center. And in New York, more than 1.25 million people visited Madison Square Garden during a five-day span just to gaze at the new Ford. Fortunately for Ford, the car more than lived up to its hype, and more than a million Model A's were sold during its first year.

Ever since that time, other companies have tried to replicate Ford's strategy of announcing a product "under development" or "in process" to build suspense and anticipation. For example, IBM followed the same approach in the 1960s in launching its 360 computer series, Nissan used the strategy successfully in 1989 in launching its Infiniti luxury cars, and Sony followed the same route when introducing its digital audio tape. And Microsoft used this marketing ploy to perfection in launching its Windows 95 software, resulting in anxious buyers lining up for blocks and people actually camping outside stores so that they could be among the first to own a copy. And each of these successes owes its inspiration to Henry Ford and his Model A.[1]

The "excitement [surrounding the introduction of the Ford Model A] could hardly have been greater had Pah-Wah, the sacred white elephant of Burma, elected to sit for seven days on the flagpole of the Woolworth Building."

Editorial in the New York World *in 1927, quoted in* Audacity, *Fall 1996, p. 36.*

I t is critically important that all managers focus on today's competitive environment and how that environment will change tomorrow. But it is also important that they use the past as context. Managers in many kinds of organizations can learn both effective and less-effective practices and strategies by understanding what managers have done in the past. Indeed, history plays an important role in many businesses today, and more and more managers are recognizing that the lessons of the past are an important ingredient of future success.

This chapter provides an overview of traditional management thought so that you, too, can better appreciate the importance of history in today's business world. We set the stage by establishing the historical context of management. We then discuss the three traditional management perspectives—classical, behavioral, and quantitative. Next we describe the systems and contingency perspectives as approaches that help integrate the three traditional perspectives. Finally, we introduce and discuss a variety of contemporary management issues and challenges.

The Role of Theory and History in Management

Practicing managers are increasingly seeing the value of theory and history in their work. This section first explains why theory and history are important and then identifies important precursors to management theory.

■ The Importance of Theory and History

Some people question the value of history and theory. Their arguments are usually based on the assumptions that history has no relevance to contemporary society and that theory is abstract and of no practical use. In reality, however, both theory and history are important to all managers today.

Why Theory?   A *theory* is simply a conceptual framework for organizing knowledge and providing a blueprint for action. Although some theories seem abstract and irrelevant, others appear very simple and practical. Management theories, used to build organizations and guide them toward their goals, are grounded in reality.[2] Practically any organization that uses assembly lines (such as Emerson Electric, Black & Decker, and Fiat) is drawing on what we describe later in this chapter as *scientific management*. Many organizations, including Kimberly-Clark, Texas Instruments, and Seiko, use the behavioral perspective (also introduced later) to improve employee satisfaction and motivation. And naming a large company that does not use one or more techniques from the quantitative management perspective would be difficult. For example, retailers such as Safeway and Target Stores routinely use operations management to determine how many check-out stands a store needs. In addition, most managers develop and refine their own theories of how they should run their organizations and manage the behavior of their employees.

No one knows the origins of Stonehenge, a mysterious circle of huge stones rising from Salisbury Plain in England. But one fact that is known is that whoever built the ancient monument must have relied heavily on a variety of management tools and techniques. For example, the stones were probably cut over 300 miles away, in Wales, and transported to Salisbury Plain. This enormous feat alone would have required careful planning and coordination and the united efforts of hundreds of laborers.

For example, Andrew Grove, CEO of Intel Corp., has developed his own operating theory of organizations. The basis of his theory is that organizations need to become more agile and responsive to their environment. By implementing his theory, Grove has transformed Intel into just such a company. As a direct result of Grove's keen understanding of his business and his ability to implement his operating theory, Intel has become the world's largest manufacturer of semiconductors.[3]

Why History?   Awareness and understanding of important historical developments are also important to contemporary managers.[4] Understanding the historical context of management provides a sense of heritage and can help managers avoid the mistakes of others. Most courses in U.S. history devote time to business and economic developments in this country, including the Industrial Revolution, the early labor movement, and the Great Depression, and to such captains of U.S. industry as Cornelius Vanderbilt (railroads), John D. Rockefeller (oil), and Andrew Carnegie (steel). The contributions of these and other industrialists left a profound imprint on contemporary culture.[5]

Many managers are also realizing that they can benefit from a greater understanding of history in general. For example, Ian M. Ross of AT&T Bell Laboratories cites *The Second World War* by Winston Churchill as a major influence on his approach to leadership. Other books that managers often mention for their relevance to today's business problems include such classics as Plato's *Republic*, Homer's *Iliad*, and Machiavelli's *The Prince*.[6] And in recent years, new business history books have been directed more at women managers and the lessons they can learn from the past.[7]

Managers at Wells Fargo & Company clearly recognize the value of history. For example, the company maintains an extensive archival library of its old banking documents and records and even employs a full-time corporate historian. As part of their orientation and training, new managers at Wells

THE WORLD OF MANAGEMENT

Management History as a Global Project

Sometimes overlooked in contemporary analysis of management history is the truly global character of that history. Although the historical examples noted in the text reflect major civilizations in several different parts of the world, a more detailed discussion could also have highlighted other civilizations—the Mayan pyramids in the West, for example, and the Great Wall of China in the East. And many of the pioneers of management discussed later in the chapter lived and worked in England, France, and Germany. Notable early writings from Japan are also just now being translated and placed into historical context. Clearly, then, contributions from every corner of the globe profoundly affected the emergence of management thinking.

> *"History tells us we used to train our managers more the way the Japanese and Germans do today."*
>
> *Alfred D. Chandler, Jr., noted business historian**

The exchange of ideas and information also flowed from the United States to other regions, as the ideas of popular American writers were also recognized abroad. The work of Frederick Taylor, for example, was as popular in Russia as in his homeland. The results of the Hawthorne studies were eagerly read throughout most of Western Europe. The human relations writings of Douglas McGregor and Abraham Maslow were also very influential in Europe. And the entire quantitative management perspective was really born during World War II as a result of international collaboration among the Allies.

Interestingly, however, the methods used to train managers in different countries have remained somewhat diverse. In the United States, for example, most managers today received their training in a college of business administration. Most such colleges, in turn, use economics as the foundation for their curriculum and stress general management skills. As a result, managers trained in the United States often have an excellent perspective of how organizations should be managed strategically but may suffer from weaker training in technical and operational areas.

In most other parts of the world, however, business schools are still the exception rather than the rule. Many students graduate with degrees in engineering or a scientific field and then receive their business "education" on the job in a manufacturing or operations setting. Although there is no real way to assess whether one system is superior to the other, it is worth noting that many foreign universities today are establishing business schools. But interestingly, these schools also tend to retain a strong focus on technology and operations, while they incorporate a much heavier dose of management history than is common in U.S. schools.

So where is management theory headed? Judging from the past, management will probably continue to evolve from a global perspective, with new ideas and concepts generated in many diverse settings. But managers in different parts of the world will continue to practice their craft in ways that seem to best fit their own unique geographic and cultural contexts. Will a unified, global management philosophy ever emerge? Perhaps one day, but a lot more water has to pass under the bridge first.

References: *V. R. Berghahn, "Making the World Safe for Competition," Audacity, Summer 1996, pp. 18–25; Alfred D. Chandler, Jr., "Why Business History?" Audacity, Fall 1992, pp. 7–15 (*quote on page 15); and Daniel Wren, The Evolution of Management Theory, 4th ed. (New York: Wiley, 1994).*

Fargo learn about the bank's history.[8] Similarly, Polaroid, Shell Oil, Levi Strauss, Ford, Lloyd's of London, Disney, Honda, and Unilever all maintain significant archives about their past and frequently evoke images from that past in their orientation and training programs, advertising campaigns, and other public relations activities.

■ Precursors to Management Theory

Even though large businesses have been around for only a few hundred years, management has been practiced for thousands of years. By examining management in antiquity and identifying some of the first management pioneers, we set the stage for a more detailed look at the emergence of management theory and practice over the last one hundred years. The international character of this historical backdrop is further highlighted in "The World of Management."

Management in Antiquity The practice of management can be traced back thousands of years. The Egyptians used the management functions of planning, organizing, and controlling when they constructed the great pyramids. Alexander the Great employed a staff organization to coordinate activities during his military campaigns. The Roman Empire developed a well-defined organizational structure that greatly facilitated communication and control. Socrates discussed management practices and concepts as early as 400 B.C., Plato described job specialization in 350 B.C., and Alfarabi listed several leadership traits in A.D. 900.[9] The simple time line in Figure 2.1 shows a few of the most important management breakthroughs and practices over the last four thousand years.

Early Management Pioneers In spite of this history, however, management per se was not given serious attention for several centuries. Indeed, the study of management did not begin until the nineteenth century. Robert Owen (1771–1858), a British industrialist and reformer, was one of the first managers to recognize the importance of an organization's human resources. Until his era, factory workers were generally viewed in much the same way that machinery and equipment were. A factory owner himself, Owen believed that workers deserved respect and dignity. He implemented better working conditions, a

FIGURE 2.1
Management in Antiquity

Management has been practiced for thousands of years. For example, the ancient Babylonians used management in governing their empire, and the ancient Romans used management to facilitate communication and control throughout their far-flung territories. The Egyptians used planning and controlling techniques in the construction of their pyramids.

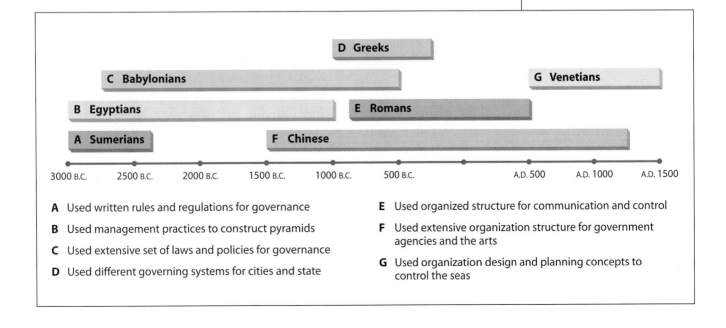

A Used written rules and regulations for governance

B Used management practices to construct pyramids

C Used extensive set of laws and policies for governance

D Used different governing systems for cities and state

E Used organized structure for communication and control

F Used extensive organization structure for government agencies and the arts

G Used organization design and planning concepts to control the seas

higher minimum working age for children, meals for employees, and fewer work hours. He assumed that giving more attention to workers would pay off in increased output.

Whereas Owen was primarily interested in employee welfare, Charles Babbage (1792–1871), an English mathematician, focused his attention on efficiencies of production. His primary contribution was his book, *On the Economy of Machinery and Manufactures.*[10] Babbage placed great faith in division of labor and advocated the application of mathematics to problems such as the efficient use of facilities and materials. In a sense, his work was a forerunner to both the classical and the quantitative management perspectives. Nor did he overlook the human element. Babbage understood that a harmonious relationship between management and labor could benefit both parties, and he favored incentives such as profit-sharing plans. In many ways, Babbage was an originator of modern management theory and practice.

MANAGEMENT IMPLICATIONS All managers should obviously focus their attention on present-day and future issues, but they should also remember the lessons from the past. An understanding of business history in general and the history of their own company in particular can help managers understand why contemporary circumstances have developed as they have, and also provide useful ideas for enhancing the effectiveness of their organization.[11] In addition, managers should recognize the value of theory as a way of organizing and thinking about information and ideas.[12]

The Classical Management Perspective

the classical management perspective Consists of two distinct branches—scientific management and administrative management

At the dawn of the twentieth century, the preliminary ideas and writings of these and other managers and theorists converged with the emergence and evolution of large-scale businesses and management practices to create interest in and focus attention on how businesses should be operated. The first important ideas to emerge are now called the **classical management perspective.** This perspective actually includes two different viewpoints: scientific management and administrative management.

■ Scientific Management

scientific management Concerned with improving the performance of individual workers

Productivity emerged as a serious business problem during the first few years of this century. Business was expanding and capital was readily available, but labor was in short supply. Hence, managers began to search for ways to use existing labor more efficiently. In response to this need, experts began to focus on ways to improve the performance of individual workers. Their work led to the development of **scientific management.** Some of the earliest advocates of scientific management included Frederick W. Taylor (1856–1915), Frank Gilbreth (1868–1924), Lillian Gilbreth (1878–1972), Henry Gantt (1861– 1919), and Harrington Emerson (1853–1931).[13] Taylor played the dominant role in this era.

Frederick W. Taylor was a pioneer in the field of labor efficiency. He introduced numerous innovations in how jobs were designed and how workers were trained to perform them. These innovations resulted in higher-quality products and improved employee morale. Taylor also formulated the basic ideas of scientific management.

One of Taylor's first jobs was as a foreman at the Midvale Steel Company in Philadelphia. It was there that he observed what he called **soldiering**—employees deliberately working at a pace slower than their capabilities. Taylor studied and timed each element of the steel-workers' jobs. He determined what each worker should be producing, and then he designed the most efficient way of doing each part of the overall task. Next he implemented a piecework pay system. Rather than paying all employees the same wage, he began increasing the pay of each worker who met and exceeded the target level of output set for his or her job.

soldiering Employees deliberately working at a pace slower than their capabilities

After Taylor left Midvale, he worked as a consultant for several companies, including Simonds Rolling Machine Company and Bethlehem Steel. At Simonds he studied and redesigned jobs, introduced rest periods to reduce fatigue, and implemented a piecework pay system. The results were higher quality and quantity of output and improved morale. At Bethlehem Steel, Taylor studied efficient ways of loading and unloading rail cars and applied his conclusions with equally impressive results. During these experiences, he formulated the basic ideas that he called *scientific management*. Figure 2.2 illustrates the basic steps Taylor suggested. He believed that managers who followed his guidelines would improve the efficiency of their workers.[14]

Taylor's work had a major impact on U.S. industry. By applying his principles, many organizations achieved major gains in efficiency. Taylor was not without his detractors, however. Labor argued that scientific management was just a device to get more work from each employee and to reduce the total number of workers needed by a firm. There was a congressional investigation into Taylor's ideas, and evidence suggests that he falsified some of his findings.[15] Nevertheless, Taylor's work left a lasting imprint on business.[16]

Frank and Lillian Gilbreth, contemporaries of Taylor, were a husband-and-wife team of industrial engineers. One of Frank Gilbreth's most interesting contributions was to the craft of bricklaying. After studying bricklayers at

FIGURE 2.2

Steps in Scientific Management

Frederick Taylor developed this system of scientific management, which he believed would lead to a more efficient and productive workforce. Bethlehem Steel was among the first organizations to profit from scientific management and still practices some parts of it today.

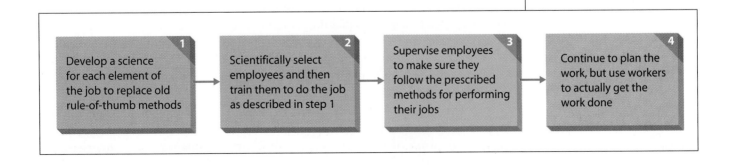

1. Develop a science for each element of the job to replace old rule-of-thumb methods

2. Scientifically select employees and then train them to do the job as described in step 1

3. Supervise employees to make sure they follow the prescribed methods for performing their jobs

4. Continue to plan the work, but use workers to actually get the work done

work, he developed several procedures for doing the job more efficiently. For example, he specified standard materials and techniques, including the positioning of the bricklayer, the bricks, and the mortar at different levels. The results of these changes were a reduction from eighteen separate physical movements to five and an increase in output of about 200 percent. Lillian Gilbreth made equally important contributions to several different areas of work, helped shape the field of industrial psychology, and made substantive contributions to the field of personnel management. Working individually and together, the Gilbreths developed numerous techniques and strategies for eliminating inefficiency. They applied many of their ideas to their family, and their experiences raising twelve children are documented in the book and movie *Cheaper by the Dozen.*

Henry Gantt, another contributor to scientific management, was an associate of Taylor at Midvale, Simonds, and Bethlehem Steel. Later, working alone, he developed other techniques for improving worker output. One, called the Gantt chart, is still used today. A Gantt chart is essentially a means of scheduling work and can be generated for each worker or for an entire complex project. Gantt also refined Taylor's ideas about piecework pay systems.

Like Taylor, the Gilbreths, and Gantt, Harrington Emerson was also a management consultant. He made quite a stir in 1910 when he appeared before the Interstate Commerce Commission to testify about a rate increase requested by the railroads. As an expert witness, Emerson asserted that the railroads could save $1 million a day by using scientific management. He was also a strong advocate of specialized management roles in organizations, believing that job specialization was as relevant to managerial work as it was to operating jobs.

■ Administrative Management

administrative management The branch of management that focuses on managing the total organization

Whereas scientific management deals with the jobs of individual employees, **administrative management** focuses on managing the total organization. The primary contributors to this approach to management were Henri Fayol (1841–1925), Lyndall Urwick (1891–1983), Max Weber (1864–1920), and Chester Barnard (1886–1961).

Henri Fayol was administrative management's most articulate spokesperson. A French industrialist, Fayol was unknown to U.S. managers and scholars until his most important work, *General and Industrial Management,* was translated into English in 1930.[17] Drawing on his own managerial experience, he attempted to systematize the practice of management to provide guidance and direction to other managers. Fayol also was the first to identify the specific managerial functions of planning, organizing, leading, and controlling. He believed that these functions accurately reflect the core of the management process. Most contemporary management books (including this one) still use this framework, and practicing managers agree that these functions are a critical part of their jobs.

After a career as a British army officer, Lyndall Urwick became a noted management theorist and consultant. He integrated scientific management with the work of Fayol and other administrative management theorists. He also advanced modern thinking about the functions of planning, organizing, and controlling. Like Fayol, he developed a list of guidelines for improving managerial effectiveness. Urwick is noted not so much for his own contributions as for his synthesis and integration of the work of others.

Although Max Weber lived and worked at the same time as Fayol and Taylor, his contributions were not recognized until some years had passed. Weber was a German sociologist, and his most important work was not translated into English until 1947.[18] Weber's work on bureaucracy laid the foundation for contemporary organization theory, discussed in detail in Chapter 12. The concept of bureaucracy, as we discuss later, is based on a rational set of guidelines for structuring organizations in the most efficient manner.

Chester Barnard, former president of New Jersey Bell Telephone Company, made notable contributions to management in his book *The Functions of the Executive*.[19] The book proposes a major theory about the acceptance of authority. The theory suggests that subordinates weigh the legitimacy of a supervisor's directives and then decide whether to accept them. An order is accepted if the subordinate understands it, is able to comply with it, and views it as appropriate. The importance of Barnard's work is enhanced by his experience as a top manager.

■ The Classical Management Perspective Today

The contributions and limitations of the classical management perspective are summarized in Table 2.1. The classical perspective is the framework from which later theories evolved, and many of its insights still hold true. For example, many of the job specialization techniques and scientific methods espoused by Taylor and his contemporaries are still reflected in the way that many industrial jobs are designed today. Moreover, many contemporary organizations still use some of the bureaucratic procedures suggested by Weber. Also, these early theorists were the first to focus attention on management as a meaning-

**TABLE 2.1
The Classical Management Perspective**

General Summary	The classical management perspective had two primary thrusts. Scientific management focused on employees within organizations and on ways to improve their productivity. Noted pioneers of scientific management were Frederick Taylor, Frank and Lillian Gilbreth, Henry Gantt, and Harrington Emerson. Administrative management focused on the total organization and on ways to make it more efficient and effective. Prominent administrative management theorists were Henri Fayol, Lyndall Urwick, Max Weber, and Chester Barnard.
Contributions	Laid the foundation for later developments in management theory.
	Identified important management processes, functions, and skills that are still recognized as such today.
	Focused attention on management as a valid subject of scientific inquiry.
Limitations	More appropriate for stable and simple organizations than for today's dynamic and complex organizations.
	Often prescribed universal procedures that are not appropriate in some settings.
	Even though some writers (such as Lillian Gilbreth and Chester Barnard) were concerned with the human element, many viewed employees as tools rather than resources.

ful field of study. Several aspects of the classical perspective are also relevant to our later discussions of planning, organizing, and controlling.

The limitations of the classical perspective, however, should not be overlooked. These early writers dealt with stable, simple organizations; many organizations today, in contrast, are changing and complex. These management theorists also proposed universal guidelines that we now recognize do not fit every organization. A third limitation of the classical management perspective is that it slighted the role of the individual in organizations. This role was much more fully developed by advocates of the behavioral management perspective.

MANAGEMENT IMPLICATIONS The classical management perspective provides many techniques and approaches to management that are relevant today. For example, thoroughly understanding the nature of work being performed, selecting the right people for that work, and approaching decisions rationally are all useful ideas—and each was developed during this period. Similarly, as long as their limitations are recognized, some of the core concepts from the bureaucratic model can still be used in the design of modern organizations.[20] Managers should also recognize that efficiency and productivity can indeed be measured and controlled in many situations. On the other hand, managers must also recognize the limitations of the classical perspective and avoid its narrow focus on efficiency to the exclusion of other important perspectives.

The Behavioral Management Perspective

the behavioral management perspective The management perspective that emphasizes individual attitudes and behaviors and group processes

Early advocates of the classical management perspective essentially viewed organizations and jobs from a mechanistic point of view: that is, they essentially sought to conceptualize organizations as machines and workers as cogs within those machines. Even though many early writers recognized the role of individuals, their focus tended to be on how managers could control and standardize the behavior of their employees. In contrast, the **behavioral management perspective** placed much more emphasis on individual attitudes and behaviors and on group processes and recognized the importance of behavioral processes in the workplace.

The behavioral management perspective was stimulated by a number of writers and theoretical movements. One of those movements was industrial psychology, the practice of applying psychological concepts to industrial settings. Hugo Munsterberg (1863–1916), a noted German psychologist, is recognized as the father of industrial psychology. He established a psychological laboratory at Harvard in 1892, and his pioneering book, *Psychology and Industrial Efficiency*, was translated into English in 1913.[21] Munsterberg suggested that psychologists could make valuable contributions to managers in the areas

WORKING WITH DIVERSITY

Rediscovering Mary Parker Follett

The business section of virtually any bookstore today carries literally dozens of books extolling the virtues of empowerment and cross-functional work teams and dozens of other books stressing the importance of knowledge-based leadership and organizational flexibility. Interestingly, however, many of these same "cutting edge" ideas were also set forth around eighty years ago by a management pioneer named Mary Parker Follett.

Follett was born in Quincy, Massachusetts, in 1868. After graduating from Radcliffe College, she taught political science for several years. During this period of her life, her social circle came to include a number of influential and wealthy philanthropists and business leaders. One of these leaders became enthralled with her ideas regarding wages and work structures and began providing her with a monthly stipend so that she could devote more time to pursuing her ideas and interests.

With her new freedom to explore her ideas, she began a long and serious study of organizations and how they functioned. One of her first messages involved worker participation. She warned, for example, that the bureaucratic model of organization just then coming into vogue might tend to bury the knowledge and ability of workers at lower levels in the hierarchy while simultaneously eliminating an important motivational factor, self-control.

Follett was also among the first to recognize the potential value of cross-functional work teams. She believed, for

> *"People often puzzle about who is the father of management. I don't know who the father was, but I have no doubt about who was the mother."*

Sir Peter Parker, London School of Economics Chairman*

example, that authority in an organization should be distributed laterally across departments, rather than vertically up and down the hierarchy. This approach, she argued, would result in collaboration based on expertise rather than on power or position. And indeed, power itself needed rethinking, at least in Follett's view. Most managers and management experts of her day thought that managers should strive to precisely define and allocate power based on hierarchical position. Follett, meanwhile, suggested that power should instead be based on knowledge and expertise—again, ideas currently popular in most modern organizations.

As her ideas began to take shape, so did her influence. She became a widely respected authority in the field and a popular speaker to business groups. And some managers no doubt tried to implement her ideas in their own organizations. Ultimately, however, Follett's views fell from favor after her death in 1933. Most experts at that time were advocating different ideas and methods, and without Follett on the scene personally to champion her ideas, they soon fell from favor and her work fell into obscurity. But today, her writings have found new favor among managers and management theorists, and she is winning the status and recognition as an important management pioneer that she so richly deserves.

References: *Dana Wechsler Linden, "The Mother of Them All," Forbes, January 16, 1995, pp. 75–76 (*quote on p. 76); and Daniel Wren, The Evolution of Management Theory, 4th ed. (New York: Wiley, 1994)*

---

of employee selection and motivation. Industrial psychology is still a major course of study at many colleges and universities. Another early advocate of the behavioral approach to management was Mary Parker Follett.[22] Follett worked during the scientific management era, but quickly came to recognize the human element in the workplace. Indeed, her work clearly anticipated the behavioral management perspective, and she appreciated the need to understand the role of behavior in organizations. Her work is highlighted in "Working with Diversity."

The Hawthorne studies were a series of early experiments that focused on behavior in the workplace. In one experiment involving this group of workers, for example, researchers monitored how productivity changed as a result of changes in working conditions. The Hawthorne studies and subsequent experiments led scientists to the conclusion that the human element is very important in the workplace.

The Hawthorne Studies

Although Munsterberg and Follett made major contributions to the development of the behavioral approach to management, its primary catalyst was a series of studies conducted near Chicago at Western Electric's Hawthorne plant between 1927 and 1932. The research, originally sponsored by General Electric, was conducted by Elton Mayo and his associates.[23] Mayo was a faculty member and consultant at Harvard. The first study involved manipulating illumination for one group of workers and comparing their subsequent productivity with the productivity of another group whose illumination was not changed. Surprisingly, when illumination was increased for the experimental group, productivity went up in both groups. Productivity continued to increase in both groups, even when the lighting for the experimental group was decreased. Not until the lighting was reduced to the level of moonlight did productivity begin to decline (and General Electric withdrew its sponsorship).

Another experiment established a piecework incentive pay plan for a group of nine men assembling terminal banks for telephone exchanges. Scientific management would have predicted that each man would try to maximize his pay by producing as many units as possible. Mayo and his associates, however, found that the group itself informally established an acceptable level of output for its members. Workers who overproduced were branded "rate busters," and underproducers were labeled "chiselers." To be accepted by the group, workers produced at the accepted level. As they approached this acceptable level of output, workers slacked off to avoid overproducing.

Other studies, including an interview program involving several thousand workers, led Mayo and his associates to conclude that human behavior was much more important in the workplace than had been previously believed. In the lighting experiment, for example, the results were attributed to the fact that both groups received special attention and sympathetic supervision for perhaps the first time. The incentive pay plans did not work because social acceptance was more important than wage incentives in determining the output of individual workers. In short, individual and social processes played a major role in shaping worker attitudes and behavior.

The Human Relations Movement

human relations movement   The perspective that workers respond primarily to the social context of the workplace

Theory X   A pessimistic and negative view of workers consistent with the views of scientific management

Theory Y   A positive view of workers; it represents the assumptions that human relations advocates make

The **human relations movement,** which grew from the Hawthorne studies and was a popular approach to management for many years, proposed that workers respond primarily to the social context of the workplace, including social conditioning, group norms, and interpersonal dynamics. A basic assumption of the human relations movement was that the manager's concern for workers would lead to increased satisfaction, which would in turn result in improved performance. Two writers who helped advance the human relations movement were Abraham Maslow and Douglas McGregor.

Theory X Assumptions	1. People do not like work and try to avoid it.
	2. People do not like work, so managers have to control, direct, coerce, and threaten employees to get them to work toward organizational goals.
	3. People prefer to be directed, to avoid responsibility, and to want security; they have little ambition.
Theory Y Assumptions	1. People do not naturally dislike work; work is a natural part of their lives.
	2. People are internally motivated to reach objectives to which they are committed.
	3. People are committed to goals to the degree that they receive personal rewards when they reach their objectives.
	4. People will both seek and accept responsibility under favorable conditions.
	5. People have the capacity to be innovative in solving organizational problems.
	6. People are bright, but under most organizational conditions their potentials are under-utilized.

In 1943, Maslow advanced a theory suggesting that people are motivated by a hierarchy of needs, including monetary incentives and social acceptance.[24] Maslow's hierarchy, perhaps the best-known human relations theory, is described in detail in Chapter 16. Meanwhile, Douglas McGregor's Theory X and Theory Y model best represents the essence of the human relations movement (see Table 2.2).[25] According to McGregor, Theory X and Theory Y reflect two extreme belief sets that different managers have about their workers. **Theory X** is a relatively negative view of workers and is consistent with the views of scientific management. **Theory Y** is more positive and represents the assumptions that human relations advocates make. In McGregor's view, Theory Y was a more appropriate philosophy for managers to adhere to. Both Maslow and McGregor notably influenced the thinking of many practicing managers.

TABLE 2.2
Theory X and Theory Y

Douglas McGregor developed Theory X and Theory Y. He argued that Theory X best represented the views of scientific management and Theory Y represented the human relations approach. McGregor believed that Theory Y was the best philosophy for all managers.

Source: Douglas McGregor, *The Human Side of Enterprise,* Copyright © 1960 by McGraw-Hill. Reprinted by permission of The McGraw-Hill Companies.

■ The Emergence of Organizational Behavior

Munsterberg, Mayo, Maslow, McGregor, and others have made valuable contributions to management. Contemporary theorists, however, have noted that many assertions of the human relationists were simplistic and inadequate descriptions of work behavior. For example, the assumption that worker satisfaction leads to improved performance has been shown to have little, if any, validity. If anything, satisfaction follows good performance, rather than precedes it. (These issues are addressed in Chapters 15 and 16.)

Current behavioral perspectives on management, known as **organizational behavior,** acknowledge that human behavior in organizations is much more complex than the human relationists realized. The field of organizational behavior draws from a broad, interdisciplinary base of psychology, sociology, anthropology, economics, and medicine. Organizational behavior takes a holistic view of behavior and addresses individual, group, and organization processes. These processes are major elements in contemporary management theory. Important topics in this field include job satisfaction, stress, motivation, leadership, group dynamics, organizational politics, interpersonal conflict, and the structure and design of organizations.[26] A contingency orientation also characterizes the field (discussed more fully later in this chapter). Our discussions of organizing (Chapters 11 through 14) and leading (Chapters 15 through 19) are heavily influenced by organizational behavior.

organizational behavior A contemporary field focusing on behavioral perspectives on management

General Summary	The behavioral management perspective focuses on employee behavior in an organizational context. Stimulated by the birth of industrial psychology, the human relations movement supplanted scientific management as the dominant approach to management in the 1930s and 1940s. Prominent contributors to this movement were Elton Mayo, Abraham Maslow, and Douglas McGregor. Organizational behavior, the contemporary outgrowth of the behavioral management perspective, draws from an interdisciplinary base and recognizes the complexities of human behavior in organizational settings.
Contributions	Provided important insights into motivation, group dynamics, and other interpersonal processes in organizations.
	Focused managerial attention on these same processes.
	Challenged the view that employees are tools and furthered the belief that employees are valuable resources.
Limitations	The complexity of individual behavior makes prediction of that behavior difficult.
	Many behavioral concepts have not yet been put to use because some managers are reluctant to adopt them.
	Contemporary research findings by behavioral scientists are often not communicated to practicing managers in an understandable form.

TABLE 2.3
The Behavioral Management Perspective

■ The Behavioral Management Perspective Today

Table 2.3 summarizes the behavioral management perspective and lists its contributions and limitations. The primary contributions relate to ways in which this approach has changed managerial thinking. Managers are now more likely to recognize the importance of behavioral processes and to view employees as valuable resources instead of mere tools. On the other hand, organizational behavior is still imprecise in its ability to predict behavior. It is not always accepted or understood by practicing managers. Hence, the potential contributions of the behavioral school have yet to be fully realized.

MANAGEMENT IMPLICATIONS Managers should remember that people are not machines and should not focus so much on the technical side of things that they ignore behavioral forces and processes in their organizations. People and their behaviors represent a powerful force that can enhance—or diminish—the effectiveness of any organization.[27] At the same time, managers should not fall prey to the common-sense fallacy that doing things to improve employee satisfaction will result in increased performance. Further, although employee morale and satisfaction are indeed important, managers should not stress these and other behavioral forces to the detriment of productivity and operating systems. ▬

The Quantitative Management Perspective

The third major school of management thought began to emerge during World War II. During the war, government officials and scientists in England

and the United States worked to help the military deploy its resources more efficiently and effectively. These groups took some of the mathematical approaches to management developed decades earlier by Taylor and Gantt and applied them to logistical problems during the war.[28] The investigators learned that problems regarding troop, equipment, and submarine deployment, for example, could all be solved through mathematical analysis. After the war, companies such as Du Pont and General Electric began to use the same techniques for deploying employees, choosing plant locations, and planning warehouses. Basically, then, this perspective is concerned with applying quantitative techniques to management. More specifically, the **quantitative management perspective** focuses on decision making, economic effectiveness, mathematical models, and the use of computers. The two branches of the quantitative approach are management science and operations management.

"Well, being single and a robot, I'm able to put in a lot of overtime."

■ Management Science

Unfortunately, the term *management science* appears to be related to scientific management, the approach developed by Taylor and others early in this century. But the two have little in common and should not be confused. **Management science** focuses specifically on the development of mathematical models. A mathematical model is a simplified representation of a system, process, or relationship.

At its most basic level, management science focuses on models, equations, and similar representations of reality. For example, managers at Detroit Edison use mathematical models to determine how best to route repair crews during blackouts. The Bank of New England uses models to figure out how many tellers need to be on duty at each location at various times throughout the day. In recent years, paralleling the advent of the personal computer, management science techniques have become increasingly sophisticated. For example, automobile manufacturers Daimler-Benz and Chrysler use realistic computer simulations to study collision damage to cars. These simulations provide precise information and enable the auto makers to avoid the costs of "crashing" so many test cars.

■ Operations Management

Operations management is somewhat less mathematical and statistically sophisticated than management science and can be applied more directly to managerial situations. Indeed, we can think of **operations management** as a form of applied management science. Operations management techniques are generally concerned with helping the organization produce its products or services more efficiently and can be applied to a wide range of problems.

For example, Rubbermaid and The Home Depot each use operations management techniques to manage their inventories (inventory management is concerned with specific inventory problems such as balancing carrying costs

Early management pioneers working during the era of the classical management perspective placed little regard on the value and importance of human behavior to organizational effectiveness. Instead, they generally viewed workers from a "machine" perspective, much like robots who were supposed to do as they were told and who were interchangeable with other workers. It wasn't until the Hawthorne studies and the emergence of the behavioral management perspective that managers came to appreciate the importance of human behavior in the workplace. Unfortunately, however, some managers today still ignore the individual needs of their workers and assume that work always takes precedence over other things.

General Summary	The quantitative management perspective focuses on applying mathematical models and processes to management situations. Management science specifically deals with the development of mathematical models to aid in decision making and problem solving. Operations management focuses more directly on the application of management science to organizations. Management information systems are developed to provide information to managers.
Contributions	Developed sophisticated quantitative techniques to assist in decision making.
	Application of models has increased our awareness and understanding of complex organizational processes and situations.
	Has been very useful in the planning and controlling processes.
Limitations	Cannot fully explain or predict the behavior of people in organizations.
	Mathematical sophistication may come at the expense of other important skills.
	Models may require unrealistic or unfounded assumptions.

TABLE 2.4
The Quantitative Management Perspective

quantitative management perspective Applies quantitative techniques to management

management science Focuses specifically on the development of mathematical models

operations management Concerned with helping the organization more efficiently produce its products or services

and ordering costs and determining the optimal order quantity). Linear programming (which involves computing simultaneous solutions to a set of linear equations) helps United Air Lines plan its flight schedules, Consolidated Freightways develop its shipping routes, and General Instrument Corporation plan which instruments to produce at various times. Other operations management techniques include queuing theory, breakeven analysis, and simulation. All these techniques and procedures apply directly to operations, but they are also helpful in areas such as finance, marketing, and human resource management.

■ The Quantitative Management Perspective Today

Like the other management perspectives, the quantitative management perspective has made important contributions and has certain limitations. Both are summarized in Table 2.4. The quantitative management perspective has provided managers with an abundance of decision-making tools and techniques and has increased understanding of overall organizational processes. It has been particularly useful in the areas of planning and controlling. On the other hand, mathematical models cannot fully account for individual behaviors and attitudes. Some experts believe that the time needed to develop competence in quantitative techniques retards the development of other managerial skills. Finally, mathematical models typically require a set of assumptions that may not be realistic.

MANAGEMENT IMPLICATIONS Managers need to learn and understand the basic mathematical techniques and procedures that have been developed within management science. Managers should also know when to use these techniques and recognize their limitations. Further, managers should avoid relying so much on quantitative results that they ignore their own experience and intuition. ■

Integrating Perspectives for Managers

Recognizing that the classical, behavioral, and quantitative approaches to management are not necessarily contradictory or mutually exclusive is important. Even though each of the three perspectives makes very different assumptions and predictions, each can also complement the others. Indeed, a complete understanding of management requires an appreciation of all three perspectives. The systems and contingency perspectives can help us integrate the earlier approaches and enlarge our understanding of all three.

■ The Systems Perspective

We briefly introduced the systems perspective in Chapter 1 in our definition of management. A **system** is an interrelated set of elements functioning as a whole.[29] As shown in Figure 2.3, by viewing an organization as a system, we can identify four basic elements: inputs, transformation processes, outputs, and feedback. First, inputs are the material, human, financial, and information resources the organization gets from its environment. Next, through technological and managerial processes, inputs are transformed into outputs. Outputs include products, services, or both (tangible and intangible); profits, losses, or both (even not-for-profit organizations must operate within their budgets); employee behaviors; and information. Finally, the environment reacts to these outputs and provides feedback to the system.

Thinking of organizations as systems provides us with a variety of important viewpoints on organizations such as the concepts of open systems, subsystems, synergy, and entropy. **Open systems** are systems that interact with their environment, whereas **closed systems** do not interact with their environment. Although organizations are open systems, some make the mistake of ignoring their environment and behaving as though their environment is not important.

The systems perspective also stresses the importance of **subsystems**—systems within a broader system. For example, the marketing, production, and finance functions within Mattel are not only systems in their own right but also subsystems within the overall organization. Because they are interdependent, a change in one subsystem can affect other subsystems as well. If the production department at Mattel lowers the quality of the toys being made (by buying lower-quality materials, for example), the effects of the change ripple down to finance (improved cash flow in the short run owing to lower costs) and to marketing (decreased sales in the long run because of customer

system   An interrelated set of elements functioning as a whole

open system   An organizational system that interacts with its environment

closed system   An organizational system that does not interact with its environment

subsystem   A system within another system

FIGURE 2.3
The Systems Perspective of Organizations

By viewing organizations as systems, managers can better understand the importance of their environment and the level of interdependence among subsystems within the organization. Managers must also understand how their decisions affect and are affected by other subsystems within the organization.

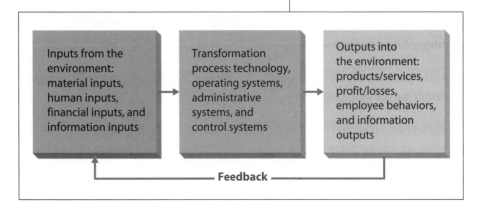

| Inputs from the environment: material inputs, human inputs, financial inputs, and information inputs | Transformation process: technology, operating systems, administrative systems, and control systems | Outputs into the environment: products/services, profit/losses, employee behaviors, and information outputs |

— **Feedback** —

Open systems are those that interact with their environment. In an age of increasing globalization and diversity, an open systems perspective is becoming increasingly important to all businesses. For example, this food service center in Singapore was created to serve Chinese, Indian, and Malay dishes. Not only does the station provide a variety of foods, but it must also offer different varieties of cutlery and other dining accoutrements as well as use signage in different languages.

synergy   Two or more subsystems working together to produce more than the total of what they might produce working alone

entropy   A normal process leading to system decline

universal perspective   An attempt to identify the one best way to do something

contingency perspective   The view that appropriate managerial behavior in a given situation depends on, or is contingent on, a wide variety of elements

dissatisfaction). Managers must therefore remember that although organizational subsystems can be managed with some degree of autonomy, their interdependence should not be overlooked.

Synergy suggests that organizational units (or subsystems) may often be more successful working together than working alone. The Walt Disney Company, for example, benefits greatly from synergy. The company's movies, theme parks, television programs, and merchandise-licensing programs all benefit one another. Children who enjoy a Disney movie such as *Hercules* want to go to Disney World and see the Hercules show there and buy stuffed animals of the film's characters. Music from the film generates additional revenues for the firm, as do computer games and other licensing arrangements for lunch boxes, clothing, and so forth. Synergy is an important concept for managers because it emphasizes the importance of working together in a cooperative and coordinated fashion.

Finally, **entropy** is a normal process that leads to system decline. When an organization does not monitor feedback from its environment and make appropriate adjustments, it may fail. For example, witness the problems of Studebaker, W. T. Grant, and Penn Central Railroad. Each of these organizations went bankrupt because it failed to revitalize itself and keep pace with changes in its environment. A primary objective of management, from a systems perspective, is to continually reenergize the organization to avoid entropy.

■ The Contingency Perspective

Another recent noteworthy addition to management thinking is the contingency perspective. The classical, behavioral, and quantitative approaches are considered **universal perspectives** because they tried to identify the "one best way" to manage organizations. The **contingency perspective,** in contrast, suggests that universal theories cannot be applied to organizations because each organization is unique. Instead, the contingency perspective suggests that appropriate managerial behavior in a given situation depends on, or is contingent on, unique elements in that situation.[30] Stated differently, effective managerial behavior in one situation cannot always be generalized to other situations. Recall, for example, that Frederick Taylor assumed that all workers would generate the highest possible level of output to maximize their own personal economic gain. We can imagine some people being motivated primarily by money—but we can just as easily imagine other people being motivated by the desire for leisure time, status, social acceptance, or any combination of these (as Mayo found at the Hawthorne plant).

■ An Integrating Framework

We noted earlier that the classical, behavioral, and quantitative management perspectives can be complementary and that the systems and contingency perspectives can help integrate them. Our framework for integrating the various approaches to management is shown in Figure 2.4. The initial premise of the framework is that before attempting to apply any specific concepts or ideas from the three major perspectives, managers must recognize the interdependence of units within the organization, the effect of environmental influences, and the need to respond to the unique characteristics of each situation. The ideas of subsystem interdependencies and environmental influences are given to us by systems theory, and the situational view of management is derived from a contingency perspective.

With these ideas as basic assumptions, the manager can use valid tools, techniques, concepts, and theories of the classical, behavioral, and quantitative management perspectives. For example, managers can still use many of the basic techniques from scientific management. In many contemporary settings, the scientific study of jobs and production techniques can enhance productivity. But managers should not rely solely on these techniques, nor should they ignore the human element. The behavioral perspective is also of use to managers today. By drawing on contemporary ideas of organizational behavior, the manager can better appreciate the role of employee needs and behaviors in the workplace. Motivation, leadership, communication, and group pro-cesses are especially important. The quantitative perspective provides the manager with a set of

FIGURE 2.4
An Integrative Framework of Management Perspectives

Each of the major perspectives on management can be useful to modern managers. Before using any of them, however, the manager should recognize the situational context within which they operate. The systems and contingency perspectives serve to integrate the classical, behavioral, and quantitative management perspectives.

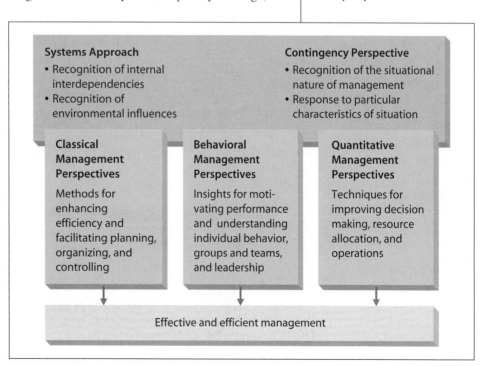

Systems Approach
• Recognition of internal interdependencies
• Recognition of environmental influences

Contingency Perspective
• Recognition of the situational nature of management
• Response to particular characteristics of situation

Classical Management Perspectives

Methods for enhancing efficiency and facilitating planning, organizing, and controlling

Behavioral Management Perspectives

Insights for motivating performance and understanding individual behavior, groups and teams, and leadership

Quantitative Management Perspectives

Techniques for improving decision making, resource allocation, and operations

Effective and efficient management

useful tools and techniques. The development and use of management science models and the application of operations management methods can help managers increase their efficiency and effectiveness.

Consider the new distribution manager of a large wholesale firm whose job is to manage one hundred truck drivers and to coordinate standard truck routes in the most efficient fashion. This new manager, with little relevant experience, might attempt to increase productivity by employing strict work specialization and close supervision (as suggested by scientific management). But doing so may decrease employee satisfaction and morale and increase turnover (as predicted by organizational behavior). The manager might also develop a statistical formula to use route driver time more efficiently (from management science). But this new system could disrupt existing work groups and social patterns (from organizational behavior). The manager might create even more problems by trying to impose programs and practices derived from her previous job. An incentive program welcomed by retail clerks, for example, might not work for truck drivers.

The manager should soon realize that a broader perspective is needed. Systems and contingency perspectives help provide broader solutions. Also, as the integrative framework in Figure 2.4 illustrates, applying techniques from several schools works better than trying to make one approach solve all problems. To solve a problem of declining productivity, the manager might look to scientific management (perhaps jobs are inefficiently designed or workers improperly trained), organizational behavior (worker motivation may be low or group norms may be limiting output), or operations management (facilities may be improperly laid out or material shortages may be resulting from poor inventory management). And before implementing any plans for improvement, the manager should try to assess their effect on other areas of the organization.

Now suppose that the same manager is involved in planning a new warehouse. She will probably consider what type of management structure to create (classical management perspective), what kinds of leaders and work-group arrangements to develop (behavioral management perspective), and how to develop a network model for designing and operating the facility itself (quantitative perspective). As a final example, if employee turnover is too high, the manager might consider an incentive system (classical perspective), plan a motivational enhancement program (behavioral perspective), or use a mathematical model (quantitative perspective) to discover that turnover costs may actually be lower than the cost of making any changes at all.

MANAGEMENT IMPLICATIONS Managers should always remember that there are no universal solutions to problems or standard responses to situations. Just as a carpenter selects certain tools for certain jobs, so should a manager carefully evaluate each situation and then select from the broad array of management techniques, models, and theories that best suit that situation. Further, managers should also keep in mind that any given situation may require multiple perspectives and viewpoints. ∎

Contemporary Management Issues and Challenges

Interest in management theory and practice has heightened in recent years as new issues and challenges have emerged. No new paradigm has been formulated that replaces the traditional views, but managers continue to look for better ways to compete and lead their organizations toward improved effectiveness. Figure 2.5 summarizes the historical development of the major models of management, described in the preceding sections, and puts into historical context the contemporary applied perspectives discussed in the next section.

■ Contemporary Applied Perspectives

In recent years, books written for the so-called popular press have also had a major impact on both the field of organizational behavior and the practice of management. This trend first became noticeable with the success of books such as William Ouchi's *Theory Z*, Thomas Peters and Robert Waterman's *In Search of Excellence*, and Terrence Deal and Allan Kennedy's *Corporate Cultures*. Each of these books, published in the early 1980s, spent time on the *New York Times* best-seller list and was virtually required reading for any manager who wanted to at least appear informed. Biographies of successful and less-than-successful executives like Lee Iacocca and Donald Trump also received widespread attention.

More recently, other applied authors have had a similar impact. Among the most popular applied authors today, along with an example of one of their recent books, are Peter Senge (*The Fifth Discipline*), Stephen Covey (*The Seven Habits of Highly Effective People*), Tom Peters (*Liberation Management: Necessary Disorganization for the Nanosecond Nineties*), Michael Porter (*The Competitive Advantage of Nations*), and Michael Hammer (*Beyond Reengineering: How the Process-Centered Organization Is Changing Our Work and Our Daily Lives*). These books highlight the management practices of successful firms such as Hewlett-Packard, Ford, IBM, and others. Scott Adams, creator of the popular comic strip "Dilbert," is also immensely popular today. Adams himself is a former communications industry worker who developed his strip to illustrate some of the absurdities that occasionally afflict contemporary organizational life. The daily strip is routinely posted outside office doors, above copy machines, and beside water coolers in hundreds of offices.

■ Contemporary Management Challenges

Managers today also face an imposing set of challenges as they guide and direct the fortunes of their companies. Coverage of each of these is thoroughly integrated throughout this book. In addition, many of them are also highlighted and/or given focused coverage in one or more special ways, such as boxed inserts, cases, and extended examples.

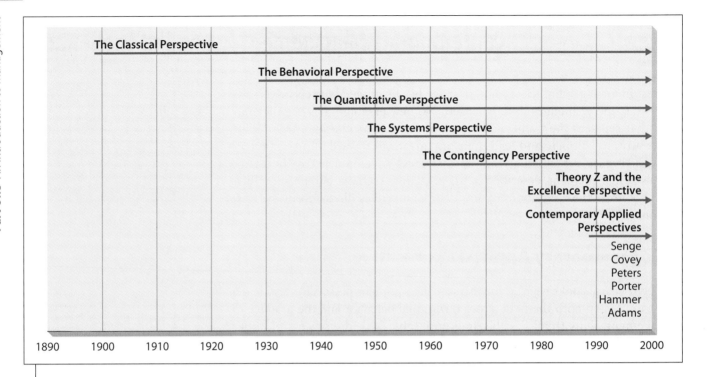

The Classical Perspective

The Behavioral Perspective

The Quantitative Perspective

The Systems Perspective

The Contingency Perspective

Theory Z and the
Excellence Perspective

Contemporary Applied
Perspectives

Senge
Covey
Peters
Porter
Hammer
Adams

1890   1900   1910   1920   1930   1940   1950   1960   1970   1980   1990   2000

FIGURE 2.5

The Emergence of Modern Management Perspectives

Most contemporary management perspectives have emerged and evolved over the last one hundred years or so. Beginning with the classical management perspective, first developed toward the end of the nineteenth century, and on through the contemporary applied perspectives of the 1990s, managers have an array of useful techniques, methods, and approaches for solving problems and enhancing the effectiveness of their organizations. Of course, managers need to also recognize that not every idea set forth is valid, and that even those that are useful are not applicable in all settings. And as we move into the twenty-first century, new methods and approaches will continue to be developed.

Downsizing is one major management challenge that is all too common today. *Downsizing* means to purposely become smaller by reducing the size of the workforce or by shedding entire divisions or businesses. From around the mid-1980s through today, it has become commonplace for firms to announce the elimination of thousands of jobs. For example, in recent years General Motors, IBM, and AT&T have each undergone major downsizing efforts involving thousands of employees. Even some Japanese firms—long thought to be immune to this challenge—have had to downsize as a result of problems in the Japanese economy. Organizations going through such downsizing have to be concerned about managing the effects of these cutbacks, not only for those who are being let go, but for those who survive—albeit with a reduced level of job security.

A second important challenge today is managing diversity. *Diversity* reflects the differences among people. Although diversity may be evident in numerous dimensions, most managers tend to focus on age, gender, ethnicity, and physical abilities and disabilities. The internationalization of businesses has also increased diversity in many organizations, carrying with it additional challenges as well as new opportunities. We cover diversity in detail in Chapter 6, as well as in several boxed features called "Working with Diversity."

Aside from demographic composition, the workforce today is also changing in other ways. It seems as if the values, goals, and ideals of each succeeding generation differ from those of its parents. Today's young workers, often called "Generation X," are sometimes stereotyped as being less devoted to long-term career prospects and less willing to accept a corporate mindset that stresses conformity and uniformity. Thus, managers are increasingly faced with the challenge of first creating an environment that will be attractive to today's worker and then finding new and different incentives to keep people motivated and interested in their work. Finally, managers must incorporate sufficient flexibility in the organization to accommodate an ever-changing set of lifestyles and preferences.

Another challenge that managers must be prepared to address is change. Organizations have always had to be concerned with managing change, but the rapid and constant environmental change faced by businesses today has made change management even more critical. Simply put, an organization that fails to monitor its environment and to change to keep pace with it is doomed to failure. But more and more managers are seeing change as an opportunity for growth, improvement, or competitive advantage, not a cause for alarm. Indeed, some managers think that if things get too calm in an organization and people start to become complacent, managers should shake things up to get everyone energized. We discuss the management of organizational change in more detail in Chapter 13.

New technology, especially as it relates to information, also poses an increasingly important management challenge. The Internet and World Wide Web, local area networks and intranets, and the increased use of e-mail and voice-mail systems are among the most recent technological changes in this area. Among the key issues associated with information technology are protecting employee privacy, improving the quality of decisions, and optimizing a firm's investments in new forms of technology as they continue to emerge. A related issue confronting managers has to do with the increased capabilities this technology provides for people to work at places other than their office. We cover information technology in Chapter 22, as well as in several boxed features called "Management InfoTech," such as the one on page 58. This box highlights some of the potential problems that might arise from relying too heavily on information technology trends such as e-mail and voice mail.

Another important management challenge today is having to choose from the complex array of new ways of organizing that managers can consider. Recall from our earlier discussion that early organization theorists such as Max Weber advocated "one best way" of organizing. These organizational prototypes generally resembled pyramids—tall structures with power controlled at the top and rigid policies and procedures governing most activities. Now, however, many organizations are seeking greater flexibility and the ability to respond more quickly to their environment by adopting flat structures. These flat structures are characterized by few levels of management; broad, wide spans of management; and fewer rules and regulations. The increased use of work teams also goes hand in hand with this new approach to organizing. These issues are given considerable attention in Chapters 12 and 19.

Globalization is yet another significant contemporary challenge for managers. Managing in a global economy poses many new challenges and opportunities. For example, at a macro level, property ownership arrangements vary widely. So do the availability of natural resources and components of the infrastructure, as well as the role of government in business. But for our purposes, a very important consideration is how behavioral processes vary widely across cultural and national boundaries. For example, values, symbols, and beliefs differ sharply among cultures. Different work norms and the role work plays in a person's life, for example, influence patterns of both work-related behavior and attitudes toward work. Cultural differences also affect the nature of

The Blessing and the Curse

Information and communication lie at the heart of what most managers do. Finding out what's going on, thinking about what it means and what else is going on, and then telling others what's going on are constant rituals that define much of the work of many managers. Today's cutting-edge information technology enables these managers to keep in constant touch with all of their information contacts at all times, regardless of time or location. Need to get a quick message to someone? Send an e-mail. Need an important document from the office? Have it faxed. Need to talk to someone right away? Use the cell phone.

Are these good things? Certainly, new information technology has enabled many managers to make decisions better and faster than ever before. And this technology also promotes more frequent communication among people, resulting in improved coordination and enhanced organizational flexibility and response times. Managers can keep in constant touch with others, and a boss, colleagues, and subordinates can get in touch with a manager anytime.

But there are trouble spots to be wary of as well. For example, information technology makes it easier than ever before for managers to suffer from information overload. One recent survey, for example, found that managers in typical large corporations send or receive an astonishing 177 messages each day. The form of these messages runs the gamut from e-mail to Post-it Notes. And many managers fall into the trap of thinking that because they can always be in touch, they must always be in touch. Thus, they check their

> *"Critical thinking and analysis get lost in an interrupt-driven workplace."*
>
> *Nancy Ozawa, consultant**

e-mail constantly, carry their cell phones on vacation or to the golf course, and keep a pager strapped around their waist at all times.

Left unchecked, these managers risk a variety of problems. From an organizational perspective, for example, people may begin to spend so much time communicating that other parts of their work suffer. And instant access to information and the pressure that accompanies modern technology may lead managers to make decisions too rapidly, without taking proper time to reflect and consider all alternatives. From an information-processing perspective alone, a single daily issue of the *New York Times* today contains more information than an average person in the seventeenth century would have encountered in a lifetime!

The pressure can have dire consequences for the individuals themselves. They risk losing balance in their lives, for example, and may be so "connected" that they are never away from their work. As a result, they become prime candidates for burnout and end up falling behind others who take a more ordered and balanced approach not only to their work but to their lives as well.

References: *"Drowning in Data,"* Newsweek, *April 28, 1997, p. 85; "E-Mail Load Turns Zap into Electronic Crawl,"* Wall Street Journal, *May 29, 1997, pp. B1, B6; Rick Tetzeli, "Surviving Information Overload,"* Fortune, *July 11, 1994, pp. 60–64; and "Memo 4/8/97, FYI: Messages Inundate Offices,"* Wall Street Journal, *April 8, 1997, pp. B1, B10 (*quote on p. B1).*

---

supervisory relationships, decision-making styles and processes, and organizational configurations. Group and intergroup processes, responses to stress, and the nature of political behaviors also differ from culture to culture. Chapter 5 is devoted to global issues, along with numerous boxed features called "The World of Management."

Another management challenge that has taken on renewed importance is ethics and social responsibility. Scandals in organizations ranging from Drexel Burnham Lambert Trading Corp. (stock market fraud) to Beech-Nut (advertising baby apple juice as being 100 percent pure when it was really chemically extended) to the Japanese firm Recruit (bribery of government officials) have made headlines around the world. From the social responsibility perspective, increasing attention has been focused on pollution and business's obligation to help clean up our environment, business contributions to social causes, and so forth. Chapter 4 covers ethics and social responsibility in more detail, as do several boxed features called "Today's Management Issues."

Quality also poses an important management challenge today. Quality is an important issue for several reasons. First, more and more organizations are using quality as a basis for competition. The newest advertising campaign from Continental Airlines stresses its recent high rankings in the J. D. Powers survey of customer satisfaction. Second, improving quality tends to increase productivity because making higher-quality products generally results in less waste and rework. Third, enhancing quality lowers costs. Whistler Corporation recently found that it was using 100 of its 250 employees to repair defective radar detectors that were built incorrectly the first time. Quality is also important because of its relationship to productivity. Quality is highlighted in Chapter 21 and boxed features called "The Quality Challenge."

Finally, the shift toward a service economy also continues to be important. Traditionally, most businesses were manufacturers—they used tangible resources such as raw materials and machinery to create tangible products such as automobiles and steel. In recent years, however, the service sector of the economy has become much more important. Indeed, services now account for well over half of the gross domestic product in the United States and play a similarly important role in many other industrialized nations. Service technology involves the use of both tangible resources (such as machinery) and intangible resources (such as intellectual property) to create intangible services (such as a haircut, insurance protection, or transportation between two cities). Although there are obviously many similarities between managing in a manufacturing and a service organization, there are also many fundamental differences.

Many businesses today are moving production to countries where labor costs are relatively low. These Indian girls, for example, are sewing soccer balls. This strategy obviously makes sense from from a cost perspective, and most companies who take this approach do so in an ethical and socially responsible way. But some firms have come under fire because their production is being done by children and/or adults who are paid wages below their local market rates and/or who work in unsafe settings. In a few cases, slave-like conditions are imposed on local workers. These issues pose significant challenges for managers and government leaders around the world.

MANAGEMENT IMPLICATIONS

Staying abreast of contemporary management issues and challenges is a bit of a juggling act for managers. On the one hand, they need to keep up with developments in their field by reading current literature. On the other hand, some of the popular press material about business and management simply describes a fad or, worse, provides an incomplete or inaccurate recipe for success.[31] Similarly, new challenges and issues often arise with little or no advance warning. Some of these remain significant and enduring, while others fall by the wayside very quickly. Thus, the astute manager will learn to take an open-minded but critical view of new ideas and issues. ▬

Summary of Key Points

Theories are important as organizers of knowledge and as road maps for action. Understanding the historical context and precursors of management and organizations provides a sense of heritage and can also help managers avoid repeating the mistakes of others. Evidence suggests that interest in management dates back thousands of years, but a scientific approach to management has emerged only in the last hundred years. During the first few decades of this century, three primary perspectives on management emerged. These are called the classical perspective, the behavioral perspective, and the quantitative perspective.

The classical management perspective had two major branches: scientific management and administrative management. Scientific management was concerned with improving efficiency and work methods for individual workers. Administrative management was more concerned with how organizations themselves should be structured and arranged for efficient operations. Both branches paid little attention to the role of the worker.

The behavioral management perspective, characterized by a concern for individual and group behavior, emerged primarily as a result of the Hawthorne studies. The human relations movement recognized the importance and potential of behavioral processes in organizations but made many overly simplistic assumptions about those processes. Organizational behavior, a more realistic outgrowth of the behavioral perspective, is of interest to many contemporary managers.

The quantitative management perspective and its two components, management science and operations management, attempt to apply quantitative techniques to decision making and problem solving. These areas are also of considerable importance to contemporary managers. Their contributions have been facilitated by the tremendous increase in the use of personal computers and integrated information networks.

The three major perspectives should be viewed in a complementary, not a contradictory, light. Each has something of value to offer. The key is understanding how to use them effectively. Two relatively recent additions to management theory, the systems and contingency perspectives, appear to have great potential both as approaches to management and as frameworks for integrating the other perspectives.

A variety of popular applied perspectives influence management practice today. Important issues and challenges facing managers include downsizing, diversity, the new workforce, organization change, ethics and social responsibility, the importance of quality, and the continued shift toward a service economy.

Discussion Questions

Questions for Review

1. Briefly summarize the classical management perspective and identify the most important contributors to each of its two branches.

2. Briefly summarize the Hawthorne studies and describe the primary conclusions of this research.

3. Describe the contingency perspective and outline its usefulness to the study and practice of management.

4. What are some contemporary issues and challenges that managers must confront?

Questions for Analysis

5. In what ways do you think management in other countries evolved in the same ways as in the United States, and in what ways do you think it may have evolved differently?

6. Explain how a manager can use tools and techniques from each of the major management perspectives in a complementary fashion.

7. Which recently published popular business books have been especially successful? Name some prominent business leaders whose ideas are widely accepted?

Questions for Application

8. Go to the library and locate material on Confucius. Outline his major ideas. Which seem to be applicable to management in the United States today?

9. Identify a local firm that has been in existence for a long time. Interview the current owner about the history of the firm and see if you can gain a better understanding of its current practices by knowing about its past.

10. Read about or study the history of a company in which you are interested. Prepare for the class a brief report that stresses the impact of the firm's history on its current practices.

**Building Effective
Decision-Making
Skills**

EXERCISE OVERVIEW

As defined in Chapter 1, decision-making skills are a manager's ability to correctly recognize and define problems and opportunities and to then select an appropriate course of action to solve problems and capitalize on opportunities. This exercise will help you develop your own decision-making skills while helping you to better understand the importance of subsystem interdependencies in organizations.

EXERCISE BACKGROUND

Assume you are the vice president of operations for a large manufacturing company. Your firm makes home office furniture and cabinets for home theater systems. Because of the growth in each product line, the firm has also grown substantially in recent years. At the same time, this growth has not gone unnoticed, and several competitors have entered the market in the last two years. Your CEO has just instructed you to determine how to cut costs by 10 percent so that the company can cut its prices by that same amount. The CEO believes that the price reduction is necessary to retain market share in the face of new competition.

You have looked closely at the situation and have decided that you can accomplish this cost reduction in three different ways. One is to begin buying slightly lower-grade materials, such as wood, glue, and stain. Another option is to lay off a portion of your workforce and then pressure the remaining workers to work harder. As part of this same option, employees hired in the future will be selected from a lower-skilled labor pool and thus be paid a lower wage. The third option is to replace your existing equipment with newer, more efficient equipment. Although this option requires a substantial up-front investment, you are certain that lower production costs can be achieved.

EXERCISE TASK

With this background in mind, respond to the following:

1. Carefully examine each of the three alternatives under consideration. In what ways might each alternative influence other parts of the organization?

2. Which is the most costly option (in terms of impact in other parts of the organization, not absolute dollars)? Which is the least costly?

3. What are the primary obstacles you might face regarding each of the three alternatives?

4. Can you think of other alternatives that might accomplish the cost-reduction goal?

Building Effective Communication & Interpersonal Skills

EXERCISE OVERVIEW

As defined in Chapter 1, communication skills are the manager's abilities to both effectively convey ideas and information to others and effectively receive ideas and information from others. Interpersonal skills are the ability to communicate with, understand, and motivate individuals and groups. This exercise applies these skills from a contingency perspective in selecting modes of communication to convey various kinds of news.

EXERCISE BACKGROUND

You are the regional branch manager for a large insurance company. For the last week you have been so tied up in meetings that you have had little opportunity to communicate with any of your subordinates. You have now caught up on things, however, and have a lot of information to convey. Specifically, here are the things that people need to know and that you need to do:

1. You need to tell three people that they are getting a pay raise of 10 percent.

2. You need to tell one person that she has been placed on probation and will lose her job if her excessive absenteeism isn't corrected.

3. You need to congratulate one person for receiving his master's degree.

4. You need to inform everyone about the schedule for the next cycle of performance reviews.

5. You need to inform two people that their requests for transfers have been approved, and you need to inform one person that his request was denied. In addition, you must tell one other person that she is being transferred, even though she did not submit a transfer request. You know that she will be unhappy.

You can convey this information via telephone calls during regular office hours, a cell phone call as you're driving home this evening, a formal written letter, a hand-written memo, a face-to-face meeting, or e-mail.

EXERCISE TASK

With this background in mind, respond to the following:

1. Choose a communication mode for each message you need to convey.

2. What factors went into your decision about each situation?

3. What would be the least appropriate communication mode for each message?

4. What would be the likely consequences for each inappropriate choice?

EXERCISE OVERVIEW

Diagnostic skills enable a manager to visualize the most appropriate response to a situation. Conceptual skills are the manager's ability to think in the abstract. This exercise will enable you to use your diagnostic and conceptual skills to extrapolate past trends to the present to the future.

Building Effective
Diagnostic
& Conceptual Skills

EXERCISE BACKGROUND

Some basic consumer products have been around for decades, but others have only recently come into being. Likewise, a variety of products that were once commonplace are no longer available. Examples of such products include the automobile crank (once used to manually start car engines before electric starters were invented) and the wooden slide rule (once used to perform calculations before electronic calculators were invented).

Working alone, identify ten products or services currently available that might not exist in the next few years. Next, form small groups of four or five. Compare your individual lists and come up with a single group list that contains the ten best examples of products or services that may not exist in the future.

EXERCISE TASK

Using the group list, respond to the questions that follow. (Your instructor will tell whether to do this exercise individually or as a group.)

1. Why might each product or service disappear?

2. Can you think of ways to prolong the existence of each product or service?

3. What advice might you give to the owner or top manager of a firm in these industries?

4. How easy or difficult was it to identify the ten requested examples? What factors made it easy or difficult?

CHAPTER CLOSING CASE

Triumph and Failure

For many years the name Triumph was synonymous with fun and high-spirited driving. Triumph sports cars were the envy of the road, and the company that made them enjoyed prestige and respect throughout the industry. But poor management eventually brought the firm to its knees, and cars that once proudly bore its name are now antique relics. The firm was originally based in Coventry, England, and was a successful manufacturer of sedans and sports cars prior to World War II. However, poor management had the firm on the brink of collapse when its plant was destroyed during the war. The Standard Motor Company purchased the Triumph name in 1944 to capitalize on the reputation that the firm had previously developed. Poorly constructed Standard-Triumph (ST) cars did not sell well, however, and the firm was already struggling when the Korean conflict resulted in widespread shortages in building materials.

The British government suggested that ST concentrate on a line of farm tractors that it was exporting successfully at the time. The firm's chairman, however, instead decided to concentrate on designing a sports car using components that were not subject to war-related demands. The result was the TR2 sports car. The new car had a sleek body built on an existing chassis and suspension from another model, with a high-performance engine developed for yet another model. Although initial public reaction was lukewarm, the firm's manufacturing strategy did enable ST to sell the TR2 at a moderate profit and to achieve moderate market success.

During the 1950s and 1960s, Triumph and the British Motor Company (BMC), maker of the MG sports car, operated as a duopoly in England. As such, they competed more on the basis of design and image than on price. Capital shortages kept Triumph in a follower role, however, and limited the firm's ability to invest in new technology. Triumph would make slight modifications in the body or engine performance or braking every couple of years and reintroduce what was essentially the same car as a new model. The TR2 became the TR3, then the TR3A, and, finally, the TR3B in 1961. Other new models introduced by the company, such as the Spitfire and the GT6, were also simply sports-car versions of the Triumph Herald, a sedan the firm introduced in the late 1950s.

Standard-Triumph hoped that the Herald would capture a sizable share of the sedan market and enable the company to achieve some financial stability. Had this happened, the firm would have funds available for the newer machinery necessary for more substantial model changes. Unfortunately, that was not to be the case, and the Herald flopped. On the verge of bankruptcy, Standard-Triumph was purchased in 1960 by Leyland Motor Corporation, Britain's largest manufacturer of trucks and buses. Managers at the new firm, Leyland-Triumph, worked to get better control over production processes and costs and to concentrate on a limited range of sports cars and one model sedan. By the early 1960s, the Triumph sports cars were becoming profitable and Leyland-Triumph was finally making money. But not for long.

By using common components, particularly for engines and chassis, assembly for both sedans and sports cars could be performed on the same lines. This held costs down and enabled prices to be competitive. However, the machinery used in the plants was old, and production and assembly techniques were not highly automated. As a result, rising labor costs began to drive costs upward again. Efforts to try to keep labor costs down led to labor unrest and unionization, which, in turn, led to new shortages and disruptions in the work flow. Parts and supplies were frequently hard to obtain or had to be back ordered for long periods of time.

Competition from U.S. and Japanese manufacturers, coupled with underdeveloped marketing and service organizations, led to still more problems and more losses. In 1968,

Leyland-Triumph and BMC merged to form the British Leyland Motor Corporation in an attempt to strengthen the position of British sports cars in the world market. The newly formed company soon found out, however, that its existing problems associated with aging equipment, a discontented workforce, limited capital, and a poor international network were not easily overcome.

To make matters worse, the British Leyland CEO failed to truly integrate the two companies. The two warring camps seemed to spend so much time battling one another that they could not effectively concentrate on running their business properly and fending off competitors. Due in large part to conflict between the two groups, the firm's big new hope, the TR7 sports car, bombed. The poorly designed, poorly manufactured, and poorly marketed car was yet another major drain on the firm's resources. The final blow was a year-long labor strike.

In 1979, as part of a major corporate consolidation plan, British Leyland began closing out many of its sports-car models. The firm could not get costs under control, and managers began to realize that profits would continue to elude them. Finally, in 1981 all of the sports cars were abandoned. In the late 1980s the firm's bus-making business was purchased by Volvo and the truck business was purchased by DAF of the Netherlands. By the early 1990s, both operations had been shut down by their new corporate owners. Ironically, the sporty two-seater pioneered by Triumph made a big comeback in the 1990s. Fueled initially by the success of the Mazda Miata, BMW, Porsche, and Mercedes have all introduced their own products for the market niche that could conceivably have still been dominated by Triumph.

Case Questions

1. What seemed to be the key reasons for the failure of Triumph?
2. What management actions might have prevented the failure of Triumph? Why and how might they have worked?
3. Could Triumph be relaunched today? Why or why not?

Case References: "Bus Stop," *New Statesman Society,* February 11, 1994, pp. 20–21; Timothy R. Whisler, "Defeating the Triumph," *Audacity,* Fall 1993, pp. 17–25; and "Triumph Before Tragedy: The Odyssey of the TR Sports Car," *Automobile Quarterly,* 1990, Vol. 28, no. 1, pp. 10–29.

CHAPTER NOTES

1. Stephen W. Sears, "The $5 Day," *Audacity*, Summer 1997, pp. 10–19; Michael Lamm, "Model Marketing," *Audacity*, Fall 1996, pp. 32–37; Robert Sobel, "The $150 Million Lemon," *Audacity*, Winter 1997, pp. 10–21; and J. M. Fenster, "Boy Wonders," *Audacity*, Spring 1997, pp. 22–31.

2. Peter F. Drucker, "The Theory of the Business," *Harvard Business Review* September–October 1994, pp. 95–104.

3. David Kirkpatrick, "Intel's Amazing Profit Machine," *Fortune*, February 17, 1997, pp. 60–72.

4. "Why Business History?" *Audacity*, Fall 1992, pp. 7–15. See also Alan L. Wilkins and Nigel J. Bristow, "For Successful Organization Culture, Honor Your Past," *Academy of Management Executive*, August 1987, pp. 221–227.

5. Daniel Wren, *The Evolution of Management Theory*, 4th ed. (New York: Wiley, 1994); and Page Smith, *The Rise of Industrial America* (New York: McGraw-Hill, 1984).

6. Martha I. Finney, "Books that Changed Careers," *HRMagazine*, June 1997, pp. 141–145.

7. See Harriet Rubin, *The Princessa: Machiavelli for Women* (New York: Doubleday/Currency, 1997). See also Nanette Fondas, "Feminization Unveiled: Management Qualities in Contemporary Writings," *Academy of Management Review*, January 1997, pp. 257–282.

8. Alan M. Kantrow (ed.), "Why History Matters to Managers," *Harvard Business Review*, January–February 1986, pp. 81–88.

9. Wren, *The Evolution of Management Theory*.

10. Charles Babbage, *On the Economy of Machinery and Manufactures* (London: Charles Knight, 1832).

11. For a recent discussion that reinforces this recommendation, see Arie de Geus, *The Living Company* (Boston: Harvard Business School Press, 1997).

12. Jac Fitz-Enz, *The 8 Practices of Exceptional Companies* (New York: American Management Association, 1997).

13. Wren, *The Evolution of Management Theory*.

14. Frederick W. Taylor, *Principles of Scientific Management* (New York: Harper and Brothers, 1911).

15. Charles D. Wrege and Amedeo G. Perroni, "Taylor's Pig-Tale: A Historical Analysis of Frederick W. Taylor's Pig-Iron Experiment," *Academy of Management Journal*, March 1974, pp. 6–27; and Charles D. Wrege and Ann Marie Stoka, "Cooke Creates a Classic: The Story Behind Taylor's Principles of Scientific Management," *Academy of Management Review*, October 1978, pp. 736–749.

16. Robert Kanigel, *The One Best Way* (New York: Viking, 1997); Oliver E. Allen, " 'This Great Mental Revolution,' " *Audacity*, Summer 1996, pp. 52–61.

17. Henri Fayol, *General and Industrial Management*, trans. J. A. Coubrough (Geneva: International Management Institute, 1930).

18. Max Weber, *Theory of Social and Economic Organizations*, trans. T. Parsons (New York: Free Press, 1947); and Richard M. Weis, "Weber on Bureaucracy: Management Consultant or Political Theorist?" *Academy of Management Review*, April 1983, pp. 242–248.

19. Chester Barnard, *The Functions of the Executive* (Cambridge, Mass.: Harvard University Press, 1938).

20. See, for example, David A. Nadler and Michael L. Tushman, *Competing by Design—The Power of Organizational Architecture* (New York: Oxford University Press, 1997).

21. Hugo Munsterberg, *Psychology and Industrial Efficiency* (Boston: Houghton Mifflin, 1913). See also Frank J. Landy, "Early Influences on the Development of Industrial and Organizational Psychology, *Journal of Applied Psychology*, 1997, Vol. 82, No. 4, pp. 467–477.

22. Wren, *The Evolution of Management Theory*, pp. 255–264.

23. Elton Mayo, *The Human Problems of an Industrial Civilization* (New York: Macmillan, 1933); and Fritz J. Roethlisberger and William J. Dickson, *Management and the Worker* (Cambridge, Mass.: Harvard University Press, 1939).

24. Abraham Maslow, "A Theory of Human Motivation," *Psychological Review*, July 1943, pp. 370–396.

25. Douglas McGregor, *The Human Side of Enterprise* (New York: McGraw-Hill, 1960).

26. For a recent review of current developments in the field of organizational behavior, see Gregory Moorhead and Ricky W. Griffin, *Organizational Behavior*, 5th ed. (Boston: Houghton Mifflin, 1998).

27. Sumantra Ghoshal and Christopher A. Bartlett, "Rebuilding Behavioral Context: A Blueprint for Corporate Renewal," *Sloan Management Review*, Winter 1996, pp. 23–36. See also "65 Years of Work in America," *Business Week*, October 17, 1994, pp. 106–117.

28. Wren, *The Evolution of Management Thought*, Chapter 21.

29. For more information on systems theory in general, see Ludwig von Bertalanffy, C. G. Hempel, R. E. Bass, and H. Jonas, "General Systems Theory: A New Approach to Unity of Science," I–VI *Human Biology*, Vol. 23, 1951, pp. 302–361. For systems theory as applied to organizations, see Fremont E. Kast and James E. Rosenzweig, "General Systems Theory: Applications for Organizations and Management," *Academy of Management Journal*, December 1972, pp. 447–465. For a recent update, see Donde P. Ashmos and George P. Huber, "The Systems Paradigm in Organization Theory: Correcting the Record and Suggesting the Future," *Academy of Management Review*, October 1987, pp. 607–621.

30. Fremont E. Kast and James E. Rosenzweig, *Contingency Views of Organization and Management* (Chicago: Science Research Associates, 1973).

31. "A Way Too Short History of Fads," *Forbes ASAP*, April 7, 1997, p. 72; "Management Theory—Or Fad of the Month?" *Business Week*, June 23, 1997, p. 47.

Effective Management Pilots Southwest Airlines

Chapter 1 details the various levels and functions of managers in organizations. This video case relates these and other concepts to a specific company.

OVERVIEW AND OBJECTIVES

After completing this video case, you should be able to:

1. More easily identify levels of managers within an organization.

2. Better relate management functions to managers at different levels.

3. Better relate skills and roles to different kinds of managers.

4. Identify linkages among schools of management thought and contemporary management issues and challenges at a company.

COMPANY BACKGROUND

Southwest Airlines is one of the most consistently profitable and effective companies in the United States. Indeed, Southwest is the only major U.S. airline to remain profitable every year since 1990 (Southwest has actually shown a profit every year since it was founded in 1967). The U.S. Department of Transportation recently concluded that Southwest has become the dominant carrier in the nation's busiest air travel markets and is the primary force behind change throughout the entire industry.

Southwest has annual revenues approaching $3.5 billion, little debt, and steadily growing profits. Southwest has 243 aircraft (all Boeing 737s) serving 50 cities in 24 states and has prospered by offering low fares and flying only short routes. There are almost 100 Southwest flights between Dallas and Houston every business day, for example, with some fares as low as $39. Like this route (Dallas and Houston are only about 250 miles apart), Southwest flights are all very short—many are less than one hour long.

A key part of Southwest's success is its ability to control costs. Southwest flies no international routes, serves no meals on any of its flights, has no first-class or assigned seats, subscribes to no computerized reservation systems, and refuses to transfer passenger baggage to other airlines. By flying only a single type of plane, maintenance and training procedures are much simpler (and cheaper) than at other companies. Because of its low fares, Southwest cannot afford to let its planes sit idle or to spend money on frills. Many airlines take an hour to clean and reboard between flights—Southwest can generally do it in less than twenty minutes.

In an industry long plagued by labor problems, Herb Kelleher, the CEO of Southwest, is affectionately known by his employees as "Uncle Herbie." One of

Kelleher's policies is that no employee will be laid off, even when times get tough. His concern and commitment to them have been repaid many times over. For example, as jet fuel prices increased during the 1990–1991 Persian Gulf crisis, more than one-third of Southwest's 8,600 employees took voluntary pay cuts to help the airline buy fuel. Wages at Southwest Airlines are only about industry average, but the employees quickly become immersed in the Southwest culture and most seem willing to put extra time, effort, and energy into their jobs.

CASE QUESTIONS

1. Identify examples of different kinds of managers that Southwest Airlines is likely to employ at different levels in its organization.

2. Discuss how managers at different levels at Southwest Airlines engage in the management functions of planning, organizing, leading, and controlling.

VIDEO REVIEW

Your instructor will now show you a video clip that provides more information about Southwest Airlines.

FOLLOW-UP QUESTIONS

1. Now provide additional and/or expanded examples to answer the Case Questions above.

2. Discuss how managers at different levels of Southwest Airlines use the various management skills identified in Chapter 1.

3. Discuss how managers at Southwest Airlines play various roles as also identified in Chapter 1.

4. Describe how each of the three major schools of management thought discussed in Chapter 2 might be used at Southwest Airlines.

5. Discuss how each of the contemporary issues and challenges noted in Chapter 2 affect Southwest Airlines.

POPULAR VIDEO FOLLOW-UP

Each of the movies listed below provides some insights and examples to illustrate various management concepts and ideas. See if you can come up with other examples.

- *Independence Day* (planning and organizing the counterattack against the aliens; the President motivating the pilots before the counterattack)

- *Titanic* (flawed control system used to monitor for icebergs)

- *Mission Impossible* (planning and organizing a mission)

- *Apollo 13* (planning and organizing a rescue operation)

- *Tucker* (planning and launching a new business)

THE FINEST SHANGHAI FOOD

良い上海料理　　良い

NEW KING TA
JEWELLERY CO.

4FL.　　　MARY BUILDING

NIC

NOBLE HOUS

Princeton
TAILOR
プリンストン

SONY

NEW KING TAI JEWELLERY CO. LTD.
K
NO: PEKING R

3

The Environment of Organizations and Managers

OBJECTIVES

After studying this chapter, you should be able to:

- Discuss the nature of the organizational environment and identify the environments of interest to most organizations.
- Describe the components of the general and task environments and discuss their impact on organizations.
- Identify the components of the internal environment and discuss their impact on organizations.
- Identify and describe how the environment affects organizations and how organizations adapt to their environment.

In the mid-1970s, more than twenty companies were manufacturing heavy equipment—the tractors used in agriculture, the bulldozers used in construction, and so forth. Today, however, just a handful remain, led by Case Corporation, Caterpillar Inc., Deere & Company, and Ingersoll-Rand Company in the United States and by Kubota Corporation in Japan. What happened to the others, and why did these particular businesses survive? The answer is surprisingly simple: for decades firms in this industry essentially ignored their environment. But recently, managers in these firms have recognized the errors of the past and focused renewed attention on the external forces that are most likely to bring them success or failure.

For example, one important business practice that plagued the industry for years was the philosophy of maintaining vast inventories of finished products—sometimes as much as a ten-month supply—and encouraging dealers to do the same. Then, when demand dropped, they would just cut prices. They also didn't worry too much about costs. Instead, when demand was strong, the manufacturers simply raised prices to cover their expenses. Further, the manufacturers gave a low priority to customer service and competed against each other mostly in their domestic markets. And few of the firms in this industry paid much attention to new technology. Instead, they simply tried to copy what their competitors were doing.

But now things have changed. Managers have come to realize that they can function more effectively with a much smaller inventory and less price cutting during down periods. This approach allows them to maintain a smoother cash flow while simultaneously keeping fewer assets tied up in idle inventory. Today's average inventory is down to less than four months. The firms remaining in the industry have also cut their operating costs substantially. Deere, for example, has slashed its workforce by half. Caterpillar and Case have also reported substantial cutbacks. As a result of these and other cost-cutting measures, operating margins throughout the industry have jumped from a meager 7 percent to a robust 13 percent.

Firms like Ingersoll-Rand and Case are also paying more attention to customer service. Service centers have been set up around the world, and top managers help maintain good relationships with big customers. And companies are investing in new technology, which has allowed them to manufacture equipment more productively than in the past and to improve the technological sophistication of their products.

International markets are also playing a bigger role in the day-to-day operations of all equipment manufacturers. Exports at Deere have increased by more than 12 percent since 1996, and Caterpillar recently sent almost $200 million in farm equipment just to the Ukraine. Similar increases also typify Ingersoll-Rand and Case. Kubota has also focused renewed attention on its foreign markets, including the United States, Europe, and South America.

But the real key to success in all of these firms, their top executives agree, is the fact that each has made flexibility and market responsiveness key business practices that permeate every aspect of the organizations. Each respects its environment more, monitors it more closely than in the past, and aggressively tries to respond to events and conditions in the environment as a way of keeping up with the pack, rather than falling so far behind that it would have no hope of ever catching up again.[1]

> *"Rigidity has been common in heavy industry. Now we're finding that we can run the business with fewer assets, lower costs, and a lot more flexibility."*
>
> *Jean-Pierre Rosso, CEO, Case Corporation, quoted in* Business Week, *August 5, 1996, p. 29.*

Managers in numerous equipment manufacturing companies made a mistake that is all too common in the business world—they failed to recognize the importance of their competitive environment and how to manage effectively within that environment. Their inventory mistakes and other basic management problems drove most of the firms in the industry out of business. Fortunately, managers at a few select firms like Deere, Caterpillar, Case, Ingersoll-Rand, and Kubota have turned things around and are once again running their respective firms with a much higher level of effectiveness.

As we note in Chapter 1, managers must have a deep understanding and appreciation of the environment in which they and their organizations function. Without this understanding managers are like one of Deere's tractors—moving along but with no way of maneuvering or changing direction. This chapter is the first of four devoted to the environmental context of management. After introducing the nature of the organization's environment, we describe first the general and then the task environments in detail. We then discuss key parts of the internal environment of an organization. We then address organization-environment relationships and, finally, how these relationships determine the effectiveness of the organization.

The Organization's Environments

To illustrate the importance of the environment to an organization, consider the analogy of a swimmer crossing a wide stream. The swimmer must assess the current, obstacles, and distance before setting out. If he or she evaluates these elements properly, the swimmer will arrive at the expected point on the far bank of the stream. But if the elements are not properly understood, the swimmer might end up too far upstream or downstream. The organization is like a swimmer, and the environment is like the stream. Thus, just as the swimmer needs to understand conditions in the water, the organization must understand the basic elements of its environment in order to maneuver properly among them.[2] More specifically, a key element in the effective management of an organization is determining the ideal alignment between the environment and the organization and then working to achieve and maintain that alignment. In order to do these things, however, the manager must first thoroughly understand the nature of the organization's environments.

external environment Everything outside an organization's boundaries that might affect it

internal environment The conditions and forces within an organization

The **external environment** is everything outside an organization's boundaries that might affect it. As shown in Figure 3.1, there are actually two separate external environments: the general environment and the task environment. An organization's **internal environment** consists of conditions and forces within the organization. Of course, not all parts of these environments are equally important for all organizations. A small two-person partnership does not have a board of directors, for example, whereas a large public corporation is required by law to have one. A private university with a large endowment (like Harvard) may be less concerned about general economic condi-

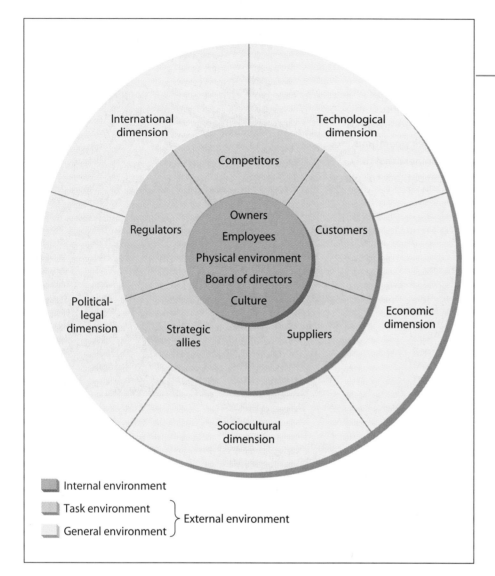

FIGURE 3.1
The Organization and Its Environments

Organizations have both an external and an internal environment. The external environment consists of two layers: the general environment and the task environment.

tions than might a state university (like the University of Missouri) that is dependent on state funding from tax revenues. Still, organizations need to fully understand which environmental forces are important and how the importance of others might increase.

MANAGEMENT
IMPLICATIONS
Managers should always be aware of the environments in which they and their organizations function. Indeed, maintaining an effective alignment between the organization and the environment is a key part of the manager's job. And manager's themselves must also be cognizant of the environment in which they as individuals and groups carry out their responsibilities. ■

Organizations have both internal and external environments. These employees work for the China Bicycle Company and are shown here doing exercises as part of the company's "morale training" activities. They live six to a room in the apartment building in the background, but also earn three times the rural mean wage for the region. Companies from other countries doing business in China must not only be aware of the external environment as it affects their operations, but should also be familiar with the internal environment that may exist within Chinese businesses serving as their competitors, suppliers, customers, and/or partners in the region.

The External Environment

general environment The set of broad dimensions and forces in an organization's surroundings that create its overall context

task environment Specific organizations or groups that affect the organization

As just noted, an organization's external environment consists of two parts. The **general environment** of an organization is the set of broad dimensions and forces in its surroundings that create its overall context. These dimensions and forces are not necessarily associated with other specific organizations. The general environment of most organizations has economic, technological, sociocultural, political-legal, and international dimensions. The other significant external environment for an organization is its task environment. The **task environment** consists of specific external organizations or groups that influence an organization.

■ The General Environment

Each of these dimensions embodies conditions and events that have the potential to influence the organization in important ways. Some examples to illustrate these dimensions as they affect McDonald's Corporation are shown in Figure 3.2.

economic dimension The overall health and vitality of the economic system in which the organization operates

The Economic Dimension The **economic dimension** of an organization's general environment is the overall health and vitality of the economic system in which the organization operates.[3] Particularly important economic factors for business are general economic growth, inflation, interest rates, and unemployment. As noted in Figure 3.2, McDonald's U.S. operation is functioning in an economy currently characterized by strong growth, low unemployment, and low inflation.[4] But economic strength sometimes has two sides. For example, low unemployment means that more people can eat out, but McDonald's also has to pay higher wages to attract new employees.[5] Similarly, low inflation means that the prices McDonald's must pay for its supplies remain relatively constant, but it also is somewhat constrained from increasing the prices it charges consumers for a hamburger or milkshake. The economic dimension is also important to nonbusiness organizations. For example, during poor economic conditions, funding for state universities drops and charitable organizations such as the Salvation Army are asked to provide greater assistance while their own incoming contributions dwindle. Hospitals are affected by the availability of government grants and the number of charitable cases they must treat for free.

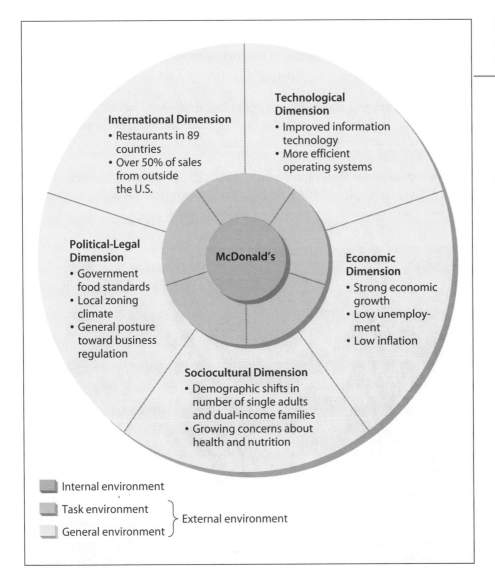

FIGURE 3.2
McDonald's General Environment

The general environment of an organization consists of technological, economic, sociocultural, political-legal, and international dimensions. This figure clearly illustrates how these dimensions are relevant to managers at McDonald's.

technological dimension   The methods available for converting resources into products or services

sociocultural dimension   The customs, mores, values, and demographic characteristics of the society in which the organization functions

Businesses face both opportunities and challenges in their external environment. For example, Marguerite Sylva, Ali Rasheed, and Neusa Benros recently opened a six-chair hair-braiding salon called the Braiderie near a predominantly black part of San Diego. The sociocultural dimension of the general environment was thus the catalyst for the identification of a large customer base in the task environment. Because the stylists only braid hair, but do not cut it or treat it, the owners thought they could sidestep local licensing requirements. Unfortunately, however, the California Barbering & Cosmetology Board (a regulatory agency reflected in the political-legal dimension of the general environment) has been pressuring the Braiderie to comply with the same licensing requirements it imposes on other hair salons and barber shops.

The Technological Dimension   The **technological dimension** of the general environment refers to the methods available for converting resources into products or services. Although technology is applied within the organization, the forms and availability of that technology come from the general environment. Computer-assisted manufacturing and design techniques, for example, allow McDonnell Douglas Corp. to simulate the three miles of hydraulic tubing that run through a DC-10. The results include decreased warehouse needs, higher-quality tube fittings, fewer employees, and major time savings. Although some people associate technology with manufacturing firms, it is also relevant in the service sector. For example, just as an automobile follows a predetermined pathway along an assembly line as it is built, a hamburger at McDonald's follows a predefined path as the meat is cooked, the burger assembled, and then wrapped and bagged for a customer.

The Sociocultural Dimension   The **sociocultural dimension** of the general environment includes the customs, mores, values, and demographic characteristics of the society in which the organization functions. Sociocultural processes are important because they determine the products, services, and standards of conduct that the society is likely to value. In some countries, for example, consumers are willing to pay premium prices for designer clothes. But the same clothes have virtually no market in other countries. Consumer tastes also change over time. Preferences for colors, styles, tastes, and so forth vary from season to season, for example. Drinking hard liquor and smoking cigarettes are far less common in the United States today than they were just a few years ago. And sociocultural factors influence how workers in a society feel about their jobs and organizations.

Appropriate standards of business conduct also vary across cultures. In the United States accepting bribes and bestowing political favors in return are

To Staple or Not to Staple ... That Is the Question

Staples, Office Depot, and OfficeMax are the three largest office supply superstore chains in the United States. Thus, a recent announcement from Staples and Office Depot regarding plans to merge attracted considerable media attention. It also attracted the scrutiny of the Federal Trade Commission, or FTC. The FTC is responsible for monitoring business practices throughout the United States in order to guard against unfair business practices and to enforce antitrust legislation.

Indeed, because of the size of the proposed merger, the two firms needed the official approval of the FTC before they could proceed. And a preliminary review by FTC representatives did indeed raise some concerns about the effects of the merger on competition in eighteen states where Staples and/or Office Depot were already dominant and where OfficeMax did not yet have any stores. The FTC feared that, under those conditions at least, the proposed merger would reduce competition and raise prices.

To help alleviate these concerns, Staples decided to sell sixty-three of its existing stores to OfficeMax, giving that firm an instant presence in key markets. Staples and Office Depot managers believed that the sale would create a more

"The FTC is venturing into new territory. It's not as black and white as before."

Washington antitrust attorney Mark Schildkraut*

level playing field by reducing their own presence in those markets and simultaneously giving their competitor significant market penetration almost overnight. Most experts believed that the FTC would be satisfied with this arrangement and approve the deal.

It was a big surprise, therefore, when the FTC rejected the merger terms, again citing antitrust concerns. Staples and Office Depot are now faced with the prospects of either abandoning their merger plans or taking the issue to court and attempting to override the FTC's ruling. And interestingly, the delayed review and decision process itself affected the competitiveness of the firms as well. Several key Office Depot managers left, for example, not wanting to face the uncertainties the merger would create for their job security. Staples delayed its expansion plans. And OfficeMax greatly accelerated its own expansion plans, picking up big chunks of market share along the way.

References: "Superstores on Notice," Business Week, March 24, 1997, pp. 32–33 (*quote on p. 32); "Staples, Office Depot to Stand Stronger Together," Discount Store News, November 4, 1996, pp. 29–30; and "Staples Merger Blocked; Appeal Unlikely," USA Today, July 1, 1997, p. 1A.

considered unethical. In other countries, however, payments to local politicians may be expected in return for a favorable response to common business transactions such as applications for zoning and operating permits. The shape of the market, the ethics of political influence, and attitudes in the workforce are only a few of the many ways in which culture can affect an organization. Figure 3.2 shows that McDonald's is clearly affected by sociocultural factors. For example, in response to growing concerns about nutrition and health, McDonald's has recently added salads to its menus and experimented with other low-fat foods. And the firm was the first fast-food chain to provide customers with information about the ingredients used in its products.

The Political-Legal Dimension The **political-legal dimension** of the general environment refers to government regulation of business and the relationship between business and government. This dimension is important for three

political-legal dimension The government regulation of business and the general relationship between business and government

basic reasons. First, the legal system partially defines what an organization can and cannot do. Although the United States is basically a free market economy, all levels of government still impose major regulations on business activity. McDonald's, for example, is subject to a variety of political and legal forces, including food preparation standards and local zoning requirements. The firm also recently lost a highly publicized lawsuit when a customer was burned by hot coffee she had purchased at a McDonald's restaurant.

Second, probusiness or antibusiness sentiment in government influences business activity. For example, during periods of probusiness sentiment, firms find it easier to compete and have fewer concerns about antitrust issues. On the other hand, during a period of antibusiness sentiment, firms may find their competitive strategies more restricted and have fewer opportunities for mergers and acquisitions because of antitrust concerns. The "Today's Management Issues" feature highlights a recent example that illustrates this point.

Finally, political stability has ramifications for planning. No company wants to set up shop in another country unless trade relationships with that country are relatively well defined and stable. Hence, U.S. firms are more likely to do business with England, Mexico, and Canada than with Haiti and El Salvador. Similar issues are also relevant to assessments of local and state governments. A new mayor or governor can affect many organizations, especially small firms that do business in only one location and are susceptible to deed and zoning restrictions, property and school taxes, and the like.

international dimension The extent to which an organization is involved in or affected by business in other countries

The International Dimension Yet another component of the general environment for many organizations is the **international dimension**, or the extent to which the organization is affected by or involved in businesses in other countries.[6] As we discuss more fully in Chapter 5, multinational firms such as General Electric, Boeing, Nestlé, Sony, Siemens, and Hyundai clearly affect and are affected by international conditions and markets. For example, as noted in Figure 3.2, McDonald's operates restaurants in 89 countries and derives more than half of its total sales outside the United States. Even firms that do business in only one country may face foreign competition at home, and they may use materials or production equipment imported from abroad. The international dimension also has implications for not-for-profit organizations. For example, the Peace Corps sends representatives to underdeveloped countries. As a result of advances in transportation and information technology in the past century, almost no part of the world is cut off from the rest. Consequently, the international dimension affects virtually every organization.[7]

■ The Task Environment

Because the impact of the general environment is often vague, imprecise, and long term, most organizations tend to focus their attention on their task environment. This environment includes competitors, customers, suppliers, regulators, and strategic allies. Although the task environment is also quite complex, it provides useful information more readily than does the general environment; as a result, managers can grapple with the environmental factors of specific interest to their organization, rather than the more abstract

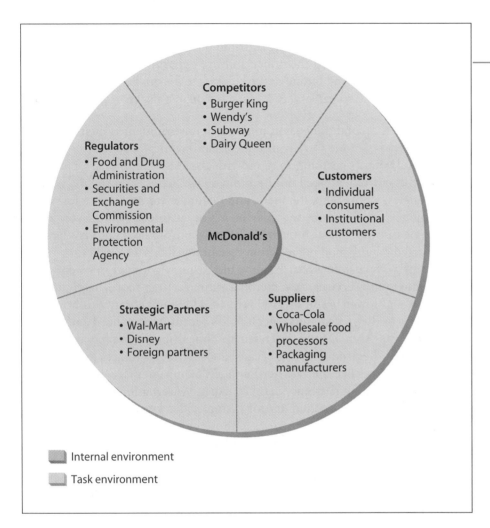

FIGURE 3.3
McDonald's Task Environment

An organization's task environment includes its competitors, customers, suppliers, strategic partners, and regulators. This figure clearly highlights how managers at McDonald's can use this framework to better identify and understand their key constituents.

dimensions of the general environment. Figure 3.3 depicts the task environment of McDonald's.

Competitors   An organization's competitors are other organizations that compete with it for resources. The most obvious resources that competitors vie for are customer dollars. Reebok, Adidas, and Nike are competitors, as are A & P, Safeway, and Kroger. McDonald's competes with other fast-food operations like Burger King, Wendy's, Subway, and Dairy Queen. But competition also occurs between substitute products. Thus, Chrysler competes with Yamaha (motorcycles) and Schwinn (bicycles) for your transportation dollars, and Walt Disney World, Club Med, and Carnival Cruise Lines compete for your vacation dollars. Nor is competition limited to business firms. Universities compete with trade schools, the military, other universities, and the external labor market to attract good students, and art galleries compete with each other to attract the best exhibits.

Organizations may also compete for resources other than consumer dollars. For example, two totally unrelated organizations may compete to acquire

competitor   An organization that competes with other organizations for resources

a loan from a bank that has only limited funds to lend. Two retailers might compete for the right to purchase a prime piece of real estate in a growing community. In a large city, the police and fire departments may compete for the same tax dollars. And businesses also compete for quality labor, technological breakthroughs and patents, and scarce raw materials.

customer Anyone who pays money to acquire an organization's products or services

Customers A second dimension of the task environment is **customers**, or anyone who pays money to acquire an organization's products or services. Most of McDonald's customers are individuals who walk into a restaurant to by food. But customers need not be individuals. Schools, hospitals, government agencies, wholesalers, retailers, and manufacturers are just a few of the many kinds of organizations that may be major customers of other organizations. Some institutional customers like schools, prisons, and hospitals have recently started buying food in bulk from restaurants like McDonald's.

Dealing with customers has become increasingly complex in recent years. New products and services, new methods of marketing, more discriminating customers, and lower brand loyalty have all added uncertainty to how businesses relate to their customers. McDonald's recently introduced a new sandwich called the Arch Deluxe intended to appeal more to adult customers. Unfortunately, the product failed because most adult customers preferred existing menu choices like the Quarter Pounder. Companies face especially critical differences among customers as they expand internationally. McDonald's sells beer in its German restaurants, for example, and wine in its French restaurants. Customers in those countries see those particular beverages as normal parts of a meal, much as customers in the United States routinely drink water, tea, or soft drinks with their meals. And the firm recently opened its first restaurant with no beef on the menu! That restaurant is in India, where beef is not a popular menu option. Instead, the local McDonald's uses lamb in its sandwiches.

supplier An organization that provides resources for other organizations

Suppliers **Suppliers** are organizations that provide resources for other organizations. McDonald's buys soft drink products from Coca-Cola; individually packaged servings of catsup from Heinz; ingredients from wholesale food processors; and napkins, sacks, and wrappers from packaging manufacturers. Common wisdom in the United States used to be that a business should try to avoid depending exclusively on particular suppliers. A firm that buys all of a certain resource from one supplier may be crippled if the supplier goes out of business or is faced with a strike. This practice can also help maintain a competitive relationship among suppliers, keeping costs down.[8] But firms eager to emulate successful Japanese firms have recently tried to change their approach. Japanese firms have a history of building major ties with only one or two major suppliers. This arrangement enables the companies to work together for their mutual benefit and makes the supplier more responsive to the customer's needs. "The World of Management" describes in more detail how this system works and relates a recent incident at Toyota that demonstrates the value of the system.

Honda picked Donnelly Corp. to make all the mirrors for its U.S.-manufactured cars. Honda chose Donnelly after learning that it did high-quality work and that its corporate culture and values were consistent with those

THE WORLD OF MANAGEMENT

Toyota's Suppliers to the Rescue

One of the key elements of the Japanese economy is the *keiretsu*. A *keiretsu* is a close-knit cluster of companies that serve as suppliers to one another. Each *keiretsu* usually includes a large bank to finance the operations of the member firms. The firms themselves are incredibly loyal to one another and often go to great lengths to help their partners remain competitive. A recent crisis at Toyota clearly illustrates the power of the *keiretsu*.

A recent fire at one of Toyota's main suppliers completely destroyed the firm's largest factory. The firm, Aisin Seiki, supplied brake valves to each of Toyota's twenty Japanese auto plants. Since Toyota only kept a four-hour inventory of valves in inventory, the auto maker had no choice but to shut down. And experts agreed that it would be weeks before the plants could reopen.

But those experts failed to account for the strength and loyalty of the thirty-six firms constituting Toyota's *keiretsu*. Within hours of the fire, engineers at Aisin began figuring out how to supply Toyota through other manufacturers. Representatives from Aisin, Toyota, and the other

"Toyota's quick recovery is attributable to the power of the group, which handled it without thinking about money or business contracts."

Yoshio Yunokawa, Toyota executive*

suppliers met and worked around the clock, figuring out the best solutions to the crisis. And the *keiretsu*'s bank opened an unlimited line of credit for all its members.

Other Toyota suppliers quickly converted some of their own manufacturing systems to produce valves, loaned machines to Aisin, and supplied their own workers to help. And none of the companies involved even asked how, when—or if—they would be compensated for their help. In the end, valves began flowing back into Toyota five days after the fire, and the firm was up and running at full capacity again in less than a week. Aisin quickly stepped in and informed the other suppliers that it would repay them for everything, including direct costs, overtime pay, lost revenues, and depreciation. And Toyota, in turn, promised a bonus of $100 million to all the other firms in its *keiretsu* as a token of its appreciation.

References: *"Toyota's Fast Rebound After Fire at Supplier Shows Why It Is Tough,"* Wall Street Journal, *May 8, 1997, pp. A1, A16 (*quote on p. A1); and Alex Taylor III, "Toyota's Boss Stands Out in a Crowd,"* Fortune, *November 25, 1996, pp. 116–122.*

endorsed by Honda. Recognizing the value of Honda as a customer, Donnelly built an entirely new plant to make the mirrors. And all this was accomplished with only a handshake. Motorola goes even further, providing its principal suppliers with access to its own renowned quality training program and evaluating the performance of each supplier as a way of helping that firm boost its own quality.[9] On the other hand, Ford recently tried to implement this approach in the development of the newest version of the Taurus. The plan failed to meet expectations, however, because Ford managers running the project continued to view their suppliers more as adversaries to be controlled than as strategic partners.[10]

Regulators **Regulators** are elements of the task environment that have the potential to control, legislate, or influence an organization's policies and practices. There are two important kinds of regulators. The first, **regulatory**

regulator A unit that has the potential to control, legislate, or otherwise influence the organization's policies and practices

regulatory agency   An agency created by the government to regulate business activities

agencies, are created by the government to protect the public from certain business practices or to protect organizations from one another.

Powerful federal regulatory agencies include the Environmental Protection Agency (EPA), the Securities and Exchange Commission (SEC), the Food and Drug Administration (FDA), and the Equal Employment Opportunity Commission (EEOC). Many of these agencies play important roles in protecting the rights of individuals. The FDA, for example, helps ensure that the food we eat is free from contaminants and thus is an important regulator for McDonald's. At the same time, many managers complain that there is too much government regulation. Most large companies must devote thousands of labor hours and hundreds of thousands of dollars a year to comply with government regulations. To complicate the lives of managers even more, different regulatory agencies sometimes provide inconsistent—or even contradictory—mandates.

For example, the *Exxon Valdez* tanker ran aground in 1989, spilling 11 million gallons of crude oil off the coast of Alaska. The EPA forced Exxon to cover the costs of the ensuing cleanup. Since many observers thought that the ship's captain was drunk at the time, the EPA also mandated that Exxon impose stricter hiring standards for employees in high-risk jobs. To comply with this mandate, Exxon adopted a policy of not assigning anyone with a history of alcohol or substance abuse to certain jobs like tanker captain. Recently, however, another regulatory agency, the EEOC, sued Exxon on the grounds that restricting people who have been rehabilitated from alcohol abuse from any job violates their rights under the 1990 Americans with Disabilities Act. Exxon was thus forced to change its policy but is now being scrutinized by the EPA again.[11] The following cartoon provides another take on this type of issue.

The regulatory environment of business imposes numerous constraints on organizations. Laws regarding employment practices have become particularly complicated in recent years. For example, a firm that uses discriminatory practices can be sued for not hiring someone or for firing a current employee. But the firm can also be penalized if it should reject or fire someone but fails to do so! Not surprisingly, then, many employment decisions today are routinely reviewed by attorneys. And the opinions of these attorneys often determine whether or not someone will be hired or fired.

"I've been speaking to my attorneys, Larson, and this time we think we've got you fired."

The regulatory environment in other countries, however, is even more stringent. When U.S. retailer Wal-Mart wants to open a new store, its regulatory requirements are actually quite low and the procedures it must follow are clearly spelled out. In a sense, within reason and general basic ground rules, the firm can open a store just about anywhere it wants and operate it in just about any manner it wants. But conditions in Germany are quite different. That country's largest retailer, Allkauf, has been trying to open a store in one town—on land that it already owns—for more than fifteen years. But the city government will not allow Allkauf to open because officials fear that local competitors will suffer. And by German law Allkauf's existing stores can be open only 68.5 hours a week; they must close no later than 6:30 P.M. on weekdays, 2:00 P.M. on Saturday, and must remain closed on Sunday. And they can hold large sales only twice a year and can never discount food items.[12]

The other basic form of regulator is the interest group. An **interest group** is organized by its members to attempt to influence organizations. Prominent interest groups include the National Organization for Women (NOW), Mothers Against Drunk Driving (MADD), the National Rifle Association (NRA), the League of Women Voters, the Sierra Club, Ralph Nader's Center for the Study of Responsive Law, Consumers Union, and industry self-regulation groups like the Council of Better Business Bureaus. Although interest groups lack the official power of government agencies, they can exert considerable influence by using the media to call attention to their positions. MADD, for example, puts considerable pressure on alcoholic-beverage producers (to put warning labels on their products), automobile companies (to make it more difficult for intoxicated people to start their cars), local governments (to stiffen drinking ordinances), and bars and restaurants (to refuse to sell alcohol to people who are drinking too much).

interest group A group formed by its own individual members to attempt to influence business

Strategic Partners A final dimension of the task environment is **strategic partners** (also called **strategic allies**)—two or more companies that work together in joint ventures or other partnerships.[13] As shown in Figure 3.3, McDonald's has several strategic partners. For example, it has one arrangement with Wal-Mart whereby small McDonald's restaurants are built in Wal-Mart stores. The firm recently signed a long-term deal with Disney: McDonald's will promote Disney movies in its stores, and Disney will build McDonald's restaurants in its theme parks. And many of the firm's foreign stores are built in collaboration with local investors. Strategic partnerships help companies get from other companies the expertise they lack. They also help spread risk and open new market opportunities. Indeed, most strategic partnerships are actually among international firms. For example, Ford has strategic partnerships with Volkswagen (sharing a distribution and service center in South America) and Nissan (building minivans in the United States).

strategic partner or ally An organization working together with one or more other organizations in a joint venture or similar arrangement

MANAGEMENT IMPLICATIONS

The external environment of an organization can appear bewilderingly complex and ambiguous. Managers can help bring order to this complexity and ambiguity by realizing that some parts of the external environment are of a more general character (the general environment), whereas others are more concrete and definable (the task environment). This understanding allows managers to monitor all parts of the environment while focusing more attention on and being more responsive to those dimensions most relevant to the organization itself. ▬

The Internal Environment

As shown earlier in Figure 3.1, organizations also have an internal environment that consists of their owners, board of directors, employees, and the physical work environment. (Another especially important part of the internal environment is the organization's culture, discussed separately in Chapter 6.)

■ Owners

owner   Anyone who can claim property rights on an organization

The owners of a business are, of course, the people who have legal property rights to that business. Owners can be a single individual who establishes and runs a small business, partners who jointly own the business, individual investors who buy stock in a corporation, or other organizations. McDonald's has 700 million shares of stock, each of which represents one unit of ownership of the firm. The family of McDonald's founder Ray Kroc stills owns a large block of this stock, as do several large institutional investors. In addition, thousands of individuals own just a few shares each. McDonald's, in turn, also owns other businesses. For example, it owns several large regional bakeries that supply its restaurants with buns. These are each incorporated as separate legal entities and managed as wholly owned subsidiaries by the parent company.

■ Board of Directors

board of directors   Governing body elected by a corporation's stockholders charged with overseeing the general management of the firm to ensure that it is being run in a way that best serves the stockholders' interests

A corporate **board of directors** is elected by the stockholders and is charged with overseeing the general management of the firm to ensure that it is being run in a way that best serves the stockholders' interests. Some boards are relatively passive. They perform a general oversight function, but seldom get actively involved in how the company is really being run. But this trend is changing, however, as more and more boards are more carefully scrutinizing the firms they oversee and exerting more influence over how they are being managed. For example, at a recent meeting of Ford's board, the firm's eleven outside directors were first surprised and then angered to learn about unexpected large losses. The losses were attributed to problems with a massive, ongoing global reorganization that was called Ford 2000. The outside directors subsequently prepared a formal letter to Ford's CEO, Alexander Trotman, calling for him to get the problems straightened out quickly. An implied message in the letter was that if he was unsuccessful he would not be retained beyond the end of his current contract.[14]

■ Employees

An organization's employees are also a major element of its internal environment. Of particular interest to managers today is the changing nature of the workforce as it becomes increasingly more diverse in terms of gender, ethnicity, age, and other dimensions. Workers are also calling for more job ownership—either partial ownership in the company or at least more say in how they perform their jobs.[15] Another trend in many firms is the increased reliance on temporary workers—individuals hired for short periods of time with no expectation of permanent employment. The usage of temporary workers has grown by over 400 percent since 1982, and almost 2.5 million temporary workers are actively involved in the workforce today. Employers like to use "temps" because they provide greater flexibility, earn lower wages, and often do not participate in benefits programs. But managers have to deal with what often amounts to a two-class workforce and with a growing number of employees who have no loyalty to the organization where they work, because they may be working for a different one tomorrow.[16]

The permanent employees of many organizations are organized into labor unions, representing yet another layer of complexity for managers. The National Labor Relations Act of 1935 requires organizations to recognize and bargain with a union if that union has been legally established by the organization's employees. Presently, around 23 percent of the U.S. labor force is represented by unions. Some large firms such as Ford, Exxon, and General Motors have several different unions. Even when an organization's labor force is not unionized, its managers do not ignore unions. For example, Kmart, J. P. Stevens, Honda of America, and Delta Air Lines all actively work to avoid unionization. And even though people think primarily of blue-collar workers as union members, many white-collar workers, such as government employees and teachers, are also represented by unions.

The internal environment consists of the owners, board of directors, employees, and physical work environment of the organization. Not surprisingly, however, the internal environment continues to change in most organizations. For example, Al West, chairman of SEI Investments, recently eliminated all secretarial positions in his firm. But he argues that productivity at SEI Investments has mushroomed since managers at the firm became responsible for their own work.

■ Physical Work Environment

A final part of the internal environment is the actual physical environment of the organization and the work that people do. Some firms have their facilities in downtown skyscrapers, usually spread across several floors. Others locate in suburban or rural settings and may have facilities more closely resembling a college campus. Some facilities have long halls lined with traditional offices.

Others have modular cubicles with partial walls and no doors. The top one hundred managers at Mars, makers of Snickers and Milky Way, all work in a single vast room. Two co-presidents are located in the very center of the room, while others are arrayed in concentric circles around them. Increasingly, newer facilities have an even more open arrangement where people work in large rooms, moving to different tables to interact with different people on different projects. Freestanding computer workstations are available for those who need them, and a few small rooms might be off to the side for private business.

MANAGEMENT IMPLICATIONS While managers strive to align their organizations with the external environment, they must also remember that their own work is carried out within the internal environment of their organizations. Owners, a corporate board of directors, employees, the physical environment, and the organization's culture interact to define the environment of managers. ▬

Organization-Environment Relationships

Our discussion to this point has identified and described the various dimensions of organizational environments. Because organizations are open systems, they interact with these various dimensions in many different ways. Hence we will now examine those interactions. First we discuss how environments affect organizations and then note a number of ways in which organizations adapt to their environments.

■ How Environments Affect Organizations

Three basic perspectives can be used to describe how environments affect organizations: environmental change and complexity, competitive forces, and environmental turbulence.[17]

Environmental Change and Complexity James D. Thompson was one of the first people to recognize the importance of the organization's environment.[18] Thompson suggests that the environment can be described along two dimensions: its degree of change and its degree of homogeneity. The degree of change is the extent to which the environment is relatively stable or relatively dynamic. The degree of homogeneity is the extent to which the environment is relatively simple (few elements, little segmentation) or relatively complex (many elements, much segmentation). These two dimensions interact to determine the level of uncertainty faced by the organization. **Uncertainty**, in turn, is a driving force that influences many organizational decisions. Figure 3.4 illustrates a simple view of the four levels of uncertainty defined by different levels of homogeneity and change.

uncertainty A major force caused by change and complexity that affects many organizational activities

The least environmental uncertainty is faced by organizations with stable and simple environments. Although no environment is totally without uncertainty, some entrenched franchised food operations (such as Subway and Taco Bell) and many container manufacturers (like Ball Corporation and Federal Paper Board) have relatively low levels of uncertainty to contend with. Subway, for example, focuses on a certain segment of the consumer market, produces a limited product line, has a constant source of suppliers, and faces relatively consistent competition.

Organizations with dynamic but simple environments generally face a moderate degree of uncertainty. Examples of organizations functioning in such environments include clothing manufacturers (targeting a certain kind of clothing buyer but sensitive to fashion-induced changes) and compact disc (CD) producers (catering to certain kinds of music buyers but alert to changing tastes in music).[19] Levi Strauss faces few competitors (Wrangler and Lee), has few suppliers and few regulators, and uses limited distribution channels. This relatively simple task environment, however, also changes quite rapidly as competitors adjust prices and styles, consumer tastes change, and new fabrics become available.

Another combination of factors is one of stability and complexity. Again, a moderate amount of uncertainty results. Ford, Chrysler, and General Motors face these basic conditions. Overall, they must interact with a myriad of suppliers, regulators, consumer groups, and competitors. Change, however, occurs quite slowly in the automobile industry. Despite many stylistic changes, cars of today still have four wheels, a steering wheel, an internal combustion engine, a glass windshield, and many of the other basic features that have characterized cars for decades.

Finally, very dynamic and complex environmental conditions yield a high degree of uncertainty. The environment has a large number of elements, and the nature of those elements is constantly changing. Intel, Compaq, IBM, Sony, and other firms in the electronics field face these conditions because of the rapid rate of technological innovation and change in consumer markets that characterize their industry, their suppliers, and their competitors.

Competitive Forces Although Thompson's general classifications are useful and provide some basic insights into organization-environment interactions, in many ways they lack the precision and specificity needed by managers who must deal with their environments on a day-to-day basis. Michael E. Porter, a Harvard professor and expert in strategic management, has proposed a more refined way to assess environments. In particular, he suggests that managers view the environment of their organizations in terms of **five competitive forces**.[20]

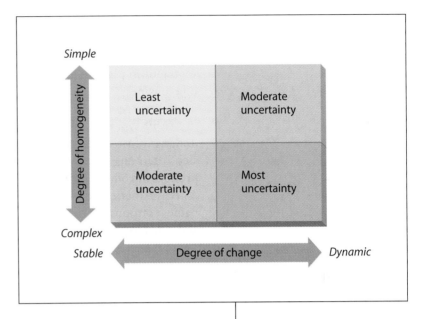

FIGURE 3.4
Environmental Change, Complexity, and Uncertainty

The degree of homogeneity and the degree of change combine to create uncertainty for organizations. For example, a simple and stable environment creates the least uncertainty, and a complex and dynamic environment creates the most uncertainty.
Source: Adapted from J. D. Thompson, *Organizations in Action.* Copyright © 1967 by McGraw-Hill. Reprinted by permission of The McGraw-Hill Companies.

five competitive forces The threat of new entrants, competitive rivalry, the threat of substitute products, the power of buyers, and the power of suppliers

The *threat of new entrants* is the extent to which new competitors can easily enter a market or market segment. It takes a relatively small amount of capital to open a dry-cleaning service or a pizza parlor, but it takes a tremendous investment in plant, equipment, and distribution systems to enter the automobile business. Thus the threat of new entrants is fairly high for a local hamburger restaurant but fairly low for Ford and Toyota.

Competitive rivalry is the nature of the competitive relationship between dominant firms in the industry. In the soft-drink industry, Coca-Cola and Pepsico often engage in intense price wars, comparative advertising, and new-product introductions. Other firms that have intense rivalries include MCI and AT&T, American Express and Visa, and Fuji and Kodak. And U.S. auto companies continually try to outmaneuver each other with warranty improvements and rebates. Local car-washing establishments, in contrast, seldom engage in such practices.

The *threat of substitute products* is the extent to which alternative products or services may supplant or diminish the need for existing products or services. The electronic calculator eliminated the need for slide rules. The advent of microcomputers, in turn, has reduced the demand for calculators as well as for typewriters and large mainframe computers. And Nutra-Sweet is a viable substitute product threatening the sugar industry.

The *power of buyers* is the extent to which buyers of the products or services in an industry have the ability to influence the suppliers. For example, a Boeing 747 has relatively few potential buyers. Only companies such as Delta, Northwest, and KLM Royal Dutch Airlines can purchase a plane. Hence, these buyers have considerable influence over the price they are willing to pay, the delivery date for the order, and so forth. On the other hand, Japanese car makers charged premium prices for their cars in the United States during the late 1970s energy crisis because if the first buyer wouldn't pay the price, two more customers were waiting in line who would. In this case, buyers had virtually no power.

The *power of suppliers* is the extent to which suppliers have the ability to influence potential buyers. The local electric company is the only source of electricity in most communities today. Subject to local or state regulation (or both), it can therefore charge what it wants for its product, provide service at its convenience, and so forth. Likewise, even though Boeing has few potential customers, those same customers have few suppliers that can sell them a 300-passenger jet. So Boeing too has power. Indeed, the firm recently exercised its power by entering into long-term, sole supplier agreements with three major U.S. airlines.[21] On the other hand, a small vegetable wholesaler has little power in selling to restaurants because if the chefs don't like the produce, they can easily find an alternative supplier.

Environmental Turbulence Although always subject to unexpected changes and upheavals, the five competitive forces can nevertheless be studied and assessed systematically and plans can be developed for dealing with them. At the same time, though, organizations also face the possibility of environmental change or turbulence, occasionally with no warning at all. The most common form of organizational turbulence is a crisis of some sort.

Until May 11, 1996, ValuJet was a star in the airline industry. Its revenues and profits were soaring, and its stock price had increased tenfold in less than a year. On that fateful day, however, a ValuJet flight crashed into the Florida Everglades, killing 110 people. Amid charges of poor maintenance practices and shoddy operating procedures, the FAA shut down ValuJet in order to study problems at the beleaguered company and to enable the company itself to get its procedures and standards in line with government requirements. The crisis precipitated a complete overhaul of virtually every part of the company. But while ValuJet was out of operation, competitors captured large blocks of its market share and its image continued to take a beating as the media reported regularly on the crash investigation and subsequent FAA investigations. The shutdown itself cost the company hundreds of millions of dollars, and it may never be able to recapture its earlier momentum and appeal.[22]

Other notable examples of crises include the crash of the space shuttle *Challenger* in 1986, which essentially paralyzed the U.S. space program for almost three years; product tampering aimed at Tylenol in 1982, which cost Johnson & Johnson $750 million in product recalls and changes in packaging and product design; and the 1995 earthquake in the industrial city of Kobe, Japan, which devastated hundreds of businesses. Yet another type of crisis that has captured the attention of managers in recent years is workplace violence—situations in which disgruntled workers or former workers assault other employees, often causing injuries and sometimes death.

Such crises affect organizations in different ways, and many organizations are developing crisis plans and teams.[23] When a Delta Air Lines plane crashed at the Dallas-Fort Worth airport a few years ago, for example, fire-fighting equipment was at the scene in minutes. Only a few flights were delayed, and none had to be canceled. Similarly, a grocery store in Boston once received a threat that someone had poisoned cans of its Campbell's tomato juice. Within six hours, a crisis team from Campbell Soup Co. removed two truckloads of juice from all eighty-four stores in the grocery chain. Still, far too few companies in the United States have a plan for dealing with major crises.

Environmental turbulence can affect organizations in devastating ways. Earthquakes, floods, and explosions can all wreck havoc on even the best-prepared businesses. The ice storm that hit Canada in early 1998 cut electric power to 3 million people and thousands of businesses. Indeed, business ground to a halt for days because people could not get to their offices, factories had no electricity, and trucks were forced to sit in parking lots because the roads were impassable.

■ How Organizations Adapt to Their Environments

Given the myriad issues, problems, and opportunities in an organization's environments, how should the organization adapt? Obviously, each organization must assess its own unique situation and then adapt according to the wisdom

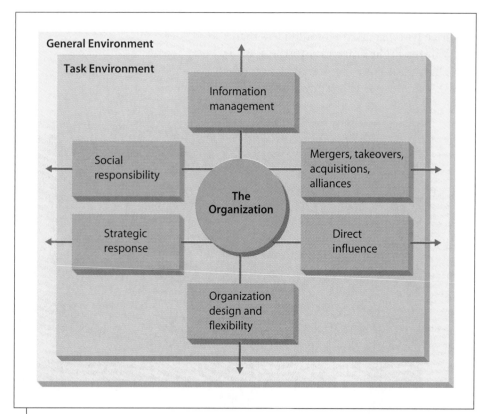

General Environment

Task Environment

- Information management
- Social responsibility
- Mergers, takeovers, acquisitions, alliances
- The Organization
- Strategic response
- Direct influence
- Organization design and flexibility

FIGURE 3.5
How Organizations Respond to Their Environments

Organizations attempt to influence their environments. The most common methods for this are through information management, strategic response, mergers, takeovers, acquisitions, alliances, organization design and flexibility, and direct influence.

of its senior management. Figure 3.5 illustrates the six basic mechanisms through which organizations adapt to their environment. One of these, social responsibility, receives special consideration in Chapter 4.

Information Management
One way organizations adapt to their environment is through information management. Information management is especially important when forming an initial understanding of the environment and when monitoring the environment for signs of change. One technique for managing information is relying on boundary spanners. A *boundary spanner* is an employee, such as a sales representative or a purchasing agent, who spends much of her time in contact with others outside the organization. Such people are in a good position to learn what other organizations are doing. All effective managers engage in *environmental scanning*, the process of actively monitoring the environment through activities such as observation and reading. Within the organization, Merrill Lynch, Federal Express, Ford, and many other firms have also established elaborate *information systems* to gather and organize relevant information for managers and to assist in summarizing that information in the form most pertinent to each manager's needs. (Information systems are covered more fully in Chapter 22.)

Strategic Response   Another way that an organization adapts to its environment is through a strategic response. Options include maintaining the status quo (for example, if its management believes that it is doing very well with its current approach), altering strategy a bit, or adopting an entirely new strategy. If the market that a company currently serves is growing rapidly, the firm might decide to invest even more heavily in products and services for that market. Likewise, if a market is shrinking or does not provide reasonable possibilities for growth, the company may decide to cut back. For example, during the mid-1990s Circuit City was enjoying rapid growth fueled by its electronics-and-appliances retail superstores. But managers also projected that the chain would reach market saturation shortly after the turn of the century. If the company wanted to continue to grow, it would need to use new strategies. Accordingly, the firm began to experiment with several new businesses: one selling new and used cars and another selling home furniture. Other options were also developed. Thus, managers were making a strategic response to their projections about the firm's likely future environment.[24]

Mergers, Takeovers, Acquisitions, and Alliances   A related strategic approach that some organizations use to adapt to their environment involves mergers, takeovers, acquisitions, and partnerships. A *merger* occurs when two or more firms combine to form a new firm. For example, fearing that industry giant American Airlines was considering major expansions, executives at Continental and Delta discussed a potential merger as a strategy for remaining competitive.[25] While this deal eventually fell through, Continental formed a strategic alliance with Northwest Airlines in 1998 for the same basic purpose. Similarly, Martin Marietta and Lockheed recently merged to create a new company. An *acquisition* occurs when one firm buys another, sometimes against its will (usually called a *hostile takeover*). The firm taken over may cease to exist and becomes part of the other company. For example, while Compaq Computer was dominating the home PC market in the mid-1990s, its managers wanted a stronger presence in key business markets. One route would have been to invest heavily and spend several years "growing" such a business from scratch. Instead, in June 1997 Compaq decided to buy an existing company that already had a strong presence in that market, Tandem Computers.[26] After a transitional period, Tandem per se will no longer exist. And in similar fashion, Compaq also acquired Digital Equipment in early 1998.

In other cases, the acquired firm often continues to operate as a subsidiary of the acquiring company. Royal Caribbean Cruise Lines recently bought controlling interest in Celebrity Cruise Lines, but intends to maintain it as a separate cruise line. And as already discussed, in a *partnership* or *alliance* the firm undertakes a new venture with another firm. A company engages in these kinds of strategies for a variety of reasons, such as easing entry into new markets or expanding its presence in a current market.

Organization Design and Flexibility   An organization may also adapt to environmental conditions by incorporating flexibility in its structural design. For example, a firm that operates in an environment with relatively low levels of uncertainty might choose to use a design with many basic rules, regulations, and standard operating procedures. Alternatively, a firm that faces a great deal of uncertainty might choose a design with relatively few standard operating procedures, instead allowing managers considerable discretion and flexibility over decisions. The former type, sometimes called a mechanistic organization design, is characterized by formal and rigid rules and relationships. The latter, sometimes called an organic design, is considerably more flexible and permits the organization to respond quickly to environmental change. These and related issues are covered in detail in Chapter 12.

Direct Influence of the Environment   Organizations are not necessarily helpless in the face of their environments. Indeed, many organizations are able to directly influence their environment in many different ways. For example, firms can influence their suppliers by signing long-term contracts with fixed prices as a hedge against inflation. Or a firm might become its own supplier. Sears, for example, owns some of the firms that produce the goods it sells, and

Campbell Soup Co. has started making its own soup cans. Similarly, almost any major activity a firm engages in affects its competitors. When JVC lowers the prices of its CD players, Sony may be forced to follow suit. Organizations also influence their customers by creating new uses for products, finding entirely new customers, and taking customers away from competitors. Organizations also influence their customers by convincing them that they need something new. Automobile manufacturers use this strategy in their advertising to convince people that they need a new car every two or three years.

Organizations influence their regulators through lobbying and bargaining. Lobbying involves sending a company or industry representative to Washington in an effort to influence relevant agencies, groups, and committees. For example, the U.S. Chamber of Commerce lobby, the nation's largest business lobby, has an annual budget of more than $100 million. The automobile companies have been successful on several occasions in bargaining with the EPA to extend deadlines for compliance with pollution control and mileage standards. Mobil Corporation has long attempted to influence public opinion and government action through an ongoing series of advertisements about the virtues of free enterprise. "The Quality Challenge" summarizes another recent instance involving an organization's ability to influence its regulatory environment.

MANAGEMENT IMPLICATIONS Managers should remember that their organization is influenced by a wide array of forces and elements in the external environment. Some of these forces and elements are relatively easy to recognize and anticipate, whereas others are more unpredictable or even impossible to anticipate. Fortunately, managers can adopt one or more strategies to adapt to their environment. Although some events are, of course, uncontrollable, managers can at least buffer their organizations to some extent through the astute use of these strategies.

The Environment and Organizational Effectiveness

Earlier in this chapter we noted the vital importance of maintaining proper alignment between the organization and its environments. The various mechanisms through which environments and organizations influence one another can cause this alignment to shift, however, and even the best managed organizations sometimes slip from their preferred environmental position. But well-managed companies recognize this problem and take corrective action to get back on track. Recall that in Chapter 1 we said that effectiveness involved doing the right things. Given the interactions between organizations and their environments, it follows that effectiveness is ultimately related to how well an organization understands, reacts to, and influences its environment.[27]

THE QUALITY CHALLENGE

Russell Stover Plays the (Chocolate) Trump Card

Like many communities, the small Texas town of Corsicana is anxious to attract new industry and create new jobs for its citizens. Sometimes, however, city officials can be too zealous in their quest for new business and unforeseen problems can result. For example, everyone was ecstatic when Russell Stover announced that it would build a $65 million candy factory, employing at least six hundred people, in Corsicana. A candy factory is a "clean" business and can even serve as a tourist stop.

Corsicana's city manager was pleased and moved aggressively ahead on locating other new businesses for the community. His next big announcement was that Griffin Industries would be building a factory a few miles from the Russell Stover site and would employ about fifty people. But then problems began to surface.

Other community leaders soon learned that the plant to be built by Griffin Industries was a rendering facility—a factory for cooking used restaurant grease and butcher waste into a product used in animal food. Next, Russell Stover announced that it was placing its plans on hold because of concerns about the rendering plant. In particular,

> *"It's an issue of simply our inability to locate in proximity to a potential odor source."*
>
> ———————————————
>
> *Tom Ward, Russell Stover executive**

> *"We're not going to emit any odors. We have to meet the state regulations with air scrubbers and so on."*
>
> ———————————————
>
> *William Shirley, Griffin Industries executive***

Russell Stover officials said that odors from the Griffin plant could permeate its candy, candy boxes and wrappers. These odors, in turn, would adversely affect the firm's products and image in the marketplace. City officials, understandably, wanted to keep Russell Stover and thus tried to block Griffin's plans through a series of legal maneuvers. Eventually, however, they appeared to have no legal way to keep Griffin out. Then Russell Stover played its trump card—it said that the town had to choose between the two firms. Faced with this dilemma, Corsicana leaders decided to buy back from Griffin Industries the land it had purchased for its factory at a premium price. Thus, Griffin made a nice profit on the deal, Russell Stover proceeded with its construction plans, and the town's city manager was soon looking for a new job.

References: *"Town May Lose Chocolate Factory If Fat Plant Is Allowed To Be Built," Associated Press news release published in the* Bryan-College Station Eagle, *June 7, 1996, pp. A9, A13 (*,** quotes on pages A9 and A13, respectively); "Russell Stover and the Chocolate Wars," Kansas City Business Journal, March 28, 1997, pp. 1–2.*

■ Models of Organizational Effectiveness

Unfortunately, there is no consensus about how to measure effectiveness. For example, an organization can make itself look extremely effective in the short term by ignoring research and development (R&D), buying cheap materials, ignoring quality control, and skimping on wages. Over time, though, the firm will no doubt falter. On the other hand, taking action consistent with a longer view such as making appropriate investments in R&D may displease investors who have a short-term outlook. Little wonder, then, that there are many different models of organizational effectiveness.

The *systems resource approach* to organizational effectiveness focuses on the extent to which the organization can acquire the resources it needs.[28] A firm that can get raw materials during a shortage is effective from this perspective. The *internal processes approach* deals with the internal mechanisms of the organization and focuses on minimizing strain, integrating individuals and the organization, and conducting smooth and efficient operations.[29] An organization that focuses primarily on maintaining employee satisfaction and morale and being efficient subscribes to this view. The *goal approach* focuses on the degree to which an organization obtains its goals.[30] When a firm establishes a goal of increasing sales by 10 percent and then achieves that increase, the goal approach maintains that the organization is effective. Finally, the *strategic constituencies approach* focuses on the groups that have a stake in the organization.[31] In this view, effectiveness is the extent to which the organization satisfies the demands and expectations of all these groups.

Although these four basic models of effectiveness are not necessarily contradictory, they do focus on different aspects of organizational performance. The systems resource approach focuses on inputs, the internal processes approach focuses on transformation processes, the goal approach focuses on outputs, and the strategic constituencies approach focuses on feedback. Thus, rather than adopting a single approach, organizational effectiveness can best

FIGURE 3.6
A Model of Organizational Effectiveness

The systems resource, internal processes, goal, and strategic constituencies each focuses on a different aspect of organizational effectiveness. Thus they can be combined to create an overall integrative perspective on effectiveness.

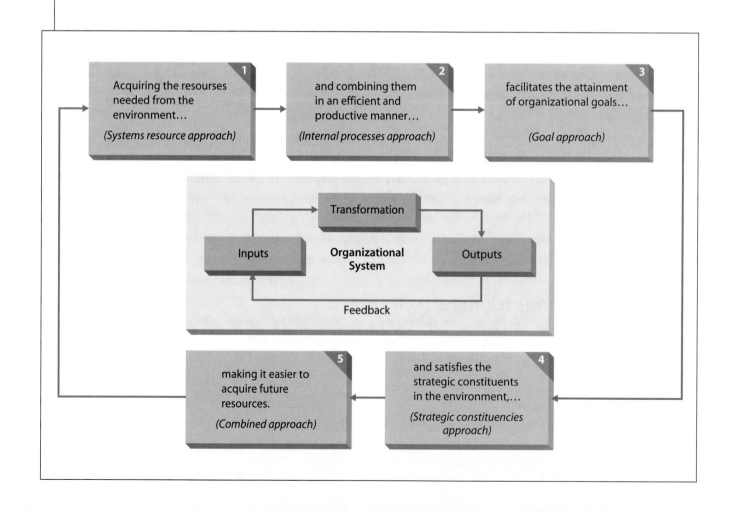

be understood by an integrated perspective such as the one illustrated in Figure 3.6. At the core of this unifying model is the organizational system, with its inputs, transformations, outputs, and feedback. Surrounding this core are the four basic approaches to effectiveness as well as a combined approach, which incorporates the other four. The basic argument is that an organization must essentially satisfy the requirements imposed on it by each of the effectiveness perspectives.

Achieving organizational effectiveness is not an easy task. The key to doing so is understanding the environment in which the organization functions. With this understanding as a foundation, managers can then chart the "correct" path for the organization as it positions itself in that environment. If managers can identify where they want the organization to be relative to other parts of their environment, and how to best get there, they stand a good chance of achieving effectiveness. On the other hand, if they pick the wrong target, or go about achieving their goals in the wrong way, they are likely to be less effective.

■ Examples of Organizational Effectiveness

Given the various models and perspectives on organizational effectiveness, it's not surprising that even the experts do not always agree on which companies are most effective. For example, for years *Fortune* has compiled an annual list of the "Most Admired" companies in the United States. Based on a large survey of leading executives, the rankings presumably reflect the organizations' ability to innovate; quality of management; value as a long-term investment; community and environmental responsibility; quality of products and services; financial soundness; use of corporate assets; and ability to attract, develop, and keep talented people. The 1998 list of *Fortune*'s ten most admired firms appears in Table 3.1.

Also in Table 3.1 is *Business Week*'s 1997 list of the ten best performing companies in the United States as determined by revenue and profit growth, return on investment, net profit margins, and return on equity over periods of one and three years. Interestingly, there are both differences and similarities between the lists. Given that "admiration" and "performance" would each seem to be highly related to effectiveness, a stronger correspondence between the two lists might have been expected. It is important to note, of course, that the magazines' editors used different variables and methods to develop their respective lists, and every firm included on one list but not the other is still a very well-managed company. But the disparities in the lists also underscore the difficulties and judgment calls that are involved when trying to really evaluate the effectiveness of any given company or organization.

Fortune's Most Admired Companies (1998)	*Business Week*'s Best Performing Companies (1998)
1. General Electric	1. Microsoft
2. Microsoft	2. Dell Computer
3. Coca-Cola	3. Cisco Systems
4. Intel	4. Intel
5. Hewlett-Packard	5. Compaq Computer
6. Southwest Airlines	6. MBNA
7. Berkshire Hathaway	7. Tellabs
8. Disney	8. EMC
9. Johnson & Johnson	9. Computer Associates Int.
10. Merck	10. Morgan Stanley Dean Witter

TABLE 3.1

Examples of Admired and High-Performing Firms

Source: "America's Most Admired Companies," *Fortune*, March 2, 1998, pp. 70–82; and "The Best Performers," *Business Week*, March 30, 1998, p. 76.

MANAGEMENT
IMPLICATIONS

Managers need to remember that the performance of their organization is best evaluated from a multifaceted and dynamic point of view. No single measure or calculation can be used to judge effectiveness. Instead, effectiveness must be approached from multiple perspectives. Moreover, managers should also keep in mind that even experts may disagree on what constitutes effectiveness and how different organizations compare to one another. ▬

Summary of Key Points

Environmental factors play a major role in determining an organization's success or failure. Managers should strive to maintain the proper alignment between their organization and its environment. All organizations have both external and internal environments.

The external environment is composed of the general and task environment layers. The general environment comprises the nonspecific elements of the organization's surroundings that might affect its activities. It consists of five dimensions: economic, technological, sociocultural, political-legal, and international. The effects of these dimensions on the organization are broad and gradual. The task environment comprises specific dimensions of the organization's surroundings that are very likely to influence the organization. It also consists of five elements: competitors, customers, suppliers, regulators, and strategic partners. Because these dimensions are associated with specific organizations in the environment, their effects are likely to be more direct and immediate.

The internal environment consists of the organization's owners, board of directors, employees, physical environment, and culture. Owners are those who have property rights claims on the organization. The board of directors, elected by stockholders, is responsible for overseeing a firm's top managers. Individual employees and the labor unions they sometimes join are other important parts of the internal environment. The physical environment, yet another part of the internal environment, varies from one organization to another.

Organizations and their environments affect each other in several ways. Environmental influences on the organization can occur through uncertainty, competitive forces, and turbulence. Organizations, in turn, use information management; strategic response; mergers, takeovers, acquisitions, and alliances; organization design and flexibility; direct influence; and social responsibility to adapt to their task environments.

One important indicator of how well an organization deals with its environment is its level of effectiveness. Organizational effectiveness requires that the organization do a good job of procuring resources, managing them properly, achieving its goals, and satisfying its constituencies. Because of the complexities associated with meeting these requirements, however, experts may disagree as to the effectiveness of any given organization at any given point in time.

Discussion Questions

Questions for Review

1. Why is an organization's environment so important? Identify and discuss each of the major dimensions of the general environment.

2. What is an organization's task environment? What are the major dimensions of that environment?

3. Name and describe the major forces that affect organization-environment relationships?

4. What is organizational effectiveness? How is it studied and assessed?

Questions for Analysis

5. Can you think of dimensions of the task environment that are not discussed in the text? Indicate their linkage to those that are discussed.

6. Some organizations come to be part-owners of other firms through mergers and acquisitions. How does the nature of partial ownership complicate the organization-environment relationship?

7. How would each dimension of an organization's task environment and internal environment assess the organization's effectiveness? Can an organization be equally effective from the perspective of each of these different groups? Why or why not?

Questions for Application

8. Go to the library and research a company. Characterize its level of effectiveness according to each of the four basic models. Share your results with the class.

9. Interview a manager from a local organization about his or her organization's environments—general, task, and internal. In the course of the interview, are all of the major dimensions identified? Why or why not?

10. Outline the several environments of your college or university. Be detailed about the dimensions and provide specific examples to illustrate how each dimension affects your institution.

Building Effective Time-Management Skills

EXERCISE OVERVIEW

Time-management skills refer to the manager's ability to prioritize work, to work efficiently, and to delegate appropriately. This exercise gives you an opportunity to relate time-management issues to environment pressures and opportunities.

EXERCISE BACKGROUND

As discussed in this chapter, managers and organizations must be sensitive to a variety of environment dimensions and forces reflected in the general, task, and internal environments. The general environment consists of the economic, technological, political-legal, sociocultural, and international dimensions. The task environment includes competitors, customers, suppliers, regulators, and strategic partners. The internal environment consists of owners, board of directors, employees, and the physical environment.

The problem faced by managers is that time is a finite resource. There are only so many hours in a day and only so many things that can be done in a given period of time. Thus, managers must constantly make choices about how they spend their time. Clearly, of course, they should try to use their time wisely and direct it at the more important challenges and opportunities they face. Spending time on a trivial issue while an important issue gets neglected is a mistake.

Time-management experts often suggest that managers begin each day by making a list of what they need to accomplish that day. After the list is compiled, the manager is advised to sort these daily tasks into three groups: tasks that must be addressed that day, tasks that should be addressed that day but which could be postponed if necessary, and tasks that can easily be postponed. The manager is then advised to perform the tasks in order of priority.

EXERCISE TASK

With the preceding background information as context, do the following:

1. Across the top of a sheet of paper, write the three priority levels noted at the beginning of this exercise.

2. Down the left side of the same sheet of paper, write the various elements and dimensions of the task and internal environment of business.

3. At the intersection of each row and column, think of an appropriate example that a manager might face. For example, think of a high-priority, a moderate-priority, and a low-priority situation involving a customer.

4. Form a small group with two or three classmates and share the examples you each developed. Focus on whether group members agree or disagree on the prioritization of each example.

Building Effective Diagnostic Skills

EXERCISE OVERVIEW

Diagnostic skills are the skills that enable a manager to visualize the most appropriate response to a situation. These skills are especially important as managers try to achieve effective environmental alignment. In some ways the various elements of the environment are like a chessboard—taking action with respect to one part of the environment may also affect other parts of the environment. Diagnostic skills can help a manager anticipate these second-level influences.

EXERCISE BACKGROUND

Assume that you are the top manager at a company very much like Merry-Go-Round in its heyday (for background, see the "Chapter Closing Case" on page 100). The firm (today) is healthy, has almost one thousand stores, and is growing rapidly. To fuel new growth, however, you want to implement some new plans. One option you are considering is launching a new chain of stores targeted at older consumers. Another option is to expand your existing stores to include nonclothing products like compact discs, videos, books, and magazines also geared to younger consumers. The logic behind this option would be to provide "one-stop shopping" for your existing customers.

EXERCISE TASK

With the preceding background information as context, do the following:

1. On a sheet of paper, list the elements that constitute an organization's task environment.

2. Beside each element write down how the first option above might affect your relationship with that part of the task environment. For example, how might option one affect your relationship with your existing suppliers?

3. Repeat this activity for the second option being considered.

EXERCISE OVERVIEW

Communication skills refer to the manager's abilities to both effectively convey ideas and information to others and effectively receive ideas and information from others. Communication skills are very important when a manager is attempting to respond to or influence some element from the organization's external environment. This exercise will help you develop your communication skills as they relate to this situation.

EXERCISE BACKGROUND

Assume that you work for a large manufacturing firm. Nine years ago, a factory owned by your company was embroiled in a major environmental disaster involving toxic waste disposal. The managers involved in the disaster, clearly your company's fault, were all fired. New procedures for dealing with waste disposal were also developed, and since that earlier situation no further problems have occurred.

The state where the factory is located is currently under fire from the Environmental Protection Agency to impose tighter environmental protection regulations on a variety of industries. The state, however, cannot afford to tighten regulations out of its existing budget. A plan recently introduced in the state legislature calls for the imposition of a new tax on all businesses found guilty of improper waste disposal, as well as other forms of pollution, anytime during the last ten years. This tax will be used to enforce the new regulations.

At the present time it is unclear as to whether the tax would apply to your firm for a single year or if it will be indefinitely imposed on any firm that initially qualifies. Your boss has told you—off the record—that the firm can live with a one-time tax. But if it will remain in place for your company indefinitely, the company will close the plant. A plant closure would also have a serious negative impact on the state's economy. The boss has also placed you in charge of media relations regarding this situation.

EXERCISE TASK

With the preceding background information as context, do the following:

1. Draft a press release stating your company's position on the potential tax.

2. Imagine that you are going to be interviewed by a reporter known to be "friendly" to your company. The reporter has agreed that you can submit potential interview questions in advance. Draft three questions and your answers to them.

3. Imagine that a reporter known to be "hostile" to your company has requested an answer. List three questions that might be asked and draft your answers to them.

Building Effective
Communication &
Interpersonal Skills

CHAPTER CLOSING CASE

When the Merry-Go-Round Stops ...

Merry-Go-Round Enterprises was once one of the most envied retailers in the United States. But because the firm lost sight of its customers' preferences, made an ill-advised acquisition, and couldn't cope with rapid growth, Merry-Go-Round fell into bankruptcy and was eventually dissolved. Indeed, it provides a classic story of how a firm can stumble when it fails to keep in contact with and to maintain proper alignment with its environment.

The firm was started in 1968 by an unorthodox entrepreneur named Leonard Weinglass. At the time Weinglass was a traveling sales representative for a clothing firm. He believed that the company he worked for, like other major retailers, was missing a bet by ignoring contemporary fashion trends among younger consumers. Thus, when he launched Merry-Go-Round, he based its product mix on trends reflected in movies and music aimed at young people.

From 1968 through the early 1990s, Merry-Go-Round was like a skyrocket. In rapid succession it hit home runs by betting on bell bottom pants (popularized by the Beatles), disco suits (John Travolta and *Saturday Night Fever*), bright leather jackets (Michael Jackson), flight jackets (Tom Cruise and *Top Gun*), parachute pants (heavy-metal band Quiet Riot), and black bustiers (Madonna). Meanwhile, the firm grew rapidly and eventually had about one thousand stores in malls across the country. And Weinglass moved to Florida, turning over operations to other managers.

But by then the firm had begun to lose touch with its market. In the early 1990s the fashion market for young consumers had started splintering into many different segments. Some retailers, like The Gap, found success by offering a more diverse product mix within its stores. Others began to offer variations in product lines in different regions of the country. But managers at Merry-Go-Round thought they knew better. Thus, in 1992 they ignored these changes in the market and made yet another big bet on a single new fad, this time based on hip-hop fashion—brightly colored, baggy clothes worn by many rap stars.

As it turned out, this decision was a big mistake. While hip-hop clothes sold well in some areas, they languished on store shelves in others. This product mistake, combined with a general downturn in retailing, caused sales throughout the Merry-Go-Round chain to decline. And managers began to search for new ways to regain the firm's momentum and growth.

In 1993, the Melville Corporation approached Merry-Go-Round about buying its 450-store Chess King clothing chain. In retrospect, the deal made no sense for Merry-Go-Round. Chess King itself was experiencing declining sales, its products were not well regarded by consumers, and its stores were in many of the same markets with existing Merry-Go-Round stores. Nevertheless, the price of $40 million was deemed a bargain and the deal was consummated.

The problems of merging the firms were greater than anticipated, however, and declining profits became mounting losses. With nearly fifteen hundred stores to oversee, rampant strife among the firm's top executives about what to do, and a cash crunch caused by the acquisition of Chess King, chaos reigned at Merry-Go-Round. In 1994, the firm had no choice but to file for protection under Chapter 11 of the bankruptcy code.

Weinglass returned to active duty in an effort to turn things around. He was out of his element in such an unwieldy and complicated situation, however, and his own mistakes compounded those already made by others. Creditors stepped in and took partial control of the firm, and one new CEO after another was brought in to try to save the firm. At one point the company went through four CEOs in eighteen months. Stores were closed and employees terminated in an effort to stem losses. Employees, meanwhile, felt that they were being treated poorly and that the firm did not appreciate their own loyalty and efforts to save the business.

Finally, on February 2, 1996, Merry-Go-Round announced that it was closing down operations for good. Within a matter of weeks it liquidated its inventory, sold its real estate holdings, and shut down its headquarters and warehouses. Indeed, the firm's total disappearance was one of the fastest in history for a company its size. Unfortunately, creditors were left with virtually nothing, and employees received only a small portion of back wages owed to them. Weinglass, meanwhile, has retired to Aspen where he runs a small diner. Once a multimillionaire, he now has no further aspirations for the big time and seems content to greet his regular customers. But this time he vows to stay in touch with them better.

Case Questions

1. Identify how each dimension of Merry-Go-Round's general environment affected the firm during both its growth and decline.

2. Describe how Merry-Go-Round's task environment affected the firm during both its growth and decline.

3. Discuss how the firm might have worked to influence its environment in more effective ways.

Case References: Justin Martin, "The Man Who Boogied Away a Billion," *Fortune,* December 23, 1996, pp. 89-100; and "About That Bonus—See You in Court," *Business Week,* February 26, 1996, p. 6.

CHAPTER NOTES

1. "Heavy Equipment Gets into Gear," *Business Week,* August 5, 1996, p. 29; *Hoover's Handbook of American Business 1997* (Austin, Texas: Hoover's Business Press, 1996), pp. 324–327, 458–459, 742–743; *Hoover's Handbook of World Business 1997* (Austin, Texas: Hoover's Business Press, 1996), pp. 296–297; and "This Cat Keeps on Purring," *Business Week,* January 20, 1997, pp. 82–84.

2. Arie de Geus, *The Living Company—Habits for Surviving in a Turbulent Business Environment* (Boston: Harvard Business School Press, 1997). See also John G. Sifonis and Beverly Goldberg, *Corporation on a Tightrope* (New York: Oxford University Press, 1996) for an interesting discussion of how organizations must navigate through the environment.

3. For a detailed analysis of linkages between economics and organizations, see Jay B. Barney and William G. Ouchi (eds.), *Organizational Economics* (San Francisco: Jossey-Bass, 1986).

4. Kim Clark, "These Are the Good Old Days," *Fortune,* June 9, 1997, pp. 74–83.

5. "Industries Crying Out for Help Wanted," *USA Today,* May 5, 1997, pp. B1, B2.

6. For an overview, see Ricky Griffin and Michael Pustay, *International Business: A Managerial Perspective,* 2nd ed.(Reading, Mass.: Addison-Wesley, 1999).

7. Warren Boeker, Jerry Goodstein, John Stephan, and Johann Peter Murmann, "Competition in a Multimarket Environment: The Case of Market Ext," *Organization Science,* March–April 1997, pp. 126–142.

8. Susan Helper, "How Much Has Really Changed between U.S. Automakers and Their Suppliers?" *Sloan Management Review,* Summer 1991, pp. 15–28.

9. Myron Magnet, "The New Golden Rule of Business," *Fortune,* February 21, 1994, pp. 60–64.

10. Mary Walton, "When Your Partner Fails You . . . " *Fortune,* May 26, 1997, pp. 151–154.

11. "Kafka Wasn't Kidding," *Forbes,* June 2, 1997, p. 160.

12. "To All U.S. Managers Upset by Regulations: Try Germany or Japan," *Wall Street Journal,* December 14, 1995, pp. A1, A5.

13. Richard N. Osborn and John Hagedoorn, "The Institutionalization and Evolutionary Dynamics of Interorganizational Alliances and Networks," *Academy of Management Journal,* April 1997, pp. 261–278.

14. "Ford: The Board Starts to Get Tough," *Business Week,* March 24, 1997, pp. 66–67.

15. Louis Richman, "The New Worker Elite," *Fortune,* August 22, 1994, pp. 56–66.

16. "Temporary Workers Getting Short Shrift," *USA Today,* April 11, 1997, pp. 1B, 2B.

17. For a recent review, see Allen C. Bluedorn, "Pilgrim's Progress: Trends and Convergence in Research on Organizational Size and Environments," *Journal of Management,* Vol. 19, No. 2, 1993, pp. 163–191.

18. James D. Thompson, *Organizations in Action* (New York: McGraw-Hill, 1967).

19. For a recent discussion of how music companies are managed, see "The Music Never Stopped," *Forbes,* March 24, 1997, pp. 90–95.

20. Michael E. Porter, *Competitive Strategy: Techniques for Analyzing Industries and Competitors* (New York: Free Press, 1980); see also Joel A.C. Baum and Helaine J. Korn, "Competitive Dynamics of Intefirm Rivalry," *Academy of Management Journal,* April 1996, pp. 255–291.

21. "Plane Maker May Not Seek More 'Sole Supplier' Deals," *USA Today,* June 26, 1997, p. 3B.

22. "Up, Up, and a Ways to Go," *Business Week,* September 16, 1996, pp. 86–88.

23. Bala Chakravarthy, "A New Strategy Framework for Coping with Turbulence," *Sloan Management Review,* Winter 1997, pp. 69–82.

24. "Sofa with Your Stereo, Sir?" *Forbes,* July 7, 1997, p. 46.

25. "Behind Talks of Delta, Continental Are Fears of Being Left Behind," *Wall Street Journal,* December 5, 1996, pp. A1, A4.

26. "Compaq Moving Beyond PCs," Associated Press wire story, as reported in the *Bryan-College Station Eagle,* June 24, 1997, p. A6; and "Aims to Ride Tandem to Top of Industry," *USA Today,* June 24, 1997, pp. 1B, 2B.

27. Gareth Jones, *Organizational Theory and Design,* 2nd ed. (Reading, Mass.: Addison-Wesley, 1998).

28. E. Yuchtman and S. Seashore, "A Systems Resource Approach to Organizational Effectiveness," *American Sociological Review,* Vol. 32, 1967, pp. 891–903.

29. B. S. Georgopoules and A. S. Tannenbaum, "The Study of Organizational Effectiveness," *American Sociological Review,* Vol. 22, 1957, pp. 534–540.

30. Jones, *Organizational Theory and Design.*

31. Anthony A. Atkinson, John H. Waterhouse, and Robert B. Wells, "A Stakeholder Approach to Strategic Performance Measurement," *Sloan Management Review,* Spring 1997, pp. 25–37.

4

The Ethical and Social Environment

OBJECTIVES

After studying this chapter, you should be able to:

- Discuss managerial ethics, three areas of special ethical concern for managers, and ways that organizations manage ethical behavior.
- Discuss the concept of social responsibility, specify to whom or what an organization might be considered responsible, and describe four types of organizational approaches to social responsibility.
- Explain the relationship between the government and organizations regarding social responsibility.
- Describe some of the activities organizations may engage in to manage social responsibility.

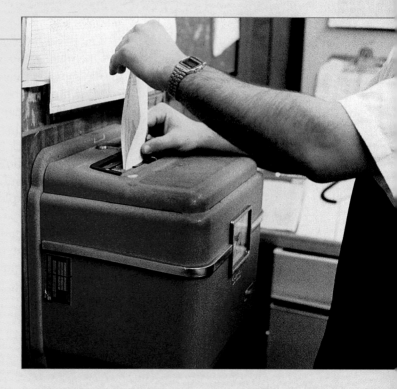

Back in 1938 the U.S. Congress passed the Fair Labor Standards Act (FLSA). Among its other provisions, the FLSA mandated that hourly employees working in excess of forty hours a week must be paid a premium wage of 1.5 times their normal hourly rate for those additional hours. The FLSA also specified that, because of the nature of their work, managerial and professional employees were exempt from this regulation. That is, because these individuals are paid salaries rather than hourly wages, they receive the same pay regardless of the number of hours they work during any given period. While the organization defines which jobs are exempt and which are not, a number of legal standards have been used over the years for making these distinctions.

Recently, however, the distinctions among exempt and nonexempt jobs have become blurred in some organizations. For example, there might be concerns that an organization could reclassify some of its wage-based, lower-level jobs as managerial positions and then refuse to pay overtime to those individuals. Even more extreme are charges that a few organizations today are pressuring hourly employees to work "off the clock"—to work when they are not being paid at all!

Because of the massive corporate downsizing programs in recent years, some firms feel that the remaining employees need to carry a greater workload. This corporate attitude means that many employees are expected to work harder and be more productive. It may also mean working longer hours. In some cases work spills over into what used to be free time. At AT&T, for example, workers are encouraged to participate in the firm's "Ambassador Program" by selling AT&T products to their friends, relatives, and neighbors during nonwork hours. Employees can win prizes for their efforts, but they are not paid for their time.

"They know . . . the first to go will be the ones the boss thinks are not giving 150%. That atmosphere makes it very difficult for most people to say, 'No, I won't work the weekend.'"

Alice Freedman, consultant, quoted in USA Today, *April 24, 1997, p. 1B.*

But other cases are more troubling. In the state of Washington, for example, a jury recently ruled that Taco Bell was guilty of pressuring its employees to do paperwork such as time sheets and schedules at home. And workers were sometimes asked to do some food preparation work before "clocking in." Mervyn's, a chain of discount stores, has been sued by a group of its lower-level managers called team coordinators. These managers charge that they were routinely ordered to work through lunch and to take paperwork home. And Albertson's, the nation's fourth-largest grocery chain, has been charged with pushing employees to work past their assigned quitting time without receiving additional wages.

In some of these cases, of course, an individual employee might simply be misinterpreting events and suggestions from his or her boss. In other situations companies charge that unions are distorting the situation to make the business look bad. And even in cases where the law is being broken, the actions might be the isolated tactics of only one or a few managers working outside formal organizational policies to get a bit more productivity out of their employees. But regardless of the circumstances, it does seem like some organizations today are seeking ways to squeeze more and more work out of fewer and fewer people. And although there may be a variety of legitimate ways to increase productivity, some managers may be crossing the line in how they are seeking to get more from their employees—without having to give anything in return.[1]

Businesses everywhere need their workers to be more productive. Asking people to give more is simply standard operating procedure in many companies today. But the issues associated with working hours and work time may blur the boundaries between appropriately encouraging people to work harder and inappropriately pressuring them to work for free. Indeed, there may be legitimate differences of opinion and perception about various cases involving work hours and compensation. Central to these opinions and perceptions—and how people and organizations respond to them—are the concepts of ethics and social responsibility.

This chapter explores the basic issues of ethics and social responsibility in detail. We first look at individual ethics and their organizational context. Next, we expand our discussion to the more general subject of social responsibility. After we explore the relationships among businesses and the government regarding socially responsible behavior, we examine the activities organizations sometimes undertake to be more socially responsible.

Individual Ethics in Organizations

ethics An individual's personal beliefs regarding what is right and wrong or good and bad

ethical behavior Behavior that conforms to generally accepted social norms

unethical behavior Behavior that does not conform to generally accepted social norms

We define **ethics** as an individual's personal beliefs about whether a behavior, action, or decision is right or wrong.[2] Note that we define ethics in the context of the individual—people have ethics; organizations do not. Likewise, what constitutes ethical behavior varies from one person to another. For example, one person who finds a $20 bill on the floor wouldn't hesitate to pocket the money, whereas another feels compelled to take the bill to the lost-and-found department. Further, although **ethical behavior** is in the eye of the beholder, it usually refers to behavior that conforms to generally accepted social norms. **Unethical behavior**, then, is behavior that does not conform to generally accepted social norms.

A society generally adopts formal laws that reflect the prevailing ethical standards—the social norms—of its citizens. For example, because most people consider theft to be unethical, laws have been passed to make such behaviors illegal and to proscribe ways of punishing those who do steal. But while laws attempt to be clear and unambiguous, their application and interpretation still lead to ethical ambiguities. For example, virtually everyone would agree that forcing employees to work excessive hours, especially for no extra compensation, is unethical. Accordingly, as noted in the "Opening Incident," a law was passed to define work and pay standards. But applying that law to organizational settings can still result in ambiguous situations that can be interpreted in different ways.

An individual's ethics are determined by a combination of factors. People start to form ethical standards as children in response to their perceptions of the behavior of their parents and/or other adults and the behaviors they are allowed to choose. As children grow and enter school, they are also influenced by peers with whom they interact every day. Dozens of important individual events also shape people's lives and contribute to their ethical beliefs and behavior as they grow into adulthood. Values and morals also contribute to ethical standards. A person who places financial gain and personal advancement at the top of her list of priorities, for example, will adopt a personal code of ethics that promotes the pursuit of wealth. Thus she may be ruthless in efforts to gain these rewards, regardless of the costs to others. In contrast, if a person's family is his top priority, he will adopt different ethical standards.

■ Managerial Ethics

Managerial ethics are the standards of behavior that guide individual managers in their work.[3] Although ethics can affect managerial work in any number of ways, three areas of special concern for managers are shown in Figure 4.1.

managerial ethics Standards of behavior that guide individual managers in their work

How an Organization Treats Its Employees One important area of managerial ethics is the way in which an organization treats its employees. This area includes things such as hiring and firing, wages and working conditions, and employee privacy and respect. For example, both ethical and legal guidelines suggest that hiring and firing decisions should be based solely on an individual's ability to perform the job. A manager who discriminates against African Americans in hiring is exhibiting both unethical and illegal behavior. But consider the case of a manager who does not discriminate in general, but occasionally hires a close friend or relative when other applicants might be more qualified. Although these hiring decisions may not be illegal, they may be objectionable on ethical grounds.

Wages and working conditions, while also tightly regulated, are also areas for potential controversy. For example, a manager's paying an employee less than he deserves, simply because the manager knows the employee cannot afford to quit or risk losing his job by complaining, might be considered unethical. Finally, most observers also would agree that an organization is obligated to protect the privacy of its employees. A manager's spreading a rumor that an employee has AIDS or is having an affair with a coworker is generally seen as an unethical breach of privacy. Likewise, the manner in which an organization responds to and addresses issues associated with sexual harassment also involves employee privacy and related rights. Unfortunately, there seems to be a growing concern that organizations may be intruding too much on employee privacy. For example, one recent survey of almost one thousand firms found that 15.7 percent of them videotaped employees performing their jobs, 14.9 percent stored and randomly reviewed their employees' e-mail, and 10.4 percent taped and reviewed telephone

Individual ethics help people decide what is right and wrong. And it is individual ethics that cause some people to generously donate their time to help others. An increasingly popular choice that some people make is a so-called "volunteer vacation"—a trip paid out of their own pocket with the goal of contributing their time, talent, and effort to help others. The people shown here, for example, are spending their vacations building a home for a poverty-stricken family in Matamoros, Mexico. Their ethics have led them to conclude that this is the "right" use of their time.

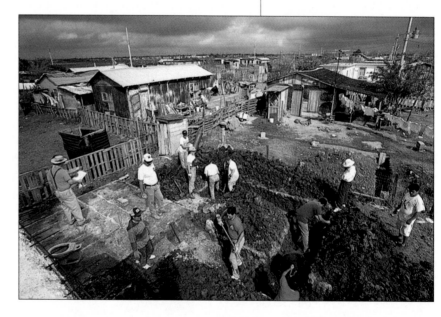

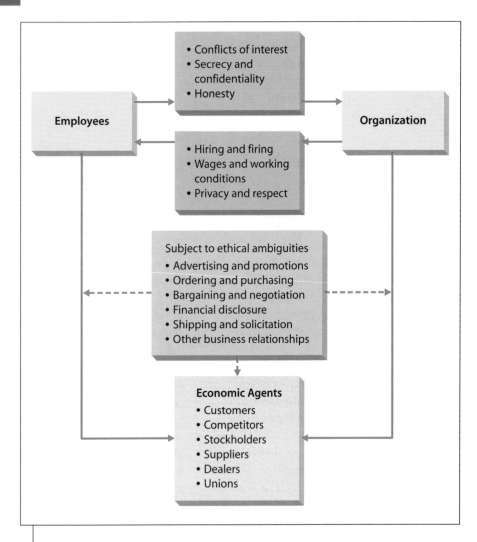

conversations.[4] The "Management InfoTech" box explores these issues in more detail.

How Employees Treat the Organization Numerous ethical issues also stem from how employees treat the organization, especially in regard to conflicts of interest, secrecy and confidentiality, and honesty. A conflict of interest occurs when a decision potentially benefits the individual to the possible detriment of the organization. For example, a buyer at J. C. Penney was recently charged with giving certain suppliers large orders in exchange for financial kickbacks to small companies he owned and with selling outright to some suppliers the bids that had been submitted to J. C. Penney by their competitors.[5] Similarly, the recent marriage of a high-ranking executive at the Limited, Inc., to the owner of a firm that was one of Limited's major suppliers raised allegations about a potential conflict of interest, eventually forcing the executive to resign her position.[6] To guard against such practices, most companies have policies that forbid their buyers from accepting gifts from suppliers.

Divulging company secrets is also clearly unethical. Employees who work for businesses in highly competitive industries—electronics, software, and fashion apparel, for example—might be tempted to sell information about company plans to competitors. In one recent case, Dow Chemical sued General Electric, alleging that GE was systematically recruiting Dow employees working on new high-tech projects with offers of higher paying jobs in order to learn the details of Dow projects.[7]

A third area of concern is honesty in general, although many companies focus their concerns here on expense accounts, or budgets they provide to their managers for travel, entertainment, and other expenses related to doing business. Some managers have admitted to routinely adding or inflating meal expenses, service charges, and car mileage to their expense account reports to unethically pad their income. They also occasionally pay more than they need to for full-fare coach airline tickets (instead of buying corporate-rate discounted coach tickets) to make upgrading them to first class easier.

FIGURE 4.1
Managerial Ethics

The three basic areas of concern for managerial ethics are the relationships of the firm to the employee, the employee to the firm, and the firm to other economic agents. Managers need to approach each set of relationships from an ethical and moral perspective.

Table 4.1 summarizes a recent survey of ethical behaviors by employees. Almost half of the 1,324 participants in this study admitted to taking unethical or illegal actions within the twelve months preceding the survey. As indicated in Table 4.1, for example, deliberately cutting corners on quality control was the most common unethical behavior. Other unethical behaviors besides those listed in the table included theft, lying to supervisors, discriminating against co-workers, forging signatures, accepting kickbacks, and having extramarital affairs.[8]

How Employees and Organizations Treat Other Economic Agents Managerial ethics also come into play in the relationship that the firm and its employees have with other economic agents. As shown in Figure 4.1, the primary agents of interest include customers, competitors, stockholders, suppliers,

MANAGEMENT INFOTECH

The Perils of E-mail

It seems as if almost overnight e-mail has become the standard method of communication in the business world. Most people enjoy its speed, ease, and casual nature. But e-mail also has its share of problems and pitfalls. One challenge, of course, is privacy. Although many people think the content of their e-mail is private, in fact, many different people may actually see it.

For example, the courts have held that e-mail messages sent and/or received during working hours and on company equipment are the property of the business. Compaq Computer, for example, has one full-time employee who does nothing but randomly scan e-mail messages that pass through the company's servers and to monitor improper Internet usage among employees. While fewer than half of the businesses in the United States have formal electronic communication policies, they do have the power of the law behind them when they establish policies or procedures.

Aside from organizational scrutiny, people also face the threat of hackers breaking into and wrecking havoc with the company's computer network, including its e-mail system. Indeed, e-mail is one of the easiest routes that hackers can use to gain access to other parts of the system. Once inside, they can also read sensitive e-mail messages, destroy those messages, or send them to other people.

And people also have reason to fear themselves. A surprisingly common error is to accidentally send an e-mail to the wrong address, or even to a large group of people. People have sent love notes to the wrong people, for example. Even worse, with a simple inadvertent click of the mouse, a sensitive or inflammable message intended for a single recipient can instead be sent to everyone in the company! Just think of the possibilities. . . .

"The only secure computer is one that is turned off, locked in a safe, and buried 20 feet down in a secret location—and I'm not completely confident of that one either."

Bruce Schneier, author*

References: *"E-Mail at Your Peril,"* Newsweek, *April 28, 1997, p. 54; and Richard Behar, "Who's Reading Your E-Mail?"* Fortune, *February 3, 1997, pp. 56-70.*

TABLE 4.1
Ethics in the Workplace

Source: USA Today, April 4, 1997, p. B1. Copyright 1997, USA Today. Reprinted with permission.

Top Ten Factors that Could Trigger Workers to Act Unethically or Illegally
• Balancing work and family • Poor internal communications • Poor leadership • Work hours and/or work load • Lack of management support • Need to meet sales, budget, or profit goals • Little or no recognition of achievements • Company politics • Personal financial worries • Insufficient resources
Top Five Types of Unethical or Illegal Behavior that Workers Say They Have Engaged in Within Twelve Months of Survey Because of These Factors
• Cut corners on quality control • Covered up incidents • Abused or lied about sick days • Lied to or deceived customers • Put inappropriate pressure on others

dealers, and unions. The behaviors between the organization and these agents that may be subject to ethical ambiguity include advertising and promotions, financial disclosures, ordering and purchasing, shipping and solicitations, bargaining and negotiation, and other business relationships.

For example, The Home Depot recently charged that one of its competitors, Rickel Home Centers, financed smear campaigns to keep a zoning board in New Jersey from giving The Home Depot permission to open a store. Toys 'R' Us Inc. has been accused of pressuring some of its suppliers to not sell their products to discounters, thereby allowing other merchants, such as Toys 'R' Us, to maintain higher prices. Some critics charge that advertisers like Disney and McDonald's inappropriately and over aggressively target young children in their advertising. And some companies like AT&T and Eastman Kodak have been criticized for using restructuring costs to perhaps artificially inflate their future earnings projections in their reports to investors.[9]

Additional complexities faced by many firms today are the variations in ethical business practices in different countries. In many countries bribes and side payments are a normal and customary part of doing business. However, U.S. laws forbid these practices, even if a firm's rivals from other countries are paying them. For example, a U.S. power-generating company lost a $320 million contract in the Middle East because government officials demanded a $3 million bribe. A Japanese firm paid the bribe and won the contract. Enron Company cancelled a big project in India because newly elected officials demanded bribes. Although these kinds of cases are clearly illegal under U.S. law, other situations are more ambiguous. In China, for example, when local journalists cover a business-sponsored news conference, they expect the host to pay for their cab fare. In Indonesia foreigners normally have to wait more than a year to get a driver's license, but they can "expedite" the process for an extra $100. And in Romania, building inspectors routinely expect a "tip" for a favorable review.[10]

■ Ethics in an Organizational Context

It is also important to note that although ethics are an individual phenomenon, ethical or unethical actions by particular managers do not occur in a vacuum. Indeed, they most often occur in an organizational context that is conducive to them. Actions of peer managers and top managers, as well as the organization's culture, all contribute to the ethical context of the organization.[11]

The starting point in understanding the ethical context of management is, of course, the individual's own ethical standards. Some people, for example, will risk personal embarrassment or lose their job before they would do something unethical. Other people are much more easily swayed by the unethical behavior they see around them and other situational factors, and they may be willing to commit major crimes to further their own careers or for financial gain. Organizational practices may strongly influence the ethical standards of employees. Some organizations openly permit unethical business practices as long as they are in the best interests of the firm.

If managers become aware of unethical practices and allow them to continue, they have contributed to an organization culture that says such activity is permitted. For example, Lars Bildman was recently fired from his post as CEO of Astra USA, a subsidiary of a large Swedish drug manufacturer, Astra AB. During his tenure with the firm, he allegedly sexually harassed dozens of Astra employees, used company funds to remodel his home, and took frequent company-paid private cruises with other company executives and prostitutes. Although only Bildman has been formally charged with criminal wrongdoing, dozens of senior managers apparently knew of the problems at Astra, and either ignored them or began to participate in similar activities themselves. Thus, their collective behaviors served to first create and then reinforce an environment that appeared to sanction those behaviors.[12]

The organization's environment also contributes to the context for ethical behavior. In a highly competitive or regulated industry, for example, a manager may feel more pressure to achieve high performance. This is at least a partial explanation for the practices described in the "Opening Incident" in this chapter—managers may feel pressure to lower costs and attempt to respond by forcing their employees to do more work for no additional wages. When managers feel pressure to meet goals or lower costs, they may explore various alternatives to help achieve these ends. And in some cases, the alternative they adopt may be unethical or even illegal.[13]

Managerial ethics must be interpreted from the point of view of their organizational context. In some organizations, for example, norms are such that people feel empowered to bend rules and to pay little or no regard to ethical conduct. But in others, norms and organization culture reinforce strictly ethical behaviors. As shown in this cartoon, if a senior executive never questions his or her own ethics—and if no one dares to question the executive's actions—the potential for ethical problems increases significantly.

"I no longer worry about what's right and what's wrong. No one would dare tell me what was wrong."

■ Managing Ethical Behavior

Spurred partially by the recent spate of ethical scandals and partially from a sense of enhanced corporate consciousness about the importance of ethical and unethical behaviors, many organizations have reemphasized ethical behavior on the part of employees.[14] This emphasis takes many forms, but any effort to enhance ethical behavior must begin with top management. It is top managers, for example, who establish the organization's culture and define what will and will not be acceptable behavior. Some companies have also started offering employees training in how to cope with ethical dilemmas. At Boeing, for example, line managers lead training sessions for other employees, and the company also has an ethics committee that reports directly to the board of directors. The training sessions involve discussions of different ethical dilemmas that employees might face and how managers might handle those dilemmas. Chemical Bank, Xerox, and McDonnell Douglas have also established ethics training programs for their managers.

Organizations are also going to greater lengths to formalize their ethical standards. Some, such as General Mills and Johnson & Johnson, have prepared guidelines that detail how employees are to treat suppliers, customers, competitors, and other constituents. Others, such as Whirlpool and Hewlett-Packard, have developed formal **codes of ethics**—written statements of the values and ethical standards that guide the firms' actions. NYNEX recently won an award from the Center for Business Ethics at Bentley College for its code of ethics and its commitment of people and resources to ensure that all employees fully understand how the code affects them.[15] The Code of Ethics of Lockheed Martin is illustrated in Figure 4.2.

Of course, no code, guideline, or training program can truly make up for the quality of an individual's personal judgment about what is right behavior and what is wrong behavior in a particular situation. Such devices may prescribe what people should do, but they often fail to help people understand and live with the consequences of their choices. Making ethical choices may lead to very unpleasant outcomes—firing, rejection by colleagues, and the forfeiture of monetary gain, to name a few. Employees at Astra who did not want to follow the firm's norms and standards either isolated themselves from senior executives or left the firm altogether. Thus managers must be prepared to confront their own consciences and weigh the options available when making difficult ethical decisions.

code of ethics   A formal, written statement of the values and ethical standards that guide a firm's actions

MANAGEMENT IMPLICATIONS

Managers need to understand the basic meanings of ethical and unethical behaviors. They also need to fully understand the various ethical linkages among the organization, its employees, and other economic agents and to ensure to the extent possible that these linkages are maintained with the proper ethical standards. Further, managers should also acknowledge the organizational context of individual ethics and be prepared to interpret ethical problems from an organizational perspective. And finally, managers should take a

Dear Colleague,

Lockheed Martin is committed to the highest standards of ethical conduct in every aspect of our dealings with all of our constituencies: employees, customers, communities, suppliers and shareholders.

As a new member of the Lockheed Martin family, you soon will receive a copy of *Setting the Standard*, Lockheed Martin's Code of Ethics and Business Conduct. The Code is also available on the Lockheed Martin Network (intranet) and on the Lockheed Martin Home Page of the World Wide Web: http://www.lmco.com

To be one of the world's premier companies of the 21st century, Lockheed Martin must set the standard for ethical business conduct in the United States and the foreign countries in which we do business. We are guided by these ethical principles and values in everything we do:

Honesty: to be truthful in all our endeavors; to be honest and forthright with one another... and with our customers, communities, suppliers and shareholders.

Integrity: to say what we mean, to deliver what we promise, and to stand for what is right.

Respect: to treat one another with dignity and fairness, appreciating the diversity of our workforce and the uniqueness of each employee.

Trust: to build confidence through teamwork and open, candid communications.

Responsibility: to speak up – without fear of retribution – and report concerns in the workplace, including violations of laws, regulations and company policies, and seek clarification and guidance whenever there is doubt.

Citizenship: to obey all the laws of the United States and the foreign countries in which we do business and to do our part to make the communities in which we live a better place to be.

Norm Augustine
Chairman

Vance Coffman
Vice Chairman
& Chief Executive Officer

LOCKHEED MARTIN

Keep this card for ready reference. Use it if you need information on how to contact your local ethics representative – or wish to discuss a matter of concern with the corporate Office of Ethics and Business Conduct.

LOCKHEED MARTIN
ETHICS HELPLINE
CALL: **800-LM ETHIC**
(800-563-8442)
For the Hearing or Speech Impaired: 800-441-7457
FAX: 805-381-1482
OR WRITE: Office of Ethics and Business Conduct
Lockheed Martin Corporation
310 North Westlake Boulevard, Suite 200
Westlake Village, CA 91362
E-MAIL: Corporate.Ethics@lmco.com

variety of measures to maintain ethical behavior by those in their organizations while also recognizing that any individual's personal actions may offset the best organizational strategies for promoting ethical conduct. ▬

FIGURE 4.2
Corporate Code of Ethics

Social Responsibility and Organizations

As we have seen, ethics relate to individuals and their decisions and behaviors. Organizations themselves do not have ethics, but do relate to their environment in ways that often involve ethical dilemmas and decisions. These situations are generally referred to within the context of the organization's social responsibility. Specifically, **social responsibility** is the set of obligations an organization has to protect and enhance the society in which it functions.

social responsibility The set of obligations an organization has to protect and enhance the societal context in which it functions

organizational stakeholders People and organizations who are directly affected by the behaviors of an organization and who have a stake in its performance

■ Areas of Social Responsibility

Organizations may exercise social responsibility toward their stakeholders, toward the natural environment, and toward general social welfare. Some organizations acknowledge their responsibilities in all three areas and strive diligently to meet each of them, whereas others emphasize only one or two areas of social responsibility. And a few acknowledge no social responsibility at all.

Organizational Stakeholders   In Chapter 3 we described the task environment as comprising those elements in an organization's external environment that directly affect the organization in one or more ways. Another way to describe these same elements is from the perspective of **organizational stakeholders**, or those people and organizations who are directly affected by the practices of an organization and that have a stake in its performance.[16] Major stakeholders are depicted in Figure 4.3.

Most companies that strive to be responsible to their stakeholders concentrate first and foremost on three main groups: customers, employees, and investors. They then select other stakeholders that are particularly relevant or important to the organization and attempt to address their needs and expectations as well.

Organizations that are responsible to their customers strive to treat them fairly and honestly. They also seek to charge fair prices, to honor warranties, to meet delivery commitments, and to stand behind the quality of the products they sell. Companies that have established excellent reputations in this area include L.L. Bean, Land's End, Dell Computer, and Johnson & Johnson.

Organizations that are socially responsible in their dealings with employees treat their workers fairly, make them a part of the team, and respect their dignity and basic human needs. Organizations such as 3M Company, Hoechst Celanese, Levi Strauss, and Southwest Airlines have all established strong reputations in this area. In addition, they also go to great lengths to find, hire, train, and promote qualified minorities.

To maintain a socially responsible stance toward investors, managers should follow proper accounting procedures, provide appropriate information to shareholders about the

FIGURE 4.3
Organizational Stakeholders

All organizations have a variety of stakeholders that are directly affected by the organization and that have a stake in its performance. These are people and organizations to whom an organization should be responsible.

financial performance of the firm, and manage the organization to protect shareholder rights and investments. Moreover, managers should be accurate and candid in their assessment of future growth and profitability. Managers should also avoid even the appearance of improprieties involving such sensitive areas as insider trading, stock price manipulation, and the withholding of financial data.

The Natural Environment   A second critical area of social responsibility relates to the natural environment. Not long ago, many organizations indiscriminately dumped sewage, waste products from production, and trash into streams and rivers, into the air, and on vacant land. When Shell Oil first explored the Amazon River basin for potential drilling sites in the late 1980s, its crews ripped down trees and left behind a trail of garbage. Now, however, many laws regulate the disposal of waste materials. In many instances, companies themselves have also become more socially responsible in their release of pollutants and general treatment of the environment. For example, when Shell recently launched a new exploration expedition into another area of the Amazon basin, the group included a biologist to oversee environmental protection and an anthropologist to help the team more effectively interact with native tribes.[17]

Still, much remains to be done. Companies need to develop economically feasible ways to avoid contributing to acid rain and global warming; to avoid depleting the ozone layer; and to develop alternative methods of handling sewage, hazardous wastes, and ordinary garbage. Procter & Gamble, for example, is an industry leader in using recycled materials for containers. Hyatt Corporation recently established a new company to help recycle waste products from its hotels. And Monsanto is launching an entire new product line aimed at improving the environment with genetically engineered crops.[18]

Companies also need to develop safety policies that cut down on accidents with potentially disastrous environmental results. When one of Ashland Oil's storage tanks ruptured several years ago, spilling more than 500,000 gallons of diesel fuel into Pennsylvania's Monongahela River, the company moved quickly to clean up the spill but was still indicted for violating U.S. environmental laws.[19] After the Exxon oil tanker *Valdez* spilled millions of gallons of oil off the coast of Alaska, the firm adopted new and more stringent procedures to keep another disaster from happening.

General Social Welfare   Some people believe that in addition to treating constituents and the environment responsibly, business organizations also should promote the general welfare of society. Examples include making contributions to charities, philanthropic organizations, and not-for-profit foundations and associations; supporting museums, symphonies, and public radio and television; and taking a role in improving public health and education. Some people also believe that organizations should act even more broadly to correct the political inequities that exist in the world. For example, these observers would argue that businesses should not conduct operations in countries with a record of human rights violations. Thus they stand in opposition to companies doing business in China and Vietnam.

■ Arguments For and Against Social Responsibility

On the surface, there seems to be little disagreement about the need for organizations to be socially responsible. In truth, though, those who oppose wide interpretations of social responsibility use several convincing arguments.[20] Some of the more salient arguments on both sides of this contemporary debate are summarized in Figure 4.4 and further explained in the following sections.

Arguments For Social Responsibility   People who argue in favor of social responsibility claim that because organizations create many of the problems that need to be addressed, such as air and water pollution and resource depletion, they should play a major role in solving them. These critics also argue that because corporations are legally defined entities with most of the same privileges as private citizens, businesses should not try to avoid their obligations as citizens. Advocates of social responsibility point out that although governmental organizations have stretched their budgets to the limit, many large businesses often have surplus revenues that could potentially be used to help solve social problems. For example, IBM routinely donates surplus computers to schools and many restaurants give leftover food to homeless shelters.

Although each of the arguments just summarized is a distinct justification for socially responsible behaviors on the part of organizations, another more general reason for social responsibility is profit itself. For example, organizations that make clear and visible contributions to society can enhance their reputations and garner greater market share for their products. Although exaggerated or untrue claims of socially responsible activities can haunt a company, claims that are true and accurate can work to the benefit of both the organization and society.

FIGURE 4.4
Arguments For and Against Social Responsibility

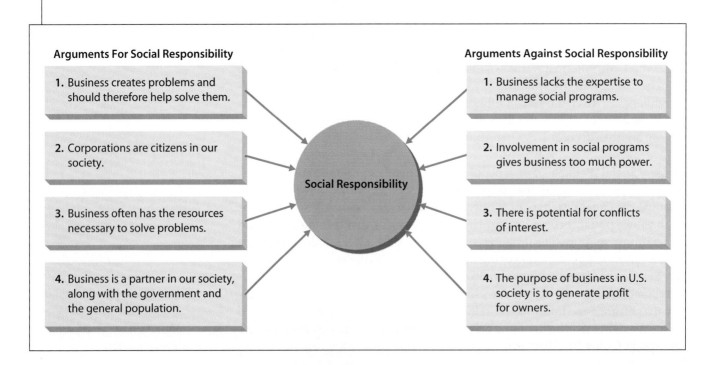

Arguments For Social Responsibility

1. Business creates problems and should therefore help solve them.

2. Corporations are citizens in our society.

3. Business often has the resources necessary to solve problems.

4. Business is a partner in our society, along with the government and the general population.

Social Responsibility

Arguments Against Social Responsibility

1. Business lacks the expertise to manage social programs.

2. Involvement in social programs gives business too much power.

3. There is potential for conflicts of interest.

4. The purpose of business in U.S. society is to generate profit for owners.

Arguments Against Social Responsibility   Some people, however, including the famous economist Milton Friedman, argue that widening the interpretation of social responsibility will undermine the U.S. economy by detracting from the basic mission of business: to earn profits for owners. For example, money that Chevron or General Electric contributes to social causes or charities is money that could otherwise be distributed to owners as a dividend. Ben & Jerry's Homemade Inc. has a very ambitious and widely touted social agenda. But some shareholders recently criticized the firm when it refused to accept a lucrative exporting deal to Japan simply because the Japanese distributor did not have a similar social agenda.[21]

Another objection to deepening the social responsibility of businesses points out that corporations already wield enormous power and that their activity in social programs gives them even more power. The "Today's Management Issues" box describes one potential example. Another argument against social responsibility focuses on the potential for conflict of interest. Suppose, for example, that one manager is in charge of deciding which local social program or charity will receive a large grant from her business. The local civic opera company (a not-for-profit organization that relies on contributions for its existence) might offer her front-row tickets for the upcoming season in exchange for her support. If opera is her favorite form of music, she might be tempted to direct the money toward the local company, when the funds might actually be needed more in other areas.[22]

Finally, critics argue that organizations lack the expertise to understand how to assess and make decisions about worthy social programs. How can a company truly know, they ask, which cause or program is most deserving of its support, or how money might best be spent? For example, Exxon recently announced a commitment to spend $5 million to help save the tiger, an endangered species that serves as the firm's corporate symbol. Exxon committed most of the money to support breeding programs in zoos and to help educate people about tigers. But conservationists criticized the firm and its plan, arguing instead that the money might have been better spent on eliminating poaching, the illegal trade of tiger fur, and the destruction of the tiger's natural habitat.[23]

■ Organizational Approaches to Social Responsibility

As we have seen, some people advocate a larger social role for organizations, and others argue that the role is already too large. Not surprisingly, organizations themselves adopt a wide range of positions on social responsibility. As Figure 4.5 illustrates, the four stances that an organization can take concerning its obligations to society fall along a continuum ranging from the lowest to the highest degree of socially responsible practices.

Obstructionist Stance   The few organizations that take what might be called an **obstructionist stance** to social responsibility usually do as little as possible to solve social or environmental problems. When they cross the ethical or

obstructionist stance   An approach to social responsibility in which firms do as little as possible to solve social or environmental problems

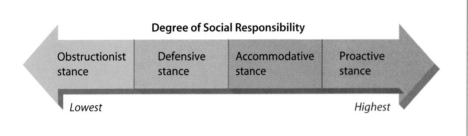

FIGURE 4.5
Approaches to Social Responsibility

Organizations can adopt a variety of approaches to social responsibility. For example, a firm that never considers the consequences of its decisions and tries to hide its transgressions is taking an obstructionist stance. At the other extreme, a firm that actively seeks to identify areas where it can help society is pursuing a proactive stance toward social responsibility.

defensive stance A social responsibility stance in which an organization does everything that is required of it legally, but nothing more

accommodative stance A social responsibility stance in which an organization meets its basic legal and ethical obligations and also goes beyond social obligation in selected cases

proactive stance A social responsibility stance in which an organization views itself as a citizen in a society and proactively seeks opportunities to contribute to that society

legal line that separates acceptable from unacceptable practices, their typical response is to deny or cover up their actions. For example, when the various problems at Astra USA, discussed earlier in the chapter, first began to surface, top officials at both that firm and its Swedish parent company denied any wrongdoing. In another now-classic instance, when officials at Beech-Nut learned that the firm was using chemical additives in its apple juice several years ago, they attempted to hide the truth. Firms that adopt this position have little regard for ethical conduct and will generally go to great lengths to hide any wrongdoing.

Defensive Stance   One step removed from the obstructionist stance is the **defensive stance**, whereby the organization will do everything that is required of it legally, but nothing more. This approach is most consistent with the arguments used against social responsibility just described. Managers in organizations that take a defensive stance insist that their job is to generate profits. For example, such a firm would install pollution control equipment dictated by law, but would not install higher-quality equipment even though it might limit pollution further. Tobacco companies such as Philip Morris take this position in their marketing efforts. In the United States, tobacco companies are legally required to include warnings to smokers on their products and to limit their advertising to prescribed media. Domestically they follow these rules to the letter of the law but use stronger marketing methods in countries that have no such rules. In many African countries, for example, cigarettes are heavily promoted, contain higher levels of tar and nicotine than those sold in the United States, and carry few or no health warning labels. Firms that take this position are also unlikely to cover up wrongdoing and will generally admit their mistakes and take appropriate corrective actions.

Accommodative Stance   A firm that adopts an **accommodative stance** meets its legal and ethical requirements but will also go beyond these requirements in selected cases. Such firms voluntarily agree to participate in social programs, but solicitors have to convince the organization that the programs are worthy of their support. Both Exxon and IBM, for example, will match contributions made by their employees to selected charitable causes. And many organizations will respond to requests for donations to Little League, Girl Scouts, youth soccer programs, and so forth. The point, though, is that someone has to knock on the door and ask—the organizations do not proactively seek such avenues for contributing.

Proactive Stance   The highest degree of social responsibility that a firm can exhibit is the **proactive stance**. Firms that adopt this approach take to heart the arguments in favor of social responsibility. They view themselves as

Volunteers? Or Draftees?

Few would argue that a business exerts a lot of influence over the people it employs. Not surprisingly, then, the latest trend in social responsibility is engendering a lot of debate because of the additional influence it may have over the employees of a business that jumps on the bandwagon. And just what is this bandwagon? Volunteerism—enticing people to use their time to help society.

For example, Shell Oil routinely pays employees to spend time helping with community service projects. A Shell attorney may devote a day to helping plant flowers in a park in a low-income neighborhood. Or a manager may tutor in a public school. The Home Depot employees recently volunteered to renovate a women's shelter in Los Angeles. And LensCrafters recently pledged volunteers to give eye care to 1 million needy people by the year 2003.

But some observers question the appropriateness of company-sponsored volunteerism programs. For example, the critics point out that some employees may feel pressured to volunteer even if they don't want to. And even if employees agree with the concept, volunteering may just be adding one more demand onto their already overloaded

"I don't want anyone thinking the company is doing this for any reason other than it's the right thing to do."

Dave Brown, CEO, LensCrafters*

"There is a great deal of pressure to do whatever the boss asks, even if the boss does not intend it that way."

Lewis Maltby, ACLU**

schedules. And there is certainly the possibility that some businesses may have more than altruism in mind and really just be seeking favorable publicity.

So how can these complications be minimized? Although there are no clear answers, experts do offer a few suggestions. For one thing, strive to ensure that participation is *truly* voluntary. One indicator of this attitude is to avoid keeping a record of who does and who does not get involved. For another, allow the volunteerism to be done during normal working hours and pay employees their normal wages, instead of asking them to work on the weekend or to volunteer their own time. And yet another guideline is to keep the program quiet. Don't trumpet the volunteers and their activities in advertising campaigns. This principal will clearly force the manager to face the real motives behind the program and keep the focus on doing good, rather than on good public relations!

References: *"Volunteers May Feel More Like Draftees,"* USA Today, *April 25, 1997, p. 1B (**quote on p. 1B); "Good Works, Good Business,"* USA Today, *April 25, 1997, pp. 1B, 2B (*quote on p. 2B); and Martha I. Finney, "Operations That Build Smiles, Confidence, Skills, and Community Goodwill,"* HRMagazine, *April 1997, pp. 110–117.*

---

citizens in a society and proactively seek opportunities to contribute. An excellent example of a proactive stance is the Ronald McDonald House program undertaken by McDonald's Corp. These houses, located close to major medical centers, can be used by families for minimal cost while their sick children are receiving medical treatment nearby. Sears offers fellowships that support promising young performers while they develop their talents. Target Stores has stopped selling guns in its stores, and some national toy retailers such as KayBee and Toys 'R' Us have voluntarily stopped selling realistic toy guns.

WORKING WITH DIVERSITY

Hiring High-Risk Employees Can Pay

Most people associate gender, skin color, or other visible differences with the word *diversity*. But in a small New England electronics firm, diversity means something else altogether—troubled people worthy of a second chance. Microboard Processing, Inc., or MPI, is owned and managed by Craig Hoekenga. Mr. Hoekenga has a strong sense of social responsibility and believes that his best way of giving back to society is by offering second chances to high-risk employees.

Almost one-third of MPI's employees might be classified as high risk and include former welfare recipients, people who have never held a steady job, convicted felons, and former drug addicts. And Hoekenga insists that at least 10 percent of each year's new hires be from a high-risk category. Although the firm also hires plenty of mainstream employees, Hoekenga considers his high-risk workers to be the backbone of the company.

For example, Ruth Tinney recently applied for a job at MPI. She had not worked for several years and had spent the last three years on welfare. Hoekenga gave her a two-week trial, and now she has a regular position as an assembly-line worker. Not all new hires succeed, of course. About two or three out of every ten fail. For example, one former drug addict who had worked at the firm for more than a year recently returned to drug abuse and went back to jail. Hoekenga also points out that he has to give people awhile to learn the ropes. Many, for example, have never held a steady job and do not understand the need for regular and prompt attendance. Therefore, MPI allows considerable latitude in absenteeism and tardiness during the first few weeks. The key is that the workers show improvement. The goal is to teach proper work habits during the first six months of employment. After that time the firm takes a much harder line and cuts people less and less slack. But the ones who do make it feel an especially strong sense of loyalty and appreciation toward Hoekenga and his company and make enormous contributions to the firm's continuing profitability and growth.

"Most employers want people with a good work ethic, social skills and an ability to produce the first day they come to work. Craig will take people who can't produce and will wait six or nine months for them to come through."

William R. Bellotti, Connecticut's deputy labor commissioner*

References: *"Making Risky Hires into Valued Workers,"* Wall Street Journal, *June 19, 1997, pp. B1, B2 (*quote on page B2).*

Another example is illustrated in the "Working With Diversity" box. These and related activities and programs exceed the accommodative stance—they indicate a sincere and potent commitment to improving the general social welfare in this country and thus represent a proactive stance to social responsibility.

Remember that these categories are not discrete, but merely define stages along a continuum of approaches. Organizations do not always fit neatly into one category. The Ronald McDonald House program has been widely applauded, for example, but McDonald's also came under fire a few years ago for allegedly misleading consumers about the nutritional value of its food products. And even though Astra and Beech-Nut took an obstructionist stance in the cases we cited, many individual employees and managers at both firms have no doubt made substantial contributions to society in a number of different ways.

Managers need to be aware of their key and relevant stakeholders and to ensure that their organization's interactions with those stakeholders, as well as their interactions with the natural environment and society in general, are handled with the appropriate level of social responsibility. Managers should also carefully weigh the various arguments for and against social responsibility and use these arguments in developing a coherent and consistent corporate stance on social responsibility.

The Government and Social Responsibility

An especially important element of social responsibility is the relationship between business and government. For example, in planned economies the government heavily regulates business activities, ostensibly to ensure that business supports some overarching set of social ideals. And even market economies experience considerable government control of business, much of it again directed at making sure that social interests are not damaged by business interests. On the other side of the coin, however, business also attempts to influence the government. Such influence attempts are usually undertaken in an effort to offset or reverse government restrictions. As Figure 4.6 shows, organizations and the government use several methods in their attempts to influence each other.

FIGURE 4.6
How Business and the Government Influence Each Other

Business and the government influence each other in a variety of ways. Government influence can be direct or indirect. Business influence relies on personal contacts, lobbying, political action committees (PACs), and favors. Federal Express, for example, has a very active PAC.

■ How Government Influences Organizations

The government attempts to shape social responsibility practices through both direct and indirect channels. Direct influence most frequently is manifested through regulation, whereas indirect influence can take a number of forms, most notably taxation policies.

Direct Regulation The government most often directly influences organizations through **regulation**, or the establishment of laws and rules that dictate what organizations can and cannot do. As noted earlier in the chapter, this regulation usually

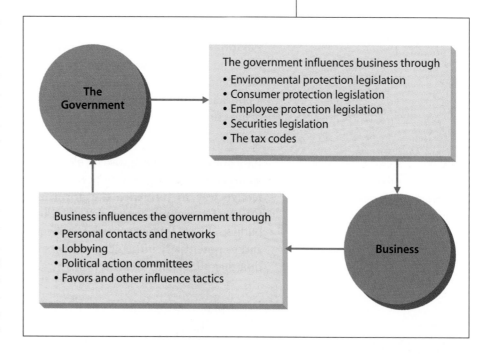

The government influences business through
• Environmental protection legislation
• Consumer protection legislation
• Employee protection legislation
• Securities legislation
• The tax codes

Business influences the government through
• Personal contacts and networks
• Lobbying
• Political action committees
• Favors and other influence tactics

The Government

Business

regulation Government's attempts to influence business by establishing laws and rules that dictate what businesses can and cannot do in prescribed areas

evolves from societal beliefs about what businesses should or should not be allowed to do. To implement legislation, the government generally creates special agencies to monitor and control certain aspects of business activity. For example, the Environmental Protection Agency handles environmental issues; the Federal Trade Commission and the Food and Drug Administration focus on consumer-related concerns; the Equal Employee Opportunity Commission, the National Labor Relations Board, and the Department of Labor help protect employees; and the Securities and Exchange Commission handles investor-related issues. These agencies have the power to levy fines or bring charges against organizations that violate regulations.

Indirect Regulation   Other forms of regulation are indirect. For example, the government can indirectly influence the social responsibility of organizations through its tax codes. In effect, the government can influence how organizations spend their social responsibility dollars by providing greater or lesser tax incentives. For instance, if the federal government wanted organizations to spend more on training the hard-core unemployed, Congress could pass laws that provided tax incentives to companies that opened new training facilities. As a result, more businesses would probably do so. Of course, some critics argue that regulation is already excessive. They maintain that a free market system would eventually accomplish the same goals as regulation with lower costs to both organizations and the government.

■ How Organizations Influence Government

As we mention in Chapter 3, organizations can influence their environment in many different ways. In particular, businesses have four main methods of addressing governmental pressures for more social responsibility.

Personal Contacts   Because many corporate executives and political leaders travel in the same social circles, personal contacts and networks offer one method of influence. A business executive, for example, may be able to contact a politician directly and present his or her case regarding a piece of legislation being considered.

lobbying The use of persons or groups to formally represent a company or group of companies before political bodies to influence legislation

Lobbying   **Lobbying**, or the use of persons or groups to formally represent an organization or group of organizations before political bodies, is also an effective way to influence the government. The National Rifle Association (NRA), for example, has a staff of lobbyists in Washington with a large annual budget. These lobbyists work to represent the NRA's position on gun control and to potentially influence members of Congress when they vote on legislation that affects the firearms industry and the rights of gun owners.

Political Action Committees   Companies themselves cannot legally make direct donations to political campaigns, so they influence the government

Organizations can attempt to influence government in a variety of ways. And some are doing just that in an effort to improve working conditions for employees in countries where few labor regulations exist. In response to scandals involving child labor and unsafe working conditions, a group of U. S. companies has formed a coalition aimed at creating a set of global labor standards. Their hope, in turn, is that these standards will result in stricter local government protection of workers in less developed parts of the word. These Malaysian workers, for example, are making clothes for Eddie Bauer, a member of the coalition.

through political action committees. **Political action committees (PACs)** are special organizations created to solicit money and then distribute it to political candidates. Employees of a firm may be encouraged to make donations to particular PACs because managers know that these PACs will support candidates with political views similar to their own. PACs, in turn, make the contributions themselves, usually to a broad slate of state and national candidates. For example, Federal Express's PAC is called Fepac. Fepac makes regular contributions to the campaign funds of political candidates who are most likely to work in the firm's best interests.

political action committee (PAC)
An organization created to solicit and distribute money to political candidates

Favors   Finally, organizations sometimes rely on favors and other influence tactics to gain support. Although these favors may be legal, they are still subject to criticism. A few years back, for example, two influential members of a House committee attending a fund-raising function in Miami were needed in Washington to finish work on a piece of legislation that Federal Express wanted the House to pass. The law being drafted would allow the company and its competitors to give their employees standby seats on airlines as a tax-free benefit. As a favor Federal Express provided one of its corporate jets to fly the committee members back to Washington. The company was eventually reimbursed for its expenses, so its assistance was not illegal, but some people argue that such actions are dangerous because of how they might be perceived. Similarly, in 1997 there were Congressional hearings into allegations that certain foreign interests had attempted to influence political elections in the United States through illegal campaign contributions.[24]

MANAGEMENT IMPLICATIONS Managers should fully understand the various ways in which business and the government influence one another. Further, while recognizing that under certain conditions endeavoring to influence the government may be both legal and appropriate, managers should also be careful to avoid crossing legal or ethical boundaries. ■

Managing Social Responsibility

The demands for social responsibility placed on contemporary organizations by an increasingly sophisticated and educated public are probably stronger than ever. As we have seen, there are pitfalls for managers who fail to adhere to high ethical standards and for companies that try to circumvent their legal obligations. Organizations therefore need to fashion an approach to social responsibility the same way that they develop any other business strategy. That is, they should view social responsibility as a major challenge that requires careful planning, decision making, consideration, and evaluation. Organizations may address this challenge through both formal and informal dimensions of managing social responsibility.

■ Formal Organizational Dimensions

Some dimensions of managing social responsibility are a formal and planned activity on the part of the organization. Formal organizational dimensions that can help manage social responsibility are legal compliance, ethical compliance, and philanthropic giving.

legal compliance The extent to which an organization complies with local, state, federal, and international laws

Legal Compliance **Legal compliance** is the extent to which the organization conforms to local, state, federal, and international laws. The task of managing legal compliance is generally assigned to the appropriate functional managers. For example, the organization's top human resource executive is responsible for ensuring compliance with regulations concerning hiring, pay, and workplace safety and health. Likewise, the top finance executive generally oversees compliance with securities and banking regulations. The organization's legal department is also likely to contribute to this effort by providing general oversight and answering queries from managers about the appropriate interpretation of laws and regulations.

ethical compliance The extent to which an organization and its members follow basic ethical standards of behavior

Ethical Compliance **Ethical compliance** is the extent to which the members of the organization follow basic ethical (and legal) standards of behavior. We noted earlier that organizations have increased their efforts in this area—

providing training in ethics and developing guidelines and codes of conduct, for example. These activities serve as vehicles for enhancing ethical compliance. Many organizations also establish a formal ethics committee, which may be asked to review proposals for new projects, help evaluate new hiring strategies, or assess a new environmental protection plan. The committee can also serve as a peer-review panel to evaluate alleged ethical misconduct by an employee.[25]

Philanthropic Giving   Finally, **philanthropic giving** is the awarding of funds or gifts to charities or other social programs. Dayton-Hudson Corp. routinely gives 5 percent of its taxable income to charity and social programs. Table 4.2 lists some of the top corporate contributors to social causes. Giving across national boundaries is also becoming more common. For example, Alcoa gave $112,000 to a small town in Brazil to build a sewage treatment plant. And Japanese firms like Sony and Mitsubishi make contributions to a number of social programs in the United States. Unfortunately, in this age of cutbacks, many corporations have also had to limit their charitable gifts over the past several years as they continue to trim their own budgets. And many firms that continue to make contributions are increasingly targeting them to programs or areas where the firm will get something in return. For example, compared to just a few years ago, firms today are more likely to give money to job training programs than to the arts. The logic is that they get a more direct payoff from the former type of contribution—in this instance, a better trained workforce from which to hire new employees.[26]

philanthropic giving   Awarding funds or gifts to charities or worthy causes

IBM	$92.7*
Microsoft Corp.	73.2*
Johnson & Johnson	72.8
Eli Lilly and Co.	71.9
Hewlett-Packard Co.	71.2†
General Motors Corp.	69.2
Philip Morris Cos. Inc.	68.0
Pfizer Inc.	60.4
Bristol-Meyers Squibb Co.	56.0
Exxon Corp.	55.4

TABLE 4.2
Top Corporate Givers 1995 (in millions)

*Fiscal year ending 6/30/96
† Fiscal year ending 10/31/95
Source: Taft Corporate Giving Directory, 18th edition. Table from *Newsweek*, September 29, 1997, p. 35.

■ Informal Organizational Dimensions

In addition to these formal dimensions for managing social responsibility, there are also informal ones. Dimensions such as leadership, organization culture, and how the organization responds to whistle blowers help shape and define people's perceptions of the organization's stance on social responsibility.

Organization Leadership and Culture   Leadership practices and organization culture can go a long way toward defining the social responsibility stance an organization and its members will adopt.[27] For example, for many years Johnson & Johnson executives provided a consistent message to employees that customers, employees, communities where the company did business, and shareholders were all important—and primarily in that order. Thus when packages of poisoned Tylenol showed up on store shelves in the 1980s, Johnson & Johnson employees didn't need to wait for orders from headquarters to know what to do: they immediately pulled all the packages from shelves before any other customers could buy them.[28] By contrast, the message sent to Astra USA employees by the actions of their top managers communicates much less regard for social responsibility.

Informal dimensions can be significant forces in social responsibility. Following the tragic death of Princess Diana, Columbia Records released a musical tribute in her honor. Columbia and most of the recording artists involved in the project indicated that their share of the proceeds would be donated to Diana's memorial fund. Following their lead, retailers like Tower Records and Virgin Megastore also committed their profits to the memorial fund as well.

Whistle Blowing   **Whistle blowing** is the disclosure by an employee of illegal or unethical conduct on the part of others within the organization.[29] How an organization responds to this practice often indicates its stance toward social responsibility. Whistle blowers may have to proceed through a number of channels to be heard, and they may even get fired for their efforts. Many organizations, however, welcome their contributions. A person who observes questionable behavior typically first reports the incident to his or her boss. If nothing is done, the whistle blower may then inform higher-level managers or an ethics committee if one exists. Eventually, the person may have to go to a regulatory agency or even the media to be heard. For example, Charles W. Robinson Jr. once worked as a director of a SmithKline lab in San Antonio. One day he noticed a suspicious billing pattern the firm was using to collect lab fees from Medicare that were considerably higher than the firm's normal charges for those same tests. He pointed out the problem to higher-level managers, but his concerns were ignored. He subsequently took his findings to the U.S. government, which sued SmithKline and eventually reached a settlement of $325 million.[30]

■ Evaluating Social Responsibility

Any organization that is serious about social responsibility must be sure that its efforts are producing the desired benefits. Essentially, this process requires applying the concept of control to social responsibility. Many organizations now require current and new employees to read their guidelines or code of ethics and then sign a statement agreeing to abide by it. An organization should also evaluate how it responds to instances of questionable legal or ethical conduct. Does it follow up immediately? Does it punish those involved? Or does it use delay and cover-up tactics? Answers to these questions can help an organization form a picture of its approach to social responsibility.

More formally, an organization may sometimes actually evaluate the effectiveness of its social responsibility efforts. For example, when Amoco recently established a job training program in Chicago, it allocated additional funds to evaluate how well the program was meeting its goals. Additionally, some organizations occasionally conduct corporate social audits. A **corporate social audit** is a formal and thorough analysis of the effectiveness of the firm's social performance. The audit is usually conducted by a task force of high-level managers from within the firm. An audit requires that the organization clearly define all its social goals, analyze the resources it devotes to each goal, determine how well it is achieving the various goals, and make recommendations about which areas need additional attention.

Ben & Jerry's conducts a formal audit of its social responsibility programs each year and publishes the results—favorable or otherwise—in its annual report. For example, one recent audit found that the firm was using a misleading label on one of its ice cream products. This criticism was published in the firm's next annual report, along with a promise to correct the error and to strive to avoid similar problems in the future.[31] Unfortunately, such audits are not conducted often because they are expensive and time consuming. Indeed, most organizations probably could do much more to evaluate the extent of their social responsibility than they do.[32]

whistle blowing The disclosing by an employee of illegal or unethical conduct on the part of others within the organization

corporate social audit A formal and thorough analysis of the effectiveness of a firm's social performance

MANAGEMENT IMPLICATIONS Managers should understand that social responsibility is not something that just happens. Instead, it must, like other organizational activities, be actively managed. Recognizing and using both formal and informal dimensions can help manage the social responsibility process, as can actually evaluating the firm's social responsibility efforts and strategies. ▬

Summary of Key Points

Ethics are an individual's personal beliefs about what constitutes right and wrong behavior. Important areas of ethical concern for managers are how the organization treats its employees, how employees treat the organization, and how the organization and its employees treat other economic agents. The ethical context of organizations consists of each manager's individual ethics and messages sent by organizational practices. Organizations use leadership, culture, training, codes, and guidelines to help them manage ethical behavior.

Social responsibility is the set of obligations an organization has to protect and enhance the society in which it functions. Organizations may be considered responsible to their stakeholders, to the natural environment, and to the general social welfare. Even so, organizations present strong arguments both for and against social responsibility. The approach an organiza-

tion adopts toward social responsibility falls along a continuum of lesser to greater commitment: the obstructionist stance, the defensive stance, the accommodative stance, and the proactive stance.

Government influences organizations through regulation, which is the establishment of laws and rules that dictate what businesses can and cannot do in prescribed areas. Organizations, in turn, rely on personal contacts, lobbying, political action committees, and favors to influence the government.

Organizations use three types of activities to formally manage social responsibility: legal compliance, ethical compliance, and philanthropic giving. Leadership, culture, and allowing for whistle blowing are informal means for managing social responsibility. Organizations should evaluate the effectiveness of their socially responsible practices as they would any other strategy.

Discussion Questions

Questions for Review

1. Do organizations have ethics? Why or why not?

2. Summarize the basic stances that an organization can take regarding social responsibility.

3. What are the arguments for and against social responsibility?

4. How does the government influence organizations? How do organizations influence the government?

Questions for Analysis

5. What is the relationship between the law and ethical behavior? Can illegal behavior possibly be ethical?

6. How are the ethics of an organization's CEO related to social responsibility?

7. How do you feel about whistle-blowing activity? If you were aware of a criminal activity taking place in your organization and if reporting it might cost you your job, what would you do?

Questions for Application

8. Refresh your memory about the *Exxon Valdez* oil spill. Evaluate the social responsibility dilemmas facing the company. For example, if Exxon had pledged unlimited resources to the cleanup, would this have been fair to the company's stockholders?

9. Assume you owned a large and highly profitable business. What stance would you take toward social responsibility? List five specific programs or causes that you might be inclined to support.

10. Review the arguments for and against social responsibility. On a scale of 1 to 10, rate the validity and importance of each point. Use these ratings to develop a position regarding how socially responsible an organization should be. Now compare your ratings and position with those of two of your classmates. Discuss your respective positions, focusing primarily on disagreements.

Building Effective Decision-Making Skills

EXERCISE OVERVIEW

Decision-making skills refer to the manager's ability to correctly recognize and define problems and opportunities and to then select an appropriate course of action to solve problems and capitalize on opportunities. Many decisions made by managers have an ethical component. This exercise will help you appreciate the potential role of ethics in making decisions.

EXERCISE BACKGROUND

Read and reflect on each of the following scenarios:

1. You are the top manager of a major international oil company. Because of a recent oil spill by another firm, all the companies in the industry have been subjected to close scrutiny regarding the safety of various work practices. Your safety manager has completed a review and informed you that your firm has one potential problem area. The manager estimates the probability of a problem within the next five years as being about 3 percent. The costs of fixing things now would be about $1.5 million. However, should you do nothing and a problem develop, the costs will be $10 million, plus your firm will receive a lot of bad publicity.

2. You manage a small fast-food restaurant. The owner has just informed you that you need to cut your payroll by 20 hours per week. You have determined that the most feasible option is to lay off one of two workers. One is a retired woman who works part-time for you. She lives on a fixed income, is raising three grandchildren, and really needs the money she earns from this job. The other is a college student who also works part-time. He is one year away from getting his degree and must work to pay his tuition and fees.

3. You have decided to donate $1,000 to a worthy cause in your neighborhood on behalf of the small business you own. Based on your own research, you have learned that the groups and charities most in need of funds are a local homeless shelter, a youth soccer league, an abortion clinic, and a tutoring program for illiterate adults.

EXERCISE TASK

With the background information above as context, do the following:

1. Make a decision between the two courses of action for scenario one.

2. Decide which of the two employees to terminate in scenario two.

3. Decide where to donate your money in scenario three.

4. What role did your own personal ethics play in making each of these decisions?

5. Compare your decisions with those of a classmate and discuss why any differences arose.

EXERCISE OVERVIEW

Building Effective Interpersonal Skills

Interpersonal skills refer to the ability to communicate with, understand, and motivate individuals and groups. Interpersonal skills may be especially important in a situation in which ethics and social responsibility issues are involved. This exercise will help you relate interpersonal skills to ethical situations.

EXERCISE BACKGROUND

Assume you are a department manager in a large retail store. Your work group recently had a problem with sexual harassment. Specifically, one of your female employees reported to you that a male employee was telling off-color jokes and making mildly suggestive comments. When you asked him about the charges, he did not deny them but instead attributed them to a misunderstanding.

He was subsequently suspended with pay while the situation was investigated. The human resource manager who interviewed both parties, as well as other employees, concluded that the male employee should not be fired, but should instead be placed on six-months probation. During this period, any further substantiated charges against him will result in immediate dismissal.

The basis for this decision included the following: (1) the male has worked in the store for more than ten years, has a good performance record, and has had no earlier problems; (2) the female indicated that she did not believe that he was directly targeting her for harassment, but instead was guilty of general insensitivity; and (3) the female did not think that his actions were sufficiently blatant to warrant dismissal but simply wanted him to stop those behaviors.

Tomorrow is to be his first day back at work. You are a bit worried about tensions that will exist in the group when he returns. You hope to minimize the tension by meeting with the female today and with the male tomorrow morning.

EXERCISE TASK

With the background information above as context, do the following:

1. Write general notes about what you will say to the female.

2. Write general notes about what you will say to the male.

3. What are the ethical issues in this situation?

4. If you have the option of having the employees work closely together or keeping them separated, which would you do? Why?

Building Effective Communication Skills

EXERCISE OVERVIEW

Communication skills refer to the manager's abilities to both effectively convey ideas and information to others and effectively receive ideas and information from others. Communication, ethics, and social responsibility are closely intertwined in certain situations. This exercise will help you relate these concepts to one another.

EXERCISE BACKGROUND

You are the public relations manager for a large chemical company. One of your foreign plants has just suffered an explosion. Although no one was killed, several dozen employees were injured. In addition, toxic chemical compounds were discharged into a nearby river and will undoubtedly cause major environmental damage. It is also clear that your company's managers at the plant are responsible for the explosion. You have learned, for example, that they took shortcuts when safety equipment was installed, used inferior materials, and failed to adequately train key employees in basic safety procedures.

Your experts' best estimates now are that it will take at least six months to clean up the river. There are also reports that the injured employees are already preparing lawsuits against the company. The local press at the plant site is also calling for an immediate and public apology and a commitment by the firm to make full restitution for all damages caused by the explosion.

A press conference has been called for one hour from now. You will be making a prepared statement about the situation and then answering questions from the reporters. Your boss, however, has given you some directions. For one thing, he says that acknowledging that six months will be needed to clean up the river will be disastrous. Instead, he wants you to indicate that cleanup will be completed in two months. He also wants you to recognize the pain caused to your injured employees and to wish them a speedy recovery, but not to acknowledge any guilt or liability on the part of your company.

EXERCISE TASK

With the background information above as context, do the following:

1. Write a press statement that meets your boss's mandate.

2. Write a press statement that is completely accurate.

3. What are the likely short- and long-term ethical implications of each statement?

4. Could you personally deliver the first statement?

CHAPTER CLOSING CASE

Juggling Global Ethics at Phillips-Van Heusen

A growing practice in business today, especially among larger companies, is moving production to foreign locations in order to capitalize on lower labor costs. For several years now this trend has affected industries ranging from automobiles to electronics to apparel. Companies that adopt this strategy, however, find that they must walk a fine line between ethically capitalizing on production efficiencies versus unethically exploiting people in less developed countries. One of the latest firms to find itself in the eye of controversy is Phillips-Van Heusen, or PVH.

PVH is one of the largest clothing manufacturers in the United States. Its most well-known brands include Izod, Gant, and Van Heusen. A few years ago the firm's board decided that it needed a new leader and a new direction. At the time, most of its production was concentrated in U.S. factories. PVH was also struggling with a chain of outlet stores it launched several years earlier.

The person selected to head PVH's turnaround was Bruce Klatsky. Klatsky, the grandson of a Russian immigrant apparel cutter, began his career with PVH as a merchandise trainee in 1972. He steadily worked himself up the organization, constantly impressing others with both his business acumen and his personal integrity. Thus, his selection as CEO came as no surprise to anyone familiar with the company.

Klatsky knew immediately that certain fundamental changes in business practices were needed to restore the firm's growth and profitability. Accordingly, he reduced PVH's investment in its outlet stores. More significantly, he also closed three U.S. shirt factories and moved their production to overseas plants. And today, PVH manufactures shirts in several countries, including Guatemala. Under Klatsky's leadership, revenues have grown from around $800 million to more than $1.5 billion in only four years.

Klatsky has been an outspoken advocate of protecting foreign workers from abuse. For example, he personally wrote and implemented a stringent code of social responsibility for the firm that stresses, among other things, that PVH will treat its employees fairly and will never violate human rights nor employ children in its factories. In Guatemala, for example, PVH's 650 workers get subsidized lunches, free on-site medical care, and school supplies for their children. Workers sit in ergonomic chairs and are paid higher wages than those paid for similar jobs elsewhere in the country. PVH has also donated more than $1.5 million to help upgrade nutrition, facilities, and teacher education at local schools.

Klatsky's efforts have attracted a lot of attention and generated much favorable publicity for both himself and his company. For example, he sits on the board of the Human Rights Watch advocacy group, as well as a White House committee set up to help eliminate sweatshops. He is also frequently asked to speak at meetings and conventions about protecting the rights of foreign workers.

Given both Klatsky's personal reputation and PVH's widely publicized efforts, then, it came as quite a surprise when the firm was recently targeted for criticism by another group, Human Rights Watch. Among other things, this group has charged that PVH actually pays its Guatemalan workers a wage that is far below the poverty level, that it hires contractors who use underage workers, and that it intimidates union organizers. The charges evolved from allegations from a number of sources ranging from local U.S. officials to a priest.

Klatsky has denied the charges, but also promised to investigate. The wage issue, meanwhile, poses the biggest ethi-cal dilemma for managers. For example, it is a documented fact that the wages paid by PVH in Guatemala are indeed higher than those paid for comparable jobs. On the other hand, it is also a documented fact that those wages are only half of what a family of five needs to be above the poverty line in Guatemala. As Klatsky himself acknowledges, it's a tough question.

Case Questions

1. What is your own assessment of the ethics of the wages PVH pays its Guatemalan workers?
2. Are any broader ethical issues associated with moving production to foreign markets to lower labor costs?
3. Use the Internet to learn more about PVH's current foreign operations, as well as current economic and labor conditions in Guatemala.

Case References: *"Critics Confront a CEO Dedicated to Human Rights,"* Wall Street Journal, *February 24, 1997;* "Made to Order," Computerworld, *April 15, 1996, p. 107.*

CHAPTER NOTES

1. "'Off-the Clock' Time: More Work for No Pay," *USA Today,* April 24, 1997, p. 1B; and "So Much for the Minimum-Wage Scare," *Business Week,* July 21, 1997, p. 19.
2. For a review of the different meanings of the word *ethics,* see Thomas M. Garrett and Richard J. Klonoski, *Business Ethics,* 3rd ed. (Englewood Cliffs, N.J.: Prentice-Hall, 1990).
3. Thomas Donaldson and Thomas W. Dunfee, "Toward a Unified Conception of Business Ethics: An Integrative Social Contracts Theory," *Academy of Management Review,* Vol. 19, No. 2, 1994, pp. 252–284.
4. "Don't Look Now, But Bosses May Be Spying," *Honolulu Advertiser,* May 23, 1997, pp. A1, A9.
5. "How a Penney Buyer Made up to $1.5 Million on Vendors' Kickbacks," *Wall Street Journal,* February 7, 1995, pp. A1, A13.
6. "A Thin Coat of Whitewash?" *Forbes,* April 8, 1996, pp. 44–47.
7. "Keeping Secrets," *USA Today,* April 10, 1997, pp. 1B, 2B (the case was settled out of court).
8. "48% of Workers Admit to Unethical or Illegal Acts," *USA Today,* April 4, 1997, pp. B1, B2.
9. "Home Depot Charges a Rival Drummed Up Opposition to Stores," *Wall Street Journal,* August 18, 1995, pp. A1, A5; "FTC Antitrust Case Accuses Toys 'R' Us," *Wall Street Journal,* May 23, 1996, pp. A3, A4; "Hey Kid, Buy This!" *Business Week,* June 30, 1997, pp. 62–69; and "Are

Companies Using Restructuring Costs to Fudge the Figures?" *Wall Street Journal,* January 30, 1996, pp. A1, A11.
10. "How U.S. Concerns Compete in Countries Where Bribes Flourish," *Wall Street Journal,* September 29, 1995, pp. A1, A14; and Patricia Digh, "Shades of Gray in the Global Marketplace," *HR Magazine,* April 1997, pp. 90–98.
11. Anthony J. Daboub, Abdul M.A. Rasheed, Richard L. Priem, and David A. Gray, "Top Management Team Characteristics and Corporate Illegal Activity," *Academy of Management Review,* 1995, Vol. 20, No. 1, pp. 138–170.
12. "Sex, Lies, and Home Improvements?" *Business Week,* March 31, 1997, p. 40; and "Abuse of Power," *Business Week,* May 13, 1996, pp. 86–98.
13. Bernhard Schwab, "A Note on Ethics and Strategy: Do Good Ethics Always Make for Good Business?" *Strategic Management Journal,* 1996, Vol. 17, pp. 499–500.
14. Alan Richter and Cynthia Barnum, "When Values Clash," *HR Magazine,* September 1994, pp. 42–45.
15. Beth Rogers, "Serious about Its Code of Ethics," *HR Magazine,* September 1994, pp. 46–48; and Kate Walter, "Values Statements That Augment Corporate Success," *HR Magazine,* October 1995, pp. 87–92.
16. Thomas Donaldson and Lee E. Preston, "The Stakeholder Theory of the Corporation: Concepts, Evidence, and Implications," *Academy of Management Review,* 1995, Vol. 20, No. 1, pp. 65–91; and Thomas M. Jones, "Instrumental Stakeholder Theory: A Synthesis of Ethics and

Economics," *Academy of Management Review*, 1995, Vol. 20, No. 2, pp. 404–437.

17. "Oil Companies Strive to Turn a New Leaf to Save Rain Forest," *Wall Street Journal*, July 17, 1997, pp. A1, A8.

18. Linda Grant, "There's Gold in Going Green," *Fortune*, April 14, 1997, pp. 116–118.

19. "Ashland Just Can't Seem to Leave Its Checkered Past Behind," *Business Week*, October 31, 1988, pp. 122–126.

20. For discussions of this debate, see Jean B. McGuire, Alison Sundgren, and Thomas Schneeweis, "Corporate Social Responsibility and Firm Financial Performance," *Academy of Management Journal*, December 1988, pp. 854–872; and Margaret A. Stroup, Ralph L. Neubert, and Jerry W. Anderson Jr., "Doing Good, Doing Better: Two Views of Social Responsibility," *Business Horizons*, March-April 1987, pp. 22–25.

21. "Is It Rainforest Crunch Time?" *Business Week*, July 15, 1996, pp. 70–71; "Yo, Ben! Yo, Jerry! It's Just Ice Cream," *Fortune*, April 28, 1997, p. 374.

22. Andrew Singer, "Can a Company Be Too Ethical?" *Across the Board*, April 1993, pp. 17–22.

23. "Help or Hype from Exxon?" *Business Week*, August 28, 1995, p. 36.

24. "1st Evidence of Foreign Campaign Money Found," *USA Today*, July 16, 1997, pp. 1A, 4A.

25. Lynn Sharp Paine, "Managing for Organizational Integrity," *Harvard Business Review*, March-April 1994, pp. 106–115.

26. "Giving—And Getting Something Back," *Business Week*, August 28, 1995, p. 81.

27. David M. Messick and Max H. Bazerman, "Ethical Leadership and the Psychology of Decision Making," *Sloan Management Review*, Winter 1996, pp. 9–22.

28. "Unfuzzing Ethics for Managers," *Fortune*, November 23, 1987, pp. 229–234.

29. For a recent review of the literature on whistle blowing, see Janet P. Near and Marcia P. Miceli, "Whistle-Blowing: Myth and Reality," *Journal of Management*, 1996, Vol. 22, No. 3, pp. 507–526.

30. "Whistle-Blowers on Trial," *Business Week*, March 24, 1997, pp. 172–178.

31. "Ben & Jerry Tell on Themselves," *Business Week*, June 26, 1995, p. 8.

32. See Michael V. Russo and Paul A. Fouts, "A Resource-Based Perspective on Corporate Environmental Performance and Profitability," *Academy of Management Journal*, June 1997, pp. 534–559.

5

The Global Environment

OBJECTIVES

After studying this chapter, you should be able to:

- Describe the nature of international business, including its meaning, recent trends, managing globalization, and managing in a global environment.
- Discuss the structure of the global economy and how it affects international management.
- Identify and discuss the environmental challenges inherent in international management.
- Describe the basic issues involved in competing in a global economy, including organization size and the management challenges in a global economy.

Hoechst AG is the world's largest chemical company, with annual revenues of more than $31 billion—exceeding those of U.S. giants Dow Chemical and Union Carbide combined. Hoechst is headquartered in Frankfurt, Germany, but has operations around the world. But although Hoechst technically remains a German company, it is also taking interesting steps to de-emphasize its German connections and to grow new businesses in other parts of the world.

The reason for Hoechst's unusual actions is really a simple one: its operating costs are too high and need to be lowered. Those costs, in turn, result from a variety of difficulties inherent in doing business in Germany today. Indeed, Germany is without a doubt one of the most difficult places in the world in which to conduct business. One primary basis for this difficulty is labor. German workers are the highest paid and—according to many experts—the most pampered in the world. For example, they receive an extra month's pay at Christmas, earn six weeks vacation per year, and receive an average hourly wage of $30. And these benefits are guaranteed by law. Moreover, firms are greatly constrained by the government in their ability to reduce their workforce and/or to lay off workers.

Environmentalism is also a major issue in Germany today. Companies in Germany face more stringent environmental controls than in any other country in the world. These controls, in turn, make it more difficult to set up business and more difficult to run a business than it is in other countries. For example, Hoechst hopes to soon begin production in a new factory that is now scheduled to open nine years later than originally planned. And all of the holdups were associated with environmental protection regulations.

"We are not merely a German company with foreign interests. One could almost say we are a nonnational company."

Juergen Dormann, Hoechst AG CEO, quoted in the Wall Street Journal, *February 18, 1997, p. A1.*

So what is Hoechst doing about these conditions? In many different fundamental ways it is moving toward becoming a global company rather than a German company. But a heavy dose of this globalization is actually focused in the United States. While most German companies restrict their management boards (similar to a board of directors) to nationals, Hoechst has an American and a Brazilian among its nine board members. Moreover, two of its six major business units are now headquartered in the United States, and Hoechst has become among the first German firms to be listed on the New York Stock Exchange. Just a few years ago more than half of Hoechst's workforce was in Germany. Now, less than one-third is in Germany. Meanwhile, the firm's workforce has grown dramatically in other parts of the world, especially in the United States.

To carry off these changes, meanwhile, has required more than a simple sleight of hand. A major part of Hoechst's strategy has involved selling off German-based businesses and buying businesses in other parts of the world. This approach has allowed the firm to shed itself of several high-cost operations and to replace them with lower-cost units. Interestingly, Germany's other large chemical companies, Bayer AG and BASF AG, have not followed Hoechst's lead and remain firmly entrenched as old-line traditional German companies. So which path is the right one? Only time will tell.[1]

International business has become a ubiquitous part of the landscape, no matter where one looks. For example, Microsoft has been aggressively seeking new business opportunities around the globe. One key player in Microsoft's expansion strategy is Rajiv Nair, shown here in his native India. Since 1990 Nair has been responsible for leading Microsoft's expansion into India, and has already created a network of 10,000 resellers in this rapidly growing market.

Although every business is unique, the challenges and opportunities facing Hoechst AG are increasingly common among today's multinational corporations. Specifically, such businesses must make critical decisions regarding how they will allocate their resources in different markets and how they will strive to gain a competitive advantage in those markets. Indeed, to be successful today, managers have to understand the global context within which they function. And this holds true regardless of whether the manager runs a *Fortune* 500 firm or a small independent company.

This chapter explores the global context of management. We start by describing the nature of international business. We then discuss the structure of the global market in terms of different economies and economic systems. The basic environmental challenges of management are introduced and discussed next. We then focus on issues of competition in a global economy. Finally, we conclude by characterizing the managerial functions of planning, organizing, leading, and controlling as management challenges in a global economy.

The Nature of International Business

As you prepared breakfast this morning, you may have plugged in a coffee pot manufactured in Asia and perhaps ironed a shirt or blouse made in Taiwan with an iron made in Mexico. The coffee you drank was probably made from beans grown in South America. To get to school, you may have driven a Japanese car. Even if you drive a Ford or Chevrolet, some of its parts were engineered or manufactured abroad. Perhaps you didn't drive a car to school but rather rode a bus (manufactured by Daimler-Benz, a German company, or by Volvo, a Swedish company) or a motorcycle (manufactured by Honda, Kawasaki, Suzuki, or Yamaha—all Japanese firms).

Businesses from around the world have a strong influence on our daily lives. But no country is unique in this respect. For instance, people drive Fords in Germany, use Compaq computers in Japan, eat McDonald's hamburgers in France, and snack on Mars candy bars in England. They drink Pepsi and wear Levi Strauss jeans in China. The Japanese buy Kodak film and use American Express credit cards. People around the world fly on American Airlines in planes made by Boeing. Their buildings are constructed with Caterpillar machinery, their factories are powered by General Electric engines, and they buy Mobil oil.

In truth, we have become part of a global village and have a global economy where no organization is insulated from the effects of foreign markets and competition.[2] Indeed, more and more firms are reshaping themselves for international competition and discovering new ways to exploit markets in every corner of the world.[3] Failure to take a global perspective is one of the biggest mistakes managers can make. Thus, we start laying the foundation of this discussion by introducing and describing the basics of international business.

■ The Meaning of International Business

There are many different forms and levels of international business. Although the lines that distinguish one from another are perhaps arbitrary, we can identify four levels of international activity that differentiate organizations.[4] These levels are illustrated in Figure 5.1. A **domestic business** acquires nearly all of its resources and sells all of its products or services within a single country. Most small businesses are essentially domestic in nature, as are many banks, retailers, agricultural enterprises, and service firms. However, very few large domestic businesses remain in the world.

Indeed, most large firms today are either international or multinational companies. An **international business** is one that is primarily based in a single country but acquires some meaningful share of its resources or revenues from other countries. Sears fits this description. Most of its stores are in the United States, for example, and the retailer earns around 90 percent of its revenues from its U.S. operations, with the remaining 10 percent coming from Sears stores in Canada and Mexico. At the same time, however, many of the products it sells, such as tools and clothing, are made abroad.[5]

A **multinational business** has a worldwide marketplace from which it buys raw materials, borrows money, and manufactures its products and to which it subsequently sells its products. Ford Motor Company is an excellent example of a multinational company. It has design and production facilities around the world. The Ford Contour,

domestic business A business that acquires all of its resources and sells all of its products or services within a single country

international business A business that is primarily based in a single country but acquires some meaningful share of its resources or revenues (or both) from other countries

multinational business A business that has a worldwide marketplace from which it buys raw materials, borrows money, and manufactures its products and to which it subsequently sells its products

FIGURE 5.1
Levels of International Business Activity

for instance, was jointly designed by European and U.S. teams and is sold with only minor variations in dozens of foreign markets. Ford makes and sells other cars in Europe that are never seen in the United States. Ford cars are designed, produced, and sold for individual markets, wherever they are and without regard for national boundaries.[6] Multinational businesses are often called *multinational corporations*, or MNCs.[7]

The final form of international business is the global business. A **global business** is one that transcends national boundaries and is not committed to a single home country. Although no business has truly achieved this level of international involvement, a few are edging closer and closer. For example, as noted in the "Opening Incident," Hoechst is portraying itself as a "nonnational company." Similarly, Unocal Corporation is legally headquartered in California. But in its company literature, Unocal says it "no longer considers itself as a U.S. company," but is, instead, a "global energy company."[8]

global business A business that transcends national boundaries and is not committed to a single home country

■ Trends in International Business

To understand why and how these different levels of international business have emerged, we must briefly look to the past. Most of the industrialized countries in Europe were devastated during World War II, and many Asian countries, especially Japan, fared no better. There were few passable roads, few standing bridges, and even fewer factories dedicated to the manufacture of peacetime products. And those regions less affected by wartime destruction— Canada, Latin America, and Africa—had not yet developed the economic muscle to threaten the economic pre-eminence of the United States.

Businesses in war-torn countries like Germany and Japan had no choice but to rebuild from scratch. Because of this position, these businesses essentially had to rethink every facet of their operations, including technology, production, finance, and marketing. Although it took many years for these countries to recover, they eventually did so, and their economic systems were subsequently poised for growth. During the same era, U.S. companies grew complacent. Their customer base was growing rapidly. Increased population spurred by the baby boom and increased affluence resulting from the postwar economic boom greatly raised the average person's standard of living and expectations. The U.S. public continually wanted new and better products and services. Many U.S. companies profited greatly from this pattern but most were also perhaps guilty of taking it for granted.

But U.S. firms are no longer isolated from global competition or the global market. A few simple numbers help tell the full story of international trade and industry. First of all, the volume of international trade increased more than 3,000 percent from 1960 to 1997. Further, although 162 of the world's largest corporations are headquartered in the United States, there are also 126 in Japan, 42 in France, 41 in Germany, and 34 in Britain.[9] Within certain industries the pre-eminence of non-U.S. firms is even more striking. For example, only one each of the world's ten largest banks and ten largest electronics companies is based in the United States. Only two of the ten largest chemical companies are U.S. firms. On the other hand, U.S. firms account for six of the eight largest aerospace companies, four of the seven largest airlines, six of the nine largest computer companies, four of the five largest diversified financial companies, and six of the ten largest retailers.[10]

U.S. firms are also finding that international operations are an increasingly important element of their sales and profits. For example, in 1995 Exxon Corporation realized 80 percent of its revenues and 66 percent of its profits abroad. For Avon Products, Inc., these percentages were 62 percent and 67 percent, respectively.[11] From any perspective, then, it is clear that we live in a truly global economy. Virtually all businesses today must be concerned with the competitive situations they face in lands far from home and with how companies from distant lands are competing in their homeland.

■ Managing the Process of Internationalization

Managers should also recognize that their global context dictates two related but distinct sets of challenges. One set of challenges must be confronted when an organization chooses to change its level of international involvement. For example, a firm that wants to move from being an international to a multinational business has to manage that transition. The other set of challenges occurs when the organization has achieved its desired level of international involvement and must then function effectively within that environment. This section highlights the first set of challenges, and the next section introduces the second set of challenges. When an organization decides to increase its level of international activity, there are several alternative strategies that can be adopted.

Importing and Exporting   Importing or exporting (or both) is usually the first type of international business in which a firm gets involved. **Exporting**, or making the product in the firm's domestic marketplace and selling it in another country, can involve both merchandise and services. **Importing** is bringing a good, service, or capital into the home country from abroad. For example, automobiles (Mazda, Ford, Volkswagen, Mercedes-Benz, Ferrari) and stereo equipment (Sony, Bang and Olufsen, Sanyo) are routinely exported by their manufacturers to other countries. Likewise, many wine distributors buy products from vineyards in France, Italy, and/or California and import them into their own countries for resale.

> **exporting**   Making a product in the firm's domestic marketplace and selling it in another country
>
> **importing**   Bringing a good, service, or capital into the home country from abroad

An import/export operation has several advantages. For example, it is the easiest way of entering a market with a small outlay of capital. Because the products are sold "as is," there is no need to adapt the product to the local conditions and little risk is involved. Nevertheless, there are also disadvantages. For example, imports and exports are subject to taxes, tariffs, and higher transportation expenses. Furthermore, products that are not adapted to local conditions may miss the needs of a large segment of the market. Finally, some products may be restricted and thus can be neither imported nor exported.

Licensing   A company may prefer to arrange for a foreign company to manufacture or market its products under a licensing agreement. Factors that may lead to this decision include excessive transportation costs, government regulations, and home production costs. **Licensing** is an arrangement whereby a

> **licensing**   An arrangement whereby one company allows another company to use its brand name, trademark, technology, patent, copyright, or other assets in exchange for a royalty based on sales

THE QUALITY CHALLENGE

Samsung Looks to Nissan for Quality Assistance

Although several Korean firms make automobiles— Hyundai, Kia, Daewoo, and Ssang Yong, for example—none has been especially successful, particularly in global markets. But a recent entry may be different. The name of that entry? Samsung, one of the world's biggest and most successful companies, with major operations in electronics, finance, machinery, and chemicals and a goal of being one of the world's largest automobile makers by the year 2010.

So why does Samsung believe that it can succeed when other Korean firms have faltered? Samsung managers believe that other Korean firms have not succeeded internationally because they have all experienced quality problems. Samsung notes, for example, that its domestic competitors usually go through a trial-and-error process of identifying and fixing problems as cars are actually being produced for sale. Thus, those cars that go out the door before a particular problem is identified and solved are almost certain to cause problems for their owners.

To combat this problem, Samsung has contracted with a powerful ally, Japan's Nissan. Nissan has agreed to share its production know-how, set up an aluminum engine plant in Korea to supply Samsung, and train one thousand

"The Korean auto industry is a bit behind the times and has been producing cheap cars. Our strategy is to make high-quality superior cars."

Kyung Choon, CEO of Samsung Motors*

Samsung engineers in modern manufacturing technology. It is also helping Samsung develop its first car, based on its own midsize Maxima. In return, Nissan will get undisclosed fees for each service it provides, plus 2 percent of the factory price for each car sold.

But Samsung is not relying just on Nissan to help it make a winner. For example, the firm has committed one full year to "practice" production, a period in which workers will learn their jobs, practice them, and get the kinks in the system straightened out. And Samsung's pockets are deep enough to provide a cushion of several years before the automobile operation must begin to show a profit. Of course, the real proof will come in a few years when the first Samsung automobiles roles off the assembly line. The industry will anxiously await the verdict—will it be another Kia or more like a Nissan? And the quality difference will no doubt make a big difference in its ultimate success.

References: *Louis Kraar, "Behind Samsung's High-Stakes Push into Cars," Fortune, May 12, 1997, pp. 119–120 (*quote on p. 120); and Hoover's Handbook of World Business 1997 (Austin, Texas: Hoover's Business Press, 1996), pp. 452–453.*

firm allows another company to use its brand name, trademark, technology, patent, copyright, or other assets. In return, the licensee pays a royalty, usually based on sales. For example, Kirin Brewery, Japan's largest producer of beer, wanted to expand its international operations but feared that the time involved in shipping the product from Japan would cause the beer to lose its freshness. Thus, Kirin has entered into a number of licensing arrangements with breweries in other markets. These brewers make beer according to strict guidelines provided by the Japanese firm and then package and market it as Kirin Beer. They then pay a royalty back to Kirin for each case sold. Molson produces Kirin in Canada under such an agreement, and the Charles Wells brewery does the same in England.[12] "The Quality Challenge" describes how Samsung licensed technology from Nissan to use in its new automobile business.

Two advantages of licensing are increased profitability and extended profitability. This strategy is frequently used for entry into less developed countries where older technology is still acceptable and, in fact, may be state of the art. A primary disadvantage of licensing is inflexibility. A firm can tie up control of its product or expertise for a long period of time. And if the licensee does not develop the market effectively, the licensing firm can lose profits. A second disadvantage is that licensees can take the knowledge and skill that they have been given access to for a foreign market and exploit them in the licensing firm's home market. In this situation what used to be a business partner becomes a business competitor.

Strategic Alliances In a **strategic alliance**, two or more firms jointly cooperate for mutual gain.[13] For example, Kodak and Fuji, along with three major Japanese camera manufacturers, recently collaborated on the development of a new film cartridge. This collaboration allowed Kodak and Fuji to share development costs, prevented an advertising war that would have resulted if the two firms had developed competing cartridges, and made it easier for the companies to introduce new cameras at the same time they introduced the new film cartridges. A **joint venture** is a special type of strategic alliance in which the partners actually share ownership of a new enterprise. General Mills and Nestlé formed a new company called Cereal Partners Worldwide (CPW). The purpose of CPW is to produce and market cereals. General Mills supplies the technology and proven formulas while Nestlé provides its international distribution network. The two partners share equally in the new enterprise. Strategic alliances have enjoyed a tremendous upsurge in the past few years. In most cases each party provides a portion of the equity or the equivalent in physical plant, raw materials, cash, or other assets. The proportion of the investment then determines the percentage of ownership in the venture.[14]

Strategic alliances have advantages as well as disadvantages. For example, they can allow quick entry into a market by taking advantage of the existing strengths of participants. Japanese automobile manufacturers employed this strategy to their advantage to enter the U.S. market by using the already established distribution systems of U.S. automobile manufacturers. Strategic alliances are also an effective way of gaining access to technology or raw materials. And they allow the firms to share the risk and cost of the new venture. One major disadvantage of this approach lies with the shared ownership of joint ventures. Although it reduces the risk for each participant, it also limits the control and the return that each firm can enjoy.[15]

Direct Investment Another level of commitment to internationalization is direct investment. **Direct investment** occurs when a firm headquartered in one country builds or purchases operating facilities or subsidiaries in a foreign country. The foreign operations then become wholly owned subsidiaries of the firm. Mercedes-Benz recently invested $1.1 billion to construct a new factory in Alabama to build its sports utility vehicle.[16] Similarly, Ford and General Motors have also recently built new plants in Brazil.[17]

A major reason many firms make direct investments is to capitalize on lower labor costs. That is, the goal is often to transfer production to locations where labor is cheap. Japanese businesses have moved much of their

strategic alliance A cooperative arrangement between two or more firms for mutual benefit

joint ventures A special type of strategic alliance in which the partners share in the ownership of an operation on an equity basis

direct investment When a firm headquartered in one country builds or purchases operating facilities or subsidiaries in a foreign country

Part Two The Environmental Context of Management

Nike Takes the Heat

One of the most compelling issues facing many international businesses today is the ethics of moving production to countries where labor costs are low, thus lowering overall production costs. And Nike, the U.S. sports apparel giant, often finds itself at the center of that controversy. About 75 percent of Nike's production is done in Indonesia, China, and Vietnam in order to capitalize on lower labor costs in those countries. But with low costs often come difficult issues.

For example, in March 1997 a U.S.-based labor group released a report condemning Nike for its labor practices in Vietnam. One charge was that 56 women were forced to run laps around the factory for wearing nonregulation shoes; twelve women reportedly fainted and had to be hospitalized. Another charge was that workers were being paid subminimum wages. Nike expressed distress when the news was released and promised a full investigation.

To help deal with the situation, Nike hired Andrew Young, former civil rights leader, mayor of Atlanta, and U.S. ambassador to the United Nations, to study and report on conditions at its overseas plants. His seventy-five-page report, unfortunately, generated even more controversy. Young basically concluded that Nike's overseas operations were in fine shape and that human rights were not being violated. For example, he found that Nike plants were clean, adequately ventilated, and well lit and that there was no pattern of widespread or systematic abuse.

But virtually ignored in Young's report was the issue of wages. His argument was that he lacked the skill to assess pay in a global economy. Moreover, he argued, Nike's pay practices are the same as dozens of other multinational firms—paying people the prevailing wages within their own country. But critics argued that he—and Nike—missed the point. They contend that companies that pay the local minimum are exploiting people and that giant corporations should be doing more to raise standards of living by paying more than minimum wages.

> *"While Nike claims it is trying to monitor and enforce its code of conduct, its current approach to monitoring and enforcement is simply not working."*
>
> *Thuyen Nguyen, Vietnam Labor Watch**

References: *"Nike to Take a Hit in Labor Report,"* USA Today, *March 27, 1997, pp. 1A, 2A (*quote on p. 2A); and "Nike Hasn't Scrubbed Its Image Yet,"* Business Week, *July 7, 1997, p. 44.*

---

maquiladoras Light-assembly plants built in northern Mexico close to the U.S. border that receive special tax breaks by the Mexican government

production to Thailand because labor costs are much lower there than in Japan. Many U.S. firms are using *maquiladoras* for the same purpose. ***Maquiladoras*** are light-assembly plants built in northern Mexico close to the U.S. border. The plants receive special tax breaks from the Mexican government, and the area is populated with workers willing to work for very low wages. More than one thousand plants in the region employ 300,000 workers, and more are planned. The plants are owned by major corporations, primarily from the United States, Japan, South Korea, and major European industrial countries. This concentrated form of direct investment benefits the country of Mexico, the companies themselves, and workers who might otherwise be without jobs. Some critics argue, however, that the low wages paid by the *maquiladoras* amount to little more than slave labor.[18] This concern is described from the point of view of one company, Nike, in "Today's Management Issues."

Like the other approaches for increasing a firm's level of internationalization, direct investment carries with it a number of benefits and liabilities. Managerial control is more complete, and profits do not have to be shared as they do in joint ventures. Purchasing an existing organization provides additional benefits in that the human resources, plant, and organizational infrastructure are already in place. Acquisition is also a way to purchase the brand-name identification of a product, which might be particularly important if the cost of introducing a new brand is high. When Nestlé bought the U.S. firm Carnation Company a few years ago, it retained the firm's brand names for all Carnation products sold in the United States. Notwithstanding these advantages, the company is now operating a part of itself entirely within the borders of a foreign country. The additional complexity in the decision making, the economic and political risks, and so forth may outweigh the advantages that can result from international expansion.

Of course, we should also note that these approaches to internationalization are not mutually exclusive. Indeed, most large firms use all of them simultaneously. MNCs have a global orientation and worldwide approach to foreign markets and production. They search for opportunities all over the world and select the best strategy to serve each market. In some settings, the firms may use direct investment, whereas in other environments licensing or strategic alliances might be more appropriate. Alternatively, the MNCs might limit their involvement to exporting and importing. The advantages and disadvantages of each approach are summarized in Table 5.1.

■ Managing in an International Market

Even when a firm is not actively seeking to increase its desired level of internationalization, its managers are still responsible for seeing that it functions effectively within whatever level of international involvement the organization

TABLE 5.1

Advantages and Disadvantages of Different Approaches to Internationalization

When organizations decide to increase their level of internationalization, they can adopt several strategies. Each strategy is a matter of degree, as opposed to being a discrete and mutually exclusive category. And each has unique advantages and disadvantages that must be considered.

Approaches to Internationalization	Advantages	Disadvantages
Importing or Exporting	1. Small cash outlay 2. Little risk 3. No adaptation necessary	1. Tariffs and taxes 2. High transportation costs 3. Government restrictions
Licensing	1. Increased profitability 2. Extended profitability	1. Inflexibility 2. Helps competitors
Strategic alliance/ Joint ventures	1. Quick market entry 2. Access to materials and technology	1. Shared ownership (limits control and profits)
Direct investment	1. Enhances control 2. Existing infrastructure	1. Complexity 2. Greater economic and political risk 3. Greater uncertainty

has achieved. In one sense, the job of a manager in an international business may not be that much different from the job of a manager in a domestic business. Each may be responsible for acquiring resources and materials, making products, providing services, developing human resources, advertising, or monitoring cash flow.

In another sense, however, the complexity associated with each of these activities may be much greater for managers in international firms. Rather than buying raw materials from sources in California, Texas, and Missouri, an international purchasing manager may buy materials from sources in Peru, India, and Spain. Rather than train managers for new plants in Michigan, Florida, and Oregon, the international human resources executive may be training new plant managers for facilities in China, Mexico, and Scotland. And instead of developing a single marketing campaign for the United States, an advertising director may be working on promotional efforts in France, Brazil, and Japan.

The key question that must be addressed by any manager trying to be effective in an international market is whether to focus on globalization or regionalism. A global thrust requires that activities be managed from an overall global perspective as part of an integrated system. Regionalism, on the other hand, involves managing within each region with less regard for the overall organization. In reality, most larger MNCs manage some activities globally (for example, finance and manufacturing) and others locally (such as human resources management and advertising). We explore these approaches more fully later.

MANAGEMENT IMPLICATIONS All managers need to understand the global environment in which they function. For managers in large multinational corporations, the global context is obvious. But even smaller domestic companies are affected by international forces. It is also important to understand the different methods for entering a foreign market and the strengths and weaknesses of each. Managers should also recognize the distinctions between the processes of internationalization and the management issues inherent in running a company with an existing international context. ▬

The Structure of the Global Economy

One way that managers seeking to operate in a global environment can improve their chances for success is to develop a clear understanding of the structure of the global economy. Although each country, and indeed many regions within any given country, are unique, we can still note some basic similarities and differences. This section describes three elements of the global economy: mature market economies and systems, high potential/high growth economies, and other economies.[19]

▮ Mature Market Economies and Systems

A **market economy** is based on the private ownership of business and allows market factors such as supply and demand to determine business strategy. Mature market economies include the United States, Japan, the United Kingdom, France, Germany, and Sweden. These countries have several things in common. For example, they tend to employ market forces in the allocation of resources. They also tend to be characterized by private ownership of property, although some variation does occur. France, for example, has a relatively high level of government ownership compared to other market economies.

U.S. managers have relatively few problems operating in market economies. Many of the business "rules of the game" that apply in the United States, for example, also apply in Germany or England. And consumers there often tend to buy the same kinds of products. For these reasons it is not unusual for U.S. firms seeking to expand geographically to begin operations in some other market economy. Although the task of managing an international business in an industrial market country is somewhat less complicated than operating in some other type of economy, the venture still poses challenges. Perhaps foremost among them is that the markets in these economies are typically quite mature. Many industries, for example, are already dominated by large and successful companies. Thus competing in these economies poses a major challenge.

The map in Figure 5.2 highlights three relatively mature market systems. **Market systems** are clusters of countries that engage in high levels of trade with each other. One mature market system is North America. The United

market economy An economy based on the private ownership of business, which allows market factors such as supply and demand to determine business strategy

market systems Clusters of countries that engage in high levels of trade with each other

FIGURE 5.2
The Global Economy

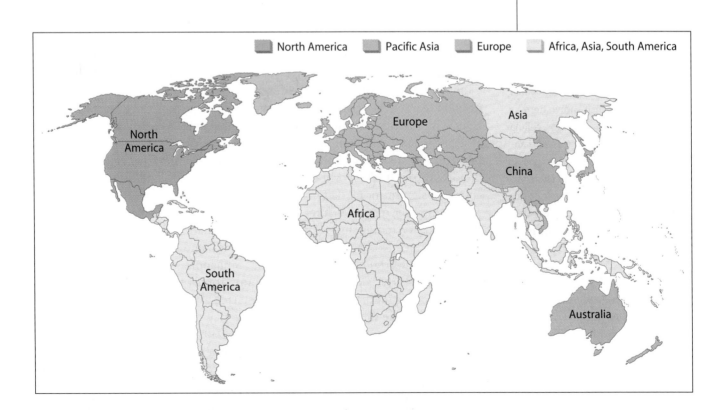

Most international business managers see the People's Republic of China as the most important emerging marketplace in the world. Its vast population and growing interest in consumerism combine to offer tremendous potential for a wide array of products and services. For example, even farmers in China's most remote regions hunger for new technology like the satellite dish shown here. Products like televisions, cellular telephones, computers, and automobiles are also experiencing strong demand as the citizens of China take their place alongside consumers from Japan, Europe, the United States, and the rest of the world.

North American Free Trade Agreement (NAFTA) An agreement between the United States, Canada, and Mexico to promote trade with one another

Pacific Asia A market system located in Southeast Asia

States, Canada, and Mexico are major trading partners; more than 70 percent of Mexico's exports go to the United States, and more than 65 percent of what Mexico imports comes from the United States. During the last several years these countries have negotiated a variety of agreements to make trade even easier. The most important of these, the **North American Free Trade Agreement**, or **NAFTA**, eliminates many of the trade barriers—quotas and tariffs, for example—that existed previously.[20]

Another mature market system is Europe. Until recently, Europe was two distinct economic areas. The eastern region consisted of communist countries such as Poland, Czechoslovakia, and Rumania. These countries relied on government ownership of business and greatly restricted trade. In contrast, western European countries with traditional market economies have been working together to promote international trade for decades. In particular, the European Union (or EU as it is often called) has long been a formidable market system. The formal members of the EU are Denmark, the United Kingdom, Portugal, the Netherlands, Belgium, Spain, Ireland, Luxembourg, France, Germany, Italy, and Greece. For years these countries followed a basic plan that led to the elimination of most trade barriers in 1992.

The European situation has recently grown more complex, however. Communism has collapsed in most eastern countries, which are now trying to develop market economies. These countries also want greater participation in trade with the western European countries. In some ways the emergence of the east has slowed and complicated business activities in the west. Long term, however, the new markets in the east are likely to make Europe an even more important part of the world economy. For example, Poland is increasingly becoming a significant market for many MNCs.

Yet another mature market system is **Pacific Asia**. As shown in Figure 5.2, this market system includes Japan, China, Thailand, Malaysia, Singapore, Indonesia, South Korea, Taiwan, the Philippines, and Australia. Whereas Japan has been a powerhouse for years, Taiwan, Singapore, Thailand, and South Korea have recently become major economic forces themselves. Trade among these nations is on the rise, and talk has started about an Asian economic community much like the EU.[21] The Asian currency crisis in 1998 was a major setback for many countries in Pacific Asia, especially Indonesia and South Korea, but most experts believe the market system as a whole will weather the storm. And even those countries most affected by the economic downturn should rebound in the next few years.

■ High Potential/High Growth Economies

In contrast to the highly developed and mature market economies just described, other countries have what is termed *high potential/high growth economies*. These economies have been relatively underdeveloped and immature and, until recently, were characterized by weak industry, weak currency, and relatively poor consumers.[22] The governments in these countries, however, have been actively working to strengthen their economies by opening their doors to foreign investment and by promoting international trade. Some of these countries have only recently adopted market economies, whereas others still use a command economy, or centrally planned system.

Even though it is technically part of Pacific Asia, the People's Republic of China is largely underdeveloped. The transfer of control of Hong Kong from Great Britain to China in 1997 focused even more attention on the market potential in the world's most populous country.[23] India is also showing signs of becoming a major market in the future.[24] Vietnam has become a potentially important market, and Brazil is also becoming more important. Likewise, Russia and the other states and republics that previously made up the Commonwealth of Independent States are also being closely watched by many companies for emerging market opportunities.[25]

The primary challenges presented by the developing economies to those interested in conducting international business there are the lack of wealth on the part of potential consumers and the underdeveloped infrastructure. Developing economies have enormous economic potential, but much of it remains untapped. Thus international firms entering these markets often have to invest heavily in distribution systems, in training consumers how to use their products, and even in providing living facilities for their workers.

■ Other Economies

Some economic systems around the world defy classification as either mature markets or high potential/high growth economies. One major area that falls outside of these categories is the oil-exporting region generally called the Middle East. The oil-exporting countries present mixed models of resource allocation, property ownership, and the development of infrastructure. These countries all have access to major amounts of crude oil, however, and thus are important players in the global economy.

These countries include Iran, Iraq, Kuwait, Saudi Arabia, Libya, Syria, and the United Arab Emirates. High oil prices in the 1970s and 1980s created enormous wealth in these countries. Many of them invested heavily in their infrastructures. Whole new cities were built, airports were constructed, and the population was educated. As oil prices have fallen, many of the oil-producing countries have been forced to cut back on these activities. Nevertheless, they are still quite wealthy. The per capita incomes of the United Arab Emirates and Qatar, for example, are among the highest in the world. Despite their great wealth, the oil-producing nations provide great challenges to managers. Political instability (as evidenced by the Persian Gulf War in 1991 and the Iraqi crisis in 1998) and tremendous cultural differences, for example, combine to make doing business in the Middle East both very risky and very difficult.

Other countries pose risks of a different sort to business. Politically and ethnically motivated violence, for example, still characterizes some countries. Foremost among these are Peru, El Salvador, Turkey, Columbia, and Northern Ireland. Cuba presents special challenges because it is so insulated from the outside world. With the fall of communism, some experts believe that Cuba will eventually join the ranks of the market economies. If so, its strategic location will quickly make it an important business center.

MANAGEMENT
IMPLICATIONS

International managers need to have a fundamental understanding of the structure of the global economy. They should also recognize the advantages and disadvantages of competing in mature market economies and systems, high potential/high growth economies, and other economies. ■—

Environmental Challenges of International Management

We noted earlier that managing in a global context both poses and creates additional challenges for the manager. As illustrated in Figure 5.3, three environmental challenges in particular warrant additional exploration at this point: the political/legal environment, the economic environment, and the cultural environment of international management.[26]

■ The Economic Environment

Every country is unique and creates a unique set of challenges for managers trying to do business there. However, three aspects of the economic environment can help managers anticipate the kinds of economic challenges they are likely to face in working abroad.

Economic System The first of these is the economic system used in the country. As we described earlier, most countries today are moving toward market economies. In a mature market economy, the key element for managers is freedom of choice. Consumers are free to decide which products they prefer to purchase, and firms are free to decide which products and services to provide. As long as both the consumer and the firm are free to decide to be in the market, then supply and demand determine which firms and which products will be available.

A related characteristic of market economies that is relevant to managers concerns the nature of property ownership. There are two pure types—complete private ownership and complete public ownership. In systems with pri-

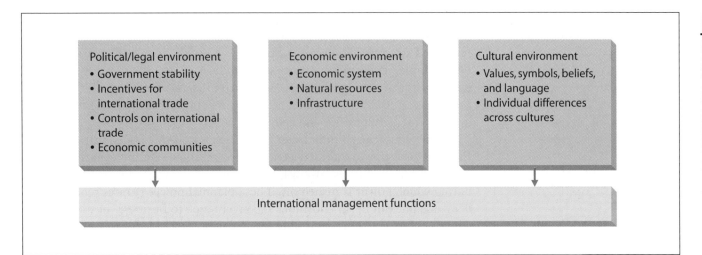

Political/legal environment	Economic environment	Cultural environment
• Government stability	• Economic system	• Values, symbols, beliefs, and language
• Incentives for international trade	• Natural resources	• Individual differences across cultures
• Controls on international trade	• Infrastructure	
• Economic communities		

International management functions

vate ownership, individuals and organizations—not the government—own and operate the companies that conduct business. In systems with public ownership, the government directly owns the companies that manufacture and sell products. Few countries have pure systems of private ownership or pure systems of public ownership. Most countries tend toward one extreme or the other, but usually a mix of public and private ownership exists.

Natural Resources   Another important aspect of the economic environment in different countries is the availability of natural resources. A very broad range of resources are available. Some countries, like Japan, have few resources of their own. Japan is thus forced to import all the oil, iron ore, and other natural resources it needs to manufacture products for its domestic and overseas markets. The United States, in contrast, has enormous natural resources and is a major producer of oil, natural gas, coal, iron ore, copper, uranium, and other metals and materials that are vital to the development of a modern economy.

One natural resource that is particularly important in the modern global economy is oil. As we noted earlier in this chapter, a small set of countries in the Middle East, including Saudi Arabia, Iraq, Iran, and Kuwait, controls a very large percentage of the world's total known reserves of crude oil. Access to this single natural resource has given these oil-producing countries enormous clout in the international economy. One of the more controversial global issues today involving natural resources is the South American rain forest. Developers and farmers in Brazil, Peru, and other countries are clearing vast areas of rain forest, arguing that its their land and they can do what they want with it. Many environmentalists, however, fear the deforestation is wiping out entire species of animals and may alter the environment enough to affect weather patterns around the world.[27]

Infrastructure   Yet another important aspect of the economic environment of relevance to international management is infrastructure. A country's

FIGURE 5.3
Environmental Challenges of International Management

Managers functioning in a global context must be aware of several environmental challenges. Three of the most important include economic, political/legal, and cultural challenges.

infrastructure The schools, hospitals, power plants, railroads, highways, ports, communication systems, air fields, and commercial distribution systems of a country

infrastructure comprises its schools, hospitals, power plants, railroads, highways, ports, communication systems, air fields, commercial distribution systems, and so forth. The United States has a highly developed infrastructure. For example, its educational system is modern, its roads and bridges are well developed, and most people have access to medical care. Overall, the United States has a relatively complete infrastructure sufficient to support most forms of economic development and activity.

Some countries, on the other hand, lack a well-developed infrastructure. In some cases they do not have enough electrical generating capacity to meet demand. Such countries—Kenya, for example—often schedule periods of time during which power is turned off. These planned power failures reduce power demands but can be an enormous inconvenience to business. In the extreme, when a country's infrastructure is greatly underdeveloped, firms interested in beginning business may have to build an entire township, including housing, schools, hospitals, and perhaps even recreation facilities, to attract a sufficient overseas work force. The "Management InfoTech" box describes how Wal-Mart is using its technology to enter new foreign markets. But Wal-Mart is able to use this technology only in more developed parts of the world.

■ The Political/Legal Environment

A second environmental challenge facing the international manager is the political/legal environment in which he or she will do business. Four important aspects of the political/legal environment of international management are government stability, incentives for multinational trade, controls on international trade, and the influence of economic communities on international trade.

Government Stability Stability can be viewed in two ways—as the ability of a given government to stay in power against other opposing factions in the country and as the permanence of government policies toward business. A country that is stable in both respects is preferable because managers have a higher probability of successfully predicting how government will affect their business. Civil war in countries such as Lebanon has made it virtually impossible for international managers to predict what government policies are likely to be and whether the government will be able to guarantee the safety of international workers. Consequently, international firms have been very reluctant to invest in Lebanon.

nationalized To be taken over by the government

In many countries—the United States, Great Britain, and Japan, for example—changes in government occur with very little disruption. In other countries—India, Argentina, and Greece, for example—changes are likely to be chaotic. Even if a country's government remains stable, the risk remains that the government might adopt new policies. In some countries foreign businesses may be **nationalized** (taken over by the government) with little or no warning. For example, a few years ago the government of Peru nationalized Perulac, a domestic milk producer owned by Nestlé, because of a local milk shortage.

MANAGEMENT INFOTECH

Technology Fuels Wal-Mart's Global Growth

Giant U.S. retailers have long sought the key to globalization. Sears, for example, opened a store in Mexico in 1947 and both Kmart and Toys 'R' Us opened overseas stores in the 1960s. But no retailer has become a true international enterprise in the same way as Ford and Toyota in automobiles, Hoechst in chemicals, and Nestlé in food products. Wal-Mart, however, is making a run at accomplishing what no other retailer has done—becoming a true multinational corporation.

"Wal-Mart is going to change the retailing landscape internationally exactly the same way it's done domestically."

Martin Terzian, CEO of Wal-Mart supplier*

Why does the Arkansas-based discounter think it can pull this off? In large part because managers at the firm have a long history of being able to pretty much do whatever they set their minds to. Indeed, Wal-Mart executives believe that international expansion will allow the firm to regain the top spot among the world's fastest growing businesses.

One key to Wal-Mart's success has been its state-of-the-art information system. Point-of-sale systems help Wal-Mart managers and buyers stay on top of what is selling, where, and for how much on virtually a daily basis. And key suppliers are tied directly into the system. For example, Black & Decker Corp. knows how much of each of its products Wal-Mart wants to have on hand. In turn, the vendor receives data from Wal-Mart's information system about sales of those products. Thus, Black & Decker is empowered to replenish Wal-Mart's inventory of Black & Decker tools as sales warrant—without waiting for Wal-Mart to authorize an actual purchase.

Wal-Mart is currently extending its information system to its foreign stores and establishing large distribution centers in each country or region. These distribution centers are wired to local stores as well as to domestic and international suppliers. Thus, as in the United States, sales information is sent to each local distribution center, and orders are placed automatically to keep store shelves stocked at adequate levels. Although Wal-Mart managers acknowledge that they need more than a fancy information system to succeed abroad, they are confident that their system will provide a basic foundation for fueling many other aspects of their international operations. And that fuel, they believe, will lead them to international retailing pre-eminence.

References: *"Wal-Mart Spoken Here,"* Business Week, *June 23, 1997, pp. 138–144 (*quote on p. 139); and* Hoover's Handbook of American Business 1997 *(Austin, Texas: Hoover's Business Press, 1996), pp. 1416–1417).*

Incentives for International Trade Another facet of the political environment is incentives to attract foreign business. For example, the state of Alabama offered Mercedes-Benz huge tax breaks and other incentives to entice the German firm to select a location in that state for a new factory. In like fashion, the French government sold land to The Walt Disney Company far below its market value and agreed to build a connecting freeway in exchange for the company's commitment to build its Disneyland Paris theme park.

Such incentives can take various forms. Some of the most common include reduced interest rates on loans, construction subsidies, and tax incentives. Less developed countries tend to offer different packages of incentives. In addition to lucrative tax breaks, for example, they can also attract investors with duty-free entry of raw materials and equipment, market protection through limitations on other importers, and the right to take profits out of the country. These countries may also have to correct deficiencies in their infrastructures, as noted earlier, to satisfy the requirements of foreign firms.

Controls on International Trade   A third element of the political environment that managers need to consider is the extent of controls on international trade. In some instances a government may decide that foreign competition is hurting domestic trade. To protect domestic business, such governments may enact barriers to international trade. These barriers include tariffs, quotas, export restraint agreements, and "buy national" laws.

tariff   A tax collected on goods shipped across national boundaries

A **tariff** is a tax collected on goods shipped across national boundaries. Tariffs can be collected by the exporting country, countries through which goods pass, and the importing country. Import tariffs, which are the most common, can be levied to protect domestic companies by increasing the cost of foreign goods. Japan charges U.S. tobacco producers a tariff on cigarettes imported into Japan as a way to keep the prices of foreign cigarettes higher than the prices charged by domestic firms. Tariffs can also be levied, usually by less developed countries, to raise money for the government.

quota   A limit on the number or value of goods that can be traded

Quotas are the most common form of trade restriction. A quota is a limit on the number or value of goods that can be traded. The quota amount is typically designed to ensure that domestic competitors will be able to maintain a certain market share. Honda is allowed to import 425,000 autos each year into the United States. This quota is one reason that Honda opened manufacturing facilities here. The quota applies to cars imported into the United States, but the company can produce as many other cars within our borders as it wants, as they are not considered imports. **Export restraint agreements** are designed to convince other governments to voluntarily limit the volume or value of goods exported to a particular country. They are, in effect, export quotas. Japanese steel producers voluntarily limit the amount of steel they send to the United States each year.

export restraint agreements
Accords reached by governments in which countries voluntarily limit the volume or value of goods they export and import from one another

Buy-national legislation gives preference to domestic producers through content or price restrictions. Several countries have this type of legislation. Brazil requires that Brazilian companies purchase only Brazilian-made computers. The United States requires that the Department of Defense purchase only military uniforms manufactured in the United States, even though the price of foreign uniforms would be half as much. Mexico requires that 50 percent of the parts of cars sold in Mexico be manufactured in Mexico.

Economic Communities   Just as government policies can either increase or decrease the political risk facing international managers, trade relations between countries can either help or hinder international business. Relations dictated by quotas, tariffs, and so forth can hurt international trade. There is currently a strong movement around the world to reduce many of these barriers. This movement takes its most obvious form in international economic communities.

economic community   A set of countries that agree to markedly reduce or eliminate trade barriers among its member nations (a formalized market system)

An international **economic community** is a set of countries that agree to markedly reduce or eliminate trade barriers among its member nations. The first, and in many ways still the most important, of these economic communities is the European Union (EU), discussed earlier. The passage of NAFTA, as also noted earlier, represents perhaps the first step toward the formation of a North American economic community. Other important economic communities include the Latin American Integration Association (Bolivia, Brazil, Colombia, Chile, Argentina, and other South American countries) and the Caribbean Common Market (the Bahamas, Belize, Jamaica, Antigua, Barbados, and twelve other countries).

■ The Cultural Environment

Another environmental challenge for the international manager is the cultural environment and how it affects business. A country's culture includes all the values, symbols, beliefs, and language that guide behavior.

Values, Symbols, Beliefs, and Language Cultural values and beliefs are often unspoken; they may even be taken for granted by those who live in a particular country. Cultural factors do not necessarily cause problems for managers when the cultures of two countries are similar. Difficulties can arise, however, when there is little overlap between the home culture of a manager and the culture of the country in which business is to be conducted. For example, most U.S. managers find the culture and traditions of England familiar. The people of both countries speak the same language and share strong historical roots, and a history of strong commerce exists between the two countries. When U.S. managers begin operations in Japan or the People's Republic of China, however, most of those commonalities disappear.

In Japanese the word *hai* (pronounced "hi") means "yes." In conversation, however, this word is used much like people in the United States use "uh-huh"; it moves a conversation along or shows the person you are talking to that you are paying attention. So when does

The economic, political/legal, and cultural environments of international business sometimes combine to produce fascinating, exciting, or sorrowful situations. For example, after South Korea's economy took a nosedive in late 1997, the International Monetary Fund had to step in and provide a $57 billion bailout package for the country. But because it feared that this would not be enough, the government of South Korea also requested help from its citizens. While Koreans have traditionally given away their children's gold rings on special occasions, these women are donating their jewelry to help the country reduce its debt to a more manageable level.

hai mean "yes" and when does it mean "uh-huh"? This question is relatively difficult to answer. If a U.S. manager asks a Japanese manager if he agrees to some trade arrangement, the Japanese manager is likely to say "hai"—which may mean "yes, I agree" or "yes, I understand" or "yes, I am listening." Many U.S. managers become frustrated in negotiations with the Japanese because they believe that the Japanese continue to raise issues that have already been settled (the Japanese managers said "yes"). What many of these managers fail to recognize is that *hai* does not always mean "yes" to the speaker.

Cultural differences between countries can have a direct impact on business practice. For example, the religion of Islam teaches that people should not make a living by exploiting the misfortune of others and that making interest payments is immoral. This means that in Saudi Arabia few businesses will provide auto-wrecking services to tow stalled cars to the garage (because that would be capitalizing on misfortune), and in the Sudan banks cannot pay or charge interest. Given these cultural and religious constraints, those two businesses—automobile towing and banking—don't seem to hold great promise for international managers in those particular countries!

Some cultural differences between countries can be even more subtle and yet have a major impact on business activities. For example, in the United States most managers clearly agree about the value of time. Most U.S. managers schedule their activities very tightly and then adhere to their schedules. Other cultures don't put such a premium on time. In the Middle East, for example, managers do not like to set appointments, and they rarely keep appointments set too far into the future. U.S. managers interacting with managers from the Middle East might misinterpret the late arrival of a potential business partner as a negotiation ploy or an insult, when it is simply a reflection of diverse views of time and its value.[28]

DILBERT by Scott Adams

Dealing with people from other cultures can be a rewarding experience, and it can also be a challenge. Language barriers, for example, pose major obstacles. Interestingly, some people believe that if they talk slower or louder, people who do not speak their language will somehow have a better understanding of what is being said. As illustrated in this cartoon, this flawed logic can even extend to electronic communication!

Language itself can be an important cultural factor in international business. Beyond the obvious and clear barriers posed by people who speak different languages, subtle differences in meaning can also play a major role. For example, Imperial Oil of Canada markets gasoline under the brand name Esso. When the firm tried to sell its gasoline in Japan, it learned that Esso means "stalled car" in Japanese. Similarly, General Motors executives couldn't understand why the Chevrolet Nova was not selling well in Latin America until they learned that, in Spanish, *no va* means "it doesn't go." The color green is used extensively in Moslem countries, but it signifies death in some other countries. The color associated with femininity in the United States is pink, but in many other countries yellow is the most feminine color.

Individual Behaviors Across Cultures   From another perspective clear differences in individual behaviors and attitudes across different cultures are also apparent. For example, Geert Hofstede, a Dutch researcher, studied 116,000 people working in dozens of different countries and found several interesting differences.[29] Hofstede's initial work identified four important dimensions

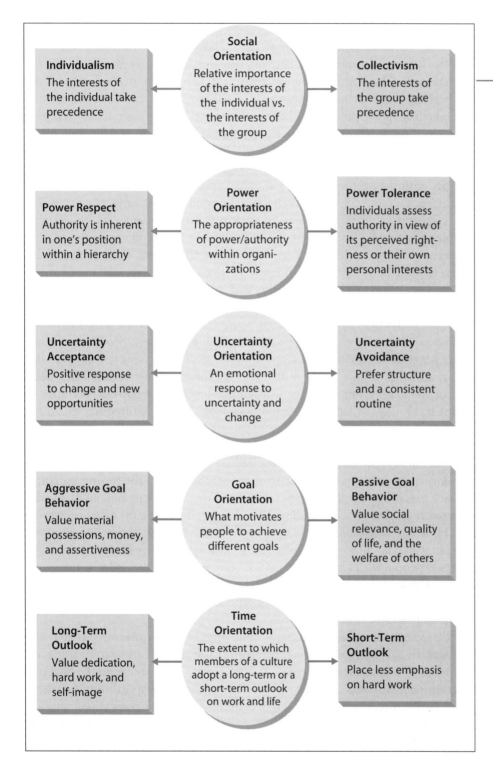

FIGURE 5.4
Individual Differences Across Cultures

Hofstede identified five fundamental differences that can be used to characterize people in different cultures. These dimensions are social orientation, power orientation, uncertainty orientation, goal orientation, and time orientation. Different levels of each dimension affect the perceptions, attitudes, values, motivation, and behaviors of people in different cultures.

Source: R. W. Griffin/M. Pustay, *International Business,* (figure 14.1, page 479)
© 1996 Addison Wesley Longman. Reprinted by permission of Addison Wesley Longman.

along which people seem to differ across cultures. More recently, he has added a fifth dimension. Figure 5.4 illustrates these dimensions.

The first dimension that Hofstede identified is social orientation.[30] **Social orientation** is a person's beliefs about the relative importance of the individual

social orientation A person's beliefs about the relative importance of the individual versus groups to which that person belongs

power orientation   The beliefs that people in a culture hold about the appropriateness of power and authority differences in hierarchies such as business organizations

uncertainty orientation   The feeling individuals have regarding uncertain and ambiguous situations

goal orientation   The manner in which people are motivated to work toward different kinds of goals

time orientation   The extent to which members of a culture adopt a long-term versus a short-term outlook on work, life, and other elements of society

versus groups to which that person belongs. The two extremes of social orientation are individualism and collectivism. *Individualism* is the cultural belief that the person comes first. Hofstede's research suggested that people in the United States, the United Kingdom, Australia, Canada, New Zealand, and the Netherlands tend to be relatively individualistic. *Collectivism*, the opposite of individualism, is the belief that the group comes first. Hofstede found that people from Mexico, Greece, Hong Kong, Taiwan, Peru, Singapore, Colombia, and Pakistan tend to be relatively collectivistic in their values. In countries with higher levels of individualism many workers may prefer reward systems that link pay with the performance of individual employees. In a more collectivistic culture such a reward system may, in fact, be counterproductive.

A second important dimension is **power orientation**, the beliefs that people in a culture hold about the appropriateness of power and authority differences in hierarchies such as business organizations. Some cultures are characterized by *power respect*. People in these cultures tend to accept the power and authority of their superiors and to respect the right of their superiors to control that power simply on the basis of their position in the hierarchy. Hofstede found that people in France, Spain, Mexico, Japan, Brazil, Indonesia, and Singapore were relatively power accepting. In contrast, people in cultures with a *power tolerance* orientation attach much less significance to a person's position in the hierarchy. These individuals are more willing to question a decision or mandate from someone at a higher level or perhaps even refuse to accept it. Hofstede's work suggested that people in the United States, Israel, Austria, Denmark, Ireland, Norway, Germany, and New Zealand tended to be more power tolerant.

The third basic dimension of individual differences studied by Hofstede was uncertainty orientation. **Uncertainty orientation** is the feeling individuals have regarding uncertain and ambiguous situations. People in cultures with *uncertainty acceptance* are stimulated by change and thrive on new opportunities. Hofstede suggested that many people from the United States, Denmark, Sweden, Canada, Singapore, Hong Kong, and Australia are in this category. In contrast, people with *uncertainty avoidance* tendencies dislike and will avoid ambiguity whenever possible. Hofstede found that many people in Israel, Austria, Japan, Italy, Colombia, France, Peru, and Germany tended to avoid uncertainty whenever possible.

The fourth dimension of cultural values that Hofstede measured is goal orientation. In this context **goal orientation** is the manner in which people are motivated to work toward different kinds of goals. One extreme on the goal orientation continuum is *aggressive goal behavior*. People who exhibit aggressive goal behaviors tend to place a high premium on material possessions, money, and assertiveness. On the other hand, people who adopt *passive goal behavior* place a higher value on social relationships, quality of life, and concern for others. According to Hofstede's research, many people in Japan tend to exhibit relatively aggressive goal behaviors, whereas many people in Germany, Mexico, Italy, and the United States reflect moderately aggressive goal behaviors. People from the Netherlands and the Scandinavian countries of Norway, Sweden, Denmark, and Finland all tend to exhibit relatively passive goal behaviors.

A recently identified fifth dimension is called **time orientation**.[31] Time orientation is the extent to which members of a culture adopt a long-term versus a short-term outlook on work, life, and other elements of society. Some cultures, such as Japan, Hong Kong, Taiwan, and South Korea, have a long-term orientation that values dedication, hard work, perseverance, and the importance of self-image. Other cultures, like Pakistan and West Africa, are more likely to have a short-term orientation. These cultures, in contrast, put considerably less emphasis on work, perseverance, and similar values. Hofstede's work suggests that the United States and Germany tend to have an intermediate time orientation.

MANAGEMENT IMPLICATIONS Managers need to understand the basic environmental challenges that confront them as they do business in international settings. These basic challenges involve political/legal differences in different countries, differences in the economic environments of different countries, and variations in the cultural environment. Each difference adds to the complexities that international managers must address. ▬

Competing in a Global Economy

Competing in a global economy is both a major challenge and an opportunity for businesses today. The nature of these challenges depends on a variety of factors, including the size of the organization. In addition, international management also has implications for the basic functions of planning, organizing, leading, and controlling.

■ Globalization and Organization Size

Although organizations of any size may compete in international markets, there are some basic differences in the challenges and opportunities faced by MNCs, medium-size organizations, and small organizations.

Multinational Corporations The large MNCs have long since made the choice to compete in a global marketplace. In general, these firms take a global perspective. They transfer capital, technology, human resources, inventory, and information from one market to another. They actively seek new expansion opportunities wherever feasible. MNCs tend to give their local managers a great deal of discretion in addressing local and regional issues. At the same time, each operation is ultimately accountable to a central authority. Managers

Rank 1996	Corporation	Country	Sales $ millions	Profits $ millions	Profits Rank	Employees Number	Employees Rank
1	General Motors	U.S.	168,369.0	4,963.0	8	647,000	3
2	Ford Motor	U.S.	146,991.0	4,446.0	11	371,702	7
3	Mitsui	Japan	144,942.8	321.9	292	41,694	276
4	Mitsubishi	Japan	140,203.7	394.1	271	35,000	308
5	Itochu	Japan	135,542.1	110.9	411	6,999	470
6	Royal Dutch/Shell Group	Brit./Neth.	128,174.5	8,887.1	1	101,000	98
7	Maruben	Japan	124,026.9	178.6	370	65,000	175
8	Exxon	U.S.	119,434.0	7,510.0	2	79,000	141
9	Sumitomo	Japan	119,281.3	1,292.8	491	26,200	354
10	Toyota Motor	Japan	108,702.0	3,426.2	18	150,736	51
11	Wal-Mart stores	U.S.	106,147.0	3,056.0	22	675,000	2
12	General Electric	U.S.	79,179.0	7,280.0	3	239,000	22
13	Nissho Iwai	Japan	78,921.2	136.9	395	17,497	407
14	Nippon Telegraph & Telephone	Japan	78,320.7	1,330.3	100	230,300	25
15	Intl. Business Machines	U.S.	75,947.0	5,429.0	6	268,648	19
16	Hitachi	Japan	75,669.0	784.2	186	330,152	10
17	AT&T	U.S.	74,525.0	5,908.0	5	130,400	65
18	Nippon Life Insurance	Japan	72,575.0	2,799.1	33	86,695	126
19	Mobil	U.S.	72,267.0	2,964.0	24	43,000	272
20	Daimler-Benz	Germany	71,589.3	1,776.1	73	290,029	12
21	British Petroleum	Britain	69,851.9	3,985.2	12	53,150	218
22	Matsushita Electric Industrial	Japan	68,147.5	1,223.9	112	270,651	18
23	Volkswagen	Germany	66,527.5	437.9	257	260,811	21
24	Daewoo	South Korea	65,160.2	468.3	250	186,314	38
25	Siemens	Germany	63,704.7	1,877.1	66	379,000	6
26	Chrysler	U.S.	61,397.0	3,529.0	16	126,000	67
27	Nissan Motor	Japan	59,118.2	690.2	203	135,331	61
28	Allianz	Germany	56,577.2	1,096.3	131	65,836	171
29	U.S. Postal Service	U.S.	56,402.0	1,567.2	82	887,546	1
30	Philip Morris	U.S.	54,553.0	6,303.0	4	154,000	48

TABLE 5.2
The World's Largest MNCs: Industrial Corporations

Source: *Fortune*, August 4, 1997, pg. F-2. *Fortune* ©1997 Time Inc. All rights reserved.

at this central authority (headquarters, a central office, etc.) are responsible for setting the overall strategic direction for the firm, making major policy decisions, and so forth. MNCs need senior managers who understand the global economy and who are comfortable dealing with executives and government officials from a variety of cultures. Table 5.2 lists the world's largest multinational enterprises.

Medium-Size Organizations   Many medium-size businesses remain primarily domestic organizations. But they still may buy and sell products made abroad and compete with businesses from other countries in their own domestic market. Increasingly, however, medium-size organizations are expanding into foreign markets as well. For example, Gold's Gym, a U.S. fitness chain, recently opened a very successful facility in Moscow.[32] In contrast to MNCs, medium-size organizations doing business abroad are much more selective about the markets they enter. They also depend more on a few international specialists to help them manage their foreign operations.

Small Organizations   More and more small organizations are also finding that they can benefit from the global economy. Some, for example, serve as local suppliers for MNCs. A dairy farmer who sells milk to Carnation Company, for example, is actually transacting business with Nestlé. Local parts suppliers also have been successfully selling products to the Toyota and Honda plants in the United States. Beyond serving as local suppliers, some small businesses also buy and sell products and services abroad. For example, the Collin Street Bakery, based in Corsicana, Texas, ships fruitcakes around the world. In 1996, the firm shipped 160,000 pounds of fruitcake to Japan. Its customers include Princess Caroline of Monaco.[33] Most small businesses rely on simple importing or exporting operations (or both) for their international sales and thus need only a few specialized management positions. Collin Street Bakery, for example, has one local manager who handles international activities. Mail-order activities within each country are subcontracted to local firms in each market.

■ Management Challenges in a Global Economy

The management functions that constitute the framework for this book—planning, organizing, leading, and controlling—are just as relevant to international managers as to domestic managers. International managers need to have a clear view of where they want their firm to be in the future; they have to organize to implement their plans, they have to motivate those who work for them, and they have to develop appropriate control mechanisms.[34]

Planning in a Global Economy   To effectively plan in a global economy, managers must have a broad-based understanding of both environmental issues and competitive issues. Global managers need to understand local market

Competing in a global economy takes skill, resources, and, on occasion, audacity. Nike, the largest sportswear company in the United States, is aggressively seeking new market opportunities in other countries. The firm recently invested $200 million to become the sponsor of Brazil's national soccer team for the next ten years. The firm hopes that this sponsorship will increase its visibility among soccer fans around the world, as well as with all sports fans in Brazil itself. Higher visibility, in turn, should lead to more sales of Nike products.

conditions and technological factors that will affect their operations. At the corporate level, executives need a great deal of information to function effectively. What markets are growing? What markets are shrinking? What are our domestic and foreign competitors doing in each market? These executives must also make a variety of strategic decisions about their organization. For example, if a firm wishes to enter the market in France, should it buy a local firm there, build a plant, or seek a strategic alliance? Critical issues include understanding environmental circumstances, the role of goals and planning in a global organization, and how decision making affects the global organization. We note special implications for global managers as we discuss planning in Chapters 7 through 10.

Organizing in a Global Economy Managers in international businesses must also attend to a variety of organizing issues. For example, General Electric has operations scattered around the globe. The firm has decided to give local managers a great deal of responsibility for how they run their business. In contrast, many Japanese firms give managers of their foreign operations relatively little responsibility. As a result, those managers must frequently travel back to Japan to present problems or get decisions approved. Managers in an international business must address the basic issues of organization structure and design, managing change, and dealing with human resources. We address the special issues of organizing the international organization in Chapters 11 through 14.

Leading in a Global Economy We noted earlier some of the cultural factors that affect international organizations. Individual managers must be prepared to deal with these and other factors as they interact with people from different cultural backgrounds. Supervising a group of five managers, each of whom is from a different state in the United States, is likely to be much simpler than supervising a group of five managers, each of whom is from a different culture. Managers must understand how cultural factors affect individuals, how motivational processes vary across cultures, the role of leadership in different cultures, how communication varies across cultures, and the nature of interpersonal and group processes in different cultures. In Chapters 15 through 19 we note special implications for international managers that relate to leading and interacting with others.

Controlling in a Global Economy Finally, managers in international organizations must also be concerned with control. Distances, time zones differences, and cultural factors also all play a role in control. For example, in some cultures close supervision is seen as being appropriate, and in other cultures it is not. Likewise, executives in the United States and Japan have trouble communicating vital information to one another because of the time zone differences. Basic control issues for the international manager revolve around operations management, productivity, quality, technology, and information systems. These issues are integrated throughout our discussion of control in Chapters 20 through 22.

MANAGEMENT IMPLICATIONS

The international challenges and opportunities facing managers in large multinational corporations, medium-size business, and small companies are subtly different. Similarly, the basic management functions of planning, organizing, leading, and controlling are also affected by the degree of internationalization of the organization. Thus, managers need to appreciate both the size of their organization and the relevant functional activities as they carry out their work in a global environment. ▬

Summary of Key Points

International business has grown to be one of the most important features of the world's economy. Learning to operate in a global economy is an important challenge facing many managers today. Businesses can be primarily domestic, international, multinational, or global in scope. Managers need to understand both the process of internationalization as well as how to manage within a given level of international activity.

To compete in the global economy, managers must understand its structure. Mature market economies and systems dominate the global economy today. North

America, the European Union, and Pacific Asia are especially important. The high potential/high growth economies in eastern Europe, Latin America, the People's Republic of China, India, and Vietnam are increasingly important to managers. The oil-exporting economies in the Middle East are also important.

Many of the challenges of management in a global context are unique issues associated with the international environmental context. These challenges reflect the economic, political/legal, and cultural environments of international management.

Basic issues of competing in a global economy vary according to whether the organization is an MNC, a medium-size organization, or a small organization. In addition, the basic managerial functions of planning, organizing, leading, and controlling must all be addressed in international organizations.

Discussion Questions

Questions for Review

1. Describe the four basic levels of international business activity. Do you think any organization will achieve the fourth level? Why or why not?

2. Summarize the basic structure of the global economy. What major changes are occurring today within that structure?

3. Briefly note some of the basic environmental challenges of international management.

4. What basic cultural differences did Hofstede identify?

Questions for Analysis

5. An organization seeking to expand its international operations must monitor several different environments. Which aspect of each environment is likely to have the greatest impact on decisions involved in such a strategic move? Why?

6. What industries do you think will have the greatest impact on international business? Are there any industries that might not be affected by the trend toward international business? If so, which ones? If there are none, why?

7. You are the CEO of an up-and-coming toy company and have plans to go international soon. What steps would you take to carry out that strategy? What areas would you stress in your decision-making process? How would you organize your company?

Questions for Application

8. Identify a local company that does business abroad. Interview an executive in that company. Why did the company go international? What major obstacles did it face? How successful has that decision been? Share your findings with the class.

9. Go to the library and find some information about the European Community's continued move toward a relaxation of trade barriers. What will be the effect of that relaxation? What will be some of the difficulties? Do you think that it is a good idea? Why or why not?

10. Many organizations fail to allow for cultural and language differences when they do business with other countries. For example, Pepsi was introduced into Asia with the slogan "Come alive with Pepsi." The slogan, however, was translated as "Bring your ancestors back from the dead with Pepsi." Go to the library and locate mistakes made by other companies entering foreign markets. What did they do wrong? How could they have prevented their mistakes?

Building **Effective**
Interpersonal
Skills

EXERCISE OVERVIEW

Interpersonal skills refer to the manager's ability to communicate with, understand, and motivate individuals and groups. Managers in international organizations must understand how culture and other factors affect how they communicate with people in different parts of the organization. This exercise enables you to learn more about your current levels of cultural understanding and develop insights into areas where you may need additional cultural awareness.

EXERCISE TASK

The "test" that follows consists of ten statements. Indicate your level of agreement with each statement as described in the instructions.

Instructions: You will agree with some of the following statements and disagree with others. In some cases, you may find it difficult to make a decision, but you should force a choice. Record your answers next to each statement according to the following scale:

4 Strongly agree   **2** Somewhat disagree
3 Somewhat agree   **1** Strongly disagree

_____ 1. Some areas of Switzerland are very much like Italy.

_____ 2. Although aspects of behavior such as motivation and attitudes within organizational settings remain quite diverse across cultures, organizations themselves appear to be increasingly similar in terms of design and technology.

_____ 3. Spain, France, Japan, Singapore, Mexico, Brazil, and Indonesia have cultures with a strong orientation toward authority.

_____ 4. Japan and Austria define male-female roles more rigidly and value qualities like forcefulness and achievement more than Norway, Sweden, Denmark, and Finland.

_____ 5. Some areas of Switzerland are very much like France.

_____ 6. Australia, Great Britain, the Netherlands, Canada, and New Zealand have cultures that view people first as individuals and place a priority on their own interests and values, whereas Colombia, Pakistan, Taiwan, Peru, Singapore, Mexico, Greece, and Hong Kong have cultures in which the good of the group or society is considered the priority.

_____ 7. The United States, Israel, Austria, Denmark, Ireland, Norway, and New Zealand have cultures with a low orientation toward authority.

_____ 8. The same manager may behave differently in different cultural settings.

_____ 9. Denmark, Canada, Norway, Singapore, Hong Kong, and Australia have cultures in which employees tolerate a high degree of uncertainty, but such levels of uncertainty are not well tolerated in Israel, Austria, Japan, Italy, Argentina, Peru, France, and Belgium.

_____ 10. Some areas of Switzerland are very much like Germany.

Building Effective Technical Skills

EXERCISE OVERVIEW

Technical skills are the skills necessary to accomplish or understand the specific kind of work being done in an organization. Some managers in international businesses must pay attention to fluctuations in currency exchange rates in the countries where the firm does business. These fluctuations affect many different kinds of financial decisions. This exercise will help you better understand the impact of exchange rates.

EXERCISE BACKGROUND

The exchange rates of most major currencies relative to the others are published regularly in newspapers such as the *Wall Street Journal, USA Today*, and the *New York Times*. Locate a recent edition of such a newspaper and determine the exchange rate on that day for U.S. dollars relative to British pounds. (Note that the pound is one of the few currencies that has a value greater than the dollar.)

Next, assume that six months have passed from the date of the exchange rate you have located. Major economic shifts have caused the exchange rate to fluctuate to a level such that one pound is worth one dollar. That is, the exchange rate six months hence will be assumed to be 1 to 1.

EXERCISE TASK

Using the information gathered above, do the following:

1. Determine the impact of this exchange rate shift on a U.S. tourist visiting England.

2. Determine the impact of the shift on an English tourist visiting the United States.

3. Determine the impact of this shift on a U.S. business that exports its products to England where they compete with locally made products.

4. Determine the impact of this shift on an English business that exports its products to the United States where they compete with locally made products.

5. Determine the impact of this shift on a U.S. business that buys raw materials in England, imports them into the United States, and makes products for shipment to Japan.

Building Effective Communication Skills

EXERCISE OVERVIEW

Communication skills refer to the manager's ability to both effectively convey ideas and information to others and effectively receive ideas and information from others. International managers have additional communication complexities due to differences in language, time zones, and so forth. This exercise enables you to enhance your communication skills by demonstrating the impact of different time zones.

EXERCISE BACKGROUND

Assume that you are a manager in a large multinational firm. Your office is located in San Francisco. You need to arrange a conference call with several other managers to discuss an upcoming strategic change by your firm. The other managers are located in New York, London, Rome, Moscow, Tokyo, Singapore, and Sydney.

EXERCISE TASK

Using the preceding information, do the following:

1. Determine the time zone differences in each of these cities.

2. Assuming that people in each city work from 8:00 A.M. to 5 P.M. (local time), determine the optimal time for your conference call. That is, what time would minimize the number of people who are inconvenienced?

3. Now assume that you need to visit each office in person. You need to spend one full day in each city. Use the Internet to review airline schedules, take into account differences in time zones, and develop an itinerary.

CHAPTER CLOSING CASE

Nestlé—Just About Everywhere!

"Going global" is one of today's hottest business trends. But amidst the hundreds of large multinationals boldly developing strategies for crossing new borders and entering new markets rests a firm that was "global" when most businesses were focused exclusively on their own domestic markets. The firm? Nestlé, a Swiss-based food processor that had international operations almost from its inception in 1866.

Just how global is Nestlé? The firm has factories in 74 of the world's 193 countries. And it sells milk, coffee, and/or chocolate bars in all of the rest! Indeed, even though Nestlé has no sales agents or distribution systems in North Korea, merchants there somehow manage to get Nestlé products on their shelves. Ninety-seven percent of Nestlé's employees are based outside of Switzerland. A recent United Nations study ranked Nestlé as having the highest level of international exposure of any business in the world. And year in and year out, Nestlé increases its market share, revenues, and profits.

So what is the key to the firm's success? Nestlé executives stress four basic operating principles. First, the firm thinks long term, rather than focusing on short-term profitability. Second, Nestlé believes in decentralization. Third, the firm sticks to what it knows best. And fourth, it recognizes the value of adapting to local tastes.

Long-term thinking shows up in many of Nestlé's decisions. For example, the firm recently paid what many observers might consider to be exorbitant prices for Perrier and Rowntree, a British-based candy maker. But Nestlé contends that although it would have obviously preferred to pay less, it nevertheless paid what it had to pay to get these prized businesses. It can afford to take this stance because investors do not expect to see a quick return. Instead, managers argue that these acquisitions will pay dividends for decades to come.

Decentralization is also a fundamental policy at Nestlé. Local managers are left alone to make decisions as they see fit. Their only reporting requirement is a one-page summary of their operations to Nestlé headquarters in Vevey, Switzerland, every quarter. Indeed, these reports cannot exceed one page in length! Somewhat more detail is required on an annual basis, but even then the reporting requirements are far lower than in virtually any other multinational corporation.

Nestlé also believes in sticking with what it does best—food processing and marketing. Whereas many other large multinationals have dabbled in far-ranging investments, Nestlé has maintained a remarkable focus on its core businesses—infant formula, powdered milk, coffee, chocolates, soups, bottled water, ice cream, cereal, and pet foods. Each of these businesses is either number one or two in worldwide market share. Indeed, its only significant operation outside of foods is a 26.3 percent investment in the cosmetics firm L'Oreal.

But even though Nestlé keeps its eye on foods, it also recognizes the importance of adapting to local tastes. For example, it stresses instant coffee in Europe and brewed coffees in the United States, both because of local tastes. Similarly, Europeans prefer soups containing meat chunks, while Japanese consumers prefer broth with no meat. Therefore, Nestlé uses different soup recipes for the products it sells in these markets.

So where does it end? Nestlé argues that it still has significant growth opportunities. For example, Nestlé gets only about 2 percent of its revenues from the Middle East, and executives see plenty of room for growth throughout the region. Moreover, there are also many more different foods and food groups for Nestlé to develop. So the future, as they say, seems to be bright for the Swiss giant.

Case Questions

1. Nestlé almost makes it seem easy. If so, why don't more firms follow the same recipe for success?

2. Do you see any hazards or problems in Nestlé's future?

3. Can you think of circumstances in which Nestlé's basic operating guidelines might conflict with one another?

Case References: *"All over the Map,"* Wall Street Journal, *September 26, 1996, pp. B1; and* Hoover's Handbook of World Business 1997 *(Austin, Texas: Hoover's Business Press, 1996), pp. 352–353.*

CHAPTER NOTES

1. "How a Chemical Giant Goes About Becoming a Lot Less German," *Wall Street Journal,* February 18, 1997, pp. A1, A14; *Hoover's Handbook of World Business 1997* (Austin, Texas: Hoover's Business Press, 1996), p. 240; and "'The German Worker is Making a Sacrifice,'" *Business Week,* July 28, 1997, pp. 46–47.

2. For an overview of international business, see Ricky W. Griffin and Michael Pustay, *International Business,* 2nd ed. (Reading, Mass.: Addison-Wesley, 1999).

3. Richard M. Steers and Edwin L. Miller, "Management in the 1990s: The International Challenge," *The Academy of Management Executive,* February 1988, pp. 21–22; and David A. Ricks, Brian Toyne, and Zaida Martinez, "Recent Developments in International Management Research," *Journal of Management,* June 1990, pp. 219–254.

4. For a more complete discussion of forms of international business, see Arvind Phatak, *International Dimensions of Management,* 3rd ed. (Boston: Kent, 1992).

5. *Hoover's Handbook of American Business 1997* (Austin, Texas: Hoover's Business Press, 1996), pp. 1196–1197.

6. Alex Taylor III, "The New Golden Age of Autos," *Fortune,* April 4, 1994, pp. 50–66.

7. John H. Dunning, *Multinational Enterprises and the Global Economy* (Wokingham, England: Addison-Wesley, 1993); and Christopher Bartlett and Sumantra Ghoshal, *Transnational Management* (Homewood, Ill.: Irwin, 1992).

8. "A Company without a Country?" *Business Week,* May 5, 1997, p. 40.

9. "The *Fortune* Global 5 Hundred—World's Largest Corporations," *Fortune,* August 4, 1997, p. F1.

10. "The *Fortune* Global 5 Hundred Ranked Within Industries," *Fortune,* August 4, 1997, pp. F16–28.

11. *Hoover's Handbook of American Business 1997* (Austin, Texas: Hoover's Business Press, 1996), pp. 212–213, 554–555.

12. "Creating a Worldwide Yen for Japanese Beer," *Financial Times,* October 7, 1994, p. 20.

13. Kenichi Ohmae, "The Global Logic of Strategic Alliances," *Harvard Business Review,* March-April 1989, pp. 143–154.

14. Jeremy Main, "Making Global Alliances Work," *Fortune,* December 17, 1990, pp. 121–126.

15. Hans Mjoen and Stephen Tallman, "Control and Performance in International Joint Ventures," *Organization Science,* May-June 1997, pp. 257–274.

16. "Mercedes Bends Rules," *USA Today,* July 16, 1997, pp. B1, B2.

17. "Conditions Ripe for a Bonanza in Car-Building," *USA Today,* July 7, 1997, pp. B1, B2.

18. "The Border," *Business Week,* May 12, 1997, pp. 64–74.

19. Griffin and Pustay, *International Business.*

20. Louis S. Richman, "How NAFTA Will Help America," *Fortune,* April 19, 1993, pp. 95–101. See also "NAFTA: Where's That 'Giant Sucking Sound'?" *Business Week,* July 7, 1997, p. 45.

21. John J. Curran, "China's Investment Boom," *Fortune,* March 7, 1994, pp. 116–124. See also Louis Kraar, "The Growing Power of Asia," *Fortune,* October 7, 1991, pp. 118–131.

22. Eileen P. Gunn, "Emerging Markets," *Fortune*, August 18, 1997, pp. 168–173.

23. "In Many Ways, Return of Hong Kong to China Has Already Happened," *Wall Street Journal*, June 9, 1997, pp. A1, A2; and "How You Can Win in China," *Business Week*, May 26, 1997, pp. 66–68.

24. "Investing in India: Not for the Fainthearted," *Business Week*, August 11, 1997, pp. 46–47.

25. "GM Is Building Plants in Developing Nations to Woo New Markets," *Wall Street Journal*, August 4, 1997, pp. A1, A4.

26. Griffin and Pustay, *International Business*.

27. "Oil Companies Strive to Turn a New Leaf to Save Rain Forest," *Wall Street Journal*, July 17, 1997, pp. A1, A8.

28. "What If There Weren't Any Clocks to Watch?" *Newsweek*, June 30, 1997, p. 14.

29. Geert Hofstede, *Culture's Consequences: International Differences in Work Related Values* (Beverly Hills, Calif.: Sage, 1980).

30. I have taken the liberty of changing the actual labels applied to each dimension for several reasons. The terms I have chosen to use are more descriptive, simpler, and more self-evident in their meaning.

31. Geert Hofstede, "The Business of International Business is Culture," *International Business Review*, Vol. 3, No. 1, 1994, pp. 1–14.

32. "Crazy for Crunchies," *Newsweek*, April 28, 1997, p. 49.

33. "Famous Bakery Keeps Business Thriving," *Corsicana Daily Sun*, June 9, 1991, p. 1C; "The World is Their Fruitcake," *Business Week*, December 25, 1995, p. 48; and new data obtained in personal correspondence with the company.

34. Stratford Sherman, "Are You as Good as the Best in the World?" *Fortune*, December 13, 1993, pp. 95–96.

6

The Cultural and Multicultural Environment

OBJECTIVES

After studying this chapter, you should be able to:

- Describe the nature of organizational and social culture.
- Discuss the importance and determinants of an organization's culture and how the culture can be managed.
- Identify and describe the major trends and dimensions of diversity and multiculturalism in organizations.
- Discuss the primary effects of diversity and multiculturalism in organizations.
- Describe individual and organizational strategies and approaches to managing diversity and multiculturalism.
- Discuss the six characteristics of the fully multicultural organization.

Women have always played an important role at Avon, the largest cosmetics firm in the United States. Starting with the first "Avon Lady" in 1886, women have been the foundation of the firm's marketing and sales efforts. And although Avon has always employed many women throughout its organization, control always remained in the hands of the handful of men who ran the company. However, a series of disastrous decisions and setbacks in the 1980s caused the firm to rethink its philosophies and to promote its best middle managers, many of them women, into the executive ranks. And as a result, Avon has turned itself around. Today the firm is known for both its exemplary financial performance and its acceptance of all people, regardless of their gender, skin color, or age.

Avon's problems started in the 1970s when its top management team tried to change the firm's strategy. This group of predominantly male managers first ignored their own marketing research about women consumers and shifting career patterns, which indicated that more women were entering the workforce and seeking professional careers. In particular, the Avon executives failed to recognize that the personal care products preferred by women were also changing. Then, in the 1980s, Avon tried to buck emerging trends and to diversify with a number of ill-conceived acquisitions. Finally, as the firm was on the brink of bankruptcy, a new top management team was brought in. Led by CEO Jim Preston, Avon refocused itself on its roots and began to again market cosmetics to a largely female market, albeit a very different market.

But this time the firm adopted new approaches. For one thing, it decided to recognize and reward managerial talent rather than the gender of the individual manager. As a result, more women were quickly promoted into higher-level positions. In addition, Preston shifted the firm's organizational cul-

ture to make it more accommodating of all its employees—to value differences among people rather than to attempt to impose a rigid and controlling model for how things were to be done. For example, the firm dropped its season ticket purchases to Knicks and Yankees games and replaced them with season tickets for the New York City Ballet and the New York Philharmonic. And the company eliminated its annual hunting retreat, a male bastion of drinking and card playing.

Avon is also moving aggressively into foreign markets. For example, Avon products are now sold in mature markets like Western Europe and Japan. But in addition, the firm sells its products throughout China, Russia, and Eastern Europe. All told, Avon manufactures its products in eighteen countries and sells them in 125. Preston credits several key female executives for championing the international push and for making sure that it was done right. And many new managers at the firm have come from international contacts, organizations, and networks that the firm did not previously see as a valuable source of executive talent.

But perhaps the biggest testament to the "new" Avon is its plans for executive succession. Four of the firm's eight top officers are women, for example, and more than 40 percent of its global managers are women. Almost half of the firm's board of directors is female. And the firm recently promoted a woman to the position of president, and another to head up worldwide sales and marketing. Clearly, then, Avon is a firm that has changed its own culture and that appreciates the power of diversity and multiculturalism.[1]

"I have the freedom to be who I am. I am no longer consumed with what I say and do and the impact it will have on my career."

Edwina D. Woodbury, Avon CFO, quoted in Fortune, *July 21, 1997, p. 78.*

Like many other organizations in the world today, Avon has seen tremendous changes in its environment during the last several decades. Market forces and industrial composition have changed, as have consumer tastes and preferences. But even more profound has been the changes Avon has made in how it runs its business and in the organizational culture it has fostered. And Avon no doubt encountered more than a few challenges along the way as it sought to address the variety of issues, opportunities, and problems that its increasingly diverse workforce has created.

This chapter is about culture in two broad forms—organizational and social. After establishing the similarities and differences among the two, we discuss organizational culture first. We then turn to diversity and multiculturalism in organizations. We begin by describing trends in diversity and multiculturalism and by identifying and discussing several common dimensions of diversity. Then we explore the effects of diversity and multiculturalism on organizations. We next address individual strategies and organizational approaches for managing diversity and multiculturalism. Finally, we characterize and describe the fully multicultural organization.

The Nature of Organization and Social Culture

organizational culture The set of values, beliefs, behaviors, customs, and attitudes that helps an organization's members understand what it stands for, how it does things, and what it considers important

At its most general level, *culture* refers to the collection of values, beliefs, behaviors, customs, and attitudes that characterize a community of people. Such a community can range from a small group of individuals to an entire nation. Our interests here start with culture at the organizational level. Thus, because the members of an organization can be viewed as a community, the organization to which they belong will have its own unique culture. **Organizational culture**, therefore, is the set of values, beliefs, behaviors, customs, and attitudes that helps the members of the organization understand what it stands for, how it does things, and what it considers important.[2]

multiculturalism The broad issues associated with differences in values, beliefs, behaviors, customs, and attitudes held by people in different cultures

diversity Exists in a group or organization when its members differ from one another along one or more important dimensions such as age, gender, or ethnicity

At a much broader level, culture can also be used to characterize the community of people who make up an entire society. Some of the basic managerial issues associated with doing business across cultures were introduced and explored in Chapter 5. But a different set of issues involving social culture also arises within the boundaries of an organization. That is, when the people who belong to an organization represent different cultures, their differences in values, beliefs, behaviors, customs, and attitudes pose unique opportunities and challenges for managers. These broad issues are generally referred to as **multiculturalism**.

A related area of interest is diversity. **Diversity** exists in a community of people when its members differ from one another along one or more important dimensions. These differences can obviously reflect the multicultural composition of a community. In the business world, however, the term *diversity* per se is more generally used to refer to demographic differences among people within a culture—differences in gender, age, and so forth. Diversity is not an absolute phenomenon, of course, wherein a group or organization is or is not diverse. Instead, diversity can be conceptualized as a continuum. If everyone in the community is exactly like everyone else, there is no diversity whatsoever. If everyone is different along every imaginable dimension, total diversity exists. In reality, of course, these extremes are more hypothetical than real. Most settings are characterized by a level of diversity somewhere between these extremes. Therefore, diversity should be thought of in terms of degree or level of diversity along relevant dimensions.

Organizational culture, multiculturalism, and diversity are closely related concepts. For example, the culture of an organization will affect the levels of diversity and multiculturalism that exist within its boundaries. Avon, for example, had to change its organizational culture before it could increase the diversity of its executive ranks. And similarities and differences arising from diversity and multicultural forces will also influence the culture of an organization. In addition, social culture and diversity are also interrelated. For example, the norms reflected in a social culture will partially determine how that culture values demographic differences among people of that culture.

Each level of culture represents important opportunities and challenges for managers. As we will see, if managers effectively understand, appreciate, and manage their organization's culture, diversity, and multiculturalism, the organization is more likely to be effective. But if managers ignore cultural forces or, even worse, attempt to circumvent or control them, then the organization is almost certain to experience serious problems.

Both organizational culture and social culture are powerful forces that can affect organizations. Many astute organizations not only recognize the importance of these cultures but also work to capitalize on them for competitive purposes. For example, as shown here, Marriott promotes multiculturalism in some of its advertising.

Managers need to have a clear understanding of organizational culture, multiculturalism, and the relationship between the two.

The Organization's Culture

Culture is an amorphous concept that defies objective measurement or observation. Nevertheless, because it is the foundation of the organization's internal environment, it plays a major role in shaping managerial behavior.[3]

■ The Importance of Organizational Culture

Several years ago, executives at Levi Strauss believed that the company had outgrown its sixty-eight-year-old building. Even though everyone enjoyed its casual and relaxed atmosphere, the company needed more space. So Levi Strauss moved into a modern office building in downtown San Francisco, where its new headquarters spread over twelve floors in a skyscraper. It quickly became apparent that the change was affecting the corporate culture—and that people did not like it. Executives felt isolated, and other managers missed the informal chance meetings in the halls. Within just a few years, Strauss moved out of the skyscraper and back into a building that fosters informality. This new site is adjacent to a park area where employees converge for lunch-time conversation. Clearly, Levi Strauss has a culture that is important to the people who work there.[4]

Culture determines the "feel" of the organization. The stereotypic image of Microsoft, for example, is a workplace where people dress very casually and work very long hours. In contrast, the image of Bank of America for some observers is a formal setting with rigid work rules and people dressed in conservative business attire. And Texas Instruments likes to talk about its "shirt sleeve" culture in which ties are avoided and few managers ever wear jackets. Southwest Airlines maintains a culture that stresses fun and excitement. The firm's CEO, Herb Kelleher, explains the company's emphasis on fun in an orientation video set to rap music.

Of course, the same culture is not necessarily found throughout an entire organization. For example, the sales and marketing department may have a culture quite different from that of the operations and manufacturing department. Regardless of its nature, however, culture is a powerful force in organizations, one that can shape the firm's overall effectiveness and long-term success. Companies that can develop and maintain a strong culture, such as Hewlett-Packard Co. and Procter & Gamble, tend to be more effective than companies that have trouble developing and maintaining a strong culture, such as Kmart Corp.[5]

■ Determinants of Organizational Culture

Where does an organization's culture come from? Typically it develops and blossoms over a long period of time. Its starting point is often the organization's founder. For example, James Cash Penney believed in treating employees and customers with respect and dignity. Employees at J. C. Penney are still called associates rather than employees (to reflect partnership), and customer satisfaction is of paramount importance. The impact of Sam Walton, Ross Perot, and Walt Disney is still felt in the organizations they founded. As an organization grows, its culture is modified, shaped, and refined by symbols, stories, heroes, slogans, and ceremonies. For example, an important value at Hewlett-Packard Co. is the avoidance of bank debt. A popular story still told at the company involves a new project being considered for several years. All objective criteria indicated that Hewlett-Packard Co. should incur bank debt to finance it, yet Bill Hewlett and David Packard rejected the project out of hand simply because "HP avoids bank debt." This story, involving two corporate heroes and based on a slogan, dictates corporate culture today. And many decisions at Walt Disney Company today are still framed by asking, "What would Walt have done?"

"I don't know how it started, either. All I know is that it's part of our corporate culture."

Corporate success and shared experiences also shape culture. For example, Hallmark Cards has a strong culture derived from its years of success in the greeting card industry. Employees speak of the Hallmark family and care deeply about the company; many of them have worked at the company for years. At Kmart, in contrast, the culture is quite weak, the management team changes rapidly, and few people sense any direction or purpose in the company. The differences in culture at Hallmark and Kmart are in part attributable to past successes and shared experiences.

■ Managing Organizational Culture

How can managers deal with culture, given its clear importance but intangible nature? Essentially, the manager must understand the current culture and then decide whether it should be maintained or changed. By understanding the organization's current culture, managers can take appropriate actions. At Hewlett-Packard Co. the values represented by "the HP way" still exist. Moreover, they guide and direct most important activities that the firm undertakes. Culture can also be maintained by rewarding and promoting people whose behaviors are consistent with the existing culture and by articulating the culture through slogans, ceremonies, and so forth. "The World of Management" describes how Merrill Lynch is working to extend its famed organizational culture into its foreign offices.

But managers must walk a fine line between maintaining a culture that still works effectively versus changing a culture that has become dysfunctional. Many of the firms already noted, as well as numerous others, take pride in perpetuating their cultures. Shell Oil Company, for example, has an elaborate display in the lobby of its Houston headquarters building that tells the story of the firm's past. But other companies may face situations in which their culture is no

An organization's culture can be determined in a variety of ways. Symbols, stories, heroes, slogans, and ceremonies, for example, all play a role in defining and continuing culture. Sometimes, however, the meaning of some element of culture can become blurred or even forgotten over time. As illustrated here, some organizations do things simply because they "always have," even to the point where these things become institutionalized standard practices. And occasionally, some of these things may even border on the absurd!

THE WORLD OF MANAGEMENT

Spreading the Merrill Lynch Culture

Merrill Lynch & Co. is the largest brokerage operation in the United States. Ever since Charles Merrill and Edmund Lynch formed the company in 1914, the firm has focused its attention on individual investors and has based its operations on customer service. A manager who has been totally immersed in the company's culture heads each local Merrill Lynch office. These managers start as assistants in existing offices to learn the ropes and then go through an extended series of training programs at the firm's training center in Princeton, New Jersey. One ongoing component of this training focuses on the firm's culture—where it started and how it is to be perpetuated.

In the last several years Merrill Lynch has been undergoing a major expansion into international markets. Fueled in part by opening new offices and in part by buying existing brokerage firms, Merrill Lynch has become one of the largest retail brokerage companies in the world. When this expansion started, many of the firm's competitors doubted that it would be able to transfer its culture abroad. But, so far, at least, these skeptics are wrong.

Merrill Lynch knew from the beginning of its internationalization efforts that sustaining its culture would be both important and difficult. Therefore, the company made the same commitment to global training as it makes to training its local managers—each and every Merrill Lynch office manager from foreign offices receives the same level of training as the firm's domestic managers receive. And like domestic managers, international managers get a continued exposure to the firm's heritage and culture. As a result, company executives say, the organizational culture of any Merrill Lynch office, regardless of where it is, remains true to the spirit of the company's founders.

> *"Visit our offices, whether it be Thailand, Malaysia, South Africa, or Germany, and you will see the same plaques on the wall with those same Merrill Principles in the local language."*
>
> *David H. Komansky, Merrill Lynch CEO**

References: *"Merrillizing the World,"* Forbes, February 10, 1997, pp. 146–151 (*quote on p. 147); and "How Merrill Lynch Is Winning the East," Business Week, September 1, 1997, pp. 79–80.

longer a strength. For example, some critics feel that Ford's culture places too much emphasis on product development and not enough on marketing. This culture sometimes results in new products that fail to live up to expectations.[6]

Culture problems sometimes arise from mergers or the growth of rival factions within an organization. For example, Wells Fargo and Company, which relies heavily on snazzy technology and automated banking services, recently acquired another large bank, First Interstate, which had focused more attention on personal services and customers satisfaction. Blending the two disparate organizational cultures has been difficult for the firm as managers have argued over how best to serve customers and operate the new enterprise.[7] Arthur Andersen, one of the Big Six accounting firms, faces a different type of cultural problem. Its relatively new Andersen Consulting Group has grown in size and importance to the point where it threatens to usurp power from the original accounting group. Differences in culture between the two groups makes reconciling their goals and agendas difficult.[8] Indeed, plans are currently being developed to split the organization into two companies. And the primary reason is cultural incompatibility.

To change culture, managers must have a clear idea of what they want to create. Schwinn Bicycle Co. has tried to redefine itself to be more competitive and to break free of its old approaches to doing business. The firm's new motto—"Established 1895. Re-established 1994"—represents an effort to create a new culture that more accurately reflects today's competitive environment in the bicycle market. Likewise, when Continental Airlines reinvented itself a few years ago, employees were invited outside the corporate headquarters building in Houston to watch as the firm's old policies and procedures manuals were set afire. The firm's new strategic direction is known throughout Continental Airlines as the "Go Forward" plan, intentionally named so as to avoid reminding people about the firm's troubled past and to, instead, focus on the future.

One major way to shape culture is by bringing outsiders into important managerial positions. The choice of a new CEO from outside the organization is often a clear signal that things will be changing. Indeed, new CEOs were the catalyst for the changes at Schwinn Bicycle and Continental Airlines noted above. Adopting new slogans, telling new stories, staging new ceremonies, and breaking with tradition can also alter culture. Culture can also be changed by methods discussed in Chapter 13.[9] We now turn our attention to other related parts of the cultural environment of management: diversity and multiculturalism.

MANAGEMENT IMPLICATIONS Managers need to have a clear understanding and appreciation of the importance of organizational culture. In addition, they need to know how culture is determined. They should also understand how to manage organizational culture and how to use organizational culture to gain competitive advantage. ▬

Diversity and Multiculturalism in Organizations

As introduced and defined earlier in this chapter, diversity and multiculturalism essentially relate to differences among people. Because organizations today are becoming more diverse and multicultural, all managers must understand the major trends and dimensions of diversity and multiculturalism.

■ Trends in Diversity and Multiculturalism

The most fundamental trend in diversity and multiculturalism is that virtually all organizations, simply put, are becoming more diverse and multicultural.

The composition of the workforce in general is changing in many ways. Figure 6.1 illustrates the basic reasons for this trend.

One factor contributing specifically to increased diversity is changing demographics in the labor force. As more women and minorities enter the labor force, for example, the available pool of talent from which organizations hire employees has changed in both size and composition. If talent within each segment of the labor pool is evenly distributed (for example, if the number of very talented men in the workforce as a percentage of all men in the workforce is the same as the number of very talented women in the labor force as a percentage of all women in the workforce), it follows logically that, over time, the composition of an organization's workforce should have proportionately more women and proportionately fewer men.

FIGURE 6.1
Reasons for Increasing Diversity and Multiculturalism

Diversity and multiculturalism are increasing in most organizations today for four basic reasons. These reasons promise to make diversity even greater in the future.

A related factor contributing to diversity is the increased awareness by organizations that they can improve the overall quality of their workforce by hiring and promoting the most talented people available. By casting a broader net in recruiting and looking beyond traditional sources for new employees, organizations are finding more broadly qualified and better qualified employees from many different segments of society. Thus these organizations are finding that diversity can be a source of competitive advantage.[10]

Another reason for the increase in diversity is that legislation and legal actions have forced organizations to hire more broadly. In earlier times, organizations in the United States were essentially free to discriminate against women, blacks, and other minorities. Thus white males dominated most organizations. But starting with the passage of the Civil Rights Act in 1964, numerous laws have outlawed discrimination against these minorities and most other groups. (The Civil Rights Act of 1964 does not prohibit discrimination on the basis of age, disability, or sexual preference.) As we describe in Chapter 14, organizations must hire and promote people today solely on the basis of their qualifications.

A final factor contributing to increased multiculturalism in particular is the globalization movement. Organizations that have opened offices and related facilities in other countries have had to learn to deal with different customs, social norms, and mores. Strategic alliances and foreign ownership also contribute as managers today are more likely to have job assignments in other countries and/or to work with foreign managers at home. As employees and managers move from assignment to assignment across national boundaries, organizations and their subsidiaries within each country thus become more diverse and multicultural.

■ Dimensions of Diversity and Multiculturalism

As we indicated earlier, many different dimensions of diversity and multiculturalism can characterize an organization. This section focuses on age, gender, ethnicity, and other dimensions of diversity.

Age Distributions   One important dimension of diversity in any organization is the age distribution of its workers. The average age of the U.S. workforce is gradually increasing and will continue to do so for the next several years. Figure 6.2 shows the age distributions for U.S. workers in 1988 and projected age distributions for the year 2000.

Several factors are contributing to this pattern. For one, the baby-boom generation (a term used to describe the unusually large number of people who were born in the twenty-year period after World War II) continues to age. Declining birth rates among the post-baby-boom generations simultaneously account for smaller percentages of new entrants into the labor force. Another factor that contributes to the aging workforce is improved health and medical care. As a result of these improvements, people are able to remain productive and active for longer periods of time. Combined with higher legal limits for mandatory retirement, more and more people are working beyond the age at which they might have retired just a few years ago.[11]

How does this trend affect organizations? Compared to their younger colleagues, older workers tend to have more experience, to be more stable, and to make greater contributions to productivity. On the other hand, despite the improvements in health and medical care, older workers are nevertheless likely to require higher levels of insurance coverage and medical benefits. And the declining labor pool of younger workers will continue to pose problems for organizations as they find fewer potential new entrants into the labor force.[12] Other issues involving the management of older workers are raised in "Today's Management Issues."

Gender   As more and more women have entered the workforce, organizations have experienced changes in the relative proportions of male and female employees. In the United States, for example, the workforce in 1964 was 66 percent male and 34 percent female. In 1994 the relative proportions had changed to 54 percent male and 46 percent female. By the year 2000 the proportions are expected to be around 52 percent male and 48 percent female.[13]

These trends aside, a major gender-related problem that many organizations face today is the so-called glass ceiling. The **glass ceiling** describes a barrier that keeps women from advancing to top management positions in many organizations.[14] This ceiling is a real barrier that is difficult to break, but it is

FIGURE 6.2
Age Distribution Trends in the U.S. Workforce

The U.S. workforce is gradually growing older. For example, by the year 2000 almost one-half of the U.S. workforce will be between the ages of thirty-five and fifty-four. These older workers have different experience and values and will want different things from their work than their younger colleagues.

Source: Data from Occupational Outlook Handbook, *published by the U. S. Bureau of Labor Statistics: Washington, DC, 1990–1991, pp. 8–12.*

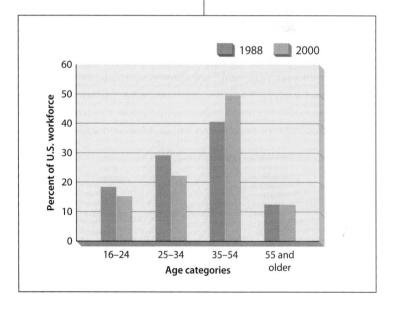

glass ceiling   A perceived barrier in some organizations that presumably keeps women from advancing to top management positions

The Dilemma of Older Workers

Phyllis Chavez was proud to still be a Wal-Mart employee at the age of seventy-one. One day recently, however, she slipped and fell in the store's receiving area where she worked, hitting her head sharply. Her supervisor wanted to take her to the hospital to be checked, but Ms. Chavez refused, insisting on first finishing her shift. A few weeks later she died from complications after surgery for a brain injury resulting from the fall. Her case illustrates one of the biggest dilemmas facing managers today—the treatment of older workers. In many companies today, significant numbers of people continue to work into their seventies. But there is considerable controversy about whether or not greater regulation of elderly workers is necessary.

On the one hand, the Age Discrimination in Employment Act of 1967 legally restricts companies from discriminating against people on the basis of their age. Employers can consider a person's ability to perform a job when making employment decisions, but cannot automatically assume that a person's age will affect his or her capacity to perform. And advocates for the elderly, such as the American Association of Retired Persons, or AARP, aggressively

> *"We've got to be sure that protective legislation will not be used against older workers."*
>
> *Sara Rix, analyst for AARP**

fight any potential employment restrictions or limitations based on age. One of the most common arguments they use is that older workers have only half as many accidents as their younger colleagues. Older workers are usually deemed to be more careful and to have more experience, thus cutting down on accidents.

But critics look at the same statistics from a different perspective. Although it is true that older workers may have fewer accidents than younger ones, the accidents older workers do have are four times more likely to result in their death. Indeed, the risks from work-related accidents begin to increase gradually around the age of forty and begin to increase sharply around the age of sixty-five. This pattern probably reflects the facts that, compared to younger people, older people recover more slowly and with more difficulty, usually have less strength and stamina, and are more prone to postaccident complications such as blood clots.

References: *"For Older Employees, On-The-Job Injuries Are More Often Deadly,"* Wall Street Journal, *June 17, 1997, pp. A1, A10 (*quote on p. A1); and "For One 73-Year-Old, Punching Timeclock Isn't Labor of Love,"* Wall Street Journal, *March 31, 1997, pp. A1, A8.*

also so subtle that it can be hard to see. Indeed, whereas almost 45 percent of all managers are women, only two females hold the title of CEO among the one thousand largest businesses in the United States. Similarly, the average pay of women in organizations is lower than that of men. Although the pay gap is gradually shrinking, inequalities are still present.

Why does the glass ceiling still seem to exist? One reason may be that real obstacles to advancement for women, such as subtle discrimination, may still exist in some organizations.[15] Another is that many talented women choose to leave their jobs in large organizations and start their own businesses. Still another factor is that some women choose to suspend or slow their career progression to have children.[16] But many talented women are continuing to work their way up the corporate ladder and are getting closer and closer to a corporate "top spot."[17]

Ethnicity A third major dimension of cultural diversity in organizations is ethnicity. **Ethnicity** refers to the ethnic composition of a group or organization. Within the United States, most organizations reflect varying degrees of ethnicity comprising whites, African Americans, Hispanics, and Asians. Figure 6.3 shows the ethnic composition of the U.S. workforce in 1988 and as projected for the year 2000 in terms of these ethnic groups.[18]

The biggest projected changes involve whites and Hispanics. In particular, the percentage of whites in the workforce is expected to drop from 79 percent to 74 percent. At the same time, the percentage of Hispanics is expected to climb from 7 percent to 10 percent. The percentage of African Americans, Asians, and others is expected to climb only about 1 percent each. As with women, members of the African American, Hispanic, and Asian groups are generally underrepresented in the executive ranks of most organizations today. And their pay is similarly lower than might be expected. But also, as is the case for women, the differences are gradually disappearing as organizations fully embrace equal employment opportunity and recognize the higher overall level of talent available to them.[19]

Other Dimensions of Diversity In addition to age, gender, and ethnicity, organizations are also confronting other dimensions of diversity. Handicapped and physically challenged employees are increasingly important in many organizations, especially since the recent passage of the Americans with Disabilities Act. Religious beliefs also constitute an important dimension of diversity. And single parents, dual-career couples, gays and lesbians, people with special dietary preferences (for example, vegetarians), and people with nontraditional political ideologies and viewpoints also represent major dimensions of diversity in today's organizations.[20]

Multicultural Differences In addition to these various diversity-related dimensions, organizations are increasingly being characterized with multicultural differences as well. Some organizations, especially international businesses, are actively seeking to enhance the multiculturalism of their workforce. But even organizations that are more passive in this regard may still become more multicultural because of changes in the external labor market. Immigration into the United States is at its highest rate since 1910, for example. More than 5 million people from Asia, Mexico, Europe, and other parts of the world entered the United States between 1991 and 1995.[21]

One of the most direct effects of this influx is a greater array of languages in many organizations. Table 6.1 shows the number of people in the United States who speak various languages and also indicates the proportions who don't speak English well or at all. For example, at the time these data were compiled, more than 17

ethnicity The ethnic composition of a group or organization

FIGURE 6.3
Racial and Ethnicity Trends in the U.S. Labor Force

The U.S. workforce is becoming ever more diverse along most dimensions of race and ethnicity. The most important trend suggests that whites will make up a significantly smaller percentage of the workforce by the year 2000 than was the case as recently as 1988. Most growth is in the Hispanic sector. Modest growth in the percentage of black and Asian workers is also expected. Managers will have to become increasingly sensitive to the needs, expectations, and aspirations of a multicultural workforce.

Source: Data from Occupational Outlook Handbook, *published by the U.S. Bureau of Labor Statistics: Washington, DC, 1990–1991, pp. 8–12.*

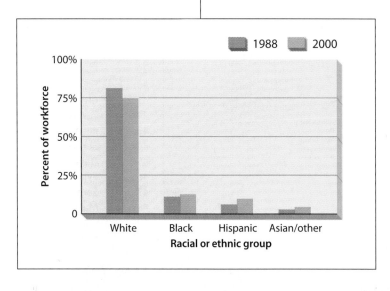

TABLE 6.1

The Top Fifty Non-English Languages Spoken in the United States

Source: USA Today, February 28, 1997, page 8A. Copyright 1997, *USA Today.* Reprinted with permission.

Rank	Language	Number of speakers	Don't speak English well/ at all
1	Spanish	17,339,172	26%
2	French	1,702,176	9%
3	German	1,547,099	7%
4	Italian	1,308,648	12%
5	Chinese	1,249,213	30%
6	Tagalog	843,251	7%
7	Polish	723,483	14%
8	Korean	626,478	30%
9	Vietnamese	507,069	28%
10	Portuguese	429,860	23%
11	Japanese	427,657	21%
12	Greek	388,260	11%
13	Arabic	355,150	11%
14	Hindi (Urdu)	331,484	9%
15	Russian	241,796	27%
16	Yiddish	213,064	8%
17	Thai (Laotian)	206,266	28%
18	Persian	201,865	12%
19	French Creole	187,658	22%
20	Armenian	149,694	26%
21	Navajo	148,530	15%
22	Hungarian	147,902	9%
23	Hebrew	144,292	5%
24	Dutch	142,684	4%
25	Mon-Khmer	127,441	43%
26	Gujarati	102,418	12%
27	Ukrainian	96,568	14%
28	Czech	92,485	6%
29	Pa. Dutch	83,525	6%
30	Miao (Hmong)	81,877	46%
31	Norwegian	80,723	5%
32	Slovak	80,388	7%
33	Swedish	77,511	4%
34	Serbo-Croatian	70,964	13%
35	Kru	65,848	3%
36	Romanian	65,265	17%
37	Lithuanian	55,781	9%
38	Finnish	54,350	6%
39	Punjabi	50,005	15%
40	Formosan	46,044	21%
41	Croatian	45,206	9%
42	Turkish	41,876	14%
43	Ilocano	41,131	20%
44	Bengali	38,101	8%
45	Danish	35,639	3%
46	Syriac	35,146	15%
47	Samoan	34,914	10%
48	Malayalam	33,949	8%
49	Cajun	33,670	7%
50	Amharic	31,505	11%

Language Barriers in the Workplace

Immigration into the United States is at its highest level since 1910. This influx of people from abroad is accompanied by an increasingly diverse workforce. Moreover, it provides employers with a substantial pool of talented workers, many of whom are eager to fill minimum-wage jobs such as washing dishes, hauling trash, and loading and unloading trucks. But language barriers have also increased, creating new problems for many employers.

For example, language difficulties can result in communication errors in memos, conversations, and letters. And people who are insecure about their language skills may be reluctant to provide information, thus impairing decision making and problem solving. Increased conflict among workers who cannot understand each other is also common. And when employees with poor English skills are in positions that interface with customers—such as drivers, waitpersons, retail clerks, and telephone operators—problems for employers can become even more severe.

"There are real, practical issues when you can't understand people you're dealing with."

Judith Langer, retail consultant*

In other situations, language barriers can be devastating. In late 1996, for example, a tanker crashed into a shopping mall built along the Mississippi River in New Orleans. The crash apparently resulted from the Chinese crew on the ship not understanding the English-language instructions being relayed by the ship's pilot.

Employers who rely on these workers face a real dilemma. On the one hand, employers cannot force their workers to learn English. Nor do employers want to be perceived as trying to eliminate a worker's cultural heritage. But companies do need their workers to be able to communicate with other workers and with the public. As a result, many companies have started to offer optional language training.

References: *"Language Proficiency Affects . . . The Workplace,"* USA Today, *February 28, 1997, p. 8A (*quote on p. 8A); and "Survival 101: Learning English,"* USA Today, *February 28, 1997, pp. 1B, 2B.*

million Spanish-speaking people lived in the United States. And 26 percent of these residents were not fluent in English. Although this language barrier may pose some obvious complications for companies, it also creates new opportunities for workers who are fluent in multiple languages. Bilingual telephone operators at Southwestern Bell in San Antonio, for example, can command a higher hourly wage than can operators who speak only English.[22] "Working with Diversity" discusses other aspects of language differences in organizations today.

MANAGEMENT IMPLICATIONS Managers should be thoroughly familiar with recent trends in diversity and multiculturalism. In addition, they should understand the basic dimensions of diversity and multiculturalism in organizations and how those dimensions affect their organizations. ▬

Effects of Diversity and Multiculturalism on Organizations

There is no question that organizations are becoming ever more diverse and multicultural. And as we see, these demographic changes provide opportunities as well as challenges for organizations. Diversity and multiculturalism both play many important roles in organizations today.

■ Multiculturalism and Competitive Advantage

Many organizations are finding that diversity and multiculturalism can be a source of competitive advantage in the marketplace. In general, six arguments have been proposed to explain how diversity and multiculturalism contribute to competitiveness.[23] These arguments are illustrated in Figure 6.4.

The *cost argument* suggests that organizations that learn to manage diversity and multiculturalism generally have higher levels of productivity and lower levels of turnover and absenteeism. Organizations that do a poor job of managing diversity and multiculturalism, on the other hand, suffer from problems of lower productivity and higher levels of turnover and absenteeism. Because each of these factors has a direct impact on costs, the former organization will remain more competitive than will the latter. For example, Ortho Pharmaceutical Corporation estimates that it has saved $500,000 by lowering turnover among women and ethnic minorities.[24] These savings can subsequently be used for additional research and development, product promotion, or other competitive purposes.

The *resource acquisition argument* suggests that organizations who manage diversity and multiculturalism effectively become known among women and minorities as good places to work. These organizations are thus better able to attract qualified employees from among these groups. Given the increased importance of these groups in the overall labor force, organizations that can attract talented employees from all segments of society are likely to be more competitive.

The *marketing argument* suggests that organizations with diverse and multicultural workforces are better able to understand different market segments than are less diverse organizations. For example, a cosmetics firm like Avon that wants to sell its products to women and blacks can better understand how to create such products and effectively market them if women and black managers are available to provide valuable suggestions and ideas regarding product development, design, packaging, advertising, and so forth.[25]

The *creativity argument* suggests that organizations with diverse and multicultural workforces are generally more creative and innovative than other organizations. If an organization is dominated by one population segment, it follows that its members will generally adhere to norms and ways of thinking that reflect that segment. Moreover, a homogenous point of view has little insight or stimulus for new ideas that might be derived from different perspectives. The diverse and multicultural organization, in contrast, is characterized by multiple perspectives and ways of thinking and is therefore more likely to generate new ideas and ways of doing things.

Related to the creativity argument is the *problem-solving argument*. Diversity and multiculturalism are accompanied by an increased pool of information. In virtually any organization, there is some information that everyone has and other information that is unique to each individual. In an organization with little diversity, the larger pool of information is common and the smaller pool is unique. But in a more diverse organization, the pool of unique information is larger. Thus, because more information can be brought to bear on a problem, there is a higher probability that better solutions can be identified.[26]

Finally, the *systems flexibility argument* suggests that organizations must become more flexible as a way of managing a diverse and multicultural workforce. As a direct consequence, the overall organizational system also becomes more flexible. As we discuss in Chapters 3 and 13, organizational flexibility enables the organization to respond more effectively to changes in its environment. Thus, by effectively managing diversity and multiculturalism within its workforce, an organization simultaneously becomes better equipped to address its environment.[27]

■ Multiculturalism and Conflict

Unfortunately, diversity and multiculturalism in an organization can also create conflict. This conflict can arise for a variety of reasons.[28] One potential avenue for conflict is when an individual thinks that someone has been hired, promoted, or fired because of her or his diversity status. For example, suppose that a male executive loses a promotion to a female executive. If he believes that she was promoted because the organization simply wanted to have more female managers, rather than because she was the better candidate for the job, he will likely feel resentful toward both her and the organization itself.

Another source of conflict stemming from diversity or multiculturalism is misunderstood, misinterpreted, or inappropriate interactions between people of different groups.[29] For example, suppose that a male executive tells a sexually explicit joke to a new female executive. He may intentionally be trying to embarrass her, he may be clumsily trying to show her that he treats everyone the same way, or he may think he is making her feel like part of the team. Regardless of his intent, however, if she finds the joke offensive she will justifiably feel anger and hostility. These feelings may be directed at only the offending individual or more generally toward the entire organization if she believes that its culture facilitates such behaviors. And, of course, sexual harassment itself is both unethical and illegal.

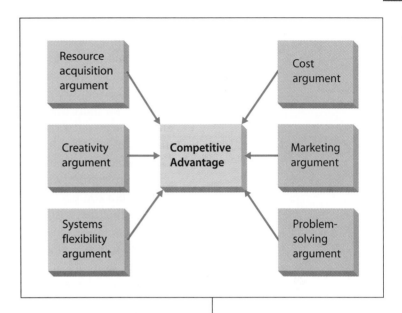

FIGURE 6.4
How Diversity and Multiculturalism Promote Competitive Advantage

Many organizations today are finding that diversity and multiculturalism can be a source of competitive advantage. Various arguments have been developed to support this viewpoint. For example, a black sales representative for Revlon helped that firm improve its packaging and promotion for its line of darker skin-tone cosmetics.

Conflict can also arise as a result of other elements of multiculturalism. For example, when a U.S. manager publicly praises a Japanese employee for his outstanding work, the action stems from the dominant cultural belief in the United States that such recognition is important and rewarding. But because the Japanese culture places a much higher premium on group loyalty and identity than on individual accomplishment, the employee will likely feel ashamed and embarrassed. Thus a well-intentioned action may backfire and result in unhappiness. A joint venture between IBM (a U.S. company), Siemens (a German company), and Toshiba (a Japanese company) has had difficulties attributed to cultural differences in work hours, working styles, interpersonal relations, and conflict.[30]

Conflict may also arise as a result of fear, distrust, or individual prejudice. Members of the dominant group in an organization may worry that newcomers from other groups pose a personal threat to their own position in the organization. For example, when U.S. firms have been taken over by Japanese firms, U.S. managers have sometimes been resentful or hostile to Japanese managers assigned to work with them. People may also be unwilling to accept coworkers who are different from themselves. And personal bias and prejudices, which are still very real among some people today, can lead to potentially harmful conflict.

Several recent high-profile problems involving diversity and multiculturalism have focused renewed attention on the potential for conflict and how important it is for managers to respond appropriately when problems occur. Shoney's, a southern restaurant chain, was charged with racism throughout its managerial ranks. Denny's, another restaurant business, was charged with similar practices. At Texaco, senior executives used racial slurs on a tape that was subsequently released to the public. And a class-action lawsuit against the financial brokerage giant Smith Barney alleges widespread hostilities and discrimination toward women throughout the firm.[31]

MANAGEMENT IMPLICATIONS   All managers need to know the effects of diversity and multiculturalism in organizations. In particular, they need to appreciate how multiculturalism can provide a basis for competitive advantage. They must also understand how multiculturalism can result in conflict. ◼

Managing Diversity and Multiculturalism in Organizations

Because of the tremendous potential that diversity and multiculturalism hold for competitive advantage, as well as the possible consequences of associated conflict, much attention has been focused in recent years on how individuals and organizations can better manage diversity and multiculturalism. In the sections that follow we first discuss individual strategies for dealing with diversity and multiculturalism and then summarize organizational approaches to managing diversity and multiculturalism.

■ Individual Strategies

One important element of managing diversity and multiculturalism in an organization relates to the attitudes and behaviors of individuals. The four basic attitudes that individuals can strive to learn are understanding, empathy, tolerance, and willingness to communicate.

Understanding   The first element is understanding the nature and meaning of diversity and multiculturalism. Some managers, for example, have taken the basic concepts of equal employment opportunity to an unnecessary extreme. They know that, by law, they cannot discriminate against people on the basis of sex, race, and so forth. Thus, in following this mandate, they believe that they must treat everyone the same.

But this belief can cause problems when translated into workplace behaviors among people after they have been hired because people are not the same. Although people need to be treated fairly and equitably, managers must understand that differences among people do, in fact, exist. Thus any effort to treat everyone the same, without regard to their fundamental human differences, will only lead to problems. Managers must understand that cultural factors cause people to behave in different ways and that these differences should be accepted.

Empathy   Related to understanding is empathy. People in an organization should try to understand the perspective of others. For example, suppose a woman joins a group that has traditionally comprised white men. Despite their good intentions, the men may not know how to help the newcomer feel comfortable. Perhaps the most effective way to welcome her might be to empathize with how she may feel. For example, she may feel disappointed or elated about her new assignment, she may be confident or nervous about her position in the group, and she may be experienced or inexperienced in working with male colleagues. By learning more about her feelings, the group members can facilitate their ability to work together effectively. Of course, at the same time, the newcomer may also feel the need to avoid revealing too much about her feelings and attitudes, at least until she becomes comfortable with her new colleagues.

Tolerance   A third related individual approach to dealing with diversity and multiculturalism is tolerance. Even though people can learn to understand others, and even though they may try to empathize with others, the fact remains that some people may still not accept or enjoy some aspect of the behaviors of others. For example, one organization recently reported that it was experiencing considerable conflict among its U.S. and Israeli employees. The Israeli employees always seemed to want to argue about every issue that arose. The U.S. managers preferred to conduct business more harmoniously and became uncomfortable with the conflict. Finally, after considerable discussion the U.S. managers learned that many Israeli employees simply enjoy arguing and see it as part of getting work done. The firm's U.S. employees still do not enjoy the arguing, but they are more willing to tolerate it as a fundamental cultural difference between themselves and their colleagues from Israel.[32]

Willingness to Communicate   A final individual approach to dealing with diversity and multiculturalism is communication. Problems are often magnified because people are afraid or otherwise unwilling to openly discuss issues that relate to diversity or multiculturalism. For example, suppose that a young employee has a habit of making jokes about the age of an elderly colleague. Perhaps the young colleague means no harm and is just engaging in what she sees as good-natured kidding. But the older employee may find the jokes offensive. If the two do not communicate, the jokes will continue and the resentment will grow. Eventually, what started as a minor problem may erupt into a much bigger one.

For communication to work, it must be two way. If a person wonders whether a certain behavior is offensive to someone else, the curious individual should just ask. Similarly, if someone is offended by the behavior of another person, he or she should explain to the offending individual how the behavior is perceived and request that it be stopped. As long as such exchanges are friendly, low key, and nonthreatening, they will generally have a positive outcome. Of course, if the same message is presented in an overly combative manner or if a person continues to engage in offensive behavior after having been asked to stop, problems are sure to escalate. At this point third parties within the organization may have to intervene. And in fact, most organizations today have one or more systems in place to address questions and problems that arise as a result of diversity. We now turn our attention to various ways that organizations can indeed better manage diversity.

■ Organizational Approaches

Whereas individuals are important in managing diversity and multiculturalism, the organization itself must play a fundamental role.[33] Through its various policies and practices, people in the organization come to understand what behaviors are and are not appropriate. Diversity and multicultural training is an even more direct method for managing diversity. And the organization's culture is the ultimate context from which diversity and multiculturalism must be addressed.

Organizational Policies   The starting point in managing diversity and multiculturalism is the policies that an organization adopts that directly or indirectly affect how people are treated. Obviously, for instance, the extent to which an organization embraces the premise of equal employment opportunity will to a large extent determine the potential diversity within an organization. But the organization that follows the law to the letter and practices only passive discrimination differs from the organization that actively seeks a diverse and varied workforce.

Another aspect of organizational policies that affects diversity and multiculturalism is how the organization addresses and responds to problems that arise from differences among people. For example, consider the example of a manager charged with sexual harassment. If the organization's policies put an excessive burden of proof on the individual being harassed and invoke only minor sanctions against the guilty party, it is sending a clear signal as to the importance of such matters. But the organization that has a balanced set of policies for addressing questions like sexual harassment sends its employees a message that diversity and individual rights and privileges are important.

Indeed, perhaps the major policy through which an organization can reflect its stance on diversity and multiculturalism is its mission statement. If the organization's mission statement articulates a clear and direct commitment to differences among people, it follows that everyone who comes into contact with that mission statement will grow to understand and accept the importance of diversity and multiculturalism, at least to that particular organization.

Organizational Practices   Organizations can also help manage diversity and multiculturalism through a variety of ongoing practices and procedures. Avon's creation of networks for various groups represents one example of an organizational practice that fosters diversity. In general, the idea is that because diversity and multiculturalism are characterized by differences among people, organizations can more effectively manage that diversity by following practices and procedures that are based on flexibility rather than rigidity.

Benefits packages, for example, can be structured to better accommodate individual situations. An employee who is part of a dual-career couple and who has no children may require relatively little insurance (perhaps because his spouse's employer provides more complete coverage) and would like to be able to schedule vacations to coincide with those of his spouse. An employee who is a single parent may need a wide variety of insurance coverage and prefer to schedule her vacation time to coincide with school holidays.

Flexible working hours are also a useful organizational practice to accommodate diversity. Differences in family arrangements, religious holidays, cultural events, and so forth may each dictate that employees have some degree of flexibility in when they work. For example, a single parent may need to leave the office everyday at 4:30 to pick up the children from their day care center. An organization that truly values diversity will make every reasonable attempt to accommodate such a need.

Organizations can also facilitate diversity and multiculturalism by making sure that its important committees and executive teams are diverse. Even if diversity exists within the broader organizational context, an organization that does not reflect diversity in groups such as committees and teams implies that diversity is not a fully ingrained element of its culture. In contrast, if all major groups and related work assignments reflect diversity, the message is quite different.

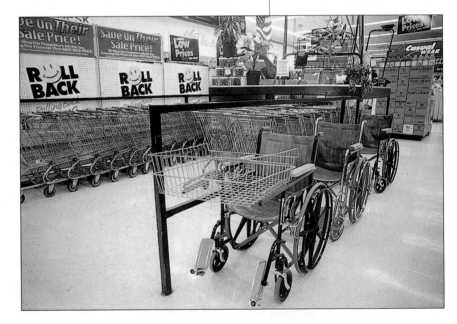

All businesses today need to acknowledge the diversity that exists among their employees and their customers. For example, many Wal-Mart stores set aside several parking spaces near their doors for shoppers with small children. And inside the stores, wheelchair-bound customers can shop from specially-designed chairs like the one shown here. Such actions not only generate additional business for the company but also send a clear message that the stores welcome all kinds of customers.

diversity and multicultural training
Training that is specifically designed to help members of an organization to function in a diverse and multicultural workforce

An organization that wants to use its own culture to reinforce multicultural issues must sometimes make difficult choices. For example, Collette Morgan and Tom Braun own a Minneapolis bookstore named Wild Rumpus. They have populated their store with a small zoo—cats, lizards, roosters, tarantulas, and songbirds, among others—to engage the excitement of their youthful customers. So important is their culture that Morgan and Braun recently rejected a very lucrative offer to open a new store in the city's massive Mall of America, arguing that they wanted to simultaneously protect their own unique organizational culture and continue to reach out to children from all backgrounds.

Diversity and Multicultural Training Many organizations are finding that **diversity and multicultural training** is an effective means for managing diversity and minimizing its associated conflict. More specifically, diversity and multicultural training is training that is specifically designed to help members of an organization to function in a diverse and multicultural workplace.[34] This training can take various forms. For example, many organizations find it useful to help people learn more about their similarities to and differences from others. Men and women can be taught to work together more effectively and can gain insights into how their own behaviors affect and are interpreted by others. In one organization a diversity training program helped male managers gain insights into how various remarks they made to one another could be interpreted by others as being sexist. In the same organization, female managers learned how to point out their discomfort with those remarks without appearing overly hostile.[35]

Similarly, white and black managers may need training to better understand each other. Managers at Mobil Corporation noticed that four black colleagues never seemed to eat lunch together. After a diversity training program, they came to realize that the black managers felt that if they ate together, their white colleagues would be overly curious about what they might be talking about. Thus they avoided close associations with one another because they feared calling attention to themselves.[36]

Some organizations even go so far as to provide language training for their employees as a vehicle for managing diversity and multiculturalism. Motorola, for example, provides English language training for its foreign employees on assignment in the United States. At Pace Foods in San Antonio, with a total payroll of 350 employees, staff meetings and employee handbooks are translated into Spanish for the benefit of the company's one hundred Hispanic employees.[37]

Organizational Culture The ultimate test of an organization's commitment to managing diversity and multiculturalism, as discussed earlier in this chapter, is its culture.[38] Regardless of what managers say or put in writing, unless they truly value diversity and multiculturalism, these concepts will never become a truly integral part of the organization. An organization that really wants to promote diversity and multiculturalism must shape its culture to clearly underscore top-management commitment to and support of diversity and multiculturalism in all forms and throughout every part of the organization. When a clear and consistent set of organizational policies and practices reinforces top-management support, diversity and multiculturalism can become a basic and fundamental part of an organization.[39]

MANAGEMENT IMPLICATIONS Managers need to appreciate the fact that diversity and multiculturalism can be managed. They should understand, for example, such individual strategies as understanding, empathy, tolerance, and a willingness to communicate can help promote diversity. Similarly, managers should also be quite familiar with such organizational strategies as organizational policies and practices, training, and organizational culture. ▬

multicultural organization An organization that has achieved high levels of diversity, is able to fully capitalize on the advantages of diversity, and has few diversity-related problems

Toward the Multicultural Organization

Many organizations today are grappling with cultural diversity. We noted in Chapter 5 that whereas many organizations are becoming increasingly global, no truly global organization exists. In similar fashion, although organizations are becoming ever more diverse, few are truly multicultural. The **multicultural organization** has achieved high levels of diversity, is able to fully capitalize on the advantages of the diversity, and has few diversity-related problems. One recent article described the six basic characteristics of such an organization.[40] These characteristics are illustrated in Figure 6.5.

First, the multicultural organization is characterized by *pluralism*, which means that every group represented in an organization works to better understand every other group. Thus black employees try to understand white employees, and white employees try just as hard to understand their black colleagues. In addition, every group represented within an organization has the potential to influence the organization's culture and its fundamental norms.

Second, the multicultural organization achieves *full structural integration*. Full structural integration suggests that the diversity within an organization is a complete and accurate reflection of the organization's external labor market. If around half of the labor market is female, then about half of the organization's employees are female. Moreover, this same proportion is reflected at all levels of the organization. There are no glass ceilings or other subtle forms of discrimination.

Third, the multicultural organization achieves *full integration of the informal network*. This characteristic suggests the absence of barriers to entry and participation in any organizational activity. For

FIGURE 6.5
The Multicultural Organization

Few, if any, organizations have become truly multicultural. At the same time, more and more organizations are moving in this direction. When an organization becomes multicultural, it reflects the six basic characteristics shown here.

Source: Based on Taylor H. Cox, "The Multicultural Organization," *Academy of Management Executive,* May 1991, pp. 34–47. Reprinted with permission.

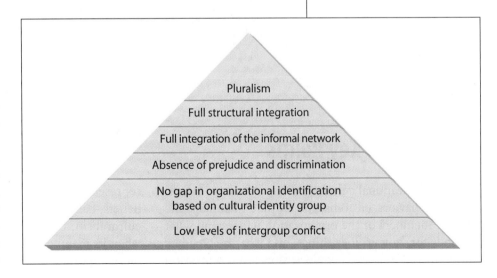

Pluralism

Full structural integration

Full integration of the informal network

Absence of prejudice and discrimination

No gap in organizational identification based on cultural identity group

Low levels of intergroup conflict

example, people enter and exit lunch groups, social networks, communication grapevines, and other informal aspects of organizational activity without regard to age, gender, ethnicity, or other dimension of diversity.

Fourth, the multicultural organization is characterized by an *absence of prejudice and discrimination*. No traces of bias exist, and prejudice is eliminated. Discrimination is not practiced in any shape, form, or fashion. And discrimination is nonexistent not because it is illegal, but because of the lack of prejudice and bias. People are valued, accepted, and rewarded purely on the basis of their skills and what they contribute to the organization.

Fifth, in the multicultural organization there is *no gap in organizational identification based on cultural identity groups*. In many organizations today people tend to make presumptions about organizational roles based on group identity. For example, many people walking into an office and seeing a man and woman conversing tend to assume that the woman is the secretary and the man is the manager. No such tendencies exist in the multicultural organization. People recognize that men and women are equally likely to be managers and secretaries.

Finally, *low levels of intergroup conflict* define the multicultural organization. We noted earlier that conflict is a likely outcome of increased diversity. The multicultural organization has evolved beyond this point to a state of virtually no conflict among people who differ. People within the organization fully understand, empathize with, have tolerance for, and openly communicate with everyone else. Values, premises, motives, attitudes, and perceptions are so well understood by everyone that any conflict that does arise is over meaningful and work-related issues, as opposed to differences in age, gender, ethnicity, or other dimensions of diversity.

MANAGEMENT IMPLICATIONS Managers should be aware of the fact that no truly multicultural organization yet exists. At the same time, though, they should be familiar with the qualities and characteristics that would typify such an organization. They should also recognize that organizations that become more multicultural are likely to be more effective than those that avoid or inhibit multiculturalism.

Summary of Key Points

Organizational culture is the set of values, beliefs, behaviors, customs, and attitudes that helps the members of the organization understand what it stands for, how it does things, and what it considers important. When the people within an organization represent different cultures, their differences in values, beliefs, behaviors, customs, and attitudes reflect multiculturalism. Diversity exists in a community of people when its members differ from one another along one or more important dimensions.

Organizational culture is an important environmental concern for managers. Managers must understand that culture is an important determinant of how well their organization will perform. Culture can be determined and managed in a number of different ways.

Diversity and multiculturalism are increasing in organizations today because of changing demographics, the desire by organizations to improve their workforce, legal pressures, and increased globalization. Diversity has several important dimensions, including age, gender, and ethnicity. The overall age of the workforce is increasing. More women are also entering the workplace, although a glass ceiling still exists in many settings. In the United States more Hispanics are also entering the workplace as the percentage of whites gradually declines.

Diversity and multiculturalism can affect an organization in a number of different ways. For example, they can be a source of competitive advantage (the cost, resource acquisition, marketing, creativity, problem-solving, and systems flexibility arguments). On the other hand, diversity and multiculturalism can also be a source of conflict in an organization.

Managing diversity and multiculturalism in organizations is the responsibility of both individuals within the organization and the organization itself. Individual approaches include understanding, empathy, tolerance, and willingness to communicate. Major organizational approaches are through policies, practices, diversity training, and culture.

Few, if any, organizations have become truly multicultural. The major dimensions that characterize organizations as they eventually achieve this state are pluralism, full structural integration, full integration of the informal network, an absence of prejudice and discrimination, no gap in organizational identification based on cultural identity group, and low levels of intergroup conflict attributable to diversity.

Discussion Questions

Questions for Review

1. How is organizational culture usually created?

2. Why are diversity and multiculturalism increasing in many organizations today?

3. Summarize the basic impact of diversity and multiculturalism on organizations.

4. Discuss the four basic individual approaches and the four basic organizational approaches to diversity and multiculturalism.

Questions for Analysis

5. Compare and contrast organizational culture and the culture of a country.

6. The text outlines many advantages of diversity and multiculturalism in organizations. Can you think of any disadvantages?

7. Which basic dimensions of diversity affect you the most?

Questions for Application

8. Visit the registrar's office or office of admissions at your college or university. Using the school's enrollment statistics, determine the relative diversity on your campus. Is the student population more or less diverse than the faculty?

9. Assume that you are starting a new organization that is likely to grow rapidly. Develop a plan for becoming a multicultural organization.

10. Assume that you work for a large multinational organization. You have just learned that you are being transferred to India. You also know that you will be the first person of your ethnicity to work there. What steps might you take before you go to minimize problems that your presence might cause?

Building Effective Technical Skills

EXERCISE OVERVIEW

Technical skills are the skills necessary to accomplish or understand the specific kind of work being done in an organization. This exercise will enable you to develop Internet skills as they relate to dealing with multicultural issues.

EXERCISE BACKGROUND

One of the most important multicultural challenges facing managers today involves language skills. Assume you are the human resource manager for a large domestic company. Your firm has recently decided to enter into a joint venture with three foreign companies, one each from France, Germany, and Korea.

The terms of this joint venture involve your three partners each sending a team of managers to your corporate headquarters for a period of two years. Your job is to make sure that your own top-management team has basic language skills in all three languages represented by your partners.

EXERCISE TASK

With the preceding background information as context, do the following:

1. Use the Internet to obtain information about language training programs and methods.

2. Obtain information about one or more program or method and decide how you should proceed.

Building Effective Diagnostic Skills

EXERCISE OVERVIEW

Diagnostic skills enable a manager to visualize the most appropriate response to a situation. This exercise gives you an opportunity to practice using diagnostic skills as they relate to organizational culture and multicultural issues and challenges.

EXERCISE BACKGROUND

Your firm has recently undergone a significant increase in its workforce. Many of the new workers you have hired are immigrants from Eastern Europe and Asia. Several do not speak English very well, but all are diligent workers who appear to be trying very hard to be successful and to fit in with their coworkers.

Recently, however, some problems have come to your attention. For one thing, several of your female workers have begun to complain about an increase in sexual harassment. For another, your supervisors have noticed an increase in tardiness and absenteeism among all of your workers.

You know that you need to take some kind of action. However, you are unsure how to proceed. Consequently, you have decided to spend a few days thinking about what to do.

EXERCISE TASK

With the preceding background information as context, do the following:

1. Think of as many causes as you can for each of the two problems you are facing.

2. Determine how you might address each problem, given the potential array of factors that might have contributed to them.

3. What role might organizational culture be playing in this situation, apart from issues of multiculturalism?

4. What role might multiculturalism be playing in this situation, apart from issues of organizational culture?

Building Effective Decision-Making Skills

EXERCISE OVERVIEW

Decision-making skills refer to the manager's ability to correctly recognize and define problems and opportunities and to then select an appropriate course of action to solve problems and capitalize on opportunities. This exercise focuses on decision making about issues related to diversity and multiculturalism.

EXERCISE BACKGROUND

For years your firm had relatively little diversity. The one thousand employees were almost exclusively white and male. But in recent years you have succeeded in increasing diversity substantially. Almost one-third of your employees are now female, and more than 40 percent are Hispanic or African American.

Unfortunately, your firm has recently faced some financial setbacks. You feel that you have no choice but to lay off about three hundred employees for a period of at least six months. If everything goes well, you also expect to be able to bring them back at that time.

EXERCISE TASK

With the preceding background information as context, do the following:

1. Develop a layoff plan that will not substantially reduce diversity in your firm.

2. Decide how you will communicate your decision to the workforce.

3. What obstacles do you foresee in implementing your decision?

CHAPTER CLOSING CASE

Porsche Shifts Gears

Porsche was a company going nowhere. And this was, of course, a strange state of affairs for one of the world's most renowned sports-car manufacturers. The firm was founded in 1929 by Ferdinand Porsche, an engineer who left Daimler-Benz with a vision to design and build racing cars. For several years, however, a lack of financial resources forced him to restrict his operation to making mass-market cars and trucks for the German military.

After World War II, however, the elder Porsche turned over the reins of the company to his son and a team of younger managers. These managers, in turn, decided the time was ripe to return to Ferdinand's original conception. Therefore, the firm began to design and build a line of sports cars that eventually became synonymous with status, speed, and mechanical precision—and, of course, extravagance, since the prices Porsche charged for its cars where far above those of mass-market cars like Fords, Nissans, and Volkswagens.

Because the market for such cars is relatively small, Porsche restricted its production and product lines, relying on large markups to generate cash flow and earn profits. Although this strategy had its ups and downs, Porsche was able to remain competitive and comfortable within its own relatively small niche.

But the automobile market changed dramatically during the early 1990s while Porsche stood still. Toyota launched its upscale Lexus line, with an impressive sports coupe, the SC400. Mazda reawakened the roadster market with its popular Miata. And Chrysler launched its Viper, a direct competitor to Porsche's products. The entire approach to making cars also changed during this time as well, emphasizing lean production and just-in-time delivery cycles.

But Porsche remained rooted in the old ways. Staid German craftsmen, for example, still built each car by hand. And massive inventories remained stored in warehouses near the Porsche plant in Stuttgart. These systems, in turn, meant that Porsche was having to keep its prices high. But customers began to wonder why they needed to pay $80,000 or more for a Porsche when they could get an SC400 for $45,000 or a Miata for $25,000.

Porsche lost $270 million between 1992 and 1995 and was actually nearing bankruptcy. Almost out of desperation, the company hired a new CEO, Wendelin Wiedeking, in an effort to save the firm. Within a few months, Wiedeking shocked the automobile industry when he turned over the operational

reins to a team of Japanese managers. These managers, in turn, came in and set in motion a veritable cultural revolution that has both reshaped and saved the company.

The first acts were symbolic. When they first entered the factory, one of the managers shouted, "We said bring us to the factory! This is a warehouse!" Wiedeking himself then took a circular saw and began cutting down the ten-foot shelving units that ran throughout the factory. The shelves had been used to store parts. But the Japanese managers knew that they also made the plant dark, foreboding, and inefficient.

Over the next few months, the new management team made more substantive changes. The corporate staff was downsized, for example, and the number of suppliers used by the firm was cut by two-thirds. The remaining suppliers were forced to commit to the just-in-time delivery philosophy that virtually every other auto maker in the world had already adopted. Workplace clutter was also cut by 20 percent, and windows were installed all around the factory. Now, each work area is light, open, and clean.

The workers themselves have also been reorganized into teams. Resistant to these changes at first, the German workers have now embraced them wholeheartedly. And the results have been impressive. The time required to produce the firm's mainstay, the Porsche 911, has been cut in half. Defect rates also plummeted. In 1994, for example, the first totally defect-free 911 rolled off the line.

Porsche is also looking ahead to the launch of a variety of new products. The first, the Boxster, has already proven to be a big hit and has a customer-waiting list of nine months. A luxury sports utility vehicle is likely to be next. All told, Porsche has doubled its output since 1995. And most experts now believe that the company has indeed turned the corner and will regain its stature as a pre-eminent manufacturer of exclusive and high-quality sports cars and related vehicles.

Case Questions

1. Characterize the old and the new cultures at Porsche.
2. What role did multiculturalism play in changing the Porsche organizational culture?
3. What organizational culture and/or multicultural problems might Porsche have to face in the future?

Case References: "Porsche Calls 911, Boxster Japanese to the Rescue," *USA Today,* April 8, 1997, pp. B1, B2; "The 25 Top Managers of the Year," *Business Week*, January 12, 1998, pp. 54–68.

CHAPTER NOTES

1. Betsy Morris, "If Women Ran the World, It Would Look a Lot Like Avon," *Fortune*, July 21, 1997, pp. 74–79; and *Hoover's Handbook of American Business 1997* (Austin, Texas: Hoover's Business Press, 1997), pp. 212–213.

2. Terrence E. Deal and Allan A. Kennedy, *Corporate Cultures: The Rights and Rituals of Corporate Life* (Reading, Mass.: Addison-Wesley, 1982).

3. Deal and Kennedy, *Corporate Cultures*.

4. Stratford Sherman, "Levi's—As Ye Sew, So Shall Ye Reap," *Fortune*, May 12, 1997, pp. 104–116.

5. Jay B. Barney, "Organizational Culture: Can It Be a Source of Sustained Competitive Advantage?" *Academy of Management Review*, July 1986, pp. 656–665.

6. "Ford's Rebates Spell Trouble As New Models Fail to Excite Buyers," *Wall Street Journal*, January 10, 1996, pp. A1, A9.

7. "Why Wells Fargo Is Circling the Wagons," *Wall Street Journal*, June 9, 1997, pp. 92–93.

8. "At Arthur Andersen, the Accountants Face an Unlikely Adversary," *Wall Street Journal*, April 23, 1997, pp. A1, A13.

9. See Tomothy Galpin, "Connecting Culture to Organizational Change," *HRMagazine*, March 1996, pp. 84–89.

10. Gail Robinson and Kathleen Dechant, "Building a Business Case for Diversity, *The Academy of Management Executive*, August 1997, pp. 21–31.

11. Walter Kiechel III, "How to Manage Older Workers," *Fortune*, November 5, 1990, pp. 183–186.

12. "The Coming Job Bottleneck," *Business Week*, March 24, 1997, pp. 184–185; Linda Thornburg, "The Age Wave Hits," *HRMagazine*, February 1995, pp. 40–46.

13. "Companies Won't Derail Diversity," *USA Today*, May 15, 1995, pp. 1B–3B.

14. Gary Powell and D. Anthony Butterfield, "Investigating the 'Glass Ceiling' Phenomenon: An Empirical Study of Actual Promotions to Top Management," *Academy of Management Journal*, 1994, Vol. 37, No. 1, pp. 68–86.

15. Karen S. Lyness and Donna E. Thompson, "Above the Glass Ceiling? A Comparison of Matched Samples of Female and Male Executives," *Journal of Applied Psychology*, 1997, Vol. 82, No. 3, pp. 359–375.

16. "Paternal, Managerial Roles Often Clash," *Wall Street Journal*, September 12, 1991, pp. B1, B4.

17. Phaedra Brotherton, "Women Make Their Mark on HR," *HRMagazine*, August 1997, pp. 74–80.

18. *Occupational Outlook Handbook* (Washington D.C.: U.S. Bureau of Labor Statistics, 1990–1991).

19. Roy S. Johnson, "The New Black Power," *Fortune*, August 4, 1997, pp. 46–47.

20. Jane Easter Bahls, "Make Room for Diverse Beliefs," *HRMagazine*, August 1997, pp. 89–95.

21. "Immigration Is on the Rise, Again," *USA Today*, February 28, 1997, p. 7A.

22. "Bilingual Employees Are Seeking More Pay, and Many Now Get It," *Wall Street Journal*, November 13, 1996, pp. A1, A6.

23. Based on Taylor H. Cox and Stacy Blake, "Managing Cultural Diversity: Implications for Organizational Competitiveness," *The Academy of Management Executive*, August 1991, pp. 45–56.

24. Michelle Neely Martinez, "Work-Life Programs Reap Business Benefits," *HRMagazine*, June 1997, pp. 110–116. See also Cox and Blake, "Managing Cultural Diversity: Implications for Organizational Competitiveness."

25. For an example, see Tim Carvell, "Spike Lee: Madison Ave.'s Gotta Have Him," *Fortune*, April 14, 1997, pp. 84–86.

26. C. Marlene Fiol, "Consensus, Diversity, and Learning in Organizations," *Organization Science*, August 1994, pp. 403–415.

27. Beatrice A. Fitzpatrick, "Make the Business Case for Diversity," *HRMagazine*, May 1997, pp. 119–123. See also Douglas Hall and Victoria Parker, "The Role of Workplace Flexibility in Managing Diversity," *Organizational Dynamics*, Summer 1993, pp. 5–14.

28. Patricia L. Nemetz and Sandra L. Christensen, "The Challenge of Cultural Diversity: Harnessing a Diversity of Views to Understand Multiculturalism," *Academy of Management Review*, 1996, Vol. 21, No. 2, pp. 434–462.

29. Christine M. Riordan and Lynn McFarlane Shores, "Demographic Diversity and Employee Attitudes: An Empirical Examination of Relational Demography within Work Units," *Journal of Applied Psychology*, 1997, Vol. 82, No. 3, pp. 342–358.

30. "Computer Chip Project Brings Rivals Together, but the Cultures Clash," *Wall Street Journal*, May 3, 1994, pp. A1, A8.

31. "How Shoney's, Belted by a Lawsuit, Found the Path to Diversity," *Wall Street Journal*, April 16, 1996, pp. A1, A6; Fay Rice, "Denny's Changes Its Spots," *Fortune*, May 13, 1996, pp. 133–142; "The Ugly Talk on the Texaco Tape," *Business Week*, November 18, 1996, p. 58; and "Smith Barney's Woman Problem," *Business Week*, June 3, 1996, pp. 102–106.

32. "Firms Address Workers' Cultural Variety," *Wall Street Journal*, February 10, 1989, p. B1.

33. Sara Rynes and Benson Rosen, "What Makes Diversity Programs Work?" *HRMagazine*, October 1994, pp. 67–75.

34. Karen Hildebrand, "Use Leadership Training to Increase Diversity," *HRMagazine*, August 1996, pp. 53–59.

35. "Learning to Accept Cultural Diversity," *Wall Street Journal*, September 12, 1990, pp. B1, B9.

36. "Firms Address Workers' Cultural Variety."

37. "Firms Grapple with Language," *Wall Street Journal*, November 7, 1989, p. B1.

38. Anthony Carneville and Susan Stone, "Diversity—Beyond the Golden Rule," *Training and Development*, October 1994, pp. 22–27.

39. Janice R. W. Joplin and Catherine S. Daus, "Challenges of Leading a Diverse Workforce," *The Academy of Management Executive*, August 1997, pp. 32–47.

40. This discussion derives heavily from Taylor H. Cox, "The Multicultural Organization," *The Academy of Management Executive*, May 1991, pp. 34–47.

Different Cultures, Same Results?

An organization's culture is the set of values that helps its members understand what an organization stands for, how it does things, and what it considers important. This video case will help you better appreciate both the differences and the importance of culture in different companies.

OVERVIEW AND OBJECTIVES

After completing this video case, you should be able to:

1. More effectively describe the culture of an organization.

2. Better appreciate differences in culture among organizations.

3. Describe how culture is formed and how it affects the daily operations of an organization.

COMPANY BACKGROUND

UOP is a large engineering firm specializing in petrochemical refining and development. The company is science-based and highly profitable. Innovation, technical specialization, and international travel are company hallmarks. Of the company's 3700 employees, 17 percent are from abroad. New hires move through orientation in teams, often working shifts together of 12 hours work and 12 hours off. The firm also enjoys especially low turnover.

Von Maur is a Midwestern department store chain. Von Maur was founded over 125 years ago, and is still run by its founding family. All employees receive intensive customer service training, and store managers are taught to make high customer service quality their most fundamental job objective. Each Saturday morning, the stores have "hero" meetings to share feedback that they have received from customers. And, unlike many other retailers, Von Maur does not extend its hours during holiday periods and actually closes early instead so that associates can be with their families.

Alligator Records was founded in the early 1970s by a frustrated music collector who had difficulty finding the blues records he enjoyed. He began to systematically obtain copyright permission to reissue old recordings himself. Operating on a shoestring budget and working alone, he started reissuing classic blues recordings and selling them at flea markets out of the trunk of his car.

The music gradually caught on, and Alligator Records has now become an important and highly successful company in its industry. The founder still runs the company, and insists on maintaining a casual and low-key work environment for everyone.

CASE QUESTIONS

1. Describe the organizational culture that you think is most likely to exist within each of these companies.

2. Identify the major similarities and differences in culture that you think exist.

VIDEO REVIEW

Your instructor will now show you a video clip that provides more information about UOP, Von Maur, and Alligator.

FOLLOW-UP QUESTIONS

1. After viewing the video, critique your own characterization (from Case Question 1) of the cultures of each of the three firms.

2. Describe the general and task environments of each of the three companies.

3. Are there any examples illustrating ethics and/or social responsibility evident in these companies?

4. What roles do global forces play in each company's business operations?

5. Do diversity and multiculturalism affect these three firms? In what ways?

POPULAR VIDEO FOLLOW-UP

Each of the movies listed below provides some insights and examples to illustrate various environmental concepts and ideas. See if you can come up with other examples.

- *The Firm* (organizational culture and ethics)

- *Rising Sun* (competitive forces, global issues, and multiculturalism)

- *Twister* (organizational crises and ethics)

- *Outbreak* (organizational crises and ethics)

- *How to Make an American Quilt* (multiculturalism)

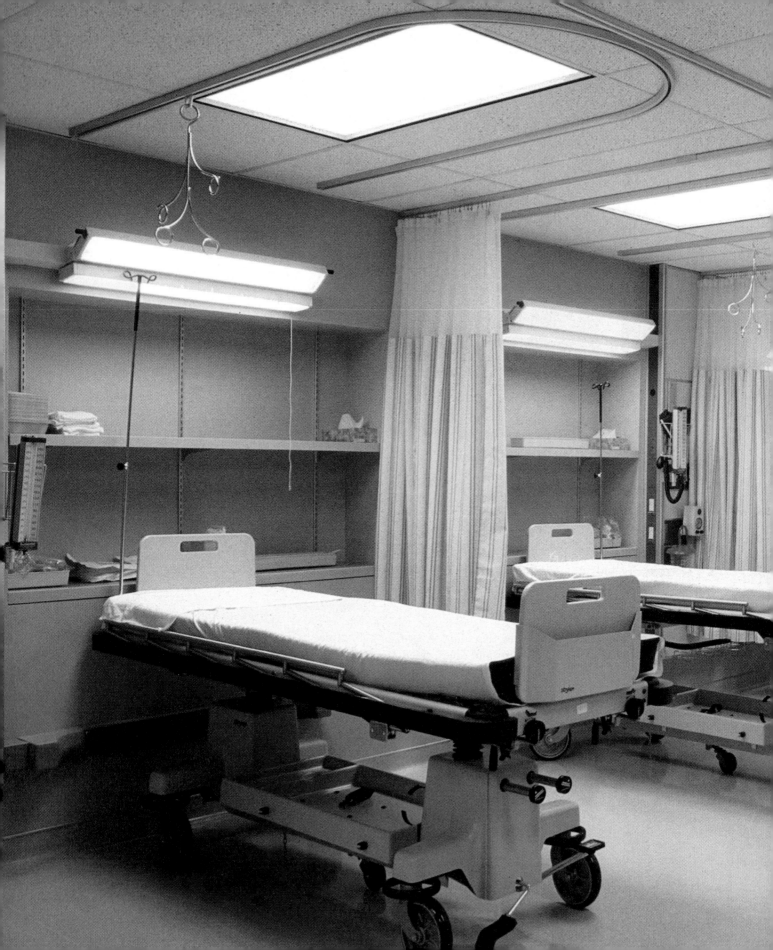

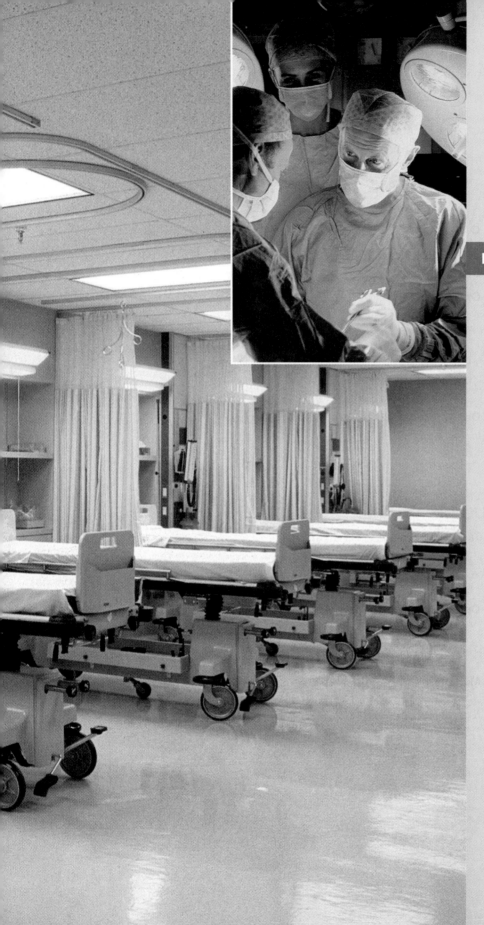

7

Basic Elements of Planning and Decision Making

OBJECTIVES

After studying this chapter, you should be able to:

- Summarize the function of decision making and the planning process.
- Discuss the purpose of organizational goals, identify different kinds of goals, discuss who sets goals, and describe how to manage multiple goals.
- Identify different kinds of organizational plans, note the time frames for planning, discuss who plans, and describe contingency planning.
- Discuss how tactical plans are developed and executed.
- Describe the basic types of operational plans used by organizations.
- Identify the major barriers to goal setting and planning, how organizations overcome those barriers, and how to use goals to implement plans.

Michael
Jordan
GUARD
CHICAGO BULLS

NIKE TOWN

Nike, of course, makes and sells more athletic shoes than any other company on Earth. But the company has recently set its sights much higher and intends to become a truly global powerhouse across a wide variety of sports-related businesses. Indeed, its lofty ambitions have earned it the spotlight throughout the sports equipment and apparel industries and in markets around the world.

In 1996, Nike was earning about $4 billion a year from its footwear business and another $2 billion from sports apparel and equipment. But Nike's chief executive officer (CEO), Philip Knight, wants more. The company's managers understand, for example, that the footwear market has become so mature, especially in the United States, that significant new growth was unlikely. At the same time, however, Nike executives see untapped potential in many new markets.

Knight stunned Nike investors and competitors when he recently announced a goal of doubling the firm's annual revenues to a staggering $12 billion by the year 2001. Although many observers thought it foolish to establish such a clear target—now everyone will know whether or not Nike reaches its lofty goal—company insiders argue that it also sends an unambiguous message as to what they see as the firm's potential and underscores the company's commitment to fulfilling that potential.

But Nike did more than simply toss out its revenue goals for people to debate. It also described in detail how it expects to achieve them. The firm actually has multiple plans to grow its revenues. One major plan relies on brand extension across a variety of sports-related equipment and apparel items. Although some people equate Nike with basketball and running shoes and apparel, other products either currently offered or planned run the gamut from eye wear (sunglasses and swim goggles) to gloves (for golf, weightlifting, and batting) to skates (both in-line and hockey). Nike is also branching out into sports-related services, including sports management, and retailing, through its growing chain of Nike Town stores.

"There isn't any market outside the U.S. where we're anywhere near our ultimate goal."

Thomas E. Clarke, Nike president, quoted in Business Week, May 12, 1997, p. 78.

Foreign expansion is also a key part of Nike's plans. As already noted, the U.S. athletic shoe market has matured. But foreign markets are still growing rapidly, and Nike sees much of its future growth coming from abroad. Michael Jordan, of course, is the firm's best known endorser in the United States. To help elevate the Nike name abroad, however, Nike has also enlisted a handball team in Germany, track and field stars in Kenya, and a women's basketball star in China.

Nike is focusing special attention on soccer. Adidas, a German sportswear company, dominates the soccer footwear and apparel markets. Given the worldwide popularity of soccer, however, Nike realizes that it must establish its own presence among aficionados of what everyone outside the U.S. calls "football" if it is to achieve its goals. Nike's first step in this direction was to outbid rival Adidas for sponsorship of the U.S. soccer team. It then followed suit with a similar deal with Brazil's national team, paying an unheard-of $200 million in sponsorship fees.

Nike has recently established another goal of becoming the world's number one supplier of soccer footwear, apparel, and equipment by the World Cup 2002 playoffs. But the going will be tough because Adidas—long content to sit back and rest on its long-standing connections—has awakened to Nike's threat and become more aggressive itself. Adidas still sponsors high-profile teams and has celebrity spokespersons in Germany, Spain, and France, and poses a major obstacle for Nike's ambitions, especially in Europe. Clearly, then, its shaping up to be a race to the goal.[1]

Nike has set some ambitious targets for its future growth. One risk that Nike managers face is the criticism they can expect and the sense of disappointment that will result if these goals are not met. No matter how well the company performs otherwise, many observers will say the company failed to reach its goals. At the same time, however, these goals do focus attention on what the firm anticipates doing and provide guidance and direction to managers throughout the firm with clear indicators of how they should manage their operations. In addition, the firm's plans for achieving its goals help guide day-to-day activities toward growth and expansion.

As we noted in Chapter 1, planning and decision making constitute the first managerial function that organizations must address. This chapter is the first of four that explore the planning process in detail. We begin by briefly examining the relationship between decision making and planning and then explaining the planning process that most organizations follow. We then discuss the nature of organizational goals and introduce the basic concepts of planning. Next we discuss tactical and operational planning more fully. Finally, we conclude with a discussion of how to manage the goal-setting and planning processes.

Decision Making and the Planning Process

Decision making is the cornerstone of planning. Consider, for example, Nike's goals and plans for doubling in size. CEO Philip Knight and other managers could have adopted an array of alternative options, including retaining the firm's current focus on athletic footwear, avoiding the soccer market because of stiff competition from Adidas, branching out into nonsportswear products such as dress shoes, seeking to grow at a faster or slower rate, and adopting a longer or shorter time frame for growth. Thus, Nike's exact mix of goals and plans for growth rates and time frames reflect choices from among a variety of alternatives.

Clearly, then, decision making is the catalyst that drives the planning process. An organization's goals follow from decisions made by various managers. Likewise, deciding on the best plan for achieving particular goals also reflects a decision to adopt one course of action as opposed to others. We discuss decision making per se in Chapter 9. Our focus here is on the planning process itself. As we discuss goal setting and planning, however, keep in mind that decision making underlies every aspect of setting goals and formulating plans.

The planning process itself can best be thought of as a generic activity. All organizations engage in planning activities, but no two organizations plan in exactly the same fashion. Figure 7.1 is a general representation of the planning process that many organizations attempt to follow. But although most firms follow this general framework, each firm also adds its own nuances and variations to the process.

As Figure 7.1 shows, all planning occurs within an environmental context. If managers do not understand this context, they are unable to develop effective plans. Thus understanding the environment is essentially the first step in planning. The four previous chapters cover many of the basic environmental issues that affect organizations and how they plan. With this understanding as a foundation, managers must then establish the organization's mission. The mission outlines the organization's purpose, premises, values, and directions. Flowing from the mission are parallel streams of goals and plans. Directly following the mission are strategic goals. These goals and the mission help determine strategic plans. Strategic goals and plans are primary inputs for developing tactical goals. Tactical goals and the original strategic plans help shape tactical plans. Tactical plans, in turn, combine with the tactical goals to shape operational goals. These goals and the appropriate tactical plans determine operational plans. Finally, goals and plans at each level can also be used as input for future activities at all levels. This chapter discusses goals and tactical and operational plans. Chapter 8 covers strategic plans.

FIGURE 7.1
The Planning Process

The planning process takes place within an environmental context. Managers must develop a complete and thorough understanding of this context to determine the organization's mission and develop its strategic, tactical, and operational goals and plans.

MANAGEMENT IMPLICATIONS Managers should recognize that decision making is the cornerstone of planning. They should also understand that although all organizations engage in planning activities, no two organizations plan in exactly the same fashion. Consequently, every manager must understand the environmental context that provides the framework for planning within her or his unique organizational setting. ▬

Organizational Goals

Goals are critical to organizational effectiveness, and they serve a number of purposes. Organizations can also have several different kinds of goals, all of which must be appropriately managed. And a number of different kinds of managers must be involved in setting goals.

■ Purposes of Goals

Goals serve four important purposes.[2] First, they provide guidance and a unified direction for people in the organization. Goals can help everyone understand where the organization is going and why getting there is important.

Several years ago Jack Welch, CEO of General Electric Co. (GE), set a goal that every business owned by the firm will be either number one or number two in its industry. This goal still helps set the tone for decisions made by GE managers as the company competes with rivals like Whirlpool and Electrolux.[3] Likewise, the goal set for Nike of doubling sales by the year 2001 helps everyone in the firm recognize the strong emphasis on growth and expansion that is driving the firm.

Second, goal-setting practices strongly affect other aspects of planning. Effective goal setting promotes good planning, and good planning facilitates future goal setting. The success of Nike demonstrates how setting goals and developing plans to reach them are complementary activities. The strong growth goal encourages managers to plan for expansion by looking for new market opportunities, for example. Similarly, managers must also always be alert for competitive threats and for new ideas that will help facilitate future expansion.

Third, goals can serve as a source of motivation to employees of the organization. Goals that are specific and moderately difficult can motivate people to work harder, especially if attaining the goal is likely to result in rewards.[4] The Italian furniture manufacturer Industrie Natuzzi SpA uses goals to motivate its workers. Each craftsperson has a goal for how long it should take to perform her or his job, such as sewing leather sheets together to make a sofa cushion or building wooden frames for chair arms. At the completion of assigned tasks, workers enter their ID numbers and job numbers into the firm's computer system. If they get a job done faster than their goal, a bonus is automatically added to their paycheck.[5] The "Management InfoTech" feature describes how Pier 1 Imports also combines technology and goals to boost motivation and performance.

Finally, goals provide an effective mechanism for evaluation and control. In other words, performance can be assessed in the future in terms of how successfully today's goals are accomplished. For example, suppose that officials of the United Way of America set a goal of collecting $250,000 from a particular community. If midway through the campaign they have raised only $50,000, they know that they need to change or intensify their efforts. If they raise only $100,000 by the end of their drive, they will need to carefully study why they did not reach their goal and what they need to do differently next year. On the other hand, if they succeed in raising $265,000, evaluations of their efforts will take on an entirely different character.

Decision making and planning are critical parts of the management process. For example, managers at Sears recently made the decision to invest heavily in the firm's home services business by creating a nationwide network of repair and service providers. Jane Thompson, shown here on the back of this van, heads up the business. Her goal is to reach $10 billion in sales. She and her management team have developed a variety of plans to help reach this goal.

MANAGEMENT INFOTECH

Pier 1 Imports Uses Technology to Meet Goals

The name of the game in retailing is sales. Virtually all measures of retailing performance revolve around sales figures—sales increases, seasonal sales fluctuations, sales compared to inventory, and so forth. One especially common performance measure is the increase in daily sales in a particular store relative to the store's sales one year before. Pier 1 Imports is using information technology to help make this performance measure, as well as others, an even more critical part of each Pier 1 store's daily business.

In the past, daily sales reports could only be calculated at the end of the day, so employees haven't known how well they were doing until it was too late to do anything about it. But now, sales figures are tabulated at each Pier 1 store on a continuous basis and displayed on a computer monitor in the employee lounge area. And Pier 1 employees are encouraged to check on the store's performance regularly. This system has allowed the firm to do an even better job of boosting sales by establishing daily improvement goals. For example, a store manager might inform employees about last year's sales figures for a given day and then set a goal of surpassing that sales level by a specific percentage.

In larger metropolitan areas, where Pier 1 has multiple stores, the same technology is being used to pit one store against the others. Each store knows not only how well it's doing, but also how the other stores in the area are doing. This knowledge allows stores to compete not only with their own sales performance from the previous year but also with other regional stores. In order to ensure that Pier 1 employees do indeed work to meet their goals, the company's incentive system ties employee bonuses to sales performance. Thus, the goals help direct employee attention and provide a clear avenue for employees to boost their income. And none of it would be possible without Pier 1's elaborate sales information system powered by local and network computer systems.

> *"Do you realize that the Green Hills store is doing just $700 a day more than us? Someday we could pass them."*
>
> *Eva Goldyn, Pier 1 store manager**

References: *"Pressure at Pier 1: Beating Sales Numbers Of Year Earlier Is a Storewide Obsession,"* Wall Street Journal, *December 7, 1995, pp. B1, B2 (*quote on page B1).*

■ Kinds of Goals

Organizations establish many different kinds of goals. In general, these goals vary by level, area, and time frame. Figure 7.2 provides examples of each type of goal for a fast-food chain.

Level Goals are set for and by different levels within an organization. As we noted earlier, the four basic levels of goals are the mission and strategic, tactical, and operational goals. An organization's **mission** is a statement of its "fundamental, unique purpose that sets a business apart from other firms of its type and identifies the scope of the business's operations in product and market terms."[6]

mission A statement of an organization's fundamental purpose

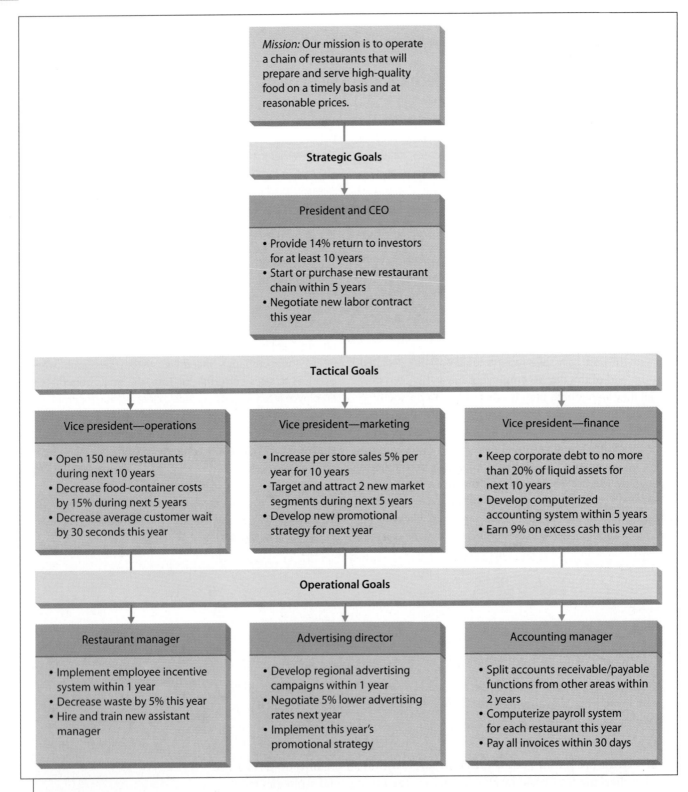

FIGURE 7.2

Kinds of Organizational Goals for a Regional Fast-Food Chain

Organizations develop many different types of goals. A regional fast-food chain, for example, might develop goals at several different levels and for several different areas.

Strategic goals are goals set by and for top management of the organization. These goals focus on broad, general issues. For example, Nike's goal of doubling sales revenues is a strategic goal. **Tactical goals** are set by and for middle managers. Tactical goals focus on how to carry out actions necessary to achieve the strategic goals. Tactical goals at Nike might center around which foreign markets to enter, which new products to launch, and so forth.

Operational goals are set by and for lower-level managers. The concern of operational goals is with shorter-term issues associated with the tactical goals. An operational goal for Nike might be a target number of new Nike Town retail outlets to be opened by the year 2000. (Some managers use the words *objective* and *goal* interchangeably. When they are differentiated, however, the term *objective* is usually used instead of *operational goal*.)

strategic goal A goal set by and for top management of the organization

tactical goal A goal set by and for middle managers of the organization

operational goal A goal set by and for lower-level managers of the organization

Area Organizations also set goals for different areas. The restaurant chain shown in Figure 7.2 has goals for operations, marketing, and finance. Hewlett-Packard Co. (H-P) routinely sets production goals for quality, productivity, and so forth. By keeping activities focused on these important areas, H-P has managed to remain competitive against organizations from around the world.[7] Human resource goals might be set for employee turnover and absenteeism. Rubbermaid and 3M set goals for product innovation. Similarly, Beth Pritchard, CEO of Bath & Body Works, has a goal that 30 percent of the products sold in the firm's retail outlets each year will be new.[8]

Time Frame Organizations also set goals across different time frames. In Figure 7.2, three goals are listed at the strategic, tactical, and operational levels. The first is a long-term goal, the second an intermediate-term goal, and the third a short-term goal. Some goals have an explicit time frame (for example, open 150 new restaurants during the next ten years), and others have an open-ended time horizon (for example, maintain 10 percent annual growth). Finally, we should also note that the meaning of different time frames varies by level. For example, at the strategic level, long-term often means ten years or longer, intermediate term around five years or so, and short-term around one year. But two or three years may be long-term at the operational level, and short-term may mean a matter of weeks or even days.

■ Responsibilities for Setting Goals

Who sets goals? The answer is actually quite simple: all managers should be involved in the goal-setting process. Each manager, however, generally has responsibilities for setting goals that correspond to his or her level in the organization. The mission and strategic goals are generally determined by the board of directors and top managers. Top and middle managers then work together to establish tactical goals. Finally, middle- and lower-level managers are jointly responsible for operational goals. Many managers also set individual goals for themselves. These goals may involve career paths, informal work-related goals outside the normal array of official goals, or just about anything of interest or concern to the manager.

Managing Multiple Goals

Organizations set many different kinds of goals and sometimes experience conflicts or contradictions among goals. Nike had problems with inconsistent goals a few years ago. The firm was producing high-quality shoes (a manufacturing goal) but they were not particularly stylish (a marketing goal). As a result, the company lost substantial market share when Reebok International started making shoes that were both high quality and fashionable. When Nike management recognized and corrected the inconsistencies, Nike regained its industry standing.[9]

optimizing Balancing and reconciling possible conflicts among goals

To address such problems, managers must understand the concept of optimizing. **Optimizing** involves balancing and reconciling possible conflicts between goals. Because goals may conflict with one another, the manager must look for inconsistencies and decide whether to pursue one goal to the exclusion of another or to find a midrange target between the extremes.[10] For example, The Home Depot has achieved dramatic success in the retailing industry by offering do-it-yourselfers high-quality home improvement products at low prices and with good service. The firm has recently announced a goal of doubling its revenues from professional contractors. Among its plans are to set up separate checkout areas and to provide special products for contractors. The challenge, however, will be to keep loyal individual customers while satisfying the unique needs of professional contractors.[11] "Today's Management Issues" illustrates another area in which managers must make trade-offs in order to optimize their goals.

MANAGEMENT IMPLICATIONS

Managers need to appreciate not only the various purposes that goals play in an organization but also the various kinds of goals that exist. No manager can avoid the goal-setting process, since all managers share responsibility for this activity. Finally, managers should also understand that because some goals may be in conflict with one another, they must be carefully optimized to serve the best overall interests of the organization. ▬

Organizational Planning

Given the clear link between organizational goals and plans, we now turn our attention to various concepts and issues associated with planning itself. In particular, this section identifies kinds of plans, time frames for planning, who is responsible for planning, and contingency planning.

Kinds of Organizational Plans

Organizations establish many different kinds of plans. At a general level, these include strategic, tactical, and operational plans.

Tradeoffs and More Tradeoffs

One of the most frustrating tradeoffs facing some managers today relates to staffing. Because unemployment is now so low, its harder than ever for some companies to hire the employees they need to remain in business. So the companies face a tradeoff of paying higher wages than they think they should versus hiring "riskier" employees—those with criminal records, poor performance histories, and so forth.

To cope with this problem, managers are resorting to a variety of strategies. One company, Metro Plastics Technologies, is paying its employees for forty hours when they only have to work thirty hours—with the one caveat that the employees must show up for work on time everyday. Other companies, such as Electronic Manufacturing Solutions, are paying the same as always but being more lenient in disciplining problem employees.

In smaller companies, the owners and/or managers who run the firms are working longer and longer hours themselves to get work done. They fill in for absent

"We're extreeemely [sic] lenient. Basically, if you just show up every day, we'll take you."

Rick James, operations manager at Electronic Manufacturing Solutions*

employees, for example, take care of various administrative chores previously delegated to others, and even answer the company telephone.

Occasionally, some businesses find they just can't solve the problem. For example, a Burger King restaurant in St. Paul recently had to close on a dozen different days simply because the manager could not hire enough people to work. After raising the starting wage from $6 to $7 an hour, the restaurant can now keep its doors open. But profit margins are down and the firm still keeps a "Help Wanted" sign on its door year-round!

References: *"As Jobs Go Begging, Bosses Toil Nights—And Improvise,"* Wall Street Journal, *March 31, 1997, pp. B1, B8 (*quote on page B1);* Justin Martin, *"So, You Want to Work for the Best …,"* Fortune, *January 12, 1998, pp. 77–80;* "Recruiters Work Hard to Showcase Fun Side of Jobs," USA Today, *December 29, 1997, p. 5B;* "High-Tech Help Wanted: No Experience Necessary," USA Today, *December 23, 1997, p. 1B.*

Strategic Plans Strategic plans are the plans developed to achieve strategic goals. More precisely, a **strategic plan** is a general plan outlining decisions of resource allocation, priorities, and action steps necessary to reach strategic goals.[12] These plans are set by the board of directors and top management; generally have an extended time horizon; and address questions of scope, resource deployment, competitive advantage, and synergy. We discuss strategic planning further in Chapter 8.

strategic plan A general plan outlining decisions of resource allocation, priorities, and action steps necessary to reach strategic goals

Tactical Plans A **tactical plan**, aimed at achieving tactical goals, is developed to implement specific parts of a strategic plan. Tactical plans typically involve upper and middle management and, compared with strategic plans, have a somewhat shorter time horizon and a more specific and concrete focus. Thus tactical plans are concerned more with actually getting things done than with deciding what to do. Tactical planning is covered in detail later in this chapter.

tactical plan A plan aimed at achieving tactical goals and implementing parts of a strategic plan

Operational Plans An **operational plan** focuses on carrying out tactical plans to achieve operational goals. Developed by middle- and lower-level

operational plan A plan that focuses on carrying out tactical plans to achieve operational goals

managers, operational plans have a short-term focus and are relatively narrow in scope. Each plan deals with a fairly small set of activities. We also cover operational planning in more detail later.

■ Time Frames for Planning

As we previously noted, strategic plans tend to have a long-term focus, tactical plans an intermediate-term focus, and operational plans a short-term focus. The sections that follow address these time frames in more detail.

Organizational planning involves developing a variety of different kinds of plans. For example, Enron, a public utility company, is expanding rapidly in a variety of foreign countries. Its managers first formulated strategic plans calling for new growth in international markets. Then they created tactical plans to help achieve their strategic goals. For example, one set of tactical plans are helping to build this power generating plant in China. And once it's up and running, a set of operational plans will help its managers run it efficiently and effectively.

Long-Range Plans A **long-range plan** covers many years, perhaps even decades. The founder of Matsushita Electric Industrial Company, Ltd., (maker of Panasonic and JVC electronic products), Konosuke Matsushita, once wrote a 250-year plan for his company.[13] Today, however, most managers recognize that environmental change makes it unfeasible to plan too far ahead, but large firms like General Motors (GM) and Exxon still routinely develop plans for ten- to twenty-year intervals. GM executives, for example, have a pretty good idea today about new car models that they plan to introduce for at least a decade in advance. The time span for long-range planning varies from one organization to another. For our purposes, we regard any plan that extends beyond five years as long-range. Managers of organizations in complex, volatile environments face a special dilemma. These organizations probably need a longer time horizon than do organizations in less dynamic environments, yet the complexity of their environment makes long-range planning difficult. Managers at these companies therefore develop long-range plans but also must constantly monitor their environment for possible changes.

Intermediate Plans An **intermediate plan** is somewhat less tentative and subject to change than is a long-range plan. Intermediate plans usually cover periods from one to five years and are especially important for middle and first-line managers. Thus intermediate plans generally parallel tactical plans. For many organizations intermediate planning has become the central focus of planning activities. Nissan, for example, has fallen far behind its domestic rivals Toyota and Honda in areas like profitability and productivity. To turn things around, the firm has developed several plans ranging in duration from two to four years, each intended to improve some part of the company's operations. One plan (three years in duration) involves updating the manufacturing technology used in each Nissan assembly factory. Another (four years in duration) calls for shifting more production to foreign plants to lower labor costs.[14]

long-range plan A plan that covers many years, perhaps even decades; common long-range plans are for five years or more

intermediate plan A plan that generally covers from one to five years

Short-Range Plans   A manager also develops a **short-range plan**, which has a time frame of one year or less. Short-range plans greatly affect the manager's day-to-day activities. There are two basic kinds of short-range plans. An **action plan** operationalizes any other kind of plan. When a specific Nissan plant is ready to have its technology overhauled, its managers focus their attention on replacing the existing equipment with new equipment as quickly and as efficiently as possible so as to minimize lost production time. In most cases the overhaul can be finished in a matter of a few months, with actual production being halted only for a few weeks. An action plan thus coordinates the actual changes at a given factory. A **reaction plan**, in turn, is a plan designed to allow the company to react to an unforeseen circumstance. At one Nissan factory the new equipment arrived earlier than expected, and plant managers had to shut down production more quickly than expected. These managers thus had to react to events beyond their control in ways that still allowed their goals to be achieved. In fact, reacting to any form of environmental turbulence, as described in Chapter 3, is a form of reaction planning.

short-range plan   A plan that generally covers a span of one year or less

action plan   A plan used to operationalize any other kind of plan

reaction plan   A plan developed to react to an unforeseen circumstance

■ Responsibilities for Planning

We earlier noted briefly the people who are responsible for setting goals. We can now expand that initial perspective a bit and examine more fully how different parts of the organization participate in the overall planning process. All managers engage in planning to some degree. Marketing sales managers develop plans for target markets, market penetration, and sales increases. Operations managers plan cost-cutting programs and better inventory control methods. As a general rule, however, the larger an organization becomes, the more the primary planning activities become associated with groups of managers rather than with individual managers.

Planning Staff   Some large organizations develop a professional planning staff. Tenneco, General Motors, General Electric, Caterpillar, Raytheon, NCR, Ford, and Boeing all have planning staffs.[15] And although the planning staff was pioneered in the United States, foreign firms such as Nippon Telegraph & Telephone have also started using them.[16] Organizations might use a

Standard operating procedures, rules, and regulations can all be useful methods for saving time, improving efficiency, and streamlining decision making and planning. But it is also helpful to periodically review SOPs, rules, and regulations to ensure that they remain useful. For example, as shown in this cartoon, a SOP for regularly ordering parts and supplies may become less effective if the demand for those parts and supplies changes.

BEETLE BAILEY   By Mort Walker

planning staff for a variety of reasons. In particular, a planning staff can reduce the workload of individual managers, help coordinate the planning activities of individual managers, bring to a particular problem many different tools and techniques, take a broader view than individual managers, and go beyond pet projects and particular departments.

Planning Task Force   Organizations sometimes use a planning task force to help develop plans. Such a task force often comprises line managers with a special interest in the relevant area of planning. The task force may also have members from the planning staff if the organization has one. A planning task force is most often created when the organization wants to address a special circumstance. For example, when Electronic Data Systems (EDS) decided to expand its information management services to Europe, managers knew that the firm's normal planning approach would not suffice, and top management created a special planning task force. The task force included representatives from each major unit within the company, the corporate planning staff, and the management team that would run the European operation. Once the plan for entering the European market was formulated and implemented, the task force was eliminated.[17]

Board of Directors   Among its other responsibilities, the board of directors establishes the corporate mission and strategy. In some companies the board takes an active role in the planning process. At CBS Inc., for example, the board of directors has traditionally played a major role in planning. In other companies the board selects a competent chief executive and delegates planning to that individual.

Chief Executive Officer   The chief executive officer is usually the president or the chair of the board of directors. The CEO is probably the single most important individual in any organization's planning process. The CEO plays a major role in the complete planning process and is responsible for implementing the strategy. The board and CEO, then, assume direct roles in planning. The other organizational components involved in the planning process have more of an advisory or consulting role.

Executive Committee   The executive committee is usually composed of the top executives in the organization working together as a group. Committee members usually meet regularly to provide input to the CEO on the proposals that affect their own units and to review the various strategic plans that develop from this input. Members of the executive committee are frequently assigned to various staff committees, subcommittees, and task forces to concentrate on specific projects or problems that might confront the entire organization at some time in the future.

Line Management   The final component of most organizations' planning activities is line management. Line managers are those persons with formal authority and responsibility for the management of the organization. They play an important role in an organization's planning process for two reasons. First, they are a valuable source of inside information for other managers as plans are formulated and implemented. Second, the line managers at the middle and lower levels of the organization usually must execute the plans developed by top management. Line management identifies, analyzes, and recommends program alternatives; develops budgets and submits them for approval; and finally sets the plans in motion.

■ Contingency Planning

Another important type of planning is **contingency planning**, or the determination of alternative courses of action to be taken if an intended plan of action is unexpectedly disrupted or rendered inappropriate.[18] Consider, for example, Nike's plans for growth. Philip Knight and his managers realize that a shift in the global economy might result in a different rate of expansion. Therefore, they might have two contingency plans based on extreme positive or negative economic shifts. First, if the economy begins to expand beyond some specific level (contingency event), then (contingency plan) the rate of the company's growth will increase. Second, if inflation increases substantially or the economy experiences a downturn, the growth rate may slow down a bit. Nike would therefore have specified two crucial contingencies (expansion or inflation in the economy outside the tolerable range) and two alternative plans (increased or decreased growth).

The mechanics of contingency planning are shown in Figure 7.3. In relation to an organization's other plans, contingency planning comes into play at four action points. At action point 1, management develops the basic plans of the organization. These may include strategic, tactical, and operational plans. As part of this development process, managers usually consider various contingency events. Some management groups even assign someone the role of devil's advocate to ask "But what if . . ." about each course of action. A variety of contingencies are usually considered.

At action point 2, the plan that management chooses is put into effect. The most important contingency events are also defined. Only the events that are

contingency planning The determination of alternative courses of action to be taken if an intended plan is unexpectedly disrupted or rendered inappropriate

FIGURE 7.3
Contingency Planning

Most organizations develop contingency plans. These plans specify alternative courses of action to be taken if an intended plan is unexpectedly disrupted or rendered inappropriate.

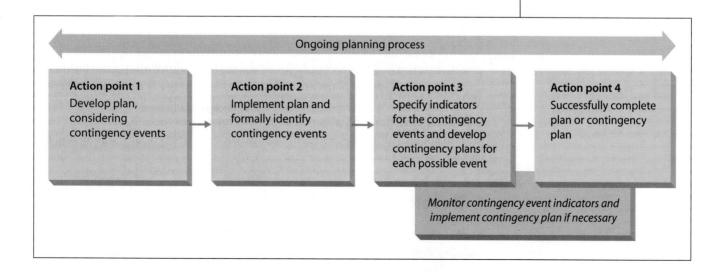

likely to occur and whose effects will have a substantial impact on the organization are used in the contingency-planning process. Next, at action point 3, the company specifies certain indicators or signs that suggest that a contingency event is about to take place. A bank might decide that a 2 percent drop in interest rates should be considered a contingency event. An indicator might be two consecutive months with a drop of .5 percent in each. As indicators of contingency events are being defined, the contingency plans themselves should also be developed. Examples of contingency plans for various situations are delaying plant construction, developing a new manufacturing process, and cutting prices.

After this stage, the managers of the organization monitor the indicators identified at action point 3. If the situation dictates, a contingency plan is implemented. Otherwise the primary plan of action continues in force. Finally, action point 4 marks the successful completion of either the original or a contingency plan.

Contingency planning is becoming increasingly important for most organizations and especially for those operating in particularly complex or dynamic environments. Few managers have such an accurate view of the future that they can anticipate and plan for everything. Contingency planning is a useful technique for helping managers cope with uncertainty and change.[19]

MANAGEMENT IMPLICATIONS

Managers should understand that organizations rely on several different kinds of plans that span different levels and different time frames. Similarly, managers should also recognize that different people are responsible for different kinds of planning activities and should be ready and prepared to play an appropriate role. In addition, all managers should understand that the potential for unexpected events makes it important to develop contingency plans. These plans should also be periodically updated and revised. ▬

Tactical Planning

As we note earlier, tactical plans are developed to implement specific parts of a strategic plan. You have probably heard the saying about winning the battle but losing the war. Tactical plans are to battles what strategy is to a war: an organized sequence of steps designed to execute strategic plans. Strategy focuses on resources, environment, and mission, whereas tactics focus primarily on people and action.[20] Figure 7.4 identifies the major elements in developing and executing tactical plans.

■ Developing Tactical Plans

Although effective tactical planning depends on many factors that vary from one situation to another, we can identify some basic guidelines. First, the manager needs to recognize that tactical planning must address a number of tactical goals derived from a broader strategic goal.[21] An occasional situation may call for a stand-alone tactical plan, but most of the time tactical plans flow from and must be consistent with a strategic plan.

For example, when Roberto Goizueta became CEO of Coca-Cola, he developed a strategic plan for carrying the firm into the twenty-first century. As part of developing the plan, Goizueta identified a critical environmental threat—considerable unrest and uncertainty among the independent bottlers who packaged and distributed Coca-Cola's products. To simultaneously counter this threat and strengthen the company's position, Coca-Cola bought several large independent bottlers and combined them into one new organization called Coca-Cola Enterprises. Selling half of the new company's stock reaped millions in profits while still effectively keeping control of the enterprise in Coca-Cola's hands. Thus the creation of the new business was a tactical plan developed to contribute to the achievement of an overarching strategic goal.[22] Following Mr. Goizueta's death in 1997, Coca-Cola managers still had a comprehensive and logical set of plans in place to help implement his vision for the firm.

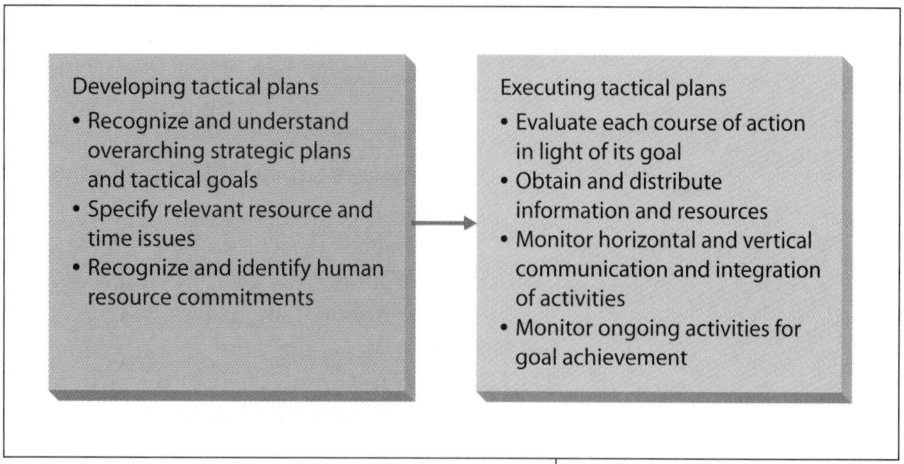

Second, although strategies are often stated in general terms, tactics must specify resources and time frames. A strategy can call for being number one in a particular market or industry, but a tactical plan must specify precisely what activities will be undertaken to achieve that goal. Consider the Coca-Cola example again. Another element of its strategic plan involves increased worldwide market share. To facilitate additional sales in Europe, managers developed tactical plans for building a new plant in the south of France to make soft-drink concentrate and for building another canning plant in Dunkirk. Building these plants represents a concrete action involving measurable resources (for example, funds to build the plants) and a clear time horizon (that is, a target date for completion).[23]

Finally, tactical planning requires the use of human resources. Managers involved in tactical planning spend a great deal of time working with other people. They must be in a position to receive information from others in and outside the organization, process that information in the most effective way, and then pass it on to others who might make use of it. Coca-Cola executives have been intensively involved in planning the new plants, setting up the new bottling venture noted earlier, and exploring a joint venture with Cadbury Schweppes in the United Kingdom. Each activity has required considerable time and effort from dozens of managers. One manager, for example, crossed the Atlantic twelve times while negotiating the Cadbury deal.

FIGURE 7.4
Developing and Executing Tactical Plans

Tactical plans are used to accomplish specific parts of a strategic plan. Each strategic plan is generally implemented through several tactical plans. Effective tactical planning involves both development and execution.

■ Executing Tactical Plans

Regardless of how well a tactical plan is formulated, its ultimate success depends on the way it is carried out. Successful implementation, in turn, depends on the astute use of resources, effective decision making, and insightful steps to ensure that the right things are done at the right time and in the right ways. A manager can see an absolutely brilliant idea fail because of improper execution.

Proper execution depends on a number of important factors. First, the manager needs to evaluate every possible course of action in light of the goal it is intended to reach. Next, he or she needs to make sure that each decision maker has the information and resources necessary to get the job done. Vertical and horizontal communication and integration of activities must be present to minimize conflict and inconsistent activities. And finally, the manager must monitor ongoing activities derived from the plan to make sure that they are achieving the desired results. This monitoring typically takes place within the context of the organization's ongoing control systems.

For example, managers at The Walt Disney Company recently developed a new strategic plan aimed at spurring growth and profits. One tactical plan developed to stimulate growth was to build a theme park dedicated to U.S. history. The first announced location for the park, outside Washington, D.C., was eventually abandoned following a barrage of protests from local residents, but Disney continues its search for a location for the park. Although building this park will be a big undertaking, it is still a tactical plan within the overall strategic plan focusing on growth.

MANAGEMENT IMPLICATIONS Although strategic planning is, of course, critical to the success of any organization, tactical planning often makes the difference in how well strategies actually work. Thus, tactical plans should be developed and executed with as much care as the organization devotes to other kinds of planning. ■

Operational Planning

Another critical element in effective organizational planning is the development and implementation of operational plans. Operational plans are derived from tactical plans and are aimed at achieving operational goals. Thus operational plans tend to be narrowly focused, have relatively short time horizons, and involve lower-level managers. Table 7.1 summarizes the two most basic forms of operational plans and the specific types of each.

■ Single-Use Plans

single-use plan A plan to carry out a course of action that is not likely to be repeated in the future

A **single-use plan** is developed to carry out a course of action that is not likely to be repeated in the future. As Disney proceeds with its expansion plans on the West Coast, it will develop numerous single-use plans for individual rides, attractions, and hotels. The two most common forms of single-use plans are programs and projects.

Programs A **program** is a single-use plan for a large set of activities. It might consist of identifying procedures for introducing a new product line, opening a new facility, or changing the organization's mission. A few years ago Black & Decker bought General Electric's small-appliance business. The deal involved the largest brand-name switch in history: 150 products were converted from GE to the Black & Decker label. Each product was carefully studied, redesigned, and reintroduced with an extended warranty. A total of 140 steps were used for each product. It took three years to convert all 150 products over to Black & Decker. The total conversion of the product line was a program.

Projects A **project** is similar to a program but is generally of less scope and complexity. A project may be a part of a broader program, or it may be a self-contained single-use plan. For Black & Decker, the conversion of each of the 150 products was a separate project in its own right. Each product had its own manager, its own schedule, and so forth. Projects are also used to introduce a new product within an existing product line or to add a new benefit option to an existing salary package.

■ Standing Plans

Whereas single-use plans are developed for nonrecurring situations, a **standing plan** is used for activities that recur regularly over a period of time. Standing plans can greatly enhance efficiency by routinizing decision making. Policies, standard operating procedures, and rules and regulations are three kinds of standing plans.[24]

Policies As a general guide for action, a policy is the most general form of standing plan. A **policy** specifies the organization's general response to a designated problem or situation. For example, McDonald's has a policy that it will not grant a franchise to an individual who already owns another fast-food restaurant. Similarly, Starbucks has a policy that it will not franchise at all; the company retains ownership of all Starbucks coffee shops. Likewise, a university admissions office might establish a policy that admission will be granted only to applicants with a minimum SAT score of 1,000 and a ranking in the top quarter of their high school class. Admissions officers may routinely deny

Plan	Description
Single-use plan	Developed to carry out a course of action not likely to be carried out in the future
Program	Single-use plan for a large set of activities
Project	Single-use plan of less scope and complexity than a program
Standing plan	Developed for activities that recur regularly over a period of time
Policy	Standing plan specifying the organization's general response to a designated problem or situation
Standard operating procedure	Standing plan outlining steps to be followed in particular circumstances
Rules and regulations	Standing plans describing exactly how specific activities are to be carried out

TABLE 7.1
Types of Operational Plans

Organizations develop various operational plans to help achieve operational goals. In general, there are two types of single-use plans and three types of standing plans.

program A single-use plan for a large set of activities
project A single-use plan of less scope and complexity than a program

standing plan A plan for activities that recur regularly over a period of time

policy A standing plan that specifies the organization's general response to a designated problem or situation

Many surgeons rely heavily on standard operating procedures. For example, these doctors specialize in hip replacement surgeries. A modified industrial robot, shown above the skeleton, is used to drill a precise hole in a femur so that the implant can be fitted exactly as the doctors want it. A clearly defined set of procedures guides the team through every surgery it conducts. At the same time, however, the doctors are also prepared to deviate from established procedures as circumstances warrant.

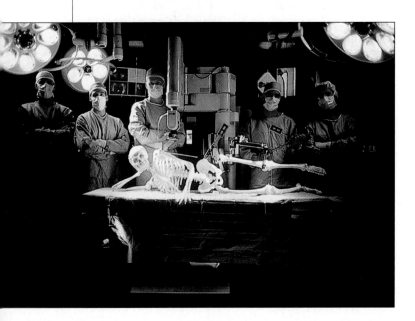

standard operating procedure (SOP) A standing plan that outlines the steps to be followed in a particular circumstance

rules and regulations Describe exactly how specific activities are to be carried out

admission to applicants who fail to reach these minimums. A policy is also likely to describe how exceptions are to be handled. The university's policy statement, for example, might create an admissions appeals committee to evaluate applicants who do not meet minimum requirements but may warrant special consideration.

Standard Operating Procedures Another type of standing plan is the **standard operating procedure**, or **SOP**. An SOP is more specific than a policy in that the former outlines the steps to be followed in particular circumstances. The admissions clerk at the university, for example, might be told that when an application is received, he or she should (1) set up a file for the applicant; (2) add test-score records, transcripts, and letters of reference to the file as they are received; and (3) give the file to the appropriate admissions director when it is complete. Gallo Vineyards in California has a three-hundred-page manual of standard operating procedures. This planning manual is credited with making Gallo one of the most efficient wine operations in the United States.[25] McDonald's has SOPs explaining exactly how Big Macs are to be cooked, how long they can stay in the warming rack, and so forth. "The Quality Challenge" describes how the up-and-coming retailer Costco uses standard operating procedures in its quest for value and customer service.

Rules and Regulations The narrowest of the standing plans, **rules and regulations** describe exactly how specific activities are to be carried out. Rather than guiding decision making, rules and regulations actually take the place of decision making in various situations. Each McDonald's restaurant has a rule prohibiting customers from using its telephones, for example. The university admissions office might have a rule stipulating that if an applicant's file is not complete two months before the beginning of a semester, the student cannot be admitted until the next semester. Of course, in most organizations a manager at a higher level can suspend or bend the rules. If the high school transcript of the child of a prominent university alumnus and donor arrives a few days late, the director of admissions would probably waive the two-month rule. Rules and regulations can become problematic if they are excessive or enforced too rigidly.

Rules and regulations and SOPs are similar in many ways. They are both relatively narrow in scope, and each can serve as a substitute for decision making. An SOP typically describes a sequence of activities, however, whereas rules and regulations focus on one activity. Recall our examples: the admissions-desk SOP consisted of three activities, whereas the two-month rule related to one activity only. In an industrial setting, the SOP for orienting a new employee could involve enrolling the person in various benefit options, introducing him or her to coworkers and supervisors, and providing a tour of the facilities. A pertinent rule for the new employee might involve when to come to work each day.

Costco Closes In

Although Wal-Mart is still the biggest bully on the retailing block, an up-and-coming upstart, Costco, has the discounting powerhouse looking over its shoulder. Costco runs a growing chain of warehouse stores, similar to Sam's Clubs (a Wal-Mart subsidiary). The numbers speak for themselves: even though Sam's has more than 40 percent more members and 70 percent more stores than Costco, Costco has higher sales revenues.

Costco has achieved this enviable status through an astute mixture of standard operating procedures geared to providing a high-quality experience to customers while maintaining an acceptable level of performance. Sam's, in contrast, pays more attention to profits and a bit less to customer service and quality.

Costco's standard operating procedures are evident in its product mix (it stocks only products that sell at a minimum level over a trial period), its inventory management

"Not respecting the customer."

Jeffrey Brotman, Costco CEO, in answer to the question: What could get a Costco employee in trouble?*

system (inventory is constantly checked and older products are quickly sold to avoid a total loss), its sales operations (point-of-sale computers constantly monitor sales figures), and even its member-screening procedures. For example, each prospective Costco member is required to complete a comprehensive membership application. Analysts then check the applicant's credit history, legal history, and income before approving the individual membership. This screening keeps bad checks to a minimum and has reduced pilferage to only 0.2 percent of sales, a phenomenally low level. And the firm uses the extra revenues that this cost-control generates to invest more and more in employee training geared to customer service.

References: *Tim W. Ferguson, "A Revolution That Has a Long Way to Go," Forbes, August 11, 1997, pp. 106–112 (*quote on page 111).*

MANAGEMENT IMPLICATIONS Managers need to understand the various kinds of operating plans that organizations use. This understanding should enable managers to better assess when to use operating plans. At the same time, managers should be flexible in how they use operating plans. ▬

Managing Goal-Setting and Planning Processes

Obviously, all of the elements of goal setting and planning discussed so far involve managing these processes in some way or another. In addition, however, because major barriers sometimes impede effective goal setting and planning, knowing how to overcome some of the barriers is important.

■ Barriers to Goal Setting and Planning

Several circumstances can serve as barriers to effective goal setting and planning; the more common ones are listed in Table 7.2.

Inappropriate Goals   Inappropriate goals come in many forms. Paying a large dividend to stockholders may be inappropriate if it comes at the expense of research and development. Goals may also be inappropriate if they are unattainable. If Chrysler set a goal of selling more cars than General Motors sells next year, people at Chrysler would probably be embarrassed because achieving such a goal would be impossible. Goals may also be inappropriate if they place too much emphasis on either quantitative or qualitative measures of success. Some goals, especially those relating to financial areas, are quantifiable, objective, and verifiable. Other goals, such as employee satisfaction and development, are difficult if not impossible to quantify. Organizations are asking for trouble if they put too much emphasis on one type of goal to the exclusion of the other.

Improper Reward System   In some settings, an improper reward system acts as a barrier to goal setting and planning. For example, people may inadvertently be rewarded for poor goal-setting behavior or go unrewarded or even be punished for proper goal-setting behavior. Suppose that a manager sets a goal of decreasing turnover next year. If turnover is decreased by even a fraction, the manager can claim success and perhaps be rewarded for the accomplishment. In contrast, a manager who attempts to decrease turnover by 5 percent but actually achieves a decrease of only 4 percent may receive a smaller reward because of her or his failure to reach the established goal. And if an organization places too much emphasis on short-term performance and results, managers may ignore longer-term issues as they set goals and formulate plans to achieve higher profits in the short-term.

TABLE 7.2
Barriers to Goal Setting and Planning

As part of managing the goal-setting and planning processes, managers must understand the barriers that can disrupt them. Managers must also know how to overcome the barriers.

Major barriers	Inappropriate goals
	Improper reward system
	Dynamic and complex environment
	Reluctance to establish goals
	Resistance to change
	Constraints
Overcoming the barriers	Understanding the purposes of goals and planning
	Communication and participation
	Consistency, revision, and updating
	Effective reward systems

Dynamic and Complex Environment   The nature of an organization's environment is also a barrier to effective goal setting and planning. Rapid change, technological innovation, and intense competition can each increase the difficulty of an organization accurately assessing future opportunities and threats. For example, when an electronics firm like IBM develops a long-range plan, it tries to take into account how much technological innovation is likely to occur during that interval. But forecasting such events is extremely difficult. During the early boom years of personal computers, data were stored primarily on floppy disks. Because these disks had a limited storage capacity, hard disks were developed. Whereas the typical floppy disk can hold hundreds of pages of information, a hard disk can store thousands of pages. Today computers increasingly store information on optical disks that hold millions of pages. The manager attempting to set goals and plan in this rapidly changing environment faces a truly formidable task.

Reluctance to Establish Goals   Another barrier to effective planning is the reluctance of some managers to establish goals for themselves and their units of responsibility. The reason for this reluctance may be lack of confidence or fear of failure. If a manager sets a goal that is specific, concise, and time related, then whether he or she attains it is obvious. Managers who consciously or unconsciously try to avoid this degree of accountability are likely to hinder the organization's planning efforts. Pfizer, a large pharmaceutical company, recently ran into problems because its managers did not set goals for research and development. Consequently, the organization fell further and further behind because managers had no way of knowing how effective their research and development efforts actually were.

Resistance to Change   Another barrier to goal setting and planning is resistance to change. Planning essentially involves changing something about the organization. As we see in Chapter 13, people tend to resist change. Avon Products almost drove itself into bankruptcy several years ago because it insisted on continuing a policy of large dividend payments to its stockholders. When profits started to fall, managers resisted cutting the dividends and started borrowing to pay them. The company's debt grew from $3 million to $1.1 billion in eight years. Eventually, managers were forced to confront the problem and cut dividends.

Constraints   Constraints that limit what an organization can do are another major obstacle to goal setting and planning. Common constraints include a lack of resources, government restrictions, and strong competition. For example, Owens Corning recently took on an enormous debt burden as part of its fight to avoid a takeover by Wickes Companies. The company now has such a large debt that it has been forced to cut back on capital expenditures and research and development. And those cutbacks have greatly constrained what the firm can plan for the future. Time constraints are also a factor. It's easy to say, "I'm too busy to plan today; I'll do it tomorrow." Effective planning takes time, energy, and an unwavering belief in its importance.

■ Overcoming the Barriers

Fortunately, there are several guidelines for making goal setting and planning effective. Some of the guidelines are also listed in Table 7.2.

Understand the Purposes of Goals and Plans   One of the best ways to facilitate the goal-setting and planning processes is to recognize their basic purposes. Managers should also recognize that there are limits to the effectiveness of setting goals and making plans. Planning is not a panacea that will solve all of an organization's problems, nor is it an iron-clad set of procedures to be followed at any cost. And effective goals and planning do not necessarily ensure success; adjustments and exceptions are to be expected as time passes. For example, Coca-Cola followed a logical and rational approach to setting goals and planning a few years ago when it introduced a new formula to combat Pepsi's increasing market share. But all the plans proved to be wrong as consumers rejected the new version of Coca-Cola. Managers quickly reversed the decision and reintroduced the old formula as Coca-Cola Classic. And it has a larger market share today than before. Thus, even though careful planning resulted in a big mistake, the company came out ahead in the long run.

Communication and Participation   Although goals and plans may be initiated at high levels in the organization, they must also be communicated to others in the organization. Everyone involved in the planning process should know what the overriding organizational strategy is, what the various functional strategies are, and how they are all to be integrated and coordinated. People responsible for achieving goals and implementing plans must have a voice in developing them from the outset. These individuals almost always have valuable information to contribute, and because they will be implementing the plans, their involvement is critical: people are usually more committed to plans that they have helped shape. Even when an organization is somewhat centralized or uses a planning staff, managers from a variety of levels in the organization should be involved in the planning process. When Compaq Computer Corp. recently set a strategic goal of moving from the number five to the number three position in the computer industry by the year 2000, the company developed a detailed brochure explaining the goal and how it was to be achieved, and distributed the brochure to every employee.

Consistency, Revision, and Updating   Goals should be consistent both horizontally and vertically. *Horizontal consistency* means that goals should be consistent across the organization, from one department to the next. *Vertical consistency* means that goals should be consistent up and down the organization—strategic, tactical, and operational goals must agree with one another. Because goal setting and planning are dynamic processes, they must also be revised and updated regularly. Many organizations are seeing the need to revise and update on an increasingly frequent basis. Citicorp, for example, used to use a three-year planning horizon for developing and providing new financial services. That cycle has been cut to two years, and the bank hopes to reduce it to one year very soon.

Effective Reward Systems   In general, people should be rewarded both for establishing effective goals and plans and for successfully achieving them. Because failure sometimes results from factors outside the manager's control, however, people should also be assured that failure to reach a goal will not necessarily bring punitive consequences. Frederick Smith, founder and CEO of Federal Express, has a stated goal of encouraging risk. Thus when Federal Express lost $233 million on an unsuccessful new service called ZapMail, no one was punished. Smith believed that the original idea was a good one but was unsuccessful for reasons beyond the company's control.

■ Using Goals to Implement Plans

Goals are often used to implement plans. One widely used method for managing the goal-setting and planning processes concurrently to ensure that both are done effectively is **management by objectives**, or **MBO**. We should also note, however, that although many firms use this basic approach, they frequently tailor it to their own special circumstances and use a special term or name for it. For example, Tenneco Inc. uses an MBO-type system but calls it the Performance Agreement System, or PAS.

The Nature and Purpose of MBO   The purpose of MBO is to give subordinates a voice in the goal-setting and planning processes and to clarify for them exactly what they are expected to accomplish in a given time span. Thus MBO is concerned with goal setting and planning for individual managers and their units or work groups.[26]

The MBO Process   The basic mechanics of the MBO process are shown in Figure 7.5. The MBO process is described here from an ideal perspective. In

management by objectives (MBO)
The process of collaborative goal setting by a manager and subordinate; the extent to which goals are accomplished is a major factor in evaluating and rewarding the subordinate's performance

FIGURE 7.5
The MBO Process

Management by objectives, or MBO, is an effective technique for integrating goal setting and planning. This figure portrays the general steps that most organizations use when they adopt MBO. Of course, most organizations adapt this general process to fit their own unique needs and circumstances.

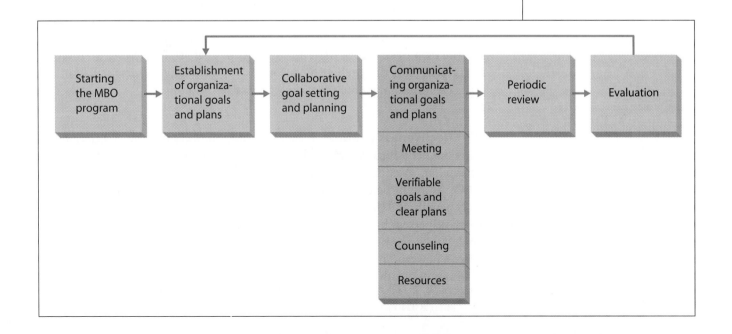

any given organization the steps of the process are likely to vary in importance and may even take a different sequence. As a starting point, however, most managers believe that if an MBO program is to be successful, it must start at the top of the organization. Top managers must communicate why they have adopted MBO, what they think it will do, and that they have accepted and are committed to MBO. Employees must also be educated about what MBO is and what their role in it will be. Having committed to MBO, managers must implement it in a way that is consistent with overall organizational goals and plans. The idea is that goals set at the top will systematically cascade down throughout the organization.

Although establishing the organization's basic goals and plans is extremely important, collaborative goal setting and planning are the essence of MBO. The collaboration involves a series of distinct steps. First, managers tell their subordinates what organizational and unit goals and plans top management has established. Then managers meet with their subordinates on a one-to-one basis to arrive at a set of goals and plans for each subordinate that both the subordinate and the manager have helped develop and to which both are committed. Next the goals are refined to be as verifiable (quantitative) as possible and to specify a time frame for their accomplishment. They should also be written. Further, the plans developed to achieve the goals need to be as clearly stated as possible and directly relate to each goal. Managers must play the role of counselors in the goal-setting and planning meeting. For example, managers must ensure that the subordinate's goals and plans are attainable and workable and that they will facilitate both the unit's and the organization's goals and plans. Finally, the meeting should spell out the resources that the subordinate will need to implement his or her plans and work effectively toward goal attainment.

Conducting periodic reviews as subordinates are working toward their goals is advisable. If the goals and plans are for a one-year period, meeting quarterly to discuss progress may be a good idea. At the end of the period, the manager meets with each subordinate again to review the degree of goal attainment. They discuss which goals were met and which were not met in the context of the original plans. The reasons for both success and failure are explored, and the employee is rewarded on the basis of goal attainment. In an ongoing MBO program, the evaluation meeting may also serve as the collaborative goal-setting and planning meeting for the next time period.

The Effectiveness of MBO   A large number of organizations, including Cypress Semiconductor, Alcoa, Tenneco, Du Pont, General Motors, Boeing, Caterpillar, Westinghouse Electric, and Black & Decker, use some form of MBO. As might be expected, MBO has both strengths and weaknesses. A primary benefit of MBO is improved employee motivation. By clarifying exactly what is expected, by allowing the employee a voice in determining expectations, and by basing rewards on the achievement of those expectations, organizations create a powerful motivational system for their employees.

Communication is also enhanced through the process of discussion and collaboration. And performance appraisals may be done more objectively, with less reliance on arbitrary or subjective assessment. MBO focuses attention on appropriate goals and plans, helps identify superior managerial talent for future promotion, and provides a systematic management philosophy that can have a positive effect on the overall organization. MBO also facilitates control. The periodic development and subsequent evaluation of individual goals and plans helps keep the organization on course toward its own long-run goals and plans.

On the other hand, MBO occasionally fails because of poor implementation. Perhaps the major problem that can derail an MBO program is lack of top-management support. Some organizations decide to use MBO, but then its implementation is delegated to lower management. This approach limits the program's effectiveness because the goals and plans cascading throughout the organization may not actually be the goals and plans of top management and because others in the organization are not motivated to accept and become committed to them. Another problem with MBO is that some firms overemphasize quantitative goals and plans and burden their systems with too much paperwork and record keeping. Some managers will not or cannot sit down and work out goals and plans with their subordinates. Rather, they "suggest" or even "assign" goals and plans to people. The result is resentment and a lack of commitment to the MBO program.[27]

MANAGEMENT IMPLICATIONS Managers need to understand that various barriers to effective goal setting and planning can exist in any organization. They should also, of course, know how to overcome these barriers. Finally, they should recognize that goals can be used to implement plans, especially through a comprehensive goal-setting system like MBO. ■

Summary of Key Points

The planning process is the first basic managerial function that organizations must address. With an understanding of the environmental context, managers develop a number of different types of goals and plans. Decision making is the underlying framework of all planning because every step of the planning process involves a decision.

Goals serve four basic purposes: to provide guidance and direction, to facilitate planning, to inspire motivation and commitment, and to promote evaluation and control. Kinds of goals can be differentiated by level, area, and time frame. All managers within an or-

ganization need to be involved in the goal-setting process. Managers need to pay special attention to the importance of managing multiple goals through optimizing and other approaches.

Goals are closely related to planning. The major types of plans are strategic, tactical, and operational. Plans are developed across a variety of time horizons, including long-range, intermediate, and short-range time frames. Essential people in an organization responsible for effective planning are the planning staff, planning task forces, the board of directors, the CEO, the executive committee, and line management. Contingency planning helps managers anticipate and plan for unexpected changes.

After plans have been developed, the manager must address how they will be achieved. This often involves tactical and operational plans. Tactical plans are at the middle of the organization and have an intermediate time horizon and moderate scope. Tactical plans are developed to implement specific parts of a strategic plan. They must flow from strategy, specify resource and time issues, and commit human resources. Tactical plans must be effectively executed.

Operational plans are at the lower levels of the organization, have a shorter time horizon, and are narrower in scope. Operational plans are derived from a tactical plan and are aimed at achieving one or more operational goals. Two major types of operational plans are single-use and standing plans. Single-use plans are designed to carry out a course of action that is not likely to be repeated in the future. Programs and projects are examples of single-use plans. Standing plans are designed to carry out a course of action that is likely to be repeated several times. Policies, standard operating procedures, and rules and regulations are all standing plans.

Several barriers exist to effective goal setting and planning. These include inappropriate goals, an improper reward system, a dynamic and complex environment, reluctance to establish goals, resistance to change, and various constraints. Methods for overcoming these barriers include understanding the purposes of goals and plans; communication and participation; consistency, revision, and updating; and an effective reward system. One particularly useful technique for managing goal setting and planning is management by objectives, or MBO. MBO is a process of collaborative goal setting and planning.

Discussion Questions

Questions for Review

1. Describe the nature of organizational goals. Be certain to include both the purposes and kinds of goals.

2. What is contingency planning? Is being flexible about your plans the same as contingency planning? Why or why not?

3. What is tactical planning? What is operational planning? What are the similarities and differences between them?

4. What are the barriers to goal setting and planning? How can they be overcome? Can you think of any ways to overcome the barriers other than the ways identified in the text?

Questions for Analysis

5. Almost by definition, organizations cannot accomplish all of their goals. Why?

6. Which kind of plan—tactical or operational— should an organization develop first? Why? Does the order of development really make a difference as long as plans of both types are made?

7. Think of examples of each type of operational plan you have used at work, in your school work, or even in your personal life.

Questions for Application

8. Interview the head of the department in which you are majoring. What kinds of goals exist for the department and for the members of the department? Share your findings with the rest of the class.

9. Interview a local small-business manager about the time frames for planning that he or she uses. How do your results compare with what you might have expected from the presentation in the textbook?

10. Interview a college or university official to determine the use of single-use and standing plans at your institution. How were these plans developed?

EXERCISE OVERVIEW

Conceptual skills refer to a person's abilities to think in the abstract. This exercise will help you develop your conceptual skills by relating your own personal goals and plans across various time frames.

EXERCISE BACKGROUND

Most people have a general idea of what they want their future to be like. However, few people actually take the time to formulate specific goals and plans for their future. To do so might provide a useful blueprint for achieving those goals and also help people better understand the likelihood of various goals actually coming to fruition.

EXERCISE TASK

With the preceding background information as context, do the following:

1. Make a list of ten goals that you want to achieve in ten years. These goals might relate to work, family, or anything else you see as important.

2. Make a list of five-year goals that you must meet to be at the halfway point in achieving your long-term goals.

3. Repeat the list for each of the next five years.

4. Evaluate the likelihood of actually being able to achieve the one-year goals, the five-year goals, and the ten-year goals.

5. How might this process be similar to and different from a manager doing the same thing for business goals?

EXERCISE OVERVIEW

Time-management skills refer to the manager's ability to prioritize work, to work efficiently, and to delegate appropriately. This exercise will help you develop your time-management skills by relating them to the process of goal optimization.

EXERCISE BACKGROUND

All managers face a myriad of goals, challenges, opportunities, and demands on their time. Juggling all of these requires a clear understanding of priorities, time availability, and related factors. Assume that you are planning to open your own business, a retail store in a local shopping mall. You are starting from scratch, with no prior business connections. You do, however, have a strong and impressive business plan that you know will work.

In planning your business, you know that you need to meet with the following parties:

- The mall manager, to negotiate a lease

- A local banker, to arrange partial financing

- An attorney, to incorporate your business

- An accountant, to set up a bookkeeping system

- Suppliers, to arrange credit terms and delivery schedules

- An advertising agency, to start promoting your business

- A staffing agency, to hire employees

- A design firm, to plan the physical layout of the store

EXERCISE TASK

With the preceding background information as context, do the following:

1. Develop a schedule listing the sequence in which you need to meet with the eight parties. Your schedule should minimize backtracking (that is, seeing one party and then having to see him or her again after seeing someone else).

2. Compare your schedule with that of a classmate and discuss differences.

3. Are different schedules equally valid?

Building Effective Communication Skills

EXERCISE OVERVIEW

Communication skills refer to the manager's abilities to both effectively convey ideas and information to others and effectively receive ideas and information from others. Communicating goals is an important part of management, and doing so requires strong communication skills.

EXERCISE BACKGROUND

Assume that you are the CEO of a large discount retailing company. You have decided that your firm needs to change its strategy in order to survive. Specifically, you want the firm to move away from discount retailing and more into specialty retailing.

To make this change, you know that you will need to close four hundred of your twelve hundred discount stores within the next year. You also need to both increase the expansion rate of your two existing specialty chains and launch one new chain. Your tentative plans call for opening three hundred new specialty stores in one business and 150 in the other next year. In addition, you want to finalize the basic concept for the new chain and to open ten stores next year. Finally, although you will be able to transfer some discount-store employees to specialty retail jobs, the new plan will put a few hundred people out of work.

EXERCISE TASK

With the preceding background information as context, do the following:

1. Write a press release that outlines these goals.

2. Determine the best way to communicate the goals to your employees.

3. Develop a contingency plan for dealing with problems.

CHAPTER CLOSING CASE

Campbell Plans for the Future

Campbell Soup Co. began in 1869 as a food canning and preserving business. Quality was a watchword from the beginning, and Campbell soon built a solid reputation as a dependable and effective enterprise. The company really took off in 1897, however, when one of its chemists discovered how to "condense" soup by removing most of the water. This condensing process allowed the company to begin selling soup in smaller and more efficient packaging options, with the consumer reconstituting the soup by adding water at home.

Campbell continued to grow slowly and steadily, and the Campbell brand name became one of the most recognized in the United States. Indeed, pop artist Andy Warhol's 1960 print illustrating a can of Campbell soup became an American icon. But although the company has always performed solidly, it never really took off with periods of rapid growth and was always seen as being an underachiever in international markets.

In the late 1980s, the firm's board of directors grew tired of its less-than-spectacular performance and decided to take drastic action. The firm concluded that there was no prime leadership candidate among Campbell's existing top managers and thus decided to look outside for help. After an extensive search, the board hired David Johnson away from Gerber Products Co. to take over as CEO and gave him a mandate to shake the firm out of the doldrums.

And so far, Johnson's efforts have resulted in dramatically improved performance. The key to the turnaround, he says, is that he focuses everything the firm does on a single overriding goal—to continually increase net earnings faster than competitors. Johnson believes that returns to shareholders is the single most important criterion of effectiveness, so he thinks it only appropriate to keep the goal of net earnings central to the firm's operations. Indeed, scoreboards comparing Campbell's earnings gains with other food processing companies are scattered throughout the company—in its corporate offices, in its factories, and in its warehouses and distribution centers. The idea is to continually remind employees of what the firm's CEO sees as important.

Of course, Johnson relies on other goals as well, but they are all developed to support the overarching goal of earnings growth. For example, he sets goals each quarter for growth in earnings per share, profitability, and overall revenue growth. He also stresses market share growth. For example, Campbell sells 80 percent of the canned soup in the United States; Johnson wants to increase share to 90 percent.

Johnson also stresses international growth. Even though the firm is doing well in its home market, international sales are still disappointing. Johnson concedes that Campbell will be hard-pressed to catch entrenched market leaders such as Nestlé and Heinz in Europe, but thinks that Asia, a market just awakening to processed foods, represents a major opportunity for the firm. Consequently, Campbell Soup has several joint ventures underway in Asia and is investing heavily in plants and distribution networks throughout the region.

To really motivate his team, Johnson has tied financial incentives to goal attainment. Indeed, the top twelve hundred managers at Campbell all have significant bonus potential tied to reaching and exceeding Johnson's yearly goals. He also requires the firm's three hundred most senior executives to hold substantial amounts of company stock, usually one-half to three times their annual salary. Johnson argues that this financial

stake will reinforce their commitment to only doing things that are in the long-term best interests of shareholders, since they themselves have a lot riding on Campbell's stock performance!

Case Questions

1. What roles are goals playing at Campbell Soup today?
2. What kinds of plans does Campbell Soup need to develop in order to meet its goals?
3. What problems might Campbell encounter in the future as a result of its emphasis on meeting financial goals?

Case References: Linda Grant, "Stirring It up at Campbell," *Fortune*, May 13, 1996, pp. 80–86; and "Changing Tastes Dent Campbell's Canned-Soup Sales," *Wall Street Journal*, April 28, 1998, pp. B1, B23.

CHAPTER NOTES

1. "The Swoosh Heard 'Round the World," *Business Week*, May 12, 1997, pp. 76–80; "Can Nike Get Unstuck?" *Time*, March 30, 1998, pp. 48–53; John Wyatt, "Is It Time to Jump on Nike?" *Fortune*, May 26, 1997, pp. 185–186; and "Nike Plans to Swoosh Into Sports Equipment But It's a Tough Game," *Wall Street Journal*, January 16, 1998, pp. A1, A10.

2. Max D. Richards, *Setting Strategic Goals and Objectives*, 2nd ed. (St. Paul, Minn.: West, 1986).

3. "GE, No. 2 in Appliances, Is Agitating to Grab Share from Whirlpool," *Wall Street Journal*, July 2, 1997, pp. A1, A6.

4. Kenneth R. Thompson, Wayne A. Hochwarter, and Nicholas J. Mathys, "Stretch Targets: What Makes Them Effective?" *Academy of Management Executive*, August 1997, pp. 48–57.

5. "A Methodical Man," *Forbes*, August 11, 1997, pp. 70–72.

6. John A. Pearce II and Fred David, "Corporate Mission Statements: The Bottom Line," *Academy of Management Executive*, May 1987, p. 109.

7. "How H-P Used Tactics of the Japanese to Beat Them at Their Game," *Wall Street Journal*, September 8, 1994, pp. A1, A6.

8. "'The McDonald's of Toiletries,'" *Business Week*, August 4, 1997, pp. 79–80.

9. "Nike Catches Up with the Trendy Frontrunner," *Business Week*, October 24, 1988, p. 88.

10. Jeffrey B. Vancouver, Roger E. Millsap, and Patricia A. Peters, "Multilevel Analysis of Organizational Goal Congruence," *Journal of Applied Psychology*, Vol. 79, No. 5, 1994, pp. 666–679.

11. "Home Depot: Beyond Do-It-Yourselfers," *Business Week*, June 30, 1997, pp. 86–88.

12. See Charles Hill and Gareth Jones, *Strategic Management*, 4th ed. (Boston: Houghton Mifflin, 1998).

13. *Hoover's Handbook of World Business 1997* (Austin, Texas: Hoover's Business Press, 1996), pp. 330.

14. "Nissan's Slow U-Turn," *Business Week*, May 12, 1997, pp. 54–55.

15. Peter Lorange and Balaji S. Chakravarthy, *Strategic Planning Systems*, 2nd ed. (Englewood Cliffs, N.J.: Prentice-Hall, 1989).

16. Carla Rapoport, "The World's Most Valuable Company," *Fortune*, October 10, 1988, pp. 92–104.

17. Richard I. Kirkland Jr., "Outsider's Guide to Europe in 1992," *Fortune*, October 24, 1988, pp. 121–127.

18. K. A. Froot, D. S. Scharfstein, and J. C. Stein, "A Framework for Risk Management," *Harvard Business Review*, November–December 1994, pp. 91–102.

19. See Donald C. Hambrick and David Lei, "Toward an Empirical Prioritization of Contingency Variables for Business Strategy," *Academy of Management Journal*, December 1985, pp. 763–788.

20. James Brian Quinn, Henry Mintzberg, and Robert M. James, *The Strategy Process* (Englewood Cliffs, N.J.: Prentice-Hall, 1988).

21. Vasudevan Ramanujam and N. Venkatraman, "Planning System Characteristics and Planning Effectiveness," *Strategic Management Journal*, Vol. 8, No. 2, 1987, pp. 453–468.

22. John Huey, "The World's Best Brand," *Fortune*, May 31, 1993, pp. 44–54.

23. J. Huey, "The World's Best Brand."

24. Thomas L. Wheelon and J. David Hunger, *Strategic Management and Business Policy*, 5th ed. (Reading, Mass.: Addison-Wesley, 1995).

25. Jaclyn Fierman, "How Gallo Crushes the Competition," *Fortune*, September 1, 1986, pp. 23–31.

26. Stephen J. Carroll and Henry L. Tosi, *Management by Objectives* (New York: Macmillan, 1973); and A. P. Raia, *Managing by Objectives* (Glenview, Ill.: Scott, Foresman, 1974).

27. For a review of the strengths and weaknesses of MBO, see Jack N. Kondrasuk, "Studies in MBO Effectiveness," *Academy of Management Review*, July 1981, pp. 419–430.

8

Managing Strategy and Strategic Planning

OBJECTIVES

After studying this chapter, you should be able to:

- Discuss the components of strategy, types of strategic alternatives, and the distinction between strategy formulation and strategy implementation.
- Describe how to use SWOT analysis in formulating strategy.
- Identify and describe various alternative approaches to business-level strategy formulation.
- Describe how business-level strategies are implemented.
- Identify and describe various alternative approaches to corporate-level strategy formulation.
- Describe how corporate-level strategies are implemented.

The 1960s were turbulent times. The war in Vietnam, college campus protests, desegregation, and the emergence of the feminist movement each contributed to a prevailing sense of unrest and social upheaval. But ubiquitous to the sixties was a set of cultural icons that today are still associated with that era: hippies, tie-died shirts, bell-bottom jeans, and the two "Beatles"—the musical group (the Beatles) and the car (the venerable Volkswagen Beetle).

Volkswagen, a German firm, hopes to recapture some of the sixties' glory when it relaunches the Beetle in 1998. But the image sought by the company this time is far different from the one it had several decades ago. To best understand what Volkswagen wants to accomplish—and why—its instructive to first examine the car's past.

Volkswagen began producing the car in 1938. The *New York Times* promptly dubbed it the Beetle because of its rounded shape and design. The first Beetles were actually shipped to the United States in 1949, selling for $800. The cars quickly became popular because of their low price and reputation for dependability. In 1968 U.S. sales of the Beetle peaked at 423,008, and four years later the 15,007,034th Beetle rolled off the assembly line, surpassing the Ford Model T as the most produced car in history. But as sales declined, Volkswagen stopped selling the Beetle in 1979, deciding instead to concentrate on newer models. The last one sold for $6,495, still among the lowest priced cars in the country at the time. But the Beetle lived on in the hearts and minds of consumers, again harkening back to the low prices and dependable service.

"We're not a real entry-level car producer anymore, as we were in the Beetle days. In the States, the perception of the customer has not followed that."

Jens Neumann, Volkswagen executive, quoted in USA Today, July 11, 1997, p. 1B.

Volkswagen's fortunes, meanwhile, began to slowly deteriorate. One model after another floundered in the U.S. market, and by 1970 its market share had dropped below 1 percent. Meanwhile, however, back in Europe Volkswagen was undergoing a very successful renaissance. The same models that were rejected in the United States were catching on in other parts of the world. In addition, the firm acquired Audi, an upscale manufacturer known in Germany for high-quality, higher-priced automobiles.

Volkswagen used the technology it acquired with Audi to continue to upgrade the quality of its other products. And slowly but surely, the firm's image gravitated upward in Europe until it became almost as respected as BMW and Mercedes-Benz. And today, Volkswagen's fortunes have improved to the point where it is both widely respected in its homeland and highly profitable throughout the world—except in the United States.

The firm is again turning its attention to the market where the Beetle once ruled. But this time Volkswagen wants to transplant its upscale image from Europe into the United States. If the company is successful, it will be able to charge higher prices for its cars and thus earn more profits. It's a calculated risk, of course, to hinge the new initiative on the car so long associated with low prices. But Volkswagen believes that the reputation of the Beetle will serve as a magnet to lure consumers from all walks of life into Volkswagen showrooms where the auto maker can display its high-quality product line.[1]

The actions taken by Volkswagen reflect one of the most critical functions that managers perform for their businesses: strategy and strategic planning. Back in the 1960s the firm had the "perfect" product, its Beetle. But as the market changed, demand for this product began to decline. Since the firm did little to change the Beetle to keep pace with the market, its fortunes suffered. But Volkswagen managers are now looking at ways to reposition the new Beetle and their other products in today's markets to better meet customer needs and preferences.

This chapter discusses how organizations manage strategy and strategic planning. We begin by examining the nature of strategic management, including its components and alternatives. We then describe the kinds of analyses needed for firms to formulate their strategies. Next we examine how organizations first formulate and then implement business-level strategies. Finally, we examine how corporate-level strategies are formulated and implemented.

The Nature of Strategic Management

strategy A comprehensive plan for accomplishing an organization's goals

strategic management A comprehensive and ongoing management process aimed at formulating and implementing effective strategies; it is a way of approaching business opportunities and challenges

effective strategy A strategy that promotes a superior alignment between the organization and its environment and the achievement of strategic goals

distinctive competence An organizational strength possessed by only a small number of competing firms

scope When applied to strategy, scope specifies the range of markets in which an organization will compete

resource deployment How an organization distributes its resources across the areas in which it competes

A **strategy** is a comprehensive plan for accomplishing an organization's goals. **Strategic management**, in turn, is a way of approaching business opportunities and challenges—it is a comprehensive and ongoing management process aimed at formulating and implementing effective strategies. Finally, **effective strategies** are those that promote a superior alignment between the organization and its environment and the achievement of strategic goals.[2]

■ The Components of Strategy

In general, a well-conceived strategy addresses three areas: distinctive competence, scope, and resource deployment. A **distinctive competence** is something the organization does exceptionally well. (We discuss distinctive competencies more fully later.) The distinctive competence of The Limited, Inc., a large clothing chain, is its speed in moving inventory. The Limited tracks consumer preferences daily with point-of-sale computers, transmits orders to suppliers in Hong Kong electronically, charters 747s to fly products to the United States, and has products in stores forty-eight hours later. Because other retailers take weeks or sometimes months to accomplish the same things, The Limited relies on this distinctive competence to stay ahead of its competition.[3]

The **scope** of a strategy specifies the range of markets in which an organization will compete. Hershey Foods has essentially restricted its scope to the confectionery business, with a few related activities in other food-processing areas. In contrast, its biggest competitor, Mars, has adopted a broader scope by competing in the pet-food business and the electronics industry, among others. Some organizations, called *conglomerates*, compete in dozens or even hundreds of markets.

A strategy should also include an outline of the organization's projected **resource deployment**—how it will distribute its resources across the areas in which it competes. General Electric Co., for example, has been using profits from its highly successful U.S. operations to invest heavily in new businesses in Europe and Asia. Alternatively, the firm might instead have chosen to invest in different industries in its domestic market and/or to invest more heavily in Latin America. The choices it made as to where and how much to invest reflect issues of resource deployment.[4]

[handwritten: A. are / B. want to be / C. How to get there]

■ Types of Strategic Alternatives

Most businesses today also develop strategies at two distinct levels. These levels provide a rich combination of strategic alternatives for organizations. The two general levels are business strategies and corporate strategies. **Business-level strategy** is the set of strategic alternatives that an organization chooses from as it conducts business in a particular industry or a particular market. Such alternatives help the organization focus its competitive efforts for each industry or market in a targeted and focused manner.

> **business-level strategy** The set of strategic alternatives that an organization chooses from as it conducts business in a particular industry or market

Corporate-level strategy is the set of strategic alternatives that an organization chooses from as it manages its operations simultaneously across several industries and several markets.[5] As we discuss later, most large companies today compete in a variety of industries and markets. Thus, although they develop business-level strategies for each industry or market, they also develop an overall strategy that helps define the mix of industries and markets that are of interest to the firm.

> **corporate-level strategy** The set of strategic alternatives that an organization chooses from as it manages its operations simultaneously across several industries and several markets

■ Strategy Formulation and Implementation

Drawing a distinction between strategy formulation and strategy implementation is also instructive. **Strategy formulation** is the set of processes involved in creating or determining the strategies of the organization, whereas **strategy implementation** is the methods by which strategies are *operationalized* or executed within the organization.[6] The primary distinction is along the lines of content versus process: the formulation stage determines what the strategy is, and the implementation stage focuses on how the strategy is achieved.

> **strategy formulation** The set of processes involved in creating or determining the strategies of the organization; it focuses on the content of strategies
>
> **strategy implementation** The methods by which strategies are operationalized or executed within the organization; it focuses on the processes through which strategies are achieved

Sometimes the processes of formulating and implementing strategies is rational, systematic, and planned. This approach is often referred to as a **deliberate strategy**—a plan chosen and implemented to support specific goals.[7] "Today's Management Issues" discusses the reemergence of deliberate strategy as an important management function. Texas Instruments Incorporated (TI) excels at formulating and implementing deliberate strategies. TI uses a planning process that assigns to most senior managers two distinct responsibilities: an operational, short-term responsibility and a strategic, long-term responsibility. Thus one manager may be responsible for both increasing the efficiency of semiconductor operations over the next year (operational, short term) and investigating new materials for semiconductor manufacture in the twenty-first century (strategic, long term). TI's objective is to help managers make short-term operational decisions while keeping in mind longer-term goals and objectives.

> **deliberate strategy** A plan of action that an organization chooses and implements to support its mission and goals

Other times, however, organizations use an **emergent strategy**—a pattern of action that develops over time in an organization in the absence of missions

> **emergent strategy** A pattern of action that develops over time in the absence of missions and goals, or despite missions and goals

TODAY'S MANAGEMENT ISSUES

The Merits of Strategy

Back in the 1970s, corporate strategy was usually seen as *the* critical, glamorous, and high-profile activity in many businesses. Highly paid MBAs prowled corporate corridors dispensing advice and offering sage proclamations about what the business should be doing. The prevailing wisdom was that businesses could carefully and deliberately figure out what they wanted to do and how to do it. And strategy consultants were turning away business because there was so much demand for their services.

But in the 1980s, new developments, such as global competition, forced many big companies to retreat from deliberate strategies. Instead, they were forced to concentrate on such tactical issues as improving quality, restructuring, downsizing, reengineering, and restoring lost productivity and competitiveness. A real watershed event occurred when Jack Welch, CEO at General Electric, disbanded that company's glorified two hundred–member planning staff in 1983. If most businesses had a strategy at all, it was often simply to pursue

> *"Most of the business managers are so busy minding their current businesses that it's hard to step out and see threats or opportunities."*
>
> *Srinivas Sukumar, Director of Strategic Planning for HP Labs**

whatever business opportunities emerged during the normal course of events.

But today, deliberate strategy is making a comeback. Bolstered by increasing efficiency and expanding global markets, many businesses are once again actively seeking to identify new market growth opportunities and to then exploit those opportunities in a rational and logical manner. But this reemergence of deliberate strategy is a bit different from earlier times. For example, rather than reconstituting large planning staffs, most companies are involving rank-and-file managers from throughout the organization in the strategic planning process. And just about everybody is committed to the idea of using caution, logic, and rationality in strategic planning, as opposed to pursuing helter-skelter growth and expansion.

References: *"Strategic,"* Business Week, *August 26, 1996, pp. 46–52 (*quote on p. 50); and Ken Blanchard, "The New Bottom Line,"* Entrepreneur, *February 1998, pp. 127–132.*

---

and goals, or despite missions and goals.[8] Implementing emergent strategies involves allocating resources even though an organization has not explicitly chosen its strategies. 3M has at times benefited from emergent strategies. The invention of invisible tape, for instance, provides a good example. Entrepreneurial engineers working independently took the invention to their boss, who concluded that it did not have major market potential because it was not part of an approved research and development plan. Only when the product was evaluated at the highest levels in the organization was it accepted and made part of 3M's product mix. Of course, 3M's Scotch tape became a major success, despite the fact that it arose outside of the firm's established practices. 3M now counts on emergent strategies to help expand its numerous businesses.[9]

SWOT An acronym that stands for strengths, weaknesses, opportunities, and threats

organizational strengths A skill or capability that enables an organization to conceive of and implement its strategies

common strength A skill or capability held by numerous competing firms

MANAGEMENT IMPLICATIONS

Managers need to appreciate the importance of strategy and strategic management in directing their organization through its competitive environment. Part of this appreciation rests on knowing the difference between business- and corporate-level strategy, and part rests on knowing the difference between deliberate and emergent strategy. ▬

Using SWOT Analysis to Formulate Strategy

The starting point in formulating strategy is usually SWOT analysis. **SWOT** is an acronym that stands for strengths, weaknesses, opportunities, and threats. As shown in Figure 8.1, SWOT analysis is a careful evaluation of an organization's internal strengths and weaknesses as well as its environmental opportunities and threats. In SWOT analysis, the best strategies accomplish an organization's mission by (1) exploiting an organization's opportunities and strengths while (2) neutralizing its threats and (3) avoiding (or correcting) its weaknesses.[10]

■ Evaluating an Organization's Strengths

Organizational strengths are skills and capabilities that enable an organization to conceive of and implement its strategies. Sears, for example, already has a network of trained service personnel in place across the country for repairing Sears appliances. Jane Thompson, a Sears executive, recently conceived of a plan to consolidate repair and home-improvement services nationwide under the well-known Sears brand name and to promote it as a general repair operation for all appliances, not just those purchased from Sears. Thus, the firm is capitalizing on existing capabilities and the strength of its name to launch a new operation.[11] Different strategies call on different skills and capabilities. For example, Matsushita Electric has demonstrated strengths in manufacturing and selling consumer electronics under the brand name Panasonic. Matsushita's strength in electronics does not ensure success, however, if the firm expands into insurance, swimming-pool manufacture, or retail. Different strategies such as these (i.e., manufacturing and selling consumer electronics versus selling insurance versus manufacturing swimming pools versus running a retail operation) require different organizational strengths. SWOT analysis divides organizational strengths into two categories: common strengths and distinctive competencies.

Common Organizational Strengths   A **common strength** is an organizational capability possessed by a large number of competing firms. For example, all the major Hollywood film studios possess common strengths in lighting, sound recording, set and costume design, and makeup. *Competitive*

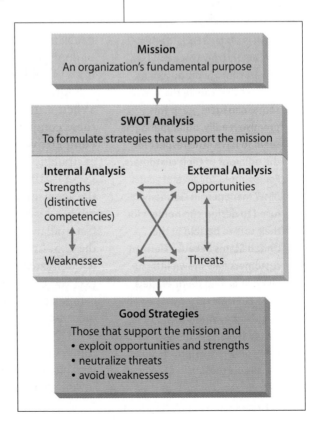

FIGURE 8.1
SWOT Analysis

SWOT analysis is one of the most important steps in formulating strategy. Using the organization's mission as a context, managers assess internal strengths (distinctive competencies) and weaknesses as well as external opportunities and threats. The goal is to then develop good strategies that exploit opportunities and strengths, neutralize threats, and avoid weaknesses.

Mission
An organization's fundamental purpose

SWOT Analysis
To formulate strategies that support the mission

Internal Analysis
Strengths
(distinctive
competencies)

Weaknesses

External Analysis
Opportunities

Threats

Good Strategies
Those that support the mission and
• exploit opportunities and strengths
• neutralize threats
• avoid weaknessess

parity exists when large numbers of competing firms are able to implement the same strategy. In this situation organizations generally attain only average levels of performance. Thus a film company that exploits only its common strengths in choosing and implementing strategies is not likely to go beyond average performance.

Distinctive Competencies A distinctive competence is a strength possessed by only a small number of competing firms. Distinctive competencies are rare among a set of competitors. George Lucas' well-known company Industrial Light and Magic (ILM), for example, has taken the cinematic art of special effects to new heights. Some of ILM's special effects can be produced by no other organization; these rare special effects are thus ILM's distinctive competencies. Organizations that exploit their distinctive competencies often obtain a *competitive advantage* and attain above-normal economic performance.[12]

Indeed, a main purpose of SWOT analysis is to discover an organization's distinctive competencies so that the organization can choose and implement strategies that exploit its unique organizational strengths.

Imitation of Distinctive Competencies An organization that possesses distinctive competencies and exploits them in the strategies it chooses can expect to obtain a competitive advantage and above-normal economic performance. However, its success will lead other organizations to duplicate these advantages. **Strategic imitation** is the practice of duplicating another firm's distinctive competence and thereby implementing a valuable strategy.

Although some distinctive competencies can be imitated, others cannot be. When a distinctive competence cannot be imitated, strategies that exploit these competencies generate sustained competitive advantages. A **sustained competitive advantage** is a competitive advantage that exists after all attempts at strategic imitation have ceased.[13]

A distinctive competence might not be imitated for three reasons. First, the acquisition or development of the distinctive competence may depend on unique historical circumstances that other organizations cannot replicate. Caterpillar Inc., for example, obtained a sustained competitive advantage when the U.S. Army granted it a long-term contract during World War II. The army felt obligated to offer this contract because of the acute international construction requirements necessary to meet the army's needs.[14] Caterpillar's current competitors, including Komatsu and Deere & Company, cannot re-create these circumstances.

Second, a distinctive competence might be difficult to imitate because competing firms might not know or understand its nature and character. The Procter & Gamble Co., for example, considers that its sustained competitive advantage is based on its manufacturing practices. Large sections of Procter &

A key part of strategic management and environmental alignment is understanding what customers truly want and how to best provide products and services that satisfy them. While some managers grasp this premise readily, other managers seem to have little respect for the opinions of their customers. For example, for several years, BMW managers in Germany refused to design cup holders for their cars to be sold in the United States because German customers had shown little interest in having them. While a cup holder is really a very small thing, some BMW dealers reported that customers opted for their competitors' products for this simple reason.

Gamble's plants are screened off to keep this information secure. Similarly, ILM refuses to disclose how it creates some of its special effects.

Finally, a distinctive competence can be difficult to imitate if it is based on complex social phenomena, such as organizational teamwork or culture. Competing organizations may know, for example, that a firm's success is directly traceable to the teamwork among its managers but, because teamwork is a difficult thing to create, organizations may not be able to imitate this distinctive competence.

strategic imitation The practice of duplicating another organization's distinctive competence and thereby implementing a valuable strategy

sustained competitive advantage A competitive advantage that exists after all attempts at strategic imitation have ceased

■ Evaluating an Organization's Weaknesses

Organizational weaknesses are skills and capabilities that do not enable an organization to choose and implement strategies that support its mission. An organization has essentially two ways of addressing weaknesses. First, it may need to make investments to obtain the strengths required to implement strategies that support its mission. Second, the organization may need to modify its mission so that it can be accomplished with the skills and capabilities that the organization already possesses.

In practice, organizations have a difficult time focusing on weaknesses, in part because organization members are often reluctant to admit that they do not possess all the skills and capabilities needed. Evaluating weaknesses also calls into question the judgment of managers who chose the organization's mission in the first place and who failed to invest in the skills and capabilities needed to accomplish it. "Working with Diversity" describes what some observers see as a long-standing weakness in some Japanese and Korean companies.

Organizations that fail either to recognize or overcome their weaknesses are likely to suffer from competitive disadvantages. An organization has a **competitive disadvantage** when it is not implementing valuable strategies that are being implemented by competing organizations. Organizations with a competitive disadvantage can expect to attain below-average levels of performance.

organizational weakness A skill or capability that does not enable an organization to choose and implement strategies that support its mission

competitive disadvantage A situation in which an organization is not implementing valuable strategies that are being implemented by competing organizations

■ Evaluating an Organization's Opportunities and Threats

Whereas evaluating strengths and weaknesses focuses attention on the internal workings of an organization, evaluating opportunities and threats requires analyzing an organization's environment. **Organizational opportunities** are areas that may generate higher performance. **Organizational threats** are areas that increase the difficulty of an organization's performing at a high level. Porter's five-forces model of the competitive environment, as discussed in Chapter 3, can be used to characterize the extent of opportunity and threat in an organization's environment.

Recall that Porter's five forces are level of rivalry, power of suppliers, power of customers, threat of substitutes, and threat of new entrants. In

organizational opportunity An area in the environment that, if exploited, may generate high performance

organizational threat An area in the environment that increases the difficulty of an organization in achieving high performance

Too Little Diversity?

Its no secret, of course, that many businesses from Japan and South Korea have been highly successful in recent years. But interestingly, some experts question whether or not the lack of diversity that exists in those firms will be an advantage or disadvantage in the future.

To see how little diversity exists in some of these businesses, consider the case of Samsung Electronics, a huge Korean business. The firm's board of directors consists of nineteen members, all male. Fifteen of them have worked for the firm for at least twenty years, and eight even attended the same university. Japan's Honda Motor Co. is quite similar—its board is all Japanese, as is every president of each Honda foreign subsidiary.

Executives at these firms defend their hiring and promotion practices. They argue, for example, that their lack of diversity reduces management conflict, smoothes decision making, and ensures that top management is both loyal to

> *"Cohesiveness of corporation is more important to Japanese. They are not well-trained in managing different nationalities. They are more comfortable in [their own] group."*
>
> *Kaoru Kobayashi, Japanese professor**

and knowledgeable about the business. It also enhances cohesiveness among key leaders, since they tend to see things in the same way and to have similar interests.

But critics point out that the lack of diversity also creates problems. For example, some experts contend that executives from Japan and Korea do not understand people from other cultures very well and thus treat them cavalierly and with disdain. By not relying more heavily on foreigners, Japanese and Korean firms may also be less knowledgeable about international laws and regulations. And some critics even predict that the lack of executive diversity may dampen creativity and innovation, potentially causing Japanese and Korean firms to be less competitive in the future.

References: *"Men's Club,"* Wall Street Journal, *September 26, 1996, pp. A1, A8 (*quote on p. A1); "Tight Little Island,"* Forbes, *January 12, 1998, pp. 52–53; and "Seoul is Still Teetering on the Edge,"* Business Week, *January 5, 1998, pp. 56–57.*

---

general, when the level of rivalry, the power of suppliers and customers, and the threat of substitutes and new entrants are all high, an industry has relatively few opportunities and numerous threats. Firms in these types of industries typically have the potential to achieve only normal economic performance. On the other hand, when the level of rivalry, the power of suppliers and customers, and the threat of substitutes and new entrants are all low, then an industry has numerous opportunities and relatively few threats. The potential for above-normal performance exists for organizations within these industries.[15]

MANAGEMENT IMPLICATIONS Managers need to understand how to perform a SWOT analysis. Understanding the differences between common organizational strengths and distinctive competencies can help managers avoid competitive parity and achieve a competitive advantage. Assessing organizational strengths and weaknesses is also a difficult—but very important—part of this process.

Formulating Business-Level Strategies

A number of frameworks have been developed for identifying the major strategic alternatives that organizations should consider when choosing their business-level strategies. Three important classification schemes are Porter's generic strategies, the Miles and Snow typology, and strategies based on the product life cycle.

■ Porter's Generic Strategies

According to Michael Porter, organizations may pursue a differentiation, overall cost leadership, or focus strategy at the business level.[16] Table 8.1 summarizes each of these strategies. An organization that pursues a **differentiation strategy** seeks to distinguish itself from competitors through the quality of its products or services. Firms that successfully implement a differentiation strategy are able to charge more than their competitors can because customers are willing to pay more to obtain the extra value they perceive.[17] Rolex pursues a differentiation strategy. Rolex watches are handmade of gold and stainless steel and are subjected to strenuous tests of quality and reliability. The firm's reputation enables it to charge thousands of dollars for its watches. Other firms that use differentiation strategies are Mercedes-Benz, Nikon, Cross, and Hewlett-Packard. This strategy is also the one that Volkswagen is attempting to adopt as it makes a new push into the U.S. automobile market.

differentiation strategy   A strategy in which an organization seeks to distinguish itself from competitors through the quality of its products or services

TABLE 8.1
Porter's Generic Strategies

Michael Porter has proposed three generic strategies. These strategies, called differentiation, overall cost leadership, and focus, are each presumed to be widely applicable to many different competitive situations.

Strategy Type	Definition	Examples
Differentiation	Distinguish products or services	Rolex (watches) Mercedes-Benz (automobiles) Nikon (cameras) Cross (writing instruments) Hewlett-Packard (hand-held calculators)
Overall cost leadership	Reduce manufacturing and other costs	Timex Hyundai Kodak Bic Texas Instruments
Focus	Concentrate on specific regional market, product market, or group of buyers	Longines Fiat, Alpha Romeo Polaroid Waterman Pens Fisher Price

overall cost leadership strategy A strategy in which an organization attempts to gain a competitive advantage by reducing its costs below the costs of competing firms

An organization implementing an **overall cost leadership strategy** attempts to gain a competitive advantage by reducing its costs below the costs of competing firms. By keeping costs low, the organization is able to sell its products at low prices and still make a profit. Timex uses an overall cost leadership strategy. For decades, this firm has specialized in manufacturing relatively simple, low-cost watches for the mass market. The price of Timex watches, starting around $29.95, is low because of the company's efficient high-volume manufacturing capacity. Other firms that implement overall cost leadership strategies are Hyundai, Eastman Kodak, Bic, and Texas Instruments. This strategy is also the one that Volkswagen used in the 1960s with its popular Beetle.

focus strategy A strategy in which an organization concentrates on a specific regional market, product line, or group of buyers

A firm pursuing a **focus strategy** concentrates on a specific regional market, product line, or group of buyers. This strategy may have either a differentiation focus, whereby the firm differentiates its products in the focus market, or an overall cost leadership focus, whereby the firm manufactures and sells its products at low cost in the focus market. In the watch industry Longines follows a focus differentiation strategy by selling highly jeweled watches to wealthy female consumers. Fiat follows a focus cost leadership strategy by selling its automobiles only in Italy and in selected regions of Europe; Alpha Romeo uses focus differentiation to sell its high-performance cars in these same markets. Fisher-Price uses focus differentiation to sell electronic calculators with large, brightly colored buttons to the parents of preschoolers. And Edward Jones is making a big splash in the stock brokerage industry by focusing on small town settings and avoiding direct competition with Wall Street powerhouses such as Merrill Lynch and Paine Webber in larger cities.[18]

■ The Miles and Snow Typology

A second classification of strategic options was developed by Raymond Miles and Charles Snow.[19] These authors suggested that business-level strategies generally fall into one of four categories: prospector, defender, analyzer, and reactor. Table 8.2 summarizes each of these strategies.

prospector strategy A strategy in which the firm encourages creativity and flexibility and is often decentralized

A firm that follows a **prospector strategy** is a highly innovative firm that is constantly seeking out new markets and new opportunities and is oriented toward growth and risk taking. Over the years, 3M has prided itself on being one of the most innovative major corporations in the world. Employees at 3M are constantly encouraged to develop new products and ideas in a creative and entrepreneurial way. This focus on innovation has led 3M to develop a wide range of new products and markets, including invisible tape and antistain fabric treatments.

defender strategy A strategy in which the firm focuses on lowering costs and improving the performance of current products

Rather than seeking new growth opportunities and innovation, a company that follows a **defender strategy** concentrates on protecting its current markets, maintaining stable growth, and serving current customers. Since the late 1970s, with the maturity of the market for writing instruments, Bic has used this approach—it has adopted a less aggressive, less entrepreneurial style of management and has chosen to defend its substantial market share in the industry. It has done so by emphasizing efficient manufacturing and customer satisfaction.

analyzer strategy A strategy in which the firm attempts to maintain its current businesses and to be somewhat innovative in new businesses

A business that uses an **analyzer strategy** combines elements of prospectors and defenders. Most large companies use this approach because they want

Strategy Type	Definition	Examples
Prospector	Is innovative and growth oriented, searches for new markets and new growth opportunities, encourages risk taking	3M Rubbermaid
Defender	Protects current markets, maintains stable growth, serves current customers	Bic Mrs. Fields
Analyzer	Maintains current markets and current customer satisfaction with moderate emphasis on innovation	IBM DuPont
Reactor	No clear strategy, reacts to changes in the environment, drifts with events	International Harvester in the 1960's and 1970's, Joseph Schlitz Brewing Co., W. T. Grant

TABLE 8.2
The Miles and Snow Typology

The Miles and Snow Typology identifies four strategic types of organizations. Three of these—the Prospector, the Defender, and the Analyzer—can each be effective in certain circumstances. The fourth type—the Reactor—represents an ineffective approach to strategy.

to both protect their base of operations and create new market opportunities. IBM uses analyzer strategies. DuPont is currently using an analyzer strategy. The firm is relying heavily on its existing chemical and fiber operations to fuel its earnings for the foreseeable future. At the same time, though, DuPont is also moving systematically into new business areas such as biotech agriculture and pharmaceuticals.[20]

Finally, a business that follows a **reactor strategy** has no consistent strategic approach; it drifts with environmental events, reacting to but failing to anticipate or influence those events. Not surprisingly, these firms usually do not perform as well as organizations that implement other strategies. Although most organizations would deny using reactor strategies, during the 1960s and 1970s International Harvester Co. (IH) clearly was a reactor. At a time when IH's market for trucks, construction equipment, and agricultural equipment was booming, IH failed to keep pace with its competitors. By the time a recession cut demand for its products, it was too late for IH to respond, and the company lost millions of dollars. The firm was forced to sell off virtually all of its businesses except its truck-manufacturing business. IH moved from being a dominant firm in trucking, agriculture, and construction to a medium-size truck manufacturer because it failed to anticipate changes in its environment.[21]

reactor strategy A strategy in which a firm has no consistent approach to strategy

■ Strategies Based on the Product Life Cycle

The **product life cycle** is a model that shows how sales volume changes over the life of products. Understanding the four stages in the product life cycle

product life cycle A model that portrays how sales volume for products changes over the life of products

FIGURE 8.2
The Product Life Cycle

Managers can use the framework of the product life cycle—introduction, growth, maturity, and decline—to plot strategy. For example, management may decide on a differentiation strategy for a product in the introduction stage and a prospector approach for a product in the growth stage. By understanding this cycle and where a particular product falls within it, managers can develop more effective strategies for extending product life.

helps managers recognize that strategies need to evolve over time. As Figure 8.2 shows, the cycle begins when a new product or technology is introduced. In this *introduction stage*, demand may be very high and sometimes outpaces the firm's ability to supply the product. At this stage, managers need to focus their efforts on "getting product out the door" without sacrificing quality. Managing growth by hiring new employees and managing inventories and cash flow are also concerns during this stage.

During the *growth stage*, more firms begin producing the product, and sales continue to grow. Important management issues include ensuring quality and delivery and beginning to differentiate an organization's product from competitors' products. New entrants into the industry during the growth stage may threaten an organization's competitive advantages; thus strategies to slow the entry of competitors are important.

After a period of growth, products enter a third phase. During this *mature stage*, overall demand growth for a product begins to slow down and the number of new firms producing the product begins to decline. The number of established firms producing the product may also begin to decline. This period of maturity is essential if an organization is going to survive in the long run. Product differentiation concerns are still important during this stage, but keeping costs low and beginning the search for new products or services are also important strategic considerations.

In the *decline stage*, demand for the product or technology decreases, the number of organizations producing the product drops, and total sales drop. Demand often declines because all those who were interested in purchasing a particular product

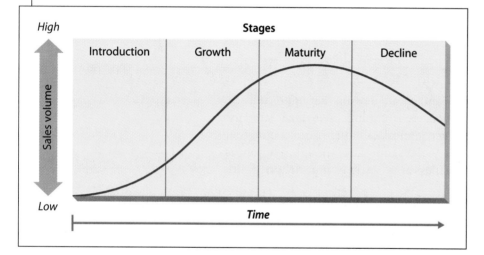

have already done so. Organizations that fail to anticipate the decline stage in earlier stages of the life cycle may go out of business. Those that differentiate their product, keep their costs low, or develop new products or services may do well during this stage. After Volkswagen stopped selling the Beetle in the United States, it continued to make them in Mexico and sell them throughout Latin America for several more years, thus extending the product's life cycle.

MANAGEMENT IMPLICATIONS Managers who formulate business-level strategies can adopt one of three competitive strategies advocated by Porter or one of the three strategies described by Miles and Snow. Managers can also use product life cycles as part of their strategy formulation process. However, they should avoid using a reactor strategy. ▬

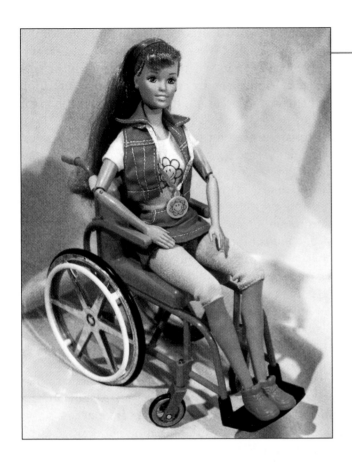

Many effective companies are able to extend the life cycles of their more successful products. The Barbie doll has been a mainstay for Mattel's toy business for years. But the firm is still looking for new opportunities to extend the product's competitive position. For example, in recent years Mattel has introduced Barbies dressed for skiing, dancing, and working out. And the firm has also introduced Barbie playmates from Asia and Latin America. One of its most recent playmates is Becky, a wheelchair-bound friend.

Implementing Business-Level Strategies

As noted earlier, after business strategies are formulated, they must then be implemented. Effective implementation requires managers to integrate the activities of several different functions. *Marketing* and *sales*, for example, are used to promote products or services and the overall public image of the organization (often through various types of advertising), price products or services, directly contact customers, and make sales. *Accounting* and *finance* control the flow of money both within the organization and from outside sources to the organization, and *manufacturing* creates the organization's products or services. Organizational *culture*, as discussed in Chapter 6, also helps firms implement their strategies.

■ Implementing Porter's Generic Strategies

Differentiation and cost leadership can each be directly implemented via these basic organizational functions. (Focus is implemented via the same approaches, but the exact method depends on whether it takes a differentiation or cost leadership perspective).

Implementing business-level strategy can be complicated, especially when it's necessary to make a change. A few years ago, Jeffrey Bezos launched Amazon.com, an Internet-based book retailer. Amazon.com built its business using a differentiation strategy, billing itself as "Earth's biggest bookstore," offering a huge selection of books, stressing ease-of-use, and relying on mail delivery service. But as other big firms, like Barnes & Noble and Amazon.com's own wholesaler, have launched Internet book selling operations themselves, Bezos has found it necessary to shift to a cost leadership strategy to protect his marketshare and fend off these new competitors.

Differentiation Strategy In general, to support differentiation, marketing and sales must emphasize the high-quality, high-value image of the organization's products or services. Neiman-Marcus, a department store for financially secure consumers, has excelled at using marketing to support its differentiation strategy. People do not go to Neiman-Marcus just to buy clothes or to shop for home electronics. Instead, a trip to Neiman-Marcus is advertised as a "total shopping experience." Customers who want to shop for $3,000 dog houses, $50,000 mink coats, and $7,000 exercise machines recognize that the store caters to their needs. Other organizations that have used their marketing function to implement a differentiation strategy include Chanel, Calvin Klein, and Bloomingdale's.

The function of accounting and finance in a business that is implementing a differentiation strategy is to control the flow of funds without discouraging the creativity needed to constantly develop new products and services to meet customer needs. If keeping track of and controlling the flow of money become more important than determining how money and resources are best spent to meet customer needs, then no organization, whether high-technology firm or fashion designer, will be able to implement a differentiation strategy effectively. In manufacturing, a firm implementing a differentiation strategy must emphasize quality and meeting specific customer needs, rather than simply reducing costs. Manufacturing may sometimes have to keep inventory on hand so that customers will have access to products when they want them. Manufacturing also may have to engage in costly customization to meet customer needs.

The culture of a firm implementing a differentiation strategy, like the firm's other functions, must also emphasize creativity, innovation, and response to customer needs. For example, the culture at Lands' End puts the needs of customers ahead of all other considerations. This firm, which sells men's and women's leisure clothes through a catalog service, offers a complete guarantee on merchandise. Dissatisfied customers may return clothes for a full refund or exchange, no questions asked. Lands' End takes orders twenty-four hours a day and will ship most orders within twenty-four hours. Lost buttons and broken zippers are replaced immediately. The priority given to customer needs is typical of an organization that is successfully implementing a differentiation strategy.

Overall Cost Leadership Strategy To support cost leadership, marketing and sales are likely to focus on simple product attributes and how these product attributes meet customer needs in a low-cost and effective manner. These organizations are very likely to engage in advertising. Throughout this effort, however, emphasis is on the value that an organization's products provide for the price, rather than on the special features of the product or service. Advertising for Bic pens ("Writes first time, every time"), Timex watches ("Takes a licking and keeps on ticking"), and Wal-Mart stores ("Always the low price leader") helps these firms implement cost leadership strategies.

Proper emphasis in accounting and finance is also pivotal. Because the success of the organization depends on having costs lower than the competitors' costs, management must take care to reduce costs wherever possible. Tight financial and accounting controls at Wal-Mart, Costco, and MCI have helped these organizations implement cost leadership strategies. Manufacturing typically helps with large runs of highly standardized products. Products are designed both to meet customer needs and to be easily manufactured. Manufacturing emphasizes increased volume of production to reduce the per unit costs of manufacturing. Organizations such as Toshiba (a Japanese semiconductor firm) and Texas Instruments have used this type of manufacturing to implement cost leadership strategies.

The culture of organizations implementing cost leadership strategies tends to focus on improving the efficiency of manufacturing, sales, and other business functions. Managers in these organizations are almost fanatical about keeping their costs low. Wal-Mart appeals to its customers to leave shopping carts in its parking lot with signs that read "Please—help us keep *your* costs low." Fujitsu Electronics, in its Tokyo manufacturing facilities, operates in plain, unpainted cinder-block and cement facilities to keep its costs as low as possible.

■ Implementing Miles and Snow's Strategies

Similarly, a variety of issues must be considered when implementing any of Miles and Snow's strategic options. (Of course, no organization would purposefully choose to implement a reactor strategy.)

Prospector Strategy An organization implementing a prospector strategy is innovative, seeks new market opportunities, and takes numerous risks. To implement this strategy, organizations need to encourage creativity and flexibility. Creativity helps an organization perceive, or even create, new opportunities in its environment; flexibility enables it to change quickly to take advantage of these new opportunities. Organizations often increase creativity and flexibility by adopting a decentralized organization structure. An organization is decentralized when major decision-making responsibility is delegated to middle- and lower-level managers. Johnson & Johnson links decentralization with a prospector strategy. Each of the firm's businesses is organized into a separate unit, and the managers of these units hold full decision-making responsibility and authority. Often these businesses develop new products for new markets. As the new products develop and sales grow, Johnson & Johnson reorganizes so that each new product is managed in a separate unit.

Defender Strategy An organization implementing a defender strategy attempts to protect its market from new competitors. It tends to downplay creativity and innovation in bringing out new products or services and to focus its efforts instead on lowering costs or improving the performance of current products. Often a firm implementing a prospector strategy will switch to a defender strategy. This change occurs when the firm successfully creates a new market or business and then attempts to protect its market from competition. A good example is Mrs. Fields Inc. One of the first firms to introduce high-quality, high-priced cookies, Mrs. Fields sold its product in special cookie stores and grew very rapidly. This success, however, encouraged numerous other companies to enter the market. Increased competition, plus reduced demand for high-priced cookies, has threatened Mrs. Fields' market position. To maintain its profitability, the firm has slowed its growth and is now focusing on making its current operation more profitable. This behavior is consistent with the defender strategy.

Analyzer Strategy An organization implementing an analyzer strategy attempts to maintain its current business and to be somewhat innovative in new businesses. Because the analyzer strategy falls somewhere between the prospector strategy (with focus on innovation) and the defender strategy (with focus on maintaining and improving current businesses), the attributes of organizations implementing the analyzer strategy tend to be similar to both of these other types of organizations. They have tight accounting and financial controls and high flexibility, efficient production and customized products, and creativity and low costs. Organizations maintain these multiple and contradictory processes with difficulty.

One organization that has been able to successfully balance the need for innovation with the need to maintain current businesses is Procter & Gamble. As a major food products company, the firm has established numerous brand-name products, such as Crest toothpaste, Tide laundry detergent, and Sure deodorant. Procter & Gamble must continue to invest in its successful products to maintain financial performance. But the firm must also encourage the development of new products and brand names. In this way, it can continue to expand its market presence and have new products to replace those whose market falls off. Through these efforts, Procter & Gamble can continue to grow.

MANAGEMENT IMPLICATIONS Managers should understand the basic concepts inherent in marketing and sales, accounting and finance, manufacturing, and organization culture. Each concept can play an important role in implementing any of the business-level strategies.

Formulating Corporate-Level Strategies

Most large organizations are engaged in several businesses, industries, and markets. Each business or set of businesses within such an organization is frequently referred to as a *strategic business unit*, or *SBU*. An organization such as General Electric operates hundreds of different businesses, making and selling products as diverse as jet engines, nuclear power plants, and light bulbs. General Electric organizes these businesses into approximately twenty SBUs. Even organizations that sell only one product may operate in several distinct markets. McDonald's sells only fast food, but it competes in markets as diverse as the United States, Europe, Russia, Japan, and South Korea.

Decisions about which businesses, industries, and markets an organization will enter, and how to manage these different businesses, are based on an organization's corporate strategy. The most important strategic issue at the corporate level concerns the extent and nature of organizational diversification. **Diversification** describes the number of different businesses that an organization is engaged in and the extent to which these businesses are related to one another. The three types of diversification strategies are single-product strategy, related diversification, and unrelated diversification.[22]

diversification The number of different businesses that an organization is engaged in and the extent to which these businesses are related to one another

■ Single-Product Strategy

An organization that pursues a **single-product strategy** manufactures just one product or service and sells it in a single geographic market. The WD-40 Company, for example, manufactures only a single product, WD-40 spray lubricant, and sells it in just one market, North America. WD-40 has considered broadening its market to Europe and Asia, but it continues to center all manufacturing, sales, and marketing efforts on one product.

single-product strategy A strategy in which an organization manufactures just one product or service and sells it in a single geographic market

The single-product strategy has one major strength and one major weakness. By concentrating its efforts so completely on one product and market, a firm is likely to be very successful in manufacturing and marketing the product. Because it has staked its survival on a single product, the organization works very hard to make sure that the product is a success. Of course, if the product is not accepted by the market or is replaced by a new one, the firm will suffer. This happened to slide-rule manufacturers when electronic calculators became widely available and to companies that manufactured only black-and-white televisions when low-priced color televisions were first mass marketed.

■ Related Diversification

Given the disadvantage of the single-product strategy, most large businesses today operate in several different businesses, industries, or markets.[23] If the businesses are somehow linked, that organization is implementing a strategy of **related diversification**. Virtually all larger businesses in the United States use related diversification.

related diversification A strategy in which an organization operates several businesses that are somehow linked with one another

Bases of Relatedness Organizations link their different businesses, industries, or markets in different ways. Table 8.3 gives some typical bases of relatedness. In companies such as Philips, a European consumer electronics company, a similar type of electronics technology underlies all the businesses. A common technology in aircraft design links Boeing's commercial and military aircraft divisions, and a common computer design technology links Digital's various computer products and peripherals.

TABLE 8.3

Bases of Relatedness in Implementing Related Diversification

Firms that implement related diversification can do so using any number of bases of relatedness. Four frequently used bases of related uses for diversification are similar technology, common distribution and marketing skills, common brand name and reputation, and common customers.

Basis of Relatedness	Examples
Similar technology	Philips, Boeing, Westinghouse, Compaq
Common distribution and marketing skills	RJR Nabisco, Philip Morris, Procter & Gamble
Common brand name and reputation	Disney, Universal
Common customers	Merck, IBM, AMF-Head

Organizations such as Philip Morris, RJR Nabisco, and Procter & Gamble operate multiple businesses related by a common distribution network (grocery stores) and common marketing skills (advertising). Disney and Universal rely on strong brand names and reputations to link their diverse businesses, which include movie studios and theme parks. Pharmaceutical firms such as Merck & Co., Inc. sell numerous products to a single set of customers: hospitals, doctors, patients, and drugstores. Similarly, AMF-Head sells snow skis, tennis rackets, and sportswear to active, athletic customers.

Advantages of Related Diversification   Pursuing a strategy of related diversification has three primary advantages. First, it reduces an organization's dependence on any one of its business activities and thus reduces economic risk. Even if one or two of a firm's businesses lose money, the organization as a whole may still survive because the healthy businesses will generate enough cash to support the others.[24] At The Limited, sales declines at Lerners (one of the firm's subsidiaries) may be offset by sales increases at Victoria's Secret (another subsidiary).

Second, by managing several businesses at the same time, an organization can reduce the overhead costs associated with managing any one business. In other words, if the normal administrative costs required to operate any business, such as legal services and accounting, can be spread over a large number of businesses, then the overhead costs *per business* will be lower than they would be if each business had to absorb all costs itself. Thus the overhead costs of businesses in a related diversified firm are usually lower than those of similar businesses that are not part of a larger corporation.[25]

Third, related diversification allows an organization to exploit its strengths and capabilities in more than one business. When organizations successfully follow this approach, they capitalize on synergies, which are complementary effects that exist among their businesses. **Synergy** exists among a set of businesses when the combined economic value of the businesses is greater than their separate economic values (recall that we introduced and defined synergy back in Chapter 2). Disney is skilled at creating and exploiting synergies. Its hit movie *The Lion King* earned almost $300 million in box office revenues. In addition, however, Disney earned hundreds of millions more from the sales of licensed Lion King toys, clothing, and video games. *The Lion King* stage show at Disney World attracts more guests to the park, and the video earned millions more for the firm. A direct-to-video sequel was also successful, as was a television show and a recently opened Broadway stage version, each contributing more money to Disney coffers.

■ Unrelated Diversification

Firms that implement a strategy of **unrelated diversification** operate multiple businesses that are not logically associated with one another. At one time, for example, Quaker Oats owned clothing chains, toy companies, and a restaurant business. Unrelated diversification was a very popular strategy in the 1960s and early 1970s. During this time, several conglomerates like ITT and Transamerica grew by acquiring literally hundreds of other organizations and then running these numerous businesses as independent entities. Even if there are important potential synergies between their different businesses, organizations implementing a strategy of unrelated diversification do not attempt to exploit them.

unrelated diversification A strategy in which an organization operates several businesses that are not associated with one another

In theory, unrelated diversification has two advantages. First, a business that uses this strategy should have stable performance over time. During any given period, if some businesses owned by the organization are in a cycle of decline, others may be in a cycle of growth. Unrelated diversification is also thought to have resource allocation advantages. Every year, when a corporation allocates capital, people, and other resources among its various businesses, it must evaluate information about the future of those businesses so that it can place its resources where they have the highest return potential. Given that it owns the businesses in question and thus has full access to information about the future of those businesses, a firm implementing unrelated diversification should be able to allocate capital to maximize corporate performance.

Despite these presumed advantages, research suggests that unrelated diversification usually does not lead to high performance. First, corporate-level managers in such a company usually do not know enough about the unrelated businesses to provide helpful strategic guidance or to allocate capital appropriately. To make strategic decisions, managers must have complete and subtle understanding of a business and its environment. Because corporate managers often have difficulty fully evaluating the economic importance of investments for all the businesses under their wing, they tend to concentrate only on a business's current performance. This narrow attention at the expense of broader planning eventually hobbles the entire organization. Many of International Harvester's problems noted earlier grew from an emphasis on current performance at the expense of investments for the future success of the firm.

Second, because organizations that implement unrelated diversification fail to exploit important synergies, they are at a competitive disadvantage compared to organizations that use related diversification. Universal Studios has been at a competitive disadvantage relative to Disney because Universal's theme parks, movie studios, and licensing divisions are less integrated and therefore achieve less synergy.

For these reasons, almost all organizations have abandoned unrelated diversification as a corporate-level strategy. ITT and Transamerica have sold off numerous businesses and now concentrate on a core set of related businesses and markets. Large corporations that have not concentrated on a core set of businesses eventually have been acquired by other companies and then broken up. Research suggests that these organizations are actually worth more when broken into smaller pieces than they are when joined.[26]

MANAGEMENT IMPLICATIONS Managers should understand the various kinds of corporate strategies that can be adopted from the perspective of strategic business units, or SBUs. Although diversification is a very common corporate-level strategy, managers should have a clear understanding of whether they should use related or unrelated diversification. Appreciating the bases for relatedness is also important.

Implementing Corporate-Level Strategies

In implementing a diversification strategy, organizations face two important questions. First, how will the organization move from a single product strategy to some form of diversification? Second, once the organization diversifies, how will it manage diversification effectively?

■ Becoming a Diversified Firm

Most organizations do not start out completely diversified. Rather, they begin operations in a single business, pursuing a particular business-level strategy. Success in this strategy then creates resources and strengths that the organization can use in related businesses.

backward vertical integration An organization's beginning the business activities formerly conducted by its suppliers

forward vertical integration An organization's beginning the business activities formerly conducted by its customers

merger The purchase of one firm by another firm of approximately the same size

acquisition The purchase of one firm by another firm that is considerably larger

Internal Development of New Products Some firms diversify by developing their own new products and services within the boundaries of their traditional business operations. Honda followed this path to diversification. Relying on its traditional strength in the motorcycle market, over the years Honda learned how to make fuel-efficient, highly reliable small engines. Honda began to apply its strengths in a new business: manufacturing small, fuel-efficient cars for the Japanese domestic market. These vehicles were first sold in the United States in the late 1960s. Honda's success in U.S. exports led the company to increase the size and improve the performance of its cars. Over the years, Honda has introduced automobiles of increasing quality, culminating in the Acura line of luxury cars. While diversifying into the market for automobiles, Honda also applied its engine-building strengths to produce a line of all-terrain vehicles, portable electric generators, and lawn mowers. In each case, Honda was able to parlay its strengths and resources into successful new businesses.

Replacement of Suppliers and Customers   Firms can also become diversified by replacing their former suppliers and customers. A company that stops buying supplies (either manufactured goods or raw materials) from other companies and begins to provide its own supplies has diversified through **backward vertical integration**. Campbell Soup once bought soup cans from several different manufacturers, but later began manufacturing its own cans. In fact, Campbell is currently one of the largest can-manufacturing companies in the world, although almost all the cans it makes are used in its soup operations.

Philip J. Purcell

An organization that stops selling to one customer and sells instead to that customer's customers has diversified through **forward vertical integration**. G.H. Bass used forward vertical integration to diversify its operations. In the past, Bass sold its shoes and other products only to retail outlets. Throughout the 1980s, however, Bass opened numerous factory outlet stores, which now sell products directly to consumers: nevertheless, Bass has not abandoned its former customers, retail outlets.

Mergers and Acquisitions   Another common way for businesses to diversify is through mergers and acquisitions—that is, through purchasing another organization. Such a purchase is called a **merger** when the two organizations being combined are approximately the same size. It is called an **acquisition** when one of the organizations is considerably larger than the other. Organizations engage in mergers and acquisitions to diversify through vertical integration by acquiring former suppliers or former customers. Mergers and acquisitions are also becoming more common in other countries such as Germany and China.[27]

Most organizations use mergers and acquisitions to acquire complementary products or complementary services, which are products or services linked by a common technology and common customers. The objective of most mergers and acquisitions is the creation or exploitation of synergies. Synergy can reduce the combined organizations' costs of doing business; it can increase revenues; and it may open the way to entirely new businesses for

Firms that choose a diversification strategy have a variety of options available to implement that strategy. One common option is to diversify through acquisition—buying other businesses. For example, Morgan Stanley, a Wall Street brokerage firm, recently embarked on a new diversification strategy. One of its first moves was to acquire Dean Witter Discover. One reason the firm wanted this business was to tap into the lucrative credit card market, and acquiring the Discover Card was the most effective way to do this.

THE WORLD OF MANAGEMENT

Blending Alcohol Giants

For years England's Grand Metropolitan PLC and Guinness PLC butted heads in the marketplace. Grand Met's Smirnoff vodka and J&B whiskey competed head-to-head with Guinness's Gordon's gin and Johnnie Walker whiskey. In addition to owning various alcohol products, Grand Met also owned Burger King, Pillsbury, and other brands and companies, and Guinness had a global brewing operation.

In April 1997, the CEOs of the two companies met for dinner. As they discussed their companies, the executives realized that it might make sense for them to consider a merger. In less than a month, they ironed out the details, and a new $21 billion company called GMG Brands was born.

> *"Our partnership has compelling strategic logic and shares management philosophies, which will create new value for our shareholders."*
>
> *Anthony Greener, Guinness Chairman**

GMG Brands is organized into four basic businesses: Pillsbury, Burger King, Guinness Brewing Worldwide, and United Distillers & Vintners. Its executives argue that the combined business will be more efficient and better able to expand into emerging global markets. At the same time, its two biggest competitors, Canada's Seagram Co. and France's LVMH Moet Hennessy Louis Vuitton, cried foul, claiming that the merger would create unfair competition in the spirits market.

References: *"Grand Met, Guinness Join Forces," USA Today, May 13, 1997, p. B1 (*quote on p. B1); and "Grand Met, Guinness to Form Liquor Colossus," Wall Street Journal, May 13, 1997, pp. B1, B8.*

---

the organization to enter.[28] "The World of Management" discusses a recent merger that was undertaken for many of the preceding reasons.

■ Managing Diversification

portfolio management technique A method that diversified organizations use to determine which businesses to engage in and how to manage these businesses to maximize corporate performance

However an organization implements diversification—whether through internal development, vertical integration, or mergers and acquisitions—it must monitor and manage its strategy. The two major tools for managing diversification are (1) organization structure and (2) portfolio management techniques. Using organization structure to manage a diversification strategy is discussed in detail in Chapter 12.[29] **Portfolio management techniques** are methods that diversified organizations use to make decisions about what businesses to engage in and how to manage these multiple businesses to maximize corporate performance. Two important portfolio management techniques are the BCG matrix and the GE Business Screen.

BCG matrix A method of evaluating businesses relative to the growth rate of their market and the organization's share of the market

BCG Matrix The **BCG** (for Boston Consulting Group) **matrix** provides a framework for evaluating the relative performance of businesses in which a diversified organization operates. It also prescribes the preferred distribution of cash and other resources among these businesses.[30] The BCG matrix uses two factors to evaluate an organization's set of businesses: the growth rate of a particular market and the organization's share of that market. The matrix suggests that fast-growing markets in which an organization has the highest market share are more attractive business opportunities than slow-growing markets in which an organization has small market share. Dividing market growth and market share into two categories (low and high) creates the simple matrix shown in Figure 8.3.

The matrix classifies the types of businesses that a diversified organization can engage in as dogs, cash cows, question marks, and stars. *Dogs* are businesses that have a very small share of a market that is not expected to grow. Because these businesses do not hold much economic promise, the BCG matrix suggests that organizations either should not invest in them or should consider selling them as soon as possible. *Cash cows* are businesses that have a large share of a market that is not expected to grow substantially. These businesses characteristically generate high profits that the organization should use to support question marks and stars. (Cash cows are "milked" for cash to support businesses in markets that have greater growth potential.) *Question marks* are businesses that have only a small share of a quickly growing market. The future performance of these businesses is uncertain. A question mark that is able to capture increasing amounts of this growing market may be very profitable. On the other hand, a question mark unable to keep up with market growth is likely to have low profits. The BCG matrix suggests that organizations should carefully invest in question marks. If their performance does not live up to expectations, question marks should be reclassified as dogs and divested. *Stars* are businesses that have the largest share of a rapidly growing market. Cash generated by cash cows should be invested in stars to ensure their pre-eminent position.

ITT invested profits from its cash cows in stars and new acquisitions and became one of the largest organizations in the world during the 1970s. However, ITT's performance in the 1980s reflects the main weakness of the BCG matrix technique: it may be too narrowly focused. Other factors besides market growth and market share determine the performance of a business. By relying so closely on the BCG matrix, ITT failed to recognize several promising opportunities in businesses that it had classified as dogs or cash cows. Other organizations recognized these opportunities and took advantage of them. Recently, ITT has explicitly abandoned the BCG matrix and no longer regards its businesses as dogs or cash cows simply on the basis of market growth and market share.

GE Business Screen In response to the narrow focus of the BCG matrix, General Electric developed the **GE Business Screen**—a more sophisticated approach to managing diversified business units. The Business Screen is a portfolio management technique that can also be represented in the form of a

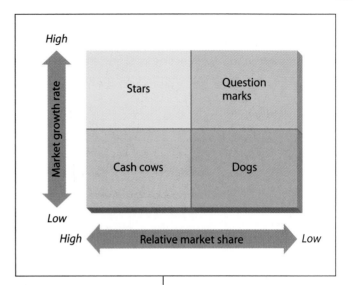

FIGURE 8.3
The BCG Matrix

The BCG matrix helps managers develop a better understanding of how different strategic business units contribute to the overall organization. By assessing each SBU on the basis of its market growth rate and relative market share, managers can make decisions about whether to commit further financial resources to the SBU or to sell or liquidate it.

Source: *Perspectives,* No. 66, "The Product Portfolio." Adapted by permission from The Boston Consulting Group, Inc., 1970.

GE Business Screen A method of evaluating businesses along two dimensions: (1) industry attractiveness and (2) competitive position; in general, the more attractive the industry and the more competitive the position, the more an organization should invest in a business

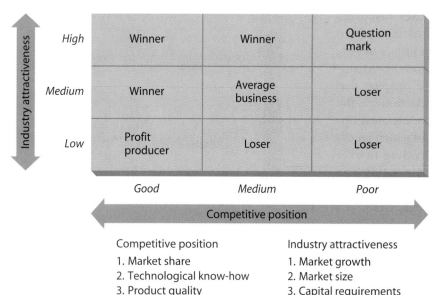

Competitive position
1. Market share
2. Technological know-how
3. Product quality
4. Service network
5. Price competitiveness
6. Operating costs

Industry attractiveness
1. Market growth
2. Market size
3. Capital requirements
4. Competitive intensity

FIGURE 8.4
The GE Business Screen

The GE Business Screen is a more sophisticated approach to portfolio management than the BCG matrix. As shown here, several factors combine to determine a business's competitive position and the attractiveness of its industry. These two dimensions, in turn, can be used to classify businesses as winners, question marks, average businesses, losers, or profit producers. Such a classification enables managers to more effectively allocate the organization's resources across various business opportunities.

From *Strategy Formulation: Analytical Concepts,* by Charles W. Hofer and Dan Schendel. Copyright 1978 West Publishing. Used by permission of South-Western College Publishing, a division of International Thomson Publishing, Inc., Cincinnati, Ohio, 45227.

matrix. Rather than focusing solely on market growth and market share, however, the GE Business Screen considers industry attractiveness and competitive position. These two factors are divided into three categories, to make the nine-cell matrix shown in Figure 8.4.[31] These cells, in turn, classify business units as winners, losers, question marks, average businesses, or profit producers.

As Figure 8.4 shows, both market growth and market share appear in a broad list of factors that determine the overall attractiveness of an industry and the overall quality of a firm's competitive position. Other determinants of an industry's attractiveness (in addition to market growth) include market size, capital requirements, and competitive intensity. In general, the greater the market growth, the larger the market, the smaller the capital requirements, and the less the competitive intensity, the more attractive an industry will be. Other determinants of an organization's competitive position in an industry (besides market share) include technological know-how, product quality, service network, price competitiveness, and operating costs. In general, businesses with large market share, technological know-how, high product quality, a quality service network, competitive prices, and low operating costs are in a favorable competitive position.

Think of the GE Business Screen as a way of applying SWOT analysis to the implementation and management of a diversification strategy. The determinants of industry attractiveness are similar to the environmental opportunities and threats in SWOT analysis, and the determinants of competitive position are similar to organizational strengths and weaknesses. By conducting this type of SWOT analysis across several businesses, a diversified organization can decide how to invest its resources to maximize corporate performance. In general, organizations should invest in winners and in question marks (where industry attractiveness and competitive position are both favorable), should maintain the market position of average businesses and profit producers (where industry attractiveness and competitive position are average), and should sell losers. For example, Unilever recently assessed its business portfolio using a similar framework and, as a result, decided to sell off several specialty chemical units that were not contributing to the firm's profitability as much as other businesses.[32]

Diversification can be achieved through the internal development of new products, replacement of suppliers and customers, and mergers and acquisitions. Managers who are pursuing a diversification strategy should know the advantages and disadvantages of each type of diversification. In addition, they should understand how to manage multiple business units by using such frameworks as the BCG matrix or the GE Business Screen. ▬

Summary of Key Points

A strategy is a comprehensive plan for accomplishing the organization's goals. Strategic management is a comprehensive and ongoing process aimed at formulating and implementing effective strategies. Effective strategies address three organizational issues: distinctive competence, scope, and resource deployment. Most large companies have both business-level and corporate-level strategies. Strategy formulation is the set of processes involved in creating or determining the strategies of an organization. Strategy implementation is the process of executing strategies.

SWOT analysis considers an organization's strengths, weaknesses, opportunities, and threats. Using SWOT analysis, an organization chooses strategies that support its mission and (1) exploit its opportunities and strengths, (2) neutralize its threats, and (3) avoid its weaknesses. Common strengths cannot be ignored, but distinctive competencies hold the greatest promise for superior performance.

A business-level strategy is the plan an organization uses to conduct business in a particular industry or market. Porter suggests that businesses may formulate a differentiation strategy, an overall cost leadership strategy, or a focus strategy at this level. According to Miles and Snow, organizations may choose one of four business-level strategies: prospector, defender, analyzer, or reactor. Business-level strategies may also take into account the stages in the product life cycle.

Strategy implementation at the business level takes place in the areas of marketing, sales, accounting and finance, and manufacturing. Culture also influences strategy implementation. Implementation of Porter's generic strategies requires different emphases in each of these organizational areas. Implementation of Miles and Snow's strategies affects organization structure and practices.

A corporate-level strategy is the plan an organization uses to manage its operations across several businesses. A firm that does not diversify is implementing a single-product strategy. An organization pursues a strategy of related diversification when it operates a set of businesses that are somehow linked. Related diversification reduces the financial risk associated with any particular product, reduces the overhead costs of each business, and enables the organization to create and exploit synergy. An organization pursues a strategy of unrelated diversification when it operates a set of businesses that are not logically associated with one another.

Strategy implementation at the corporate level addresses two issues: how the organization will go about its diversification and the way that an organization is managed once it has diversified. Businesses accomplish diversification in three ways: developing new products internally, replacing suppliers (backward vertical integration) or customers (forward vertical integration), and engaging in mergers and acquisitions. Organizations manage diversification through the organization structure that they adopt and through portfolio management techniques. The BCG matrix classifies an organization's diversified businesses as dogs, cash cows, question marks, or stars according to market share and market growth rate. The GE Business Screen classifies businesses as winners, losers, question marks, average businesses, or profit producers according to industry attractiveness and competitive position.

Discussion Questions

Questions for Review

1. What are the two main types of strategic alternatives available to an organization?

2. How does a deliberate strategy differ from an emergent strategy?

3. List and describe Porter's generic strategies and the Miles and Snow typology of strategies.

4. What is the difference between a single-product strategy, a related diversification strategy, and an unrelated diversification strategy?

Questions for Analysis

5. Common strengths among firms cannot give one firm a competitive advantage. Does this mean that an organization should actually ignore its common strengths in choosing and implementing its strategies? Why or why not?

6. Suppose that an organization does not have any distinctive competencies. If the organization is able to acquire some distinctive competencies, how long are these strengths likely to remain distinctive competencies? Why?

8. Suppose that an organization moves from a single-product strategy to a strategy of related

diversification. How might the organization use SWOT analysis to select attributes of its current business to serve as bases of relatedness among its newly acquired businesses?

9. For decades now, Ivory Soap has advertised that it is 99 percent pure. Ivory has refused to add deodorants, facial creams, or colors to its soap. It also packages its soap in plain paper wrappers—no foil or fancy printing. Is Ivory implementing product differentiation, low cost, focus strategy, or some combination? Explain your answer.

Questions for Application

10. Interview a manager and categorize the business- and corporate-level strategies of his or her organization according to Porter's generic strategies, the Miles and Snow typology, and extent of diversification.

11. Is implementing a differentiation strategy always going to improve an organization's performance? Give three real-world examples in which differentiation did not seem to improve an organization's performance, and describe why it did not. What do these "errors" have in common?

Building Effective Decision-Making Skills

EXERCISE OVERVIEW

Decision-making skills refer to the manager's ability to correctly recognize and define problems and opportunities and to then select an appropriate course of action to solve problems and capitalize on opportunities. As noted in the chapter, many organizations use SWOT analysis as part of the process of strategy formulation. This exercise will help you understand how managers obtain the information they need to perform such an analysis and use it as a framework for making decisions.

EXERCISE BACKGROUND

SWOT is an acronym for strengths, weaknesses, opportunities, and threats. Good strategies are those that exploit an organization's opportunities and strengths while neutralizing threats and avoiding or correcting weaknesses.

Assume that you have just been hired to run a medium-size manufacturing company. The firm has been manufacturing electric motors, circuit breakers, and similar electronic components for industrial use. In recent years, the firm's financial performance has gradually eroded. You have been hired to turn things around.

Meetings with both current and former top managers of the firm have led you to believe that a new strategy is needed. In earlier times the firm was successful in part because its products were of top quality. This differentiation strategy allowed the company to charge premium prices for them. Recently, however, various cost-cutting measures have resulted in a decrease in quality. Moreover, competition has also increased. As a result, your firm no longer has a reputation for top-quality products, but your manufacturing costs are still relatively high. The next thing you want to do is to conduct a SWOT analysis.

EXERCISE TASK

With the preceding background information as context, do the following:

1. List the sources you will use to obtain information about the firm's strengths, weaknesses, opportunities, and threats.

2. Rate each source in terms of its probable reliability.

3. Rate each source in terms of how easy or difficult it will be to access.

4. How confident should you be in making decisions based on the information obtained?

EXERCISE OVERVIEW

Conceptual skills refer to the manager's ability to think in the abstract. This exercise gives you some experience in using your conceptual skills on real business opportunities and potential.

Building Effective
Conceptual
Skills

EXERCISE BACKGROUND

Many successful managers have at one time or another had an idea for using an existing product for new purposes or in new markets. For example, Arm & Hammer Baking Soda (a food product used in cooking) is now also widely used to absorb odors in refrigerators. Commercials advise consumers to simply open a box of Arm & Hammer and place it in their refrigerator. This promotion has led to a big increase in sales of the baking soda.

In other situations, managers have extended product life cycles of products by taking them into new markets. The most common example today involves products that are becoming obsolete in more industrialized countries and introducing them in less industrialized countries.

EXERCISE TASK

Apply your conceptual skills by doing each of the following:

1. Make a list of ten simple products that have relatively straightforward purposes (for example, a pencil, which is used for writing).

2. Try to identify two or three alternative uses for each product (for example, a pencil can be used as a splint for a broken finger in an emergency).

3. Evaluate the market potential for each alternative product use as high, moderate, or low (for example, the market potential for pencils as splints is probably low).

4. Form small groups of two or three members each and pool your ideas. Each group should choose two or three ideas to present to the class.

EXERCISE OVERVIEW

Technical skills are necessary for the manager to accomplish or understand the specific kind of work being done in an organization. This exercise will enable you to sharpen your technical skills with regard to using the Internet and to see how the Internet can facilitate strategic planning.

EXERCISE BACKGROUND

Select a company in which you have some interest. It might be a firm that you would like to work for, one where someone you know works, or a firm that is simply in the news a lot. Next, identify the two or three firms that you see as being the firm's biggest competitors. Visit the web sites of the company you originally selected and the competitors you subsequently identified.

EXERCISE TASK

With the preceding background information as context, do the following:

1. Analyze the business and corporate strategies being used by the firm you originally selected.

2. Analyze the business and corporate strategies being used by its competitors.

3. Evaluate the effectiveness of each firm's strategies.

CHAPTER CLOSING CASE

Pepsi Changes Its Strategy

Pepsi-Cola was invented in 1898 by a pharmacist in North Carolina. While his claims that it had medicinal value were never proven and quickly dropped from advertisements, Pepsi continued to grow in popularity and eventually became a strong national brand. While Pepsi-Cola has never been able to catch up to Coca-Cola, it has been a strong number two for several years.

In 1965 Pepsi Cola company executives decided to diversify as a means for new growth. They acquired snack foods giant Frito-Lay, the maker of products such as Fritos, Lay's Potato Chips, Doritos, and Tostitos. They also changed the company's name to PepsiCo to reflect its broader product line. Almost from the date of the acquisition, Frito-Lay has been a major and successful component of the company.

Indeed, PepsiCo executives were so happy with the combined firm that several years later they decided to expand again. This time the strategy called for acquisitions in the restaurant industry. As a result, PepsiCo acquired Pizza Hut in 1977, Taco Bell in 1978, and Kentucky Fried Chicken in 1986. These three businesses made PepsiCo the largest restaurant company in the world.

The logic behind these acquisitions seemed to make a lot of sense. For example, PepsiCo managers argued that the restaurants would all sell Pepsi Cola beverages and Frito-Lay chips. Similarly, grocery stores and other retailers could presumably sponsor joint promotions of Frito-Lay snack products and Pepsi beverages. And for several years things seemed to be working well.

But in the early 1990s, Pepsi's strategy started to unravel. Coca-Cola began an aggressive push into both existing and emerging foreign markets, for example, and to chip away at Pepsi Cola's domestic market share. Coke's U.S. share rose almost 2 percent in 1996 while Pepsi's dropped by 1 percent. Unfortunately, Pepsi managers found that they were constrained in their ability to fight back. These constraints, in turn, were generally tied to the restaurant business.

Because the restaurant business is so competitive and profit margins in that business are so small, PepsiCo was having to devote a disproportionate amount of attention to managing restaurant operations. Ironically, PepsiCo itself had created part of the problem when it introduced so-called value meal pricing at Taco Bell in the late 1980s. This and similar pricing strategies cut profit margins even further, but also became so ingrained that virtually every company in the industry was using it. Consequently, PepsiCo didn't have the resources to focus additional attention and energy on its besieged soft drink business.

In early 1997, PepsiCo executives reached a critical juncture. They realized that either they had to stand back and allow Coca-Cola to pull far ahead in the soft drink market or they had to get out of the restaurant business altogether. After considerable deliberation they decided to adopt the latter strategy— to divest themselves of the restaurant operation and concentrate on soft drinks and on the snack foods market, a market they dominated.

To prepare for this move, Pepsi first sold some of its company-owned restaurants to franchisees. Then, in late 1997, the restaurant operations were legally restructured as a separate corporation, with shares available on the open market. PepsiCo decided to maintain control of a large block of stock in the new restaurant business, both to keep stock prices higher and to protect its exclusive arrangements for selling Pepsi products in the restaurants. But actual management of the new enterprise will be autonomous, and PepsiCo intends to gradually sell off most, if not all, of its ownership.

Case Questions

1. Was Pepsi's original strategy closer to related or to unrelated diversification?

2. What can be learned about the relationships among business- and corporate-level strategies from PepsiCo's experiences?

3. Do you think PepsiCo should also shed its snack food operations? Why or why not?

References: *Hoover's Handbook of American Business 1998* (Austin, Texas: Hoover's Business Press, 1998), pp. 1074–1075; "PepsiCo Takes Restaurants off Menu," *USA Today,* January 24, 1997, pp. 1B, 2B.

CHAPTER NOTES

1. "New Bug Goes Upscale But Draws on Nostalgia," *USA Today*, January 6, 1998, pp.1B, 2B; "VW Longs for Life in Luxury Lane," *USA Today*, July 11, 1997, pp. 1B, 2B; "VW's U.S. Comeback Rides on Restyled Beetle," *Wall Street Journal*, May 6, 1997, pp. B1, B2; "Can VW Revive Beetlemania?" *Business Week*, January 12, 1998, p. 46; and "New Bug Goes Upscale But Draws on Nostalgia," *USA Today*, January 6, 1998, pp. 1B, 2B.

2. For early discussions of strategic management, see Kenneth Andrews, *The Concept of Corporate Strategy*, rev. ed. (Homewood, Ill.: Dow Jones-Irwin, 1980); and Igor Ansoff, *Corporate Strategy* (New York: McGraw-Hill, 1965). For more recent perspectives, see Michael E. Porter, "What Is Strategy?" *Harvard Business Review*, November–December 1996, pp. 61–78.

3. *Hoover's Handbook of American Business 1997* (Austin, Texas: Hoover's Business Press, 1996), pp. 832–833

4. Peter Koenig, "If Europe's Dead, Why Is GE Investing Billions There?" *Fortune*, September 9, 1996, pp. 114–118; and "Jack Welch's Secret," *Forbes*, January 26, 1998, p. 44.

5. For a discussion of the distinction between business- and corporate-level strategies, see Charles Hill and Gareth Jones, *Strategic Management: An Integrated Approach*, 4th ed. (Boston: Houghton Mifflin, 1998).

6. See David Barry and Michael Elmes, "Strategy Retold: Toward a Narrative View of Strategic Discourse," *Academy of Management Review*, April 1997, pp. 429–452; and Dennis P. Slevin and Jeffrey G. Covin, "Strategy Formation Patterns, Performance, and the Significance of Context," *Journal of Management*, Vol. 23, No. 2, 1997, pp. 189–209.

7. See Gary Hamel, "Strategy as Revolution," *Harvard Business Review*, July–August 1996, pp. 69–82.

8. See Henry Mintzberg, "Patterns in Strategy Formulation," *Management Science*, October 1978, pp. 934–948; and Henry Mintzberg, "Strategy Making in Three Modes," *California Management Review*, 1973, pp. 44–53.

9. "The Drought Is Over at 3M," *Business Week*, November 7, 1994, pp. 140–141.

10. For a recent discussion, see Elaine Mosakowski, "Strategy Making under Causal Ambiguity: Conceptual Issues and Empirical Evidence," *Organization Science*, July–August 1997, pp. 414–423.

11. "If It's on the Fritz, Take It to Jane," *Business Week*, January 27, 1997, pp. 74–75.

12. Jay Barney, "Firm Resources and Sustained Competitive Advantage," *Journal of Management*, June 1991, pp. 99–120.

13. Jay Barney, "Strategic Factor Markets," *Management Science*, December 1986, pp. 1231–1241.

14. "This Cat Keeps on Purring," *Business Week*, January 20, 1997, pp. 82–84.

15. See Michael Porter, *Competitive Strategy* (New York: Free Press, 1980).

16. Porter, *Competitive Strategy*.

17. Ian C. MacMillan and Rita Gunther McGrath, "Discovering New Points of Differentiation," *Harvard Business Review*, July–August 1997, pp. 133–136.

18. Richard Teitelbaum, "The Wal-Mart of Wall Street," *Fortune*, October 13, 1997, pp. 128–130; and "Friendly Enemies," *Fortune*, February 2, 1998, pp. 102–104.

19. Raymond E. Miles and Charles C. Snow, *Organizational Strategy, Structure, and Process* (New York: McGraw-Hill, 1978).

20. "At DuPont, Time to Both Sow and Reap," *Business Week*, September 29, 1991, pp. 107–108.

21. E. P. Learned, C. R. Christensen, K. R. Andrews, and W. D. Guth, *Business Policy* (Homewood, Ill.: Irwin, 1969), pp. 758–792.

22. Alfred Chandler, *Strategy and Structure: Chapters in the History of the American Industrial Enterprise* (Cambridge, Mass.: MIT Press, 1962); Richard Rumelt, *Strategy, Structure, and Economic Performance* (Cambridge, Mass.: Division of Research, Graduate School of Business Administration, Harvard University, 1974); and Oliver Williamson, *Markets and Hierarchies* (New York: Free Press, 1975).

23. K. L. Stimpert and Irene M. Duhaime, "Seeing the Big Picture: The Influence of Industry, Diversification, and Business Strategy on Performance," *Academy of Management Journal*, Vol. 40, No. 3, 1997, pp. 560–583.

24. See Chandler, *Strategy and Structure*; and Yakov Amihud and Baruch Lev, "Risk Reduction as a Managerial Motive for Conglomerate Mergers," *Bell Journal of Economics*, 1981, pp. 605–617.

25. Chandler, *Strategy and Structure*; and Williamson, *Markets and Hierarchies*.

26. For a discussion of the limitations of unrelated diversification, see Jay Barney and William G. Ouchi, *Organizational Economics* (San Francisco: Jossey-Bass, 1986).

27. "Latest Merger Boom Is Happening in China, and Bears Watching," *Wall Street Journal*, July 30, 1997, pp. A1, A9; "A Breakthrough in Bavaria," *Business Week*, August 4, 1997, p. 54.

28. Terence Pare, "The New Merger Boom," *Fortune*, November 28, 1994, pp. 95–106.

29. See Constantinoes C. Markides and Peter J. Williamson, "Corporate Diversification and Organizational Structure:

A Resource-Based View," *Academy of Management Journal*, April 1996, pp. 340–367.

30. See Barry Hedley, "A Fundamental Approach to Strategy Development," *Long Range Planning*, December 1976, pp. 2–11; and Bruce Henderson, "The Experience Curve-Reviewed IV: The Growth Share Matrix of the Product Portfolio," *Perspectives*, No. 135 (Boston: Boston Consulting Group, 1973).

31. Michael G. Allen, "Diagramming G.E.'s Planning for What's WATT," in Robert J. Allio and Malcolm W. Pen-

nington (eds.), *Corporate Planning: Techniques and Applications* (New York: AMACOM, 1979). Limits of this approach are discussed in R. A. Bettis and W. K. Hall, "The Business Portfolio Approach: Where It Falls Down in Practice," *Long Range Planning*, March 1983, pp. 95–105.

32. "Unilever to Sell Specialty-Chemical Unit to ICI of the U.K. for About $8 Billion," *Wall Street Journal*, May 7, 1997, pp. A3, A12.

9

Managing Decision Making and Problem Solving

OBJECTIVES

After studying this chapter, you should be able to:

■ Define decision making and discuss types of decisions and decision-making conditions.

■ Discuss rational perspectives on decision making, including the steps in decision making.

■ Describe the behavioral nature of decision making.

■ Discuss group and team decision making, including the advantages and disadvantages of group and team decision making and how it can be more effectively managed.

Well-defined seminal moments in the histories of most companies usually determine their future successes and failures. A good case in point is Kimberly-Clark Corporation. Indeed, two critical decisions coming twenty years apart have indelibly defined the company's current competitive strategies and its future directions.

In the mid-1970s Kimberly basically had its feet planted firmly in two disparate businesses. Its core business was forestry products—trees and paper—and pulp-making operations, and it was here that the company had committed most of its capital. But most of the firm's profits came from its disposable tissue business. Indeed, the name "Kleenex" was virtually synonymous with Kimberly-Clark and has almost become a generic term for facial tissues.

Company officials determined that their strategy was a barrier to future growth—low growth and low profits in the forestry businesses constrained expansion in those markets. Moreover, these operations were requiring so much capital that the company lacked the resources to fuel growth in other areas. Consequently, Kimberly management made the decision to sell off major portions of the forestry operations and use the funds this step generated to expand into consumer products such as disposable diapers and paper towels.

Over the course of the next several years, therefore, Kimberly sold one forestry business after another and carefully and calculatedly launched a variety of new products. Unfortunately, however, Kimberly found it tough competing against the entrenched industry giant Procter & Gamble. Its vast size and sophisticated distribution network prevented competitors such as Kimberly from gaining significant market share. At the same time, Procter & Gamble was also beginning to move into the facial tissue market, putting Kleenex in a vulnerable position.

The next major watershed event for the firm occurred in 1995 when its managers made the decision to buy Scott Paper Company for $9.4 billion. This acquisition gave Kimberly-Clark new market share in a number of different markets. For example, Kimberly's share of the bathroom tissue market jumped from 5 percent to 31 percent, and its share of the home paper towel market more than tripled to 18 percent.

Even more important, the Scott acquisition gave Kimberly major positions in several foreign markets. Scott was the dominant tissue products company in Mexico, for example, enjoying near-monopoly status. Kimberly was also now able to use its new clout to compete with Procter & Gamble on a more even basis. Indeed, their international competition has produced some interesting twists and turns.

For example, when Kimberly entered the French market in 1994, ruthless price cutting between the two giants inadvertently pushed their largest French competitor, Peaudouce, to the edge of bankruptcy. Its savior? Kimberly-Clark. And the next year, the same scenario was played out in Argentina, with Kimberly-Clark again landing the wounded domestic competitor. Although the winner has not yet been determined, Kimberly-Clark is clearly making is presence felt. And it all started with a decision to sell some trees and make more tissue.[1]

> **"Every morning I look in the mirror and ask how I can beat the hell out of P&G [Procter & Gamble]. And I want every one of my employees to do the same."**
>
> Wayne Sanders, Kimberly-Clark chief executive, quoted in Forbes, March 24, 1997, p. 100.

The opening incident portrays two significant decisions made by Kimberly-Clark executives that have essentially reshaped the entire character of their firm. But in addition to the two decisions highlighted here, they have made many, many more decisions as well, some also very important (such as which foreign markets to enter and how and when to enter those markets), some of moderate importance (such as package design for tissues products and color choices for tissue products), and others of perhaps relatively low importance (such as the exact numbers of tissues to put in a box of Kleenex). Some experts believe that decision making is the most basic and fundamental of all managerial activities.[2] Thus we discuss it here in the context of the first management function, planning. Keep in mind, however, that although decision making is perhaps most closely linked to the planning function, it is also part of organizing, leading, and controlling.

We begin our discussion by exploring the nature of decision making. We then describe rational perspectives on decision making. Behavioral aspects of decision making are then introduced and described. We conclude with a discussion of group and team decision making.

The Nature of Decision Making

Managers at BMW recently made the decision to build a new manufacturing plant in South Carolina at a cost of more than $600 million. At about the same time, the manager at the BMW dealership in Bryan, Texas, made a decision to sponsor a local youth soccer team for $150. Each of these examples includes a decision, but the decisions differ in many ways. Thus as a starting point in understanding decision making, we must first explore the meaning of decision making as well as types of decisions and conditions under which decisions are made.[3]

■ Decision Making Defined

decision making The act of choosing one alternative from among a set of alternatives

decision-making process Recognizing and defining the nature of a decision situation, identifying alternatives, choosing the "best" alternative, and putting it into practice

Decision making can refer to either a specific act or a general process. **Decision making** per se is the act of choosing one alternative from among a set of alternatives. The decision-making process, however, is much more elaborate. One step of the process, for example, is that the person making the decision must recognize that a decision is necessary and identify the set of feasible alternatives before selecting one. Hence, the **decision-making process** includes recognizing and defining the nature of a decision situation, identifying alternatives, choosing the "best" alternative, and putting it into practice.[4]

The word *best* implies effectiveness. Effective decision making requires the decision maker to understand the situation driving the decision. Most people would consider an effective decision to be one that optimizes some set of factors such as profits, sales, employee welfare, and market share. In some situations, though, an effective decision may be one that minimizes loss, expenses,

When Time Is of the Essence

Sometimes decisions can be made over a long and extended time frame during which the manager has the luxury of carefully and thoroughly gathering information and assessing alternatives. But other times managers have to act quickly, before they are truly prepared, and hope that they are making the right decisions. Gerhard Cromme recently faced such a case.

Cromme is the CEO of Krupp, one of Germany's largest manufacturers. Krupp has 140 subsidiaries and affiliates worldwide, with steel production as its core business. In early 1997 Cromme decided to plan an acquisition—he proposed to make a bid to take over Thyssen, Germany's largest steel company (Krupp was second). He also in-

"He had to give up or act."

Unidentified business associate of Gerhard Cromme, CEO of Germany's Krupp group*

tended to spend several months formulating the bid and ensuring that it was really the correct decision.

However, in March 1997 an unknown Krupp insider leaked word of the potential planned takeover to the press. The ensuing publicity forced Cromme into an unpleasant situation: he knew that he had to proceed with the takeover bid immediately or else drop his plan altogether. After deliberating for twenty-four hours, he made his decision and announced a formal bid to buy Thyssen for $8 billion.

References: *"The Long Arms of Krupp,"* Business Week, *March 31, 1997, p. 53 (*quote on p. 53); and "Exaggerated Rumours of a Death,"* Economist, *March 22, 1997, pp. 79–80.*

or employee turnover. It may even mean selecting the best method for going out of business, laying off employees, or terminating a contract.

We should also note that managers make decisions about both problems and opportunities. For example, making decisions about how to cut costs by 10 percent reflects a problem—an undesired situation that requires a solution. But decisions are also necessary in situations of opportunity. Learning that the firm is earning higher-than-projected profits, for example, requires a subsequent decision. Should the extra funds be used to increase shareholder dividends, reinvested in current operations, or used to expand into new markets?

Of course, a manager may have to wait a long time to know whether he or she made the correct decision. For example, when George Fisher took over as CEO of Kodak, he made several major decisions that will affect the company for decades. Among other things, for example, he sold off several chemical- and health-related businesses, reduced the firm's debt by $7 billion in the process, launched a major new line of advanced cameras and film called Advantix, and made major new investments in emerging technology such as digital photography. But analysts believe that the payoffs from these decisions will not be known for at least ten years.[5] "The World of Management" feature describes how one German manager, Gerhard Cromme, the CEO of Krupp, also had to make a decision with long-term consequences. His decision to buy a competitor had to be made more quickly than planned, and, as with the Kodak situation, cannot be evaluated for quite some time.

programmed decision A decision that is fairly structured or recurs with some frequency (or both)

nonprogrammed decision A decision that is relatively unstructured; occurs much less often than a programmed decision

FIGURE 9.1
Decision-Making Conditions

Most major decisions in organizations today are made under a state of uncertainty. Managers making decisions in these circumstances must be sure to learn as much as possible about the situation and approach the decision from a logical and rational perspective.

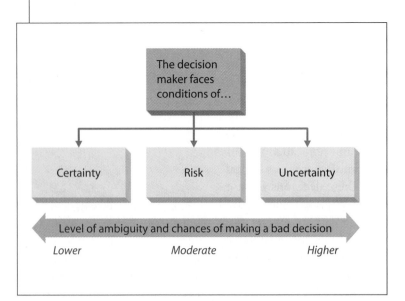

Types of Decisions

Managers must make many types of decisions. In general, however, most decisions fall into one of two categories: programmed and nonprogrammed.[6] A **programmed decision** is one that is fairly structured or recurs with some frequency (or both). Kimberly-Clark uses programmed decisions to purchase new supplies of wood pulp, dyes and chemicals, and packaging materials for its tissue products. For example, a plant manager may need to keep a ten-day supply of packaging on hand, and know that it takes three days to get the packaging from the supplier. Thus, whenever the on-hand supply of packaging reaches thirteen days, a new order is placed. Likewise, the Bryan BMW dealer made a decision to sponsor a youth soccer team each year. Thus when the soccer club president calls, the dealer already knows what he will do. Many decisions regarding basic operating systems and procedures and standard organizational transactions are of this variety and can therefore be programmed.

Nonprogrammed decisions, on the other hand, are relatively unstructured and occur much less often. Kimberly-Clark's earlier decision to change its emphasis from wood products to consumer products and its more recent decision to acquire Scott Paper were both nonprogrammed decisions. Managers faced with such decisions must treat each one as unique, investing enormous amounts of time, energy, and resources into exploring the situation from all perspectives. Intuition and experience are major factors in nonprogrammed decisions. Most decisions made by top managers involving strategy (including mergers, acquisitions, and takeovers), organization design, new facilities, new products, labor contracts, and legal issues are nonprogrammed.

Decision-Making Conditions

Just as there are different kinds of decisions, there are also different conditions in which decisions must be made. The managers who made Kimberly-Clark's decision to move from wood to consumer products had little idea what to expect as a result. Alternatively, the managers who decided to buy Scott Paper knew details about Scott's current products, their market share, and so forth, and could thus estimate with reasonable assurance how the two firms together would stack up in the marketplace. Managers sometimes have an almost perfect understanding of conditions surrounding a decision, but at other times they have few clues about those conditions. In general, as shown in Figure 9.1, the circumstances that exist for the decision maker are conditions of certainty, risk, or uncertainty.[7]

Decision Making Under Certainty When the decision maker knows with reasonable certainty what the alternatives are and what conditions are associated with each alternative, a **state of certainty** exists. Suppose, for example, that Singapore Airlines needs to buy five new jumbo jets. The decision is from whom to buy them. Singapore has only two choices: The Boeing Co. (a U.S. firm) and Airbus (a European consortium). Each has proven products and will specify prices and delivery dates. The airline thus knows the alternative conditions associated with each. There is little ambiguity and a relatively low chance of making a bad decision.

Few organizational decisions are made under conditions of true certainty.[8] The complexity and turbulence of the contemporary business world make such situations rare. Even the airplane purchase decision we just considered has less certainty than it appears. The aircraft companies may not be able to guarantee delivery dates so they may write cost-increase or inflation clauses into contracts. Thus the airline may not be truly certain of the conditions surrounding each alternative.

Decision Making Under Risk   A more common decision-making condition is a state of risk. Under a **state of risk**, the availability of each alternative and its potential payoffs and costs are all associated with probability estimates.[9] Suppose, for example, that a labor contract negotiator for a company receives a "final" offer from the union just before a strike deadline. The negotiator has two alternatives: to accept or to reject the offer. The risk centers on whether the union representatives are bluffing. If the company negotiator accepts the offer, she avoids a strike but commits to a costly labor contract. If she rejects the contract, she may get a more favorable contract if the union is bluffing; she may provoke a strike if it is not.

On the basis of past experiences, relevant information, the advice of others, and her own intuition, she may believe that there is about a 75 percent chance that the union is bluffing and about a 25 percent chance that it will back up its threats. Thus the negotiator can base a calculated decision on the two alternatives (accept or reject the contract demands) and their probable consequences. When making decisions under a state of risk, managers must accurately determine the probabilities associated with each alternative. For example, if the union negotiators are committed to a strike if their demands are not met and the company negotiator rejects their demands because she guesses they will not strike, her miscalculation will prove costly. As indicated in Figure 9.1, decision making under conditions of risk is accompanied by moderate ambiguity and chances of a bad decision.[10] Kimberly-Clark's decision to acquire Scott Paper was made under conditions of risk. Similarly, "Working with Diversity" describes how Loida Lewis recently made several tough decisions under conditions of risk since she took over the reins of TLC Beatrice.

Managers occasionally have to make non-programmed and unstructured decisions. NASA's successful Rover mission to Mars in 1997 was largely driven by non-programmed decisions. Obviously, the original decision itself to initiate the mission was a non-programmed decision. After all, managers don't send something to Mars every day! But non-programmed decisions continued to dominate the mission, right down to the time when Rover got stuck on rocks and these mission control managers had to carefully figure out how to maneuver the craft back onto level ground!

state of certainty   A condition in which the decision maker knows with reasonable certainty what the alternatives are and what conditions are associated with each alternative

state of risk   A condition in which the availability of each alternative and its potential payoffs and costs are all associated with probability estimates

Making the Tough Decisions

Reginald Lewis made national headlines several years ago when he bought TLC Beatrice International Holdings for $1 billion. Although the size of the deal was impressive, the headlines were prompted by the fact that Lewis was African-American and Beatrice thus became the largest minority-owned business in the United States. He subsequently ran the firm with an extravagant and flamboyant style for a few years, and made it a high priority to support African-American causes and to hire and promote as many African-Americans as possible.

Unfortunately, Lewis died in 1993, leaving the management of the firm to his half-brother and its ownership in the hands of his wife, Loida Lewis. Most observers assumed that Ms. Lewis, a Filipino immigration lawyer with no management experience, would remain in the background. But less than a year later she became so concerned about the firm's performance that she took over its reins.

Among her first actions were to sell off several underperforming businesses. Interestingly, although Beatrice is a U.S. firm, it owns no businesses inside the United States—all of its holdings are in Europe. She also eliminated numerous expensive perks that her husband had acquired, including a corporate jet, a fleet of limousines, and a lavish apartment in Paris that Reginald had used when he traveled there. Loida, on the other hand, focused more attention on the bottom line and restored the company's financial performance to all-time high levels.

> *"I know where I want this company to go, and I know how I want this company to get there."*
>
> *Loida Lewis, CEO of TLC Beatrice**

But her actions have not been without controversy. The most stunning decision she made was to sever many of the ties that Reginald had forged with the African-American community, eliminating most of the contributions he provided to more than fifty black charities and foundations. Although African-American leaders widely criticized this step, Loida argues that her decisions have simply been tough—and correct—business decisions.

References: *"A Woman's Touch,"* Time, October 28, 1996, pp. 60–62 (*quote on page 61); Derek Dingle, *"Not Business as Usual,"* Black Enterprise, June 1996, pp. 105–138; and Jolie Solomon, *"Operation Rescue,"* Working Woman, May 1996, pp. 54–59.

---

state of uncertainty A condition in which the decision maker does not know all the alternatives, the risks associated with each, or the consequences each alternative is likely to have

Decision Making Under Uncertainty Most of the major decision making in contemporary organizations is done under a **state of uncertainty**. The decision maker does not know all the alternatives, the risks associated with each, or the likely consequences of each alternative.[11] This uncertainty stems from the complexity and dynamism of contemporary organizations and their environments. Consider, for example, Kimberly-Clark's decision to move from wood to consumer products. Because many of the alternatives, risks, and consequences were unknown, considerable uncertainty accompanied this decision. Indeed, many of the decisions already noted—BMW's decision to build a new plant and Kodak's decision to invest in digital photography—were made under conditions of uncertainty. To make effective decisions in these circumstances, managers must acquire as much relevant information as possible and approach the situation from a logical and rational perspective. Intuition, judgment, and experience always play major roles in the decision-making process under conditions of uncertainty. Even so, uncertainty is the most ambiguous condition for managers and the one most prone to error.

MANAGEMENT IMPLICATIONS	Managers should remember that decision making is the foundation of much of their work. It is also important to understand the distinction between programmed and nonprogrammed decisions and the different conditions—certainty, risk, and uncertainty—that surround decision-making situations. ■

classical decision model A prescriptive approach to decision making that tells managers how they should make decisions. It assumes that managers are logical and rational and that their decisions will be in the best interests of the organization

Rational Perspectives on Decision Making

Most managers like to think of themselves as rational decision makers. And indeed, many experts argue that managers should try to be as rational as possible in making decisions.[12]

■ The Classical Model of Decision Making

The **classical decision model** is a prescriptive approach that tells managers how they should make decisions. It rests on the assumptions that managers are logical and rational and that they make decisions that are in the best interests of the organization. Figure 9.2 shows how the classical model views the decision-making process: (1) Decision makers have complete information about the decision situation and possible alternatives. (2) They can effectively eliminate uncertainty to achieve a decision condition of certainty. (3) They evaluate all aspects of the decision situation logically and rationally. As we see later, these conditions rarely, if ever, actually exist.

■ Steps in Rational Decision Making

A manager who really wants to approach a decision rationally and logically should try to follow the **steps in rational decision making**, listed in Table 9.1. These steps in rational decision making help keep the decision maker focused on facts and logic and help guard against inappropriate assumptions and pitfalls.

steps in rational decision making Recognize and define the decision situation; identify appropriate alternatives; evaluate each alternative in terms of its feasibility, satisfactoriness, and consequences; select the best alternative; implement the chosen alternative; follow-up and evaluate the results of the chosen alternative

FIGURE 9.2
The Classical Model of Decision Making

The classical model of decision making assumes that managers are rational and logical. It attempts to prescribe how managers should approach decision situations.

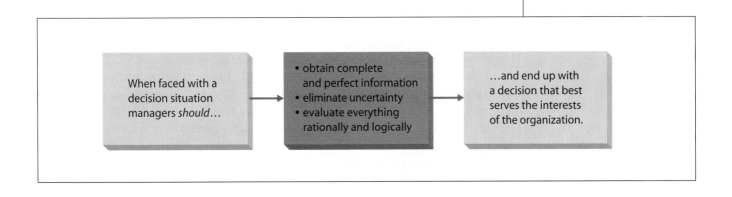

Step	Detail	Example
1. Recognizing and defining the decision situation	Some stimulus indicates that a decision must be made. The stimulus may be positive or negative.	A plant manager sees that employee turnover has increased by 5 percent.
2. Identifying alternatives	Both obvious and creative alternatives are desired. In general, the more important the decision, the more alternatives should be generated.	The plant manager can increase wages, increase benefits, or change hiring standards.
3. Evaluating alternatives	Each alternative is evaluated to determine its feasibility, its satisfactoriness, and its consequences.	Increasing benefits may not be feasible. Increasing wages and changing hiring standards may satisfy all conditions.
4. Selecting the best alternative	Consider all situational factors, and choose the alternative that best fits the manager's situation.	Changing hiring standards will take an extended period of time to cut turnover, so increase wages.
5. Implementing the chosen alternative	The chosen alternative is implemented into the organizational system.	The plant manager may need permission of corporate headquarters. The human resource department establishes a new wage structure.
6. Following up and evaluating the results	At some time in the future, the manager should ascertain the extent to which the alternative chosen in step 4 and implemented in step 5 has worked.	The plant manager notes that, six months later, turnover dropped to its previous level.

TABLE 9.1
Steps in the Rational Decision-Making Process

Although the presumptions of the classical decision model rarely exist, managers can approach decision making with rationality. By following the steps of rational decision making, managers ensure that they are learning as much as possible about the decision situation and its alternatives.

Recognizing and Defining the Decision Situation The first step in rational decision making is recognizing that a decision is necessary—that is, there must be some stimulus or spark to initiate the process. For many decisions and problem situations, the stimulus may occur without any prior warning. When equipment malfunctions, the manager must decide whether to repair or replace it. Or when a major crisis erupts such as damage from the ice storms that plagued the Northeast U.S. in 1998 or an explosion at a factory, as described in Chapter 3, the manager must quickly decide how to deal with it. As we already note, the stimulus for a decision may be either positive or negative. A manager who must decide how to invest surplus funds, for example, faces a positive decision situation. A negative financial stimulus could involve having to trim budgets because of cost overruns. The "Management InfoTech" feature discusses how National Semiconductor is using information obtained from the Internet to frame and define decision situations. For example, increased interest in a product might cause managers to look more closely at potential new demand.

Inherent in problem recognition is the need to define precisely what the problem is. The manager must develop a complete understanding of the problem, its causes, and its relationship to other factors. This understanding comes from careful analysis and thoughtful consideration of the situation. Consider the recent situation faced by Olin Pool Products. Even though Olin controlled half the market for chlorine-based pool treatment systems, its profits were slipping and it was rapidly losing market share to new competitors. These indicators provided clear evidence to General Manager Doug Cahill that something needed to be done. He went on to define the problem as a need to restore profitability and regain lost market share.[13]

Identifying Alternatives   Once the decision situation has been recognized and defined, the second step is to identify alternative courses of effective action. Developing both obvious, standard alternatives and creative, innovative alternatives is generally useful. In general, the more important the decision, the more attention is directed to developing alternatives. If the decision involves a multimillion-dollar relocation, a great deal of time and expertise will be devoted to identifying the best locations; for example, J. C. Penney Company spent two years searching before selecting the Dallas-Fort Worth area for its new corporate headquarters. If the problem is to choose a color for the company softball team uniforms, less time and expertise will be brought to bear.

Although managers should seek creative solutions, they must also recognize that various constraints often limit their alternatives. Common constraints include legal restrictions, moral and ethical norms, authority constraints, or constraints imposed by the power and authority of the manager, available technology, economic considerations, and unofficial social norms. Doug Cahill at

MANAGEMENT INFOTECH

Using the Web to Improve Decisions

Just about everyone these days talks about using the Web to gather information and make decisions. It is debatable, however, how many companies and managers are actually using the Web effectively. But one thing that's not debatable is how well National Semiconductor is using the Web.

National makes thousands of electronic parts, components, and products and is a prime source for engineers seeking the latest technology. The company has been posting product descriptions and ordering information directly on the Web for several years. The firm's Web site gets more than 6 million hits a month and fields another one thousand product queries daily. A National executive recently came up with a great idea—track the hits received by various products and use that information as a basis for forecasting future demand.

> *"Customers won't wait for us to catch up to their component requirements. They will find another supplier."*
>
> *Paul Brockett, executive VP of worldwide sales and marketing at National Semiconductor**

So far, at least, the strategy seems to be working extremely well. For example, National managers recently observed that interest in a small, $2 heat-sensing device was increasing dramatically. They quickly determined that the device had potential for cooling the microprocessors in multimedia laptop computers. National made some minor modifications to the product and began to promote it on the Web site for that very purpose. And today that small device generates more than $100 million a year in sales revenue!

References: *"Using the Web to Push Key Data to Decision Makers,"* Fortune, *September 29, 1997, p. 254 (*quote on p. 254); "A Network for Mom and Pop,"* Business Week, *January 19, 1998, p. 16; and Peter Keating, "Coming off the Ropes, These Techs Pack Punch,"* Money, *December 1996, pp. 76–78.*

Olin identified several alternatives that might help his firm: seek a bigger firm to take control of Olin and inject new resources, buy one or more competitors to increase Olin's own size, maintain the status quo and hope that competitors stubbed their toes, or overhaul the organization to become more competitive.

Evaluating Alternatives   The third step in the decision-making process is evaluating each of the alternatives. Figure 9.3 presents a decision tree that can be used to judge different alternatives. The figure suggests that each alternative be evaluated in terms of its feasibility, its satisfactoriness, and its consequences. The first question to ask is whether an alternative is feasible. Is it within the realm of probability and practicality? For a small, struggling firm, an alternative requiring a huge financial outlay is probably out of the question. Some alternatives may not be feasible because of legal barriers. And limited human, material, and information resources may make other alternatives impractical.

When an alternative has passed the test of feasibility, it must next be examined to see how well it satisfies the conditions of the decision situation. For example, a manager searching for ways to double production capacity might consider purchasing an existing plant from another company. If closer examination reveals that the new plant would increase production capacity by only 35 percent, this alternative may not be satisfactory. Finally, when an alternative has proven both feasible and satisfactory, its probable consequences must still be assessed. To what extent will a particular alternative influence other parts of the organization? What financial and nonfinancial costs will be associated with such influences? For example, a plan to boost sales by cutting prices may disrupt cash flows, need a new advertising program, and alter the behavior of sales representatives because it requires a different commission structure. The manager, then, must put "price tags" on the consequences of each alternative. Even an alternative that is both feasible and satisfactory must be eliminated if its consequences are too expensive for the total system. Cahill decided that being taken over would cause too great a loss of autonomy (consequences not affordable), that buying a competitor was too expensive (not feasible), and that doing nothing would not solve the problem (not satisfactory).

FIGURE 9.3
Evaluating Alternatives in the Decision-Making Process

Managers must thoroughly evaluate all the alternatives, which increases the chances that the alternative finally chosen will be successful. Failure to evaluate an alternative's feasibility, satisfactoriness, and consequences can lead to a wrong decision.

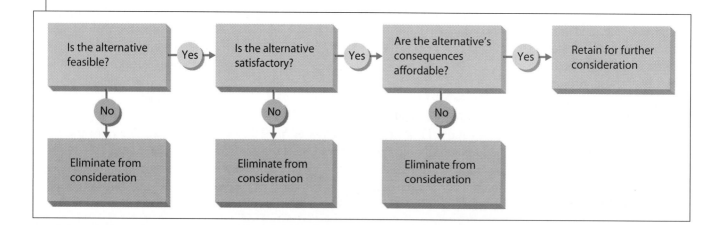

Selecting the Best Alternative   Even though many alternatives fail to pass the triple tests of feasibility, satisfactoriness, and affordable consequences, two or more alternatives may remain. Choosing the best of these is the real crux of decision making. One approach is to choose the alternative with the highest combined level of feasibility, satisfactoriness, and affordable consequences. Even though most situations do not lend themselves to objective, mathematical analysis, the manager can often develop subjective estimates and weights for choosing an alternative.

Optimization is also a frequent goal. Because a decision is likely to affect several individuals or subunits, any feasible alternative will probably not maximize all of the relevant goals. Suppose that the manager of the Kansas City Royals needs to select one new outfielder for the next baseball season. Bill hits .350 but is barely able to catch a fly ball; Joe hits only .175 but is outstanding in the field; and Sam hits .290 and is a solid but not outstanding fielder. The manager would probably select Sam because of the optimal balance of hitting and fielding. Decision makers should also remember that finding multiple acceptable alternatives may be possible—selecting just one alternative and rejecting all the others may not be necessary. For example, the Royals' manager might decide that Sam will start each game, Bill will be retained as a pinch hitter, and Joe will be retained as a defensive substitute. In many hiring decisions, the candidates remaining after evaluation are ranked. If the top candidate rejects the offer, it may be automatically extended to the number two candidate, and, if necessary, to the remaining candidates in order. Olin Pool Products' managers selected the alternative of overhauling the organization to become more competitive.

Implementing the Chosen Alternative   After an alternative has been selected, the manager must put it into effect. In some decision situations, implementation is fairly easy; in others, it is more difficult. In the case of an acquisition, for example, managers must decide how to integrate all the activities of the new business, including purchasing, human resource practices, and distribution, into an ongoing organizational framework. For example, after Kimberly-Clark acquired Scott Paper, it took more than a year to integrate the two firms into a single business unit. Operational plans, which we discussed in Chapter 7, are useful in implementing alternatives.

When they are implementing decisions, managers must also consider people's resistance to change. The reasons for such resistance include insecurity, inconvenience, and fear of the unknown. When J. C. Penney decided to move its headquarters from New York to Texas, many employees chose to resign, rather than to relocate. Managers should anticipate potential resistance at various stages of the implementation process. (Resistance to change is covered in Chapter 13.) Managers should also recognize that, even when all alternatives have been evaluated as precisely as possible and the consequences of each alternative weighed, unanticipated consequences are still likely. Any number of things—unexpected cost increases, a less-than-perfect fit with existing organizational subsystems, or unpredicted effects on cash flow or operating expenses, for example—could develop after implementation begins. Greg Cahill eliminated several levels of management at Olin, combined fourteen departments into eight, gave new authority to every manager, and empowered employees to take greater control over their work.

Following Up and Evaluating the Results The final step in the decision-making process requires managers to evaluate the effectiveness of their decision—that is, they should make sure that the chosen alternative has served its original purpose. If an implemented alternative appears not to be working, the manager can respond in several ways. Another previously identified alternative (the second or third choice) could be adopted. Or the manager might recognize that the situation was not correctly defined to start with and begin the process all over again. Finally, the manager might decide that the original alternative is in fact appropriate but has not yet had time to work or should be implemented in a different way.

Failure to evaluate decision effectiveness may have serious consequences. The Pentagon spent $1.8 billion and eight years developing the Sergeant York antiaircraft gun. From the beginning, tests revealed major problems with the weapon system, but not until it was in its final stages, when it was demonstrated to be completely ineffective, was the project scrapped.[14] In a classic case of poor decision making, managers at Coca-Cola decided to change the formula for the soft drink. Consumer response was extremely negative. In contrast to the Pentagon, however, Coca-Cola immediately reacted: it reintroduced the old formula within three months as Coca-Cola Classic and quickly recovered from its mistake.[15] Had managers stubbornly stuck with their decision and failed to evaluate its effectiveness, the results would have been disastrous. Greg Cahill's decisions at Olin are paying big dividends—the firm's profits are back up and most of the market share it recently lost has been regained as well.

MANAGEMENT IMPLICATIONS Whenever possible managers should strive to apply rationality and logic to the decisions they make. By following the logical sequence of steps in the classical model, managers can lessen risk and reduce uncertainty in many decision-making situations. Of course, at the same time managers should also recognize the "prescriptive" nature of this approach and not adhere to it so rigidly that they fail to consider their own experience and intuition. Finally, they should also know that even using the classical model effectively does not guarantee success. ▬

Behavioral Aspects of Decision Making

If all decision situations were approached as logically as those described in the preceding section, more decisions would prove to be successful. Yet decisions are often made with little consideration for logic and rationality. Some experts have estimated that U.S. companies use rational decision-making techniques less than 20 percent of the time.[16] And even when organizations try to be logical, they sometimes fail. For example, managers at Coca-Cola decided to change Coke's formula after four years of extensive marketing research, taste tests, and rational deliberation—but the decision was still wrong. On the other hand, sometimes when a decision is made with little regard for logic, it can still turn out to be correct. An important ingredient in how these forces work is the behavioral aspect of decision making. The administrative model better reflects these subjective considerations. Other behavioral aspects include political forces, intuition and escalation of commitment, risk propensity, and ethics.

■ The Administrative Model

Herbert A. Simon was one of the first experts to recognize that decisions are not always made with rationality and logic.[17] Simon was subsequently awarded the Nobel Prize in economics. Rather than prescribing how decisions should be made, his view of decision making, now called the **administrative model**, describes how decisions often actually are made. As illustrated in Figure 9.4, the model holds that managers (1) have incomplete and imperfect information, (2) are constrained by bounded rationality, and (3) tend to satisfice when making decisions.

Bounded rationality suggests that decision makers are limited by their values and unconscious reflexes, skills, and habits. They are also limited by less than complete information and knowledge. Bounded rationality partially explains how U.S. auto executives allowed Japanese auto makers to get such a strong foothold in the U.S. market. For years, executives at GM, Ford, and Chrysler compared their companies' performance to one another and ignored foreign imports. The U.S. companies did not acknowledge the foreign "threat" until the domestic auto market had been changed forever. If managers had gathered complete information from the beginning, they might have been better able to thwart foreign competitors. Essentially, then, the concept of bounded rationality suggests that although people try to be rational decision makers, their rationality has limits.

Another important part of the administrative model is **satisficing**. This concept suggests that rather than conducting an exhaustive search for the best possible alternative, decision makers tend to search only until they identify an alternative that meets some minimum standard of sufficiency. A manager looking for a site for a new plant, for example, may select the first site she finds that meets basic requirements for transportation, utilities, and price, even though

administrative model A decision-making model that argues that decision makers (1) have incomplete and imperfect information, (2) are constrained by bounded rationality, and (3) tend to satisfice when making decisions

bounded rationality A concept suggesting that decision makers are limited by their values and unconscious reflexes, skills, and habits

satisficing The tendency to search for alternatives only until one is found that meets some minimum standard of sufficiency

FIGURE 9.4

The Administrative Model of Decision Making

The administrative model is based on behavioral processes that affect how managers make decisions. Rather than prescribing how decisions should be made, it focuses more on describing how they are made.

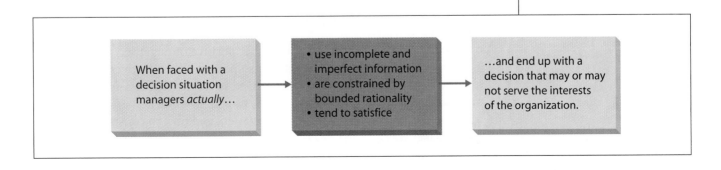

further search might yield a better location. People satisfice for a variety of reasons. Managers may simply be unwilling to ignore their own motives (such as reluctance to spend time making a decision) and therefore not be able to continue searching after a minimally acceptable alternative is identified. The decision maker may be unable to weigh and evaluate large numbers of alternatives and criteria. Also, subjective and personal considerations often intervene in decision situations.

Because of the inherent imperfection of information, bounded rationality, and satisficing, the decisions made by a manager may or may not actually be in the best interests of the organization. A manager may choose a particular location for the new plant because the site offers the lowest price and best availability of utilities and transportation. Or she may choose the location because it's in a community in which she wants to live.

In summary, then, the classical and administrative models paint quite different pictures of decision making. Which is more correct? Actually, each can be used to better understand how managers make decisions. The classical model is prescriptive: it explains how managers can at least attempt to be more rational and logical in their approach to decisions. The administrative model can be used by managers to develop a better understanding of their inherent biases and limitations.[18] In the following sections, we describe more fully other behavioral forces that can influence decisions.

■ Political Forces in Decision Making

Political forces are another major element that contributes to the behavioral nature of decision making. Organizational politics is covered in Chapter 17, but one major element of politics, coalitions, is especially relevant to decision making. A **coalition** is an informal alliance of individuals or groups formed to achieve a common goal. This common goal is often a preferred decision alternative. For example, coalitions of stockholders frequently band together to force a board of directors to make a certain decision.

Coalitions led to the formation of Unisys Corporation, a large computer firm. Sperry was once one of the computer giants of the United States, but a series of poor decisions put the company on the edge of bankruptcy. Two major executives waged battle for three years over what to do. One wanted to get out of the computer business altogether, and the other wanted to stay in. Finally, the manager who wanted to remain in the computer business garnered enough support to earn promotion to the corporation's presidency. The other manager took early retirement. Shortly thereafter, Sperry agreed to be acquired by Burroughs Corporation. The resulting combined company is called Unisys.[19]

The impact of coalitions can be either positive or negative. They can help astute managers get the organization on a path toward effectiveness and profitability, or they can strangle well-conceived strategies and decisions. Managers must recognize when to use coalitions, how to assess whether coalitions are acting in the best interests of the organization, and how to constrain their dysfunctional effects.

coalition An informal alliance of individuals or groups formed to achieve a common goal

■ Intuition and Escalation of Commitment

Two other important decision processes that go beyond logic and rationality are intuition and escalation of commitment to a chosen course of action.

Intuition   **Intuition** is an innate belief about something without conscious consideration. Managers sometimes decide to do something because it "feels right" or they have a hunch. This feeling is usually not arbitrary, however. Rather, it is based on years of experience and practice in making decisions in similar situations. An inner sense may help managers make an occasional decision without going through a full-blown rational sequence of steps. For example, the New York Yankees recently called three major sneaker manufacturers—Nike, Reebok, and Adidas—and informed them that the team wanted to make a sponsorship deal. While Nike and Reebok were carefully and rationally assessing the possibilities, managers at Adidas quickly realized that a partnership with the Yankees made a lot of sense for them. Adidas executives responded very quickly to the idea and ended up hammering out a contract while their competitors were still analyzing details.[20] Of course, all managers, but most especially inexperienced ones, should be careful not to rely on intuition too heavily. If rationality and logic are continually flaunted for what "feels right," the odds are that disaster will strike one day.

intuition   An innate belief about something without conscious consideration

Risk propensity is an important behavioral process that affects many decisions. When Harlem entrepreneur Melba Wilson was looking for new business opportunities, she could have pursued any number of relatively "safe" possibilities. Instead, however, she chose to gamble on a risky course of action—reopening Minton's Playhouse, a famous jazz club that had been shuttered for decades.

Escalation of Commitment   Another important behavioral process that influences decision making is **escalation of commitment** to a chosen course of action. In particular, decision makers sometimes make decisions and then become so committed to the course of action suggested by that decision that they stay with it, even when it appears to have been wrong.[21] For example, when people buy stock in a company, they sometimes refuse to sell it even after repeated drops in price. They chose a course of action—buying the stock in anticipation of making a profit—and then stay with it even in the face of increasing losses.

For years Pan American World Airways ruled the skies and used its profits to diversify into real estate and other businesses. But with the advent of deregulation, Pan Am began to struggle and lose market share to other carriers. Because the Pan Am executives still saw the company as first and foremost an airline, when they finally realized how ineffective the airline operations had become they began to slowly sell off the firm's profitable holdings to keep the airline flying. Experts today, though, point out that the "rational" decision

escalation of commitment   A decision maker's staying with a decision even when it appears to be wrong

would have been to sell off the remaining airline operations and concentrate on the firm's more profitable businesses. Eventually, the company was left with nothing but an ineffective and inefficient airline and then had to sell off its more profitable routes before eventually being taken over by Delta. Had Pan Am managers made the more rational decision years earlier, chances are the firm could still be a profitable enterprise today, albeit one with no involvement in the airline industry.[22]

Thus decision makers must walk a fine line. On the one hand, they must guard against sticking with an incorrect decision too long. To do so can bring about financial decline. Chrysler's recent decision to abandon the production of a new luxury car, as described more fully in "The Quality Challenge" box, illustrates a case of managers abandoning a course of action deemed to no longer be effective. On the other hand, managers should not bail out of a seemingly incorrect decision too soon, as did Adidas several years ago. Adidas once dominated the market for professional athletic shoes. It subsequently entered the market for amateur sports shoes and did well there also. But managers interpreted a sales slowdown as a sign that the boom in athletic shoes was over. They thought that they had made the wrong decision and ordered drastic cutbacks. The market took off again with Nike at the head of the pack, and Adidas never recovered. Fortunately, a new management team has changed the way Adidas makes decisions and, as illustrated earlier, the firm is again on its way to becoming a force in the athletic shoe and apparel markets.

■ Risk Propensity and Decision Making

risk propensity The extent to which a decision maker is willing to gamble in making a decision

The behavioral element of **risk propensity** is the extent to which a decision maker is willing to gamble when making a decision. Some managers are cautious about every decision they make. They try to adhere to the rational model and are extremely conservative in what they do. Such managers are more likely to avoid mistakes, and they infrequently make decisions that lead to big losses. Other managers are extremely aggressive in making decisions and are willing to take risks. They rely heavily on intuition, reach decisions quickly, and often risk big investments on their decisions. As in gambling, these managers are more likely than their conservative counterparts to achieve big successes with their decisions; they are also more likely to incur greater losses. The organization's culture is a prime ingredient in fostering different levels of risk propensity.

■ Ethics and Decision Making

As we mentioned in Chapter 4, individual ethics are personal beliefs about right and wrong behavior. Ethics are clearly related to decision making in a number of ways. For example, suppose that after careful analysis a manager realizes that her company could save money by closing her department and subcontracting with a supplier for the same services. But to recommend this course of action would result in the loss of several jobs, including her own. Her own ethical stan-

Knowing When to Stop

I ts often hard to stop something that has momentum. Managers make a decision, a new project is initiated, it takes on a life of its own, and even though circumstances might change, the company continues to support the project until it's finished. But managers at Chrysler recently made an important decision that runs counter to this trend—they actually decided to stop a popular project that no longer seemed to make sense.

Several years ago Chrysler executives decided to build and manufacture a new luxury car to compete with Cadillac, BMW, Jaguar, and Lexus. The car would be called the Chrysler LX. Chrysler spent more than four years planning the car and had created a design that company executives found very exciting. The design team had developed engineering specifications, and production managers had created space in Chrysler factories to build the car.

At the point when production schedules were actually being outlined, however, company executives decided to

> *"We're convinced we made the right decision. We're convinced of our ability to qualitatively reassess decisions. . . ."*
>
> *Robert Lutz, president of Chrysler**

take one last look at the project before proceeding. And it was at this very last step that they realized conditions had changed and that the Chrysler LX no longer made sense. Specifically, several new entrants to the market had lowered everyone's sales and profit margins, and at the same time, many upscale consumers were shifting to sports utility vehicles. They also realized that to meet necessary levels of profitability they would need to sacrifice quality and productivity, a choice they were not willing to make. As a result, Chrysler executives made the critical decision to pull the plug on their pet project, probably saving the company millions of dollars.

References: *"The Car Chrysler Didn't Build,"* Forbes, *August 12, 1996, pp. 89–91 (*quote on p. 91); and* Hoover's Handbook of American Business 1998 *(Austin, Texas: Hoover's Business Press, 1998), pp. 349–350.*

dards will clearly shape how she proceeds.[23] Indeed, each component of managerial ethics (relationships of the firm to its employees, of employees to the firm, and of the firm to other economic agents) involves a wide variety of decisions, all of which are likely to have an ethical component. A manager must remember, then, that just as behavioral processes such as politics and risk propensity affect the decisions she makes, so too do her ethical beliefs.

MANAGEMENT IMPLICATIONS Managers must understand that various behavioral processes affect how decisions are made. Their own bounded rationality and satisficing tendencies, for example, should be acknowledged. In addition, managers should also be on the alert for political forces as they relate to decision making and to the role of intuition, escalation of commitment, risk propensity, and ethics. ■

Group and Team Decision Making in Organizations

In more and more organizations today, important decisions are made by groups and teams rather than by individuals. Examples include the executive committee of General Motors, product design teams at Texas Instruments, and marketing planning groups at Compaq Computer. Managers can typically choose whether to have individuals or groups and teams make a particular decision. Thus knowing about forms of group and team decision making and their advantages and disadvantages is important.[24]

■ Forms of Group and Team Decision Making

The most common methods of group and team decision making are interacting groups, Delphi groups, and nominal groups.

Interacting Groups and Teams **Interacting groups and teams** are the most common form of decision-making group. The format is simple—either an existing or a newly designated group or team is asked to make a decision. Existing groups or teams might be functional departments, regular work teams, or standing committees. Newly designated groups or teams can be ad hoc committees, task forces, or newly constituted work teams. The group or team members talk among themselves, argue, agree, argue some more, form internal coalitions, and so forth. Finally, after some period of deliberation, the group or team makes its decision. An advantage of this method is that the interaction between people often sparks new ideas and promotes understanding. A major disadvantage, though, is that political processes can play too big a role.

More and more often these days, businesses are relying on groups and teams to make critical decisions. Hewlett-Packard recently announced an ambitious program to dramatically improve customer satisfaction with its products. HP assigned the program to two managers, Mei-Lin Cheng and Julie Anderson, and their team. But HP left all the details and major decisions associated with meeting its customer satisfaction goals in the hands of the team.

Delphi Groups A **Delphi group** is sometimes used for developing a consensus of expert opinion. Developed by the Rand Corporation, the Delphi procedure solicits input from a panel of experts who contribute individually. Their opinions are combined and, in effect, averaged. Assume, for example, that the problem is to establish an expected date for a major technological breakthrough in converting coal into usable energy. The first step in using the Delphi procedure is to obtain the cooperation of a panel of experts. For this situation, experts might include various research scientists, university researchers, and executives in a relevant energy industry. At first, the experts are asked to anonymously predict a time frame for the expected breakthrough. The persons coordinating the Delphi group collect the responses, average them, and ask the experts for another prediction. In this round, the experts who provided unusual or extreme predictions may be asked to justify them. These explanations may then be relayed to the other experts. When the predictions stabilize, the average prediction is taken to represent the decision of the "group" of experts. The time, expense, and logistics of the Delphi technique rule out its use for routine, everyday decisions, but it has been successfully used for forecasting technological breakthroughs at Boeing, market potential for new products at General Motors, research and development patterns at Eli Lilly and Company (a major drug company), and future economic conditions by the U.S. government.[25]

Nominal Groups Another useful group and team decision-making technique occasionally used is the **nominal group**. Unlike the Delphi method, where group members do not see one another, nominal group members are brought together. The members represent a group in name only, however; they do not talk to one another freely like the members of interacting groups. Nominal groups are used most often to generate creative and innovative alternatives or ideas. To begin, the manager assembles a group of knowledgeable people and outlines the problem to them. The group members are then asked to individually write down as many alternatives as they can think of. The members then take turns stating their ideas, which are recorded on a flip chart or blackboard at the front of the room. Discussion is limited to simple clarification. After all alternatives have been listed, more open discussion takes place. Group members then vote, usually by rank-ordering the various alternatives. The highest ranking alternative represents the decision of the group. Of course, the manager in charge may retain the authority to accept or reject the group decision.

■ Advantages of Group and Team Decision Making

The advantages and disadvantages of group and team decision making relative to individual decision making are summarized in Table 9.2. One advantage is simply that more information is available in a group or team setting—as suggested by the old axiom "Two heads are better than one." A group or team represents a variety of educational backgrounds, experiences, and perspectives. Partly as a result of this increased information, groups and teams typically can identify and evaluate more alternatives than can one person.[26] The people involved in a group or team decision understand the logic and rationale behind it, are more likely to accept it, and are equipped to communicate the decision to their work groups or departments.[27] Finally, research evidence suggests that groups may make better decisions than individuals.[28]

interacting group or team A decision-making group or team in which members openly discuss, argue about, and agree on the best alternative

Delphi group A form of group decision making in which a group is used to achieve a consensus of expert opinion

nominal group A structured technique used to generate creative and innovative alternatives or ideas

TABLE 9.2
Advantages and Disadvantages of Group and Team Decision Making

To increase the chances that a group or team decision will be successful, managers must learn how to manage the process of group and team decision making. Westinghouse, Federal Express, and IBM are increasingly using groups and teams in the decision-making process.

Advantages	Disadvantages
1. More information and knowledge are available.	1. The process takes longer than individual decision making, so it is costlier.
2. More alternatives are likely to be generated.	2. Compromise decisions resulting from indecisiveness may emerge.
3. More acceptance of the final decision is likely.	3. One person may dominate the group.
4. Enhanced communication of the decision may result.	4. Groupthink may occur.
5. Better decisions generally emerge.	

■ Disadvantages of Group and Team Decision Making

Perhaps the biggest drawback of group and team decision making is the additional time and (hence) the greater expense entailed. The increased time stems from interaction and discussion among group or team members. If a given manager's time is worth $50 an hour and if the manager spends two hours making a decision, the decision "costs" the organization $100. For the same decision, a group of five managers might require three hours of time. At the same $50-an-hour rate, the decision "costs" the organization $750. Assuming that the group or team makes the "best" decision, the additional expense may be justified, but the fact remains that group and team decision making is more costly than asking one person to make a decision.

Group or team decisions may also represent undesirable compromises.[29] For example, hiring a compromise top manager may be a bad decision in the long run because he or she may not be able to respond adequately to various subunits in the organization nor have everyone's complete support. Sometimes one individual dominates the group process to the point where others cannot make a full contribution. This dominance may stem from a desire for power or from a naturally dominant personality. The problem is that what appears to emerge as a group decision may actually be the decision of one person.

Finally, a group or team may succumb to a phenomenon known as groupthink. **Groupthink** occurs when the desire for consensus and cohesiveness overwhelms the goal of reaching the best possible decision.[30] Under the influence of groupthink, the group may arrive at decisions that are not in the best interest of either the group or the organization, but rather avoid conflict among group members. One of the clearest documented examples of groupthink involved the space shuttle *Challenger* disaster. As NASA was preparing to launch the shuttle, numerous problems and questions arose. At each step of the way, however, decision makers argued that there was no reason to delay and that everything would be fine. Shortly after the launch on January 28, 1986, the shuttle exploded, killing all seven crew members.

groupthink A situation that occurs when a group or team's desire for consensus and cohesiveness overwhelms its desire to reach the best possible decision

■ Managing Group and Team Decision-Making Processes

Managers can do several things to help promote the effectiveness of group and team decision making. One is simply being aware of the pros and cons of having a group or team make a decision. Time and cost can be managed by setting a deadline by which the decision must be made final. Dominance can be at least partially avoided if a special group is formed just to make the decision. An astute manager, for example, should know who in the organization may try to dominate and can either avoid putting that person in the group or put several strong-willed people together.

To avoid groupthink, each member of the group or team should critically evaluate all alternatives. So that members present divergent viewpoints, the leader should not make his or her own position known too early. At least one member of the group or team might be assigned the role of devil's advocate.

And after reaching a preliminary decision, the group or team should hold a follow-up meeting wherein divergent viewpoints can be raised again if any group members wish to do so.[31] Gould Paper Company used these methods by assigning managers to two different teams. The teams then spent an entire day in a structured debate presenting the pros and cons of each side of an issue to ensure the best possible decision. Sun Microsystems makes most of its major decisions using this same approach.

MANAGEMENT IMPLICATIONS

Managers usually have the option of having a decision made by an individual or by a group or team. They should therefore assess the relative advantages and disadvantages of each approach when deciding how to make a particular decision, as well as the different methods by which groups or teams can be used. If groups or teams are being used, the managers should also take appropriate steps to manage the decision-making process so as to enhance its effectiveness.

Decision making is a pervasive part of most managerial activities. Virtually everything that happens in a company involves making a decision or implementing a decision that has been made. While some decisions are grand and significant in scope, others, such as the ones shown in the center panel of this cartoon, involve more routine, day-to-day activities. And still others, illustrated in the right panel, deal with what to have for lunch or when to take a break. Regardless of their goals, however, the people making the decisions need to take them seriously and do what they believe to be best for the company.

Summary of Key Points

Decisions are an integral part of all managerial activities, but they are perhaps most central to the planning process. Decision making is the act of choosing one alternative from among a set of alternatives. The decision-making process includes recognizing and defining the nature of a decision situation, identifying alternatives, choosing the "best" alternative, and putting it into practice. Two common types of decisions are programmed and nonprogrammed. Decisions may be made under states of certainty, risk, or uncertainty.

Rational perspectives on decision making rest on the classical model. This model assumes that managers have complete information and that they will behave in a rational manner. The primary steps in rational decision making are (1) recognizing and defining the situation, (2) identifying alternatives, (3) evaluating alternatives, (4) selecting the best alternative, (5) implementing the chosen alternative, and (6) following up and evaluating the effectiveness of the alternative after it is implemented.

Behavioral aspects of decision making rely on the administrative model. This model recognizes that managers will have incomplete information and that they will not always behave rationally. The administrative model also recognizes the concepts of bounded rationality and satisficing. Political activities by coalitions, managerial intuition, and the tendency to become increasingly committed to a chosen course of action are all important. Risk propensity is also an important behavioral perspective on decision making. Finally, ethics also affect how managers make decisions.

To help enhance decision-making effectiveness, managers often use interacting, Delphi, or nominal groups or teams. Group and team decision making in general has several advantages as well as disadvantages relative to individual decision making. Managers can adopt a number of strategies to help groups and teams make better decisions.

Discussion Questions

Questions for Review

1. Describe the nature of decision making.

2. What are the main features of the classical model of the decision-making process? What are the main features of the administrative model?

3. What are the steps in rational decision making? Which step do you think is the most difficult to carry out? Why?

4. Describe the behavioral nature of decision making. Be certain to provide some detail about political forces, risk propensity, ethics, and commitment in your description.

Questions for Analysis

5. Was your decision about what college or university to attend a rational decision? Did you go through each step in rational decision making? If not, why not?

6. Can any decision be purely rational, or are all decisions at least partially behavioral in nature? Defend your answer against alternatives.

7. Under what conditions would you expect group or team decision making to be preferable to individual decision making, and vice versa? Why?

Questions for Application

8. Interview a local business manager about a major decision that he or she made recently. Try to determine whether the manager used each of the steps in rational decision making. If not, which were omitted? Why might the manager have omitted those steps?

9. Interview a local business manager about a major decision that he or she made recently. Try to determine whether aspects of the behavioral nature of decision making were involved. If so, which were involved? Why might this have occurred?

10. Interview a department head at your college or university to determine whether group or team decision making is used at all. If it is, for what types of decisions is it used?

Building Effective Decision-Making Skills

EXERCISE OVERVIEW

Decision-making skills refer to the manager's ability to correctly recognize and define problems and opportunities and to then select an appropriate course of action to solve problems and capitalize on opportunities. Communication skills refer to the manager's abilities to both effectively convey ideas and information to others and effectively receive ideas and information from others. Not surprisingly, these skills can be highly interrelated. This exercise will give you insights into some of those interrelations.

EXERCISE BACKGROUND

Identify a decision that you will need to make sometime in the near future. If you work in a managerial position, you might select a real problem or issue to address. For example, you might use the selection or termination of an employee, the allocation of pay raises, or the selection of someone for a promotion.

If you do not work in a managerial position, you might instead select an upcoming decision related to your academic work, for example, what major to select, whether to attend summer school or to work, which job to select, whether to live on or off campus next year. Be sure to select a decision that you have not yet made.

EXERCISE TASK

Using the decision you selected, do each of the following:

1. On a sheet of paper, list the kinds of information that you will most likely use in making your decision. Beside each entry, make notes as to where you can obtain the information, what form the information will be presented in, the reliability of the information, and other characteristics of the information that you deem to be relevant.

2. Assume that you have used the information obtained above and have now made the decision. (It might be helpful at this point to select a hypothetical decision situation and resultant choice to frame your answers.) On the other side of the paper, list the various communication consequences that come with your decision. For example, if your choice involves an academic major, you may need to inform your advisor and your family. List as many consequences as you can. Beside each one, make notes as to how you would communicate with each party, the timeliness of your communication, and other factors that seem to be relevant.

3. What behavioral forces might play a role in your decision?

EXERCISE OVERVIEW

Interpersonal skills refer to the manager's ability to understand and motivate individuals and groups. This exercise enables you to practice your interpersonal skills in a role-playing exercise.

Building Effective Interpersonal Skills

EXERCISE BACKGROUND

You supervise a group of six employees who work in an indoor facility in a relatively isolated location. The company you work for has recently adopted an ambiguous policy regarding smoking. Essentially, the policy states that all company work sites are to be smoke free unless the employees at a specific site choose differently and at the discretion of the site supervisor.

Four members of the work group you supervise are smokers. They have presented the argument that because they constitute the majority they should be allowed to smoke at work. The other two members of the group, both non-smokers, argue that the health-related consequences of secondary smoke should outweigh the preferences of the majority.

To compound the problem further, your boss wrote the new policy and is quite defensive about it—numerous individuals have already criticized the policy. You know that your boss will get very angry with you if you also raise concerns about the policy. Finally, you are personally indifferent about the issue. You do not smoke yourself, but your spouse does smoke. Secondary smoke does not bother you, and you do not have strong opinions about it. Still, you have to make a decision about what to do. You see that your choices are to (1) mandate a smoke-free environment, (2) allow smoking in the facility, or (3) ask your boss to clarify the policy.

EXERCISE TASK

Based on the preceding background information as context, assume that you are the supervisor and do the following:

1. Assume that you have chosen option one. Write an outline that you will use to announce your decision to the four smokers.

2. Assume that you have chosen option two. Write an outline that you will use to announce your decision to the two nonsmokers.

3. Assume that you have chosen option three. Write an outline that you will use when you meet with your boss.

4. Are there other alternatives?

5. What would you do if you were actually the group supervisor?

EXERCISE OVERVIEW

Technical skills are the skills necessary to accomplish or understand the specific kind of work being done in an organization. This exercise enables you to practice technical skills using the Internet to obtain information for making a decision.

EXERCISE BACKGROUND

Assume that you are a business owner seeking a location for a new factory. Your company makes products that are relatively "clean"—that is, they do not pollute the environment, nor will your factory produce any dangerous waste products. Thus, most communities would welcome your plant.

You are seeking a place that has a stable and well-educated workforce, a good quality of life, good health care, and a good educational system. You have narrowed your choice to these towns:

1. Columbia, Missouri

2. Madison, Wisconsin

3. Manhattan, Kansas

4. College Station, Texas

5. Baton Rouge, Louisiana

6. Athens, Georgia

EXERCISE TASK

With the preceding background information as context, do the following:

1. Use the Internet to research each of these cities.

2. Rank-order each city on the basis of the criteria noted above.

3. Select the "best" city for your new factory.

CHAPTER CLOSING CASE

The Path Not Taken

Sears, Roebuck and Co. and Montgomery Ward were founded just a few years apart (Ward in 1872 and Sears in 1893), and together they controlled the retailing landscape in the United States for more than half a century. For decades their growth and competitive strategies were mirror images of one another. For example, their department stores dominated downtown areas and were often located within a city block of each other. Reading their mail-order catalogs became a ubiquitous part of growing up. They even shared the same corporate headquarters location, Chicago. But after decades of parallel strategies and growth, critical decisions at each firm, coming at just about the same time, put them on dramatically different paths, one to fortune and success and one to the brink of ruin.

These decisions came immediately after the end of World War II. Executives at Sears looked carefully at demographic data and patterns and concluded that the citizens of the United States were on the verge of a massive exodus away from central downtown areas to the suburbs. These same executives decided to invest in this trend by moving along with the families who were becoming "suburbanites." Sears began opening all of its new stores in suburban locations, for example, and the stores were usually an anchor in an emerging new form of retailing—the enclosed shopping mall.

Ward, however, followed a different course. Ward's CEO at the time was Sewell Avery. Avery believed that the suburbs were a "fad." More significantly, he also believed a distorted view of economic history, which seemed to suggest that a major depression had followed every war since the time of Napoleon. Because World War II had just ended, Avery reasoned, a major depression was about to strike. And indeed, Sears was stretched so thin by its expansion that if a depression had occurred, the firm would have gone under.

But the depression never came, and Sears flourished. Between 1946, when its expansion started, and 1956, Sears' revenues more than doubled, and it became the undisputed leader in the retailing industry. Although the firm hit some snags in the 1980s and was overtaken by Wal-Mart, Sears has maintained its place as a major force in the retailing industry and today remains profitable and financially healthy.

But Montgomery Ward never recovered from its decision to remain entrenched in the inner cities. Even worse, however, was Sewell Avery's steadfast commitment to his beliefs and his unwillingness to even consider that perhaps he was wrong. Amazingly, Ward did not open a single new store between the years of 1941 and 1957. And during this entire era, Avery clung to his beliefs that a depression was imminent, Sears would collapse, and Ward would be able to buy its competitor at a fraction of its worth!

Ward's board finally gave up on Avery's vision in 1955 and forced him out. But by then it was too late. Sears and J. C. Penney had sewn up the best suburban locations and established themselves in the minds of suburbanites as "the" department stores. And Ward was never really able to break back into the mix. The firm has continued to stumble along, reaching its nadir in 1997 when it was finally forced to file for protection

from its creditors under bankruptcy laws. Whether or not the venerable retailer will be able to figure out how to reinvent itself, of course, remains to be seen. But whatever the outcome, Ward's insiders can only think about what might have been if Avery Sewell had been willing to reconsider his decision half a century earlier.

Case Questions

1. Describe the decision-making processes that likely took place at Sears and Montgomery Ward in the 1940s.
2. Discuss how behavioral processes affected decisions at Montgomery Ward.
3. Under what circumstances might group decision making at Montgomery Ward have resulted in the same outcome? A better outcome?

Case References: "You Snooze, You Lose," *Newsweek*, July 21, 1997, p. 50; *Hoover's Handbook of American Business 1998* (Austin, Texas: Hoover's Business Press, 1998), pp. 946–947; 1198–1199.

CHAPTER NOTES

1. "The Battle of the Bottoms," *Forbes*, March 24, 1997, pp. 98–103; "Strength Ahead?" *Barrons*, July 28, 1997, p. 13; and Linda Grant, "Outmarketing P&G," *Fortune*, January 12, 1998, pp. 150–153.
2. Richard Priem, "Executive Judgment, Organizational Congruence, and Firm Performance," *Organization Science*, August 1994, pp. 421–432.
3. Paul Nutt, "The Formulation Processes and Tactics Used in Organizational Decision Making," *Organization Science*, May 1993, pp. 226–240.
4. For recent reviews of decision making, see E. Frank Harrison, *The Managerial Decision Making Process*, 4th ed. (Boston: Houghton Mifflin, 1995).
5. "Kodak Moment Came Early for CEO Fisher, Who Takes a Stumble," *Wall Street Journal*, July 25, 1997, pp. A1, A6.
6. George P. Huber, *Managerial Decision Making* (Glenview, Ill.: Scott, Foresman, 1980).
7. Huber, *Managerial Decision Making*. See also David W. Miller and Martin K. Starr, *The Structure of Human Decisions* (Englewood Cliffs, N.J.: Prentice-Hall, 1976); and Alvar Elbing, *Behavioral Decisions in Organizations*, 2nd ed. (Glenview, Ill: Scott, Foresman, 1978).
8. Huber, *Managerial Decision Making*.
9. See Bart Nooteboom, Hans Berger, and Niels G. Noorderhaven, "Effects of Trust and Governance on Relational Risk," *Academy of Management Journal*, Vol. 40, No. 2, 1997, pp. 308–338. See also Avi Fiegenbaum and Howard Thomas, "Attitudes toward Risk and the Risk-Return Paradox: Prospect Theory Explanations," *Academy of Management Journal*, March 1988, pp. 85–106; Jitendra V. Singh, "Performance, Slack, and Risk Taking in Organizational Decision Making," *Academy of Management Journal*, September 1986, pp. 562–585; and James G. March and Zur Shapira, "Managerial Perspectives on Risk and Risk Taking," *Management Science*, November 1987, pp. 1404–1418.
10. "Taking the Angst out of Taking a Gamble," *Business Week*, July 14, 1997, pp. 52–53.
11. See Richard M. Cyert and Morris H. DeGroot, "The Maximization Process under Uncertainty," in Patrick D. Larkey and Lee S. Sproull, eds., *Information Processing in Organizations* (Greenwich, Conn.: JAI Press, 1984), pp. 47–61.
12. Glen Whyte, "Decision Failures: Why They Occur and How to Prevent Them," *Academy of Management Executive*, August 1991, pp. 23–31.
13. Thomas Stewart, "How to Lead a Revolution," *Fortune*, November 28, 1994, pp. 48–61.
14. Kenneth Labich, "Coups and Catastrophes," *Fortune*, December 23, 1985, p. 125.

15. "You Snooze, You Lose," *Newsweek*, July 21, 1997, p. 50.

16. "The Wisdom of Solomon," *Newsweek*, August 17, 1987, pp. 62–63.

17. Herbert A. Simon, *Administrative Behavior* (New York: Free Press, 1945). Simon's ideas have been recently refined and updated in Herbert A. Simon, *Administrative Behavior*, 3rd ed. (New York: Free Press, 1976) and in Herbert A. Simon, "Making Management Decisions: The Role of Intuition and Emotion," *Academy of Management Executive*, February 1987, pp. 57–63.

18. Patricia Corner, Angelo Kinicki, and Barbara Keats, "Integrating Organizational and Individual Information Processing Perspectives on Choice," *Organization Science*, August 1994, pp. 294–302.

19 "Unisys: So Far, So Good—But the Real Test Is Yet to Come," *Business Week*, March 2, 1987, pp. 84–86; and "So Far, Married Life Seems to Agree with Unisys," *Business Week*, October 3, 1988, pp. 122–126.

20. Charles P. Wallace, "Adidas—Back in the Game," *Fortune*, August 18, 1997, pp. 176–182.

21. Barry M. Staw and Jerry Ross, "Good Money after Bad," *Psychology Today*, February 1988, pp. 30–33; and D. Ramona Bobocel and John Meyer, "Escalating Commitment to a Failing Course of Action: Separating the Roles of Choice and Justification," *Journal of Applied Psychology*, Vol.79, No. 3, 1994, pp. 360–363.

22. "You Snooze, You Lose," *Newsweek*, July 21, 1997, p. 50.

23. Martha I. Finney, "The Catbert Dilemma—The Human Side of Tough Decisions," *HRMagazine*, February 1997, pp. 70–76.

24. Edwin A. Locke, David M. Schweiger, and Gary P. Latham, "Participation in Decision Making: When Should It Be Used?" *Organizational Dynamics*, Winter 1986, pp. 65–79; and Nicholas Baloff and Elizabeth M. Doherty, "Potential Pitfalls in Employee Participation," *Organizational Dynamics*, Winter 1989, pp. 51–62.

25. Andre L. Delbecq, Andrew H. Van de Ven, and David H. Gustafson, *Group Techniques for Program Planning* (Glenview, Ill.: Scott, Foresman, 1975); and Michael J. Prietula and Herbert A. Simon, "The Experts in Your Midst," *Harvard Business Review*, January–February 1989, pp. 120–124.

26. Norman P. R. Maier, "Assets and Liabilities in Group Problem Solving: The Need for an Integrative Function," in J. Richard Hackman, Edward E. Lawler III, and Lyman W. Porter, eds., *Perspectives on Business in Organizations*, 2nd ed. (New York: McGraw-Hill, 1983), pp. 385–392.

27. Anthony L. Iaquinto and James W. Fredrickson, "Top Management Team Agreement about the Strategic Decision Process: A Test of Some of Its Determinants and Consequences," *Strategic Management Journal*, Vol. 18, 1997, pp. 63–75.

28. James H. Davis, *Group Performance* (Reading, Mass.: Addison-Wesley, 1969).

29. Richard A. Cosier and Charles R. Schwenk, "Agreement and Thinking Alike: Ingredients for Poor Decisions," *Academy of Management Executive*, February 1990, pp. 69–78.

30. Irving L. Janis, *Groupthink*, 2nd ed. (Boston: Houghton Mifflin, 1982).

31. Janis, *Groupthink*.

10

Managing Entrepreneurship and New Venture Formation

OBJECTIVES

After studying this chapter, you should be able to:

- Discuss the nature of entrepreneurship.
- Describe the roles of entrepreneurs in society.
- Understand the major issues involved in choosing strategies for small firms and the role of international management in entrepreneurship.
- Discuss the structural challenges unique to entrepreneurial firms.
- Describe the determinants of performance of small firms.

I n 1984, James Koch was a high-flying management consultant pulling in $250,000 a year. To the surprise of his family and friends, however, he quit this job and invested his life's savings in starting a new business from scratch and going head-to-head with international competitors in a market that had not had a truly successful specialty product in decades. And to their bigger surprise, he succeeded!

The company Koch founded is Boston Beer Co., and its flagship product is a premium beer called Samuel Adams. Koch's family had actually been brewing beer for generations, and he started with a recipe developed by his great-great-grandfather, who in the 1870s had sold the beer in St. Louis under the name Louis Koch Lager. To fund his operation, Koch used $100,000 in personal savings and another $300,000 invested by his friends.

James Koch set up shop in an old warehouse in Boston, bought some surplus brewing equipment from a large brewery, and started operations. Because his beer used only the highest quality ingredients, he needed to price it at about $1 more per case than such premium imports as Heineken. Boston-area distributors, meanwhile, doubted that consumers would pay $6 per six-pack for an American beer, and most refused to carry it. Thus, Koch began selling the beer directly to retailers and bars himself.

But his big break came when he entered Samuel Adams Lager in the Great American Beer Festival, where it won the consumer preference poll—the industry's equivalent of the Oscar. Koch then started using this victory as his advertising mantra, proclaiming Samuel Adams as "The Best Beer in America." Sales began to take off, and national distributors began calling for the beer. In order to meet surging demand, Koch contracted part of the brewing to a near-deserted Stroh's brewery in Pittsburgh.

During the early 1990s, sales of Samuel Adams products grew at an annual rate of more than 57 percent, and in 1996 sales topped $214 million. Koch, meanwhile, has retained

controlling interests in the business and still oversees the day-to-day brewing operations. Indeed, he claims that he has sampled at least one of the firm's products every day since the business started, primarily as a way of monitoring quality.

But Koch's success has not gone unnoticed, especially by industry giant Anheuser-Busch Companies, Inc. Anheuser-Busch and other national brewers have recently seen their sales take a hit from so-called microbreweries, small regional or local companies that sell esoteric brews made in small quantities and deriving cache from their very scarcity. The Boston Beer Co. was the first of these to make it big, and most others are trying to follow in its footsteps. Obviously, therefore, Anheuser-Busch has a vested interest in not letting these smaller start-ups gain too much market share, most of which would come at its own expense.

Recently, for example, Koch learned that Anheuser-Busch had inquired about buying the entire crop from a German hops farmer who has an exclusive arrangement with Boston Beer. Had Anheuser-Busch succeeded, Koch says, he would have been put out of business. Anheuser-Busch has also complained that the labeling on Samuel Adams is misleading, hiding the fact the beer made in Pittsburgh is actually being brewed under contract by Stroh's, not Boston Beer. And the industry giant has even tried to convince wholesalers, who are highly dependent on Anheuser-Busch products such as Budweiser, to stop selling specialty beers like Samuel Adams. Koch, meanwhile, simply sees all this attention as a clear sign that he has made it.[1]

"You don't create a whole new national market in the beer business by being frightened."

James Koch, owner, Boston Beer Co., quoted in Fortune, March 31, 1997, p. 85.

Just like James Koch, thousands of people all over the world start new businesses each year. And like the Boston Beer Co., some of these businesses succeed while, unfortunately, many others fail. Some of the people who fail in a new business try again, and sometimes it takes two or more failures before a successful business gets under way. Henry Ford, for example, went bankrupt twice before succeeding with the Ford Motor Co.

This process of starting a new business, sometimes failing and sometimes succeeding, is part of what is called *entrepreneurship*, the subject of this chapter. We begin by exploring the nature of entrepreneurship. We then examine the role of entrepreneurship in the business world and discuss strategies for entrepreneurial organizations. We then describe the structure and performance of entrepreneurial organizations.

The Nature of Entrepreneurship

entrepreneurship   The process of planning, organizing, operating, and assuming the risk of a business venture

entrepreneur   Someone who engages in entrepreneurship

Entrepreneurship is the process of planning, organizing, operating, and assuming the risk of a business venture. An **entrepreneur**, in turn, is someone who engages in entrepreneurship. James Koch, as highlighted in the opening incident fits this description. He put his own resources on the line and took a personal stake in the success or failure of his budding enterprise. Business owners who hire professional managers to run their businesses and then turn their attention to other interests are not entrepreneurs. Although they are assuming the risk of the venture, they are not actively involved in organizing or operat-

Entrepreneurs find new business through many different approaches. For example, take Dineh Mohajer. A few years ago, when she was studying pre-med at USC, she wanted some blue nail polish to wear to a party but couldn't find just the right shade, so she made it herself. She subsequently decided there is a market among Generation X-ers like herself for new approaches to cosmetics and toiletries. So, she dropped out of school and founded Hard Candy and started marketing nail polish with names like Pimp and Porno. Mohajer's firm now has 25 employees and sales of over $10 million a year.

ing it. Likewise, professional managers whose job is running someone else's business are not entrepreneurs, for they assume less-than-total personal risk for the success or failure of the business.

Entrepreneurs start small businesses. We define a **small business** as one that is privately owned by one individual or a small group of individuals and which has sales and assets that are not large enough to influence its environment. A small two-person software development company with annual sales of $100,000 would clearly be a small business, whereas Microsoft Corporation is just as clearly a large business. But the boundaries are not always this clear cut. For example, a regional retailing chain with twenty stores and annual revenues of $30 million may sound large but is really very small when compared to giants such as Wal-Mart and Sears.

small business A business that is privately owned by one individual or a small group of individuals; it has sales and assets that are not large enough to influence its environment

MANAGEMENT IMPLICATIONS Managers should understand the nature and meaning of entrepreneurship and what differentiates it from management. ▬

The Role of Entrepreneurship in Society

The history of entrepreneurship and of the development of new businesses is in many ways the history of great wealth and of great failure. Some entrepreneurs have been very successful and have accumulated vast fortunes from their entrepreneurial efforts. For example, when Microsoft Corporation sold its

Identifying market niches and then providing products or services to fill them underlies the role of entrepreneurship in society. Take something as innocuous as Beanie Babies, for example. These small plush animals introduced a few years ago have become collector's items, with some discontinued models selling on secondary markets for hundreds of dollars. While those who aren't interested in Beanie Babies may scoff, the premise is the same as for limited edition books, signed and numbered prints, and autographed baseballs—by creating an innovative product that appeals to some people and then creating at least an image of scarcity or limited availability, entrepreneurs can increase their prospects for success.

FIGURE 10.1
**Trends in Women-Owned
Small Business**

The percentage of women-
owned businesses in the United
States continues to escalate dramatically. Although there are
still relatively few women who
own businesses in industries
such as agriculture or forestry,
their presence is quite large in
other industries such as wholesaling, retailing, and services.
Source: Reprinted from April 18, 1994
issue of *Business Week* by special permission. Copyright © 1994 by The
McGraw-Hill Companies.

stock to the public in 1986, Bill Gates, then just thirty years old, received $350 million for his share of Microsoft.[2] Today, his holdings—valued at $9 billion— make him one of the richest people in the world. Many more entrepreneurs, however, have lost a great deal of money. Research suggests that most new businesses fail within the first three years of founding.[3] Many that last longer do so only because the entrepreneurs themselves work long hours for very lit- tle income.

Increasingly, small businesses in the United States are being spearheaded by women.[4] There are many reasons for this trend, two of which we give here. First, some women, frustrated by what they see as limited promotion opportu- nities in large organizations, believe that starting their own business is the best route to success. Second, some women see owning their own business as a good way to combine their careers with the responsibilities of motherhood. Figure 10.1 shows the dramatic increase in women-owned proprietorships in various industries between 1980 and 1990. "Working with Diversity" tells the story of one successful woman entrepreneur.

The experiences of individuals who win (and lose) fortunes as a result of their entrepreneurial activities may make fascinating stories, but the vital role that entrepreneurship plays in our society and our economy is even more telling. More than 99 percent of the nation's 16 million businesses are small. More than six hundred thousand new businesses are incorporated each year. Their vibrant, almost countless activi- ties influence a number of economic areas, including in- novation, job creation, and contributions to large busi- nesses.[5]

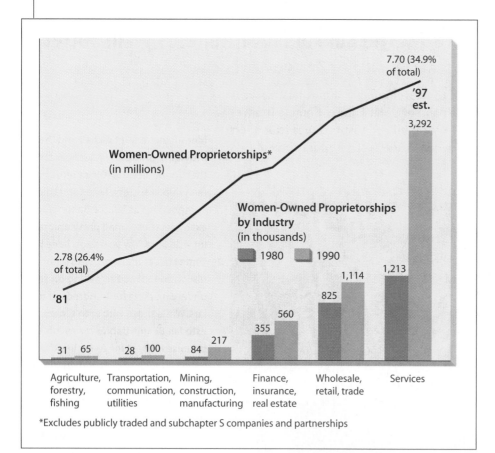

*Excludes publicly traded and subchapter S companies and partnerships

■ Innovation

The resourcefulness and inge- nuity typical of small business have spawned new industries and contributed a great many innovative ideas and techno- logical breakthroughs to our society. Small businesses or in- dividuals working alone in- vented, among other things, the personal computer, the transistor radio, the photocopying machine, the jet engine, and the instant photograph. They also gave us the pocket calculator, power steering,

Chucking It All to Have It All

Kathy Dawson seemed to have it all—she was a major executive in a fast-growing company earning a big salary. Trouble is, she wanted more— more time for herself and for her children, that is. Her executive job required her to work long hours, often until late in the evening, and to be away from home several nights a month. Ms. Dawson eventually became concerned that she was not spending enough time with her children. She was also frustrated because her business associates seemed to be insensitive to her situation—they were all male and most were unmarried.

So, a few years ago, she left the corporate world and founded the Dawson Group, a human resource consulting business. By being her own boss, she both avoided the frustrations of the corporate environment she left behind and created much more flexibility for herself—she can more easily take work home now and can bring her kids into the

> *"High-achieving women are leaving corporations to start their own businesses, mainly because they feel it gives them control of their lives."*
>
> Sharon Hadary, executive director of the National Foundation for Women Business owners*

office if she wants or needs to. And sometimes she even gets her children to help stuff envelopes or make copies!

Of course, Ms. Dawson has paid a price for her independence. Her income is still only half of her former salary, for example, and she still has to travel more than she would like. And although some of her friends and associates applaud her actions, others worry that she has sent a signal to the corporate world that the old stereotypes about women may not be all wrong. But on balance, she thinks the tradeoff has been worth it. Indeed, her only regret seems to be that she didn't take this plunge earlier.

References: *"More Women Quit Lucrative Jobs to Start Their Own Businesses,"* Wall Street Journal, *November 11, 1996, pp. A1, A8 (*quote on p. A1);"Banking on Female Entrepreneurs,"* Bank Management, *May–June 1996, pp. 20–25; and "A Cool Billion for Women,"* Working Woman, *February 1996, p. 54.*

automatic transmission, air conditioning, and even the nineteen-cent ballpoint pen. Some scholars believe that entrepreneurs and small businesses are the driving force behind innovation in a society. As entrepreneurs seek the income and wealth associated with successful innovation, they create new technologies and products that displace older technologies and products.[6]

■ Job Creation

Small businesses create more new jobs than do larger businesses. One study suggested that small businesses may account for as much as 66 percent of all new employment in the United States each year. In another study, the U.S. Department of Commerce found that small, young, high-technology businesses created new jobs at a much faster rate than did larger, older businesses. The new jobs created by small businesses come in small bites. When a new restaurant opens, it may employ fifteen persons. When a new retail specialty store opens, it may employ twenty persons. Because so many new businesses are created each year, however, the cumulative impact on employment is significant.

■ Contributions to Large Businesses

Small businesses are the primary suppliers and distributors for the products of large businesses. General Motors (GM), for example, buys materials from more than twenty-five thousand suppliers, most of them small businesses. GM also distributes its products through small businesses—independent dealers. Likewise, Sony buys supplies from thousands of small businesses, distributes its electronic products through numerous small distributors and its movies through numerous independent movie theaters, and sells its records through independent record stores.

> **MANAGEMENT IMPLICATIONS**
>
> All managers, regardless of the size of their organization, should recognize the important roles that entrepreneurs play in the areas of innovation, job creation, and supporting large businesses. ■

Strategy for Entrepreneurial Organizations

One of the most basic challenges facing an entrepreneurial organization is choosing a strategy. The three strategic challenges facing small firms, in turn, are choosing an industry in which to compete, emphasizing distinctive competencies, and writing a business plan.[7]

■ Choosing an Industry

As we discussed in Chapter 3, we can apply Michael Porter's five forces framework to estimate the average economic performance of the firms in an industry. In general, an industry characterized by high levels of rivalry, strong substitutes, a strong threat of entry, and powerful suppliers and buyers has lower return potential for firms than do industries without these characteristics.[8]

Entrepreneurs seeking to begin small-business operations should generally look to industries with favorable industry attributes. Thus, for example, entrepreneurs who start a business based on a technology with few rivals or substitutes and a low threat of entry usually earn higher rates of return than entrepreneurs who start a business without these advantages.

Examples of small businesses that chose a high-potential industry are Microsoft and Lotus, both very successful computer software companies. These companies have developed personal computer software that dominates their respective market segments (Microsoft in operating systems; Lotus in spreadsheet software). Because these firms are so dominant in their segments, there is low rivalry in their industries. Because of the skills that computer users have developed in applying these particular software packages, there are few substitutes. And because of the reputation and success of these firms, entry into these software segments is unlikely (although certainly not impossible). Examples of small businesses that begin operations in an industry with lower return potential are independent video rental stores. Because of the large number of video rental stores and because all stores carry many of the same videos, rivalry in this industry is intense. Substitutes in the form of cable television, movie theaters, network television, and even books are common. Because the cost of entering this industry is relatively low (the cost of videos plus a lease and computer software), entry into the video rental business is easy. For these reasons, independent video rental operations are often marginal financial performers, although as members of national chains, video stores can be profitable.

Industries in Which Small Businesses Are Strong Small businesses tend to do well in the service, retail, and wholesale industries. Service organizations are perhaps the most common type of entrepreneurial business because they require a fairly small capital investment to start up.[9] A certified public accountant, for example, can open a business simply by renting an office and hanging out a sign. The number of small businesses in the service industry including video rental shops, hair salons, and tax preparation services has significantly increased in recent years, all because the costs of the physical assets needed to start these businesses are relatively low.

Entrepreneurs are also effective in the area of specialty retailing. Specialty retailers cater to specific customer groups such as golfers, college students, and people who do their own automobile repairs. Often, the number of these special consumers is relatively small, and thus the dollar size of the market associated with these consumers is small. Although large organizations may be unwilling to enter a business where the market is so small, small businesses may be very successful in these industries.[10]

Wholesalers buy products from large manufacturers and resell them to retailers. Small businesses dominate the wholesale industry because they are often able to develop personal working relationships with several sellers and several buyers. A wholesale supplier of computer equipment may have to develop supply relationships with five or six floppy disk manufacturers, six or seven hard disk manufacturers, and five or six video screen manufacturers to have the inventory it needs to respond to the needs of its retail customers. If this wholesaler was not "independent," but instead was part of a larger electronics company, it would have supply relationships with only one supplier of floppy disks, one supplier of hard disks, and one maker of video screens. As long as end users want many supply options, the independent wholesaler can play an important economic role.

FIGURE 10.2

Economies of Scale in Small Business Organizations

Small businesses sometimes find it difficult to compete in manufacturing-related industries because of the economies of scale associated with plant, equipment, and technology. As shown in (a), firms that produce a large number of units (that is, larger businesses) can do so at a lower per unit cost. At the same time, however, new forms of technology occasionally cause the economies-of-scale curve to shift, as illustrated in (b). In this case, smaller firms may be able to compete more effectively with larger ones because of the drop in per unit manufacturing cost.

Industries in Which Small Businesses Are Weak   Small organizations have difficulty succeeding in certain other industries. Foremost among them are industries dominated by large-scale manufacturing and agriculture, which is an industry in transition from domination by small family farms to domination by large corporate farms.

Research has shown that manufacturing costs often fall as the number of units produced by an organization increases. This relationship between cost and production is called an *economy of scale*.[11] Small organizations usually cannot compete effectively on the basis of economies of scale. As depicted in panel A of Figure 10.2, organizations with higher levels of production have a major cost advantage over those with lower levels of production. Given the cost positions of small and large firms when there are strong economies of scale in manufacturing, it is not surprising that small manufacturing organizations generally do not do as well as large ones.

Interestingly, when technology in an industry changes, it often shifts the economies-of-scale curve, thereby creating opportunities for smaller organizations. For example, steel manufacturing was historically dominated by a few large companies that owned several huge facilities. With the development of minimill technology, however, extracting economies of scale at a much smaller level of production became possible. This type of shift is depicted in panel B of Figure 10.2. Point A in this panel is the low-cost point with the original economies of scale. Point B is the low-cost point with the economies of scale brought on by the new technology. Notice that the number of units needed for low costs is considerably lower for the new technology than for the old. This characteristic has allowed numerous smaller firms to enter the steel industry. Such entry would not have been possible with the older technology.

Of course, not all manufacturing is capital intensive. Some manufacturing can be done with minimal plant and equipment. This kind of light industry is

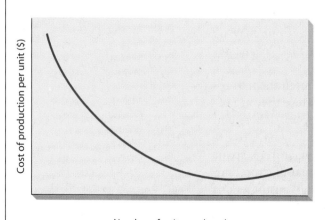

(a) Standard economies-of-scale curve

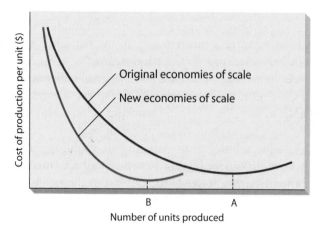

(b) Change in technology that shifts economies of scale and may make small business production possible typical of some parts of the computer industry and some parts of the plastic fabrication industry, in printing, and elsewhere. Small organizations can excel in these industries. Agriculture is an industry in transition. Small family farms were among the first small businesses in the world, and until recently they were among the most successful. Economies of scale and high equipment prices, however, have forced many small farmers out of business. Giant agribusiness enterprises and corporate farms are gradually replacing them. These multifarm businesses own and farm millions of acres and are large enough to fully exploit economies of scale by purchasing and sharing the most modern farm equipment, applying the latest scientific methods in farming, and even influencing government policy to favor farmers.

■ Emphasizing Distinctive Competencies

As we explained in Chapter 8, an organization's distinctive competencies are the aspects of business that the firm performs better than its competitors. The distinctive competencies of small business usually fall into three areas: the ability to identify new niches in established markets, the ability to identify new markets, and the ability to move quickly to take advantage of new opportunities.

Identifying Niches in Established Markets An **established market** is one in which several large firms compete according to relatively well-defined criteria. For example, throughout the 1970s several well-known computer-manufacturing companies, including IBM, Digital Equipment, and Hewlett-Packard, competed according to three product criteria: computing power, service, and price. Over the years, the computing power and quality of service delivered by these firms continued to improve while prices (especially relative to computing power) continued to drop.

Enter Apple Computer and the personal computer. For Apple, user friendliness, not computing power, service, and price, was to be the basis of competition. Apple targeted every manager, every student, and every home as the owner of a personal computer. The major entrepreneurial act of Apple was not to invent a new technology (indeed, the first Apple computers used all standard parts) but to recognize a new kind of computer and a new way to compete in the computer industry.

Apple's approach to competition was to identify a new niche in an established market. A **niche** is simply a segment of a market that is not currently being exploited. In general, small entrepreneurial businesses are better at discovering these niches than are larger organizations. Large organizations

Entrepreneurs who successfully identify and exploit their distinctive competencies have a good chance for success. Douglas Becker and R. Christopher Hoehn-Saric have built Sylvan Learning Centers, specializing in tutoring school-age children in math, science, and other basics. Using what they learned from this business, Sylvan recently has started administering tests like the GRE and GMAT for Educational Testing Services. They are also experimenting with learning centers inside public schools. By relying on its distinctive competencies, Sylvan is now generating about $250 million in revenues each year.

established market A market in which several large firms compete according to well-defined criteria
niche A segment of a market not currently being exploited

The Big Picture

The Toronto-based Imax Corporation is on a roll. Although many people associate Imax with tourist-oriented fare (Imax theaters are located in the Smithsonian, for example, and across from the Alamo), the company is expanding rapidly around the world and moving more into mainstream film presentation.

Imax was founded in 1967 using a patented technology to project huge images onto giant screens with little or no loss in clarity or brightness. More than one hundred special films have been made for Imax screens, most with themes such as science, nature, or history. Unfortunately, Imax never really had sufficient funding to expand rapidly or to move into other entertainment venues. This situation changed in 1993, however, when two deep-pocketed investors bought the firm.

The new owners, former Wall Street partners, have unveiled a sweeping new strategy to grow the firm. For one thing, they intend to double the number of theaters the company currently owns by getting other movie chains to include one Imax auditorium in new multiplexes. Second, they also want to expand internationally, with a goal of more than doubling the sixty-three theaters currently in operation in North America. And third, they are actively working with major film studios to figure out how to make new movies compatible with both conventional and Imax projection systems. One of their major partners in this area, Sony, has several new films in development that can be shown on both kinds of screens. Apparently, then, Imax's new owners have seen "the big picture," and its green!

> *". . .you're going to see more people making movies for those [Imax] screens."*
>
> *George Lucas, noted producer and director**

References: *"Now Showing in Imax: Money!"* Business Week, *March 31, 1997, p. 80 (*quote on p. 80); and "Maxed Out,"* Canadian Business, *April 1996, p. 18.*

---

usually have so many resources committed to older, established business practices that they may be unaware of new opportunities. Entrepreneurs can see these opportunities and move quickly to take advantage of them.[12] "The World of Management" describes a promising market niche currently being developed by Imax.

Identifying New Markets Successful entrepreneurs also excel at discovering whole new markets. Discovery can happen in at least two ways. First, an entrepreneur can transfer a product or service that is well established in one geographic market to a second market. This is what Marcel Bich did with ballpoint pens, which occupied a well-established market in Europe before Bich introduced them to this country. Bich's company, Bic Corp., eventually came to dominate the U.S. market.

Second, entrepreneurs can sometimes create entire industries. Entrepreneurial inventions of the dry paper copying process and the semiconductor have created vast new industries. Not only have the first companies into these markets been very successful (Xerox and National Semiconductor, respectively), but their entrepreneurial activity has spawned the development of hundreds of thousands of other companies and hundreds of thousands of jobs. Again, because entrepreneurs are not encumbered with a history of doing business in a particular way, they are usually better at discovering new markets than are larger, more mature organizations.

First-Mover Advantages   A **first-mover advantage** is any advantage that comes to a firm because it exploits an opportunity before any other firm does. Sometimes large firms discover niches within existing markets or new markets at just about the same time as small entrepreneurial firms do but are not able to move as quickly as small companies to take advantage of these opportunities.

first-mover advantage   Any advantage that comes to a firm because it exploits an opportunity before any other firm does

There are numerous reasons for this difference. For example, many large organizations make decisions slowly because each of their many layers of hierarchy has to approve an action before it can be implemented. Also, large organizations may sometimes put a great deal of their assets at risk when they take advantage of new opportunities. Every time Boeing decides to build a new model of a commercial jet, it is making a decision that could literally bankrupt the company if it does not turn out well. The size of the risk may make large organizations cautious. The dollar value of the assets at risk in a small organization, in contrast, is quite small. Managers may be willing to "bet the company" when the value of the company is only $100,000. They might be unwilling to bet the company when the value of the company is $1 billion.

■ Writing a Business Plan

Once an entrepreneur has chosen an industry to compete in and determined which distinctive competencies to emphasize, these choices are usually included in a document called a *business plan*. In a **business plan** the entrepreneur summarizes the business strategy and how that strategy is to be implemented. The very act of preparing a business plan forces prospective entrepreneurs to crystallize their thinking about what they must do to launch their business successfully and obliges them to develop their business on paper before investing time and money in it. The idea of a business plan is not new. What is new is the growing use of specialized business plans by entrepreneurs, mostly because creditors and investors demand them for use in deciding whether to help finance a small business.

business plan   A document that summarizes the business strategy and structure

The plan should describe the match between the entrepreneur's abilities and the requirements for producing and marketing a particular product or service. It should define strategies for production and marketing, legal aspects and organization, and accounting and finance. In particular, it should answer three questions: (1) What are the entrepreneur's goals and objectives? (2) What strategies will the entrepreneur use to obtain these goals and objectives? (3) How will the entrepreneur implement these strategies?

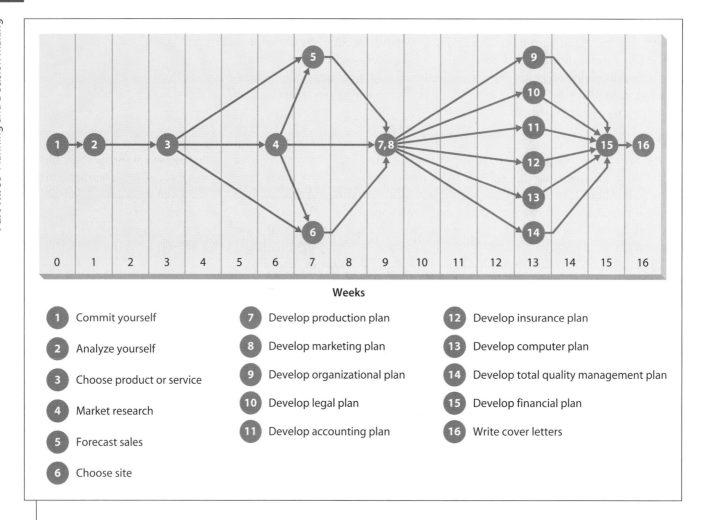

1 Commit yourself

2 Analyze yourself

3 Choose product or service

4 Market research

5 Forecast sales

6 Choose site

7 Develop production plan

8 Develop marketing plan

9 Develop organizational plan

10 Develop legal plan

11 Develop accounting plan

12 Develop insurance plan

13 Develop computer plan

14 Develop total quality management plan

15 Develop financial plan

16 Write cover letters

FIGURE 10.3

A PERT Diagram for Business Planning

Business planning involves a number of very specific activities and events, as shown in this PERT diagram. Following a logical and systematic process such as the one shown here will enhance the chances for success.

Source: Figure "A PERT Diagram for Business Planning" from Nicholas C. Siropolis, *Small Business Management,* 5th ed. Copyright © 1994 by Houghton Mifflin Company. Used by permission.

Some idea of the complexity of planning a new business may be gleaned from the PERT diagram shown in Figure 10.3. The diagram shows the major steps in planning the launch of a new business. Notice that the development of a business plan consists of a set of specific activities, perhaps none of which is more pivotal than marketing research—the systematic and intensive study of all the facts, opinions, and judgments that bear on the successful marketing of a product or service.

Figure 10.3 also shows the sequential nature of much strategic decision making in small businesses. For example, entrepreneurs cannot forecast sales revenues without first researching markets. The sales forecast itself is one of the most important elements in the business plan. Without such forecasts, it is all but impossible to estimate intelligently the size of a plant, store, or office or to determine how much inventory to carry or how many employees to hire.

Another important business activity is financial planning, which translates all other activities into dollars. Generally, the financial plan is made up of a cash budget, an income statement, balance sheets, and a breakeven chart. The most important of these statements is the cash budget because it tells entrepreneurs how much money they need before they open for business and how much money they need to keep the business operating.

Entrepreneurship and International Management

Finally, whereas many people associate international management with big business, many smaller companies are also finding expansion and growth opportunities in foreign countries. For example, Fuci Metals, a small but growing enterprise, buys metal from remote locations in areas such as Siberia and Africa and then sells them to big auto makers like Ford and Toyota. Similarly, California-based Gold's Gym is expanding into foreign countries, and has been especially successful in Russia.[13] Although considerable risks accompany such ventures, they also give entrepreneurs new opportunities and can be a real catalyst for success.

MANAGEMENT IMPLICATIONS Entrepreneurs should exercise caution when selecting an industry, recognizing that some are easier and others more difficult for a small business. By emphasizing distinctive competencies and relying on a well-formulated business plan, entrepreneurs can increase their chances for success. Small businesses should also give full consideration to international opportunities. ▬

Structure of Entrepreneurial Organizations

With a strategy in place and a business plan in hand, the entrepreneur can then proceed to devise a structure that turns the vision of the business plan into a reality. Many of the concerns in structuring any business, which are described in the next four chapters of this book, are also relevant to small businesses. For example, entrepreneurs need to consider organization design and develop job descriptions, organization charts, and management control systems. Small businesses do have some special concerns relating to structure, however, including the form of ownership and sources of financing, methods for starting the business, and sources of management help.

Forms of Ownership and Sources of Financing

Ownership structure specifies who possesses legal title to an organization's assets and who has a claim on any economic profits generated by a firm. Financing a small business involves decisions concerning the sources of capital that will be used to start the business and what claims (if any) these sources have on the organization's profits. A number of alternatives are available for both ownership structure and sources of financing, and each option has advantages and disadvantages.

Business ownership can take a variety of forms. For example, the Mississippi Band of Choctaw Indians owns and operates several successful businesses, including one that makes wire harnesses for automotive electronics and another, in partnership with American Greetings, that makes greeting cards. Indeed, the tribe's holdings have become so successful that they are the region's largest employer and rely on non-Indians to fill about half the jobs in the Choctaw's various enterprises.

Forms of Ownership A popular form of legal ownership for many new businesses is the **sole proprietorship** in which legal title to all assets and claims on all future economic profits are controlled by a single individual. About 70 percent of all U.S. businesses are sole proprietorships. The major advantages of a sole proprietorship are that the individual entrepreneur has total freedom in conducting business, start-up is simple and inexpensive, and business profits are taxed as ordinary income to the proprietor. The disadvantages are that the proprietor has unlimited liability (his or her personal assets are at risk to cover business debts) and the business ends when the proprietor retires or dies.

Another form of ownership is the **partnership**, in which two or more persons agree to be partners in a business, share title in the assets of the firm, be held jointly liable for a firm's debts, and share a firm's profits. The least common form of ownership, partnerships are often used by accounting, legal, and architectural firms. These types of organizations are highly dependent on the professional skills of individuals, and partnerships tend to foster the professional mutual respect that is essential in these business activities. Partnerships provide a larger pool of talent and capital to start a business than do sole proprietorships, but they are just as easy to form and they offer the same tax benefits. They also have similar disadvantages: liability and no legal continuance if the partnership is dissolved. An added difficulty may be conflict or tension between partners.

Most large, and some smaller, organizations use the corporation as the basis for ownership. A **corporation** is a legal entity created under the law that is independent of any single individual. Like an individual, a corporation can borrow money, enter into contracts, own property, sue, and be sued. Its owners are the stockholders. An advantage that distinguishes the corporation from sole proprietorships and partnerships is that it is responsible for its own liabilities, so the owners have limited liability. A corporation continues to exist despite the retirement or death of any of its owners, and it can often borrow money easily. Corporations have higher start-up costs, however, and they are subject to increased regulation and double taxation (that is, the corporation pays taxes on its profits, and then stockholders pay taxes on their dividends).

A few other special forms of ownership also exist. *Master limited partnerships* and *subchapter S corporations* provide many of the advantages of corporations without double taxation. *Cooperatives* enable a number of small organizations to pool resources and share markets. Ocean Spray Cranberries is a cooperative that is made up of seven hundred independent cranberry growers and one hundred citrus growers.

Sources of Financing An important issue confronting all entrepreneurs is locating the money necessary to open and operate the business. Personal resources (savings and money borrowed from friends or family) are the most common sources of new-business financing. Personal resources are often the most important source because they reinforce the entrepreneur's personal commitment to the venture. Many entrepreneurs also take advantage of various lending programs and assistance provided by lending institutions and government agencies.[14] Government programs are especially interested in helping women and minority entrepreneurs.

Another common source of funds is venture capitalists. A **venture capitalist** is someone who actively seeks to invest in new businesses. The advantage of this approach is that it gives entrepreneurs access to a large resource base with fewer restrictions than might be imposed by the government or by banks. In return, however, the entrepreneur must relinquish to the venture capitalist a portion of the profits or share ownership.[15]

■ Methods for Starting a New Business

Another set of questions that an entrepreneur must address when organizing a business is whether to buy an existing business, start a new one, or seek a franchising agreement.

Buying an Existing Business Buying an existing business offers many advantages. Because the entrepreneur can examine the business's historical records to determine the pattern of revenue and profit and the type of cash flow, he or she can eliminate much guesswork about what to expect. The entrepreneur also acquires existing supplier, distributor, and customer networks. On the negative side, the entrepreneur inherits whatever problems the business may already have and may be forced to accept existing contractual agreements. Howard Schultz bought Starbucks Corporation when it was a small, struggling outfit and turned it into a big successful company.

Starting a New Business Starting a new business from scratch allows the owner to avoid the shortcomings of an existing business and to put his or her personal stamp on the enterprise. James Koch used this method to start the Boston Beer Co. The entrepreneur also has the opportunity to choose suppliers, bankers, lawyers, and employees without worrying about existing agreements or contractual arrangements.[16] More uncertainty is involved in starting a new business, however, than in taking over an existing one. The entrepreneur starts out with less information about projected revenues and cash flow, has to build a customer base from zero, and may be forced to accept unfavorable credit terms from suppliers. Because it is an unknown quantity, a new business may have difficulty borrowing money.

Franchising An alternative to buying an existing business or starting one from scratch is entering into a **franchising agreement**. The entrepreneur pays

sole proprietorship A form of ownership in which one individual controls legal title to all assets and claims or all future profits

partnership A form of ownership in which two or more persons agree to be partners, to share title of firm assets, to be held jointly liable for firm debts, and to share firm profits

corporation A legal entity that is created under the law, and which is independent of any single individual, for the sole purpose of business ownership and control

venture capitalist Someone who actively seeks to invest in new businesses

franchising agreement A contract between an entrepreneur (the **franchisee**) and a parent company (the **franchiser**); the entrepreneur pays the parent company for the use of the trademarks, products, formulas, and business plans

TODAY'S MANAGEMENT ISSUES

Big Mac Attack?

McDonald's Corporation and its "golden arches" have made many individual entrepreneurs quite wealthy. The average McDonald's franchisee, for example, nets about $100,000 a year, and many earn substantially more. Further, many franchisees own multiple restaurants. So why would any of these franchisees have reason to be unhappy? Actually, many longtime McDonald's franchisees are up in arms about what they see as inappropriate treatment at the hands of the hamburger giant. Two big issues seem to be at the heart of the matter.

For one thing, for the last several years McDonald's has been aggressively seeking new market share via rapid expansion. But since there are already so many McDonald's restaurants in most markets, many of the new ones are popping up close to existing ones, in some cases just a few streets away. The worst-case scenario for a franchisee occurs when McDonald's awards ownership of a new restaurant a few blocks away to a newcomer. But even if the existing franchisee gets the new award, its revenues are still likely to be earned, at least in part, at the expense of the existing outlet.

> *"You work and work to build up your business, and they can take a piece away."*
>
> *Disgruntled McDonald's franchisee**

The other problem voiced by the franchisees is the parent company's inability to pump up same-store sales. The owners argue, for example, that the chain's menu has grown a bit long in the tooth, and most of the new products the firm has attempted in recent years—the McLean Deluxe and the Arch Deluxe come to mind—have flopped. Meanwhile, rival Burger King has launched several successful new products during that same span. McDonald's further angered its franchisees when it recently announced major price cuts on Big Macs and other popular sandwiches without first informing the franchisees! Still, most franchisees are happy with the firm and realize they are getting a good return on their investments. But the firm's critics are also becoming more numerous and more vocal.

References: *"Fast-Food Fight," Business Week, June 2, 1997, pp. 34–36 (*quote on p. 34); "Some Franchisees Say Moves by McDonald's Hurt Their Operations," Wall Street Journal, April 17, 1996, pp. A1, A8; and Shelly Branch, "What's Eating McDonald's?" Fortune, October 31, 1997, pp. 122–125.*

---

a parent company (the **franchiser**) a flat fee or a share of the income from the business. In return the entrepreneur (the **franchisee**) is allowed to use the company's trademarks, products, formulas, and business plan. Industries within which franchising is common include fast foods (McDonald's), specialty retail clothing stores (Benetton), personal computer stores (ComputerLand), and local automobile dealerships.[17]

Franchising may reduce the entrepreneur's financial risk because many parent companies provide advice and assistance. They also provide proven production, sales, and marketing methods; training; financial support; and an established identity and image. Some franchisers also allow successful individual franchisees to grow by opening multiple outlets.

On the negative side, some franchises are expensive. A McDonald's franchise costs several hundred thousand dollars. Also, the parent company often restricts the franchisee to certain types of products. A McDonald's franchisee cannot change the formula for milkshakes, alter the preparation of Big Macs, or purchase supplies from any other company. Some franchise agreements are difficult to terminate.[18] "Today's Management Issues" explores other controversies currently surrounding McDonald's and its franchisees.

Despite the drawbacks, franchising is growing by leaps and bounds. Presently, more than one-third of U.S. retail sales go through franchises, and that figure is expected to climb to one-half by the end of this century.[19] Much of the attraction of franchising is that this approach to starting a new business involves limited risks. At the same time, however, also remember that no form of business is completely risk free.

■ Sources of Management Help

Since the 1950s, the idea that small businesses benefit from management assistance has grown widely. Table 10.1 lists the many sources of management help now offered at little or no cost to entrepreneurs, both before and after they embark on a new business. Because of the extent of management sophistication needed to launch a venture such as microcomputer manufacture, special services are available to entrepreneurs who go into a high-technology business.[20]

Table 10.1 covers not only federal help but also help from sources such as community colleges and universities, the Department of Commerce, and other organizations made up of small businesses. Heading the list is the Small Business Administration (SBA). Many entrepreneurs have the mistaken view that the SBA only lends money or guarantees repayment of loans made by commercial banks. Even more important are SBA efforts to help entrepreneurs manage their businesses effectively and spend their money wisely.

The SBA offers entrepreneurs four major cost-free management-assistance programs: Service Corps of Retired Executives (SCORE), Active Corps of Executives (ACE), Small Business Institute (SBI), and Small Business Development Centers (SBDC). Under the SCORE and ACE programs, the SBA tries to match an expert to the need. If an entrepreneur needs a marketing plan but does not know how to put one together, the SBA pulls from its list of SCORE or ACE counselors someone with marketing knowledge and experience. SCORE counselors are retired executives. ACE offers the assistance of currently practicing executives. The SBI program taps the talents available at colleges and universities. This program involves not only professors of business administration but also students working for advanced degrees. Under a professor's guidance, such students work with entrepreneurs to help solve their management problems. Finally, the SBDC program assembles the resources and skills needed by entrepreneurs at a single location where entrepreneurs can go to receive instruction and training in management and technical skills.

MANAGEMENT IMPLICATIONS Entrepreneurs should carefully weigh the advantages and disadvantages of the various forms of legal organization for their business. They should also carefully weigh the advantages and disadvantages of different methods for starting a business and be aware of the various sources of information available to them. ■

TABLE 10.1   Sources of Help for Entrepreneurs

Management Help Offered by	Where Available	Before They Go into a Business Whose Technology Is		After They Go into a Business Whose Technology Is	
		High	Low	High	Low
U.S. Small Business Administration counseling by					
Staff	N				✓
Service Corps of Retired Executives (SCORE)	N				✓
Active Corps of Executives (ACE)	N				✓
Small Business Institute (SBI)	N			✓	✓
Small Business Development Center (SBDC)	S	✓	✓	✓	✓
Prebusiness workshops	N		✓		
Nonaccredited courses and seminars	N				✓
Publications	N		✓		✓
U.S. Department of Commerce					
Seminars and workshops	N			✓	✓
Publications	N	✓	✓	✓	✓
Other federal agencies (such as the IRS[a])					
Seminars and workshops	N				✓
Publications	N				✓
State, county, and local governments					
Counseling	S				✓
Seminars and workshops	S				✓
Publications	S				✓
Local development corporations and the like					
Counseling	N				✓
Seminars and workshops	N				✓
Universities					
Accredited courses	S	✓	✓	✓	✓
Nonaccredited courses and seminars	S				✓
Publications	S	✓	✓	✓	✓
Counseling	S				
Community colleges					
Accredited courses	S				✓
Nonaccredited courses and seminars	N				✓
Counseling	S				✓
Small-business groups (such as the NFIB[b])					
Seminars and workshops	S				✓
Counseling	S				✓
Publications	N				✓
Large corporations (such as the Bank-America Corp.)					
Publications	N		✓		✓
Counseling	S				✓
Trade associations					
Publications	N			✓	✓
Seminars and workshops	N			✓	✓

N = nationally; S = some parts of nation.   [a]U.S. Internal Revenue Service.   [b]National Federation of Independent Business.

The Performance of Entrepreneurial Organizations

The formulation and implementation of an effective strategy plays a major role in determining the overall performance of an entrepreneurial organization.[21] This section examines how entrepreneurial firms evolve over time and the attributes of these firms that enhance their chance for success.

The Life Cycle of Entrepreneurial Firms

The entrepreneurial life cycle is a series of predictable stages that small businesses pass through. A common pattern of evolution for entrepreneurial organizations is depicted in Figure 10.4. This pattern is similar to the product life cycle discussed in Chapter 8, but it refers specifically to the challenges and changes in small entrepreneurial firms.

First comes the acceptance stage, in which the small business struggles to break even and survive. Entrepreneurial firms are usually small enough at this stage that they can spot obstacles to success and act quickly to remove them. Moreover, entrepreneurs usually have the skills needed to modify their products or services as required by customers during this stage. Such modifications are often necessary for small firms struggling to obtain enough cash from sales and other sources to continue operations. Many small organizations, despite the skill and effort of entrepreneurs, never emerge from the acceptance stage.

FIGURE 10.4

Stages of Evolution for Entrepreneurial Firms

Entrepreneurial firms often follow a pattern of evolution that resembles this curve. After an initial period of acceptance, during which the firm struggles and experiences low cash flow, the breakthrough stage is achieved. During this period, the firm experiences rapid sales growth and must focus on managing growth. When the maturity stage is reached, growth becomes more stable and the entrepreneur must begin to focus more attention on the actual management of the enterprise.

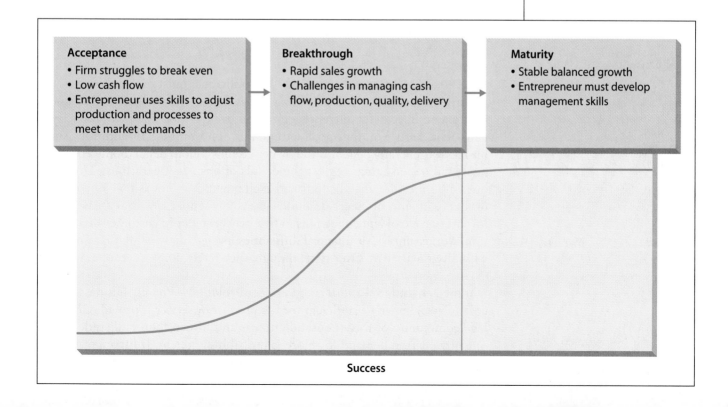

Acceptance
- Firm struggles to break even
- Low cash flow
- Entrepreneur uses skills to adjust production and processes to meet market demands

Breakthrough
- Rapid sales growth
- Challenges in managing cash flow, production, quality, delivery

Maturity
- Stable balanced growth
- Entrepreneur must develop management skills

Success

The breakthrough stage follows. In the preceding stage, the rate of growth is slow—so slow that it is often unnoticed. But in the breakthrough stage, growth is so fast and unpredictable that many entrepreneurs fail to keep pace with it. Caught unprepared, they blunder. Sales revenues spiral upward as problems begin to surface with cash flow, production, quality, and delivery. At the same time, competition may become more severe.

In the face of these pressures, entrepreneurs may apply hasty, ill-conceived solutions to problems. For example, if sales begin to level off or slip, entrepreneurs may hire specialists such as an accountant, a quality-control analyst, or a customer services representative to relieve the problem. As a result, costs go up, squeezing profits further. The best way to become alerted to the problems presented by rapid growth is to continue updating the business plan. With a thorough, updated business plan in place, entrepreneurs are less likely to be surprised by breakthroughs.

In the mature stage a more stable, balanced period of steady growth replaces the lack of control of the breakthrough stage. Organizations that survive to the mature stage can continue to grow for many years. In this last stage, however, entrepreneurs often face another challenge. Although they usually have the technical skills required during the acceptance stage, they often do not possess the managerial skills required during the mature stage. Entrepreneurs without these skills either have to develop them or turn the day-to-day operations of their organization over to professional managers and concentrate on new business opportunities or the creation of new organizations.[22]

■ Reasons for Entrepreneurial Success

Many organizations successfully move through the stages listed in Figure 10.4 to become stable and mature organizations. Many factors contribute to this success, and six of the most common ones are described in the following sections.[23]

Hard Work, Drive, and Dedication   An individual must have a strong desire to work independently and be willing to put in long hours to succeed as an entrepreneur. Successful entrepreneurs tend to be reasonable risk takers, self-confident, hard working, goal setters, and innovators.[24] In addition, small businesses generally benefit if the owner attends well to detail. Some entrepreneurs fail because they neglect the details of business operations. They may open a business for the glamour and excitement of it, but as the concomitant drudgery of entrepreneurship builds, they may ignore essential areas such as inventory control and collections. They may also ignore customer dissatisfaction, worker unrest, or financial difficulties, preferring to think that problems will solve themselves. Over time, though, they rarely do.

Market Demand for Products or Services Provided   For any business to succeed, demand must be sufficient for the product or service it provides. If a college community of fifty thousand citizens and fifteen thousand students has one pizza parlor, demand for more is probably sufficient. If fifteen pizza parlors are already in operation, however, a new one will have to serve especially good pizza or offer something else unique if it is to succeed. Liz Claiborne's clothing business was successful because there was unmet demand for clothing for working women; Apple Computer was initially successful because there was unmet demand for personal computers.

Managerial Competence   The entrepreneur must possess basic managerial competence. He or she needs to know how to select business locations and facilities, acquire financing, and hire and evaluate employees. The entrepreneur must also be able to manage growth, control costs, negotiate contracts, and make difficult choices and decisions. An entrepreneur who has a product for which there is tremendous demand might be able to survive for a while without managerial skills. Over time, and especially in the mature stage of the life cycle, however, the manager who lacks these skills is unlikely to succeed.

Luck   Some small businesses succeed purely because of luck. There was an element of luck in Alan McKim's success with Clean Harbors, an environmental "clean up" organization based in New England. McKim formed this business just as the federal government committed $1.6 billion to help clean up toxic waste. Although McKim might have succeeded anyway, the extra revenue generated by the government Superfund no doubt contributed to this success.[25]

THE FAR SIDE   By GARY LARSON

© 1985 FarWorks, Inc./Dist. by Universal Press Syndicate   Larson

Early business failures

Strong Control Systems   Small businesses, like all organizations, need strong control systems. Small businesses can be ruined by weak control. For example, too many slow-paying customers can reduce a small business's cash flow to a trickle. Excess inventory, employee theft, poor-quality products, plummeting sales, and insufficient profit margins can have equally disastrous effects. If the control system either does not alert the entrepreneur to these problems or alerts the entrepreneur too late, recovery may be difficult or impossible. (Control systems are discussed more fully in Part VI of the book.)

Sufficient Capitalization   Small businesses need sufficient funds to survive start-up and growth. One rule of thumb is that an entrepreneur should have sufficient personal funds when starting out to be able to live with no business income for a year. The entrepreneur needs to be able to maintain his or her personal life, cover all operating expenses, and still have an allowance for unexpected contingencies. An entrepreneur who is planning to pay next month's rent from a new business's profits may be courting disaster.

As noted in the text, successful entrepreneurs must choose an industry, emphasize their distinctive competencies, and develop an effective business plan. Unfortunately, entrepreneurs frequently misjudge or do not effectively implement one or more of these activities. As illustrated in this cartoon, for example, providing a product that people do not really want is almost certain to result in failure. Chocolate confections, sausages, and corn-on-the-cob are often popular treats served on sticks at athletic events, fairs, festivals, and carnivals—but cucumbers, peaches, and porcupines are not as well-received!

MANAGEMENT IMPLICATIONS   Entrepreneurs should understand the typical life cycle of a new business and be prepared to manage their business accordingly. In addition, they should also fully understand the basic factors that contribute to entrepreneurial success. ▬

Summary of Key Points

Entrepreneurship is the process of planning, organizing, operating, and assuming the risk of a business venture. An entrepreneur is someone who engages in entrepreneurship. In general, entrepreneurs start small businesses. Small businesses are an important source of innovation, create numerous jobs, and contribute to the success of large businesses.

In choosing strategies, entrepreneurs have to consider the characteristics of the industry in which they are going to conduct business. Entrepreneurs can use Porter's five forces framework to choose their industry. A small business must also emphasize its distinctive competencies. Small businesses generally have several distinctive competencies that they should exploit in choosing their strategy. Small businesses are usually skilled at identifying niches in established markets, identifying new markets, and acting quickly to obtain first-mover advantages. Small businesses are usually not skilled at exploiting economies of scale. Once an entrepreneur has chosen a strategy, the strategy is normally written down in a business plan. Writing a business plan forces an entrepreneur to plan thoroughly and to anticipate problems that might occur.

With a strategy and business plan in place, entrepreneurs must choose a structure to implement them.

All the structural issues summarized in the next four chapters of this book are relevant to the entrepreneur. In addition, the entrepreneur has some unique structural decisions to make. In determining ownership and financial structure, the entrepreneur can choose a sole proprietorship, a partnership, a corporation, a master limited partnership, a subchapter S corporation, or a cooperative. In determining financial structure, an entrepreneur has to decide how much personal capital to invest in an organization, how much bank and government support to obtain, and whether to encourage venture capital firms to invest. Finally, entrepreneurs have to choose among the options of buying an existing business, starting a new business from scratch, or entering into a franchising agreement.

Most small businesses experience a three-phase life cycle: acceptance, breakthrough, and maturity. There are several reasons why successful small businesses are able to move through all three of these stages of development: hard work, drive, and dedication; market demand for products or services provided; managerial competence; luck; strong control systems; and sufficient capitalization.

Discussion Questions

Questions for Review

1. Why are entrepreneurs and small businesses important to society?

2. In which types of industries do small firms often excel? In which types of industries do small firms struggle?

3. List the ownership options available to entrepreneurs. What are the advantages and disadvantages of each?

4. What are the elements of success for small businesses?

Questions for Analysis

5. Entrepreneurs and small businesses play important roles in society. If these roles are so important, should the government do more to encourage the development of small business? Why or why not?

6. Franchising agreements seem to be particularly popular ways of starting a new business in industries in which retail outlets are geographically widely spread and where the quality of goods or services purchased can be evaluated only after the purchase has occurred. For example, a hamburger

may look tasty, but you know for sure that it is well made only after you buy it and eat it. By going to a McDonald's, you know exactly the kind and quality of hamburger you will receive, even before you walk in the door. What makes franchise arrangements so popular under these conditions?

7. If employing family members can cause problems in a small organization, why is this practice so common?

8. What steps might an entrepreneur take before deciding to expand into a foreign market?

Questions for Application

9. Interview the owner of a small business in your town. Evaluate how successful this small business has been. Using the criteria presented in this chapter, explain its success (or lack of success).

10. Using the information on managing a small business in this chapter, analyze whether you would like to work in a small business—as an employee or as a founder. Given your personality, background, and experience, does working in or starting a new business appeal to you? Why?

Building Effective Communication Skills

EXERCISE OVERVIEW

Communication skills refer to the manager's abilities to both effectively convey ideas and information to others and to effectively receive ideas and information from others. Although communication skills are important to all organizations, some entrepreneurs argue that they are even more important in smaller organizations than they are in larger ones. This exercise will help you understand some of the complexities in communicating in smaller businesses.

EXERCISE BACKGROUND

Assume that you are the owner/manager of a small retail chain. Your company sells moderate-priced apparel for professional men and women. You have ten stores located in the Midwest. Each store has a general manager responsible for the overall management of that specific store. Each store also has one assistant manager.

In addition, your corporate office is staffed by a human resource manager, an advertising specialist, and two buyers. In the past, each store was managed at the total discretion of its local manager. As a result, each store had a different layout, a different culture, and different policies and procedures.

You have decided that you want to begin opening more stores at a rapid pace. To expedite this process, however, you also want to standardize your stores. Unfortunately, however, you realize that this decision is bound to make many of your current managers unhappy. They will see it as a loss of authority and managerial discretion. Nevertheless, you believe that it is important to achieve standardization in all areas.

Your plans are to remodel all the stores to fit a standard layout. You also intend to develop a companywide policy and operations manual that each store must adhere to. This manual will specify exactly how each store will be managed. You plan to inform your managers of this plan first in a memo and then in a follow-up meeting to discuss questions and concerns.

EXERCISE TASK

With the preceding background information as context, do the following:

1. Draft a memo that explains your intentions to the store managers.

2. Make a list of the primary objections you anticipate.

3. Outline an agenda for the meeting in which you plan to address the managers' questions and concerns.

4. Do you personally agree with this communication strategy? Why or why not?

Building Effective Technical Skills

EXERCISE OVERVIEW

Technical skills are the skills necessary to accomplish or understand the specific work being done in an organization. This exercise will allow you to gain insights into your own technical skills and the relative importance of technical skills in different kinds of organizations.

EXERCISE BACKGROUND

Some entrepreneurs have the technical skills they need to open and run their business successfully. For example, a hair stylist who opens a hair salon, an architect who starts a residential design firm, and a chef who launches a new restaurant are all likely to have the technical skills needed to do the work of the organization (hair styling, blue print rendering, and cooking, respectively).

In other cases, the entrepreneur who starts the organization may have general management skills but essentially "buy" required technical skills in the labor market. For example, an entrepreneur might start a new restaurant without knowing how to cook by hiring a professional chef to perform this function.

EXERCISE TASK

With the preceding background information as context, do the following:

1. Examine the following list of ten small businesses that an individual entrepreneur might conceivably launch. Spend a few minutes thinking about each business. (Hint: try to conceptualize an existing local business that might generally fit the description.)

2. Make notes about the specific technical skills required for each business.

3. For each business, decide whether the entrepreneur actually needs to possess the technical skills or whether it is feasible to consider hiring others who possess the skills instead.

4. What are some major factors that determine the viability of buying technical skills in the labor market?

New Businesses:

    a. clothing retail store

    b. computer clone assembly business

    c. tavern

    d. sports card retail store

    e. aluminum recycling operation

    f. used compact disk retail store

    g. drop-in health-care clinic

    h. gourmet coffee bean shop

    i. business services operation

    j. appliance repair shop

Building Effective Conceptual Skills

EXERCISE OVERVIEW

Conceptual skills refer to the manager's ability to think in the abstract. This exercise will help you relate conceptual skills to entrepreneurship.

EXERCISE BACKGROUND

Assume that you have decided to open a small business in the local business community when you graduate (the community where you are attending college, not your home). Assume that you have funds to start a business without having to worry about finding other investors.

Without regard to market potential, profitability, or similar considerations, list five businesses that you might want to open and operate based solely on your personal interests. For example, if you enjoy bicycling, you might enjoy opening a shop that caters to cyclists.

Next, without regard to personal attractiveness or interests, list five businesses that you might want to open and operate based solely on market opportunities. Evaluate the prospects for success of each of the ten businesses.

EXERCISE TASK

With the preceding background information as context, do the following:

1. Form a small group with three or four classmates and discuss your respective lists. Look for instances of where the same type of business appears on either the same or alternative lists. Also look for cases where the same business appears with similar or dissimilar prospects for success.

2. How important is personal interest in small business success?

3. How important is market potential in small business success?

CHAPTER CLOSING CASE

Many Young Entrepreneurs Seek Foreign Venues

I n today's competitive business environment, more and more entrepreneurs are looking to foreign ports-of-call for business opportunities. Indeed, the U.S. Census Bureau estimates that as many as 250,000 U.S. citizens leave the country to live abroad each year, with many of them expecting to start their own business when they arrive at their foreign destination.

For example, Michael Giles, a graduate of the Columbia law school, moved to a black township named Soweto, right outside of Johannesburg, South Africa. Giles determined that only four launderettes were in business to serve the needs of 4.5 million residents. He arranged to get a loan from the U.S. government's Overseas Private Investment Corporation and has launched a chain of 198 coin-operated launderettes throughout many of South Africa's black townships.

Mike DeNoma left a lucrative job at Kentucky Fried Chicken and launched his own chain of Chinese fast-food restaurants in Hong Kong. Eugene Matthews, another lawyer, has shipped twenty thousand cows to Vietnam and set up two modern dairy farms in that country. Lisa Frankenberg has started her own newspaper in Prague. Robert Brooker and Adam Haven-Weiss opened a chain of bagel shops in Eastern Europe.

Of course, entrepreneurs from the United States are not the only ones seeking business opportunities abroad. Indeed, one of the most successful young international entrepreneurs is England's Matthew Stillman, the founder and owner of one of Europe's most successful film production companies, Stillking Productions. In 1992 Stillman spent a week in Prague on vacation. He had been trying to break into the movie business back home in London for years but had achieved only marginal success.

In Prague, however, Stillman saw an opportunity that he couldn't pass up. He and a friend founded Stillking Productions with only $500 between them. They bought a used typewriter and answering machine and rented an abandoned office in a crumbling film studio for $150 a month. To support their fledgling enterprise, they worked in the evenings managing a local nightclub. When they had earned enough money for an airline ticket, Stillman took a trip to Los Angeles looking for customers. As it turned out, pop singer k.d. lang was looking for a central European location for her next music video and gave the contract to Stillman.

Later, Stillking got its first big job, making commercials for a Japanese firm. This job led to an even bigger contract making commercials to commemorate the fiftieth anniversary of the United Nations. Things continued to snowball, and Stillking quickly enlisted many large international clients intent on selling products and making commercials in Europe. Today, the firm has a production schedule set more than a year in advance and is turning away business. Although commercials are still the bedrock of the company, Stillman eventually wants to break into the movie-making business.

Of course, there is no such thing as a sure thing. Many would-be entrepreneurs have also failed in their quest to launch new enterprises in foreign markets. And many others found success to be less than they had imagined, giving up and eventually returning home. The struggles of opening a business in a foreign country are indeed a challenge. Most emerging markets lack an effective infrastructure, for example, and getting even routine things done can take far longer than one might expect. A four-month wait for a telephone hook-up in many countries is not uncommon, for example.

People who want to try this route to success need to remember several important things. First, they must tailor their products and services to the local market. Second, they should not expect to get rich, but instead must be willing to work long and hard just to make ends meet. A certain degree of luck is also needed, as is a fair measure of perseverance. And market opportunities are where you find them—many successful entrepreneurs in foreign countries have found their market niche by providing products and services for other entrepreneurs.

Case Questions

1. What factors most likely contribute to success and failure in international start-up companies such as Stillking Productions?
2. What countries or regions today do you think are most amenable to start-up operations by foreign entrepreneurs?
3. If you wanted to move to another country and start a business, where would you go and what would you do?

Case References: "Go East," *Forbes,* December 2, 1996, pp. 80–82; and William Echikson, "Young Americans Go Abroad to Strike It Rich," *Fortune,* October 17, 1994, pp. 185–195.

CHAPTER NOTES

1. Ronald B. Lieber, "Beating the Odds," *Fortune*, March 31, 1997, pp. 82–90; and "Flashbacks," *Forbes*, April 7, 1997, p. 143.

2. Bro Uttal, "Inside the Deal That Made Bill Gates $350,000,000," *Fortune*, July 21, 1986, pp. 23–33.

3. Murray B. Low and Ian MacMillan, "Entrepreneurship: Past Research and Future Challenges," *Journal of Management*, June 1988, pp. 139–159.

4. "Women Entrepreneurs," *Business Week*, April 18, 1994, pp. 104–110.

5. Scott Shane, "Explaining Variation in Rates of Entrepreneurship in the United States: 1899–1988," *Journal of Management*, Vol. 22, No. 5, 1996, pp. 747–781.

6. "Big vs. Small," *Time*, September 5, 1988, pp. 48–50; and J. A. Schumpeter, *Capitalism, Socialism, and Democracy*, 3rd ed. (New York: Harper & Row, 1950).

7. Amar Bhide, "How Entrepreneurs Craft Strategies That Work," *Harvard Business Review*, March–April 1994, pp. 150–163.

8. Michael Porter, *Competitive Strategy* (New York: Free Press, 1980).

9. "Hot Growth Companies," *Business Week*, May 26, 1997, pp. 90–102.

10. See Faye Brookman, "Specialty Cosmetic Stores: A Hit with Frustrated Consumers," *Advertising Age*, March 4, 1991, p. 32; and Laurie Freeman, "Department Stores in Fight for Their Lives," *Advertising Age*, March 4, 1991, p. 29.

11. F. M. Scherer, *Industrial Market Structure and Economic Performance*, 2nd ed. (Boston: Houghton Mifflin, 1980).

12. The importance of discovering niches is emphasized in Charles Hill and Gareth Jones, *Strategic Management: An Integrative Approach*, 4th ed. (Boston: Houghton Mifflin, 1998).

13. Gregory Patterson, "An American in...Siberia?" *Fortune*, August 4, 1997, p. 63; and "Crazy for Crunchies," *Newsweek*, April 28, 1997, p. 49.

14. "Persistence Pays in Search of Funds," *USA Today*, May 11, 1987, p. 3E.

15. Daniel M. Cable and Scott Shane, "A Prisoner's Dilemma Approach to Entrepreneur-Venture Capitalist Relationships," *Academy of Management Review*, January 1997, pp. 142–176. See also "New Breed of Investor Brings More Than Cash to Hopeful Start-Ups," *Wall Street Journal*, August 25, 1997, pp. A1, A11.

16. Gary J. Castrogiovanni, "Pre Start-Up Planning and the Survival of New Small Businesses: Theoretical Linkages," *Journal of Management*, Vol. 22, No. 6, 1996, pp. 801–822.

17. Faye Rice, "How to Succeed at Cloning a Small Business," *Fortune*, October 28, 1985, pp. 60–66; and "Franchising Tries to Divvy Up Risk," *USA Today*, May 11, 1987, p. 5E.

18. "Businesses Vie for More Control," *USA Today*, January 5, 1993, pp. 1B, 2B.

19. Rice, "How to Succeed at Cloning a Small Business."

20. "We Cure Small-Business Headaches," *Forbes*, October 20, 1997, pp. 168–169.

21. Charles Burck, "The Real World of the Entrepreneur," *Fortune*, April 5, 1993, pp. 62–80.

22. Ibid.

23. John B. Miner, "The Expanded Horizon for Achieving Entrepreneurial Success," *Organizational Dynamics*, Winter 1997, pp. 54–67.

24. Amar Bhide, "The Questions Every Entrepreneur Must Answer," *Harvard Business Review*, November–December 1996, pp. 120–132. See also " 'Career Opportunity: Long Hours, Good Pay'," *Forbes*, May 19, 1997, pp. 102–103.

25. See Jay Barney, "Strategic Factor Markets: Expectations, Luck, and Business Strategy," *Management Science*, October 1986, pp. 1231–1241.

Building Global Strategies

The global environment of business is playing an increasingly important role in the strategies of all businesses—domestic and multinational, large and small, manufacturing and service. This video case relates to the global business environment and how a variety of different types of businesses can use it as a framework for growth and expansion.

OVERVIEW AND OBJECTIVES

After completing this video case, you should be able to:

1. Better understand the complexities and opportunities that the global environment provides a business and its strategic managers.

2. More easily see the different ways that a business can take advantage of opportunities in the global environment.

3. Better appreciate how tactical planning, decision making, and entrepreneurship relate to the global environment.

COMPANY BACKGROUND

Texas Instruments is a huge multinational firm headquartered in Dallas, Texas. TI, as it is more commonly known, once relied heavily on related diversification to fuel its growth. For example, in the 1970s, the firm operated electronics development and manufacturing businesses, consumer electronics businesses, defense electronics businesses, and semiconductor chemical businesses. But in recent years, TI has sold many of these holdings in order to concentrate more completely on its semiconductor business and related operations. The key to success in this business is volume—in general, the more chips a company can make, the lower its costs per chip. In 1997, TI posted sales of almost $10 billion, with about half coming from North America, a third from East Asia, and the rest from Europe.

In contrast to Texas Instruments, Dat'l Do-It is a small business located in central Florida. Dat'l Do-It specializes in hot sauces, and is one of Tobasco's biggest rivals in the United States. The key part of Dat'l Do-It's operations is a rare, very hot pepper that only grows in the region around its headquarters. Its products are emblazoned with a cute, animated alligator that is the firm's corporate symbol.

Pier 1 Imports lies somewhere in between Texas Instruments and Dat'l Do-It in terms of size and scope. Pier 1 is a U.S. specialty retailer that sells household and decorating goods that are almost exclusively made in other countries. A small network of 10 buyers scours the globe, searching for interesting products that can be shipped to Pier 1 stores in the United States for resale.

CASE QUESTIONS

1. Speculate as to the role of the global business environment in the success of Texas Instruments, Dat'l Do-It, and Pier 1 Imports.

2. How do you think managers at each company might be able to capitalize on global markets and opportunities?

VIDEO REVIEW

Your instructor will now show you a video clip that provides more information about TI, Dat'l Do-It, and Pier 1 Imports.

FOLLOW-UP QUESTIONS

1. After viewing the video, identify the major strengths, weaknesses, opportunities, and threats facing each of the three firms described above.

2. Describe the corporate and business strategies being pursued by each firm.

3. Identify and discuss the tactical and operational plans of each firm.

4. Describe the issues involved in making decisions about global markets for each firm.

5. What relationships do you see between the global environment and entrepreneurship?

POPULAR VIDEO FOLLOW-UP

Each of the movies listed below provides some insights and examples that illustrate planning and decision-making concepts and ideas. Try to come up with other examples.

- *Star Wars* (planning a military mission)

- *The American President* (goals, optimization, and operational planning)

- *Broken Arrow* (operational planning)

- *Jumanji* (operational planning and decision making)

- *Crimson Tide* (decision making under uncertainty)

11

Basic Elements of Organizing

OBJECTIVES

After studying this chapter, you should be able to:

- Identify the basic elements of organizations.
- Describe alternative approaches to designing jobs.
- Discuss the rationale and the most common bases for grouping jobs into departments.
- Describe the basic elements involved in establishing reporting relationships.
- Discuss how authority is distributed in organizations.
- Discuss the basic coordinating activities undertaken by organizations.
- Describe basic ways in which positions within an organization can be differentiated.

H. J. Heinz is one of the world's largest food processing companies. Heinz makes literally thousands of products and markets them around the world. The firm started about a 150 years ago when a youngster named Henry J. Heinz began selling surplus vegetables from the family's backyard garden to his neighbors. When Henry became an adult, he and a friend started making processed horseradish, packaging it in glass containers, and selling it to neighborhood grocery stores.

From that modest beginning, Heinz grew steadily for many decades. Among the firm's key highlights were inventing tomato ketchup and sweet pickles. The firm's long-standing slogan—*57 Varieties*—was coined to promote Heinz's line of pickles at the 1893 Chicago World's Fair. Heinz was selling its products on four continents in 1900 and started making food products in the United Kingdom in 1905.

Today Heinz is organized into six basic divisions. The food service division sells packaged food products to restaurants and hotels—small packets of ketchup, for example, as well as jellies, syrups, and similar condiments. The infant foods division sells baby food products under the brand names Heinz, Farley's, and Pablum. The ketchup and condiments division also uses the Heinz name on its ketchup, steak sauces, pickles, relishes, and other products.

Star-Kist tuna is the fourth division at Heinz. A fifth division makes pet foods and sells them under such popular brand names as 9 Lives, Gravy Train, Ken-L-Ration, and Kibbles 'n Bits. Finally, Heinz's sixth major division is its line of Weight Watcher's foods and programs, purchased in 1978.

Since the earliest days of the company's international expansion more than a century ago, a key hallmark of Heinz's approach to management has been decentralization—allowing managers at each production and/or marketing site to make all key decisions about running the firm's operation there.

> *"This plan will make Heinz one of the three pre-eminent branded food companies in the world."*
>
> Anthony O'Reilly, Heinz CEO, quoted in *Cincinnati Inquirer, March 15, 1997, p. B14.*

These site managers thus had substantial responsibility and authority to make decisions and to do what they believed was best for the company.

In recent times, however, Heinz has been stumbling badly. Its profits have been declining, for example, and competitors have been gaining market share in key markets. The firm's Weight Watcher's division has been especially hard hit. While its operating costs have continued to escalate, Nestlé's Lean Cuisine and ConAgra's Healthy Choice lines have become formidable competitors.

Heinz executives have finally decided that they have to make some changes to turn things around. The centerpiece of their efforts involves the systematic centralization of the firm's international operations. Specifically, key decision-making responsibility and authority is being taken away from operations managers in other countries and relocated to the firm's corporate headquarters staff in Pittsburgh. As part of this program, the firm will also be eliminating several thousand jobs, many of them staff-level positions in distant facilities.

Heinz will also be focusing specific attention on the Weight Watcher's division. Among other things, the firm is selling off company-owned meeting spaces for its Weight Watcher's offices and moving the meetings back into rental space. A new marketing effort featuring Sarah Ferguson has been launched in an effort to return the division to the top of its market. If these efforts are unsuccessful, Heinz executives will consider selling the division. After all, where better to shrink?[1]

The H.J. Heinz company has a long and well-established way of getting things done, and this system has served it well. But the firm's managers have made the critical decision to make major changes in key parts of the organization. Managing the basic framework organizations use to get their work done—their structure—is a fundamental part of the management process.

This chapter discusses many of the critical elements of organization structure that managers can control. It is the first of four chapters devoted to organizing, which is the second basic managerial function identified in Chapter 1. In Part III we described managerial planning—deciding what to do. Organizing, the subject of Part IV, focuses on how to do it. We first elaborate on the meaning of *organization structure*. Subsequent sections of this chapter explore the basic elements that managers use to create an organization.

The Elements of Organizing

Imagine asking a child to build a castle with a set of building blocks. He selects a few small blocks and some larger ones. He uses some square ones, some round ones, and some triangular ones. When he finishes, he has his own castle, unlike any other. Another child, presented with the same task, constructs a different castle. She will select different blocks, for example, and combine them in different ways. The childrens' activities—choosing certain combinations of blocks and then putting them together in unique ways—are analogous to the manager's job of organizing.

organizing Deciding how best to group organizational activities and resources

Organizing is deciding the best way to group organizational elements.[2] Just as children select different kinds of building blocks, managers can choose from various structural possibilities. And just as the children can assemble the blocks in any number of ways, so too can managers put the organization together in many different ways. Understanding the nature of these building blocks and the different ways in which they can be configured can have a powerful impact on a firm's competitiveness.[3] In this chapter, our focus is on the building blocks themselves—**organization structure**. In Chapter 12 we focus on how the blocks can be put together—organization design.

organization structure The set of elements that can be used to configure an organization

Managers can use six basic building blocks to construct an organization: designing jobs, grouping jobs, establishing reporting relationships between jobs, distributing authority among jobs, coordinating activities between jobs, and differentiating between positions. The logical starting point is the first building block—designing jobs for people within the organization.

MANAGEMENT IMPLICATIONS

Managers should understand the basic building blocks of organization structure and recognize that part of the organizing function is knowing how to best assemble these building blocks into an efficient overall structure for the firm. ■

Designing Jobs

The first building block of organization structure is job design. **Job design** is the determination of an individual's work-related responsibilities.[4] For a machinist at Caterpillar Inc., job design might specify what machines are to be operated, how they are to be operated, and what performance standards are expected. For a manager at Caterpillar, job design might involve defining areas of decision-making responsibility, identifying goals and expectations, and establishing appropriate indicators of success. The natural starting point for designing jobs is determining the level of desired specialization.

job design The determination of an individual's work-related responsibilities

◼ Job Specialization

Job specialization is the degree to which the overall task of the organization is broken down and divided into smaller component parts. Job specialization evolved from the concept of *division of labor*. Adam Smith, an eighteenth-century economist, described how a pin factory used division of labor to improve productivity.[5] One man drew the wire, another straightened it, a third cut it, a fourth ground the point, and so on. Smith claimed that ten men working in this fashion were able to produce forty-eight thousand pins in a day, whereas each man working alone could produce only twenty pins per day.

job specialization The degree to which the overall task of the organization is broken down and divided into smaller component parts

More recently, the best example of the impact of specialization is the automobile assembly line pioneered by Henry Ford and his contemporaries. Mass-production capabilities stemming from job specialization techniques have had a profound impact throughout the world. High levels of low-cost production transformed U.S. society during the first several decades of this century into one of the strongest economies in the history of the world.

Job specialization is a normal extension of organizational growth. For example, when Walt Disney started his company, he did everything himself—wrote cartoons, drew them, and then marketed them to theaters. As the business grew, he eventually hired others to perform many of these functions. As growth continued, so did specialization. For example, an animation artist working on Disney movies today may specialize in drawing only a single character. And today, The Walt Disney Company has thousands of specialized jobs; clearly, no one person could perform them all.

◼ Benefits and Limitations of Specialization

Job specialization provides four benefits to organizations.[6] First, workers performing small, simple tasks will become very proficient at that task. Second, transfer time between tasks decreases. If employees perform several different tasks, they inevitably lose some time as they switch from one to another. Third, the more narrowly defined a job is, the easier it is to develop specialized equipment to assist with that job. Fourth, when an employee who performs a highly specialized job is absent or resigns, the manager is able to train someone new at relatively low cost. Although specialization is generally thought of in terms of operating jobs, many organizations have extended the basic elements of specialization to managerial and professional levels as well.[7]

On the other hand, job specialization can have negative consequences. The foremost criticism is that workers who perform highly specialized jobs may become bored and dissatisfied. The job may be so specialized that it offers no challenge or stimulation. Boredom and monotony set in, absenteeism rises, and the quality of the work may suffer. Furthermore, the anticipated benefits of specialization do not always occur. For example, a study conducted at Maytag found that the time spent moving work-in-process from one worker to another was greater than the time needed for the same individual to change from job to job.[8] Thus, although some degree of specialization is necessary, it should not be carried to extremes because of the possible negative consequences. Managers must be sensitive to situations in which extreme specialization should be avoided. And indeed, several alternative approaches to designing jobs have been developed in recent years.

■ Alternatives to Specialization

To counter the problems associated with specialization, managers have sought other approaches to job design that achieve a better balance between organizational demands for efficiency and productivity and individual needs for creativity and autonomy. Five alternative approaches are job rotation, job enlargement, job enrichment, the job characteristics approach, and work teams.[9]

job rotation An alternative to job specialization that involves systematically moving employees from one job to another

Job Rotation   **Job rotation** involves systematically moving employees from one job to another. A worker in a warehouse might unload trucks on Monday, carry incoming inventory to storage on Tuesday, verify invoices on Wednesday, pull outgoing inventory from storage on Thursday, and load trucks on Friday. Thus the jobs do not change but, instead, workers move from job to job. Unfortunately, for this very reason, job rotation has not been very successful in enhancing employee motivation or satisfaction. Jobs that are amenable to rotation tend to be relatively standard and routine. Workers who are rotated to a "new" job may be more satisfied at first, but satisfaction soon wanes. Although many companies (among them American Cyanamid, Bethlehem Steel, Ford, Prudential Insurance, TRW, and Western Electric) have tried job rotation, it is most often used today as a training device to improve worker skills and flexibility.

job enlargement An alternative to job specialization that involves giving the employee more tasks to perform

Job Enlargement   On the assumption that doing the same basic task over and over is the primary cause of worker dissatisfaction, **job enlargement** was developed to increase the total number of tasks workers perform. As a result, all workers perform a wide variety of tasks, which presumably reduces the level of job dissatisfaction. Many organizations have used job enlargement, including IBM, Detroit Edison, AT&T, the U.S. Civil Service, and Maytag. At Maytag, for example, the assembly line for producing washing-machine water pumps was systematically changed so that work that had originally been performed by six workers, who passed the work sequentially from one person to another, was performed by four workers, each of whom assembled a complete pump.[10]

MANAGEMENT INFOTECH

Working from Home at Compaq

Like many big companies, Compaq Computer maintains a large sales force to assist in marketing and selling its products and servicing customers after they buy the firm's products. And until 1993, also like many other companies, Compaq's sales force worked out of regional and/or local headquarters facilities, traveling to and from their office each day.

"The only traffic I have to avoid is my 4-year-old."

Compaq sales representative*

But in 1993, Compaq decided to change the way it organized its sales function. For one thing, it wanted to cut the size of the group by one-third. For another, it wanted to reduce its overhead expenses. And for yet another, the company wanted to enrich the jobs of the sales reps to make them more motivating and engaging. The key, managers realized, was to allow the sales representatives to work from home offices, eliminating both their commute time and the need to maintain a company office for them.

In addition, the job itself was changed. Customers had complained that their sales representative was often too busy to help. And the reps themselves complained that they were so busy answering telephone calls and dealing with routine e-mail that they couldn't adequately service their customers. Compaq decided to split the sales function into two parts. All customers were given toll-free numbers staffed by trained specialists. These specialists, in turn, handled all routine and day-to-day calls and queries.

The true sales representatives were thus given more time to really seek out new customers and establish new accounts. Each sales rep also had his or her home office equipped with state-of-the-art telecommunications equipment. This system allows the reps to communicate with their customers, their bosses, and each other with less travel and hassle. The bottom line, therefore, was improved productivity and more customer satisfaction.

References: *"Compaq Computer Corp.—Company of the Year,"* Forbes, *January 12, 1998, pp. 90–94; "The Office That Never Closes,"* Forbes, *May 23, 1994, pp. 212–213 (*quote on p. 212);* Hoover's Handbook of American Business 1998 *(Austin, Texas: Hoover's Business Press, 1998), pp. 398–399; and David Kirkpatrick, "Houston, We Have Some Problems,"* Fortune, *June 23, 1997, pp. 102–103.*

Unfortunately, although job enlargement does have some positive consequences, they are often offset by several disadvantages: (1) training costs usually rise, (2) unions have argued that pay should increase because the worker is doing more tasks, and (3) in many cases the work remains boring and routine even after job enlargement.

Job Enrichment A more comprehensive approach, **job enrichment**, assumes that increasing the range and variety of tasks is not sufficient by itself to improve employee motivation.[11] Thus job enrichment attempts to increase both the number of tasks a worker does and the control the worker has over the job. To implement job enrichment managers remove some controls from the job, delegate more authority to employees, and structure the work in complete, natural units. These changes increase subordinates' sense of responsibility. Another part of job enrichment is to continually assign new and challenging tasks, thereby increasing employees' opportunity for growth and advancement. The "Management InfoTech" box describes how Compaq Computer achieved job enrichment in its sales force.

job enrichment An alternative to job specialization that involves increasing both the number of tasks the worker does and the control the worker has over the job

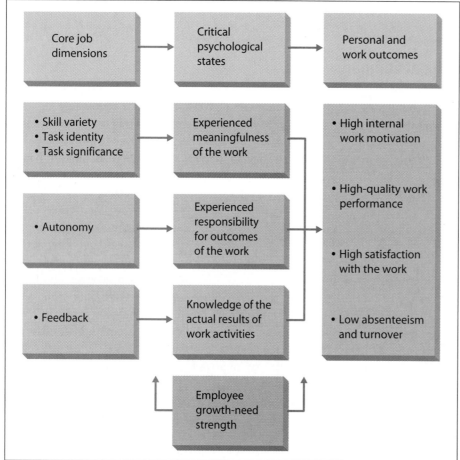

FIGURE 11.1
The Job Characteristics Approach

The job characteristics approach to job design provides a viable alternative to job specialization. Five core job dimensions may lead to critical psychological states that, in turn, may enhance motivation, performance, and satisfaction while also reducing absenteeism and turnover.

Source: J. R. Hackman and G. R. Oldham, "Motivation Through the Design of Work: Test of a Theory," *Organizational Behavior and Human Performance,* Vol. 16 (1976), pp. 250–279. Copyright © Academic Press, Inc. Reprinted by permission of Academic Press and the authors.

AT&T was one of the first companies to try job enrichment. In one experiment, eight typists in a service unit prepared customer service orders. Faced with low output and high turnover, management determined that the typists felt little responsibility to clients and received little feedback. The unit was changed to create a typing team. Typists were matched with designated service representatives, the task was changed from ten specific steps to three more general steps, and job titles were upgraded. As a result, the frequency of order processing increased from 27 percent to 90 percent, the need for messenger service was eliminated, accuracy improved, and turnover became practically nil.[12] Other organizations that have tried job enrichment include Texas Instruments, IBM, and General Foods. This approach, however, also has disadvantages. For example, work systems should be analyzed before enrichment, but this seldom happens, and managers rarely ask for employee preferences when enriching jobs.

Job Characteristics Approach The **job characteristics approach** is an alternative to job specialization that does take into account the work system and employee preferences.[13] As illustrated in Figure 11.1, the job characteristics approach suggests that jobs should be diagnosed and improved along five core dimensions:

1. *Skill variety:* the number of things a person does in a job
2. *Task identity:* the extent to which the worker does a complete or identifiable portion of the total job
3. *Task significance:* the perceived importance of the task
4. *Autonomy:* the degree of control the worker has over how the work is performed
5. *Feedback:* the extent to which the worker knows how well the job is being performed

The higher a job rates on those dimensions, the more employees will experience various psychological states. Experiencing these states, in turn, presumably leads to high motivation, high-quality performance, high satisfaction, and low absenteeism and turnover. Finally, a variable called *growth-need strength* is presumed to affect how the model works for different people. People with a strong desire to grow, develop, and expand their capabilities (indicative of high growth-need strength) are expected to respond strongly to the presence or absence of the basic job characteristics; individuals with low growth-need strength are expected not to respond as strongly or consistently.

Researchers have conducted many studies to test the usefulness of the job characteristics approach. The Southwestern Division of Prudential Insurance, for example, used this approach in its claims division. Results included moderate declines in turnover and a small but measurable improvement in work quality. Other research findings have not supported this approach as strongly. Thus, although the job characteristics approach is one of the most promising alternatives to job specialization, it is probably not the final answer.

job characteristics approach An alternative to job specialization that suggests that jobs should be diagnosed and improved along five core dimensions, taking into account both the work system and employee preferences

Work Teams Another alternative to job specialization is **work teams**. Under this arrangement, a group is given responsibility for designing the work system to be used in performing an interrelated set of jobs. In the typical assembly-line system, the work flows from one worker to the next, and each worker has a specified job to perform. In a work team, however, the group itself decides how jobs will be allocated. For example, the work team assigns specific tasks to members, monitors and controls its own performance, and has autonomy over work scheduling.[14] We discuss work teams more fully in Chapter 19.

work team An alternative to job specialization that allows an entire group to design the work system it will use to perform an interrelated set of tasks

**MANAGEMENT
IMPLICATIONS**
Managers should know that they have several job design alternatives at their disposal. They should also know the benefits and limitations of each alternative as they decide how to most appropriately design jobs within their organization. ▬

Managers are always on the alert for new and better ways to design jobs for employees. One of the newest strategies is called cell manufacturing. Cell manufacturing is a flexible system that uses elements from job enrichment and the job characteristics theory to give workers more control over their jobs while simultaneously improving flexibility for the company by allowing it to more easily alter the products being made by a given worker. This employee is assembling computers for Compaq, a pioneer in cell manufacturing.

Grouping Jobs: Departmentalization

departmentalization The process of grouping jobs according to some logical arrangement

The second building block of organization structure is the grouping of jobs according to some logical arrangement. This process is called **departmentalization**. After establishing the basic rationale for departmentalization, we identify some common bases along which departments are created.

■ Rationale for Departmentalization

FIGURE 11.2
Bases for Departmentalization: Apex Computers

Organizations group jobs into departments. Apex—a hypothetical organization—uses all four of the primary bases of departmentalization—function, product, customer, and location. Like Apex, most large organizations use more than one type of departmentalization.

When organizations are small, the owner-manager can personally oversee every worker. As an organization grows, however, personally supervising all the employees becomes more and more difficult for the owner-manager. Consequently, new managerial positions are created to supervise the work of others. Employees are not assigned to particular managers randomly. Rather, jobs are grouped according to some plan. The logic embodied in such a plan is the basis for all departmentalization.[15]

■ Common Bases for Departmentalization

Figure 11.2 presents a partial organizational chart for Apex Computers, a hypothetical firm that manufactures and sells computers and software. The chart

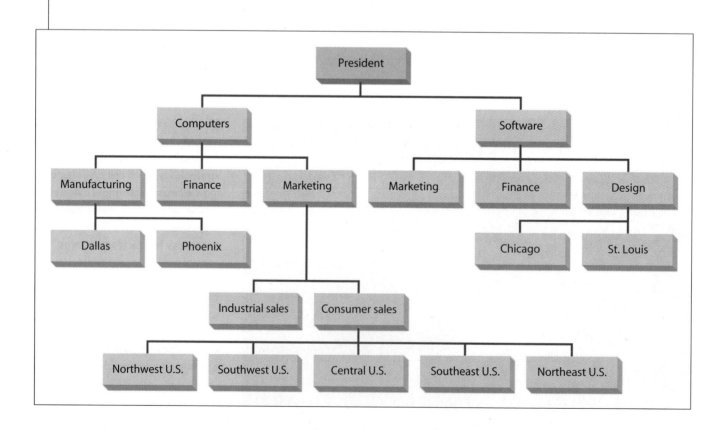

shows that Apex uses all four of the most common bases for departmentalization: function, product, customer, and location.

Functional Departmentalization The most common base for departmentalization, especially among smaller organizations, is by function. **Functional departmentalization** groups together those jobs involving the same or similar activities. (In this context the word *function* means organizational functions such as finance and production, rather than the basic managerial functions such as planning or controlling.) The computer department at Apex has manufacturing, finance, and marketing departments.

This approach has three primary advantages. First, experts in a particular functional area can staff that department. Marketing experts can run the marketing function, for example. Second, supervision is also facilitated because an individual manager needs to be familiar with only a relatively narrow set of skills. And third, coordinating activities inside each department is easier than in the other forms of departmentalization discussed later.

On the other hand, as an organization begins to grow, several disadvantages of this approach may emerge. For one, decision making tends to become slower and more bureaucratic. Employees may also begin to concentrate too narrowly on their own units and lose sight of the total organizational system. Finally, accountability and performance become increasingly difficult to monitor. For example, determining whether a new product fails because of production deficiencies or a poorly received marketing campaign may not be possible.

Product Departmentalization **Product departmentalization**, a second common approach, involves grouping and arranging activities around products or product groups. Apex Computers has two product-based departments at the highest level of the firm. One is responsible for all activities associated with Apex's personal computer business, and the other handles the software business. Most larger businesses adopt this form of departmentalization for grouping activities at the business or corporate level.

Product departmentalization has three major advantages. First, all activities associated with one product or product group can be easily integrated and coordinated. Second, the speed and effectiveness of decision making are enhanced. Third, the performance of individual products or product groups can be assessed more easily and objectively, thereby making departments clearly accountable for the results of their activities.

Product departmentalization also has two major disadvantages. For one, managers in each department may focus on their own product or product group to the exclusion of the rest of the organization. That is, a marketing manager may see her or his primary duty as helping the group, rather than helping the overall organization. For another, administrative costs rise because each department must have its own functional specialists in areas like marketing research and financial analysis.

Customer Departmentalization Under **customer departmentalization**, the organization structures its activities to respond to and interact with specific customers or customer groups. The lending activities in most banks, for example, are usually tailored to meet the needs of different kinds of customers (for

functional departmentalization
Grouping jobs involving the same or similar activities

product departmentalization
Grouping jobs around products or product groups

customer departmentalization
Grouping jobs to respond to and interact with specific customers or customer groups

example, business, consumer, mortgage, and agricultural loans). Figure 11.2 shows that the marketing branch of Apex's computer business has two distinct departments—industrial sales and consumer sales. The industrial sales department handles marketing activities aimed at business customers, whereas the consumer sales department is responsible for wholesaling computers to retail stores catering to individual purchasers.

The basic advantage of this approach is that the organization is able to use skilled specialists to deal with unique customers or customer groups. It takes one set of skills to evaluate a balance sheet and lend a business $50,000 for operating capital and a different set of skills to evaluate an individual's creditworthiness and lend $10,000 for a new car. However, a fairly large administrative staff is required to integrate the activities of the various departments. In banks, for example, coordination is necessary to make sure that the organization does not overcommit itself in any one area and to handle collections on delinquent accounts from a diverse set of customers.

location departmentalization

Grouping jobs on the basis of defined geographic sites or areas

Location Departmentalization **Location departmentalization** groups jobs on the basis of defined geographic sites or areas. The defined sites or areas may range in size from a hemisphere to only a few blocks of a large city. The manufacturing branch of Apex's computer business has two plants—one in Dallas and another in Phoenix. Similarly, the design division of its software design unit has two labs—one in Chicago and the other in St. Louis. Apex's consumer sales group has five sales territories corresponding to different regions of the United States. Transportation companies, police departments (precincts represent geographic areas of a city), and the Federal Reserve Bank all use location departmentalization.

The primary advantage of location departmentalization is that it enables the organization to respond easily to unique customer and environmental characteristics in the various regions. On the negative side, a larger administrative staff may be required if the organization must keep track of units in scattered locations.

Other Forms of Departmentalization Although most organizations are departmentalized by function, product, location, or customer, other forms are occasionally used. Some organizations group certain activities by time. One of the machine shops of Baker Hughes, Inc., in Houston, for example, operates on three shifts. Each shift has a superintendent who reports to the plant manager, and each shift has its own functional departments. Time is thus the framework for many organizational activities. Other organizations that use time as a basis for grouping jobs include some hospitals and many airlines. In other situations, departmentalization by sequence is appropriate. Many college students, for instance, must register in sequence: last names starting with A through E register in line 1, F through L in line 2, and so on. Other areas that may be organized in sequence include credit departments (specific employees run credit checks according to customer name) and insurance claims divisions (by policy number).

Other Considerations Two final points about job grouping remain to be made. First, departments are often called something entirely different—

divisions, units, sections, and bureaus are all common synonyms. The higher we look in an organization, the more likely we are to find *departments* referred to as *divisions*. H.J. Heinz, for example, is organized into six major divisions. Nevertheless, the underlying logic behind all the labels is the same: they represent groups of jobs that have been yoked together according to some unifying principle. Second, almost any organization is likely to employ multiple bases of departmentalization, depending on level. Although Apex Computer is a hypothetical firm we created to explain departmentalization, it is quite similar to many real organizations in that it uses a variety of bases of departmentalization for different levels and different sets of activities.

MANAGEMENT IMPLICATIONS Managers need to thoroughly understand the strengths and weaknesses of each common method or approach to departmentalization. This knowledge will enable them to select the best approach to departmentalization for their own unique circumstances. ■

Establishing Reporting Relationships

The third basic element of organizing is the establishment of reporting relationships among positions. Suppose, for example, that the owner-manager of a small business has just hired two new employees, one to handle marketing and one to handle production. Will the marketing manager report to the production manager, will the production manager report to the marketing manager, or will each report directly to the owner-manager? These questions reflect the basic issues involved in establishing reporting relationships: clarifying the chain of command and the span of management.

Clear and precise reporting relationships are important in organizations. Police officers need formally defined reporting relationships so that they know who is in charge during a hostage crisis, a burglary investigation, or a drug bust.

■ Chain of Command

Chain of command is an old concept, first popularized in the early years of this century. For example, early writers about the chain of command argued that clear and distinct lines of authority need to be established among all positions in the organization. The chain of command actually has two components. The first, called *unity of command*, suggests that each person within an organization must have a clear reporting relationship to one and only one boss (as we see in Chapter 12, newer models of organization design successfully violate this premise). The second, called the *scalar*

Bridgestone Organizes the World

Although its name sounds decidedly western, Bridgestone Corporation is, in fact, a large Japanese tire company. The firm has eighty-three plants worldwide. In addition to its flagship Bridgestone label, the company also owns Firestone and makes private label products for Sears, Montgomery Ward, and other automobile retailers. Bridgestone is the number-two tire company in both North America (after Goodyear) and Europe (after Michelin) and the largest in Asia.

But the big tire company stumbled badly in the early 1990s, especially in North America, following its acquisition of Firestone. Merging the two companies was more difficult than managers had anticipated, for example, and there was a bit of a backlash from General Motors, Firestone's largest single customer. To turn things around, the company named Yoichiro Kaizaki as president and sent him to the United States.

> *"The Buck Stops Here."*
>
> *Former U.S. president Harry Truman, quoted on a sign given to Bridgestone division presidents*

Kaizaki was initially frustrated because he could not always figure out reporting relationships and lines of authority. To remedy the situation, he divided the company into twenty-one operating units and named a president for each one. Then he gave each new president a desk plaque with Harry Truman's famous quote "The Buck Stops Here" emblazoned across it. Finally, he tied each president's pay directly to the performance of his or her business unit in relation to its goals.

Almost immediately business started to improve. The parent company pumped in some money to upgrade North American factories, and sales and profits started to increase. After defeating a costly strike by the United Rubber Workers in 1994, Bridgestone is well on its way toward becoming the world's largest tire maker by the year 2000.

References: *"The Buck Stops Here," Forbes, March 10, 1997, pp. 44–45; and* Hoover's Handbook of World Business 1998 *(Austin, Texas: Hoover's Business Press, 1998), pp. 140–141.*

---

chain of command A clear and distinct line of authority among the positions in an organization

principle, suggests that a clear and unbroken line of authority must extend from the lowest to the highest position in the organization. The popular saying "The buck stops here" is derived from this idea—someone in the organization must ultimately be responsible for every decision. This slogan has recently found its way inside the culture of Bridgestone Corporation, as described in "The World of Management."

■ Narrow Versus Wide Spans

span of management The number of people who report to a particular manager

Another part of establishing reporting relationships is determining how many people will report to each manager, that is, determining the **span of management** (sometimes called the *span of control*). For years managers and researchers sought to determine the optimal span of management. For example, should it be relatively narrow (with few subordinates per manager) or relatively wide (with many subordinates)? One early writer, A. V. Graicunas, went so far as to quantify span of management issues.[16] Graicunas noted that a manager must deal with three kinds of interactions with and among subordinates: direct (the manager's one-to-one relationship with each subordinate), cross (among the subordinates themselves), and group (between groups of subordinates). The number of possible interactions of all types between a manager and subordinates can be determined by the following formula:

$$I = N (2^N/2 + N - 1)$$

where I is the total number of interactions with and among subordinates and N is the number of subordinates.

If a manager has only two subordinates, six potential interactions exist. If the number of subordinates increases to three, the possible interactions total eighteen. With five subordinates there are one hundred possible interactions. Although Graicunas offers no prescription for what N should be, his ideas demonstrate how complex the relationships become when more subordinates are added. The important point is that each additional subordinate adds more complexity than the previous one did. Going from nine to ten subordinates is very different from going from three to four.

Another early writer, Ralph C. Davis, described two kinds of spans: an operative span for lower-level managers and an executive span for middle and top managers. He argued that operative spans could approach thirty subordinates, whereas executive spans should be limited to between three and nine (depending on the nature of the managers' jobs, the growth rate of the company, and similar factors). Lyndall F. Urwick suggested that an executive span should never exceed six subordinates, and General Ian Hamilton reached the same conclusion.[17] Today we recognize that the span of management is a crucial factor in structuring organizations but that there are no universal prescriptions for an ideal or optimal span.[18] Later we summarize some important variables that influence the appropriate span of management in a particular situation. First, however, we describe how the span of management affects the overall structure of an organization.

Distributing authority is a key building block in creating an effective organization. Unfortunately, some managers prefer to avoid accountability for decisions and work to ensure that someone else can always be held responsible for mistakes and errors. This Dilbert cartoon, for instance, illustrates a whimsical view of a manager teaching others how to avoid accountability and pass the buck on to others.

■ Tall Versus Flat Organizations

Imagine an organization with thirty-one managers and a narrow span of management. As shown in Figure 11.3, the result is a relatively tall organization with five layers of management. With a somewhat wider span of control, however, the flat organization shown in Figure 11.3 emerges. This configuration has only three layers of management.

What difference does the height of an organization make to its operations? One early study at Sears, Roebuck and Co. found that a flat structure led to higher levels of employee morale and productivity.[19] Researchers have also argued that a tall structure is more expensive (because of the larger number of managers involved) and that it fosters more communication problems (because of the increased number of people through whom information must pass). On the other hand, a wide span of management in a flat organization may result in a manager's having more administrative responsibility (because there are fewer managers) and more supervisory responsibility (because more subordinates are reporting to each manager). If these additional responsibilities become excessive, the flat organization may suffer.[20]

Many experts agree that businesses can function effectively with fewer layers of organization than they currently have. The Franklin Mint, for example, reduced its number of management layers from six to four. At the same time, CEO Stewart Resnick increased his span of management from six to twelve. Similarly, IBM has eliminated several layers of management. "The Quality Challenge" describes how Andersen Windows has boosted its service quality in

FIGURE 11.3
Tall Versus Flat Organizations

Wide spans of management result in flat organizations, which may lead to improved employee morale and productivity as well as increased managerial responsibility. Many organizations today, including IBM and General Electric, are moving toward flat structures to improve communication and flexibility.

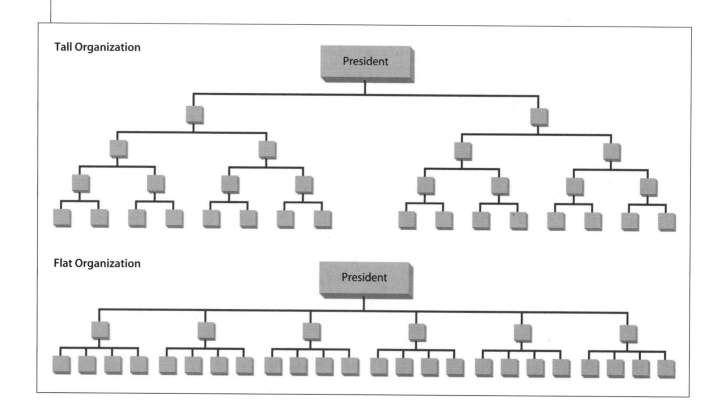

Tall Organization

Flat Organization

THE QUALITY CHALLENGE

Boosting Quality at Andersen Windows

Andersen Windows has been in business for nearly a century, specializing in mass-produced wooden windows. Until 1980, the firm made standardized products in large batches, and customers chose their windows from detailed catalog descriptions. But at about that time the market began to shift as more customers began to request custom-made windows.

In making the transition to custom-order production, however, Andersen encountered some quality problems. Price calculations for a custom window might take several hours to compute and could be as long as fifteen pages, for example, and by 1991 about 20 percent of Andersen's shipments contained at least one order discrepancy. Several layers of management were created to oversee and control activities. As customer frustration mounted, however, Andersen managers knew that they had to do something.

In response to its service quality problems, Andersen decided to reduce bureaucracy and streamline its order-

"People don't want their windows to look like their neighbor's windows, or anyone else's in the world for that matter."

Mike Tremblay, Andersen Windows executive*

processing system by developing an electronic ordering and inventory management system. Instead of using paper documents to route orders through as many as a dozen different locations and across several layers of hierarchy, for example, customers can now create custom window treatments at dealers' computers, get price quotes almost instantaneously, and place orders on the spot—dealing with a single contact rather than with several bureaucratic layers. Order discrepancies have also dropped substantially. As a result, Andersen now can offer almost two hundred thousand products (up from twenty-five thousand in 1985), make them quicker, and ship the windows with virtually no errors!

References: *Justin Martin, "Are You as Good as You Think You Are?"* Fortune, *September 30, 1996, pp. 142–152 (*quote on p. 143); Regis McKenna,* Real Time *(Boston: Harvard Business School Press, 1997); and Jeffrey Pfeiffer,* The Human Equation *(Boston: Harvard Business School Press, 1998).*

part by reducing layers in its hierarchy. One additional reason for this trend is that improved organizational communication networks allow managers to stay in touch with more subordinates than was possible even just a few years ago.[21]

■ Determining the Appropriate Span

Of course, the initial question remains: How do managers determine the appropriate span for their unique situations? Although no perfect formula exists, researchers have identified a set of factors that influence the span for a particular circumstance.[22] Some of these factors are listed in Table 11.1. For example, if the manager and subordinates are competent and well trained, a wide span may be effective. Physical dispersion is also important. The more widely subordinates are scattered, the narrower the span should be. On the other hand, if all the subordinates are in one location, the span can be somewhat wider. The amount of nonsupervisory work expected of the manager is also relevant. Some managers, especially at the lower levels of an organization, spend most or all of

1. Competence of supervisor and subordinates (the greater the competence, the wider the potential span)

2. Physical dispersion of subordinates (the greater the dispersion, the narrower the potential span)

3. Extent of nonsupervisory work in manager's job (the more nonsupervisory work, the narrower the potential span)

4. Degree of required interaction (the less required interaction, the wider the potential span)

5. Extent of standardized procedures (the more procedures, the wider the potential span)

6. Similarity of tasks being supervised (the more similar the tasks, the wider the potential span)

7. Frequency of new problems (the higher the frequency, the narrower the potential span)

8. Preferences of supervisors and subordinates

TABLE 11.1

Factors Influencing the Span of Management

Although researchers have found advantages to the flat organization (less expensive, fewer communication problems than a tall organization, for example), a number of factors may favor a tall organization.

their time supervising subordinates. Other managers spend a lot of time doing paperwork, planning, and engaging in other managerial activities. Thus these managers may need a narrower span.

Some job situations also require a great deal of interaction between supervisor and subordinates. In general, the more interaction that is required, the narrower the span should be. Similarly, if the organization follows a fairly comprehensive set of standard procedures, a relatively wide span is possible. If only a few standard procedures exist, however, the supervisor usually has to play a larger role in overseeing day-to-day activities and may find a narrower span more efficient. Task similarity is also important. If most of the jobs being supervised are similar, a supervisor can handle a wider span. When each employee is performing a different task, more of the supervisor's time is spent on individual supervision. Likewise, if new problems that require supervisory assistance arise frequently, a narrower span may be called for. If new problems are relatively rare, though, a wider span can be established. Finally, the preferences of both supervisor and subordinates may affect the optimal span. Some managers prefer to spend less time actively supervising their employees, and many employees prefer to be more self-directed in their jobs. A wider span may be possible in these situations.[23]

In some organizational settings other factors may influence the optimal span of management. The relative importance of each factor also varies from setting to setting. It is unlikely that all eight factors will suggest the same span; some may suggest a wider span, and others may indicate a need for a narrow span. Hence managers must assess the relative weight of each factor or set of factors when deciding on the optimal span of management for their unique situation.

MANAGEMENT IMPLICATIONS

Managers should understand the various circumstances that affect the appropriate span of management. In addition, they should be aware of how the span of management specifically results in a relatively taller or flatter organization, as well as the implications of these effects.

Distributing Authority

Another important building block in structuring organizations is the determination of how authority is to be distributed among positions. **Authority** is power that has been legitimized by the organization.[24] Distributing authority is another normal outgrowth of increasing organizational size. For example, when an owner-manager hires a sales representative to market her products, she needs to give the new employee appropriate authority to make decisions about delivery dates, discounts, and so forth. If every decision requires the approval of the owner-manager, she is no better off than she was before she hired the sales representative. The power given to the sales representative to make certain kinds of decisions, then, represents the establishment of a pattern of authority—the sales representative can make some decisions alone, can make others in consultation with coworkers, and must defer some decisions to the boss. Two specific issues that managers must address when distributing authority are delegation and decentralization.[25]

authority Power that has been legitimized by the organization

delegation The process by which a manager assigns a portion of his or her total workload to others

■ The Delegation Process

Delegation is the establishment of a pattern of authority between a superior and one or more subordinates. Specifically, **delegation** is the process by which managers assign a portion of their total workload to others.[26]

Reasons for Delegation   The primary reason for delegation is to enable the manager to get more work done. Subordinates help ease the manager's burden by doing major portions of the organization's work. In some instances, a subordinate may have more expertise in addressing a particular problem than the manager does. For example, the subordinate may have had special training in developing information systems or may be more familiar with a particular product line or geographic area. Delegation also helps develop subordinates. By participating in decision making and problem solving, subordinates learn about overall operations and improve their managerial skills.

Parts of the Delegation Process   In theory, as shown in Figure 11.4, the delegation process involves three steps. First, the manager assigns responsibility, or gives the subordinate a job to do. The assignment of responsibility might range from telling a subordinate to prepare a report to placing the person in charge of a task force. Along with the assignment, the individual is also given the authority to do the job. The manager may give the subordinate the power to requisition needed

FIGURE 11.4
Steps in the Delegation Process

Good communication skills can help a manager successfully delegate responsibility to subordinates. A manager must not be reluctant to delegate, nor must he or she fear that the subordinate will do the job so well that the manager's advancement is threatened.

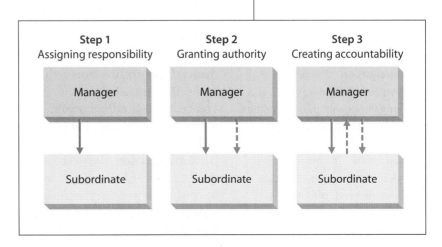

Step 1 Assigning responsibility	Step 2 Granting authority	Step 3 Creating accountability
Manager	Manager	Manager
Subordinate	Subordinate	Subordinate

information from confidential files or to direct a group of other workers. Finally, the manager establishes the subordinate's accountability—that is, the subordinate accepts an obligation to carry out the task assigned by the manager.

These three steps do not occur mechanically, however. Indeed, when a manager and a subordinate have developed a good working relationship, the major parts of the process may be implied rather than stated. The manager may simply mention that a particular job must be done. A perceptive subordinate may realize that the manager is actually assigning the job to him. From past experience with the boss, the worker may also know, without being told, that he has the necessary authority to do the job and that he is accountable to the boss for finishing the job as "agreed."

Problems in Delegation Unfortunately, problems often arise in the delegation process. For example, a manager may be reluctant to delegate. Some managers are so disorganized that they are unable to plan work in advance and, as a result, cannot delegate appropriately. Similarly, some managers may worry that subordinates will do too well and pose a threat to their own advancement. And finally, managers may not trust the subordinate to do the job well. Similarly, some subordinates are reluctant to accept delegation. They may be afraid that failure will result in a reprimand. They may also perceive that there are no rewards for accepting additional responsibility. Or they may simply prefer to avoid risk and, therefore, want their boss to take all responsibility.

There are no quick fixes for these problems. The basic issue is communication. Subordinates must understand their own responsibility, authority, and accountability, and the manager must come to recognize the value of effective delegation. Eventually, subordinates should be able to make substantial contributions to the organization. At the same time, managers should recognize that a subordinate's satisfactory performance is not a threat to their own career, but an accomplishment by both the subordinate who did the job and the manager who trained the subordinate and was astute enough to entrust the subordinate with the project. Ultimate responsibility for the outcome, however, continues to reside with the manager.

■ Decentralization and Centralization

Just as authority can be delegated from one individual to another, organizations also develop patterns of authority across a wide variety of positions and departments. **Decentralization** is the process of systematically delegating power and authority throughout the organization to middle and lower-level managers. Hence, a decentralized organization is one in which decision-making power and authority are delegated as far down the chain of command as possible. Decentralization, of course, is just one end of a continuum anchored at the other end by **centralization**, the process of systematically retaining power and authority in the hands of higher-level managers. In a centralized organization decision-making power and authority are retained at the higher levels of management. When H. Ross Perot ran EDS he practiced centralization; his successors have used decentralization.

decentralization The process of systematically delegating power and authority throughout the organization to middle and lower-level managers

centralization The process of systematically retaining power and authority in the hands of higher-level managers

No organization is ever completely decentralized or completely centralized: some firms position themselves toward one end of the continuum, and some lean the other way.[27]

What factors determine an organization's position on the decentralization-centralization continuum? One common determinant is the organization's external environment. Usually, the greater the complexity and uncertainty of the environment, the greater is the tendency to decentralize. Another crucial factor is the history of the organization. Firms tend to do what they have done in the past, so there is likely to be some relationship between what an organization did in its early history and what it chooses to do today in terms of centralization or decentralization. The nature of the decisions being made is also considered. The costlier and riskier the decision, the more pressure there is to centralize. Organizations also consider the abilities of lower-level managers. If lower-level managers do not have the ability to make high-quality decisions, there is likely to be a high level of centralization. If lower-level managers are well qualified, top management can take advantage of those talents by decentralizing; in fact, if top management doesn't, talented lower-level managers may leave the organization.[28]

A manager has no clear-cut guidelines for determining whether to centralize or decentralize. Many successful organizations such as Sears and General Electric are quite decentralized. Equally successful firms such as McDonald's and Kmart have remained centralized. IBM has recently undergone a transformation from using a highly centralized approach to a much more decentralized approach to managing its operations. A great deal of decision-making authority was passed from the hands of a select group of top executives down to six product and marketing groups. The reason for the move was to speed the company's ability to make decisions, introduce new products, and respond to customers. For years, most Japanese firms have been highly centralized. Recently, though, many leading Japanese firms have moved toward decentralization.

MANAGEMENT IMPLICATIONS All managers should know the steps in the delegation process. In addition, they should also be aware of problems that can occur as a result of ineffective delegation. Finally, they should know how the distribution of authority results in centralization or decentralization and the factors that affect each. ▬

Coordinating Activities

A fifth major element of organizing is coordination. As we discussed earlier, job specialization and departmentalization involve breaking down jobs into small units and then combining those jobs into departments. After this task is accomplished, the activities of the departments must be linked—systems must

coordination   The process of linking the activities of the various departments of the organization

Coordination is an important part of organizing. For example, Sue Hayes and Kathy Van Wieren work for Herman Miller, a large office furniture company. As they lift these large panels, both workers must know when to lift, how to lift, and where they are going. Without such co-ordination, they could drop the panel, damaging it and/or injuring themselves. In similar fashion, many managerial tasks must be coordinated with other tasks to ensure that they are being performed efficiently and effectively.

be put into place to keep the activities of each department focused on the attainment of organizational goals. The key ingredient is **coordination**—the process of linking the activities of the various departments of the organization.[29]

■ The Need for Coordination

The primary reason for coordination is that departments and work groups are interdependent—they depend on each other for information and resources to perform their respective activities. The greater the interdependence between departments, the more coordination the organization requires if departments are to be able to perform effectively. There are three major forms of interdependence: pooled, sequential, and reciprocal.[30]

Pooled interdependence represents the lowest level of interdependence. Units with pooled interdependence operate with little interaction—the output of the units is pooled at the organizational level. The Gap clothing stores operate with pooled interdependence. The parent organization treats each store as a department. Each store has its own operating budget, staff, and so forth. The profits or losses from each store are "added together" at the organizational level. The stores are interdependent to the extent that the final success or failure of one store affects the others, but they do not generally interact on a day-to-day basis.

In **sequential interdependence**, the output of one unit becomes the input for another in a sequential fashion. This approach creates a moderate level of interdependence. At Nissan, for example, one plant assembles engines and then ships them to a final assembly site at another plant where the cars are completed. The plants are interdependent in that the final assembly plant must have the engines from engine assembly before it can perform its primary function of producing finished automobiles. But the level of interdependence is generally one way—the engine plant is not necessarily dependent on the final assembly plant.

Reciprocal interdependence exists when activities flow both ways between units. This form is clearly the most complex. Within a Marriott Hotel, for example, the reservations department, front-desk check-in, and housekeeping are all reciprocally interdependent. Reservations has to provide front-desk employees with information about how many guests to expect each day, and housekeeping needs to know which rooms require priority cleaning. If any of the three units does not do its job properly, the others will all be affected.

■ Structural Coordination Techniques

Because of the obvious coordination requirements that characterize most organizations, many techniques for achieving coordination have been developed. Some of the most useful devices for maintaining coordination among interdependent units are the managerial hierarchy, rules and procedures, liaison roles, task forces, and integrating departments.[31]

The Managerial Hierarchy Organizations that use the hierarchy to achieve coordination place one manager in charge of interdependent departments or units. In Kmart distribution centers, major activities include receiving and unloading bulk shipments from railroad cars and loading other shipments onto trucks for distribution to retail outlets. The two groups (receiving and shipping) are interdependent in that they share the loading docks and some equipment. To ensure coordination and minimize conflict, one manager is in charge of the whole operation.

Rules and Procedures Routine coordination activities can be handled via rules and standard procedures. In the Kmart distribution center, an outgoing truck shipment has priority over an incoming rail shipment. Thus when trucks are to be loaded, the shipping unit is given access to all of the center's auxiliary forklifts. This priority is specifically stated in a rule. But, as useful as rules and procedures often are in routine situations, they are not particularly effective when coordination problems are complex or unusual.

Liaison Roles We introduced the liaison role of management in Chapter 1. As a device for coordination, a manager in a liaison role coordinates interdependent units by acting as a common point of contact. This individual may not have any formal authority over the groups but instead simply facilitates the flow of information between units. Two engineering groups working on component systems for a large project might interact through a liaison. The liaison maintains familiarity with each group as well as with the overall project. She can answer questions and otherwise serve to integrate the activities of all the groups.

Task Forces A task force may be created when the need for coordination is acute. When interdependence is complex and several units are involved, a single liaison person may not be sufficient. Instead, a task force might be assembled by drawing one representative from each group. The coordination function is thus spread across several individuals, each of whom has special information about one of the groups involved. When the project is completed, task force members return to their original positions. For example, a college overhauling its degree requirements might establish a task force made up of representatives from each department affected by the change. Each person retains her or his regular departmental affiliation and duties but also serves on the special task force. After the new requirements are agreed on, the task force is dissolved.

pooled interdependence When units operate with little interaction, their output is simply pooled

sequential interdependence When the output of one unit becomes the input of another in sequential fashion

reciprocal interdependence When activities flow both ways between units

Integrating Departments Integrating departments are occasionally used for coordination. These are somewhat similar to task forces but are more permanent. An integrating department generally has some permanent members as well as members who are assigned temporarily from units that are particularly in need of coordination. One study found that successful firms in the plastics industry, which is characterized by complex and dynamic environments, used integrating departments to maintain internal integration and coordination.[32] An integrating department usually has more authority than a task force and may even be given some budgetary control by the organization.

In general, the greater the degree of interdependence, the more attention the organization must devote to coordination. When interdependence is pooled or simple sequential, the managerial hierarchy or rules and procedures are often sufficient. When more complex forms of sequential or simpler forms of reciprocal interdependence exist, liaisons or task forces may be more useful. When reciprocal interdependence is complex, task forces or integrating departments are needed. Of course, the manager must also rely on her or his own experience and insights when choosing coordination techniques for the organization.

MANAGEMENT IMPLICATIONS Managers need to understand how varying degrees of interdependence determine the need for coordination within their organization. In addition, they also need to know how to use various structural techniques to facilitate coordination. ▬

Differentiating Between Positions

line position A position in the direct chain of command that is responsible for the achievement of an organization's goals

staff position A position intended to provide expertise, advice, and support for line positions

The last building block of organization structure is differentiating between line and staff positions in the organization. A **line position** is a position in the direct chain of command that is responsible for the achievement of an organization's goals. A **staff position** is intended to provide expertise, advice, and support for line positions.

■ Differences Between Line and Staff

The most obvious difference between line and staff is purpose—line managers work directly toward organizational goals, whereas staff managers advise and assist. But other distinctions exist as well. One important difference is authority. Line authority is generally thought of as the formal or legitimate authority created by the organizational hierarchy. Staff authority is less concrete and may take various forms. One form is the authority to advise. In this instance, the line manager can choose whether to seek or to avoid input from the staff; even when advice is sought, the manager might choose to ignore it.

Another form of staff authority is called compulsory advice. In this case the line manager must listen to the advice but can choose to heed it or ignore it. For example, the Pope is expected to listen to the advice of the Sacred College when dealing with church doctrine, but he may follow his own beliefs when making decisions. Perhaps the most important form of staff authority is called functional authority—formal or legitimate authority over activities related to the staff member's specialty. For example, a human resource staff manager may have functional authority when there is a question of discrimination in hiring. Conferring functional authority is probably the most effective way to use staff positions because the organization is able to take advantage of specialized expertise while maintaining a chain of command.

■ Administrative Intensity

Organizations sometimes attempt to balance their emphasis on line versus staff positions in terms of administrative intensity. **Administrative intensity** is the degree to which managerial positions are concentrated in staff positions. An organization with a high administrative intensity has many staff positions relative to the number of line positions; low administrative intensity reflects relatively more line positions. Although staff positions are important in many different areas, they tend to proliferate unnecessarily. All else being equal, organizations would like to spend most of their human resource dollars on line managers because by definition they contribute to the organization's basic goals. A surplus of staff positions represents a drain on an organization's cash and an inefficient use of resources.

Many organizations have recently reduced their administrative intensity by eliminating staff positions. CBS has cut hundreds of staff positions at its New York headquarters, and IBM has cut its corporate staff workforce from seven thousand to twenty-three hundred. Burlington Northern generates almost $7 billion in annual sales and manages a workforce of forty-three thousand with a corporate staff of only seventy-seven managers!

In many work settings, managers must ensure a clear differentiation between various positions. At the Beverly Hills Hotel, for example, this maitre d' is responsible for managing an important hotel function. Here he inspects his staff and makes sure that everyone knows what to do in order for things to go smoothly. Everyone knows that he is in charge, and each knows his or her own responsibilities.

MANAGEMENT IMPLICATIONS

All managers need to understand the fundamental differences that exist between line positions and staff positions in organizations in general and their organization in particular. Managers should also understand the meaning of administrative intensity and how to manage it effectively. ■

administrative intensity The degree to which managerial positions are concentrated in staff positions

Summary of Key Points

Organizations are made up of a series of elements. The most common of these involve designing jobs, grouping jobs, establishing reporting relationships, distributing authority, coordinating activities, and differentiating between positions.

Job design is the determination of an individual's work-related responsibilities. The most common form is job specialization. Because of various drawbacks to job specialization, managers have experimented with job rotation, job enlargement, job enrichment, the job characteristics approach, and work teams as alternatives.

After jobs are designed, they are grouped into departments. The most common bases for departmentalization are function, product, customer, and location. Each approach has unique advantages and disadvantages. Large organizations employ multiple bases of departmentalization at different levels.

Establishing reporting relationships starts with clarifying the chain of command. The span of management partially dictates whether the organization is relatively tall or flat. The trend in recent years has been toward flatter organizations. Several situational factors influence the ideal span.

Distributing authority starts with delegation. Delegation is the process by which the manager assigns a portion of his or her total workload to others. Systematic delegation throughout the organization is decentralization. Centralization involves keeping power and authority at the top of the organization. Several factors influence the appropriate degree of decentralization.

Coordination is the process of linking the activities of the various departments of the organization. Pooled, sequential, or reciprocal interdependence among departments is a primary reason for coordination. Managers can draw on several techniques to help achieve coordination.

A line position is a position in the direct chain of command that is responsible for achieving an organization's goals. In contrast, a staff position provides expertise, advice, and support for line positions. Administrative intensity is the degree to which managerial positions are concentrated in staff positions.

Discussion Questions

Questions for Review

1. What is job specialization? What are its advantages and disadvantages?

2. What is departmentalization? Why and how is departmentalization carried out?

3. In what general ways can organizations be shaped? What implications does each of these ways have with regard to the distribution of authority within the organization?

4. How are positions differentiated in organizations? What are the advantages and disadvantages of such differentiation?

Questions for Analysis

5. Seeing how specialization can be utilized in manufacturing organizations is easy. How can it be used by other types of organizations such as hospitals, churches, schools, and restaurants? Should those organizations use specialization? Why or why not?

6. Try to develop a different way to departmentalize your college or university, a local fast-food restaurant, a manufacturing firm, or some other organization. What might be the advantages of your form of organization?

7. Which type of position (line, staff, administrative) is most important to an organization? Why? Could

an organization function without any of them? Why or why not?

Questions for Application

8. Go to the library and locate organization charts for ten different organizations. Look for similarities and differences among them and try to account for what you find.

9. Contact two very different local organizations (for example, a retailing firm, a manufacturing firm, a church, a civic club) and interview top managers to develop organization charts for each organization. How do you account for the similarities and differences between them?

10. How many people does the head of your academic department supervise? the dean of your college? the president of your university or college? Why do different spans of management exist among these officials? How might you find out if the spans are appropriate in size?

Building Effective
Time-Management Skills

EXERCISE OVERVIEW

Time-management skills refer to the manager's ability to prioritize work, to work efficiently, and to delegate appropriately. As noted in this chapter, various situational factors affect the appropriate span of management that is optimal for a particular situation. This exercise relates time-management issues with the appropriate span of management.

EXERCISE BACKGROUND

Many factors affect the appropriate span of management for a particular situation. These are noted and summarized in Table 11.1. The span of management has a direct relationship to the efficient use of the manager's time. That is, a less-than-optimal span of management is likely to result in an inefficient use of time. If the span is too narrow, the manager may have too little work to do, but if the span is too wide, the manager's other work may get neglected.

EXERCISE TASK

Considering the various factors that influence an optimal span, respond to the following:

1. Describe how a span inappropriately matched with each factor will result in inefficiencies for both managers and subordinates.

2. If situational factors and the existing span of management are inappropriately matched, it might be possible to change one or the other to achieve a better fit. Examine each factor and decide whether it would be easier to change the factor or the span of management to improve fit.

3. Now assume that you are a manager. Assess the relative importance that you would place on each situational factor to define your own span of management.

Building Effective Diagnostic Skills

EXERCISE OVERVIEW

Diagnostic skills enable a manager to visualize the most appropriate response to a situation. This exercise will help you develop your diagnostic skills as they relate to issues of centralization and decentralization in an organization.

EXERCISE BACKGROUND

Managers must often change the degree of centralization or decentralization in their organization. Begin this exercise by reflecting on two very different scenarios. In scenario A, assume that you are the top manager in a large organization. The organization has a long and well-known history of being very centralized. For valid reasons beyond the scope of this exercise, assume that you have decided to make the firm much more decentralized. For scenario B, assume the exact opposite situation. That is, you are the top manager of a firm that has always used decentralization but has now decided to become much more centralized.

EXERCISE TASK

With the preceding background information as context, do the following:

1. Make a list of the major barriers you see to implementing decentralization in scenario A.

2. Make a list of the major barriers you see to implementing centralization in scenario B.

3. Which scenario do you think would be easiest to actually implement? That is, is it likely to be easier to move from centralization to decentralization or from decentralization to centralization? Why?

4. Given a choice of starting your own career in a firm that is either highly centralized or highly decentralized, which do you think you would prefer? Why?

Building Effective Conceptual Skills

EXERCISE OVERVIEW

Conceptual skills refer to a person's abilities to think in the abstract. This exercise will help you develop your conceptual skills as they relate to designing jobs.

EXERCISE BACKGROUND

Begin by thinking of three different jobs, one that appears to have virtually no enrichment, one that appears to have moderate enrichment, and one that appears to have a great deal of enrichment. These jobs might be ones that you have personally held, or ones that you have observed and about which you can make some educated or informed judgments.

Evaluate each job along the five dimensions described in the job characteristics theory. Now see whether you can identify ways to improve each dimension for each job. That is, see whether you can determine how to enrich the jobs using the job characteristics theory as a framework.

Finally, meet with a classmate and share results. See whether you can improve your job enrichment strategy based on the critique offered by your classmate.

EXERCISE TASK

With the preceding background information as context, do the following:

1. What job qualities make some jobs easier to enrich than others?

2. Can all jobs be enriched?

3. Even if a particular job can be enriched, does that always mean that it should be enriched?

4. Under what circumstances might an individual prefer to have a routine and unenriched job?

CHAPTER CLOSING CASE

3M Organizes for Innovation

Minnesota Mining and Manufacturing, better known as 3M, is among the most innovative and profitable companies in the world today. Among its best-known products are Post-It Notes, Scotch Magic tape, and Scotchguard Fabric Protection. But beyond these household phrases, 3M makes more than sixty thousand individual products. The firm also has the ambitious goal of deriving 30 percent of its sales each year from products that are less than four years old.

One key to 3M's amazing success is its unusual structure. If asked, 3M executives can produce an organization chart that shows a neat and tidy arrangement for positions, departments, and reporting relationships that looks as traditional as any hierarchy in existence. Underneath the president, for example, are three major divisions: one for consumer products, one for industrial products, and one for the firm's international business activities. Within each division is the standard array of corporate functions, such as finance and marketing.

But 3M executives are also quick to add that although their firm can be drawn like a traditional and hierarchical pyramid, that's far from how things actually work at the company. In-deed, managers describe the firm's "real" structure as looking something like an upside-down table with hundreds of legs. The table top itself, again residing on the bottom, consists of thirty-three technology platforms—a technology from which the firm can develop multiple products for multiple markets.

The legs growing up from the platforms are actually businesses derived from one or more technologies. No one really knows how many legs—or businesses—exist at any given time, but top managers estimate the number at between five hundred and one thousand. Wrapped around the legs are three sets of overriding elements that tie together the entire company—its financial goals and disciplines, its human resource philosophies, and its corporate values.

Another interesting part of 3M's success is what it calls "bootleg time." Each manager and scientist at the company is expected to spend approximately 15 percent of her or his time just tinkering with products—trying to figure out new uses for them, ways of making them faster, or ways of making them cheaper, for example.

A good example of how this approach has helped the company is the now legendary story of the invention of Post-It

Notes. It seems that one research scientist was working on a new glue but couldn't get it to bond properly. He vented his frustrations to his colleagues and then put the project aside. A few weeks later another scientist was trying to figure out how he could attach written notes to the pages of his church hymnal without permanently damaging the pages. He borrowed some of the glue from the first scientist, brushed it on the back of his notes, and found that he could later remove them without damaging either the notes or his hymnal. And today, Post-It products account for almost $1 billion in annual revenues for the firm.

But the structure that pulls all this off is bewildering, sometimes even to 3M itself. As already noted, for example, top managers profess to not really know how many businesses exist within the corporation at any given time. Likewise, they claim to not know how many labs the firm has. What they do know, however, is that the firm has one huge central lab where scientists can test ideas and where the accumulated knowledge of the firm is stored. Satellite labs are testing grounds, meanwhile, where scientists first develop ideas. And when scientists can't get funding from their own business, they are encouraged to shop their ideas to other 3M businesses. Confusing? No doubt. But also enormously profitable.

Case Questions

1. Identify the key parts of 3M's organization structure.
2. Why doesn't 3M use a more conventional structure?
3. Why don't more firms use 3M's model for organization structure?

Case References: Thomas A. Stewart, "3M Fights Back," *Fortune,* February 5, 1996, pp. 94–99; *Hoover's Handbook of American Business 1998* (Austin, Texas: Hoover's Business Press, 1998), pp. 934–935.

CHAPTER NOTES

1. "Highly Paid, High-Profile Heinz CEO Ends Reign, Era," *USA Today*, December 3, 1997, pp. 1B, 2B; "57 Varieties of Challenges," *Business Week*, March 24, 1997, p. 44; *Hoover's Handbook of American Business 1997* (Austin, Texas: Hoover's Business Press, 1996), pp. 708–709; and "The CEO and the Board," *Business Week*, September 15, 1997, pp. 107–116.

2. Gareth Jones, *Organization Theory*, 2nd ed. (Reading, Mass.: Addison-Wesley, 1997).

3. David A. Nadler and Michael L. Tushman, *Competing by Design—the Power of Organizational Architecture* (New York: Oxford University Press, 1997).

4. Ricky W. Griffin and Gary McMahan, "Motivation through Job Design," in *Organizational Behavior—The State of the Science*, ed. Jerald Greenberg (Hillsdale, N.J.: Lawrance Erlbaum Associates, 1994), pp. 23–44.

5. Adam Smith, *Wealth of Nations* (New York: Modern Library, 1937; originally published in 1776).

6. Ricky W. Griffin, *Task Design* (Glenview, Ill.: Scott, Foresman, 1982).

7. Anne S. Miner, "Idiosyncratic Jobs in Formal Organizations," *Administrative Science Quarterly*, September 1987, pp. 327–351.

8. M. D. Kilbridge, "Reduced Costs through Job Enlargement: A Case," *Journal of Business*, 1960, Vol. 33, pp. 357–362.

9. Griffin and McMahan, "Motivation through Job Enrichment."

10. Kilbridge, "Reduced Costs through Job Enrichment: A Case."

11. Frederick Herzberg, *Work and the Nature of Man* (Cleveland: World Press, 1966).

12. Robert Ford, "Job Enrichment Lessons from AT&T," *Harvard Business Review*, January–February 1973, pp. 96–106.

13. J. Richard Hackman and Greg R. Oldham, *Work Redesign* (Reading, Mass.: Addison-Wesley, 1980).

14. "Some Plants Tear Out Long Assembly Lines, Switch to Craft Work," *Wall Street Journal*, October 24, 1994, pp. A1, A4.

15. Richard L. Daft, *Organization Theory and Design*, 6th ed. (St. Paul, Minn.: West, 1998).

16. A.V. Graicunas, "Relationships in Organizations," *Bulletin of the International Management Institute*, March 7, 1933, pp. 39–42.

17. Ralph C. Davis, *Fundamentals of Top Management* (New York: Harper & Row, 1951); Lyndall F. Urwick, *Scientific Principles and Organization* (New York: American Management Association, 1938), p. 8; and Ian Hamilton, *The Soul and Body of an Army* (London: Edward Arnold, 1921), pp. 229–230.

18. David D. Van Fleet and Arthur G. Bedeian, "A History of the Span of Management," *Academy of Management Review*, 1977, pp. 356–372.

19. James C. Worthy, "Factors Influencing Employee Morale," *Harvard Business Review*, January 1950, pp. 61–73.

20. Dan R. Dalton, William D. Todor, Michael J. Spendolini, Gordon J. Fielding, and Lyman W. Porter, "Organization Structure and Performance: A Critical Review," *Academy of Management Review*, January 1980, pp. 49–64.

21. Brian Dumaine, "The Bureaucracy Busters," *Fortune*, June 17, 1991, pp. 36–50.

22. David Van Fleet, "Span of Management Research and Issues," *Academy of Management Journal*, September 1983, pp. 546–552.

23. For a recent analysis of these and other factors that can influence the appropriate span of management, see Edward E. Lawler III, "Substitutes for Hierarchy," *Organizational Dynamics*, Summer 1988, pp. 4–15.

24. See Daft, *Organization Theory and Design*.

25. William Kahn and Kathy Kram, "Authority at Work: Internal Models and Their Organizational Consequences," *Academy of Management Review*, 1994, Vol. 19, No. 1, pp. 17–50.

26. Carrie R. Leana, "Predictors and Consequences of Delegation," *Academy of Management Journal*, December 1986, pp. 754–774.

27. "Remote Control," *HRMagazine*, August 1997, pp. 82–90.

28. "Toppling the Pyramids," *Canadian Business*, May 1993, pp. 61–65.

29. Kevin Crowston, "A Coordination Theory Approach to Organizational Process Design," *Organization Science*, March–April 1997, pp. 157–166.

30. James Thompson, *Organizations in Action* (New York: McGraw-Hill, 1967). For a recent discussion, see Bart Victor and Richard S. Blackburn, "Interdependence: An Alternative Conceptualization," *Academy of Management Review*, July 1987, pp. 486–498.

31. Jay R. Galbraith, *Designing Complex Organizations* (Reading, Mass.: Addison-Wesley, 1973); and Jay R. Galbraith, *Organizational Design* (Reading, Mass.: Addison-Wesley, 1977).

32. Paul R. Lawrence and Jay W. Lorsch, "Differentiation and Integration in Complex Organizations," *Administrative Science Quarterly*, March 1967, pp. 1–47.

12

Managing Organization Design

OBJECTIVES

After studying this chapter, you should be able to:

- Describe the basic nature of organization design.
- Identify and explain the two basic universal perspectives on organization design.
- Identify and explain several situational influences on organization design.
- Discuss how an organization's strategy and its design are interrelated.
- Describe the basic forms of organization design that characterize many organizations.
- Describe emerging issues in organization design.

For decades The Boeing Co. has been the world's largest manufacturer of commercial aircraft. And almost since its inception in 1916, Boeing has been a hierarchical, bureaucratic firm bound by rules, regulations, and procedures. But as the twentieth century draws to a close, Boeing is remaking itself into a sleek and flexible organization that is in every way the antithesis of its former self.

Top managers at Boeing recognized several warning signals that changes were needed. For one thing, a long and bitter strike by the International Association of Machinists & Aerospace Workers revealed just how much distrust existed between the firm's workers and its managers. And for another, airline customers have become increasingly vocal in their criticism of the firm's delivery schedules and price structures.

As CEO Frank Shrontz was retiring, he named Philip Condit as his successor and challenged him to remake Boeing into a firm that would continue its legacy of engineering, technology, and industry leadership while simultaneously adopting many of the organization design features popularized by new high-technology companies like Microsoft and Compaq Computer.

Condit started by carefully analyzing every facet of how Boeing conducted its operations. He concluded that the firm's antiquated functional organization design was its biggest impediment. In a functional design, functional specialists in areas like engineering, finance, and marketing are grouped together into departments. Each department, in turn, is responsible for its own unique functional area.

For example, at Boeing, the work of design engineers was totally independent of production and operations people responsible for actually constructing airplanes and their component parts. That is, the engineer drew plans and then turned them over to the manufacturers, who had had no opportunity for input whatsoever. Similarly, if tool builders found a problem in a design for a new part for an airplane, they had to report it to their supervisor, who took it up the ladder until the informa-

tion finally reached the senior engineer who had originally diagrammed the tools. The engineer would then respond to the question and pass the information laboriously back down the chain of command.

Condit realized that the old system wasn't working. As a result, he threw out Boeing's old-fashioned functional design and replaced it with an organic and flexible model based on products. Under the new design, representatives from every relevant functional department work together from the inception of a project until its completion. Suppose, for example, that Boeing wanted to develop a new modular luggage storage compartment for its aircraft. Managers would create an organization-within-an-organization to get the project completed. The group would have design engineers, manufacturing managers, industrial marketing managers, financial experts, and even a human resource specialist to provide employment services for the group.

By using the new approach, Boeing can move people and their talents in response to current needs. Moreover, organizational barriers are broken down as people communicate with one another more frequently and more directly. For example, if tool builders have a problem with a design now, they can pick up a telephone and call the engineer who designed the part. Or, just as likely, they will see the designer in a product meeting and can ask their question directly. And so far, at least, Boeing's managers think that with their new organization design in place, the sky's the limit![1]

"We're trying to destroy all of the old functional hierarchies."

Ron Woodard, Boeing executive, quoted in Forbes, June 3, 1996, p. 64.

One of the major ingredients in managing any business is the creation of an organization design to link the various elements that constitute the organization. Managers in any given organization can select its design from a wide range of alternatives. Philip Condit and his executive team at Boeing are remaking one of the largest major corporations in the world. The basis for this makeover is the firm's organization design; the reasons behind the change involve the firm's environment and its strategy.

In Chapter 11, we identified the basic elements that go into creating an organization. In this chapter we explore how those elements can be combined to create an overall design for the organization. We first discuss the nature of organization design. We then describe early approaches aimed at identifying universal models of organization design. Situational factors, such as technology, environment, size, and life cycle, are then introduced. Next we discuss the relationship between an organization's strategy and its structure. Basic forms of organization design are described next. We conclude by presenting four emerging issues in organization design.

organization design The overall set of structural elements and the relationships among those elements used to manage the total organization

The Nature of Organization Design

What is organization design? In Chapter 11 we noted that job specialization and span of management are among the common elements of organization structure. We also described how both the appropriate degree of specialization and the appropriate span of management can vary. Not really addressed, however, were questions of the relationship between specialization and span. For example, should a high level of specialization be matched with a certain span? And will different combinations of each work best with different bases of departmentalization? These and related issues are associated with questions of organization design.[2]

Organization design is the overall set of structural elements and the relationships among those elements used to manage the total organization. Thus organization design is a means to implement strategies and plans to achieve organizational goals. As we discuss organization design, keep in mind two important points. First, organizations are not designed and then left intact. Most organizations change almost continuously as a result of factors such as events and people. (The processes of organization change are discussed in Chapter 13.) Second, organization design for larger organizations is complex and has so many nuances and

Organization design is a complex and an ever changing process. Take what might appear to be a simple organization—the Atlanta Braves baseball team. The Braves' management team must create a structure that works best for the team itself. They must also include stadium management systems, minor league operations, media contract functions, a licensing group, and a variety of other activities. The design they use is different from all other sports teams, as well as from all other organizations in general.

variations that their descriptions must be considerably simplified to be explained in basic terms.

| MANAGEMENT IMPLICATIONS | Managers should know that designing an organization is an ongoing process that is never really finished and should recognize that organization |

design for larger organizations is extremely complex. ▬

Universal Perspectives on Organization Design

In Chapter 2, we made the distinction between contingency and universal approaches to solving management problems. Recall, for example, that universal perspectives try to identify the "one best way" to manage organizations; on the other hand, contingency perspectives suggest that appropriate managerial behavior in a given situation depends on, or is contingent on, unique elements in that situation. The foundation of contemporary thinking about organization design can be traced to two early universal perspectives: the bureaucratic model and the behavioral model.

■ Bureaucratic Model

We also noted in Chapter 2 that Max Weber, an influential German sociologist, was a pioneer of classical organization theory. At the core of Weber's writings was the bureaucratic model of organizations.[3] The Weberian perspective suggests that a **bureaucracy** is a model of organization design based on a legitimate and formal system of authority. Many people associate bureaucracy with red tape, rigidity, and passing the buck. For example, how many times have you heard people refer disparagingly to "the federal bureaucracy"? And many U.S. managers believe that bureaucracy in the Japanese government is a major impediment to U.S. firms' ability to do business there.

Weber viewed the bureaucratic form of organization as logical, rational, and efficient. He offered the model as a framework to which all organizations should aspire; the "one best way" of doing things. According to Weber, the ideal bureaucracy exhibits five basic characteristics:

bureaucracy A model of organization design based on a legitimate and formal system of authority

1. The organization should adopt a distinct division of labor, and each position should be filled by an expert.

2. The organization should develop a consistent set of rules to ensure that task performance is uniform.

3. The organization should establish a hierarchy of positions or offices that creates a chain of command from the top of the organization to the bottom.

Shedding Bureaucracy at Toyota

Japanese organizations have a long-standing tradition of being tall, hierarchical, and mechanistic. Although teamwork dominates most manufacturing settings, managers have been forced to follow rigid chains of command and adhere to detailed rules and procedures. This approach to organization design has enabled the organizations to keep costs low and efficiency high; however, it has also tended to stifle creativity and make decision making a slow and laborious process.

> *"I would like to see fast change. If we fall behind competitors in reform, we will lose out in the competition."*
>
> *Hiroshi Okuda, president of Toyota**

Japan's biggest auto maker, Toyota, recently decided to break with tradition and move toward a flatter and more organic form of organization design. The stimuli for this move were a slowdown in organizational growth and concerns that its foreign competitors like General Motors, Ford, and BMW were gaining market share and product quality.

To get things turned around, Toyota promoted Hiroshi Okuda to the position of president. Okuda is the first person from outside the Toyoda family to run the firm in more than three decades. His mandate was to eliminate the bureaucracy that was choking organizational flexibility and to make Toyota more responsive and nimble. Accordingly, he eliminated several layers of the hierarchy, eliminated many antiquated procedures, and placed renewed emphasis on speed and time-to-market. For example, even though Toyota already was the world leader in the time needed to get a new model into production, Okuda challenged his engineers to cut the time from a fast twenty-seven months to an unheard-of eighteen months. Although it's still too soon to know the effects of these changes, so far, at least, Okuda seems to have Toyota well on the road to recovery.

References: Alex Taylor III, "How Toyota Defies Gravity," Fortune, December 8, 1997, pp. 100–108; "Shaking up an Old Giant," Forbes, May 20, 1996, pp. 68–80 (*quote on p. 69); Alex Taylor III, "Toyota's Boss Stands out in a Crowd," Fortune, November 25, 1996, pp. 116–119; and "Toyota Names a Chief Likely to Shake Up Global Auto Business," Wall Street Journal, August 11, 1995, pp. A1, A5.

---

4. Managers should conduct business in an impersonal way and maintain an appropriate social distance between themselves and their subordinates.

5. Employment and advancement in the organization should be based on technical expertise, and employees should be protected from arbitrary dismissal.

Perhaps the best examples of bureaucracies today are government agencies and universities. Consider, for example, the steps you must go through and the forms you must fill out to apply for admission to college, request housing, register each semester, change majors, submit a degree plan, substitute a course, and file for graduation. The reason these procedures are necessary is that universities deal with large numbers of people who must be treated equally and fairly. Hence rules, regulations, and standard operating procedures are needed. Large labor unions are also usually organized as bureaucracies.[4] Some bureaucracies, such as the U.S. Postal Service, are trying to portray themselves as less mechanistic and impersonal. The strategy of the Postal Service is to become more service oriented as a way to compete against rivals such as Federal Express and UPS. "The World of Management" discusses how Toyota is also working to become less bureaucratic.

A primary strength of the bureaucratic model is that several of its elements (such as reliance on rules and employment based on expertise) do, in fact, often improve efficiency. Bureaucracies also help prevent favoritism (because everyone must follow the rules) and make procedures and practices very clear to everyone. Unfortunately, however, this approach also has several disadvantages. One major disadvantage is that the bureaucratic model results in inflexibility and rigidity. After rules are created and put into place, making exceptions or changing them is often difficult. In addition, the bureaucracy often results in the neglect of human and social processes within the organization.

■ Behavioral Model

Another important universal model of organization design was the **behavioral model**, which paralleled the emergence of the human relations school of management thought. Rensis Likert, a management researcher, studied several large organizations to determine why some were more effective than others.[5] He found that the organizations in his sample that used the bureaucratic model of design tended to be less effective than those that used a more behaviorally oriented model consistent with the emerging human relations movement—in other words, organizations that paid more attention to developing work groups and were more concerned about interpersonal processes were more effective than those that didn't.

Likert developed a framework that characterized organizations in terms of eight important processes: leadership, motivation, communication, interactions, decision making, goal setting, control, and performance goals. Likert believed that all organizations could be measured and categorized along a continuum associated with each of these dimensions. He argued that the basic bureaucratic form of organization, which he called a **System 1 design**, anchored one end of each dimension. The characteristics of the System 1 organization in Likert's framework are summarized in Table 12.1.

Also summarized in this table are characteristics of Likert's other extreme form of organization design, called **System 4 design**, which was based on the behavioral model. For example, a System 4 organization uses a wide array of motivational processes, and its interaction processes are open and extensive. Other distinctions between System 1 and System 4 organizations are equally obvious. In between the System 1 and System 4 extremes lie the System 2 and System 3 organizations. Likert argued that System 4 should be adopted by all organizations. He suggested that managers should emphasize supportive relationships, establish high performance goals, and practice group decision making to achieve a System 4 organization. Many organizations attempted to adopt the System 4 design during its period of peak popularity. In 1969, General Motors converted a plant in the Atlanta area from a System 2 to a System 4 organization. Over the next three years, direct and indirect labor efficiency improved, as did tool-breakage rates, scrap costs, and quality.[6]

Like the bureaucratic model, the behavioral approach has both strengths and weaknesses. Its major strength is that it emphasizes human behavior by

behavioral model A model of organization design consistent with the human relations movement and stressing attention to developing work groups and concern with interpersonal processes

System 1 design Similar to the bureaucratic model

System 4 design Similar to the behavioral model

System 1 Organization	System 4 Organization
1. Leadership process includes no perceived confidence and trust. Subordinates do not feel free to discuss job problems with their superiors, who in turn do not solicit their ideas and opinions.	1. Leadership process includes perceived confidence and trust between superiors and subordinates in all matters. Subordinates feel free to discuss job problems with their superiors, who in turn solicit their ideas and opinions.
2. Motivational process taps only physical, security, and economic motives through the use of fear and sanctions. Unfavorable attitudes toward the organization prevail among employees.	2. Motivational process taps a full range of motives through participatory methods. Attitudes are favorable toward the organization and its goals.
3. Communication process is such that information flows downward and tends to be distorted, inaccurate, and viewed with suspicion by subordinates.	3. Communication process is such that information flows freely throughout the organization—upward, downward, and laterally. The information is accurate and undistorted.
4. Interaction process is closed and restricted. Subordinates have little effect on departmental goals, methods, and activities.	4. Interaction process is open and extensive. Both superiors and subordinates are able to affect departmental goals, methods, and activities.
5. Decision process occurs only at the top of the organization; it is relatively centralized.	5. Decision process occurs at all levels through group processes; it is relatively decentralized.
6. Goal-setting process is located at the top of the organization; discourages group participation.	6. Goal-setting process encourages group participation in setting high, realistic objectives.
7. Control process is centralized and emphasizes fixing of blame for mistakes.	7. Control process is dispersed throughout the organization and emphasizes self-control and problem solving.
8. Performance goals are low and passively sought by managers who make no commitment to developing the human resources of the organization.	8. Performance goals are high and actively sought by superiors who recognize the necessity for making a full commitment to developing, through training, the human resources of the organization.

TABLE 12.1

System 1 and System 4 Organizations

The behavioral model identifies two extreme types of organization design called System 1 and System 4. The two designs vary in eight fundamental processes. The System 1 design is considered to be somewhat rigid and inflexible.

Adapted from Rensis Likert, *The Human Organization.* Copyright © 1967 by The McGraw-Hill Companies. Reprinted by permission of The McGraw-Hill Companies.

stressing the value of an organization's employees. Likert and his associates thus paved the way for a more humanistic approach to designing organizations. Unfortunately, the behavioral approach also argues that there is one best way to design organizations—as a System 4. As we see, however, evidence is strong that there is no one best approach to organization design.[7] What works for one organization may not work for another, and what works for one organization may change as that organization's situation changes. Hence universal models like bureaucracy and System 4 have been largely supplanted by newer models that take contingency factors into account. In the next section we identify a number of factors that help determine the best organization design for a particular situation.

MANAGEMENT
IMPLICATIONS

Managers should understand the basic concepts inherent in the bureaucratic and behavioral models of organization design. While appreciating the strengths and weaknesses of these models, managers should also remember that universal models such as these are not truly applicable to to-day's organization and that different approaches are needed. ▬

Situational Influences on Organization Design

The **situational view of organization design** is based on the assumption that the optimal design for any given organization depends on a set of relevant situational factors.[8] That is, situational factors play a role in determining the best organization design for any particular circumstance. Four such factors—technology, environment, size, and organizational life cycle—are discussed here. Another, strategy, is described in the next section.

situational view of organization design Based on the assumption that the optimal design for any given organization depends on a set of relevant situational factors

■ Core Technology

Technology is the conversion processes used to transform inputs (such as materials or information) into outputs (such as products or services). Most organizations use multiple technologies, but an organization's most important one is called its *core technology*. Although most people visualize assembly lines and machinery when they think of technology, the term can also be applied to service organizations. For example, a brokerage firm like Merrill Lynch uses technology to transform investment dollars into income in much the same way that Union Carbide Corp. uses natural resources to manufacture chemical products.

The link between technology and organization design was first recognized by Joan Woodward.[9] Woodward studied one hundred manufacturing firms in southern England. She collected information about such things as the history of each organization, its manufacturing processes, its forms and procedures, and its financial performance. Woodward expected to find a relationship between the size of an organization and its design, but no such relationship emerged. As a result, she began to seek other explanations for differences. Close scrutiny of the firms in her sample suggested a potential relationship between technology and organization design. This follow-up analysis led Woodward to first classify the organizations according to their technology. She identified three basic forms of technology:

1. *Unit or small-batch technology.* The product is custom-made to customer specifications, or it is produced in small quantities. Organizations using

Small-batch technology can affect organization design in a number of ways. Shanghai Tang is a Hong Kong-based operation that makes custom suits and dresses. The firm's tailors use modern technology, rely on traditional styling, and have a reputation for high-quality work that has resulted in rapid growth. By using new flexible manufacturing methods, the company can deliver most custom-tailored apparel in as fast as 24 hours.

technology Conversion processes used to transform inputs into outputs

this form of technology include a tailor shop like Brooks Brothers (custom suits), a printing shop like Kinko's (business cards, company stationery), and a photography studio.

2. *Large-batch or mass-production technology.* The product is manufactured in assembly-line fashion by combining component parts into another part or finished product. Examples include automobile manufacturers like Subaru, washing-machine companies like Whirlpool Corporation, and electronics firms like Philips.

3. *Continuous-process technology.* Raw materials are transformed to a finished product by a series of machine or process transformations. The composition of the materials themselves is changed. Examples include petroleum refineries like Exxon and Shell and chemical refineries like Dow Chemical and Hoechst Celanese.

These forms of technology are listed in order of their assumed levels of complexity. That is, unit or small-batch technology is presumed to be the least complex, and continuous-process technology the most complex. Woodward found that different configurations of organization design were associated with each technology.

As technology became more complex in Woodward's sample, the number of levels of management increased (that is, the organization was taller). The executive span of management also increased, as did the relative size of its staff component. The supervisory span of management, however, first increased and then decreased as technology became more complex, primarily because much of the work in continuous-process technologies is automated. Fewer workers are needed, but the skills necessary to do the job increase. These findings are consistent with the discussion of the span of management in Chapter 11—the more complex the job, the narrower the span should be.

At a more general level of analysis, Woodward found that the two extremes (unit or small-batch technology and continuous-process technology) tended to be very similar to Likert's System 4 organization, whereas the middle-range organizations (large-batch or mass-production technology) were much more like bureaucracies or System 1. The large-batch and mass-production organizations also had a higher level of specialization.[10] Finally, Woodward found that organizational success was related to the extent to which organizations followed the typical pattern. For example, successful continuous-process organizations tended to be more like System 4 organizations, whereas less-successful firms with the same technology were less like System 4 organizations.

Thus technology clearly appears to play an important role in determining organization design. As future technologies become more diverse and complex, managers will have to be even more aware of the impact of technology on the design of organizations. For example, the increased use of robotics may necessitate alterations in organization design to better accommodate different assembly methods. Likewise, increased use of new forms of information technology will almost certainly cause organizations to redefine the nature of work and the reporting relationships among individuals.[11] Indeed, "Management InfoTech" discusses the so-called wired organization in this context.

MANAGEMENT INFOTECH

The Wired Organization

Some are calling it the most profound advancement in organization design since the evolution of the modern corporation. The so-called wired organization is promising to reshape how people work and how they relate to one another. This revolution in organization design is fueled, of course, by advances in information technology such as the Internet, intranets, e-mail, and the myriad other forms of communication technology that are so popular today.

With sophisticated communication networks, everyone in an organization can be plugged into data sources and have the means to access that data, interpret it, and send it on to others. Modern communication networks also alter other linkages throughout the organization. Now people can always reach their boss, for example, and individuals at different locations (or even in different countries) can work on the same group project from their own personal computer.

Bosses also change how they manage, usually preferring to be informal, casual, and relaxed. Corporate boundaries become fuzzy, and the traditional chain of command becomes truly obsolete. So how do organizations create this new type of design? They probably don't create it in a planned and orderly fashion. Instead, it is more likely to evolve as the people of the organization itself create the design that works best for them.

> *"When work is carried out through networks, an organization's structure changes whether you want it to or not. I can't find a single case where it doesn't happen."*
>
> *Susan Falzon, partner at a Cambridge research and consulting company**

References: *Thomas A. Stewart, "Managing in a Wired Company," Fortune, July 11, 1994, pp. 44–56 (*quote on p. 56); and "When Software Is More Than Just Software," Fortune, December 8, 1997, pp. 222–226.*

■ Environment

In addition to the various relationships described in Chapter 3, environmental elements and organization design are specifically linked in a number of ways. The first widely recognized analysis of environment-organization design linkages was provided by Tom Burns and G. M. Stalker.[12] Like Woodward, Burns and Stalker worked in England. Their first step was identifying two extreme forms of organizational environment: stable (one that remains relatively constant over time) and unstable (subject to uncertainty and rapid change). Next they studied the designs of organizations in each type of environment. Not surprisingly, they found that organizations in stable environments tended to have a different kind of design from organizations in unstable environments. The two kinds of design that emerged were called mechanistic and organic organization.

A **mechanistic organization**, quite similar to the bureaucratic or System 1 model, was most frequently found in stable environments. Free from uncertainty, organizations structured their activities in rather predictable ways by means of rules, specialized jobs, and centralized authority. Mechanistic orga-

mechanistic organization Similar to the bureaucratic or System 1 model, most frequently found in stable environments

organic organization Very flexible and informal model of organization design, most often found in unstable and unpredictable environments

nizations are also quite similar in nature to bureaucracies. Although no environment is completely stable, Kmart and Wendy's use mechanistic designs. Each Kmart store, for example, has prescribed methods for store design and merchandise-ordering processes. No deviations are allowed from these methods. An **organic organization**, on the other hand, was most often found in unstable and unpredictable environments, in which constant change and uncertainty usually dictate a much higher level of fluidity and flexibility. Motorola (facing rapid technological change) and The Limited (facing constant change in consumer tastes) use organic designs. A manager at Motorola, for example, has considerable discretion over how work is performed and how problems can be solved.

These ideas were extended in the United States by Paul R. Lawrence and Jay W. Lorsch.[13] They agreed with Burns and Stalker that environmental factors influence organization design but believed that this influence varies between different units of the same organization. In fact, they predicted that each organizational unit has its own unique environment and responds by developing unique attributes. Lawrence and Lorsch suggested that organizations could be characterized along two primary dimensions.

differentiation Extent to which the organization is broken down into subunits

integration Degree to which the various subunits must work together in a coordinated fashion

One of these dimensions, **differentiation**, is the extent to which the organization is broken down into subunits. A firm with many subunits is highly differentiated; one with few subunits has a low level of differentiation. The second dimension, **integration**, is the degree to which the various subunits must work together in a coordinated fashion. For example, if each unit competes in a different market and has its own production facilities, they may need little integration. Lawrence and Lorsch reasoned that the degree of differentiation and integration needed by an organization depends on the stability of the environments that its subunits face.[14]

■ Organizational Size

organizational size Total number of full-time or full-time–equivalent employees

The size of an organization is yet another factor that affects its design.[15] Although several definitions of size exist, we define **organizational size** as the total number of full-time or full-time–equivalent employees. A team of researchers at the University of Aston in Birmingham, England, believed that Woodward had failed to find a size-structure relationship (which was her original expectation) because almost all the organizations she studied were relatively small (three-fourths had fewer than five hundred employees).[16] Thus the researchers decided to undertake a study of a wider array of organizations to determine how size and technology both individually and jointly affect an organization's design.

Their primary finding was that technology did in fact influence structural variables in small firms, probably because all the firms' activities tended to be centered around the core technology. In large firms, however, the strong technology-design link broke down, most likely because technology is not as central to on-going activities in large organizations. The Aston studies yielded a number of basic generalizations: when compared to small organizations, large organizations tend to be characterized by higher levels of job specialization, more standard operating procedures, more rules, more regulations, and a greater degree of decentralization.

■ Organizational Life Cycle

Of course, size is not constant. As we note in Chapter 10, for example, some small businesses are formed but soon disappear. Others remain as small, independently operated enterprises as long as their owner-manager lives. A few, such as Compaq Computer, Dell Computer, Liz Claiborne, and Reebok, skyrocket to become organizational giants. And occasionally large organizations reduce their size through layoffs or divestitures. For example, Navistar is today far smaller than was its previous incarnation as International Harvester Co.

Although no clear pattern explains changes in size, many organizations progress through a four-stage **organizational life cycle**.[17] The first stage is the *birth* of the organization. The second stage, *youth*, is characterized by growth and the expansion of organizational resources. *Midlife* is a period of gradual growth evolving eventually into stability. Finally, *maturity* is a period of stability, perhaps eventually evolving into decline. Montgomery Ward is an example of a mature organization—it is experiencing little or no growth and appears to be falling behind the rest of the retailing industry.

Managers must confront a number of organization design issues as the organization progresses through these stages. In general, as an organization passes from one stage to the next, it becomes bigger, more mechanistic, and more decentralized. It also becomes more specialized, devotes more attention to planning, and takes on an increasingly large staff component. Finally, demands for coordination increase, formalization increases, organizational units become geographically more dispersed, and control systems become more extensive. Thus an organization's size and design are clearly linked, and this link is dynamic because of the organizational life cycle.[18]

organizational life cycle Progression through which organizations evolve as they grow and mature

MANAGEMENT IMPLICATIONS Managers should remember that organization design is neither static nor universal. Therefore, they must also understand how situational factors such as environment, technology, size, and life cycle should be considered when designing an organization. ■

Strategy and Organization Design

Another important determinant of an organization's design is the strategy adopted by its top managers.[19] In general, both corporate and business strategies affect organization design. Basic organizational functions such as finance and marketing can also affect organization design in some cases.

Many successful firms ensure that their strategy and organization design are complementary. Consider Great Plains Software and its CEO, Doug Burgum. Like his competitors, Burgum's operation has a software support center. But Great Plains took a novel twist by linking price and service. Customers who pay a premium for their service contracts get rapid call-backs (less than 30 minutes) and usually work with the same support personnel all the time. Customers who pay the standard rate get call-backs in about an hour, and again speak to the same person. Customers who pay the economy rate get call-backs within two hours, and usually speak to a different person each time.

Corporate-Level Strategy

As we noted in Chapter 8, an organization can adopt various corporate-level strategies. Its choice will partially determine what type of design will be most effective. For example, a firm that pursues a single-product strategy likely relies on functional departmentalization and can use a mechanistic design. If either unrelated or related diversification is used to spur growth, managers need to decide how to arrange the various units within the organizational umbrella. For example, if the firm is using related diversification, it needs to maintain a high level of coordination among the various units to capitalize on the presumed synergistic opportunities inherent in this strategy. On the other hand, firms using unrelated diversification are more likely to rely on a strong hierarchical reporting system so that corporate managers can better monitor the performance of individual units within the firm.

An organization that adopts the portfolio approach to implement its corporate-level strategies must also ensure that its design fits its strategy. For example, each strategic business unit may remain a relatively autonomous unit within the organization. But managers at the corporate level need to decide how much decision-making latitude to give the heads of each unit (a question of decentralization), how many corporate-level executives are needed to oversee the operations of various units (a question of span of management), and how much information is shared among the units (a question of coordination).[20]

Business-Level Strategy

Business-level strategies affect the design of individual businesses within the organization as well as the overall organization itself. An organization pursuing a defender strategy, for example, is likely to be somewhat tall and centralized, have narrow spans of management, and perhaps take a functional approach to departmentalization. Thus it may generally follow the bureaucratic approach to organization design.

In contrast, a prospecting type of organization is more likely to be flatter and decentralized. With wider spans of management, it tries to be very flexible and adaptable in its approach to doing business. A business that uses an analyzer strategy is likely to have an organization design somewhere in between these two extremes (perhaps being a System 2 or 3 organization). Given that a reactor is essentially a strategic failure, its presumed strategy is probably not logically connected to its design.

Generic competitive strategies can also affect organization design. A firm using a differentiation strategy, for example, may structure departments around whatever it is using as a basis for differentiating its products (marketing, perhaps, in the case of image or manufacturing in the case of quality). A cost leadership strategy necessitates a strong commitment to efficiency and control. Thus such a firm is more centralized as it attempts to control costs. And a firm using a focus strategy may design itself around the direction of its focus (for example, location departmentalization if its focus is geographic region; customer departmentalization if its focus is customer groups).

■ Organizational Functions

The relationship between an organization's functional strategies and its design is less obvious and may be subsumed under corporate- or business-level concerns. A firm whose marketing strategy calls for aggressive marketing and promotion may need separate departments for advertising, direct sales, and promotion. If its financial strategy calls for low debt, it may need only a small finance department. If production strategy calls for manufacturing in diverse locations, organization design arrangements need to account for this geographic dispersion. Human resource strategy may call for greater or lesser degrees of decentralization as a way to develop skills of new managers at lower levels in the organization. And research and development (R&D) strategy may dictate various designs for managing the R&D function itself. A heavy commitment to R&D, for example, may require a separate unit with a vice president in charge. A lesser commitment to R&D may be achieved with a director and a small staff.

MANAGEMENT IMPLICATIONS
Strategy is also an important factor in determining the best design for a particular organization. Thus, managers should clearly understand both their corporate, business, and functional strategies and how those strategies impinge on the organization design that is best for the situation. ▬

Basic Forms of Organization Design

Because technology, environment, size, life cycle, and strategy can all influence organization design, it should come as no surprise that organizations adopt many different kinds of designs. Most designs, however, fall into one of four basic categories. Others are hybrids based on two or more of the basic forms.

■ Functional (U-Form) Design

The **functional design** is an arrangement based on the functional approach to departmentalization as detailed in Chapter 11. This design has been termed the **U-form** (for unitary) by the noted economist Oliver E. Williamson.[21]

U-form or **functional design**
Based on the functional approach to departmentalization

Under the U-form arrangement, the members and units in the organization are grouped into functional departments such as marketing and production.

To operate efficiently in this design, an organization must maintain considerable coordination across departments. This integration and coordination are most commonly the responsibility of the CEO and members of senior management. Figure 12.1 shows the U-form design as applied to the corporate level of a small manufacturing company. In a U-form organization, none of the functional areas can survive without the others. Marketing, for example, needs products from operations to sell and funds from finance to pay for advertising. The WD-40 Company, which makes a popular lubricating oil, and the McIlhenny Company, which makes Tabasco sauce, are examples of firms that use the U-form design.

In general, this approach shares the basic advantages and disadvantages of functional departmentalization. Thus the U-form design allows the organization to staff all important positions with functional experts and facilitates coordination and integration. On the other hand, this approach promotes a functional, rather than an organizational, focus and tends to promote centralization. And as we noted in Chapter 11, functionally based designs are most commonly used in small organizations because an individual CEO can easily oversee and coordinate the entire organization. As an organization grows, the CEO finds that staying on top of all functional areas is increasingly difficult.

■ Conglomerate (H-Form) Design

Another common form of organization design is the conglomerate, or **H-form**, approach.[22] An organization made up of a set of unrelated businesses

FIGURE 12.1
Functional U-Form Design for a Small Manufacturing Company

The U-form design is based on functional departmentalization. This small manufacturing firm uses managers at the vice presidential level to coordinate activities within each functional area of the organization. Note that each functional area is dependent on the others.

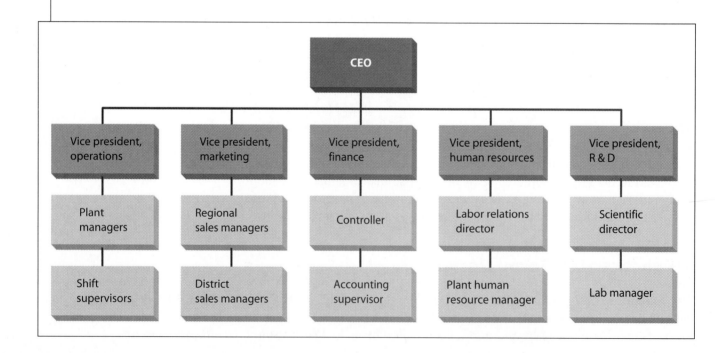

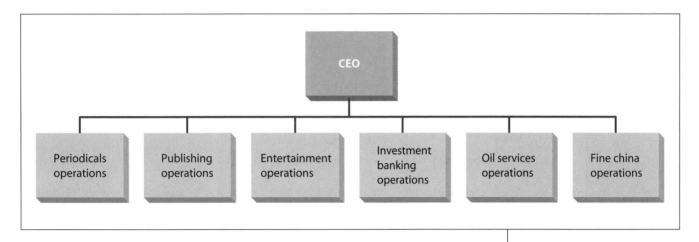

usually uses the **conglomerate** design. Thus the H-form design is essentially a holding company that results from unrelated diversification. (The *H* in this term stands for "holding.")

This approach is based loosely on the product form of departmentalization (see Chapter 11). A general manager operates each business or set of businesses and is responsible for its profits or losses, and each general manager functions independently of the others. Pearson PLC, a British firm, uses the H-form design. As illustrated in Figure 12.2, Pearson consists of six business groups. Although its periodicals and publishing operations are related to one another, all of its other businesses are clearly unrelated. Other firms that use the H-form design include General Electric (aircraft engines, appliances, broadcasting, financial services, lighting products, plastics, and other unrelated businesses) and Tenneco (pipelines, auto parts, shipbuilding, financial services, and other unrelated businesses).

In an H-form organization, a corporate staff usually evaluates the performance of each business, allocates corporate resources across companies, and shapes decisions about buying and selling businesses. The basic shortcoming of the H-form design is the complexity associated with holding diverse and unrelated businesses. Managers usually find comparing and integrating activities across a large number of diverse operations difficult. Michael Porter's research suggests that many organizations following this approach achieve only average-to-weak financial performance.[23] Thus, although some U.S. firms are still using the H-form design, many have abandoned it for other approaches.

FIGURE 12.2
Conglomerate (H-Form) Design at Pearson PLC

Pearson PLC, a British firm, uses the conglomerate form of organization design. This design, which results from a strategy of unrelated diversification, is a complex one to manage. Managers find that comparing and integrating activities among the dissimilar operations are difficult. Companies may abandon this design for another approach, such as the M-form design.

H-form or conglomerate design
Used by an organization made up of a set of unrelated businesses

■ Divisional (M-Form) Design

In the divisional design, which is becoming increasingly popular, a product form of organization is also used; in contrast to the H-form, however, the divisions are related. Thus the **divisional design**, or **M-form** (for multidivisional), is based on multiple businesses in related areas operating within a larger organizational framework. This design results from a strategy of related diversification.

M-Form or divisional design Based on multiple businesses in related areas operating within a larger organizational framework

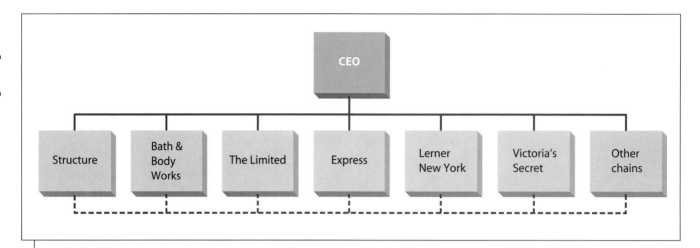

CEO

| Structure | Bath & Body Works | The Limited | Express | Lerner New York | Victoria's Secret | Other chains |

FIGURE 12.3
Multidivisional (M-Form) Design at The Limited, Inc.

The Limited, Inc., uses the multidivisional approach to organization design. Although each unit operates with relative autonomy, all units function in the same general market. This design resulted from a strategy of related diversification. Other firms that use M-form designs include PepsiCo and Woolworth Corporation.

Some activities are extremely decentralized down to the divisional level; others are centralized at the corporate level.[24] For example, as shown in Figure 12.3, The Limited, Inc., uses this approach. A general manager heads each Limited division, and each division operates with reasonable autonomy; however, the divisions also coordinate their activities as is appropriate. Other firms that use this approach are The Walt Disney Company (theme parks, movies, and merchandising units, all interrelated) and Hewlett-Packard (computers, printers, scanners, electronic medical equipment, and other electronic instrumentation).

The opportunities for coordination and shared resources represent one of the biggest advantages of the M-form design. The Limited's marketing research and purchasing departments are centralized. Thus a buyer can inspect a manufacturer's entire product line, buy some designs for The Limited chain, others for Express, and still others for Lerner New York. The M-form design's basic objective is to optimize internal competition and cooperation. Healthy competition among divisions for resources can enhance effectiveness, but cooperation should also be promoted. Research suggests that the M-form organization that can achieve and maintain this balance will outperform large U-form and all H-form organizations.[25]

■ Matrix Design

matrix design Based on two overlapping bases of departmentalization

The **matrix design**, another common approach to organization design, is based on two overlapping bases of departmentalization.[26] The foundation of a matrix is a set of functional departments. A set of product groups, or temporary departments, is then superimposed across the functional departments. Employees in a matrix are simultaneously members of a functional department (such as engineering) and of a project team.

Figure 12.4 shows a basic matrix design. Vice presidents of engineering, production, finance, and marketing head the functional units at the top of the organization. Each manager has several subordinates. Along the side of the organization are a number of positions called *project manager*. Each project manager heads a project group composed of representatives or workers from the functional departments. Note from the figure that a matrix reflects a *multiple-command structure*—any given individual reports to both a functional superior and one or more project managers.

The project groups, or teams, are assigned to designated projects or programs. For example, if the company is developing a new product, representatives from each functional area work as a team on the new product. These team members also retain membership in their original functional group. At any given time a person may be a member of several teams as well as a member of a functional group. Ford used this approach in creating its popular Taurus automobile. It formed a group—called "Team Taurus"—made up of designers, engineers, production specialists, marketing specialists, and other experts from different areas of the company. Team Taurus enabled Ford to get a very successful product to market at least a year earlier than would have been possible using the auto maker's traditional approaches. More recently, Ford used the same approach to create the newest version of the Mustang.

Many organizations have used the matrix design. Notable among them are American Cyanamid, Monsanto Company, NCR, The Chase Manhattan Bank, Prudential, General Motors, and several state and federal government agencies. Some organizations, however, such as Citibank and the Dutch firm

FIGURE 12.4
A Matrix Organization

A matrix organization design is created by superimposing a product form of departmentalization onto an existing functional organization. Project managers coordinate teams of employees drawn from different functional departments. Thus a matrix relies on a multiple-command structure.

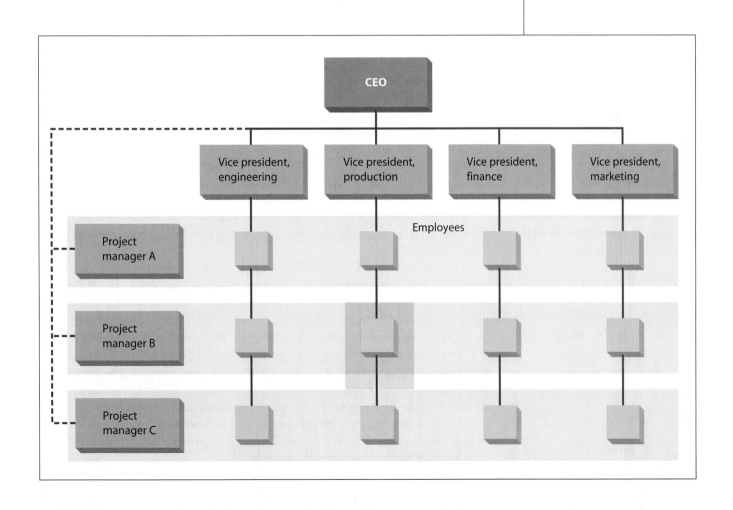

Philips, adopted and then dropped the matrix design. Thus managers should recognize that a matrix design is not always appropriate.

The matrix form of organization design is most often used in one of three situations.[27] First, a matrix may work when there is strong pressure from the environment. For example, intense external competition may dictate the sort of strong marketing thrust that is best spearheaded by a functional department, but the diversity of a company's products may argue for product departments. Second, a matrix may be appropriate when large amounts of information need to be processed. For example, creating lateral relationships by means of a matrix is one effective way to increase the organization's capacity to process information. Third, the matrix design may work when there is pressure for shared resources. For example, a company with ten product departments may have resources for only three marketing specialists. A matrix design would allow all the departments to share the company's scarce marketing resource.

Responsibility and accountability are important considerations in organizations. A potential shortcoming in the matrix form of organization design is that responsibilities can become blurred and accountability can be difficult to trace. In this cartoon, Dagwood's boss, Mr. Dithers, is attempting to shift responsibility and accountability in order to protect himself in the event that things go wrong! While few managers are likely to be this candid about their motives, a few might nevertheless be tempted to use this tactic as a way of deflecting fault or blame to their subordinates.

Researchers have observed six primary advantages of the matrix design. First, it enhances flexibility because teams can be created, redefined, and dissolved as needed. Second, because they assume a major role in decision making, team members are likely to be highly motivated and committed to the organization. Third, employees in a matrix organization have considerable opportunity to learn new skills. The fourth advantage of a matrix design is that it provides an efficient way for the organization to take full advantage of its human resources. Fifth, team members retain membership in their functional unit so that they can serve as a bridge between the functional unit and the team, enhancing cooperation. Sixth, the matrix design gives top management a useful vehicle for decentralization. After the day-to-day operations are delegated, top management can devote more attention to areas such as long-range planning.

On the other hand, the matrix design has some major disadvantages. Employees may be uncertain about reporting relationships, especially if they are simultaneously assigned to a functional manager and to several project managers. "Today's Management Issues" also notes how individuals must sometime struggle with personal versus team loyalties in situations like a matrix design. To complicate matters, some managers see the matrix as a form of anarchy in which they have unlimited freedom. Another set of problems is associated with the dynamics of group behavior. Groups take longer than individuals to make decisions, may be dominated by one individual, and may compromise too much. They may also get bogged down in discussion and not focus on their primary objectives. Finally, a matrix organization may have to devote more time to coordinating task-related activities.[28]

The Individual or the Team?

Some U.S. managers today are facing a real dilemma. The cultural norms that have guided them during much of their careers have stressed individual achievement and accomplishment. People are supposed to work hard toward their own goals—both personal and professional—and organizations are supposed to recognize and reward the fruits of their labors. And indeed, most companies today still rely heavily on individually based systems for evaluating performance and providing rewards. In addition, many organizations are also stressing to their employees the importance of personal career management.

But this approach to doing business often runs counter to teamwork. Within the context of a team, individuals are supposed to subordinate their own work goals, for example, and do what's best for the team—regardless of how it affects them personally. Thus individual performance may be optimized to help the team, and an individual may have little to personally show for his or her special contributions. In addition, organizations have trouble assessing team performance and providing team-based rewards.

"Talk about individual responsibility— it's absolutely important. But you're part of a team—that's absolutely important. But has anybody married that?"

David Witte, CEO of Ward Howell International, an executive search firm*

So managers may have to make tough decisions. Do I do what's best for me, in terms of personal rewards, recognition, and career development opportunities, even if it compromises my contributions to my team? Or do I selflessly do what's best for my team, even if it means that my own performance gets understated and my career development opportunities are constrained?

To make the team concept really work, an organization must alter the way it treats people. In particular, the organization that wants to use teams effectively has to find ways to allow individual team members to meet their own goals, continue to learn new skills, and to maintain and improve their standing in the labor market.

References: *Thomas A. Stewart, "The Great Conundrum—You vs. the Team," Fortune, November 25, 1996, pp. 165–166 (*quote on p. 165); and Mary Cianni and Donna Wnuck, "Individual Growth and Team Enhancement: Moving Toward a New Model of Career Development,"* Academy of Management Executive, *February 1997, pp. 105–115.*

■ Hybrid Designs

Some organizations use a design that represents a hybrid of two or more of the common forms of organization design. For example, an organization may have five related divisions and one unrelated division, making its design a cross between an M-form and an H-form. Indeed, few companies use a design in its pure form; most firms, in fact, have one basic organization design as a foundation but maintain sufficient flexibility so that they can make temporary or permanent modifications for strategic purposes. Ford, for example, used the matrix approach to design the Taurus and the Mustang, but the company is basically a U-form organization showing signs of moving to an M-form design. As we noted earlier, any combination of factors may dictate the appropriate form of design for any particular company.

Managers need to understand the various basic forms of organization design, as well as the strengths and weaknesses of each form. In addition key decision makers must know the best circumstances for using each approach. Further, they should not follow any given approach too rigidly. Instead, consistent with the hybrid model, managers should pick and choose the most appropriate features from each model of organization design. ▬

Emerging Issues in Organization Design

Finally, in today's complex and ever-changing environment, managers must continue to learn about and experiment with new forms of organization design. Many organizations are creating designs for themselves that maximize their ability to adapt to changing circumstances and to a changing environment. They try to accomplish this goal by not becoming too compartmentalized or too rigid. As we noted earlier, bureaucratic organizations are slow, inflexible, and hard to change. To avoid these problems, then, organizations can try to be as different from bureaucracies as possible—operating with relatively few rules, general job descriptions, and so forth. This final section highlights some of the more important emerging issues.[29]

■ The Team Organization

team organization An approach to organization design that relies almost exclusively on project-type teams, with little or no underlying functional hierarchy

Some organizations today are using the **team organization**, an approach to organization design that relies almost exclusively on project-type teams, with little or no underlying functional hierarchy. Within such an organization people float from project to project, according to their skills and the demands of those projects. At Cypress Semiconductor, T. J. Rodgers refuses to allow the organization to grow so large that it can't function this way. Whenever a unit or group starts getting too large, he simply splits it into smaller units. Consequently, all units within the organization are small. This design allows them to change direction, explore new ideas, and try new methods without dealing with a rigid bureaucratic organizational context. Although few organizations have actually reached this level of adaptability, Hewlett-Packard and Xerox are among those moving toward it.[30]

■ The Virtual Organization

virtual organization An approach to organization design that has little or no formal structure

Closely related to the team organization is the virtual organization. A **virtual organization** has little or no formal structure. Such an organization typically has only a handful of permanent employees and a very small staff and administrative headquarters facility. As the needs of the organization change, its managers bring in temporary workers, lease facilities, and outsource basic support services to meet the demands. As the situation changes, the temporary work-force also changes, with some people leaving the organization and others entering. Facilities and the services subcontracted to others change as well. Thus, the organization exists only in response to its needs. For example, Global Research Consortium (GRC) is a virtual organization. GRC offers research and consulting services to firms doing business in Asia. As clients request various services GRC's staff of three permanent employees subcontract the work to an appropriate set of several dozen independent consultants and/or researchers with whom it has relationships. At any given time, therefore, GRC may have several projects underway and twenty or thirty people working on projects. As the projects change, so does the composition of the organization.

■ The Learning Organization

Another recent approach to organization design is the so-called learning organization. Organizations that adopt this approach work to integrate their own improvement with ongoing employee learning and development. Specifically, a **learning organization** is one that works to facilitate the lifelong learning and personal development of all of its employees while continually transforming itself to respond to changing demands and needs.[31]

learning organization An approach to organization design that works to facilitate the lifelong learning and personal development of all of its employees while continually transforming itself to respond to changing demands and needs

Although managers might approach the concept of a learning organization from a variety of perspectives, improved quality, continuous improvement, and performance measurement are frequent goals. The basic premise is that the most consistent and logical strategy for achieving continuous improvement is by constantly upgrading employee talent, skill, and knowledge. For example, if each employee in an organization learns one new thing each day and can translate that knowledge into work-related practice, continuous improvement will logically follow. Indeed, organizations that wholeheartedly embrace this approach believe that only way to achieve continuous improvement is to ensure constant learning by employees.

In recent years many organizations have implemented this approach. For example, the Shell Oil Company recently purchased an executive conference center north of its headquarters in Houston. The center boasts state-of-the-art classrooms and instructional technology, lodging facilities, a restaurant, and recreational amenities such as a golf course, swimming pool, and tennis courts. Line managers at the firm rotate through the Shell Learning Center, as the facility has been renamed, and serve as teaching faculty. Such teaching assignments last from a few days to several months. All Shell employees routinely attend training programs, seminars, and related activities, all the while learning the latest information they need to contribute more effectively to the firm. Recent seminars have covered topics as diverse as time management, implications of the Americans with Disabilities Act, balancing work and family demands, and international trade theory.

■ Issues in International Organization Design

Another emerging issue in organization design is the trend toward the internationalization of business. As we discussed in Chapter 5, most businesses today interact with suppliers, customers, or competitors (or all three) from other countries. The relevant issue for organization design is how to design the firm to deal most effectively with international forces and compete in global markets. For example, consider a moderate-size company that has just decided to "go international." Should it set up an international division, retain its current structure and establish an international operating group, or make its international operations an autonomous subunit?[32]

Figure 12.5 illustrates four of the most common approaches to organization design used for international purposes. Design A is the simplest, relying on a separate international division; Levi Strauss & Co. uses this approach. Design B, used by Ford Motor Co., is an extension of location departmentalization to international settings. An extension of product departmentalization, with each product manager being responsible for all product-related activities regardless of location, is shown in design C. Finally, design D, most typical of larger multinational corporations, is an extension of the multidivisional structure with branches located in various foreign markets; Nestlé and Unilever use design D.

MANAGEMENT IMPLICATIONS

Managers should be aware of emerging issues in organization design and be prepared to capitalize on the newest thinking and breakthroughs to keep pace with their competitors. Of course, managers should also be wary of jumping on any bandwagon too quickly and falling victim to an ineffective fad. ▬

Firms that want to expand internationally often find it necessary to alter their organization design as they grow. For example, Invacare is a growing manufacturer of wheelchairs and other equipment for disabled workers. But because of different working conditions and government regulations in different countries, Invacare has different units for designing and constructing its wheelchairs bound for such countries and Germany, Great Britain, and France.

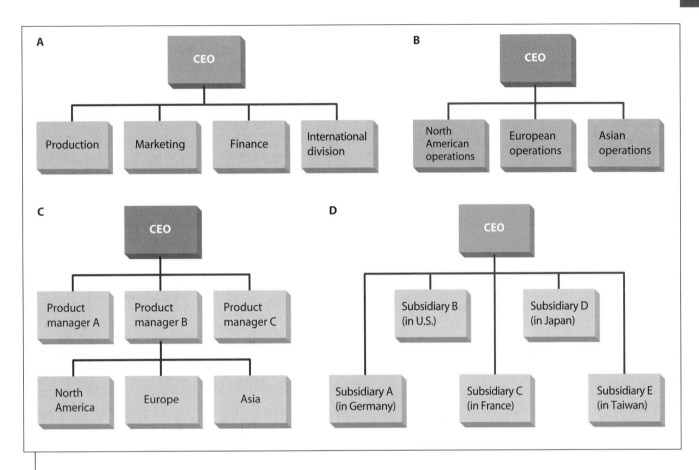

FIGURE 12.5
Common Organization Designs for International Organizations

Companies that compete in international markets must create an organization design that fits their own unique circumstances. These four general designs are representative of what many international organizations use. Each is derived from one of the basic forms of organization design.

Summary of Key Points

Organization design is the overall set of structural elements and the relationships among those elements used to manage the total organization. Two early universal models of organization design were the bureaucratic model and the behavioral model. These models attempted to prescribe how all organizations should be designed.

The situational view of organization design is based on the assumption that the optimal organization design is a function of situational factors. Four important situational factors are technology, environment, size, and organizational life cycle. Each of these factors plays a role in determining how an organization should be designed.

An organization's strategy also helps shape its design. In various ways both corporate- and business-level strategies affect organization design. Basic organizational functions such as marketing and finance also play a role in shaping design.

Many organizations today adopt one of four basic organization designs: functional (U-form), conglomerate (H-form), divisional (M-form), or matrix. Other organizations use a hybrid design derived from two or more of these basic designs.

Four emerging issues in organization design are the team organization, the virtual organization, the learning organization, the design of international businesses.

Discussion Questions

Questions for Review

1. Compare and contrast the bureaucratic and behavioral models of organization design. What are the advantages and disadvantages of each?

2. Describe the basic situational factors that affect an organization's design.

3. How are an organization's strategy and its structure related?

4. Describe the basic forms of organization design. Outline the advantages and disadvantages of each.

Questions for Analysis

5. Can bureaucratic organizations avoid the problems usually associated with bureaucracies? If so, how? If not, why not? Do you think bureaucracies are still necessary? Why or why not? Is retaining the desirable aspects of bureaucracy and eliminating the undesirable ones possible? Why or why not?

6. The matrix organization design is complex and difficult to implement successfully. Why then do so many organizations use it?

7. Identify the problems in organization design that are common and unique to international businesses versus domestic businesses.

Questions for Application

8. What form of organization does your university or college use? What form does your city or town government use? What form do other organizations with which you are familiar use? What similarities and differences do you see? Why?

9. Interview the manager of a local small business and obtain a description of his or her organization design. Can you identify any links between the manager's strategy and the structure of his or her organization? Share your findings with the class.

10. Interview members of a local organization (a fast-food chain, department store, book store, bank, church, school association) to ascertain how adaptable they perceive their organization to be.

Building Effective Communication Skills

EXERCISE OVERVIEW

Communication skills refer to the manager's abilities to effectively convey ideas and information to others and to effectively receive ideas and information from others. This exercise shows you how communication works in various kinds of organization design.

EXERCISE BACKGROUND

Given that organization design defines, at least in part, the interrelationships among jobs and positions within the organization, the organization design and communication patterns should be interrelated. On a sheet of paper, sketch basic organization designs based on the bureaucratic, U-form, M-form, H-form, and matrix designs. Each design should be several levels high and several positions wide.

EXERCISE TASK

With the preceding background information as context, do the following:

1. Identify a single position toward the middle of each design you have drawn and assume that you are holding that position in the organization.

2. Think of a circumstance in which you might need to communicate with four other individuals in the organization—all from different areas and levels.

3. Describe the processes you might need to follow for each communication. That is, consider issues such as chain of command, reporting relationships, and so forth.

4. Decide which forms of organization design are most conducive to communication and which are least conducive.

5. Does the content of the message matter? In what ways?

Building Effective Conceptual Skills

EXERCISE OVERVIEW

Conceptual skills refer to a manager's ability to think in the abstract. This exercise will encourage you to apply your conceptual skills to the concepts associated with the situational influences on organization design.

EXERCISE BACKGROUND

Several factors affect the appropriate design of an organization. The key factors discussed in this chapter are core technology, the organization's environment, its size, and its life cycle. The text does not provide detail, however, as to how the situational factors working together in various combinations might affect organization design. For example, how might a particular form of technology and certain environmental forces together influence organization design?

The text also notes several basic forms of organization design, such as the functional, conglomerate, divisional, and matrix approaches. Some implications are also drawn as to how situational factors relate to each design.

EXERCISE TASK

With these ideas in mind, do the following:

1. Identify a firm that uses each of the four basic forms of organization design. Assess the technology, environment, size, and life cycle for the four firms.

2. Relate each situational factor to the design used by each firm.

3. Form an opinion as to the actual relation between each factor and the design used by each firm. That is, do you think that each firm's design is directly determined by its environment, or is the relationship you observe coincidental?

4. Can you prioritize the relative importance of the situational factors across the firms? Does the rank-order importance of the factors vary in any systematic way?

Building Effective Decision-Making Skills

EXERCISE OVERVIEW

Decision-making skills refer to the manager's ability to correctly recognize and define problems and opportunities and to then select an appropriate course of action to solve problems and capitalize on opportunities. The purpose of this exercise is to give you insights into how managers must make decisions within the context of creating an organization design.

EXERCISE BACKGROUND

Assume that you have decided to open a casual sportswear business in your local community. Your products will be athletic caps, shirts, shorts, and sweats emblazoned with the logos of your college and local high schools. You are a talented designer and have developed some ideas that will make your products unique and very popular. You also have inherited enough money to get your business up and running and to cover about one year of living expenses (that is, you do not need to pay yourself a salary).

You intend to buy sportswear in various sizes and styles from other suppliers. Your firm will then use silk-screen processes and add the logos and other decorative touches to the products. Local clothing store owners have seen samples of your products and have indicated a keen interest in selling them. You know, however, that you will still need to service accounts and keep your customers happy.

You are now trying to determine how many people you need to get your business going and how to most effectively group them into an organization. You realize that you can start out quite small and then expand as sales warrant. However, you also worry that if you are continually adding people and rearranging your organization that confusion and inefficiency will result.

EXERCISE TASK

Step One: Under each of the following scenarios, decide how to best design your organization. Sketch a basic organization chart to show your thoughts.

Scenario 1—You will sell the products yourself, and you intend to start with a workforce of five people.

Scenario 2—You intend to oversee production yourself, and you intend to start with a workforce of nine people.

Scenario 3—You do not intend to handle any one function yourself, but you will oversee the entire operation; you intend to start with a workforce of fifteen people.

Step Two: Form small groups of four to five people each. Compare your various organization charts, focusing on similarities and differences.

Step Three: Working in the same group, assume that five years have passed and your business has been a big success. You have a large plant for making your products and are shipping them to fifteen states. You employ almost five hundred people. Create an organization design that you think best fits this organization.

FOLLOW-UP QUESTIONS

1. How clear or ambiguous were the decisions about organization design?

2. What are your thoughts about starting out too large so as to maintain stability, as opposed to starting small and then growing?

3. Which basic factors did you consider in choosing a design?

CHAPTER CLOSING CASE

The Big Overhaul at American Express

As most people know, the ubiquitous phrase "Don't Leave Home Without It" refers to the American Express card. But American Express Company is really more than just a charge card business—it is an international financial services powerhouse with several businesses scattered around the world. And like other diversified global companies, American Express has to continually evaluate its operations and change the way it does business in order to remain competitive.

A good case in point is a recent overhaul in the organization design of the firm's American Express Financial Advisors division, headquartered in Minneapolis. AEFA, as the division is known inside the company, is a network of financial planners who sell American Express products such as mutual funds, insurance, and investment certificates to middle-income investors.

Until recently, AEFA was organized in a functional design, just like most of its competitors. Planners were rewarded for bringing in new business (usually through cold calls to prospects and leads generated by mailing lists and referrals). New customers were then passed on to the sales support staff, which was responsible for maintaining client records, answering questions, and handling routine transactions. Clear chains of command and a network of rules and procedures guided most of the firm's activities.

But in the early 1990s, AEFA managers became concerned about the future of their business. Although the group was growing at a rate of more than 20 percent a year and generating huge profits for its corporate parent, key decision makers recognized that cold calling was becoming so widespread that a backlash from customers was emerging. Moreover, Internet-based competitors were beginning to emerge, and AEFA feared that these upstarts would change the rules of the business.

As a result of these concerns and motivated to protect their business position, AEFA executives decided to overhaul their entire business approach. Their starting point was a new organization design intended to promote flexibility and responsiveness. AEFA started by eliminating the venerable position of general sales manager—one key executive ultimately responsible for all business sales and to whom all sales employees were accountable. After reorganization, these responsibilities were spread across seven different remaining positions.

Each of these seven key executives has a vertical operation defined as a geographic region. For example, one manager might be responsible for the southeast part of the United States while another might be responsible for the northwest states. In addition, each key executive has horizontal responsibility for one process that spans the entire company. For example, one of the seven key executives has companywide responsibility for client satisfaction. Another is responsible for companywide account management systems.

One level below the seven key executives, 180 departments have been reconfigured into forty-five process-oriented clusters, each led by a vice president. For example, one cluster is responsible for training and integrating new planners into the company; another is responsible for conducting customer satisfaction surveys and sending the results to managers. The commission system for planners has also been changed: both new business and client satisfaction now affect an individual planner's commission. Thus, planners are motivated not only to generate new business but also to satisfy their existing accounts.

So far, at least, the new system seems to be working quite well. The business is still growing, its costs are down, and most planners believe that they now have a better understanding of how to keep clients happy after they make their first purchase from AEFA. But the company faced a few rough spots during the transition as various individuals had to give up power or control over something they valued. In addition, although the current organization design seems to be working well within existing markets, it provides little incentive or catalyst for international growth.

Case Questions

1. Diagram AEFA's old and new organization designs. Compare and contrast them.
2. What do you think are the advantages and disadvantages of both the old and new organization designs at AEFA?
3. Why does AEFA's new organization design appear to be limiting the firm's international growth? How might this situation be changed?

Case References: "How Rising Star Quit at American Express and Took Staff Along," *Wall Street Journal*, December 12, 1997, pp. A1, A12; *Hoover's Handbook of American Business 1997* (Austin, Texas: Hoover's Business Press, 1996), pp. 132–133; Rahul Jacob, "The Struggle to Create an Organization for the 21st Century," *Fortune*, April 3, 1995, pp. 90–99; and Raymond E. Miles, Charles C. Snow, John A. Mathews, Grant Miles, and Henry J. Coleman Jr., "Organizing in the Knowledge Age: Anticipating the Cellular Form," *Academy of Management Executive*, November 1997, pp. 7–24.

CHAPTER NOTES

1. Ronald Henkoff, "Boeing's Big Problem," *Fortune*, January 12, 1998, pp. 96–103; "Destroying the Old Hierarchies," *Forbes*, June 3, 1996, pp. 62–72; and "Booming Boeing," *Business Week*, September 30, 1996, pp. 118–125.
2. See Richard L. Daft, *Organization Theory & Design*, 6th ed. (St. Paul, Minn.: West, 1998); and Gareth Jones, *Organization Theory*, 2nd ed. (Reading, Mass.: Addison-Wesley, 1998).
3. Max Weber, *Theory of Social and Economic Organizations*, trans. by T. Parsons (New York: Free Press, 1947).
4. Paul Jarley, Jack Fiorito, and John Thomas Delany, "A Structural Contingency Approach to Bureaucracy and Democracy in U.S. National Unions," *Academy of Management Journal*, 1997, Vol. 40, No. 4, pp. 831–861.
5. Rensis Likert, *New Patterns in Management* (New York: McGraw-Hill, 1961); and Rensis Likert, *The Human Organization* (New York: McGraw-Hill, 1967).
6. William F. Dowling, "At General Motors: System 4 Builds Performance and Profits," *Organizational Dynamics*, Winter 1975, pp. 23–28.
7. Daft, *Organization Theory & Design*.
8. For descriptions of situational factors, see Robert K. Kazanjian and Robert Drazin, "Implementing Internal Diversification: Contingency Factors for Organization Design Choices," *Academy of Management Review*, April 1987, pp.

342–354; Allen Bluedorn, "Pilgrim's Progress: Trends and Convergence in Research on Organizational Size and Environments," *Journal of Management*, Summer 1993, pp. 163–191; and Jones, *Organization Theory*.
9. Joan Woodward, *Industrial Organization: Theory and Practice* (London: Oxford University Press, 1965).
10. Joan Woodward, *Management and Technology, Problems of Progress Industry*, No. 3 (London: Her Majesty's Stationery Office, 1958).
11. William Bridges, "The End of the Job," *Fortune*, September 19, 1994, pp. 62–74.
12. Tom Burns and G. M. Stalker, *The Management of Innovation* (London: Tavistock, 1961).
13. Paul R. Lawrence and Jay W. Lorsch, *Organization and Environment* (Homewood, Ill.: Irwin, 1967).
14. For detailed discussions of the environment-organization design relationship, see Masoud Yasai-Ardekani, "Structural Adaptations to Environments," *Academy of Management Review*, January 1986, pp. 9–21; Christine S. Koberg and Geraldo R. Ungson, "The Effects of Environmental Uncertainty and Dependence on Organizational Performance: A Comparative Study," *Journal of Management*, Winter 1987, pp. 725–737; and Barbara W. Keats and Michael A. Hitt, "A Causal Model of Linkages among Environmental Dimensions, Macro Organizational Characteristics, and

Performance," *Academy of Management Journal*, September 1988, pp. 570–598.

15. Edward E. Lawler III, "Rethinking Organization Size," *Organizational Dynamics*, Autumn 1997, pp. 24–33.

16. Derek S. Pugh and David J. Hickson, *Organization Structure in Its Context: The Aston Program I* (Lexington, Mass.: D. C. Heath, 1976).

17. Robert H. Miles and Associates, *The Organizational Life Cycle* (San Francisco: Jossey-Bass, 1980). See also "Is Your Company Too Big?" *Business Week*, March 27, 1989, pp. 84–94.

18. Douglas Baker and John Cullen, "Administrative Reorganization and Configurational Context: The Contingent Effects of Age, Size, and Change in Size," *Academy of Management Journal*, 1993, Vol. 36, No. 6, pp. 1251–1277. See also Kevin Crowston, "A Coordination Theory Approach to Organizational Process Design," *Organization Science*, March–April 1997, pp. 157–168.

19. See Charles W. L. Hill and Gareth Jones, *Strategic Management: An Analytic Approach*, 4th ed. (Boston: Houghton Mifflin Co., 1998).

20. Richard D'Aveni and David Ravenscraft, "Economies of Integration versus Bureaucrat Costs: Does Vertical Integration Improve Performance?" *Academy of Management Journal*, 1994, Vol. 37, No. 5, pp. 1167–1206.

21. Oliver E. Williamson, *Markets and Hierarchies* (New York: Free Press, 1975).

22. Williamson, *Markets and Hierarchies*.

23. Michael E. Porter, "From Competitive Advantage to Corporate Strategy," *Harvard Business Review*, May–June 1987, pp. 43–59.

24. Williamson, *Markets and Hierarchies*.

25. Jay B. Barney and William G. Ouchi, eds., *Organizational Economics* (San Francisco: Jossey-Bass, 1986); and Robert E. Hoskisson, "Multidivisional Structure and Performance:

The Contingency of Diversification Strategy," *Academy of Management Journal*, December 1987, pp. 625–644. See also Bruce Lamont, Robert Williams, and James Hoffman, "Performance during 'M-Form' Reorganization and Recovery Time: The Effects of Prior Strategy and Implementation Speed," *Academy of Management Journal*, 1994, Vol. 37, No. 1, pp. 153–166.

26. Stanley M. Davis and Paul R. Lawrence, *Matrix* (Reading, Mass.: Addison-Wesley, 1977).

27. Davis and Lawrence, *Matrix*.

28. See Lawton Burns and Douglas Wholey, "Adoption and Abandonment of Matrix Management Programs: Effects of Organizational Characteristics and Interorganizational Networks," *Academy of Management Journal*, Vol. 36, No. 1, pp. 106–138.

29. Raymond E. Miles, Charles C. Snow, John A. Mathews, Grant Miles, and Henry J. Coleman Jr., "Organizing in the Knowledge Age: Anticipating the Cellular Form," *Academy of Management Executive*, November 1997, pp. 7–24.

30. "The Horizontal Corporation," *Business Week*, December 20, 1993, pp. 76–81; and Shawn Tully, "The Modular Corporation," *Fortune*, February 8, 1993, pp. 106–114.

31. Peter Senge, *The Fifth Discipline* (New York: The Free Press, 1993). See also Alessandro Lomi, Erik R. Larsen, and Ari Ginsberg, "Adaptive Learning in Organizations: A System Dynamics-Based Exploration," *Journal of Management*, 1997, Vol. 23, No. 4, pp. 561–582.

32. For a recent discussion of these issues, see William G. Egelhoff, "Strategy and Structure in Multinational Corporations: A Revision of the Stopford and Wells Model," *Strategic Management Journal*, Vol. 9, 1988, pp. 1–14. See also Ricky W. Griffin and Michael Pustay, *International Business—A Managerial Perspective*, 2nd ed. (Reading, Mass.: Addision Wesley, 1999).

13

Managing Organization Change and Innovation

OBJECTIVES

After studying this chapter, you should be able to:

- Describe the nature of organization change, including forces for change and planned versus reactive change.
- Discuss the steps in organization change and how to manage resistance to change.
- Identify and describe major areas of organization change.
- Discuss the assumptions, techniques, and effectiveness of organization development.
- Describe the innovation process, various forms of innovation, the failure to innovate, and how organizations can promote innovation.

Daimler-Benz is Germany's largest industrial firm and one of its most important. The firm is best known among consumers for its line of luxury cars sold under the name Mercedes Benz. Indeed, the Mercedes division is the world's oldest auto maker. In addition to its preeminent passenger cars, Mercedes also manufactures commercial vans, trucks, buses, and industrial diesel engines.

A few years ago Daimler-Benz managers, concerned that the firm was perhaps too reliant on its Mercedes division, decided to diversify. Through an aggressive strategy based in part on acquiring new firms and in part on growing other existing Daimler-Benz businesses, the company was quickly transformed into a diversified conglomerate. One division consisted of various aerospace businesses. A second was created for financial services. A third included a variety of industrial and manufacturing units dealing with automation and rail systems. Mercedes-Benz made up the fourth division.

Unfortunately, the diversified Daimler-Benz never lived up to its promise. Despite its major investments and managerial commitments, the firm continued to struggle as it attempted to bring each business up to an acceptable level of profitability. Especially problematic were the aerospace and financial services units that continued to lose money at an alarming pace. Indeed, the losses in these two units were so great in 1995 that the entire corporation lost money for the first time in decades.

That same year, the board promoted Jurgen Schrempp to the position of CEO and gave him a mandate to turn things around—and quickly. One of his first major moves, in turn, also proved to be very controversial and ultimately cost the firm one of its most highly-regarded executives. Up until Daimler's recent problems, the Mercedes unit operated with virtual autonomy. Mercedes-Benz, for example, had its own CEO, Helmut Werner. And indeed, many observers had been surprised that Daimler's board had tapped Schrempp over Werner to take the top spot.

"In such a situation, you either run away

or fix it yourself."

Jurgen Schrempp, CEO of Daimler-Benz, quoted in Fortune, November 10, 1997, p. 146.

Schrempp decided almost immediately that to achieve his mandate, Mercedes would need to be folded into Daimler's corporate structure. His arguments were (1) that the firm's other units needed more access to the managerial, technical, and operational expertise at Mercedes and (2) that costs could be lowered by consolidating administrative expenses. Not surprisingly, Werner opposed this move. Although he had several reasonable arguments for keeping Mercedes independent, it was also clearly the case that Schrempp's proposal would undermine Werner's authority in the company.

Both high-powered executives had their own supporters on Daimler's board of directors, but Schrempp eventually prevailed. Although he tried to talk Werner into staying on as the number-two executive in the company, the defeated executive quickly left the firm. Schrempp, meanwhile, forged ahead at full speed: Mercedes was incorporated into Daimler, and several underperforming businesses were closed or sold. Daimler's pending merger with Chrysler, announced in mid-1998, reflected the firm's new commitment to growth.

Schrempp also supported the building of the first Mercedes factory outside of Germany—in the state of Alabama—and arranged for Daimler-Benz to become the first German firm to be listed on the New York Stock Exchange. Within two years his managerial moves had begun to pay dividends. Profits began to surge once more, and new Mercedes products became the talk of the industry. But to make these dreams a reality, Schrempp had to basically dismantle and then reassemble his firm so that it more closely resembles one of its high-powered roadsters than one of its busses.[1]

Managers at Daimler-Benz have had to grapple with something all managers must eventually confront: the need for change. They first perceived that they needed to make certain changes aimed at fostering diversification. Later, they realized that this strategy was not working and that other changes were necessary to get the firm back on track. Making these changes, however, required the CEO to overcome internal corporate politics. The changes were costly in a variety of ways, but they seem to be paying off now as the firm has regained its financial vitality.

Understanding when and how to implement change is a vital part of management. This chapter describes how organizations manage change. We first examine the nature of organization change and identify the basic issues of managing change. We then identify and describe major areas of change, including reengineering, a major type of change that many firms have recently undertaken. We also examine organization development and conclude by discussing a related area, organizational innovation.

The Nature of Organization Change

organization change Any substantive modification to some part of the organization

Organization change is any substantive modification to some part of the organization.[2] Thus change can involve virtually any aspect of an organization: work schedules, bases for departmentalization, span of management, machinery, organization design, people themselves, and so on. The effects of any change in an organization often extend beyond the actual area where the change is implemented. For example, when Northrup Grumman recently installed a new computerized production system at one of its plants, employees were trained to operate new equipment, the compensation system was adjusted to reflect new skill levels, the span of management of supervisors was altered, and several related jobs were redesigned. Selection criteria for new employees were also changed, and a new quality control system was installed.[3] In addition, multiple organization-change activities can occur simultaneously.[4]

■ Forces for Change

The basic reason that organizations make changes is that something relevant to the organization either has changed or is going to change. The organization consequently has little choice but to change as well. Indeed, a primary reason for the problems that organizations often face is failure to anticipate or respond properly to changing circumstances. Forces for change may be external or internal to the organization.[5]

External Forces   External forces for change derive from the organization's general and task environments. For example, two energy crises, an aggressive Japanese automobile industry, floating currency exchange rates, and floating international interest rates—all manifestations of the international dimension of the general environment—profoundly influenced U.S. auto makers. New rules of production and competition forced them to dramatically alter the way they do business. In the political arena new laws, court decisions, and regulations affect organizations. The technological dimension may yield new production techniques that the organization needs to explore. The economic dimension is affected by inflation, the cost of living, and money supplies. The sociocultural dimension, reflecting societal values, determines what kinds of products or services will be accepted in the market.

Change comes in all forms and fashions, and affects organizations everywhere. For example, these Palestinian Boy Scouts from Hebron are having lunch with Israeli students in Haifa. As the world continues to become a global village, people everywhere will need to learn about new cultures and become more tolerant and open to new ideas. And managers will need to take this same path as they guide change in their own organizations as these social forces move into the workplace.

Because of its proximity to the organization, the task environment is an even more powerful force for change than the general environment is. Competitors influence an organization through their price structures and product lines. When Compaq lowers the prices it charges for computers, Dell and IBM have little choice but to follow suit. Because customers determine what products can be sold at what prices, organizations must be concerned with consumer tastes and preferences. Suppliers affect organizations by raising or lowering prices or changing product lines. Regulators can have dramatic effects on an organization. For example, if OSHA rules that a particular production process is dangerous to workers, the regulation can force a firm to close a plant until it meets higher safety standards. Unions can force change when they negotiate for higher wages or strike.[6]

Internal Forces A variety of forces inside the organization may cause change. If top management revises the organization's strategy, organization change is likely to result. A decision by an electronics company to enter the home computer market or a decision to increase a ten-year product sales goal by 3 percent would occasion many organization changes. Other internal forces for change may be reflections of external forces. As sociocultural values shift, for example, workers' attitudes toward their jobs may also shift—and workers may demand a change in working hours or working conditions. In such a case, even though the force is rooted in the external environment, the organization must respond directly to the internal pressure it generates.[7]

■ Planned Versus Reactive Change

Some change is planned well in advance; other change comes about as a reaction to unexpected events. **Planned change** is designed and implemented in an orderly and timely fashion in anticipation of future events. On the other

planned change Change that is designed and implemented in an orderly and timely fashion in anticipation of future events

reactive change A piecemeal response to circumstances as they develop

hand, **reactive change** is a piecemeal response to events as they occur. Because reactive change may be hurried, the potential for poorly conceived and executed change is increased. Planned change is almost always preferable to reactive change.[8]

Georgia-Pacific, a large forest-products business, is an excellent example of a firm that recently went through a planned and well-managed change process. When the current CEO, A. D. Correll, took over the firm's leadership in 1991, he quickly became alarmed at the firm's high accident rate—nine serious injuries per one hundred employees each year and twenty-six deaths during the most recent five-year period. Even though the forest-products business is inherently dangerous, Correll believed that the accident rate was far too high and began a major change effort to improve the situation. He and other top managers developed a multistage change program in-

Change is a common event in most organizations today. And while much of this change is necessary and beneficial, managers sometimes engage in change activities that are either unnecessary or poorly conceived. When this happens, it increases the chances that employees will resist the change—they will experience uncertainty, threatened self-interests, different perceptions, and/or feelings of loss. Indeed, as shown in this cartoon, change can be so poorly managed that employees sense it before it even occurs and develop resistance without even knowing the details.

tended to educate workers about safety, improve safety equipment in the plant, and eliminate a long-standing part of the firm's culture that made injuries almost a badge of courage. Just seven years later Georgia-Pacific has the best safety record in the industry, with relatively few injuries.[9]

A few years ago, on the other hand, Caterpillar was caught flat-footed by a worldwide recession in the construction industry, suffered enormous losses, and took several years to recover. Had managers at Caterpillar anticipated the need for change earlier, they might have been able to respond more quickly. More recently, Kodak announced plans to cut several thousand jobs, a reaction to sluggish sales and profits.[10] Again, better anticipation might have forestalled these job cuts. The importance of approaching change from a planned perspective is reinforced by the frequency of organization change. Most companies or divisions of large companies implement some form of moderate change at least every year and one or more major changes every four to five years.[11] Managers who sit back and respond only when they have to are likely to spend a lot of time hastily changing and rechanging things. A more effective approach is to anticipate forces urging change and plan ahead to deal with them.

MANAGEMENT IMPLICATIONS Managers should understand the meaning and pervasiveness of change, as well as its potential impact throughout their organization. They should also realize that change seldom stops and that multiple simultaneous changes may be necessary. Managers should also recognize that both external and internal forces can spark the need for change. Moreover, managers should value the importance of planned versus reactive change. Their goal should be to plan for change whenever possible. ▬

Managing Change in Organizations

Organization change is a complex phenomenon. A manager cannot simply wave a wand and implement a planned change like magic. Instead, any change must be systematic and logical if it is to have a realistic opportunity to succeed. Consequently, the manager needs to understand the steps of effective change and how to counter employee resistance to change.

■ Steps in the Change Process

Many researchers have developed models or frameworks outlining steps for change.[12] The Lewin model was one of the first, although a more comprehensive approach is usually more useful.

The Lewin Model Kurt Lewin, a noted organizational theorist, suggested that every change requires three steps.[13] The first step is *unfreezing*—individuals who will be affected by the impending change must be shown why the change is necessary. Next the *change itself* is implemented. Finally, *refreezing* involves reinforcing and supporting the change so that it becomes a part of the system. For example, one of the changes Caterpillar faced in response to the recession involved a massive workforce reduction. The first step (unfreezing) was convincing the United Auto Workers to support the reduction because of its importance to long-term effectiveness. After this step was accomplished, thirty thousand jobs were eliminated (implementation). Then Caterpillar worked to improve its damaged relationship with its workers (refreezing) by guaranteeing future pay hikes and promising no more cutbacks. As interesting as Lewin's model is, it unfortunately lacks operational specificity. Thus organizations often need a more comprehensive perspective.

A Comprehensive Approach to Change The comprehensive approach to change takes a systems view and delineates a series of specific steps that often lead to successful change. This expanded model is illustrated in

Managing change is an important function for many managers. One important change, of course, is the increasing diversity that is becoming more apparent in companies today. Women who have made it to the top, however, face a continuing struggle. On the one hand, their jobs are demanding and take much of their time and energy. On the other hand, however, many feel an obligation to mentor their junior colleagues. Finding the right balance is a difficult and elusive undertaking, and both sets of pressures reflect change that warrants consideration and attention.

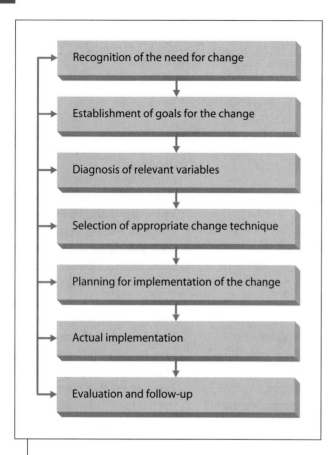

FIGURE 13.1

Steps in the Change Process

Managers must understand how and why to implement change. A manager who, when implementing change, follows a logical and orderly sequence such as the one shown here is more likely to succeed than a manager whose change process is haphazard and poorly conceived.

Figure 13.1. The first step is recognizing the need for change. Reactive change might be triggered by employee complaints, declines in productivity or turnover, court injunctions, sales slumps, or labor strikes. Recognition may simply be managers' awareness that change in a certain area is inevitable. For example, managers may be aware of the general frequency of organizational change undertaken by most organizations and recognize that their organization should probably follow the same pattern. The immediate stimulus might be the result of a forecast indicating new market potential, the accumulation of cash surplus for possible investment, or an opportunity to achieve and capitalize on a major technological breakthrough. Managers might also initiate change today because indicators suggest that it will be necessary in the near future.

Managers must next set goals for the change. To increase market share, to enter new markets, to restore employee morale, to settle a strike, and to identify investment opportunities are all goals for change. Third, managers must diagnose what brought on the need for change. Turnover, for example, might be caused by low pay, poor working conditions, poor supervisors, or employee dissatisfaction. Thus, although turnover may be the immediate stimulus for change, managers must understand its causes to make the right changes.

The next step is to select a change technique that will accomplish the intended goals. If low pay is causing high turnover, the organization might need a new reward system. If the cause is poor supervision, interpersonal skills training may be called for. (Various change techniques are summarized later in this chapter.) After they choose the appropriate technique, managers must plan its implementation. Issues to consider include the costs of the change, its effects on other areas of the organization, and the degree of employee participation appropriate for the situation. If the change is implemented as planned, the results should then be evaluated. If the change was intended to reduce turnover, managers must check turnover after the change has been in effect for a while. If turnover is still too high, other changes may be necessary.[14]

■ Understanding Resistance to Change

Another element in the effective management of change is understanding the resistance that often greets change.[15] Managers need to know why people resist change and what can be done about their resistance. When Westinghouse replaced all its typewriters with personal computers several years ago, most people responded favorably. One manager, however, resisted the change to the point where he began leaving work every day at noon. It was some time before he began staying in the office all day again. Resistance to change has many causes. "Management InfoTech" explores this phenomenon in more detail.

MANAGEMENT INFOTECH

Teaching Old Dogs New Tricks Isn't Easy!

The personal computer has substantially changed the way that most managers work. But a few holdouts have not yet taken the electronic plunge. A good example is Jean-Pierre Rosso, CEO of Case Corp., the big farm-equipment manufacturer. Even though Case now has a requirement that all new white-collar employees must be computer literate, Rosso himself doesn't know how to use one. He relies on his secretary to read and respond to his e-mail and to search the Internet for information he may need.

But Rosso isn't alone. One study, for example, found that 20 percent of the executives surveyed didn't have a PC on their desks. Among the top managers who make little use of computers are Jack Welch (CEO of General Electric),

> *"I think I can survive the current era [without computer literacy]. But there's no question that I am a dinosaur."*
>
> *Jean-Pierre Rosso, Case Corp. CEO**

Lawrence Bossidy (CEO of Allied Signal), and Rand Araskog (CEO of ITT).

What explains this apparent technophobia? One explanation is that since most older managers never learned to type, they have spent their careers relying on a secretary or assistant to do their clerical work for them. Some top managers argue that they are simply too busy doing other things. And still others admit they are simply afraid to try something as exotic and complicated as a computer. But one CEO did recently admit that his five-year-old daughter was teaching him how to use the Internet.

References: *"Computer Illiterates Still Roam Executive Suites,"* Wall Street Journal, *June 24, 1996, pp. B1, B8 (*quote on p. B1).*

Uncertainty   Perhaps the biggest cause of employee resistance to change is uncertainty. In the face of impending change, employees may become anxious and nervous. They may worry about their ability to meet new job demands, they may think that their job security is threatened, or they may simply dislike ambiguity. RJR Nabisco was the target of an extended and confusing takeover battle a few years ago, and during the entire time employees were nervous about the impending change. The *Wall Street Journal* described them this way: "Many are angry at their leaders and fearful for their jobs. They are swapping rumors and spinning scenarios for the ultimate outcome of the battle for the tobacco and food giant. Headquarters staffers in Atlanta know so little about what's happening in New York that some call their office 'the mushroom complex,' where they are kept in the dark."[16]

Threatened Self-Interests   Many impending changes threaten the self-interests of some managers within the organization. A change might potentially diminish their power or influence within the company, so they fight it. Managers at Sears, Roebuck and Co. recently developed a plan calling for a new type of store. The new stores would be somewhat smaller than typical Sears stores and would not be located in large shopping malls. Instead, they would be located in smaller strip centers. They would carry clothes and other "soft goods," but not hardware, appliances, furniture, or automotive products.

When executives in charge of the excluded product lines heard about the plan, they raised such strong objections that the plan was put on hold.

Different Perceptions   A third reason that people resist change is a difference in perception. A manager may make a decision and recommend a plan for change on the basis of her own assessment of a situation. Others in the organization may resist the change because they perceive the situation differently or do not agree with the manager's assessment.[17] Executives at 7-Eleven are currently battling this problem as they attempt to enact a major organizational change. The corporation wants to make its convenience stores a bit "upscale" by selling fancy fresh foods to go, the newest hard-cover novels, and some gourmet products. But many franchisees are balking because they see this move as taking the firm away from its core blue-collar customers.[18]

Feelings of Loss   Many changes involve altering work arrangements in ways that disrupt existing social networks. Because social relationships are important, most people resist any change that might adversely affect those relationships. Other intangibles threatened by change include power, status, security, familiarity with existing procedures, and self-confidence. As described in the opening incident of this chapter, Daimler-Benz recently lost a key executive because of a power struggle involving a change.

■ Overcoming Resistance to Change

Of course, a manager should not give up in the face of resistance to change. Although there are no sure-fire cures, several techniques at least have the potential to overcome resistance.[19]

Participation   Participation is often the most effective technique for overcoming resistance to change. Employees who participate in planning and implementing a change are better able to understand the reasons for the change. Uncertainty is reduced, and self-interests and social relationships are less threatened.

Employees are more likely to accept the change gracefully when they have an opportunity to express their ideas and assume the perspectives of others. A classic study of participation monitored the introduction of a change in production methods among four groups in a Virginia pajama factory.[20] The two groups that were allowed to fully participate in planning and implementing the change improved their productivity and satisfaction significantly when compared to the two groups that did not participate. In another example, 3M Company recently attributed $10 million in cost savings to employee participation in several organization-change activities.[21]

Education and Communication   Educating employees about the need for and the expected results of an impending change should reduce their resistance to it. Establishing and maintaining open communication during the change process helps to minimize uncertainty. Caterpillar used these methods during many of its cutbacks to reduce resistance. First, it educated UAW representa-

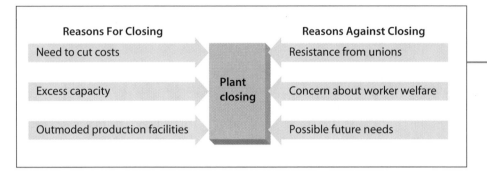

FIGURE 13.2
Force-Field Analysis for Plant Closing at Chrysler

A force-field analysis can help a manager facilitate change. A manager able to identify forces acting both for and against a change can see where to focus efforts to remove barriers to change (such as offering training and relocation to displaced workers). Removing the forces against the change can at least partially overcome resistance.

tives about the need for and potential value of the planned changes. Then management told all employees what was happening, when it would happen, and how it would affect them individually.

Facilitation   Several facilitation procedures can also reduce resistance to change; for example, making only necessary changes, announcing those changes well in advance, and allowing time for people to adjust to new ways of doing business.[22] One manager at a Prudential regional office spent several months systematically planning a change in work procedures and job design. He then became too hurried, coming in over the weekend with a work crew and rearranging the office layout. When employees walked in on Monday morning, they were hostile, anxious, and resentful. What was a promising change became a disaster, and the manager had to scrap the entire plan.

Force-Field Analysis   Although force-field analysis may sound like something out of a Star Trek movie, it can help overcome resistance to change. In almost any change situation, forces are acting for and against the change. To facilitate the change, managers start by listing each set of forces and then trying to tip the balance so that the forces facilitating the change outweigh those hindering the change. It is especially important to try to remove or at least minimize some of the forces acting against the change. Suppose, for example, that Chrysler is considering a plant closing as part of a change. As shown in Figure 13.2, three factors are reinforcing the change: Chrysler needs to cut costs, it has excess capacity, and the plant has outmoded production facilities. At the same time, there is resistance from the UAW, concern for workers being put out of their jobs, and a feeling that the plant might be needed again in the future. Chrysler might start by convincing the UAW that the closing is necessary by presenting profit and loss figures. It could then offer relocation and retraining to displaced workers. And it might shut down the plant and put it in "moth balls" so that it could be renovated later. The three major factors hindering the change are thus eliminated or reduced in importance.

MANAGEMENT IMPLICATIONS   Managers should approach change from a logical and rational perspective and understand how to proceed through a progression of events as they enact change. They should also understand that some people are likely to resist change but that certain techniques at least partially overcome this resistance. ■

Areas of Organization Change

Although change can involve virtually any part of an organization, most change interventions affect organization structure and design, technology and operations, or people. The most common areas of change within each of these broad categories are listed in Table 13.1.

■ Changing Structure and Design

Organization change might be focused on any of the basic components of organization structure or on the organization's overall design. Thus the organization might change the way it designs its jobs or its bases of departmentalization. Likewise, it might change reporting relationships or the distribution of authority. For example, we noted in Chapter 11 the trend toward flatter organizations. Coordination mechanisms and line and staff configurations are also subject to change. On a larger scale, the organization might change its overall design. For example, a growing business could decide to drop its functional design and adopt a divisional design, or it might transform itself into a matrix. Finally, the organization might change any part of its human resource management system, such as its selection criteria, its performance appraisal methods, or its compensation package.[23]

Organization Structure and Design	Technology and Operations	People
Job design	Information technologies	Abilities and skills
Departmentalization	Equipment	Performance
Reporting relationships	Work processes	Perceptions
Authority distribution	Work sequences	Expectations
Coordination mechanisms	Control systems	Attitudes
Line-staff structure		Values
Overall design		
Culture		
Human resource management		

TABLE 13.1
Areas of Organization Change

Organization change can affect any part, area, or component of an organization. Most change, however, fits into one of three general areas: organization structure and design, technology and operations, and people.

■ Changing Technology and Operations

Technology is the conversion process used by an organization to transform inputs into outputs. Because of the rapid rate of all technological innovation, technological changes are becoming increasingly important to many organizations. Table 13.1 lists several areas that are likely to experience technological change. One important area of change revolves around information technology. The adoption and institutionalization of information technology innovations is almost constant in most firms today. Another important form of technological change involves equipment. To keep pace with competitors, firms periodically need to replace existing machinery and equipment with newer models.

A change in work processes or work activities may be necessary if new equipment is introduced or new products are manufactured. In manufacturing industries, the major reason for changing a work process is to accommodate a change in the materials used to produce a finished product. Consider a firm that manufactures battery-operated flashlights. For many years flashlights were made of metal, but now most are made of plastic. A firm might decide to move from metal to plastic flashlights because of consumer preferences, raw materials costs, or other reasons. Whatever the reason, the technology necessary to make flashlights from plastic differs importantly from that used to make flashlights from metal. Work process changes may occur in service organizations as well as in manufacturing firms. As unisex hair salons replace traditional barber shops and beauty parlors, for example, the hybrid organizations have to develop new methods for handling appointments and setting prices.

A change in work sequence may or may not accompany a change in equipment or a change in work processes. Making a change in work sequence means altering the order or sequence of the work stations involved in a particular manufacturing process. For example, a manufacturer might have two parallel assembly lines producing two similar sets of machine parts. The lines might converge at one central quality control unit where inspectors verify tolerances. The manager, however, might decide to change to periodic, rather than final, inspection. Under this arrangement, one or more inspections are established farther up the line.

Work sequence changes can also be made in service organizations. The processing of insurance claims, for example, could be changed. The sequence of logging and verifying claims, requesting checks, getting countersignatures, and mailing checks could be altered in several ways, such as combining the first two steps or routing the claims through one person while another handles checks. Organizational control systems may also be targets of change.[24]

■ Changing People

A third area of organization change has to do with human resources. For example, an organization might decide to change the skill level of its workforce. This change might be prompted by changes in technology or by a general desire to upgrade the quality of the workforce. Thus training programs and new selection criteria might be needed. The organization might also decide to improve its workers performance level. In this instance, a new incentive system or performance-based training might be in order.

Perceptions and expectations are also a common focus of organization change. Workers in an organization might believe that their wages and benefits are not as high as they should be. Management, however, might have evidence that shows the firm is paying a competitive wage and providing a superior benefit package. The change, then, would be centered on informing and educating the workforce about the comparative value of its compensation package. A common approach is to publish a statement that places an actual dollar value on each benefit and compares that amount to the benefits at other local organizations.

Changing Attitudes and Behaviors About Diversity

Texaco executives made headlines a few years ago when a tape-recorded conversation in which they made racially insulting remarks was made public. About the same time AT&T came under fire when a company newsletter used images of monkeys to represent people in Africa. And Denny's, the popular restaurant chain, attracted national attention over charges that it discriminated against minority customers and employees.

In each case, company officials made public apologies and offered restitution to those who were most directly offended. Another response from each company was an announced requirement that key managers throughout the firm would need to participate in diversity training. *Diversity training*, as the term suggests, is a training activity designed to help people understand the beliefs, values, and lifestyles of others and to make them more tolerant and accepting of diverse points of view.

Many experts believe that a well-planned and delivered diversity training program can indeed help people become more tolerant of others. On the other hand, some critics believe that such training addresses only surface-level issues. For example, some of the terms the Texaco executives were using in a negative manner had actually been learned in a diversity program!

> *"The objective is to help managers and supervisors to understand how unconscious behavior can impact employees, how differences can get in the way of productivity in the workplace and how to leverage diversity as a competitive advantage."*
>
> Edward N. Gadsden Jr., Texaco's diversity director*

References: *"Do Diversity Programs Make a Difference?"* Wall Street Journal, *December 4, 1996, p. B1 (*quote on p. B1); "Texaco Tapes Raise Scrutiny Over Diversity Training,"* USA Today, *November 11, 1996, p. 2B; and David A. Thomas and Suzy Wetkaufer, "A Question of Color: A Debate on Race in the U.S. Workplace,"* Harvard Business Review, *September–October 1997, pp. 118–128.*

Change can also be directed at employee attitudes and values. In many organizations today, managers are trying to eliminate adversarial relationships with workers and adopt a more collaborative relationship. "Working with Diversity" describes how some firms are using diversity training for this purpose. In many ways, changing attitudes and values is perhaps the hardest change to make.

■ Reengineering in Organizations

Many organizations today have also gone through a massive and comprehensive change program involving all aspects of organization design, technology, and people. Although various terms are used, the term currently in vogue for these changes is *reengineering*. Specifically, **reengineering** is the radical redesign of all aspects of a business to achieve major gains in cost, service, or time.[25]

reengineering The radical redesign of all aspects of a business to achieve major gains in cost, service, or time

The Need for Reengineering   Why are so many organizations finding it necessary to reengineer themselves? We noted in Chapter 2 that all systems, including organizations, are subject to entropy—a normal process leading to system decline. An organization is behaving most typically when it maintains the status quo, doesn't change in sync with its environment, and starts consuming its own resources to survive. In a sense, that is what IBM did. The firm's managers grew complacent and assumed that IBM's historic prosperity would continue and that they need not worry about environmental shifts, foreign competition, and so forth—and entropy set in. The key is to recognize the beginning of the decline and to move immediately toward reengineering. Major problems occur when managers either don't recognize the onset of entropy until it is well advanced or else are complacent in taking steps to correct it.

Approaches to Reengineering   Figure 13.3 shows the general steps in reengineering. The first step is setting goals and developing a strategy for reengineering. The organization must know in advance what reengineering is supposed to accomplish and how those accomplishments will be achieved. Next, top managers must begin and direct the reengineering effort. If a CEO announces that reengineering is to occur, but does nothing else, the program is not likely to succeed. But if the CEO is constantly involved in the process, underscoring its importance and taking the lead, reengineering stands a much better chance of success.

Most experts also agree that a sense of urgency usually accompanies successful reengineering. People in the organization must see the clear and present need for the changes being implemented and appreciate their importance. In addition, most successful reengineering efforts start with a new, clean slate. That is, rather than assuming that the existing organization is a starting point and then trying to modify it, reengineering usually starts by asking questions such as, How are customers best served? and How are competitors best neutralized? New approaches and systems are then created and imposed in place of existing ones.

Finally, reengineering requires a careful blend of top-down and bottom-up involvement. On the one hand, strong leadership is necessary, but too much involvement by top management can make the changes seem autocratic. Similarly, employee participation is also important, but too little involvement by leaders can undermine the program's importance and create a sense that top managers don't care. Thus care must be taken to carefully balance these two countervailing forces.

MANAGEMENT IMPLICATIONS   Managers need to understand the breadth of areas in which organization change can be necessary. More important, they should also note the potential areas of interdependence among areas of change. For example, a change in technology may also necessitate a change in organization structure and people. Finally,

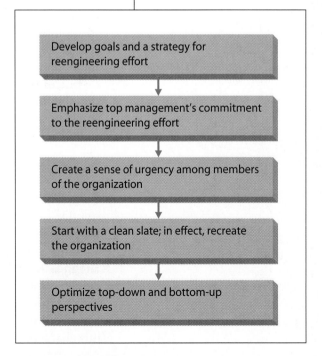

FIGURE 13.3
The Reengineering Process

Reengineering is a major redesign of all areas of an organization. To be successful, reengineering requires a systematic and comprehensive assessment of the entire organization. Goals, top management support, and a sense of urgency help the organization re-create itself and blend both top-level and bottom-up perspectives.

Develop goals and a strategy for reengineering effort

Emphasize top management's commitment to the reengineering effort

Create a sense of urgency among members of the organization

Start with a clean slate; in effect, recreate the organization

Optimize top-down and bottom-up perspectives

managers should also understand reengineering, a relatively recent perspective on change that involves massive and total change throughout an organization, spanning all three of the traditional change areas of organization design, technology, and people. ▬

Organization Development

We note in several places the importance of people and change. A special area of interest that focuses almost exclusively on people is organization development (OD).

■ Organization Development Assumptions

organization development An effort that is planned, organization wide, and managed from the top; it is intended to increase organization effectiveness and health through planned interventions in the organization's process, using behavioral science knowledge

Organization development is concerned with changing attitudes, perceptions, behaviors, and expectations. More precisely, **organization development** is a planned effort that is organization-wide and that is managed from the top; it is intended to increase organization effectiveness and health through planned interventions in the organization's "process," using behavioral science knowledge.[26] The theory and practice of OD are based on several very important assumptions. The first is that employees have a desire to grow and develop. Another is that employees have a strong need to be accepted by others within the organization. Another critical assumption of OD is that the total organization and the way it is designed will influence the behavior of individuals and groups within the organization. Thus some form of collaboration between managers and their employees is necessary to (1) take advantage of the skills and abilities of the employees and (2) eliminate aspects of the organization that retard employee growth, development, and group acceptance. Because of the intense personal nature of many OD activities, many large organizations rely on one or more OD consultants (either full-time employees assigned to this function or outside experts hired specifically for OD purposes) to implement and manage their OD program.[27]

■ Organization Development Techniques

Several kinds of interventions or activities are generally considered to be part of OD.[28] Some OD programs may use only one or a few of these; other programs use several of them at once.

Diagnostic Activities   Just as a physician examines patients to diagnose their current condition, an OD diagnosis analyzes the current condition of an organization. To carry out this diagnosis, managers use questionnaires, opinion or attitude surveys, interviews, archival data, and meetings to assess various characteristics of the organization. The results from this diagnosis may generate profiles of the organization's activities, which managers can then use to identify areas in need of correction.

Team Building   The purpose of team-building activities is to enhance the effectiveness and satisfaction of individuals who work in groups or teams and to promote overall group effectiveness. Given the widespread use of teams today, these activities have taken on increased importance. An OD consultant might interview team members to determine how they feel about the group; then an off-site meeting could be held to discuss the issues that surfaced and to iron out any problem areas or member concerns. Caterpillar used team building as one method for changing the working relationships between workers and supervisors from confrontational to cooperative.[29]

Survey Feedback   In survey feedback, each employee responds to a questionnaire intended to measure perceptions and attitudes (for example, satisfaction and supervisory style). Everyone involved, including the supervisor, receives the results of the survey. The aim of this approach is usually to change the behavior of supervisors by showing them how their subordinates view them. After the feedback has been provided, workshops may be conducted to evaluate results and suggest constructive changes.

Education   Educational activities focus on classroom training. Although such activities can be used for technical or skill-related purposes, an OD educational activity typically focuses on "sensitivity skills"—that is, it teaches employees to be more considerate and understanding of the people they work with. Participants often go through a series of experiential or role-playing exercises to learn how others in the organization feel.

Intergroup Activities   Intergroup activities focus on improving the relationships between two or more groups. We noted in Chapter 11 that as group interdependence increases, so do coordination difficulties. Intergroup OD activities are designed to promote cooperation or resolve conflicts that arose as a result of interdependence. Experiential or role-playing activities are often used to achieve this goal.

Third-Party Peacemaking   Another approach to OD is through third-party peacemaking, which is most often used when substantial conflict exists within the organization. Third-party peacemaking can be appropriate on the individual, group, or organization level. The third party, usually an OD consultant, uses various mediation or negotiation techniques to resolve problems and conflicts between individuals or groups.

Technostructural Activities   Technostructural activities are concerned with the design of the organization, the technology of the organization, and the interrelationship of design and technology with people on the job. A structural change such as an increase in decentralization, a job design change such as an increase in the use of automation, and a technological change involving a modification in work flow qualify as technostructural OD activities if their objective is to improve group and interpersonal relationships within the organization.

Process Consultation   In process consultation an OD consultant observes groups in the organization to develop an understanding of their communication patterns, decision-making and leadership processes, and methods of cooperation and conflict resolution. The consultant then provides feedback to the involved parties about the observed processes. The goal of this form of intervention is to improve the observed processes. A leader who is presented with feedback outlining deficiencies in his or her leadership style, for example, might be expected to change that style.

Life and Career Planning   Life and career planning helps employees formulate their personal goals and evaluate strategies for integrating their goals with the goals of the organization. Such activities might include specification of training needs and plotting a career map. General Electric has a reputation for doing an outstanding job in this area.

Coaching and Counseling   Coaching and counseling provide nonevaluative feedback to individuals. The purpose is to help people develop a better sense of how others see them and to learn behaviors that will assist others in achieving their work-related goals. The focus is not on how the individual is performing today; instead, it is on how the person can perform better in the future.

Planning and Goal Setting   More pragmatically oriented than many other interventions are activities designed to help managers improve their planning and goal setting. Emphasis still falls on the individual, however, because the intent is to help individuals and groups integrate themselves into the overall planning process. The OD consultant might use the same approach as he or she used for process consultation, but the focus is on the mechanics of planning and goal setting.

■ The Effectiveness of Organization Development

Given the range of activities that OD encompasses, reports of mixed results from various OD interventions should not be surprising. Many well-known organizations, including American Airlines, Texas Instruments, Procter & Gamble, ITT Corporation, Polaroid, and B.F. Goodrich, actively practice some form of OD. Goodrich, for example, has trained sixty people in OD processes and techniques. These trained experts have subsequently become internal OD consultants; their job is to assist other managers in applying OD techniques.[30] In contrast, managers at other companies have tried OD and decided to discard it.[31]

OD will probably remain an important part of management theory and practice. Of course, there are no sure things when dealing with social systems such as organizations, and the effectiveness of many OD techniques is difficult to evaluate. Because all organizations are open systems interacting with their environments, an improvement in an organization after an OD intervention may be attributable to the intervention, but it may also be attributable to changes in economic conditions, luck, or other factors.[32]

MANAGEMENT IMPLICATIONS Organization development is an important form of organization change that focuses on process issues. Managers should recognize the nature of OD before attempting to use any given OD technique. Top management support is necessary for OD to be successful, but managers also need to realize that no matter how well planned it is, OD may not work in every situation or for every organization. ▬

Organizational Innovation

The final element of organization change that we address is innovation. **Innovation** is the managed effort of an organization to develop new products, new services, or new uses for existing products or services. Innovation is clearly important because without new products or services, any organization will fall behind its competition.[33]

innovation The managed effort of an organization to develop new products or services or new uses for existing products or services

■ The Innovation Process

The organizational innovation process consists of developing, applying, launching, growing, and managing the maturity and decline of creative ideas.[34] Figure 13.4 depicts this process.

Innovation Development Innovation development involves the evaluation, modification, and improvement of creative ideas. Innovation development can transform a product or service with only modest potential into a product or service with significant potential. Parker Brothers, for example, decided during innovation development not to market an indoor volleyball game, but

FIGURE 13.4
The Innovation Process

Organizations actively seek to manage the innovation process. These steps illustrate the general life cycle that characterizes most innovations. Of course, as with creativity, the innovation process will suffer if it is approached too mechanically and rigidly.

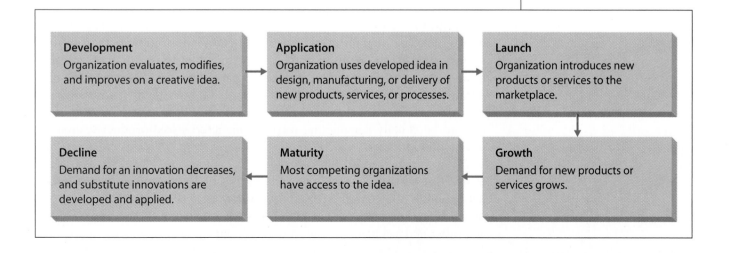

Development	Application	Launch
Organization evaluates, modifies, and improves on a creative idea.	Organization uses developed idea in design, manufacturing, or delivery of new products, services, or processes.	Organization introduces new products or services to the marketplace.

Decline	Maturity	Growth
Demand for an innovation decreases, and substitute innovations are developed and applied.	Most competing organizations have access to the idea.	Demand for new products or services grows.

MISSION: To design a new generation space launch vehicle that will dramatically reduce the cost and complexity of going into orbit. That will enable private companies to launch countless space-based businesses and take advantage of a whole new universe of opportunities in the century ahead—just as private enterprise helped the aviation industry take off during *this* century.

Quite possibly the most far-fetched idea since the airplane.

LOCKHEED MARTIN

SUCCESS: Lockheed Martin and our teammates have created an innovative yet practical design called VentureStar, a reusable, single-stage-to-orbit vehicle. The first step is to begin building, and will soon fly, a 1/2-scale demonstrator—the X-33—to validate the vehicle's advanced technologies and capabilities. That energy we, as a global technology leader, are helping to launch the future.

Innovation is the lifeblood of many companies. Lockheed Martin, for example, relies heavily on new products to remain strong and profitable. This potential product, for example, is called the VentureStar. Managers at Lockheed Martin see the VentureStar as a potential replacement for the Space Shuttle. At the present time, VentureStar is in the innovation development stage as a small-scale demonstrator is being constructed to validate the craft's basic design.

instead to sell separately the appealing little foam ball designed for the game. The firm will never know how well the volleyball game would have sold, but the Nerf ball and numerous related products have generated millions of dollars in revenues.[35]

Innovation Application   In the innovation application stage, an organization uses a developed idea in the design, manufacturing, or delivery of new products, services, or processes. At this point the innovation emerges from the laboratory and is transformed into tangible goods or services. One example of innovation application is the use of radar-based focusing systems in Polaroid's instant cameras. The idea of using radio waves to discover the location, speed, and direction of moving objects was first applied extensively by Allied forces during World War II. As radar technology developed, the electrical components became smaller and more streamlined. Researchers at Polaroid applied this well-developed technology in a new way.[36]

Application Launch   Application launch is the stage in which an organization introduces new products or services to the marketplace. The important question is not, Does the innovation work? but rather, Will customers want to purchase the innovative product and service? History is full of creative ideas that did not generate enough customer interest to be successful. Some notable innovation failures include Sony's seat warmer, the Edsel automobile, and Polaroid's SX-70 instant camera (which cost $3 billion to develop, but never sold more than one hundred thousand units in a year).[37] Thus despite development and application, new products and services can still fail at the launch phase.

Application Growth   After an innovation has been successfully launched, it enters the stage of application growth. This period is one of high economic performance for an organization because demand for the product or service is often greater than supply. Organizations that fail to anticipate this stage may unintentionally limit their growth, as Gillette did by not anticipating demand for its Sensor razor blades. However, overestimating demand for a new product can be equally detrimental to performance. Unsold products can sit in warehouses for years.

Innovation Maturity   After a period of growing demand, an innovative product or service often enters a period of maturity. Innovation maturity is the stage in which most organizations in an industry have access to an innovation—either as a result of developing the innovation on their own or copying the innovation of others—and are applying it in approximately the same way. The technological application of an innovation during this stage can be very sophisticated, but because of its widespread use, the innovation no longer provides a competitive advantage.

The time that elapses between innovation development and innovation maturity depends on the particular product or service. Whenever an innovation involves the use of complex skills (such as a complicated manufacturing process or highly sophisticated teamwork), moving from the growth phase to the maturity phase tends to take more time. In addition, if the skills needed to implement these innovations are rare and difficult to imitate, then strategic imitation may be delayed and the originating organization may enjoy a period of sustained competitive advantage.

Innovation Decline Every successful innovation bears its own seeds of decline. Because an organization does not gain a competitive advantage from an innovation at maturity, it must encourage its creative scientists, engineers, and managers to begin looking for new innovations. The continued search for competitive advantage usually leads new products and services to move from the creative process through innovation maturity and finally to innovation decline. Innovation decline is the stage during which demand for an innovation decreases and substitute innovations are developed and applied.

■ Forms of Innovation

Each creative idea an organization develops poses a different challenge for the innovation process. Innovations can be radical or incremental, technical or managerial, and product or process.

Radical Versus Incremental Innovations **Radical innovations** are new products or technologies developed by an organization that completely replace the existing products or technologies in an industry. **Incremental innovations** are new products or processes that modify existing ones. Firms that implement radical innovations fundamentally shift the nature of competition and the interaction of firms within their environments. Firms that implement incremental innovations alter, but do not fundamentally change, competitive interaction in an industry.

radical innovation A new product, service, or technology, that completely replaces an existing one

incremental innovation A new product, service, or technology that modifies an existing one

Over the last several years, organizations have introduced many radical innovations. For example, compact disk technology has virtually replaced long-playing vinyl records in the recording industry, and high-definition television seems likely to replace traditional television technology (color as well as black and white) in the near future. Whereas radical innovations like these tend to be very visible and public, incremental innovations actually are more numerous. One example is Ford's sports utility vehicle, Explorer. Although other companies had similar products, Ford more effectively combined the styling and engineering that generated increased demand for all sports utility vehicles.

Technical Versus Managerial Innovations **Technical innovations** are changes in the physical appearance or performance of a product or service or

technical innovation A change in appearance or performance of products or services or the physical processes through which a product or service passes

managerial innovation A change in the management process in an organization

product innovation A change in the physical characteristics of a product or service or the creation of a new one

process innovation A change in the way a product or service is manufactured, created, or distributed

FIGURE 13.5
Effects of Product and Process Innovation on Economic Return

As the innovation process moves from development to decline, the economic return from product innovations gradually declines. In contrast, the economic return from process innovations increases during this same process.

in the physical processes through which a product or service is manufactured. Many of the most important innovations over the last fifty years have been technical. For example, the serial replacement of the vacuum tube with the transistor, the transistor with the integrated circuit, and the integrated circuit with the microchip has greatly enhanced the power, ease of use, and speed of operation of a wide variety of electronic products.

Not all innovations developed by organizations are technical, however. **Managerial innovations** are changes in the management process by which products and services are conceived, built, and delivered to customers. Managerial innovations do not necessarily affect the physical appearance or performance of products or services directly. In effect, reengineering, as we discussed earlier in this chapter, represents a managerial innovation.

Product Versus Process Innovations   Perhaps the two most important types of technical innovations are product innovations and process innovations. **Product innovations** are changes in the physical characteristics or performance of existing products or services or the creation of brand-new products or services. **Process innovations** are changes in the way products or services are manufactured, created, or distributed. Whereas managerial innovations generally affect the broader context of development, process innovations directly affect manufacturing.

The implementation of robotics, for example, is a process innovation. As Figure 13.5 shows, the effect of product and process innovations on economic return depends on the stage of the innovation process that a new product or service occupies. At first, during development, application, and launch, the physical attributes and capabilities of an innovation most affect organizational performance. Thus product innovations are particularly important during these beginning phases. Later, as an innovation enters the phases of growth, maturity, and decline, an organization's ability to develop process innovations such as fine-tuning manufacturing, increasing product quality, and improving product distribution becomes important to maintaining economic return.

Japanese organizations often excel at process innovation. For example, the market for 35mm cameras was dominated by German and other European manufacturers when, in the early 1960s, Japanese organizations such as Canon and Nikon began making cameras. Some of the early Japanese products were

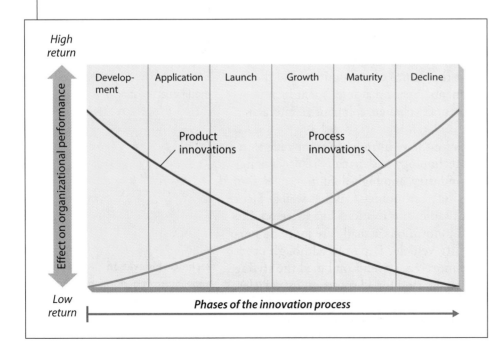

High return

Development | Application | Launch | Growth | Maturity | Decline

Product innovations

Process innovations

Effect on organizational performance

Low return

Phases of the innovation process

Fixing Philips

For years and years Philips Electronics has disappointed investors across Europe. The Dutch firm has a history of incredible innovation—creating everything from the cassette tape to the compact disk—but has also displayed a near-remarkable propensity for throwing away one business opportunity after another and for failing to capitalize on its innovations. The basic mistakes seem to follow a near-predictable process: Philips engineers create a new technology, the firm invests too much money in it with no regard for consumer preferences or tastes, and then marketing managers do a poor job of introducing and promoting it.

A good case in point was a product Philips developed and introduced in the early 1990s called the CD-i. This advanced device focused on interactivity between CD-ROMs and a television, instead of a computer. At the time analysts believed that the CD-i would be enormously successful. But through a combination of poor marketing, bumbling promotion, and a total disregard for consumers, Philips created a monumental product disaster that resulted in a loss of over $1 billion.

> *"If we want to come even close to the middle range of the companies we compare ourselves with, it's going to be quite an operation."*
>
> *Cor Boonstra, Philips' CEO**

Finally, after a series of internally developed CEOs had failed to change the course, Philips hired a newcomer to the industry, Cor Boonstra, to lead a turn around. Boonstra had spent twenty years at Sara Lee in the United States, had no electronics industry experience, but was believed to be a great manager.

Once on the job, he went right to work. Within six months he sold eighteen Philips' companies, for example, and announced both a major corporate restructuring and a new corporate strategy. His short-term goal is simply to get Philips to the middle of the industry. Then, he says, he can concentrate on becoming truly competitive. But observers say that his biggest challenge will be overcoming and reshaping the dysfunctional culture that pervades the company. Only then, they warn, can Philips truly break away from the pack.

References: *Charles P. Wallace, "Can He Fix Philips?"* Fortune, *March 31, 1997, pp. 98–99 (* quote on page 99); and* Hoover's Handbook of World Business 1998 *(Austin, Texas: Hoover's Business Press, 1998), pp. 404–405.*

not very successful, but these companies continued to invest in their process technology and eventually were able to increase quality and decrease manufacturing costs. Now Canon and Nikon dominate the worldwide market for 35mm cameras, and the German companies, because they were not able to maintain the same pace of process innovation, are struggling to maintain market share and profitability.

■ The Failure to Innovate

To remain competitive in today's economy, organizations must be innovative. And yet many organizations that should be innovative are not successful at bringing out new products or services, or do so only after innovations created by others are very mature. "The World of Management" describes how Philips

Electronics is attempting to overcome recent failures to innovate. Organizations may fail to innovate for at least three reasons.

Lack of Resources   Innovation is expensive in terms of dollars, time, and energy. If a firm does not have sufficient money to fund a program of innovation or does not currently employ the kinds of employees it needs to be innovative, it may lag behind in innovation. Even highly innovative organizations cannot become involved in every new product or service their employees think up. For example, numerous other commitments in the electronic instruments and computer industry delayed Hewlett-Packard's entry into the personal computer market. Because firms do not have infinite resources of money, time, and technical and managerial expertise, they have to make some difficult choices about which innovations to invest in.

Failure to Recognize Opportunities   Because firms cannot pursue all innovations, they need to learn how to carefully evaluate innovations and to select the ones that hold the greatest potential. To obtain a competitive advantage, an organization usually must make investment decisions before the innovation process reaches the mature stage. The earlier the investment, however, the greater the risk. If organizations are not skilled at recognizing and evaluating opportunities, they may be overly cautious and fail to invest in innovations that turn out later to be successful for other firms.

Resistance to Change   Innovation means giving up old products and old ways of doing things in favor of new products and new ways of doing things. These kinds of changes can be personally difficult for members of an organization. Thus resistance to change can slow the innovation process.

■ Promoting Innovation in Organizations

Many ideas for promoting innovation in organizations have been developed over the years. Three specific ways for promoting innovation are through the reward system, through the organizational culture, and through a process called intrapreneurship.[38]

The Reward System   A firm's reward system is the means by which it encourages and discourages certain behaviors by employees. Major components of the reward system include salaries, bonuses, and perquisites. Using the reward system to promote innovation is a fairly mechanical, but nevertheless effective, management technique. The idea is to provide financial and nonfinancial rewards to people and groups that develop innovative ideas. When the members of an organization understand that they will be rewarded for such activities, they are more likely to work creatively. With this end in mind, Monsanto Company gives a $50,000 award each year to the scientist or group of scientists that develops the biggest commercial breakthrough.

Managers also need to be very careful in responding to innovative failure. If innovative failure is due to incompetence, systematic errors, or managerial sloppiness, then a firm should respond appropriately—perhaps by withholding raises or reducing promotion opportunities. On the other hand, people who act in good faith to develop an innovation that does not work out should not be punished for failure. If they are, they will probably not be creative in the future. A punitive reward system will discourage people from taking risks and therefore reduce the organization's ability to obtain competitive advantages.

Many new product ideas simply do not work out in the marketplace. The creative and innovative processes are fraught with too many uncertainties to generate positive results every time. An individual may have prepared herself to be creative, but an insight may not be forthcoming. Or managers may attempt to apply a developed innovation, only to recognize that it does not work. Indeed, some organizations believe that if all their innovative efforts succeed, then they are probably not taking enough risks in research and development. At 3M, for example, nearly 60 percent of the creative ideas suggested each year do not succeed in the marketplace.

Organizational Culture An organization's culture is the set of values, beliefs, and symbols that help guide behavior. A strong, appropriately focused organizational culture can be used to support innovative activity. A well-managed culture can communicate a sense that innovation is valued and will be rewarded and that occasional failure in the pursuit of new ideas is not only acceptable but even expected. Firms such as 3M, Corning, Monsanto, Procter & Gamble, Texas Instruments, Johnson & Johnson, and Merck have strong, innovation-oriented cultures that value individual creativity, risk taking, and inventiveness.[39]

Intrapreneurship in Larger Organizations In recent years, many large businesses have realized that the entrepreneurial spirit that propelled their growth becomes stagnant after they transform themselves from a small but growing concern into a larger one. To help revitalize this spirit, some firms today encourage "intrapreneurship." **Intrapreneurs** are similar to entrepreneurs except that they develop a new business in the context of a large organization. There are three intrapreneurial roles in large organizations.[40] To successfully use intrapreneurship to encourage creativity and innovation, the organization must find one or more individuals to perform these roles.

The *inventor* is the person who actually conceives of and develops the new idea, product, or service by means of the creative process. Because the inventor may lack the expertise or motivation to oversee the transformation of the product or service from an idea into a marketable entity, however, a second role comes into play. A *product champion* is usually a middle manager who learns about the project and becomes committed to it. He or she helps overcome organizational resistance and convinces others to take the innovation seriously. The product champion may have only limited understanding of the technological aspects of the innovation. Nevertheless, product champions are skilled at knowing how the organization works, whose support is needed to push the

intrapreneurs Similar to entrepreneurs except that intrapreneurs develop a new business in the context of a large organization

project forward, and where to go to secure the resources necessary for successful development. A *sponsor* is a top-level manager who approves of and supports a project. This person may fight for the budget needed to develop an idea, overcome arguments against a project, and use organizational politics to ensure the project's survival. With a sponsor in place, the inventor's idea has a much better chance of being successfully developed.

Several firms have embraced intrapreneurship as a way to encourage creativity and innovation. Colgate-Palmolive has a separate unit, Colgate Venture Company, staffed with intrapreneurs who develop new products. General Foods developed the Culinova Group as a unit to which employees can take their ideas for possible development. S.C. Johnson & Sons, Inc., established a $250,000 fund to support new product ideas, and Texas Instruments refuses to approve a new innovative project unless it has an acknowledged inventor, champion, and sponsor.

MANAGEMENT IMPLICATIONS Managers need to realize that innovation is the lifeblood of most organizations and is a process that can be successfully managed. To do so, however, managers must understand the various forms of innovation, the reasons that some organizations fail to innovate, and some techniques that promote and stimulate innovation. ▬

Summary of Key Points

Organization change is any substantive modification to some part of the organization. Change may be prompted by forces internal or external to the organization. In general, planned change is preferable to reactive change.

Managing the change process is very important. The Lewin model provides a general perspective on the steps involved in change, although a comprehensive model is usually more effective. People tend to resist change because of uncertainty, threatened self-interests, different perceptions, and feelings of loss. Participation, education and communication, facilitation, and force-field analysis are methods for overcoming this resistance.

Many change techniques or interventions are in use. The most common ones involve changing organizational structure and design, technology, and people. Each of these broad categories comprises several specific areas of change. Reengineering is the radical redesign of all aspects of a business to achieve major gains in cost, service, or time. It is occasionally needed to offset entropy. The basic steps are developing goals and strate-

gies, conveying the involvement of top management, creating a sense of urgency, starting with a clean slate, and balancing top-down and bottom-up perspectives.

Organization development is concerned with changing attitudes, perceptions, behaviors, and expectations. Its effective use relies on an important set of assumptions. Conflicting opinions exist about the effectiveness of several organization development techniques.

The innovation process has six steps: development, application, launch, growth, maturity, and decline. Basic categories of innovation include radical, incremental, technical, managerial, product, and process innovations. Despite the importance of innovation, many organizations fail to innovate. They may lack the required creative individuals, be committed to too many other creative activities, fail to recognize opportunities, or resist the change that innovation requires. Organizations can use various tools to overcome these problems, including the reward system, organizational culture, and intrapreneurship.

Discussion Questions

Questions for Review

1. What forces or kinds of events lead to organization change? Identify each force or event as planned or reactive change.

2. How is each step in the process of organization change implemented? Are some of the steps likely to meet with more resistance than others? Why or why not?

3. What are the various areas of organization change? In what ways are they similar and in what ways do they differ?

4. What are the steps in the innovation process?

Questions for Analysis

5. Could reactive change of the type identified in question 1 have been planned for ahead of time? Why or why not? Should all organization change be planned? Why or why not?

6. A company has recently purchased equipment that, when installed, will do the work of one hundred employees. The workforce of the company is very concerned and is threatening to take some kind of action. If you were the human resource manager, what would you try to do to satisfy all parties concerned? Why?

7. Think of several relatively new products or services that you use. What form of innovation does each represent?

Questions for Application

8. Some people resist change while others welcome change enthusiastically. To deal with the first group, one needs to overcome resistance to change; to deal with the second, one needs to overcome resistance to stability. What advice can you give a manager facing the latter situation?

9. Can a change made in one area of an organization—in technology, for instance—not lead to change in other areas? Why or why not?

10. Find out more about one of the techniques for organization development presented in this chapter. What are the advantages and disadvantages of that technique relative to other techniques?

EXERCISE OVERVIEW

Time management skills refer to the manager's ability to prioritize work, to work efficiently, and to delegate appropriately. Using time management skills wisely can change how a person works.

Building Effective
Time-Management Skills

EXERCISE BACKGROUND

Almost every task you perform can theoretically be performed more efficiently. The next time you work on a particular task, such as studying for a test, writing a paper, or working on a project, take note of your work habits. You might even consider videotaping yourself while you work, and reviewing the tape later.

   Take special note of the things you do that appear to not contribute to task performance. Examples might include going to the refrigerator and getting food, watching television while you are working, daydreaming, making an unnecessary telephone call, and so forth. Next, estimate how much of the total "work" time was actually spent doing things besides working.

EXERCISE TASK

With the preceding background information as context, do the following:

1. Assess the extent to which each nonwork activity was actually wasted effort or actually contributed in some way to task performance.

2. Describe how the work might have been completed had you not done any of the nonwork activities.

3. Describe a change approach that might help you use your work time more efficiently.

Building Effective Interpersonal Skills

EXERCISE OVERVIEW

A manager's interpersonal skills are her or his ability to understand and motivate individuals and groups. These abilities are especially important during a period of change. Thus, this exercise will help you understand how to apply your interpersonal skills to a change situation.

EXERCISE BACKGROUND

Assume that you are the manager of a retail store in a local shopping mall. Your staff consists of seven full-time and ten part-time employees. The full-time employees have worked together as a team for three years. The part-timers are all local college students; a few of them have worked in the store for more than a year, but there tends to be a lot of turnover among this group.

Your boss, the regional manager, has just informed you that the national chain that owns your store is planning to open a second store in the same mall. She has also informed you that you must plan and implement the following changes:

1. You will serve as manager of both stores until the sales volume of the new store warrants its own full-time manager.

2. You are to designate one of the full-time employees in your present store as the assistant manager, since you will be in the store less often now.

3. To have experienced workers in the new store, you are to select three of your current full-time workers to move to the new store, one of whom should also be appointed as assistant manager of that store.

4. You can hire three new people to replace those transferred from your existing store and three new people to work at the new store.

5. You can decide for yourself how to deploy your part-timers, but you will need a total of ten in the existing store and eight at the new store.

You realize that many of your employees will be unhappy with these changes. They all know each other and work well together. However, the new store will be in a new section of the mall and will be a very nice place to work.

EXERCISE TASK

With this background information in mind, do the following:

1. Determine the likely reasons for resistance to this change from your workers.

2. Determine how you will decide about promotions and transfers (make whatever assumptions you think are warranted).

3. Outline how you will inform your employees about the change.

4. An alternative strategy would involve keeping the existing staff intact and hiring new employees for the new store. Outline a persuasion strategy for trying to convince your boss that this option is better.

EXERCISE OVERVIEW

Diagnostic skills help a manager visualize the most appropriate response to a situation. Diagnostic skills are especially important during a period of organization change.

Building Effective Diagnostic Skills

EXERCISE BACKGROUND

Assume that you are the general manager of a hotel located on a tropical island. The hotel is situated along a beautiful stretch of beach and is one of six large resorts in the area. The hotel, owned by a group of foreign investors, is one of the oldest on the island. For several years, the hotel has been operated as a franchise unit of a large international hotel chain, as are all of the other hotels on the island.

For the last few years, the hotel's owners have been taking most of the profits for themselves and putting relatively little back into the hotel. They also have let you know that their business is not in good financial health; the money earned from your hotel is being used to offset their other losses. In contrast, most of the other hotels around you have recently been refurbished, and plans have just been announced to build two new ones in the near future.

A team of executives from franchise headquarters has just visited your hotel. The executives expressed considerable disappointment in the property.

They feel that it has not kept pace with the other resorts on the island. They also informed you that if the property is not brought up to their standards, the franchise agreement, up for review in a year, will be revoked. You see this situation as potentially disastrous, since the hotel would lose its "brand name," access to the franchisor's reservation system, and so forth.

Sitting alone in your office, you have identified several viable alternatives:

1. Try to convince the owners to remodel the hotel. You estimate that it will take $5 million to meet the franchisor's minimum standards and another $5 million to bring the hotel up to the standards of the top resort on the island.

2. Try to convince the franchisor to give you more time and more options to upgrade the facility.

3. Allow the franchise agreement to terminate and try to succeed as an independent hotel.

4. Assume that the hotel is going to fail and start looking for another job. You have a good reputation, although you might have to start at a lower level with another firm (perhaps as an assistant manager).

EXERCISE TASK

With the preceding background information as context, do the following:

1. Rank the four alternatives in terms of their potential success (make assumptions as appropriate).

2. Identify other alternatives not noted here.

3. Can any alternatives be pursued simultaneously?

4. Develop an overall strategy for trying to save the hotel while also protecting your own self-interests.

CHAPTER CLOSING CASE

Levi Strauss Hikes Up Its Pants

Levi Strauss & Co. and the ubiquitous denim blue jeans it sells around the world have been industry icons for years. The firm can trace its roots back to the mid-19th century when its namesake immigrated to the United States from Bavaria. Shortly after arriving in San Francisco during the California gold rush, Levi Strauss decided that it was a safer bet to produce equipment for other miners than it was to set out with his own pick and shovel. Work pants crafted from heavy canvas proved to be his most successful product, and the rest, as they say, is history.

Strauss began coloring the pants with blue pigments and enlisted the aid of a friend to provide what would become the trademark rivets to key stress points. The firm grew slowly but surely for decades, always led by one of Strauss' direct descendants. But Levi's real growth started in the 1950s when its pants became an essential uniform for the youth of the United States.

The momentum continued into the 1960s as denim took its place alongside incense, tie-died shirts, and long hair as symbols of a rebellious youth. And as the baby boomers, who were the youth of the 1950s and 1960s, grew into adulthood, Levi's jeans became their fashion mainstay. The name Levi's became almost synonymous with blue jeans. During the 1970s through the 1990s, Levi also expanded rapidly overseas, and today the brand is sold in more than seventy countries.

Under the leadership of Robert Hass (Levi Strauss' great-great-grandnephew), Levi also forged an innovative relationship with its employees. High levels of job security, an innovative reward structure, and an open and participative approach to management created a loyal and dedicated workforce that helped keep the organization at the top of its industry.

But as the 1990s grew to a close, Levi Strauss seemed to hit a wall. And as a result, the firm has had to reexamine every aspect of its business operations and simultaneously redefine its relationship with its workforce. The catalyst for change was an almost-sudden drop in market share. For example, in 1990 Levi held 30.9 percent of the jeans market in the United States. But by 1997 that figure had plummeted to just 18.7 percent. Similarly, the firm's market share among fifteen- to nineteen-year-old consumers dropped from 33 percent in 1993 to 26 percent in 1997.

As a result of this alarming trend, company executives faced an intense and detailed period of introspection to find out what was happening to the company. Their conclusion was that Levi Strauss had been so successful with its core baby-boomer consumers that it had essentially neglected younger consumers. As a result, top-end designers such as Tommy Hilfiger and Ralph Lauren and discounted store brands sold at Sears and J. C. Penney took market share from Levi. Similarly,

the jeans giant had also ignored emerging fashion trends like wide-legged and baggy jeans.

Once they saw their problem, executives took quick action on a number of fronts. Most painfully, the company announced that it was closing eleven U.S. factories and laying off one-third of its North American workforce. Needless to say, this step served to dramatically and unalterably change its relationship with its workforce. The company also acknowledged that it needed to alter the composition of its executive team to boost creativity and market knowledge. Too many company officials, it said, had come up through the ranks and knew only one way of doing things—the old tried-and-true Levi's way. Thus one goal now is to fill 30 percent of all new management jobs with outsiders. Experts agree that Levi will need some time to get its act together again, but they also acknowledge that the changes seem to fit the situation as well as a pair of the firm's jeans fit after a long day at the office.

Case Questions

1. What forces led to the need for change at Levi Strauss?
2. What kinds of changes can you identify at Levi?
3. One mistake a firm can make is failing to change when it needs to; another is changing too quickly. How can managers like those at Levi best position themselves to change when they need to—not too quickly, but not too late either?

Case References: "Levi's Is Hiking up Its Pants," *Business Week*, December 1, 1997, pp. 70–75; "Its Share Shrinking, Levi Strauss Lays Off 6,395," *Wall Street Journal*, November 4, 1997, pp. B1, B8; and "Levi's Gets the Blues," *Time*, November 17, 1997, p. 66.

CHAPTER NOTES

1. Alex Taylor III, "'Neutron Jurgen Ignites a Revolution at Daimler-Benz," *Fortune*, November 10, 1997, pp. 144–152; "A Tough Deadline," *Forbes*, April 22, 1996, pp. 165–173; and "Dustup at Daimler," *Business Week*, February 3, 1997, pp. 52–53.

2. For excellent reviews of this area, see Richard W. Woodman, "Organization Change and Development: New Arenas for Inquiry and Action," *Journal of Management*, June 1989, pp. 205–228; William Pasmore and Mary Fagans, "Participation, Individual Development, and Organizational Change: A Review and Synthesis," *Journal of Management*, June 1992, pp. 375–397; and Richard Pascale, Mark Millemann, and Linda Gioja, "Changing the Way We Change," *Harvard Business Review*, November–December 1997, pp. 126–139.

3. For additional insights into how technological change affects other parts of the organization, see P. Robert Duimering, Frank Safayeni, and Lyn Purdy, "Integrated Manufacturing: Redesign the Organization Before Implementing Flexible Technology," *Sloan Management Review*, Summer 1993, pp. 47–56.

4. Joel Cutcher-Gershenfeld, Ellen Ernst Kossek, and Heidi Sandling, "Managing Concurrent Change Initiatives," *Organizational Dynamics*, Winter 1997, pp. 21–38.

5. Thomas A. Stewart, "How to Lead a Revolution," *Fortune*, November 28, 1994, pp. 48–61.

6. See Warren Boeker, "Strategic Change: The Influence of Managerial Characteristics and Organizational Growth," *Academy of Management Journal*, 1997, Vol. 40, No. 1, pp. 152–170.

7. Alan L. Frohman, "Igniting Organizational Change from Below: The Power of Personal Initiative," *Organizational Dynamics*, Winter 1997, pp. 39–53.

8. Nandini Rajagopalan and Gretchen M. Spreitzer, "Toward a Theory of Strategic Change: A Multi-Lens Perspective and Integrative Framework," *Academy of Management Review*, 1997, Vol. 22, No. 1, pp. 48–79.

9. Anne Fisher, "Danger Zone," *Fortune*, September 8, 1997, pp. 165–167.

10. "Kodak to Cut 10,000 Jobs," Associated Press story reported in *The Bryan-College Station Eagle*, November 12, 1997, p. A6.

11. John P. Kotter and Leonard A. Schlesinger, "Choosing Strategies for Change," *Harvard Business Review*, March–April 1979, p. 106.

12. Erik Brynjolfsson, Amy Austin Renshaw, and Marshall Van Alstyne, "The Matrix of Change," *Sloan Management Review*, Winter 1997, pp. 37–54.

13. Kurt Lewin, "Frontiers in Group Dynamics: Concept, Method, and Reality in Social Science," *Human Relations*, June 1947, pp. 5–41.

14. See Connie J. G. Gersick, "Revolutionary Change Theories: A Multilevel Exploration of the Punctuated Equilibrium Paradigm," *Academy of Management Review*, January 1991, pp. 10–36.

15. For a good illustration of how resistance emerges, see Gerald Andrews, "Mistrust, the Hidden Obstacle to Empowerment, *HR Magazine*, November 1994, pp. 66–74.

16. "RJR Employees Fight Distraction Amid Buy-out Talks," *Wall Street Journal*, November 1, 1988, p. A8.

17. Arnon E. Reichers, John P. Wanous, and James T. Austin, "Understanding and Managing Cynicism about Organizational Change," *Academy of Management Executive*, February 1997, pp. 48–59.

18. "How Classy Can 7-Eleven Get?" *Business Week*, September 1, 1997, pp. 74–75.

19. For a classic discussion, see Paul R. Lawrence, "How to Deal with Resistance to Change," *Harvard Business Review*, January–February 1969, pp. 4–12, 166–176.

20. Lester Coch and John R. P. French Jr., "Overcoming Resistance to Change," *Human Relations*, August 1948, pp. 512–532.

21. Charles K. Day Jr., "Management's Mindless Mistakes,"

Industry Week, May 29, 1987, p. 42. See also "Inspection from the Plant Floor," *Business Week*, April 10, 1989, pp. 60–61.

22. Benjamin Schneider, Arthur P. Brief, and Richard A. Guzzo, "Creating a Climate and Culture for Sustainable Organizational Change," *Organizational Dynamics*, Spring 1996, pp. 7–19.

23. David A. Nadler, "The Effective Management of Organizational Change," in *Handbook of Organizational Behavior*, ed. Jay W. Lorsch (Englewood Cliffs, N.J.: Prentice-Hall, 1987), pp. 358–369.

24. Jeffrey A. Alexander, "Adaptive Change in Corporate Control Practices," *Academy of Management Journal*, March 1991, pp. 162–193.

25. Thomas A. Stewart, "Reengineering—the Hot New Managing Tool," *Fortune*, August 23, 1993, pp. 41–48.

26. Richard Beckhard, *Organization Development: Strategies and Models* (Reading, Mass.: Addison-Wesley, 1969), p. 9.

27. W. Warner Burke, "The New Agenda for Organization Development," *Organizational Dynamics*, Summer 1997, pp. 7–20.

28. Wendell L. French and Cecil H. Bell Jr., *Organization Development: Behavioral Science Interventions for Organization Improvement*, 2nd ed. (Englewood Cliffs, N.J.: Prentice-Hall, 1978).

29. William G. Dyer, *Team Building Issues and Alternatives* (Reading, Mass.: Addison-Wesley, 1980).

30. Roger J. Hower, Mark G. Mindell, and Donna L. Simmons, "Introducing Innovation Through OD," *Management Review*, February 1978, pp. 52–56.

31. "Is Organization Development Catching On? A Personnel Symposium," *Personnel*, November–December 1977, pp. 10–22.

32. For a recent discussion on the effectiveness of various OD techniques in different organizations, see John M. Nicholas, "The Comparative Impact of Organization Development Interventions on Hard Criteria Measures," *Academy of Management Review*, October 1982, pp. 531–542.

33. Constantinos Markides, "Strategic Innovation," *Sloan Management Review*, Spring 1997, pp. 9–24.

34. L. B. Mohr, "Determinants of Innovation in Organizations," *American Political Science Review*, 1969, pp. 111–126; G. A. Steiner, *The Creative Organization* (Chicago: University of Chicago Press, 1965); R. Duncan and A. Weiss, "Organizational Learning: Implications for Organizational Design," in *Research in Organizational Behavior*, Vol. 1, ed. B. M. Staw (Greenwich, Conn.: JAI Press, 1979), pp. 75–123; and J. E. Ettlie, "Adequacy of Stage Models for Decisions on Adoption of Innovation," *Psychological Reports*, 1980, pp. 991–995.

35. Beth Wolfensberger, "Trouble in Toyland," *New England Business*, September 1990, pp. 28–36.

36. See Alan Patz, "Managing Innovation in High Technology Industries," *New Management*, September 1986, pp. 54–59.

37. "Flops," *Business Week*, August 16, 1993, pp. 76–82.

38. Dorothy Leonard and Jeffrey F. Rayport, "Spark Innovation through Empathic Design," *Harvard Business Review*, November–December 1997, pp. 102–115.

39. See Steven P. Feldman, "How Organizational Culture Can Affect Innovation," *Organizational Dynamics*, Summer 1988, pp. 57–68.

40. See Gifford Pinchot III, *Intrapreneuring* (New York: Harper and Row, 1985).

14

Managing Human Resources in Organizations

OBJECTIVES

After studying this chapter, you should be able to:

■ Describe the environmental context of human resource management, including its strategic importance and its relationship with legal and social factors.

■ Discuss how organizations attract human resources, including human resource planning, recruiting, and selecting.

■ Describe how organizations develop human resources, including training and development, performance appraisal, and performance feedback.

■ Discuss how organizations maintain human resources, including the determination of compensation and benefits and career planning.

■ Discuss labor relations, including how employees form unions and the mechanics of collective bargaining.

Cisco Systems is one of the hottest companies in California's fabled Silicon Valley. Founded in 1984 by two enterprising Stanford University employees, Cisco specializes in technology and technological systems to link computer networks. By 1997 the firm's annual sales exceeded $6 billion, and it was selling its products in over seventy-five countries.

To maintain its dizzying growth level, Cisco has had to add new employees at a steady pace. For example, the company recently doubled the size of its workforce in an eighteen-month period. In some areas and in some industries, this level of growth would be easy to manage. But in the Silicon Valley and in the world of high-technology, finding and keeping bright and talented people is difficult even during periods of normal growth.

But Cisco has been able to identify, hire, and—most important of all—retain the best employees through the use of a well-developed and executed human resource recruiting strategy. The strategy began when top managers at Cisco clearly defined the kinds of employees they wanted to hire for the firm. In particular, they set a goal of hiring only from among the top 15 percent of the people currently working in the industry.

Next, they studied exactly how this caliber of person goes about looking for a job. For example, Cisco prefers to hire exceptional, high-caliber employees who are relatively content with their present jobs but are willing to consider challenging, exciting, and rewarding alternatives. These kinds of people often dislike actually looking for new jobs, and instead are more likely to be enticed by Internet Web sites that are enhanced with interesting graphics and images.

And finally, Cisco executives developed innovative hiring procedures for getting these people interested in working for Cisco. For example, potential new recruits can actually indicate their interest in Cisco electronically. And the firm will also reply to them electronically and provide answers to most of their most common questions, such as pay, benefits, and opportunities for advancement.

Of course, after the firm hires these employees, it must still work to keep them. Thus, Cisco offers among the highest salaries in the industry. It also provides an exhaustive set of leading-edge benefits for its employees; for example, Cisco has an innovative and rewarding profit-sharing program, flexible work schedules, and a pleasant work environment. Cisco also maintains a casual and relaxing corporate culture.

As a result, Cisco's turnover rate is among the lowest in its industry. And Cisco managers believe that these loyal and talented employees will help keep the firm on top for many years.[1] Thus, the firm realizes that its people represent an important competitive advantage and that by investing heavily in them it is enhancing its potential long-term success.

"Our philosophy is very simple—if you get the best people in the industry to fit into your culture and you motivate them properly, then you're going to be an industry leader."

John Chambers, Cisco CEO, quoted in Fortune, September 29, 1997, p. 275.

Cisco Systems is one of the most successful businesses around these days, and its human resources are clearly an integral part of Cisco's success. From its earliest days, the firm's managers made a strategic commitment to identify, hire, and retain the best and brightest people. Moreover, the firm has been able to maintain this strategy and today is the employer of choice for many talented people in California's Silicon Valley.

This chapter is about how organizations manage the people that comprise them. This set of processes is called human resource management, or HRM. We start by describing the environmental context of HRM. We then discuss how organizations attract human resources. Next we describe how organizations seek to further develop the capacities of their human resources. We then examine how high-quality human resources are maintained by organizations and conclude by discussing labor relations.

The Environmental Context of Human Resource Management

human resource management
The set of organizational activities directed at attracting, developing, and maintaining an effective workforce

Human resource management (HRM) is the set of organizational activities directed at attracting, developing, and maintaining an effective workforce.[2] Human resource management takes place within a complex and ever-changing environmental context. Three particularly vital components of this context are HRM's strategic importance and the legal and social environment of HRM.

■ The Strategic Importance of Human Resource Management

Human resources are critical for effective organizational functioning.[3] HRM (or personnel, as it is sometimes called) was once relegated to second-class status in many organizations, but its importance has grown dramatically in the last two decades. Its new importance stems from increased legal complexities, the recognition that human resources are a valuable means for improving productivity, and the awareness today of the costs associated with poor human resource management.[4]

Indeed, managers now realize that the effectiveness of their HR (human resource) function has a substantial impact on the bottom-line performance of the firm. Poor human resource planning can result in spurts of hiring followed by layoffs—costly in terms of unemployment compensation payments, training expenses, and morale. Haphazard compensation systems do not attract, keep, and motivate good employees, and outmoded recruitment practices can expose the firm to expensive and embarrassing discrimination lawsuits. Consequently, the chief human resource executive of most large businesses is a vice president directly accountable to the CEO, and many firms are developing strategic HR plans and are integrating those plans with other strategic planning activities.[5]

Even organizations with as few as two hundred employees usually have a human resource manager and a human resource department charged with overseeing these activities. Responsibility for HR activities, however, is shared between the HR department and line managers. The HR department may recruit and initially screen candidates, but the final selection is usually made by managers in the department where the new employee will work. Similarly, although the HR department may establish performance appraisal policies and procedures, the actual evaluating and coaching of employees is done by their immediate superiors.

The Legal Environment of Human Resource Management

A number of laws regulate various aspects of employee-employer relations, especially in the areas of equal employment opportunity, compensation and benefits, labor relations, and occupational safety and health. Table 14.1 summarizes the major employment-related laws.

TABLE 14.1
The Legal Environment of Human Resource Management

As much as any area of management, HRM is subject to wide-ranging laws and court decisions. These laws and decisions affect the human resource function in many areas. For example, AT&T was once fined several million dollars for violating Title VII of the Civil Rights Act of 1964.

Equal Employment Opportunity

Title VII of the Civil Rights Act of 1964 (as amended by the *Equal Employment Opportunity Act of 1972*): forbids discrimination in all areas of the employment relationship

Age Discrimination in Employment Act: outlaws discrimination against people older than forty years

Various executive orders, especially *Executive Order 11246* in 1965: requires employers with government contracts to engage in affirmative action

Pregnancy Discrimination Act: specifically outlaws discrimination on the basis of pregnancy

Vietnam Era Veterans Readjustment Assistance Act: extends affirmative action mandate to military veterans who served during the Vietnam War

Americans with Disabilities Act: specifically outlaws discrimination against disabled persons

Civil Rights Act of 1991: makes it easier for employees to sue an organization for discrimination but limits punitive damage awards if they win

Compensation and Benefits

Fair Labor Standards Act: establishes minimum wage and mandated overtime pay for work in excess of forty hours per week

Equal Pay Act: requires that men and women be paid the same amount for doing the same jobs

Employee Retirement Income Security Act: regulates how organizations manage their pension funds

Family and Medical Leave Act of 1993: requires employers to provide up to twelve weeks of unpaid leave for family and medical emergencies

Labor Relations

National Labor Relations Act: spells out procedures by which employees can establish labor unions and requires organizations to bargain collectively with legally formed unions; also known as the *Wagner Act*

Labor-Management Relations Act: limits union power and specifies management rights during a union-organizing campaign; also known as the *Taft-Hartley Act*

Health and Safety

Occupational Safety and Health Act: mandates the provision of safe working conditions

Title VII of the Civil Rights Act of 1964 Forbids discrimination on the basis of sex, race, color, religion, or national origin in all areas of the employment relationship

adverse impact When minority group members pass a selection standard at a rate less than 80 percent of the pass rate of majority group members

Equal Employment Opportunity Commission Charged with enforcing Title VII of the Civil Rights Act of 1964

Age Discrimination in Employment Act Outlaws discrimination against people older than forty years; passed in 1967, amended in 1978 and 1986

affirmative action Intentionally seeking and hiring qualified or qualifiable employees from racial, sexual, and ethnic groups that are underrepresented in the organization

Americans With Disabilities Act Prohibits discrimination against people with disabilities

Civil Rights Act of 1991 Amends the original Civil Rights Act, making it easier to bring discrimination lawsuits while limiting punitive damages

Fair Labor Standards Act Sets a minimum wage and requires overtime pay for work in excess of forty hours per week; passed in 1938 and amended frequently since then

Equal Pay Act of 1963 Requires that men and women be paid the same amount for doing the same jobs

Equal Employment Opportunity **Title VII of the Civil Rights Act of 1964** forbids discrimination in all areas of the employment relationship. The intent of Title VII is to ensure that employment decisions are based on an individual's qualifications rather than personal biases. The law has reduced direct forms of discrimination (refusing to promote blacks into management, failing to hire men as flight attendants, refusing to hire women as construction workers) as well as indirect forms of discrimination (using employment tests that whites pass at a higher rate than blacks do).

Employment requirements such as test scores or other qualifications are legally defined as having an **adverse impact** on minorities and women when such individuals meet or pass the requirement at a rate less than 80 percent of the rate of majority group members. Criteria that have an adverse impact on protected groups can be used only when solid evidence proves that the criteria effectively identify individuals who are better able than others to do the job. The **Equal Employment Opportunity Commission** (EEOC) is charged with enforcing Title VII as well as several other employment-related laws. The EEOC recently had a backlog of almost one hundred thousand claims waiting to be resolved.[6]

The **Age Discrimination in Employment Act**, passed in 1967, amended in 1978, and amended again in 1986, is an attempt to prevent organizations from discriminating against older workers. In its current form, this law outlaws discrimination against people older than forty years. Both the Age Discrimination Act and Title VII require passive nondiscrimination, or equal employment opportunity. Employers are not required to seek out and hire minorities, but they must treat fairly all who apply.

Several executive orders, however, require that employers holding government contracts engage in **affirmative action**—intentionally seeking and hiring employees from groups that are underrepresented in the organization. These organizations must have a written affirmative action plan that spells out employment goals for underutilized groups and how those goals will be met. These employers are also required to act affirmatively in hiring Vietnam-era veterans and qualified handicapped individuals.

In 1990, Congress passed the **Americans with Disabilities Act** that forbids discrimination on the basis of disabilities and requires employers to provide reasonable accommodations for disabled employees. More recently, the **Civil Rights Act of 1991** amended the original Civil Rights Act as well as other related laws by making it easier to bring discrimination lawsuits (which partially explains the aforementioned backlog of cases) and simultaneously limiting the amount of punitive damages that can be awarded in those lawsuits.

Compensation and Benefits Laws also regulate compensation and benefits. The **Fair Labor Standards Act**, passed in 1938 and amended frequently since then, sets a minimum wage and requires the payment of overtime rates for work in excess of forty hours per week. Salaried professional, executive, and administrative employees are exempt from the minimum hourly wage and overtime provisions. The **Equal Pay Act of 1963** requires that men and women be paid the same amount for doing the same jobs. Attempts to circumvent the law by having different job titles and pay rates for men and women who perform the same work are also illegal. Basing an employee's pay on seniority or performance is legal, however, even if it means that a man and woman are paid different amounts for doing the same job.

The provision of benefits is also regulated in some ways by state and federal laws. Certain benefits are mandatory—for example, worker's compensation insurance for employees who are injured on the job. Employers who provide a pension plan for their employees are regulated by the **Employee Retirement Income Security Act of 1974 (ERISA)**. The purpose of this act is to help ensure the financial security of pension funds by regulating how they can be invested. The **Family and Medical Leave Act of 1993** requires employers to provide up to twelve weeks of unpaid leave for family and medical emergencies.

Employee Retirement Income Security Act of 1974 (ERISA) Sets standards for pension plan management and provides federal insurance if pension funds go bankrupt

Family and Medical Leave Act of 1993 Requires employers to provide up to twelve weeks of unpaid leave for family and medical emergencies

Labor Relations Union activities and management's behavior toward unions constitute another heavily regulated area. The **National Labor Relations Act** (also known as the *Wagner Act*), passed in 1935, sets up a procedure for employees of a firm to vote on whether to have a union. If they vote for a union, management is required to bargain collectively with the union. The **National Labor Relations Board** was established by the Wagner Act to enforce its provisions. Following a series of severe strikes in 1946, the **Labor-Management Relations Act** (also known as the *Taft-Hartley Act*) was passed in 1947 to limit union power. The law increases management's rights during an organizing campaign. The Taft-Hartley Act also contains the *National Emergency Strike* provision, which allows the president of the United States to prevent or end a strike that endangers national security. Taken together, those laws balance union and management power. Employees can be represented by a properly constituted union, but management can make nonemployee-related business decisions without interference from an employee union.

National Labor Relations Act Passed in 1935 to set up procedures for employees to vote on whether to have a union; also known as the Wagner Act

National Labor Relations Board Established by the Wagner Act to enforce its provisions

Labor-Management Relations Act Passed in 1947 to limit union power; also known as the Taft-Hartley Act

Health and Safety The **Occupational Safety and Health Act of 1970** directly mandates the provision of safe working conditions. It requires that

Occupational Safety and Health Act of 1970 Directly mandates the provision of safe working conditions

Employee safety and health have become major issues for organizations and their human resource managers. For example, Karen Vanderstoep's job at Hormel requires that she lift heavy pieces of meat and operate dangerous equipment. Note that she is wearing a hard hat, ear protectors, and a heavy apron and gloves. She also stands on a springy rubber mat to reduce fatigue and strain on her knees. These and myriad other improvements have dramatically reduced injuries at the Hormel facility.

employers (1) provide a place of employment that is free from hazards that may cause death or serious physical harm and (2) obey the safety and health standards established by the *Occupational Safety and Health Administration* (OSHA). Safety standards are intended to prevent accidents, whereas occupational health standards are concerned with preventing occupational disease. For example, standards limit the concentration of cotton dust in the air because this contaminant has been associated with lung disease in textile workers. The standards are enforced by OSHA inspections, which are conducted when an employee files a complaint of unsafe conditions or when a serious accident occurs. OSHA also performs spot inspections of plants in especially hazardous industries such as mining and chemicals. Employers who fail to meet OSHA standards may be fined.

Emerging Legal Issues   Several other areas of legal concern have emerged during the past few years. One is sexual harassment. Although sexual harassment is forbidden under Title VII, it has received additional attention in the courts recently as more and more victims have decided to publicly confront the problem. Another emerging human resource management issue is alcohol and drug abuse. Both alcoholism and drug dependence are major problems today. Recent court rulings have tended to define alcoholics and drug addicts as disabled, protecting them under the same laws that protect other handicapped people. Finally, AIDS has emerged as an important legal issue as well. AIDS victims too are most often protected under various laws protecting the disabled.[7]

■ Change and Human Resource Management

Beyond the objective legal context of HRM, various social changes are also affecting how organizations interact with their employees. First, many organizations are now using more and more temporary workers. This trend allows them to add workers as necessary without the risk that they may have to eliminate those jobs in the future. This approach also cuts labor costs because temporary workers earn no benefits and their pay is often less than the pay of permanent workers. On the other hand, temporary workers also tend to be less loyal to an organization and may lack the job-specific skills to perform at a high level. Still, the number of temporary workers continues to increase rapidly and may be as high as two million employees per day.[8]

Second, dual-career families are much more common today than just a few years ago. Organizations are finding that they must make accommodations for employees who are dual career partners. These accommodations may include delaying transfers, offering employment to the spouses of current employees to retain them, and providing more flexible work schedules and benefits packages. A related aspect of social change and HRM, workforce diversity, was covered more fully in Chapter 6.

Employment-at-will is also becoming an important issue. Although employment-at-will has legal implications, its emergence as an issue is socially driven. **Employment-at-will** is a traditional view of the workplace that says

employment-at-will   A traditional view of the workplace that says organizations can fire their employees for any reason; recent court judgments are limiting employment-at-will

organizations can fire an employee for any reason. Increasingly, however, people are arguing that organizations should be able to fire only people who are poor performers or who violate rules and, conversely, not be able to fire people who report safety violations to OSHA or refuse to perform unethical activities. Several court cases in recent years have upheld this emerging view that permits organizations to terminate employees only in cases that show clear and just cause or as part of an organization-wide cutback.

MANAGEMENT IMPLICATIONS Managers need to understand and appreciate the value of human resources as perhaps the most important determinant of an organization's success. Taking a strategic orientation to human resource management is also becoming more popular. In addition, managers must also be familiar with the various laws and related regulations that govern human resource practices. The role of change and HR must also be carefully acknowledged. ▬

Attracting Human Resources

With an understanding of the environmental context of human resource management as a foundation, we are now ready to address its first substantive concern—attracting qualified people who are interested in employment with the organization.

■ Human Resource Planning

The starting point in attracting qualified human resources is planning. HR planning, in turn, involves job analysis and forecasting the demand and supply of labor.

Job Analysis **Job analysis** is a systematic analysis of jobs within an organization. A job analysis is made up of two parts. The *job description* lists the duties of a job; the job's working conditions; and the tools, materials, and equipment used to perform it. The *job specification* lists the skills, abilities, and other credentials needed to do the job. Job analysis information is used in many human resource activities. For instance, knowing about job content and job requirements is necessary to develop appropriate selection methods and job-relevant performance appraisal systems and to set equitable compensation rates.[9]

job analysis A systematized procedure for collecting and recording information about jobs

Forecasting Human Resource Demand and Supply After managers fully understand the jobs to be performed within the organization, they can start

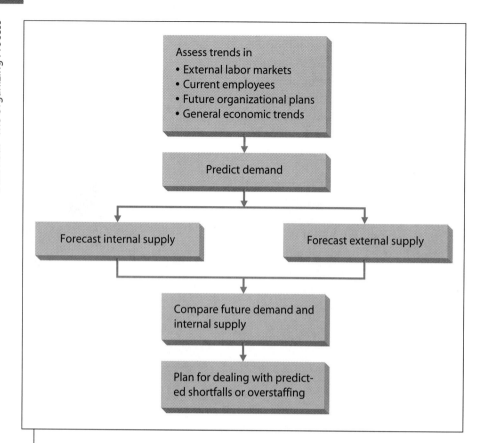

Assess trends in
• External labor markets
• Current employees
• Future organizational plans
• General economic trends

Predict demand

Forecast internal supply

Forecast external supply

Compare future demand and internal supply

Plan for dealing with predicted shortfalls or overstaffing

FIGURE 14.1
Human Resource Planning

Attracting human resources cannot be left to chance if an organization expects to function at peak efficiency. Human resource planning involves assessing trends, forecasting supply and demand of labor, and then developing appropriate strategies for addressing any differences.

replacement chart Lists each important managerial position in the organization, who occupies it, how long he or she will probably remain in the position, and who is or will be a qualified replacement

employee information system (skills inventory) Contains information on each employee's education, skills, experience, and career aspirations; usually computerized

planning for the organization's future human resource needs. Figure 14.1 summarizes the steps most often followed. The manager starts by assessing trends in past human resources usage, future organizational plans, and general economic trends. A good sales forecast is often the foundation, especially for smaller organizations. Historical ratios can then be used to predict demand for employees such as operating employees and sales representatives. Of course, large organizations use much more complicated models to predict their future human resource needs.

Forecasting the supply of labor is really two tasks: forecasting the internal supply (the number and type of employees who will be in the firm at some future date) and forecasting the external supply (the number and type of people who will be available for hiring in the labor market at large). The simplest approach merely adjusts present staffing levels for anticipated turnover and promotions. Again, though, large organizations use extremely sophisticated models to make these forecasts.

Union Oil Company of California, for example, has a complex forecasting system for keeping track of the present and future distributions of professionals and managers. The Union Oil system can spot areas where there will eventually be too many qualified professionals competing for too few promotions or, conversely, too few good people available to fill important positions.

At higher levels of the organization, managers plan for specific people and positions. The technique most commonly used is the **replacement chart**, which lists each important managerial position, who occupies it, how long he or she will probably stay in it before moving on, and who (by name) is now qualified or soon will be qualified to move into the position. This technique allows ample time to plan developmental experiences for persons identified as potential successors to critical managerial jobs. Charles Knight, CEO of Emerson Electric Co., has an entire room dedicated to posting the credentials of his top seven hundred executives.

To facilitate both planning and identifying persons for current transfer or promotion, some organizations also have an **employee information system**, or **skills inventory**. Such systems are usually computerized and contain information on each employee's education, skills, work experience, and career aspirations. Such a system can quickly locate all the employees in the organization who are qualified to fill a position requiring, for instance, a degree in chemical

Selecting the right person for a job is an important function for human resource managers. Sometimes, however, managers succeed at this function by being extra creative. For example, Mills College needed to remove some flammable brush from its Oakland campus. Hiring humans for the job would have been problematic—the brush was on a steep hillside, removing the brush would have been a challenge, and neighbors would have complained about the noise of heavy equipment. Mills' solution, shown here, was simple—instead of hiring people for the dangerous and unpleasant job, it rented a herd of goats!

engineering, three years of experience in an oil refinery, and fluency in Spanish.

Forecasting the external supply of labor is a different problem altogether. How does a manager, for example, predict how many electrical engineers will be seeking work in Georgia three years from now? To get an idea of the future availability of labor, planners must rely on information from outside sources such as state employment commissions, government reports, and figures supplied by colleges on the number of students in major fields.

Matching Human Resource Supply and Demand   After comparing future demand and internal supply, managers can make plans to manage predicted shortfalls or overstaffing. If a shortfall is predicted, new employees can be hired, present employees can be retrained and transferred into the understaffed area, individuals approaching retirement can be convinced to stay on, or labor-saving or productivity-enhancing systems can be installed.

If the organization needs to hire, the external labor supply forecast helps managers plan how to recruit, based on whether the type of person needed is readily available or scarce in the labor market. As we note earlier, the trend in temporary workers also gives staffing managers extra flexibility. If overstaffing is expected to be a problem, the main options are transferring the extra employees, not replacing individuals who quit, encouraging early retirement, and laying off people.[10]

■ Recruiting Human Resources

When an organization has an idea of its future human resource needs, the next phase is usually recruiting new employees. **Recruiting** is the process of

recruiting   The process of attracting individuals to apply for jobs that are open

Low Pay, or No Pay?

Marriott International, one of the world's largest hotel chains, is going to some unusual lengths to attract new employees. Among its recent hires, for example, are a woman severely beaten by her boyfriend, a man who did time for manslaughter, an addict who relapsed, and people evicted from homeless shelters. The company trains these people to be productive workers and then puts them to work—usually in menial, minimum-wage jobs. Why does Marriott follow this plan? One reason is that a widespread labor shortage is forcing Marriott (and many other companies) to go to great lengths to find new employees. For another, the company argues that it is providing an important social benefit by helping relatively unproductive people get off the welfare rolls and become contributing members of society. Critics, on the other hand, charge Marriott and other companies with exploiting people and seeking ways to employ as many workers as possible while paying them only the bare minimum. In addition, critics point out that

> *"If we pay wages in excess of the productive contribution of our people, we will become noncompetitive ourselves."*
>
> *J.W. Marriott Jr., CEO Marriott International, Inc.**

the U.S. government is helping to subsidize Marriott's training costs.

Marriott, for its part, also points out that it incurs extra work and costs in its efforts to rehabilitate workers. In addition to job skills, for example, the firm must also teach people the basic requirements of keeping a job—reporting to work on time, maintaining proper grooming and hygiene, and so forth. The company trainers have had to contend with fights, tardiness, and workers with so few job skills that they simply could not find a job—any job—for those individuals. All in all, then, it looks like Marriott is working in ways that benefit society. And if it gets some extra benefits along the way, is that really so bad?

References: *"Low-Wage Lessons,"* Business Week, *November 11, 1996, pp. 108–116 (*quote on p. 109); and "Hiring Welfare People, Hotel Chain Finds, Is Tough but Rewarding,"* Wall Street Journal, *October 31, 1996, pp. A1, A14.*

---

attracting qualified persons to apply for the available jobs. Where do recruits come from? Some recruits are found internally; others come from outside of the organization. "Today's Management Issues" describes one interesting, and somewhat controversial, recruiting strategy that Marriott International is using.

Internal recruiting means considering present employees as candidates for openings. Promotion from within can help build morale and keep high-quality employees from leaving the firm. In unionized firms, the procedures for notifying employees of internal job change opportunities are usually spelled out in the union contract. For higher-level positions, a skills inventory system may be used to identify internal candidates, or managers may be asked to recommend individuals who should be considered. One disadvantage of internal recruiting is its "ripple effect." When an employee moves to a different job, someone else must be found to take his or her old job. In one organization, 454 job movements were necessary as a result of filling 195 initial openings![11]

internal recruiting Considering current employees as applicants for higher-level jobs in the organization

External recruiting involves attracting persons outside the organization to apply for jobs. External recruiting methods include advertising, campus interviews, employment agencies or executive search firms, union hiring halls, referrals by present employees, and hiring "walk ins" or "gate hires" (people who show up without being solicited). Of course, a manager must select the most appropriate methods, using the state employment service to find maintenance workers, but not a nuclear physicist, for example. Private employment agencies can be a good source of clerical and technical employees, and executive search firms specialize in locating top-management talent. Newspaper ads are often used because they reach a wide audience and thus allow minorities "equal opportunity" to find out about and apply for job openings. The Internet is also becoming an important recruiting tool, as more and more companies are posting job openings on their web pages and more and more job seekers are scanning the Internet for openings.

> **external recruiting** Getting people from outside the organization to apply for jobs

The organization must also keep in mind that recruiting decisions often go both ways—the organization is recruiting an employee, but the prospective employee is also selecting a job.[12] Thus the organization wants to put its best foot forward, treat all applicants with dignity, and strive for a good person-job fit. Recent estimates suggest that hiring the "wrong" operating employee—one who flops and either quits or must be fired—generally costs the organization $5,000 in lost productivity and training. Hiring the wrong manager can cost the organization as much as $75,000.[13]

One generally successful method for facilitating a good person-job fit is through the so-called **realistic job preview (RJP)**. As the term suggests, the RJP involves providing the applicant with a real picture of performing the job. RJPs are accomplished by insuring that verbal and written descriptions of jobs are accurate, by allowing applicants to view current employees at work, and other methods.

> **realistic job preview (RJP)** Provides the applicant with a real picture of what performing the job the organization is trying to fill would be like

■ Selecting Human Resources

Once the recruiting process has attracted a pool of applicants, the next step is to select whom to hire. The intent of the selection process is to gather from applicants information that will predict their job success and then to hire the candidates likely to be most successful. "The World of Management" describes Toyota's complex—and thorough—selection process. Of course, the organization can gather information only about factors that are predictive of future performance. The process of determining the predictive value of information is called **validation.**

> **validation** Determining the extent to which a selection device is really predictive of future job performance

Two basic approaches to validation are predictive validation and content validation. *Predictive validation* involves collecting the scores of employees or applicants on the device to be validated and correlating their scores with actual job performance. A significant correlation means that the selection device is a valid predictor of job performance. *Content validation* uses logic and job analysis data to establish that the selection device measures the exact skills needed for successful job performance. The most critical part of content validation is a careful job analysis showing exactly what duties are to be per-

THE WORLD OF MANAGEMENT

Toyota Seeks the Best

When Toyota decided to open its first automobile assembly plant in the United States several years ago, the firm knew it faced real challenges in staffing the facility. In Toyota's home country, Japan, many high school students go through special training programs funded by businesses to teach them various work skills. And high school graduates not heading off to college usually enroll in apprenticeship programs to further develop their skills. Because no such programs exist in the United States, Toyota realized that it would not have as large and as talented a labor pool from which to hire as it had back home.

The firm initially had more than one hundred thousand applicants for twenty-seven hundred production jobs. Many were initially screened out because they didn't have the necessary education and/or experience. Most of the remaining applicants underwent more than fourteen hours of testing. Finalists from this pool then participated in various work simulations under the watchful eyes of Toyota managers. And after all this, only the very best were hired.

"Those exercises are pretty close to what they'll experience on the assembly line."

Mark Daugherty, Toyota assistant personnel manager*

All told, Toyota estimated that it spent over $13,000 hiring each worker for the factory.

After the plant was up and running, however, Toyota didn't slack off in its hiring rigor. Indeed, it still maintains the same high standards. For example, applicants who meet minimum education and experience qualifications are invited to the factory for a difficult twelve-hour assessment the company calls the "Day of Work." Throughout this day the applicants simulate work in various settings, meet with existing employees, and undergo detailed tests. The plant's managers try to make the work simulations as realistic as possible, and they hire only those employees who perform at the very highest levels. Does Toyota's rigorous hiring process pay off? Managers believe that it does and, as evidence, point to the fact that product quality in the United States is comparable to product quality in Japan.

References: *"Toyota Devices Grueling Workout for Job Seekers,"* USA Today, *August 11, 1997, p. 3B (*quote on 3B); and "Toyota Takes Pains, and Time, Filling Jobs at its Kentucky Plant,"* Wall Street Journal, *December 1, 1987, pp. 1, 29.*

formed. The test is then developed to measure the applicant's ability to perform those duties.

Applications   The first step in selection is usually asking the candidate to fill out an application. Applications are an efficient way to gather information about the applicant's previous work history, educational background, and other job-related demographic data. They should not contain questions about areas not related to the job such as gender, religion, or national origin. This information is generally used informally to decide whether a candidate merits further evaluation, and interviewers use applications to learn about candidates before interviewing them.

Tests   Tests of ability, skill, aptitude, or knowledge that is relevant to the particular job are usually the best predictors of job success, although tests of general intelligence or personality are occasionally useful as well. In addition to being validated, tests should be administered and scored consistently. All candidates should be given the same directions, should be allowed the same amount of time, and should experience the same testing environment (temperature, lighting, distractions).[14]

Interviews Although a popular selection device, interviews are sometimes poor predictors of job success. For example, biases inherent in the way people perceive and judge others on first meeting affect subsequent evaluations by the interviewer. Interview validity can be improved by training interviewers to be aware of potential biases and by increasing the structure of the interview. In a structured interview, questions are written in advance and all interviewers follow the same question list with each candidate they interview. This procedure introduces consistency into the interview procedure and allows the organization to validate the content of the questions.[15]

For interviewing managerial or professional candidates, a somewhat less structured approach can be used. Question areas and information-gathering objectives are still planned in advance, but the specific questions vary with the candidates' backgrounds. Trammell Crow Real Estate Investors uses a novel approach in hiring managers. Each applicant is interviewed not only by two or three managers but also by a secretary or young leasing agent. This approach provides information about how the prospective manager relates to nonmanagers.[16]

Assessment Centers Assessment centers are a popular method used to select managers and are particularly good for selecting current employees for promotion. The assessment center is a content-valid simulation of major parts of the managerial job. A typical center lasts two to three days, with groups of six to twelve persons participating in a variety of managerial exercises. Centers may also include interviews, public speaking, and standardized ability tests. Candidates are assessed by several trained observers, usually managers several levels above the job for which the candidates are being considered. Assessment centers are quite valid if properly designed and are fair to members of minority groups and women.[17] Assessment activities can be performed in a multipurpose location, such as a conference room, or in a permanent facility created specifically for these activities. AT&T pioneered the assessment center concept. For years the firm has used assessment centers to make virtually all of its selection decisions for management positions.

Other Techniques Organizations also use other selection techniques depending on the circumstances. Polygraph tests, once popular, are declining in use. On the other hand, more and more organizations are requiring that applicants in whom they are interested take physical exams. Organizations are also increasingly using drug tests, especially in situations in which drug-related performance problems could create serious safety hazards.[18] For example, applicants for jobs in a nuclear power plant would likely be tested for drug use. And some organizations today even run credit checks on prospective employees.

MANAGEMENT
IMPLICATIONS

Managers need to remember that attracting the best possible human resources is an important part of organizational effectiveness. Planning is the first step: it tells managers how many people the organization will need in the future and the array of skills those people will need to possess. Recruiting a pool of qualified applicants and then using the optimal combination of selection techniques to hire the best applicants can significantly affect the success of the organization. ▬

Developing Human Resources

Regardless of how effective a selection system is, however, most employees need additional training if they are to grow and develop in their jobs. Evaluating their performance and providing feedback are also necessary.

■ Training and Development

training Teaching operational or technical employees how to do the job for which they were hired

development Teaching managers and professionals the skills needed for both present and future jobs

In HRM, **training** usually refers to teaching operational or technical employees how to do the job for which they were hired. **Development** refers to teaching managers and professionals the skills needed for both present and future jobs. Most organizations provide regular training and development programs for managers and employees.[19] For example, IBM spends more than $700 million annually on training programs and has a vice president in charge of employee education. U.S. businesses spend more than $30 billion annually on training and development programs away from the workplace. And this figure doesn't include wages and benefits paid to employees while they are participating in such programs.[20]

Assessing Training Needs The first step in developing a training plan is to determine what needs exist. For example, if employees do not know how to operate the machinery necessary to do their jobs, a training program on how to operate the machinery is clearly needed. On the other hand, when a group of office workers is performing poorly, training may not be the answer. The problem could be motivation, aging equipment, poor supervision, inefficient work design, or a deficiency of skills and knowledge. Only the last factor can be remedied by training. As training programs are being developed, the manager should set specific and measurable goals specifying what participants are to learn. Managers should also plan to evaluate the training program after employees complete it. Figure 14.2 diagrams the training process from start to finish.

Common Training Methods Selecting a training method depends on many factors, but perhaps the most important is training content. When the training content is factual material (such as company rules or explanations of how to fill out forms), assigned reading, programmed learning, and lecture methods work

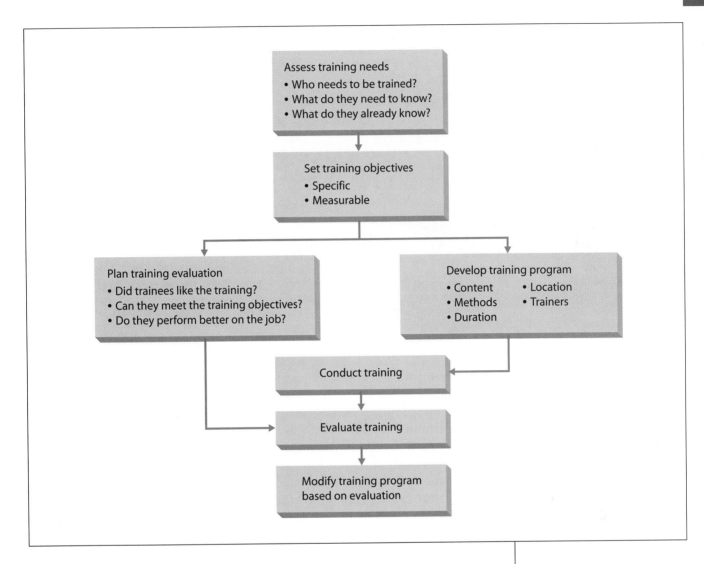

FIGURE 14.2
The Training Process

Managing the training process can go a long way toward enhancing its effectiveness. If training programs are well conceived and well executed, both the organization and its employees benefit. Following a comprehensive process helps managers meet the objectives of the training program.

well. When the content is interpersonal relations or group decision making, however, firms must use a method that allows interpersonal contact such as role-playing or case discussion groups. When employees must learn a physical skill, methods allowing practice and the actual use of tools and material are needed, as in on-the-job training or vestibule training. (*Vestibule training* enables participants to focus on safety, learning, and feedback, rather than on productivity.) CD-ROM-based training is also becoming popular. Xerox, Massachusetts Mutual Life Insurance, and Ford have all reported tremendous success with this method.[21] Most training programs actually rely on a mix of methods. Boeing, for example, sends managers to an intensive two-week training seminar involving tests, simulations, role-playing exercises, and CD-ROM flight simulation exercises.[22]

Evaluation of Training   Training and development programs should always be evaluated. Typical evaluation approaches include measuring one or more relevant criteria (such as attitudes or performance) before and after the

training and determining whether the criteria changed. Evaluation measures collected at the end of training are easy to get, but actual performance measures collected when the trainee is on the job are more important. Trainees may say that they enjoyed the training and learned a lot, but the true test is whether their job performance improves after training.

■ Performance Appraisal

When employees are trained and settled into their jobs, one of management's next concerns is performance appraisal. **Performance appraisal** is a formal assessment of how well employees are doing their job. Employees' performance should be evaluated regularly for many reasons. One reason is that performance appraisal may be necessary for validating selection devices or assessing the impact of training programs. A second reason is administrative—to aid in making decisions about pay raises, promotions, and training. Still another reason is to provide feedback to employees to help them improve their perform-ance and plan future careers.

Because performance evaluations often help determine wages and promotions, they must be fair and nondiscriminatory. In the case of appraisals, content validation is used to show that the appraisal system accurately measures performance on important job elements and does not measure traits or behavior that are irrelevant to job performance.

Training and developing people is an important part of human resource management. Canon, for example, invests heavily in training its employees as part of its goal to remain a leading manufacturer of photography equipment. One of its biggest problems has been trying to balance the trend toward moving production to cheaper labor markets while maintaining high performance levels. One tactic Canon uses is to send its newly hired Malaysian workers to one of its plants in Japan for training. After these workers have gained proficiency, they are sent back to Malaysia to work in Canon's factory there.

performance appraisal   A formal assessment of how well an employee is doing his or her job

Common Appraisal Methods   Two basic categories of appraisal methods commonly used in organizations are objective methods and judgmental methods. Objective measures of performance include actual output (that is, number of units produced), scrap rate (such as materials wasted or defective items produced), dollar volume of sales, and number of claims processed. Objective performance measures may be contaminated by "opportunity bias" if some workers have a better chance to perform than others. For example, a sales representative has a greater opportunity to sell snow blowers in Michigan than does a colleague selling the same product in Florida. Fortunately, adjusting raw performance figures for the effect of opportunity bias and thereby arriving at figures that accurately represent each individual's performance is often possible.

Another type of objective measure, the special performance test, assesses each employee under standardized conditions. This kind of appraisal also eliminates opportunity bias. For example, GTE Southwest Inc. has a series of prerecorded calls that operators in a test booth answer. The operators are graded on speed, accuracy, and courtesy in handling the calls. Performance tests measure ability, but do not measure the extent to which someone is motivated to use that ability on a daily basis. (A high-ability person may be a lazy performer except when being tested.) Special performance tests must therefore be supplemented by other appraisal methods to provide a complete picture of performance.

Judgmental methods, including ranking and rating techniques, are the most common way to measure performance. Ranking compares employees directly with each other and orders them from best to worst. Ranking has a number of drawbacks. Ranking is difficult for large groups because the people in the middle of the distribution may be hard to distinguish from one another accurately. Comparisons of people in different work groups are also difficult. For example, an employee ranked third in a strong group may be more valuable than an employee ranked first in a weak group. Another criticism of ranking is that the manager must rank people on the basis of overall performance, although each person is likely to have both strengths and weaknesses. Furthermore, rankings do not provide useful information for feedback. To be told that you are ranked third is not nearly as helpful as being told that the quality of your work is outstanding, its quantity is satisfactory, your punctuality could use improvement, and your paperwork is seriously deficient.

Rating differs from *ranking* in that rating compares each employee with a fixed standard, rather than with other employees. A rating scale provides the standard. Figure 14.3 gives examples of three graphic rating scales for a bank teller. Each consists of a performance dimension to be rated (punctuality, congeniality, and accuracy) followed by a scale on which to make the rating. In constructing graphic rating scales, HR managers must select performance dimensions that are relevant to job performance. In particular, they should focus on job behaviors and results, rather than on personality traits or attitudes.

The **Behaviorally Anchored Rating Scale (BARS)** is a sophisticated and useful rating method. Supervisors construct rating scales with associated behavioral anchors. They first identify relevant performance dimensions and then generate

Behaviorally Anchored Rating Scale (BARS) A sophisticated rating method in which supervisors construct a rating scale associated with behavioral anchors

FIGURE 14.3
Graphic Rating Scales for a Bank Teller

Graphic rating scales are a very common method for evaluating employee performance. The manager who is doing the rating circles the point on each scale that best reflects her or his assessment of the employee on that scale. Graphic rating scales are widely used for many different kinds of jobs.

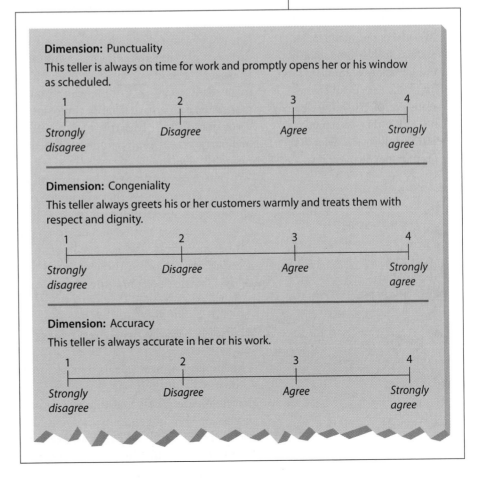

Dimension: Punctuality
This teller is always on time for work and promptly opens her or his window as scheduled.

1	2	3	4
Strongly disagree	Disagree	Agree	Strongly agree

Dimension: Congeniality
This teller always greets his or her customers warmly and treats them with respect and dignity.

1	2	3	4
Strongly disagree	Disagree	Agree	Strongly agree

Dimension: Accuracy
This teller is always accurate in her or his work.

1	2	3	4
Strongly disagree	Disagree	Agree	Strongly agree

Job: Specialty store manager
Dimension: Inventory control

7 — Always orders in the right quantities and at the right time

6 — Almost always orders at the right time but occasionally orders too much or too little of a particular item

5 — Usually orders at the right time and almost always in the right quantities

4 — Often orders in the right quantities and at the right time

3 — Occasionally orders at the right time but usually not in the right quantities

2 — Occasionally orders in the right quantities but usually not at the right time

1 — Never orders in the right quantities or at the right time

FIGURE 14.4
Behaviorally Anchored Rating Scale

Behaviorally anchored rating scales help overcome some of the limitations of standard rating scales. Each point on the scale is accompanied by a behavioral anchor—a summary of an employee behavior that fits that spot on the scale.

anchors—specific, observable behaviors typical of each performance level. Figure 14.4 shows an example of a behaviorally anchored rating scale for the dimension "inventory control."

The other scales in this set, developed for the job of department manager in a chain of specialty stores, include handling customer complaints, planning special promotions, following company procedures, supervising sales personnel, and diagnosing and solving special problems. BARS can be effective because it requires that management take proper care in constructing the scales and it provides useful anchors for supervisors to use in evaluating people. It is costly, however, because outside expertise is usually needed and because scales must be developed for each job within the organization.

Errors in Performance Appraisal   Errors or biases can occur in any kind of rating or ranking system. One common problem is *recency error*—the tendency to base judgments on the subordinate's most recent performance because it is most easily recalled. Often a rating or ranking is intended to evaluate performance over an entire time period, such as six months or a year, so the recency error does introduce error into the judgment. Other errors include overuse of one part of the scale—being too lenient, being too severe, or giving everyone a rating of "average."

Halo error is allowing the assessment of an employee on one dimension to "spread" to ratings of that employee on other dimensions. For instance, if an employee is outstanding on quality of output, a rater might tend to give that employee higher marks than deserved on other dimensions. Errors can also occur because of race, sex, or age discrimination, intentionally or unintentionally. The best way to offset these errors is to ensure that a valid rating system is developed at the outset and then to train managers in its use.

■ Performance Feedback

The last step in most performance appraisal systems is giving feedback to subordinates about their performance. The feedback interview usually occurs in a private meeting between the person being evaluated and his or her boss. The discussion should generally be focused on the facts—the assessed level of performance, how and why that assessment was made, and how performance can be improved in the future. Feedback interviews are not easy to conduct. Many managers are uncomfortable with the task, especially if the feedback is negative and subordinates are disappointed with the appraisal. Properly training managers, however, can help these managers conduct more effective feedback interviews.[23]

A recent innovation in performance appraisal is called "360 degree" feedback: managers are evaluated by everyone around them—their boss, their peers, and their subordinates. Such a complete and thorough approach provides people with a far richer array of information about their performance than does a conventional boss-to-employee appraisal. Of course, such a system also takes considerable time and must be handled to not breed fear and mistrust in the workplace.[24]

MANAGEMENT IMPLICATIONS Managers need to remember that even though they may hire outstanding applicants as employees, it is still usually necessary to develop their skills through training and development. Moreover, managers must also understand the purpose and techniques of performance appraisal. Especially important, in addition, is providing performance feedback to employees after appraisals have been conducted. ▬

Maintaining Human Resources

After organizations have attracted and developed an effective workforce, they must also make every effort to maintain that workforce. To do so requires effective compensation and benefits as well as career planning.

■ Determining Compensation

Compensation is the financial remuneration the organization gives to its employees in exchange for their work. There are three basic forms of compensation. *Wages* are the hourly compensation paid to operating employees. The minimum hourly wage paid in the United States in 1997 was $5.15. *Salary* refers to compensation paid for total contributions, as opposed to being based on hours worked. For example, managers earn an annual salary, usually paid monthly. They receive the salary regardless of the number of hours they work. Some firms have started paying all their employees a salary, instead of hourly wages. For example, all entry-level operating employees at Chaparral Steel Company earn a salary, starting at $18,000 a year. Finally, *incentives* represent special compensation opportunities that are usually tied to performance. Sales commissions and bonuses are among the most common incentives.

Compensation is an important and complex part of the organization-employee relationship. Basic compensation is necessary to provide employees with the means to maintain a reasonable standard of living. Beyond this, how-

compensation The financial remuneration given by the organization to its employees in exchange for their work

ever, compensation also provides a tangible measure of the value of the individual to the organization. If employees do not earn enough to meet their basic economic goals, they will seek employment elsewhere. Likewise, if they believe that their contributions are undervalued by the organization, they may leave or exhibit poor work habits, low morale, and little commitment to the organization. Thus designing an effective compensation system is clearly in the organization's best interests.[25]

A good compensation system can help attract qualified applicants, retain present employees, and stimulate high performance at a cost reasonable for the industry and geographic area. To set up a successful system, management must make decisions about wage levels, the wage structure, and the individual wage determination system.

Wage-Level Decision The wage-level decision is a management policy decision about whether the firm wants to pay above, at, or below the going rate for labor in the industry or the geographic area.[26] Most firms choose to pay near the average. Those that cannot afford more pay below average. Large, successful firms may try to cultivate the image of being "wage leaders" by intentionally paying more than average and thus attracting and keeping high-quality employees. IBM, for example, pays top dollar to get the new employees it wants. As noted in this chapter's Opening Incident, Cisco Systems also uses this approach. McDonald's, on the other hand, often pays close to the minimum wage. The level of unemployment in the labor force also affects wage levels. Pay declines when labor is plentiful and increases when labor is scarce.

After managers make the wage-level decision, they need information to help set actual wage rates. Managers need to know what the maximum, minimum, and average wages are for particular jobs in the appropriate labor market. This information is collected by means of a wage survey. Area wage surveys can be conducted by individual firms or by local HR or business associations. Professional and industry associations often conduct surveys and make the results available to employers.

job evaluation An attempt to assess the worth of each job relative to other jobs

benefits Things of value other than compensation that an organization provides to its workers

Wage-Structure Decision Wage structures are usually set up through a procedure called **job evaluation**—an attempt to assess the worth of each job relative to other jobs.[27] At Ben & Jerry's Homemade Inc., company policy dictates that the highest-paid employee in the firm cannot earn more than seven times what the lowest-paid employee earns. The simplest method for creating a wage structure is to rank jobs from those that should be paid the most (for example, the president) to those that should be paid the least (for example, a mail clerk or a janitor).

In a smaller firm with few jobs (like Ben & Jerry's, for example), this method is quick and practical, but larger firms with many job titles require more sophisticated methods. The next step is setting actual wage rates on the basis of a combination of survey data and the wage structure that results from job evaluation. Jobs of equal value are often grouped into wage grades for ease of administration.

Individual Wage Decisions After wage-level and wage-structure decisions are made, the individual wage decision must be addressed. This decision concerns how much to pay each employee in a particular job. Although the easiest decision is to pay a single rate for each job, more typically a range of pay rates is associated with each job. For example, the pay range for an individual job might be $5.85 to $6.39 per hour, with different employees earning different rates within the range.

A system is then needed for setting individual rates. Individual rates may be set on the basis of seniority (enter the job at $6.85, for example, and increase ten cents per hour every six months on the job), initial qualifications (inexperienced people start at $6.85; more experienced workers start at a higher rate), or merit (raises above the entering rate are given for good performance). Combinations of these methods may also be used.

■ Determining Benefits

Benefits are things of value other than compensation that the organization provides to its workers. The average company spends an amount equal to more than one-third of its cash payroll on employee benefits. Thus, an employee who earns $18,000 per year averages about $6,588 more per year in benefits.

Benefits come in several forms. Pay for time not worked includes sick leave, vacation, holidays, and unemployment compensation. Insurance benefits often include life and health insurance for employees and their dependents. Workers' compensation is a legally required insurance benefit that provides medical care and disability income for employees injured on the job. Social security is a government pension plan to which both employers and employees contribute. Many employers also provide a private pension plan to which they and their employees contribute. Employee service benefits may also include items such as tuition reimbursement and recreational opportunities.

Some organizations have instituted "cafeteria benefit plans," whereby basic coverage is provided for all employees but employees are then allowed to choose which additional benefits they want (up to a cost limit based on salary). An employee with five children might choose medical and dental coverage for dependents, a single employee might prefer more vacation time, and an older employee might elect increased pension benefits. Flexible systems are expected to encourage people to stay in the organization and even help the company attract new employees.[28]

Human resource managers must develop effective and equitable compensation strategies if they want to attract and retain good employees. Marriott has an innovative program it calls Marriott Pathways, created to help get people off welfare and into productive jobs. Michael Bradford, for example, spent much of his life on welfare, and served a short stint in prison. But after completing Pathways, he now works for a Marriott hotel where he earns $7.60 an hour and has full benefits such as health insurance. HR managers at the company have pegged this compensation to be cost-effective for Marriott while also being fair for the person doing the job.

WORKING WITH DIVERSITY

Trends in Domestic Partner Benefits

For decades most larger companies have offered their employees an array of benefits ranging from vacation time to sick leave to group insurance coverage. Traditionally, benefits such as insurance have been extended to the employee's immediate family as well. But *family* has been defined as the employee's husband or wife and their children.

In recent years, however, many companies have redefined the term *family* to encompass unmarried, gay, and/or lesbian couples as well. Several factors have prompted this trend. One is simply an awareness on the part of some managers that this practice is fair and just in today's world. Other companies have taken this step in order to remain competitive in the labor market. For example, although Disney received a lot of publicity when it extended benefits to domestic partners, the firm was actually only re-

"It's not an avalanche of companies, but we're seeing improvement, and much of it has come in the last year to 18 months."

Liz Winfield, author and consultant*

sponding to similar moves by Universal, Paramount, Sony, and Warner Bros. For other employers, extending benefits to domestic partners is a legal requirement. For example, the city of San Francisco mandates this practice to all companies that do business with the city.

How widespread has this practice become? One recent survey suggests that about 10 percent of the businesses in the United States offer benefit coverage to same-sex and/or opposite-sex partners. Of the ones that don't, most cited cost as the biggest reason for not extending benefit coverage to domestic partners. Meanwhile, 20 percent objected on the basis of moral concerns.

References: *"One in 10 Firms Extend Benefits to Life Partners,"* USA Today, *January 24, 1997, p. A1 (*quote on p. A1); and "Domestic Partner Benefits on Rise,"* USA Today, *October 14, 1997, p. 8B.*

In recent years companies have also started offering even more innovative benefits as a way of accommodating different needs. On-site childcare, mortgage assistance, and generous paid leave programs are becoming popular.[29] "Working with Diversity" discusses another interesting trend in benefits. At the same time, however, J. C. Penney, Chrysler, Allied-Signal, Genentech, and other companies have started eliminating some benefits because of the escalating cost of insurance.[30] Of course, eliminating benefits can create resentment among employees.

A good benefits plan may encourage people to join and stay with an organization, but it seldom stimulates high performance because benefits are tied more to membership in the organization than to performance. To manage their benefits programs effectively, companies should shop carefully, avoid redundant coverage, and provide only those benefits that employees want. Benefits programs should also be explained to employees in clear and straightforward language so that they can use the benefits appropriately and appreciate what the company is providing.

"Your thirty-five years of hard work, sacrifice, and devotion
to duty won't go unrewarded, Erickson —
go ahead and pick a duck."

Organizations offer a wide array of compensation and benefits to their employees. Many also provide extra incentives for key employees who remain with the company for an extended time. Longevity pay, for example, is used in some settings, while other organizations reward their more senior employees with pins, plaques, watches, or even cash bonuses. But as illustrated in this cartoon, such rewards are meaningful and effective only if they provide something of real value to the employee. Trivial or meaningless tokens or rewards can even backfire, causing employees to feel unappreciated.

■ Career Planning

A final aspect of maintaining human resources is career planning. Few people work in the same jobs for their entire career. Some people change jobs within one organization, others change organizations, and many do both. When these movements are haphazard and poorly conceived, both the individual and the organization suffer. Thus planning career progressions in advance is in everyone's best interest.[31] Of course, planing a thirty-year career for a newcomer just joining the organization is difficult. But planning can help map out what areas the individual is most interested in and help the person see what opportunities are available within the organization.

MANAGEMENT IMPLICATIONS Managers should recognize the critical importance of compensation and benefits. On the one hand, these represent significant costs for the organization and should therefore be carefully monitored and controlled. On the other hand, compensation and benefits are also tangible indicators to the employee of his or her value to the organization and so should be fair and equitable. Career planning is also something all managers should consider for both themselves and their employees. ■

labor relations The process of dealing with employees when they are represented by a union

Managing Labor Relations

Labor relations is the process of dealing with employees who are represented by a union.[32] Managing labor relations is an important part of HRM.

collective bargaining The process of agreeing on a satisfactory labor contract between management and a union

Managing labor relations is a complex and challenging job. Dating back to the pioneering efforts of Cesar Chavez, for example, labor relations among migrant farm workers in California remains a contentious issue for workers and employers alike. The United Farm Workers Union is actively working to improve the working conditions of these strawberry pickers in Ventura County. The workers receive relatively low wages and have little job security. But local farmers who hire the migrant workers argue that their profit margins are already razor-thin and that they face just as much uncertainty as the workers.

■ How Employees Form Unions

For employees to form a new local union, several things must occur. First, employees must become interested in having a union. Nonemployees who are professional organizers employed by a national union (such as the Teamsters or United Auto Workers) may generate interest by making speeches and distributing literature outside the workplace. Inside, employees who want a union try to convince other workers of the benefits of a union.

The second step is to collect employees' signatures on authorization cards. These cards state that the signer wishes to vote to determine whether the union will represent him or her. Thirty percent of the employees in the potential bargaining unit must sign these cards to show the National Labor Relations Board (NLRB) that interest is sufficient to justify holding an election. Before an election can be held, however, the bargaining unit must be defined. The bargaining unit consists of all employees who will be eligible to vote in the election and to join and be represented by the union if one is formed.

The election is supervised by an NLRB representative (or if both parties agree, by the American Arbitration Association—a professional association of arbitrators) and is conducted by secret ballot. If a simple majority of those voting (not of all those eligible to vote) vote for the union, then the union becomes certified as the official representative of the bargaining unit.[33] The new union then organizes itself by officially signing up members and electing officers; it will soon be ready to negotiate the first contract. The union-organizing process is diagrammed in Figure 14.5. If workers become disgruntled with their union, or if management presents strong evidence that the union is not representing workers appropriately, the NLRB can arrange a decertification election. The results of such an election determine whether the union remains certified.

Organizations usually prefer that employees not be unionized, because unions limit management's freedom in many areas. Management may thus wage its own campaign to convince employees to vote against the union. "Unfair labor practices" are often committed at this point. For instance, it is an unfair labor practice for management to promise to give employees a raise (or any other benefit) if the union is defeated. Experts agree that the best way to avoid unionization is to practice good employee relations all the time—not just when threatened by a union election. Providing absolutely fair treatment with clear standards in the areas of pay, promotion, layoff, and discipline; having a complaint or appeal system for persons who feel unfairly treated; and avoiding any kind of favoritism will help make employees feel that a union is unnecessary.

■ Collective Bargaining

The intent of **collective bargaining** is to agree on a labor contract between management and the union that is satisfactory to both parties. The contract contains agreements such as wages, hours, about conditions of employment promotion, layoff, discipline, benefits, methods of allocating overtime, vacations, rest periods, and the grievance procedure. The process of bargaining may go on for weeks, months, or longer, with representatives of management and the union meeting to make proposals and counterproposals. The resulting agreement must be ratified by the union membership. If it is not approved, the union may strike to put pressure on management or may choose not to strike and simply continue negotiating until a more acceptable agreement is reached.

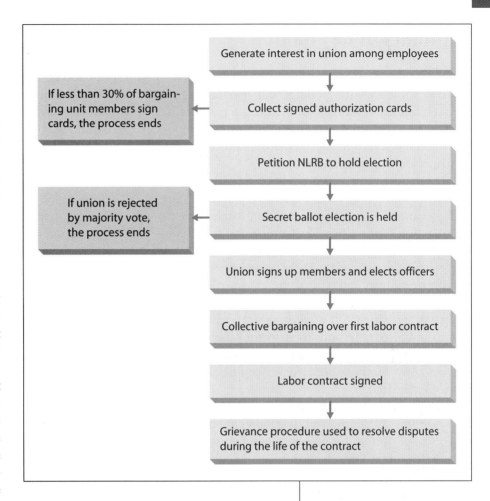

The **grievance procedure** is the means by which the contract is enforced. Most provisions in a contract concern how management will treat employees. When employees believe that they have not been treated fairly under the contract, they file a grievance to correct the problem. The first step in a grievance procedure is for the aggrieved employee to discuss the alleged contract violation with her immediate superior. Often the grievance is resolved at this stage. If the employee still believes that she is being mistreated, however, the grievance can be appealed to the next level. A union official can help an aggrieved employee present her case. If the manager's decision is also unsatisfactory to the employee, additional appeals to successively higher levels are made, until finally all in-company steps are exhausted. The final step is to submit the grievance to binding arbitration. An arbitrator is a labor-law expert who is paid jointly by the union and management. The arbitrator studies the contract, hears both sides of the case, and renders a decision that both parties must obey. The grievance system for resolving disputes about contract enforcement prevents any need to strike during the term of the contract.[34]

FIGURE 14.5
The Union-Organizing Process

If employees of an organization want to form a union, the law prescribes a specific set of procedures that both employees and the organization must follow. Assuming that these procedures are followed and the union is approved, the organization must engage in collective bargaining with the new union.

grievance procedure The means by which a labor contract is enforced

---

MANAGEMENT
IMPLICATIONS

Labor relations are important in human resource management. Managers must understand the legal and procedural elements of unionization, the process of collective bargaining, and the importance of a grievance system. ■

Summary of Key Points

Human resource management is concerned with attracting, developing, and maintaining the human resources an organization needs. Its environmental context consists of its strategic importance and the legal and social environments that affect human resource management.

Attracting human resources is an important part of the HRM function. Human resource planning starts with job analysis and then focuses on forecasting the organization's future need for employees, forecasting the availability of employees both within and outside the organization, and planning programs to ensure that the proper number and type of employees will be available when needed. Recruitment and selection are the processes by which job applicants are attracted, assessed, and hired. Methods for selecting applicants include applications, tests, interviews, and assessment centers. Any method used for selection should be properly validated.

Organizations must also work to develop their human resources. Training and development enable employees to perform their present jobs effectively and to prepare for future jobs. Performance appraisals are im-

portant for validating selection devices, assessing the impact of training programs, deciding on pay raises and promotions, and determining training needs. Both objective and judgmental methods of appraisal can be applied, and a good system usually includes several methods. The validity of appraisal information is always a concern because accurately evaluating the many aspects of a person's job performance is difficult.

Maintaining human resources is also important. Compensation rates must be fair compared with rates for other jobs within the organization and with rates for the same or similar jobs in other organizations in the labor market. Properly designed incentive or merit pay systems can encourage high performance, and a good benefits program can help attract and retain employees. Career planning is also a major aspect of human resource management.

If a majority of a company's nonmanagement employees so desire, they have the right to be represented by a union. Management must engage in collective bargaining with the union in an effort to agree on a contract. While the contract is in effect, the grievance system is used to settle disputes with management.

Discussion Questions

Questions for Review

1. What is job analysis and how is it related to human resource planning?

2. Describe recruiting and selection. What are the major sources for recruits? What are the common selection methods?

3. What is the role of compensation and benefits in organizations? How should the amount of compensation and benefits be determined?

4. What basic steps can employees follow if they wish to unionize?

Questions for Analysis

5. What are the advantages and disadvantages of internal and external recruiting? Which method do

you feel is best in the long term? Why? Be sure to think about this issue from the standpoint of both the organization and individuals (whether inside or outside of the organization) who might be considered for positions.

6. How do you know whether a selection device is valid? What are the possible consequences of using invalid selection methods? How can an organization ensure that its selection methods are valid?

7. Are benefits more important than compensation to an organization? To an individual? Why?

Questions for Application

8. Write a description and specifications for a job that you have held (office worker, checkout clerk, salesperson, lifeguard). Then contact a company with

such a job and obtain an actual description and specification from that firm. In what ways are your description and specification like theirs? In what ways are they different?

9. Contact a local organization to determine how it evaluates the performance of employees in complex jobs such as middle or higher-level manager, scientist, lawyer, or market researcher. What problems with performance appraisal can you note?

10. Interview someone who is or has been a member of a union to determine his or her reasons for joining. Would you join a union? Why or why not?

Building Effective Technical Skills

EXERCISE OVERVIEW

Technical skills refer to the manager's abilities to accomplish or understand work done in an organization. Many managers must have technical skills to hire appropriate people to work in the organization. This exercise will help you use technical skills as part of the selection process.

EXERCISE BACKGROUND

Variation one: If you currently work full-time, or have worked full-time in the past, select two jobs with which you have some familiarity. Select one job that is relatively low in skill level, responsibility, required education, and pay and one job that is relatively high in skill level, responsibility, required education, and pay. The exercise will be more useful to you if you use real jobs that you can relate to at a personal level.

Variation two: If you have never worked full-time, or if you are not personally familiar with an array of jobs, assume that you are a manager for a small manufacturing facility. You need to hire individuals to fill two jobs. One job is for the position of plant custodian. This individual will sweep floors, clean bathrooms, empty trash cans, and so forth. The other person will be office manager. This individual will supervise a staff of three clerks and secretaries, administer the plant payroll, and coordinate the administrative operations of the plan.

EXERCISE TASK

With the preceding information as background, do the following:

1. Identify the most basic skills that you think are necessary for someone to perform each job effectively.

2. Identify the general indicators or predictors of whether or not a given individual can perform each job.

3. Develop a brief set of interview questions that you might use to determine whether or not an applicant has the qualifications to perform each job.

4. How important is it that a manager hiring employees to perform a job have the technical skills to do that job him- or herself?

Building Effective Communication Skills

EXERCISE OVERVIEW

All managers must be able to communicate effectively with others in the organization. Communication is especially important in the human resource area, since people are the domain of human resource management.

EXERCISE BACKGROUND

Many companies provide various benefits to their workers. These benefits may include pay for time not worked, insurance coverage, pension and retirement savings plans, and so forth, and are often very costly to the organization. As noted in the text, for example, benefits often equal around one-third of what employees are paid in wages and salaries. In some countries, such as Germany, the figures are even higher.

Yet many employees often fail to appreciate the actual value of the benefits their employers provide for them. For example, employees frequently underestimate the dollar value of their benefits. And when comparing their income to that of others or when comparing alternative job offers, many people focus almost entirely on direct compensation—wages and salaries directly paid to the individual.

For example, consider a college graduate who has two offers. One job offer is for $20,000 a year, and the other is for $22,000. The individual is likely to see the second offer as being more attractive, even if the first offer has sufficiently more attractive benefits to make the total compensation packages equivalent.

EXERCISE TASK

With this information as context, respond to the following:

1. Why do you think most people focus on pay when assessing their compensation?

2. If you were the human resource manager for a firm, how would you communicate benefit value to your employees?

3. Suppose an employee tells you that he is thinking about leaving for a "better job." You then learn that he is defining "better" only in terms of higher pay. How might you help him compare total compensation (including benefits)?

4. Some firms today are cutting their benefits. How would you communicate a benefit cut to your employees?

Building Effective Decision-Making Skills

EXERCISE OVERVIEW

Decision-making skills include the manager's ability to correctly recognize and define problems and opportunities and to then select an appropriate course of action to solve problems and capitalize on opportunities. This exercise will help you develop decision-making skills by applying them to a human resource problem. Managers must frequently select one or more employees for termination, layoffs, special recognition, training, or promotion. Each such selection represents a decision.

EXERCISE TASK

Your company recently developed a plan to identify and train top hourly employees for promotion to first-line supervisor. As part of this program, your boss has requested a ranking of the six hourly employees who report to you with respect to their promotion potential. Given their biographical data, rank them in the order in which you would select them for promotion to first-line supervisor; that is, the person ranked number one would be first in line for promotion. Repeat this process in a group with three or four of your classmates.

Biographical Data

1. *Sam Nelson:* White male, age forty-five, married, with four children. Sam has been with the company for five years, and his performance evaluations have been average to above average. He is well liked by the other employees in the department. He devotes his spare time to farming and plans to farm after retirement.

2. *Ruth Hornsby:* White female, age thirty-two, married, with no children; husband has a management-level job with a power company. Ruth has been with the company for two years and has received above-average performance evaluations. She is very quiet and keeps to herself at work. She says she is working to save for a down payment on a new house.

3. *Joe Washington:* Black male, age twenty-six, single. Joe has been with the company for three years and has received high performance evaluations. He is always willing to take on new assignments and to work overtime. He is attending college in the evenings and someday wants to start his own business. He is well liked by the other employees in the department.

4. *Ronald Smith:* White male, age thirty-five, recently divorced, with one child, age four. Ronald has received excellent performance evaluations during his two years with the company. He seems to like his present job but has removed himself from the line of progression. He seems to have personality conflicts with some of the employees in the department.

5. *Betty Norris:* Black female, age forty-four, married, with one grown child. Betty has been with the company for ten years and is well liked by fellow employees. Her performance evaluations have been average to below-average, and her advancement has been limited by a lack of formal education. She has participated in a number of technical training programs conducted by the company.

6. *Roy Davis:* White male, age thirty-six, married, with two teenage children. Roy has been with the company for ten years and has received excellent performance evaluations until last year. His most recent evaluation was average. He is friendly and well liked by his fellow employees. One of his children has had a serious illness for over a year, resulting in a number of large medical expenses. Roy is working a second job on weekends to help with these expenses. He has expressed a serious interest in promotion to first-line supervisor.

Source: From *Supervisory Management: The Art of Working With and Through People*, 3/e, by Donald C. Mosley, Leon C. Megginson, and Paul H. Pietri, Jr. Copyright 1993. Used by permission of South-Western College Publishing, a division of International Thomson Publishing, Inc., Cincinnati, Ohio 45227.

CHAPTER CLOSING CASE

The Labor Standoff at UPS

T he ubiquitous brown trucks that constitute the fleet of United Parcel Service, or UPS, have become a common scene on the U.S. landscape. The huge parcel delivery service has dominated its industry for years, moving millions of packages every day of the year. One key ingredient to UPS's long-standing success has been a strong and loyal relationship with its employees. The firm has a history of promoting from within, paying well, and treating its employees fairly and justly. Even though the firm's drivers have long been organized by the Teamsters Union, labor relations have been generally calm and amicable.

But all that changed in 1997 when UPS drivers walked out on strike, bringing the company to its knees and allowing UPS competitors like Federal Express and the U.S. Postal Service to seize market share that would be hard for UPS to recapture. The story of what prompted the strike and how it ended provides useful and interesting insights into an array of human resource management practices and issues.

The wedge between UPS and the Teamsters was created by two fundamental issues. One was the firm's growing reliance on part-time workers. UPS had started using more and more part-time workers, often replacing a retired employee with two or more part-timers. This practice gave the firm greater staffing flexibility and held down wage and benefits costs. For example, its full-time employees earned $19.95 an hour, whereas part-timers received half that amount. The Teamsters, meanwhile, argued that this hiring practice was actually intended to undercut the job security of the firm's full-time employees and weaken the power of the union itself. At the time of the strike, UPS employed 105,000 part-time workers.

The other issue related to the firm's pension plan. At the time of the strike, the Teamsters had managed to create a "standard" pension plan for several larger companies whose employees the union represented. UPS, meanwhile, wanted to pull out of the multi-employer plan and create its own plan just for UPS workers. UPS argued that it could provide a comparable plan at a lower price, whereas the union argued that the company was taking the first step toward a reduced plan for retired employees.

The two sides bargained extensively for months, and nearly reached an agreement on several different occasions. But one or another problem also came up, and the two sides eventually became more and more antagonistic. Finally, UPS workers went out on strike on August 3, 1997. The strike had immediate and dramatic effects, not only on UPS but all across the country. The firm tried to maintain operations with managers and nonunion employees, but could handle only about 5 percent of the volume. And other companies—especially small ones—complained long and loudly that the strike was putting them out of business. President Clinton considered intervening, but eventually decided to stay out of the fray.

Meanwhile, much to the firm's dismay, surveys found dramatic public support for the striking workers. In addition, many long-standing and loyal customers were transferring their business to other carriers. Finally, two weeks after the strike started, UPS essentially threw in the towel and the striking workers went back to work. Among the concessions the firm made were an agreement to convert ten thousand part-time jobs to full-time at double the pay; to drop plans to pull out of the Teamsters multi-employer pension plan; and to boost employee pay over a five-year period by an average of 15 percent for full-time employees and 35 percent for part-timers. The Teamsters, meanwhile, agreed to a five-year contract instead of their preferred three-year deal.

But even after the striking workers returned to work, UPS faced an uphill battle. For one thing, its public image had been irreparably tarnished. For another, it had lost 10 percent of its market share, and those customers who had switched showed no indication of returning to a firm that some felt had betrayed them. And finally, managers had to figure out how to cover more than $1 billion in additional costs the new contract would add to the company's income statement.

Case Questions

1. Identify as many human resource issues as possible in this case.
2. How might the UPS strike have been averted? Which side "won" the strike? Why?
3. Are strikes always bad? Under what circumstances might a strike be beneficial to a company?

Case References: "A Wake-up Call for Business," *Business Week*, September 1, 1997, pp. 28–29; "This Package Is a Heavy One for the Teamsters," *Business Week*, August 25, 1997, pp. 40–41; "UPS Pact Fails to Shift Balance of Power Back Toward U.S. Workers," *Wall Street Journal*, August 20, 1997, pp. A1, A6.

CHAPTER NOTES

1. "The ASAP Dynamic 100," *Forbes ASAP*, February 23, 1998, pp. 51–52; Patricia Nakache, "Cisco's Recruiting Edge," *Fortune*, September 29, 1997, pp. 275–276; and Michelle Neely Martinez, "How Top Recruiters Snag New Grads," *HRMagazine*, August 1997, pp. 61–64.

2. For a complete review of human resource management, see Cynthia D. Fisher, Lyle F. Schoenfeldt, and James B. Shaw, *Human Resource Management*, 4th ed. (Boston: Houghton Mifflin, 1999).

3. David Terpstra and Elizabeth Rozell, "The Relationship of Staffing Practices to Organizational Level Measures of Performance," *Personnel Psychology*, Spring 1993, pp. 27–38.

4. Patrick Wright and Gary McMahan, "Strategic Human Resources Management: A Review of the Literature," *Journal of Management*, June 1992, pp. 280–319.

5. Augustine Lado and Mary Wilson, "Human Resource Systems and Sustained Competitive Advantage: A Competency-Based Perspective," *Academy of Management Review*, 1994, Vol. 19, No. 4, pp. 699–727.

6. "Silver Lining," *Forbes*, November 21, 1994, pp. 124–125.

7. Romuald Stone, "AIDS in the Workplace: An Executive Update," *Academy of Management Executive*, August 1994, pp. 52–64.

8. Jaclyn Fierman, "The Contingency Work Force," *Fortune*, January 24, 1994, pp. 30–36.

9. David Bowen, Gerald Ledford, and Barry Nathan, "Hiring for the Organization, Not the Job," *Academy of Management Executive*, November 1991, pp. 35–45; see also Frederick P. Morgeson and Michael A. Campion, "Social and Cognitive Sources of Potential Inaccuracy in Job Analysis," *Journal of Applied Psychology*, 1997, Vol. 82, No. 5, pp. 627–655.

10 Leonard Greenhalgh, Anne T. Lawrence, and Robert I. Sutton, "Determinants of Work Force Reduction Strategies in Declining Organizations," *Academy of Management Review*, April 1988, pp. 241–254.

11. Michael R. Carrell and Frank E. Kuzmits, *Personnel: Human Resource Management*, 3rd ed. (New York: Merrill, 1989).

12. Robert Gatewood, Mary Gowan, and Gary Lautenschlager, "Corporate Image, Recruitment Image, and Initial Job Choice Decisions," *Academy of Management Journal*, 1993, Vol. 36, No. 2, pp. 414–427.

13. Brian Dumaine, "The New Art of Hiring Smart," *Fortune*, August 17, 1987, pp. 78–81.

14. Frank L. Schmidt and John E. Hunter, "Employment Testing: Old Theories and New Research Findings," *American Psychologist*, October 1981, 1128–1137; see also "New Test Quantifies the Way We Work," *Wall Street Journal*, February 7, 1990, p. B1.

15. Robert Liden, Christopher Martin, and Charles Parsons, "Interviewer and Applicant Behaviors in Employment Interviews," *Academy of Management Journal*, 1993, Vol. 36, No. 2, pp. 372–386.

16. Dumaine, "The New Art of Hiring Smart."

17. Paul R. Sackett, "Assessment Centers and Content Validity: Some Neglected Issues," *Personnel Psychology*, Vol. 40, 1987, pp. 13–25.

18. Abby Brown, "To Test or Not to Test," *Personnel Administrator*, March 1987, pp. 67–70.

19. For a recent review, see Bernard Keys and Joseph Wolfe, "Management Education and Development: Current Issues and Emerging Trends," *Journal of Management*, June 1988, pp. 205–229.

20. Michael Brody, "Helping Workers to Work Smarter," *Fortune*, June 8, 1987, pp. 86–88.

21. "Videos Are Starring in More and More Training Programs," *Business Week*, September 7, 1987, pp. 108–110.

22. "'Boeing U': Flying by the Book," *USA Today*, October 6, 1997, pp. 1B, 2B.

23. Barry R. Nathan, Allan Mohrman, and John Milliman, "Interpersonal Relations as a Context for the Effects of Appraisal Interviews on Performance and Satisfaction: A Longitudinal Study," *Academy of Management Journal*, June 1991, pp. 352–369.

24. Brian O'Reilly, "360 Feedback Can Change Your Life," *Fortune*, October 17, 1994, pp. 93–100.

25. Jaclyn Fierman, "The Perilous New World of Fair Pay," *Fortune*, June 13, 1994, pp. 57–64.

26. Caroline L. Weber and Sara L. Rynes, "Effects of Compensation Strategy on Job Pay Decisions," *Academy of Management Journal*, March 1991, pp. 86–109.

27. Peter Cappelli and Wayne F. Cascio, "Why Some Jobs Command Wage Premiums: A Test of Career Tournament and Internal Labor Market Hypotheses," *Academy of Management Journal*, December 1991, pp. 848–868.

28. "To Each According to His Needs: Flexible Benefits Plans Gain Favor," *Wall Street Journal*, September 16, 1986, p. 29.

29. "The Future Look of Employee Benefits," *Wall Street Journal*, September 7, 1988, p. 21.

30. "Firms Forced to Cut Back on Benefits," *USA Today*, November 29, 1988, pp. 1B, 2B.

31. Robert Waterman, Judith Waterman, and Betsy Collard, "Toward a Career-Resilient Workforce," *Harvard Business Review*, July–August 1994, pp. 87–95.

32. Barbara Presley Nobel, "Reinventing Labor," *Harvard Business Review*, July–August 1993, pp. 115–125.

33. John A. Fossum, "Labor Relations: Research and Practice in Transition," *Journal of Management*, Summer 1987, pp. 281–300.

34. For recent research on collective bargaining, see Wallace N. Davidson III, Dan L. Worrell, and Sharon H. Garrison, "Effect of Strike Activity on Firm Value," *Academy of Management Journal*, June 1988, pp. 387–394; John M. Magenau, James E. Martin, and Melanie M. Peterson, "Dual and Unilateral Commitment Among Stewards and Rank-and-File Union Members," *Academy of Management Journal*, June 1988, pp. 359–376; and Brian E. Becker, "Concession Bargaining: The Meaning of Union Gains," *Academy of Management Journal*, June 1988, pp. 377–387.

Organizing for Success

Organizing is the second major functional area of management. Just as a gardener decides what to plant, when to plant, and how to arrange the things that are being planted, so too does a manager decide how to structure jobs, how to group jobs, and how to arrange relationships among jobs and groups of jobs. This video case relates the organizing function to four different companies.

OVERVIEW AND OBJECTIVES

After completing this video case, you should be able to:

1. Better understand the complexities inherent in the organizing process.

2. More easily see the different ways that a business can be organized.

3. Better appreciate the role of change and change management in organizing.

COMPANY BACKGROUND

The Ritz-Carlton is a premium hotel chain known for its amazing service, luxurious rooms and amenities, and high prices. But the people who can afford to stay at a Ritz-Carlton seldom complain about the prices. They recognize that they are getting unsurpassed service for their money. And the Ritz-Carlton, similarly, understands that if it wants to continue its enviable record of sales and profit, it must continue to cater to the individual needs, preferences, and whims of the well-heeled clients it serves. Accordingly, each hotel within the company functions as an autonomous enterprise with a manager totally responsible for its performance.

General Mills is a major food products company. The firm is the second largest in the breakfast cereal market, its biggest business (Kellogg's is a bit larger). But General Mills also has an enviable array of other profitable product lines as well. For example, General Mills also makes Betty Crocker bakery products, Yoplait yogurts, Bugles snack foods, and Gold Medal flour, and operates the Red Lobster and Olive Garden restaurant chains.

Xerox Corporation, as virtually everyone knows, makes photocopying machines. But Xerox aspires to be much more, now calling itself "The Document Company." The firm has recently tried to focus its attention on being the premier provider of equipment and services for all phases of document proc-essing—from document creation to storage to formatting and printing to distribution. It sees its major clients as being other businesses, hospitals, educational organizations, and the government—in short, any other entity that uses documents in any form.

TGI Friday is a fast-growing restaurant chain. At the present time, the company has about 320 restaurants scattered all across the country, and another 75 in 35 other countries. TGI Friday tries to provide the same basic menu in each country, with only minor modifications for local tastes. It hires all of its employees from the areas around its restaurants and then teaches those employees how to conduct business the "Friday" way.

CASE QUESTIONS

1. How do you think each of the four businesses described above might best be organized? (For Ritz-Carlton, focus on a single hotel.)

2. What role do you think change plays in each company?

VIDEO REVIEW

Your instructor will now show you a video clip that provides more information about Ritz-Carlton, General Mills, Xerox, and TGI Friday.

FOLLOW-UP QUESTIONS

1. After viewing the video, compare the methods of organization used at each company with your prediction in Case Question 1.

2. Why do you think each firm uses its own particular method of organization design?

3. Describe the role of change in each company.

4. What alternative methods of organizing might be called for in the future at each company?

5. Speculate as to the role of human resource management at each firm.

POPULAR VIDEO FOLLOW-UP

Each of the movies listed below provides some insights and examples to illustrate various organizing concepts and ideas. See if you can come up with other examples.

- *Courage Under Fire* (accountability and delegation)

- *James and the Giant Peach* (responsibility, authority, and delegation)

- *Broadcast News* (various organizing concepts)

- *The Rock* (organization, human resource selection)

- *Norma Rae* (labor relations)

15

Basic Elements of Individual Behavior in Organizations

OBJECTIVES

After studying this chapter, you should be able to:

- Explain the nature of the individual-organization relationship.
- Define personality and describe personality attributes that affect behavior in organizations.
- Discuss individual attitudes in organizations and how they affect behavior.
- Describe basic perceptual processes and the role of attributions in organizations.
- Discuss the causes and consequences of stress and describe how it can be managed.
- Describe creativity and its role in organizations.
- Explain how workplace behaviors can directly or indirectly influence organizational effectiveness.

Delta Airlines has long been one of the flagships of the U.S. air industry. Delta's image has been based on clean planes, plush amenities, and a distinctly warm and highly personalized service. Its employees have been treated exceptionally well, paid among the highest wages in the industry, and provided high levels of job security. As a result, the firm has had a proud and stable work force, which, in turn, was pleased to deliver high-quality service to Delta passengers.

In response to competition from low-cost carriers like ValuJet and Southwest Airlines, executives at Delta launched a dramatic three-year cost-cutting program. One area that received major attention was the work force as the firm shrunk by approximately eighty thousand employees. Many of these employees had twenty-five years or more experience with the firm. The airline then hired outside contractors to handle jobs such as airplane cleaning, maintenance and ground support, and baggage loading.

As a consequence of these steps, Delta's profit picture has improved immensely. At the same time, however, its image has been tarnished, and many of the remaining employees feel resentful and bitter. For example, prior to the cost-cutting measures, Delta maintained one full-time mechanic at each gate. This mechanic was ready to solve any routine problem that existed on an arriving aircraft. Now, however, the firm has one mechanic for every three or four gates. Thus, the individual mechanic must often move quickly between gates. As a result, some flights are delayed, some problems go uncorrected, and the mechanics complain about their workload.

To make matters worse, many of the new contract employees do not have the same level of commitment to Delta as their full-time predecessors had. For example, during East Coast winter storms in 1995, many newly hired contract workers at Delta's primary hub, Atlanta, simply didn't show up for work. To make matters worse, the airline's reduced staff of baggage handlers was totally overwhelmed by their job. At one point more than

"This has tested our people. There have been some morale problems. But so be it."

Ronald Allen, Delta CEO, quoted in the Wall Street Journal, *June 20, 1996, p. A8.*

five thousand bags were sitting in Atlanta when they needed to be somewhere else. Meanwhile, inside the airport long lines of angry passengers stood impatiently waiting for someone to help them. In the old days, experienced loyal Delta employees would have gone out of their way to make these passengers feel better. At the new Delta part-time employees, with no understanding of the organization's heritage, stood in their place and often offered curt and/or incorrect suggestions to people.

Even in-flight service has been diminished. Delta has eliminated one flight attendant from virtually every aircraft it flies. For example, whereas the firm once used three flight attendants in coach on its Boeing 727s, the standard staffing is now two flight attendants, the FAA minimum. Similarly, in earlier times cabin cleaning was performed by in-house crews who earned almost $8 an hour and who enjoyed full health benefits and travel privileges. Outside contractors now do the work, and many customers have started to complain about poor quality cleaning, soiled carpets, and sticky tray tables.

Will Delta be able to overcome these problems? The firm's CEO acknowledges that the cost cutting has been anything but smooth. Moreover, he also acknowledges that the firm may have cut too deeply and eliminated people that it should have retained. Nevertheless, he says, the days of high-cost benevolent operations are over. The firm has to remain cost focused and bottom-lined oriented if it is to survive.[1]

psychological contract The overall set of expectations held by an individual with respect to what he or she will contribute to the organization and what the organization will provide to the individual

contributions What the individual provides to the organization

elta Airlines and its employees are in the process of redefining their relationship. To do so, the parties are having to each assess how well their respective needs and capabilities match. And the many unique attributes that characterize each employee affects how they feel about these changes, how they will alter their future attitudes about the firm, and how they perform their jobs. These attributes reflect the basic elements of individual behavior in organizations.

This chapter describes several of these basic elements and is the first of five chapters designed to develop a more complete perspective on the *leading* function of management. In the first section of this chapter we investigate the psychological nature of individuals in organizations. The next section of the chapter introduces the concept of personality and discusses several important personality attributes that can influence behavior in organizations. We then examine individual attitudes and their role in organizations, the role of stress in the workplace, and the role of individual creativity. Finally, we describe some basic individual behaviors that are important to organizations.

Understanding Individuals in Organizations

As a starting point in understanding human behavior in the workplace, we must consider the basic nature of the relationship between individuals and organizations. We must also gain an appreciation of the nature of individual differences.

FIGURE 15.1
The Psychological Contract

Psychological contracts are the basic assumptions that individuals have about their relationships with their organization. Such contracts are defined in terms of contributions by the individual relative to inducements from the organization.

■ The Psychological Contract

Most people have a basic understanding of a contract. Whenever we buy a car or sell a house, for example, both buyer and seller sign a contract that specifies the terms of the agreement. A psychological contract is similar in some ways to a standard legal contract, but is less formal and not as well defined. In particular, a **psychological contract** is the overall set of expectations held by an individual with respect to what he or she will contribute to the organization and what the organization will provide in return.[2] Thus, a psychological contract is not written on paper nor are all of its terms explicitly negotiated.

The essential nature of a psychological contract is illustrated in Figure 15.1. The individual makes a variety of **contributions** to the organization—effort, skills, ability, time, loyalty, and so forth. These contributions presumably satisfy various needs and requirements of the organization. That is, because the organization may have hired the person because of her skills, it is

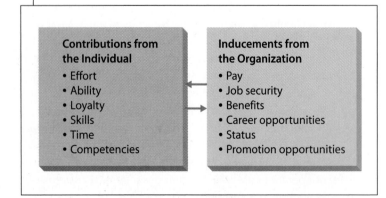

Contributions from the Individual	Inducements from the Organization
• Effort	• Pay
• Ability	• Job security
• Loyalty	• Benefits
• Skills	• Career opportunities
• Time	• Status
• Competencies	• Promotion opportunities

reasonable for the organization to expect that she will subsequently display those skills in the performance of her job.

In return for these contributions, the organization provides **inducements** to the individual. Some inducements, such as pay and career opportunities, are tangible rewards. Others, such as job security and status, are intangible. Just as the contributions available from the individual must satisfy needs of the organization, the inducements offered by the organization must serve the needs of the individual. That is, if a person accepts employment with an organization because he thinks he will earn an attractive salary and have an opportunity to advance, he will subsequently expect those rewards to be forthcoming.

If both the individual and organization perceive that the psychological contract is fair and equitable, they will be satisfied with the relationship and will likely continue it. On the other hand, if either party sees an imbalance or inequity in the contract, that party may initiate a change. For example, the individual may request a pay raise or promotion, decrease her contributed effort, or look for a better job elsewhere. The organization can also initiate change by requesting that the individual improve his skills through training, transfer the person to another job, or terminate the person's employment altogether.

A basic challenge faced by the organization, then, is to manage psychological contracts. The organization must ensure that it is getting value from its employees. At the same time, it must also be sure that it is providing employees with appropriate inducements. If the organization is underpaying its employees for their contributions, for example, they may perform poorly or leave for better jobs elsewhere. On the other hand, if they are being overpaid relative to their contributions, the organization is incurring unnecessary costs.[3]

inducements What the organization provides to the individual

person-job fit The extent to which the contributions made by the individual match the inducements offered by the organization

The person-job fit is an important relationship in any organizational setting. For example, many people would balk at the idea of cleaning the outside windows on the top of a skyscraper, of cutting logs in harsh weather, or, as shown here, trying to train a white tiger. But for Gregg Lee, the animal trainer at Marine World Africa USA in California, it's just all in a day's work!

■ The Person-Job Fit

One specific aspect of managing psychological contracts is managing the person-job fit. **Person-job fit** is the extent to which the contributions made by the individual match the inducements offered by the organization. In theory, each employee has a specific set of needs to be fulfilled and a set of job-related behaviors and abilities to contribute. Thus, if the organization can take perfect advantage of those behaviors and abilities and exactly fulfill his needs, it will have achieved a perfect person-job fit.

Of course, such a precise level of person-job fit rarely occurs. One reason for the disparity is that organizational selection procedures are imperfect. Organizations can only estimate the skill level of job candidates when making hiring decisions. But even simple performance dimensions are hard to measure objectively and validly.

Another reason for imprecise person-job fits is that people and organizations change. An individual who finds a new job stimulating and exciting may find the same job boring and monotonous after a few years of performing it. And when the

Modeling Human Behavior

People are people, and machines are machines, right? Yes, of course. But some interesting work going on now has the potential to help managers use machines to improve their understanding of how and why people behave as they do. Whereas machines function in perfectly logical, rational, and precise ways, human behavior is subject to the influences of individual differences.

Modeling technology started in consumer research. Marketing researchers have found that they can construct a virtual "sample" of individuals, each imbued with ages, incomes, spending patterns, and so forth. These characteristics have, in turn, been modeled within the sample, following statistical profiles of a relevant population. Thus, a consumer products firm can electronically introduce into the virtual sample two different products and then see which one sells the best.

Computer modeling has recently been extended to workplace and management issues. For example, one deci-

> *"Companies will choose to model reality differently, because we all have different assumptions about how people behave."*
>
> Michael Schrage, technology consultant*

sion managers must make is how much to invest in training employees. If a company invests too little, it will have an unproductive workforce; however, if it invests too much, competitors will start systematically raiding the firm to hire its well-trained workers. A firm can use computer modeling tools to help determine the optimal range of training investment.

Other related applications include helping a company configure the best compensation and benefits packages for its employees, the best approach for recruiting, and the best approach for structuring teams and work groups. Will computers ever be able to precisely model and predict the behaviors of a real person? Probably not, but they seem to be getting closer and closer.

References: *"Playing the Game of Life,"* Forbes, April 7, 1997, pp. 100–108 (*quote on p. 100); and James Henderson, *"Breakthroughs in Modeling Human Behavior,"* Science Digest, June 1997, pp. 88–105.

organization adopts new technology, it changes the skills it needs from its employees. Still another reason for imprecision in the person-job fit is that each individual is unique. Measuring skills and performance is difficult enough. Assessing needs, attitudes, and personality is far more complex. Each of these individual differences serves to make matching individuals with jobs a difficult and complex process.

■ The Nature of Individual Differences

individual differences Personal attributes that vary from one person to another

Individual differences are personal attributes that vary from one person to another. Individual differences may be physical, psychological, and emotional. Taken together, all the traits that characterize any specific person serve to make that individual unique. Much of the remainder of this chapter is devoted to individual differences. Before proceeding, however, we must also note the importance of the situation in assessing the behavior of individuals.

Are specific differences that characterize a given individual good or bad? Do they contribute to or detract from performance? The answer, of course, is that it depends on the circumstances. One person may be very dissatisfied, withdrawn, and negative in one job setting but very satisfied, outgoing, and positive in another. Working conditions, coworkers, and leadership are all important ingredients in determining the impact of any given set of individual differences and how a person will react and respond to a job setting. "Management InfoTech" describes how some experts are working toward computer simulations that may one day improve our understanding of the nature and scope of individual differences in organizations.

Thus, whenever an organization attempts to assess or account for individual differences among its employees, it must also be sure to consider the situation in which behavior occurs. Individuals who are satisfied or productive workers in one context may become dissatisfied or unproductive workers in another context. Attempting to consider both individual differences and contributions in relation to inducements and contexts, then, is a major challenge for organizations as they attempt to establish effective psychological contracts with their employees and achieve optimal fits between people and jobs.

MANAGEMENT IMPLICATIONS Managers should understand the psychological contracts they establish with their employees and take care to be fair and equitable. Managers also need to realize that people may not be precisely matched with their jobs, but still attempt to do as good a job as possible in optimizing this relationship. Finally, managers should also recognize and appreciate the fact that every individual is unique.

Personality and Individual Behavior

Personality traits represent some of the most fundamental sets of individual differences in organizations. **Personality** is the relatively stable set of psychological attributes that distinguish one person from another.[4] Managers should strive to understand basic personality attributes and the ways they can affect people's behavior in organizational situations, not to mention their perceptions of and attitudes toward the organization.

personality The relatively permanent set of psychological and behavioral attributes that distinguish one person from another

■ The "Big Five" Personality Traits

Psychologists have identified literally thousands of personality traits and dimensions that differentiate one person from another. But in recent years, researchers have identified five fundamental personality traits that are especially relevant to organizations. Because these five traits are so important and because they are

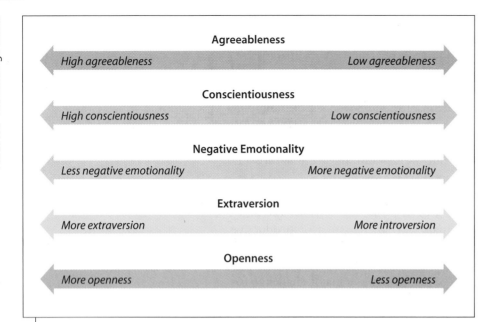

FIGURE 15.2

The "Big Five" Model of Personality

The "big-five" personality model represents an increasingly accepted framework for understanding personality traits in organizational settings. In general, experts tend to agree that personality traits toward the left end of each dimension, as illustrated in this figure, are more positive in organizational settings, whereas traits closer to the right are less positive.

"big five" personality traits   A popular personality framework based on five key traits

agreeableness   A person's ability to get along with others

conscientiousness   The number of goals on which a person focuses

negative emotionality   Extent to which a person is poised, calm, resilient, and secure

extraversion   a person's comfort level with relationships

currently the subject of so much attention, they are commonly referred to as the **"big five" personality traits**.[5] Figure 15.2 illustrates the "big five" traits.

Agreeableness refers to a person's ability to get along with others. Agreeableness causes some people to be gentle, cooperative, forgiving, understanding, and good-natured in their dealings with others. But it results in others being irritable, short-tempered, uncooperative, and generally antagonistic toward other people. Although research has not yet fully investigated the effects of agreeableness, logic suggests that highly agreeable people are likely to develop good working relationships with coworkers, subordinates, and higher-level managers, whereas less agreeable people will not have particularly good working relationships. This same pattern might also extend to relationships with customers, suppliers, and other key organizational constituents.

Conscientiousness refers to the number of goals on which a person focuses. People who focus on relatively few goals at one time are likely to be organized, systematic, careful, thorough, responsible, and self-disciplined as they work to pursue those goals. Others, however, tend to take on a wider array of goals and, as a result, to be more disorganized, careless, and irresponsible, as well as less thorough and self-disciplined. Research has found that more-conscientious people tend to be higher performers than less conscientious people across a variety of different jobs. This pattern seems logical, of course, since more-conscientious people will take their jobs seriously and will approach the performance of their jobs in a highly responsible fashion.

The third of the big-five personality dimensions is **negative emotionality**. People with less negative emotionality will be relatively poised, calm, resilient and secure. But people with more negative emotionality will be more excitable, insecure, reactive, and subject to extreme mood swings. People with less negative emotionality might be expected to handle job stress, pressure, and tension relatively well. Their stability might also lead them to be seen as being more reliable than their less stable counterparts.

Extraversion refers to a person's comfort level with relationships. People who are called extraverts are sociable, talkative, assertive, and open to establishing new relationships. But introverts are much less sociable, talkative, assertive, and less open to establishing new relationships. Research suggests that, compared to introverts, extraverts tend to be higher overall job performers and that they are also more likely to be attracted to jobs based on personal relationships like sales and marketing positions.

Finally, **openness** refers to a person's rigidity of beliefs and range of interests. People with high levels of openness are willing to listen to new ideas and to change their own ideas, beliefs, and attitudes as a result of new information. They also tend to have broad interests and to be curious, imaginative, and creative. On the other hand, people with low levels of openness tend to be less receptive to new ideas and less willing to change their minds. Further, they also tend to have fewer and narrower interests and to be less curious and creative. People with more openness might be expected to be better performers, owing to their flexibility and the likelihood that they will be better accepted by others in the organization. Openness may also encompass an individual's willingness to accept change. For example, people with high levels of openness may be relatively receptive to change, whereas people with low levels of openness may be more likely to resist change.

openness A person's rigidity of beliefs and range of interests

The big-five framework continues to attract the attention of both researchers and managers. The potential value of this framework is that it encompasses an integrated set of traits that appear to be valid predictors of certain behaviors in certain situations. Thus, managers who can develop both an understanding of the framework and the ability to assess these traits in their employees will be in a good position to understand how and why they behave as they do.[6] On the other hand, managers must also be careful to not overestimate their ability to assess the "big five" traits in others. Even assessment using the most rigorous and valid measures, for instance, is still likely to be somewhat imprecise. Another limitation of the big-five framework is that is primarily based on research conducted in the United States. Thus, there are unanswered questions as to its relevance to other cultures. And even within the United States, various other factors and traits are also likely to affect behavior in organizations.

■ Other Personality Traits at Work

In addition to the big five, several other personality traits influence behavior in organizations. Among the most important are locus of control, self-efficacy, authoritarianism, Machiavellianism, self-esteem, and risk propensity.

Locus of control is the extent to which people believe that their behavior has a real affect on what happens to them.[7] Some people, for example, believe that if they work hard they will succeed. They also may believe that people fail because they lack ability or motivation. People who believe that individuals are in control of their lives are said to have an *internal locus of control*. Other people think that fate, chance, luck, or other people's behavior determines what happens to them. For example, an employee who fails to get a promotion may attribute that failure to a politically motivated boss or just bad luck, rather than to her or his own lack of skills or poor performance record. People who think that forces beyond their control dictate what happens to them are said to have an *external locus of control*.

locus of control The degree to which an individual believes that behavior has a direct impact on the consequences of that behavior

Self-efficacy is a related but subtly different personality characteristic. Self-efficacy is a person's beliefs about his or her capabilities to perform a task.[8] People with high self-efficacy believe that they can perform well on a

self-efficacy An individual's beliefs about her or his capabilities to perform a task

Individual personality traits are a major contributor to job selection and work performance. Take Izabel Lam, for example. Her company makes dinnerware and cutlery inspired by under water imagery. To deal with design piracy, Ms. Lam has frequently had to file lawsuits and report counterfeiters to authorities. She even hired a private detective agency to track down design pirates in Thailand. Only someone with a clearly internal locus of control and strong self-efficacy, risk propensity, and self-esteem would go to these lengths to protect her interests.

specific task, whereas people with low self-efficacy tend to doubt their ability to perform a specific task. While self-assessments of ability contribute to self-efficacy, so does the individual's personality. Some people simply have more self-confidence than do others. This belief in their ability to perform a task effectively results in their being more self-assured and more able to focus their attention on performance.

Another important personality characteristic is **authoritarianism**, the extent to which an individual believes that power and status differences are appropriate within hierarchical social systems like organizations.[9] For example, a person who is highly authoritarian may accept directives or orders from someone with more authority purely because the other person is "the boss." On the other hand, although a person who is not highly authoritarian may still carry out appropriate and reasonable directives from the boss, he or she is also more likely to question things, express disagreement with the boss, and even to refuse to carry out orders if they are for some reason objectionable. A highly authoritarian manager may be autocratic and demanding, and highly authoritarian subordinates will be more likely to accept this behavior from their leader. On the other hand, a less authoritarian manager may allow subordinates a bigger role in making decisions, and less authoritarian subordinates will respond positively to this behavior.

Machiavellianism is another important personality trait. This concept is named after Niccolo Machiavelli, a sixteenth-century author. In his book *The Prince*, Machiavelli explained how the nobility could more easily gain and use power. Machiavellianism is now used to describe behavior directed at gaining power and controlling the behavior of others. Research suggests that Machiavellianism is a personality trait that varies from person to person. More-Machiavellian individuals tend to be rational and nonemotional, may be willing to lie to attain their personal goals, put little weight on loyalty and friendship, and enjoy manipulating others' behavior. Less-Machiavellian individuals are more emotional, less willing to lie to succeed, value loyalty and friendship highly, and get little personal pleasure from manipulating others.

Self-esteem is the extent to which a person believes that she is a worthwhile and deserving individual.[10] A person with high self-esteem is more likely to seek higher-status jobs, be more confident in his ability to achieve higher levels of performance, and derive greater intrinsic satisfaction from his accomplishments. In contrast, a person with less self-esteem may be more content to remain in a lower-level job, be less confident of her ability, and focus more on extrinsic rewards. Among the major personality dimensions, self-esteem is the one that has been most widely studied in other countries. Although more research is clearly needed, the published evidence suggests that self-esteem as a personality trait does indeed exist in many countries and that its role in organizations is reasonably important across different cultures.[11]

Risk propensity is the degree to which an individual is willing to take chances and make risky decisions. A manager with a high risk propensity, for example, might be expected to experiment with new ideas and gamble on new products. He might also lead the organization in new and different directions. This manager might also be a catalyst for innovation. On the other hand, the same individual might also jeopardize the continued well-being of the organization if the risky decisions prove to be bad ones. A manager with low risk propensity might lead to a stagnant and overly conservative organization, or help the organization successfully weather turbulent and unpredictable times by maintaining stability and calm. Thus, the potential consequences of risk propensity to an organization are heavily dependent on that organization's environment.

MANAGEMENT IMPLICATIONS Managers need to realize that people vary along a wide array of personality traits. The big-five and other traits provide useful frameworks for understanding how and why people differ. At the same time, managers should realize that many other traits also exist and that assessing and understanding precisely how a given trait affects behavior is difficult, at best.

authoritarianism The extent to which an individual believes that power and status differences are appropriate within hierarchical social systems like organizations

Machiavellianism Behavior directed at gaining power and controlling the behavior of others

self-esteem The extent to which a person believes that he or she is a worthwhile and deserving individual

risk propensity The degree to which an individual is willing to take chances and make risky decisions

Attitudes and Individual Behavior

Another important element of individual behavior in organizations is attitudes. **Attitudes** are complexes of beliefs and feelings that people have about specific ideas, situations, or other people. Attitudes are important because they are the mechanism through which most people express their feelings. An employee's statement that he feels underpaid by the organization reflects his feelings about his pay. Similarly, when a manager says that she likes the new advertising campaign, she is expressing her feelings about the organization's marketing efforts.

Attitudes have three components. The *affective component* of an attitude reflects feelings and emotions an individual has toward a situation. The *cognitive component* of an attitude is derived from knowledge an individual has about a situation. It is important to note that cognition is subject to individual perceptions (something we discuss more fully later). Thus, one person might "know" that a certain political candidate is better than another while someone else may "know" just the opposite. Finally, the *intentional component* of an attitude reflects how an individual expects to behave toward or in the situation.

To illustrate these three components, consider the case of a manager who places an order for some supplies for his organization from a new office supply firm. Suppose many of the items he orders are out of stock, others are overpriced, and still others arrive damaged. When he calls someone at the supply firm for assistance, he is treated rudely and gets disconnected before his claim is resolved. When asked how he feels about the new office supply firm, he might respond, "I don't like that company (affective component). It is the

attitudes Complexes of beliefs and feelings that people have about specific ideas, situations, or other people

worst office supply firm I've ever dealt with (cognitive component). I'll never do business with that company again (intentional component)."

People try to maintain consistency among the three components of their attitudes as well as among all their attitudes. However, circumstances sometimes arise that lead to conflicts. The conflict individuals may experience among their own attitudes is called **cognitive dissonance**.[12] Say, for example, an individual who has vowed never to work for a big, impersonal corporation intends instead to open her own business and be her own boss. Unfortunately, a series of financial setbacks forces her to take a job with a large company and work for someone else. Thus cognitive dissonance occurs: the affective and cognitive components of the individual's attitude conflict with intended behavior. To reduce cognitive dissonance, which is usually an uncomfortable experience for most people, the individual described above might tell herself the situation is only temporary and that she can go back out on her own in the near future. Or she might revise her cognitions and decide that working for a large company is more pleasant than she had ever expected.

cognitive dissonance Caused when an individual has conflicting attitudes

■ Work-Related Attitudes

People in organizations form attitudes about many different things. For example, employees are likely to have attitudes about their salary, promotion possibilities, their boss, employee benefits, the food in the company cafeteria, and the color of the company softball team uniforms. Of course, some of these attitudes are more important than others. Especially important attitudes are job satisfaction or dissatisfaction and organizational commitment.

Job Satisfaction or Dissatisfaction **Job satisfaction** or **dissatisfaction** is an attitude that reflects the extent to which an individual is gratified by or fulfilled in his or her work. Extensive research conducted on job satisfaction indicates that personal factors such as an individual's needs and aspirations determine this attitude, along with group and organizational factors such as relationships with coworkers and supervisors, working conditions, work policies, and compensation.[13]

job satisfaction or **dissatisfaction** An attitude that reflects the extent to which an individual is gratified by or fulfilled in his or her work

A satisfied employee also tends to be absent less often, to make positive contributions, and to stay with the organization. In contrast, a dissatisfied employee may be absent more often, may experience stress that disrupts coworkers, and may be continually looking for another job. Contrary to what many managers believe, however, high levels of job satisfaction do not necessarily lead to higher levels of performance. One survey also indicates that contrary to popular opinion, Japanese workers are less satisfied with their jobs than are their counterparts in the United States.[14]

Organizational Commitment **Organizational commitment** is an attitude that reflects an individual's identification with and attachment to the organization itself. A person with a high level of commitment is likely to see herself as a true member of the organization (for example, referring to the organization in personal terms such as "we make high-quality products"), to overlook minor sources of dissatisfaction with the organization, and to see herself remaining a

organizational commitment An attitude that reflects an individual's identification with and attachment to the organization itself

THE QUALITY CHALLENGE

Restoring Positive Attitudes at Continental

For years Continental Airlines wallowed in red ink and had perhaps the poorest reputation of any carrier in the airline industry. Continental's pilots and rank-and-file workers endured layoffs, wage cuts, poor benefits, and broken promises by management, and were frequently embarrassed to tell people where they worked. But when Gordon Bethune took over as CEO a few years ago, things began to change. While Bethune knew that he needed to change many of the firm's operations, he also knew that employee attitudes and morale were at the root of many of the company's problems.

One of Bethune's first actions was to change the reward system for pilots to boost on-time performance. Bethune knew that the improved performance was saving the firm millions of dollars because when planes are late an airline must often pay for passengers' meals and hotel rooms and for booking them onto other airlines. He divided the total savings by the number of employees and sent each of them a check for that amount—$65 per employee. Although not a big sum, this gesture proved that he was willing to share success with everyone. Bethune also an-

> *"Getting the plane off the gate isn't my job or your job. We act like it's everybody's job."*
>
> *Mark Bindley, Continental baggage handler**

nounced that henceforth each employee would receive a check for $65 every month that Continental was in the top five in on-time performance and a check for $100 when the company was in the top three.

Bethune also wanted to improve communication throughout Continental. He set up a toll-free number for employees to call with complaints and problems and created a committee to respond to every call within forty-eight hours. He also gave employees his voice-mail number and personally returns most of their calls. And today he is careful to refer to Continental's employees as his "coworkers." Once the joke of the airline industry, Continental is now among the most profitable carriers in the world, and its reputation among business travelers has soared to near the top of the ratings.

References: *"Piloted by Bethune, Continental Air Lifts Its Workers' Morale,"* Wall Street Journal, *May 15, 1996, pp. A1, A8 (*quote on page A1);* Hoover's Handbook of American Business 1998 *(Austin, Texas: Hoover's Business Press, 1998), pp. 418–419; and Gordon Bethune, "Communication Is Essential,"* Profiles, *November 1996, p. 8.*

member of the organization. In contrast, a person with less organizational commitment is more likely to see himself as an outsider (for example, referring to the organization in less personal terms such as "they don't pay their employees very well"), to express more dissatisfaction about things, and to not see himself as a long-term member of the organization. Research suggests that Japanese workers may be more committed to their organizations than are American workers.[15]

Research also suggests that commitment strengthens with an individual's age, years with the organization, sense of job security, and participation in decision making.[16] Employees who feel committed to an organization have highly reliable habits, plan a long tenure with the organization, and muster more effort in performance. Although organizations can do few definitive things to promote commitment, some specific guidelines are available. For one thing, if the organization treats its employees fairly and provides reasonable rewards and job security, those employees are more likely to be satisfied and committed. Allowing employees to have a say in how things are done can also promote all three attitudes. "The Quality Challenge" describes how employees at Continental Airlines have become more committed and satisfied in recent years and how, as a result, the firm's performance has improved dramatically.

■ Affect and Mood in Organizations

Researchers have recently started to focus renewed interest on the affective component of attitudes. Recall from our discussion above that the affect component of an attitude reflects our feelings and emotions. Managers once believed that emotion and feelings varied among people from day to day; however, current research suggests that although some short-term fluctuation does indeed occur, underlying stable predispositions maintain fairly constant and predictable moods and emotional states.[17]

positive affectivity   A tendency to be relatively upbeat and optimistic, have an overall sense of well-being, see things in a positive light, and seem to be in a good mood

Some people, for example, tend to have a higher degree of **positive affectivity;** they are relatively upbeat and optimistic, have an overall sense of well-being, and usually see things in a positive light. Thus, they always seem to be in a good mood. Other people, those with more **negative affectivity**, are just the opposite. They are generally downbeat and pessimistic, and they usually see things in a negative way. They seem to be in a bad mood most of the time.

negative affectivity   A tendency to be generally downbeat and pessimistic, see things in a negative way, and seem to be in a bad mood

Of course, as noted above, short-term variations can occur among even the most extreme types. People with a lot of positive affectivity, for example, may still be in a bad mood if they have just received some bad news—being passed over for a promotion, getting extremely negative performance feedback, or being laid off or fired, for instance. Similarly, those with negative affectivity may still be in a good mood—at least for a short time—if they have just been promoted, received very positive performance feedback, or had other good things befall them. After the initial impact of these events wears off, however, those with positive affectivity will generally return to their normal positive mood, whereas those with negative affectivity will gravitate back to their normal bad mood.

MANAGEMENT IMPLICATIONS   All managers should appreciate the importance of attitudes in organizations. Managers should be especially concerned with such job-related attitudes as job satisfaction and dissastisfaction and organizational commitment. Understanding the causes and consequences of these attitudes is also helpful. ■

Perception and Individual Behavior

As noted earlier, an important element of an attitude is the individual's perception of the object about which the attitude is formed. Since perception plays a role in various other workplace behaviors, managers need to have a general understanding of basic perceptual processes.[18] The role of attributions is also important.

■ Basic Perceptual Processes

Perception is the set of processes by which an individual becomes aware of and interprets information about the environment. As shown in Figure 15.3, basic perceptual processes that are particularly relevant to organizations are selective perception and stereotyping.

Selective Perception   **Selective perception** is the process of screening out information that we are uncomfortable with or that contradicts our beliefs. For example, suppose a manager is exceptionally fond of a particular worker. The manager has a very positive attitude about the worker and thinks he is a top performer. One day the manager notices that the worker seems to be goofing off. Selective perception may cause the manager to quickly forget what he observed. Similarly, suppose a manager has formed a very negative image of a particular worker. She thinks this worker is a poor performer and never does a good job. When she happens to observe an example of high performance from the worker, she, too, may not remember it for very long. In one sense, selective perception is beneficial because it allows us to disregard minor bits of information. Of course, this rule holds true only if our basic perception is accurate. If selective perception causes us to ignore important information, however, it can become quite detrimental.

Stereotyping   **Stereotyping** is the process of categorizing or labeling people on the basis of a single attribute. Common attributes from which people often stereotype are race and gender. Of course, stereotypes along these lines are inaccurate and can be harmful. For example, suppose a manager forms the stereotype that only women can perform certain tasks and that men are best suited for other tasks. To the extent that this stereotype affects the manager's hiring practices, the manager is (1) costing the organization valuable talent for both sets of jobs, (2) violating federal law, and (3) behaving unethically.

On the other hand, certain forms of stereotyping can be useful and efficient. Suppose, for example, that a manager believes that communication skills are important for a particular job and that speech communication majors tend to have exceptionally good communication skills. As a result, whenever he interviews candidates for jobs, he pays especially close attention to speech communication majors. To the extent that communication skills truly predict job performance and that majoring in speech communication does indeed provide those skills, this form of stereotyping can be beneficial.

perception   The set of processes by which an individual becomes aware of and interprets information about the environment

selective perception   The process of screening out information that we are uncomfortable with or which contradicts our beliefs

stereotyping   The process of categorizing or labeling people on the basis of a single attribute

FIGURE 15.3
Perceptual Processes

Two of the most basic perceptual processes are selective perception and stereotyping. As shown here, selective perception occurs when we screen out information (represented by the – symbols) that causes us discomfort or that contradicts our beliefs. Stereotyping occurs when we categorize or label people on the basis of a single attribute, illustrated here by color.

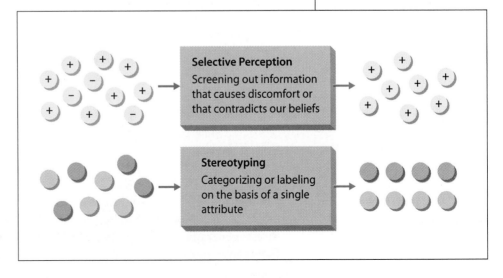

Selective Perception
Screening out information that causes discomfort or that contradicts our beliefs

Stereotyping
Categorizing or labeling on the basis of a single attribute

■ Perception and Attribution

attribution   The process of observing behavior and attributing causes to it

Perception is also closely linked with another process called attribution. **Attribution** is a mechanism through which we observe behavior and then attribute causes to it.[19] The behavior that is observed may be our own or that of others. For example, suppose someone realizes one day that she is working fewer hours than before, that she talks less about her work, and that she calls in sick more frequently. She might conclude that she has become disenchanted with her job and subsequently decide to quit. Thus, she observed her own behavior, attributed a cause to it, and developed what she thought was a consistent response.

More common is attributing cause to the behavior of others. For example, if the manager of the individual described above has observed the same behavior, he might form exactly the same attribution. On the other hand, he might instead decide that she has a serious illness, that he is driving her too hard, that she is experiencing too much stress, that she has a drug problem, or that she is having family problems.

The basic framework around which we form attributions is *consensus* (the extent to which other people in the same situation behave the same way), *consistency* (the extent to which the same person behaves in the same way in the same situation at different times), and *distinctiveness* (the extent to which the same person behaves in the same way in other situations). For example, suppose a manager observes that an employee is late for a meeting. The manager might further realize that the employee is the only one who is late (low consensus), recall that he is often late for other meetings (high consistency), and subsequently realize that the same employee is sometimes late for work and returning from lunch (low distinctiveness). This pattern of attributions might cause the manager to decide that the individual's behavior is something that should be changed. As a result, the manager might meet with the subordinate and establish some punitive consequences for future tardiness.

MANAGEMENT IMPLICATIONS   Managers need to recognize the role of perception in organizational behavior. Specifically, they should know how selective perception and stereotyping affect not only the behavior of others, but their own behavior as well. Understanding the attribution process is also helpful. ■

Stress and Individual Behavior

stress   An individual's response to a strong stimulus, which is called a **stressor**

Another important element of behavior in organizations is stress. **Stress** is an individual's response to a strong stimulus.[20] This stimulus is called a **stressor**. Stress generally follows a cycle referred to as the **General Adaptation Syndrome**, or GAS,[21] shown in Figure 15.4. According to this view, when an individual first encounters a stressor, the GAS is initiated and the first stage, alarm, is activated. He may feel panic, may wonder how to cope, and may feel helpless. For example, suppose a manager is told to prepare a detailed evaluation of a plan by his firm to buy one of its competitors. His first reaction may be to ask, "How will I ever get this done by tomorrow?"

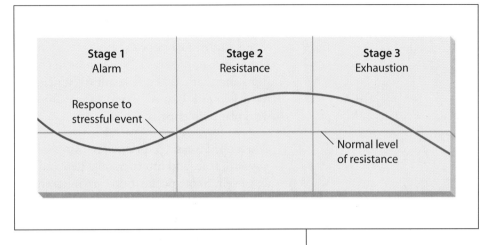

FIGURE 15.4
The General Adaptation Syndrome

The General Adaptation Syndrome represents the normal process by which we react to stressful events. At stage 1—alarm—we feel panic and alarm and our level of resistance to stress drops. Stage 2—resistance—represents our efforts to confront and control the stressful circumstance. If we fail, we may eventually reach stage 3—exhaustion—and just give up or quit.

If the stressor is too intense, the individual may feel unable to cope and never really try to respond to its demands. In most cases, however, after a short period of alarm, the individual gathers some strength and starts to resist the negative effects of the stressor. For example, the manager with the evaluation to write may calm down, call home to say he's working late, role up his sleeves, order some coffee, and get to work. Thus, at stage 2 of the GAS, the person is resisting the effects of the stressor.

In many cases, the resistance phase may end the GAS. If the manager is able to complete the evaluation earlier than expected, he may drop it in his briefcase, smile to himself, and head home tired but satisfied. On the other hand, prolonged exposure to a stressor without resolution may bring on stage 3 of the GAS—exhaustion. At this stage, the individual literally gives up and can no longer resist the stressor. The manager, for example, might fall asleep at his desk at 3 A.M. and never finish the evaluation.

We should note that stress is not all bad. In the absence of stress, we may experience lethargy and stagnation. An optimal level of stress, on the other hand, can result in motivation and excitement. Too much stress, however, can have negative consequences. It is also important to understand that stress can be caused by "good" as well as "bad" things. Excessive pressure, unreasonable demands on our time, and bad news can all cause stress. But receiving a bonus and then having to decide what to do with the money can be stressful as well. So, too, can receiving a promotion, gaining recognition, and similar positive events.

One important line of thinking about stress focuses on **Type A** and **Type B** personalities.[22] Type A individuals are extremely competitive, very devoted to work, and have a strong sense of time urgency. They are likely to be aggressive, impatient, and very work oriented. They have a lot of drive and want to accomplish as much as possible as quickly as possible. Compared to Type A individuals, Type Bs are less competitive, less devoted to work, and have a weaker sense of time urgency. Type Bs are less likely to experience conflict with other people and more likely to have a balanced, relaxed approach to life. They are able to work at a constant pace without time urgency. Type B people are not necessarily more or less successful than are Type A people, but they are less likely to experience stress.

General Adaptation Syndrome
General cycle of the stress process

Type A Individuals who are extremely competitive, very devoted to work, and have a strong sense of time urgency

Type B Individuals who are less competitive, less devoted to work, and have a weaker sense of time urgency

■ Causes and Consequences of Stress

Stress is obviously not a simple phenomenon. Figure 15.5 depicts several different causes of stress. Note that this list includes only work-related conditions and that stress can result from personal circumstances as well.[23] "Today's Management Issues" explores yet another serious consequence of stress, workplace violence.

Causes of Stress   Work-related stressors fall into one of four categories: task, physical, role, and interpersonal demands. *Task demands* are associated with the task itself. Some occupations are inherently more stressful than others. Having to make fast decisions, decisions with less than complete information, or decisions that have relatively serious consequences are some of the things that can make some jobs stressful. The jobs of surgeon, airline pilot, and stock broker are relatively more stressful than the jobs of general practitioner, airplane baggage loader, and office receptionist. Although general practitioners make important decisions, they are also likely to have time to make a considered diagnosis and fully explore various treatments. But during surgery, surgeons must make decisions quickly while realizing that the wrong one may endanger the life of a patient.

Physical demands are stressors associated with the job setting. Working outdoors in extremely hot or cold temperatures, or even in an improperly heated or cooled office, can lead to stress. A poorly designed office, which makes it difficult for people to have privacy or promotes too little social interaction, can result in stress, as can poor lighting and inadequate work surfaces. Even more severe are actual threats to health. Examples include jobs like coal mining, poultry processing, and toxic waste handling.

Role demands can also cause stress. (Roles are discussed more fully in Chapter 19). A role is a set of expected behaviors associated with a position in a group or organization. Stress can result from either role ambiguity or role conflict that people can experience in groups. For example, an employee who is feeling pressure from her boss to work longer hours while also being asked by her family for more time at home will almost certainly experience stress. Similarly, a new employee experiencing role ambiguity because of poor orientation and training practices by the organization will also suffer from stress.

FIGURE 15.5
Causes of Work Stress

There are several causes of work stress in organizations. Four general sets of organizational stressors are task demands, physical demands, role demands, and interpersonal demands.

Organizational Stressors			
Task Demands	**Physical Demands**	**Role Demands**	**Interpersonal Demands**
• Quick decisions	• Temperature extremes	• Role ambiguity	• Group pressures
• Critical decisions	• Poorly designed office	• Role conflict	• Leadership styles
• Incomplete information for decisions	• Threats to health		• Conflicting personalities

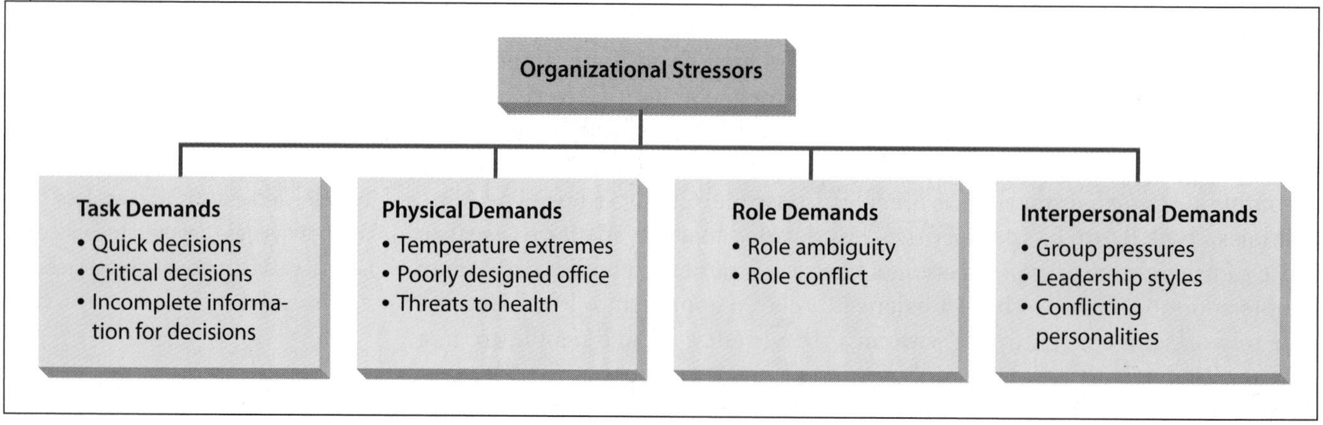

TODAY'S MANAGEMENT ISSUES

Stress and Workplace Violence

Almost everyone experiences stress in one form or another. Stress may cause such things as anxiety or high blood pressure. Occasionally, however, the level of stress experienced by an individual may become so great that it pushes that person over the edge. He or she may then take action that results in destruction or even death. For example, consider the case of James Daniel Simpson, a quiet and reserved young man who no one ever expected to cause trouble.

"He really seemed like a regular guy. He was quiet, and mostly kept to himself. I would never have dreamed that he could do something like this."

Anonymous Rossler employee*

Throughout his high school years in El Paso, Simpson was quiet and reserved. He never caused any problems, but made few friends. Classmates and neighbors recall him as being polite and dependable. They also note that he didn't talk much and usually kept to himself. He moved to Corpus Christi in 1992 and went to work for the Walter Rossler Company. Rossler performs consulting work for area refinery industries and specializes in ultrasonic inspections. Rossler paid $1,900 for Simpson to enroll in some training courses at a local college. Like other employees who took advantage of Rossler's training incentive, Simpson signed an agreement to repay the money if he left the company for any reason within three years of the date of the agreement. The agreement itself was dated November 3, 1993.

By all accounts Simpson was an average worker—his work was acceptable, but he did not distinguish himself in any way. He occasionally came to work late, but his overall performance was satisfactory. The only complaint that Simpson himself voiced was to object to the company's policy requiring employees to come and go through the back door. He resented this policy because a few managers and secretaries were "exempt" and were allowed to use the front door. In September 1994 he quit his job at Rossler and began to look for other work. After repeated attempts to recover the money it had spent for Simpson's training, Rossler filed a lawsuit against him on November 1, 1994. The suit was eventually settled out of court with Simpson agreeing to repay $700 of the total amount. Rossler also provided unsatisfactory references for Simpson as he continued to search for a new job.

Over the next six months, Simpson's savings dwindled, and his prospects for work disappeared. In February 1995 he purchased two guns from a local dealer. Shortly thereafter, he ran out of money and pawned his television, one of his last assets. On the afternoon of Monday, April 3, 1995, Simpson drove to a local park and fired several shots into the air. After leaving the park, he drove to the offices of Walter Rossler Company and parked in front of the building. His former coworkers at Rossler had often chided him for using an antitheft alarm in his old, beat-up Subaru. On this day, however, he did not bother to set the alarm.

He walked directly to the building and entered through the front door. Once inside, he systematically walked through the facility, shooting and killing five people. It appeared that he was seeking out specific targets. As he approached each one, Simpson first cursed them and then shot them. Along the way, he bypassed at least two employees without so much as a second glance. He also spared Lisa Rossler, daughter of the owners, and her infant son. Simpson then walked out through the back door of the building and into a small shed. Once inside, he killed himself with a single shot to the head.

Sources: *"Employers on Guard for Violence,"* Wall Street Journal, *April 5, 1995, pp. 3A; "Dialing the Stress-Meter Down,"* Newsweek, *March 6, 1995, p. 62; and personal research by the author.*

Interpersonal demands are stressors associated with relationships that confront people in organizations. For example, group pressures regarding restriction of output and norm conformity can lead to stress. Leadership style may

Psychological contracts help define mutual understandings between people and their employers in terms of what inducements the organization will provide in return for contributions from individuals. In general, the higher the inducements, the greater the contributions that are expected, and vice versa. Psychological contracts are often more central to people than to organizations, however. As illustrated in this cartoon, managers often bring work home—sometimes tangible work and other times things that are more intangible. If they feel they are being properly rewarded, these managers will continue to provide this extra level of support. But if they feel their extra efforts are not appreciated, they are inclined to cut back on these extra contributions.

also cause stress. Employees who feel a strong need to participate in decision making may feel stress if their boss refuses to allow participation. And individuals with conflicting personalities may experience stress if required to work too closely together. A person with an internal locus of control might be frustrated when working with someone who prefers to wait and just let things happen.

Consequences of Stress As noted earlier, the results of stress may be positive or negative. The negative consequences may be behavioral, psychological, or medical. Behaviorally, for example, stress may lead to detrimental or harmful actions, such as smoking, alcoholism, overeating, and drug abuse. Other stress-induced behaviors are accident proneness, violence toward self or others, and appetite disorders.

Psychological consequences of stress interfere with an individual's mental health and well-being. These outcomes include sleep disturbances, depression, family problems, and sexual dysfunction. Managers are especially prone to sleep disturbances when they experience stress at work.[24] Medical consequences of stress affect an individual's physiological well-being. Heart disease and stroke have been linked to stress, as have headaches, backaches, ulcers and related disorders, and skin conditions such as acne and hives.

Individual stress also has direct consequences for businesses. For an operating employee stress may translate into poor quality work and lower productivity. For a manager stress may mean faulty decision making and disruptions in working relationships. Withdrawal behaviors can also result from stress. People who are having difficulties with stress in their jobs are more likely to call in sick or to leave the organization. More subtle forms of withdrawal may also occur. A manager may start missing deadlines, for example, or taking longer lunch breaks. Employees may also withdraw by developing feelings of indifference. The irritation displayed by people under great stress can make them difficult to get along with. Job satisfaction, morale, and commitment can all suffer as a result of excessive levels of stress. So, too, can motivation to perform.

burnout A feeling of exhaustion that may develop when someone experiences too much stress for an extended period of time

Another consequence of stress is **burnout**—a feeling of exhaustion that may develop when someone experiences too much stress for an extended period of time. Burnout results in constant fatigue, frustration, and helplessness. Increased rigidity follows, as does a loss of self-confidence and psychological withdrawal. The individual dreads going to work, often puts in longer hours but get less accomplished than before, and exhibits signs of mental and physical exhaustion. Because of the damaging effects of burnout, some firms are taking steps to help avoid it. For example, British Airways trains its employees to recognize the symptoms of burnout and to develop strategies for avoiding it.

■ Managing Stress

Given the potential negative consequences of stress, people and organizations should be concerned about how to limit its more damaging effects. Many approaches have been developed to help people and organizations manage stress.[25]

One way people manage stress is through exercise. People who exercise regularly feel less tension and stress, are more self-confident, and more optimistic. Their better physical condition also makes them less susceptible to many common illnesses. People who don't exercise regularly, on the other hand, tend to feel more stress and are more likely to be depressed. They are also more likely to have heart attacks. And because of their physical condition, they are more likely to contract illnesses.

Another method people use to manage stress is relaxation. Relaxation allows individuals to adapt to, and therefore better deal with, their stress. Relaxation comes in many forms, such as taking regular vacations. A recent study found that people's attitudes toward a variety of workplace characteristics improved significantly following a vacation. People can also learn to relax at work. For example, some experts recommend that people take regular rest breaks during their normal workday.

People can also use time management to control stress. The idea behind time management is that many daily pressures can be reduced or eliminated if individuals do a better job of managing time. One approach to time management is to make a list every morning of the things to be done that day. The items on the list are then grouped into three categories: critical activities that must be performed, important activities that should be performed, and optional or trivial things that can be delegated or postponed. The individual performs the items on the list in their order of importance.

Finally, people can manage stress through support groups. A support group can be as simple as a group of family members or friends to enjoy leisure time with. Going out after work with a couple of coworkers to a basketball game or a movie, for example, can help relieve stress built up during the day. Family and friends can help people cope with stress on an ongoing basis and during times of crisis. For example, an employee who has just learned that she did not get the promotion she has been working toward for months may find it helpful to have a good friend to lean on, to talk to, or to yell at. People also may make use of more elaborate and formal support groups. Community centers or religious institutions, for example, may sponsor support groups for people who have recently gone through a divorce, the death of a loved one, or some other tragedy.

Stress can be a powerful force in organizations. Dr. Madan Kataria has founded 37 "laughing clubs" to help people in high-stress jobs cope with pressure and tension. His approach includes deep breathing exercises and yoga, but also relies heavily on laughter.

Organizations are also beginning to realize that they should be involved in helping employees cope with stress. One argument is that because the business is at least partially responsible for stress, the business should also help relieve it. Another argument is that stress-related insurance claims by employees can be expensive for the organization. Still another reason that business should be involved in helping employees cope with stress is that workers experiencing lower levels of detrimental stress will be able to function more effectively. AT&T has initiated a series of seminars and workshops to help its employees cope with the stress they face in their jobs. The firm was prompted to develop these seminars for these three reasons.

A wellness stress program is a special part of the organization specifically created to help deal with stress. Organizations have adopted stress management programs, health promotion programs, and other kinds of programs for this purpose. The AT&T seminar program noted earlier is similar to this idea, but true wellness programs are ongoing activities that have many components. They commonly include exercise-related activities as well as classroom instruction dealing with smoking cessation, weight reduction, and general stress management.

Some companies are developing their own programs or using existing programs of this type. Johns-Manville, for example, has a gym at its corporate headquarters. Other firms negotiate discounted health club membership rates with local establishments. For the instructional part of the program, the organization can sponsor its own training or perhaps jointly sponsor seminars with a local YMCA, civic organization, or religious institution. Organization-based fitness programs facilitate employee exercise, a very positive consideration, but such programs are also quite costly. Nevertheless, more and more companies are developing fitness programs for their employees.

MANAGEMENT IMPLICATIONS Managers should know the processes through which stress affects people. Being able to assess and deal with the causes and consequences of stress is especially important. Knowing whether people are more prone toward Type A or Type B behavior is also of value to managers. Finally, managers need to recognize that they have the capacity to help themselves and others cope with work-related stress.

Creativity in Organizations

creativity The ability of an individual to generate new ideas or to conceive of new perspectives on existing ideas

Creativity is yet another important component of individual behavior in organizations. **Creativity** is the ability of an individual to generate new ideas or to conceive of new perspectives on existing ideas. What makes a person creative? How do people become creative? How does the creative process work?

Although psychologists have not yet discovered complete answers to these questions, examining a few general patterns can help us understand the sources of individual creativity within organizations.[26]

■ The Creative Individual

Numerous researchers have focused their efforts on attempting to describe the common attributes of creative individuals. These attributes generally fall into three categories: background experiences, personal traits, and cognitive abilities.

Background Experiences and Creativity   Researchers have observed that many creative individuals were raised in an environment in which creativity was nurtured. Mozart was raised in a family of musicians and began composing and performing music at age six. Pierre and Marie Curie, great scientists in their own right, also raised a daughter, Irene, who won the Nobel Prize in chemistry. Thomas Edison's creativity was nurtured by his mother. However, people with background experiences very different from theirs have also been creative. The African-American abolitionist and writer Frederick Douglass was born into slavery in Tuckahoe, Maryland, and had very limited opportunities for education. Nonetheless, his creative thinking and powerful oratory helped lead to the Emancipation Proclamation, which outlawed slavery in the United States.

Personal Traits and Creativity   Certain personal traits have also been linked to creativity in individuals. The traits shared by most creative people are openness, an attraction to complexity, high levels of energy, independence and autonomy, strong self-confidence, and a strong belief that one is, in fact, creative. Individuals who possess these traits are more likely to be creative than are those who do not have them.

Cognitive Abilities and Creativity   Cognitive abilities are an individual's power to think intelligently and to analyze situations and data effectively. Intelligence may be a precondition for individual creativity—although most creative people are highly intelligent, not all intelligent people necessarily are creative. Creativity is also linked with the ability to think divergently and convergently. *Divergent thinking* is a skill that allows people to see differences between situations, phenomena, or events. *Convergent thinking* is a skill that allows people to see similarities between situations, phenomena, or events. Creative people are generally very skilled at both divergent and convergent thinking.

Interestingly, Japanese managers have recently questioned their own creative ability. The concern is that their emphasis on group harmony has perhaps stifled individual initiative and hampered the development of individual creativity. As a result, many Japanese firms, including Omron Corporation, Fuji Photo, and Shimizu Corporation, have launched employee training programs intended to boost the creativity of their employees.[27]

■ The Creative Process

Although creative people often report that ideas seem to come to them "in a flash," individual creative activity actually tends to progress through a series of stages. While not all creative activity has to follow these four stages, much of it does.

Preparation   The creative process normally begins with a period of *preparation*. Formal education and training are usually the most efficient ways of becoming familiar with this vast amount of research and knowledge. To make a creative contribution to business management or business services, individuals must usually receive formal training and education in business, which is one reason for the strong demand for undergraduate and master's level business education. Formal business education can be an effective way for an individual to get up to speed and begin making creative contributions quickly. Experiences that managers have on the job after their formal training has finished can also contribute to the creative process. In an important sense the education and training of creative people never really ends. It continues as long as they remain interested in the world and curious about the way things work.

Incubation   The second phase of the creative process is *incubation*—a period of less intense conscious concentration during which the knowledge and ideas acquired during preparation mature and develop. A curious aspect of incubation is that it is often helped along by pauses in concentrated rational thought. Some creative people rely on physical activity such as jogging or swimming to provide a "break" from thinking. Others may read or listen to music. Sometimes sleep may even supply the needed pause.

While out rowing one day, David Morse, a research scientist at Corning, hit on the answer to a difficult product improvement. Morse had a special interest in a new line of cookware called Visions. These glass pots and pans had many advantages over traditional cookware, but no one at Corning had yet succeeded in putting a nonstick surface on the glass. Looking for a solution to this problem, Morse put in many long days in the laboratory, but it was during his hours of rowing that the ideas and concepts that would enable him to devise a nonstick coating began to come together and mature. Morse may never have been able to solve this technical problem if he had not taken the time to let his ideas incubate.

Insight   Usually occurring after preparation and incubation, *insight* is a spontaneous breakthrough in which the creative person achieves a new understanding of some problem or situation. Insight represents a coming together of all

Creativity is an important ingredient in business success. Managers at Kimberly-Clark were looking for new product ideas when they were interviewing parents who were toilet training their toddlers. The parents expressed frustration at existing products, so Kimberly-Clark developed Pull-Ups—a disposable diaper which can be pulled down and then pulled back up during training. Pull-Ups have been so successful that they now bring in $500 million a year for the company.

the scattered thoughts and ideas that were maturing during incubation. It may occur suddenly or develop slowly over time. Insight can be triggered by some external event, such as a new experience or an encounter with new data that forces the individual to think about old issues and problems in new ways, or it can be a completely internal event in which patterns of thought finally coalesce in ways that generate new understanding.

One manager's key insight led to a complete restructuring of Citibank's back room operations. (*Back room operations* refers to the enormous avalanche of paperwork that a bank must process in order to serve its customers—listing checks and deposits, updating accounts, and preparing bank statements.) Historically, back room operations at Citibank had been managed as if they were part of the regular banking operation. When John Reed arrived on the scene as vice president, he realized that back room operations had less to do with banking and more to do with manufacturing. Reed's insight was that back room operations could be managed as a paper-manufacturing process. On the basis of this insight, he hired former manufacturing managers from Ford and other automobile companies. By reconceptualizing the nature of back room operations, Reed was able to substantially reduce the costs of these operations for Citibank.

Verification   Once an insight has occurred, *verification* determines the validity or truthfulness of the insight. For many creative ideas, verification includes scientific experiments to determine whether or not the insight actually leads to the results expected. In David Morse's case, the insight concerning how to apply a nonstick coating on glass pots was verified in several important experiments and practical trials. Without these experiments and trials, Morse's idea would have remained an interesting concept with little practical application. Verification may also include the development of a product or service prototype. A *prototype* is one (or a very small number) of products built just to see whether the ideas behind this new product actually work. Product prototypes are rarely sold to the public but are very valuable in verifying the insights developed in the creative process. After the new product or service is developed, verification in the marketplace is the ultimate test of the creative idea behind it.

■ Enhancing Creativity in Organizations

Managers who wish to enhance and promote creativity in their organization can do so in a variety of ways.[28] One important method for enhancing creativity is to make it a part of the organization's culture, often through explicit goals. Firms that truly want to stress creativity, such as 3M and Rubbermaid, state goals that some percent of future revenues are to be gained from new products. This statement clearly communicates that creativity and innovation are valued.

Another important part of enhancing creativity is to reward creative successes while being careful to not punish creative failures. Many ideas that seem worthwhile on paper fail to pan out in reality. If the first person to come up with an idea that fails is fired or otherwise punished, others in the organization will become more cautious in their own work. And as a result, fewer creative ideas will emerge.

Managers need to understand the creative process. The ability to recognize and nurture creativity in others can be especially valuable, as can creating an environment through which creativity is more likely to emerge. ■

Types of Workplace Behaviors

workplace behavior A pattern of action by the members of an organization that directly or indirectly influences organizational effectiveness

Now that we have looked closely at how individual differences can influence behavior in organizations, let's turn our attention to what we mean by workplace behavior. **Workplace behavior** is a pattern of action by the members of an organization that directly or indirectly influences organizational effectiveness. Important workplace behaviors include performance and productivity, absenteeism and turnover, and organizational citizenship.

■ Performance Behaviors

performance behaviors The total set of work-related behaviors that the organization expects the individual to display

Performance behaviors are the total set of work-related behaviors that the organization expects the individual to display. Thus, they derive from the psychological contract. For some jobs performance behaviors can be narrowly defined and easily measured. For example, an assembly line worker who attaches parts to a product as it passes by on a moving conveyor has relatively few performance behaviors. He or she is expected to remain at the work station and correctly attach the parts. Performance can often be assessed quantitatively by counting the percentage of parts correctly attached.

For many other jobs, however, performance behaviors are more diverse and much more difficult to assess. For example, consider the case of a research and development scientist at Merck. The scientist works in a lab trying to find new scientific breakthroughs that have commercial potential. The scientist must apply knowledge learned in graduate school with experience gained from previous research. Intuition and creativity are also important elements. And the desired breakthrough may take months or even years to accomplish. As we discussed in Chapter 14, organizations use many techniques to evaluate performance. The key, of course, is to match the evaluation mechanism with the job being performed.

■ Withdrawal Behavior

absenteeism When an individual does not show up for work

Another important type of work-related behavior results in withdrawal—absenteeism and turnover. **Absenteeism** occurs when an individual does not show up for work. The cause may be legitimate (illness, jury duty, death in the family, and so on) or feigned (reported as legitimate but actually just an excuse not to come to work). When an employee is absent, her or his work does not get done at all or a substitute must be hired to do it. In either case the quantity or quality of actual output is likely to suffer. Obviously, some absenteeism is expected. The key concern of organizations is to minimize feigned absenteeism and reduce legitimate absences as much as possible. High absenteeism may be a symptom of other problems as well, such as job dissatisfaction and low morale.

Turnover occurs when people quit their jobs. An organization usually incurs costs in replacing individuals who have quit, but turnover that involves especially productive people is even more costly. Turnover seems to result from a number of factors including aspects of the job, the organization, the individual, the labor market, and family influences. In general, a poor person-job fit is also a likely cause of turnover.

turnover When people quit their jobs

Efforts to directly manage turnover are frequently fraught with difficulty, even in organizations that concentrate on rewarding good performers. Of course, some turnover is inevitable, and in some cases it may even be desirable. For example, if the organization is trying to cut costs by reducing its staff, having people leave voluntarily is preferable to having to terminate them. And if the people who choose to leave are low performers or express high levels of job dissatisfaction, the organization may also benefit from turnover.

■ Organizational Citizenship

Organizational citizenship refers to the behavior that makes a positive overall contribution to the organization.[29] Consider, for example, an employee who does work that is acceptable in terms of quantity and quality. However, she refuses to work overtime, she won't help newcomers learn the ropes, and she is generally unwilling to make any contribution to the organization beyond the strict performance of her job. Although she might be seen as a good performer, she is not likely to be seen as a good organizational citizen. Another employee may exhibit a comparable level of performance. In addition, however, he will always work late when the boss asks him to, he takes time to help newcomers learn their way around, and he is perceived as being helpful and committed to the organization's success. Although his level of performance may be seen as equal to that of the first worker, he is also likely to be seen as a better organizational citizen.

organizational citizenship The behavior of individuals that makes a positive overall contribution to the organization

The determinant of organizational citizenship behaviors is likely to be a complex mosaic of individual, social, and organizational variables. For example, the personality, attitudes, and needs of the individual will have to be consistent with citizenship behaviors. Similarly, the social context, or work group, in which the individual works will need to facilitate and promote such behaviors. (We discuss group dynamics in Chapter 19.) And the organization itself, especially its culture, must be capable of promoting, recognizing, and rewarding these types of behaviors if they are to be maintained. Although the study of organizational citizenship is still in its infancy, preliminary research suggests that it may play a powerful role in organizational effectiveness.[30]

MANAGEMENT IMPLICATIONS Managers should realize that employees can exhibit a wide array of workplace behaviors. Managers should try to determine which behaviors are most important and seek ways of encouraging those behaviors, instead of alternative behaviors. ■

Summary of Key Points

Understanding individuals in organizations is an important consideration for all managers. A basic framework that can be used to facilitate this understanding is the psychological contract—the set of expectations held by people with respect to what they will contribute to the organization and what they expect to get in return. Organizations strive to achieve an optimal person-job fit, but this process is complicated by the existence of individual differences.

Personality is the relatively stable set of psychological and behavioral attributes that distinguish one person from another. The big-five personality traits are agreeableness, conscientiousness, negative emotionality, extraversion, and openness. Other important traits are locus of control, self-efficacy, authoritarianism, Machiavellianism, self-esteem, and risk propensity.

Attitudes are based on emotion, knowledge, and intended behavior. Whereas personality is relatively stable, some attitudes can be formed and changed easily. Others are more constant. Job satisfaction or dissatisfaction and organizational commitment are important work-related attitudes.

Perception is the set of processes by which an individual becomes aware of and interprets information about the environment. Basic perceptual processes include selective perception and stereotyping. Perception and attribution are also closely related.

Stress is an individual's response to a strong stimulus. The General Adaptation Syndrome outlines the basic stress process. Stress can be caused by task, physical, role, and interpersonal demands. Consequences of stress include certain outcomes most relevant to individuals and other outcomes most relevant to organizations, as well as burnout. Several things can be done to manage stress.

Creativity is the capacity to generate new ideas. Creative people tend to have certain profiles of background experiences, personal traits, and cognitive abilities. The creative process itself includes preparation, incubation, insight, and verification.

Workplace behavior is a pattern of action by the members of an organization that directly or indirectly influences organizational effectiveness. Performance behaviors are the set of work-related behaviors the organization expects the individual to display in order to fulfill the psychological contract. Basic withdrawal behaviors are absenteeism and turnover. Organizational citizenship refers to behavior that makes a positive overall contribution to the organization.

Discussion Questions

Questions for Review

1. What is a psychological contract? Why is it important?

2. Identify and describe five basic personality attributes.

3. Identify and discuss the steps in the creative process.

4. Identify and describe several important workplace behaviors.

Questions for Analysis

5. An individual described someone else as having "no personality." What is wrong with this statement? What did the individual actually mean?

6. Describe a circumstance in which you formed a new attitude about something.

7. As a manager, how would you go about trying to make someone a better organizational citizen?

Questions for Application

8. Write the psychological contract you have in this class. That is, what do you contribute, and what inducements are available? Compare your contract with those of some of your classmates. In what ways are they similar, and in what ways is your unique?

9. Assume you are going to hire three new employees for the department store you manage, one will sell shoes, one will manage the toy department, and one

will work in the stockroom. Identify the basic characteristics each person should have to achieve a good person-job fit.

10. Make a list of the things that cause stress for the typical college student. Now make a list of how college students manage stress. Compare your lists with those of three of your classmates.

Building Effective Diagnostic & Conceptual Skills

EXERCISE OVERVIEW

Conceptual skills refer to a manager's ability to think in the abstract, whereas diagnostic skills focus on responses to situations. These skills must frequently be used together to better understand the behavior of others in the organization, as illustrated by this exercise.

EXERCISE BACKGROUND

Human behavior is a complex phenomenon in any setting, but especially so in organizations. Understanding how and why people choose particular behaviors can be difficult and frustrating, but quite important. Consider, for example, the following scenario.

Sandra Buckley has worked in your department for several years. Until recently, she has been a "model" employee. She was always on time, or early, for work and stayed late whenever necessary to get her work done. She was upbeat, cheerful, and worked very hard. She frequently said that the company was the best place she had ever worked and that you were the perfect boss.

About six months ago, however, you began to see changes in Sandra's behavior. She occasionally comes in late, and you cannot remember the last time she agreed to work past 5:00. She also complains a lot. Other workers have started to avoid her, because she is so negative all the time. You also suspect that she may be looking for a new job.

EXERCISE TASK

Using the preceding scenario as background, do the following:

1. Assume that you have done some background work to find out what has happened. Write a brief scenario with more information that might explain why Sandra's behavior has changed (for example, your case might include the fact that you recently promoted someone else when Sandra might have expected to get the job). Make your scenario as descriptive as possible.

2. Relate elements of your case to the various behavioral concepts discussed in this chapter.

3. Decide whether or not you might be able to resolve things with Sandra to overcome whatever issues have arisen. That is, do you think you can correct the situation?

4. Which behavioral process or concept discussed in this chapter is easiest to change? Which is the most difficult to change?

Building Effective Time-Management Skills

EXERCISE OVERVIEW

Time-management skills help people prioritize work, work more efficiently, and delegate appropriately. Poor time management, in turn, may result in stress. This exercise will help you relate time-management skills to stress reduction.

EXERCISE BACKGROUND

Make a list of several of the major things that cause stress for you. Stressors might involve school (for example, hard classes, too many exams), work (for example, financial pressures, demanding work schedule), and/or personal circumstances (for example, friends, romance, family). Try to be as specific as possible. Also try to identify at least ten different stressors.

EXERCISE TASK

Use your list to do each of the following:

1. Evaluate the extent to which poor time management on your part plays a role in how each stressor affects you. For example, do exams cause stress because you delay studying?

2. Develop a strategy for dealing with each time-related stressor.

3. Note interrelationships among different kinds of stressors and time. For example, financial pressures may cause you to work, but work may interfere with school. Can any of these interrelationships be more effectively managed vis-à-vis time?

4. How do you manage the stress in your life? Is it possible to manage stress in a more time-effective manner?

Building Effective Interpersonal Skills

EXERCISE OVERVIEW

Interpersonal skills refer to the ability to communicate with, understand, and motivate individuals and groups. Implicit in this definition is the notion that a manager should try to understand important characteristics of others, including their personalities. This exercise will give you insights into both the importance of personality in the workplace as well as some of the difficulties associated with assessing personality traits.

EXERCISE BACKGROUND

You will first try to determine which personality traits are most relevant for different jobs. You will then write a series of questions that you think may help assess or measure those traits in prospective employees. First, read each of the following job descriptions:

Sales representative: This position involves calling on existing customers to ensure that they are happy with the firm's products. It also requires the sales representative to work to get customers to increase the quantity of your products they are buying, as well as attracting new customers. A sales representative must be aggressive, but not pushy.

Office manager: The office manager oversees the work of a staff of twenty secretaries, receptionists, and clerks. The manager hires them, trains them, evaluates their performance, and sets their pay. The manager also schedules working hours and, when necessary, disciplines or fires workers.

Warehouse worker: Warehouse workers unload trucks and carry shipments to shelves for storage. They also pull customer orders from shelves and take products for packing. The job requires workers to follow orders precisely and has little room for autonomy or interaction with others during work.

EXERCISE TASK

Working alone, identify a single personality trait that you think is especially important for a person to be able to effectively perform each of these three jobs. Next, write five questions, which, when answered by a job applicant, will help you assess how that applicant scores on that particular trait. These questions should be of the type that can be answered on a five-point scale (for example, strongly agree, agree, neither agree or disagree, disagree, strongly disagree).

Exchange questions with a classmate. Pretend you are a job applicant. Provide honest and truthful answers to each question. Discuss the traits each of you identified for each position. How well you think your classmate's questions actually measure those traits?

Conclude by addressing the following questions:

1. How easy is it to measure personality?

2. How important do you believe it is for organizations to consider personality in hiring decisions?

3. Do perception and attitudes affect how people answer personality questions?

CHAPTER CLOSING CASE

Hard Work or Dead End?

People everywhere seem to be working longer hours. Sometimes they do it to survive, sometimes because they want to, and sometimes because they see it as a means to an end. Consider, for example, Julie Herendeen, Richard Thibeault, and Josh McIntyre. Ms. Herendeen has an MBA from Harvard and is considered to be one of the best and the brightest young managers at Netscape. Herendeen's workday starts at 6:30 A.M. when she checks her e-mail from her home computer.

By 8:30, Julie is in her office cubicle. She immediately turns on her computer and discovers a new string of e-mails that have arrived since she last checked only an hour and a half earlier. She eats fast-food breakfast at her computer while she answers these messages. Throughout the day, Herendeen attends a variety of meetings and conferences. Finally, around 5:00 in the evening when many workers in other industries are headed home, Julie escapes the endless litany of meetings and conversations and finally makes it to her own desk again where she can begin to work. At 8:30 that evening, she's still working. During the last 3¹/2 hours, she has continued to respond to e-mail and voice mail. She also developed an outline of a sales presentation. Finally, at 9:00 she leaves her office. Ms. Herendeen says she loves her work and can't see doing anything else.

Richard Thibeault also works long hours. Thibeault manages an Au Bon Pain bakery café in Boston. But much of what he has to do doesn't seem like management at all. Like many other businesses, Au Bon Pain has cut back on its workforce and is holding store managers strictly accountable for keeping costs in line. Thus Richard now does a lot of work that he once had employees to do. For example, he is often at work at 3:00 A.M. to start baking rolls and pastries. During the day he also empties trash, fills in at the cash register when his employees take a lunch break, and cleans tables.

Because Au Bon Pain does little evening business, he can often get off around 4:00 or so in the afternoon during the week. He also works long hours on Saturday and Sunday. Mr. Thibeault recently calculated that he was working around seventy hours a week and earning the equivalent of $7.83 an hour—scarcely more than the wages his part-time workers make. But he is under constant pressure from the home office to shave costs and boost revenues. He doesn't know how much longer he can keep it up, though. His doctor is already telling him he needs to quit before he suffers serious health problems.

Finally, Josh McIntyre works at a small electronics factory in California. He has a law degree and started out as an attorney with a major law firm in a big city. But from the day he started he was miserable. Although the pay was good, the pressure was unrelenting. He routinely worked seventy or more hours a week and sometimes exceeded one hundred hours. He was doing very well; he received regular feedback that the partners were very pleased with his work and that big things were on the horizon.

One night, however, as he was walking to his car at 10:00, he realized that it was his birthday. No one had known it, and it had passed without fanfare. Indeed, he had not talked to anyone outside his law practice for weeks—had not watched television, had not exercised, had not read a novel. In short, all he was doing was working. The next day, he tendered his resignation and moved to a small town near his family home. Josh's brother helped him get a job assembling electrical components. He makes an hourly wage, but works only forty hours a week.

McIntyre says that he is happier now than he's ever been in his life. He isn't making much money, but he has plenty of personal time to do the things he enjoys. For example, he has learned to play the guitar and is taking up gardening. He still thinks about law, however, and intends to get back into it soon. However, his plan is to start a small practice in a rural community where he can avoid the big-city pressures and stress that drove him away in the first place.

Case Questions

1. What individual differences might explain the three people discussed in this case?

2. Why do you think these three individuals have made certain choices, but not others?

3. Identify causes and consequences of stress that might be relevant for each of these three people.

Case References: Stratford Sherman, "A Day in the Life of a Netscape Exec," *Fortune*, May 13, 1996, pp. 124–130; and "For Richard Thibeault, Being a 'Manager' Is a Blue-Collar Life," *Wall Street Journal*, October 1, 1996, pp. A1, A12.

CHAPTER NOTES

1. "Cost Cutting at Delta Raises the Stock Price but Lowers the Service," *Wall Street Journal*, June 20, 1996, pp. A1, A8; and *Hoover's Handbook of American Business 1998* (Austin, Texas: The Reference Press, 1998), pp. 468–469.

2. Lynn McGarlane Shore and Lois Tetrick, "The Psychological Contract as an Explanatory Framework in the Employment Relationship," in *Trends in Organizational Behavior*, eds. C. L. Cooper and D. M. Rousseau (London: John Wiley & Sons Ltd., 1994), pp. 91–110.

3. Elizabeth Wolfe Morrison and Sandra L. Robinson, "When Employees Feel Betrayed: A Model of How Psychological Contract Violation Develops," *Academy of Management Review*, January 1997, pp. 226–256. See also Gary Powell, "The Simultaneous Pursuit of Person-Organization Fit and Diversity," *Organizational Dynamics*, Winter 1998, pp. 50–61.

4. Lawrence Pervin, "Personality" in *Annual Review of Psychology*, Vol. 36, eds. Mark Rosenzweig and Lyman Porter (Palo Alto, Calif.: Annual Reviews, 1985), pp. 83–114; and S. R. Maddi, *Personality Theories: A Comparative Analysis*, 4th ed. (Homewood, Ill.: Dorsey, 1980).

5. L. R. Goldberg, "An Alternative 'Description of Personality': The Big Five Factor Structure," *Journal of Personality and Social Psychology*, 1990, Vol. 59, pp. 1216–1229.

6. Michael K. Mount, Murray R. Barrick, and J. Perkins Strauss, "Validity of Observer Ratings of the Big Five Personality Factors," *Journal of Applied Psychology*, 1994, Vol. 79, No. 2, pp. 272–280; and Timothy A. Judge, Joseph J. Martocchio, and Carl J. Thoreson, "Five-Factor Model of Personality and Employee Absence," *Journal of Applied Psychology*, 1997, Vol. 82, No. 5, pp. 745–755.

7. J. B. Rotter, "Generalized Expectancies for Internal vs. External Control of Reinforcement," *Psychological Monographs*, 1966, Vol. 80, pp. 1–28.

8. Marilyn E. Gist and Terence R. Mitchell, "Self-Efficacy: A Theoretical Analysis of Its Determinants and Malleability," *Academy of Management Review*, April 1992, pp. 183–211.

9. T. W. Adorno, E. Frenkel-Brunswick, D. J. Levinson, and R. N. Sanford, *The Authoritarian Personality* (New York: Harper & Row, 1950).

10. Jon L. Pierce, Donald G. Gardner, and Larry L. Cummings, "Organization-Based Self-Esteem: Construct Definition, Measurement, and Validation," *Academy of Management Journal*, 1989, Vol. 32, pp. 622–648.

11. Michael Harris Bond and Peter B. Smith, "Cross-Cultural Social and Organizational Psychology," in *Annual Review of Psychology*, Vol. 47, ed. Janet Spence (Palo Alto, Calif.: Annual Reviews, 1996), pp. 205–235.

12. Leon Festinger, *A Theory of Cognitive Dissonance* (Palo Alto, Calif.: Stanford University Press, 1957).

13. Patricia C. Smith, L. M. Kendall, and Charles Hulin, *The Measurement of Satisfaction in Work and Behavior* (Chicago: Rand-McNally, 1969).

14. James R. Lincoln, "Employee Work Attitudes and Management Practice in the U.S. and Japan: Evidence from a Large Comparative Study," *California Management Review*, Fall 1989, pp. 89–106.

15. Lincoln, "Employee Work Attitudes and Management Practice in the U.S. and Japan: Evidence from a Large Comparative Study."

16. Richard M. Steers, "Antecedents and Outcomes of Organizational Commitment," *Administrative Science Quarterly*, 1977, Vol. 22, pp. 46–56. See also Karen E. Mishra, Gretchen M. Spreitzer, and Aneil K. Mishra, "Preserving Employee Morale during Downsizing," *Sloan Management Review*, Winter 1998, pp. 83–95.

17. For research work in this area, see Jennifer M. George and Gareth R. Jones, "The Experience of Mood and Turnover Intentions: Interactive Effects of Value Attainment, Job Satisfaction, and Positive Mood," *Journal of Applied Psychology*, 1996, Vol. 81, No. 3, pp. 318–325; and Larry J. Williams, Mark B. Gavin, and Margaret Williams, "Measurement and Nonmeasurement Processes with Negative Affectivity and Employee Attitudes," *Journal of Applied Psychology*, 1996, Vol. 81, No. 1, pp. 88–101.

18. Kathleen Sutcliffe, "What Executives Notice: Accurate Perceptions in Top Management Teams," *Academy of Management Journal*, 1994, Vol. 37, No. 5, pp. 1360–1378.

19. For a classic treatment of attribution, see H. H. Kelley, *Attribution in Social Interaction* (Morristown, N.J.: General Learning Press, 1971).

20. For a recent overview of the stress literature, see Frank Landy, James Campbell Quick, and Stanislav Kasl, "Work, Stress, and Well-Being," *International Journal of Stress Management*, 1994, Vol. 1, No. 1, pp. 33–73.

21. Hans Selye, *The Stress of Life* (New York: McGraw-Hill, 1976).

22. M. Friedman and R. H. Rosenman, *Type A Behavior and Your Heart* (New York: Alfred A. Knopf, 1974).

23. "Work & Family," *Business Week*, June 28, 1993, pp. 80–88.

24. "Breaking Point," *Newsweek*, March 6, 1995, pp. 56–62.

25. John M. Kelly, "Get a Grip on Stress," *HRMagazine*, February 1997, pp. 51–58.

26. See Richard W. Woodman, John E. Sawyer, and Ricky W. Griffin, "Toward a Theory of Organizational Creativity," *Academy of Management Review*, April 1993, pp. 293–321.

27. Emily Thornton, "Japan's Struggle to Be Creative," *Fortune*, April 19, 1993, pp. 129–134.

28. Filiz Tabak, "Employee Creative Performance: What Makes It Happen?" *Academy of Management Executive*, 1997, Vol. 11, No. 1, pp. 119–122.

29. For recent findings regarding this behavior, see Dennis W. Organ, "Personality and Organizational Citizenship Behavior," *Journal of Management*, 1994, Vol. 20, No.2, pp. 465–478.

30. Mary Konovsky and S. Douglas Pugh, "Citizenship Behavior and Social Exchange," *Academy of Management Journal*, 1994, Vol. 37, No. 3, pp. 656–669; and Philip M. Podsakoff, Michael Ahearne, and Scott B. MacKenzie, "Organizational Citizenship Behavior and the Quantity and Quality of Work Group Performance," *Journal of Applied Psychology*, Vol. 82, No. 2, pp. 262–270.

16

Managing Employee Motivation and Performance

OBJECTIVES

After studying this chapter, you should be able to:

- Characterize the nature of motivation, including its importance and basic historical perspectives.
- Identify and describe the major content perspectives on motivation.
- Identify and describe the major process perspectives on motivation.
- Describe reinforcement perspectives on motivation.
- Identify and describe popular motivational strategies.
- Describe the role of organizational reward systems in motivation.

OUTLINE

Changing the work-related needs, motives, and values of an individual in an organization is, on its own merits, a daunting challenge. Consider, then, the difficulties inherent in trying to change the needs, motives, and values of an entire population. This is exactly the task being confronted by businesses in Saudi Arabia. For decades Saudi Arabia relied heavily on so-called guest workers to perform most of its menial and service-oriented jobs. People from Pakistan, Egypt, and the Philippines, for example, could easily enter Saudi Arabia and find steady work performing jobs that were unattractive to locals. And companies in Saudi Arabia took advantage of this situation by routinely hiring these guest workers for less attractive jobs and paying them relatively low wages. Most guest workers found jobs in restaurants, as security guards, as custodians and maintenance people, and as package couriers.

Recently, however, the government of Saudi Arabia has changed its liberal guest-worker policy. For one thing, a huge baby boom of Saudis is now reaching employment age and there aren't enough jobs to go around. For another, the government, a large employer itself, is in the midst of downsizing and has fewer jobs to offer citizens. Officials are now taking a much harder stance regarding guest workers. For example, few new guest workers are being admitted. And as current workers' visas expire, they are not being renewed, forcing those workers to leave the country. One new law bans foreign workers from owning cars. In some cities in Saudi Arabia, authorities can automatically close down a retail store if someone other than a Saudi national is working behind the counter. And the government has ordered all companies to increase their native workforce by 5 percent each year.

"If I'm supposed to be here at 8 and I come in at 9, why can't I stay until 3:30 instead of 2:30?"

Khalid Al Sharif, Saudi worker fired for coming to work late, quoted in the Wall Street Journal, *September 12, 1996, p. A1.*

A problem, however, arises from the prevailing work ethic reflected by the preceding quotation. Because most Saudi workers have grown up in a privileged setting and have had autonomy over where and when they worked, they have trouble adjusting to more regimented and routine work situations. While progress is being made in some companies, others still face major motivational challenges. For example, McDonald's is having a difficult time attracting enough qualified Saudis to hold management positions in its restaurants. Most Saudis consider restaurant work demeaning, regardless of the actual position held.

And even though many workers are trying, they still have trouble adjusting to a traditional work environment. For example, when beginning higher-level business dealings in Saudi Arabia, managers typically spend a considerable amount of time exchanging information and asking questions about one another's families. Many young Saudis who are working in lower-level positions now still adhere to this practice; they may trade as many as a dozen pleasantries before getting down to business. And they are also prone to showing unfailing hospitality to visitors. Although this approach is desirable in some situations, in others it can be counterproductive. For example, Saudi workers have been known to walk off their job at a busy airline counter to have tea with a friend who has strolled up— Saudis consider it rude to not be sociable with visitors, regardless of the circumstance![1]

Like employees throughout the world, workers in Saudi Arabia are motivated by fundamental needs, motives, and values. But as society changes, these workers are also having to change. These dynamics—the needs of the employees and how organizations can and cannot satisfy them—are fundamental concepts in employee motivation. Virtually any organization can have a motivated workforce. The trick is figuring how to create a system in which employees can receive rewards that they genuinely want by performing in ways that fit the organization's goals and objectives.

In most settings, people can choose how hard they work and how much effort they expend. Thus, managers need to understand how and why employees make different choices regarding their own performance. The key ingredient behind this choice is motivation, the subject of this chapter. We first examine the nature of employee motivation and then explore the major perspectives on motivation. Newly emerging approaches are then discussed. We conclude with a description of rewards and their role in motivation.

The Nature of Motivation

motivation The set of forces that cause people to behave in certain ways

Motivation is the set of forces that cause people to behave in certain ways.[2] On any given day, an employee may choose to work as hard as possible at a job, to work just hard enough to avoid a reprimand, or to do as little as possible. The goal for the manager is to maximize the likelihood of the first behavior and minimize the likelihood of the last one. This goal becomes all the more important when we understand the significance of motivation in the workplace.

■ The Importance of Employee Motivation in the Workplace

Individual performance is generally determined by three things: motivation (the desire to do the job), ability (the capability to do the job), and the work environment (the resources needed to do the job). If an employee lacks ability, the manager can provide training or replace the worker. If there is a resource problem, the manager can correct it. But if motivation is the problem, the task for the manager is more challenging. Individual behavior is a complex phenomenon, and the manager may be hard-pressed to figure out the precise nature of the problem and how to solve it.

FIGURE 16.1
The Motivation Framework

The motivation process progresses through a series of discrete steps. Content, process, and reinforcement perspectives on motivation address different parts of this process.

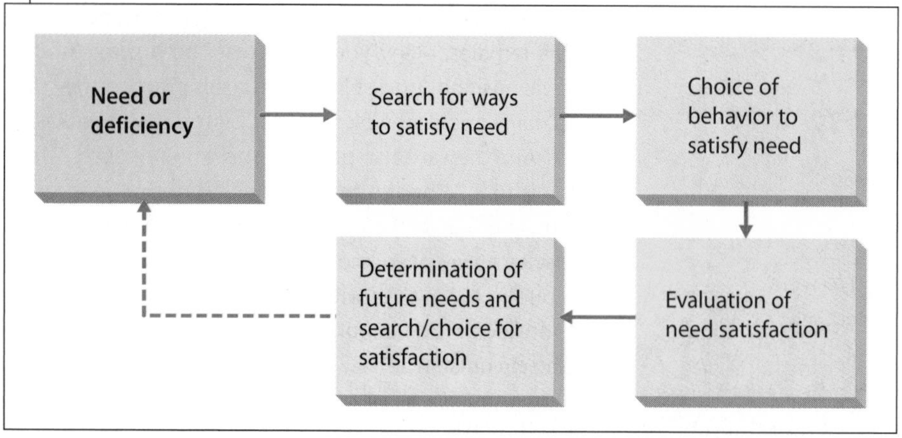

Need or deficiency → Search for ways to satisfy need → Choice of behavior to satisfy need → Evaluation of need satisfaction → Determination of future needs and search/choice for satisfaction ⤏ (back to Need or deficiency)

Thus, motivation is important because of its significance as a determinant of performance and because of its intangible character.

The motivation framework in Figure 16.1 is a good starting point for understanding how motivated behavior occurs. The motivation process begins with a need deficiency. For example, when a worker believes that she is underpaid, she experiences a need for more income. In response, the worker searches for ways to satisfy the need, such as working harder to try to earn a raise or seeking a new job. Next, she chooses an option to pursue. After carrying out the chosen option—working harder and putting in more hours for a reasonable period of time, for example—she then evaluates her success. If her hard work resulted in a pay raise, she probably feels good about things and will continue to work hard. But if she wasn't rewarded with a raise, she is likely to try another option.

■ Historical Perspectives on Motivation

To appreciate what we know about employee motivation, it is helpful to review some historical perspectives. The traditional, human relations, and human resource approaches have each shed partial light on motivation.

The Traditional Approach   The traditional approach is best represented by the work of Frederick W. Taylor.[3] As noted in Chapter 2, Taylor advocated an incentive pay system. He believed that managers knew more about the jobs being performed than did workers, and he assumed that economic gain was the primary thing that motivated everyone. Other assumptions of the traditional approach were that work is inherently unpleasant for most people and that the money they earn is more important to employees than the nature of the job they are performing. Hence, people could be expected to perform any kind of job if they were paid enough. Although the role of money as a motivating factor cannot be dismissed, proponents of the traditional approach took too narrow a view of the role of monetary compensation and also failed to consider other motivational factors.

People can be motivated by a wide array of factors, some of them obvious (such as money or prestige), but others more subtle. For example, Scott Coleman is an air-traffic controller and an amateur pilot. He is one of over 800 volunteer pilots across the United States who donate their time, planes, and fuel to transport patients to hospitals. Coleman is shown here preparing to take young Erika Carlson and her mother to a hospital in Boston where Erika will undergo a week of medical tests and treatment. Coleman is motivated simply by his desire to help others.

The Human Relations Approach   The human relations approach was also summarized in Chapter 2.[4] The human relationists emphasized the role of social processes in the workplace. Their basic assumptions were that employees want to feel useful and important, that employees have strong social needs, and that these needs are more important than money in motivating employees. Advocates of the human relations approach advised managers to make workers feel important and allow them a modicum of self-direction and self-control in carrying out routine activities. The illusion of involvement and importance were expected to satisfy workers' basic social needs and result in higher motivation to perform. For example, a manager might allow a work group to participate in making a decision, even though he or she had already determined what the decision would be. The symbolic gesture of seeming to allow participation was expected to enhance motivation, even though no real participation took place.

The Human Resource Approach   The human resource approach to motivation carries the concepts of needs and motivation one step farther. Whereas the human relationists believed that the illusion of contribution and participation would enhance motivation, the human resource view assumes that the contributions themselves are valuable to both individuals and organizations. It assumes that people want to contribute and are able to make genuine contributions. Management's task, then, is to encourage participation and to create a work environment that makes full use of the human resources available. This philosophy guides most contemporary thinking about employee motivation. At Ford, Westinghouse, Texas Instruments, and Hewlett-Packard, for example, work teams are being called upon to solve a variety of problems and to make substantive contributions to the organization.

MANAGEMENT IMPLICATIONS   Managers should understand the central role that motivation plays in determining employee job performance. They should also be familiar with traditional approaches to motivation.

Content Perspectives on Motivation

content perspectives   Approaches to motivation that try to answer the question, What factor or factors motivate people?

Content perspectives on motivation deal with the first part of the motivation process—needs and need deficiencies. More specially, **content perspectives** address the question, What factors in the workplace motivate people? Labor leaders often argue that workers can be motivated by more pay, shorter working hours, and improved working conditions. Meanwhile, some experts suggest that motivation can be enhanced by providing employees with more autonomy and greater responsibility. Both views represent content views of motivation. The former asserts that motivation is a function of pay, working hours, and working conditions; the latter suggests that autonomy and responsibility are the causes of motivation. Two widely known content perspectives on motivation are the need hierarchy and the two-factor theory.

■ The Need Hierarchy Approach

Many theorists support the need hierarchy approach. Need hierarchies assume that people have different needs that can be arranged in a hierarchy of importance. The two best-known theories are Maslow's hierarchy of needs and the ERG theory.

Maslow's Hierarchy of Needs   Abraham Maslow, a human relationist, argued that people are motivated to satisfy five need levels.[5] **Maslow's hierarchy of needs** is shown in Figure 16.2. At the bottom of the hierarchy are the *physiological needs*—things like food, sex, and air that represent basic issues of survival and biological function. In organizations these needs are generally satisfied by adequate wages and the work environment itself, which provides restrooms, adequate lighting, comfortable temperatures, and ventilation.

Next are the *security needs* for a secure physical and emotional environment. Examples include the desire for housing and clothing and the need to be free from worry about money and job security. These needs can be satisfied in the workplace by job continuity (no layoffs), a grievance system (to protect against arbitrary supervisory actions), and an adequate insurance and retirement benefit package (for security against illness and provision of income in later life). Even today, however, depressed industries and economic decline can put people out of work and restore the primacy of security needs.

Belongingness needs relate to social processes. They include the need for love and affection and the need to be accepted by one's peers. These needs are satisfied for most people by family and community relationships outside of work and friendships on the job. A manager can help satisfy these needs by allowing social interaction and by making employees feel like part of a team or work group.

Esteem needs actually comprise two different sets of needs: the need for a positive self-image and self-respect and the need for recognition and respect from others. A manager can help address these needs by providing various extrinsic symbols of accomplishment such as job titles, nice offices, and rewards for excellence. At a more intrinsic level, the manager can provide challenging job assignments and opportunities for the employee to feel a sense of accomplishment.

At the top of the hierarchy are the *self-actualization needs*. These involve realizing one's potential for continued growth and individual development. The self-actualization needs are perhaps the most difficult for a manager to address. In fact, it can be argued that these needs must be met entirely from within the individual. But a manager can help by promoting a culture wherein self-actualization is possible. For instance, a manager could give employees a chance to participate in making decisions about their work and the opportunity to learn new skills.

Maslow's hierarchy of needs   Suggests that people must satisfy five groups of needs in order—physiological, security, belongingness, esteem, and self-actualization

FIGURE 16.2
Maslow's Hierarchy of Needs

Maslow's hierarchy suggests that human needs can be classified into five categories and that these categories can be arranged in a hierarchy of importance. A manager should understand that an employee may not be satisfied with only a salary and benefits; he or she may also need challenging job opportunities to experience self-growth and satisfaction.

Source: Adapted from Abraham H. Maslow, "A Theory of Human Motivation," *Psychological Review,* 1943, Vol. 50, pp. 370–396.

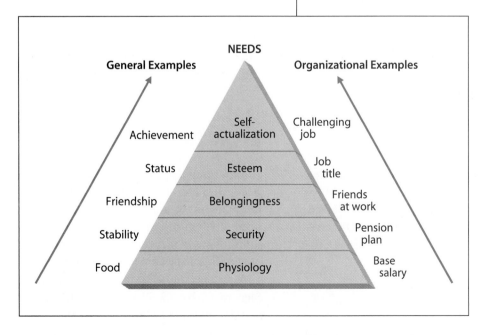

NEEDS

General Examples — Organizational Examples

General Examples	Needs	Organizational Examples
Achievement	Self-actualization	Challenging job
Status	Esteem	Job title
Friendship	Belongingness	Friends at work
Stability	Security	Pension plan
Food	Physiology	Base salary

Maslow suggests that the five need categories constitute a hierarchy. An individual is motivated first and foremost to satisfy physiological needs. As long as they remain unsatisfied, the individual is motivated only to fulfill them. When satisfaction of physiological needs is achieved, they cease to act as primary motivational factors and the individual moves "up" the hierarchy and becomes concerned with security needs. This process continues until the individual reaches the self-actualization level. Maslow's concept of the need hierarchy has a certain intuitive logic and has been accepted by many managers. But research has revealed certain shortcomings and defects in the theory. Some research has found that five levels of need are not always present and that the order of the levels is not always the same as postulated by Maslow.[6] In addition, people from different cultures are likely to have different need categories and hierarchies.

The ERG Theory   In response to these and similar criticisms, an alternative hierarchy of needs called the **ERG theory of motivation** was developed.[7] This theory collapses the need hierarchy developed by Maslow into three levels. *Existence needs* correspond to the physiological and security needs. *Relatedness needs* focus on how people relate to their social environment. In Maslow's hierarchy they would encompass both the need to belong and the need to earn the esteem of others. *Growth needs*, the highest level in this schema, include the needs for self-esteem and self-actualization.

Although the ERG theory assumes that motivated behavior follows a hierarchy in somewhat the same fashion as suggested by Maslow, there are two important differences. First, the ERG theory suggests that more than one level of need can cause motivation at the same time. For example, it suggests that people can be motivated by a desire for money (existence), friendship (relatedness), and the opportunity to learn new skills (growth) all at once. Second, the ERG theory has what has been called a *frustration-regression* element: if needs remain unsatisfied the individual will become frustrated, regress to a lower level, and begin to pursue those things again. For example, a worker previously motivated by money (existence needs) may have just been awarded a pay raise sufficient to satisfy those needs. Suppose that he then attempts to establish more friendships to satisfy relatedness needs. If for some reason he cannot establish those friendships in the workplace, he eventually gets frustrated and regresses to being motivated to earn even more money.

■ The Two-Factor Theory

Another popular content perspective on motivation is the **two-factor theory**.[8] Frederick Herzberg developed his theory by interviewing two hundred accountants and engineers. He asked them to recall occasions when they had been satisfied and motivated and occasions when they had been dissatisfied and unmotivated. Surprisingly, he found that different sets of factors were associated with satisfaction and with dissatisfaction—that is, a person might identify "low pay" as causing dissatisfaction but would not necessarily mention "high pay" as a cause of satisfaction. Instead, different factors—such as recognition or accomplishment—were cited as causing satisfaction and motivation.

ERG theory of motivation   Suggests that people's needs are grouped into three possibly overlapping categories—existence, relatedness, and growth

two-factor theory of motivation   Suggests that people's satisfaction and dissatisfaction are influenced by two independent sets of factors—motivation factors and hygiene factors

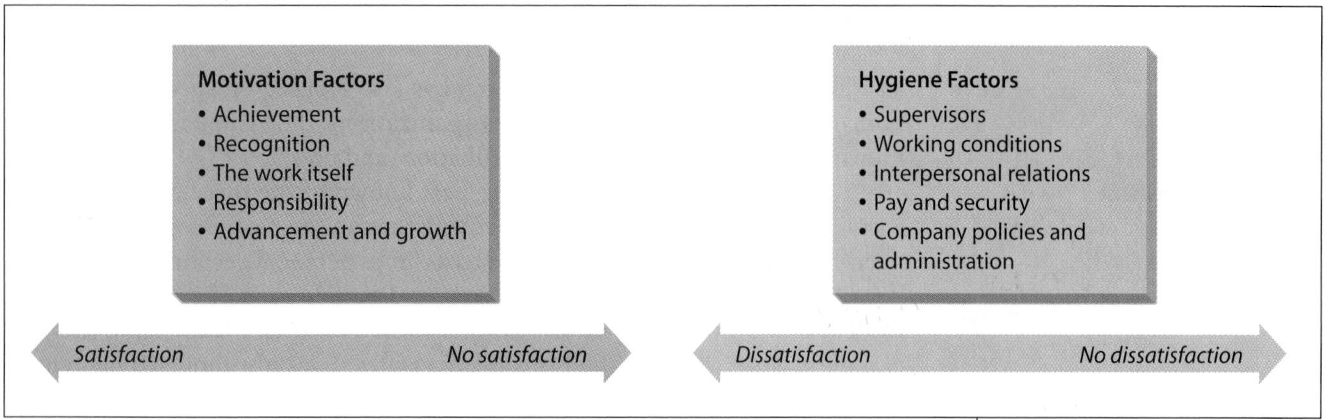

FIGURE 16.3
The Two-Factor Theory of Motivation

The two-factor theory suggests that job satisfaction has two dimensions. A manager who tries to motivate an employee using only hygiene factors such as pay and good working conditions will likely not succeed. To motivate employees and produce a high level of satisfaction, managers must also offer factors such as responsibility and the opportunity for advancement (motivation factors).

This finding led Herzberg to conclude that the traditional view of job satisfaction was incomplete. That view assumed that satisfaction and dissatisfaction are at opposite ends of a single continuum. People might be satisfied, dissatisfied, or somewhere in between. But Herzberg's interviews identified two different dimensions altogether: one ranging from satisfaction to no satisfaction and the other ranging from dissatisfaction to no dissatisfaction. This perspective, along with several examples of factors that affect each continuum, is shown in Figure 16.3. Note that the factors influencing the satisfaction continuum—called motivation factors—are related specifically to the work content. The factors presumed to cause dissatisfaction—called hygiene factors—are related to the work environment.

Based on these findings, Herzberg argues that the process of motivating employees has two stages. First, managers must ensure that the hygiene factors are not deficient. Pay and security must be appropriate, working conditions must be safe, technical supervision must be acceptable, and so on. By providing hygiene factors at an appropriate level, managers do not stimulate motivation but merely ensure that employees are "not dissatisfied." Employees whom managers attempt to "satisfy" through hygiene factors alone will usually do just enough to get by. Thus, managers should proceed to the second stage: giving employees the opportunity to experience motivation factors such as achievement and recognition. Herzberg's theory suggests that this approach will result in a high level of satisfaction and motivation.

Herzberg also describes exactly how to use the two-factor theory in the workplace. Specifically, he recommends job enrichment, as discussed in Chapter 11. He argues that jobs should be redesigned to provide higher levels of the motivation factors.

Although widely accepted by many managers, Herzberg's two-factor theory is not without its critics. One criticism is that the findings in Herzberg's initial interviews are subject to other explanations. Another charge is that his sample was not representative of the general population and that subsequent research often failed to uphold the theory.[9] At the present time, researchers in the field do not hold Herzberg's theory in high esteem. However, it has had a major impact on managers and has played a key role in increasing their awareness of motivation and its importance in the workplace.

■ Individual Human Needs

In addition to these theories, research has also focused on specific individual human needs that are important in organizations. The three most important individual needs are achievement, affiliation, and power.[10]

need for achievement The desire to accomplish a goal or task more effectively than in the past

The **need for achievement**, the best known of the three, is the desire to accomplish a goal or task more effectively than in the past. People with a high need for achievement have a desire to assume personal responsibility, a tendency to set moderately difficult goals, a desire for specific and immediate feedback, and a preoccupation with their task. David C. McClelland, the psychologist who first identified this need, argues that only about 10 percent of the U.S. population has a high need for achievement. In contrast, almost 25 percent of the workers in Japan have a high need for achievement.

need for affiliation The desire for human companionship and acceptance

The **need for affiliation** is less well understood. Like Maslow's belongingness need, the need for affiliation is a desire for human companionship and acceptance. People with a strong need for affiliation are likely to prefer (and perform better in) a job that entails a lot of social interaction and offers opportunities to make friends. The need for power has also received considerable attention as an important ingredient in managerial success.

need for power The desire to be influential in a group and to control one's environment

The **need for power** is the desire to be influential in a group and to control one's environment. Research has shown that people with a strong need for power are likely to be superior performers, have good attendance records, and occupy supervisory positions. One study found that managers as a group tend to have a stronger power motive than the general population and that successful managers tend to have stronger power motives than less successful managers.[11]

process perspectives Approaches to motivation that focus on why people choose certain behavioral options to fulfill their needs and how they evaluate their satisfaction after they have attained these goals

MANAGEMENT IMPLICATIONS

Managers should remember that Maslow's need hierarchy, the ERG theory, the two-factor theory, and the needs for achievement, affiliation, and power all provide useful insights into factors that cause motivation. What they do not do is shed much light on the process of motivation. They do not explain why people are motivated by one factor rather than by another at a given level or how people try to satisfy the different needs. These questions involve behaviors or actions, goals, and feelings of satisfaction—concepts that the various process perspectives on motivation address. ■

Process Perspectives on Motivation

Process perspectives are concerned with how motivation occurs. Rather than attempting to identify motivational stimuli, **process perspectives** focus on why people choose certain behavioral options to satisfy their needs and how they evaluate their satisfaction after they have attained these goals. Three useful process perspectives on motivation are the expectancy, equity, and goal-setting theories.

■ Expectancy Theory

Expectancy theory suggests that motivation depends on two things—how much we want something and how likely we think we are to get it.[12] Assume that you are approaching graduation and looking for a job. You see in the want ads that Exxon is seeking a new vice president with a starting salary of $350,000 per year. Even though you might want the job, you will not apply because you realize that you have little chance of getting it. The next ad you see is for someone to scrape bubble gum from underneath theater seats for a starting wage of $5.20 an hour. Even though you could probably get this job, you do not apply because you do not want it. Then you see an ad for a management trainee for a big company with a starting salary of $25,000. You will probably apply for this job because you want it and because you think you have a reasonable chance of getting it.

Expectancy theory rests on four basic assumptions. First, it assumes that behavior is determined by a combination of forces in the individual and in the environment. Second, it assumes that people make decisions about their own behavior in organizations. Third, it assumes that different people have different types of needs, desires, and goals. Fourth, it assumes that people make choices from among alternative plans of behavior based on their perceptions of the extent to which a given behavior will lead to desired outcomes.

Figure 16.4 summarizes the basic expectancy model. The model suggests that motivation leads to effort and that effort, combined with employee ability

expectancy theory Suggests that motivation depends on two things—how much we want something and how likely we think we are to get it

FIGURE 16.4
The Expectancy Model of Motivation

The expectancy model of motivation is a complex but relatively accurate portrayal of how motivation occurs. According to this model, a manager must understand what employees want (such as pay, promotions, or status) to begin to motivate them.

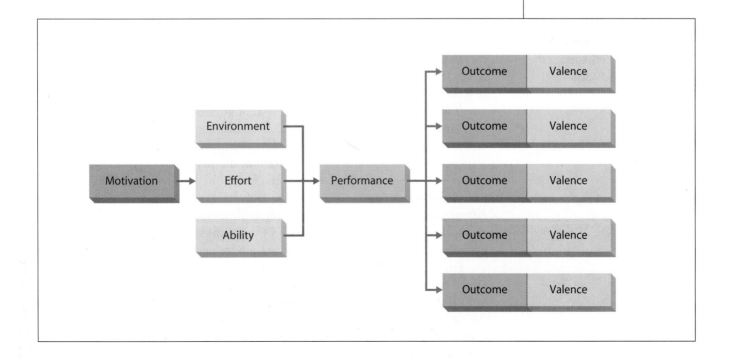

and environmental factors, results in performance. Performance, in turn, leads to various outcomes, each of which has an associated value called its valence. The most important parts of the expectancy model cannot be shown in the figure, however. These are the individual's expectation that effort will lead to high performance, that performance will lead to outcomes, and that each outcome will have some kind of value.

effort-to-performance expectancy The individual's perception of the probability that his or her effort will lead to high performance

Effort-to-Performance Expectancy The **effort-to-performance expectancy** is the individual's perception of the probability that effort will lead to high performance. When the individual believes that effort will lead directly to high performance, expectancy will be quite strong (close to 1.00). When the individual believes that effort and performance are unrelated, the effort-to-performance expectancy is very weak (close to 0). The belief that effort is somewhat, but not strongly, related to performance carries with it a moderate expectancy (somewhere between 0 and 1).

performance-to-outcome expectancy The individual's perception that her or his performance will lead to a specific outcome

Performance-to-Outcome Expectancy The **performance-to-outcome expectancy** is the individual's perception that performance will lead to a specific outcome. For example, if the individual believes that high performance will result in a pay raise, the performance-to-outcome expectancy is high (approaching 1.00). The individual who believes that high performance may lead to a pay raise has a moderate expectancy (between 1.00 and 0). The individual who believes that performance has no relationship with rewards has a low performance-to-outcome expectancy (close to 0).

outcomes Consequences of behaviors in an organizational setting, usually rewards

valence An index of how much an individual desires a particular outcome; it is the attractiveness of the outcome to the individual

Outcomes and Valences Expectancy theory recognizes that an individual's behavior results in a variety of **outcomes**, or consequences, in an organizational setting. A high performer, for example, may get bigger pay raises, faster promotions, and more praise from the boss. On the other hand, she may also be subject to more stress and incur resentment from coworkers. Each of these outcomes also has an associated value, or **valence**—an index of how much an individual values a particular outcome. If the individual wants the outcome, its valence is positive; if the individual does not want the outcome, its valence is negative; and if the individual is indifferent to the outcome, its valence is zero.

It is this part of expectancy theory that goes beyond the content perspectives on motivation. Different people have different needs, and they will try to satisfy these needs in different ways. For an employee who has a high need for achievement and a low need for affiliation, the pay raise and promotions cited above as outcomes of high performance might have positive valences, the praise and resentment zero valences, and the stress a negative valence. For a different employee with a low need for achievement and a high need for affiliation, the pay raise, promotions, and praise might all have positive valences, whereas both resentment and stress could have negative valences.

For motivated behavior to occur, three conditions must be met. First, the effort-to-performance expectancy must be greater than zero (the individual must believe that if effort is expended, high performance will result). The performance-to-outcome expectancy must also be greater than zero (the individual must believe that if high performance is achieved, certain outcomes will

THE QUALITY CHALLENGE

Adjusting Quality and Pay

For decades Cleveland-based Lincoln Electric has been recognized for its innovative and influential reward system. All Lincoln employees have been treated as individual entrepreneurs, with total responsibility for their own work and earnings. Base pay has been low, but workers have been able to earn exceptionally large bonuses as a result of their contributions to the firm's bottom line. For example, Lincoln workers earn an average of $16.54 an hour, which is about $2 more than the average pay for manufacturing work in Cleveland. And some individuals earn as much as $100,000 a year by putting in overtime and pushing the limits on how much they can produce.

Unfortunately, things have not gone well at Lincoln in recent years. One major problem is that competitors have surpassed Lincoln's quality levels. Another is simply that increased competition has shaved profit margins throughout the industry. To address the environmental pressures, Lincoln is slowly but surely modifying its pay system to focus more on quality improvement and productivity. For example, base pay has been increased, and bonus pay has been cut. The new pay plan allows the firm to keep its costs under tighter control. It also allows Lincoln to identify quality problems more readily and deal with them in a more direct fashion. Although remnants of the firm's classic incentive system remain, concerns for quality and productivity have redefined its scope and boundaries

"The bonus is a good program, and it has worked well, but it's got to be modified some."

David C. Lincoln, company director*

References: *"A Model Incentive Plan Gets Caught in a Vise,"* Business Week, *January 22, 1996, pp. 89–92 (*quote on p. 89); and Richard M. Hodgetts, "A Conversation with Donald F. Hastings of the Lincoln Electric Company,"* Organizational Dynamics, *Winter 1997, pp. 68–74.*

---

follow). And the sum of the valences for the outcomes must be greater than zero. (One or more outcomes may have negative valences if they are more than offset by the positive valences of other outcomes. For example, the attractiveness of a pay raise, a promotion, and praise from the boss may outweigh the unattractiveness of more stress and resentment from coworkers.) Expectancy theory suggests that when these conditions are met, the individual is motivated to expend effort.

Starbucks credits its unique stock ownership program with maintaining a dedicated and motivated workforce. Based on the fundamental concepts of expectancy theory, Starbucks employees earn stock as a function of their seniority and performance. Thus, their hard work helps them earn shares of ownership in the company.[13] On the other hand, "The Quality Challenge" illustrates how one firm has had to modify its reward system in order to keep quality in line with costs.

The Porter-Lawler Extension   An interesting extension of expectancy theory has been proposed by Porter and Lawler.[14] Recall from Chapter 2 that the human relationists assumed that employee satisfaction causes good performance. We also noted that research has not supported such a relationship. Porter and

equity theory Suggests that people are motivated to seek social equity in the rewards they receive for performance

Lawler suggest that a relationship may indeed exist between satisfaction and performance but that it goes in the opposite direction—that is, high performance may lead to high satisfaction. Figure 16.5 summarizes Porter and Lawler's logic. Performance results in rewards for an individual. Some of these are extrinsic (such as pay and promotions); others are intrinsic (such as self-esteem and accomplishment). The individual evaluates the equity, or fairness, of the rewards relative to the effort expended and the level of performance attained. If the rewards are perceived to be equitable, the individual is satisfied.

■ Equity Theory

After needs have stimulated the motivation process and the individual has chosen an action that is expected to satisfy those needs, the individual assesses the fairness, or equity, of the outcome. **Equity theory** contends that people are motivated to seek social equity in the rewards they receive for performance.[15] Equity is an individual's belief that the treatment he or she is receiving is fair relative to the treatment that others receive. According to equity theory, outcomes from a job include pay, recognition, promotions, social relationships, and intrinsic rewards. To get these rewards, the individual makes inputs to the job, such as time, experience, effort, education, and loyalty. The theory suggests that people view their outcomes and inputs as a ratio and then compare it to the ratio of someone else. This other "person" may be someone in the work group or some sort of group average or composite. The process of comparison looks like this:

$$\frac{\text{outcomes (self)}}{\text{inputs (self)}} \overset{?}{=} \frac{\text{outcomes (other)}}{\text{inputs (other)}}$$

Both the formulation of the ratios and comparisons between them are very subjective and are based on individual perceptions. As a result of comparisons, three conditions may result: the individual may feel equitably rewarded, underrewarded, or overrewarded. A feeling of equity will result when the two ratios are equal. This condition may occur even though the other person's outcomes are greater than the individual's own outcomes—provided that the other's inputs are also proportionately greater. Suppose that Mark has a high school education and earns $25,000. He may still feel equitably treated relative to Susan, who earns $30,000, because she has a college degree.

People who feel underrewarded try to reduce the inequity. Such an individual might decrease her inputs by exerting less effort, increase her outcomes by asking for a raise, distort the original

FIGURE 16.5
The Porter-Lawler Extension of Expectancy Theory

The Porter-Lawler extension of expectancy theory suggests that if performance results in equitable rewards, people will be more satisfied. Thus performance can lead to satisfaction. Managers must therefore be sure that any system of motivation includes rewards that are fair, or equitable, for all.

Source: Edward E. Lawler III and Lyman W. Porter, "The Effect of Performance on Job Satisfaction," *Industrial Relations,* October 1967, p. 23. Used with permission of the University of California.

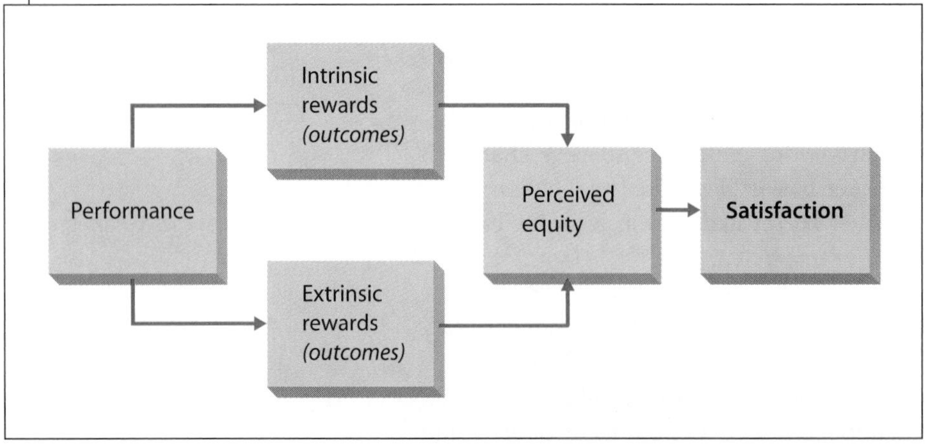

ratios by rationalizing, try to get the other person to change her or his outcomes or inputs, leave the situation, or change the object of comparison. An individual may also feel overrewarded relative to another person. This perception is not likely to be terribly disturbing to most people, but research suggests that some people who experience inequity under these conditions are somewhat motivated to reduce it. Under such a circumstance the person might increase his inputs by exerting more effort, reduce his outcomes by producing fewer units (if paid on a per unit basis), distort the original ratios by rationalizing, or try to reduce the inputs or increase the outcomes of the other person.

■ Goal-Setting Theory

The goal-setting theory of motivation assumes that behavior is a result of conscious goals and intentions.[16] Therefore, by setting goals for people in the organization, a manager should be able to influence their behavior. Given this premise, the challenge is to develop a thorough understanding of the processes by which people set goals and then work to reach them. In the original version of the goal-setting theory, two specific goal characteristics—goal difficulty and goal specificity—were expected to shape performance.

Goal Difficulty   *Goal difficulty* is the extent to which a goal is challenging and requires effort. If people work to achieve goals, they will probably work harder to achieve more difficult goals. But a goal must not be so difficult that it is unattainable. If a new manager asks her sales force to increase sales by 300 percent, the group may become disillusioned. A more realistic but still difficult goal—perhaps a 30 percent increase—would be a better incentive. A substantial body of research supports the importance of goal difficulty. In one study, for example, managers at Weyerhaeuser Co. set difficult goals for truck drivers hauling loads of timber from cutting sites to wood yards. Over a nine-month period, the drivers increased the quantity of wood they delivered by an amount that would have required $250,000 worth of new trucks at the previous per truck average load.[17]

Goal Specificity   *Goal specificity* is the clarity and precision of the goal. A goal of "increasing productivity" is not very specific; a goal of "increasing productivity by 3 percent in the next six months" is quite specific. Some goals, such as those involving costs, output, profitability, and growth are readily amenable to specificity. Other goals, however, such as improving employee job satisfaction, morale, company image and reputation, ethics, and socially responsible behavior may be much harder to state in specific terms. Like difficulty, specificity has also been shown to be consistently related to performance. The study of timber truck drivers mentioned in the preceding paragraph, for example, also examined goal specificity. The initial loads the truck drivers were carrying were found to be 60 percent of the maximum weight each truck could haul. The managers set a new goal for drivers of 94 percent, which the drivers were soon able to reach. Thus, the goal was both specific and difficult.

Because the theory attracted so much widespread interest and research support from researchers and managers alike, an expanded model of the

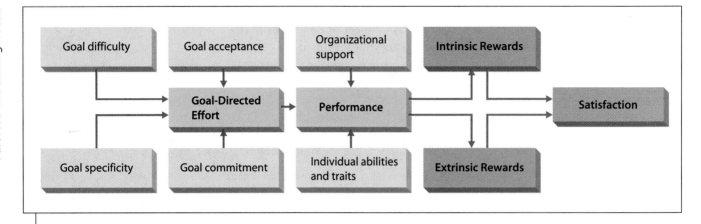

reinforcement theory Approach to motivation that explains the role of rewards as they cause behavior to change or remain the same over time
positive reinforcement A method of strengthening behavior with rewards or positive outcomes after a desired behavior is performed

goal-setting process was eventually proposed. The expanded model, shown in Figure 16.6, attempts to capture more fully the complexities of goal setting in organizations.

The expanded theory argues that goal-directed effort is a function of four goal attributes: difficulty and specificity, as already discussed, and acceptance and commitment. *Goal acceptance* is the extent to which a person accepts a goal as his or her own. *Goal commitment* is the extent to which she or he is personally interested in reaching the goal. The manager who vows to take whatever steps are necessary to cut costs by 10 percent has made a commitment to achieve the goal. Factors that can foster goal acceptance and commitment include participating in the goal-setting process, making goals challenging but realistic, and believing that goal achievement will lead to valued rewards.

The interaction of goal-directed effort, organizational support, and individual abilities and traits determine actual performance. Organizational support is whatever the organization does to help or hinder performance. Positive support might mean making available adequate personnel and a sufficient supply of raw materials; negative support might mean failing to fix damaged equipment. Individual abilities and traits are the skills and other personal characteristics necessary for doing a job. As a result of performance, a person receives various intrinsic and extrinsic rewards, which in turn influence satisfaction. Note that the latter stages of this model are quite similar to the Porter and Lawler expectancy model discussed earlier.

MANAGEMENT IMPLICATIONS Expectancy theory can be useful for managers who are trying to improve the motivation of their subordinates. Managers can follow a series of steps to implement the basic ideas of the theory. First, figure out the outcomes each employee is likely to want. Second, decide what kinds and levels of performance are needed to meet organizational goals. Then make sure that the desired levels of performance are attainable and that desired outcomes and desired performance are linked. Next, analyze the complete situation for conflicting expectancies and ensure that the rewards are large enough. Finally, make sure the total system is equitable (fair to all). The most important idea for managers to remember from equity theory is that if rewards are to motivate employees, they must be perceived as being equitable and fair. A second implication is that managers need to consider the nature of the "other" to whom the employee is comparing herself or himself. Goal-setting theory can be used to implement both expectancy and equity theory concepts. ▬

Reinforcement Perspectives on Motivation

A third element of the motivational process addresses why some behaviors are maintained over time and why other behaviors change. As we have seen, content perspectives deal with needs, whereas process perspectives explain why people choose various behaviors to satisfy needs and how they evaluate the equity of the rewards they get for those behaviors. Reinforcement perspectives explain the role of those rewards as they cause behavior to change or remain the same over time. Specifically, **reinforcement theory** argues that behavior that results in rewarding consequences is likely to be repeated, whereas behavior that results in punishing consequences is less likely to be repeated.[18]

▪ Kinds of Reinforcement in Organizations

Table 16.1 summarizes the four basic kinds of reinforcement that can result from behavior: positive reinforcement, avoidance, punishment, and extinction.[19] Two kinds of reinforcement strengthen or maintain behavior, whereas the other two weaken or decrease behavior.

Positive reinforcement, a method of strengthening behavior, is a reward or a positive outcome after a desired behavior is performed. When a manager observes an employee doing an especially good job and offers praise, the praise

TABLE 16.1
Elements of Reinforcement Theory

A manager who wants the best chance of reinforcing a behavior would likely offer the employee a positive reinforcement after a variable number of behaviors (variable-ratio reinforcement). For example, the manager could praise the employee after the third credit card application was received. Additional praise might be offered after the next five applications, then again after the next three, the next seven, the next four, and so on.

Arrangement of the Reinforcement Contingencies

1. **Positive reinforcement.** Strengthens behavior by providing a desirable consequence.

2. **Avoidance.** Strengthens behavior by allowing escape from an undesirable consequence.

3. **Punishment.** Weakens behavior by providing an undesirable consequence.

4. **Extinction.** Weakens behavior by not providing a desirable consequence.

Schedules for Applying Reinforcement

1. **Fixed interval.** Reinforcement applied at fixed time intervals, regardless of behavior.

2. **Variable interval.** Reinforcement applied at variable time ber

3. **Fixed ratio.** Reinforcement applied after a fixed number of behaviors, regardless of time.

4. **Variable ratio.** Reinforcement applied after a variable num-

avoidance   Used to strengthen behavior by avoiding unpleasant consequences that would result if the behavior were not performed

punishment   Used to weaken undesired behaviors by using negative outcomes or unpleasant consequences when the behavior is performed

extinction   Used to weaken undesired behaviors by simply ignoring or not reinforcing that behavior

serves to positively reinforce the behavior of good work. Other positive reinforcers in organizations include pay raises, promotions, and awards. Employees who work at General Electric's customer service center receive clothing, sporting goods, and even trips to Disney World as rewards for outstanding performance. The other method of strengthening desired behavior is through **avoidance**. An employee may come to work on time to avoid a reprimand. In this instance the employee is motivated to perform the behavior of punctuality to avoid an unpleasant consequence that is likely to follow tardiness.

Some managers use **punishment** to weaken undesired behaviors. When an employee is loafing, coming to work late, doing poor work, or interfering with the work of others, the manager might resort to reprimands, discipline, or fines. The logic is that the unpleasant consequence will reduce the likelihood that the employee will repeat that particular behavior. Given the counterproductive side effects of punishment (such as resentment and hostility), it is often advisable to use the other kinds of reinforcement if at all possible. **Extinction** can also be used to weaken behavior, especially behavior that has previously been rewarded. When an employee tells an off-color joke and the boss laughs, the laughter reinforces the behavior and the employee may continue to tell off-color jokes. By simply ignoring this behavior and not reinforcing it, the boss can cause the behavior to subside and eventually become "extinct."

■ Providing Reinforcement in Organizations

fixed-interval schedules   Provide reinforcement at fixed intervals of time, such as regular weekly pay checks

variable-interval schedules   Provide reinforcement at varying intervals of time, such as occasional visits by the supervisor

fixed-ratio schedules   Provide reinforcement after a fixed number of behaviors regardless of the time interval involved, such as a bonus for every fifth sale

variable-ratio schedules   Provide reinforcement after varying numbers of behaviors are performed, such as the use of complements by a supervisor on an irregular basis

The timing and frequency of reinforcement are also important elements of reinforcement theory. The various scheduling strategies for providing reinforcement are listed in Table 16.1. The **fixed-interval schedule** provides reinforcement at fixed intervals of time regardless of behavior. A good example of this schedule is the weekly or monthly paycheck. This method provides the least incentive for good work because employees know they will be paid regularly regardless of their effort. A **variable-interval schedule** also uses time as the basis for reinforcement, but the time interval varies from one reinforcement to the next. This schedule is appropriate for praise or other rewards based on visits or inspections. When employees do not know when the boss is going to drop by, they tend to maintain a reasonably high level of effort all the time.

A **fixed-ratio schedule** gives reinforcement after a fixed number of behaviors, regardless of the time that elapses between behaviors. This approach results in an even higher level of effort. For example, when Sears is recruiting new credit-card customers, salespersons get a small bonus for every fifth application returned from their department. This arrangement keeps motivation high because each application gets the person closer to the next bonus. The **variable-ratio schedule**, the most powerful schedule in terms of maintaining desired behaviors, varies the number of behaviors needed for each reinforcement. A supervisor who praises an employee for her second order, the seventh order after that, the ninth after that, then the fifth, and then the third is using a variable-ratio schedule. The employee is motivated to increase the frequency of the desired behavior because each performance increases the probability of receiving a reward. Of course, a variable-ratio schedule is difficult (if not impossible) to use for formal rewards such as pay because it would be too complicated to administer.

Managers wanting to explicitly use reinforcement theory to motivate their employees generally do so with a technique called **behavior modification**, or **OB Mod**.[20] An OB Mod program starts by specifying behaviors that are to be increased (such as producing more units) or decreased (such as coming to work late). These target behaviors are then tied to specific forms of kinds of reinforcement. Although many organizations (such as Procter & Gamble and Ford) have used OB Mod, the best-known application has been at Emery Air Freight. Management believed that the containers used to consolidate small shipments into fewer, larger shipments were not being packed efficiently. Through a system of self-monitored feedback and rewards, Emery increased container usage from 45 percent to 95 percent and saved more than $3 million during the first three years of the program.[21]

behavior modification, or **OB Mod** Method for applying the basic elements of reinforcement theory in an organizational setting

MANAGEMENT IMPLICATIONS Managers should be familiar with the role of reinforcement in motivation. Specifically, they should understand how various forms of reinforcement affect behavior and the different schedules that can be used to provide reinforcement to employees in organizations. ▬

Popular Motivational Strategies

Although these theories provide a solid explanation for motivation, managers must use various techniques and strategies to actually apply them. Among the most popular motivational strategies today are empowerment, participation, and alternative forms of work arrangements.

■ Empowerment and Participation

Empowerment and participation represent important methods that managers can use to enhance employee motivation. **Empowerment** is the process of enabling workers to set their own work goals, make decisions, and solve problems within their sphere of responsibility and authority. **Participation** is the process of giving employees a voice in making decisions about their own work. Thus, empowerment is a somewhat broader concept that promotes participation in many areas, including, but not limited to, work itself, work context, and work environment.[22]

The role of participation and empowerment in motivation can be expressed in terms of both the content perspectives and the expectancy theory. Employees who participate in decision making may be more committed to executing decisions properly. Furthermore, the successful process of making a

empowerment The process of enabling workers to set their own work goals, make decisions, and solve problems within their sphere of responsibility and authority

participation The process of giving employees a voice in making decisions about their own work

decision, executing it, and then seeing the positive consequences can help satisfy a person's need for achievement, provide recognition and responsibility, and enhance self-esteem. Simply being asked to participate in organizational decision making also may enhance an employee's self-esteem. In addition, participation should help clarify expectancies; that is, by participating in decision making, employees may better understand the linkage between their performance and the rewards they want most.

Areas of Participation   At one level, employees can participate in addressing questions and making decisions about their own jobs. Instead of just telling them how to do their jobs, for example, managers can ask employees to make their own decisions about how to do them. Based on their own expertise and experience with their tasks, workers might be able to improve their own productivity. In many situations, they might also be well qualified to make decisions about what materials to use, what tools to use, and so forth.

It might also be helpful to let workers make decisions about administrative matters, such as work schedules. If jobs are relatively independent of one another, employees might decide when to change shifts, take breaks, go to lunch, and so forth. A work group or team might also be able to schedule vacations and days off for all of its members. Furthermore, employees are getting increasing opportunities to participate in broader issues of product quality. Such participation has become a hallmark of successful Japanese and other international firms, and many U.S. companies have followed suit.

Techniques and Issues in Empowerment   In recent years many organizations have actively sought ways to extend participation beyond the traditional areas. Simple techniques such as suggestion boxes and question-and-answer meetings allow a certain degree of participation, for example. The basic motive has been to capitalize on the assets and capabilities inherent in all employees. Many managers today prefer the term *empowerment* to *participation* because the first term is more comprehensive.

One method of empowering workers is through work teams. Such teams are collections of employees empowered to plan, organize, direct, and control their own work. Their supervisor, rather than being a traditional "boss," assumes the role of a coach. The other method for empowerment is to change the firm's overall method of organizing. The basic pattern is for an organization to eliminate layers from its hierarchy, thereby become much more decentralized. Power, responsibility, and authority are delegated as far down the organization as possible, placing the control over work squarely in the hands of those who actually do it.[23]

Regardless of the specific technique or method used, however, empowerment will only enhance organizational effectiveness if certain conditions exist. First of all, the organization must be sincere in its efforts to spread power and autonomy to lower levels of the organization. Token efforts to promote participation in only a few areas are not likely to succeed. Second, the organization must be committed to maintaining participation and empowerment. Workers will be resentful if they are given more control, only to later have it reduced or taken away altogether. Third, the organization must be systematic and patient in its efforts to empower workers. Turning over too much control too quickly

To Empower or Not to Empower—That Is the Question

Empowerment is a major motivational innovation being used by many organizations today. Its proponents argue that effective empowerment can result in a workforce that is more highly motivated and does higher quality work than less empowered workers. And advocates urge all companies—big or small—to embrace empowerment and what it represents. Some advocates even suggest that empowerment is the only motivational strategy that makes sense in today's business world.

However, as it turns out, empowerment isn't for everyone. Indeed, a significant number of employees seem to prefer to put in their eight hours a day, have someone else make all the decisions, and simply draw their paycheck and go home. Some of these individuals don't want to work in the group or team context that almost always accompanies empowerment. Others don't want the accountability that usually goes with empowerment. And still others simply value other things more highly than having a voice in how they work.

Hence, in reality managers need to carefully assess the nature of their organization and the nature of their workforce. Empowerment can indeed work wonders—in the right settings. But trying to force empowerment into organizations where it doesn't fit or onto workers who don't want it can backfire. And backfiring empowerment can badly burn an unsuspecting organization!

> *"The admission ticket for this kind of responsibility is accountability—and not everyone necessarily wants accountability."*
>
> *Alexander M. Cutler, CEO of EatonCorp**

References: *"Not All Workers Find Empowerment as Neat as It Sounds,"* Wall Street Journal, *September 8, 1997, pp. A1, A13 (*quote on p. A1); and Robert E. Quinn and Gretchen M. Spreitzer, "The Road to Empowerment: Seven Questions Every Leader Should Consider,"* Organizational Dynamics, *Autumn 1997, pp. 37–46.*

can spell disaster. And finally, the organization must be prepared to increase its commitment to training. Employees being given more freedom in how they work are likely to need additional training to help them exercise that freedom most effectively. "Today's Management Issues" discusses another interesting issue regarding employee empowerment.

■ New Forms of Working Arrangements

Many organizations today are also experimenting with alternative work arrangements. These alternative arrangements are generally intended to enhance employee motivation and performance by providing greater flexibility in how and when people work. Among the more popular alternative work arrangements are variable work schedules, flexible work schedules, job sharing, and telecommuting.[24]

Variable Work Schedules   In spite of many exceptions, the traditional work schedule starts at 8:00 or 9:00 in the morning and ends at 5:00 in the evening, five days a week (and of course, many managers work additional hours outside of these times). Unfortunately, this schedule prevents many employees from

Flexible work schedules can be a powerful motivational strategy. Consider, for example, Tina Willford and her employer, First Tennessee Bank. The bank allows Willford to leave work early each day so that she can spend time with her young children. She makes up the time after her children are in bed. First Tennessee considers Willford to be a rising star, and is interested in doing whatever it can to both motivate her and keep her satisfied.

compressed work schedule   Working a full forty-hour week in fewer than the traditional five days

flexible work schedules or **flexitime**   Allowing employees to select, within broad parameters, the hours they work

attending to routine personal business—going to the bank, seeing a doctor or dentist for a routine checkup, having a parent-teacher conference, getting an automobile serviced, and so forth. At a surface level, then, employees locked into this sort of an arrangement may decide to take a sick or vacation day to handle these activities. At a more unconscious level, some people may also feel so powerless and constrained by a fixed traditional job schedule as to become resentful and frustrated.

To help counter these problems, some businesses have adopted a **compressed work schedule**, working a full forty-hour week in fewer than the traditional five days.[25] One approach involves working ten hours a day for four days, leaving an extra day off. Another alternative is for employees to work slightly less than ten hours a day but to complete the forty hours by lunch time on Friday. And a few firms have tried having employees work twelve hours a day for three days, followed by four days off. Organizations that have used these forms of compressed workweeks include John Hancock Mutual Life Insurance Co., Atlantic Richfield Co., and R.J. Reynolds Tobacco Co. One problem with this schedule is that when employees put in too much time in a single day, they tend to get tired and perform at a lower level later in the day.

Another schedule that some organizations are beginning to use is called a "nine-eighty" schedule. Under this arrangement an employee works a traditional schedule one week, and a compressed schedule the next, getting every other Friday off. That is, a person works eighty hours (the equivalent of two weeks of full-time work) in nine days. By alternating the regular and compressed schedules across half the work force, the organization can be fully staffed at all times and still give employees two full days off each month. Shell Oil and Amoco Corporation are two of the firms that currently use this schedule.

Flexible Work Schedules   Another promising alternative work arrangement is **flexible work schedules**, sometimes called **flexitime**. Flexitime gives employees more personal control over the times they work. The workday is broken down into two categories: flexible time and core time. All employees must be at work during core time, but they can choose their own schedules during flexible time. Thus, one employee may choose to start work early in the morning and leave in midafternoon, another to start in the late morning and work until late afternoon, and still another to start early in the morning, take a long lunch break, and work until late afternoon. Organizations that have used the flexible work schedule method include Control Data Corporation, DuPont, Metropolitan Life, Texaco, and some offices of the federal government.

Job Sharing   In **job sharing** two part-time employees share one full-time job. One person may perform the job from 8:00 A.M. to noon and the other from 1:00 P.M. to 5:00 P.M. Job sharing may be desirable for people who want to work only part-time or when job markets are tight. For its part, the organization can accommodate the preferences of a broader range of employees and may benefit from the talents of more people.

job sharing   When two part-time employees share one full-time job

Telecommuting   A relatively new approach to alternative work arrangements is **telecommuting**—allowing employees to spend part of their time working off-site, usually at home. By using e-mail, the Internet, and other up-to-the-minute technology, many employees can maintain close contact with their organization while they perform some of their job functions at home. The increased power and sophistication of modern communication technology is making telecommuting easier and easier.

telecommuting   Allowing employees to spend part of their time working off-site, usually at home

MANAGEMENT IMPLICATIONS   Managers need to be familiar with various motivation strategies and techniques that can be used to improve performance. Those interested in enhancing the motivation of their subordinates should understand empowerment, participation, and various alternative work arrangements.

Using Reward Systems to Motivate Performance

Aside from these types of motivational strategies, an organization's reward system is its most basic tool for managing employee motivation. An organizational **reward system** is the formal and informal mechanisms by which employee performance is defined, evaluated, and rewarded.

reward systems   The formal and informal mechanisms by which employee performance is defined, evaluated, and rewarded

■ Effects of Organizational Rewards

Organizational rewards can affect attitudes, behaviors, and motivation. Thus managers should clearly understand and appreciate their importance.[26]

Effect of Rewards on Attitudes   Although employee attitudes such as satisfaction are not a major determinant of job performance, they are nonetheless important. They contribute to (or discourage) absenteeism and affect turnover, and they help establish the culture of the organization. We can draw four major generalizations about employee attitudes and rewards.[27] First, employee satisfaction is influenced by how much is received and how much the individual thinks should be received. Second, employee satisfaction is affected by comparisons with what happens to others. Third, employees often misperceive the rewards of others. When an employee believes that someone else is making more

"I think I should warn you that the flip side of our generous bonus-incentive program is capital punishment."

Organizations provide rewards and incentives that can serve as positive reinforcement to desired behavior. Similarly, most also have various forms of punishment that can be used to weaken or eliminate undesired behaviors. While not as extreme as the humorous example shown here, positive reinforcement and punishment that are clearly linked to desired and undesired behaviors can play a major role in boosting employee performance and organizational effectiveness.

money than that person really makes, the potential for dissatisfaction increases. Fourth, overall job satisfaction is affected by how satisfied employees are with both the extrinsic and the intrinsic rewards they derive from their jobs. Drawing from the content theories and expectancy theory, this conclusion suggests that a variety of needs may cause behavior and that behavior may be channeled toward a variety of goals.

Effect of Rewards on Behaviors   An organization's primary purpose in giving rewards is to influence employee behavior. Extrinsic rewards affect employee satisfaction, which, in turn, plays a major role in determining whether an employee will remain on the job or seek a new job. Reward systems also influence patterns of attendance and absenteeism; and if rewards are based on actual performance, employees tend to work harder to earn those rewards.

Effect of Rewards on Motivation   Reward systems are clearly related to the expectancy theory of motivation. The effort-to-performance expectancy is strongly influenced by the performance appraisal that is often a part of the reward system. Employees are likely to put forth extra effort if they know that performance will be measured, evaluated, and rewarded. The performance-to-outcome expectancy is affected by the extent to which employees believe that performance will be followed by rewards. Finally, as expectancy theory predicts, each reward or potential reward has a somewhat different value for each individual. One person may want a promotion more than he or she wants benefits; someone else may want just the opposite.

■ Designing Effective Reward Systems

What are the elements of an effective reward system? Experts agree that they have four major characteristics.[28] First, the reward system must meet the needs of the person for basic necessities. Next, the rewards should compare favorably with those offered by other organizations. Unfavorable comparisons with people in other settings could result in feelings of inequity. Third, the distribution of rewards within the organization must be equitable. And fourth, the reward system must recognize that different people have different needs and choose different paths to satisfy those needs. Content theories and expectancy theory contribute to this conclusion. Insofar as possible, a variety of rewards and methods for achieving them should be made available to employees.

■ New Approaches to Rewarding Employees

Organizational reward systems have traditionally been of two kinds: a fixed hourly or monthly rate or an incentive system. Fixed-rate systems are familiar to most people. Hourly employees are paid a specific wage (based on job demands, experience, or other factors) for each hour they work. Salaried employees receive a fixed sum of money on a weekly or monthly basis. Although some reductions may be made for absences, the amount is usually the same regardless of whether the individual works less than or more than a normal amount of time.[29]

From a motivational perspective such rewards can be tied more directly to performance through merit pay raises. In a **merit system** an employee's annual pay raise is based on the person's overall job performance.[30] When the organ-ization's performance appraisal system is appropriately designed, merit pay is a good system for maintaining long-term performance. Increasingly, however, organizations are experimenting with various kinds of incentive systems.

Incentive systems attempt to reward employees in proportion to what they do. A piece-rate pay plan is a good example of an incentive system. In a factory that manufactures luggage, for example, each worker may be paid fifty cents for each handle and set of locks installed on a piece of luggage. Hence, the employee has an incentive to work hard: the more units produced, the higher the pay. Four increasingly popular incentive systems are profit sharing, gain sharing, lump-sum bonuses, and pay-for-knowledge.

Profit sharing provides a varying annual bonus to employees based on corporate profits. This system unites workers and management toward the same goal—higher profits. Ford, USX, and Alcoa all have profit-sharing plans. Gain sharing is a group-based incentive system in which all group members get bonuses when the group exceeds predetermined performance levels. The lump-sum bonus plan gives each employee a one-time cash bonus, rather than a base salary increase. Finally, pay-for-knowledge systems pay the individual, rather than the job. Thus, a firm using this approach would determine a person's pay based on that individual's total set of skills and work-related knowledge, rather than on the basis of the specific job the employee might be performing at any given time.

Organizations can use a variety of rewards to motivate high performance and to recognize those who do well. For example, the Long Beach Convention & Entertainment Center selects an "Employee of the Month" based on performance, effort, and dedication to the job. By displaying the individual's name in lights outside the center, managers affirm the employee's importance and motivate others to strive for the same recognition.

merit system A reward system whereby people get different pay raises at the end of the year depending on their overall job performance

incentive system A reward system whereby people get different pay amounts at each pay period based on what they produce

MANAGEMENT IMPLICATIONS

Managers need to know how rewards affect employee attitudes, behaviors, and motivation. In addition, they should know how to design reward systems and be familiar with new approaches to rewarding employees. ▬

Summary of Key Points

Motivation is the set of forces that cause people to behave in certain ways. Managers need to know about motivation because it, along with ability and environmental factors, determines individual performance. The basic historical perspectives on motivation are the traditional view, the human relations approach, and the human resource view.

Content perspectives on motivation are concerned with what factor or factors motivate people. Popular content theories include Maslow's need hierarchy, the ERG theory, and Herzberg's two-factor theory. In addition to these theories, the needs for achievement, affiliation, and power are important considerations as well.

Process perspectives on motivation deal with how motivation occurs. Expectancy theory suggests that people are motivated to perform if they believe that their effort will result in high performance, that this performance will lead to rewards, and that the positive aspects of the outcomes outweigh the negative aspects. Equity theory is based on the premise that people are motivated to achieve and maintain social equity. Attribution theory is a new process theory.

The reinforcement perspective focuses on how motivation is maintained. Its basic assumption is that behavior that results in rewarding consequences is likely to be repeated, whereas behavior resulting in negative consequences is less likely to be repeated. Reinforcement contingencies can be arranged in the form of positive reinforcement, avoidance, punishment, and extinction, and they can be provided on fixed-interval, variable-interval, fixed-ratio, or variable-ratio schedules.

Two newly emerging approaches to employee motivation are goal-setting theory and the Japanese approach. Managers often adopt behavior modification, modified work schedules, work redesign, and participation programs to enhance motivation.

Organizational reward systems are the primary mechanisms managers have for managing motivation. Properly designed systems can improve attitudes, motivation, and behaviors. Effective reward systems must provide sufficient rewards on an equitable basis at the individual level. Contemporary reward systems include merit systems and various kinds of incentive systems.

Discussion Questions

Questions for Review

1. What were the basic historical perspectives on motivation?

2. Compare and contrast content, process, and reinforcement perspectives on motivation.

3. In what ways are the emerging perspectives on motivation like the content, process, and reinforcement perspectives? In what ways are they different?

4. Compare and contrast the various motivational strategies described in this chapter.

Questions for Analysis

5. Compare and contrast the different content theories. Can you think of any ways in which the theories are contradictory?

6. Expectancy theory seems to make a great deal of sense, but it is complicated. Some people argue that its complexity reduces its value to practicing managers. Do you agree or disagree?

7. Offer examples other than those from this chapter to illustrate positive reinforcement, avoidance, punishment, and extinction.

Questions for Application

8. Think about the worst job you ever had. What approach to motivation did that organization use? Now think about the best job you ever had. What approach to motivation was used there? What conclusions can you draw from this limited information?

9. Interview managers and workers (or administrators and faculty) from a local organization. What views

of or approaches to motivation seem to be in use in that organization?

10. Can you locate any local organizations that have implemented or are implementing any of the motivational strategies discussed in this chapter? If so, interview a manager and a worker to obtain their views on the program.

Building Effective Interpersonal Skills

EXERCISE OVERVIEW

Interpersonal skills—the ability to understand and motivate individuals and groups—are especially critical when managers attempt to deal with issues associated with equity and justice in the workplace. This exercise will provide you with insights into how these skills may be used.

EXERCISE BACKGROUND

You are the manager of a group of professional employees in the electronics industry. One of your employees, David Brown, has asked to meet with you. You think you know what David wants to discuss, and you are unsure as to how to proceed.

You hired David about ten years ago. During his time in your group he has been a solid, but not outstanding, employee. His performance, for example, has been satisfactory in every respect, but seldom outstanding. As a result, he has consistently received average performance evaluations, pay increases, and so forth. Indeed, he actually makes somewhat less today than do a couple of people with less tenure in the group but with stronger performance records.

The company has just announced an opening for a team leader position in your group, and you know that David wants the job. He feels that he has earned the opportunity to have the job on the basis of his consistent efforts. Unfortunately, you see things a bit differently. You really want to appoint another individual, Becky Thomas, to the job. Becky has worked for the firm for only six years but is your top performer. You want to reward her performance and think that she will do an excellent job. On the other hand, you do not want to lose David because he is a solid member of the group.

EXERCISE TASK

Using the information above, respond to the following:

1. Using equity theory as a framework, how are David and Becky likely to see the situation?

2. Outline a conversation with David in which you tell him that you are offering the job to Becky.

3. What advice might you offer Becky, in her new job, about interacting with David?

4. What other rewards might you offer David to keep him motivated?

Building Effective Decision-Making Skills

EXERCISE OVERVIEW

Decision-making skills include the manager's ability to correctly recognize and define situations and to select courses of action. This exercise will allow you use expectancy theory as part of a hypothetical decision-making situation.

EXERCISE BACKGROUND

Assume that you are about to graduate from college and have received three job offers, as summarized below:

1. The first offer is an entry-level position in a large company. The salary offer is $22,000, and you will begin work in a very attractive location. However, you also see promotion prospects as being relatively limited, and you know that you are likely to have to move frequently.

2. The second offer is a position with a start-up company. The salary offer is $19,000. You know that you will have to work especially long hours. If the company survives for a year, however, opportunities there are unlimited. You may need to move occasionally, but not for a few years.

3. The third offer is a position in your family's business. The salary is $25,000, and you start as a middle manager. You know that you can control your own transfers, but you also know that some people in the company may resent you because of your family ties.

EXERCISE TASK

Using the three job offers as a framework, do the following.

1. Using expectancy theory as a framework, assess your own personal valence for each outcome in selecting a job.

2. Evaluate the three jobs in terms of their outcomes and associated valences.

3. Which job would you select from among these three?

4. What other outcomes will be important to you in selecting a job?

Building Effective Conceptual Skills

EXERCISE OVERVIEW

Conceptual skills refer to the manager's ability to think in the abstract. This exercise will enable you to develop your conceptual skills by relating theory to reality in a personal way.

EXERCISE BACKGROUND

First, you will develop a list of things you want from life. Then you will categorize them according to one of the theories in the chapter. Next, you will discuss your results with a small group of classmates.

EXERCISE TASK

1. Prepare a list of approximately fifteen things you want from life. These can be very specific (such as a new car) or very general (such as a feeling of accomplishment in school). Try to include some things you want right now and other things you want later in life. Next, choose the one motivational theory discussed in this chapter that best fits your set of needs. Classify each item from your "wish list" in terms of the need or needs it might satisfy.

2. Your instructor will then divide the class into groups of three. Spend a few minutes in the group discussing each person's list and its classification according to needs.

3. After the small-group discussions, your instructor will reconvene the entire class. Discussion should center on the extent to which each theory can serve as a useful framework for classifying individual needs. Students who found that their needs could be neatly categorized or those who found little correlation between their needs and the theories are especially encouraged to share their results.

4. As a result of this exercise, do you place more or less trust in the need theories as viable management tools?

5. Could a manager use some form of this exercise in an organizational setting to enhance employee motivation?

CHAPTER CLOSING CASE

Gambling with Motivation

People who frequent gambling casinos usually do so because they find the activity of wagering to be a pleasurable one. These people often forget, however, that gambling itself is a big business, a business that must be effectively managed if its owners are to remain in operation. Just as any business relies on people to carry out its work, casinos need employees to manage and work in hotel operations, entertainment venues, gift shops, parking operations, and the gaming areas. Moreover, owners rely on their managers to oversee the marketing, financial, and human resource functions. Although people may debate the morality of legalized gambling, no one can question its profitability.

One of the most successful businesses in the gambling industry today is Mirage Resorts, Incorporated. Stephen Wynn is the primary owner and chief executive officer of Mirage Resorts. The company is best known for its elaborate Mirage and Treasure Island Resorts in Las Vegas. The Mirage Resort, for example, has 3,030 hotel rooms and a ninety-five thousand square foot casino; the hotel features such attractions as Siegfried and Roy's white tigers and a dolphin exhibit. The Treasure Island Resort includes full-size replicas of a British frigate and a pirate ship that engage in live sea battles.

The company also owns the Golden Nugget casinos in Las Vegas and Laughlin and has a 50 percent stake in the Casino Iguazu in Argentina. In addition, Mirage has new projects under development for other areas in Nevada as well as in New Jersey and Mississippi. Most industry observers credit the success of Mirage to Wynn and his innovative management practices. Wynn, for example, has all the characteristics of a charismatic and inspirational leader. He is interesting, well informed, and can inspire others to follow his lead.

Another integral part of Mirage's success has been Wynn's approach to dealing with his employees. For example, he recently observed, "I have found that you can never go wrong indulging your employees." Thus, throughout his company he regularly strives for ways to recognize superior performance.

One routine part of this management system is what Wynn calls his "Gotcha" awards. These awards can be handed out at the discretion of a first-line supervisor to any employee observed doing his or her job in an exceptionally competent manner. The most common Gotcha awards are an extra day off with pay or a gift certificate good for merchandise at one of Mirage's gift shops or restaurants.

Employees and supervisors of the year at each Mirage casino are treated to Hawaiian vacations and a banquet that costs the company about $400,000. In addition, although entertainment operations like hotels frequently give employees free food, most of Wynn's competitors use leftovers from the guest buffet for this purpose. Mirage workers enjoy fresh and free meals in gleaming new cafeterias.

Another management innovation pioneered by Wynn is what he calls "planned insubordination." Essentially, managers at Mirage Resorts are required to explain why any given task needs to be accomplished. If subordinates find the explanation to be unconvincing, they are not required to perform the task. This practice causes managers to carefully consider the reasons behind their decisions before announcing them and helps subordinates more fully understand how the business is being managed.

And what are the effects of these benevolent human resource strategies? For one thing, Mirage's turnover rate of 12 percent is less than half the industry average. Moreover, despite the fact that almost half of Mirage's workers belong to unions, no grievances have been filed against the firm for more than four years. Because the company has a reputation as being an attractive place to work, Mirage can attract good employees and pay them at or even sometimes below market rates.

Case Questions

1. What motivational theories and techniques does Wynn use?
2. How well do you think Wynn's management style would work in other settings?
3. If you were one of Wynn's competitors, how would you deal with the fact he is the employer of choice among casino workers in Las Vegas today?

Case References: "Picasso Among the High Rollers," *Forbes*, May 19, 1997, pp. 44–46; Kenneth Labich, "Gambling's Kings," *Fortune*, July 22, 1996, pp. 80–88; and Patrick J. Spain and James R. Talbot (eds.), *Hoover's Handbook of American Business 1997* (Austin, Texas: The Reference Press, 1996), pp. 1002–1003.

CHAPTER NOTES

1. "Certain Work Is Foreign to Saudis, but That's Changing," *Wall Street Journal*, September 12, 1996, pp. A1, A4; and Ricky W. Griffin and Michael W. Pustay, *International Business: A Managerial Perspective*, 2nd ed., Chapter 14 (Reading, Mass.: Addison-Wesley), 1999.
2. Richard M. Steers and Lyman W. Porter (Eds.), *Motivation and Work Behavior*, 5th ed. (New York: McGraw-Hill, 1991).
3. Frederick W. Taylor, *Principles of Scientific Management* (New York: Harper and Brothers, 1911).
4. Elton Mayo, *The Social Problems of an Industrial Civilization* (Boston: Harvard University Press, 1945); and Fritz J. Rothlisberger and W. J. Dickson, *Management and the Worker* (Boston: Harvard University Press, 1939).
5. Abraham H. Maslow, "A Theory of Human Motivation," *Psychological Review*, 1943, Vol. 50, pp. 370–396; and Abraham H. Maslow, *Motivation and Personality* (New York: Harper & Row, 1954).
6. For a review, see Craig Pinder, *Work Motivation* (Glenview, Ill.: Scott, Foresman, 1984). See also Steers and Porter, *Motivation and Work Behavior*.
7. Clayton P. Alderfer, *Existence, Relatedness, and Growth* (New York: Free Press, 1972).
8. Frederick Herzberg, Bernard Mausner, and Barbara Snyderman, *The Motivation to Work* (New York: Wiley, 1959); and Frederick Herzberg, "One More Time: How Do You Motivate Employees?" *Harvard Business Review*, January–February 1987, pp. 109–120.
9. Robert J. House and Lawrence A. Wigdor, "Herzberg's Dual-Factor Theory of Job Satisfaction and Motivation: A Review of the Evidence and a Criticism," *Personnel Psychology*, Winter 1967, pp. 369–389; and Victor H. Vroom, *Work and Motivation* (New York: Wiley, 1964). See also Pinder, *Work Motivation*.
10. David C. McClelland, *The Achieving Society* (Princeton, N.J.: Van Nostrand, 1961); and David C. McClelland, *Power: The Inner Experience* (New York: Irvington, 1975).
11. David McClelland and David H. Burnham, "Power Is the Great Motivator," *Harvard Business Review*, March–April 1976, pp. 100–110.
12. Victor H. Vroom, *Work and Motivation*.
13. "Starbucks' Secret Weapon," *Fortune*, September 29, 1997, p. 268.
14. Lyman W. Porter and Edward E. Lawler III, *Managerial Attitudes and Performance* (Homewood, Ill.: Dorsey Press, 1968).

15. J. Stacy Adams, "Towards an Understanding of Inequity," *Journal of Abnormal and Social Psychology*, November 1963, pp. 422–436; and Richard T. Mowday, "Equity Theory Predictions of Behavior in Organizations," in *Motivation and Work Behavior*, eds. Steers and Porter, pp. 91–113.

16. See Edwin A. Locke, "Toward a Theory of Task Performance and Incentives," *Organizational Behavior and Human Performance*, 1968, Vol. 3, pp. 157–189.

17. Gary P. Lathm and J. J. Baldes, "The Practical Significance of Locke's Theory of Goal Setting," *Journal of Applied Psychology*, 1975, Vol. 60, pp. 187–191.

18. B. F. Skinner, *Beyond Freedom and Dignity* (New York: Knopf, 1971).

19. Fred Luthans and Robert Kreitner, *Organizational Behavior Modification and Beyond: An Operant and Social Learning Approach* (Glenview, Ill.: Scott, Foresman, 1985).

20. Luthans and Kreitner, *Organizational Behavior Modification and Beyond*; and W. Clay Hamner and Ellen P. Hamner, "Behavior Modification on the Bottom Line," *Organizational Dynamics*, Spring 1976, pp. 2–21.

21. "At Emery Air Freight: Positive Reinforcement Boosts Performance," *Organizational Dynamics*, Winter 1973, pp. 41–50; for a recent update, see Alexander D. Stajkovic and Fred Luthans, "A Meta-Analysis of the Effects of Organizational Behavior Modification on Task Performance, 1975–95," *Academy of Management Journal*, 1997, Vol. 40, No. 5, pp. 1122–1149.

22. David J. Glew, Anne M. O'Leary-Kelly, Ricky W. Griffin, and David D. Van Fleet, "Participation in Organizations: A Preview of the Issues and Proposed Framework for Future Analysis," *Journal of Management*, 1995, Vol. 21, No. 3, pp. 395–421.

23. Robert E. Quinn and Gretchen M. Spreitzer, "The Road to Empowerment: Seven Questions Every Leader Should Consider," *Organizational Dynamics*, Autumn 1997, pp. 37–40.

24. Baxter W. Graham, "The Business Argument for Flexibility, *HRMagazine*, May 1996, pp. 104–110.

25. A. R. Cohen and H. Gadon, *Alternative Work Schedules: Integrating Individual and Organizational Needs* (Reading, Mass.: Addison-Wesley, 1978).

26. Michelle Neely Martinez, "Rewards Given the Right Way," *HRMagazine*, May 1997, pp. 109–118.

27. Edward E. Lawler III, *Pay and Organizational Development* (Reading, Mass.: Addison-Wesley, 1981). See also Edward E. Lawler III, *Pay and Organizational Effectiveness: A Psychological View* (New York: McGraw-Hill, 1971).

28. Lawler, *Pay and Organizational Development*.

29. Bill Leonard, "New Ways to Pay Employees," *HRMagazine*, February 1994, pp. 61–69.

30. "Grading 'Merit Pay,' " *Newsweek*, November 14, 1988, pp. 45–46; and Frederick S. Hills, K. Dow Scott, Steven E. Markham, and Michael J. Vest, "Merit Pay: Just or Unjust Desserts," *Personnel Administrator*, September 1987, pp. 53–59.

17

Managing Leadership and Influence Processes

OBJECTIVES

After studying this chapter, you should be able to:

■ Describe the nature of leadership and distinguish leadership from management.

■ Discuss and evaluate the trait approach to leadership.

■ Discuss and evaluate models of leadership that focus on behaviors.

■ Identify and describe the major situational approaches to leadership.

■ Identify and describe three related perspectives on leadership.

■ Discuss political behavior in organizations and how it can be managed.

Even though Compaq Computer was formed less than two decades ago, the firm seems to have already had two distinct lives. The first started when Rod Canion and two other former Texas Instruments engineers launched the firm in 1982. Their first product design was sketched on a paper place mat in a restaurant where they agreed to go into business together. Led by Canion's rational and deliberate decision-making style, Compaq did all the right things and in 1988 became the youngest firm to ever enter the *Fortune* 500.

It appeared for awhile that the firm's management could do no wrong. But, unfortunately, things have a way of changing in the computer business. Canion's strategy for Compaq was to sell primarily to big businesses and to act in a relatively slow and deliberate fashion so as to avoid mistakes. When Compaq began to falter in 1991, Canion was at a loss as to how to proceed and was eventually forced out by the firm's board of directors.

To get the firm back on track, the board tapped Eckhard Pfeiffer, a German marketing specialist who had previously headed Compaq's very successful European operations. Pfeiffer wasted little time in revamping the way that the firm did business. In short order he mandated that the firm develop and launch dozens of new products, that manufacturing become more efficient so that costs could be lowered, and that the dealer network selling Compaq computers be enlarged. He also announced new initiatives directed at selling computers to individual consumers and to schools, domains previously controlled by Dell and Apple, respectively.

Even the wildest optimist could not have predicted how successful Pfeiffer's approach would turn out to be. Since he took over, for example, Compaq has more than tripled its share of the PC market, moving from 3.8 percent to 12 percent. Moreover, its profits in 1996 exceeded those of IBM and Apple combined. But Pfeiffer does not believe in standing still. Indeed, his ideas and strategies are keeping the firm in a constant state of flux. He continues to push for ever lower costs, ever greater productivity, and constant increases in market share, sales, and profits.

More recently, Pfeiffer has taken Compaq into new markets and still encourages managers to constantly be on the alert for new market opportunities. Indeed, in every business where it competes, Compaq is growing at a faster pace than the market itself. Pfeiffer recently announced a goal of transforming Compaq into a $40 billion Goliath by the turn of the century.

How does he do it? His colleagues believe that Pfeiffer has two qualities that allowed him to first turn things around and then set forth in bold new directions at Compaq. The first is that he was able to clearly communicate his vision for the company to each of its managers and employees. The second is that he is able to impart a sense of urgency—a feeling that things have to be done *now*.

This latter characteristic has facilitated the ongoing sense of change that he believes must drive Compaq in the years to come. And he sees plenty of changes on the horizon—lower prices, more powerful machines, and technology unheard of today are all right around the corner. And many experts believe that Pfeiffer will lead Compaq around that corner first.[1]

> *"We've seen the long-term potential. It's stronger than we had anticipated, much stronger than others have recognized."*

Eckhard Pfeiffer, Compaq CEO, quoted in Business Week, *February 17, 1997, p. 72.*

Eckhard Pfeiffer has a relatively rare combination of skills that set him apart from many others: he is both an astute leader and a fine manager, and he recognizes many of the challenges necessary to play both roles. He knows when to make tough decisions, when to lead and encourage his employees, and when to stand back and let them do their jobs. And thus far Compaq is reaping big payoffs from his efforts.

This chapter examines people like Pfeiffer more carefully—by focusing on leadership and its role in management. We characterize the nature of leadership and trace the three major approaches to studying leadership—traits, behaviors, and situations. After examining several other perspectives on leadership, we conclude by describing another approach to influencing others—political behavior in organizations.

The Nature of Leadership

In Chapter 16, we described various models and perspectives on employee motivation. From the manager's standpoint, trying to motivate people is an attempt to influence their behavior. In many ways leadership, too, is an attempt to influence the behavior of others. In this section, we first define leadership, then differentiate it from management, and conclude by relating it to power.

■ The Meaning of Leadership

leadership As a process, the use of noncoercive influence to shape the group's or organization's goals, motivate behavior toward the achievement of those goals, and help define group or organization culture; as a property, the set of characteristics attributed to individuals who are perceived to be leaders

leaders People who can influence the behaviors of others without having to rely on force; those accepted by others as leaders

Leadership is both a process and a property.[2] As a process—focusing on what leaders actually do—leadership is the use of noncoercive influence to shape the group's or organization's goals, motivate behavior toward the achievement of those goals, and help define group or organization culture.[3] As a property, leadership is the set of characteristics attributed to individuals who are perceived to be leaders. Thus **leaders** are people who can influence the behaviors of others without having to rely on force; leaders are people whom others accept as leaders.

■ Leadership Versus Management

These definitions clearly show that although leadership and management are related, they are not the same. A person can be a manager, a leader, both, or neither.[4] Some of the basic distinctions between the two are summarized in Table 17.1. At the left side of the table are four elements that differentiate leadership from management. The two columns show how each element differs when considered from a management and a leadership point of view. For example, when executing plans, managers focus on monitoring results, comparing them with goals, and correcting deviations. In contrast, leaders focus on energizing people to overcome bureaucratic hurdles to help reach goals. Thus when Eckhard Pfeiffer monitors the performance of his employees, he is

Activity	Management	Leadership
Creating an agenda	**Planning and budgeting.** Establishing detailed steps and timetables for achieving needed results; allocating the resources necessary to make those needed results happen.	**Establishing direction.** Developing a vision of the future, often the distant future, and strategies for producing the changes needed to achieve that vision.
Developing a human network for achieving the agenda	**Organizing and staffing.** Establishing some structure for accomplishing plan requirements, staffing that structure with individuals, delegating responsibility and authority for carrying out the plan, providing policies and procedures to help guide people, and creating methods or systems to monitor implementation.	**Aligning people.** Communicating the direction by words and deeds to everyone whose cooperation may be needed to influence the creation of teams and coalitions that understand the vision and strategies and accept their validity.
Executing plans	**Controlling and problem solving.** Monitoring results versus planning in some detail, identifying deviations, and then planning and organizing to solve these problems.	**Motivating and inspiring.** Energizing people to overcome major political, bureaucratic, and resource barriers by satisfying very basic, but often unfulfilled, human needs.
Outcomes	Produces a degree of predictability and order and has the potential to consistently produce major results expected by various stakeholders (for example, for customers, always being on time; for stockholders, being on budget).	Produces change, often to a dramatic degree, and has the potential to produce extremely useful change (for example, new products that customers want, new approaches to labor relations that help make a firm more competitive).

playing the role of manager. But when he inspires them to work harder at achieving their goals, he is a leader.

Organizations need both management and leadership if they are to be effective. Leadership is necessary to create change, and management is necessary to achieve orderly results. Management in conjunction with leadership can produce orderly change, and leadership in conjunction with management can keep the organization properly aligned with its environment. Indeed, organizations are so strongly motivated to attract effective leaders that they sometimes go to extreme measures, as discussed in "Today's Management Issues." An excellent example of an individual who is clearly both an outstanding manager and an exemplary leader is Kenneth Chenault, president of American Express Company. Chenault excels at the more routine tasks of a senior manager, but also inspires great confidence and motivation in his followers.[5]

■ Power and Leadership

To fully understand leadership, it is necessary to understand power. **Power** is the ability to affect the behavior of others. One can have power without actually using it. For example, a football coach has the power to bench a player who is not performing up to par. The coach seldom has to use this power because players recognize that the power exists and work hard to keep their starting position. In organizational settings we can usually identify five kinds of power: legitimate, reward, coercive, referent, and expert power.[6]

TABLE 17.1

Distinctions Between Management and Leadership

Management and leadership are related, but distinct, constructs. Managers and leaders differ in how they go about creating an agenda, developing a rationale for achieving the agenda, executing plans, and in the types of outcomes they achieve.

Source: Reprinted with permission of The Free Press, a division of Simon & Schuster Inc. from *A Force for Change: How Leadership Differs from Management* by John P. Kotter. Copyright © 1990 by John P. Kotter, Inc.

power The ability to affect the behavior of others

Golden Parachutes or Golden Eggs?

Imagine getting forced out of your job, and receiving more than $90 million in severance pay! That's just what happened when Michael Ovitz was asked to leave his job as president of The Walt Disney Company. But although this "going away package" was in a class by itself, attractive exit packages for executives have become the norm, rather than the exception today.

For example, John Ameriman recently retired as CEO at Mattel. But whereas retirement to some might mean rocking on the porch, Ameriman still receives over $1 million in annual salary as an adviser to the new CEO. Phillip Rooney left WMX Technologies but will receive severance pay of $12.5 million paid out over five years. And Joel Alvord retired as chair of Shawmut after it was acquired by Fleet Financial and was rewarded with $15.5 million in exit pay.

Such arrangements are often called "golden parachutes." The idea is that to attract high-profile executives with proven track records a firm may have to guarantee

"People are being allowed to dictate terms that give huge rewards under all [situations], including abject failure."

Graef Crystal, compensation consultant*

them some package of benefits if they are terminated, asked to retire prematurely, or lose their job as a result of a merger. And most experts agree that such compensation is generally appropriate and fair. For example, Michael Ovitz gave up controlling interest in another major business in order to take the job at Disney.

At the same time, critics believe that these parachutes may have gotten out of hand. For example, its one thing to promise a reasonable exit package to cover the executive until she or he finds a new job, but its altogether different to provide multiyear, multimillion-dollar packages. Even worse, critics contend, is giving such packages to managers who do a poor job and who are leaving simply so the company can hire a better replacement.

References: *"Where Parting Is Such a Sweet Deal,"* Business Week, *March 31, 1997, pp. 42–45; "Do You Need an Expert on Widgets to Head a Widget Company?"* Wall Street Journal, *January 21, 1998, pp. A1, A10.*

---

legitimate power The power granted through the organizational hierarchy to people occupying particular positions

Legitimate Power **Legitimate power** is power granted through the organizational hierarchy; it is the power accorded people occupying a particular position as defined by the organization. A manager can assign tasks to a subordinate, and a subordinate who refuses to do them can be reprimanded or even fired. Such outcomes stem from the manager's legitimate power as defined and vested in her or him by the organization. Legitimate power, then, is authority. All managers have legitimate power over their subordinates. The mere possession of legitimate power, however, does not by itself make someone a leader. Some subordinates follow only orders that are strictly within the letter of organizational rules and policies. If asked to do something not in their job description, they refuse or do a poor job. The manager of such employees is exercising authority but not leadership.

reward power The power to give or withhold rewards, such as salary increases, bonuses, promotions, praise, recognition, and interesting job assignments

Reward Power **Reward power** is the power to give or withhold rewards. Rewards that a manager may control include salary increases, bonuses, promotion recommendations, praise, recognition, and interesting job assignments. In general, the greater the number of rewards a manager controls and the more important the rewards are to subordinates, the greater is the manager's reward power. If the subordinate sees as valuable only the formal organizational rewards provided by the manager, then the manager is not a leader. If the subordinate also wants and appreciates the manager's informal rewards like praise, gratitude, and recognition, however, then the manager is also exercising leadership.

Coercive Power **Coercive power** is the power to force compliance by means of psychological, emotional, or physical threat. In the past physical coercion in organizations was relatively common. In most organizations today, however, coercion is limited to verbal reprimands, written reprimands, disciplinary layoffs, fines, demotion, and termination. Some managers occasionally go so far as to use verbal abuse, humiliation, and psychological coercion in an attempt to manipulate subordinates. (Of course, most people would agree that these are not appropriate managerial behaviors.) James Dutt, former CEO of Beatrice Company, once told a subordinate that if his wife and family got in the way of his working twenty-four hours a day, seven days a week, he should get rid of them.[7] The more punitive the elements under a manager's control and the more important they are to subordinates, the more coercive power the manager possesses. On the other hand, the more a manager uses coercive power, the more likely he is to provoke resentment and hostility and the less likely he is to be seen as a leader.

Referent Power Compared with legitimate, reward, and coercive power, which are relatively concrete and grounded in objective facets of organizational life, **referent power** is abstract. It is based on identification, imitation, loyalty, or charisma. Followers may react favorably because they identify in some way with a leader, who may be like them in personality, background, or attitudes. In other situations followers might choose to imitate a leader with referent power by wearing the same kinds of clothes, working the same hours, or espousing the same management philosophy. Referent power may also take the form of charisma, an intangible attribute of the leader that inspires loyalty and enthusiasm. Thus a manager might have referent power, but it is more likely to be associated with leadership.

Expert Power **Expert power** is derived from information or expertise. A manager who knows how to interact with an eccentric but important customer, a scientist who knows how to achieve an important technical breakthrough that no one else has dreamed of, and a secretary who knows how to unravel bureaucratic red tape have expert power over anyone who needs that information. The more important the information and the fewer the people who have access to it, the greater is the degree of expert power possessed by any one individual. In general, people who are both leaders and managers tend to have a lot of expert power.

coercive power The power to force compliance by means of psychological, emotional, or physical threat

referent power The personal power that accrues to someone based on identification, imitation, loyalty, or charisma

expert power The personal power that accrues to someone based on the information or expertise that they possess

Expert power is often an important ingredient in the success of many people. Dr. Susan Love, for example, is a world-renowned expert on women's health in general and breast cancer in particular. Her work is widely recognized and cited, giving her the power to influence public opinion, government health policy, and the daily health habits of millions of women.

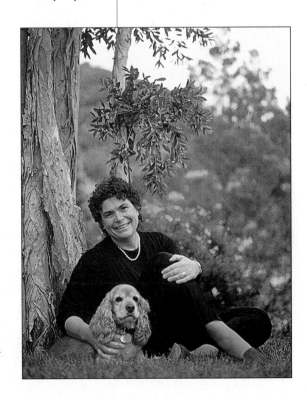

Using Power   How does a manager or leader use power? Several methods have been identified.[8] (Understanding these methods is the objective of a "Building Skills" exercise at the end of this chapter.) One method is the *legitimate request*, which is based on legitimate power. The manager requests that the subordinate comply because the subordinate recognizes that the organization has given the manager the right to make the request. Most day-to-day interactions between manager and subordinate are of this type. Another use of power is *instrumental compliance*, which is based on the reinforcement theory of motivation. In this form of exchange, a subordinate complies to get the reward the manager controls. Suppose that a manager asks a subordinate to do something outside the range of the subordinate's normal duties, such as working extra hours on the weekend, terminating a relationship with a long-standing buyer, or delivering bad news. The subordinate complies and, as a direct result, reaps praise and a bonus from the manager. The next time the subordinate is asked to perform a similar activity, that subordinate will recognize that compliance will be instrumental in her getting more rewards. Hence the basis of instrumental compliance is clarifying important performance-reward contingencies.

A manager is using *coercion* when he suggests or implies that the subordinate will be punished, fired, or reprimanded if he does not do something. *Rational persuasion* occurs when the manager can convince the subordinate that compliance is in the subordinate's best interest. For example, a manager might argue that the subordinate should accept a transfer because it would be good for the subordinate's career. In some ways rational persuasion is like reward power except that the manager does not really control the reward.

Still another way a manager can use power is through *personal identification*. A manager who recognizes that she has referent power over a subordinate can shape the behavior of that subordinate by engaging in desired behaviors: the manager consciously becomes a model for the subordinate and exploits personal identification. Sometimes a manager can induce a subordinate to do something consistent with a set of higher ideals or values through *inspirational appeal*. For example, a plea for loyalty represents an inspirational appeal. Referent power plays a role in determining the extent to which an inspirational appeal is successful because its effectiveness depends at least in part on the persuasive abilities of the leader.

A dubious method of using power is through *information distortion*. The manager withholds or distorts information to influence subordinates' behavior. For example, if a manager has agreed to allow everyone to participate in choosing a new group member but subsequently finds one individual whom she really prefers, she might withhold some of the credentials of other qualified applicants so that the group "selects" her candidate. This use of power is dangerous. It may be unethical, and if subordinates find out that the manager has deliberately misled them, they will lose their confidence and trust in that manager's leadership.[9]

MANAGEMENT IMPLICATIONS   Managers need to recognize the distinctions between leadership as a process and as a property. They should also appreciate the differences between leadership and management. Finally, managers need to know the most common bases of power and how to use them most effectively. ▄

The Search for Leadership Traits

The first organized approach to studying leadership analyzed the personal, psychological, and physical traits of strong leaders. The trait approach assumed that some basic trait or set of traits differentiated leaders from nonleaders. If those traits could be defined, potential leaders could be identified. Researchers thought that leadership traits might include intelligence, assertiveness, above-average height, good vocabulary, attractiveness, self-confidence, and similar attributes.[10]

During the first several decades of this century, researchers conducted hundreds of studies in an attempt to identify important leadership traits. For the most part the results of the studies were disappointing. For every set of leaders who possessed a common trait, a long list of exceptions was also found, and the list of suggested traits soon grew so long that it had little practical value. Alternative explanations usually existed even for relations between traits

The trait approach to leadership assumes that some basic trait or traits differentiates leaders from non-leaders. For example, many people in Great Britain assume that members of the royal family will be great leaders simply by virtue of their lineage. Thus, they expect Prince Charles to be a strong and effective leader, and publically express their dismay or outrage whenever he makes a mistake or fails to meet their expectations.

Japan's Greatest Leader?

Although it is not exactly a household name, Konosuke Matsushita may have been the greatest business leader in the history of Japan. Many consumers today know Matsushita as the company that makes such well-known brand-name products as Panasonic, Quasar, JVC, and Technics. And Matsushita is the world's largest consumer products maker.

Matsushita got his start in 1917. At the time he worked for Osaka Light, an electric utility. But he quit his job when his boss refused to listen to his ideas about a new type of electric socket. He subsequently invested 200 yen (about $50)—his entire life savings—to start a small electric business. His first workers contributed their time for free because he could not afford to pay them. After a shaky start, his company began to introduce one or two new products a month. His first "indulgences" were to pay his workers and to start hiring new employees.

In 1922 he got his big break. At the time bicycle lights were powered either by candles or large, bulky batteries.

"Cut production by half, starting now, but don't dismiss any employees. We'll reduce output not by laying off workers, but by having them work half-days. We will continue to pay the same wages they are getting now, but we will eliminate all holidays. We'll ask all the workers to do their best to try to sell the stock backlog."

Konosuke Matsushita*

Matsushita developed a new battery that was smaller, lighter, and much longer lasting than conventional ones. With this new product Matsushita Electric took off. But the cornerstone of his business remained the loyal and dedicated employees who believed in his ability and integrity.

Even during the Great Depression of 1929, Matsushita refused to lay off workers. And when the world economy recovered, his firm again took off on its path to multinational status. Even though Matsushita died in 1989, the firm that bears his name remains firmly entrenched atop its industry. And its concerns for its workers has remained a central and enduring part of the firm's corporate culture.

References: *John P. Kotter, "Matsushita: The World's Greatest Entrepreneur?"* Fortune, *March 31, 1997, pp. 105–111; John P. Kotter,* Matsushita Leadership *(New York: Free Press, 1997); and* Hoover's Handbook of World Business 1998 *(Austin, Texas: Hoover's Business Press, 1998), pp. 334–335.*

and leadership that initially appeared valid. For example, many leaders have good communication skills and are assertive. Rather than those traits being the cause of leadership, however, successful leaders may begin to display those traits after they have achieved leadership positions.

Although most researchers gave up trying to identify traits as predictors of leadership ability, many people still explicitly or implicitly adopt a trait orientation.[11] For example, politicians are frequently elected on the basis of personal appearance, speaking ability, or an aura of self-confidence. In addition, as discussed in "The World of Management," traits such as honesty and integrity may very well be fundamental leadership traits that do serve an important purpose.

| MANAGEMENT IMPLICATIONS | Managers need to understand the concept of leadership traits, but should pay most attention to avoiding the pitfalls of relying on or making inferences about a person's leadership ability based on various traits. ▬ |

Leadership Behaviors

Spurred on by their lack of success in identifying useful leadership traits, researchers soon began to investigate other variables, especially the behaviors or actions of leaders. The new hypothesis was that effective leaders somehow behaved differently than less-effective leaders. Thus the goal was to develop a fuller understanding of leadership behaviors.

■ Michigan Studies

Researchers at the University of Michigan, led by Rensis Likert, began studying leadership in the late 1940s.[12] Based on extensive interviews with both leaders (managers) and followers (subordinates), this research identified two basic forms of leader behavior: job centered and employee centered. Managers using **job-centered leader behavior** pay close attention to subordinates' work, explain work procedures, and are keenly interested in performance. Managers using **employee-centered leader behavior** are interested in developing a cohesive work group and ensuring that employees are satisfied with their jobs. Their primary concern is the welfare of subordinates.

job-centered leader behavior The behavior of leaders who pay close attention to the job and work procedures involved with that job

employee-centered leader behavior The behavior of leaders who develop cohesive work groups and ensure employee satisfaction

The two styles of leader behavior were presumed to be at the ends of a single continuum. Although this view suggests that leaders may be extremely job-centered, extremely employee-centered, or somewhere in between, Likert studied only the two end styles for contrast. He argued that employee-centered leader behavior generally tended to be more effective. We should also note the similarities between Likert's leadership research and his Systems 1 through 4 organization design (discussed in Chapter 12). Job-centered leader behavior is consistent with the System 1 design (rigid and bureaucratic), whereas employee-centered leader behavior is consistent with the System 4 design (organic and flexible). When Likert advocates moving organizations from System 1 to System 4, he is also advocating a transition from job-centered to employee-centered leader behavior.

■ Ohio State Studies

At about the same time that Likert was beginning his leadership studies at the University of Michigan, a group of researchers at Ohio State also began studying leadership.[13] The extensive questionnaire surveys conducted during the

FIGURE 17.1
The Leadership Grid®

The Leadership Grid® is a method of evaluating leadership styles. The overall objective of an organization using the Grid® is to train its managers using OD techniques so that they are simultaneously more concerned for both people and production (9, 9 style on the Grid®).

Source: From *Leadership Dilemmas-Grid Solutions* by Robert R. Blake and Anne Adams McCanse. (Formerly the Managerial Grid by Robert R. Blake and Jane S. Mouton.) Houston: Gulf Publishing Company, p. 29. Copyright © 1991 by Scientific Methods, Inc. Reproduced by permission of the owners.

Ohio State studies also suggested that there are two basic leader behaviors or styles: initiating-structure behavior and consideration behavior. When using **initiating-structure behavior,** the leader clearly defines the leader-subordinate role so that everyone knows what is expected, establishes formal lines of communication, and determines how tasks will be performed. Leaders using **consideration behavior** show concern for subordinates and attempt to establish a friendly and supportive climate. The behaviors identified at Ohio State are similar to those described at Michigan, but there are important differences. One major difference is that the Ohio State researchers did not interpret leader behavior as being one-dimensional: each behavior was assumed to be independent. Presumably, then, a leader could simultaneously exhibit varying levels of initiating structure and varying levels of consideration.

At first, the Ohio State researchers thought that leaders who exhibit high levels of both behaviors would tend to be more effective than other leaders. A study at International Harvester Co. (now Navistar International Corp.), however, suggested a more complicated pattern.[14] The researchers found that employees of supervisors who ranked high on initiating structure were high performers but expressed low levels of satisfaction and had a higher absence rate. Conversely, employees of supervisors who ranked high on consideration had low performance ratings but high levels of satisfaction and few absences from work. Later research isolated other variables that make consistent prediction difficult and determined that situational influences also occurred. (This body of research is discussed in the section on situational approaches to leadership.)

■ Leadership Grid®

Yet another behavioral approach to leadership is the Leadership Grid®.[15] The Leadership Grid provides a means for evaluating leadership styles and then training managers to move toward an ideal style of behavior. The Leadership Grid is shown in Figure 17.1. The horizontal axis represents **concern for production** (similar to job-centered and initiating-structure behaviors), and the vertical axis represents **concern for people** (similar to employee-centered and consideration behavior). Note the five extremes of managerial behavior: the 1,1 manager (impover-

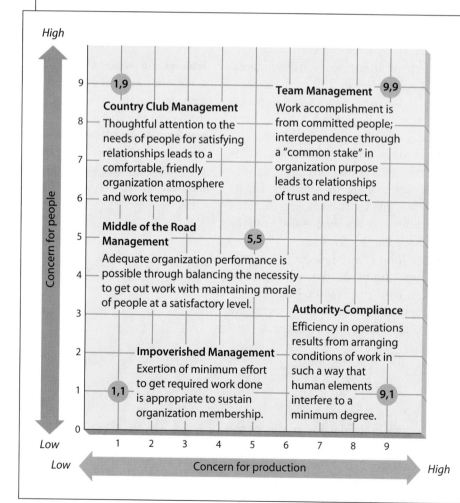

ished management) who exhibits minimal concern for both production and people; the 9,1 manager (authority-compliance) who is highly concerned about production but exhibits little concern for people; the 1,9 manager (country club management) whose concerns are exactly opposite the concerns of the 9,1 manager; the 5,5 manager (middle-of-the-road management) who maintains adequate concern for both people and production; and the 9,9 manager (team management) who exhibits maximum concern for both people and production.

According to this approach, the ideal style of leadership behavior is the 9,9 approach. The individuals who developed the Leadership Grid have gone so far as to market a comprehensive training program that purports to help move a company's managers toward the 9,9 approach to leadership. A.G. Edwards, Westinghouse, the Federal Aviation Authority, Equicor, and other companies have used this program with reasonable success. However, there is little published scientific data regarding its true effectiveness.

The leader-behavior theories have played an important role in the development of contemporary thinking about leadership. In particular, they urge us not to be preoccupied with what leaders *are* (the trait approach) but to concentrate on what leaders *do* (their behaviors). Unfortunately, these theories also make universal prescriptions about what constitutes effective leadership.

When we are dealing with complex social systems composed of complex individuals, few if any relationships are consistently predictable and certainly no formulas for success are infallible. Yet the behavior theorists tried to identify consistent relationships between leader behaviors and employee responses in the hope of finding a dependable prescription for effective leadership. As we might expect, they often failed. Other approaches to understanding leadership were therefore needed.

The catalyst for these new approaches was the realization that, although interpersonal and task-oriented dimensions might be useful to describe the behavior of leaders, they were not useful for predicting or prescribing it. The next step in the evolution of leadership theory was the creation of situational models.

concern for production The part of the Leadership Grid that deals with the job and task aspects of leader behavior

concern for people The part of the Leadership Grid that deals with the human aspects of leader behavior

initiating-structure behavior The behavior of leaders who define the leader-subordinate role so that everyone knows what is expected, establish formal lines of communication, and determine how tasks will be performed

consideration behavior The behavior of leaders who show concern for subordinates and attempt to establish a warm, friendly, and supportive climate

MANAGEMENT IMPLICATIONS Managers should appreciate the importance of leadership behaviors and also be familiar with the basic kinds of leadership behaviors. At the same time managers should also recognize that universal or "one best way" models of leadership are of dubious value. ▬

Situational Approaches to Leadership

Situational models assume that appropriate leader behavior varies from one situation to another. The goal of a situational theory, then, is to identify key situational factors and to specify how they interact to determine appropriate

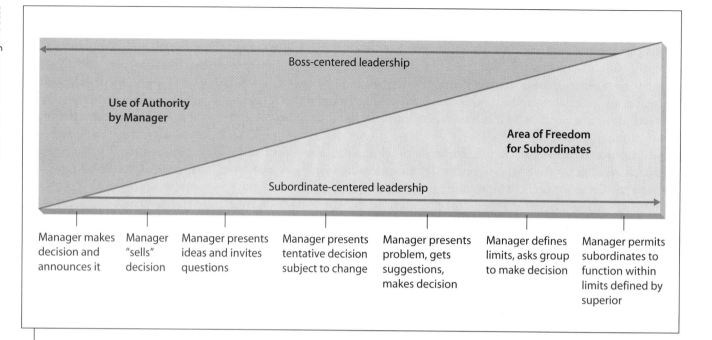

Boss-centered leadership

Use of Authority
by Manager

Area of Freedom
for Subordinates

Subordinate-centered leadership

| Manager makes decision and announces it | Manager "sells" decision | Manager presents ideas and invites questions | Manager presents tentative decision subject to change | Manager presents problem, gets suggestions, makes decision | Manager defines limits, asks group to make decision | Manager permits subordinates to function within limits defined by superior |

FIGURE 17.2
Tannenbaum and Schmidt's Leadership Continuum

The Tannenbaum and Schmidt leadership continuum was an important precursor to modern situational approaches to leadership. The continuum identifies seven levels of leadership that range between the extremes of boss-centered and subordinate-centered leadership.

Source: Reprinted by permission of the *Harvard Business Review*. An exhibit from "How to Choose a Leadership Pattern" by Robert Tannenbaum and Warren Schmidt (May–June 1973). Copyright © 1973 by the President and Fellows of Harvard College; all rights reserved.

leader behavior. Before discussing the three major situational theories, we should first discuss an important early model that laid the foundation for subsequent developments. In a 1958 study of the decision-making process, Robert Tannenbaum and Warren H. Schmidt proposed a continuum of leadership behavior. Their model is much like the original Michigan framework.[16] Besides purely job-centered behavior (or "boss centered" behavior, as they termed it) and employee-centered ("subordinate centered") behavior, however, they identified several intermediate behaviors that a manager might consider. These are shown on the leadership continuum in Figure 17.2.

This continuum of behavior moves from the one extreme of having the manager make the decision alone to the other extreme of having the employees make the decision with minimal guidance. Each point on the continuum is influenced by characteristics of the manager, subordinates, and the situation. Managerial characteristics include the manager's value system, confidence in subordinates, personal inclinations, and feelings of security. Subordinate characteristics include the subordinates' need for independence, readiness to assume responsibility, tolerance for ambiguity, interest in the problem, understanding of goals, knowledge, experience, and expectations. Situational characteristics that affect decision making include the type of organization, group effectiveness, the problem itself, and time pressures. Although this framework pointed out the importance of situational factors, it was only speculative. It remained for others to develop more comprehensive and integrated theories. In the following sections, we describe the three most important and most widely accepted situational theories of leadership: the LPC theory, the path-goal theory, and the Vroom-Yetton-Jago model.

■ Least-Preferred Coworker (LPC) Theory

The **LPC theory**, developed by Fred Fiedler, was the first true situational theory of leadership.[17] As we discuss later, LPC stands for least-preferred coworker. Beginning with a combined trait and behavior approach, Fiedler identified two styles of leadership: task oriented (analogous to job-centered and initiating-structure behavior) and relationship oriented (similar to employee-centered and consideration behavior). He went beyond the earlier behavioral approaches by arguing that the style of behavior is a reflection of the leader's personality, and that most personalities naturally fall into one of his two categories: task oriented or relationship oriented. Fiedler measures leader style by means of a controversial questionnaire called the **least-preferred coworker (LPC)** measure. To use the measure, a manager or leader is asked to describe the specific person with whom he or she is able to work least well—the LPC—by filling in a set of sixteen scales anchored at each end by a positive or negative adjective. Three of the sixteen scales follow.

LPC theory A theory of leadership that suggests that the appropriate style of leadership varies with situational favorableness

least-preferred coworker (LPC) The measuring scale that asks leaders to describe the person with whom he or she is able to work least well

Helpful __ __ __ __ __ __ __ __ Frustrating
           8 7 6 5 4 3 2 1

Tense __ __ __ __ __ __ __ __ Relaxed
           1 2 3 4 5 6 7 8

Boring __ __ __ __ __ __ __ __ Interesting
           1 2 3 4 5 6 7 8

The leader's LPC score is then calculated by totaling the numbers checked on each scale. Note in these three examples that the higher numbers are associated with the positive qualities (helpful, relaxed, and interesting), whereas the negative qualities (frustrating, tense, and boring) have low point values. A high total score is assumed to reflect a relationship orientation and a low score a task orientation on the part of the leader. The LPC measure is controversial because researchers disagree about its validity. Some critics question exactly what an LPC measure reflects and whether the score is an index of behavior, personality, or some other factor.[18]

Favorableness of the Situation The underlying assumption of situational models of leadership is that appropriate leader behavior varies from one situation to another. According to Fiedler, the key situational factor is the favorableness of the situation from the leader's point of view. This factor is determined by leader-member relations, task structure, and position power.

Leader-member relations refer to the nature of the relationship between the leader and the work group. If the leader and the group have a high degree of mutual trust, respect, and confidence and if they like one another, relations are assumed to be good. If there is little trust, respect, or confidence and if they do not like each other, relations are poor. Naturally, good relations are more favorable.

Task structure is the degree to which the group's task is well defined. The task is structured when it is routine, easily understood, and unambiguous and

FIGURE 17.3

The Least-Preferred Coworker Theory of Leadership

Fiedler's LPC theory of leadership suggests that appropriate leader behavior varies as a function of the favorableness of the situation. Favorableness, in turn, is defined by task structure, leader-member relations, and the leader's position power. According to LPC theory, the most and least favorable situations call for task-oriented leadership, whereas moderately favorable situations suggest the need for relationship-oriented leadership.

when the group has standard procedures and precedents to rely on. An unstructured task is nonroutine, ambiguous, and complex, with no standard procedures or precedents. You can see that high structure is more favorable for the leader, whereas low structure is less favorable. For example, if the task is unstructured, the group will not know what to do and the leader will have to play a major role in guiding and directing its activities. If the task is structured, the leader will not have to get so involved and can devote time to nonsupervisory activities.

Position power is the power vested in the leader's position. If the leader has the power to assign work and to reward and punish employees, position power is assumed to be strong. But if the leader must get job assignments approved by someone else and does not administer rewards and punishment, position power is weak and it is more difficult to accomplish goals. From the leader's point of view, strong position power is clearly preferable to weak position. However, position power is not as important as task structure and leader-member relations.

Favorableness and Leader Style   Fiedler and his associates conducted numerous studies linking the favorableness of various situations to leader style and the effectiveness of the group.[19] The results of these studies—and the overall framework of the theory—are shown in Figure 17.3. To interpret the model, look first at the situational factors at the top of the figure: good or bad leader-member relations, high or low task structure, and strong or weak leader-position power can be combined to yield eight unique situations. For example, good leader-member relations, high task structure, and strong leader-position power (at the far left) are presumed to define the most favorable situation; bad leader-member relations, low task structure, and weak leader-power (at the far right) are the least favorable. The other combinations reflect intermediate levels of favorableness.

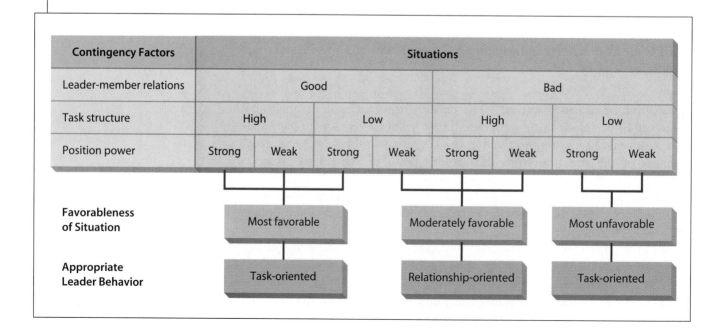

Below each set of situations is shown the degree of favorableness and the form of leader behavior found to be most strongly associated with effective group performance for those situations. When the situation is most and least favorable, Fiedler has found that a task-oriented leader is most effective. When the situation is only moderately favorable, however, a relationship-oriented leader is predicted to be most effective.

Flexibility of Leader Style   Fiedler argued that, for any given individual, leader style is essentially fixed and cannot be changed: leaders cannot change their behavior to fit a particular situation because it is linked to their particular personality traits. Thus when a leader's style and the situation do not match, Fiedler argued that the situation should be changed to fit the leader's style. When leader-member relations are good, task structure low, and position power weak, the leader style most likely to be effective is relationship oriented. If the leader is task oriented, a mismatch exists. According to Fiedler, the leader can make the elements of the situation more congruent by structuring the task (by developing guidelines and procedures, for instance) and increasing power (by requesting additional authority or by other means).

Fiedler's contingency theory has been attacked on the grounds that it is not always supported by research, that his findings are subject to other interpretations, that the LPC measure lacks validity, and that his assumptions about the inflexibility of leader behavior are unrealistic.[20] However, Fiedler's theory was one of the first to adopt a situational perspective on leadership. It has helped many managers recognize the important situational factors they must contend with, and it has fostered additional thinking about the situational nature of leadership. Moreover, in recent years Fiedler has attempted to address some of the concerns about his theory by revising it and adding such additional elements as cognitive resources.

■ Path-Goal Theory

The path-goal theory of leadership—associated most closely with Martin Evans and Robert House—is a direct extension of the expectancy theory of motivation discussed in Chapter 16.[21] Recall that the primary components of expectancy theory included the likelihood of attaining various outcomes and the value associated with those outcomes. The **path-goal theory** of leadership suggests that the primary functions of a leader are to make valued or desired rewards available in the workplace and to clarify for the subordinate the kinds of behavior that will lead to goal accomplishment and valued rewards—that is, the leader should clarify the paths to goal attainment.

Leader Behavior   The most fully developed version of path-goal theory identifies four kinds of leader behavior. *Directive leader behavior* is letting subordinates know what is expected of them, giving guidance and direction, and scheduling work. *Supportive leader behavior* is being friendly and approachable, showing concern for subordinate welfare, and treating members as equals. *Participative leader behavior* is consulting subordinates, soliciting suggestions, and allowing participation in decision making. *Achievement-oriented leader* behavior

path-goal theory   A theory of leadership suggesting that the primary functions of a leader are to make valued or desired rewards available in the workplace and to clarify for the subordinate the kinds of behavior that will lead to those rewards

is setting challenging goals, expecting subordinates to perform at high levels, encouraging subordinates, and showing confidence in subordinates' abilities.

In contrast to Fiedler's theory, path-goal theory assumes that leaders can change their style or behavior to meet the demands of a particular situation. For example, when encountering a new group of subordinates and a new project, the leader may be directive in establishing work procedures and in outlining what needs to be done. Next, the leader may adopt supportive behavior to foster group cohesiveness and a positive climate. As the group becomes familiar with the task and as new problems are encountered, the leader may exhibit participative behavior to enhance group members' motivation. Finally, achievement-oriented behavior may be used to encourage continued high performance.

Situational Factors   Like other situational theories of leadership, path-goal theory suggests that appropriate leader style depends on situational factors. Path-goal theory focuses on the situational factors of the personal characteristics of subordinates and environmental characteristics of the workplace.

Important personal characteristics include the subordinates' perception of their own ability and their locus of control. If people perceive that they are lacking in ability, they may prefer directive leadership to help them understand path-goal relationships better. If they perceive themselves to have a lot of ability, however, employees may resent directive leadership. Locus of control is a personality trait. People who have an internal locus of control believe that what happens to them is a function of their own efforts and behavior. Those who have an external locus of control assume that fate, luck, or "the system" determines what happens to them. A person with an internal locus of control may prefer participative leadership, whereas a person with an external locus of control may prefer directive leadership. Managers can do little or nothing to influence the personal characteristics of subordinates, but they can shape the environment to take advantage of these personal characteristics by providing rewards and structuring tasks, for example.

Environmental characteristics include factors outside the subordinate's control. Task structure is one such factor. When structure is high, directive leadership is less effective than when structure is low. Subordinates do not usu-

Most effective leaders demonstrate sincere interest in the personal welfare of their followers. This interest can extend to concern about their families and personal lives as well. When the interest is real, employees may feel more valued and appreciated by their leader and develop stronger job satisfaction and dedication. But if the leader's interest is superficial and is an obvious ploy to show interest, employees will likely see what's going on and come to resent and lose respect for the leader.

ally need their boss to continually tell them how to do an extremely routine job. The formal authority system is another important environmental characteristic. Again, the higher the degree of formality, the less directive is the leader behavior that subordinates will accept. The nature of the work group also affects appropriate leader behavior. When the work group provides the employee with social support and satisfaction, supportive leader behavior is less critical. When social support and satisfaction cannot be derived from the group, the worker may look to the leader for this support.

The basic path-goal framework as illustrated in Figure 17.4 shows that different leader behaviors affect a subordinate's motivation to perform. Personal and environmental characteristics are seen as defining which behaviors lead to which outcomes. The path-goal theory of leadership is a dynamic and incomplete model. The original intent was to state the theory in general terms so that future research could explore a variety of interrelationships and modify the theory. Research results suggest that the path-goal theory is a reasonably good description of the leadership process and that future investigations along these lines should enable us to discover more about the link between leadership and motivation.[22]

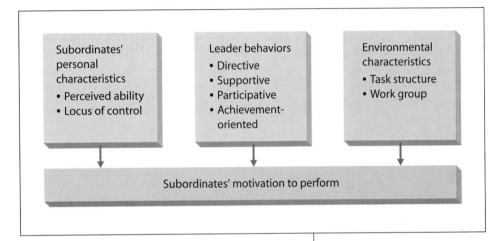

FIGURE 17.4
The Path-Goal Framework

The path-goal theory of leadership suggests that managers can use four types of leader behavior to clarify subordinates' paths to goal attainment. Personal characteristics of the subordinate and environmental characteristics within the organization both must be taken into account when determining which style of leadership will work best for a particular situation.

Vroom-Yetton-Jago (VYJ) model
Predicts what kinds of situations call for what degrees of group participation

■ Vroom-Yetton-Jago Model

The **Vroom-Yetton-Jago (VYJ) model** predicts what kinds of situations call for what degrees of group participation. The VYJ model, then, sets norms or standards for including subordinates in decision making. The model was first proposed by Victor Vroom and Philip Yetton in 1973 and was revised and expanded in 1988 by Vroom and Arthur G. Jago.[23] The VYJ model is somewhat narrower than the other situational theories in that it focuses on only one part of the leadership process—how much decision-making participation to allow subordinates.

Basic Premises   The VYJ model argues that decision effectiveness is best gauged by the quality of the decision and by employee acceptance of the decision. Decision quality is the objective effect of the decision on performance. Decision acceptance is the extent to which employees accept and are committed to the decision. To maximize decision effectiveness, the VYJ model suggests that, depending on the situation, managers adopt one of five

TABLE 17.2
**Decision Styles in the
Vroom-Yetton-Jago Model**

The difference between these styles
is the degree of participation they
provide for subordinates. The extreme forms are purely autocratic
(AI) and total participation (GII). The
other three styles fall between these
extremes.

Source: Reprinted with permission of the
University of Pittsburgh Press from *Leadership
and Decision-Making* by Victor H. Vroom and
Philip W. Yetton. Copyright © 1973 by the
University of Pittsburgh Press.

Decision Style	Definition
AI	Manager makes the decision alone.
AII	Manager asks for information from subordinates but makes the decision alone. Subordinates may or may not be informed about what the situation is.
CI	Manager shares the situation with individual subordinates and asks for information and evaluation. Subordinates do not meet as a group, and the manager alone makes the decision.
CII	Manager and subordinates meet as a group to discuss the situation, but the manager makes the decision.
GII	Manager and subordinates meet as a group to discuss the situation, and the group makes the decision.

A = autocratic; C = consultative; G = group

decision-making styles. Table 17.2 summarizes the two autocratic styles (AI and AII), two consultative styles (CI and CII), and one group style (GII).

The situation that is presumed to dictate an appropriate decision-making style is defined by a series of questions about the characteristics or attributes of the problem under consideration. To address the questions, the manager uses one of four decision trees. Two of the trees are used when the problem affects the entire group, and the other two are appropriate when the problem relates to an individual. One of each is to be used when the time necessary to reach a decision is important, and the others are to be used when time is less important but the manager wants to develop subordinates' decision-making abilities.

Figure 17.5 shows the tree for time-driven group problems. The problem attributes defining the situation are arranged along the top of the tree and are expressed as questions. To use the tree, the manager starts on the left side and asks the first question. Thus the manager first decides whether the problem involves a quality requirement—that is, whether there are quality differences in the alternatives and whether they matter. The answer determines the path to the second node, where the manager ask another question. The manager continues in this fashion until a terminal node is reached and an appropriate decision style is indicated. Each prescribed decision style is designed to protect the original goals of the process (decision quality and subordinate acceptance) within the context of the group versus individual and time versus development framework.

Evaluation The original version of the VYJ model has been widely tested. Indeed, one recent review concluded that it had received more scientific support than any other leadership theory.[24] The inherent complexity of the model presents a problem for many managers, however. Even the original version was criticized because of its complexity, and the revised VYJ model is far more complex than the original. Managers can use special computer software to define their situation, answer questions about problem attributes, and develop a strategy for decision-making participation.[25]

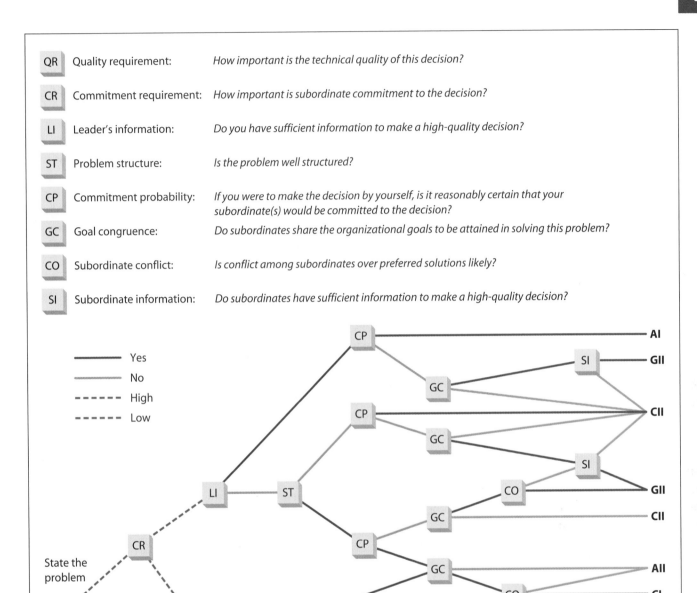

QR	Quality requirement:	*How important is the technical quality of this decision?*
CR	Commitment requirement:	*How important is subordinate commitment to the decision?*
LI	Leader's information:	*Do you have sufficient information to make a high-quality decision?*
ST	Problem structure:	*Is the problem well structured?*
CP	Commitment probability:	*If you were to make the decision by yourself, is it reasonably certain that your subordinate(s) would be committed to the decision?*
GC	Goal congruence:	*Do subordinates share the organizational goals to be attained in solving this problem?*
CO	Subordinate conflict:	*Is conflict among subordinates over preferred solutions likely?*
SI	Subordinate information:	*Do subordinates have sufficient information to make a high-quality decision?*

FIGURE 17.5

Time-Driven Group Problem Decision Tree for VYJ Model

To use this decision tree, the manager asks a series of questions about the problem situation. The answers lead the manager through the tree. The recommended decision style (see Table 17.2) at each endpoint is predicted to enhance decision quality and acceptance.

Adapted and reprinted from *Leadership and Decision-Making* by Victor H. Vroom and Philip W. Yetton, by permission of the University of Pittsburgh Press. Copyright © 1973 by University of Pittsburgh Press.

■ Other Situational Approaches

In addition to the major theories, other situational models have been developed in recent years. Here, we discuss the leader-member exchange model and the life cycle model.

leader-member exchange (LMX) model Stresses that leaders have different kinds of relationships with different subordinates

The Leader-Member Exchange Model The **leader-member exchange (LMX) model** stresses that leaders have different kinds of relationships with different subordinates.[26] Each manager-subordinate relationship represents one vertical dyad. The model suggests that leaders establish special working relationships with a handful of subordinates called the "in-group." Other subordinates remain in the "out-group." Those in the in-group receive more of the manager's time and attention and also tend to be better performers. Early research on this model is quite promising.[27]

life cycle theory A model suggesting that appropriate leader behavior depends on the maturity of the follower

Life Cycle Model Another well-known situational theory is the **life cycle theory**, which suggests that appropriate leader behavior depends on the maturity of the followers.[28] In this context maturity includes motivation, competence, and experience. The theory suggests that as followers become more mature, the leader needs to gradually move from a high level of task orientation to a low level. Simultaneously, employee-oriented behavior should start low, increase at a moderate rate, and then decline again. This theory is well known among practicing managers, but it has received little scientific support from researchers.[29]

MANAGEMENT IMPLICATIONS The most important thing for managers to remember about the situational theories is their underlying assumption that appropriate leadership behavior depends on elements of the situation. The LPC theory points to some of these situational factors. The path-goal theory stresses that leaders can change their behaviors to best match the situation. And the VYJ model provides clear guidance about employee participation in decision making. ■

Related Perspectives on Leadership

Because of its importance to organizational effectiveness, leadership continues to be the focus of a great deal of research and theory building. New approaches that have attracted much attention are the concepts of substitutes for leadership and transformational leadership.

substitutes for leadership A concept that identifies situations in which leader behaviors are neutralized or replaced by characteristics of subordinates, the task, and the organization

■ Substitutes for Leadership

The concept of **substitutes for leadership** was developed because existing leadership models and theories do not account for situations in which leadership is not needed.[30] They simply try to specify what kind of leader behavior is appropriate. The substitute concept, however, identifies situations in which leader behaviors are neutralized or replaced by characteristics of the subordinate, the task, and the organization. For example, when a patient arrives in a hospital emergency room, the professionals on duty do not wait for a leader to tell them what to. Nurses, doctors, and attendants go into action without waiting for directive or supportive leader behavior from the emergency-room supervisor.

Characteristics of the subordinate that may serve to neutralize leader behavior include ability, experience, need for independence, professional orientation, and indifference toward organizational rewards. For example, employees with a high level of ability and experience may not need to be told what to do. Similarly, a subordinate's strong need for independence may render leader behavior ineffective. Task characteristics that may substitute for leadership include routines, the availability of feedback, and intrinsic satisfaction. When the job is routine and simple, the subordinate may not need direction. When the task is challenging and intrinsically satisfying, the subordinate may not need or want social support from a leader.

Organizational characteristics that may substitute for leadership include formalization, group cohesion, inflexibility, and a rigid reward structure. Leadership may not be necessary when policies and practices are formal and inflexible, for example. Similarly, a rigid reward system may rob the leader of reward power and thereby decrease the importance of the role. Preliminary research has shown that substitutes for leadership do indeed exist and that they function generally as predicted.[31]

■ Charismatic Leadership

The concept of **charismatic leadership**, like trait theories, assumes that charisma is an individual characteristic of the leader. **Charisma** is a form of interpersonal attraction that inspires support and acceptance. All else being equal, someone with charisma is more likely to be able to influence others than is someone without charisma. For example, compared to a supervisor who lacks charisma, a highly charismatic supervisor will be more successful in influencing subordinate behavior. Thus, influence is again a fundamental element of this perspective. An excellent example of charismatic leadership is the subject of "Working with Diversity."

Robert House first proposed a theory of charismatic leadership in 1977, based on research findings from various social science disciplines.[32] His theory suggests that charismatic leaders are likely to have a lot of self-confidence, a firm conviction in their beliefs and ideals, and a strong need to influence people. They also tend to communicate high expectations about follower performance and express confidence in followers. Donald Trump is an excellent example of a charismatic leader. Even though he has made his share of mistakes and generally is perceived as only an "average" manager, many people view him as larger than life.[33]

Most experts today acknowledge three elements of charismatic leadership in organizations.[34] First, the leader needs to be able to envision the future, to set high expectation, and to model behaviors consistent with meeting those

charismatic leadership Assumes that charisma is an individual characteristic of the leader

charisma A form of interpersonal attraction that inspires support and acceptance

WORKING WITH DIVERSITY

Organizing Low-Paid Workers

Talk about challenges! First, as part of the Hispanic culture, Mexican men are generally unenthusiastic about following the lead of a woman. Second, low-wage employees are often reluctant to make waves because they know they can be easily replaced. So why is Yanira Merino one of the most respected (or feared, depending on your point of view) labor organizers today? Merino, an immigrant from El Salvador, specializes in organizing low-wage employees in such industries as food processing, which is staffed largely by immigrant workers.

Part of the answer is her charisma. She speaks eloquently and with passion. She also takes risks, and others are willing to follow her lead. And finally, she fights for downtrodden workers in places where they have traditionally been treated with little respect and given few opportunities for advancement. For example, the first plant she organized

"You know the risks we are taking. If we are caught, we could lose our jobs. But we want to make a change. We want to go for it."

Yanira Merino, union organizer*

was a tuna-processing factory in California. The plant's divisive bonus policy pitted one worker against another, and the supervisors routinely told ethnic jokes and made sexually harassing comments.

From there, she moved on to a poultry factory in North Carolina. There, workers were treated with little respect, and working conditions were abysmal. And again, Merino's organizing efforts paid off; the workers are now represented by a union. She subsequently returned to southern California and is working to organize immigrant manufacturing workers. Who knows, admirers say, she may end up being the next Mother Jones.

References: *"Can Unions Organize Low-Paid Workers? Watch This Woman,"* Wall Street Journal, *October 23, 1995, pp. A1, A10 (*quote on p. A1); and "Shattering the AFL-CIO's Glass Ceiling,"* Business Week, *November 13, 1995, p. 46.*

---

expectations. Next, the charismatic leader must be able to energize others through a demonstration of personal excitement, personal confidence, and patterns of success. And finally, the charismatic leader enables others by supporting them, by empathizing with them, and by expressing confidence in them.

Charismatic leadership ideas are quite popular among managers and are the subject of numerous books and articles. Unfortunately, few studies have specifically attempted to test the meaning and impact of charismatic leadership. In addition, lingering ethical issues about charismatic leadership trouble some people.

transformational leadership Leadership that goes beyond ordinary expectations by transmitting a sense of mission, stimulating learning experiences, and inspiring new ways of thinking

■ Transformational Leadership

Another new perspective on leadership has been called by a number of labels: charismatic leadership, inspirational leadership, symbolic leadership, and transformational leadership. We use the term **transformational leadership** and define it as leadership that goes beyond ordinary expectations by transmitting a sense of mission, stimulating learning experiences, and inspiring new ways of thinking.[35] Because of rapid change and turbulent environments, transformational leaders are increasingly being seen as vital to the success of business.

A recent popular-press article identified seven keys to successful leadership: trusting one's subordinates, developing a vision, keeping cool, encouraging risk, being an expert, inviting dissent, and simplifying things.[36] Although this list was the result of a simplistic survey of the leadership literature, it is nevertheless consistent with the premises underlying transformational leadership. So, too, are recent examples cited as effective leadership. Take, for example, the case of General Electric. When Jack Welch assumed the position of CEO, GE was a lethargic behemoth composed of more than one hundred businesses. Decision making was slow, and bureaucracy stifled individual initiative. Welch stripped away the bureaucracy, streamlined the entire organization, sold dozens of business, and bought many new ones. He literally re-created the organization, and today GE is one of the most admired and profitable firms in the world. Transformational leadership was the basis for all of Welch's changes.

Jackie Thomas, Nike's associate director of sports marketing, is a charismatic leader. She is a fierce competitor, both in the executive suite and, as shown here, on the basketball court. Ms. Thomas leads by example, inspires loyalty and dedication from her subordinates, and is very effective at planning and implementing new programs and initiatives. She is recognized throughout Nike as one of the firm's strongest and most capable managers and leaders.

MANAGEMENT IMPLICATIONS Managers should appreciate the basic nature of charisma in organizations. In addition, they should also be fully aware of the distinctions between transformational leadership and what experts call transactional leadership—routine and administrative activities generally associated with management. ▬

Political Behavior in Organizations

Another common influence on behavior is politics and political behavior. **Political behavior** describes activities carried out for the specific purpose of acquiring, developing, and using power and other resources to obtain one's preferred outcomes.[37] Political behavior may be undertaken by managers dealing with their subordinates, subordinates dealing with their managers, and managers and subordinates dealing with others at the same level. In other words, it may be directed upward, downward, or laterally. Decisions ranging from where to locate a manufacturing plant to where to put the company

political behavior The activities carried out for the specific purpose of acquiring, developing, and using power and other resources to obtain one's preferred outcomes

coffeepot are subject to political action. In any situation individuals may engage in political behavior to further their own ends, to protect themselves from others, to further goals they sincerely believe to be in the organization's best interest, or to simply acquire and exercise power. And individuals, groups of individuals, or groups of groups may seek power.[38]

Although political behavior is difficult to study because of its sensitive nature, one early survey found that many managers believed that politics influenced salary and hiring decisions in their firms. Many also believed that the incidence of political behavior was greater at the upper levels of their organizations and less at the lower levels. More than one-half of the respondents felt that organizational politics was bad, unfair, unhealthy, and irrational but most suggested that successful executives have to be good politicians and be political to "get ahead."[39]

■ Common Political Behaviors

Research has identified four basic forms of political behavior widely practiced in organizations.[40] One form is *inducement*, which occurs when a manager offers to give something to someone else in return for that individual's support. For example, one product manager might suggest to another product manager that she will put in a good word with his boss if he supports a new marketing plan that she has developed. A second tactic is *persuasion*, which relies on both emotion and logic. An operations manager wanting to construct a new plant on a certain site might persuade others to support his goal on grounds that are objective and logical (it is less expensive and has lower taxes than alternative sites) as well as subjective and personal (it has nice weather and is close to cultural attractions).

A third political behavior involves the *creation of an obligation*. For example, one manager might support a recommendation made by another manager for a new advertising campaign. Although he may really have no opinion on the new campaign, he may think that by going along he is incurring a debt from the other manager and will be able to "call in" that debt when he needs additional support to get something done. *Coercion* is the use of force to get one's way. For example, a manager may threaten to withhold support, rewards, or other resources as a way to influence someone else.

Impression management is a subtle form of political behavior that deserves special mention. **Impression management** is a direct and intentional effort by someone to enhance his or her image in the eyes of others. People engage in impression management for a variety of reasons. For one thing, they may do so in order to further their own career. By making themselves look good, they think they are more likely to receive rewards, to be given attractive job assignments, and to receive promotions. They may also engage in impression management to boost their own self-esteem. When people have a solid image in an organization, others make them aware of it through compliments, respect, and so forth. Still another reason people use impression management is in an effort to acquire more power and hence more control.

People attempt to manage how others perceive them through various

impression management A direct and intentional effort by someone to enhance his or her image in the eyes of others

mechanisms. Appearance is one of the first things people think of. Hence, a person motivated by impression management will pay close attention to choice of attire, selection of language, and the use of manners and body posture. People interested in impression management are also likely to jockey to be associated only with successful projects. By being assigned to high-profile projects led by highly successful managers, a person can begin to link his or her own name with such projects in the minds of others.

Sometimes people too strongly motivated by impression management become obsessed by it and may resort to dishonest and/or unethical means. For example, some people have been known to take credit for others' work in an effort to make themselves look better. People have also been known to exaggerate or even falsify their personal accomplishments in an effort to build an enhanced image.[41]

Managing Political Behavior

By its very nature, political behavior is tricky to approach in a rational and systematic way. But managers can handle political behavior so that it does not do excessive damage. First, managers should be aware that even if their actions are not politically motivated, others may assume that they are. Second, by providing subordinates with autonomy, responsibility, challenge, and feedback, managers reduce the likelihood of political behavior by subordinates. Third, managers should avoid using power if they want to avoid charges of political motivation. Fourth, managers should get disagreements out in the open so that subordinates will have less opportunity for political behavior, using conflict for their own purposes. Finally, managers should avoid covert activities. Behind-the-scene activities give the impression of political intent even if none really exists.[42] Other guidelines include clearly communicating the bases and processes for performance evaluation, tying rewards directly to performance, and minimizing competition among managers for resources.[43]

Of course, those guidelines are a lot easier to list than they are to implement. The well-informed manager should not assume that political behavior does not exist or, worse yet, attempt to eliminate it by issuing orders or commands. Instead, the manager must recognize that political behavior exists in virtually all organizations and that it cannot be ignored or stamped out. It can, however, be managed so that it will seldom inflict serious damage on the organization. It may even play a useful role in some situations.[44] For example, a manager may be able to use his or her political influence to stimulate a greater sense of social responsibility or to heighten awareness of the ethical implications of a decision.

MANAGEMENT IMPLICATIONS Managers need to understand the dynamics of political behavior in organizations. In particular, they should know the more common political behaviors, including impression management, as well as methods for managing political behavior. ■

Summary of Key Points

As a process, leadership is the use of noncoercive influence to shape the group's or organization's goals, motivate behavior toward the achievement of those goals, and help define group or organization culture. As a property, leadership is the set of characteristics attributed to those who are perceived to be leaders. Leadership and management are often related but are also different. Managers and leaders use legitimate, reward, coercive, referent, and expert power.

The trait approach to leadership assumed that some basic trait or set of traits differentiated leaders from nonleaders. The leadership-behavior approach to leadership assumed that the behavior of effective leaders was somehow different from the behavior of nonleaders. Research at the University of Michigan and Ohio State identified two basic forms of leadership behavior—one concentrating on work and performance and the other concentrating on employee welfare and support. The Leadership Grid attempts to train managers to exhibit high levels of both forms of behavior.

Situational approaches to leadership recognize that appropriate forms of leadership behavior are not universally applicable and attempt to specify situations in which various behaviors are appropriate. The LPC theory suggests that a leader's behaviors should be either task oriented or relationship oriented, depending on the favorableness of the situation. The path-goal theory suggests that directive, supportive, participative, or achievement-oriented leader behaviors may be appropriate, depending on the personal characteristics of subordinates and the environment. The Vroom-Yetton-Jago model maintains that leaders should vary the extent to which they allow subordinates to participate in making decisions as a function of problem attributes. The leader-member exchange model and the life cycle theory are two new situational theories.

Related leadership perspectives are the concept of substitutes for leadership, charismatic leadership, and the role of transformational leadership in organizations.

Political behavior is another type of influence that managers in organizations frequently use. Impression management, one especially important form of political behavior, is a direct and intentional effort by someone to enhance his or her image in the eyes of others. Managers can take steps to limit the effects of political behavior.

Discussion Questions

Questions for Review

1. Could someone be a manager but not a leader? a leader but not a manager? both a leader and a manager? Explain.

2. What were the major findings of the Michigan and Ohio State studies of leadership behaviors? Briefly describe each group of studies and compare and contrast their findings.

3. What are the situational approaches to leadership? Briefly describe each one and compare and contrast their findings.

4. Describe charismatic and transformation perspectives on leadership. How can they be integrated with existing approaches to leadership?

Questions for Analysis

5. How can a leader be both task oriented and employee oriented at the same time? Can you think of other forms of leader behavior that would be important to a manager? If so, share your thoughts with your class.

6. When all or most of the leadership substitutes are present, does the follower no longer need a leader? Why or why not?

7. Why should members of an organization be aware that political behavior may be going on within the organization? What might occur if they did not recognize this behavior?

Questions for Application

8. What traits seem best to describe student leaders? military leaders? business leaders? political leaders? religious leaders? What might account for the similarities and differences in your lists of traits?

9. Think about a decision that would affect you as a student. Use the Vroom-Yetton-Jago model to decide whether the administrator making that decision should involve students in the decision. Which parts of the model seem most important in making that decision? Why?

10. How do you know whether transformational leadership is present in a group or organization? Could transformational leadership ever lead to dysfunctional outcomes for individuals or organizations? If so, why? If not, why not?

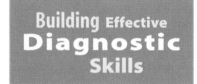

Building Effective
Diagnostic
Skills

EXERCISE OVERVIEW

Diagnostic skills help a manager visualize appropriate responses to a situation. One situation managers often face is deciding whether to use power to solve a problem. This exercise will help you develop your diagnostic skills as they relate to using different types of power in different situations.

EXERCISE BACKGROUND

Earlier in this chapter, in the "Using Power" section, several methods have been identified for using power. These include the following:

1. Legitimate request

2. Instrumental compliance

3. Coercion

4. Rational persuasion

5. Personal identification

6. Inspirational appeal

EXERCISE TASK

With these ideas in mind, do the following:

1. Relate each use of power listed here to the five types of power identified in the chapter. That is, indicate which type(s) of power is most closely associated with each use of power, which type(s) may be related to each use of power, and which type(s) are unrelated to each use of power.

2. Is a manager more likely to be using multiple forms of power simultaneously or to be using a single type of power?

3. Identify other methods and approaches to using power.

4. What are some of the dangers and pitfalls associated with using power?

**Building Effective
Decision-Making
Skills**

EXERCISE OVERVIEW

The Vroom-Yetton-Jago (VYJ) model of leadership is an effective method for determining how much participation a manager might allow his or her subordinates in making a decision. This exercise will enable you to refine your decision-making skills by applying the VYJ model to a hypothetical situation.

EXERCISE BACKGROUND

Assume that you are the branch manager of the West Coast region of the United States for an international manufacturing and sales company. The company is making a major effort to control costs and boost efficiency. As part of this effort, the firm recently installed a networked computer system linking sales representatives, customer service employees, and other sales support staff. The goal of this network was to increase sales while cutting sales expenses.

Unfortunately, just the opposite has resulted—sales are down slightly, while expenses are increasing. You have looked into this problem, and believe that the computer hardware people are using is fine. You also believe, however, that the software used to run the system is flawed. You believe it to be too hard to use and that it provides incomplete information.

Your employees disagree with your assessment, however. They believe that the entire system is fine. They attribute the problems to poor training in how to use the system and a lack of incentive for using it to solve many problems that they already know how to handle using other methods. Some of them also think that their colleagues are just resisting change.

Your boss has just called and instructed you to "solve the problem." She indicated that she has complete faith in your ability to do so, expects you to decide how to proceed, and wants a report suggesting a course of action in five days.

EXERCISE TASK

Using the preceding background information, do the following:

1. Using your own personal preferences and intuition, describe how you would proceed.

2. Now use the VYJ model to determine a course of action.

3. Compare and contrast your initial approach and the approach suggested by the VYJ model.

**Building Effective
Conceptual
Skills**

EXERCISE OVERVIEW

Conceptual skills refer to the manager's ability to think in the abstract. This exercise will enable you to apply your conceptual skills to the identification of leadership qualities in others.

EXERCISE TASK

1. Working alone, list the names of ten people you think of as leaders. Note that the names should not necessarily be confined to "good" leaders, but instead should identify "strong" leaders.

2. Form small groups with three or four classmates and compare lists. Focus on common and unique examples, as well as the kinds of individuals listed (male versus female, contemporary versus historical, business versus non-business, and so on).

3. From all the lists, choose two leaders whom most people in the group consider to be the most successful and least successful.

4. Identify similarities and differences between the two successful leaders and between the two less successful leaders.

5. Relate the successes and failures to at least one theory or perspective discussed in the chapter.

6. Select one group member to report your findings to the rest of the class.

CHAPTER CLOSING CASE

Big Turnaround at Adidas

Adidas was founded in 1948 by Adi Dassler, a brilliant Bavarian shoe designer, and for years the company ruled the market for athletic sportswear. Virtually every athlete who competed in the 1956 Olympics wore Adidas shoes. And no less a player than Kareem Abdul-Jabbar wore Adidas shoes when he dominated the NBA. But bumbling management and internal problems seriously weakened the firm and allowed Nike to swoop in and take control.

First, Adi's brother Rudolf left to form his firm, Puma. Adi's son Horst also split from the family and started another competing manufacturer. Horst later returned to the fold and took over the firm's management in 1985. Neglect and the onslaught of Nike and Reebok had taken their toll. When Horst died in 1987, Adidas's market share had fallen from a high of 70 percent to just 2 percent. And no one in the family was prepared to step in and take over.

Horst's sisters sold the company to a French financier named Bernard Tapie in 1989 for a paltry $320 million. Tapie professed to have big plans for the firm and promised to bring in $100 million in new investment to get the firm back on its feet. Unfortunately, Tapie became so involved in politics that

he, too, paid the firm little attention. He subsequently became embroiled in a soccer-fixing scandal while serving as France's Urban Affairs Minister, was sentenced to prison, declared bankruptcy, and turned Adidas over to his creditors.

The creditors, in turn, turned to Robert Louis-Dreyfuss, another French financier, and asked him to take over control of the company. Louis-Dreyfuss had no experience in the shoe or sportswear businesses, but he did have a sterling reputation as a turnaround artist. And now, under his leadership, Adidas is beginning to show signs of making the sneaker wars a real battle.

As soon as he moved into the president's office, he was astonished to be asked to personally approve a sales representative's expense account for $300. He knew at that moment that his challenges centered around bureaucracy and old-fashioned business practices. Almost immediately Louis-Dreyfuss replaced the entire top-management team at Adidas, all of whom were German. He brought in new executives from other countries and designated English as the firm's official language. He also renegotiated all existing manufacturing contracts to get costs in line with those of Nike and Reebok. And as he got costs under control, he then turned to marketing.

Louis-Dreyfuss doubled the firm's marketing budget and instructed managers in that department to get busy with new, innovative, and aggressive ideas for taking back market share previously lost to competitors. These managers, in turn, enlisted the endorsements of sports stars like Steffi Graf and Kobe Bryant. The marketing department's biggest coup, however, was getting the New York Yankees to strike a deal that required all players on the team to wear Adidas shoes.

Adidas still faces an uphill battle. But Louis-Dreyfuss has shown remarkable acumen for managing in a highly competitive industry. Among his more recent victories have been signing up the several major national soccer teams and acquiring Salomon, a major ski equipment manufacturer. Moreover, he believes that the firm will continue its renaissance and that will soon take what he sees as its rightful place alongside Nike—and ahead of Reebok and other competitors—at the top of the athletic apparel industry.

Case Questions

1. What leadership theory or concept best explains Louis-Dreyfuss's success at Adidas?

2. What can other leaders learn from Louis-Dreyfuss?

3. Do you think Adidas can overtake Nike? Why or why not?

Case References: "An Adrenaline Rush at Adidas," *Business Week*, September 29, 1997, p. 136; Charles P. Wallace, "Adidas—Back in the Game," *Fortune*, August 18, 1997, pp. 176–182.

CHAPTER NOTES

1. "Compaq: There's No End to Its Drive," *Business Week*, February 17, 1997, pp. 72–73; Stephanie Losee, "How Compaq Keeps the Magic Going," *Fortune*, February 21, 1994, pp. 90–92; and *Hoover's Handbook of American Business 1997* (Austin, Texas: Hoover's Business Press, 1996), pp. 390–391.

2. See Ronald A. Heifetz and Donald L. Laurie, "The Work of Leadership," *Harvard Business Review*, January–February 1997, pp. 124–134. See also Arthur G. Jago, "Leadership: Perspectives in Theory and Research," *Management Science*, March 1982, pp. 315–336.

3. Gary A. Yukl, *Leadership in Organizations*, 3rd ed. (Englewood Cliffs, N.J.: Prentice-Hall, 1994), p. 5.

4. See John P. Kotter, "What Leaders Really Do," *Harvard Business Review*, May–June 1990, pp. 103–111.

5. "Leader, Not Boss," *Forbes*, December 1, 1997, pp. 52–54. See also Michael E. McGill and John W. Slocum, Jr., "A *Little* Leadership, Please?" *Organizational Dynamics*, Winter 1998, pp. 39–49.

6. John R. P. French and Bertram Raven, "The Bases of Social Power," in *Studies in Social Power*, ed. Dorwin Cartwright (Ann Arbor, Mich.: University of Michigan Press, 1959), pp. 150–167.

7. Hugh D. Menzies, "The Ten Toughest Bosses," *Fortune*, April 21, 1980, pp. 62–73.

8. Thomas A. Stewart, "Get with the New Power Game," *Fortune*, January 13, 1997, pp. 58–62.

9. For more information on the bases and uses of power, see Philip M. Podsakoff and Chester A. Schriesheim, "Field Studies of French and Raven's Bases of Power: Critique, Reanalysis, and Suggestions for Future Research," *Psychological Bulletin*, 1985, Vol. 97, pp. 387–411; Robert C. Benfari, Harry E. Wilkinson, and Charles D. Orth, "The Effective Use of Power," *Business Horizons*, May–June 1986, pp. 12–16; and Yukl, *Leadership in Organizations*.

10. Bernard M. Bass, *Bass & Stogdill's Handbook of Leadership*, 3rd. ed. (Riverside, N.J.: Free Press, 1990).

11. Shelley A. Kirkpatrick and Edwin A. Locke, "Leadership: Do Traits Matter?" *Academy of Management Executive*, May 1991, pp. 48–60; see also Robert J. Sternberg, "Managerial Intelligence: Why IQ Isn't Enough," *Journal of Management*, 1997, Vol. 23, No. 3, pp. 475–493.

12. Rensis Likert, *New Patterns of Management* (New York: McGraw-Hill, 1961); and Rensis Likert, *The Human Organization* (New York: McGraw-Hill, 1967).

13. The Ohio State studies stimulated many articles, monographs, and books. A good overall reference is Ralph M. Stogdill and A. E. Coons, eds., *Leader Behavior: Its Description and Measurement* (Columbus, Ohio: Bureau of Business Research, Ohio State University, 1957).

14. Edwin A. Fleishman, E. F. Harris, and H. E. Burt, *Leadership and Supervision in Industry* (Columbus, Ohio: Bureau of Business Research, Ohio State University, 1955).

15. Robert R. Blake and Jane S. Mouton, *The Managerial Grid* (Houston: Gulf Publishing, 1964); and Robert R. Blake and Jane S. Mouton, *The Versatile Manager: A Grid Profile* (Homewood, Ill.: Dow Jones-Irwin, 1981).

16. Robert Tannenbaum and Warren H. Schmidt, "How to Choose a Leadership Pattern," *Harvard Business Review*, March–April 1958, pp. 95–101.

17. Fred E. Fiedler, *A Theory of Leadership Effectiveness* (New York: McGraw-Hill, 1967).

18. Chester A. Schriesheim, Bennett J. Tepper, and Linda A. Tetrault, "Least Preferred Co-Worker Score, Situational

Control, and Leadership Effectiveness: A Meta-Analysis of Contingency Model Performance Predictions," *Journal of Applied Psychology*, 1994, Vol. 79, No. 4, pp. 561–573.

19. Fiedler, *A Theory of Leadership Effectiveness*; and Fred E. Fiedler and M. M. Chemers, *Leadership and Effective Management* (Glenview, Ill.: Scott, Foresman, 1974).

20. For recent reviews and updates, see Lawrence H. Peters, Darrell D. Hartke, and John T. Pohlmann, "Fiedler's Contingency Theory of Leadership: An Application of the Meta-Analysis Procedures of Schmidt and Hunter," *Psychological Bulletin*, Vol. 97, pp. 274–285; and Fred E. Fiedler, "When to Lead, When to Stand Back," *Psychology Today*, September 1987, pp. 26–27.

21. Martin G. Evans, "The Effects of Supervisory Behavior on the Path-Goal Relationship," *Organizational Behavior and Human Performance*, May 1970, pp. 277–298; and Robert J. House and Terence R. Mitchell, "Path-Goal Theory of Leadership," *Journal of Contemporary Business*, Autumn 1974, pp. 81–98. See also Yukl, *Leadership in Organizations*.

22. For a recent review, see J. C. Wofford and Laurie Z. Liska, "Path-Goal Theories of Leadership: A Meta-Analysis," *Journal of Management*, 1993, Vol. 19, No. 4, pp. 857–876.

23. Victor H. Vroom and Philip H. Yetton, *Leadership and Decision-making* (Pittsburgh: University of Pittsburgh Press, 1973); and Victor H. Vroom and Arthur G. Jago, *The New Leadership* (Englewood Cliffs, N.J.: Prentice-Hall, 1988).

24. Yukl, *Leadership in Organizations*.

25. Vroom and Jago, *The New Leadership*.

26. Fred Dansereau, George Graen, and W. J. Haga, "A Vertical-Dyad Linkage Approach to Leadership within Formal Organizations: A Longitudinal Investigation of the Role-Make Process," *Organizational Behavior and Human Performance*, 1975, Vol. 15, pp. 46–78; and Richard M. Dienesch and Robert C. Liden, "Leader-Member Exchange Model of Leadership: A Critique and Further Development," *Academy of Management Review*, July 1986, pp. 618–634.

27. Antoinette Phillips and Arthur Bedeian, "Leader-Follower Exchange Quality: The Role of Personal and Interpersonal Attributes," *Academy of Management Journal*, 1994, Vol. 37, No. 4, pp. 990–1001.

28. Paul Hersey and Kenneth H. Blanchard, *Management of Organizational Behavior*, 3rd ed. (Englewood Cliffs, N.J.: Prentice-Hall, 1977).

29. Yukl, *Leadership in Organizations*.

30. Steven Kerr and John M. Jermier, "Substitutes for Leadership: Their Meaning and Measurement," *Organizational Behavior and Human Performance*, December 1978, pp. 375–403.

31. See Charles C. Manz and Henry P. Sims Jr., "Leading Workers to Lead Themselves: The External Leadership of Self-Managing Work Teams," *Administrative Science Quarterly*, March 1987, pp. 106–129.

32. See Robert J. House, "A 1976 Theory of Charismatic Leadership," in *Leadership: The Cutting Edge*, eds. J. G. Hunt and L. L. Larson (Carbondale, Ill.: Southern Illinois University Press, 1977), pp. 189–207. See also Jay A. Conger and Rabindra N. Kanungo, "Toward a Behavioral Theory of Charismatic Leadership in Organizational Settings," *Academy of Management Review*, October 1987, pp. 637–647.

33. Stratford P. Sherman, "Donald Trump Just Won't Die," *Fortune*, August 13, 1990, pp. 75–79.

34. David A. Nadler and Michael L. Tushman, "Beyond the Charismatic Leader: Leadership and Organizational Change," *California Management Review*, Winter 1990, pp. 77–97.

35. James MacGregor Burns, *Leadership* (New York: Harper & Row, 1978). See also Badrinarayan Shankar Pawar and Kenneth K. Eastman, "The Nature and Implications of Contextual Influences on Transformational Leadership: A Conceptual Examination," *Academy of Management Review*, 1997, Vol. 22, No. 1, pp. 80–109.

36. Labich, "The Seven Keys to Business Leadership."

37. Jeffrey Pfeffer, *Power in Organizations* (Marshfield, Mass.: Pitman Publishing, 1981), p. 7.

38. Timothy Judge and Robert Bretz, "Political Influence Behavior and Career Success," *Journal of Management*, 1994, Vol. 20, No. 1, pp. 43–65.

39. Victor Murray and Jeffrey Gandz, "Games Executives Play: Politics at Work," *Business Horizons*, December 1980, pp. 11–23; and Jeffrey Gandz and Victor Murray, "The Experience of Workplace Politics," *Academy of Management Journal*, June 1980, pp. 237–251.

40. Don R. Beeman and Thomas W. Sharkey, "The Use and Abuse of Corporate Power," *Business Horizons*, March–April 1987, pp. 26–30.

41. See William L. Gardner, "Lessons in Organizational Dramaturgy: The Art of Impression Management," *Organizational Dynamics*, Summer 1992, pp. 51–63; and Elizabeth Wolf Morrison and Robert J. Bies, "Impression Management in the Feedback-Seeking Process: A Literature Review and Research Agenda," *Academy of Management Review*, July 1991, pp. 522–541.

42. Murray and Gandz, "Games Executives Play."

43. Beeman and Sharkey, "The Use and Abuse of Corporate Power."

44. Stefanie Ann Lenway and Kathleen Rehbein, "Leaders, Followers, and Free Riders: An Empirical Test of Variation in Corporate Political Involvement," *Academy of Management Journal*, December 1991, pp. 893–905.

18

Managing Interpersonal Relations and Communication

OBJECTIVES

After studying this chapter, you should be able to:

- Describe the interpersonal nature of organizations.
- Describe the role and importance of communication in the manager's job.
- Identify the basic forms of communication in organizations.
- Discuss informal communication, including its various forms and types.
- Describe how the communication process can be managed so as to recognize and overcome barriers.

Kmart had its brief moment in the spotlight and then seemed to fade from the scene. But a new CEO is bent on restoring the firm's lost luster and on again making Kmart both a name respected by customers and an industry powerhouse to be reckoned with by competitors. Unfortunately, he faces quite a challenge.

Kmart was the first big retailer to make a successful plunge into discounting. During the 1970s Kmart opened more than one hundred stores a year and was clearly and unambiguously focused on passing Sears to become the biggest retailer in the world. But the firm was so fixated on who was ahead of it—Sears, J. C. Penney, and Montgomery Ward—that it paid too little attention to who was behind it—Sam Walton and Wal-Mart. Kmart did indeed pass the "big three" retailers and take the top spot, but only for a short time.

Even as Wal-Mart was moving past Kmart to become the largest retailer, the firm's managers essentially chose to ignore this formidable competitor and to instead embark on a diversification program into other areas of retailing. Kmart allowed its core discounting business to drift and flounder while it invested in retailers such as OfficeMax, Borders Bookstores, the Sports Authority, Builders Square, and others. But the poorly managed amalgam began to fall apart almost as quickly as it was built, and one CEO after another failed to turn things around.

Finally, however, the firm may have found the right person for the job. As the firm bordered on bankruptcy, its board knew it had to find a real superstar to run the business. Floyd Hall was named to the top spot at Kmart in 1995 and given a sweeping mandate to restore the firm's long-lost competitiveness. His previous jobs had included stints as manager of a Montgomery Ward store; president of B. Dalton bookstores;

president of Target, a rival discount chain; and founder of his own retail chain, The Museum Company. Hall came in as one of the most respected executives in retailing.

According to his supporters, Hall seems to have brought two great strengths to his new job. First, he is an excellent listener. Many top managers either believe they already have all the answers or are too impatient to really listen to anyone else. Hall, however, will listen to anybody who has something meaningful to say. He calls it "filling up his knowledge jar." During his first year on the job, he held weekly meetings with employees, customers, and suppliers, listening intently as they described what they liked and disliked about Kmart.

In addition to being an effective listener, Hall is also an excellent communicator. He selects just the right words to capture what he wants to say and knows just how and when to say them for maximum impact. For example, after one early briefing with stock market analysts, several brokers who had previously discouraged their clients from investing in retailing stocks started to encourage investment in Kmart stock. But Hall is far more than talk. He has sold off several underperforming units, for example, and is frantically transforming many run-down Kmart stores into modern, bright, and efficient operations. Although Kmart has a long way to go, it does appear, at least for now, that its stores will remain "open for business."[1]

> *"I see no reason why Kmart can't be as*
>
> *good a retailer as anybody in the country."*

Floyd Hall, Kmart CEO, quoted in USA Today, *April 9, 1997, p. 1B.*

Floyd Hall seems to have a surprisingly rare combination of communication skills and managerial acumen. Communication is a vital part of managerial work. Indeed, managers around the world agree that communication is one of their most important tasks. Managers must be able to convey their vision and goals for the organization to others. And others must communicate with managers so that they will better understand what's going on in their environment and how they and their organizations can become more effective.

This chapter is the first of two that focus on interpersonal processes in organizations. This chapter establishes the interpersonal nature of organizations and then discusses communication, one of the most basic forms of interaction among people. We begin the discussion in this chapter by examining communication in the context of the manager's job. Next we identify and discuss forms of interpersonal, group, and organizational communication. Then we describe techniques for managing organizational communication. Chapter 19 continues this theme with a discussion of two other elements of interpersonal relations: group and team processes and conflict.

The Interpersonal Nature of Organizations

In Chapter 1, we noted that much of a manager's job involves scheduled and unscheduled meetings, telephone calls, and related activities. Indeed, a great deal of what all managers do involves interacting with other people, both inside and outside the organization. The schedule that follows is a typical day for the president of a Houston-based company, part of a larger firm whose headquarters are in California. He kept a log of his activities for several days so you could better appreciate the nature of managerial work.

8:00–8:15 A.M. Arrive at work; review mail sorted by secretary.

8:15–8:30 A.M. Read the *Wall Street Journal*; read and respond to e-mail.

8:30–9:15 A.M. Meet with labor officials and plant manager to resolve minor labor disputes.

9:15–9:30 A.M. Review internal report and dictate correspondence for secretary to type.

9:30–10:00 A.M. Meet with two marketing executives to review advertising campaign; instruct them to fax approvals to advertising agency.

10:00–noon Meet with company executive committee to discuss strategy, budgetary issues, and competition (this committee meets weekly).

12:00–1:15 P.M. Lunch with the financial vice president and two executives from another subsidiary of the parent corporation. Primary topic of discussion is the Houston Rockets basketball team. Place two calls from cellular phone en route to lunch and receive one call en route back to office.

1:15–2:00 P.M. Meet with human resource director and assistant about a recent OSHA inspection; establish a task force to investigate the problems identified and to suggest solutions.

2:00–2:30 P.M. Conference call with four other company presidents.

2:30–3:00 P.M. Meet with financial vice president about a confidential issue that came up at lunch (unscheduled).

3:00–3:30 P.M. Work alone in office; read and respond to new e-mail.

3:30–4:15 P.M. Meet with a group of sales representatives and the company purchasing agent.

4:15–5:30 P.M. Work alone in office.

5:30–7:00 P.M. Play racquetball at nearby athletic club with marketing vice president.

This manager spent most of his time communicating and interacting with other people. And this compressed daily schedule does not include several other brief telephone calls, brief conversations with his secretary, and brief conversations with other managers. Clearly, interpersonal relations, communication, and group processes are a pervasive part of all organizations and a vital part of all managerial activities.[2]

■ Interpersonal Dynamics

The nature of interpersonal relations in an organization is as varied as the individual members themselves. At one extreme, interpersonal relations can be personal and positive, particularly when the two parties know each other, have mutual respect and affection, and enjoy interacting with one another. Two managers who have known each other for years, play golf together on weekends, and are close personal friends will likely interact at work in a positive fashion. At the other extreme, interpersonal dynamics can be personal but negative. This situation is most likely to occur when the parties dislike one another, do not have mutual respect, and do not enjoy interacting with one another. Suppose a manager has fought openly for years to block the promotion of another manager within the organization. Over the objections of the first manager, however, the other manager eventually gets promoted to the same rank. When the two of them must interact, it will most likely be in a negative manner.

Most interactions fall between these extremes, as members of the organization interact in a professional way focused primarily on goal accomplishment. The interaction deals with the job at hand, is relatively formal and structured, and is task directed. Two managers may respect each other's work and recognize the professional competence

Interpersonal dynamics are a major part of organizational life. Much of the work people do involves interacting with others— sometimes in positive ways, sometimes in negative ways. These executives are attending a company party at the Boston Children's Museum. While they are obviously enjoying themselves, their interactions will also affect their working relationships after the party has ended.

that each brings to the job. However, they may also have few common interests and little to talk about besides the job they are doing. These different types of interaction may occur between individuals, between groups, or between individuals and groups, and they can change over time. The two managers in the second scenario, for example, might decide to bury the hatchet and adopt a detached, professional manner. The two managers in the third example could find more common ground than they anticipated, and their working relationship might evolve into a personal and positive interaction.

■ Outcomes of Interpersonal Behaviors

A variety of things can happen as a result of interpersonal behaviors. Recall from Chapter 16, for example, that numerous perspectives on motivation suggest that people have social needs. Interpersonal relations in organizations can be a primary source of need satisfaction for many people. For people with a strong need for affiliation, high-quality interpersonal relations can be an important positive element in the workplace. However, when this same person is confronted with poor-quality working relationships, the effect can be just as great in the other direction.

Interpersonal relations also serve as a solid basis for social support. Suppose that an employee receives a poor performance evaluation or is denied a promotion. Others in the organization can lend support because they share a common frame of reference—an understanding of the causes and consequences of what happened. Good interpersonal relations throughout an organization can also be a source of synergy. People who support one another and who work well together can accomplish much more than people who do not support one another and who do not work well together. Another outcome, implied earlier, is conflict—people may leave an interpersonal exchange feeling angry or hostile. But a common thread is woven throughout all of these outcomes—communication between and among people in the organization.

MANAGEMENT IMPLICATIONS Managers need to keep in mind that interpersonal dynamics form the crux of most managerial work. Moreover, managers should be aware that the outcomes of interpersonal behaviors and interactions can take various forms, some good and some not so good. ■

Communication and the Manager's Job

As evidenced by the daily log presented earlier, a typical day for a manager includes doing desk work, attending scheduled meetings, placing and receiving telephone calls, reading correspondence, answering correspondence, attending unscheduled meetings, and tours.[3] Most of these activities involve communication. In fact, managers usually spend more than half of their time on some form of communication. Communication always involves two or more people, so other behavioral processes such as motivation, leadership, and group and team processes all come into play. To be true leaders, top executives must handle communication effectively.

■ A Definition of Communication

Imagine three managers working in an office building. The first is all alone but is nevertheless yelling for a subordinate to come help. No one appears, but he continues to yell. The second is talking on the telephone to a subordinate, but static on the line causes the subordinate to misunderstand some important numbers. As a result, the subordinate sends 1,500 crates of eggs to 150 Fifth Street, when he should have sent 150 crates of eggs to 1500 Fifteenth Street. The third manager is talking in her office with a subordinate who clearly hears and understands what is being said. Each of these managers is attempting to communicate but with different results.

Communication is the process of transmitting information from one person to another. Did any of our three managers communicate? The last one did, and the first did not. How about the second? In fact, she did communicate. She transmitted information and information was received. The problem was that the message transmitted and the message received were not the same. The words spoken by the manager were distorted by static and noise. **Effective communication,** then, is the process of sending a message so that the message received is as close in meaning as possible to the message intended. Although the second manager engaged in communication, it was not effective.

Our definition of effective communication is based on the ideas of meaning and consistency of meaning. *Meaning* is the idea that the individual who initiates the communication exchange wishes to convey. In effective communication, the meaning is transmitted in such a way that the receiving person understands it. For example, consider these four messages:

1. The high today will be only forty degrees.
2. It will be cold today.
3. Ceteris paribus
4. Xnlgp bo5cz4ik abl9

You probably understand the meaning of the first statement. The second statement may seem clear at first, but it is somewhat less clear than the first statement; *cold* is a relative condition, and the word can mean different things to different people. Fewer still understand the third statement because it is written in Latin. None of you understand the last statement; it is written in a secret code that your author developed as a child.

communication The process of transmitting information from one person to another

effective communication The process of sending a message in such a way that the message received is as close in meaning as possible to the message intended

■ The Role of Communication in Management

We noted earlier the variety of activities that fill a manager's day. Meetings, telephone calls, and correspondence are all a necessary part of every manager's

THE QUALITY CHALLENGE

Open Book Management at Chaparral Steel

Although few people have heard of Chaparral Steel Corp., the company enjoys a strong reputation as one of the most effective firms in the steel industry. Chaparral was founded in 1973, and today enjoys annual sales of over $450 million. In earlier times most steel companies were large, bureaucratic operations like U.S. Steel (now USX) and Bethlehem Steel. However, increased competition from low-cost foreign steel firms—especially those in Japan and Korea—caused major problems for these manufacturers with their high overhead costs and inflexible modes of operation.

These competitive pressures, in turn, led to the formation of so-called minimills like Chaparral. Because of their size, technology, and flexibility, these firms can maintain much lower production costs and respond more quickly to customer requests. And today Chaparral is recognized as one of the best of this new breed of steel companies. For example, whereas most mills produce an average of one ton of steel with 3 to 5 labor-hours, Chaparral produces a ton with less than 1.4 labor-hours.

Since its inception, Chaparral has been led by Gordon Forward. Forward knew he would have to use novel management techniques for Chaparral to succeed. One of the first things he decided to do was to break down the traditional barriers between management and labor. Thus, he mandated that there would be neither reserved parking spaces nor separate dining area for managers. He also insisted that all employees be paid on a salary basis—no time clocks or time sheets for anyone. He also pioneered a concept called "open book management"—any employee can see any document, record, or other piece of information.

Forward believes in trusting everyone in the organization. When the firm recently needed a new rolling mill lathe, it budgeted $1 million for its purchase and then put the purchase decision in the hands of an operating machinist. The machinist, in turn, investigated various options, visited other mills in Japan and Europe, and then recommended an alternative piece of machinery costing less than half of the budgeted amount.

Forward also recognizes the importance of investing in and rewarding people. Continuous education is an integral part of Chaparral's culture, with a variety of classes being offered all the time. Everyone also participates in the good—and bad—times. For example, workers have a guaranteed base salary that is adequate but below the standard market rate. In addition, however, each employee gets a pay-for-performance bonus based on his or her individual achievements. Finally, companywide bonuses are paid to everyone on a quarterly basis. These bonuses are tied to overall company performance.

> *"We encourage people at all organizational levels to have face-to-face dialogues."*
>
> *Dennis Beach, Chaparral Executive Vice President*

References: *John Case, "Opening the Books,"* Harvard Business Review, *March–April 1997, pp. 118–129, Brian Dumaine, "Chaparral Steel: Unleash Workers and Cut Costs,"* Fortune, *May 18, 1992, pp. 88; and Ricky W. Griffin and Ronald J. Ebert,* Business Essentials, *2nd ed. (Englewood Cliffs, N.J.: Prentice-Hall, 1998), p. 119.*

job—and all clearly involve communication. On a typical Monday, Nolan Archibald, CEO of Black & Decker Corp., attended five scheduled meetings and two unscheduled meetings; had fifteen telephone conversations; received twenty-nine letters, memos, and reports; and dictated ten letters.

To better understand the linkages between communication and management, recall the variety of roles that managers must fill. Each of the ten basic managerial roles discussed in Chapter 1 (see Table 1.2) would be impossible to fill without communication.[4] Interpersonal roles involve interacting with supervisors, subordinates, peers, and others outside the organization. Decisional roles require managers to seek out information to use in making decisions and then to communicate those decisions to others. Informational roles focus specifically on the acquiring and disseminating of information.

Communication also relates directly to the basic management functions of planning, organizing, leading, and controlling. Environmental scanning, integrating planning-time horizons, and decision making, for example, all necessitate communication. Delegation, coordination, and organization change and development also entail communication. Developing reward systems and interacting with subordinates as a part of the leading function would be impossible without some form of communication. And communication is essential to establishing standards, monitoring performance, and taking corrective actions as a part of control. Clearly, then, communication is a pervasive part of virtually all managerial activities. "The Quality Challenge" portrays in even more detail how the concept of open book management has contributed to the success of Chaparral Steel.

The Communication Process

Figure 18.1 illustrates how communication generally takes place between people. The process of communication begins when one person (the sender) wants to transmit a fact, idea, opinion, or other information to someone else (the receiver). This fact, idea, or opinion has meaning to the sender, whether it be simple and concrete or complex and abstract. For example, Linda Porter, a marketing representative at Xerox, recently landed a new account and wanted to tell her boss about it. This fact and her motivation to tell her boss represented meaning.

The next step is to encode the meaning into a form appropriate to the situation. The encoding might take the form of words, facial expressions, gestures, or even artistic expressions and physical actions. For example, the Xerox representative might have said, "I just landed the Acme account," "We just got some good news from Acme," "I just spoiled Canon's day," "Acme just made the right decision," or any number of other things. She actually chose the second

FIGURE 18.1
The Communication Process

As the figure shows, noise can disrupt the communication process at any step. Managers must therefore understand that a conversation in the next office, a fax machine out of paper, and the receiver's worries may all thwart the manager's best attempts to communicate.

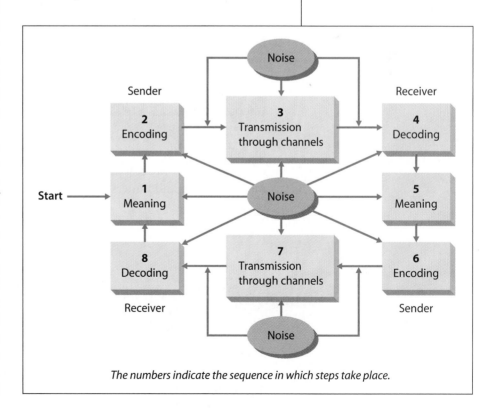

The numbers indicate the sequence in which steps take place.

message. Clearly, the encoding process is influenced by the content of the message, the familiarity of sender and receiver, and other situational factors.

After the message has been encoded, it is transmitted through the appropriate channel or medium. The channel by which the present encoded message is being transmitted to you is the printed page. Common channels in organizations include meetings, e-mail, memos, letters, reports, and telephone calls. Linda Porter might have written her boss a note, sent him an e-mail, called him on the telephone, or dropped by his office to convey the news in person. Because both she and her boss were out of the office when Linda got the news, she called and left him a voice-mail message.

After the message is received, it is decoded back into a form that has meaning for the receiver. As noted earlier, the consistency of this meaning can vary dramatically. Upon hearing about the Acme deal, the sales manager at Xerox might have thought, "This'll mean a big promotion for both of us," "This is great news for the company," or "She's blowing her own horn too much again." His actual feelings were closest to the second statement. In many cases, the meaning prompts a response, and the cycle is continued when a new message is sent by the same steps back to the original sender. The manager might have called the sales representative to offer congratulations, written her a personal note of praise, offered praise in an e-mail, or sent a formal letter of acknowledgment. Linda's boss wrote her a personal note.

"Noise" may disrupt communication anywhere along the way. Noise can be the sound of someone coughing, a truck driving by, or two people talking close at hand. It can also include disruptions such as a letter being lost in the mail, a telephone line going dead, an e-mail getting misrouted, or one of the participants in a conversation being called away before the communication process is completed. If the note written by Linda's boss had gotten lost, she might have felt unappreciated. As it was, his actions positively reinforced not only her efforts at Acme but also her effort to keep him informed.

MANAGEMENT IMPLICATIONS Managers must clearly understand and appreciate the differences between communication and effective communication and the pervasive role of communication in their work. They should also be familiar with the basic communication process as a mechanism for making their communication more effective and understanding why communication mistakes sometimes occur. ▬

Forms of Communication in Organizations

Managers need to understand several kinds of communication that are common in organizations today. These include interpersonal communication, communication in networks and teams, organizational communication, and electronic communication.

▪ Interpersonal Communication

Interpersonal communication is generally either oral or written. Each mode has clear strengths and weaknesses.

Oral Communication **Oral communication** takes place in face-to-face conversation, group discussions, telephone calls, and other circumstances in which the spoken word is used to express meaning. Henry Mintzberg demonstrated the importance of oral communication when he found that most managers spend between 50 and 90 percent of their time talking to people.[5]

The primary advantage of oral communication is that it promotes prompt feedback and interchange in the form of verbal questions or agreement, facial expressions, and gestures. Oral communication is also easy (all the sender needs to do is talk), and it can be done with little preparation (though careful preparation is advisable in certain situations). The sender does not need pencil and paper, typewriter, or other equipment. In one survey 55 percent of the executives sampled believed that their own written communication skills were fair or poor, so they chose oral communication to avoid embarrassment![6]

However, oral communication also has drawbacks. It may suffer from problems of inaccuracy if the speaker chooses the wrong words to convey meaning or leaves out pertinent details, if noise disrupts the process, or if the receiver forgets part or all of the message. A two-way discussion seldom allows time for a thoughtful, considered response or for introducing many new facts, and there is no permanent record of what has been said. In addition, although most managers are comfortable talking to people individually or in small groups, few enjoy speaking to larger audiences.[7]

Written Communication "Putting it in writing" can solve many of the problems inherent in oral communication. Nevertheless, and perhaps surprisingly, **written communication** is not as common as one might imagine, nor is it a mode of communication much respected by managers. One sample of managers indicated that only 13 percent of the mail they received was of immediate use to them.[8] More than 80 percent of the managers who responded to another survey indicated that the written communication they received was of fair or poor quality.[9]

The biggest single drawback of written communication is that it inhibits feedback and interchange. When one manager sends another manager a letter, it must be written or dictated, typed, mailed, received, routed, opened, and read. If there is a misunderstanding, it may take several days for it to be

oral communication Face-to-face conversation, group discussions, telephone calls, and other circumstances in which the spoken word is used to transmit meaning

People communicate with one another in a variety of ways and in many different settings. Consider this team of Netscape employees. They are using oral communication as they talk while they eat lunch. They are also using written communication from the papers stacked on the table and electronic communication in the form of e-mail. Moreover, they are using nonverbal communication with their body language and facial expressions.

written communication Memos, letters, reports, notes, and other circumstances in which the written word is used to transmit meaning

Loose Lips Can Sink Ships

It's no secret that Eastman Kodak Company has been struggling in recent times. Its core businesses have mature markets with little growth opportunity, and the firm's recent ventures into new areas have generally been disappointing. To counter its problems, the firm has implemented a major cost-cutting program and hired a new CEO, George Fisher. Fisher had previously earned high marks for his leadership at Motorola.

Kodak's chief operating officer is Leo Thomas. Thomas has a long-standing reputation in the company for being tough-minded and bold in his approach to problems. He states his mind clearly—sometimes bluntly—and pays little attention to what others think about him or the way he handles himself. In general, most executives at the firm give him high marks for his executive skills, but a few have expressed concern about his interpersonal style and worry that his bluntness may backfire.

In 1994 just such an incident happened. As the fourth quarter of the year approached, the company's financial managers realized that Kodak was not going to meet its profit goals. Thomas responded by writing a blistering memo in which he mandated severe cost cuts. For example, he ordered that travel and entertainment budgets be cut in half, banned personal computer purchases, and cut research and development spending budgets.

Unfortunately for Kodak, someone leaked the memo to the press. The press, in turn, reported the contents of the letter. The news caused a near panic among analysts and

> *"People have told Jack that these things are bound to leak, but he doesn't seem to care."*
>
> *A former Kodak executive, referring to Leo Thomas, Kodak chief operating officer,* Business Week, *October 31, 1994, p. 52*

investors who were holding Kodak stock. Fearing that bad financial news was looming, large numbers of shareholders sold out. The net result was that the market capitalization of Kodak (that is, the total value of its stock) dropped $1.1 billion in two days.

After the carnage, there were differences of opinion as to what it all meant. Many insiders felt that the market had overreacted. They reasoned, for example, that Thomas often wrote such memos, frequently sending them to hundreds of managers. But others criticized him for having written the memo to begin with. They argued that it had only been a matter of time before one of his memos was leaked to the outside business community.

Of equal interest to some people was why Thomas had written the memo to begin with. One popular theory was that he was feeling heat from Fisher, his new boss. Fisher was known to be pressuring managers to meet their profit goals, and Thomas may have simply been trying to show Fisher that he was doing his best to keep things on track. Regardless of the reasons or other explanations, however, one thing was clear: the memo wrecked havoc with the financial community's opinion of Kodak. Of course, as time passes the damage inflicted by this event will diminish and the firm will again be judged on its actual performance in the marketplace.

References: *"Loose Lips Sink Stock Prices,"* Business Week, *October 31, 1994, p. 52; and* Hoover's Handbook of American Business 1998 *(Austin, Texas: Hoover's Business Press, 1998), pp. 508–509.*

recognized, let alone rectified. A phone call could settle the whole matter in just a few minutes. Thus, written communication often inhibits feedback and interchange and is usually more difficult and time consuming than oral communication. "Today's Management Issues" describes an unfortunate situation involving written communication.

Of course, written communication offers some advantages. It can be quite accurate and provides a permanent record of the exchange. The sender can take the time to collect and assimilate the information and can draft and revise it before it is transmitted. The receiver can take the time to read it carefully and can refer to it repeatedly, as needed. For these reasons, written communication is generally preferable when important details are involved. At times it is important to one or both parties to have a written record available as evidence of exactly what took place. Julie Regan, founder of Toucan-Do, an importing company based in Honolulu, relies heavily on formal business letters in establishing contacts and buying merchandise from vendors in Southeast Asia. She believes that such letters give her an opportunity to carefully think through what she wants to say, to tailor her message to each individual, and to avoid misunderstandings later.

Choosing the Right Form   Which form of interpersonal communication should the manager use? The best medium will be determined by the situation. Oral communication is often preferred when the message is personal, nonroutine, and brief. Written communication is usually best when the message is more impersonal, routine, and longer. The manager can also combine media to capitalize on the advantages of each. For example, a quick telephone call to set up a meeting is easy and gets an immediate response. Following up the call with a reminder note helps ensure that the recipient will remember the meeting, and it provides a record of the meeting having been called. Electronic communication, discussed more fully later, blurs the differences between oral and written communication and can help each be more effective.

communication network   The pattern through which the members of a group communicate

■ Communication in Networks and Work Teams

Whereas communication among team members in an organization is clearly interpersonal in nature, substantial research also exists focusing specifically upon how people in networks and work teams communicate with one another. A **communication network** is the pattern through which the members of a group or team communicate. Researchers studying group dynamics have discovered several typical networks in groups and teams consisting of three, four, and five members. Representative networks among members of five-member teams are shown in Figure 18.2.[10]

   In the wheel pattern all communication flows through one central person who is probably the group's leader. In a sense the wheel is the most centralized

FIGURE 18.2
Types of Communication Networks

Research on communication networks has identified five basic networks for five-person groups. These vary in terms of information flow, position of the leader, and effectiveness for different types of tasks. Managers might strive to create centralized networks when group tasks are simple and routine. Alternatively, managers can foster decentralized groups when group tasks are complex and nonroutine.

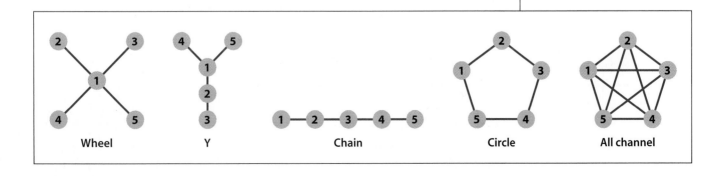

Wheel   Y   Chain   Circle   All channel

network because one person receives and disseminates all information. The Y pattern is slightly less centralized—two persons interact with more than one other person, while three people interact with only one person each. The chain offers a more even flow of information among members, although two people (the ones at each end) interact with only one other person. This path is closed in the circle pattern. Finally, the all-channel network, the most decentralized, allows a free flow of information among all group members. Everyone participates equally, and the group's leader, if there is one, is not likely to have excessive power.

Research conducted on networks suggests some interesting connections between the type of network and group performance. For example, when the group's task is relatively simple and routine, centralized networks tend to perform with greatest efficiency and accuracy. The dominant leader facilitates performance by coordinating the flow of information. For example when a group of accounting clerks is logging incoming invoices and distributing them for payment, one centralized leader can efficiently coordinate the entire process. When the task is complex and nonroutine, such as making a major decision about organizational strategy, decentralized networks tend to be most effective because open channels of communication permit more interaction and a more efficient sharing of relevant information. Managers should recognize the effects of communication networks on group and organizational performance and should try to structure networks appropriately.

■ Organizational Communication

Still other forms of communication in organizations flows among and between organizational units or groups. Each involves oral or written communication but also extends to broad patterns of communication across the organization.[11] As shown in Figure 18.3, some forms of communication follow vertical and horizontal linkages in the organization.

FIGURE 18.3

Formal Communication in Organizations

Formal communication in organizations follows official reporting relationships and/or prescribed channels. For example, vertical communication, shown here with dashed lines, flows between levels in the organization and involves subordinates and their managers. Horizontal communication flows between people at the same level and is usually used to facilitate coordination.

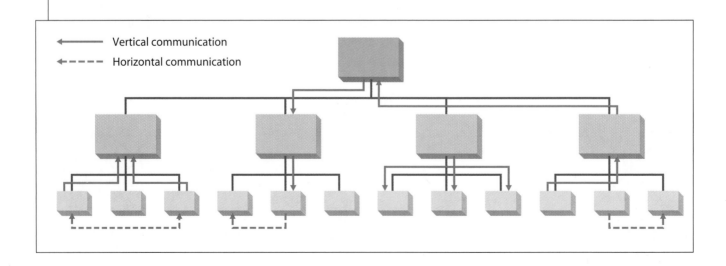

Vertical communication
Horizontal communication

Vertical Communication   **Vertical communication** flows both up and down the organization, usually along formal reporting lines—that is, it is the communication that takes place between managers and their superiors and subordinates. Vertical communication may involve only two people, or it may flow through several organizational levels.

Upward communication consists of messages from subordinates to superiors. This flow is usually from subordinates to their direct superior, then to that person's direct superior, and so on up the hierarchy. Occasionally, a message might bypass a particular superior. The typical content of upward communication is requests, information that the lower-level manager thinks is of importance to the higher-level manager, responses to requests from the higher-level manager, suggestions, complaints, and financial information. Research has shown that upward communication is more subject to distortion than is downward communication. Subordinates are likely to withhold or distort information that makes them look bad. The greater the degree of difference in status between superior and subordinate and the greater the degree of distrust, the more likely the subordinate is to suppress or distort information.[12] For example, when Harold Geneen was CEO of ITT, subordinates routinely withheld information about problems if they thought the news would make him angry and if they thought they could solve the problem themselves without his ever knowing about it.[13]

Downward communication occurs when information flows down the hierarchy from superiors to subordinates. The typical content of these messages is directives on how something is to be done, the assignment of new responsibilities, performance feedback, and general information that the higher-level manager thinks will be of value to the lower-level manager. Leo Thomas's memo at Kodak to other managers regarding cost cutting, discussed in "Today's Management Issues," was downward communication. Vertical communication can, and usually should, be two way. That is, give-and-take communication with active feedback is generally likely to be more effective than one-way communication.[14]

Horizontal Communication   Whereas vertical communication involves a superior and a subordinate, **horizontal communication** involves colleagues and peers at the same level of the organization. For example, an operations manager might communicate to a marketing manager that inventory levels are running low and that projected delivery dates should be extended by two weeks. Horizontal communication probably occurs more among managers than among nonmanagers.

This type of communication serves a number of purposes. It facilitates coordination among interdependent units. For example, a manager at Motorola was once researching the strategies of Japanese semiconductor firms in Europe. He found a great deal of information that was relevant to his assignment. He also uncovered some additional information that was potentially important to another department; so he passed it along to a colleague in that department, who used it to improve his own operations.[15] Horizontal communication can also be used for joint problem solving, as when two plant managers at Northrup Grumman got together to work out a new method to improve productivity. Finally, horizontal communication plays a major role in work teams whose members are drawn from several departments.

vertical communication Communication that flows up and down the organization usually along formal reporting lines; it takes place between managers and their subordinates and may involve several different levels of the organization

horizontal communication Communication that flows laterally within the organization; it involves colleagues and peers at the same level of the organization and may involve individuals from several different organizational units

■ Electronic Communication

Finally, electronic communication has taken on much greater importance in organizations in recent times. Both formal information systems and personal information technology have reshaped how managers communicate with one another.

Formal Information Systems   Another increasingly important method of organizational communication is the use of information systems. An organization that wants to rely heavily on information systems usually does so through either a managerial approach or an operational approach. The managerial approach involves the creation of a position usually called the chief information officer, or CIO. Unisys, General Mills, and Burlington Industries have all created such a position. The CIO is responsible for determining the information-processing needs and requirements of the organization and then putting in place systems that facilitate smooth and efficient organizational communication.

The operational approach, often a part of the CIO's efforts, involves the creation of one or more formal information systems linking all relevant managers, departments, and facilities in the organization. In the absence of such a system, a marketing manager, for example, may need to call a warehouse manager to find out how much of a particular product is in stock before promising shipping dates to a customer. An effective formal information system enables the marketing manager to get the information more quickly, and probably more accurately, by plugging directly into a computerized information system. Because of the increased emphasis and importance of these kinds of information systems, we cover them in detail in Chapter 22.

Personal Electronic Technology   In recent years, the nature of organizational communication has changed dramatically, mainly because of breakthroughs in personal electronic communication technology, and the future promises even more change. Electronic typewriters and photocopying machines were early breakthroughs. The photocopier, for example, permits a manager to distribute a printed report to many people in an extremely short time. Personal computers have accelerated the process even more. E-mail systems, the Internet, and corporate intranets promise to carry communication technology even further in the years to come.[16]

It is now possible to have teleconferences in which managers stay at their own locations (such as offices in different cities) but are seen on television monitors as they "meet." A manager in New York can keyboard a letter or memorandum at her personal computer, point and click with a mouse, and have the message delivered to hundreds or even thousands of colleagues around the world in a matter of seconds. Highly detailed information can be retrieved with ease from large electronic databanks. This technology has given rise to a new version of an old work arrangement—telecommuting is the label given to a new electronic cottage industry. In a cottage industry people work at home (in their cottages) and periodically take the product of their labor to the company. Telecommuters work at home on their computers and transmit their work to the company by means of telephone modems.

For example, David L. Hoffman, a partner in a Chicago law firm, lives in Telluride, Colorado. He consults with clients over the phone, sends them re-

MANAGEMENT INFOTECH

Cellular Phones Take a Toll

One of the most ubiquitous devices in organizations today is the cellular telephone. It seems like only a few years ago that cell phones were a rarity. Now, however, in any large airport or business center, a casual observer can easily spot dozens of people sitting in chairs, leaning against the wall, or strolling around as they conduct business on their cell phones.

The advent of cell phones has afforded many managers the opportunity to become considerably more productive. It's easier for them to make telephone calls on the road, to stay in touch with clients and customers, and to maintain contact with their office. At the same time, however, cell phones also pose some problems for many busy executives. Specifically, because these executives are always available for contact, they have less "downtime" and less opportunity to disengage from their work.

In the past, for example, managers had free time when they were traveling to and from work or when they were

"My cell phone is like ice cream—most of the time I love it, but I'm not sure its always good for me."

Anonymous Shell executive

away from their offices at lunch. Now, however, many are readily accessible during these times because of the cell phones that they carry with them. Thus what might have once been a refreshing one-hour lunch break may now simply be a continuation of work as the individual makes and receives telephone calls while eating at the corner deli.

The astute manager who wants to regain some control over this aspect of his or her work life really has more control than might be expected. Simply put, all the manager has to do is to turn off the cell phone. Obviously, if the individual is expecting a very important and urgent telephone call, taking the cellular telephone to lunch might not be a bad idea. But if nothing pressing is on the horizon, perhaps the manager should instead simply leave the phone behind and take advantage of a few minutes of rest from the ongoing demands of the executive's life.

References: *"Drowning in Data,"* Newsweek, *April 28, 1997, p. 85; and* "Stress Busters for Busy Execs," Fortune, *July 8, 1996, p. 37.*

---

ports through the telephone lines with his modem or by Federal Express, and has calls to his Chicago office electronically routed to Telluride. Recent estimates suggest that as many as fifteen million Americans use telephones, computers, and couriers to work outside their conventional offices.

Cellular telephones and facsimile machines have made it even easier for managers to communicate. Many now use cellular phones to make calls while commuting to and from work and carry them in briefcases so they can receive calls while at lunch. Facsimile machines make it easy for people to use written communication media and get rapid feedback.

Psychologists, however, are beginning to associate some problems with these communication advances. For one thing, managers who are seldom in their "real" offices are likely to fall behind in their fields and to be victimized by organizational politics because they are not present to keep in touch with what's going on and to protect themselves. They drop out of the organizational grapevine and miss out on much of the informal communication that takes place. Moreover, the use of electronic communication at the expense of face-to-face meetings and conversations makes it hard to build a strong culture, develop solid working relationships, and create a mutually supportive atmosphere of trust and cooperation.[17] "Management InfoTech" explores this phenomenon in more detail.

grapevine An informal communication network among people in an organization

Managers should realize that they have more modes of communication available to them today than at any time in history. A plethora of interpersonal, team-based, organizational, and electronic communication channels make it easier than ever before to keep in contact with others and to procure and distribute information. However, managers should also be aware of pitfalls inherent in various communication methods. ▬

Informal Communication in Organizations

FIGURE 18.4
Informal Communication in Organizations

Informal communication in organizations may or may not follow official reporting relationships and/or prescribed channels. It may cross different levels and different departments or work units, and may or may not have anything to do with official organizational business.

The aforementioned forms of organizational communication represent planned, formal communication mechanisms. However, in many cases much of the communication that takes place in an organization transcends these formal channels and instead follows any of several informal methods. Figure 18.4 illustrates numerous paths of informal communication. Common forms of informal communication in organizations include the grapevine, management by wandering around, and nonverbal communication.

■ The Grapevine

The **grapevine** is an informal communication network that can permeate an entire organization. Grapevines are found in all organizations except the very smallest, but they do not always follow the same patterns as, nor do they necessarily coincide with, formal channels of authority and communication. Research has identified several kinds of grapevine chains.[18] The two most

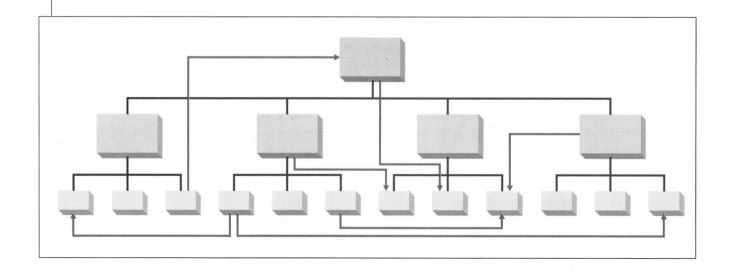

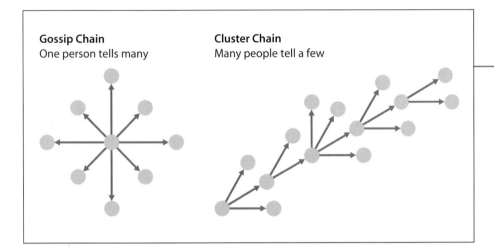

Gossip Chain
One person tells many

Cluster Chain
Many people tell a few

FIGURE 18.5
Common Grapevine Chains Found in Organizations

The two most common grapevine chains in organizations are the gossip chain (in which one person communicates messages to many others) and the cluster chain (in which many people pass messages to a few others).
Source: Adapted from *Human Behavior at Work: Organizational Behavior,* Eighth Edition, by Keith Davis and John W. Newstrom. Copyright ©1989 by The McGraw-Hill Companies. Reprinted by permission of The McGraw-Hill Companies.

common are illustrated in Figure 18.5. The gossip chain occurs when one person spreads the message to many other people. Each one, in turn, may either keep the information confidential or pass it on to others. The gossip chain is likely to carry personal information. The other common grapevine is the cluster chain in which one person passes the information to a few selected individuals. Some of the receivers pass the information to a few other individuals; the rest keep it to themselves.

Although not everyone agrees on the accuracy of the information carried by the grapevine, research is increasingly finding it to be fairly accurate, especially when the information is based on fact rather than speculation. One recent study found that the grapevine may be between 75 percent and 95 percent accurate.[19] That same study also found that informal communication is increasing in many organizations for two basic reasons. One contributing factor is the recent increase in merger, acquisition, and takeover activity. Because such activity can greatly affect the people within an organization, they are likely to spend more time talking about it.[20] The second contributing factor is that as more and more corporations move their facilities from traditional downtown locations to suburbs, employees tend to talk less and less to others outside the organization and more and more to each other. When businesses are concentrated in downtown locations, for example, people often lunch with friends from other companies located across the street or on the next block. But because suburban locations tend to be in less concentrated areas, there are likely to be fewer other businesses nearby. Consequently, people will be more likely to spend their time with their co-workers from the same workplace.

Attempts to eliminate the grapevine are fruitless, but fortunately the manager does have some control over it. By maintaining open channels of communication and responding vigorously to inaccurate information, the manager can minimize the damage the grapevine can do. The grapevine can actually be an asset. By learning who the key people in the grapevine are, for example, the manager can partially control the information they receive and use the grapevine to sound out employee reactions to new ideas such as a change in human resource policies or benefit packages. The manager can also get valuable information from the grapevine and use it to improve decision making.

management by wandering around An approach to communication that involves the manager literally wandering around and having spontaneous conversations with others

■ Management by Wandering Around

Another increasingly popular form of informal communication is called **management by wandering around.**[21] The basic idea is that some managers keep in touch with what's going on by wandering around and talking with people—immediate subordinates, subordinates far down the organizational hierarchy, delivery people, customers, or anyone else who is involved with the company in some way. Bill Marriott, for example, frequently visits the kitchens, loading docks, and custodial work areas whenever he tours a Marriott hotel. He claims that by talking with employees throughout the hotel, he gets new ideas and has a better feel for the entire company.

A related form of organizational communication that really has no specific name is the informal interchange that happens outside the normal work setting. Employees attending the company picnic, playing on the company softball team, or taking fishing trips together will almost always spend part of their time talking about work. For example, Texas Instruments engineers at TI's Lewisville, Texas, facility often frequent a local bar in town after work. On any given evening they talk about the Dallas Cowboys, the company's newest government contract, the weather, their boss, the company's stock price, local politics, and problems at work. There is no set agenda, and the key topics of discussion vary from group to group and from day to day. Still, the social gatherings serve an important role. They promote a strong culture and enhance understanding of how the organization works.

nonverbal communication Any communication exchange that does not use words or that uses words to carry more meaning than the strict definition of the words themselves

■ Nonverbal Communication

Nonverbal communication is a communication exchange that does not use words or that uses words to carry more meaning than the strict definition of the words themselves. Nonverbal communication is a powerful but little-understood form of communication in organizations. It often relies on facial expression, body movements, physical contact, and gestures. One study found that as much as 55 percent of the content of a message is transmitted by facial expression and body posture and that another 38 percent derives from inflection and tone. Words themselves account for only 7 percent of the content of the message.[22]

Communication is a powerful force in organizations. Nonverbal communication can be especially important. As shown in this cartoon, some organizations are experimenting with meetings in rooms with no furniture. The logic is two-fold: without status symbols like traditional seating arrangements, better communication may result (leaders usually sit at the head of the table) and meetings may be more efficient if people can't get too comfortable (since they have no place to sit). But some managers might still attempt to circumvent the goals of this approach by seeking other ways to maintain their status.

Research has identified three kinds of nonverbal communication practiced by managers—images, settings, and body language.[23] In this context, *images* are the kinds of words people elect to use. "Damn the torpedoes, full speed ahead" and "Even though there are some potential hazards, we should proceed with this course of action" may convey the same meaning. Yet the person who uses the first expression may be perceived as a maverick, a courageous hero, an individualist, or a reckless and foolhardy adventurer. The person who uses the second might be described as aggressive, forceful, diligent, or narrow-minded and resistant to change. In short, our choice of words conveys much more than just the strict meaning of the words themselves.

The setting for communication also plays a major role in nonverbal communication. Boundaries, familiarity, the home turf, and other elements of the setting are all important. Much has been written about the symbols of power in organizations. The size and location of an office, the kinds of furniture in the office, and the accessibility of the person in the office all communicate useful information. For example, H. Ross Perot positions his desk so that it is always between him and a visitor. This arrangement keeps him in charge. When he wants a less formal dialogue, he moves around to the front of the desk and sits beside his visitor. Jim Treybig of Tandem Computers has his desk facing a side window so that when he turns around to greet a visitor there is never anything between them.[24]

A third form of nonverbal communication is body language.[25] The distance we stand from someone as we speak has meaning. In the United States standing very close to someone you are talking to generally signals either familiarity or aggression. The English and Germans stand farther apart than Americans when talking, whereas the Arabs, Japanese, and Mexicans stand closer together.[26] Eye contact is another effective means of nonverbal communication. For example, prolonged eye contact might suggest either hostility or romantic interest. Other kinds of body language include body and arm movement, pauses in speech, and mode of dress.

The manager should be aware of the importance of nonverbal communication and recognize its potential impact. Giving an employee good news about a reward with the wrong nonverbal cues can destroy the reinforcement value of the reward. Likewise, reprimanding an employee but providing inconsistent nonverbal cues can limit the effectiveness of the sanctions. The tone of the message, where and how the message is delivered, facial expressions, and gestures can all amplify, or weaken the message or change the message altogether.

MANAGEMENT IMPLICATIONS

Managers need to appreciate the power and pervasiveness of informal communication. The grapevine, for example, can be a powerful force with which managers must contend. Management by wandering around can be an effective way of learning about what's going on in the organization and what people are talking about. And nonverbal communication can frequently convey a great deal of information.

Managing Organizational Communication

In view of the importance and pervasiveness of communication in organizations, it is vital for managers to understand how to manage the communication process.[27] Managers should understand how to maximize the potential benefits of communication and minimize the potential problems. We begin our discussion of communication management by considering the factors that might disrupt effective communication and how to deal with them.

■ Barriers to Communication

Several factors may disrupt the communication process or serve as barriers to effective communication.[28] As shown in Table 18.1, these may be divided into two classes: individual barriers and organizational barriers.

Individual Barriers Several individual barriers may disrupt effective communication. One common problem is conflicting or inconsistent signals. Another is lack of credibility. A manager is sending conflicting signals when she says on Monday that things should be done one way but then prescribes an entirely different procedure on Wednesday. A manager is also sending inconsistent signals when he says that he has an "open door" policy and wants his subordinates to drop by but keeps his door closed and becomes irritated whenever someone stops in. Credibility problems arise when the sender is not considered a reliable source of information. He may not be trusted or may not be perceived as knowledgeable about the subject at hand. When a politician is caught withholding information or when a manager makes a series of bad decisions, the extent to which that person will be listened to and believed thereafter diminishes. In extreme cases, people may talk about something they obviously know little or nothing about. Some people are simply reluctant to initiate a communication exchange. This reluctance may occur for a variety of reasons. A manager may be reluctant to tell subordinates about an impending budget cut because

TABLE 18.1
Barriers to Effective Communication

Numerous barriers can disrupt effective communication. Some of these barriers involve individual characteristics and processes. Others are a function of the organizational context in which communication is taking place.

Individual Barriers	Organizational Barriers
Conflicting or inconsistent cues	Semantics
Credibility about the subject	Status or power differences
Reluctance to communicate	Different perceptions
Poor listening skills	Noise
Predispositions about the subject	Overload

he knows they will be unhappy about it. Likewise, a subordinate may be reluctant to transmit information upward for fear of reprisal or because she feels that such an effort would be futile.

Two other individual barriers to effective communication are poor listening habits and predispositions about the subject at hand. Some people are poor listeners. When someone is talking to them, they may be daydreaming, looking around, reading, or listening to another conversation. Because they are not concentrating on what is being said, they may not comprehend part or all of the message. They may even think that they really are paying attention, only to realize later that they cannot remember parts of the conversation. Receivers may also bring certain predispositions to the communication process. They may already have their minds made up, firmly set in a certain way. For example, a manager may have heard that his new boss is unpleasant and hard to work with. When she calls him in for an introductory meeting, he may go into that meeting predisposed to dislike her and discount what she has to say.

Organizational Barriers   Other barriers to effective communication involve the organizational context in which the communication occurs. Semantics problems arise when words have different meanings for different people. Words and phrases such as *profit, increased output*, and *return on investment* may have positive meanings for managers but less positive meanings for labor. Communication problems may arise when people from different levels of power or status try to communicate with each other. For example, the company president may discount a suggestion from an operating employee, thinking "How can someone at that level help me run my business?" Or factory workers may be reluctant to offer suggestions when the president arrives to inspect a new plant. The marketing vice president may have more power than the human resource vice president and consequently may not pay much attention to a staffing report submitted by the human resource department.

People who perceive a situation differently may have difficulty communicating with one another. When two managers observe that a third manager has not spent much time in her office lately, one may believe that she has been to several important meetings while the other may think she is "hiding out." If they need to talk about her in some official capacity, problems may arise because one has a positive impression and the other a negative impression.

Environmental factors may also disrupt effective communication. As mentioned earlier, noise can affect communication in many ways. Similarly, overload may be a problem when the receiver is being sent more information than he or she can effectively handle. When a manager assigns many jobs to a subordinate whose family and friends are pressuring him or her to do other things, overload may result and communication effectiveness diminish.

■ Improving Communication Effectiveness

Considering how many factors can disrupt communication, managers are fortunate to have several techniques for improving communication effective-

Individual Skills	Organizational Skills
Develop good listening skills	Follow up
Encourage two-way communication	Regulate information flows
Be aware of language and meaning	Understand the richness of media
Maintain credibility	
Be sensitive to receiver's perspective	
Be sensitive to sender's perspective	

TABLE 18.2
Overcoming Barriers to Communication

Because communication is so important, managers have developed a number of methods for overcoming barriers to effective communication. Some of these methods involve individual skills, whereas others are based on organizational skills.

ness.[29] As shown in Table 18.2, these techniques include both individual and organizational skills.

Individual Skills   The most important individual skill for improving communication effectiveness is being a good listener. Being a good listener requires that the individual be prepared to listen, not interrupt the speaker, concentrate on both the words and the meaning being conveyed, be patient, and ask questions as appropriate.[30] So important are good listening skills that companies like Delta, IBM, and Unisys conduct programs to train their managers to be better listeners. Figure 18.6 illustrates the characteristics of poor listeners versus good listeners.

In addition to being a good listener, several other individual skills can also promote effective communication. Feedback, one of the most important, is facilitated by two-way communication. Two-way communication allows the receiver to ask questions, request clarification, and express opinions that let the sender know whether he or she has been understood. In general, the more complicated the message, the more useful two-way communication is. In addition, the sender should be aware of the meanings that different receivers might attach to various words. For example, the phrase *increasing profits* may have positive connotations to shareholders (because they will be the beneficiaries) but negative connotations to labor leaders (because they may fear that the firm will seek to achieve those profits via cutbacks and downsizing and/or realize that wage increases will not be available).

FIGURE 18.6
More and Less Effective Listening Skills

Effective listening skills are a vital part of communicaiton in organizations. There are several things that can contribute to poor listening skills by individuals in organizations. Fortunately, there are also several things people can do to improve their listening skills.

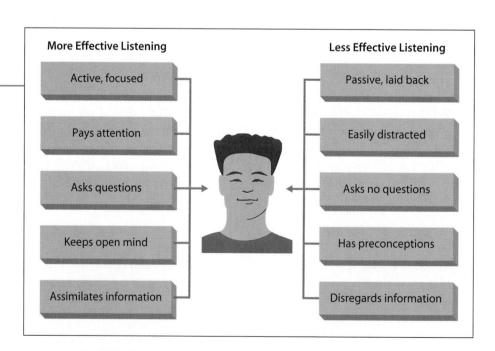

Furthermore, the sender should try to maintain credibility. This can be accomplished by not pretending to be an expert when one is not, by "doing one's homework" and checking facts, and by otherwise being as accurate and honest as possible. The sender should also try to be sensitive to the receiver's perspective. A manager who must tell a subordinate that she has not been recommended for a promotion should recognize that the subordinate will be frustrated and unhappy. The content of the message and its method of delivery should be chosen accordingly. The manager should be primed to accept a reasonable degree of hostility and bitterness without getting angry in return.[31] Finally, the receiver should also try to be sensitive to the sender's point of view. Suppose that a manager has just received some bad news—for example, that his position is being eliminated next year. Others should understand that he may be disappointed, angry, or even depressed for a while. Thus they might make a special effort not to take too much offense if he snaps at them, and they might look for signals that he needs someone to talk to.

Managing organizational communication takes a variety of innovative forms. For example, managers at Interim Services, a Florida-based temp company, believe that it is important that they know all their employees. To facilitate this, all new employees are given a "passport" when they start work at Interim. They are expected to visit all the firm's department managers during their first month at work. Each manager "stamps" the employee's passport after they have met. Employees turn their passports in when they are completed, and then proceed to the next stage in their orientation program, a series of workshops.

Organizational Skills Three useful organizational skills can also enhance communication effectiveness for both the sender and the receiver—following up, regulating information flow, and understanding the richness of different media. *Following up* simply involves checking at a later time to be sure that a message has been received and understood. After a manager mails a report to a colleague, she might call a few days later to make sure the report has arrived. If it has, the manager might ask whether the colleague has any questions about it.

Regulating information flow means that the sender or receiver takes steps to ensure that overload does not occur. For the sender, avoiding overload could mean not passing too much information through the system at one time. For the receiver, it might mean calling attention to the fact that he is being asked to do too many things at once. Many managers limit the influx of information by periodically weeding out the list of journals and routine reports they receive, or they train a secretary to screen phone calls and visitors.

Both senders and receivers should also understand the richness associated with different media. When a manager is going to lay off a subordinate temporarily, the manager should deliver the message in person. A face-to-face meeting enables the manager to explain the situation and answer questions. When the purpose of the message is to grant a pay increase, written communication may be appropriate because it can be more objective and precise. The manager could then follow up the written notice with personal congratulations.

MANAGEMENT IMPLICATIONS Managers need to be aware of the many forces that can disrupt communication in their organizations. Just as important, managers should also know how to overcome those barriers, and they should use these techniques and methods as much as possible. ■

Summary of Key Points

Communication is the process of transmitting information from one person to another. Effective communication is the process of sending a message so that the message received is as close in meaning as possible to the message intended.

Communication is a pervasive and important part of the manager's world. The communication process consists of a sender encoding meaning and transmitting it to one or more receivers, who receive the message and decode it into meaning. In two-way communication the process continues with the roles reversed. Noise can disrupt any part of the overall process.

Several forms of organizational communication exist. Interpersonal communication focuses on communication among a small number of people. Two important forms of interpersonal communication, oral and written, offer unique advantages and disadvantages. Thus, the manager should weigh the pros and cons of each when choosing a medium for communication. Communication networks are recurring patterns of communication among members of a group or work team. Vertical communication between superiors and subordinates may flow upward or downward. Horizontal communication involves peers and colleagues at the same level in the organization. Organizations also use information systems to manage communication. Electronic communications is having a profound effect on managerial and organizational communication.

A great deal of informal communication also goes on in organizations. The grapevine is the informal communication network among people in an organization. Management by wandering around is also a popular informal method of communication. Nonverbal communication includes facial expressions, body movement, physical contact, gestures, and inflection and tone.

Managing the communication process necessitates recognizing the barriers to effective communication and understanding how to overcome them. Barriers can be identified at both the individual and organizational level. Likewise, both individual and organizational skills can be used to overcome these barriers.

Discussion Questions

Questions for Review

1. Define communication. What are the components of the communication process?

2. Which form of interpersonal communication is best for long-term retention? Why? Which form is best for getting across subtle nuances of meaning? Why?

3. Describe three communication networks. Which type of network seems to most accurately describe the grapevine? Why?

4. What are the informal methods of communication? Give five examples of nonverbal communication that you have recently observed.

Questions for Analysis

5. Is it possible for an organization to function without communication? Why or why not?

6. At what points in the communication process can problems occur? Give examples of communication problems and indicate ways to prevent or alleviate them.

7. In terms of the barriers most likely to be encountered, what are the differences between horizontal and vertical communication in an organization? How might a formal information system be designed to reduce such barriers?

Questions for Application

8. What forms of communication have you experienced today? What form of communication is involved in a face-to-face conversation with a friend? A telephone call from a customer? A traffic light or crossing signal? A picture of a cigarette in a circle with a slash across it? An area around machinery defined by a yellow line painted on the floor?

9. Interview a local manager to determine what forms of communication are used in his or her organization. Arrange to observe that manager for a couple of hours. What forms of communication did you observe?

10. How are electronic communication devices likely to affect the communication process in the future? Why? Interview someone from a local organization who uses electronic communications to see whether she or he agrees with you.

Building Effective Technical Skills

EXERCISE OVERVIEW

Technical skills are the skills necessary to perform the work of the organization. This exercise will help you develop and apply technical skills involving the Internet and its potential for gathering information relevant to making important decisions.

EXERCISE BACKGROUND

Assume that you are a manager for a large national retailer. You have been assigned the responsibility for identifying potential locations for the construction of a warehouse and distribution center. The idea behind such a center is that the firm can use its enormous purchasing power to buy many products in large, bulk quantities at relatively low prices. Individual stores can then order specific quantities they need from the warehouse.

The location will need an abundance of land. The warehouse itself, for example, will cover more than four square acres. In addition, it needs to be close to railroads and major highways because shipments will be arriving by both rail and trucks, although outbound shipments will be exclusively by truck. Other important considerations are that land prices and the cost of living should be relatively low and that weather conditions should be mild (so as to minimize disruptions to shipments).

The firm's general experience is that small to midsize communities work best. Moreover, warehouses are already in place in the western and eastern parts of the United States, so this new one will most likely be in the central or south-central area. Your boss has asked to identify three or four possible sites.

EXERCISE TASK

With the preceding information as a framework, do the following:

1. Use the Internet to identify as many as ten possible locations.

2. Use additional information from the Internet to narrow the set of possible locations to three or four.

3. Use the Internet to find out as much as possible about the potential locations.

Building Effective Communication Skills

EXERCISE OVERVIEW

Communication skills refer to a manager's ability to effectively convey ideas and information to others and to effectively receive ideas and information from others. This exercise focuses on communication skills as they involve deciding how to best convey information.

EXERCISE BACKGROUND

Assume that you are a middle manager for a large electronics firm. People in your organization generally use one of three means for communicating with one another. The most common way is verbal communication, either face to face or by telephone. Electronic mail is also widely used. Finally, a surprisingly large amount of communication is still done with paper, such as memos, reports, or letters.

During a typical day you receive and send a variety of messages and other communication, and you generally use some combination of all three communication methods. Here are some of the things that you need to communicate today:

1. You need to schedule a meeting with five subordinates.

2. You need to congratulate a coworker who just had a baby.

3. You need to reprimand a staff assistant who has been coming in to work late for the last several days.

4. You need to inform the warehouse staff that several customers have recently complained because their shipments were not properly packed.

5. You need to schedule a meeting with your boss.

6. You need to announce two promotions.

7. You need to fire someone who has been performing poorly for some time.

8. You need to inform several individuals about a set of new government regulations that will soon affect them.

9. You need to inform a supplier that your company will soon be cutting back on its purchases because you plan to shift more of your business to a supplier offering lower prices.

10. You need to resolve a disagreement between two subordinates who want to take their vacation at the same time.

EXERCISE TASK

Using the preceding information, do the following:

1. Indicate which methods of communication would be appropriate for each situation.

2. Rank the methods for each communication situation from best to worst.

3. Compare your rankings with those of a classmate and discuss any differences.

EXERCISE OVERVIEW

Time-management skills refer to the manager's ability to prioritize work, to work efficiently, and to delegate appropriately. This exercise will help you develop your time-management skills as they relate to communication.

EXERCISE BACKGROUND

Communication is a vital and necessary part not only of management but of our daily lives as well. We benefit when communication takes place in effective ways. But ineffective communication can be a major source of wasted time and energy.

EXERCISE TASK

With this idea as context, do the following:

1. Consider your verbal communication activities for one day. Recall who you talked to, when, for how long, and about what subjects.

2. Do the same for mail you received and mail you sent.

3. Evaluate each communication exchange as being more valuable or less valuable.

4. Estimate how much time you spent on less valuable communication.

5. Decide how you could have either avoided those less valuable communication exchanges or made them more valuable.

6. Consider how much control we really do have over our communication.

Building Effective Time-Management Skills

CHAPTER CLOSING CASE

Exxon's Communication Failure

Exxon Corporation is one of the oldest businesses in the United States, tracing its roots to 1863 when John D. Rockefeller opened an oil refinery that would eventually become Standard Oil Company. The U.S. Department of Justice broke up Standard Oil under antitrust legislation in 1911. One surviving piece eventually became Exxon, which is now the largest U.S. oil company and one of the largest industrial companies in the country. But just because it is large and successful does not mean that it handles crisis communication well.

In 1989 an Exxon oil tanker, the *Exxon Valdez*, ran aground in Prince William Sound, Alaska, spilling nearly eleven million barrels of oil and causing tremendous environmental damage. Exxon's poor handling of the crisis sent a message to corporations worldwide that they needed to have better and more effective crisis-communication plans.

After the *Valdez* incident Exxon was attacked for being too slow to respond, too slow to accept its responsibility, and for providing inadequate cleanup efforts. In a crisis situation such as the *Valdez* disaster, the primary task of management is to inform the public—through the media—about what has happened. Exxon's then-CEO, Lawrence Rawl, however, made no comment for nearly a week after the incident and instead relied on his staff to handle early communications. When he finally did make a public appearance, he seemed uninformed and unsure of the details of what was happening, which further fueled negative reactions.

For example, Exxon claimed that the damage was minimal, but newscasts were clearly showing pictures of oil-covered beaches and rocks covered with thousands of dead birds and fish. The media essentially suggested that Exxon was not being completely honest and candid in its statements and public relations releases. Differences between accounts provided by Exxon and as covered by the media led to a negative public reaction and distrust of Exxon.

Delays, errors, and contradictions seemed to demonstrate that Exxon was arrogant, uncaring, and unaware of the environment in which it operated. The public quickly became outraged. Customers threatened a boycott and thousands of them even returned their credit cards (the actual impact of these actions, however, was virtually negligible). Nevertheless, in a full-page newspaper advertisement ten days after the crisis, Rawl claimed that the company had acted swiftly and competently.

Unfortunately, Exxon's crisis communications problems were confounded by internal problems of its own making. As it was still dealing with its environmental disaster, Exxon laid off more than seventy-five thousand workers and reduced training for those that remained. Employees were asked to take early retirement or to relocate when Exxon moved to Texas from New York. Consequently, many Exxon employees were unhappy or worried about their own future. As a result, they were not particularly motivated or excited about helping the company overcome its problems.

Thus, although the press coverage of the *Valdez* crisis emphasized Rawl's difficulties in responding to the public outcry over the oil spill, morale and attitude problems among its employees also played a role. Exxon seemed to have image problems both within and without the company and was having communication problems of varying kinds.

Has Exxon ever learned its lesson? It does appear to finally be getting the message. For example, its crisis-communication plan now involves having video and telecommunications resources, senior executives trained in dealing with a hostile media, contacts with print and broadcast media, and a clear spokesperson, the new CEO, Lee Raymond, in place and prepared to deal with any situation imaginable. In the event of another disaster, the crisis team will meet every hour after a disaster occurs until it is resolved. The plan has also been tested in mock disaster drills and simulations. Had Exxon had such a plan ten years ago, most of its problems from the *Valdez* crisis could have been averted.

Case Questions

1. In what ways did Exxon not handle the communication process very well in the *Valdez* crisis?

2. What barriers to communication seemed to be involved in Exxon's response? Why or in what way?

3. What unintended messages did Exxon send as a result of the way it handled the *Valdez* crisis? How might it prevent any negative communication problems from such crises in the future?

Case References: *Hoover's Handbook of American Business 1998* (Austin, Texas: Hoover's Business Press, 1998), pp. 558–559; Daniel G. Johnson, "Crisis Management: Forewarned is Forearmed," *Journal of Business Strategy,* March–April 1993, pp. 58–64; "Exxon Stops the Flow," *Time,* March 25, 1991, p. 51; Peter Nulty, "Exxon's Problem: Not What You Think," *Fortune,* April 23, 1990, pp. 202–204; and Sue Stephenson, "The Media and You," *HRMagazine,* June 1997, pp. 146–155.

CHAPTER NOTES

1. "Shoppers Get Kmart's Attention," *USA Today,* April 9, 1997, pp. 1B, 2B; "Kmart Chief Known for Plain Talk, Bold Action," *USA Today,* April 9, 1997, p. 2B; and *Hoover's Handbook of American Business 1998* (Austin, Texas: Hoover's Business Press, 1998), pp. 812–813.

2. See John J. Gabarro, "The Development of Working Relationships," in *Handbook of Organizational Behavior,* ed. Jay W. Lorsch (Englewood Cliffs, N.J.: Prentice-Hall, 1987), pp. 172–189; see also "Team Efforts, Technology, Add New Reasons to Meet," *USA Today,* December 8, 1997, pp. 1A, 2A.

3. Henry Mintzberg, *The Nature of Managerial Work* (New York: Harper & Row, 1973).

4. Mintzberg, *The Nature of Managerial Work.*

5. Mintzberg, *The Nature of Managerial Work.*

6. Walter Kiechel III, "The Big Presentation," *Fortune,* July 26, 1982, pp. 98–100.

7. "Executives Who Dread Public Speaking Learn to Keep Their Cool in the Spotlight," *Wall Street Journal,* May 4, 1990, pp. B1, B6.

8. Mintzberg, *The Nature of Managerial Work.*

9. Kiechel, "The Big Presentation."

10. A. Vavelas, "Communication Patterns in Task-Oriented Groups," *Journal of the Acoustical Society of America*, 1950, Vol. 22, pp. 725–730; and Jerry Wofford, Edwin Gerloff, and Robert Cummins, *Organizational Communication* (New York: McGraw Hill, 1977).

11. Nelson Phillips and John Brown, "Analyzing Communications in and around Organizations: A Critical Hermeneutic Approach," *Academy of Management Journal*, 1993, Vol. 36, No. 6, pp. 1547–1576.

12. Walter Kiechel III, "Breaking Bad News to the Boss," *Fortune*, April 9, 1990, pp. 111–112.

13. Myron Magnet, "Is ITT Fighting Shadows—or Raiders?" *Fortune*, November 11, 1985, pp. 25–28.

14. Mary Young and James Post, "How Leading Companies Communicate with Employees," *Organizational Dynamics*, Summer 1993, pp. 31–43.

15. Brian Dumaine, "Corporate Spies Snoop to Conquer," *Fortune*, November 7, 1988, pp. 68–76.

16. "Here Comes the Intranet," *Business Week*, February 26, 1996, pp. 76–84.

17. Walter Kiechel III, "Hold for the Communicaholic Manager," *Fortune*, January 2, 1989, pp. 107–108.

18. Keith Davis, "Management Communication and the Grapevine," *Harvard Business Review*, September-October 1953, pp. 43–49.

19. "Spread the Word: Gossip Is Good," *Wall Street Journal*, October 4, 1988, p. B1.

20. See David M. Schweiger and Angelo S. DeNisi, "Communication with Employees Following a Merger: A Longitudinal Field Experiment," *Academy of Management Journal*, March 1991, pp. 110–135.

21. See Tom Peters and Nancy Austin, *A Passion for Excellence* (New York: Random House, 1985).

22. Albert Mehrabian, *Non-verbal Communication* (Chicago: Aldine, 1972).

23. Michael B. McCaskey, "The Hidden Messages Managers Send," *Harvard Business Review*, November-December 1979, pp. 135–148.

24. Thomas Moore, "Make-or-Break Time for General Motors," *Fortune*, February 15, 1988, pp. 32–42; and Brian O'Reilly, "How Jimmy Treybig Turned Tough," *Fortune*, May 25, 1987, pp. 102–104.

25. David Givens, "What Body Language Can Tell You That Words Cannot," *U.S. News & World Report*, November 19, 1984, p. 100.

26. Edward J. Hall, *The Hidden Dimension* (New York: Doubleday, 1966).

27. For a detailed discussion of improving communication effectiveness, see Courtland L. Bove and John V. Thill, *Business Communication Today*, 3rd ed. (New York: McGraw-Hill, 1992).

28. See Otis W. Baskin and Craig E. Aronoff, *Interpersonal Communication in Organizations* (Glenview, Ill.: Scott, Foresman, 1980).

29. Joseph Allen and Bennett P. Lientz, *Effective Business Communication* (Santa Monica, Calif.: Goodyear, 1979).

30. Boyd A. Vander Houwen, "Less Talking, More Listening," *HRMagazine*, April 1997, pp. 53–58.

31. For a recent discussion of these and related issues, see Eric M. Eisenberg and Marsha G. Witten, "Reconsidering Openness in Organizational Communication," *Academy of Management Review*, July 1987, pp. 418–426.

19

Managing Work Groups and Teams

OBJECTIVES

After studying this chapter, you should be able to:

- Define and identify types of groups and teams in organizations.
- Discuss reasons people join groups and teams.
- Describe the stages of group and team development.
- Identify and discuss four essential characteristics of groups and teams.
- Discuss interpersonal and intergroup conflict in organizations.
- Describe how organizations manage conflict.

OUTLINE

Few people have ever heard of a small company called Fastener Supply. The twenty-three-year-old, sixteen-employee company based in Reading, Massachusetts, distributes eighteen thousand types of metal, rubber, and nylon fasteners—devices used to hold together the parts that constitute everything from automobiles to personal computers to bug zappers. Motorola, Polaroid, and Lucent Technologies are the biggest of the company's 350 or so customers.

No one at Fastener Supply believed that the firm had a quality problem. Nevertheless, CEO George Danis was aware of recent trends and concerns in quality management and knew that his firm needed to be ahead of the industry, not behind it. A small firm like Fastener Supply can really suffer from the loss of only one big customer, so Danis decided to be proactive on the issue of quality.

An initial quality audit revealed no significant customer complaints. And on a percentage basis, things seemed to be fine. For example, significantly less than 1 percent of the firm's fasteners failed to meet customer standards. But in absolute terms the numbers didn't look quite so good. Because the firm ships more than 70 million units a year, about 112,000 fasteners could be returned each year because of a quality problem. Danis decided to cut that rate to 500 defects per million.

To tackle this problem, Danis created a team of three employees, one each from purchasing, sales, and quality control. The group was named the Continuous Improvement Team, or CIT, and was charged with reducing the customer rejection rate by 50 percent. The team members were initially concerned about meeting such an ambitious goal but quickly set to work.

They decided to focus their efforts on three areas: supplier quality, customer feedback, and training. Fastener Supply doesn't actually make fasteners at all, but instead buys them from various fastener manufacturers. The CIT instructed each of the firm's suppliers to improve its standards for production and delivery or risk losing business. Some suppliers did indeed balk, and 37 were dropped from Fastener Supply's

supplier network. But about 250 met the new standards and continued to have a strong relationship with the firm.

The CIT also sought feedback about areas where customers were not unhappy, but where there was still room for improvement. The team received and implemented almost forty useful suggestions. For example, one suggestion was that a Fastener Supply representative inform customers of all shipping delays. Because the firm already had a policy of informing customers about extended delays, it was easy enough to tell them when a shipment would be delayed for a day or two. Finally, the CIT also suggested that all employees at Fastener Supply receive more training in every phase of the operation, ranging from packing and loading boxes to logging inventory in computers. As a result, virtually all phases of the firm's operations improved. For example, the year after shipping employees received better training, only two of the seven thousand boxes shipped were returned with parts damaged because of bad packing.

By virtually any measure, the CIT has been a big success for Fastener Supply. It actually beat Danis' lofty quality improvement goal by driving defects down to only 216 per million, a phenomenally low level. In addition, the firm's business has been increasing at a rapid pace as word of its quality spreads throughout the industry. But neither the firm nor the CIT are finished. Indeed, the mantra heard throughout Fastener Supply today is achieving the ultimate—zero defects. Although this ideal may never truly be reached, Fastener Supply's CIT vows to keep working toward it.[1]

> ## "Staying still wasn't going to cut it anymore."
>
> *John Jenkins, president of Fastener Supply, quoted in USA Today, May 2, 1997, p. 9B.*

George Danis at Fastener Supply recognized and took advantage of what many experts are increasingly seeing as a tremendous resource for all organizations—the power of groups and teams. When he needed to make some changes at his firm, Danis could have mandated them himself. Or he could have hired an outside consulting firm to tell his employees how to improve. Instead, he created a team of employees and empowered it to resolve the problem.

This chapter is about processes that lead to and follow from activities like those at Fastener Supply. In our last chapter we established the interpersonal nature of organizations. We extend that discussion by first introducing basic concepts of group and team dynamics. Subsequent sections explain the characteristics of groups and teams in organizations. We then describe interpersonal and intergroup conflict and conclude with a discussion of ways to manage conflict.

Groups and Teams in Organizations

group Two or more people who interact regularly to accomplish a common purpose or goal

Groups are a ubiquitous part of organizational life. They are the basis for much of the work that gets done, and they evolve both inside and outside the normal structural boundaries of the organization. In this context a **group** is two or more people who interact regularly to accomplish a common purpose or goal.[2] The purpose of a group or team may range from preparing a new advertising campaign to informally sharing information to making important decisions to fulfilling social needs.

■ Types of Groups and Teams

In general, three basic kinds of groups are found in organizations—functional groups, task groups and teams, and informal or interest groups.[3] These are illustrated in Figure 19.1.

functional group A group created by the organization to accomplish a number of tasks with an indefinite time horizon

Functional Groups A **functional group** is a permanent group created by the organization to accomplish a number of tasks for an unspecified time. The marketing department of Kmart, the management department of the University of North Texas, and the nursing staff of the Mayo Clinic are functional groups. The marketing department at Kmart, for example, seeks to plan effective advertising campaigns, increase sales, run in-store promotions, and develop a unique identity for the company. Functional groups remain in existence after they attain their current objectives—those objectives are simply replaced by new ones.

informal or **interest group** Created by its members for purposes that may or may not be relevant to those of the organization

Informal or Interest Groups An **informal** or **interest group** is created by its own members for purposes that may or may not be relevant to organiza-

FIGURE 19.1
Types of Groups in Organizations

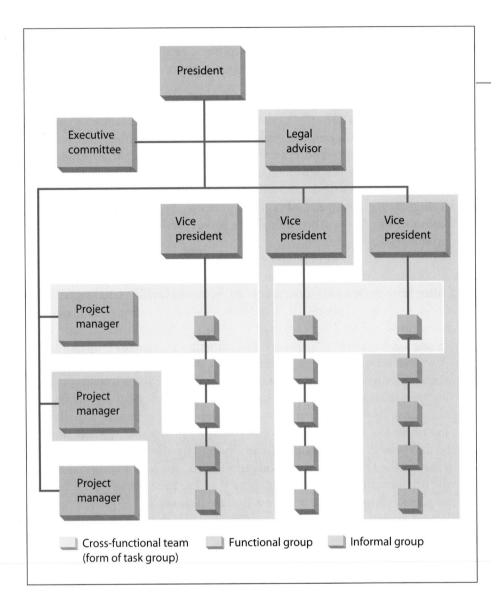

Every organization has many different types of groups. In this hypothetical organization, a functional group is shown within the blue area, a cross-functional group within the yellow area, and an informal group within the green area.

☐ Cross-functional team (form of task group)   ☐ Functional group   ☐ Informal group

tional goals. It also has an unspecified time horizon. A group of employees who lunch together everyday may be discussing how to improve productivity, how to embezzle money, or local politics and sports. As long as the group members enjoy eating together, they will probably continue to do so. When lunches cease to be pleasant, they will seek other company or a different activity.

Informal groups can be a powerful force that managers cannot ignore. One writer described how a group of employees at a furniture factory subverted its boss's efforts to increase production. The group members tacitly agreed to produce a reasonable amount of work, but not to work too hard. One man kept a stockpile of completed work hidden as a backup in case he got too far behind. In another example auto workers described how they left out gaskets and seals and put soft-drink bottles inside doors.[4] Of course, informal groups can also be a positive force, as demonstrated recently when Continental Airline's employees worked together to buy a new motorcycle for Gordon Bethune, the company's CEO, to show their support and gratitude for his excellent leadership.

task group A group created by the organization to accomplish a relatively narrow range of goals within a stated or implied time horizon

Task Groups A **task group** is a group created by the organization to accomplish a relatively narrow range of goals within a stated or implied time horizon. Most committees and task forces are task groups. The organization specifies group membership and assigns the goals, such as developing a new product or evaluating a proposed grievance procedure. The time horizon for accomplishing these goals is either specified (a committee may be asked to make a recommendation within 60 days) or implied (the project team will disband when the new product is developed).

team A group of workers who function as a unit, often with little or no supervision, to carry out work-related tasks, functions, and activities

Teams are a special form of task group that have become increasingly popular. In the sense used here, a **team** is a group of workers who function as a unit, often with little or no supervision, to carry out work-related tasks, functions, and activities. Table 19.1 lists and defines some of the types of teams that are being used today. Earlier forms of teams included autonomous work groups and quality circles. Teams are also sometimes called *self-managed teams*, *cross-functional teams*, or *high-performance teams*. Many firms today are routinely using teams to carry out most of their daily operations.[5]

Organizations create teams for various reasons. For one thing, teams give more responsibility for task performance to the workers who are actually performing the tasks. They also empower workers by giving them greater authority and decision-making freedom. In addition, they allow the organization to capitalize on the knowledge and motivation of its workers. Finally, teams enable the organization to shed its bureaucracy and to promote flexibility and responsiveness.[6] Ford used a team to design its new F-150 pickup truck.[7] Similarly, General Motors used a team to develop the newest model of the Chevrolet Malibu.[8]

When an organization decides to use teams, it is essentially implementing a major form of organization change, as discussed in Chapter 13. Thus it is important to follow a logical and systematic approach to planning and integrating teams into an existing organization design. It is also important that managers and

TABLE 19.1
Types of Teams

Source: "Types of Teams" adapted from Brian Dumaine, "The Trouble With Teams," *Fortune*, September 5, 1994. Copyright © 1994 Time Inc. All rights reserved.

Problem-solving team   Most popular type of team; comprises knowledge workers who gather to solve a specific problem and then disband

Management team   Consists mainly of managers from various functions like sales and production; coordinates work among other teams

Work team   An increasingly popular type of team, work teams are responsible for the daily work of the organization; when empowered, they are self-managed teams

Virtual team   A new type of work team that interacts by computer; members enter and leave the network as needed and may take turns serving as leader

Quality circle   Declining in popularity, quality circles, comprising workers and supervisors, meet intermittently to discuss workplace problems

"We work 24 hours a day."

Advanced Systems Development Corporation (ASDC)
Beijing, China

IBM emerging markets software development team
Seattle, Washington

team members recognize that resistance may be encountered, especially from first-line managers who will be giving up much of their authority to the team. Many organizations find that they must change the whole management philosophy of such managers from being a supervisor to being a coach or facilitator.[9]

Managers should monitor the contributions of the teams and how effectively they are functioning. In the best circumstance teams will become very cohesive groups with high performance norms. To achieve this state, the manager can use any or all of the techniques described later in this chapter for enhancing cohesiveness. If implemented properly, and with the support of the workers themselves, performance norms are likely to be relatively high. That is, if the change is properly implemented, the team participants will understand the value and potential of teams and the rewards they may expect to get as a result of their contributions. On the other hand, poorly designed and implemented teams will do a less effective job and may detract from organizational performance.[10]

■ Why People Join Groups and Teams

People join groups and teams for many reasons. They join functional groups simply by virtue of joining organizations. People accept employment to earn money or to practice their chosen profession. Once inside the organization, they are assigned to jobs and roles and thus become members of functional groups. People in existing functional groups are told, are asked, or volunteer to

Teams have become a ubiquitous part of most organizations. They are used to create products, provide customer service, solve problems, and myriad other purposes. IBM is using a global system of interrelated teams to establish Java as the standard for network applications. The software development team shown here on the right is based in Seattle. When its workday ends, the project is electronically transmitted to a counterpart team in Beijing, shown on the left. They continue work on the project, and transmit it back to Seattle in time for the next workday!

TODAY'S MANAGEMENT ISSUES

The Legality of Teams

Managers who use teams must be careful to not cross an important legal boundary—a line that many people do not even know exists. This legal boundary dates back to the Wagner Act, or National Labor Relations Act of 1935, discussed in Chapter 14. Among its other provisions, this law made it illegal for managers to set up worker organizations, or sham unions, to undercut legitimate ones. This practice was common in the 1930s; businesses used it to keep unions out.

> *"Having management on both sides is what the law is designed to prevent."*
>
> *AFL-CIO attorney**

Although the Wagner Act was not intended to deal directly with practices such as work teams, organized labor has recently invoked that law to charge management with the illegal use of such teams. The fundamental issue is the domain of the team. If the team is working on work-related problems that affect the performance of its own members, most labor unions see no problem. But if the team is working on broad, general issues, and especially if those issues deal with things like pay, working conditions, and so forth, then problems may exist in some cases.

If the firm is already unionized, such general and broad issue-oriented teams may still be acceptable. In most such cases the union will have to agree to the teams to begin with, and the union cannot claim that the teams are surrogate unions, since legitimate ones already exist. But if the company is not unionized, organized labor is quick to argue that broad and general unions cannot be used. Their use could be construed as a direct and demonstrable attempt to keep unions out. In such cases, unions argue, managers can suggest to workers that they can form their own teams, but the managers themselves cannot play a role in creating them or setting their agenda. To do so would be a violation of the Wagner Act. And so far, at least, the courts agree.

References: *Mary E. Pivec and Howard Z. Robbins, "Employee Involvement Remains Controversial,"* HRMagazine, *November 1996, pp. 145–149; and "Putting a Damper on That Old Team Spirit,"* Business Week, *May 4, 1992, p. 60 (*quote on p. 60).*

serve on committees, task forces, and teams. "Today's Management Issues" discusses one recent controversy regarding team formation. Similarly, people join informal or interest groups for various reasons, most of them quite complex.[11]

Interpersonal Attraction   One reason people choose to form informal or interest groups is that they are attracted to each other. Many factors contribute to interpersonal attraction. When people see a lot of each other, pure proximity increases the likelihood that interpersonal attraction will develop. Attraction is increased when people have similar attitudes, personality, or economic standing.

Group Activities   Individuals may also be motivated to join a group because the activities of the group appeal to them. Jogging, playing bridge, bowling, discussing poetry, playing war games, and flying model airplanes are all activities that some people enjoy. Many of them are more enjoyable to participate in as a member of a group, and most require more than one person. Many large firms like Exxon and Apple have a league of football, softball, or bowling teams. A person may join a bowling team not because of any noticeable attraction to other group members, but simply because being a member of the group allows that person to participate in a pleasant activity. Of course, if the level of interpersonal attraction of the group is very low, a person may choose to forgo the activity rather than join the group.

Group Goals   The goals of a group may also motivate people to join. The Sierra Club, which is dedicated to environmental conservation, is a good example of this kind of interest group. Various fund-raising groups are another illustration. Members may or may not be personally attracted to the other fundraisers, and they probably do not enjoy the activity of knocking on doors asking for money, but they join the group because they subscribe to its goal. Workers join unions such as the United Auto Workers because they support its goals.

Need Satisfaction   Still another reason for joining a group is to satisfy the need for affiliation. New residents in a community may join the Newcomers Club partially as a way to meet new people and partially just to be around other people. Likewise, newly divorced individuals often join support groups as a way to have companionship.

Instrumental Benefits   A final reason people join groups is that membership may be instrumental in providing other benefits. For example, college students entering their senior year frequently join several professional clubs or associations because they think that listing such memberships on a résumé will enhance their chances of getting a good job. Similarly, a manager might join a certain racquet club not because she is attracted to its members (although she might be) and not because of the opportunity to play tennis (although she may enjoy it), but because she believes that being a member of this club will lead to important and useful business contacts. Many people maintain memberships in civic groups such as Kiwanis and Rotary for similar reasons.

■ Stages of Group and Team Development

Imagine the differences between a collection of five people who have just been brought together to form a group or team and a group or team that has functioned like a well-oiled machine for years. Members of a new group or team are unfamiliar with how they will function together and are tentative in their interactions. In a group or team with considerable experience, members are familiar with one another's strengths and weaknesses and are more secure in their role in the group. The former group or team is generally considered to be immature; the latter, mature. To progress from the immature phase to the

FIGURE 19.2
Stages of Group Development

As groups mature, they tend to evolve through four distinct stages of development. Managers must understand that group members need time to become acquainted, accept each other, develop a group structure, and become comfortable with their roles in the group before they can begin to work directly to accomplish goals.

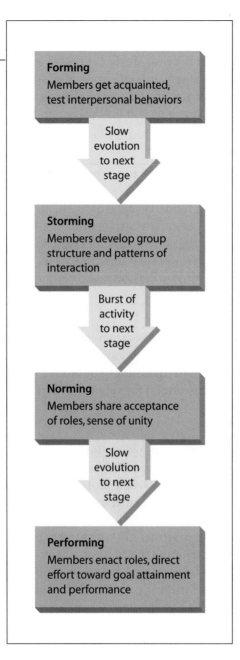

Forming
Members get acquainted, test interpersonal behaviors

Slow evolution to next stage

Storming
Members develop group structure and patterns of interaction

Burst of activity to next stage

Norming
Members share acceptance of roles, sense of unity

Slow evolution to next stage

Performing
Members enact roles, direct effort toward goal attainment and performance

mature phase, a group or team must go through certain stages of development, as shown in Figure 19.2.[12]

The first stage of development is called *forming*. The members of the group or team get acquainted and begin to test which interpersonal behaviors are acceptable and which are unacceptable to the other members. The members are very dependent on others at this point to provide cues about what is acceptable. The basic ground rules for the group or team are established and a tentative group structure may emerge. At Reebok, for example, a merchandising team was created to handle its sportswear business. The team leader and his members were barely acquainted and had to spend a few weeks getting to know one another.

The second stage of development, often slow to emerge, is *storming*. This stage may be characterized by general lack of unity and uneven interaction patterns. At the same time, however, some members of the group or team may begin to exert themselves to become recognized as the group leader or at least to play a major role in shaping the group's agenda. In Reebok's team some members advocated a rapid expansion into the marketplace; others argued for a slower entry. The first faction won, with disastrous results. Because of the rush, product quality was poor and deliveries were late. As a result, the team leader was fired and a new manager placed in charge.

The third stage in group development, called *norming*, usually begins with a burst of activity. During this stage each person begins to recognize and accept her or his role and to understand the roles of others. Members also begin to accept one another and to develop a sense of unity. There may also be temporary regressions to the previous stage. For example, the group or team might begin to accept one particular member as the leader. If this person later violates important norms and otherwise jeopardizes his or her claim to leadership, conflict might reemerge as the group rejects this leader and searches for another. Reebok's new leader transferred several people away from the team and set up a new management system and structure. The remaining employees accepted his new approach and settled into doing their jobs.

Performing, the final stage of group or team development, is again slow to develop. The team really begins to focus on the problem at hand. The members enact the roles they have accepted, interaction occurs, and the efforts of the group are directed toward goal attainment. The basic structure of the group or team is no longer an issue but has become a mechanism for accomplishing the purpose of the group. Reebok's sportswear business is now growing consistently and has successfully avoided the problems that plagued it at first. "Management InfoTech" discusses how teams at this level of maturity may need different kinds of physical work space in order to work most effectively.

MANAGEMENT INFOTECH

Redefining the Office

The recent trend toward the heavy use of work teams in organizations has produced an interesting by-product: corresponding changes in offices and office space. Offices were traditionally laid out in geometric and symmetrical fashion. Specialists were grouped together, for example, with marketing managers in one location, finance managers in another, and so forth. Individual managers also had their own offices. Meetings were held in conference rooms scattered around the building.

"It's tough to have an effective team if the vast majority of your floor plan is turned over to private offices grouped by job title."

Fritz Steel, organizational consultant*

But this physical arrangement often creates problems for teams. A marketing manager, for example, is likely to interact more with team members from design, manufacturing, and quality control than with other marketing managers. And meetings are so commonplace that teams may have to struggle to find an available meeting space.

To make a work space that is more conducive to teams, some organizations are building new facilities or remodeling older ones. These new work spaces have fewer interior walls but a lot more open space. In many businesses like Hewlett-Packard and Northern Telecom, large open spaces dominate buildings and other facilities; employees cluster around work tables and sit in comfortable chairs as they work together on projects. Their individual offices tend to be much smaller and become more of a place to store materials and make private telephone calls.

In some organizations, the "office" environment has changed even more. For example, at Chiat/Day, an advertising agency, workers do not have offices or even assigned workspaces. Mobile computer workstations are scattered throughout the facility. Employees simply take any empty seat, log on, and go to work. As they finish, they move to a lounge area or other open space. They can sit at an individual work table and work alone or around a table and work with others. These new office topographies are becoming increasingly popular as more and more businesses seek to capitalize fully on the power of work teams and social interaction at work.

References: Ronald Lieber, "Cool Offices," Fortune, December 9, 1996, pp. 204–210 (*quote on p. 204); and "Team Efforts, Technology Add New Reasons to Meet," USA Today, December 8, 1997, pp. 1A, 2A.

Managers should recognize the variety of groups that can exist in an organization. Knowledge about teams is especially important in many modern organizations. In addition, managers should understand and appreciate the various reasons that people join groups and teams. Finally, managers should also understand and be able to recognize the stages of development that a newly created group passes through as it becomes more mature. ▬

Characteristics of Groups and Teams

roles The parts individuals play in groups in helping the group reach its goals

role structure The set of defined roles and interrelationships among those roles that the group members define and accept

As groups and teams mature and pass through the four basic stages of development, they begin to take on four important characteristics—a role structure, norms, cohesiveness, and informal leadership.[13]

■ Role Structures

Each individual in a team has a part—or **role**—to play, in helping the group reach its goals. Some people are leaders, some do the work, some interface with other teams, and so on. Indeed, a person may take on a *task-specialist role* (concentrating on getting the group's task accomplished) or a *socioemotional role* (providing social and emotional support to others on the team). A few people, usually the leaders, perform both roles; a few others may do neither. The group's **role structure** is the set of defined roles and interrelationships among those roles that the group or team members define and accept. Each of us belongs to many groups and therefore plays multiple roles—in work groups, classes, families, and social organizations.[14]

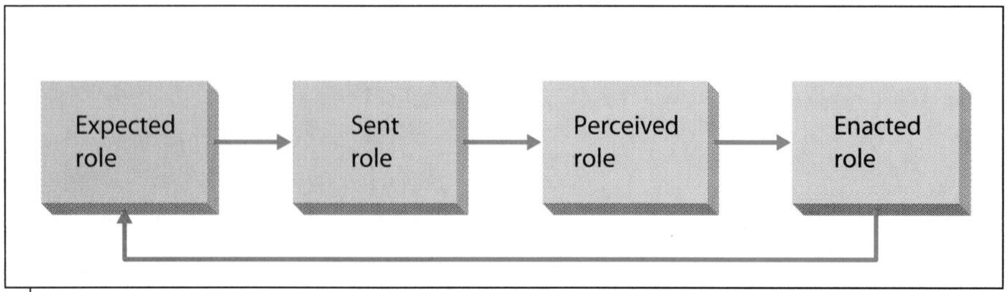

FIGURE 19.3
The Development of a Role

Roles and role structures within a group generally evolve through a series of role episodes. The first two stages of role development are group processes as the group members let individuals know what is expected of them. The other two parts are individual processes as the new group members perceive and enact their roles.

Role structures emerge as a result of role episodes, as shown in Figure 19.3. The process begins with the *expected role*—what other members of the team expect the individual to do. The expected role gets translated into the *sent role*—the messages and cues that team members use to communicate the expected role to the individual. The *perceived role* is what the individual perceives the sent role to mean. Finally, the *enacted role* is what the individual actually does in the role. The enacted role, in turn, influences future expectations of the team. Of course, role episodes seldom unfold this easily. When major disruptions occur, individuals may experience role ambiguity, conflict, or overload.

Role Ambiguity **Role ambiguity** arises when the sent role is unclear. If your instructor tells you to write a term paper but refuses to provide more information, you will probably experience role ambiguity. You do not know what the topic is, how long the paper should be, what format to use, or when the paper is due. In work settings role ambiguity can stem from poor job descriptions, vague instructions from a supervisor, or unclear cues from coworkers. The result is likely to be a subordinate who does not know what to do. Role ambiguity can be a significant problem for both the individual who must contend with it and the organization that expects the employee to perform.

role ambiguity Arises when the sent role is unclear and the individual does not know what is expected of him or her

Role Conflict **Role conflict** occurs when the messages and cues composing the sent role are clear but contradictory or mutually exclusive.[15] One common form is *interrole conflict*—conflict between roles. For example, if a person's boss says that to get ahead one must work overtime and on weekends and that person's spouse says that he or she needs to spend more time at home with the family, conflict may result. In a matrix organization interrole conflict often arises between the roles people play on various teams as well as between team roles and the person's permanent role in a functional group.

role conflict Occurs when the messages and cues that make up the sent role are clear but contradictory or mutually exclusive

Intrarole conflict may occur when the person gets conflicting demands from different sources within the context of the same role. A manager's boss may tell her that she needs to put more pressure on subordinates to follow new work rules. At the same time, her subordinates may indicate that they expect her to get the rules changed. Thus, the cues are in conflict, and the manager may be unsure about which course to follow.

Intrasender conflict occurs when a single source sends clear but contradictory messages. This situation might arise if one morning the boss announces the elimination of overtime for the next month but after lunch tells someone to work late that same evening.

Person-role conflict results from a discrepancy between the role requirements and the individual's personal values, attitudes, and needs. If a person is told to do something unethical or illegal or if the work is distasteful (for example, firing a close friend), person-role conflict is likely. Role conflict of all varieties is of particular concern to managers. Research has shown that conflict may occur in many situations and lead to various adverse consequences, including stress, poor performance, and rapid turnover.

Role Overload A final consequence of a weak role structure is **role overload**, which occurs when expectations for the role exceed the individual's capabilities. When a manager gives an employee several major assignments at once while increasing the person's regular workload, the employee will probably experience role overload. Role overload may also result when an individual takes on too many roles at one time. For example, a person trying to work extra hard at his job, run for election to the school board, serve on a committee in church, coach Little League baseball, maintain an active exercise program, and be a contributing member to his family will probably encounter role overload.

role overload Occurs when expectations for the role exceed the individual's capabilities to perform

In a functional group or team, the manager can take steps to avoid role ambiguity, conflict, and overload. Having clear and reasonable expectations and sending clear and straightforward cues go a long way toward eliminating role ambiguity. Consistent expectations that take into account the employee's other roles and personal value system may minimize role conflict. Role overload can be avoided simply by recognizing the individual's capabilities and limits. In friendship and interest groups, role structures are likely to be less formal; hence the possibility of role ambiguity, conflict, or overload may not be so great. However, if one or more of these problems do occur, they may be difficult to handle. Because roles in friendship and interest groups are less likely to be partially defined by a formal authority structure or written job descriptions, the individual cannot turn to these sources to clarify a role.

■ Behavioral Norms

norms Standards of behavior that the group accepts and expects of its members

Norms are standards of behavior that the group or team accepts for its members. Most committees, for example, develop norms governing their discussions. A person who talks too much is perceived as doing so to make a good impression or to get his or her own way. Other members may not talk much to this person, may not sit nearby, may glare at the person, and may otherwise "punish" the individual for violating the norm. Norms, then, define the boundaries between acceptable and unacceptable behavior.[16] Some groups develop norms that limit the upper bounds of behavior to "make life easier" for the group. In general, these norms are counterproductive—don't make more than two comments in a committee discussion or don't produce any more than you have to. Other groups may develop norms that limit the lower bounds of behavior. These norms tend to reflect motivation, commitment, and high performance—don't come to meetings unless you've read the reports to be discussed or do produce as much as you can. Managers can sometimes use norms to improve the organization. For example, Kodak has successfully used group norms to reduce injuries in some of its plants.[17]

Norm Generalization   The norms of one group cannot always be generalized to another group. Some academic departments, for example, have a norm that suggests that faculty members dress up on teaching days. People who fail to observe this norm are "punished" by sarcastic remarks or even formal reprimands. In other departments the norm may be casual clothes, and the person unfortunate enough to wear dress clothes may be punished just as vehemently. Even within the same work area, similar groups or teams can develop different norms. One team may strive always to produce above its assigned quota; another may maintain productivity just below its quota. The norm of one team may be to be friendly and cordial to its supervisor; that of another team may be to remain aloof and distant. Some differences are due primarily to the composition of the teams.

Norm Variation   Norm variation within a group or team can also occur. A common norm is that the least senior member of a group is expected to perform unpleasant or trivial tasks for the rest of the group. These tasks might be to wait on customers who are known to be small tippers (in a restaurant), to deal with complaining customers (in a department store), or to handle the low-commission line of merchandise (in a sales department). Another example is when certain individuals, especially informal leaders, may violate some norms. If the team is going to meet at eight o'clock, anyone arriving late will be chastised. Occasionally, however, the informal leader may arrive a few minutes late. As long as this behavior does not occur too often, the group will probably ignore it.

Norm Conformity Four sets of factors contribute to norm conformity. First, factors associated with the group are important. For example, some groups or teams may exert more pressure for conformity than others exert. Second, the initial stimulus that prompts behavior can affect conformity. The more ambiguous the stimulus (for example, news that the team is going to be transferred to a new unit), the more pressure there is to conform. Third, individual traits determine the individual's propensity to conform (for example, more intelligent people are often less susceptible to pressure to conform). Finally, situational factors such as team size and unanimity influence conformity. As an individual learns the group's norms, he can do several different things. The most obvious is to adopt the norms. For example, the new male professor who notices that all the other men in the department dress up to teach can also start wearing a suit. A variation is to try to obey the "spirit" of the norm while retaining individuality. The professor may recognize that the norm is actually to wear a tie; thus he might succeed by wearing a tie with his sport shirt, jeans, and sneakers.

The individual may also ignore the norm. When a person does not conform, several things can happen. At first the group may increase its communication with the deviant individual to try to bring her back in line. If this technique does not work, communication may decline. The group may eventually begin to exclude the individual from its activities and, in effect, ostracize the person.

Finally, we need to briefly consider another aspect of norm conformity—socialization. **Socialization** is generalized norm conformity that occurs as a person makes the transition from being an outsider to being an insider. A newcomer to an organization, for example, gradually begins to learn the norms about such things as dress, working hours, and interpersonal relations. As the newcomer adopts these norms, she is being socialized into the organizational culture. Some organizations, like Texas Instruments, work to actively manage the socialization process; others leave it to happenstance.

■ Cohesiveness

A third important team characteristic is cohesiveness. **Cohesiveness** is the extent to which members are loyal and committed to the group. In a highly

THE FAR SIDE By GARY LARSON

© 1987 FarWorks, Inc./Dist. by Universal Press Syndicate   4-12

Groups and teams are powerful forces in many organizations. People working together in a coordinated and integrated way can often accomplish far more than they could working alone. One problem that can arise, however, is called "free-riding." Free-riding occurs when someone in a group or team fails to carry out his or her responsibilities and lets others do all the work. As illustrated in this cartoon, the Viking in the back of the boat is neglecting his work, and letting the rest of the group carry his weight. Thus, he is a free rider!

socialization Generalized norm conformity that occurs as a person makes the transition from being an outsider to being an insider in the organization

cohesiveness The extent to which members are loyal and committed to the group; the degree of mutual attractiveness within the group

TABLE 19.2
Factors that Influence Group Cohesiveness

Several different factors can potentially influence the cohesiveness of a group. For example, a manager can establish intergroup competition, assign compatible members to the group, create opportunities for success, establish acceptable goals, and foster interaction to increase cohesiveness. Other factors can be used to decrease cohesiveness.

Factors that Increase Cohesiveness	Factors that Reduce Cohesiveness
Intergroup competition	Group size
Personal attraction	Disagreement on goals
Favorable evaluation	Intragroup competition
Agreement on goals	Domination
Interaction	Unpleasant experiences

cohesive team, the members work well together, support and trust one another, and are generally effective at achieving their chosen goal.[18] In contrast, a team that lacks cohesiveness is not very coordinated, and its members do not necessarily support one another fully and may have trouble reaching goals. Of particular interest are the factors that increase and reduce cohesiveness and the consequences of team cohesiveness. These are listed in Table 19.2.

Factors that Increase Cohesiveness   Five factors can increase the level of cohesiveness in a group or team. One of the strongest is intergroup competition. When two or more groups are in direct competition (for example, three sales groups competing for top sales honors or two football teams competing for a conference championship), each group is likely to become more cohesive. Second, just as personal attraction plays a role in causing a group to form, so too does attraction seem to enhance cohesiveness. Third, favorable evaluation of the entire group by outsiders can increase cohesiveness. Thus, a group's winning a sales contest or a conference title or receiving recognition and praise from a superior will tend to increase cohesiveness.

Similarly, if all the members of the group or team agree on their goals, cohesiveness is likely to increase.[19] And the more frequently members of the group interact with each other, the more likely the group is to become cohesive. A manager who wants to foster a high level of cohesiveness in a team might do well to establish some form of intergroup competition, assign members to the group who are likely to be attracted to one another, provide opportunities for success, establish goals that all members are likely to accept, and allow ample opportunity for interaction.

Factors that Reduce Cohesiveness   There are also five factors that are known to reduce team cohesiveness. First, cohesiveness tends to decline as a group increases in size. Second, when members of a team disagree on the group's goals, cohesiveness may decrease. For example, when some members believe the group should maximize output and others think output should be restricted, cohesiveness declines. Third, intragroup competition reduces cohesiveness. When members are competing among themselves, they focus more on their own actions and behaviors than on those of the group.

Fourth, domination by one or more persons in the group or team may reduce overall cohesiveness. Other members may feel that they do not have an opportunity to interact and contribute, and they may become less attracted to the group as a consequence. Finally, unpleasant experiences that result from group membership may reduce cohesiveness. A sales group that comes in last in a sales contest, an athletic team that sustains a long losing streak, and a work group reprimanded for poor-quality work may all become less cohesive as a result of their unpleasant experience.

Consequences of Cohesiveness In general, as teams become more cohesive their members tend to interact more frequently, conform more to norms, and become more satisfied with the team. Cohesiveness may also influence team performance. However, performance is also influenced by the team's performance norms. Figure 19.4 shows how cohesiveness and performance norms interact to help shape team performance.

When both cohesiveness and performance norms are high, high performance should result because the team wants to perform at a high level (norms) and its members are working together toward that end (cohesiveness). When norms are high and cohesiveness is low, performance will be moderate. Although the team wants to perform at a high level, its members are not necessarily working well together. When norms are low, performance will be low, regardless of whether group cohesiveness is high or low.

The least desirable situation occurs when low performance norms are combined with high cohesiveness. In this case all team members embrace the standard of restricting performance (owing to the low performance norm), and the group is united in its efforts to maintain that standard (owing to the high cohesiveness). If cohesiveness is low, the manager might be able to raise performance norms by establishing high goals and rewarding goal attainment or by bringing in new group members who are high performers. But a highly cohesive group is likely to resist these interventions.[20]

Cohesive teams can be highly effective contributors to the success of any organization. This team, for example, consists of doctors and nurses working together to lower costs at Methodist Healthcare System in San Antonio. The team members share the same performance norms, and their close personal relationships have led the team to become more cohesive as they find new answers and help reach their goal. To date, the overall cost reduction program to which they belong has yielded savings of over $60 million.

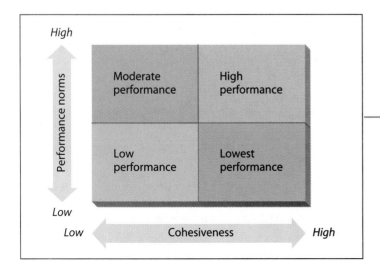

FIGURE 19.4

The Interaction Between Cohesiveness and Performance Norms

Group cohesiveness and performance norms interact to determine group performance. From the manager's perspective, high cohesiveness combined with high performance norms is the best situation, and high cohesiveness with low performance norms is the worst situation. Managers who can influence the level of cohesiveness and performance norms can greatly improve the effectiveness of a work group.

■ Formal and Informal Leadership

informal leader   A person who engages in leadership activities but whose right to do so has not been formally recognized by the organization or group

Most functional groups and teams have a formal leader—that is, one appointed by the organization or chosen or elected by the members of the group. Because friendship and interest groups are formed by the members themselves, however, any formal leader must be elected or designated by the members. Although some groups do designate such a leader (a softball team may elect a captain, for example), many do not. Moreover, even when a formal leader is designated, the group or team may also look to others for leadership. An **informal leader** is a person who engages in leadership activities but whose right to do so has not been formally recognized. The formal and the informal leader in any group or team may be the same person, or they may be different people. Earlier in the chapter we noted the distinction between the task-specialist and socioemotional roles within groups. An informal leader is likely to be a person capable of carrying out both roles effectively. If the formal leader can fulfill only one of these roles, an informal leader often emerges to supplement the formal leader's functions. If the formal leader cannot fill either role, one or more informal leaders may emerge to carry out both sets of functions.

Is informal leadership desirable? Informal leaders can be quite powerful because they draw from referent or expert power. When they are working in the best interest of the organization, they can be a tremendous asset. Notable athletes such as Brett Favre and Rebecca Lobo are classic examples of informal leaders. However, when informal leaders work counter to the goals of the organization, they can cause significant difficulties. Such leaders may lower performance norms, instigate walkouts or wildcat strikes, or otherwise disrupt the organization.

MANAGEMENT IMPLICATIONS   Managers need to clearly understand the four basic characteristics of groups and teams. Specifically, they need to understand and know how to manage role structures so as to minimize role ambiguity, conflict, and overload. The importance of behavioral norms also cannot be overlooked. Managers should also understand the power of cohesiveness, the factors that can increase and decrease it, and how it interacts with performance norms. Finally, managers should also know the difference between formal and informal leadership and be able to identify their key informal leaders. ■

Interpersonal and Intergroup Conflict

Of course, when people work together in an organization, things do not always go smoothly. Indeed, conflict is an inevitable element of interpersonal relationships in organizations. In this section we consider how conflict affects overall performance. We also explore the causes of conflict between individuals, between groups, and between an organization and its environment.

■ The Nature of Conflict

Conflict is a disagreement among two or more individuals, groups, or organizations. This disagreement may be relatively superficial or very strong. It may be short-lived or exist for months or even years, and it may be work related or personal. Conflict may manifest itself in various ways. People may compete with one another, glare at one another, shout, or withdraw. Groups may band together to protect popular members or oust unpopular members. Organizations may seek legal remedy.

conflict A disagreement between two or more individuals or groups

Most people assume that conflict is something to be avoided because it connotes antagonism, hostility, unpleasantness, and dissension. Indeed, managers and management theorists have traditionally viewed conflict as a problem to be avoided.[21] In recent years, however, we have come to recognize that although conflict can be a major problem, certain kinds of conflict may also be beneficial.[22] For example, when two members of a site selection committee disagree over the best location for a new plant, each may be forced to more thoroughly study and defend his or her preferred alternative. As a result of more systematic analysis and discussion, the committee may make a better decision and be better prepared to justify it to others than if everyone had agreed from the outset and accepted an alternative that was perhaps less well analyzed.

As long as conflict is being handled in a cordial and constructive manner, it is probably serving a useful purpose in the organization. On the other hand, when working relationships are being disrupted and the conflict reaches destructive levels, it should be addressed.[23] We discuss ways of dealing with such conflict later in this chapter.

Figure 19.5 depicts the general relationship between conflict and performance for a group or organization. If the group or organization experiences absolutely no conflict, its members may become complacent and apathetic. As a result, group or organizational performance and innovation may begin to suffer. A moderate level of conflict among group or organizational members, on the other hand, can spark motivation, creativity, innovation, and initiative and raise performance. Too much conflict, though, can produce such undesirable results as hostility and lack of cooperation, which lower performance. The key for managers is to find and maintain the optimal amount of conflict that fosters high performance. Of course, what constitutes optimal conflict varies with the situation and the people involved.[24]

FIGURE 19.5
The Nature of Organizational Conflict

Either too much or too little conflict can be dysfunctional for an organization. In either case performance may be low. However, an optimal level of conflict that sparks motivation, creativity, innovation, and initiative can result in higher levels of performance. T. J. Rodgers, CEO of Cypress Semiconductor, maintains a moderate level of conflict in his organization as a way of keeping people energized and motivated.

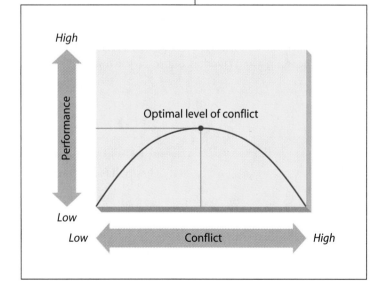

■ Causes of Conflict

Conflict may arise in both interpersonal and intergroup relationships. Occasionally conflict between individuals and groups may be caused by particular organizational strategies and practices. A third arena for conflict is between an

Diversity at Marriott

Diversity is a fact of life in organizations today. And although it provides many benefits, the potential for conflict increases significantly. Different backgrounds, perspectives, customs, and values combine to make it ever more likely that people will disagree and see things in different ways.

For example, take the Marriott Marquis Hotel in New York's Time Square. The hotel employs seventeen hundred people from seventy countries and who speak forty-seven different languages. One major reason for the hotel's diversity is its labor pool—the surrounding neighborhood is home to a diverse group of immigrants, and it is often these residents who apply for jobs. The hotel believes a diverse workforce is an asset, in part because it fits the hotel's multicultural clientele.

But managing the diversity at Marriott can be a challenge. For example, consider the case of Jessica Brown, an African-American quality-assurance manager responsible for housekeeping. Ms. Brown says that when she rewards other African-American's, some of her Hispanic employees criticize her for playing favorites. But when she rewards the

". . . all you can really do is hope [the resentment] goes away eventually. And it usually does."

—————————————

Cynthia Keating, Marriott manager*

Hispanics, some African-Americans accuse her of ignoring them.

Balancing religious practices against the needs of the company is also complicated. One manager, Victor Aragona, recently sought out a room attendant to fix an overflowing bathtub. Aragona found the attendant prostrate on a towel in the housekeeper's closet, bowing to Mecca and saying his daily Islamic prayers. Rather than disturb him, Aragona fixed the bathtub himself.

To help cope with these challenges, Marriott offers frequent training programs in multiculturalism and conflict management. These courses, required for all managers, are also open to most nonmanagers. Even so, the hotel still has to offer periodic and regular refresher courses to help people work together with a minimum of conflict.

References: *"How One Hotel Manages Staff Diversity,"* Wall Street Journal, *November 20, 1996, pp. B1, B11 (*quote on p. B11); and* Hoover's Handbook of American Business 1998 *(Austin, Texas: Hoover's Business Press, 1998), pp. 872–873.*

organization and its environment. "Working with Diversity" describes how diversity has led to conflict at a large Marriott hotel.

Interpersonal Conflict. Conflict between two or more individuals is almost certain to occur in any organization, given the great variety in perceptions, goals, attitudes, and so forth among its members. William Gates, founder and CEO of Microsoft, and Kazuhiko Nishi, a former business associate from Japan, ended a long-term business relationship because of interpersonal conflict. Nishi accused Gates of becoming too political, whereas Gates charged that Nishi's behavior became too unpredictable and erratic.

A frequent source of interpersonal conflict in organizations is what many people call a personality clash—when two people distrust each other's motives, dislike one another, or for some other reason simply can't get along.[25]

Conflict also may arise between people who have different beliefs or perceptions about some aspect of their work or their organization. For example, one manager may want the organization to require all employees to use Microsoft Office software because she thinks standardization will enhance productivity. Another manager may believe that individuals should be able to use any software package they prefer, as long as they can get their work done effectively. Similarly, a male manager may disagree with his female colleague over whether the organization is guilty of discriminating against women in promotion decisions.

Conflict also can result from excess competitiveness among individuals. Two people vying for the same job, for example, may resort to political behavior in an effort to gain an advantage. If either competitor sees the other's behavior as inappropriate, accusations are likely to result. Even after the "winner" of the job is determined, such conflict may continue to undermine interpersonal relationships, especially if the reasons given in selecting one candidate are ambiguous or open to alternative explanations. Robert W. Allen recently resigned as CEO of Delta Airlines because he disagreed with other key executives over how best to reduce the carrier's costs. After he began looking for a replacement for one of his rivals without the approval of the firm's board of directors, the resultant conflict and controversy left him no choice but to leave.[26]

Intergroup Conflict.   Conflict between two or more organizational groups is also quite common. For example, the members of a firm's marketing group may disagree with the production group over product quality and delivery schedules. Two sales groups may disagree over how to meet sales goals, and two groups of managers may have different ideas about the best way to allocate organizational resources.

Many intergroup conflicts arise more from organizational causes than from interpersonal causes. In Chapter 11 we described three forms of group interdependence—pooled, sequential, and reciprocal. Just as increased interdependence makes coordination more difficult, it also increases the potential for conflict. For example, recall that in sequential interdependence work is passed from one unit to another. Intergroup conflict may arise if the first group turns out too much work (the second group will fall behind), too little work (the second group will not meet its own goals), or poor-quality work.

At a J. C. Penney department store, conflict recently arose between stockroom employees and sales associates. The sales associates claimed that the stockroom employees were slow in delivering merchandise to the sales floor so that it could be priced and shelved. The stockroom employees, in turn, claimed that the sales associates were not giving them enough lead time to get the merchandise delivered and failed to understand that they had additional duties besides carrying merchandise to the sales floor.

Just like people, different departments often have different goals. Further, these goals may often be incompatible. A marketing goal of maximizing sales, achieved partially by offering many products in a wide variety of sizes, shapes, colors, and models, probably conflicts with a production goal of minimizing costs, achieved partially by long production runs of a few items. Reebok recently confronted this very situation. One group of managers wanted to introduce a new sportswear line as quickly as possible while other managers wanted to expand more deliberately and cautiously. Because the two groups were not able to reconcile their differences effectively, conflict between the two factions led to quality problems and delivery delays that plagued the firm for months.

Competition for scarce resources can also lead to intergroup conflict. Most organizations—especially universities, hospitals, government agencies, and businesses in depressed industries—do not have unlimited resources. In one New England town, for example, the public works department and the library recently battled over funds from a federal construction grant. The Oldsmobile, Pontiac, and Chevrolet divisions of General Motors have frequently fought over the rights to manufacture various new products developed by the company.

Conflict Between Organization and Environment. Conflict that arises between one organization and another is called interorganizational conflict. A moderate amount of interorganizational conflict resulting from business competition is, of course, expected, but sometimes conflict becomes more extreme. For example, the owners of Jordache Enterprises, Inc., and Guess? Inc., have been battling in court for years over ownership of the Guess label, allegations of design theft, and several other issues.[27] Similarly, General Motors and Volkswagen only recently resolved a bitter four-year-old conflict that started when a key GM executive, Jose Ignacio Lopez de Arriortua, left for a position at Volkswagen. The U.S. company claimed that he took with him key secrets that could benefit its German competitor. After the messy departure, the two firms traded dozens of charges and countercharges, and only a court settlement was able to end the conflict.[28]

Conflict can also arise between an organization and other elements of its environment. For example, an organization may engage in conflict with a consumer group over claims about its products. McDonald's faced this problem a few years ago when it published nutritional information about its products that omitted details about fat content. A manufacturer might engage in conflict with a governmental agency such as OSHA. For example, the firm's management may believe it is in compliance with OSHA regulations, whereas agency officials believe that the firm is not in compliance. Or a firm might engage in conflict with a supplier over the quality of raw materials. The firm may think the supplier is providing inferior materials while the supplier thinks the materials are adequate. Finally, individual managers may obviously have disagreements with groups of workers. For example, a manager may think her workers are doing poor quality work and that they are unmotivated. The workers, on the other hand, may believe they are doing a good job and that the manager is doing a poor job of leading them.

MANAGEMENT IMPLICATIONS Managers need to have a thorough understanding of conflict. In particular, they need to understand the nature of conflict and the primary forces that may cause various forms of conflict to arise in their organizations. ▬

Managing Conflict in Organizations

How do managers cope with all this potential conflict? Fortunately, as Table 19.3 shows, managers can use various techniques to stimulate conflict for constructive ends, to control conflict before it gets out of hand, and to resolve it if it does. This section looks at ways of managing conflict.

■ Stimulating Conflict

An organization may decide to stimulate conflict by placing individual employees or groups in competitive situations. Managers can establish sales contests, incentive plans, bonuses, or other competitive stimuli to spark competition. As long as the ground rules are equitable and all participants perceive the contest as fair, the conflict created by the competition is likely to be constructive because each participant will work hard to win (thereby enhancing some aspect of organizational performance).

Another useful method for stimulating conflict is to bring in one or more outsiders who will shake things up and present a new perspective on organizational practices. Outsiders may be new employees, current employees assigned to an existing work group, or consultants or advisers hired on a temporary basis. Of course, this action can also provoke resentment from insiders who feel they were qualified for the position. The Beecham Group, a British company, once hired an executive from the United States as its CEO expressly to change how the company did business. His arrival brought with it new ways of doing things and a new enthusiasm for competitiveness. Unfortunately, some valued employees also chose to leave Beecham because they resented the changes.

Changing established procedures, especially procedures that have outlived their usefulness, can also stimulate conflict. Such actions cause people to reassess how they perform their job and whether they perform them correctly. For example, one university president announced that all vacant staff positions

---

Stimulating conflict
Increase competition among individuals and teams
Hire outsiders to shape things up
Change established procedures
Controlling conflict
Expand resource base
Enhance coordination of interdependence
Set supraordinate goals
Match personalities and work habits of employees
Resolving and eliminating conflict
Avoid conflict
Convince conflicting parties to compromise
Bring conflicting parties together to confront and negotiate conflict

TABLE 19.3
Methods for Managing Conflict

Conflict is a powerful force in organizations, and has both negative and positive consequences. Thus, managers can draw upon several different techniques to stimulate, control, resolve, or eliminate conflict, depending on their unique circumstances.

could be filled only after written justification had received his approval. Conflict arose between the president and the department heads who felt they were having to provide unnecessary paperwork. Most requests were granted, but because department heads now had to think through their staffing needs, a few unnecessary positions were appropriately eliminated.

■ Controlling Conflict

One method of controlling conflict is to expand the resource base. Suppose a top manager receives two budget requests for $100,000 each. If she has only $180,000 to distribute, the stage is set for conflict because each group will feel its proposal is worth funding and will be unhappy if it is not fully funded. If both proposals are indeed worthwhile, the manager may be able to come up with the extra $20,000 from some other source and thereby avoid difficulty.

Pooled, sequential, and reciprocal interdependence can all result in conflict. If managers use an appropriate technique for enhancing coordination, they can reduce the probability that conflict will arise. Techniques for coordination (described in Chapter 11) include using the managerial hierarchy, relying on rules and procedures, enlisting liaison persons, forming task forces, and integrating departments. At the J. C. Penney store mentioned earlier in the chapter, managers addressed conflict by providing sales people with clearer forms on which to specify the merchandise they needed and in what sequence. If one coordination technique does not have the desired effect, a manager might shift to another approach.

Competing goals can also be a potential source of conflict among individuals and groups. Managers can sometimes focus employee attention on higher-level, or superordinate, goals as a way of eliminating lower-level conflict. When labor unions such as the United Auto Workers make wage concessions to ensure survival of the automobile industry, they are responding to a superordinate goal. Their immediate goal may be higher wages for members, but they realize that without the automobile industry, their members would not even have jobs.

Finally, managers should try to match the personalities and work habits of employees so as to avoid conflict between individuals. For instance, two valuable subordinates, one a chain smoker and the other a vehement antismoker, should probably not be required to work together in an enclosed space. If conflict does arise between incompatible individuals, a manager might seek an equitable transfer for one or both of them to other units.

■ Resolving and Eliminating Conflict

Despite everyone's best intentions, conflict will sometimes flare up. If it is disrupting the workplace, creating too much hostility and tension, or otherwise harming the organization, attempts must be made to resolve it. Some managers who are uncomfortable dealing with conflict choose to avoid the conflict and hope it will go away. Avoidance may sometimes be effective in the short run for some kinds of interpersonal disagreements, but it does little to resolve long-run or chronic conflict. Even more inadvisable, though, is "smoothing"—minimizing the conflict and telling everyone that things will get better. Often the conflict will only worsen as people continue to brood over it.

Compromise is striking a middle-range position between two extremes. This approach can work if it is used with care, but in most compromise situations someone wins and someone loses. Budget problems are one of the few areas amenable to compromise because of their objective nature. Assume, for example, that additional resources are not available to the manager mentioned earlier. She has $180,000

to divide, and each of two groups claims to need $100,000. If the manager believes that both projects warrant funding, she can allocate $90,000 to each. The fact that the two groups have at least been treated equally may minimize the potential conflict.

The confrontation approach to conflict resolution—also called interpersonal problem solving—consists of bringing the parties together to confront the conflict. The parties discuss the nature of their conflict and attempt to reach an agreement or a solution. Confrontation requires a reasonable degree of maturity on the part of the participants, and the manager must structure the situation carefully. If handled well, this approach can be an effective means of resolving conflict. In recent years many organizations have experimented with a technique called alternative dispute resolution, using a team of employees to arbitrate conflict in this way.[29]

Regardless of the approach, organizations and their managers must address conflict if it is to serve constructive purposes and not have destructive consequences. Conflict is inevitable in organizations, but its effects can be constrained with proper attention. For example, Union Carbide once sent two hundred of its managers to a three-day workshop on conflict management. The managers engaged in a variety of exercises and discussions to learn with whom they were most likely to come into conflict and how they should try to resolve it. As a result, managers at the firm later reported that hostility and resentment in the organization had been greatly diminished and that people in the firm reported more pleasant working relationships.[30]

Managing conflict in organizations is an important—and often delicate—process. After Brown University attempted to eliminate several of its women's athletic programs, members of the affected teams filed a lawsuit against the university. The athletes believed that this action violated Title IX, a 1972 law that requires equal funding for women's and men's athletics in colleges and universities. Discussions, appeals, and mediation had failed to resolve the conflict, so women athletes finally decided that litigation was their only option. The U. S. Supreme Court sided with the athletes in 1997, and required that Brown reinstate its full slate of athletics for men and women.

MANAGEMENT IMPLICATIONS

Managers should understand that conflict may need to be stimulated, controlled, and/or resolved and eliminated. They should thus be familiar with the various conflict-management techniques and understand their respective benefits and weaknesses.

Summary of Key Points

group is two or more people who interact regularly to accomplish a common purpose or goal. Organizations have functional groups, task groups and teams, and informal or interest groups. A team is a group of workers who function as a unit, often with little or no supervision, to carry out organizational functions.

People join functional groups and teams to pursue a career. Their reasons for joining informal or interest groups include interpersonal attraction, group activities, group goals, need satisfaction, and potential instrumental benefits. The stages of team development include testing and dependence, intragroup conflict and hostility, development of group cohesion, and focusing on the problem at hand.

Four important characteristics of teams are role structures, behavioral norms, cohesiveness, and informal leadership. Role structures define task and socioemotional specialists and may be victimized by role ambiguity, role conflict, or role overload. Norms are standards of behavior for group members. Cohesiveness is the extent to which members are loyal and committed to the team and to one another. Several factors can increase or reduce team cohesiveness. The relationship between performance norms and cohesiveness is especially important. Informal leaders are those whom the group members themselves choose to follow.

Conflict is a disagreement between two or more people, groups, and/or organizations. Too little or too much conflict may hurt performance, but an optimal level of conflict may improve performance. Interpersonal and intergroup conflict in organizations may be caused by personality differences or by particular organizational strategies and practices.

Organizations may encounter conflict with one another and with various elements of the environment. Three methods of managing conflict are to stimulate it, control it, or resolve and eliminate it.

Discussion Questions

Questions for Review

1. What is a group? Describe the several different types of groups and indicate the similarities and differences between them.

2. Why do people join groups? Do all teams develop through all of the stages discussed in this chapter? Why or why not?

3. Describe the characteristics of teams. How might the management of a mature team differ from the management of teams that are not yet mature?

4. Describe the nature and causes of conflict in organizations. Is conflict always bad? Why or why not?

Questions for Analysis

5. Is it possible for a group to be of more than one type at the same time? If so, under what circumstances? If not, why not?

6. Think of several groups of which you have been a member. Why did you join each? Did each group progress through the stages of development discussed in this chapter? If not, why not?

7. Do you think teams are a valuable new management technique that will endure, or are they just a fad that will be replaced with something else in the near future?

Questions for Application

8. Try to find local organizations that regularly use groups in their operations. What kinds of groups do they use? How do they use the groups? Is that use effective? Why or why not?

9. Try to find a local business that is using teams. Talk to a manager or team participant at the company and learn about their experiences.

10. Would a manager ever want to stimulate conflict in his or her organization? Why or why not? Interview several managers of local business organizations to obtain their views on the use of conflict. Compare their answers to your answer to this question.

EXERCISE OVERVIEW

A manager's interpersonal skills refer to her or his ability to understand and motivate individuals and groups. Clearly, then, interpersonal skills play a major role in determining how well a manager can interact with others in a group setting. This exercise enables you to practice your interpersonal skills in a group setting.

EXERCISE BACKGROUND

You have just been transferred to a new position in which you supervise a group of five employees. The business you work for is fairly small and has few rules and regulations. Unfortunately, the lack of rules and regulations is creating a problem that you must now address.

Specifically, two of the group members are nonsmokers. They are becoming increasingly vocal about the fact that two other members of the group smoke at work. These two workers believe that the secondary smoke in the workplace is endangering their health and want to establish a nonsmoking policy like that of many large businesses today.

The two smokers, however, argue that because the firm did not have such a policy when they started working there, imposing such a policy on them now would be unfair. One smoker, in particular, says that he turned down an attractive job with another company because he wanted to work in a place where he could smoke.

The fifth worker, a nonsmoker, says that smoking doesn't bother her. Her husband smokes at home, so she is used to being around smokers. You suspect that if the two vocal nonsmokers are not appeased, they may leave. You also believe that the two smokers will leave if you mandate a no-smoking policy. All five people do good work, and you do not want to lose any of them.

EXERCISE TASK

With this information as context, do the following:

1. Explain the nature of the conflict that exists in this work group.

2. Develop a course of action for dealing with the situation.

EXERCISE OVERVIEW

Groups and teams are becoming ever more important in organizations. This exercise will allow you to practice your conceptual skills as they apply to work teams in organizations.

EXERCISE BACKGROUND

Many highly effective groups exist outside the boundaries of typical business organizations (see "Chapter Closing Case" on page 601). For example, each of the following represents a team:

A basketball team

An elite military squadron

A government policy group such as the presidential cabinet

A student planning committee

EXERCISE TASK

1. Give an example of a real team, such as one of the above. Choose a team that (1) is not part of a normal business, (2) you can argue is highly effective, and (3) was not discussed in the closing case.

2. Determine the reasons for the team's effectiveness.

3. Determine what a manager can learn from this particular team and how he or she can use its success determinants in a business setting.

Building Effective Time-Management Skills

EXERCISE OVERVIEW

Time-management skills refer to the manager's ability to prioritize work, to work efficiently, and to delegate appropriately. This exercise will enable you to develop time-management skills as they relate to running team meetings.

EXERCISE BACKGROUND

Although teams and team meetings are becoming more and more common, some managers worry that they waste too much time. Here are ten suggestions for making meetings more efficient:

1. Have an agenda.

2. Only meet when there is a reason.

3. Set a clear starting and ending time.

4. Put a clock in front of everyone.

5. Take away all the chairs and make people stand.

6. Lock the door at starting time to "punish" latecomers.

7. Give everyone a role in the meeting.

8. Use visual aids.

9. Have a recording secretary to document what transpires.

10. Have a one-day-a-week meeting "holiday"—a day on which no one can schedule a meeting.

EXERCISE TASK

With the preceding information as context, do the following:

1.   Evaluate the likely effectiveness of each suggestion.

2.   Rank the suggestions in terms of their likely value.

3.   Add at least three other suggestions for improving the efficiency of a team meeting.

CHAPTER CLOSING CASE

Elite Teams

Some managers think of work teams as a new innovation. They think that "quality circles" were the first work teams and that no real teams existed more than just a few years ago. In reality, however, teams have been around in many work settings for years. Managers can learn a great deal about teams in their own organizations by observing how other organizations create and manage elite teams. These teams can be found in a wide variety of settings and doing a wide variety of work.

Take the Navy Seals, for example. This elite group demands absolute and total commitment to the group. A grueling and exhausting training camp culminates with hell week—a five-day period during which recruits run endless miles over wet sand wearing combat boots, swim countless miles carrying a full backpack, run obstacles courses over and over again, and perform rigorous calisthenics while instructors yell insults at them. They get perhaps a total of four hours of sleep during this period. But at the end, after three months of training, those who remain have been molded into a highly cohesive group in which every member is totally committed to the others. Although only three out of ten make it, those who do have accomplished something special.

Or take the Tokyo String Quartet, universally recognized as one of the best musical ensembles in the world. Its members have played together for decades, and each one knows exactly how the moods, talents, and preferences of the others will affect the decisions the group makes and the performances they create. Although each musician is a virtuoso in

his own right, each is also willing—indeed, even anxious—to make his own ego and recognition secondary to the good of the group.

Another shining example of teamwork in action is the University of North Carolina women's soccer team. The team coach, Anson Dorrance, knows the importance of understanding each individual member of the team and what motivates her to perform at her best. He builds individual self-confidence by constant practice and encouragement, yet melds his charges into a well-oiled machine by teaching them to depend on one another. The results have been remarkable: UNC is the most dominant college athletic program in history, with a winning percentage of 94.5 and twelve national titles in the last twenty years.

Yet another fine example of teamwork is the emergency room staff at Massachusetts General Hospital in Boston. Considered one of the best teaching hospitals in the world, the emergency room team is one of Mass General's strengths. Around two hundred patients show up for emergency treatment every day. A team of doctors, nurses, and technicians—each with a specific role to play—surrounds the gurney of every patient who needs emergency surgery. One starts an IV, one cuts away clothing from wounds or burns, one tries to soothe the patient, and others begin to assess the damage and decide what to do. The lead role, in turn, may be played by an attending physician or senior resident, but everyone is free to offer suggestions and point out alternative treatment options. The result is an impressive survival rate and the recognition from other hospitals that Mass General's emergency team is the best in the business.

Managers can learn valuable lessons from other elite teams as well. For example, the top NBA basketball teams function flawlessly as they run fast breaks or a full-court pressure defense. Members of police SWAT teams have to depend on one another and have a clear understanding of their roles. The offensive linemen of a football team must learn different blocking schemes and be able to help one another pick up a blitz or double team an especially effective rusher. And the engineers at Houston's Boots & Coots who travel the world to extinguish oil-well fires must have absolute confidence and trust in one another as they undertake their hazardous jobs in conditions that are often dangerous and far removed from the comforts of home.

Case Questions

1. What can managers learn from each of the elite teams identified in this case?

2. Can you identify other kinds of elite teams that managers might learn from?

3. What characteristics and elements of these teams cannot be generalized to organizations?

Case References: Kenneth Labich, "Elite Teams," *Fortune*, February 19, 1996, pp. 90–99; Gregory Moorhead and Ricky W. Griffin, *Organizational Behavior*, 5th Ed. (Boston: Houghton Mifflin, 1998), Chapter 12.

CHAPTER NOTES

1. "Fastener's 3-Prong Plan Yields Perfection," *USA Today*, May 2, 1997, p. 9B.

2. For a review of definitions of groups, see Gregory Moorhead and Ricky W. Griffin, *Organizational Behavior*, 5th ed. (Boston: Houghton Mifflin, 1998).

3. Dorwin Cartwright and Alvin Zander, eds., *Group Dynamics: Research and Theory*, 3rd ed. (New York: Harper & Row, 1968).

4. Robert Schrank, *Ten Thousand Working Days* (Cambridge, Mass.: MIT Press, 1978); Bill Watson, "Counter Planning on the Shop Floor," in *Organizational Reality*, 2nd ed., eds. Peter Frost, Vance Mitchell, and Walter Nord (Glenview, Ill.: Scott, Foresman, 1982), pp. 286–294.

5. Brian Dumaine, "Payoff from the New Management," *Fortune*, December 13, 1993, pp. 103–110.

6. Glenn Parker, "Cross-Functional Collaboration," *Training & Development*, October 1994, pp. 49–58.

7. "How Ford's F-150 Lapped the Competition," *Business Week*, July 29, 1996, pp. 74–76.

8. "Struggle to Remake the Malibu Says a Lot about Remaking GM," *Wall Street Journal*, March 27, 1997, pp. A1, A8.

9. "Why Teams Fail," *USA Today*, February 25, 1997, pp. 1B, 2B.

10. Brian Dumaine, "The Trouble with Teams," *Fortune*, September 5, 1994, pp. 86–92. See also Susan G. Cohen and Diane E. Bailey, "What Makes Teams Work: Group Effectiveness Research from the Shop Floor to the Executive Suite," *Journal of Management*, 1997, Vol. 23, No. 3, pp. 239–290.

11. Marvin E. Shaw, *Group Dynamics—The Psychology of Small Group Behavior*, 4th ed. (New York: McGraw-Hill, 1985).

12. See Connie Gersick, "Marking Time: Predictable Transitions in Task Groups," *Academy of Management Journal*, June 1989, pp. 274–309.

13. For a review of other team characteristics, see Michael Campion, Gina Medsker, and A. Catherine Higgs, "Relations between Work Group Characteristics and Effectiveness: Implications for Designing Effective Work Groups," *Personnel Psychology*, Winter 1993, pp. 823–850.

14. David Katz and Robert L. Kahn, *The Social Psychology of Organizations*, 2nd ed. (New York: Wiley, 1978), pp. 187–221.

15. Robert L. Kahn, D. M. Wolfe, R. P. Quinn, J. D. Snoek, and R. A. Rosenthal, *Organizational Stress: Studies in Role Conflict and Role Ambiguity* (New York: Wiley, 1964).

16. Daniel C. Feldman, "The Development and Enforcement of Group Norms," *Academy of Management Review*, January 1984, pp. 47–53.

17. "Companies Turn to Peer Pressure to Cut Injuries as Psychologists Join the Battle," *Wall Street Journal*, March 29, 1991, pp. B1, B3.

18. James Wallace Bishop and K. Dow Scott, "How Commitment Affects Team Performance," *HRMagazine*, February 1997, pp. 107–115.

19. Anne O'Leary-Kelly, Joseph Martocchio, and Dwight Frink, "A Review of the Influence of Group Goals on Group Performance," *Academy of Management Journal*, 1994, Vol. 37, No. 5, pp. 1285–1301.

20. Philip M. Podsakoff, Michael Ahearne, and Scott B. MacKenzie, "Organizational Citizenship Behavior and the Quantity and Quality of Work Group Performance, *Journal of Applied Psychology*, 1997, Vol. 82, No. 2, pp. 262–270.

21. Clayton P. Alderfer, "An Intergroup Perspective on Group

Dynamics," in *Handbook of Organizational Behavior*, ed. Jay W. Lorsch (Englewood Cliffs, N.J.: Prentice-Hall, 1987), pp. 190–222. See also Eugene Owens and E. Leroy Plumlee, "Intraorganizational Competition and Interorganizational Conflict: More Than a Matter of Semantics," *Business Review*, Winter 1988, pp. 28–32; and Dina Lynch, "Unresolved Conflicts Affect the Bottom Line," *HRMagazine*, May 1997, pp. 49–55.

22. Kathleen M. Eisenhardt, Jean L. Kahwajy, and L. J. Bourgeois III, "How Management Teams Can Have a Good Fight," *Harvard Business Review*, July–August 1997, pp. 77–89.

23. Thomas Bergmann and Roger Volkema, "Issues, Behavioral Responses and Consequences in Interpersonal Conflicts," *Journal of Organizational Behavior*, 1994, Vol. 15, pp. 467–471.

24. Robin Pinkley and Gregory Northcraft, "Conflict Frames of Reference: Implications for Dispute Processes and Outcomes," *Academy of Management Journal*, 1994, Vol. 37, No. 1, pp. 193–205.

25. Bruce Barry and Greg L. Stewart, "Composition, Process, and Performance in Self-Managed Groups: The Role of Personality," *Journal of Applied Psychology*, 1997, Vol. 82, No. 1, pp. 62–78.

26. "Delta CEO Resigns after Clashes with Board," *USA Today*, May 13, 1997, p. B1.

27. "A 'Blood War' in the Jeans Trade," *Business Week*, November 13, 1989, pp. 74–81.

28. Peter Elkind, "Blood Feud," *Fortune*, April 14, 1997, pp. 90–102.

29. "Solving Conflicts in the Workplace without Making Losers," *Wall Street Journal*, May 27, 1997, p. B1.

30. "Teaching How to Cope with Workplace Conflicts," *Business Week*, February 18, 1980, pp. 136, 139.

Motivating for Success at World Book International

The function of leading is a critical component of the management process. And motivating employees to perform well is one of the most important parts of leading. This video case relates to motivating employees in today's competitive business environment.

OVERVIEW AND OBJECTIVES

After completing this video case, you should be able to:

1. Understand how different needs affect work behavior.

2. Describe fundamental motivational processes in organizations.

3. Discuss how managers can apply different motivational perspectives to enhance the performance of their employees.

4. Recognize the role of other parts of the leading process and how they might relate to motivation.

COMPANY BACKGROUND

Many adults can recall using the World Book Encyclopedias when they were youngsters in grade school. The easy-to-use and clearly written books that comprised the encyclopedia set made them a favorite among educators around the world. Today, World Book International has grown into a thriving multinational enterprise. Its books are translated into more than a dozen languages, and tens of thousands of sales representatives around the globe market the firm's products in diverse regions and to diverse people. And, being more than just an encyclopedia company, World Book publishes a complete line of reference and educational books and computer software.

CASE QUESTIONS

1. Discuss how you think Maslow's hierarchy of needs might relate to World Book International employees.

2. Discuss the role of equity theory in a firm like World Book.

3. Describe how expectancy theory might be applied to World Book.

VIDEO REVIEW

Your instructor will now show you a brief video clip that provides more information about motivation at World Book International.

FOLLOW-UP QUESTIONS

1. Assess your responses to the first set of Case Questions above and modify your answers as needed.

2. How general (or how situation-specific) are the motivational practices at World Book?

3. Describe how individual differences are reflected at World Book.

4. Discuss how leadership and influence processes affect World Book.

5. Describe how group and team processes affect World Book.

POPULAR VIDEO FOLLOW-UP

Each of the movies listed below provides some insights and examples to illustrate various leading concepts and ideas. See if you can come up with other examples.

- *Falling Down* (individual differences and stress)

- *Jurassic Park* (motivation, leadership, and power)

- *Aliens* (leadership)

- *Dave* (interpersonal relations and communication)

- *Twelve Angry Men* and *The Joy Luck Club* (group processes)

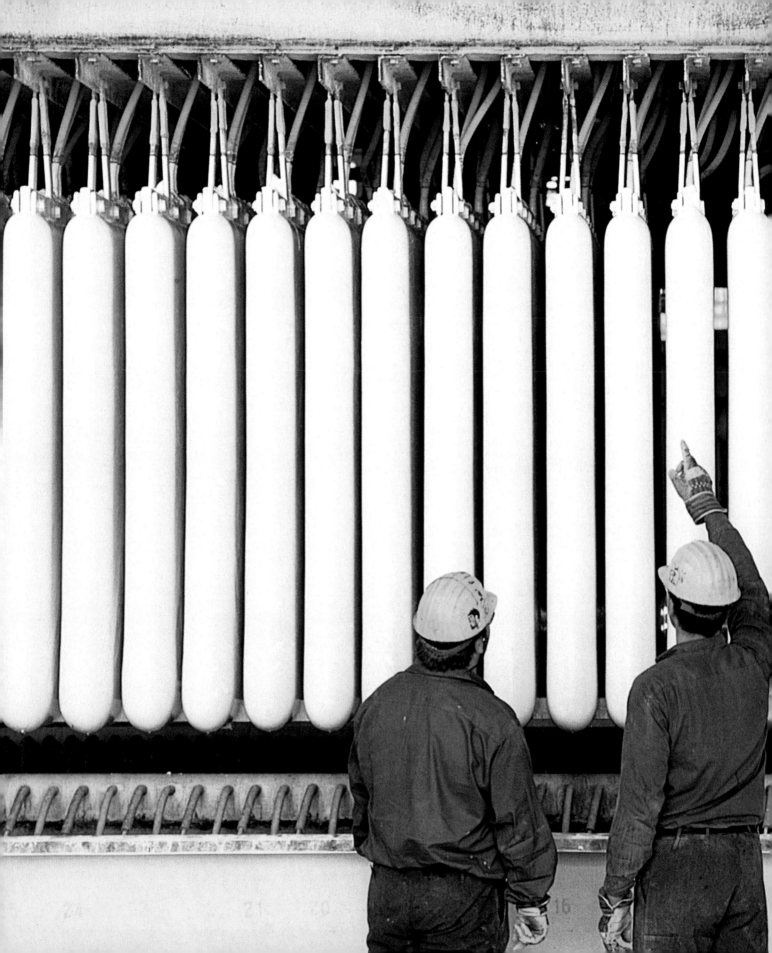

20

Basic Elements of Control

OBJECTIVES

After studying this chapter, you should be able to:

■ Explain the purpose of control, identify different types of control, and describe the steps in the control process.

■ Identify and explain the three forms of operations control.

■ Describe budgets and other tools of financial control.

■ Identify and distinguish between two opposing forms of structural control.

■ Discuss the relationship between strategy and control, including international strategic control.

■ Identify characteristics of effective control, why people resist control, and how managers can overcome this resistance.

The name Abercrombie & Fitch goes back to the days when Teddy Roosevelt and Admiral Byrd chose the small Manhattan emporium to outfit their expeditions. Its more recent incarnation, however, has been in the form of a thriving specialty shop under the umbrella of retailer Goliath Limited, Inc. Limited acquired the twenty-five-store chain in 1988 and planned to use it to gain entree into the men's fashion market. The corporation's own Limited, Express, Lerner, Victoria Secret, and Lane Bryant had a strong presence in various segments of the women's fashion market, so the firm was looking to the men's market for future growth.

Limited appointed Sally Frame Kasaks to head Abercrombie & Fitch. She set the firm on its expansion path and developed its basic product mix before leaving Limited in 1992 to take over Ann Taylor Stores. Limited then recruited Mike Jeffries from another retailer to take her place. He took the basic concepts Ms. Kasaks had envisioned, modified them a bit, and then implemented them throughout all Abercrombie & Fitch stores. He also put into place his own near-fanatical control orientation.

For example, each week the company's home office sends each store a detailed "time line." This time line specifies minute tasks to be performed each day, including how to arrange clothes on racks and how many hours and store employees each such task should require. Merchandise display techniques are also spelled out in detail. For example, sweaters are not to be stacked higher than four to a pile. Moreover, men's sweaters are to be arranged with larger sizes on top, while women's sweaters have the smaller sizes on top. Blouses displayed on hangers are to have the top button undone, but if the blouse is folded then the top two buttons are to be kept undone.

"This is very much a military operation.

It is very disciplined and very controlled."

Mike Jeffries, CEO of Abercrombie & Fitch, quoted in the Wall Street Journal, *October 7, 1997, p. B1.*

Mr. Jeffries' fashion design team at headquarters also dispatches detailed plans and layouts for each table on the sales floor, along with specific weekly sales and profit goals. For example, a table near the door and in the center of the sales floor is supposed to generate, on average, $2,800 in sales each week.

But Abercrombie & Fitch doesn't stop with merchandise. Jeffries also has a twenty-nine-page "look book"—detailed specifications for dress and appearance of the firm's sales staff. For example, men cannot wear necklaces or have facial hair. Women can wear nail polish only in "natural colors," and the nails themselves cannot extend more than a quarter-inch beyond the fingertip. The only "piercing" allowed is for earrings—men can wear one, and women can wear two. But no earring can be larger than a dime.

So far, at least, Jeffries' efforts have been paying off in a big way. Since he took over, for example, the number of Abercrombie & Fitch stores has quadrupled. And his chain is far and away the most profitable of the Limited's holdings. Although whether his plans can withstand the next wave of fickle fashion trends remains to be seen, for the time being, at least, Jeffries clearly has Abercrombie & Fitch on the right path—a path that he has blazed and from which he doesn't intend to stray.[1]

Mike Jeffries is relying on one of the four fundamental functions of management to keep Abercrombie & Fitch on its path to growth and profitability—control. He decided where he wanted the business to go, pointed it in that direction, and created systems to keep it on track. Any business can enhance its financial health by taking the same steps, although each organization must work with its own particular configuration of revenues and costs. The general framework for achieving and maintaining financial health is control.

As we discussed in Chapter 1, control is one of the four basic managerial functions that provide the organizing framework for this book. This chapter is the first three devoted to this important area. In the first section of the chapter, we explain the purpose of control. We then look at types of control and the steps in the control process. The rest of the chapter examines the four levels of control most organizations must employ to remain effective: operations, financial, structural, and strategic control. We conclude by discussing the characteristics of effective control, noting why some people resist control and describing what organizations can do to overcome this resistance. The remaining two chapters in this part focus on managing for total quality and managing information.

control   The regulation of organizational activities so as to facilitate goal attainment

The Nature of Control in Organizations

FIGURE 20.1
The Purpose of Control

Control is one of the four basic management functions in organizations. The control function, in turn, has four basic purposes. Properly designed control systems are able to fulfill each of these purposes.

Control is the regulation of organizational activities so that some targeted element of performance remains within acceptable limits. Without this regulation, organizations have no indication of how well they perform in relation to their goals. Control, like a ship's rudder, keeps the organization moving in the proper direction. At any point in time, it compares where the organization is in terms of performance (financial, productive, or otherwise) to where it is supposed to be. Like a rudder, control provides an organization with a mechanism for adjusting its course if performance falls outside of acceptable boundaries. For example, Federal Express has a performance goal of delivering 99 percent of its packages on time. If on-time deliveries fall to 97 percent, control systems will signal the problem to managers so they can make necessary adjustments in operations to regain the target level of performance. An organization without effective control procedures is not likely to reach its goals—or, if it does reach them, to know that it has!

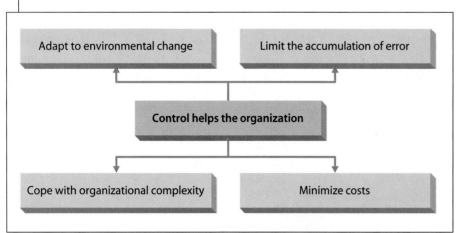

THE QUALITY CHALLENGE

Using Control to Boost Quality at American Standard

American Standard is a diversified manufacturer that makes parts and systems for air conditioners and heating units. In addition, it makes plumbing parts and supplies and truck brakes. In 1988 the firm went private and took on an enormous debt load to fend off a hostile takeover bid by Black & Decker.

As the dust settled, however, the firm realized that it was in a difficult spot. In addition to unacceptably high levels of debt, American Standard was also inefficient and several of its businesses were not doing well. Faced with this daunting challenge, the firm promoted Emmanuel A. Kampouris to the job of CEO and gave him a mandate to get things back on track.

Kampouris quickly sold off several underperforming units and used the cash to both reduce the firm's debt and jump start the businesses he kept. And along the way he totally overhauled American Standard's manufacturing systems and processes. The firm is now the most efficient company in its industry and among the most efficient in the country.

The key has been streamlining everything from purchasing to production to inventory to distribution. This new simplification enabled managers to implement tighter controls throughout the organization, and these controls, in turn, have boosted productivity and efficiency. For example, the firm's bathroom fixtures plant in England, which formerly needed three weeks to make a sink or commode, can now produce the same products in four days. And customers are happy about these changes. Home Depot, for example, used to wait for several weeks to receive an order from American Standard; the retailer now gets its orders in just a few days.

> *"They've learned how to take a manufacturing business and run it like a bat out of hell."*
>
> *Michael Hammer, management consultant**

References: *"American Standard Wises Up,"* Business Week, *November 18, 1996, pp. 70–71 (*quote on p. 70); and* Hoover's Handbook of American Business 1998 *(Austin, Texas: Hoover's Business Press, 1998), pp. 148–149.*

▊ The Purpose of Control

As Figure 20.1 illustrates, control provides an organization with ways to adapt to environmental change, to limit the accumulation of error, to cope with organizational complexity, and to minimize costs. These four functions of control are worth a closer look.

Adapting to Environmental Change In today's complex and turbulent business environment, all organizations must contend with change.[2] If managers could establish goals and achieve them instantaneously, control would not be needed. But between the time a goal is established and the time it is reached, many things can happen in the organization and its environment to disrupt movement toward the goal—or even to change the goal itself. A properly designed control system can help managers anticipate, monitor, and respond to changing circumstances.[3] In contrast, an improperly designed system can result in organizational performance that falls far below acceptable levels. "The Quality Challenge" discusses how one firm, American Standard, has used control to boost its quality, productivity, and profitability.

Similarly, Michigan-based Metalloy, a forty-three-year-old family-run metalcasting company, signed a contract to make engine-seal castings for NOK, a big Japanese auto parts maker. Metalloy was satisfied when its first five thousand unit production ran yielded 4,985 acceptable castings and only fifteen defective ones. NOK, however, was quite unhappy with this performance and insisted that Metalloy raise its standards. In short, global quality standards had shifted so dramatically that managers at Metalloy had lost touch with how high their own standards had to be in order to remain competitive. A properly designed control system, on the other hand, would have kept Metalloy's managers better attuned to rising standards.

Limiting the Accumulation of Error   Small mistakes and errors do not often seriously damage the financial health of an organization. Over time, however, small errors may accumulate and become very serious. For example, Whistler Corporation, a large radar detector manufacturer, once faced such rapidly escalating demand that it essentially stopped worrying about quality. The defect rate rose from 4 percent to 9 percent to 15 percent and eventually reached 25 percent. One day, a manager realized that 100 of the firm's 250 employees were spending all their time fixing defective units and that $2 million worth of inventory was awaiting repair. Had the company adequately controlled quality as it responded to increased demand, the problem would have never reached such proportions.

Coping with Organizational Complexity   When a firm purchases only one raw material, produces one product, has a simple organization design, and enjoys constant demand for its product, its managers can maintain control with a very basic and simple system. But a business that produces many products from multiple raw materials and that has a large market area, a complicated organization design, and many competitors needs a sophisticated system in order to maintain adequate control. Emery Air Freight was quite profitable until it bought Purolator Courier Corporation. The new Emery that resulted from the acquisition was much bigger and more complex, but no new controls were added to operations. Consequently, Emery began to lose money and market share, costs increased, and service deteriorated until the company was on the verge of bankruptcy. Some question remains as to whether Emery will ever regain its former levels of performance.

Minimizing Costs   When it is practiced effectively, control can also help reduce costs and boost output. For example, Georgia-Pacific Corporation, a large wood products company, learned that a new technology could make thinner blades for its saws. The firm used its control system to calculate the amount of wood that could be saved from each cut made by the thinner blades relative to the cost of replacing the existing blades. The results have been impressive—the new blades save enough wood each year to fill eight hundred rail cars. As Georgia-Pacific discovered, effective control systems can eliminate waste, reduce labor costs, and improve output per unit of input. Similarly, the CEO of Travelers Group Inc. recently decided that the $60,000 cost for repairing a broken fountain in front of company headquarters was excessive and instead spent only $20,000 to have it filled and planted

Corporate Anorexia?

Throughout the 1980s and 1990s, a key watchword in U.S. companies has been downsizing. Diet metaphors abound: cut the fat, get lean, trim down. But recently, another diet metaphor has also emerged—*corporate anorexia.* The concern is that although many companies may have indeed needed to cut back a bit, some may have gone too far and cut into the muscle of their organization. And a few may have gotten so addicted to the ideas of controlling expenses, eliminating jobs, and slashing inventories that they have forgotten how to take risks, grow, and innovate.

What kinds of problems can result from corporate anorexia? One potential problem is an attitude among survivors that only costs matter. Overburdened staff members may start only going through the motions of their work—doing the bare minimum just to get by. They avoid all risks, and managers continually cut back on innovation and development as a way of cutting short-terms costs. In the long-term, however, these attitudes and behaviors can be deadly for a company.

Another problem with cutting too far is that the organ-

> *"You can't shrink to greatness."*
>
> *Jim Stanford, president of Petro-Canada, a Calgary-based oil and gas giant**

ization may hamper its ability to compete—to do the jobs that are necessary to the firm's survival. For example, if the sales staff is too lean, customers will eventually begin to lose touch with the firm and take their business elsewhere. A smaller engineering staff may be unable to devote adequate attention to developing and refining products, and the firm may gradually lose its presence in the marketplace. And a smaller human resource staff may not be able to adequately recruit new employees and provide the support needed to maintain and develop existing ones.

The challenge, then, is both clear and daunting. On the one hand, managers should clearly be on the alert for inefficiencies and excess costs. But on the other hand, pruning should be done with caution and from a long-term perspective. The key, of course, is finding this ideal balance without tipping too far in either direction.

References: *"Some Companies Cut Costs Too Far, Suffer 'Corporate Anorexia,'"* Wall Street Journal, *July 5, 1995, pp. A1, A5 (*quote on p. A5); and "Call It Dumbsizing: Why Some Companies Regret Cost-Cutting,"* Wall Street Journal, *May 14, 1996, pp. A1, A6.*

with a low-maintenance tree.[4] On the other hand, "Today's Management Issues" provides some warnings against taking cost control too far.

■ Types of Control

The preceding examples of control illustrate the regulation of several organizational activities, from producing quality products to coordinating complex organizations. Organizations practice control in a number of different areas and at different levels, and the responsibility for managing control is widespread.

Areas of Control Control can focus on any area of an organization. Most organizations define areas of control in terms of the four basic types of resources they use: physical, human, information, and financial resources.[5] Control of physical resources includes inventory management (stocking neither too few

operations control Focuses on the processes the organization uses to transform resources into products or services

financial control Concerned with the organization's financial resources

structural control Concerned with how the elements of the organization's structure are serving their intended purpose

strategic control Focuses on how effectively the organization's strategies are helping the organization meet its goals

nor too many units in inventory), quality control (maintaining appropriate levels of output quality), and equipment control (supplying the necessary facilities and machinery). Control of human resources includes selection and placement, training and development, performance appraisal, and compensation. Control of information resources includes sales and marketing forecasting, environmental analysis, public relations, production scheduling, and economic forecasting. Financial control involves managing the organization's debt so that it does not become excessive, ensuring that the firm always has enough cash on hand to meet its obligations but that it does not have excess cash in a checking account, and that receivables are collected and bills paid on a timely basis.

Control of financial resources is the most important area of control because financial resources are related to the control of all the other resources in an organization: too much inventory leads to storage costs; poor selection of personnel leads to termination and rehiring expenses; inaccurate sales forecasts lead to disruptions in cash flows and other financial effects. Financial issues tend to pervade most control-related activities. Indeed, financial issues are the basic problem faced by Emery Air Freight. Various inefficiencies and operating blunders put the company in a position where it lacked the money to service its debt (make interest payments on loans), had little working capital (cash to cover daily operating expenses), and was too heavily leveraged (excessive debt) to borrow more money.

FIGURE 20.2
Levels of Control

Managers use control at a number of different levels. The most basic levels of control in organizations are strategic, structural, operations, and financial control. Each level must be properly managed if control is to be most effective.

Levels of Control Just as control can be broken down by area, as Figure 20.2 shows it can also be broken down by level within the organizational system. **Operations control** focuses on the processes the organization uses to transform resources into products or services (quality control is one type of operations control).[6] **Financial control** is concerned with the organization's financial resources (monitoring receivables to make sure customers are paying their bills on time is an example of financial control). **Structural control** is concerned with how the elements of the organization's structure are serving their intended purposes (monitoring the administrative ratio to make sure staff expenses do not become excessive is an example of structural control). Finally, **strategic control** focuses on how effectively the organization's corporate, business, and functional strategies are succeeding in helping the organization meet its goals. (For example, if a corporation has been unsuccessful in implementing its strategy of related diversification, its managers need to identify the reasons and either change the strategy or renew their efforts to implement it.) We discuss these four levels of control more fully later in this chapter.

Responsibilities for Control Traditionally, managers have been responsible for overseeing the wide array of control systems and concerns in organizations. Managers decide which types of control the organization will use, implement control systems, and take actions based on the information provided by control systems. Thus, ultimate responsibility for control rests with all managers throughout an organization.

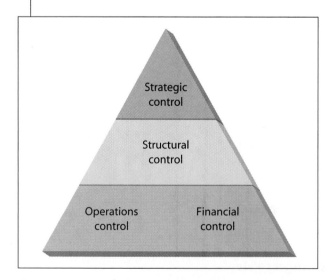

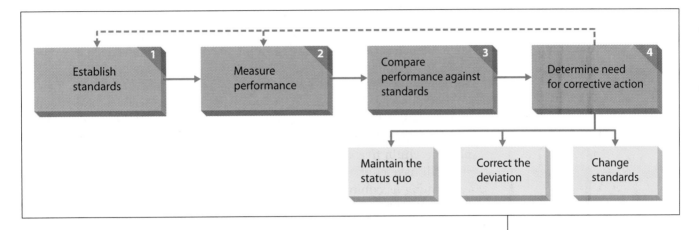

FIGURE 20.3
Steps in the Control Process

Having an effective control system can help ensure that an organization achieves its goals. Implementing a control system, however, is a systematic process that generally proceeds through four interrelated steps.

Most larger organizations also have one or more specialized managerial positions called controller. A **controller** is responsible for helping line managers with their control activities, for coordinating the organization's overall control system, and for gathering and assimilating relevant information. Many businesses that use an H-form or M-form organization design have several controllers: one for the corporation and one for each division. The job of controller is especially important in organizations that have complex control systems.[7]

In addition, many organizations are beginning to use operating employees to help maintain effective control. Indeed, employee participation is often used as a vehicle for allowing operating employees an opportunity to help facilitate organizational effectiveness. For example, Whistler Corporation increased employee participation in an effort to fix its quality problems. The first step was to eliminate the quality control unit that had been responsible for checking product quality at the end of the assembly process. Next, all operating employees were encouraged to check their own work and told that they would be responsible for correcting their own errors. As a result, Whistler has eliminated its quality problems and is highly profitable once again.

controller A position in organizations that helps line managers with their control activities

■ Steps in the Control Process

Regardless of the type or levels of control systems an organization needs, every control process has four fundamental steps.[8] These are illustrated in Figure 20.3.

Establish Standards The first step in the control process is to establish standards. A **control standard** is a target against which subsequent performance will be compared.[9] Employees at Taco Bell fast-food restaurant, for example, work toward the following three service standards:

control standard A target against which subsequent performance will be compared

1. A minimum of 95 percent of all customers will be greeted within three minutes of their arrival.
2. Preheated tortilla chips will not sit in the warmer more than thirty minutes before they are served to customers.
3. Empty tables will be cleaned within five minutes after being vacated.

Control standards should be expressed in measurable terms. Note that Taco Bell's first standard has a time limit of three minutes and an objective target of 95 percent of all customers. In the third item the objective target is implied: "all" empty tables.

Control standards should also be consistent with the organization's goals. Taco Bell has organizational goals involving customer service, food quality, and restaurant cleanliness. A control standard for a retailer like Home Depot should be consistent with its goal of increasing its annual sales volume by 25 percent within five years. A hospital trying to shorten the average hospital stay will have control standards that reflect current averages. A university reaffirming its commitment to academic excellence might adopt a standard of graduating 80 percent of its student athletes within five years of their enrollment. Control standards can be as narrow or as broad as the level of activity to which they apply and must follow logically from organizational goals and objectives.

A final aspect of establishing standards is to identify performance indicators. Performance indicators are measures of performance that provide information that is directly relevant to what is being controlled. For example, suppose an organization is following a tight schedule in building a new plant. Relevant performance indicators could be buying a site, selecting a building contractor, and ordering equipment. Monthly sales increases are not, however, directly relevant. On the other hand, if control is being focused on revenue, monthly sales increases are relevant, whereas buying land for a new plant is less relevant.

Measure Performance   The second step in the control process is to measure performance. Performance measurement is a constant, ongoing activity for most organizations. For control to be effective, performance measures must be valid. Daily, weekly, and monthly sales figures measure sales performance, and production performance may be expressed in terms of unit cost, product quality, or volume produced. Employees performance is often measured in terms of quality or quantity of output, but for many jobs measuring performance is not so straightforward.

A research and development scientist at Merck & Co., Inc., for example, may spend years working on a single project before achieving a breakthrough. A manager who takes over a business on the brink of failure may need months or even years to turn things around. Valid performance measurement, however difficult to obtain, is nevertheless vital in maintaining effective control, and appropriate performance indicators usually can be developed. The scientist's progress, for example, may be partially assessed by peer review, and the manager's success may be evaluated by her ability to convince creditors that she will eventually be able to restore profitability.

Compare Performance Against Standards   The third step in the control process is to compare performance against established standards. Performance may be higher than, lower than, or identical to the standard. In some cases comparison is easy. The goal of each product manager at General Electric is to make the product either number one or number two (on the basis of total sales) in its market. This standard is clear, and total sales are easy to calculate; therefore, determining whether this standard has been met is relatively simple. Sometimes, however, comparisons are less clear-cut. If performance is lower than expected, the question is how much deviation from standards to allow before taking remedial action. For example, is increasing sales by 7.9 percent, when the standard was 8 percent, close enough?

The timetable for comparing performance to standards depends on a variety of factors, including the importance and complexity of what is being controlled. For longer-run and higher-level standards, annual comparisons may be appropriate. Other circumstances may require more frequent comparisons. For example, a business with a cash shortage may need to monitor its on-hand cash reserves daily. We noted earlier the cash-flow problems Emery Air Freight faced after it purchased Purolator Courier. As part of their efforts to improve the firm's control, Emery's managers eventually started monitoring their cash reserves weekly.

Determine Need for Corrective Action The final step in the control process is to determine the need for corrective action. Decisions regarding corrective actions draw heavily on a manager's analytic and diagnostic skills. After comparing performance against control standards, one of three actions is appropriate: maintain the status quo (do nothing), correct the deviation, or change the standard. Maintaining the status quo is preferable when performance essentially matches the standard, but it is more likely that some action will be needed to correct a deviation from the standard.

Performance that is higher than expected may also cause problems for organizations. For example, when Chrysler first introduced both the Viper and the Prowler, demand was so strong that there were waiting lists and many customers were willing to pay more than the suggested retail price to obtain a car. The company was reluctant to increase production, primarily because it feared demand would eventually drop, but it didn't want to alienate potential customers. Consequently, Chrysler decided to reduce its advertising. This simple step curtailed demand a bit and limited customer frustration.

Changing an established standard usually is necessary if it was set too high or too low at the outset. This error is apparent if large numbers of employees routinely beat the standard by a wide margin or if no employees ever meet the standard. Also, standards that were perfectly appropriate when they were established may need to be adjusted if business conditions change.

MANAGEMENT IMPLICATIONS Managers should understand the various fundamental purposes of control. In addition, they should be familiar with the types of control in organizations, especially those which are most relevant to their own work. Managers should also accept responsibility for their role in the organization's control functions. Finally, they should be thoroughly knowledgeable about the steps in the control process. ▬

Operations Control

preliminary control Attempts to monitor the quality or quantity of financial, physical, human, and information resources before they actually become part of the system

screening control Relies heavily on feedback processes during the transformation process

FIGURE 20.4
Forms of Operations Control

Most organizations develop multiple control systems that incorporate all three basic forms of control. For example, the publishing company that produced this book screens inputs by hiring only qualified persons, typesetters, and printers (preliminary control). In addition, quality is checked during the transformation process such as after the manuscript is typeset (screening control), and the outputs—printed and bound books—are checked before they are shipped from the bindery (postaction control).

One of the four levels of control practiced by most organizations, operations control, is concerned with the processes the organization uses to transform resources into products or services. As Figure 20.4 shows, the three forms of operations control—preliminary, screening, and postaction—occur at different points in relation to the transformation processes used by the organization.

■ Preliminary Control

Preliminary control concentrates on the resources—financial, material, human, and information—the organization brings in from the environment. Preliminary control attempts to monitor the quality or quantity of these resources before they enter the organization. Firms like PepsiCo and General Mills hire only college graduates for their management training program, and even then only after applicants satisfy several interviewers and selection criteria. In this way the firms control the quality of the human resources entering the organization. When Sears orders merchandise to be manufactured under its own brand name, it specifies rigid standards of quality, thereby controlling physical inputs. Organizations also control financial and information resources. For example, privately held companies like UPS and Mars limit the extent to which outsiders can buy their stock, and television networks verify the accuracy of news stories before they are broadcast.

■ Screening Control

Screening control focuses on meeting standards for product and/or service quality or quantity during the actual transformation process. Screening control relies heavily on feedback processes. For example, in a Compaq Computer factory computer system components are checked periodically as each unit is being assembled. This type of screening ensures that all the components that have been assembled up to that point are working properly. The periodic quality checks provide feedback to workers so they know what, if any, corrective actions to take. Because they are useful in identifying the cause of problems, screening controls tend to be used more often than other forms of control.

More and more companies are adopting screening controls

Feedback

| Inputs | → | Transformation | → | Outputs |

Preliminary control
Focus is on inputs to the organizational system

Screening control
Focus is on how inputs are being transformed into outputs

Postaction control
Focus is on outputs from the organizational system

Companies use a variety of forms of operations control. Manchester Plastics, for example, makes instrument panels for the Ford Taurus and Mercury Sable. This worker is inspecting what is called cluster trim appliqués—plastic based components that are combined to create the external surface of the instrument panels. Since her inspection is taking place within the overall assembly process, it represents screening control. Meanwhile, because Ford requires its suppliers to meet exacting quality standards, Manchester's efforts also serve as preliminary control for Ford, since the automaker knows that the instrument panels it receives from Manchester will meet or exceed the standards that Ford has imposed.

because they are an effective way to promote employee participation and catch problems early in the overall transformation process. For example, Corning recently adopted screening controls for use in manufacturing television glass. In the past only finished television screens were inspected. Unfortunately, more than 4 percent of them were later returned by customers because of defects. Now the glass screens are inspected at each step in the production process rather than at the end, and the return rate from customers has dropped to .03 percent.

▪ Postaction Control

Postaction control focuses on the outputs of the organization after the transformation process is complete. Corning's old system was postaction control—final inspection after the product is completed. Although Corning abandoned its postaction control system, this method of control may still be effective, primarily if a product can be manufactured in only one or two steps or if the service is fairly simple and routine. Although postaction control alone may not be as effective as preliminary or screening control, it can provide management with information for future planning. For example, if a quality check of finished goods indicates an unacceptably high defective rate, the production manager knows that he or she must identify the causes and take steps to eliminate them. Postaction control also provides a basis for rewarding employees. Recognizing that an employee has exceeded personal sales goals by a wide margin, for example, may alert the manager that a bonus or promotion is in order.

Most organizations use more than one form of operations control. For example, Honda's preliminary control includes hiring only qualified employees and specifying strict quality standards when ordering parts from other

postaction control Monitors the outputs or results of the organization after the transformation process is complete

manufacturers. Honda also uses numerous screening controls to check the quality of components going into its cars. A final inspection and test drive as each car rolls off the assembly line is part of the company's postaction control.

| MANAGEMENT IMPLICATIONS | Managers should know the four basic levels of control used in organizations. They should also understand how organizations can use multiple |

levels of control simultaneously to enhance their effectiveness. ▬

Financial Control

Financial control is the control of financial resources as they flow into the organization (revenues, shareholder investments); are held by the organization (working capital, retained earnings); and flow out of the organization (expenses). Businesses must manage their finances so that revenues are sufficient to cover expenses and still return a profit to the firm's owners. Not-for-profit organizations such as universities have the same concerns: their revenues (from tax dollars or tuition) must cover operating expenses and overhead. Dickson Poon is a Chinese investor who has profited by relying heavily on financial control. He buys distressed up-scale retailers like Britain's Harvey Nichols and the U.S.'s Barney's, imposes strict financial controls, and begins generating hefty profits.[10] A complete discussion of financial management is beyond the scope of this book, but we will examine the control provided by budgets and other financial control tools.

■ Budgetary Control

budget A plan expressed in numerical terms

A **budget** is a plan expressed in numerical terms.[11] Organizations establish budgets for work groups, departments, divisions, and the whole organization. The usual time period for a budget is one year, although breakdowns of budgets by the quarter or month are also common. Budgets are generally expressed in financial terms, but they may occasionally be expressed in units of output, time, or other quantifiable factors.

Because of their quantitative nature, budgets provide yardsticks for measuring performance and facilitate comparisons across departments, between levels in the organization, and from one time period to another. Budgets serve four primary purposes. They help managers coordinate resources and projects (because they use a common denominator, usually dollars). Budgets help define the established standards for control. They also provide guidelines about the organization's resources and expectations. Finally, budgets

Type of Budget	What Budget Shows
Financial budget	**Sources and uses of cash**
Cash-flow or cash budget	All sources of cash income and cash expenditures in monthly, weekly, or daily periods
Capital expenditures budget	Costs of major assets such as a new plant, machinery, or land
Balance sheet budget	Forecast of the organization's assets and liabilities in the event all other budgets are met
Operating budget	**Planned operations in financial terms**
Sales or revenue budget	Income the organization expects to receive from normal operations
Expense budget	Anticipated expenses for the organization during the coming time period
Profit budget	Anticipated differences between sales or revenues and expenses
Nonmonetary budget	**Planned operations in nonfinancial terms**
Labor budget	Hours of direct labor available for use
Space budget	Square feet or meters of space available for various functions
Production budget	Number of units to be produced during the coming time period

TABLE 20.1
Types of Budgets

Organizations use a variety of types of budgets to help manage their control function. The three major categories of budgets are financial, operating, and nonmonetary budgets. There are several different types of budgets in each category. Each budget must be carefully matched with the specific function being controlled in order to be most effective.

enable the organization to evaluate the performance of managers and organizational units.

Types of Budgets   Most organizations develop and use three different kinds of budgets—financial, operating, and nonmonetary. Table 20.1 summarizes the characteristics of each type of budget.

A financial budget indicates where the organization expects to get its cash for the coming time period and how it plans to use it. Because financial resources are critically important, the organization needs to know where those resources will be coming from and how they are to be used. The financial budget provides answers to both questions. Usual sources of cash include sales revenue, short- and long-term loans, the sale of assets, and the issuance of new stock.

For years Exxon's capital budget has been very conservative. As a result, the firm has amassed a huge financial reserve but has been overtaken in sales by Royal Dutch/Shell. Exxon recently decided to loosen its purse strings and begin budgeting more for capital expenditures. For example, whereas Exxon's capital budget was less than $8 billion in 1994, managers increased this budget to $9.2 billion in 1996 and plan to increase to around $11 billion by the year 2000.[12]

An operating budget is concerned with planned operations within the organization. It outlines what quantities of products and/or services the

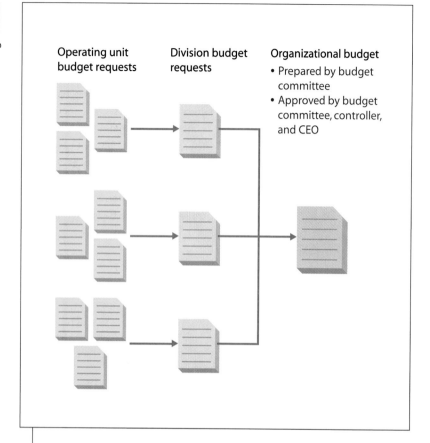

Operating unit
budget requests

Division budget
requests

Organizational budget
- Prepared by budget
  committee
- Approved by budget
  committee, controller,
  and CEO

FIGURE 20.5

Developing Budgets in Organizations

Most organizations use the same basic process to develop budgets. Operating units are requested to submit their budget requests to divisions. These divisions, in turn, compile unit budgets and submit their own budgets to the organization. An organizational budget is then compiled for approval by the budget committee, controller, and CEO.

organization intends to create and what resources will be used to create them. IBM creates an operating budget that specifies how many of each model of its personal computer will be produced each quarter.

A nonmonetary budget is simply a budget expressed in nonfinancial terms, such as units of output, hours of direct labor, machine hours, or square-foot allocations. Nonmonetary budgets are most commonly used by managers at the lower levels of an organization. For example, a plant manager can schedule work more effectively knowing that he or she has eight thousand labor hours to allocate in a week, rather than trying to determine how to best spend $76,451 in wages in a week.

Developing Budgets Traditionally, budgets were developed by top management and the controller and then imposed on lower-level managers. Although some organizations still follow this pattern, many organizations now expect all managers to participate in the budget process. As a starting point, top management generally issues a call for budget requests, accompanied by an indication of overall patterns the budgets may take. For example, if sales are expected to drop in the next year, managers may be told to prepare for cuts in operating budgets.

As Figure 20.5 shows, the heads of each operating unit typically submit budget requests to the head of their division. An operating unit head might be a department manager in a manufacturing or wholesaling firm or a program director in a social service agency. The division heads might include plant managers, regional sales managers, or college deans. The division head integrates and consolidates the budget requests from operating unit heads into one overall division budget request. A great deal of interaction among managers usually takes place at this stage, as the division head coordinates the budgetary needs of the various departments.

Division budget requests are then forwarded to a budget committee, which is usually composed of top managers. The committee reviews budget requests from several divisions and, once again, duplications and inconsistencies are corrected. Depending upon the nature and magnitude of these duplications and corrections, the committee may either make them itself or send the budgets back to division managers for revision. Finally, the budget committee, the controller, and the CEO review and agree on the overall budget for the organization as well as specific budgets for each operating unit. These decisions are then communicated back to each manager.

Strengths and Weaknesses of Budgeting   Budgets offer a number of advantages, but they have several weaknesses as well. On the plus side, budgets facilitate effective control. Placing dollar values on operations enables managers to monitor operations better and pinpoint problem areas. Budgets also facilitate coordination and communication between departments because they express diverse activities in a common denominator (dollars). Budgets help maintain records of organizational performance and are a logical complement to planning. That is, as managers develop plans they should simultaneously consider control measures to accompany them. Organizations can use budgets to link plans and control by first developing budgets as part of the plan and then using those budgets as a part of control.

On the other hand, some managers apply budgets too rigidly. Budgets are intended to serve as frameworks, but managers sometimes fail to recognize that changing circumstances may warrant budget adjustments. The process of developing budgets can also be very time consuming. Finally, budgets may limit innovation and change. When all available funds are allocated to specific operating budgets, it may be impossible to procure additional funds to take advantage of an unexpected opportunity.

Indeed, for these very reasons some organizations are working to scale back their budgeting system. Although most organizations are likely to continue to use budgets, the goal is to make them less confining and rigid. For example, Xerox, 3M, and Digital Equipment have cut back on their budgeting systems by reducing the number of budgets they generate and by injecting more flexibility into the budgeting process.[13]

■ Other Tools of Financial Control

Although budgets are the most common means of financial control, other useful tools are financial statements, ratio analysis, and financial audits.

Well-established and monitored financial regulations in most of today's developed economies ensure that financial control systems can be easily followed and readily interpreted and evaluated. But less certainty exists in some of today's developing economies. The Almaty stock exchange in Kazakhstan is subject to few rules and has no operating procedures. Not surprisingly, the exchange has had difficulty in attracting foreign investors. But as these economies mature and continue to develop, new controls will be created and investors can have more faith in the financial information they are given.

financial statement A profile of some aspect of an organization's financial circumstances

balance sheet List of assets and liabilities of an organization at a specific point in time

income statement A summary of financial performance over a period of time

ratio analysis The calculation of one or more financial ratios to assess some aspect of the organization's financial health

audits An independent appraisal of an organization's accounting, financial, and operational systems

Financial Statements A **financial statement** is a profile of some aspect of an organization's financial circumstances. Financial statements are generally prepared and presented according to commonly accepted accounting procedures.[14] The two most basic financial statements prepared and used by virtually all organizations are a balance sheet and an income statement.

The **balance sheet** lists the assets and liabilities of the organization at a specific point in time, usually the last day of an organization's fiscal year. For example, the balance sheet may summarize the financial condition of an organ-ization on December 31, 1999. Most balance sheets are divided into current assets (assets that are relatively liquid, or easily convertible into cash), fixed assets (assets that are longer term and less liquid), current liabilities (debts and other obligations that must be paid in the near future), long-term liabilities (payable over an extended period of time), and stockholders' equity (the owners' claims against the assets).

Whereas the balance sheet reflects a snapshot profile of an organizations financial position at a single point in time, the **income statement** summarizes financial performance over a period of time, usually one year. For example, the income statement might be for the period January 1, 1999, through December 31, 1999. The income statement summarizes the firm's revenues less its expenses to report net income (that is, profit or loss) for the period. Information from the balance sheet and income statement is used in computing important financial ratios.

Ratio Analysis Financial ratios compare various elements within a balance sheet, income statement, or both. **Ratio analysis** is the calculation of one or more financial ratios to assess some aspect of the financial health of an organization. Organizations use a variety of financial ratios as part of financial control. For example, *liquidity ratios* indicate how liquid (easily converted into cash) an organization's assets are. *Debt ratios* reflect the ability to meet long-term financial obligations. *Return ratios* show managers and investors how much return the organization is generating relative to its assets. *Coverage ratios* help estimate the organization's ability to cover interest expenses on borrowed capital. *Operating ratios* indicate the effectiveness of specific functional areas rather than the effectiveness of the total organization. The Walt Disney Company relies heavily on financial ratios to keep its financial operations on track.[15]

Financial Audits **Audits** are independent appraisals of an organization's accounting, financial, and operational systems. The two major types of financial audit are the external audit and the internal audit.

External audits are financial appraisals conducted by experts who are not employees of the organization.[16] External audits are typically concerned with ensuring that the organization's accounting procedures and financial statements are compiled in an objective and verifiable fashion. The organization contracts with certified public accountants (CPAs) for this service. The CPA's main objective is to verify for stockholders, the IRS, and other interested parties that the methods by which the organization's financial managers and accountants prepare documents and reports are legal and proper. External audits are so important that publicly held corporations are required by law to have external audits regularly, as assurance to investors that the financial reports are reliable. An external audit at U.S. Shoe Corporation once discovered some significant accounting irregularities in one of the firm's divisions. As a result, the firm was fined by the Securities and Exchange Commission and had to revamp its entire accounting system.[17]

Some organizations are also starting to employ external auditors to review other aspects of their financial operations. For example, some auditing firms now specialize in checking corporate legal bills. An auditor for the Fireman's Fund Insurance Corporation uncovered several thousands of dollars in legal fee errors. Other auditors are beginning to specialize in real estate, employee benefits, and pension plan investments.[18]

Whereas external audits are conducted by external accountants, an *internal audit* is handled by employees of the organization. Its objective is the same as that of an external audit—to verify the accuracy of financial and accounting procedures used by the organization. Internal audits also examine the efficiency and appropriateness of financial and accounting procedures. Because the staff members who conduct them are a permanent part of the organization, internal audits tend to be more expensive than external audits. But employees, who are familiar with the organization's practices, may also point out significant aspects of the accounting system besides its technical correctness. For example, they may be able to suggest more effective and efficient ways of communicating pertinent financial information to various managers in the firm. Large organizations such as Dresser Industries and Ford have internal auditing staffs that spend all their time conducting audits of different divisions and functional areas of the organizations. Smaller organizations may assign accountants to an internal audit group on a temporary or rotating basis.

MANAGEMENT IMPLICATIONS Regardless of their area of responsibility, all managers should understand the basics of financial control. In particular, they need to know how budgets are developed and used for control and about the use of other tools of financial control. ■

Structural Control

Organizations can create designs for themselves that result in very different approaches to control. Two major forms of structural control—bureaucratic control and clan control—represent opposite ends of a continuum, as shown

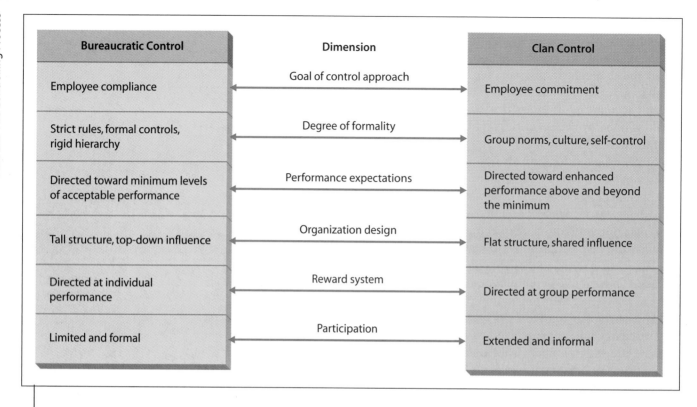

FIGURE 20.6
Organizational Control

Organizational control generally falls somewhere between the two extremes of bureaucratic and clan control. NBC Television uses bureaucratic control, whereas Levi Strauss uses clan control.

bureaucratic control A form of organizational control characterized by formal and mechanistic structural arrangements

in Figure 20.6.[19] The six dimensions shown in the figure represent perspectives adopted by the two extreme types of structural control. That is, they have different goals, degrees of formality, performance focus, organization designs, reward systems, and levels of participation. Although a few organizations fall precisely at one extreme or the other, most tend toward one end but may have specific characteristics of either.

■ Bureaucratic Control

Bureaucratic control is an approach to organization design characterized by formal and mechanistic structural arrangements. As the term suggests, it follows the bureaucratic model. The goal of bureaucratic control is employee compliance. Organizations that use it rely on strict rules and a rigid hierarchy, insist that employees meet minimally acceptable levels of performance, and often have a tall structure. Their rewards focus on individual performance and allow only limited and formal employee participation.

NBC Television applies structural controls that reflect many elements of bureaucracy. The organization relies on numerous rules to regulate employee travel, expense accounts, and other expenses. A new performance appraisal system precisely specifies minimally acceptable levels of performance for everyone. The organization's structure is considerably taller than those of the other major networks, and rewards are based on individual contributions. Perhaps most significantly, many NBC employees have argued that they have too small a voice in how the organization is managed.

Abercrombie & Fitch also uses bureaucratic control. In yet another example, a large oil company recently decided to allow employees to wear casual attire to work. But a committee then spent weeks developing a twenty-page manual that described what was and was not acceptable. For example, denim pants are not allowed, although casual cotton pants are fine. Similarly, athletic shoes may be worn as long as they are not white, and all shirts must have a collar.

■ Clan Control

Clan control, in contrast, is an approach to organizational design characterized by informal and organic structural arrangements. As Figure 20.6 shows, its goal is employee commitment to the organization. Accordingly, it relies heavily on group norms and a strong corporate culture, and gives employees the responsibility for controlling themselves. Employees are encouraged to perform beyond minimally acceptable levels. Organizations using this approach are usually relatively flat. They direct reward at group performance and favor widespread employee participation.

clan control An approach to organizational control based on informal and organic structural arrangements

Levi Strauss is a firm that practices clan control. The firm's managers use groups as the basis for work and have created a culture wherein group norms help facilitate high performance. Rewards are subsequently provided to the higher performing groups and teams. The company's culture also reinforces contributions to the overall team effort, and employees have a strong sense of loyalty to the organization. Levi Strauss has a flat structure, and power is widely shared. Employee participation is encouraged in all areas of operation. Another company that uses this approach is Southwest Airlines. When Southwest decided to "go casual," the firm resisted the temptation to develop dress guidelines. Instead, managers decided to allow employees to exercise discretion over their attire and to deal with clearly inappropriate situations on a case-by-case basis.

MANAGEMENT IMPLICATIONS Managers should be familiar with the two basic forms of structural control used by organizations. They should also recognize which form their own organization uses, as well as why that particular form of control has evolved. ■

Strategic Control

Given the obvious importance of an organization's strategy, it is also important to assess how effective that strategy is in helping the organization meet its goals.[20] To do so requires the organization to integrate its strategy and control systems. The importance of linking strategy and control is especially pronounced for international and multinational companies.

■ Integrating Strategy and Control

Strategic control generally focuses on five aspects of organizations—structure, leadership, technology, human resources, and information and operational control systems. For example, an organization should periodically examine its structure to determine whether or not it is facilitating the attainment of the organization's strategic goals. Suppose a firm using a functional (U-form) design has an established goal of achieving a 20 percent sales growth rate per year. However, performance indicators show a current growth rate of only 10 percent per year. Detailed analysis might reveal that the current structure is inhibiting growth in some way (for example, by slowing decision making and inhibiting innovation) and that a divisional (M-form) design is more likely to bring about the desired growth (by speeding decision making and promoting innovation).

In this way, strategic control focuses on the extent to which implemented strategy achieves the organization's strategic goals. If, as outlined above, one or more avenues of implementation are inhibiting the attainment of goals, that avenue should be changed. Consequently, the firm might need to alter its structure, replace key leaders, adopt new technology, modify its human resources, or change its information and operational control systems. For example, Ikea, the Swedish furniture manufacturer, has experienced disappointing performance from its internationalization strategy. As a result, the company has recently announced a major change in how it will manage its international operations.[21]

Strategic control is critical to the success of many businesses. Take Minnesota-based Fastenal Co. Its CEO, Bob Kierlin, shown here with a team of employees, has made a strategic decision to provide his employees with few perks and no pensions. However, he believes strongly in extreme decentralization. He gives employees tremendous decision-making authority to carry out their jobs. Kierlin thinks that highly motivated employees prefer the power to work with almost total independence over more traditional kinds of rewards like extra vacation time or fitness centers. He ties pay raises and stock ownership to long-term performance and gives employees open access to information, which gives them the opportunity and the motivation to work in the best interests of the firm.

■ International Strategic Control

Because of both their relatively large size and the increased complexity associated with international business, global organizations must take an especially pronounced strategic view of their control systems. One very basic question that has to be addressed is whether to manage control from a centralized or decentralized perspective.[22] Under a centralized system, each organizational unit around the world is responsible for frequently reporting the results of its performance to headquarters. Managers from the home office often visit foreign branches to observe firsthand how the units are functioning.

British Petroleum, Unilever, Procter & Gamble, and Sony use this approach. They believe centralized control is effective because it allows the home office to keep better informed of the performance of foreign units and to maintain more control over how decisions are made. For example, British Petroleum discovered that its Australian subsidiary was not billing customers for charges as quickly as its competitors were. By shortening the billing cycle,

THE WORLD OF MANAGEMENT

Weak International Controls Can Spell Trouble

Control is important for any business, but especially one with international operations. Control is also especially important for small businesses. Take a small business with international operations, then, and you have a case where control is critical. And lessons learned the hard way can be expensive. For example, consider the case of Azon USA, Inc., a Michigan-based supplier of machinery and chemicals used by makers of aluminum windows.

When Azon set up its first international office in the United Kingdom, Azon's CEO, James Dunstan, was able to hire an experienced manager who already worked in an Azon subsidiary to head up the new office. Dunstan visits the UK once a year, and the UK manager also makes one trip to Michigan a year. A brief quarterly financial report is the only other formal communication between the two operations, and the UK office has grown constantly in both sales and profits.

> *"The autonomy that I gave the guy in Britain didn't work with the other guy."*
>
> *James M. Dunstan, CEO of Azon**

But when Dunstan decided to set up shop in another European country, he had an altogether different experience. He hired someone he did not know very well but tried to use the same casual reporting relationship that had worked in the UK. After two years, however, he discovered that although the new manager was traveling constantly, staying in five-star hotels, and draining his substantial expense accounts, he was generating very little new business. All told, the new operation ended up losing more than $750,000 before Dunstan closed it. Although the firm was not in jeopardy of going under, it nevertheless had some tight moments before effective control was reestablished. And Mr. Dunstan vows to keep a closer watch on things in the future!

References: *"Small Firms, Big Hurdles,"* Wall Street Journal, *September 26, 1996, pp. R1, R2 (*quote on p. R2), Joan Magretta, "Governing the Family-Owned Enterprise,"* Harvard Business Review, *January–February 1998, pp. 112–123.*

British Petroleum now receives customer payments five days faster than before. Managers believe that they discovered this oversight only because of a centralized financial control system.

Organizations that use a decentralized control system require foreign branches to report on their performance and activities less frequently and in less detail. For example, each unit may submit summary performance statements on a quarterly basis and provide full statements only once a year. Similarly, visits from the home office are less frequent and less concerned with monitoring and assessing performance. IBM, Ford, and Shell use this approach. Because Ford practices decentralized control of its design function, European designers have developed several innovative automobile design features. Managers believe that if they had been more centralized, designers would not have had the freedom to develop their new ideas. "The World of Management" describes the experiences of one small firm that erred in how it managed its international control.

MANAGEMENT IMPLICATIONS   Managers need to understand the relationship between control and strategy. In addition, managers in companies with international operations need to be familiar with the special control issues that they face. ■

Managing Control in Organizations

Effective control, whether at the operations, financial, structural, or strategic level, successfully regulates and monitors organizational activities. To use the control process, managers must recognize the characteristics of effective control and understand how to identify and overcome occasional resistance to control.[23]

■ Characteristics of Effective Control

Control systems tend to be most effective when they are integrated with planning and are when they are flexible, accurate, timely, and objective.

Integration with Planning   Control should be linked with planning. The more explicit and precise this linkage, the more effective the control system. The best way to integrate planning and control is to account for control as plans develop. In other words, as goals are set during the planning process, attention should be paid to developing standards that will reflect how well the plan is realized. Managers at Champion Spark Plug Company decided to broaden their product line to include a full range of automotive accessories—a total of twenty-one new products. As a part of this plan, managers decided in advance what level of sales they wanted to realize from each product for each of the next five years. These sales goals became the standards against which actual sales would be compared. Thus, by accounting for their control system as they developed their plan, managers at Champion did an excellent job of integrating planning and control.

Flexibility   The control system itself must be flexible enough to accommodate change. Consider, for example, an organization whose diverse product line requires seventy-five raw materials. The company's inventory control system must be able to manage and monitor current levels of inventory for all seventy-five materials. When a change in product line changes the number of raw materials or when the required quantities of the existing materials change, the control system should be flexible enough to handle the revised requirements. The alternative—designing and implementing a new control system—is an avoidable expense. Champion's control system includes a mechanism that automatically ships products to major customers to keep their inventory at predetermined levels. The firm had to adjust this system when one of its biggest customers, Montgomery Ward, decided not to stock the full line of Champion products. Because its control system was flexible, modifying it for Montgomery Ward was relatively simple.

Accuracy Managers make a surprisingly large number of decisions based on inaccurate information. Field representatives may hedge their sales estimates to make themselves look better. Production managers may hide costs to meet their targets. Human resource managers may overestimate their minority recruiting prospects to meet affirmative action goals. In each case the information other managers receive is inaccurate, and the results of inaccurate information may be quite dramatic. If sales projections are inflated, a manager might cut advertising (thinking it is no longer needed) or increase advertising (to further build momentum). Similarly, a production manager unaware of hidden costs may quote a sales price much lower than desirable. Or a human resources manager may speak out publicly on the effectiveness of the company's minority recruiting, only to learn that these prospects have been overestimated. In each case the result of inaccurate information is inappropriate managerial action.

Timeliness Timeliness does not necessarily mean quickness. Rather, it describes a control system that provides information as often as is necessary. Because Champion has a wealth of historical data on its spark plug sales, it does not need information on spark plugs as frequently as it needs sales feedback for its newer products. Retail organizations usually need sales results daily so that they can manage cash flow and adjust advertising and promotion. In contrast, they may require information about physical inventory only quarterly or annually. In general, the more uncertain and unstable the circumstances, the more frequently measurement is needed.

Objectivity The control system should provide information that is as objective as possible. To appreciate this statement, imagine the task of a manager responsible for control of his organization's human resources. He asks two plant managers to submit reports. One manager notes that morale at his plant is "okay," that grievances are "about where they should be," and that turnover is "under control." The other reports that absenteeism at her plant is running at 4 percent, that sixteen grievances were filed this year (compared with twenty-four last year), and that turnover is 12 percent. The second report will almost always be more useful than the first. Of course, managers also need to look beyond the numbers when assessing performance. For example, a plant manager may be boosting productivity and profit margins by putting too much pressure on workers and using poor quality materials. As a result, impressive short-run gains may be overshadowed by longer run increases in employee turnover and customer complaints.

■ Resistance to Control

Managers may sometimes make the mistake of assuming that the value of an effective control system is self-evident to employees. This is not always so, however. Many employees resist control, especially if they feel overcontrolled, if they think control is inappropriately focused or that it rewards inefficiency, or if they are uncomfortable with accountability.

Overcontrol Occasionally, organizations try to control too many things. This situation becomes especially problematic when the control directly affects employee behavior. An organization that instructs its employees when to come to work, where to park, when to have morning coffee, and when to leave for the day exerts considerable control over people's daily activities. Yet many organizations attempt to control not only these but other aspects of work behavior as well. Troubles arise when employees perceive these attempts to limit their behavior as unreasonable. A company that tells its employees how to dress, how to arrange their desks, and how to wear their hair may meet with more resistance. Employees at Chrysler used to complain because they were forced to park their non-Chrysler vehicles in a distant parking lot. People felt that these efforts to control their personal behavior (for example, what kind of car to drive) were excessive. Managers eventually removed these controls and now allow open parking. Some employees at Abercrombie & Fitch might also feel that the firm is guilty of overcontrol.

Inappropriate Focus The control system may be too narrow or it may focus too much on quantifiable variables and leave no room for analysis or interpretation. A sales standard that encourages high-pressure tactics to maximize short-run sales may sacrifice goodwill from long-term customers. Such a standard is too narrow. A university reward system that encourages faculty members to publish large numbers of articles but fails to consider the quality of the work is also inappropriately focused. Employees resist the intent of the control system by focusing their effort only on the performance indicators being used.

Rewards for Inefficiency Imagine two operating departments that are approaching the end of the fiscal year. Department one expects to have $5,000 of its budget left over; department two is already $3,000 in the red. As a result, department one is likely to have its budget cut for the next year ("They had money left, so they obviously got too much to begin with") and department two is likely to get a budget increase ("They obviously haven't been getting enough money"). Thus department one is punished for being efficient, and department two is rewarded for being inefficient. (No wonder departments commonly hasten to deplete their budgets as the end of the year approaches!) As with inappropriate focus, people resist the intent of this control and behave in ways that run counter to the organization's intent.

Too Much Accountability Effective controls allow managers to determine whether or not employees successfully discharge their responsibilities. If standards are properly set and performance accurately measured, managers know when problems arise and which departments and individuals are responsible.

Managing control is important in virtually all organizations. A particularly sensitive control issue facing managers today involves electronic communication such as e-mail. Too little control may allow employees to waste vast amounts of time e-mailing their friends and family, conducting personal business on the Internet, and so forth. But too much control may restrict personal freedom and create an oppressive culture that stifles employee motivation and creativity. Thus, the key is finding the right balance.

People who do not want to be answerable for their mistakes or who do not want to work as hard as their boss might like therefore resist control. For example, American Express has a system that provides daily information on how many calls each of its operators handles. If one operator typically works at a slower pace and handles fewer calls than other operators, that individual's deficient performance is easy to pinpoint.

■ Overcoming Resistance to Control

Perhaps the best way to overcome resistance to control is to create effective control to begin with. If control systems are properly integrated with organizational planning and if the controls are flexible, accurate, timely, and objective, the organization will be less likely to overcontrol, to focus on inappropriate standards, or to reward inefficiency. Two other ways to overcome resistance are encouraging participation and developing verification procedures.

Encourage Employee Participation   Chapter 13 noted that participation can help overcome resistance to change. By the same token, when employees are involved with planning and implementing the control system, they are less likely to resist it. For instance, employee participation in planning, decision making, and quality control at the Chevrolet gear axle plant in Detroit has resulted in increased employee concern for quality and a greater commitment to meeting standards.

Develop Verification Procedures   Multiple standards and information systems provide checks and balances in control and allow the organization to verify the accuracy of performance indicators. Suppose a production manager argues that she failed to meet a certain cost standard because of increased prices of raw materials. A properly designed inventory control system will either support or contradict her explanation. Suppose that an employee who was fired for excessive absences argues that he was not absent "for a long time." An effective human resource control system should have records that support the termination. Resistance to control declines because these verification procedures protect both employees and management. If inventory control records support the production manager's claim about the rising cost of raw materials, she will not be held solely accountable for failing to meet the cost standard and some action will probably be taken to lower the cost of raw materials.

"You've got to really wonder just how many more cut-backs this department can absorb!"

In recent years, many organizations have sought ways to lower their costs through cost-cutting programs. They have reduced their workforces, eliminated perquisites, and outsourced services that independent contractors can do for a lower price. But some experts worry that many organizations have cut too much, increasing pressure and stress on the employees who are left. While it is doubtful that any organization has gone to the lengths illustrated in this cartoon, many employees nevertheless are feeling the consequences of these cutbacks.

MANAGEMENT
IMPLICATIONS   Managers should know the basic characteristics of effective control. They should also understand why employees are likely to resist control, as well as techniques that can be used to overcome this resistance. ▬

Summary of Key Points

Control is the regulation of organizational activities so that some targeted element of performance remains within acceptable limits. Control provides ways to adapt to environmental change, to limit the accumulation of errors, to cope with organizational complexity, and to minimize costs. Control can focus on financial, physical, information, and human resources and includes operations, financial, structural, and strategic levels. Control is the function of managers, of the controller, and, increasingly, of operating employees.

Steps in the control process are (1) establish standards of expected performance (2) measure actual performance (3) compare performance to the standards, and (4) evaluate the comparison and take appropriate action.

Operations control focuses on the processes the organization uses to transform resources into products or services. Preliminary control is concerned with the resources that serve as inputs to the system. Screening control is concerned with the organization's transformation processes. Postaction control is concerned with the outputs of the organization. Most organizations need multiple control systems because no one system alone can provide adequate control.

Financial control focuses on controlling the organization's financial resources. The foundation of financial control is budgets, or plans expressed in numerical terms. Most organizations rely on financial, operating, and nonmonetary budgets. Financial statements, various kinds of ratios, and external and internal audits are

also important tools organizations use as part of financial control.

Structural control addresses how well an organization's structural elements serve their intended purpose. Two basic forms of structural control are bureaucratic and clan control. Bureaucratic control is relatively formal and mechanistic, whereas clan control is informal and organic. Most organizations use a form of organizational control that falls somewhere between these two extremes.

Strategic control focuses on whether the organization's strategies are effectively helping the organization meet its goals. The integration of strategy and control is generally achieved through organization structure, leadership, technology, human resources, and information and operational control systems. International strategic control is also important for multinational organizations. The foundation of international strategic control is whether to practice centralized or decentralized control.

One way to increase the effectiveness of control is to fully integrate planning and control. The control system should also be flexible, accurate, timely, and as objective as possible. Employees may resist organizational controls because of overcontrol, inappropriate focus, rewards for inefficiency, and a desire to avoid accountability. Managers can overcome this resistance by improving the effectiveness of controls, by allowing employee participation, and by developing verification procedures.

Discussion Questions

Questions for Review

1. What is the purpose of organizational control? Why is it important?

2. What are the steps in the control process? Which step is likely to be the most difficult to perform? Why?

3. What are the similarities and differences between the various forms of operations control? What are the costs and benefits of each form?

4. How can a manager understand and overcome resistance and make control effective?

Questions for Analysis

5. How is the controlling process related to the functions of planning, organizing, and leading?

6. Are the differences in bureaucratic control and clan control related to differences in organization structure? If so, how? If not, why not? (Note that the

terms are similar to those used to discuss the organizing process.)

7. Do you use a budget for your personal finances? Relate your experiences with budgeting to the discussion in the chapter.

Questions for Application

8. Does your college or university have a controller? If so, find out how the position fits into the organization's design. If not, why do you think such a position has not been created?

9. Interview several local managers to determine which form of operations control they most frequently use—preliminary, screening, postaction, or multiple. How might you account for what you found?

10. Ask managers from different parts of the same organization or from different organizations what makes controls effective. How do their views compare with those presented in this chapter? Why might differences exist?

Building Effective Time-Management Skills

EXERCISE OVERVIEW

Time-management skills—a manager's abilities to prioritize work, to work efficiently, and to delegate appropriately—play a major role in the control function. That is, a manager can use time-management skills to more effectively control his or her own work. This exercise demonstrates the relationship between time-management skills and control.

EXERCISE BACKGROUND

You are a middle manager in a small manufacturing plant. Today is Monday, and you have just returned from a one-week vacation. The first thing you discover is that your secretary will not be in today. His aunt died, and he is out of town at the funeral. He did, however, leave you the following note:

Dear Boss:
Sorry about not being here today. I will be back tomorrow. In the meantime, here are some things you need to know:

1. Ms. Glinski (your boss) wants to see you today at 4:00.

2. The shop steward wants to see you ASAP about a labor problem.

3. Mr. Bateman (one of your big customers) has a complaint about a recent shipment.

4. Ms. Ferris (one of your major suppliers) wants to discuss a change in the delivery schedule.

5. Mr. Prescott from the chamber of commerce wants you to attend a breakfast meeting on Wednesday and discuss our expansion plans.

6. The legal office wants to discuss our upcoming OSHA inspection.

7. Human resources wants to know when you can interview someone for the new supervisor's position.

8. Jack Williams, the machinist you fired last month, has been hanging around the parking lot.

EXERCISE TASK

With the preceding information as a framework, do the following:

1. Prioritize the work into three categories: very timely, moderately timely, and less timely. (Are importance and timeliness the same thing?)

2. Decide what additional information you need before you can really begin to prioritize this work?

3. Explain how your approach would differ if your secretary was at work today?

Building Effective Diagnostic Skills

EXERCISE OVERVIEW

Diagnostic skills enable managers to visualize responses to situations. Given that control focuses on regulating organizational activities, diagnostic skills are clearly important to the determination of what activities should be regulated, how to best assess activities, and how to respond to deviations. This exercise demonstrates this relationship.

EXERCISE BACKGROUND

You are the manager of a popular, locally owned restaurant. Your restaurant competes with chains such as Chili's, Bennigan's, and Applebee's. However, you have been able to maintain your marketshare in light of increased competition from these outlets by concentrating on providing exceptional service.

Recently, you have become aware of three trends that concern you. First, your costs are increasing. Monthly charges for food purchases seem to be growing at an exceptionally rapid pace. Second, customer complaints are also increasing, even though the actual number of complaints is still quite small. And finally, turnover among your employees is also increasing. Although turnover in the restaurant business is almost always very high, the recent increase is in marked contrast to your historical patterns.

EXERCISE TASK

Using the preceding information, do the following:

1. Identify as many potential causes as possible for each problem area.

2. Group each cause into one of two categories: more likely and less likely.

3. Develop at least one potential action that you might take to address each cause.

Building Effective Decision-Making Skills

EXERCISE OVERVIEW

Decision-making skills refer to the manager's ability to correctly recognize and define problems and opportunities and to then select an appropriate course of action to solve problems and capitalize on opportunities. This exercise will enable you to practice your decision-making skills in relation to organizational control.

EXERCISE BACKGROUND

Assume that you are the top manager of a medium-size, family-owned manufacturing company. Several family members work in various managerial positions, but you have just been hired to run the company. The company has a long-standing tradition of avoiding debt and owns several smaller businesses in related industries.

Over the last few years the company has lagged in productivity and efficiency and now finds itself in desperate straits. Profits have just about disappeared, and one of your bigger competitors may be planning an attempt to take over the business. You have asked a consulting firm to help you identify alternatives for turning things around. The primary options are as follows:

1. Issue a public stock offering (IPO) to raise funds.

2. Borrow money from a bank to finance a turnaround.

3. Sell several of the smaller operations to fund a turnaround.

4. Seek a buyer for the entire firm.

EXERCISE TASK

With the preceding background information as context, do the following:

1. Evaluate each options from a strategic standpoint.

2. Explain how each option relates to control.

3. Select the option that you like the best.

4. Describe the barriers you will probably encounter with the option you have chosen.

CHAPTER CLOSING CASE

Ford Cuts Its Costs

A s U.S. auto makers have gradually regained their competitive positions in the global marketplace, first one and then another has taken the occasional misstep and fallen back—as in the old adage of two steps forward and then one back again. The latest to drop behind by a step has been Ford. While General Motors and Chrysler were charging ahead in the mid-1990s, Ford's costs had gotten out of line. Managers knew that Ford needed to take significant steps for the firm to catch up with its rivals.

Jacques A. Nasser, a company executive from Australia, was installed as president of Ford in 1996 and given a mandate to cut costs. Nasser, in turn, readily accepted the challenge and quickly put into motion a variety of plans and ideas that he had already been formulating. His background is in engineering, and he is skilled in getting to the heart of an issue and taking quick and decisive action.

One of his immediate steps was to eliminate several unprofitable models from Ford's product line. Managers had been loathe to drop the slow-selling Thunderbird, for example, because the name plate had long been part of the sporty image that Ford had tried to cultivate. But Nasser quickly—and with little sentiment—halted production and announced that the Thunderbird was dead. However, he left the door open for possibly reintroducing a newly designed and reengineered Thunderbird in the future.

As he was shutting down slow-selling products, he simultaneously boosted production on Ford's faster- selling products. For example, the Ford Expedition—a full-size sports utility vehicle that got off to a quick start—was not being produced in sufficient numbers to meet demand. Nasser ordered an entire Michigan factory to be turned over to the production of the Expedition and its $10,000 per unit profit margins.

Nasser also implemented a broad-based plan of cost reductions. The Ford culture had long supported free spending; for example, its executives traveled first class and had virtually unlimited expense accounts. In addition, most top managers had discretionary spending accounts, which they could use for virtually any purpose remotely related to work (to support golf club memberships or to buy expensive gifts for associates, for example). Nasser moved quickly to cut travel budgets and restrict access to first-class travel privileges. He also froze all discretionary spending accounts until new policies could be developed to regulate their use.

But Nasser's biggest undertaking was a make over of Ford's entire organization design. Alexander Trotman, the firm's CEO, had previously launched an ambitious plan he called Ford 2000. This plan called for centralizing most international operations in Ford's Dearborn headquarters, with the goal of achieving worldwide efficiencies and coordination. But Nasser was already aware that Ford 2000 was not working out as well as expected. Working behind the scenes so as not to embarrass Trotman, Nasser quietly but firmly began to dismantle the Ford 2000 plan and to reverse its course by restoring control to regional operations in major marketplaces around the world.

So how have things worked out? So far, at least, Nasser's plans seem to be paying big dividends. For example, at the beginning of 1997 Ford announced a cost-reduction goal for the year of $1 billion. But as the year unfolded, Ford found its costs dropping more than expected and raised the goal to reductions in excess of $3 billion. Amazingly, 1997 was the first year in Ford's history that its annual costs dropped. One key part of Ford's success was its European operations, which exceeded its own $500 million cost-reduction goal. Ford's executives now want to cut another $3 billion in 1998.

Case Questions

1. Identify as many forms of control as possible in this case.
2. Which forms of control seem to be working the best? Which are more and less likely to contribute to Ford's long-term success?
3. Use the Internet to learn how well Ford is performing today.

Case References: "Ford Has a Tiger in Its Tank," *Business Week*, July 14, 1997, p. 30; and "Ford Triples Its Billion-Dollar Cost-Cutting Goal," *USA Today*, December 15, 1997, p. 1B.

CHAPTER NOTES

1. "No Detail Escapes the Attention of Abercrombie & Fitch's Chief," *Wall Street Journal*, October 7, 1997, pp. B1, B20; and *Hoover's Handbook of American Business 1997* (Austin, Texas: Hoover's Business Press, 1996), pp. 832–833.

2. Thomas A. Stewart, "Welcome to the Revolution," *Fortune*, December 13, 1993, pp. 66–77.

3. William Taylor, "Control in an Age of Chaos," *Harvard Business Review*, November–December 1994, pp. 64–70.

4. "At Travelers, It's Trim, Trim, Trim," *Business Week*, February 10, 1997, p. 101.

5. Mark Kroll, Peter Wright, Leslie Toombs, and Hadley Leavell, "Form of Control: A Critical Determinant of Acquisition Performance and CEO Rewards," *Strategic Management Journal*, 1997, Vol. 18, No. 2, pp. 85–96.

6. Sim Sitkin, Kathleen Sutcliffe, and Roger Schroeder, "Distinguishing Control from Learning in Total Quality Management: A Contingency Perspective," *Academy of Management Review*, 1994, Vol. 19, No. 3, pp. 537–564.

7. Robert Lusch and Michael Harvey, "The Case for an Off-Balance-Sheet Controller," *Sloan Management Review*, Winter 1994, pp. 101–110.

8. Edward E. Lawler III and John G. Rhode, *Information and Control in Organizations* (Pacific Palisades, Calif.: Goodyear, 1976).

9. Charles W. L. Hill, "Establishing a Standard: Competitive Strategy and Technological Standards in Winner-Take-All Industries," *Academy of Management Executive*, 1997, Vol. 11, No. 2, pp. 7–16.

10. "Luxury's Mandarin," *Newsweek*, August 25, 1997, p. 43.

11. See Belverd E. Needles Jr., Henry R. Anderson, and James C. Caldwell, *Principles of Accounting*, 7th ed. (Boston: Houghton Mifflin, 1999).

12. "The Tiger is on the Prowl," *Forbes*, April 21, 1997, pp. 42–43.

13. Thomas A. Stewart, "Why Budgets Are Bad for Business," *Fortune*, June 4, 1990, pp. 179–190.

14. Needles, Anderson, and Caldwell, *Principles of Accounting.*

15. "Mickey Mouse, CPA," *Forbes*, March 10, 1997, pp. 42–43.

16. Needles, Anderson, and Caldwell, *Principles of Accounting.*

17. "Questions about U.S. Shoe Corp. Continue to Mount," *Wall Street Journal*, April 5, 1990, p. A4.

18. "Auditors of Corporate Legal Bills Thrive," *Wall Street Journal*, February 13, 1991, p. B1.

19. William G. Ouchi, "The Transmission of Control through Organizational Hierarchy," *Academy of Management Journal*, June 1978, pp. 173–192; and Richard E. Walton, "From Control to Commitment in the Workplace," *Harvard Business Review*, March–April 1985, pp. 76–84.

20. Peter Lorange, Michael F. Scott Morton, and Sumantra Ghoshal, *Strategic Control* (St. Paul, Minn: West, 1986). See also Joseph C. Picken and Gregory G. Dess, "Out of (Strategic) Control," *Organizational Dynamics*, Summer 1997, pp. 35–45.

21. "Ikea's New Game Plan," *Business Week*, October 6, 1997, pp. 99–102.

22. See Hans Mjoen and Stephen Tallman, "Control and Performance in International Joint Ventures," *Organization Science*, May–June 1997, pp. 257–265.

23. For a recent study of effective control, see Diana Robertson and Erin Anderson, "Control System and Task Environment Effects on Ethical Judgment: An Exploratory Study of Industrial Salespeople," *Organization Science*, November 1993, pp. 617–629.

21

Managing for Total Quality in Organizations

OBJECTIVES

After studying this chapter, you should be able to:

■ Explain the meaning and importance of managing quality and total quality management.
■ Explain the meaning and importance of managing productivity, productivity trends, and ways to improve productivity.
■ Explain the nature of operations management and its role in managing quality.
■ Identify and discuss the components involved in designing operations systems for quality.
■ Discuss technology and its role in operations management.
■ Identify and discuss the components involved in using operations systems for quality.

Young Joseph Hartmann immigrated to the United States from Bavaria in 1877. Soon after arriving he started a small trunk-making company, using the skills he had learned in his homeland. Today, Hartmann Luggage, based in Lebanon, Tennessee, is among the most respected names in the luggage industry.

The firm makes a full line of luggage products, ranging from business cases to suitcases to computer cases. Hartmann luggage is also among the most expensive in the industry—even a small bag costs hundreds of dollars. So why are consumers willing to pay such a premium price for a suitcase? One reason is the quality that characterizes Hartmann bags.

Virtually all the work on a Hartmann bag is done by hand by trained workers who excel at their craft. The company uses only the highest quality materials, ranging from industrial strength belting leather to the strongest cloth and metal hinges.

But it is in the testing lab that Hartmann truly excels. Every new case or bag Hartmann intends to make is first tested for a lifetime of use before going into production. And most of this testing is done with special machines that Hartmann managers have conceptualized and constructed.

One of its machines resembles a Ferris wheel. A bag is placed inside the so-called tumble tester, and it slowly begins to turn. The bag tumbles like a towel in a clothes dryer, crashing against metal protrusions to simulate the treatment luggage typically receives in an airport baggage-handling system.

> ### "We have repaired or refurbished bags that are 40 years old."

Gail Jamison, Hartmann repair section chief, quoted in USA Today, *September 23, 1997, p. 12E.*

Each test run is for seven thousand turns, the equivalent of five years of bouncing and abuse.

Another testing machine lifts a briefcase up and down every few seconds, as many as one hundred thousand times. This test measures the wear and tear that lifting creates on the briefcase handle. If the wear is excessive, stronger leather is used. Another machine tests the amount of energy or tension needed to pull apart the stitches that hold a bag together. Among the most interesting machines Hartmann uses is a treadmill-like device that simulates asphalt, tile, and carpet—testing how a bag holds up to being dragged or pulled from an airport to a parking lot. Other machines test wheel strength; the durability of shoulder straps; and how well a bag stands up to ultraviolet rays, rain, humidity, heat, and ice.

Given the extensive battery of tests that Hartmann bags must pass, it's little wonder that the firm backs them with such a praiseworthy guarantee. And there's little wonder that consumers who can afford to pay the price are eager to own the firm's products.[1]

Managers at Hartmann Luggage have made quality a hallmark of their company's operations. This quality, in turn, allows them to charge premium prices and earn superior profits. But to be successful with this strategy, the firm must know that its products can withstand the demands of consumers and the rigors of daily and business use.

In this chapter we explore quality and its role in business today. We first discuss managing for total quality. We then discuss productivity, which is closely related to quality. Next we introduce operations management and its role in improving quality. The remaining two sections of the chapter cover designing operations systems and using operations systems for quality.

Managing Total Quality

Quality and productivity are major determinants of business success or failure today and are central issues in managing organizations.[2] But as we will see, achieving high levels of quality is not an easy accomplishment. Simply ordering that quality be improved is about as effective as waving a magic wand.[3]

The catalyst for the emergence of quality as a mainstream management concern was foreign business, especially Japanese. And nowhere was it more visible than in the auto industry. During the energy crisis in the late 1970s, many people bought Toyotas, Hondas, and Nissans because they were more fuel efficient than U.S. cars. Consumers soon found, however, that the Japanese cars were also of higher quality than U.S. cars. Parts fit together better, the trim work was neater, and the cars were more reliable. Thus, after the energy crisis subsided, Japanese cars remained formidable competitors because of their proven quality.

■ The Meaning of Quality

quality The totality of features and characteristics of a product or service that bear on its ability to satisfy stated or implied needs

The American Society for Quality Control defines **quality** as the totality of features and characteristics of a product or service that bear on its ability to satisfy stated or implied needs.[4] Quality has several attributes. Table 21.1 lists eight basic dimensions that determine the quality of a particular product or service. For example, a product that has durability and is reliable is of higher quality than a product with less durability and reliability.

Quality is also relative. For example, a Lincoln Continental is a higher-grade car than a Ford Taurus, which, in turn, is a higher-grade car than a Ford Escort. The difference in quality stems from differences in design and other features. The Escort, however, is considered a high-quality car relative to its engineering specifications and price. Likewise, the Taurus and Continental may also be high-quality cars, given their standards and prices. Thus, quality is both an absolute and a relative concept.

Quality is relevant for both products and services. Although its importance for products like cars and computers was perhaps recognized first, service firms ranging from airlines to restaurants have also come to see that quality is a vi-

1. **Performance.** A product's primary operating characteristic. Examples are automobile acceleration and a television set's picture clarity.
2. **Features.** Supplements to a product's basic functioning characteristics, such as power windows on a car.
3. **Reliability.** A probability of not malfunctioning during a specified period.
4. **Conformance.** The degree to which a product's design and operating characteristics meet established standards.
5. **Durability.** A measure of product life.
6. **Serviceability.** The speed and ease of repair.
7. **Aesthetics.** How a product looks, feels, tastes, and smells.
8. **Perceived quality.** As seen by a customer.

TABLE 21.1
Eight Dimensions of Quality

These eight dimensions generally capture the meaning of quality, which is a critically important ingredient to organizational success today. Understanding the basic meaning of quality is a good first step to more effectively managing it.

Source: Adapted and reprinted by permission of *Harvard Business Review,* from "Competing on the Eight Dimensions of Quality," by David Garvin, November/December 1987. Copyright © 1987 by the President and Fellows of Harvard College, all rights reserved.

tally important determinant of their success or failure. Service quality, as we will discuss later in this chapter, has thus also become a major competitive issue in U.S. industry today.

■ The Importance of Quality

To help underscore the importance of quality, the U.S. government created the **Malcolm Baldrige Award,** named for the former Secretary of Commerce who championed quality in U.S. industry. The award, administered by an agency of the Department of Commerce, is given annually to firms that achieve major improvements in the quality of their products or services. That is, the award is based on changes in quality, as opposed to absolute quality.

Recent winners of the Baldrige Award include Motorola; the Cadillac division of General Motors; and divisions of Texas Instruments, AT&T, Xerox, and Westinghouse. In addition, numerous other quality awards have been created. For example, the Rochester Institute of Technology and *USA Today* award their Quality Cup to individual teams of workers within organizations, not to entire organizations. Quality is also an important concern for individual manager and organizations for three very specific reasons: competition, productivity, and costs.[5]

Malcolm Baldrige Award   Named after a former Secretary of Commerce, this prestigious award is given to firms that achieve major quality improvements

Competition   Quality has become one of the most competitive points in business today. Among Ford, Chrysler, and General Motors, each argues, for example, that its cars are higher in quality than the cars of the others. Similarly, among American, United, and Delta airlines, each argues that it provides the best and most reliable service. Indeed, it seems that virtually every U.S. business has adopted quality as a major point of competition. Thus a business that fails to keep pace may find itself falling behind not only foreign competition but also other U.S. firms.[6]

Productivity   Managers also now recognize that quality and productivity are related. In the past many managers thought that they could increase output (productivity) only by decreasing quality. Managers today have learned the hard way that such an assumption is almost always wrong. If a firm installs a meaningful quality enhancement program, three things are likely to result. First, the number of defects is likely to decrease, causing fewer returns from customers. Second, because the number of defects goes down, resources (materials and people) dedicated to reworking flawed output will be decreased. Third, because making employees responsible for quality reduces the need for quality inspectors, the organization can produce more units with fewer resources.

Costs Improved quality also lowers costs. Poor quality results in higher returns from customers, high warranty costs, and lawsuits from customers injured by faulty products. Future sales are lost because of disgruntled customers. An organization with quality problems often has to increase inspection expenses just to catch defective products. We noted in Chapter 20, for example, how Whistler Corporation was using 100 of its 250 employees just to fix poorly assembled radar detectors.[7]

TQM A strategic commitment by top management to make quality a guiding factor in everything it does

FIGURE 21.1
Total Quality Management

Quality is one of the most important issues facing organizations today. Total quality management, or TQM, is a comprehensive effort to enhance an organization's product or service quality. TQM involves the five basic dimensions shown here. Each is important and must be effectively addressed if the organization truly expects to increase quality.

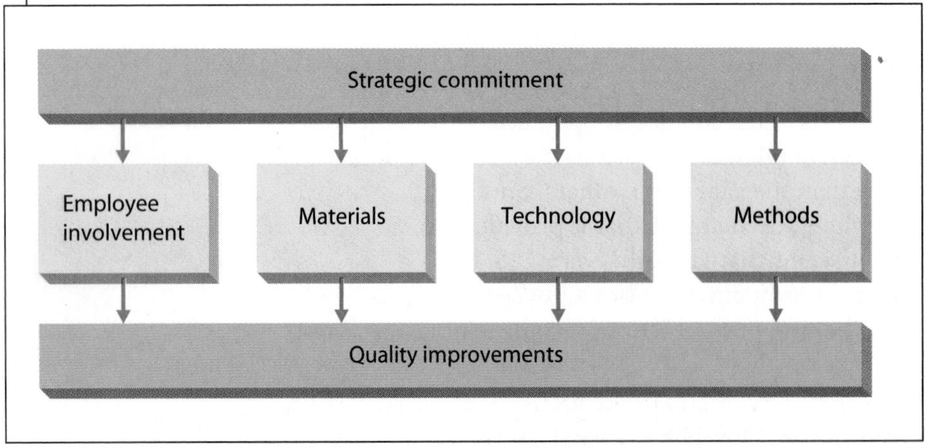

■ Total Quality Management

Once an organization decides to enhance the quality of its products and services, it must implement the decision. The most pervasive approach to managing quality has been called **total quality management,** or **TQM**—a real and meaningful effort by an organization to change its whole approach to business to make quality a guiding factor in everything the organization does.[8] Figure 21.1 highlights the major ingredients in TQM.

Strategic Commitment The starting point for TQM is a strategic commitment by top management. Such commitment is important for several reasons. First, the organizational culture must change to recognize that quality is not just an ideal but is instead an objective goal that must be pursued.[9] Second, a decision to pursue the goal of quality carries with it some real costs—for expenditures such as new equipment and facilities. Thus, without a commitment from top management, quality improvement will prove to be just a slogan or gimmick, with little or no real change.

Employee Involvement Employee involvement is another critical ingredient in TQM. Virtually all successful quality

Strategic commitment → Employee involvement, Materials, Technology, Methods → Quality improvements

remodeled plant. The company also wiped out the need for approvals by eliminating most managerial positions and set up teams as a basis for organizing work. In another example, stressing the importance of the schedule helped Motorola build a new plant and start production of a new product in only eighteen months.

ISO 9000   Still another useful technique for improving quality is ISO 9000. **ISO 9000** refers to a set of quality standards created by the International Organization for Standardization (ISO). These standards cover such areas as product testing, employee training, record keeping, supplier relations, and repair polices and procedures. Firms that want to meet these standards apply for certification and are audited by a firm chosen by the ISO's domestic affiliate (in the United States, the American National Standards Institute). The ISO auditors review every aspect of the candidate's business operations in relation to the standards. Many firms report that merely preparing for an ISO 9000 audit has been helpful by pointing out obvious areas where quality can be improved. In addition, firms such as General Electric, DuPont, Eastman Kodak, British Telecom, and Philips Electronics are urging—or in some cases requiring—their suppliers to attain ISO 9000 certification.[15]

ISO 9000 is an increasingly important TQM tool in may organizations. These workers are employed at National Steel. Here they celebrate the announcement that their division, Pace, has met ISO 9000 standards and is now certified under all quality requirements imposed by the ISO. The firm believes that this designation will improve its competitiveness and generate new business.

Statistical Quality Control   A final quality control technique is **statistical quality control (SQC).** As the term suggests, SQC is primarily concerned with managing quality.[16] Moreover, it is a set of specific statistical techniques that can be used to monitor quality. *Acceptance sampling* involves sampling finished goods to ensure that quality standards have been met. Acceptance sampling is effective only when the correct percentage of products that should be tested (for example, 2, 5, or 25 percent) is determined. This decision is especially important when the test renders the product useless. Flash cubes, wine, and collapsible steering wheels, for example, are consumed or destroyed during testing. Another SQC method is in-process sampling. *In-process sampling* involves evaluating products during production so that needed changes can be made. The painting department of a furniture company might periodically check the tint of the paint it is using. The company can then adjust the color to conform to customer standards. The advantage of in-process sampling is that it allows companies to detect problems before they accumulate.

speed   The time an organization needs to accomplish its activities, including developing, making, and distributing its products or services

ISO 9000   A set of quality standards created by the International Organization for Standardization

SQC   A set of specific statistical techniques that can be used to monitor quality; includes acceptance sampling and in-process sampling

MANAGEMENT
IMPLICATIONS

All managers today need to understand and appreciate the importance of total quality. Specifically, they need to understand the meaning of quality as well as its role in competitive strategy. The ingredients of total quality management are also important in many organizations today. Various TQM tools and techniques are also useful for improving quality. ▬

Managing Productivity

Although the current focus on quality by American companies is a relatively recent phenomenon, managers have been aware of the importance of productivity for many years. The stimulus for this attention was a recognition that the gap between productivity in the United States and productivity in other industrialized countries was narrowing. This section describes the meaning of productivity and underscores its importance. After summarizing recent productivity trends, we suggest ways that organizations can increase their productivity.

■ The Meaning of Productivity

productivity An economic measure of efficiency that summarizes what is produced relative to the resources used to produce it

In a general sense, **productivity** is an economic measure of efficiency that summarizes the value of outputs relative to the value of the inputs used to create them.[17] Productivity can be and often is assessed at different levels of analysis and in different forms.

Levels of Productivity *Level of productivity* means the units of analysis used to calculate or define productivity. For example, aggregate productivity is the total level of productivity achieved by a country. Industry productivity is the total productivity achieved by all the firms in a particular industry. Company productivity, just as the term suggests, is the level of productivity achieved by an individual company. Unit and individual productivity refer to the productivity achieved by a unit or department within an organization and the level of productivity attained by a single person.

Forms of Productivity There are many different forms of productivity. Total factor productivity is defined by the following formula:

$$\text{Productivity} = \frac{\text{Outputs}}{\text{Inputs}}$$

Total factor productivity is an overall indicator of how well an organization uses all of its resources, such as labor, capital, materials, and energy to create all of its products and services. The biggest problem with total factor productivity is that all the ingredients must be expressed in the same terms—dollars (it is difficult to add hours of labor to number of units of a raw material in a meaningful way). Total factor productivity also gives little insight into how things can be changed to improve productivity. Consequently, most organizations prefer to calculate a partial productivity ratio that uses only one category of resource. For example, labor productivity could be calculated by this simple formula:

$$\text{Labor Productivity} = \frac{\text{Outputs}}{\text{Direct Labor}}$$

This method has two advantages. First, it is not necessary to transform the units of input into some other unit. Second, this method provides managers with specific insights into how changing different resource inputs affects productivity. Suppose that an organization can manufacture 100 units of a particular product with twenty hours of direct labor. The organization's labor productivity index is five (or five units per labor hour). Now suppose that worker efficiency is increased (through one of the ways to be discussed later in this chapter) so that the same twenty hours of labor results in the manufacture of 120 units of the product. The labor productivity index increases to six (six units per labor hour), and the firm can see the direct results of a specific managerial action.

■ The Importance of Productivity

Managers have various reasons for wanting their firms to maintain high levels of productivity. Firm productivity is a primary determinant of an organization's level of profitability and, ultimately, its ability to survive. An organization that is more productive than another will have more products to sell at lower prices and have more profits to reinvest in other areas. Productivity also partially determines people's standards of living within a particular country. At an economic level, businesses consume resources and produce goods and services. In turn, the goods and services created within a country can be used by that country's own citizens or exported for sale in other countries. The more goods and services the businesses within a country can produce, the more goods and services the country's citizens will have. Even goods that are exported result in financial resources flowing back into the home country. Thus the citizens of a highly productive country are likely to have notably higher standards of living than are the citizens of a country with low productivity.

■ Productivity Trends

The United States has the highest level of productivity in the world. For example, Japanese workers produce only about 76 percent as much as U.S. workers, whereas German workers produce about 84 percent as much.[18] But in recent years other countries have been closing the gap.[19] This trend was a primary factor in the decisions made by U.S. businesses to retrench, retool, and become more competitive in the world marketplace. For example, General Electric's dishwasher plant in Louisville has cut its inventory requirements by 50 percent, reduced labor costs from 15 percent to only 10 percent of total manufacturing costs, and cut product development time in half. As a result of these kinds of efforts, productivity trends have now leveled out and U.S. workers are generally maintaining their lead in most industries.

One important factor that has hurt U.S. productivity has been the tremendous growth of the service sector in the United States. While this sector grew, its productivity levels did not. One part of this problem relates to measurement. For example, it is fairly easy to calculate the number of tons of steel produced at a Bethlehem Steel mill and divide it by the number of labor hours used; it is more difficult to determine the output of an attorney or a Certified Public Accountant. Still, virtually everyone agrees that improving service-sector productivity is the next major hurdle facing U.S. business.[20]

Figure 21.2 illustrates recent trends in productivity growth for both the total U.S. economy and broken down into manufacturing and services (agricultural productivity is not included). As you can see, manufacturing productivity stalled from the mid-1970s to the early 1980s but has been increasing since that time. Service sector productivity, meanwhile, has remained relatively stable. Total productivity, therefore, has been increasing but only at a modest pace.

■ Improving Productivity

How does a business or industry improve its productivity? Numerous specific suggestions made by experts generally fall into two broad categories: improving operations and increasing employee involvement.

Improving Operations   One way that firms can improve operations is by spending more on research and development. R&D spending helps identify new products, new uses for existing products, and new methods for making products. Each of these contributes to productivity. For example, Bausch & Lomb almost missed the boat on extended-wear contact lenses because the company had neglected R&D. When the firm realized that its major competitors were almost a year ahead in developing the new lenses, management made R&D a top-priority concern. As a result, the company made several scientific breakthroughs, shortened the time needed to introduce new products, and greatly enhanced both total sales and profits—and all with a smaller work force than the company used to employ. Even though other countries are greatly increasing their R&D spending, the United States continues to be the world leader in this area.

Another way firms can boost productivity through operations is by reassessing and revamping their transformation facilities. We noted earlier how one of GE's modernized plants does a better job than six antiquated ones. Just building a new factory is no guarantee of success, but IBM, Ford, Allen-Bradley, Caterpillar, and many other businesses have achieved dramatic productivity gains by revamping their production facilities. Facilities refinements are not limited to manufacturers. Most McDonald's restaurants now have drive-through windows, and many are moving soft-drink dispensers out to the restaurant floor so that customers can get their own drinks. Each of these moves is an attempt to increase the speed with which customers can be served and thus to increase productivity.

FIGURE 21.2
Manufacturing and Service Productivity Growth Trends (1970–1993)

Both manufacturing productivity and service productivity in the United States continue to grow, although manufacturing productivity is growing at a faster pace. Total productivity, therefore, also continues to grow.

Source: Graph "Productivity Growth" from Myron Magnet, "The Productivity Payoff Arrives," *Fortune,* June 27, 1994, p. 79. © 1995 Time Inc. All rights reserved. Used by permission.

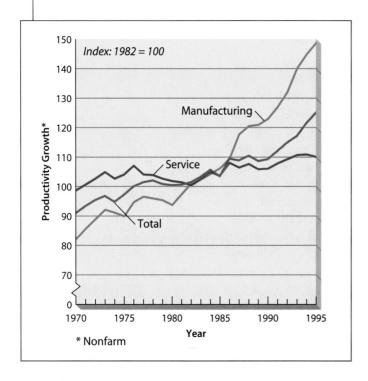

Increasing Employee Involvement The other major thrust in productivity enhancement has been toward employee involvement. We noted earlier that participation can enhance quality. So, too, can it boost productivity. Examples of this involvement are an individual worker being given a bigger voice in how she does her job, a formal agreement of cooperation between management and labor, and total involvement throughout the organization.[21] GE eliminated most of the supervisors at its one new circuit-breaker plant and put control in the hands of workers.

Another method popular in the United States is increasing the flexibility of an organization's work force by training employees to perform a number of different jobs. Such cross-training allows the firm to function with fewer workers because workers can be transferred easily to areas where they are most needed. Being proficient in more jobs and having a better understanding of how the overall firm operates, in turn, can result in employees being more satisfied with their work and more involved with the company. For example, the Lechmere department store in Sarasota, Florida, encourages workers to learn numerous jobs within the store. One person in the store can operate a forklift in the stockroom, serve as a cashier, or provide customer service on the sales floor. At a Motorola plant, 397 of 400 employees have learned at least two skills under a similar program.

Rewards are essential to making employee involvement work. Firms must reward people for learning new skills and using them proficiently. At Motorola, for example, workers who master a new skill are assigned for five days to a job requiring them to use that skill. If they perform with no defects, they are moved to a higher pay grade, and then they move back and forth between jobs as they are needed. If there is a performance problem, they receive more training and practice. This approach is fairly new, but preliminary indicators suggest that it can increase productivity significantly. Many unions resist such programs because they threaten job security and reduce a person's identification with one skill or craft.

MANAGEMENT IMPLICATIONS Managers should understand the concept of productivity and appreciate its importance. In addition, they should be familiar with productivity trends and with common methods for improving productivity.

Managing Quality Through Operations Management

We noted earlier that both quality and productivity can be enhanced through various elements of operations. But what exactly are operations? And how are they managed? **Operations management** is the set of managerial activities that an organization uses to transform resource inputs into products and services. When IBM buys electronic components, assembles them into computers,

operations management The total set of managerial activities that an organization uses to transform resource inputs into products, services, or both

Manufacturing and production are frequently key components of a company's quality management efforts. IGT Corporation makes electronic slot machines that are sold to casinos and other gambling operations around the world. Because of the stringent government regulations that affect this industry, and the potential costs that errors might create, it is extremely important that all machines be of the highest quality. Thus this inspector is closely examining a transparent cover sheet which will announce whether or not the gambler has struck it rich!

and then ships them to customers, it is relying on operations management. When a Pizza Hut employee orders food and paper products and then combines dough, cheese, and tomato paste to create a pizza, he or she is using operations management.

■ The Importance of Operations

Operations is an important functional concern for organizations because efficient and effective management of operations goes a long way toward ensuring quality and productivity. Inefficient or ineffective operations management, on the other hand, will almost inevitably lead to lower levels of both quality and productivity. In an economic sense, operations management provides utility, or value, of one type or another, depending on the nature of the firm's products or services. If the product is a physical good, such as a Yamaha motorcycle, operations provides *form utility* by combining many dissimilar inputs (sheet metal, rubber, paint, combustion engines, and human craftsmanship) to produce the desired output. The inputs are converted from their incoming forms into a new physical form. This conversion is typical of manufacturing operations and essentially reflects the organization's technology.

In contrast, the operations activities of American Airlines provide *time and place utility* through its services. The airline transports passengers and freight according to agreed-on departure and arrival places and times. Other service operations, such as a Coors Brothers Beer distributorship or The Gap retail chain, provide place and possession utility by bringing the customer and products made by others together. Although the organizations in these examples produce different kinds of products or services, their operations processes share many important features.[22]

■ Manufacturing and Production

manufacturing A form of business that combines and transforms resource inputs into tangible outcomes

Because manufacturing once dominated U.S. industry, the entire area of operations management used to be called production management. **Manufacturing** is a form of business that combines and transforms resources into tangible outcomes that are then sold to others. The Goodyear Tire and Rubber Company is a manufacturer because it combines rubber and chemical compounds and uses blending equipment and molding machines to ultimately create tires. Broyhill is a manufacturer because it buys wood and metal components, pads, and fabric and then combines them into furniture.

During the 1970s, manufacturing entered a long period of decline in the United States, primarily because of foreign competition. U.S. firms had grown lax and sluggish, and new foreign competitors came onto the scene with new equipment and much higher levels of efficiency. For example, steel companies in the Far East were able to produce high-quality steel for much lower prices than were U.S. companies like Bethlehem Steel and U.S. Steel (now USX Corporation). Faced with a battle for survival, many companies underwent a long and difficult period of change by eliminating waste and transforming themselves into leaner and more efficient and responsive entities. They reduced their work forces dramatically, closed antiquated or unnecessary plants, and modernized their remaining plants. In recent years, their efforts have started to pay dividends as U.S. business has regained its competitive position in many different industries. Although manufacturers from other parts of the world are still formidable competitors and U.S. firms may never again be competitive in some markets, the overall picture is much better than it was just a few years ago. And prospects continue to look bright.

■ Service Operations

During the decline of the manufacturing sector, a tremendous growth in the service sector kept the U.S. economy from declining at the same rate. A **service organization** is one that transforms resources into an intangible output and creates time or place utility for its customers. For example, Merrill Lynch Co. makes stock transactions for its customers, Avis leases cars to its customers, and your local hairdresser cuts your hair. In 1947 the service sector was responsible for less than half of the U.S. gross national product (GNP). By 1975, however, this figure reached 65 percent, and by 1995 it was more than 75 percent. The service sector has been responsible for almost 90 percent of all new jobs created in the United States during the 1990s. Managers have learned that many of the tools, techniques, and methods used in a factory are also useful to a service firm. For example, managers of automobile plants and hair salons have to decide how to design their facility, identify the best location for it, determine optimal capacity, make decisions about inventory storage, set procedures for purchasing raw materials, and set standards for productivity and quality. "The Quality Challenge" describes the interrelationship between quality and services at Air France.

service organization An organization that transforms resources into services

■ The Role of Operations in Organizational Strategy

Operations management is clearly very important to organizations. Beyond its direct impact on quality and productivity, it also directly influences the organization's overall level of effectiveness. For example, the deceptively simple strategic decision of whether to stress high quality regardless of cost, lowest possible cost regardless of quality, or some combination of the two, has

Air France Boosts Service Quality and Productivity

In the international airline industry most of the press is usually devoted to British Air, American Airlines, Lufthansa, and KLM—huge companies with a reputation for exemplary passenger service and a record of profitability. Often lost in the shuffle is Air France, generally overlooked because of its history of indifferent service and weak financial performance.

But Air France has recently been trying mightily to change its image. It wants to become a more attractive carrier to well-heeled business travelers and jet-setters, for example, and to enhance its earnings and market share. And it's trying to increase both its service quality and its productivity simultaneously.

On the service side, Air France has mandated extensive new service training for all its employees. It has also improved its meal service and on-board amenities—especially in its business-class and first-class compartments—and

"Air France is making an awful lot of progress in a very difficult environment, which France is."

Jon Ash, airline industry expert*

launched major new advertising campaigns to lure more business travelers to its international flights.

On the productivity side, like many other firms Air France is trying to do more with less. It has cut its route structure, for example, from 220 locations in 106 countries in 1991 to 197 locations in 98 countries today. The firm has also reduced its payroll by 5 percent. Moreover, Air France has been working diligently to cut stifling work rules and to reduce its internal bureaucracy. And the company has been investing heavily in automation and other new technology to become more competitive with other major international carriers. Thus it seems that Air France may be just about ready to take off.

References: *"Air France's Restructuring Taking Off,"* USA Today, January 2, 1997, p. 6B (*quote on p. 6B); and *"Can Air France Make Its Connection?"* Business Week, June 17, 1996, p. 126.

numerous implications. A highest-possible-quality strategy will dictate state-of-the-art technology and rigorous control of product design and materials specifications. A combination strategy might call for lower-grade technology and less concern about product design and materials specifications. Just as strategy affects operations management, so too does operations management affect strategy. Suppose that a firm decides to upgrade the quality of its products or services. The organization's ability to implement the decision depends in part on current production capabilities and other resources. If existing technology will not permit higher-quality work and if the organization lacks the resources to replace its technology, increasing quality to the desired new standards will be difficult.

MANAGEMENT IMPLICATIONS The importance of operations management should be obvious to all managers. They should also understand the similarities and differences between manufacturing and service businesses. Finally, managers need to know the role of operations management in their firm's strategy. ■

Designing Operations Systems for Quality

The problems that operations managers face as they attempt to improve quality revolve around the acquisition and utilization of resources for conversion. Their goals include both efficiency and effectiveness. As they design their operations systems, operations managers must address a number of issues. The most basic considerations are product-service mix, capacity, and facilities.

Product-Service Mix

A natural starting point in designing operations systems to enhance quality and productivity is determining the **product-service mix.** This decision flows from corporate, business, and marketing strategies. Managers have to make a number of decisions about their products and services, starting with how many and what kinds to offer. The Procter & Gamble Co., for example, makes regular, tartar-control, and gel formulas of Crest toothpaste and packages them in several different sizes of tubes and pumps. Decisions also have to be made regarding the level of quality desired, the optimal cost of each product or service, and exactly how each is to be designed. GE, for example, reduced the number of parts in its industrial circuit breakers from 28,000 to 1,275. The whole process involved product design.

product-service mix How many and what kinds of products or services (or both) to offer

Capacity

The **capacity** decision involves choosing the amount of products, services, or both that can be produced by the organization. Determining whether to build a factory capable of making five thousand or eight thousand units per day is a capacity decision. So, too, is deciding whether to build a restaurant with 100 or 150 seats or a bank with five or ten teller stations. The capacity decision is truly a high-risk one because of the uncertainties of future product demand and the large monetary stakes involved. An organization that builds capacity exceeding its needs may commit resources (capital investment) that will never be recovered. Many firms made this mistake during the 1960s and 1970s. Alternatively, an organization can build a facility with a capacity that is smaller than the expected demand. Doing so may result in lost market opportunities, but it may also free capital resources for use elsewhere in the organization.

A major consideration in determining capacity is demand. A company operating with fairly constant monthly demand might build a plant capable of producing an amount each month roughly equivalent to its demand. But if its market is characterized by seasonal fluctuations, building a smaller plant to meet normal demand and then adding extra shifts during peak periods might be the most effective choice. Likewise, a restaurant that needs 150 seats for Saturday night but never needs more than 100 at any other time during the week would probably be foolish to expand to 150 seats. During the rest of the week, it must still pay to light, heat, cool, and clean the excess capacity.

capacity The amount of products, services, or both that an organization can produce

Properly designed operations systems can dictate the potential quality levels an organization can achieve. At Ipsilon Networks, for example, managers are hard at work creating new forms of network software that might one day challenge Cisco Systems for industry leadership. An open workplace where engineers work in cubicles is generally thought to be the most cost-effective way to facilitate interaction among engineers. As a prank, however, CEO Brian Nesmith and founder Tom Lyon recently built a temporary "office" for an engineer who complained about the lack of privacy in his cubicle.

■ Facilities

Facilities are the physical locations where products or services are created, stored, and distributed. Major decisions pertain to location and layout.

Location   **Location** is the physical positioning or geographic site of facilities; it must be determined by the needs and requirements of the organization. A company that relies heavily on railroads for transportation needs to be located close to rail facilities. GE decided that it did not need six plants to make circuit breakers, so it invested heavily in automating one plant and closed the other five. Different organizations in the same industry may have different facilities requirements. Benetton Group SPA uses only one distribution center for the entire world, whereas Kmart Corp. has several distribution centers in the United States alone. A retail business must choose its location very carefully to be convenient for consumers.

Layout   The choice of physical configuration, or the **layout,** of facilities is closely related to other operations decisions. The three entirely different layout alternatives shown in Figure 21.3 help demonstrate the importance of the layout decision. A **product layout** is appropriate when large quantities of a single product are needed. It makes sense to custom design a straight-line flow of work for a product when a specific task is performed at each work station as each unit flows past. Most assembly lines use this format. For example, IBM's personal computer factories use a product layout.

Process layouts are used in operations settings that create or process a variety of products. Auto repair shops and health-care clinics are good examples. Each car and each person is a separate "product." The needs of each incoming job are diagnosed as it enters the operations system, and the job is routed through the unique sequence of work stations needed to create the desired finished product. In a process layout each type of conversion task is centralized in a single work station or department. All welding is done in one designated shop location, and any car that requires welding is moved to that area. This setup is in contrast to the product layout in which several different work stations may perform welding operations if the conversion task sequence so dictates.

The **fixed-position layout** is used when the organization is creating a few very large and complex products. Aircraft manufacturers like the Boeing Co. and shipbuilders like Newport News use this method. An assembly line capable of moving a 747 would require an enormous plant; instead, the airplane itself remains stationary, and people and machines move around it as it is assembled.

MANAGEMENT IMPLICATIONS Managers need to be familiar with how the product-service mix, capacity, and facilities decisions and issues contribute to total quality management and organizational effectiveness. ▬

Technology and Quality

A related element of operations management that affects quality is technology. In Chapter 3 we defined **technology** as the set of processes and systems that organizations use to convert resources into products or services.

■ Manufacturing Technology

Organizations use numerous forms of manufacturing technology. In Chapter 12 we discussed the research of Joan Woodward in which she identified three forms of technology—unit or small batch, large batch or mass production, and

facilities The physical locations where products or services are created, stored, and distributed

location The physical positioning or geographic site of facilities

layout The physical configuration of facilities, the arrangement of equipment within facilities, or both

product layout A physical configuration of facilities arranged around the product; used when large quantities of a single product are needed

process layout A physical configuration of facilities arranged around the process; used in facilities that create or process a variety of products

fixed-position layout A physical configuration of facilities arranged around a single work area; used for the manufacture of large and complex products such as airplanes

technology The set of processes and systems used by organizations to convert resources into products or services

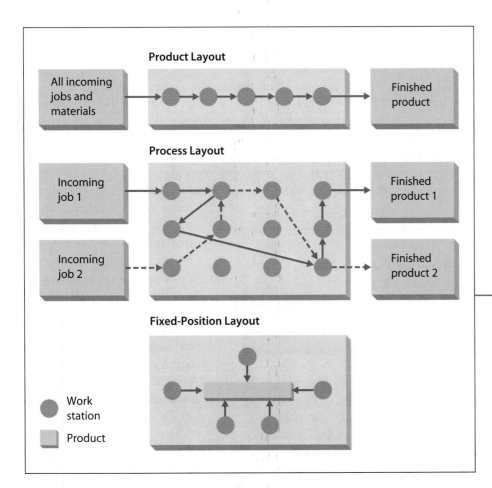

FIGURE 21.3
Approaches to Facilities Layout

When a manufacturer produces large quantities of a product (such as cars or computers), it may arrange its facilities into an assembly line (product layout). In a process layout, the work (such as patients in a hospital or custom pieces of furniture) moves through a variety of work stations. Locomotives and bridges are both manufactured in a fixed-position layout.

continuous process.[23] She also found that each form of technology was associated with a specific type of organization structure. Of course, newer forms of technology, which Woodward did not consider, also warrant attention. Two of these are automation and computer-assisted manufacturing.

Automation **Automation** is the process of designing work so that it can be completely or almost completely performed by machines. Because automated machines operate quickly and make few errors, they increase the amount of work that can be done. Thus, automation helps to improve products and services, and it fosters innovation. Automation is the most recent step in the development of machines and machine-controlling devices, although such devices have been around since the 1700s. James Watt, a Scottish engineer, invented a mechanical speed control to regulate the speed of steam engines in 1787. The Jacquard loom, developed by a French inventor, was controlled by paper cards with holes punched in them. Early accounting and computing equipment was controlled by similar punched cards.

automation The process of designing work so that it can be completely or almost completely performed by machines

Automation relies on feedback, information, sensors, and a control mechanism. Feedback is the flow of information from the machine to the sensor. Sensors are the parts of the system that gather information and compare it to some preset standards. The control mechanism is the device that sends instructions to the automatic machine. Early automatic machines were primitive, and the use of automation was relatively slow to develop. The example in Figure 21.4 illustrates these elements. A thermostat has sensors that monitor air temperature and compare it to a preset low value. If the air temperature falls below the preset value, the thermostat sends an electrical signal to the furnace, turning it on. The furnace heats the air. When the sensors detect that the air temperature has reached a value higher than the low preset value, the thermostat stops the furnace. The last step (shutting off the furnace) is known as feedback, a critical component of any automated operation.

The big move to automate factories began during World War II. The shortage of skilled workers and the development of high-speed computers combined to bring about a tremendous interest in automation. Programmable automation (the use of computers to control machines) was introduced during this era, far outstripping conventional automation (the use of mechanical or electromechanical devices to control machines).[24] The automobile industry began to use automatic machines for a variety of jobs. In fact, the term *automation* came into use in the 1950s in the automobile industry. The chemical and oil-refining industries also began to use computers to regulate production. This type of

FIGURE 21.4
A Simple Automatic Control Mechanism

All automation includes feedback, information, sensors, and a control mechanism. A simple thermostat is an example of automation. Another example is Benetton's distribution center in Italy. Orders are received, items pulled from stock and packaged for shipment, and invoices are prepared and transmitted with no human intervention.

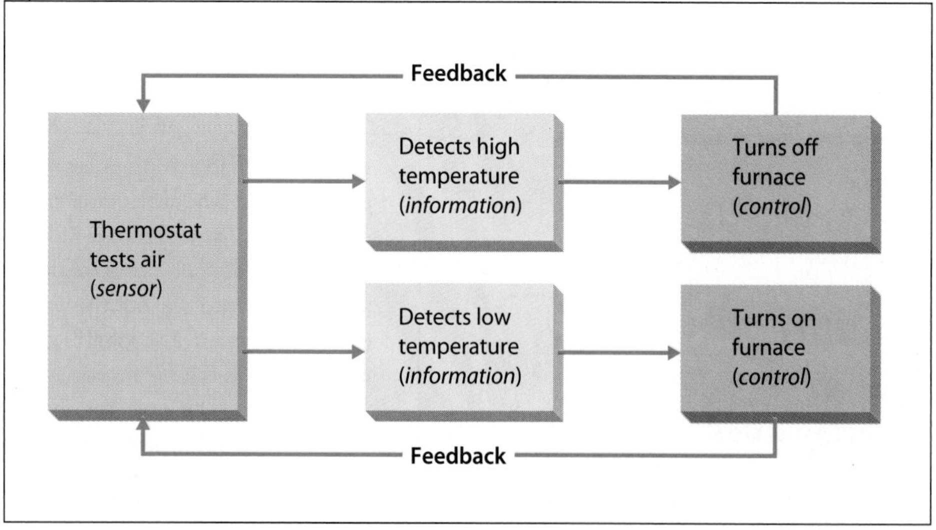

computerized, or programmable, automation presents the greatest opportunities and challenges for management today.

The impact of automation on people in the workplace is complex. In the short term people whose jobs are automated find themselves without jobs. In the long term, however, more jobs are created than are lost. Nevertheless, not all companies can help displaced workers find new jobs, so the human costs of automation are sometimes high. In the coal industry, for instance, automation has been used primarily in mining. The output per miner has risen dramatically from the 1950s on. The demand for coal, however, has decreased, and productivity gains resulting from automation have lessened the need for miners. Consequently, a lot of workers have lost their jobs, and the industry has not been able to absorb them. In contrast, in the electronics industry the rising demand for products has led to increasing employment opportunities despite the use of automation.

Computer-Assisted Manufacturing   Current extensions of automation generally revolve around computer-assisted manufacturing. *Computer-assisted manufacturing* is technology that relies on computers to design or manufacture products. One type of computer-assisted manufacturing is *computer-aided design* (CAD)—the use of computers to design parts and complete products and to simulate performance so that engineers and designers do not need to build prototypes. McDonnell Douglas uses CAD to study hydraulic tubing in DC-10s. Japan's automotive industry uses it to speed up car design. GE used CAD to change the design of circuit breakers, and Benetton uses CAD to design new styles and products. Oneida Ltd., the table flatware firm, used CAD to design a new spoon in only two days.[25]

CAD is usually combined with *computer-aided manufacturing (CAM)* to ensure that the design moves smoothly to production. The production computer shares the design computer's information and is able to have machines with the proper settings ready when production is needed. A CAM system is especially useful for reorders because the computer can quickly produce the desired product, prepare labels and copies of orders, and ship the product to the customer.

Closely aligned with this approach is *computer-integrated manufacturing (CIM)*. In CIM, CAD and CAM are linked together, and computers adjust machine placements and settings automatically to enhance both the complexity and the flexibility of scheduling. The computer controls all manufacturing activities. Because the computer can access the company's other information systems, CIM is a powerful and complex management control tool.[26]

A *flexible manufacturing system (FMS)* usually has robotic work units or workstations, assembly lines, and robotic carts or some other form of computer-controlled transport system to move material as needed from one part of the system to another. FMSs, such as the one at Lexmark's manufacturing facility in Lexington, Kentucky, rely on computers to coordinate and integrate automated production and materials handling.[27]

These systems are not without disadvantages, however.[28] For example, because they represent fundamental change, they also generate resistance. Additionally, because of their tremendous complexity, CAD systems are not always reliable. CIM systems are so expensive that they raise the breakeven point for

robot Any artificial device that can perform functions ordinarily thought to be appropriate for human beings

firms using them.[29] Consequently, the firm must operate at high levels of production and sales to be able to afford the systems.

Robotics   One of the newest trends in manufacturing technology is robotics. A **robot** is any artificial device that performs functions ordinarily thought to be appropriate for human beings. Robotics refers to the science and technology of the construction, maintenance, and use of robots. The use of industrial robots has steadily increased since 1980 and is expected to continue to increase slowly as more companies recognize the benefits that accrue to users of industrial robots.

Welding was one of the first applications for robots and it continues to be the area for most applications. In second place and close behind is materials handling. Other applications include machine loading and unloading; painting and finishing; assembly; casting; and machining applications such as cutting, grinding, polishing, drilling, sanding, buffing, and deburring. Chrysler, for instance, replaced about two hundred welders with fifty robots on an assembly line and increased productivity about 20 percent.[30] The use of robots in inspection work is increasing. They can check for cracks and holes, and they can be equipped with vision systems to perform visual inspections.

Robots are also beginning to move from the factory floor to all manner of other applications. The Dallas police used a robot to apprehend a suspect who had barricaded himself in an apartment building. The robot smashed a window and reached with its mechanical arm into the building. The suspect panicked and ran outside. At the Long Beach Memorial Hospital in California, brain surgeons are assisted by a robot arm that drills into the patient's skull with excellent precision. Some newer applications involve remote work. For example, the use of robot submersibles controlled from the surface can help divers in remote locations. Surveillance robots fitted with microwave sensors can do things that a human guard cannot do, such as "seeing" through nonmetallic walls and in the dark. In other applications automated farming ("agrimation") uses robot harvesters to pick fruit from trees.[31]

Some small manufacturers also use robots. For example, at an upholstery shop a robot slices carpeting to fit the inside of custom vans, and a novelties company uses a robot to stretch balloons flat so that they can be spray painted with slogans. At a jewelry company a robot assists in the process of laser engraving class rings. The robots in these examples are lighter, faster, stronger, and more intelligent than those used in heavy manufacturing and are the types that more and more organizations will be using in the future.[32]

■ Service Technology

Service technology is also changing rapidly. And it, too, is moving more and more toward automated systems and procedures. In banking, for example, new technological breakthroughs have led to automated teller machines and made it much easier to move funds between accounts or between different banks. Some people now have their pay checks deposited directly into a checking account from which many of their bills are then automatically paid. And credit card transactions by Visa customers are recorded and billed electronically.

Hotels use increasingly sophisticated technology to accept and record room reservations. Universities use new technologies to electronically store and provide access to a wide range of books, scientific journals, government reports, and articles. Hospitals and other health-care organizations use new forms of service technology to manage patient records, dispatch ambulances, and monitor vital signs. Restaurants use technology to record and fill customer orders, order food and supplies, and prepare food. Given the increased role that service organizations are playing in today's economy, even more technological innovations are likely to be developed in the years to come.[33]

MANAGEMENT IMPLICATIONS Managers should be knowledgeable about the basic forms and dimensions of manufacturing technology, both those that their organizations currently use and those their organizations might use in the future. In addition, managers should be familiar with service technology and its relevance to operations management and to total quality management.

Using Operations Systems for Quality

After operations systems have been properly designed, the organization must put them into use. Their basic functional purpose is to control transformation processes to ensure that relevant goals are achieved in areas such as quality and costs. Operations has a number of special purposes within this control framework, including purchasing and inventory management.

■ Operations Management as Control

One way of using operations management as control is to coordinate it with other functions. Monsanto Company, for example, established a consumer products division that produces and distributes fertilizers and lawn chemicals. To facilitate control, the operations function was organized as an autonomous profit center. This approach is effective for Monsanto because its manufacturing division has the authority to determine not only the costs of creating the product but also the product price and the marketing programs.

In terms of overall organizational control, such a division should be held accountable only for the activities over which it has decision-making authority. It would be inappropriate, of course, to make operations accountable for profitability in an organization that stresses sales and market share over quality and productivity. Misplaced accountability results in ineffective organizational control, to say nothing of hostility and conflict. Depending on the strategic role of operations, then, operations managers are accountable for different kinds of results. For example, in an organization using bureaucratic control, account-

MANAGEMENT INFOTECH

Using the Internet for Corporate Purchasing

A few years ago, Thayer Stewart, an American Express executive, had an intriguing idea. He was pondering the enormous costs that many companies incur as part of their purchasing activities. The costs of ordering paper clips, pens, pencils, and myriad other supplies often exceed those of the supplies themselves. These costs include the time spent submitting orders, checking them after they are received, processing payments, and the capital tied up in maintaining an adequate inventory.

Stewart realized that American Express could profit by enabling businesses to order supplies on-line, with American Express, of course, managing the purchasing system. Working with a consultant from MIT, Stewart and his group created an online catalog filled with the basic supplies most businesses routinely use.

> "Trying to hold on to a proprietary advantage on the Internet is like putting up a dam after the river has run dry."
>
> *Thayer Stewart, American Express executive**

American Express provided the financing for the consultant to leave MIT and start his own operation called SupplyWorks. The key to SupplyWorks was generic software and operating systems that could interface with most proprietary systems already in use in different businesses. Without such easy access, businesses would have little incentive to switch from their current systems. But by offering an easy-to-use interface and low prices, SupplyWorks has been able to quickly attain the dominant position in a small but growing market.

References: *Mary J. Cronin, "Setting Standards for Corporate Purchasing on the Internet,"* Fortune, *September 8, 1997, pp. 156–158 (*quote on p. 158); and* Hoover's Handbook of American Business 1998 *(Austin, Texas: Hoover's Business Press, 1998), pp. 136–137.*

ability will be spelled out in rules and regulations. In a clan system it is likely to be understood and accepted by everyone.

Within operations, managerial control ensures that resources and activities achieve primary goals such as a high percentage of on-time deliveries, low unit-production cost, or high product reliability. Any control system should focus on the elements that are most crucial to goal attainment. For example, firms in which product quality is a major concern (as it is at Rolex), might adopt a screening control system to monitor the product as it is being created. If quantity is a pressing issue (as it is at Timex), a postaction system might be used to identify defects at the end of the system without disrupting the manufacturing process itself.

■ Purchasing Management

purchasing management Buying materials and resources needed to produce products and services

Purchasing management is concerned with buying the materials and resources needed to create products and services. Thus the purchasing manager for a retailer like Sears, Roebuck and Co. is responsible for buying the merchandise the store will sell. The purchasing manager for a manufacturer buys raw materials, parts, and machines for the organization, and he or she must balance a number of constraints. Buying too much ties up capital and increases storage costs. Buying too little might lead to shortages and high reordering costs. The manager must also make sure that the quality of what is purchased meets the organization's needs, that the supplier is reliable, and that the best financial terms are negotiated. "Management InfoTech" discusses one new innovation in purchasing management.

Many firms have recently changed their approach to purchasing as a means to lower costs and improve quality and productivity. In particular, rather than relying on hundreds or even thousands of suppliers, many companies are reducing their number of suppliers and negotiating special production-delivery arrangements. For example, the Honda plant in Marysville, Ohio, found a local business owner looking for a new opportunity. Honda negotiated an agreement whereby he would start a new company to mount car stereo speakers into plastic moldings. He delivers finished goods to the plant three times a day, and Honda buys all that he can manufacture. Thus the business owner has a stable sales base, Honda has a local and reliable supplier, and both companies benefit.

inventory control Managing the organization's raw materials, work-in-process, finished goods, and products in transit

just-in-time (JIT) method An inventory system that has necessary materials arriving as soon as they are needed (just in time) so that the production process is not interrupted

■ Inventory Management

Inventory control, also called materials control, is essential for effective operations management. The four basic kinds of inventories are *raw materials,* *work-in-process, finished-goods,* and *in-transit* inventories. As shown in Table 21.3, the sources of control over these inventories are as different as their purposes. Work-in-process inventories, for example, are made up of partially completed products that need further processing; they are controlled by the shop floor system. In contrast, the quantities and costs of finished-goods inventories are under the control of the overall production scheduling system, which is determined by high-level planning decisions. In-transit inventories are controlled by the transportation and distribution systems.

Like most other areas of operations management, inventory management has changed notably in recent years. One particularly important breakthrough is the **just-in-time (JIT) method.** First popularized by the Japanese, the JIT system reduces the organization's investment in storage space for raw materials and in the materials themselves. Historically, manufacturers built large storage areas and filled them with materials, parts, and supplies that would be needed days, weeks, and even months in

TABLE 21.3
Inventory Types, Purposes, and Sources of Control

JIT is a recent breakthrough in inventory management. With JIT inventory systems, materials arrive just as they are needed. JIT therefore helps an organization control its raw materials inventory by reducing the amount of space it must devote to storage.

Type	Purpose	Source of Control
Raw materials	Provide the materials needed to make the product	Purchasing models and systems
Work-in-process	Enables overall production to be divided into stages of the manageable size	Shop-floor control systems
Finished goods	Provide ready supply of products on customer demand and enable long, efficient production runs	High-level production scheduling systems in conjunction with marketing
In-transit (pipeline)	Distributes products to customers	Transportation and distribution control systems

Just-in-time inventory management is very popular in many firms today. GATX Logistics manages a portion of Mitsubishi's inventory for its factory in Normal, Illinois. GATX purchases and stores short-term quantities of parts such as the wheel covers shown here. GATX employees then transport the covers to the Mitsubishi factory across the street just as they are needed—a dozen or so cars' worth at a time. This allows Mitsubishi to devote far less space to storage and fewer of its employees to moving parts and supplies.

the future. A manager using the JIT approach orders materials and parts more often and in smaller quantities, thereby reducing investment in both storage space and actual inventory. The ideal arrangement is for materials to arrive as they are needed—or "just in time."

Recall our example about the small firm that assembles stereo speakers for Honda and delivers them three times a day so that Honda does not need to carry the speakers in inventory. In an even more striking example, Johnson Controls Inc. makes automobile seats for Chrysler and ships them by small truckloads to a Chrysler plant seventy-five miles away. Each shipment is scheduled to arrive two hours before it is needed. Clearly, the JIT approach requires high levels of coordination and cooperation between the company and its suppliers. If shipments arrive too early, Chrysler has no place to store them. If they arrive too late, the entire assembly line may have to be shut down, resulting in an enormous expense. When properly designed and used, the JIT method controls inventory very effectively.

MANAGEMENT IMPLICATIONS

Managers should understand how operations systems can be used to enhance quality. In particular, managers should be familiar with the role of operations management as control and the importance of purchasing and inventory management.

Summary of Key Points

Quality is a major consideration for all managers today. Quality is important because it affects competition, productivity, and costs. Total quality management is a comprehensive, organization-wide effort to enhance quality through a variety of avenues.

Productivity is also a major concern to managers. Productivity is a measure of how efficiently an organization is using its resources to create products or services. The United States still leads the world in individual productivity, but other industrialized nations are catching up.

Quality and productivity are often addressed via operations management, the set of managerial activities that organizations use in creating their products and services. Operations management is important to both manufacturing and service organizations. It plays an important role in an organization's strategy.

The starting point in using operations management to improve quality is by designing appropriate operations systems. Key areas of concern are product and service design, capacity, and facilities.

Technology also plays an important role in quality. Automation is especially important today. Numerous computer-aided manufacturing techniques are widely practiced. Robotics is also a growing area. Technology is as relevant to service organizations as to manufacturing organizations.

After an operations system has been designed and put into place, it serves a critical role in quality control. Major areas of interest during the use of operations systems are purchasing and inventory management.

Discussion Questions

Questions for Review

1. What is quality? Why is it so important today?

2. What is productivity? How can it be increased?

3. What is the relationship of operations management to overall organizational strategy? Where do productivity and quality fit into that relationship?

4. What are the major components of operations systems? How are they designed?

Questions for Analysis

5. How might the management functions of planning, organizing, and leading relate to the management of quality and productivity?

6. Some people argue that quality and productivity are inversely related; as one goes up, the other goes down. How can that argument be refuted?

7. Is operations management most closely linked to corporate-level, business-level, or functional strategies? Why or in what way?

Questions for Application

8. Interview local managers in different kinds of organizations (business, service, religious) to determine how they deal with quality and productivity.

9. Consider your college or university as an organization. How might it go about developing a TQM program?

10. Go to the library and locate information on several different organizations' uses of operations management. What similarities and differences do you find? Why do you think those similarities and differences exist?

Building Effective Conceptual Skills

EXERCISE OVERVIEW

A manager's conceptual skills are her or his ability to think in the abstract. This exercise demonstrates the relationship that often exists between the conceptual skills of key managers in an organization and that organization's ability to implement total quality initiatives.

EXERCISE BACKGROUND

Conceptual skills may help managers learn how to improve some aspect of their own operations from observations or experiences gleaned from dealings with other organizations.

To begin this exercise, carefully recall the last time you ate in a restaurant that involved some degree of self-service. Examples might include a fast-food restaurant like McDonald's, a cafeteria, or even a traditional restaurant with a salad bar. Recall as much about the experience as possible, and develop some ideas as to why the restaurant is organized and laid out as it is.

Now carefully recall the last time you purchased something in a retail outlet. Possible examples might be an article of clothing from a specialty store, a book from a bookstore, or some software from a computer store. Again recall as much about the experience as possible, and develop some ideas as to why the store is organized and laid out as it is.

Building Effective Technical Skills

EXERCISE OVERVIEW

Technical skills are the skills necessary to accomplish or understand the specific kind of work being done in an organization. This exercise will help you see how technical skills relate to quality, productivity, and operations management.

EXERCISE BACKGROUND

Select a product that you use on a regular basis, for example, computers, compact disks, books, or apparel. Next, learn as much as you can about how that product is designed, produced, and distributed to consumers.

Assume that you have decided to go into business to make the selected product. Create two columns on a sheet of paper. In one column list all the activities necessary to produce the product that you know how to do (for example, install software on a computer or sew two pieces of fabric together). Then list in the next column the activities that you do not know how to do.

EXERCISE TASK

With the preceding background information as context, do the following:

1. Specify where people might learn the skills necessary to perform all the activities for the product you intend to make.

2. Rank the importance of the skills regarding the product.

3. Determine how many people you will need to employ to have a full skill set available.

EXERCISE TASK

Using these two examples, do the following:

1. Identify three or four elements of the service received at each location that you think most directly influenced—either positively or negatively—the quality and efficiency of the experience there.

2. Analyze the service elements from one organization and see if they can somehow be used by the other.

3. Now repeat the process for the second organization.

EXERCISE OVERVIEW

As noted in this chapter, the quality of a product or service is relative to price and expectations. A manager's diagnostic skills—the ability to visualize responses to a situation—can be useful in helping to best position quality relative to price and expectations.

EXERCISE BACKGROUND

Think of a recent occasion in which you purchased a tangible product. For example, think about clothing, electronic equipment, luggage, or professional supplies that you subsequently came to feel to be of especially high quality. Now recall another product that you evaluated as having appropriate or adequate quality and a third that you felt had low or poor quality.

Next, recall parallel experiences involving purchases of services. Examples might include an airline, train, or bus trip; a meal in a restaurant; a haircut; or an oil change for your car.

Finally, recall three experiences in which both products and services were involved. Examples might include having questions answered by someone about a product you were buying or returning a defective or broken product for a refund or warranty repair. Try to recall instances in which there was an apparent disparity between product and service quality (that is, a poor-quality product accompanied by outstanding service or a high-quality product with mediocre service).

EXERCISE TASK

Using the nine examples you just identified, do the following:

1. Assess the extent to which the quality you associated with each was a function of price and your expectations.

2. Consider whether the quality of each be improved without greatly affecting price. If so, how?

3. Consider these questions: Can high-quality service offset only adequate or even poor product quality? Can outstanding product quality offset only adequate or even poor-quality service?

Building Effective
Diagnostic
Skills

CHAPTER CLOSING CASE

Honda Emphasizes Quality

Honda Motor Company, of course, is among the most successful and respected firms in the global automobile industry. Although Honda is only the ninth-largest firm in its industry, and just the third-largest in Japan, the company enjoys a stellar reputation for producing high-quality cars in ways that are innovative and cost efficient. Indeed, Honda is at the forefront of the industry in its operations management practices.

The foundation of Honda's operations management strategy has long been the basic formula of well-engineered cars created to match consumer preferences and produced in an efficient manner. But like all companies, Honda has had to occasionally adjust its processes. For example, its new products in the early 1990s were a bit off the mark with consumers, and sales dropped in both Japan and the United States. Its costs were also a bit higher than normal.

To get things back on track, Honda managers have begun to focus more on new product design and new methods for improving productivity. Among the newest wave of Honda products, for example, are so-called recreational vehicles, smaller and more nimble than conventional sports utility vehicles but with the same characteristics and qualities of their larger brethren. The Odyssey, the CR-V, and the Orthia are three of Honda's very popular RVs.

Another interesting strategy Honda is implementing is to develop the capability to design and manufacture a so-called world car. Most cars today are made for specific countries or regions, with considerable differences across regions. These differences reflect variations in consumer tastes, environmental restrictions, preferred options, disposable income, and so forth. Honda's Accord, for example is among the best-selling cars in the United States, but its styling does not have wide appeal in Japan.

Auto makers know that a car they could sell essentially unchanged around the world would be enormously profitable thanks to economies of scale. Ford has attempted to develop a world car twice, failing with the Escort but coming a bit closer with the Contour. Honda, meanwhile, is feverishly trying to make its Accord universally appealing.

Honda's strategy hinges on the distinction between engineering and design. The firm plans to use the chassis, engine, and other "mechanics" everywhere. But it also intends to customize the exterior design to meet local tastes. Thus, Accords sold in the United States, Europe, and Japan will look very different on the outside but will be essentially the same on the inside. By using the same platform in all markets, Honda will save millions of dollars.

Another key part of Honda's approach is based on speed. Honda can get new designs to market faster and adjust its production more quickly than any other car manufacturer in the world. For example, the firm recently made a changeover from producing 1997 Accords to 1998 Accords at its Maryville, Ohio, factory in less than twelve hours. Rivals often spend weeks or even months in changing over between model years.

Such successes are necessary for Honda if it's to keep its place in the industry. Because Honda has far fewer models than its bigger rivals, it depends more on its core models like Accord and Civic than its competitors depend on a single model. Indeed, Accord accounts for half of Honda's sales in the United States and more than a quarter of its worldwide production. But at least for now, Honda seems to be on the right track!

Case Questions:

1. How does operations management contribute to Honda's success?
2. Describe Honda's apparent views on product quality.
3. Do you think a "world car" is really feasible? Why or why not?

Case References: "Can Honda Build a World Car?" *Business Week,* September 8, 1997, pp. 100–108; Alex Taylor III, "The Man Who Put Honda Back on Track," *Fortune,* September 9, 1996, pp. 92–100; and "Quick-Change Artists," *Newsweek,* September 1, 1997, p. 47.

CHAPTER NOTES

1. "The Quest for Quality Is in the Bag(gage)," *USA Today,* September 23, 1997, p. 12E.
2. "Quality—How to Make It Pay," *Business Week,* August 8, 1994, pp. 54–59.
3. Rhonda Reger, Loren Gustafson, Samuel DeMarie, and John Mullane, "Reframing the Organization: Why Implementing Total Quality Is Easier Said Than Done," *Academy of Management Review,* 1994, Vol. 19, No. 3, pp. 565–584.

4. Ross Johnson and William O. Winchell, *Management and Quality* (Milwaukee: American Society for Quality Control, 1989). See also Carol Reeves and David Bednar, "Defining Quality: Alternatives and Implications," *Academy of Management Review*, 1994, Vol. 19, No. 3, pp. 419–445.

5. W. Edwards Deming, *Out of the Crisis* (Cambridge, Mass.: MIT Press, 1986).

6. David Waldman, "The Contributions of Total Quality Management to a Theory of Work Performance," *Academy of Management Review*, 1994, Vol. 19, No. 3, p. 510–536.

7. Joel Dreyfuss, "Victories in the Quality Crusade," *Fortune*, October 10, 1988, pp. 80–88.

8. Thomas Y. Choi and Orlando C. Behling, "Top Managers and TQM Success: One More Look after All These Years," *Academy of Management Executive*, 1997, Vol. 11, No. 1, pp. 37–48.

9. James Dean and David Bowen, "Management Theory and Total Quality: Improving Research and Practice through Theory Development," *Academy of Management Review*, 1994, Vol. 19, No. 3, pp. 392–418.

10. Edward E. Lawler, "Total Quality Management and Employee Involvement: Are They Compatible?" *Academy of Management Executive*, 1994, Vol. 8, No. 1, pp. 68–79.

11. "Quality Is Becoming Job One in the Office, Too," *Business Week*, April 29, 1991, pp. 52–56.

12. Jeremy Main, "How to Steal the Best Ideas Around," *Fortune*, October 19, 1992, pp. 102–106.

13. James Brian Quinn and Frederick Hilmer, "Strategic Outsourcing," *Sloan Management Review*, Summer 1994, pp. 43–55.

14. Thomas Robertson, "How to Reduce Market Penetration Cycle Times," *Sloan Management Review*, Fall 1993, pp. 87–96.

15. Ronald Henkoff, "The Hot New Seal of Quality," *Fortune*, June 28, 1993, pp. 116–120. See also Mustafa V. Uzumeri, "ISO 9000 and Other Metastandards: Principles for Management Practice?" *Academy of Management Executive*, 1997, Vol. 11, No. 1, pp. 21–28.

16. Paula C. Morrow, "The Measurement of TQM Principles and Work-Related Outcomes," *Journal of Organizational Behavior*, July 1997, pp. 363–376.

17. John W. Kendrick, *Understanding Productivity: An Introduction to the Dynamics of Productivity Change* (Baltimore: Johns Hopkins, 1977).

18. "The Productivity Payoff Arrives," *Fortune*, June 27, 1994, pp. 79–84.

19. "Study: USA Losing Competitive Edge," *USA Today*, April 25, 1997, p. 9D.

20. Michael van Biema and Bruce Greenwald, "Managing Our Way to Higher Service-Sector Productivity," *Harvard Business Review*, July–August 1997, pp. 87–98.

21. David Wright and Paul Brauchle, "Teaming Up for Quality," *Training & Development*, September 1994, pp. 67–75.

22. Paul M. Swamidass, "Empirical Science: New Frontier in Operations Management Research," *Academy of Management Review*, October 1991, pp. 793–814.

23. Joan Woodward, *Industrial Organization: Theory and Practice* (London: Oxford University Press, 1965).

24. Paul D. Collins, Jerald Hage, and Frank M. Hull, "Organizational and Technological Predictors of Change in Automaticity," *Academy of Management Journal*, September 1988, pp. 512–543.

25. "Computers Speed the Design of More Workaday Products," *Wall Street Journal*, January 18, 1985, p. 25.

26. Robert Bonsack, "Executive Checklist: Are You Ready for CIM?" *CIM Review*, Summer 1987, pp. 35–38.

27. M. Sepehri, "IBM's Automated Lexington Factory Focuses on Quality and Cost Effectiveness," *Industrial Engineering*, February 1987, pp. 66–74.

28. "Computers Speed the Design of More Workaday Products."

29. "How Automation Could Save the Day," *Business Week*, March 3, 1986, pp. 72–74.

30. Otto Friedrich, "The Robot Revolution," *Time*, December 8, 1980, pp. 72–83.

31. "Robots Head for the Farm," *Business Week*, September 8, 1986, pp. 66–67.

32. "Boldly Going Where No Robot Has Gone Before," *Business Week*, December 22, 1986, p. 45.

33. James Brian Quinn and Martin Neil Baily, "Information Technology: Increasing Productivity in Services," *Academy of Management Executive*, 1994, Vol. 8, No. 3, pp. 28–37.

22

Managing Information and Information Technology

OBJECTIVES

After studying this chapter, you should be able to:

■ Describe the role and importance of information in the manager's job.

■ Identify the basic building blocks of information technology.

■ Discuss the basic factors that determine an organization's information technology needs.

■ Describe the basic kinds of information systems used by organizations.

■ Discuss how information systems can be managed.

■ Describe how information systems affect organizations.

■ Identify recent advances in information technology.

Texas Instruments (TI) has operations around the world. While the firm's operations are concentrated in the state that is its namesake, TI also has facilities in more than thirty countries scattered across Europe, Asia, and South America. Particularly important in recent years has been a facility in India, created to take advantage of a high-quality but relatively inexpensive labor pool of talented engineers in that country.

The firm has long been a leader in integrated global design. Until recently, however, global design teams were relatively inefficient. Days at a time were lost as detailed engineering drawings traveled between countries. Even facsimile technology did not help greatly, because the images were often blurred and the drawings themselves were very large—drawings were sometimes cut into small pieces, each piece was faxed separately, and someone on the other end taped them together.

Eventually, the firm began to transmit images and other data electronically through integrated computer information networks—*intranets*—linked by satellites. This new technology, increasingly referred to as rapid manufacturing, allowed TI engineers in facilities around the globe to work on the same project simultaneously—to communicate just as easily as if they were sitting in the same room. Almost immediately after this system was implemented, the time needed to develop a new calculator dropped by 20 percent. Later improvements shaving another 17 percent off development time soon followed.

In some parts of the world, TI has had to go to great lengths to get its information technology in place. For example, the firm wanted to set up a satellite dish at its Bangalore, India, facility so that its engineers there could interface with TI engineers in other locations. The only way to get the dish to

Bangalore was to haul it in by oxcart, but it appears to have been a worthwhile investment. Engineers there are now able to uplink with their counterparts in the United States and Japan and have made numerous contributions to the development of new forms of microchips.

One TI group that has taken special advantage of information technology and rapid manufacturing has been the Texas Instruments Registration and Identification System (Tiris) group. This group is managed in England, develops products in the Netherlands and Germany, and produces those products in Japan and Malaysia. The TI communication network has made it easier than anyone might have imagined for these engineers to work together, to communicate, and to coordinate their efforts. Indeed, Tiris management strongly feels that the system has given them a significant competitive advantage.

The system has also allowed the firm to expand the boundaries of its workday by taking advantage of different time zones. A U.S. financial exchange recently asked TI for a price quote on some new equipment. A group of managers in Dallas started work late in the afternoon; at quitting time they forwarded the files to their counterparts in Tokyo. Managers there took up the project, spent their day on it, and then passed the task on to managers in Nice, France. Managers there finished the job and sent the information back to Dallas. Within twenty-four hours of getting the request, TI could show the customer the price quote—and a computer-generated image from rapid manufacturing of exactly what the product would look like.[1]

> ### "In two or three years rapid manufacturing will be on everybody's lips."
>
> Unidentified Texas Instruments executive, quoted in *Fortune, January 12, 1998, p. 120D.*

Texas Instruments is aggressively using the latest technology for competitive advantage. And increasingly, that technology is helping firms like TI manage the information that is so vital to their daily operations and strategic management. Information comes in a variety of forms and in large quantities. If organizations aren't careful, they can lose control of how they manage the information they need to conduct business efficiently and effectively. Consequently, in recent years businesses like TI have recognized that they need better ways to manage their information.

This chapter is about advances in information management. We describe the role and importance of information to managers, the characteristics of useful information, and information management as control and then identify the basic building blocks of information systems. We discuss the general and specific determinants of information technology needs. We then consider the primary kinds of information technology used in organizations and describe how this technology is managed.

Information and the Manager

Information has always been an integral part of every manager's job. Its importance, however, and therefore the need to manage it continue to grow at a rapid clip. To appreciate this trend, we need to understand the role of information in the manager's job, characteristics of useful information, and the nature of information management as control.

■ The Role of Information in the Manager's Job

In Chapters 1 and 18 we highlighted the role of communication in the manager's job. Given that information is a vital part of communication, it follows that management and information are closely related. Indeed, we can conceptualize management as a series of steps involving the reception, processing, and dissemination of information. As illustrated in Figure 22.1, the manager is constantly bombarded with data and information (the difference between the two is noted later).

Suppose that Bob Henderson is an operations manager for a large manufacturing firm. During the course of a normal day, Bob receives a great many pieces of information from both formal and informal conversations and meetings, telephone calls, personal observation, e-mails, letters, reports, memos, and trade publications. He gets a report from a subordinate that explains exactly how to solve a pressing problem, so he calls the subordinate and tells him to put the solution into effect immediately. He scans a copy of a report prepared for another manager, sees that it has no relevance to him, and discards it. He sees a *Wall Street Journal* article that he knows Sara Ferris in marketing should see, so he passes it on to her. He gets an electronic summary of yesterday's production report, but since he knows he won't need to analyze it for another week, he stores it. He observes a worker doing a job incorrectly and realizes that the incorrect method is associated with a mysterious quality problem that someone told him about last week.

A key part of information-processing activity is differentiating between data and information. **Data** are raw figures and facts reflecting a single aspect of reality. The facts that a plant has thirty-five machines, that each machine can produce one thousand units of output per day, that current and projected future demand for the units is thirty thousand per day, and that workers sufficiently skilled to run the machines make $15 an hour are data.

Information is data presented in a way or form that has meaning. Thus, summarizing the preceding four pieces of data provides information—the plant has excess capacity and is therefore incurring unnecessary costs. Information has meaning to a manager and provides a basis for action. The plant manager might use the information and decide to sell four machines (keeping one as a backup) and transfer five operators to other jobs.

A related term is **information technology**, or **IT**. Information technology refers to the resources used by an organization to manage information that it needs to carry out its mission. IT may consist of computers, computer networks, telephones, facsimile machines, and other pieces of hardware. In addition, IT involves software that facilitates the system's abilities to manage information in a way that is useful for managers.[2]

The grocery industry uses data, information, and information technology to automate inventory and check-out facilities. The average Kroger store, for example, carries twenty-one thousand items. Computerized scanning machines at the check-out counters provide daily sales figures for any product; these figures alone are data and have little meaning in their pure form. Information is compiled from this data by another computerized system. Using this IT system, managers can identify how any given product or product line is selling in any number of stores over any meaningful period of time.[3]

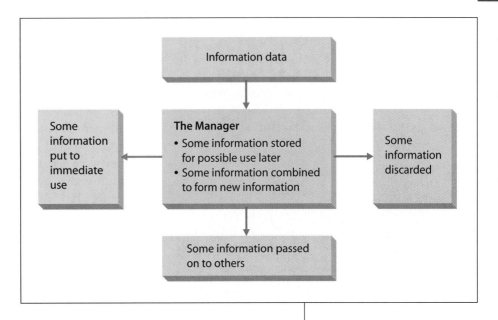

FIGURE 22.1
Managers as Information Processors

Managers who receive information and data must decide what to do with it. Some is stored for possible later use, and other information is combined to form new information. Subsequently, some is used immediately, some is passed on to others, and some is discarded.

data   Raw figures and facts reflecting a single aspect of reality

information   Data presented in a way or form that has meaning

information technology or **IT**   Refers to the resources an organization uses to manage information that it needs to carry out its mission

■ Characteristics of Useful Information

What factors differentiate information that is useful from information that is not? In general, information is useful if it is accurate, timely, complete, and relevant.

Information and the manager's job have long been interrelated, but they are becoming even more intertwined. For example, consider the success enjoyed by Atcom/Info. Atcom/Info is placing kiosks in airports, convention centers, and business hotels throught the United States. In the "old days," a manager might seek out a pay telephone, swipe a calling card through the machine, and place a call. Atcom/Info provides the same ease of use, but with e-mail instead! The manager swipes a credit card through the machine, and then uses the keyboard to send e-mail! The advantages of this method, of course, are that it is fast, cheap, and avoids the problems of missed telephone calls and busy signals.

Accurate For information to be of real value to a manager, it must be accurate. Accuracy means that the information must provide a valid and reliable reflection of reality. A Japanese construction company once bought information from a consulting firm about a possible building site in London. The Japanese were told that the land, which would be sold in a sealed bid auction, would attract bids of close to $250 million. They were also told that the land currently held an old building that could easily be demolished. Thus the Japanese bid $255 million—which ended up being $90 million more than the next-highest bid. A few days later the British government declared the building historic, preempting any thought of demolition. Clearly, the Japanese acted on information that was less than accurate.[4]

Timely Information also needs to be timely. Timeliness does not necessarily mean speediness; it means only that information needs to be available in time for appropriate managerial action. What constitutes timeliness is a function of the situation facing the manager. When Marriott was gathering information for its Fairfield Inn project, managers projected a six-month window for data collection. They felt this would give them an opportunity to do a good job of getting the information they needed about launching an economy motel business without delaying the project. In contrast, Marriott's computerized reservation and accounting system can provide a manager with the previous night's occupancy level at any Marriott facility.[5]

Complete Information must tell a complete story for it to be useful to a manager. If it is less than complete, the manager is likely to get an inaccurate or distorted picture of reality. For example, managers at Kroger used to think that house-brand products were more profitable than national brands because they yielded higher unit profits. On the basis of this information, they gave house brands a lot of shelf space and centered a lot of promotional activities around them. As Kroger's managers became more sophisticated in understanding their information, however, they realized that national brands were actually more profitable over time because national brands outsold housebrands during any given period of time. Although a store might sell ten cans of Kroger coffee in a day with a profit of twenty-five cents per can (total profit of $2.50), it would also sell fifteen cans of Maxwell House coffee with a profit of twenty cents per can (total profit of $3.00).

Relevant Finally, information must be relevant if it is to be useful to managers. Relevance, like timeliness, is defined according to the needs and circumstances of a particular manager. Operations managers need information on costs and productivity; human resource managers need information on hiring needs and turnover rates; and marketing managers need information on sales projections and advertising rates. As Wal-Mart contemplates countries for possible expansion opportunities, it gathers information about local regulations, customs, and so forth. But the information about any given country isn't really relevant until the decision is made to enter that market.

■ Information Management as Control

The manager also needs to appreciate the role of information in control—indeed, to see information management as a vital part of the control process in the organization.[6] As already noted, managers receive much more data and information than they need or can use. Accordingly, deciding how to handle each piece of data and information involves a form of control.[7]

The control perspective on information management is illustrated in Figure 22.2. Information enters, is used by, and leaves the organization. For example, Marriott took great pains to make sure it got all the information it needed to plan for and enter the economy-lodging business. Once this preliminary information was gathered, it was necessary to make sure that the information was made available in the proper form to everyone who needed it. In general, the effort to ensure that information is accurate, timely, complete, and relevant is a form of screening control. Finally, Marriott wanted to make sure that its competitors did not learn about its Fairfield Inn plans until the last possible minute. It also wanted to time and orchestrate news releases, public announcements, and advertising for maximum benefit. These efforts thus served a postaction control function.

MANAGEMENT IMPLICATIONS

Managers need to understand and appreciate the role of information in their jobs. In addition, they should know the characteristics that typify useful information and understand the control function that is served by effective information management. ▬

accurate information Provides a valid and reliable reflection of reality

timely information Available in time for appropriate managerial action

complete information Provides managers with all the information they need

relevant information Assures managers that the information is useful to them in their particular circumstances for their particular needs

FIGURE 22.2
Information Management as Control

Information management can be a part of the control system via preliminary, screening, and/or postaction control mechanisms. Because information from the environment is just as much a resource as raw materials or finances, it must be monitored and managed to promote its efficient and effective utilization.

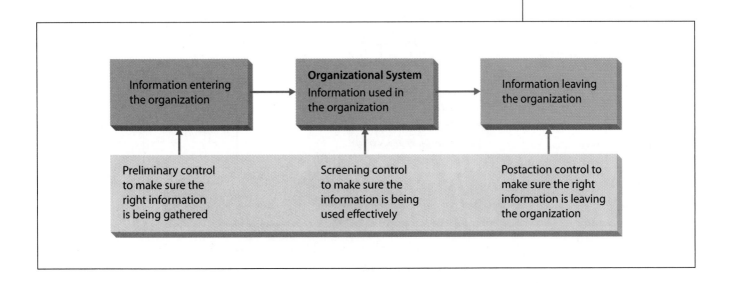

Building Blocks of Information Technology

Information technology is generally of two types—manual or computer based. All information technology, and the systems that it defines, has five basic parts. Figure 22.3 diagrams these parts for a computer-based information technology system. The *input medium* is the device that is used to add data and information into the system. For example, the optical scanner at Kroger enters point-of-sale information. Alternatively, someone can enter data through a keyboard.

The data that are entered into the system typically flow first to a processor. The *processor* is the part of the system that is capable of organizing, manipulating, sorting, or performing calculations or other transformations with the data. Most systems also have one or more *storage devices*—a place where data can be stored for later use. Floppy disks, hard drives, CD-ROM disks, magnetic tapes, and optical disks are common forms of storage devices. As data are transformed into usable information, the resultant information must be communicated to the appropriate person by means of an *output medium*. Common ways to display output are video displays, printers, other computers, and facsimile machines.

Finally, the entire information technology system is operated by a *control system*—most often software of one form or another. Simple systems in smaller organizations can use off-the-shelf software. Microsoft Windows 95 or 98, DOS, and OS-2 are general operating systems that control more specialized types of software. WordPerfect and Microsoft Word are popular systems for word processing. Lotus 1-2-3 and Excel are popular spreadsheet programs, and dBASE III is frequently used for database management. Of course, elabo-

FIGURE 22.3

Building Blocks of a Computer-Based Information System

Computer-based information systems generally have five basic components—an input medium, a processor, an output medium, a storage device, and a control system. Non-computer–based systems use parallel components for the same basic purposes.

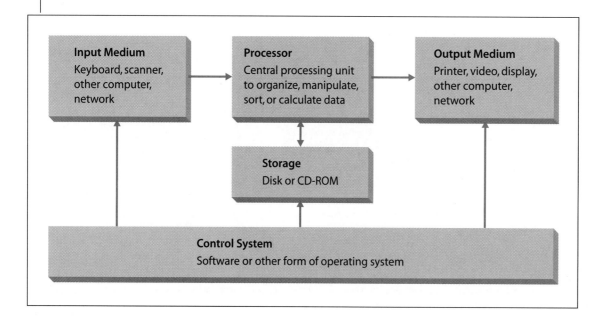

rate systems of the type used by large businesses require a special customized operating system. When organizations start to link computers together into a network, the operating system must be even more complex.

As we noted earlier, information technology systems need not be computerized. Many small organizations still function quite well with a manual system using paper documents, routing slips, paper clips, file folders, file cabinets, and typewriters. Increasingly, however, even small businesses are abandoning their manual systems for computerized ones. As hardware prices continue to drop and software becomes more and more powerful, computerized information systems will likely be within the reach of any business that wants to have one.

MANAGEMENT IMPLICATIONS   Managers should be familiar with the basic components that constitute an information system and how they relate to one another. ▬

Determinants of Information Technology Needs

What determines whether an organization needs an information system, and how do these factors help define the organization's information technology needs? In general, the key factors that determine these needs fall into two categories: general determinants and specific determinants.[8] These are illustrated in Figure 22.4.

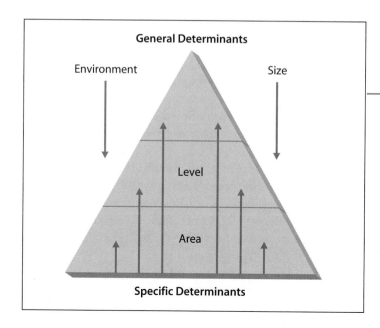

FIGURE 22.4
Determinants of an Organization's Information-Processing Needs

Information-processing needs are determined by such general organizational factors as the environment and the organization's size and such specific managerial factors as their area and level in the organization.

The environment is a major determinant of a company's information system requirements. Colleges and universities have become the dominant training ground to prepare tomorrow's workforce to better use electronic communication technology. Most campuses today invest heavily in new equipment and software to ensure that their graduates will be properly prepared. For several years, some smaller institutions have even been requiring their students to purchase a computer as a condition of admission. This trend was recently taken to a new level, however, when the huge state-supported University of Florida imposed a similar requirement on its next entering class.

■ General Determinants

Two general factors help define an organization's information technology needs. These factors are the environment and the size of the organization.

Environment In Chapters 3 and 12 we noted that the environment of an organization affects that organization in many different ways. Still another way that the environment affects an organization is as a determinant of its information technology needs. In general, the more uncertain and complex the environment, the greater is the need to formally manage information. Given that virtually all organizations face at least some degree of uncertainty, it can be argued that all organizations need to worry about managing their information. However, an organization like Hewlett-Packard or IBM that operates in an extremely uncertain environment has very strong needs for elaborate information technology.

Size Size is another general determinant of an organization's information technology needs. All else being equal, the larger an organization is, the greater are its needs to manage its information systematically. Thus, General Motors has greater information technology needs than does its Cadillac division alone, and each has greater needs than does a single Cadillac dealership. The effects of organizational size can also be either slightly constrained or greatly accentuated by the diversity of the organization. A large organization that is essentially a single division, for example, has less pressure for sophisticated information technology than does a firm of the same size that comprises several different divisions.

■ Specific Determinants

Two other factors serve to define the information technology needs of an organization. These factors are the area and level of the organization.

Area By area, we mean basic functional areas like finance, operations, marketing, or human resources. Each of these areas has a unique set of information technology needs. Human resources, for example, needs complete demographic data on all current employees, job-grade information, affirmative action statistics, and so forth. Marketing needs data on current prices, market share, and advertising expenditures.

Another key ingredient is the extent to which the various areas within an organization work in an integrated and coordinated fashion. If each acts totally on its own, with coordination handled by the managerial hierarchy, each area can survive with its own information system. But if different areas are expected to coordinate their activities, then their information systems need to be coordinated. For example, the marketing system may be updated to include a projection for 10 percent more sales next year than previously expected. An integrated information system could use that information to provide the operations manager with an indication that additional output will be needed, to provide the human resource manager with an indication of how many additional workers will be needed, and to provide the financial manager with an indication of how much additional working capital will be needed to support higher wage and materials costs.

Level Organizational level also helps determine the information technology requirements of the organization. Managers at the top of the organization need broad, general kinds of information across a variety of time frames to help them with strategic planning. Middle managers need information of somewhat more specificity and with a shorter time frame. Lower-level managers need highly specific information with a very short time frame. For example, the vice president of marketing at General Mills might want to know projected demand for eight different cereal products over the next five years. A divisional sales manager might need to know projected demand for two of those cereal products for the next one-year period. A district sales manager might need to know how much of one cereal is likely to be sold next month.

MANAGEMENT IMPLICATIONS Managers should be knowledgeable about how environment and organizational size—general factors—affect their information technology needs. They should also know how area and level—specific factors—affect information technology needs as well.

Basic Kinds of Information Systems

Organizations that use information systems, especially large organizations, often find that they need several kinds of systems to manage their information effectively. The six most general kinds of information systems are transaction-processing systems, basic management information systems, decision support systems, executive information systems, intranets, and expert systems.

■ Transaction-Processing Systems

Transaction-processing systems were the first computerized form of information system adopted by many businesses. A **transaction-processing system**, or **TPS**, is a system designed to handle routine and recurring transactions within the business. Visa uses a TPS to record charges to individual credit accounts, credit payments made on the accounts, and send monthly bills to

transaction-processing system or **TPS** A system designed to handle a business's routine and recurring transactions

management information system or **MIS** A system that gathers more comprehensive data, organizes and summarizes it in a form of value to managers, and provides those managers with the information they need to do their work

customers. In general, a TPS is most useful when the organization has a large number of highly similar transactions to process. Thus, most forms of customer billings, bank transactions, and point-of-sale records are amenable to this form of information system. The automated scanners at Kroger that record each unit sold and its price are a form of TPS.

A TPS is especially helpful in aggregating large amounts of data into more manageable forms of information summaries. For example, a bank manager probably cares little about any given Visa transaction recorded for any single cardholder. More useful is information about the average number of purchases made by each cardholder, their average daily balances, average monthly finance charges assessed, and so forth. In general, a TPS is most useful to lower-level managers. Even though this approach was the earliest, it is still of considerable use and relevance to many organizations. Many of these organizations, however, have also found it necessary to develop more sophisticated systems.

■ Basic Management Information Systems

The next step in the evolution of information management is generally called the **management information system**, or **MIS**. An MIS is a system that gathers more comprehensive data, organizes and summarizes it in a form that is of value to functional managers, and then provides those same managers with the information they need to do their work. Figure 22.5 shows how such a system might work.

An MIS for a manufacturing firm might develop a computerized inventory system that keeps track of both anticipated orders and inventory on hand. A marketing representative talking to a customer about anticipated delivery dates can "plug into the system" and get a good idea of when an order can be shipped. Likewise, the plant manager can use the system to help determine how much of each of the firm's products to manufacture next week or next month. Seminole Manufacturing Co. uses a variation on the standard MIS called an EDE—electronic data exchange. Seminole supplies Wal-Mart with men's pants. The EDE system ties Seminole directly into Wal-Mart's computerized inventory system to check current sales levels and stock on hand. Wal-Mart can then transmit new orders directly into Seminole's system—and managers there are already geared up to start working on it. As a result, delivery times have been cut in half and sales are up 31 percent.[9] A similar concept is explained in "Today's Management Issues."

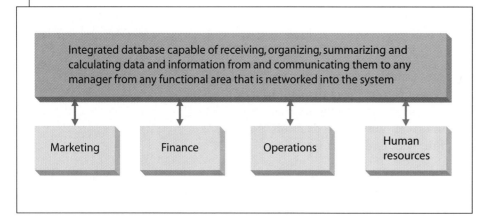

TODAY'S MANAGEMENT ISSUES

Inventory? Or Information?

Once upon a time, businesses were in the inventory business. They produced their goods on an almost continuous basis and then stockpiled them in massive warehouses. When an order came in, someone would go to the warehouse and pull the goods that had been ordered. Then someone else would pack them into boxes and crates. And finally, someone else would ship them to the customer.

Although many businesses still use this process, others are trying to break away. The problems with maintaining inventory are obvious—inventory ties up capital; goods in inventory are subject to damage, theft, and obsolescence; and numerous jobs are associated with maintaining it. Some firms, however, are trying to break away from the inventory trap by conceptually replacing it with information—information about who wants what, where it is, and how can it be sent there the fastest and easiest way?

A good example of the new approach to inventory management is the partnership between Compaq Computer and a logistics firm called Skyway. In the past Compaq shipped monitors, modems, keyboards, and other computer components to a central distribution center where finished systems were assembled and packed. But now, Skyway picks up those components from their respective factories and ships them directly to the customer. Thus, Compaq avoids a large inventory in its distribution center, and the customer gets a computer much faster than before.

> *"We want to replace inventory with information, and once you have all this data percolating up, you have to be able to manage it differently."*
>
> *Kip Hawley, Skyway CEO**

Similarly, a subsidiary of UPS helps Cisco Systems ship tons of routers to Europe each week. The bar-code tracking system at UPS and its integrated information network enable the shipper to perform this function faster—and less expensively—than Cisco could under its old system. A FedEx subsidiary does similar work for Apple Computer. Suppose, for example, that an Apple customer reports that the monitor on a new computer system is defective. FedEx picks up the new monitor from Apple and ships it to the customer. The customer packs the defective monitor into the same box, FedEx picks it up, and then ships it to a repair shop near a FedEx terminal. The monitor is fixed and then shipped to the next customer who needs a replacement.

Information, of course, is the raw material that makes these linkages work: Skyway is linked directly to Compaq, UPS is linked directly to Cisco, and FedEx is linked directly to Apple. Even though the Apple customer actually calls Apple, for example, Apple does not have to contact FedEx; the shipper already knows what to do because it gets the same information as Apple gets. Such seamless inventory management is allowing many companies to hold down costs and provide better service.

References: *"Replacing Inventory with Information,"* Forbes, *March 24, 1998, pp. 54–58 (*quote on p. 56); and* Hoover's Handbook of American Business 1998 *(Austin, Texas: Hoover's Business Press, 1996), pp. 178–179.*

■ Decision Support Systems

An increasingly common information system is called a **decision support system,** or **DSS**. A DSS is both very elaborate and quite powerful. Such a system can automatically search for, manipulate, and summarize information needed by managers for specific decisions. A DSS is much more flexible than a traditional MIS and can help cope with nonroutine problems and decisions.

A manager might be interested in knowing the likely effects of a price increase for a particular product sold by the firm. Thus, she might decide to

decision support system or **DSS**
A system that automatically searches for, manipulates, and summarizes information needed by managers for use in making specific decisions

query the DSS to determine potential outcomes for price increases of 5, 7, and 10 percent. The DSS knows the pricing history for the product, the prices charged by competitors, their most recent price changes, the effects of price on sales, seasonal variations in demand and price, inflation rates, and virtually any other relevant piece of information that might have been determined. The system calculates projected sales, market share, and profit profiles for the potential price-increase levels and provides them to the manager.

Decision support systems are complex. They take time and resources to develop and more time and resources to maintain and teach managers to use effectively. They also seem to hold considerable potential for improving the quality of information available to managers as they make important decisions. Frito-Lay makes extensive use of decision support systems in marketing its products. As sales data is received, managers are cued as to what products are selling above and below normal, as well as a number of other points. They can then cut prices, increase shipments, or take whatever action is suggested by the information.

■ Executive Information Systems

executive information system or **EIS** A system designed to meet the special information-processing needs of top managers

intranet A communication network similar to the Internet but operating within the boundaries of a single organization

expert system An information system created to duplicate or imitate the thought processes of a human expert

Executive information systems are the newest form of information system. An **executive information system**, or **EIS**, is a system designed to meet the special information-processing needs of top managers. Because many top managers lack basic computer skills and because they need highly specialized information not readily available in conventional systems, many executives were reluctant to use their organizations' information system.

An EIS is constructed to be very user-friendly. That is, technical knowledge is not necessary to use it. Instead, such systems generally use icons and symbols and require very few commands. The information they provide allows managers to bypass details and get directly to overall trends and patterns that may affect strategic decision making. The EIS summarizes information for managers; it does not provide specific details. It also tailors the information to the specific needs of the manager.[10]

Information has become a major component in the work of all managers and the activities of all organizations. Indeed, new and exciting methods and sources for gathering and analyzing information are appearing almost daily. Of course, as as shown here in this amusing cartoon, managers must insure that they are getting the information they truly need and that it is of sufficient quality to meet their needs. Flawed or old information may do more harm than no information at all!

■ Intranets

Many larger organizations today are also developing **intranets**, communication networks similar to the Internet but operating within the boundaries of a single organization. Such systems enable every business unit or division within the organization to compile information about itself and to make it available to employees in the business units or divisions. Specific functional groups can use an intranet for communication. For example, human resources can post job openings and describe benefit options, and marketing can outline details of upcoming promotional activities. Interest groups can use an intranet to post announcements. In addition, rather than print company newsletters on paper, the material can be made available electronically.[11]

■ Expert Systems

Expert systems are also becoming more and more practical. An **expert system** is an information system created to duplicate, or at least imitate, the thought processes of a human being. The starting point in developing an expert system is to identify all the "if then" contingencies that pertain to a given situation. These contingencies form the knowledge base for the system. For example, Table 22.1 summarizes the knowledge base for a hypothetical firm's pricing policy. The facts and if-then contingencies outlined in the table determine the pricing policy. The statements in bold type represent the current situation facing the company. Thus a manager could query the system like this: "What is price-policy?" The system would respond, "Price-policy is increase-price." The manager could then ask why, and the system would answer, "Price-policy is increase-price because margin is low and demand is strong."

Organizations have developed considerably more complex and useful expert systems. For example, Campbell's developed an expert system to re-create the thought processes of one of its key employees, a manager who was very familiar with operations of the seven-story soup kettles used to cook soup. The manager, Aldo Cimino, knew so much about how the kettles worked that the company feared no one else could learn the job as well as he. So it hired Texas Instruments to study his job, interview him and observe his work, and create an expert system that could mimic his experience. The resulting system, containing more than 150 if-then rules, helps operate the kettles today.[12]

MANAGEMENT IMPLICATIONS Managers should be familiar with the six basic kinds of information systems that organizations use. In addition, they should understand the basic functions, benefits, and limitations of each. ■

Factual Knowledge
Price is $50.
Cost $45.
Demand is 1,121.
Margin is (price – cost).

Process Knowledge

1. If margin is high and demand is weak, then price-policy is decrease-price.
2. If margin is normal and demand is steady, then price-policy is maintain-price.
3. **If margin is low and demand is strong, then price-policy is increase-price.**
4. If margin is greater-than 25, then margin is high.
5. **If margin is less-than 10, then margin is low.**
6. If margin is-not high and margin is-not low, then margin is normal.
7. **If demand is greater-than 1,100, then demand is strong.**
8. If demand is less-than 900, then demand is weak.
9. If demand is-not strong and demand is-not weak, then demand is steady.

TABLE 22.1

An Example Knowledge Base for a Firm's Pricing Policy

Expert systems imitate human thought processes. This sample knowledge base for an expert system summarizes both factual knowledge relevant to the system as well as process knowledge that guides the system to various decisions. For example, Singapore's container cargo port handles more than 60 containers per ship per hour. Its expert system routes incoming ships to empty berths and then automatically schedules loading and unloading equipment, storage facilities, and so forth.

Source: David B. Paradice and James F. Courtney, Jr., "Intelligent Organizations," *Texas A&M Business Forum,* Fall 1988, pp. 18–22. Reprinted with permission.

Managing Information Systems

At this point the value and importance of information systems should be apparent. There are still important questions to be answered, however. How are such systems developed, and how are they used on a day-to-day basis? This section provides insights into these issues and related areas.

■ Establishing Information Systems

The basic steps involved in creating an information system are outlined in Figure 22.6. The first step is to determine the information needs of the organization and to establish goals for what the proposed system should achieve. It is absolutely imperative that the project have full support and an appropriate financial commitment from top management if it is to be successful. Once the decision has been made to develop and install an information system, a task force is usually constituted to oversee everything. Target users must be well represented on such a task force.

Next, three tasks can be done simultaneously. One task is to assemble a database. Most organizations already possess the information they need for an information system, but it is often not in the correct form. The Pentagon is spending large sums of money to transform all of its paper records into computer records. Many other branches of the government are also working hard to computerize their data.[13]

While the database is being assembled, the organization also needs to determine its hardware needs and acquire the appropriate equipment. Some systems rely solely on one large mainframe computer; others are increasingly using personal computers. Equipment is usually obtained from large manufacturers like IBM, Compaq, and Sun. Finally, software needs must also be determined and an appropriate operating system obtained. Again, off-the-shelf packages will sometimes work, although most companies end up doing some customization.

The actual information system is created by integrating the database, the hardware, and the software. Obviously, the mechanics of creating an information system are beyond the scope of this discussion. However, the company usually has to rely on the expertise of outside consulting firms, along with various vendors, to put it all together. During this phase the equipment is installed, cables are strung between units, the data are entered into the system, the operating system is installed and tested, and so forth. System controls are also installed. A control is simply a characteristic of the system that limits certain forms of access or limits what a person can do with the system. For example, top managers may want to limit access to certain sensitive data to a few key people, who then enter private codes before they can access the data. It is also important to make sure that data cannot be accidentally erased by someone who happens to press the wrong key.

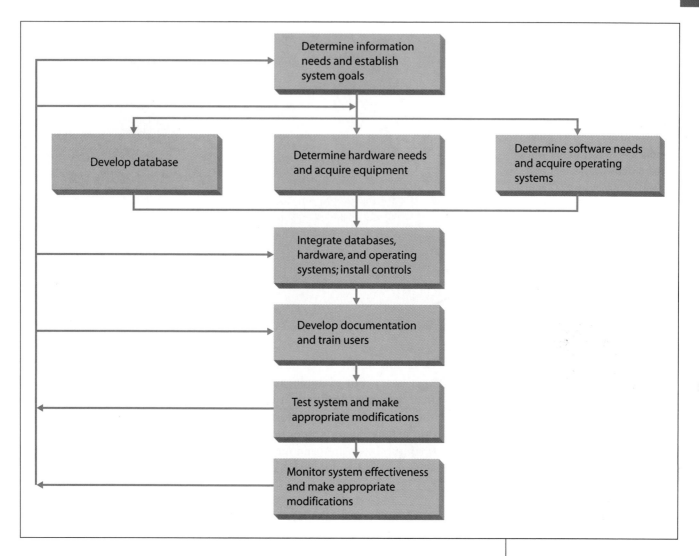

The next step is to develop documentation of how the system works and to train people to use it. Documentation refers to manuals, computerized help programs, diagrams, and instruction sheets. Essentially, it tells people how to use the system for different purposes. Beyond pure documentation, however, training sessions are also common. Such sessions allow people to practice using the system under the watchful eye of experts.

The system must then be tested and appropriate modifications made. Regardless of how well planned an information system is, some glitches will always develop. For example, the system may be unable to generate a report that needs to be made available to certain managers. Or the report may not be in the appropriate format. Or certain people may be unable to access data that they need in order to get other information from the system. In most cases the consultants or internal group that installed the system will be able to make such modifications as the need arises.

The organization must recognize that information management needs will change over time. Hence, even though the glitches get straightened out and

FIGURE 22.6
Establishing an Information System

Establishing an information system is a complex procedure. Managers must realize, however, that the organization's information management needs will change over time, and some steps of the process may have to be done again in the future.

One of the biggest and most ambitious urban renewal projects in years is the ongoing transformation of New York's seedy 42nd Street from a neighborhood of porno palaces and bars into a family-friendly mecca featuring Disney stores, Broadway theaters, and similar venues. Disney and other investors, of course, had to rely heavily on information as they made decisions about huge financial commitments. Much of this information was obtained, analyzed, and presented in electronic form to managers at Disney and officials in the city and state governments of New York.

the information system is put into normal operation, future modifications may still be necessary. For example, after Black & Decker acquired General Electric's small-appliance business, it had to overhaul its own information system to accommodate all the new information associated with its new business. Information management is a continuous process. Even if an effective information system can be created and put into use, there is still an good chance that it will need to be modified occasionally to fit changing circumstances.

■ Integrating Information Systems

In very large and complex organizations, information systems must also be integrated. This integration may involve linkages between different information systems within the same organization or between different organizations altogether.[14] Within an organization, for example, the marketing system and the operations system should be able to communicate with one another.

Linking systems together is not as easy as it might seem. A company might install its first information system in operations using a Sun system. A couple of years later, it might put a system into marketing but decide for some reason to use IBM equipment. When a decision is made still later to integrate the two systems, differences in technology and operating systems might make such integration difficult or even impossible.

One way to overcome this problem is to develop everything at once. Unfortunately, doing so is expensive, and sometimes managers simply can't anticipate their future needs accurately. Another method is to adopt a standard type of system at the beginning so that subsequent additions fit properly. Even then, however, breakthroughs in information system technology may still make it necessary to change approaches in midstream.

The **information superhighway**, or **Internet**, is an emerging example of a vast, integrated information system that is changing the way people com-

information superhighway

(**Internet**)   An emerging integrated information system that can be accessed by anyone with a computer and a modem

municate. Everyday, more and more people tie into the Internet to access information about topics such as weather, sports, business, hobbies, and leisure activities.[15]

■ Using Information Systems

The real test of the value of an information system is how it can be used. Ideally, an information system should be simple to use and nontechnical—that is, someone should not have to be a computer expert to use the system. In theory, a manager should be able to access a modern information system by turning on a computer and pressing certain keys in response to menu prompts. The manager should also be able to enter appropriate new data or request certain kinds of information. The requested information might first be displayed on a computer screen or monitor. When the manager is satisfied, the information can then be printed out on a standard printer, stored in the system for possible future use or for use by others, or both.

The Travelers Group has made effective use of its information system to improve its efficiency. The firm started by hiring a team of trained nurses to review health-insurance claims. These nurses tap into the company's regular information system and analyze the medical diagnoses that accompany each claim. The nurses use this information to determine whether to require a second opinion before approving a particular surgical procedure. They enter their decision directly into the system. The printed claim form tells the claimant whether he or she must seek a second opinion before proceeding.

MANAGEMENT IMPLICATIONS Managers should know the processes involved in establishing an information system. They should also know how to integrate and use information systems as they are being created and after they have been implemented. ■

The Impact of Information Systems on Organizations

Information systems are clearly an important part of most modern organizations. Their effects are felt in a variety of ways. In particular, information systems affect performance, the organization itself, and people within the organization. Information systems also have clear limits to what they can do.

■ Performance Effects

Organizations install information systems because they think they will make the organization more effective and efficient. During the 1980s, for example,

WORKING WITH DIVERSITY

Women in the Valley

White males still dominate the executive suites of many old-line businesses—oil, steel, and automobile manufacturing, for example. A primary reason for this situation is that when these companies were founded a hundred or more years ago few women or minorities had employment opportunities. It was a "man's world," so to speak, and the Carnegies, Rockefellers, Fords, and Vanderbilts that launched the heavy manufacturing industries that until recently dominated the U.S. economy wanted to keep it that way. The organizational cultures and practices that grew from their views thus served as barriers to women and minorities. And even though this scenario may have changed recently, relatively few women and minorities have had the chance to break into the top managerial ranks of companies like Mobil, Bethlehem Steel, and General Motors.

But newer high-tech industries such as computer manufacturing, software development, and information technology don't have this long legacy of male dominance. Not surprisingly, then, women and minorities are finding it much easier to excel in these areas than in old-line manufacturing companies. Indeed, high-tech hotbeds like Austin,

> *"In the tech industry people don't care how old you are, what color you are, or what sex you are."*
>
> *Christina Jones, high-tech entrepreneur**

Texas, and Silicon Valley in California are just as open and receptive to women and minority executives and entrepreneurs as they are to white males.

For example, Christina Jones cofounded Trilogy Development Group in Austin and then left to start another company called pcOrder.com, Inc. The first business was a software development company, and the second helps computer and software companies market their products over the Internet. More than half of her sixty employees are women.

In California, success stories are even more abundant. Mary Ann Byrnes, for example, has started a successful company that uses submarine recognition technology to disconnect stolen cellular telephones. Lounette Dyer owns a growing company that helps marketers refine and get more information from their customer databases. And Maureen Lawrence's business is at the forefront of developing the next generation of data-networking equipment. Clearly, then, diversity and high tech seem to go hand-in-hand.

References: *"Women of the Valley,"* Forbes, *December 30, 1996, pp. 102–108 (*quote on p. 102); and "The Best Entrepreneurs,"* Business Week, *January 12, 1998, pp. 70–73.*

almost 40 percent of all capital spending by U.S. companies on information systems technology—close to a trillion dollars. Since 1990, meanwhile, U.S. companies have spent more on information technology than on capital equipment.[16] And some experts believe that in the early years of the twenty-first century investments in information technology will grow even faster. "Working with Diversity" discusses how many successful female entrepreneurs are getting in on this trend.

Has the expenditure been worthwhile? Some experts say yes; others have their doubts. The problem is that although information systems can speed up an organization's ability to crunch numbers and generate documents, it is difficult to measure whether the increased speed is justified in light of the enormous costs involved. Many organizations, ranging from General Electric to Kmart to American Airlines, claim that their information systems have made them enormously successful. Indeed, there seems to be a growing consensus that information systems do pay for themselves over time, although an organization may have to wait many years for the pay back.

A good example of a highly effective system is the one developed by the U.S. Forest Service. The Forest Service used to have a policy of attacking every forest fire by 10 A.M. the day after it was reported. Costs could run as high as $10 million for a major fire. The service now uses computer models as a part of its information system to determine how important containment really is. For example, rivers often provide a natural barrier that stops fires from spreading. An Idaho blaze was determined to fit just such a pattern. Under the old plan, the service would have spent an estimated $3.7 million to extinguish the blaze. But understanding how a river would halt the fire's spread resulted in expenses of only $400,000. Information is made available to firefighters in the field through hand-held programmable computers tied into a master information system. Although not every organization will be as satisfied as the Forest Service is with its information system, more and more firms are telling comparable success stories.

Organizational Effects

Information systems affect the organization's basic structure and design. These effects generally happen in two ways. First, most organizations decide to create a separate unit to handle the information management system; some even create a new top-management position, usually called the chief information officer, or CIO. This manager and her or his staff is responsible for maintaining the information system, upgrading it as appropriate, finding new uses for it, and training people in its use.[17]

The second way in which information affects organizations is by allowing companies to eliminate layers in the managerial hierarchy. As discussed in Chapter 11, information systems allow managers to stay in touch with large numbers of subordinates, thereby eliminating the need for hierarchical control. IBM, for example, eliminated a layer of management because of improved efficiencies achieved through its information management system. Some experts have suggested that in the future managers will be able to coordinate as many as two hundred subordinates at one time.

Behavioral Effects

Information systems affect the behaviors of people in organizations. Some of these effects are positive; others can be negative. On the plus side information systems usually

Information technology can have profound effects on an organization. Consider the success enjoyed by Michael Fields. Fields worked for Oracle's software guru Larry Ellison for three years, but could ever quite agree on new product development priorities. Ellison preferred the most glamorous businesses such as hotel and airline reservation systems and on-line retailing opportunities. Fields, however, saw greater prospects in less glamorous areas, such as information storage backup and network security. Eventually, Fields cashed in his stock options and launched his own business, Open Vision Technologies. And so far, at least, Open Vision has been a resounding success.

TABLE 22.2

Limitations of Information Systems

Although information systems play a vital role in modern organizations, they are not without their limitations. In particular, information systems have six basic limitations. For example, one major limitation of installing an information system is cost. For a large company, an information system might cost several million dollars.

1. Information systems are expensive and difficult to develop and implement.

2. Information systems are not suitable for all tasks or problems.

3. Managers sometimes rely on information systems too much.

4. Information provided to managers may not be as accurate, timely, complete, or relevant as it appears.

5. Managers may have unrealistic expectations of what the information system can do.

6. The information system may be subject to sabotage, computer viruses, or downtime.

improve individual efficiency. Some people also enjoy their work more because they have fun using the new technology. As a result of computerized bulletin boards and e-mail, groups can form across organizational boundaries.

On the negative side, information systems can lead to isolation as people have everything they need to do their jobs without interacting with others. Managers can work at home easily, with the possible side effects of making them unavailable to others who need them or removing them from key parts of the social system. Computerized working arrangements also tend to be much less personal than other methods. For example, a computer-transmitted "pat on the back" will likely mean less than a real one. Researchers are just beginning to determine the impact of information systems on individual behaviors and attitudes.[18]

■ Information System Limitations

It is also necessary to recognize the limits of information systems. Several of these are listed in Table 22.2. First, as already noted, information systems are expensive and difficult to develop. Thus organizations may try to cut corners or install a system in such a piecemeal fashion that its effectiveness suffers.

Information systems simply are not suitable for some tasks or problems. Complex problems requiring human judgment must still be addressed by humans. Information systems are often a useful tool for managers, but they can seldom actually replace managers. Managers also may come to rely too much on information systems. As a consequence, the manager may lose touch with the real-world problems he or she needs to be concerned about.

Information may not be as accurate, timely, complete, or relevant as it appears. People have a strong tendency to think that because a computer performed the calculations, the answer must be correct—especially if the answer is calculated to several decimal places. However, if the initial information was flawed, all subsequent computations using it are likely to be flawed as well.

Managers sometimes have unrealistic expectations about what an information system can accomplish. They may believe that the first stage of implementation will result in a full-blown Orwellian communication network that a child could use. When the manager sees the flaws and limits of the system, she or he may be disappointed and as a result not use the system effectively. Finally, the information system may be subject to sabotage, computer viruses, or downtime. Disgruntled employees have been known to deliberately enter false data. And a company that relies too much on a computerized information system may become totally paralyzed in the event of a simple power outage.

MANAGEMENT IMPLICATIONS Managers should know that information technology has the potential to affect performance, the organization itself, and the behaviors of its employees. Managers should also remember these effects can be positive or negative. ▬

Summary of Key Points

Information is a vital part of every manager's job. For information to be useful, it must be accurate, timely, complete, and accurate. Information technology is best conceived of as part of the control process.

Information technology systems contain five basic components. These are an input medium, a processor, storage, a control system, and an output medium. Although the forms vary, both manual and computerized information systems have these components.

Four factors determine an organization's information technology requirements. Two general factors are the environment and size of the organization. Two specific factors are area and level of the organization. Each factor must be weighed in planning an information system.

There are four basic kinds of information systems—transaction-processing systems, basic management information systems, decision support systems, and executive information systems. Each provides certain types of information and is most valuable for specific types of managers.

Managing information systems involves three basic elements. The first is deciding how to establish information systems. Of course, this step actually involves a wide array of specific activities and steps. The systems must then be integrated. Finally, managers must be able to use them.

Information systems affect organizations in various ways. Major influences are on performance, the organization itself, and behavior within the organization. There are also limitations to the effectiveness of information systems. Managers should understand these limitations so as to not have unrealistic expectations.

Recent advances in information technology include breakthroughs in telecommunications, networks, and expert systems. Each promises to further enhance an organization's ability to manage information effectively.

Discussion Questions

Questions for Review

1. What are the characteristics of useful information? How can information management aid in organizational control?

2. What are the building blocks of information systems? How are they related to one another?

3. What is a management information system? How can such a system be used to benefit an organization?

4. What is an expert system? Do such systems have any significant potential for use by business organizations? Why or why not?

Questions for Analysis

5. In what ways is a management information system like an inventory control system or a production control system? In what ways is it different?

6. It has been said that the information revolution now occurring is like the industrial revolution in terms of the magnitude of its impact on organizations and society. What leads to such a view? Why might that view be an overstatement?

7. Is it possible for the chief information officer of an organization to become too powerful? If so, how might the situation be prevented? If not, why not?

Questions for Application

8. Interview a local business manager about the use of information in his or her organization. How is information managed? Is a computer system used? How well does the information system seem to be integrated with other aspects of organizational control?

9. Your college or university library deals in information. What kind of information system is used? Is it computerized? How might the information system be redesigned to be of more value to you?

10. Go to the library and try to find information about a business that is using an expert system. If you can get the information, share it with the class. Why might this be a difficult assignment?

Building Effective Communication Skills

EXERCISE OVERVIEW

Communication skills refer to the manager's abilities to effectively convey ideas and information to others and to effectively receive ideas and information from others. This exercise demonstrates how communication skills relate to information technology.

EXERCISE BACKGROUND

Newer forms of information technology like e-mail and cellular telephones are changing the ways that managers communicate with one another. In some ways these forms of communication are similar to earlier forms, but in other ways they are fundamentally different.

Go to your library and research the business literature from the 1960s. Look specifically for "how to" articles dealing with telephone etiquette and letter-writing fundamentals. Find at least one list of "do's and don'ts" about each form of communication.

EXERCISE TASK

With the preceding background information as context, do the following:

1. Identify suggestions from each list that seem to be just as applicable to modern forms of information technology as they were in the 1960s.

2. Identify suggestions from each list that do not seem to be applicable to modern forms of information technology.

3. Compile your own new how-to lists for using information technology.

4. Add to your lists suggestions for using other forms of information technology such as facsimile machines and voice-mail systems.

EXERCISE OVERVIEW

Interpersonal skills refer to the ability to communicate with, understand, and motivate individuals and groups. Information technology has obvious linkages with interpersonal skills.

EXERCISE BACKGROUND

Your company is at the forefront of modern information technology. All your managers have voice mail and e-mail, all are networked, and many have started working at home. They point out that they are more productive there and don't really need to come into the office every day to get their work done. And, indeed, productivity is booming.

But you recently discovered a situation that has caused you some concern. Specifically, you have learned that you have two employees who have each worked for you for almost six months and who communicate with one another on a regular basis—but have never met in person. Because you consider your company a warm and friendly place to work, you are alarmed by this lack of personal interaction.

EXERCISE TASK

With the preceding background information as context, do the following:

1. Decide whether or not face-to-face communication is important today.

2. If so, develop a plan for enhancing interpersonal relations among your employees without losing the competitive advantage you have gained from information technology.

3. If not, develop a rationale that you might use to placate or comfort an employee who complains about the lack of interpersonal relations.

EXERCISE OVERVIEW

Time-management skills refer to the manager's ability to prioritize work, to work efficiently, and to delegate appropriately. This exercise focuses on how time management and information technology may relate to one another.

EXERCISE BACKGROUND

One of the biggest implied advantages of modern information technology today is time management—modern technology is supposed to make us more productive and more efficient and make it easier to communicate with one another. At the same time most people acknowledge that information technology can also get out of hand.

Here are five forms of information technology. Start this exercise by thinking of ways that each form can both save and waste time.

1. Cellular telephone
2. E-mail
3. Voice mail
4. Internet
5. Facsimile machine

EXERCISE TASK

With the preceding background information as context, do the following:

1. Describe what a manager can do to capitalize more on the advantages and minimize the disadvantages of each form of information technology in terms of time-management.

2. Some managers have argued that they have become more efficient by turning off one or more of these information technology devices. Critique this idea from a time management perspective.

3. Identify two other forms of information technology you use and characterize them in terms of time management.

CHAPTER CLOSING CASE

Information Drives Big Retailers

When many people think of sophisticated information systems they think of high-tech companies such as IBM and Compaq and firms that have a strong reliance on information such as FedEx and UPS. These individuals might be surprised to learn that many retailers also rely heavily on information systems to help them keep track of inventory, sales, and reordering cycles.

For example, the king of retailing, Wal-Mart, has relied heavily on information technology for years. Indeed, even though the firm opened its first store in 1962, it didn't really take off until 1970. And the catalyst for that growth was new investments in information technology. For one thing, Wal-Mart began building heavily automated distribution centers that cut shipping costs and time. For another, it implemented a computerized inventory system to speed up checkout and reordering.

Wal-Mart has continued to rely on information, spending as much as half a billion dollars a year on information technology. Indeed, its current information storage capacity of twenty-four terabytes is second only to the U.S. government. Of course, all this information is useless unless it is shared, so Wal-Mart also makes sure that all its associates (the term it uses for employees) have the information they need to compete most effectively.

Wal-Mart managers get weekly Top 50 reports detailing the top-selling items of the week by number of units sold, total dollars, and profits. And all department managers carry scanners; running the scanner over any product's bar code can tell them how many of that item sold the day before, the week before, and for the same periods last year. The scanners can also tell them how many of every item they have in stock, how many are on the way, and how many are in stock at nearby stores in case they need to borrow some.

Wal-Mart also continually analyzes its ninety million weekly transactions to look for purchasing patterns. For example, although most retailers display charcoal, grills, and grilling supplies close together, Wal-Mart has also learned to place packages of small baggies next to pretzels—many parents, it turns out, pack pretzels in baggies for school lunches. Information technology like this helps Wal-Mart remain the king of retailing.

But what about the previous king, Sears? Just a few years ago, most experts were writing Sears off as an also-ran. Among the reasons for its fall from grace were callous disregard for customers and disdain for modern management methods such as information technology. But under new CEO Arthur Martinez, Sears has come storming back and restaked its claim as one of the best—even if not the biggest—retailers around. And in doing so, Sears has taken several pages from Wal-Mart's playbook.

For example, Sears is vigorously investing in information technology to track sales and learn more about its customers. Sears is developing large databases that track customer purchases; it also maintains complete records on all service work it performs. Thus, if an ice maker breaks during its warranty period, the customer won't be required to produce any sort of proof-of-purchase—Sears will already know when it was bought, how much it cost, and if any other service work has been performed on it.

International retailers are also getting into the act. Consider, for example, how 7-Eleven Japan manages its information. Every 7-Eleven store in Japan has a powerful, custom-made NEC computer. The computer controls store equipment such as refrigerators and air conditioners and automatically notifies maintenance companies if anything needs servicing. Sales information is presented to managers in a format that is easy to read, understand, and use. The information shows which products sell best at different times of day and under different weather conditions.

When it is time to reorder, the manager uses a hand-held terminal so that he or she can freely move around the store while doing the reordering. That terminal can also receive messages from the central office, informing the store manager, for instance, of new products or specials that should be considered in restocking. The company also shares information with its suppliers. The moment a customer buys a soft drink or a can of beer, the information goes directly to the bottler or brewery. Suppliers can use the information to forecast demand for their products and thus more carefully match their production to sales. They can use the information to develop new products for changing customer tastes. Supplying 7-Eleven stores is such a sought after arrangement that more than thirty-five companies now have special factories to produce items exclusively for 7-Eleven Japan. In addition, the suppliers coordinate their deliveries so that only twelve, rather than thirty-four, trucks makes deliveries each day.

Case Questions

1. Describe the role of information in retailing.
2. Can you think of other kinds of information that might benefit a retailer?
3. Can a retailer have too much information? Why or why not?

Case References: "Believe in Yourself, Believe in Your Merchandise," *Forbes*, September 8, 1997, pp. 118–124; Patricia Sellers, "Sears: The Turnaround Is Ending; The Revolution Has Begun," *Fortune*, April 28, 1997, pp. 106–118; and "Reinventing Sears," *Time*, December 23, 1996, pp. 53–55.

CHAPTER NOTES

1. Gene Bylinsky, "Industry's Amazing Instant Prototypes," *Fortune*, January 12, 1998, pp. 120B–120D; Thomas Stewart, "Managing in a Wired Company," *Fortune*, July 11, 1994, pp. 44–56; and *Hoover's Handbook of American Business 1998* (Austin, Texas: Hoover's Business Press, 1998), pp. 1294–1295.

2. Christopher P. Holland and A. Geoffrey Lockett, "Mixed Mode Network Structures: The Strategic Use of Electronic Communication by Organizations," *Organization Science*, September–October 1997, pp. 475–488.

3. "At Today's Supermarket, the Computer Is Doing It All," *Business Week*, August 11, 1996, pp. 64–66.

4. Carla Rapoport, "Great Japanese Mistakes," *Fortune*, February 13, 1989, pp. 108–111.

5. Edward W. Desmond, "How Your Data May Soon Seek You Out," *Fortune*, September 1997, pp. 149–154.

6. William J. Bruns Jr. and F. Warren McFarlin, "Information Technology Puts Power in Control Systems," *Harvard Business Review*, September–October 1987, pp. 89–94.

7. N. Venkatraman, "IT-Enabled Business Transformation: From Automation to Business Scope Redefinition," *Sloan Management Review*, Winter 1994, pp. 73–84.

8. Marianne Broadbent and Peter Weill, "Management by Maxim: How Business and IT Managers Can Create IT Infrastructures," *Sloan Management Review*, Spring 1997, pp. 77–89.

9. "Believe in Yourself, Believe in the Merchandise," *Forbes*, September 8, 1997, pp. 118–124.

10. Jeremy Main, "At Last, Software CEOs Can Use," *Fortune*, March 13, 1989, pp. 77–83.

11. "Get What You Want from the Web," *Fortune*, October 27, 1997, pp. 283–284.

12. "Turning an Expert's Skills into Computer Software," *Business Week*, October 7, 1985, pp. 104–108.

13. "The Messy Business of Culling Company Files," *Wall Street Journal*, May 22, 1997, pp. B1, B2.

14. "How Do You Build an Information Highway?" *Business Week*, September 16, 1991, pp. 108–112.

15. "Getting Your Company's Internet Strategy Right," *Fortune*, March 18, 1996, pp. 72–78.

16. "The Information Age in Charts," *Fortune*, April 4, 1994, p. 77.

17. "The New Enablers—Chief Information Officers," *Forbes*, June 2, 1997, pp. 138–143.

18. "Worksite Face-Off: Techie vs. User," *USA Today*, June 17, 1997, pp. B1, B2.

Control and Information Management Can Breed Success

Control is the fourth fundamental management function; information management plays a key role in effective control. Just as a pilot works to keep a plane on course, so too does a manager use control to guide an organization toward its goals and through the successful implementation of its strategies. This video case illustrates how control and information can be managed to enhance organizational effectiveness.

OVERVIEW AND OBJECTIVES

After completing this video case you should be able to:

1. Better appreciate the information management issues that exist in different organizations.

2. More easily recognize the role of information and information management in effective control.

COMPANY BACKGROUND

Assume that you are a top manager in one of the following three kinds of organizations:

Information Resources is in the data and information business. Your company takes the data from optical scanning devices in supermarkets and drug stores, transforms it into usable information, and then sells that information to consumer products firms like Nestlé and Procter & Gamble and retailers like Kroger and Albertson's.

The second firm is called the Armes Agency. Headquartered in El Paso, Texas and run by Jay J. Armes, this firm is primarily in the intelligence business. The firm gathers information for its clients, undertakes electronic surveillances, and trains security officers of big companies and detectives for other private agencies.

Finally, CSX Corporation is one of the world's largest railroad companies. CSX owns and manages fleets of trains, engines, and railcars throughout the United States. The firm is also a major player in ocean container-shipping and barge transportation. CSX resources transport gravel, chemicals, automobiles and trucks, grains, and a variety of other products and commodities.

CASE QUESTIONS

1. Identify the kinds of control systems that each of these organizations is likely to use.

2. Describe the kinds of information that each firm uses.

3. How are information and control related in each firm?

VIDEO REVIEW

Your instructor will now show you a video clip that provides more information about Information Resources, the Armes Agency, and CSX.

FOLLOW-UP QUESTIONS

1. After viewing the video, revise your answers to the Case Questions above as needed.

2. Identify the similarities and differences in control at the three firms.

3. Identify the similarities and differences in information management at the three firms.

4. What role does quality play in each of these firms?

POPULAR VIDEO FOLLOW-UP

Each of the movies listed below provides some insights and examples to illustrate various control concepts and ideas. See if you can come up with other examples.

■ *Air Force One* (control)

■ *Apollo 13* (control)

■ *Die Hard With a Vengeance* (control and operations management)

■ *The Sting* (information management)

■ *While You Were Sleeping* (information management)

Tools for Planning and Decision Making

This appendix discusses a number of the basic tools and techniques that managers can use to enhance the efficiency and effectiveness of planning and decision making. We first describe forecasting, an extremely important tool, and then discuss several other planning techniques. Next we discuss several tools that relate more to decision making. We conclude by assessing the strengths and weaknesses of the various tools and techniques.

Forecasting

To plan, managers must make assumptions about future events. But unlike wizards of old, planners cannot simply look into a crystal ball. Instead, they must develop forecasts of probable future circumstances. **Forecasting** is the process of developing assumptions or premises about the future that managers can use in planning or decision making.

forecasting The process of developing assumptions or premises about the future that managers can use in planning or decision making

■ Sales and Revenue Forecasting

As the term implies, **sales forecasting** is concerned with predicting future sales. Because monetary resources (derived mainly from sales) are necessary to finance both current and future operations, knowledge of future sales is of vital importance. Sales forecasting is something that every business, from Exxon to a neighborhood pizza parlor, must do. Consider, for example, the following questions that a manager might need to answer:

sales forecasting The prediction of future sales

1. How much of each of our products should we produce next week? next month? next year?
2. How much money will we have available to spend on research and development and on new-product test marketing?
3. When and to what degree will we need to expand our existing production facilities?
4. How should we respond to union demands for a 15 percent pay increase?
5. If we borrow money for expansion, can we pay it back?

None of these questions can be adequately answered without some notion of what future revenues are likely to be. Thus sales forecasting is generally one of the first steps in planning.

Unfortunately, the term *sales forecasting* suggests that this form of forecasting is appropriate only for organizations that have something to sell. But other kinds of organizations also depend on financial resources, and so they also must forecast. The University of South Carolina, for example, must forecast future state aid before planning course offerings, staff size, and so on. Hospitals must forecast their future income from patient fees, insurance payments, and other sources to assess their ability to expand. Although we will continue to use the conventional term, keep in mind that what is really at issue is **revenue forecasting**.

revenue forecasting The prediction of future revenues from all sources

Several sources of information are used to develop a sales forecast. Previous sales figures and any obvious trends, such as the company's growth or stability, usually serve as the base. General economic indicators, technological improvements, new marketing strategies, and the competition's behavior all may be added together to ensure an accurate forecast. Once projected, the sales (or revenues) forecast becomes a guiding framework for a variety of other activities. Raw-material expenditures, advertising budgets, sales-commission structures, and similar operating costs are all based on projected sales figures.

Organizations often forecast sales across several time horizons. The longer-run forecasts may then be updated and refined as various shorter-run cycles are completed. For obvious reasons, a forecast should be as accurate as possible, and the accuracy of sales forecasting tends to increase as organizations learn from their previous forecasting experience. But the more uncertain and complex future conditions are likely to be, the more difficult it is to develop accurate forecasts. To partially offset these problems, forecasts are more useful to managers if they are expressed as a range rather than as an absolute index or number. If projected sales increases are expected to be in the range of 10 to 12 percent, a manager can consider all the implications for the entire range. A 10 percent increase could dictate one set of activities; a 12 percent increase could call for a different set of activities.

■ Technological Forecasting

technological forecasting The prediction of what future technologies are likely to emerge and when they are likely to be economically feasible

Technological forecasting is another type of forecasting used by many organizations. It focuses on predicting what future technologies are likely to emerge and when they are likely to be economically feasible. In an era when technological breakthrough and innovation have become the rule rather than the exception, it is important that managers be able to anticipate new developments. If a manager invests heavily in existing technology (such as production processes, equipment, and computer systems) and the technology becomes obsolete in the near future, the company has wasted its resources.

The most striking technological innovations in recent years have been in electronics, especially semiconductors. Home computers, electronic games, and sophisticated communications equipment are all evidence of the electronics explosion. Given the increasing importance of technology and the rapid pace of technological innovation, it follows that managers will grow increasingly concerned with technological forecasting in the years to come.

■ Other Types of Forecasting

Other types of forecasting are also important to many organizations. Resource forecasting projects the organization's future needs for and the availability of human resources, raw materials, and other resources. General economic conditions are the subject of economic forecasts. For example, some organizations undertake population or market-size forecasting. Some organizations also attempt to forecast future government fiscal policy and various government regulations that might be put into practice. Indeed, virtually any component in an organization's environment may be an appropriate area for forecasting.

■ Forecasting Techniques

To carry out the various kinds of forecasting we have identified, managers use several different techniques.[1] Time-series analysis and causal modeling are two common quantitative techniques.

Time-Series Analysis   The underlying assumption of **time-series analysis** is that the past is a good predictor of the future. This technique is most useful when the manager has a lot of historical data available and when stable trends and patterns are apparent. In a time-series analysis, the variable under consideration (such as sales or enrollment) is plotted across time, and a "best fit" line is identified.[2] Figure A.1 shows how a time-series analysis might look. The dots represent the number of units sold for each year from 1993 through 2001. The best-fit line has also been drawn in. It is the line around which the dots cluster with the least variability. A manager who wants to know what sales to expect in 2002 simply extends the line. In this case the projection would be around eighty-two hundred units.

Real time-series analysis involves much more than simply plotting sales data and then using a ruler and a pencil to draw and extend the line. Sophisticated mathematical procedures, among other things, are necessary to account for seasonal and cyclical fluctuations and to identify the true best-fit line. In real situations data seldom follow the neat pattern found in Figure A.1. Indeed, the data points may be so widely dispersed that they mask meaningful trends from all but painstaking, computer-assisted inspection.

time-series analysis   A forecasting technique that extends past information into the future through the calculation of a best-fit line

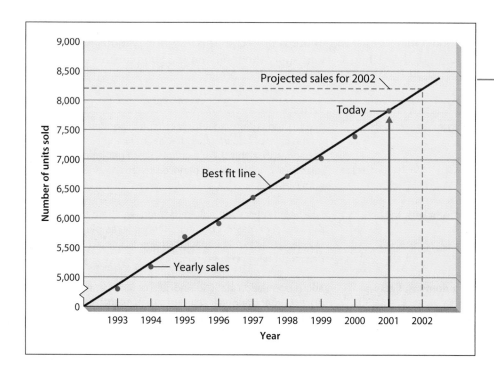

FIGURE A.1

An Example of Time-Series Analysis

Because time-series analysis assumes that the past is a good predictor of the future, it is most useful when historical data are available, trends are stable, and patterns are apparent. For example, it can be used for projecting estimated sales for products like shampoo, pens, and automobile tires.

causal modeling A group of different techniques that determine causal relationships between different variables

regression model An equation that uses one set of variables to predict another variable

econometric model A causal model that predicts major economic shifts and their impact on the organization

Causal Modeling Another useful forecasting technique is **causal modeling**. Actually, the term *causal modeling* represents a group of several techniques. Table A.1 summarizes three of the most useful approaches. **Regression models** are equations created to predict a variable (such as sales volume) that depends on a number of other variables (such as price and advertising). The variable being predicted is called the *dependent variable*; the variables used to make the prediction are called *independent variables*. A typical regression equation used by a small business might take this form:

$$y = ax_1 + bx_2 + cx_3 + d$$

where

y = the dependent variable (sales in this case)

x_1, x_2, and x_3 = independent variables (advertising budget, price, and commissions)

a, b, and c = weights for the independent variables calculated during development of the regression model

d = a constant

To use the model, a manager can insert various alternatives for advertising budget, price, and commissions into the equation and then compute y. The calculated value of y represents the forecasted level of sales, given various levels of advertising, price, and commissions.[3]

Econometric models employ regression techniques at a much more complex level. **Econometric models** attempt to predict major economic shifts and the potential impact of those shifts on the organization. They might be used to predict various age, ethnic, and economic groups that will characterize different regions of the United States in the year 2000 and to further predict the kinds of products and services these groups may want. A complete econometric model may consist of hundreds or even thousands of equations. Computers are almost always necessary to apply them. Given the complexities involved in

TABLE A.1
Summary of Causal Modeling Forecasting Techniques

Managers use several different types of causal models in planning and decision making. Three popular models are regression models, econometric models, and economic indicators.

Regression models	Used to predict one variable (called the dependent variable) on the basis of known or assumed other variables (called independent variables). For example, we might predict future sales based on the values of price, advertising, and economic levels.
Econometric models	Make use of several multiple-regression equations to consider the impact of major economic shifts. For example, we might want to predict what impact the migration toward the Sun Belt might have on our organization.
Economic indicators	Various population statistics, indexes, or parameters that predict organizationally relevant variables such as discretionary income. Examples include cost-of-living index, inflation rate, and level of unemployment.

developing econometric models, many firms that decide to use them rely on outside consultants specializing in this approach.

Economic indicators, another form of causal model, are population statistics or indexes that reflect the economic well-being of a population. Examples of widely used economic indicators include the current rates of national productivity, inflation, and unemployment. In using such indicators, the manager draws on past experiences that have revealed a relationship between a certain indicator and some facet of the company's operations. Pitney Bowes Data Documents Division, for example, can predict future sales of its business forms largely on the basis of current GNP estimates and other economic growth indexes.

economic indicator A key population statistic or index that reflects the economic well-being of a population

Qualitative Forecasting Techniques Organizations also use several qualitative techniques to develop their forecasts. A **qualitative forecasting technique** relies more on individual or group judgment or opinion rather than on sophisticated mathematical analyses. The Delphi procedure, described in Chapter 9 as a mechanism for managing group decision-making activities, can also be used to develop forecasts. A variation of it—the *jury-of-expert-opinion* approach—involves using the basic Delphi process with members of top management. In this instance top management serves as a collection of experts asked to make a prediction about something—competitive behavior, trends in product demand, and so forth. Either a pure Delphi or a jury-of-expert-opinion approach might be useful in technological forecasting.

qualitative forecasting technique One of several techniques that rely on individual or group judgment rather than on mathematical analyses

The *sales-force-composition* method of sales forecasting is a pooling of the predictions and opinions of experienced salespeople. Because of their experience, these individuals are often able to forecast quite accurately what various customers will do. Management combines these forecasts and interprets the data to create plans. Textbook publishers use this procedure to project how many copies of a new title they might sell.

The *customer evaluation* technique goes beyond an organization's sales force and collects data from customers of the organization. The customers provide estimates of their own future needs for the goods and services that the organization supplies. Managers must combine, interpret, and act on this information. This approach, however, has two major limitations. Customers may be less interested in taking time to develop accurate predictions than are members of the organization itself, and the method makes no provision for including any new customers that the organization may acquire. Wal-Mart helps its suppliers use this approach by providing them with detailed projections regarding what it intends to buy several months in advance.

Selecting an appropriate forecasting technique can be as important as applying it correctly. Some techniques are appropriate only for specific circumstances. For example, the sales-force-composition technique is good only for sales forecasting. Other techniques, like the Delphi method, are useful in a variety of situations. Some techniques, such as the econometric models, require extensive use of computers, whereas others, such as customer evaluation models, can be used with little mathematical expertise. For the most part selection of a particular technique depends on the nature of the problem, the experience and preferences of the manager, and available resources.[4]

Other Planning Techniques

Of course, planning involves more than just forecasting. Other tools and techniques that are useful for planning purposes include linear programming, breakeven analysis, and simulations.

■ Linear Programming

linear programming A planning technique that determines the optimal combination of resources and activities

Linear programming is one of the most widely used quantitative tools for planning. **Linear programming** is a procedure for calculating the optimal combination of resources and activities. It is appropriate when there is some objective to be met (such as a sales quota or a certain production level) within a set of constraints (such as a limited advertising budget or limited production capabilities).

To illustrate how linear programming can be used, assume that a small electronics company produces two basic products—a high-quality cable television tuner and a high-quality receiver for picking up television audio and playing it through a stereo amplifier. Both products go through the same two departments, first production and then inspection and testing. Each product has a known profit margin and a high level of demand. The production manager's job is to produce the optimal combination of tuners (T) and receivers (R) in order to maximize profits and use the time in production (PR) and in inspection and testing (IT) most efficiently. Table A.2 gives the information needed for the use of linear programming to solve this problem.

The *objective function* is an equation that represents what we want to achieve. In technical terms it is a mathematical representation of the desirability of the consequences of a particular decision. In our example, the objective function can be represented as follows:

$$\text{Maximize profit} = \$30X_T + \$20X_R$$

where

R = the number of receivers to be produced

T = the number of tuners to be produced

TABLE A.2
Production Data for Tuners and Receivers

Linear programming can be used to determine the optimal number of tuners and receivers an organization might make. Essential information needed to perform this analysis includes the number of hours each product spends in each department, the production capacity for each department, and the profit margin for each product.

The $30 and $20 figures are the respective profit margins of the tuner and receiver, as noted in Table A.2. The objective, then, is to maximize profits.

However, this objective must be accomplished within a specific set of constraints. In our example, the constraints are the time required to produce each product in each department and the total amount of time avail-

Department	Number of Hours Required per Unit		Production Capacity for Day (in Hours)
	Tuners (T)	Receivers (R)	
Production (PR)	10	6	150
Inspection and testing (IT)	4	4	80
Profit margin	$30	$20	

able. These data are also found in Table A.2 and can be used to construct the relevant constraint equations:

$$10T + 6R \leq 150$$

$$4T + 4R \leq 80$$

(that is, we cannot use more capacity than is available), and of course,

$$T \geq 0$$

$$R \geq 0$$

The set of equations consisting of the objective function and constraints can be solved graphically. To start, we first assume that production of each product is maximized when production of the other is at zero. The resultant solutions are then plotted on a coordinate axis. In the PR department, if $T = 0$ then:

$$10T + 6R \leq 150$$

$$10(0) + 6R \leq 150$$

$$R \leq 25$$

In the same department, if $R = 0$ then:

$$10T + 6(R) \leq 150$$

$$10T + 6(0) \leq 150$$

$$T \leq 15$$

Similarly, in the IT department, if no tuners are produced,

$$4T + 4R \leq 80$$

$$4(0) + 4R \leq 80$$

$$R \leq 20$$

and, if no receivers are produced,

$$4T + 4R \leq 80$$

$$4T + 4(0) \leq 80$$

$$T \leq 20$$

The four resulting inequalities are graphed in Figure A.2. The shaded region represents the feasibility space, or production combinations that do not exceed the capacity of either department. The optimal number of products will be defined at one of the four corners of the shaded area—that is, the firm should produce twenty receivers only (point C), fifteen tuners only (point B), thirteen receivers and seven tuners (point E), or no products at all. With the constraint that production of both tuners and receivers must be greater than zero, it follows that point E is the optimal solution. That combination requires 148 hours in PR and 80 hours in IT and yields $470 in profit.

FIGURE A.2

The Graphical Solution of a Linear Programming Problem

Finding the solution to a linear programming problem graphically is useful when only two alternatives are being considered. When problems are more complex, computers that can execute hundreds of equations and variables are necessary. Virtually all large firms, such as General Motors, Texaco, and Sears, use linear programming.

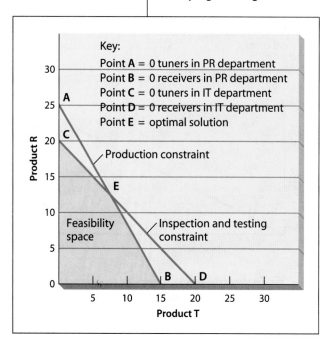

Key:
Point A = 0 tuners in PR department
Point B = 0 receivers in PR department
Point C = 0 tuners in IT department
Point D = 0 receivers in IT department
Point E = optimal solution

(Note that if only receivers were produced, the profit would be $400; producing only tuners would mean $450 in profit.)

Unfortunately, only two alternatives can be handled by the graphical method, and our example was extremely simple. When there are other alternatives, a complex algebraic method must be employed. Real-world problems may require several hundred equations and variables. Clearly, computers are necessary to execute such sophisticated analyses. Linear programming is a powerful technique, playing a key role in both planning and decision making. It can be used to schedule production, select an optimal portfolio of investments, allocate sales representatives to territories, or produce an item at some minimum cost.

■ Breakeven Analysis

Linear programming is called a *normative procedure* because it prescribes the optimal solution to a problem. Breakeven analysis is a *descriptive procedure* because it simply describes relationships among variables; then it is up to the manager to make decisions. We can define **breakeven analysis** as a procedure for identifying the point at which revenues start covering their associated costs. It might be used to analyze the effects on profits of different price and output combinations or various levels of output.

Figure A.3 represents the key cost variables in breakeven analysis. Creating most products or services includes three types of costs: fixed costs, variable costs, and total costs. *Fixed costs* are costs that are incurred regardless of what volume of output is being generated. They include rent or mortgage payments on the building, managerial salaries, and depreciation of plant and equipment. *Variable costs* vary with the number of units produced, such as the cost of raw materials and direct labor used to make each unit. *Total costs* are fixed costs plus variable costs. Note that because of fixed costs, the line for total costs never begins at zero.

Other important factors in breakeven analysis are revenue and profit. *Revenue*, the total dollar amount of sales, is computed by multiplying the number of units sold by the sales price of each unit. *Profit* is then determined by subtracting total costs from total revenues. When revenues and total costs are plotted on the same axes, the breakeven graph shown in Figure A.4 emerges. The point at which the lines representing total costs and total revenues cross is the breakeven point. If the company represented in Figure A.4 sells more units than are represented by point A, it will realize a profit; selling below that level will result in a loss.

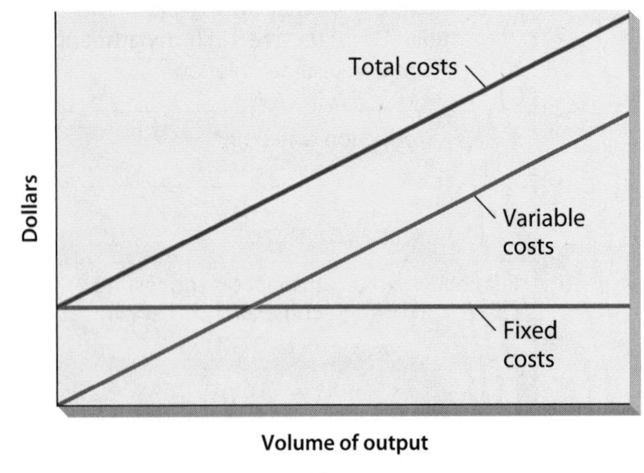

Mathematically, the breakeven point (expressed as units of production or volume) is shown by the formula

$$BP = \frac{TFC}{P - VC}$$

breakeven analysis A procedure for identifying the point at which revenues start covering costs

FIGURE A.3
An Example of Cost Factors for Breakeven Analysis

To determine the breakeven point for profit on sales for a product or service, the manager first must determine both fixed and variable costs. These costs are then combined to show total costs.

where

BP = breakeven point

TFC = total fixed costs

P = price per unit

VC = variable cost per unit

Assume that you are considering the production of a new garden hoe with a curved handle. You have determined that an acceptable selling price will be $20. You have also determined that the variable costs per hoe will be $15, and you have total fixed costs of $400,000 per year. The question is, How many hoes must you sell each year to break even? Using the breakeven model, you find that

$$BP = \frac{TFC}{P-VC}$$

$$BP = \frac{400,000}{20-15}$$

$$BP = 80,000 \text{ units}$$

Thus, you must sell eighty thousand hoes to break even. Further analysis would also show that if you could raise your price to $25 per hoe, you would need to sell only forty thousand to break even, and so on.

The state of New York used a breakeven analysis to evaluate seven variations of prior approvals for its Medicaid service. Comparisons were conducted of the costs involved in each variation against savings gained from efficiency and improved quality of service. The state found that only three of the variations were cost effective.[5]

Breakeven analysis is a popular and important planning technique, but it also has noteworthy weaknesses. It considers revenues only up to the breakeven point, and it makes no allowance for the time value of money. For example, because the funds used to cover fixed and variable costs could be used for other purposes (such as investment), the organization is losing interest income by tying up its money prior to reaching the breakeven point. Thus, managers often used breakeven analysis as only the first step in planning. After the preliminary analysis has been completed, more sophisticated techniques (such as rate-of-return analysis or discounted-present-value

FIGURE A.4
Breakeven Analysis

After total costs are determined and graphed, the manager then graphs the total revenues that will be earned on different levels of sales. The regions defined by the intersection of the two graphs show loss and profit areas. The intersection itself shows the breakeven point—the level of sales at which all costs are covered but no profits are earned.

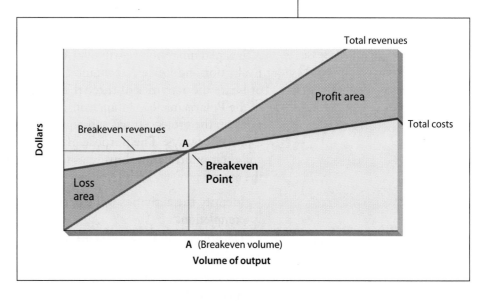

analysis) are used. Those techniques can help the manager decide whether to proceed or to divert resources into other areas.

■ Simulations

organizational simulation A model of a real-world situation that can be manipulated to discover how it functions

Another useful planning device is simulation. The word *simulate* means to copy or to represent. An **organizational simulation** is a model of a real-world situation that can be manipulated to discover how it functions. Simulation is a descriptive, rather than a prescriptive, technique. Northern Research & Engineering Corporation is an engineering consulting firm that helps clients plan new factories. By using a sophisticated factory simulation model, the firm recently helped a client cut several machines and operations from a new plant and to save over $750,000.

To consider another example, suppose the city of Houston was going to build a new airport. Issues to be addressed might include the number of runways, the direction of those runways, the number of terminals and gates, the allocation of various carriers among the terminals and gates, and the technology and human resources needed to achieve a target frequency of takeoffs and landings. (Of course, actually planning such an airport would involve many more variables than these.) A model could be constructed to simulate these factors, as well as their interrelationships. The planner could then insert several different values for each factor and observe the probable results.

Simulation problems are in some ways similar to those addressed by linear programming, but simulation is more useful in very complex situations characterized by diverse constraints and opportunities. The development of sophisticated simulation models may require the expertise of outside specialists or consultants, and the complexity of simulation almost always necessitates the use of a computer. For these reasons simulation is most likely to be used as a technique for planning in large organizations that have the required resources.

■ PERT

PERT A planning tool that uses a network to plan projects involving numerous activities and their interrelationships

A final planning tool we will discuss is PERT. **PERT**, an acronym for Program Evaluation and Review Technique, was developed by the U.S. Navy to help coordinate the activities of three thousand contractors during the development of the Polaris nuclear submarine, and it was credited with saving two years of work on the project. It has subsequently been used by most large companies in a variety of ways. The purpose of PERT is to develop a network of activities and their interrelationships so as to highlight critical time intervals that affect the overall project. PERT follows six basic steps:

1. Identify the activities to be performed and the events that will mark their completion.
2. Develop a network showing the relationships among the activities and events.
3. Calculate the time needed for each event and the time necessary to get from each event to the next.

4. Identify within the network the longest path that leads to completion of the project. This path is called the critical path.

5. Refine the network.

6. Use the network to control the project.

Suppose that a marketing manager wants to use PERT to plan the test marketing and nationwide introduction of a new product. Table A.3 identifies the basic steps involved in carrying out this project. The activities are then arranged in a network like the one shown in Figure A.5. In the figure each completed event is represented by a number in a circle. The activities are indicated by letters on the lines connecting the events. Notice that some activities are performed independently of one another and that others must be performed in sequence. For example, test production (activity a) and test site location (activity c) can be done at the same time, but test site location has to be done before actual testing (activities f and g) can be done.

The time needed to get from one activity to another is then determined. The normal way to calculate the time between each activity is to average the

Activities		Events	
a	Produce limited quantity for test marketing.	1	Origin of project.
		2	Completion of production for test marketing.
b	Design preliminary package.	3	Completion of design for preliminary package.
c	Locate test market.	4	Test market located.
d	Obtain local merchant cooperation.	5	Local merchant cooperation obtained.
e	Ship product to selected retail outlets.	6	Product for test marketing shipped to retail outlets.
f	Monitor sales and customer reactions.	7	Sales and customer reactions monitored.
g	Survey customers in test-market area	8	Customers in test-market area surveyed.
h	Make needed product changes.	9	Product changes made.
l	Make needed package changes.	10	Package changes made.
j	Mass produce the product.	11	Product mass produced.
k	Begin national advertising.	12	National advertising carried out.
l	Begin national distribution.	13	National distribution completed.

TABLE A.3
Activities and Events for Introducing a New Product

PERT is used to plan schedules for projects and it is particularly useful when many activities with critical time intervals must be coordinated. Besides launching a new product, PERT is useful for projects like constructing a new factory or building, remodeling an office, or opening a new store.

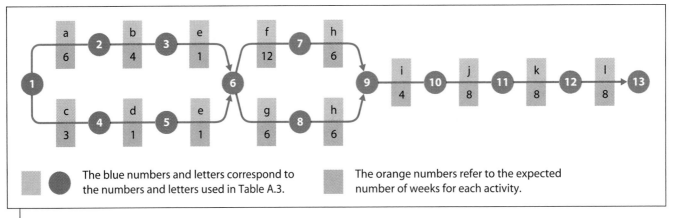

The blue numbers and letters correspond to the numbers and letters used in Table A.3.

The orange numbers refer to the expected number of weeks for each activity.

FIGURE A.5

A PERT Network for Introducing a New Product

most optimistic, most pessimistic, and most likely times, with the most likely time weighted by 4. Time is usually calculated with the following formula:

$$\text{Expected time} = \frac{a + 4b + c}{6}$$

where

a = optimistic time

b = most likely time

c = pessimistic time

critical path   The longest path through a PERT network

The expected number of weeks for each activity in our example is shown in parentheses along each path in Figure A.5. The **critical path**—or the longest path through the network—is then identified. This path is considered critical because it shows the shortest time in which the project can be completed. In our example the critical path is 1-2-3-6-7-9-10-11-12-13, totaling fifty-seven weeks. PERT thus tells the manager that the project will take fifty-seven weeks to complete.

The first network may be refined. If fifty-seven weeks to completion is too long a time, the manager might decide to begin preliminary package design before the test products are finished. Or the manager might decide that ten weeks rather than twelve is a sufficient time period to monitor sales. The idea is that if the critical path can be shortened, so too can the overall duration of the project. The PERT network serves as an ongoing framework for both planning and control throughout the project. For example, the manager can use it to monitor where the project is relative to where it needs to be. Thus, if an activity on the critical path takes longer than planned, the manager needs to make up the time elsewhere or live with the fact that the entire project will be late.

Decision-Making Tools

Managers can also use a number of tools that relate more specifically to decision making than to planning. Two commonly used decision-making tools are payoff matrices and decision trees.

■ Payoff Matrices

A **payoff matrix** specifies the probable value of different alternatives, depending on different possible outcomes associated with each. The use of a payoff matrix requires that several alternatives be available, that several different events could occur, and that the consequences depend on which alternative is selected and on which event or set of events occurs. An important concept in understanding the payoff matrix, then, is probability. A **probability** is the likelihood, expressed as a percentage, that a particular event will or will not occur. If we believe that a particular event will occur seventy-five times out of one hundred, we can say that the probability of its occurring is 75 percent, or .75. Probabilities range in value from 0 (no chance of occurrence) to 1.00 (certain occurrence—also referred to as 100 percent). In the business world, there are few probabilities of either 0 or 1.00. Most probabilities that managers use are based on subjective judgment, intuition, and historical data.

payoff matrix A decision-making tool that specifies the probable value of different alternatives depending on different possible outcomes associated with each

probability The likelihood, expressed as a percentage, that a particular event will or will not occur

The **expected value** of an alternative course of action is the sum of all possible values of outcomes due to that action multiplied by their respective probabilities. Suppose, for example, that a venture capitalist is considering investing in a new company. If he believes there is a .40 probability of making $100,000, a .30 probability of making $30,000, and a .30 probability of losing $20,000, the expected value (EV) of this alternative is

expected value When applied to alternative courses of action, the sum of all possible values of outcomes from that action multiplied by their respective probabilities

$$EV = .40(100,000) + .30(30,000) + .30(-20,000)$$

$$EV = 40,000 + 9,000 - 6,000$$

$$EV = \$43,000$$

The investor can then weigh the expected value of this investment against the expected values of other available alternatives. The highest EV signals the investment that should most likely be selected.

For example, suppose another venture capitalist wants to invest $20,000 in a new business. She has identified three possible alternatives: a leisure products company, an energy enhancement company, and a food-producing company. Because the expected value of each alternative depends on short-run changes in the economy, especially inflation, she decides to develop a payoff matrix. She estimates that the probability of high inflation is .30 and the probability of low inflation is .70. She then estimates the probable returns for each investment in the event of both high and low inflation. Figure A.6 shows what the payoff matrix might look like (a minus sign indicates a loss). The expected value of investing in the leisure products company is

$$EV = .30(-10,000) + .70(50,000)$$

$$EV = -3,000 + 35,000$$

$$EV = \$32,000$$

Similarly, the expected value of investing in the energy enhancement company is

$$EV = .30(90,000) + .70(-15,000)$$

$$EV = 27,000 + (-10,500)$$

$$EV = \$16,500$$

FIGURE A.6

An Example of a Payoff Matrix

A payoff matrix helps the manager determine the expected value of different alternatives. A payoff matrix is effective only if the manager ensures that probability estimates are as accurate as possible.

		High inflation (*Probability of .30*)	Low inflation (*Probability of .70*)
Investment alternative **1**	Leisure products company	–$10,000	+$50,000
Investment alternative **2**	Energy enhancement company	+$90,000	–$15,000
Investment alternative **3**	Food-processing company	+$30,000	+$25,000

And, finally, the expected value of investing in the food-processing company is

$$EV = .30(30,000) + .70(25,000)$$

$$EV = 9,000 + 17,500$$

$$EV = \$26,500$$

Investing in the leisure products company, then, has the highest expected value.

Other potential uses for payoff matrices include determining optimal order quantities, deciding whether to repair or replace broken machinery, and deciding which of several new products to introduce. Of course, the real key to effectively using payoff matrices is making accurate estimates of the relevant probabilities.

■ Decision Trees

decision tree A planning tool that extends the concept of a payoff matrix through a sequence of decisions

Decision trees are like payoff matrices in that they enhance a manager's ability to evaluate alternatives by making use of expected values. However, they are most appropriate when there are a number of decisions to be made in sequence.

Figure A.7 illustrates a hypothetical decision tree. The firm represented wants to begin exporting its products to a foreign market, but limited capacity restricts it to only one market at first. Managers feel that either France or China would be the best place to start. Whichever alternative is selected, sales for the product in that country may turn out to be high or low. In France, there is a .80 chance of high sales and a .20 chance of low sales. The anticipated payoffs in these situations are predicted to be $20 million and $3 million, respectively. In China, the probabilities of high versus low sales are .60 and .40, respectively, and the associated payoffs are presumed to be $25 million and $6 million. As shown in Figure A.7, the expected value of shipping to France is $16,600,000, whereas the expected value of shipping to China is $17,400,000.

The astute reader will note that this part of the decision could have been set up as a payoff matrix. However, the value of decision trees is that we can extend the model to include subsequent decisions. Assume, for example, that the company begins shipping to China. If high sales do in fact materialize, the

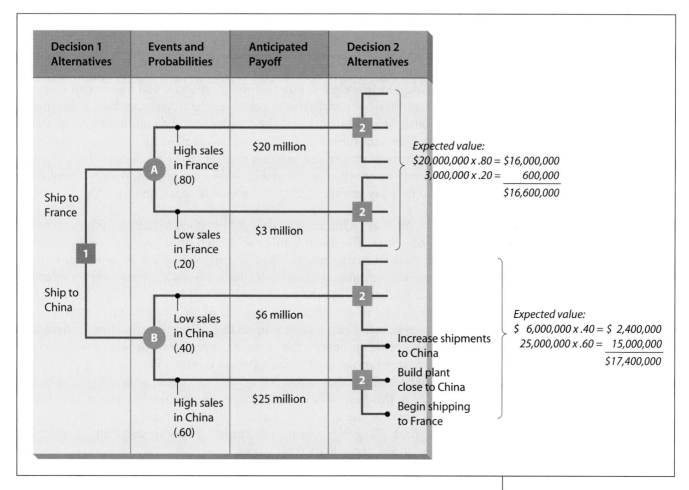

Decision 1 Alternatives	Events and Probabilities	Anticipated Payoff	Decision 2 Alternatives

Ship to France

A — High sales in France (.80) — $20 million — 2

Low sales in France (.20) — $3 million — 2

Expected value:
$20,000,000 x .80 = $16,000,000
3,000,000 x .20 = 600,000
$16,600,000

1

Ship to China

B — Low sales in China (.40) — $6 million — 2

High sales in China (.60) — $25 million — 2

Increase shipments to China

Build plant close to China

Begin shipping to France

Expected value:
$ 6,000,000 x .40 = $ 2,400,000
25,000,000 x .60 = 15,000,000
$17,400,000

company will soon reach another decision situation. It might use the extra revenues to (1) increase shipments to China, (2) build a plant close to China in order to cut shipping costs, or (3) begin shipping to France. Various outcomes are possible for each decision, and each outcome will also have both a probability and an anticipated payoff. It is therefore possible to compute expected values back through several tiers of decisions all the way to the initial one. As it is with payoff matrices, determining probabilities accurately is the crucial element in the process. Properly used, however, decision trees can provide managers with a useful road map through complex decision situations.

■ Other Techniques

In addition to payoff matrices and decision trees, a number of other quantitative methods are also available to facilitate decision making.

Inventory Models   **Inventory models** are techniques that help the manager decide how much inventory to maintain. Target Stores uses inventory models to help determine how much merchandise to order, when to order it, and so forth. Inventory consists of both raw materials (inputs) and finished goods (outputs). Polaroid, for example, maintains a supply of the chemicals that it uses to make film, the cartons it packs film in, and packaged film ready to be shipped. For finished goods both extremes are bad: excess inventory ties up

FIGURE A.7
An Example of a Decision Tree

A decision tree extends the basic concepts of a payoff matrix through multiple decisions. This tree shows the possible outcomes of two levels of decisions. The first decision is whether to expand to China or France. The second decision, assuming that the company expands to China, is whether to increase shipments to China, build a plant close to China, or initiate shipping to France.

inventory model A technique that helps managers decide how much inventory to maintain

just-in-time (JIT) An inventory management technique in which materials are scheduled to arrive in small batches as they are needed, eliminating the need for resources such as big reserves and warehouse space

queuing model A model used to optimize waiting lines in organizations

distribution model A model used to determine the optimal pattern of distribution across different carriers and routes

game theory A planning tool used to predict how competitors will respond to different actions the organization might take

capital, whereas a small inventory may result in shortages and customer dissatisfaction. The same holds for raw materials: too much inventory ties up capital, but if a company runs out of resources, work stoppages may occur. Finally, because the process of placing an order for raw materials and supplies has associated costs (such as clerical time, shipping expenses, and higher unit costs for small quantities), it is important to minimize the frequency of ordering. Inventory models help the manager make decisions so as to optimize the size of inventory. New innovations in inventory management such as **just-in-time**, or **JIT**, rely heavily on decision-making models. A JIT system involves scheduling materials to arrive in short batches as they are needed, thereby eliminating the need for a big reserve inventory, warehouse space, and so forth.[6]

Queuing Models **Queuing models** are intended to help organizations manage waiting lines. We are all familiar with such situations: shoppers waiting to pay for groceries at Kroger, drivers waiting to buy gas at an Exxon station, travelers calling American Airlines for reservations, and customers waiting for a teller at Citibank. Take the Kroger example. If a store manager has only one check-out stand in operation, the store's cost for check-out personnel is very low; however, many customers are upset by the long line that frequently develops. To solve the problem, the store manager could decide to keep twenty check-out stands open at all times. Customers would like the short waiting period, but personnel costs would be very high. A queuing model would be appropriate in this case to help the manager determine the optimal number of check-out stands: the number that would balance personnel costs and customer waiting time. Target Stores uses queuing models to determine how many check-out lanes to put in its retail stores.

Distribution Models A decision facing many marketing managers relates to the distribution of the organization's products. Specifically, the manager must decide where the products should go and how to transport them. Railroads, trucking, and air freight have associated shipping costs, and each mode of transportation follows different schedules and routes. The problem is to identify the combination of routes that optimize distribution effectiveness and distribution costs. **Distribution models** help managers determine this optimal pattern of distribution.

Game Theory **Game theory** was originally developed to predict the effect of one company's decisions on competitors. Models developed from game theory are intended to predict how a competitor will react to various activities that an organization might undertake, such as price changes, promotional changes, and the introduction of new products. If Bank of America were considering raising its prime lending rate by 1 percent, it might use a game theory model to predict whether Citicorp would follow suit. If the model revealed that Citicorp would do so, Bank of America would probably proceed; otherwise, it would probably maintain the current interest rates. Unfortunately, game theory is not yet as useful as it was originally expected to be. The complexities of the real world combined with the limitation of the technique itself restrict its applicability. Game theory, however, does provide a useful conceptual framework for analyzing competitive behavior, and its usefulness may be improved in the future.

Artificial Intelligence A fairly new addition to the manager's quantitative tool kit is **artificial intelligence (AI)**. The most useful form of AI is the expert system.[7] An expert system is essentially a computer program that tries to duplicate the thought processes of experienced decision makers. For example, Digital Equipment has developed an expert system that checks sales orders for new computer systems and then designs preliminary layouts for those new systems. Digital can now ship the computer to a customer in components for final assembly on site. This approach has enabled the company to cut back on its own final-assembly facilities.

artificial intelligence (AI) A computer program that attempts to duplicate the thought processes of experienced decision makers

Strengths and Weaknesses of Planning Tools

Like all issues confronting management, planning tools of the type described here have a number of strengths and weaknesses.

■ Weaknesses and Problems

One weakness of the planning and decision-making tools discussed in this appendix is that they may not always adequately reflect reality. Even with the most sophisticated and powerful computer-assisted technique, reality must often be simplified. Many problems are also not amenable to quantitative analysis because important elements of them are intangible or nonquantifiable. Employee morale or satisfaction, for example, is often a major factor in managerial decisions.

The use of these tools and techniques may also be quite costly. For example, only larger companies can afford to develop their own econometric models. Even though the computer explosion has increased the availability of quantitative aids, some expense is still involved and it will take time for many of these techniques to become widely used. Resistance to change also limits the use of planning tools in some settings. If a manager for a retail chain has always based decisions for new locations on personal visits, observations, and intuition, she or he may be less than eager to begin using a computer-based model for evaluating and selecting sites. Finally, problems may arise when managers have to rely on technical specialists to use sophisticated models. Experts trained in the use of complex mathematical procedures may not understand or appreciate other aspects of management.

■ Strengths and Advantages

On the plus side, planning and decision-making tools offer many advantages. For situations that are amenable to quantification, they can bring sophisticated mathematical processes to bear on planning and decision making. Properly designed models and formulas also help decision makers "see reason." For example, a manager might not be inclined to introduce a new product line simply because she or he doesn't think it will be profitable. After seeing a forecast predicting first-year sales of one hundred thousand units coupled with a breakeven analysis showing profitability after only twenty thousand, however, the manager will probably change her or his mind. Thus rational planning tools and techniques force the manager to look beyond personal prejudices and predispositions. Finally, the computer explosion is rapidly making sophisticated planning techniques available in a wider range of settings than ever before.

The crucial point to remember is that planning tools and techniques are a means to an end, not an end in themselves. Just as a carpenter uses a hand saw in some situations and an electric saw in others, a manager must recognize that a particular model may be useful in some situations but not in others that may call for a different approach. Knowing the difference is one mark of a good manager.

Summary of Key Points

Managers often use a variety of tools and techniques as they develop plans and make decisions. Forecasting is one widely used method. Forecasting is the process of developing assumptions or premises about the future. Sales or revenue forecasting is especially important. Many organizations also rely heavily on technological forecasting. Time-series analysis and causal modeling are important forecasting techniques. Qualitative techniques are also widely used.

Managers also use other planning tools and techniques in different circumstances. Linear programming helps optimize resources and activities. Breakeven analysis helps identify how many products or services must be sold to cover costs. Simulations model reality. PERT helps plan how much time a project will require.

Other tools and techniques are useful for decision making. Constructing a payoff matrix, for example, helps a manager assess the expected value of different alternatives. Decision trees are used to extend expected values across multiple decisions. Other popular decision-making tools and techniques include inventory models, queuing models, distribution models, game theory, and artificial intelligence.

Various strengths and weaknesses are associated with each of these tools and techniques, as well as with their use by a manager. The key to success is knowing when each should and should not be used and knowing how to use and interpret the results that each provides.

APPENDIX NOTES

1. For a classic review, see John C. Chambers, S. K. Mullick, and D. Smith, "How to Choose the Right Forecasting Technique," *Harvard Business Review*, July–August 1971, pp. 45–74.

2. Charles Ostrom, *Time-Series Analysis: Regression Techniques* (Beverly Hills, Calif.: Sage Publications, 1980).

3. Fred Kerlinger and Elazar Pedhazur, *Multiple Regression in Behavioral Research* (New York: Holt, 1973).

4. Chambers, Mullick, and Smith, "How to Choose the Right Forecasting Technique"; see also J. Scott Armstrong, *Long-Range Forecasting: From Crystal Ball to Computers* (New York: Wiley, 1978).

5. Edward Hannan, Linda Ryan, and Richard Van Orden, "A Cost-Benefit Analysis of Prior Approvals for Medicaid Services in New York State," *Socio-Economic Planning Sciences*, 1984, Vol. 18, pp. 1–14.

6. Ramon L. Alonso and Cline W. Fraser, "JIT Hits Home: A Case Study in Reducing Management Delays," *Sloan Management Review*, Summer 1991, pp. 59–68.

7. Beau Sheil, "Thinking about Artificial Intelligence," *Harvard Business Review*, July-August 1987, pp. 91-97; and Dorothy Leonard-Barton and John J. Sviokla, "Putting Expert Systems to Work," *Harvard Business Review*, March–April 1988, pp. 91–98.

Photo and Cartoon Credits (continued)

Powell/Allsport; *Chapter 18*: p. 545: Courtesy of Kmart Corp.; p. 547: Ken Martin/Impact Visuals; p. 553: Olivier Laude/The Gamma-Liaison Network; p. 562: Reprinted with special permission of King Feature Syndicate, Inc.; p. 567: C. J. Walker; *Chapter 19*: p. 575: Courtesy of Fastener Supply Company; p. 579: Courtesy of IBM Corp.; p. 587: THE FAR SIDE © 1998 FARWORKS, INC. Used by permission of UNIVERSAL PRESS SYNDI-CATE. All rights reserved,: p. 589: Will Panich/Courtesy of Baxter International; p. 597: Ilene Perlman; *Chapter 20*: p. 609: Carol Lundeen; p. 619: Roger Ball/Courtesy of Collins and Aikman; p. 623: Nikolai Ignatiev/Network/SABA Press Photos; p. 628: Christopher Hornsby; p. 632: Photo by Wyatt McSpadden/FORTUNE, © 1997 Time Inc. All rights reserved.; p. 633: Cartoons by Bradford Veley; *Chapter 21*: p. 641: Courtesy of Hartmann Luggage; p. 646: DILBERT by Scott Adams © 1994 United Feature Syndicate, Inc.; p. 647: Courtesy of National Steel; p. 652: Mark Richards/PhotoEdit; p. 656: Andy Freeberg; p. 664: Todd Buchanan/Black Star; *Chapter 22*: p. 671: Courtesy of Texas Instruments; p. 674: Robbie McClaran/SABA Press Photos; p. 678: James D. Wilson/The Gamma-Liaison Network; p. 682: Roz Chast © 1996 from The New Yorker Collection. All rights reserved.; p. 686: Peter Aaron/ESTO; p. 689: Andy Freeberg.

Name Index

Organization and Product Index

Subject Index

SKILL-BUILDING EXERCISES AT A GLANCE

Building Effective
Technical Skills

Building Effective
Diagnostic/Conceptual Skills

Building Effective
Time-Management Skills

Building Effective
Decision-Making Skills

Building Effective
Communication/Interpersonal Skills